GALE
ENCYCLOPEDIA OF
MULTICULTURAL
AMERICA

GALE
ENCYCLOPEDIA OF
MULTICULTURAL
AMERICA
SECOND EDITION

volume 3
Oneidas – Yupiat

Contributing Editor
ROBERT VON DASSANOWSKY

Author of Introduction
RUDOLPH J. VECOLI

Edited by
JEFFREY LEHMAN

Endorsed by the Ethnic and Multicultural
Information Exchange Round Table,
American Library Association.

GALE GROUP

Detroit
San Francisco
London
Boston
Woodbridge, CT

Jeffrey Lehman, *Editor*
Elizabeth Shaw, *Associate Editor*
Gloria Lam, *Assistant Editor*
Linda S. Hubbard, *Managing Editor*
Contributing editors: Ashyia N. Henderson, Brian Koski, Allison McClintic Marion,
Mark F. Mikula, David G. Oblender, Patrick Politano

Maria Franklin, *Permissions Manager*
Margaret A. Chamberlain, *Permissions Specialist*

Mary Beth Trimper, *Production Director*
Evi Seoud, *Assistant Production Manager*

Cynthia Baldwin, *Product Design Manager*
Barbara J. Yarrow, *Imaging and Multimedia Content Manager*
Randy Bassett, *Image Database Supervisor*
Pamela A. Reed, *Imaging Coordinator*
Robert Duncan, *Senior Imaging Specialist*

Library of Congress Cataloging-in-Publication Data

Gale encyclopedia of multicultural America / contributing editor, Robert von
Dassanowsky ; edited by Jeffrey Lehman.— 2nd ed.
    p. cm.
    Includes bibliographical references and index.
    Summary: Essays on approximately 150 culture groups of the U.S., from Acadians to
Yupiats, covering their history, acculturation and assimilation, family and community
dynamics, language and religion.
    ISBN 0-7876-3986-9 (set : alk. paper) — ISBN 0-7876-3987-7 (vol. 1 : alk. paper) —
    ISBN 0-7876-3988-5 (vol. 2 : alk. paper) — ISBN 0-7876-3989-3 (vol. 3 : alk. paper)
    1. Pluralism (Social sciences)—United States—Encyclopedias, Juvenile. 2.
Ethnology—United States—Encyclopedias, Juvenile. 3. Minorities—United
States—Encyclopedias, Juvenile. 4. United States—Ethnic relations—Encyclopedias. 5.
United States—Race relations—Encyclopedias, Juvenile. [1. Ethnology—Encyclopedias.
2. Minorities—Encyclopedias.] I. Dassanowsky, Robert. II. Lehman, Jeffrey, 1969-

E184.A1 G14 1999
305.8'00973'03—dc21   99-044226

CONTENTS

Volume 1

Volume II

Volume III

The first edition of the *Gale Encyclopedia of Multicultural America*, with 101 essays on different culture groups in the United States, filled a need in the reference collection for a single, comprehensive source of extensive information about ethnicities in the United States. Its contents satisfied high school and college students, librarians, and general reference seekers alike. The American Library Association's Ethnic Materials and Information Exchange Round Table *Bulletin* endorsed it as an exceptionally useful reference product and the Reference Users and Services Association honored it with a RUSA award.

The second edition of the *Gale Encyclopedia of Multicultural America* has been endorsed by the Ethnic and Multicultural Information Exchange Round Table of the American Library Association

This second edition adds to and improves upon the original. The demand for more current and comprehensive multicultural reference products in public, high school, and academic libraries remains strong. Topics related to ethnic issues, immigration, and acculturation continue to make headlines. People from Latin America, Africa, and Asia represent higher percentages of the new arrivals and increase the diversity of our population. The new *Gale Encyclopedia of Multicultural America*, with 152 essays, more than 250 images, a general bibliography updated by Vladimir Wertsman, and an improved general subject index, covers 50 percent more groups. Both new and revised essays received the scrutiny of scholars. Approximately 50 essays received significant textual updating to reflect changing conditions at the end of the century in America. In all essays, we updated the directory information for media, organizations, and museums by adding e-mail addresses and URLs, by deleting defunct groups, and by adding new groups or more accurate contact information. We have also created fresher suggested readings lists.

SCOPE

The three volumes of this edition address 152 ethnic, ethnoreligious, and Native American cultures currently residing in the United States. The average essay length is 8,000 words, but ranges from slightly less than 3,000 to more than 20,000 words, depending on the amount of information available. Essays are arranged alphabetically by the most-commonly cited name for the group—although such terms as

Sioux and Gypsy may be offensive to some members of the groups themselves, as noted in the essays.

Every essay in the first edition appears in the second edition of *Gale Encyclopedia of Multicultural America*, though some are in a different form. For example, the Lebanese Americans and Syrian Americans originally were covered in a single essay on Syrian/Lebanese Americans; in this book, they are separate entries. Additionally, the editors selected 50 more cultures based on the original volume's two main criteria: size of the group according to 1990 U.S. Census data and the recommendations of the advisory board. The advisors chose groups likely to be studied in high school and college classrooms. Because of the greater number of groups covered, some essays new to this edition are about groups that still have not established large enough populations to be much recognized outside of their immediate locations of settlement. This lower "visibility" means that few radio, television, or newspaper media report on events specific to very small minority groups. As a result, many of the essays are shorter in length.

The *Gale Encyclopedia of Multicultural America*'s essays cover a wide range of national and other culture groups, including those from Europe, Africa, Central America, South America, the Caribbean, the Middle East, Asia, Oceania, and North America, as well as several ethnoreligious groups. This book centers on communities as they exist in the United States, however. Thus, the encyclopedia recognizes the history, culture, and contributions of the first settlers—such as English Americans and French Americans—as well as newer Americans who have been overlooked in previous studies—such as Garifuna Americans, Georgian Americans, and Mongolian Americans. Moreover, such ethnoreligious groups as the Amish and the Druze are presented.

The various cultures that make up the American mosaic are not limited to immigrant groups, though. The Native Americans can more accurately be referred to as First Americans because of their primacy throughout the entire Western hemisphere. This rich heritage should not be undervalued and their contributions to the tapestry of U.S. history is equally noteworthy. Therefore, we felt it imperative to include essays on Native American peoples. Many attempts at a full-scale treatment of Native America have been made, including the *Gale Encyclopedia of Native American Tribes*, but such thorough coverage could not be included here for reasons of space. With the help of experts and advisors, the second edition added six new essays on Indian groups, again selected for their cultural diversity and geographical representation, bringing the total to 18.

The first edition contained two chapters devoted to peoples from Subsaharan Africa. Because the vast majority of people in the United States from this region identified themselves as African American in the 1990 U.S. Census, there is a lengthy essay entitled "African Americans" that represents persons of multiple ancestry. The census also indicated that Nigerian Americans—at 91,688 people—outnumbered all other individual national groups from Africa. This second edition adds nine more essays on peoples of African origin, most of whom are significantly less populous than Nigerian Americans. Nevertheless, the variety of customs evident in these cultures and the growing proportion of immigrants from Africa to America make it necessary and beneficial to increase coverage.

We also attempted to improve the overall demographic coverage. *Gale Encyclopedia of Multicultural America* now has 12 more essays on Asians/Pacific Islanders; five more on Hispanics, Central Americans, or South Americans; nine more on Middle Eastern/North Africans; and eight more on European peoples. The 49 essays on European immigrants treat them as separate groups with separate experiences to dispel the popular notions of a generic European American culture.

FORMAT

While each essay in the *Gale Encyclopedia of Multicultural America* includes information on the country of origin and circumstances surrounding major immigration waves (if applicable), they focus primarily on the group's experiences in the United States, specifically in the areas of acculturation and assimilation, family and community dynamics, language, religion, employment and economic traditions, politics and government, and significant contributions to American society. Wherever possible, each entry also features directory listings of periodicals, broadcast and Internet media, organizations and associations, and museums and research centers to aid the user in conducting additional research. Each entry also cites sources for further study that are current, useful, and accessible. Every essay contains clearly-marked, standardized headings and subheadings designed to locate specific types of information within each essay while also facilitating cross-cultural comparisons.

ADDITIONAL FEATURES

The improved general subject index in *Gale Encyclopedia of Multicultural America* still provides reference to significant terms, people, places, movements, and events, but also contains concepts pertinent to multicultural studies. Vladimir Wertsman, former librarian at the New York Public Library and member of the Ethnic and Multicultural Information Exchange Round Table of the American Library Association, has updated the valuable general bibliography. Its sources augment the further readings suggested in the text without duplicating them by listing general multicultural studies works. Finally, more than 250 images highlight the essays.

A companion volume, the *Gale Encyclopedia of Multicultural America: Primary Documents*, brings history to life through a wide variety of representative documents. More than 200 documents—ranging in type from periodical articles and autobiographies to political cartoons and recipes—give readers a more personal perspective on key events in history as well as the everyday lives of 90 different cultures.

ACKNOWLEDGMENTS

The editor must thank all the people whose efforts, talents, and time improved this project beyond measure. Contributing editor Professor Robert von Dassanowsky made the marathon run from beginning to end, all the while offering his insights, feedback, and unsolicited attention to details that could have been overlooked by a less observant eye; he made clear distinctions about how to treat many of the newer, lesser-known groups being added; he provided his expertise on 13 original essays and 12 new essays in the form of review and update recommendations; and he constantly served as an extra editorial opinion. The entire advisory board deserves a round of applause for

their quick and invaluable feedback, but especially Vladimir Wertsman, who once again served as GEMA's exemplary advisor, tirelessly providing me with needed guidance and words of encouragement, review and update of key essays, and an updated general bibliography. The Multicultural team also aided this process considerably: especially Liz Shaw for just about everything, including accepting most of the responsibilities for other projects so that I could focus on *Gale Encyclopedia of Multicultural America*; handling the ever-changing photo permissions and selection; and coordinating the assignment, review, and clean-up inherent in having 152 essays written or updated. Also noteworthy is Gloria Lam, who took on some of Liz's tasks when necessary. I thank Mark Mikula and Bernard Grunow for helping out in a pinch with their technological prowess; the expert reviewers, including Dean T. Alegado, Timothy Dunnigan, Truong Buu Lam, Vasudha Narayanan, Albert Valdman, Vladimir Wertsman, and Kevin Scott Wong; and Rebecca Forgette, who deserves accolades for the improvement of the index.

Even though I laud the highly professional contributions of these individuals, I understand that as the editor, this publication is my responsibility.

SUGGESTIONS ARE WELCOME

The editor welcomes your suggestions on any aspect of this work. Please mail comments, suggestions, or criticisms to: The Editor, *Gale Encyclopedia of Multicultural America*, The Gale Group, 27500 Drake Road, Farmington Hills, MI 48331-3535; call 1-800-877-GALE [877-4253]; fax to (248) 699-8062; or e-mail galegroup.com.

The editors wish to thank the permissions managers of the companies that assisted us in securing reprint rights. The following list acknowledges the copyright holders who have granted us permission to reprint material in this second edition of the *Gale Encyclopedia of Multicultural America*. Every effort has been made to trace the copyright holders, but if omissions have occured, please contact the editor.

COPYRIGHTED IMAGES

The photographs and illustrations appearing in the *Gale Encyclopedia of Multicultural America*, were received from the following sources:

Cover photographs: **The Joy of Citizenship,** UPI/Bettmann; **Against the Sky,** UPI/Bettmann; **Leaving Ellis Island,** The Bettmann Archive.

Acadian man dumping bucket of crayfish into red sack, 1980s-1990s, Acadian Village, near Lafayette, Louisiana, photograph by Philip Gould. Corbis. **Acadian people dancing outdoors at the Acadian Festival,** c.1997, Lafayette, Louisiana, photograph by Philip Gould. Corbis. **Acadians** (re-enactment of early Acadian family), photograph. Village Historique Acadien. **African American family,** photograph by Ken Estell. **African American; Lunch counter segregation protest,** Raleigh, North Carolina, 1960, photograph. AP/Wide World Photos. **African American Rabbi,** photograph by John Duprey. ©New York Daily News, L.P. **African American school room in Missouri, c.1930,** photograph. Corbis-Bettmann Archive. **Albanian Harry Bajraktari** (Albanian American publisher, holding newspaper), photograph. AP/Wide World Photos. **Albanian woman** (shawl draped over her head), photograph. Corbis-Bettmann. **Amish boys** (five boys and a horse), photograph. AP/Wide World Photos. **Amish families** gathering to eat a traditional Amish meal in New Holland, Pennsylvania, photograph by David Johnson. **Amish farmers** (two men, woman, and horses), photograph. AP/Wide World Photos. **Apache boys and girls** (conducting physics experiments), Carlisle Indian School, Pennsylvania, c.1915, photograph. National Archives and Records Administration. **Apache Devil Dancers** (group of dancers), photograph. AP/Wide World Photos. **Apaches holding their last tribal meeting at Mescalera, NM,** 1919, photograph. Corbis-Bettmann. **Arab American woman in traditional Arab clothing** (blues and gold) riding a purebred Arabian horse, 1984, Los Angeles, California, photograph. Corbis/Kit Houghton Photography. **Arab Americans** (two women and five children, crossing the street), photograph. AP/Wide World Photos. **Arab; Alixa Naff,** sitting with Arab-American artifacts, photograph by Doug Mills. AP/Wide World Photo. **Young Arab girl/woman** (wearing yellow hairbow), 1998, Los Angeles, California, photograph by Catherine Karnow. Corbis. **Argentinean dancers,** Hispanic Parade, New York, photograph by Frances M. Roberts. Levine & Roberts Stock Photography. **Argentinean; Geraldo Hernandez,** (on float at Hispanic American Parade), photograph by Joe Comunale. AP/Wide World Photos. **Armenian rug making,** Jarjorian, Victoria, and Mrs. Paul Sherkerjian, with two women and children demonstrating Armenian rug making (in traditional garb), 1919, Chicago, Illinois, photograph. Corbis-Bettmann. **Armenian; Maro Partamian,** (back turned to choir), New York City, 1999, photograph by Bebeto Matthews. AP/Wide World Photos. **Armenian; Norik Shahbazian,** (showing tray of baklava), Los Angeles, California, 1998, photograph by Reed Saxon. AP/Wide World Photos. **Asian Indian woman, holding plate of food,** Rockville, Maryland, 1993, photograph by Catherine Karnow. Corbis. **Asian Indian; Three generations of an East Indian family** (sitting under trees), c.1991, Pomo, California, photograph by Joseph Sohm. Corbis/ChromoSohm Inc. **Australian; Marko Johnson,** (seated holding Australian instrument, didjeridoo, which he crafted, collection behind), 1998, Salt Lake City, Utah, photograph. AP/Wide World Photos. **Austrian; Arnold Schwarzenegger,** sitting and talking to President Gerorge Bush, photograph. AP/Wide World Photos. **Basque children wearing traditional costumes,** c.1996, Boise, Idaho, photograph by Jan Butchofsky-Houser. Corbis. **Basque couple wearing traditional costumes,** Boise, Idaho, photograph by Buddy Mays. Corbis. **Belgian; Waiter serving food in Belgian restaurant** (wearing black uniform), photograph by Jeff Christensen. Archive Photos. **Blackfoot Indians burial platform** (father mourning his son), 1912, photograph by Roland Reed. The Library of Congress. **Blackfoot Indians chasing buffalo,** photograph by John M. Stanley. National Archives and Records Administration. **Bolivian; Gladys Gomez,** (holding U.S. and Bolivian flags), New York City, 1962, photograph by Marty Hanley. Corbis/Bettmann. **Bosnian refugees,** Slavica Cvijetinovic, her son Ivan, and Svemir Ilic (in apartment), 1998, Clarkston, Georgia, photograph. AP/Wide World Photos. **Brazilian Street Festival,** Jesus, Michelle, and Adenilson Daros (on vacation from Brazil) dancing together, 15th Brazil Street Festival, 1998, New York, photograph. AP/Wide World Photos. **Brazilian; Tatiana Lima,** (wearing Carnival costume), photograph by Jeff Christensen. Archive Photos. **Bulgarian American artist, Christo** (kneeling, left hand in front of

painting), New York City, c.1983, photograph by Jacques M.Chenet. Corbis. **Bulgarian; Bishop Andrey Velichky,** (receiving cross from swimmer), Santa Monica, California, 1939, photograph. Corbis/Bettmann. **Burmese Chart** (chart depicting the pronunciation and script for numbers and expressions), illustration. Eastword Publications Development. The Gale Group. **Cambodian girls standing on porch steps,** 1994, Seattle, Washington, photograph by Dan Lamont. Corbis. **Cambodian child, Angelina Melendez,** (standing in front of chart), photograph. AP/Wide World Photos. **Cambodian; Virak Ui,** (sitting on bed), photograph. AP/Wide World Photos. **Canadian American farmers in a field with a truck,** Sweetgrass, Montana, 1983, photograph by Michael S. Yamashita. Corbis. **Canadian; Donald and Kiefer Sutherland,** (standing together), Los Angeles, California, 1995, photograph by Kurt Kireger. Corbis. **Cape Verdean Henry Andrade** (preparing to represent Cape Verde in Atlanta Olympics), 1996, Cerritos, California, photograph. AP/Wide World Photos. **Cherokee boy and girl** (in traditional dress), c.1939, photograph. National Archives and Records Administration. **Cherokee woman with child on her back fishing,** photograph. Corbis-Bettmann. **Chilean; Hispanic Columbus Day parade** (children dancing in the street), photograph by Richard I. Harbus. AP/Wide World Photos. **Chinese Chart** (depicting examples of pictographs, ideographs, ideographic combinations, ideograph/sound characters, transferable characters, and loan characters), illustration. Eastword Publications Development. The Gale Group. **Chinese Dragon Parade** (two people dressed in dragon costumes), photograph by Frank Polich. AP/Wide World Photos. **Choctaw family standing at Chucalissa,** photograph. The Library of Congress. **Choctaw school children and their teacher** (standing outside of Bascome School), Pittsburg County, photograph. National Archives and Records Administration. **Colombian Americans perform during the Orange Bowl Parade** (women wearing long skirts and blouses), photograph by Alan Diaz. AP/Wide World Photos. **Creek Council House** (delegates from 34 tribes in front of large house), Indian Territory, 1880, photograph. National Archives and Records Administration. **Creek; Marion McGhee (Wild Horse),** doing Fluff Dance, photograph. AP/Wide World Photos. **Creole; elderly white woman holding Creole baby on her lap,** 1953, Saba Island, Netherlands Antilles, photograph by Bradley Smith. Corbis. **Creole; Mardi Gras** (Krewe of Rex floats travelling through street), photograph by Drew Story. Archive Photos. **Creole; Two men presenting the Creole flag,**

Zydeco Festival, c.1990, Plaisance, Louisiana, photograph by Philip Gould. Corbis. **Creole woman quilting** (red and white quilt, in 19th century garb), Amand Broussard House, Vermillionville Cajun/Creole Folk Village, Lafayette, Louisiana, c.1997, photograph by Dave G. Houser. Corbis. **Croatian Americans** (man with child), photograph. Aneal Vohra/Unicorn Stock Photos. **Croatian boy holding ends of scissors-like oyster rake,** 1938, Olga, Louisiana, photograph by Russell Lee. Corbis. **Cuban Americans** (holding crosses representing loved ones who died in Cuba), photograph by Alan Diaz. AP/Wide World Photos. **Cuban family reunited in Miami, Florida,** 1980, photograph. AP/Wide World Photos. **Cuban refugees** (older man and woman and three younger women), photograph. Reuters/Corbis-Bettmann. **Cuban children marching in Calle Ocho Parade,** photograph © by Steven Ferry. **Czech Americans** (at Czech festival), photograph. Aneal Vohra/Unicorn Stock Photos. **Czech immigrants** (six women and one child), photograph. UPI/Corbis-Bettmann. **Czech women,** standing in front of brick wall, Ellis Island, New York City, 1920, photograph. Corbis/ Bettmann. **Danish American women** (at ethnic festival), photograph. © Aneal Vohra/Unicorn Stock Photos. **Danish Americans** (women and their daughters at Dana College), photograph. Dana College, Blair Nebraska. **Dominican; Ysaes Amaro** (dancing, wearing mask with long horns), New York City, 1999, photograph by Mitch Jacobson. AP/Wide World Photos. **Dominican; Hispanic Parade,** Dominican women dancing in front of building (holding flower baskets), photograph © Charlotte Kahler. **Dutch Americans** (Klompen dancers perform circle dance), Tulip Festival, Holland, Michigan, photograph. © Dennis MacDonald/Photo Edit. **Dutch immigrants** (mother and children), photograph. UPI/Corbis-Bettmann. **Dutch; Micah Zantingh,** (looking at tulips, in traditional Dutch garb), Tulip Festival, 1996, Pella, Iowa, photograph. AP/Wide World Photos. **English; Morris Dancers** (performing), photograph. Rich Baker/Unicorn Stock Photos. **English; British pub patrons,** Marty Flicker, Steve Jones, Phil Elwell, and Alan Shadrake (at British pub "The King's Head"), photograph by Bob Galbraith. AP/Wide World Photos. **Eritreans demonstrating against Ethiopian aggression,** in front of White House, 1997-1998, Washington, D.C., photograph by Lee Snider. Corbis. **Estonian Americans** (family sitting at table peeling apples), photograph. Library of Congress/Corbis. **Estonian Americans** (group of people, eight men, three woman and one little girl), photograph. UPI/Corbis-Bettmann. **Ethiopian; Berhanu Adanne** (front left), surrounded by Ethiopian immigrants Yeneneh Adugna (back left) and Halile Bekele (right front), celebrating his win of the Bolder Boulder 10-Kilometer Race, 1999, Boulder, Colorado, photograph. AP/Wide World Photos. **Filipino Immigrants,** photograph. Photo by Gene Viernes Collection **Filipino; Lotus Festival** (Fil-Am family, holding large feather and flower fans), photograph by Tara Farrell. AP/Wide World Photos. **Finnish Americans** (proponents of socialism with their families), photograph. The Tuomi Family Photographs/Balch Institute for Ethnic Studies. **Finnish Americans** (standing in line at festival), photograph.© Gary Conner /Photo Edit. **Finnish; Three generations of Finnish Americans,** Rebecca Hoekstra (l to r), Margaret Mattila, Joanna Hoekstra, with newspaper at kitchen table), 1999, Painesville, Michigan, photograph. AP/Wide World Photos. **French Americans** (woman playing an accordian) , photograph. © Joe Sohm/Unicorn Stock Photos. **French children in parade at Cape Vincent's French Festival,** photograph. Cape Vincent Chamber of Commerce. **French; Sally Eustice** (wearing French bride costume, white lace bonnet, royal blue dress), Michilimackinac, Michigan, c.1985, photograph by Macduff Everton. Corbis. **French-Canadian farmers,** waiting for their potatoes to be weighed (by woodpile), 1940, Arostook County, Maine, photograph. Corbis. **French-Canadian farmer sitting on digger,** Caribou, Maine, 1940, photograph by Jack Delano. Corbis. **French-Canadian; Grandmother of Patrick Dumond Family** (wearing white blouse, print apron), photograph. The Library of Congress. **French-Canadian; Two young boys** (standing on road), photograph. The Library of Congress. **German immigrants** (little girl holding doll), photograph. UPI/Corbis-Bettmann. **German people dancing at Heritagefest,** photograph. Minnesota Office of Tourism. © Minnesota Office of Tourism. **German; Steuben Day Parade** (German Tricentennial Multicycle), photograph. AP/Wide World Photos. **Greek American** (girl at Greek parade), photograph. Kelly-Mooney Photography/Corbis. **Greek American altar boys** (at church, lighting candles), photograph © Audrey Gottlieb 1992. **Greek; Theo Koulianos,** (holding cross thrown in water by Greek Orthodox Archbishop), photograph by Chris O'Meara. AP/Wide World Photos. **Guamanian boy in striped shirt leaning against doorjamb,** c.1950, photograph. Corbis/Hulton-Deutsch Collection. **Guatemalan boy and girl riding on top of van** (ethnic pride parade), 1995, Chicago, Illinois, photograph by Sandy Felsenthal. Corbis. **Guatemalan girls in traditional dress,** at ethnic pride parade, 1995, Chicago, Illinois, photograph by Sandy Felsenthal. Corbis. **Guatemalan; Julio Recinos,**

(covering banana boxes), Los Angeles, California, 1998, photograph by Damian Dovargnes. AP/Wide World Photos. **Gypsies; Flamenco** (wedding party group), photograph. UPI/Corbis-Bettmann. **Gypsy woman** (performing traditional dance), photograph. © Russell Grundke/Unicorn Stock Photos. **Haitian; Edwidge Danticat,** Ixel Cervera (Danticat signing her book for Cervera), New York City, 1998, photograph by Bebeto Matthews. AP/Wide World Photos. **Haitian; Fernande Maxton with Joseph Nelian Strong** (holding photo of Aristide), photograph by Bebeto Matthews. AP/Wide World Photos. **Haitian; Sauveur St. Cyr,** (standing to the right of alter), New York City, 1998, photograph by Lynsey Addario. AP/Wide World Photos. **Hawaiian children wearing leis in Lei Day celebration, Hawaii,** 1985, photograph by Morton Beebe. Corbis. **Hawaiian group singing at luau, Milolii, Hawaii,** 1969, photograph by James L. Amos. Corbis. **Hawaiian man checking fish trap,** photograph. The Library of Congress. **Hawaiian women dancing,** Washington D.C., 1998, photograph by Khue Bui. AP/Wide World Photos. **Hmong; Vang Alben** (pointing to portion of Hmong story quilt), Fresno, California, 1998, photograph by Gary Kazanjian. AP/Wide World Photos. **Hmong; Moua Vang** (holding fringed parasol), Fresno, California, 1996, photograph by Thor Swift. AP/Wide World Photos. **Hopi dancer at El Tovar, Grand Canyon,** photograph. Corbis-Bettmann. **Hopi women's dance,** 1879, photograph by John K. Hillers. National Archives and Records Administration. **Hungarian American debutante ball,** photograph by Contessa Photography **Hungarian Americans** (man reunited with his family), photograph. Special Collections and University Archives, Rutgers University. **Hungarian refugees** (large group on ship deck), photograph. UPI/Corbis-Bettmann. **Icelanders** (five women sitting outside of Cabin), photograph. North Dakota Institute for Regional Studies and Archives/North Dakota State University. **Icelandic girl kneeling, picking cranberries,** c.1990, Half Moon Lake, Wisconsin, photograph by Tom Bean. Corbis. **Indonesian; Balinese dancer wearing white mask, gold headdress and embroidered collar,** 1980-1995, Bali, Indonesia, photograph. CORBIS/David Cumming; Ubiquitous. **Indonesian; two Balinese dancers** (in gold silk, tall headdresses, with fans), Bali, Indonesia, photograph by Dennis Degnan. Corbis. **Indonesian; Wayang Golek puppets** (with helmets, gold trimmed coats), 1970-1995, Indonesia, photograph by Sean Kielty. Corbis. **Inuit dance orchestra,** 1935, photograph by Stanley Morgan. National Archives and Records Administration. **Inuit dancer and drummers,** Nome, Alaska, c.1910, photograph. Corbis/Michael Maslan Historic Photographs. **Inuit wedding people,** posing outside of Saint Michael's Church, Saint Michael, Alaska, 1906, photograph by Huey & Laws. Corbis. **IIranian; Persian New Year celebrations,** among expatriate community (boy running through bonfire), c.1995, Sydney, Australia, photograph by Paul A. Souders. Corbis. **Irish girls performing step dancing in Boston St. Patrick's Day Parade,** 1996, photograph. AP/Wide World Photos. **Irish immigrants** (woman and nine children), photograph. UPI/Corbis-Bettmann. **Irish; Bernie Hurley,** (dressed like leprechaun, rollerblading), Denver, St. Patrick's Day Parade, 1998, photograph. AP/Wide World Photos. **Irish; Bill Pesature,** (shamrock on his forehead), photograph. AP/Wide World Photos. **Iroquois steel workers at construction site,** 1925, photograph. Corbis-Bettmann. **Iroquois tribe members,** unearthing bones of their ancestors, photograph. Corbis-Bettmann. **Israeli; "Salute to Israel" parade,** children holding up Israeli Flag, photograph by David Karp. AP/Wide World Photos. **Israeli; "Salute to Israel" parade,** Yemenite banner, New York, photograph by Richard B. Levine. Levine & Roberts Stock Photography **Italian Americans** (men walking in Italian parade), photograph. Robert Brenner/Photo Edit. **Italian immigrants** (mother and three children), photograph. Corbis-Bettmann. **Italian railway workers,** Lebanon Springs, New York, c.1900, photograph by H. M. Gillet. Corbis/Michael Maslan Histrorical Photographs. **Jamaican women playing steel drums in Labor Day parade** (wearing red, yellow drums), 1978, Brooklyn, New York, photograph by Ted Spiegel. Corbis **Jamaican; Three female Caribbean dancers at Liberty Weekend Festival** (in ruffled dresses and beaded hats), 1986, New York, photograph by Joseph Sohm. Corbis/ChromoSohm Inc. **Japanese American children,** eating special obento lunches from their lunchboxes on Children's Day, 1985, at the Japanese American Community and Cultural Center, Little Tokyo, Los Angeles, California, photograph by Michael Yamashita. Corbis. **Japanese American girl with baggage** (awaiting internment), April, 1942, photograph. National Archives and Records Administration. **Japanese American girls,** wearing traditional kimonos at a cherry blossom festival, San Francisco, California, photograph by Nik Wheeler. Corbis. **Japanese immigrants** (dressed as samurai), photograph. National Archives and Records Administration. **Jewish; Bar Mitzvah** (boy reading from the Torah), photograph. © Nathan Nourok/Photo Edit. **Jewish; Orthodox Jews** (burning hametz in preparation of Passover), photograph by Ed Bailey. AP/Wide World Photos. **Jewish; Senator Alfonse D'Amato with Jackie Mason** (at

Salute to Israel Parade), photograph. AP/Wide World Photos. **Kenyan; David Lichoro,** (wearing "God has been good to me!" T-shirt), 1998, Iowa State University, Ames, Iowa, photograph. AP/Wide World Photos. **Kenyan; Samb Aminata** (with Kenyan sculptures for sale), 24th Annual Afro American Festival, 1997, Detroit Michigan, photograph. AP/Wide World Photos. **Korean American boy,** holding Korean flag, photograph by Richard B. Levine. Levine & Roberts Stock Photography. **Korean basic alphabet,** illustration. Eastword Publications Development. The Gale Group. **Korean; signs in Koreatown, NY** (Korean signs, people in lower left corner of photo), photograph. AP/Wide World Photos. **Laotian women** (standing around Vietnam Veterans Memorial, wearing traditional Laos costumes), photograph by Mark Wilson. Archive Photos. **Laotian; Chia Hang, Pahoua Yang** (daughter holding mother's shoulders), Brooklyn Center, Minnesota, 1999, photograph by Dawn Villella. AP/Wide World Photos. **Latvian Americans** (mother, father, 11 children), photograph. UPI/Corbis-Bettmann. **Latvian; Karl Zarins,** (Latvian immigrant holding his daughter), photograph. UPI/Corbis-Bettmann. **Lebanese Americans,** demonstrating, Washington D. C., 1996, photograph by Jeff Elsayed. AP/Wide World Photos. **Liberian; Michael Rhodes,** (examining Liberian Passport Masks), at the 1999 New York International Tribal Antiques Show, Park Avenue Armory, New York, photograph. AP/Wide World Photos. **Lithuanian Americans** (family of 12, men, women and children), photograph. UPI/Corbis-Bettmann. **Lithuanian Americans** (protesting on Capitol steps), photograph. UPI/Corbis-Bettmann. **Malaysian float at Pasadena Rose Parade, Pasadena, California,** c.1990, photograph Dave G. Houser. Corbis. **Maltese Americans** (girls in Maltese parade), photograph. © Robert Brenner/Photo Edit. **Maltese immigrant woman at parade,** New York City, photograph by Richard B. Levine. Levine & Roberts Stock Photography. **Mexican Celebration of the Day of the Dead festival** (seated women, flowers, food), c.1970-1995, photograph by Charles & Josette Lenars. Corbis. **Mexican soccer fans dancing outside Washington's RFK Stadium,** photograph by Damian Dovarganes. AP/Wide World Photos. **Mongolian "throat singer," Ondar,** performing at the Telluride Bluegrass Festival, 1999, Telluride, Colorado, photograph. AP/Wide World Photos. **Mongolian wedding gown being modeled,** at the end of the showing of Mary McFadden's 1999 Fall and Winter Collection, New York, photograph. AP/Wide World Photos. **"Mormon emigrants," covered wagon caravan,** photograph by C. W. Carver. National Archives and Records Adminis-

tration. **Mormon family in front of log cabin,** 1875, photograph. Corbis-Bettmann. **Mormon Women** (tacking a quilt), photograph. The Library of Congress. **Moroccan; Lofti's Restaurant,** New York City, 1995, photograph by Ed Malitsky. Corbis. **Navajo family courtyard** (one man, one child, two women in foreground), photograph. Corbis-Bettmann. **Navajo protesters,** marched two miles to present grievances to tribal officals, photograph. AP/Wide World Photos. **Navajo protesters** (walking, three holding large banner), 1976, Arizona, photograph. AP/Wide World Photos. **Nepalese; Gelmu Sherpa rubbing "singing bowl,"** May 20, 1998, photograph by Suzanne Plunkett. AP/Wide World Photos. **Nez Perce family in a three-seated car,** 1916, photograph by Frank Palmer. The Library of Congress. **Nez Perce man in ceremonial dress** (right profile), c.1996, Idaho, photograph by Dave G. Houser. Corbis. **Nicaraguan girls in a Cinco de Mayo parade** (flower in hair, wearing peasant blouses), c.1997, New York, photograph by Catherine Karnow. Corbis. **Nicaraguan; Dennis Martinez,** (playing baseball), photograph by Tami L. Chappell. Archive Photos. **Norwegian Americans** (gathered around table, some seated and some standing), photograph. UPI/Corbis-Bettmann. **Norwegian Americans** (Leikarring Norwegian dancers), photograph. © Jeff Greenberg/Photo Edit. **Ojibwa woman and child,** lithograph. The Library of Congress. **Ojibwa woman and papoose,** color lithograph by Bowen's, 1837. The Library of Congress **Paiute drawing his bow and arrow** (two others in festive costume), 1872, photograph by John K. Hillers. National Archives and Records Administration. **Paiute woman** (grinding seeds in hut doorway), 1872, photograph by John K. Hillers. National Archives and Records Administration. **Paiute; Revival of the Ghost Dance,** being performed by women, photograph. Richard Erdoes. Reproduced by permission. **Pakistani American family in traditional dress,** photograph by Shazia Rafi. **Palestinean; Jacob Ratisi,** with brother John Ratisi (standing inside their restaurant), photograph by Mark Elias. AP/Wide World Photos. **Palestinian; Faras Warde,** (holding up leaflets and poster), Boston, Massachusetts, 1998, photograph by Kuni. AP/Wide World Photos. **Peruvian shepherd immobilizes sheep while preparing an inoculation,** 1995, Bridgeport, California, photograph by Phil Schermeister. Corbis. **Polish Americans** (woman and her three sons), photograph. UPI/Corbis-Bettmann. **Polish; Kanosky Family,** (posing for a picture), August, 1941. Reproduced by permission of Stella McDermott. **Polish; Leonard Sikorasky and Julia Wesoly,** (at Polish parade), photograph. UPI/Corbis-Bettmann. **Portuguese American** (man fishing), photograph. © 1994 Gale Zucker. **Portuguese Americans** (children in traditional Portuguese dress), photograph. © Robert Brenner/Photo Edit. **Pueblo mother with her children** (on ladder by house), Taos, New Mexico, photograph. Corbis-Bettmann. **Pueblo; Row of drummers and row of dancers,** under cloudy sky, photograph by Craig Aurness. Corbis. **Pueblo; Taos Indians performing at dance festival,** c.1969, New Mexico, photograph by Adam Woolfit. Corbis. **Puerto Rican Day Parade** (crowd of people waving flags), photograph by David A.Cantor. AP/Wide World Photos. **Puerto Rican; 20th Annual Three Kings Day Parade** (over-life-size magi figures, Puerto Rican celebration of Epiphany), 1997, El Museo del Barrio, East Harlem, New York, photograph. AP/Wide World Photos. **Puerto Rican; Puerto Rican New Progressive Party,** photograph. AP/Wide World Photos. **Romanian Priests** (leading congregation in prayer), photograph. AP/Wide World Photos. **Romanian; Regina Kohn,** (holding violin), photograph. UPI/Corbis-Bettmann. **Russian Americans** (five women sitting in wagon), photograph. UPI/Corbis-Bettmann. **Russian; Lev Vinjica,** (standing in his handicraft booth), photograph. AP/Wide World Photos. **Russian; Olesa Zaharova,** (standing in front of chalkboard, playing hangman), Gambell, Alaska, 1992, photograph by Natalie Fobes. Corbis. **Salvadoran; Ricardo Zelada,** (standing, right arm around woman, left around girl), Los Angeles, California, 1983, photograph by Nik Wheeler. Corbis. **Samoan woman playing ukulele,** sitting at base of tree, Honolulu, Oahu, Hawaii, 1960's-1990's, photograph by Ted Streshinsky. Corbis. **Samoan men, standing in front of sign reading "Talofa . . . Samoa,"** Laie, Oahu, Hawaii, 1996, photograph by Catherine Karnow. Corbis. **Scottish Americans** (bagpipers), photograph. © Tony Freeman/Photo Edit. **Scottish Americans** (girl performing Scottish sword dance), photograph. © Jim Shiopee/Unicorn Stock Photos. **Scottish; David Barron** (swinging a weight, in kilt), 25th Annual Quechee Scottish Festival, 1997, Quechee, Vermont, photograph. AP/Wide World Photos. **Serbian; Jelena Mladenovic,** (lighting candle), New York City, 1999, photograph by Lynsey Addario. AP/Wide World Photos. **Serbian; Jim Pigford,** (proof-reading newspaper pages), Pittsburgh, Pennsylvania, 1999, photograph by Gene J. Puskar. AP/Wide World Photos. **Sicilian Archbishop Iakovos** (standing in front of stage, spreading incense), photograph by Mark Cardwell. Archive Photos. **Sioux girl** (sitting, wearing long light colored fringed clothing), photograph. The Library of Congress. **Sioux Police,** (on horseback, in front of buildings), photograph. National Archives and Records Administration. **Slovak immigrant** (woman at Ellis Island), photograph. Corbis-Bettmann. **Slovenian; Bob Dole** (listening to singing group), Cleveland, Ohio, 1996, photograph by Mark Duncan. AP/Wide World Photos. **Spanish American; Isabel Arevalo** (Spanish American), photograph. Corbis-Bettmann. **Spanish; United Hispanic American Parade** (group performing in the street, playing musical instruments), photograph by Joe Comunale. AP/Wide World Photos. **Swedish; Ingrid and Astrid Sjdbeck,** (sitting on a bench), photograph. UPI/Corbis-Bettmann. **Swedish; young girl and boy in traditional Swedish clothing,** 1979, Minneapolis, Minnesota, photograph by Raymond Gehman. Corbis. **Swiss; Dr. Hans Kung,** (signing book for Scott Forsyth), 1993, Chicago, photograph. AP/Wide World Photos. **Swiss; Ida Zahler,** (arriving from Switzerland with her eleven children), photograph. UPI/Corbis-Bettmann. **Syrian children in New York City** (in rows on steps), 1908-1915, photograph. Corbis. **Syrian man with a food cart,** peddles his food to two men on the streets of New York, early 20th century, photograph. Corbis. **Syrian man selling cold drinks in the Syrian quarter,** c.1900, New York, photograph. Corbis. **"Taiwan Independence, No Chinese Empire"** Demonstration, protesters sitting on street, New York City, 1997, photograph by Adam Nadel. AP/Wide World Photos. **Thai; Christie Wong, Julie Trung, and Susan Lond** (working on float that will be in the Tournament of the Roses Parade), photograph by Fred Prouser. Archive Photos. **Tibetan Black Hat Dancers,** two men wearing identical costumes, Newark, New Jersey, 1981, photograph by Sheldan Collins. Corbis-Bettmann. **Tibetan Buddhist monk at Lollapalooza,** 1994, near Los Angeles, California, photograph by Henry Diltz. Corbis. **Tibetan; Kalachakra Initiation Dancers,** dancing, holding up right hands, Madison, Wisconsin, 1981, photograph by Sheldan Collins. Corbis. **Tibetan; Tenzin Choezam** (demonstrating outside the Chinese Consulate, "Free Tibet...,"), 1999, Houston, Texas, photograph. AP/Wide World Photos. **Tlingit girls wearing nose rings,** photograph by Miles Brothers. National Archives and Records Administration. **Tlingit mother and child,** wearing tribal regalia, Alaska/Petersburg, photograph by Jeff Greenberg. Archive Photos. **Tlingit;** attending potlach ceremony in dugout canoes, 1895, photograph by Winter & Pont. Corbis. **Tongan man at luau, adorned with leaves,** Lahaina, Hawaii, 1994, photograph by Robert Holmes. Corbis. **Trinidadian; West Indian American Day parade** (woman wearing colorful costume, dancing in the street), photograph by Carol Cleere. Archive Photos. **Turkish Parade**

(Turkish band members), photograph. AP/Wide World Photos. **Turkish; Heripsima Hovnanian,** (Turkish immigrant, with family members), photograph. UPI/Corbis-Bettmann. **Ukrainian Americans** (dance the Zaporozhian Knight's Battle), photograph. UPI/Corbis-Bettmann. **Ukrainian; Oksana Roshetsky,** (displaying Ukrainian Easter eggs), photograph. UPI/Corbis-Bettmann. **Vietnamese dance troupe** (dancing in the street), photograph by Nick Ut. AP/Wide World Photos. **Vietnamese refugee to Lo Huyhn** (with daughter, Hanh), photograph. AP/Wide World Photos. **Vietnamese; Christina Pham,** (holding large fan), photograph. AP/Wide World Photos. **Virgin Islander schoolchildren standing on school steps,** Charlotte Amalie, Virgin Island, photograph. Corbis/Hulton-Deutsch Collection. **Welsh; Tom Jones,** photograph. AP/Wide World Photos.

ADVISORY BOARD

CONTRIBUTORS

Nabeel Abraham
Professor of Anthropology
Henry Ford Community College
Dearborn, Michigan

June Granatir Alexander
Assistant Professor
Russian and East European Studies
University of Cincinnati
Cincinnati, Ohio

Donald Altschiller
Freelance writer, Cambridge, Massachusetts

Diane Andreassi
Freelance writer, Livonia, Michigan

Carl L. Bankston III
Professor, Department of Sociology
Louisiana State University
Baton Rouge, Louisiana

Diane E. Benson ('Lxeis')
Tlingit actress and writer, Eagle River, Alaska

Barbara C. Bigelow
Freelance writer, White Lake, Michigan

D. L. Birchfield
Editor and writer, Oklahoma City, Oklahoma

Herbert J. Brinks
Professor, Department of History
Calvin College
Grand Rapids, Michigan

Sean T. Buffington
Professor, Department of Ethnic Studies
University of Michigan
Ann Arbor, Michigan

Phyllis J. Burson
Independent consultant, Silver Spring, Maryland

Kimberly Burton
Freelance copyeditor, Ann Arbor, Michigan

Helen Bush Caver
Associate Professor and Librarian
Jacksonville State University
Jacksonville, Alabama

Cida S. Chase
Professor of Spanish, Oklahoma State University
Stillwater, Oklahoma

Clark Colahan
Professor of Spanish, Whitman College
Walla Walla, Washington

Robert J. Conley
Freelance writer, Tahlequah, Oklahoma

Jane Stewart Cook
Freelance writer, Green Bay, Wisconsin

Amy Cooper
Freelance writer, Ann Arbor, Michigan

Paul Cox
Dean, General Education and Honors
Brigham Young University
Provo, Utah

Ken Cuthbertson
Queen's Alumni Review
Queen's University
Kingston, Ontario, Canada

Rosetta Sharp Dean
Counselor and writer, Anniston, Alabama

Stanley E. Easton
Professor of Japanese
University of Tennessee
Chattanooga, Tennessee

Tim Eigo
Freelance writer, Phoenix, Arizona

Lucien Ellington
Freelance writer

Jessie L. Embry
Oral History Program Director
Charles Redd Center for Western Studies
Brigham Young University
Provo, Utah

Allen Englekirk
Chairperson, Modern Languages and Literature
Gonzaga University
Spokane, Washington

Marianne P. Fedunkiw
Freelance writer, Toronto, Ontario, Canada

Ellen French
Freelance writer, Murrieta, California

Mary Gillis
Freelance writer, Huntington Woods, Michigan

Edward Gobetz
Executive Director
Slovenian Research Center of America, Inc.
Willoughby Hills, Ohio

Mark A. Granquist
Assistant Professor of Religion
Saint Olaf College
Northfield, Minnesota

Derek Green
Freelance writer, Ann Arbor, Michigan

Paula Hajar
Freelance writer, New York, New York

Loretta Hall
Freelance writer, Albuquerque, New Mexico

Francesca Hampton
Freelance writer, Santa Cruz, California

Richard C. Hanes
Freelance writer, Eugene, Oregon

Sheldon Hanft
Professor, Department of History
Appalachian State University
Boone, North Carolina

James Heiberg
Freelance writer, Minneapolis, Minnesota

Karl Heil
Freelance writer, Ann Arbor, Michigan

Evan Heimlich
Assistant Coordinator, Multicultural Resource
    Center
University of Kansas
Lawrence, Kansas

Angela Washburn Heisey
Freelance writer

Mary A. Hess
Teaching Assistant, Integrated Arts and
    Humanities
Michigan State University
Lansing, Michigan

Laurie Collier Hillstrom
Freelance writer, Pleasant Ridge, Michigan

Maria Hong
Freelance writer, Austin, Texas

Edward Ifkovič
Writer and lecturer, Hartford, Connecticut

Alphine W. Jefferson
Professor, Department of History
College of Wooster
Wooster, Ohio

Charlie Jones
Librarian, Plymouth-Canton High School
Canton, Michigan

J. Sydney Jones
Freelance writer, Soquel, California

Jane Jurgens
Assistant Professor, Learning Resources Center
St. Cloud State University
St. Cloud, Minnesota

Jim Kamp
Freelance writer and editor, Royal Oak, Michigan

John Kane
Freelance writer and copyeditor, Branford,
    Connecticut

Oscar Kawagley
Assistant Professor of Education
University of Alaska
Fairbanks, Alaska

Vituat Kipal
Librarian, Slavic and Baltic Division
New York Public Library

Judson Knight
Freelance writer, Atlanta, Georgia

Paul Kobel
Freelance writer, North Tonawanda, New York

Donald B. Kraybill
Professor, Department of Sociology
Elizabethtown College
Elizabethtown, Pennsylvania

Ken Kurson
Freelance writer, New York, New York

Odd S. Lovoll
Professor of Scandinavian American Studies
Saint Olaf College
Northfield, Minnesota

Lorna Mabunda
Freelance writer, Ann Arbor, Michigan

Paul Robert Magocsi
Director and Chief Executive Officer
Multicultural History Society of Ontario
Toronto, Ontario, Canada

Marguertie Marín
Freelance writer

William Maxwell
Contributing Editor
A Gathering of the Tribes Magazine
New York, New York

Jacqueline A. McLeod
Freelance writer, East Lansing, Michigan

Mary C. Sengstock
Professor, Department of Sociology
Wayne State University
Detroit, Michigan

Elizabeth Shostak
Freelance writer, Cambridge, Massachusetts

Stefan Smagula
Freelance writer, Austin, Texas

Keith Snyder
Freelance copyeditor, Washington, DC

Jane E. Spear
Freelance writer, Canton, Ohio

Janet Stamatel
Freelance copyeditor, Detroit, Michigan

Bosiljka Stevanovič
Principal Librarian, Donnell Library Center
World Languages Collection
New York Public Library

Andris Straumanis
Freelance writer, New Brighton, Minnesota

Pamela Sturner
Freelance writer, New Haven, Connecticut

Liz Swain
Freelance writer, San Diego, California

Mark Swartz
Manuscript editor
University of Chicago Press
Chicago, Illinois

Thomas Szendrey
Freelance writer

Harold Takooshian
Professor, Division of Social Studies
Fordham University
New York, New York

Baatar Tsend
Mongolian Scholar
Indiana University
Bloomington, Indiana

Felix Eme Unaeze
Head Librarian
Reference and Instructional
    Services Department
Timme Library, Ferris State University
Big Rapids, Michigan

Steven Béla Várdy
Professor and Director, Department of History
Duquesne University
Pittsburgh, Pennsylvania

Drew Walker
Freelance writer, New York, New York

Ling-chi Wang
Professor, Asian American Studies
Department of Ethnic Studies
University of California
Berkeley, California

K. Marianne Wargelin
Freelance writer, Minneapolis, Minnesota

Ken R. Wells
Freelance writer, Aliso Viejo, California

Vladimir F. Wertsman
Chair, Publishing and Multicultural
    Materials Committee
American Library Association

Mary T. Williams
Associate Professor
Jacksonville State University
Jacksonville, Alabama

Elaine Winters
Freelance writer, Berkeley, California

Eveline Yang
Manager, Information Delivery Program
Auraria Library
Denver, Colorado

Eleanor Yu
Deputy news Editor
Courtroom Television Network
New York, New York

INTRODUCTION

RUDOLPH J. VECOLI

The term multiculturalism has recently come into usage to describe a society characterized by a diversity of cultures. Religion, language, customs, traditions, and values are some of the components of culture, but more importantly culture is the lens through which one perceives and interprets the world. When a shared culture forms the basis for a "sense of peoplehood," based on consciousness of a common past, we can speak of a group possessing an ethnicity. As employed here, ethnicity is not transmitted genetically from generation to generation; nor is it unchanging over time. Rather, ethnicity is invented or constructed in response to particular historical circumstances and changes as circumstances change. "Race," a sub-category of ethnicity, is not a biological reality but a cultural construction. While in its most intimate form an ethnic group may be based on face-to-face relationships, a politicized ethnicity mobilizes its followers far beyond the circle of personal acquaintances. Joined with aspirations for political self-determination, ethnicity can become full-blown nationalism. In this essay, ethnicity will be used to identify groups or communities that are differentiated by religious, racial, or cultural characteristics and that possess a sense of peoplehood.

The "Multicultural America" to which this encyclopedia is dedicated is the product of the mingling of many different peoples over the course of several hundred years in what is now the United States. Cultural diversity was characteristic of this continent prior to the coming of European colonists and African slaves. The indigenous inhabitants of North America who numbered an estimated 4.5 million in 1500 were divided into hundreds of tribes with distinctive cultures, languages, and religions. Although the numbers of "Indians," as they were named by Europeans, declined precipitously through the nineteenth century, their population has rebounded in the twentieth century. Both as members of their particular tribes (a form of ethnicity), Navajo, Ojibwa, Choctaw, etc., and as American Indians (a form of panethnicity), they are very much a part of today's cultural and ethnic pluralism.

Most Americans, however, are descendants of immigrants. Since the sixteenth century, from the earliest Spanish settlement at St. Augustine, Florida, the process of repeopling this continent has gone on apace. Some 600,000 Europeans and Africans were recruited or enslaved and transported across the Atlantic Ocean in the colonial period to what was to become the United States. The first census of 1790 revealed the high degree of diversity that already marked the American population. Almost 19 percent were of African ancestry, another 12 percent Scottish and Scotch-Irish, ten percent German, with smaller numbers of French, Irish, Welsh, and Sephardic Jews. The census did not include American Indians. The English, sometimes described as the "founding people," only comprised 48 percent of the total. At the time of its birth in 1776, the United States was already a "complex ethnic mosaic," with a wide variety of communities differentiated by culture, language, race, and religion.

The present United States includes not only the original 13 colonies, but lands that were subsequently purchased or conquered. Through this territorial expansion, other peoples were brought within the boundaries of the republic; these included, in addition to many Native American tribes, French, Hawaiian, Inuit, Mexican, and Puerto Rican, among others. Since 1790, population growth, other than by natural increase, has come primarily through three massive waves of immigration. During the first wave (1841-1890), almost 15 million immigrants arrived: over four million Germans, three million each of Irish and British (English, Scottish, and Welsh), and one million Scandinavians. A second wave (1891-1920) brought an additional 18 million immigrants: almost four million from Italy, 3.6 million from Austria-Hungary, and three million from Russia. In addition, over two million Canadians, Anglo and French, immigrated prior to 1920. The intervening decades, from 1920 to 1945, marked a hiatus in immigration due to restrictive policies, economic depression, and war. A modest post-World War II influx of refugees was followed by a new surge

subsequent to changes in immigration policy in 1965. Totalling approximately 16 million—and still in progress, this third wave encompassed some four million from Mexico, another four million from Central and South America and the Caribbean, and roughly six million from Asia. While almost 90 percent of the first two waves originated in Europe, only 12 percent of the third did.

Immigration has introduced an enormous diversity of cultures into American society. The 1990 U.S. Census report on ancestry provides a fascinating portrait of the complex ethnic origins of the American people. Responses to the question, "What is your ancestry or ethnic origin?," were tabulated for 215 ancestry groups. The largest ancestry groups reported were, in order of magnitude, German, Irish, English, and African American, all more than 20 million.

Other groups reporting over six million were Italian, Mexican, French, Polish, Native American, Dutch, and Scotch-Irish, while another 28 groups reported over one million each. Scanning the roster of ancestries one is struck by the plethora of smaller groups: Hmong, Maltese, Honduran, Carpatho-Rusyns, and Nigerian, among scores of others. Interestingly enough, only five percent identified themselves simply as "American"—and less than one percent as "white."

Immigration also contributed to the transformation of the religious character of the United States. Its original Protestantism (itself divided among many denominations and sects) was both reinforced by the arrival of millions of Lutherans, Methodists, Presbyterians, etc., and diluted by the heavy influx of Roman Catholics—first the Irish and Germans, then Eastern Europeans and Italians, and more recently Hispanics. These immigrants have made Roman Catholicism the largest single denomination in the country. Meanwhile, Slavic Christian and Jewish immigrants from Central and Eastern Europe established Judaism and Orthodoxy as major American religious bodies. As a consequence of Near Eastern immigration—and the conversion of many African Americans to Islam—there are currently some three million Muslims in the United States. Smaller numbers of Buddhists, Hindus, and followers of other religions have also arrived. In many American cities, houses of worship now include mosques and temples as well as churches and synagogues. Such religious pluralism is an important source of American multiculturalism.

The immigration and naturalization policies pursued by a country are a key to understanding its self-conception as a nation. By determining who to admit to residence and citizenship, the dominant element defines the future ethnic and racial composition of the population and the body politic. Each of the three great waves of immigration inspired much soul-searching and intense debate over the consequences for the republic. If the capacity of American society to absorb some 55 million immigrants over the course of a century and a half is impressive, it is also true that American history has been punctuated by ugly episodes of nativism and xenophobia. With the possible exception of the British, it is difficult to find an immigrant group that has not been subject to some degree of prejudice and discrimination. From their early encounters with Native Americans and Africans, Anglo-Americans established "whiteness" as an essential marker of difference and superiority. The Naturalization Act of 1790, for example, specified that citizenship was to be available to "any alien, being a free white person." By this provision not only were blacks ineligible for naturalization, but also future immigrants who were deemed not to be "white." The greater the likeness of immigrants to the Anglo-American type (e.g., British Protestants), the more readily they were welcomed.

Not all Anglo-Americans were racists or xenophobes. Citing Christian and democratic ideals of universal brotherhood, many advocated the abolition of slavery and the rights of freedmen—freedom of religion and cultural tolerance. Debates over immigration policy brought these contrasting views of the republic into collision. The ideal of America as an asylum for the oppressed of the world has exerted a powerful influence for a liberal reception of newcomers. Emma Lazarus's sonnet, which began "Give me your tired, your poor, your huddled masses yearning to breathe free, the wretched refuse of your teeming shore," struck a responsive chord among many Anglo-Americans. Moreover, American capitalism depended upon the rural workers of Europe, French Canada, Mexico, and Asia to man its factories and mines. Nonetheless, many Americans have regarded immigration as posing a threat to social stability, the jobs of native white workers, honest politics, and American cultural—even biological—integrity. The strength of anti-immigrant movements has waxed and waned with the volume of immigration, but even more with fluctuations in the state of the economy and society. Although the targets of nativist attacks have changed over time, a constant theme has been the danger posed by foreigners to American values and institutions.

Irish Catholics, for example, were viewed as minions of the Pope and enemies of the Protestant character of the country. A Protestant Crusade culminated with the formation of the American (or "Know-Nothing") Party in 1854, whose battle cry was "America for the Americans!" While the Know-Nothing movement was swallowed up by sectional conflict culminating in the Civil War, anti-Catholicism continued to be a powerful strain of nativism well into the twentieth century.

Despite such episodes of xenophobia, during its first century of existence, the United States welcomed all newcomers with minimal regulation. In 1882, however, two laws initiated a progressive tightening of restrictions upon immigration. The first established qualitative health and moral standards by excluding criminals, prostitutes, lunatics, idiots, and paupers. The second, the Chinese Exclusion Act, the culmination of an anti-Chinese movement centered on the West Coast, denied admission to Chinese laborers and barred Chinese immigrants from acquiring citizenship. Following the enactment of this law, agitation for exclusion of Asians continued as the Japanese and others arrived, culminating in the provision of the Immigration Law of 1924, which denied entry to aliens ineligible for citizenship (those who were not deemed "white"). It was not until 1952 that a combination of international politics and democratic idealism finally resulted in the elimination of all racial restrictions from American immigration and naturalization policies.

In the late nineteenth century, "scientific" racialism, which asserted the superiority of Anglo-Saxons, was embraced by many Americans as justification for imperialism and immigration restriction. At that time a second immigrant wave was beginning to bring peoples from eastern Europe, the Balkans, and the Mediterranean into the country. Nativists campaigned for a literacy test and other measures to restrict the entry of these "inferior races." Proponents of a liberal immigration policy defeated such efforts until World War I created a xenophobic climate which not only insured the passage of the literacy test, but prepared the way for the Immigration Acts of 1921 and 1924. Inspired by racialist ideas, these laws established national quota systems designed to drastically reduce the number of southern and eastern Europeans entering the United States and to bar Asians entirely. In essence, the statutes sought to freeze the biological and ethnic identity of the American people by protecting them from contamination from abroad.

Until 1965 the United States pursued this restrictive and racist immigration policy. The Immigration Act of 1965 did away with the national origins quota system and opened the country to immigration from throughout the world, establishing preferences for family members of American citizens and resident aliens, skilled workers, and refugees. The unforeseen consequence of the law of 1965 was the third wave of immigration. Not only did the annual volume of immigration increase steadily to the current level of one million or more arrivals each year, but the majority of the immigrants now came from Asia and Latin America. During the 1980s, they accounted for 85 percent of the total number of immigrants, with Mexicans, Chinese, Filipinos, and Koreans being the largest contingents.

The cumulative impact of an immigration of 16 plus millions since 1965 has aroused intense concerns regarding the demographic, cultural, and racial future of the American people. The skin color, languages, and lifestyles of the newcomers triggered a latent xenophobia in the American psyche. While eschewing the overt racism of earlier years, advocates of tighter restriction have warned that if current rates of immigration continue, the "minorities" (persons of African, Asian, and "Hispanic" ancestry) will make up about half of the American population by the year 2050.

A particular cause of anxiety is the number of undocumented immigrants (estimated at 200,000-300,000 per year). Contrary to popular belief, the majority of these individuals do not cross the border from Mexico, but enter the country with either student or tourist visas and simply stay—many are Europeans and Asians. The Immigration Reform and Control Act (IRCA) of 1986 sought to solve the problem by extending amnesty for undocumented immigrants under certain conditions and imposing penalties on employers who hired undocumented immigrants, while making special provisions for temporary agricultural migrant workers. Although over three million persons qualified for consideration for amnesty, employer sanctions failed for lack of effective enforcement, and the number of undocumented immigrants has not decreased. Congress subsequently enacted the Immigration Act of 1990, which established a cap of 700,000 immigrants per year, maintained preferences based on family reunification, and expanded the number of skilled workers to be admitted. Immigration, however, has continued to be a hotly debated issue. Responding to the nativist mood of the country, politicians have advocated measures to limit access of legal as well as undocumented immigrants to Medicare and other welfare benefits. A constitutional amendment was even proposed that would deny citizenship to American-born children of undocumented residents.

Forebodings about an "unprecedented immigrant invasion," however, appear exaggerated. In the early 1900s, the rate of immigration (the number of immigrants measured against the total population) was ten per every thousand; in the 1980s the rate was only 3.5 per every thousand. While the number of foreign-born individuals in the United States reached an all-time high of almost 20 million in 1990, they accounted for only eight percent of the population as compared with 14.7 per cent in 1910. In other words, the statistical impact of contemporary immigration has been of a much smaller magnitude than that of the past. A persuasive argument has also been made that immigrants, legal and undocumented, contribute more than they take from the American economy and that they pay more in taxes than they receive in social services. As in the past, immigrants are being made scapegoats for the country's problems.

Among the most difficult questions facing students of American history are: how have these tens of millions of immigrants with such differing cultures incorporated into American society?; and what changes have they wrought in the character of that society? The concepts of acculturation and assimilation are helpful in understanding the processes whereby immigrants have adapted to the new society. Applying Milton Gordon's theory, acculturation is the process whereby newcomers assume American cultural attributes, such as the English language, manners, and values, while assimilation is the process of their incorporation into the social networks (work, residence, leisure, families) of the host society. These changes have not come quickly or easily. Many immigrants have experienced only limited acculturation and practically no assimilation during their lifetimes. Among the factors that have affected these processes are race, ethnicity, class, gender, and character of settlement.

The most important factor, however, has been the willingness of the dominant ethnic group (Anglo-Americans) to accept the foreigners. Since they have wielded political and social power, Anglo-Americans have been able to decide who to include and who to exclude. Race (essentially skin color) has been the major barrier to acceptance; thus Asians and Mexicans, as well as African Americans and Native Americans, have in the past been excluded from full integration into the mainstream. At various times, religion, language, and nationality have constituted impediments to incorporation. Social class has also strongly affected interactions among various ethnic groups. Historically, American society has been highly stratified with a close congruence between class and ethnicity, i.e., Anglo-Americans tend to belong to the upper class, northern and western Europeans to the middle class, and southern and eastern Europeans and African Americans to the working class. The metaphor of a "vertical mosaic" has utility in conceptualizing American society. A high degree of segregation (residential, occupational, leisure) within the vertical mosaic has severely limited acculturation and assimilation across class and ethnic lines. However, within a particular social class, various immigrant groups have often interacted at work, in neighborhoods, at churches and saloons, and in the process have engaged in what one historian has described as "Americanization from the bottom UP."

Gender has also been a factor since the status of women within the general American society, as well as within their particular ethnic groups, has affected their assimilative and acculturative experiences. Wide variations exist among groups as to the degree to which women are restricted to traditional roles or have freedom to pursue opportunities in the larger society. The density and location of immigrant settlements have also influenced the rate and character of incorporation into the mainstream culture. Concentrated urban settlements and isolated rural settlements, by limiting contacts between the immigrants and others, tend to inhibit the processes of acculturation and assimilation.

An independent variable in these processes, however, is the determination of immigrants themselves whether or not to shed their cultures and become simply Americans. By and large, they are not willing or able to do so. Rather, they cling, often tenaciously, to their old world traditions, languages, and beliefs. Through chain migrations, relatives and friends have regrouped in cities, towns, and the countryside for mutual assistance and to maintain their customary ways. Establishing churches, societies, newspapers, and other institutions, they have built communities and have developed an enlarged sense of peoplehood. Thus, ethnicity (although related to nationalist movements in countries of origin) in large part has emerged from the immigrants' attempt to cope with life in this pluralist society. While they cannot transplant their Old Country ways intact to the Dakota prairie or the Chicago slums, theirs is a selective adaptation, in which they have taken from American culture that which they needed and have kept from their traditional culture that which they valued. Rather than becoming Anglo-Americans, they became ethnic Americans of various kinds.

Assimilation and acculturation have progressed over the course of several generations. The children and grandchildren of immigrants have retained less of their ancestral cultures (languages are first to go; customs and traditions often follow) and have assumed more mainstream attributes. Yet many have retained, to a greater or lesser degree, a sense of identity and affiliation with a particular ethnic group. Conceived of not as a finite culture

brought over in immigrant trunks, but as a mode of accommodation to the dominant culture, ethnicity persists even when the cultural content changes.

We might also ask to what have the descendants been assimilating and acculturating. Some have argued that there is an American core culture, essentially British in origin, in which immigrants and their offspring are absorbed. However, if one compares the "mainstream culture" of Americans today (music, food, literature, mass media) with that of one or two centuries ago, it is obvious that it is not Anglo-American (even the American English language has undergone enormous changes from British English). Rather, mainstream culture embodies and reflects the spectrum of immigrant and indigenous ethnic cultures that make up American society. It is the product of syncretism, the melding of different, sometimes contradictory and discordant elements. Multiculturalism is not a museum of immigrant cultures, but rather this complex of the living, vibrant ethnicities of contemporary America.

If Americans share an ideological heritage deriving from the ideals of the American Revolution, such ideals have not been merely abstract principles handed down unchanged from the eighteenth century to the present. Immigrant and indigenous ethnic groups, taking these ideals at face value, have employed them as weapons to combat ethnic and racial prejudice and economic exploitation. If America was the Promised Land, for many the promise was realized only after prolonged and collective struggles. Through labor and civil rights movements, they have contributed to keeping alive and enlarging the ideals of justice, freedom, and equality. If America transformed the immigrants and indigenous ethnic groups, they have also transformed America.

How have Americans conceived of this polyglot, kaleidoscopic society? Over the centuries, several models of a social order, comprised of a variety of ethnic and racial groups, have competed for dominance. An early form was a society based on caste—a society divided into those who were free and those who were not free. Such a social order existed in the South for two hundred years. While the Civil War destroyed slavery, the Jim Crow system of racial segregation maintained a caste system for another hundred years. But the caste model was not limited to black-white relations in the southern states. Industrial capitalism also created a caste-like structure in the North. For a century prior to the New Deal, power, wealth, and status were concentrated in the hands of an Anglo-American elite, while the workers, comprised largely of immigrants and their children, were the helots of the farms and the factories.

The caste model collapsed in both the North and the South in the twentieth century before the onslaught of economic expansion, technological change, and geographic and social mobility.

Anglo-conformity has been a favored model through much of our history. Convinced of their cultural and even biological superiority, Anglo-Americans have demanded that Native Americans, African Americans, and immigrants abandon their distinctive linguistic, cultural, and religious traits and conform (in so far as they are capable) to the Anglo model. But at the same time that they demanded conformity to their values and lifestyles, Anglo-Americans erected barriers that severely limited social intercourse with those they regarded as inferior. The ideology of Anglo-conformity has particularly influenced educational policies. A prime objective of the American public school system has been the assimilation of "alien" children to Anglo-American middle class values and behaviors. In recent years, Anglo-conformity has taken the form of opposition to bilingual education. A vigorous campaign has been waged for a constitutional amendment that would make English the official language of the United States.

A competing model, the Melting Pot, symbolized the process whereby the foreign elements were to be transmuted into a new American race. There have been many variants of this ideology of assimilation, including one in which the Anglo-American is the cook stirring and determining the ingredients, but the prevailing concept has been that a distinctive amalgam of all the varied cultures and peoples would emerge from the crucible. Expressing confidence in the capacity of America to assimilate all newcomers, the Melting Pot ideology provided the rationale for a liberal immigration policy. Although the Melting Pot ideology came under sharp attack in the 1960s as a coercive policy of assimilation, the increased immigration of recent years and the related anxiety over national unity has brought it back into favor in certain academic and political circles.

In response to pressures for 100 percent Americanization during World War I, the model of Cultural Pluralism has been offered as an alternative to the Melting Pot. In this model, while sharing a common American citizenship and loyalty, ethnic groups would maintain and foster their particular languages and cultures. The metaphors employed for the cultural pluralism model have included a symphony orchestra, a flower garden, a mosaic, and a stew or salad. All suggest a reconciliation of diversity with an encompassing harmony and coherence. The fortunes of the Pluralist model have fluctuated with the national mood. During the 1930s, when cultural democracy was in vogue, pluralist ideas were popular. Again during the period of the "new ethnicity" of the 1960s and the 1970s, cultural pluralism attracted a considerable following. In recent years, heightened fears that American society was fragmenting caused many to reject pluralism for a return to the Melting Pot.

As the United States enters the twenty-first century its future as an ethnically plural society is hotly contested. Is the United States more diverse today than in the past? Is the unity of society threatened by its diversity? Are the centrifugal forces in American society more powerful than the centripetal? The old models of Angloconformity, the Melting Pot, and Cultural Pluralism have lost their explanatory and symbolic value. We need a new model, a new definition of our identity as a people, which will encompass our expanding multiculturalism and which will define us as a multiethnic people in the context of a multiethnic world. We need a compelling paradigm that will command the faith of all Americans because it embraces them in their many splendored diversity within a just society.

SUGGESTED READINGS

On acculturation and assimilation, Milton Gordon's *Assimilation in American Life: The Role of Race, Religion, and National Origins* (1964) provides a useful theoretical framework. For a discussion of the concept of ethnicity, see Kathleen Neils Conzen, et al. "The Invention of Ethnicity: A Perspective from the USA," *Journal of American Ethnic History*, 12 (Fall 1992). *Harvard Encyclopedia of American Ethnic Groups*, edited by Stephan Thernstrorn (Cambridge, MA, 1980) is a standard reference work with articles on themes as well as specific groups; see especially the essay by Philip Gleason, "American Identity and Americanization." Roger Daniels's *Coming to America: A History of Immigration and Ethnicity in American Life* (New York, 1991) is the most comprehensive and up-to-date history. For a comparative history of ethnic groups see Ronald Takaki's *A Different Mirror: A History of Multicultural America* (1993). On post-1965 immigration, David Reimers's *Still the Golden Door: The Third World Comes to America* (1985), is an excellent overview. A classic work on nativism is John Higham's, *Strangers in the Land: Patterns of American Nativism: 1860-1925* (1963), but see also David H. Bennett's *The Party of Fear: From Nativist Movements to the New Right in American History* (1988). On the Anglo-American elite see E. Digby Baltzell's *The Protestant Establishment: Aristocracy and Caste in America* (1964).

ONEIDAS

by

Angela Washburn Heisey
and Richard C. Hanes

Throughout much of the twentieth century the Oneidas of New York and Wisconsin lobbied the federal government and fought legal battles to regain land lost in previous centuries and to prevent further loss of land through land allotment and assimilationist policies.

OVERVIEW

The name Oneida (oh-NI-duh), or Onyotaa:ka, as they call themselves, means "people of the stone set up." The Oneida language belongs to the Iroquoian language family, which also includes the Mohawk, Onondaga, Cayuga, and Seneca tongues. The tribes formed a confederacy centuries ago known as the Five Nations, or Ho'da'sho'ne, "People of the Long House." Each group lived in a distinct territory, with the Mohawk residing east of the Oneidas and the other three residing to the west. The confederacy became The Six Nations when the Oneidas granted shelter and later admission into the League of the linguistically and culturally related Tuscaroras. The Tuscaroras were fleeing north from war in the Carolinas in 1722. The Oneidas were once a strong and flourishing traditional native society living in what is now in modern-day central New York State, and their territory stretched from the St. Lawrence River in the north southward to the border of what is now Pennsylvania. During the seventeenth and eighteenth centuries, the Oneidas suffered significant population losses from smallpox epidemics and warfare over fur trade territories. In 1677, the Oneida population was estimated at only about 1,000. The population has rebounded to more than 11,300 Oneidas in the 1990s. Many reside in the United States, living on Oneida reservations in Wisconsin and New York, and while another 600 live in Ontario, Canada.

HISTORY

European contact with the Oneida people, who traditionally lived in a single principal village, occurred early in the seventeenth century, possibly as early as 1616. The Oneidas became fur traders to obtain European goods, which led to the abandonment and loss of many of their old skills. Jack Campisi in the *Handbook of North American Indians* reported that by 1640 two trade networks competed, one made up of the Algonquin, Huron, and French, and the other consisting of the Oneidas, Dutch, and English. These two trade networks warred up until the beginning of the eighteenth century.

During the American Revolutionary War, the Oneidas fought with the Continental army against the British and supplied George Washington's starving army with hundreds of bushels of corn during the winter of 1777–1778 at Valley Forge. Their alliance with the Americans did not bode well for their relationships with other Iroquois tribes who were sympathetic to the British. For that reason, many Iroquois moved to Canada following the war. However, in payment for their assistance, the Treaty of Fort Stanwix in 1784 offered the Oneidas a guarantee of their claim to their traditional lands. The treaty between the U.S. Continental Congress and the Oneida Nation provided that the Oneidas "shall be secure in the possession of the lands on which they are settled." This guarantee was again stated in the 1789 Treaty of Fort Harmar. However, between these two treaties, the state of New York forced tribal land cessions via the 1785 Treaty at Fort Herkimer and 1788 Treaty of Fort Schuyler. Through these two treaties, the Oneidas lost most of their ancestral lands, reducing the Oneida territory from the more than six million original acres to about 300,000 acres. In 1790, the U.S. Congress passed the Indian Trade and Non-Intercourse Act, forbidding purchases of Indian land without prior federal consent. In 1794, the Treaty of Canandaigua and the Veterans' Treaty were signed to protect the then-present boundaries of the occupied Oneida lands. Nevertheless, the state of New York continued to ignore federal efforts to protect the Indian lands. State and local governments imposed a total of 26 treaties (all later ruled illegal) and the Oneida territory was further reduced to only a few hundred acres.

In 1822, Chief Shenandoah of the Oneidas purchased rights from the Menominee in the Wisconsin Territory to settle on their lands. Between 1823 and 1838, close to 700 Oneidas relocated to a four-million-acre tract in Wisconsin, which President James Monroe soon reduced to half a million acres. Then, in 1838, according to Jack Campisi, the Treaty of Buffalo Creek directed the removal of all Iroquois from New York State while the Wisconsin land base was further decreasing to only 65,000 acres near Green Bay. In reaction, more than two hundred Oneidas sold their New York land in 1839 and jointly purchased 5,200 acres near London, Ontario. During the early 1840s, more than 400 Oneidas moved north into Ontario, reuniting with members of the Iroquois League who earlier had fled their traditional New York lands. Only about 200 Oneidas were left in New York. Some settled around the town of Oneida, while many moved onto the Onondaga reservation near Syracuse.

MODERN ERA

Throughout much of the twentieth century, the Oneidas of New York and Wisconsin lobbied the federal government and fought legal battles to regain land lost in previous centuries and to prevent further loss of land through land allotment and assimilationist policies. A significant blow to long-term tribal prosperity in Wisconsin was the allotment of reservation lands under authority of the General Allotment Act of 1887. By 1908, the entire reservation had been divided up among individual tribal members. Those over 18 years of age received 40 acres of land each; those under 18, 26 acres. Often the parcels of individual tribal families were not adjoining, further hampering farming efforts. Because the new tax burdens were too heavy, by the mid-1920s, most lands had passed out of tribal ownership through foreclosures, and only a few hundred acres remained. The tribal government ceased operation, and many Oneidas moved to urban areas for wage employment in factories. The federal government repurchased some of the lost lands after the tribe formed a new government in the 1930s. By the 1970s, the Wisconsin Oneidas owned 2,200 acres in scattered panels, interspersed with non-Indian ownership.

Following World War II, the United States adopted an Indian "termination," or assimilationist, policy. Proponents of the policy rationalized this scheme of taking tribal lands and eliminating government services as a way to forcibly assimilate Oneidas into mainstream American society. Despite prior internal political divisions, the Oneidas of Wisconsin united in the effort to resist the federal government's attempts to sell off what tribal lands they still held. Wisconsin Oneida leaders such as Dennison Hill, Irene Moore, Charles A. Hill, Mamie Smith, Oscar Archiquette, and Morris Wheelock united to battle against termination legislation of the late 1940s and early 1950s. The Oneidas also struggled to preserve the terms of the 1794 Canandaigua Treaty, which called for a government annuity to the Oneidas. The U.S. government attempted to pay it off in a lump sum. By 1956, government pressures began to lessen, and the threat passed. Two buildings in Oneida, Wisconsin, are named for two of the key figures of this period in Oneida land claims history: Irene Moore and Oscar Archiquette.

In 1974, and again in 1985, the U.S. Supreme Court ruled that the 1790 Non-Intercourse Act negated the earlier treaties between the Oneidas and New York state. The 1985 decision known as *County of Oneida v. Oneida Indian Nation* ruled that the 270,000 acres of Oneida lands that were transferred more than 175 years earlier had violated the Indian Non-Intercourse Act. In a landmark decision in American Indian law, the court's opinion found no applicable statute of limitations and no legal basis to deny the Oneidas' land claim. The Court had found that the Oneidas held a right to a large amount of land in central New York State in Oneida and Madison Counties. The case established an important legal precedent that potentially applies to all pending and future eastern Indian land claims.

Taking their case before the federal courts brought together the three separate groups of Oneidas. Beginning in 1987, the Oneidas and the state of New York attempted to negotiate a settlement following the Court decision, but with no success. Finally, in 1998, the Oneida Indian Nation, the Oneida tribe of Wisconsin, and the Oneida band of the Thames of Ontario filed a lawsuit against the state in an effort to end the case. To assert their right to repossess the lands illegally taken two centuries before, the suit named the thousands of landowners in the contested region as defendants. The U.S. government joined the suit on behalf of the tribes in late 1998. With the case still pending at the end of the twentieth century, the Oneidas in New York continued a policy of reacquiring lands as they became available on the open market. Their initial purchase was 42 acres of land near the city of Oneida.

SETTLEMENT PATTERNS

The Oneidas today comprise three separately recognized groups, the Oneida Indian Nation of New York, the Oneida tribe of Wisconsin, and the Oneida Band of the Thames of Ontario, Canada. Each of the three groups has its own government independent of the others. By 1990 approximately 700 Oneidas lived on the 32-acre reservation in central New York, with a total tribal enrollment in the Oneida Nation of New York of 1,543. In Wisconsin more than 4,800 Oneidas lived on a 2,200-acre reservation, and overall tribal enrollment in the Oneida tribe of Wisconsin was more than 10,000. The Ontario branch had approximately 4,000 members. The settlement pattern of the Oneidas in Wisconsin was largely based on religion. In eight small communities, the Anglicans settled on the northern portion of the reserve and Methodists to the south.

ACCULTURATION AND ASSIMILATION

TRADITIONS, CUSTOMS, AND BELIEFS

Through all of their moves and changes in economy, the Oneida were able to preserve certain traditions while others faded from use. The Iroquois traditionally lived in longhouses, impressively striking in appearance. According to William M. Fenton, a longhouse typically held from six to ten nuclear families, each of about five or six persons, and two families shared every fire. The size of the longhouses depended on the number of families they sheltered, but each was about 25 feet wide, and the average length was about 80 feet. For each fire, a two-apartment section added about 25 feet to the length of the longhouse. These apartment sections had low flat platforms walled off at both ends by a partition and open in the center, where a fire was shared with the opposite apartment. Food and personal items were stored on long shelves above the platforms, dried food and corn were stored in large bark bins between apartments, and firewood was stacked near the end doors.

Today the Oneida Nation of New York manages a housing program designed to eventually provide single-family homes on aboriginal lands for all the members who want them. Since September of 1994, single-family houses have been built ranging from two to four bedrooms, in addition to duplexes for tribal elders at the Village of the White Pines.

The Oneidas are a matrilineal society, and clan membership follows the mother's family line; however, the Wisconsin Oneida also trace patrilineal descent. Three clans compose Oneida society: the Turtle Clan, the Wolf Clan, and the Bear Clan. The Turtle teaches patience and endurance and represents strength and solidarity; he is old, wise, and well-respected. The Wolf demonstrates keen observation skills in listening and watching and illustrates strong sense of family. The Bear exemplifies gentleness and strength, displaying discipline and control. The Oneida culture also views the eagle as a protector, possessing great vision to watch over all the nations and warn them of danger. The Tree of Peace, a great white pine, is believed by the Iroquois to have been planted by the Peacemaker, who originally inspired the formation of the Iroquois Confederacy centuries before. The roots of this great tree spread out in all four directions, and all the weapons of the Iroquois nations were buried there to create an everlasting peace.

The gift of a *wampum* belt traditionally accompanied a message of truth, importance, and great significance. A wampum of dark color signaled a serious purpose, sadness, or perhaps great political importance. The Two Row Wampum symbolizes the agreement and conditions under which the Iroquois welcomed the Europeans to this land. Its message: "You say that you are our Father and I am your son. We say, We will not be like father and son, but like Brothers. This wampum belt confirms our words. These two rows will symbolize two paths or two vessels, traveling down the same river side by side. One, a birch bark canoe, for the Indian People, their laws, their customs and their ways. We shall each travel the river together, side by side, but each foot in our own boat. Neither of us will make compulsory laws or interfere in the internal affairs of the other. Neither of us will try to steer the other's vessel."

In 1975, Northeast Wisconsin In-school Telecommunications at the University of Wisconsin at Green Bay produced *Forest Spirits*, a series of seven half-hour programs concerning various aspects of Oneida and Menominee cultural heritage.

TRADITIONAL FOODS

The interplanting of corn, pole beans, and squash, referred to as the "Three Sisters," was a key characteristic of Oneida and other Iroquois horticultural practices. The pole beans grew up the corn stalks, providing cover for the squash. Bacteria colonies on the bean roots capture nitrogen for the special needs of the corn. The Three Sisters were central to the spiritual well-being of the Oneidas, protected by Three Sister spirits. Considered special gifts, the three were grown and eaten together, and celebrated together in thanksgiving traditions. The Oneidas also grew some of their own tobacco for ceremonial smoking.

MUSIC

Percussion instruments were predominant in traditional music, which involved narrow melodic lines. Traditional musical instruments included rattles, which were prominent in ceremonies. Some were made from snapping turtles or hickory bark used for the Feather Dance. More commonly, cowhorn rattles with wooden handles and water drums were used. Rasps were another commonly used traditional instrument in dances.

TRADITIONAL DRESS

Buckskin clothing, simple in design, was the traditional dress. Women wore a skirt and jacket, men a loincloth with leggings and shirts for cooler weather. Both wore moccasins, sometimes made from cornhusks. Clothing was at times decorated with paint or porcupine-quill embroidery. By the eighteenth century, many Iroquois had adapted European fabrics to their dress. The most common traditional dress of the Iroquois was the women's ribbon dress. Shorter ribbon shirts were worn by men, which were stitched out of printed fabrics and decorated with ribbons, across the upper chest and back, hanging loosely down the front. The Oneida ribbon shirt has become a Pan-Indian garment, worn particularly at pow-wows and other gatherings.

The *kostoweh* is the traditional Iroquois headdress. Made from an ash splint frame, it is decorated with turkey feathers. Deer horns are mounted on top of a kostoweh worn by a leader.

The Oneidas also did a lot of beadwork. In the late nineteenth and early twentieth centuries, Oneida women earned a good income by selling beadwork to non-natives at tourist centers. They began to make floral designs with their glass beads and applied these new shapes to many useful things, including pincushions, handbags, sewing cases, and clothing. Oneidas traditionally consider bead working a special gift to share and use often. Bead working, it is believed, came from the Creator to teach patience and humility.

DANCES AND SONGS

It was believed that ceremonial singing or dancing increased an individual's power. Medicine societies related to healing are prominent in the culture. Traditional dances include the Fish Dance, Women's Dance, and various stomp dances. A Personal Chant form of song, used more recently for thanksgiving, is reminiscent of warrior death songs of the past. The Condolence ceremony, for installing new leaders or for mourning, is also maintained. The Wisconsin Oneida hold the Oneida Powwow annually in July.

HEALTH ISSUES

Jack Campisi reported two Oneida medicine societies, the False Face and Little Water. To become part of one of these societies an individual either had to be cured one of the societies or had to have dreamed of becoming a part of it. Dreaming was a large part of healing for the Oneidas; an ability to dream and know the future commanded respect. Dreamers were often asked and consulted on different cures for specific ailments. Some belief also existed in different types of witchcraft and magic potions for healing. The Wisconsin Oneida are now served by the Oneida Community Health Center. With revenues from Turning Stone Casino Resort, the New York Oneidas have established a Health Services Department, which treats all Native Americans from a six-county region in central New York State. A wide range of services and preventive care programs are offered.

LANGUAGE

According to the Summer Institute of Linguistics, a linguistics forum of Wycliff Translators, in 1977, only 250 speakers of Oneidas remained out of a total population of 7,000. The native speakers included members of all three branches, the Oneidas of central New York, eastern Wisconsin, and Ontario. An Iroquoian language, Oneida is most closely related to Mohawk.

The Oneida people consider their language as one of their most precious traditions. Language programs among Oneida communities foster the passing of the language to young people by older members. The Oneidas have produced audio tapes, CD-ROMs, and booklets to teach the traditional language. The dream of many Oneidas is that one day most members will be able to speak the language fluently.

GREETINGS AND COMMON TERMS

Common Oneida and Iroquoian expressions include: *i-kê* —I am walking; *ikkehe*—I see it; *o-nyohsa* —squash; *oga-oh*—it tastes good; *kalo-ya* —sky or heaven; *ganoonyok*—thanksgiving speech; *onéo*—corn; *o'gyo-dyo-h*—It is snowing; *agatho-de*—I hear it; and, *o-ge-k*—I ate it.

FAMILY AND COMMUNITY DYNAMICS

EDUCATION

Like many Native American groups in the late twentieth century, the Oneidas use educational programs as a primary means of maintaining or restoring traditional tribal customs. Gaming revenues in Wisconsin and New York provide substantial fund-ing to support educational initiatives. In the late 1990s, the New York Oneidas established the goal for lifelong learning as a key to continued economic prosperity. Beginning with the Early Learning Center for young children, programs are available for tribal members throughout their lives, including educational programs as part of elders' services. Oneida culture and language are key aspects of the education offered, particularly for the youth programs. The Oneida Education Department sponsors programs for students and adults, including college and career counseling. In a unique partnership with the State University of New York at Morrisville, a degree program in casino management is offered to train future leaders of the Oneida resort. The old tribal bingo hall, replaced by Turning Stone Casino Resort, has been converted into an Educational Resource Center, housing a tribal library, language facility, career resource center, and an adult learning center. In Wisconsin, the Oneida Tribal School (for kindergarten through eighth grade), located in the town of Oneida, is operated under direction of the U.S. Bureau of Indian Affairs (BIA).

"There is a matriarchal tradition at Oneida. Women are prominent. One of our first tribal chairpersons in the 1940s was a woman..."

Roberta Hill Whiteman, (from an interview on July 29, 1991).

THE ROLE OF WOMEN

Oneida women primarily planted and gathered various plant species, while men cleared forests, constructed houses, hunted, or fought. The women gathered strawberries, huckleberries, blackberries, raspberries, greens, hickory nuts, walnuts, beechnuts, chestnuts, acorns, roots, skunk cabbage, poke, milkweed, and other edibles. Many berries were dried and packed for winter, and several of the nuts were used for their oils as well as for food. Women also gathered firewood and prepared skins and made clothing. A thin cornmeal soup was frequently made, to which pieces of meat, fish, or other foods could be added.

FUNERALS

The Condolence ceremony for mourning is an important event in Iroquois society and is influenced by the Hurons' Feast of the Dead. At its height, the Feast of the Dead was held once a decade and involved a ten-day feast. Traditionally, the dead were removed from individual graves and reburied at a common location. Much of the time was spent preparing the corpses for their final placement. Presents brought by friends of the dead were redistributed among those in attendance. Taboos forbade the use of the deceased's name too soon for naming new family members. The modern Feast of the Dead is much less complex.

The Condolence ceremony focuses on deceased leaders and raising up their successors. The ceremony is still practiced where hereditary leaders still persist, such as the Oneidas of the Thames. In the late twentieth century, the ceremony lasts from early afternoon into the evening. A set of rites is performed, including the Condoling Song, which consisted of a hymn of farewell composed of six or more verses. The song is often followed by the Requickening Address, symbolic for restoring life. Most of the ceremony is conducted in a longhouse.

INTERACTIONS WITH OTHER TRIBES

The Oneidas are members of the Iroquois Confederacy, also known as the League of the *Haudenosaunee*, or Six Nations. The other nations include the Mohawk, Onondaga, Cayuga, Seneca, and Tuscarora. The confederacy acts through a combined legislative body, the Grand Council. The confederacy was formed centuries ago at the urging of an influential Native American, Peacemaker, who encouraged the union after a vision showing it to be the way to be secure from future threats. The nations also shared a common traditional religion known as the Longhouse Religion, introduced by Seneca prophet Handsome Lake, who died in 1815.

RELIGION

The Oneidas have been influenced by many different religious traditions. At the dawn of the nineteenth century, Handsome Lake, an Iroquoian prophet, experienced visions that formed the basis of what became the Longhouse religion. This monotheistic Native American religion was strongly based on a Christian model, with some ancestral ceremonies included. The Christian influence in the Longhouse religion came from years of contact with neighboring Quakers, Catholics, and Protestants. According to Anthony F. C. Wallace in the *Handbook of North American Indians,* Handsome Lake's visions were put into a moral code, which outlawed drunkenness, gambling, quarreling, sexual promiscuity, wife-beating, and witchcraft. Although Handsome Lake did not directly come to the Oneidas, some Wisconsin and Canadian Oneidas became believers. The prophet had more visions and kept advising the Iroquois, including on the continuation of celebrating the traditional Oneida religious ceremonies.

The Oneidas were also influenced strongly by Presbyterian minister Samuel Kirkland. The minister established a church among the Oneidas and lived with the tribe for more than 40 years, until his death in 1808. French entrepreneur Pierre Penet established a Catholic mission among the Oneidas. However, the governor of New York removed Penet and the Catholic mission shortly after.

Although many Wisconsin Oneidas have been members of Episcopal and Methodist churches throughout the twentieth century, others continue to adhere to the Longhouse Religion of Handsome Lake.

EMPLOYMENT AND ECONOMIC TRADITIONS

The traditional economy of the Oneidas included the cultivation of corn, beans, and squash; an extensive hunting territory; fishing stations on Oneida Lake; and the collection of various wild plants such as berries. The Oneidas seasonally hunted deer, bear, and nearly all small mammals, usually using a bow and arrow. They also utilized two kinds of traps, the deadfall and the twitch-up snare. The Iroquoian diet varied enormously, including every kind of mammal, fish, bird, or reptile. After the harvest, hunting parties with all the men and some women left the villages, set up camp, and hunted for days, drying and packing the meat for the upcoming winter.

The American Revolutionary War disrupted the Oneidas' existing economy significantly. Afterwards, communities and fields needed restoration. A massive influx of non-Indians onto Oneida lands also followed the war. Through a series of treaties and agreements, the tribal lands of the Oneidas of New York were reduced to a 32-acre parcel by the end of the nineteenth century. The Oneidas suffered from lack of improvements such as water and septic systems, unpaved narrow roads, and rundown housing.

After passage of the Indian Gaming Act of 1988, the Oneidas of Wisconsin opened a 2,000-slot-machine gambling complex outside Green Bay. They established the Oneida Nation Electronics (ONE) Corporation to manage the facility's electronics systems. The gaming income provided capital for other long-term business ventures. In 1997, the tribe through ONE signed an agreement with Plexus, an electronics manufacturing company, to build a $22 million plant on reservation lands. The plant was to be owned and financed by the Oneidas but operated by Plexus, with the profits shared. The Wisconsin Oneidas have already invested and managed an industrial park, printing company, a bank, hotel, and convenience stores on the reservation. The tribal government uses casino revenues to provide services to Oneida members, such as subsidized housing, health care, and student counseling. Valuing the education of its children, the tribe invested monies in building a day care facility and an elementary school in the shape of a turtle, namesake of an Oneida clan and a familiar character of Oneida oral literature. The tribe has also invested heavily in reviving its culture and language among its youth, through activities such as the creation of a new written form of the Oneida language and the production of a CD-ROM featuring oral literature told by Oneida elders.

In July 1993, the Oneida Indian Nation of New York opened the Turning Stone Casino, which employs nearly 2,000 people. The casino and resort is billed as a world-class tourist destination. It is the only legal casino in New York State. The resort includes a 285-room luxury hotel, five restaurants, several retail establishments known as the Shoppes At Turning Stone, and a recreational park. The addition of a golf course and convention center was planned. In 1998, the resort accommodated well over three million visitors. The resort has been credited with the stimulation of substantial economic growth in central New York.

Through the years the Oneidas have maintained a tenuous relationship with the U.S. government. One issue of continued conflict has been the obligation of the federal government to provide social services to the Oneidas, despite their very small land base. The resort enabled the Oneidas to begin providing long-overdue social programs for their people. Today, the Oneida Nation currently offers numerous programs to its members, including a housing project, Nation Elders' Program, health care, education scholarships and incentive programs, heating assistance, youth programs, and a job network to help members gain employment. The Elders' Program provides rides for elders to the Oneida Nation cookhouse for a luncheon three days a week as well as for museum visits, shopping excursions, and places to visit overnight. The Oneida Nation acquired several businesses in the 1990s, including a textile factory, a recreational vehicle park with a convenience and gift store, a newly built gas station, and a smoke shop. Oneida leaders sought diversity in their business interests as a means to maintain a healthy economy on the reservation, even if casino benefits were to wane or cease altogether. The nation created almost 3,000 jobs directly and claims to have stimulated the creation of another 2,000 jobs in the region. The nation's local payroll in 1998 was more than $82 million. In lieu of paying local taxes due to their sovereign status, the Oneidas provide hundreds of thousands of dollars in grants to local school districts and municipalities.

The pace of economic recovery for the New York Oneidas was staggering. Through the 1990s, the Oneida Indian Nation of New York progressed from employing only a handful of people in two businesses to becoming the largest employer in the Oneida and Madison counties of central New York. The Oneidas became a major tourism promoter for the region. In fact, the economic picture for the Oneidas in New York improved so significantly that the tribe requested the Bureau of Indian Affairs to allocate certain funds earmarked for services for their tribe to other more needy tribes in 1998 and 1999. By the late 1990s, the tribe was providing more than 60 programs and services for tribal members, including a new housing program, a child learning center, elder-care programs, community and development centers, and educational scholarship programs.

When the Oneidas of the Thames moved to Canada in the 1840s to the newly purchased reserve, they were allowed to claim as many acres as they could feasibly clear and farm. Several small communities grew up on the reserve. Through the nineteenth century, subsistence farming was the primary economic pursuit of the tribe, augmented by seasonal lumbering employment. By the twentieth century, however, farming had waned, and members sought wage-labor jobs in white communities. Less fortunate economically than the Oneidas in New York and Wisconsin, the Ontario group still relies on governmental support for basic services.

POLITICS AND GOVERNMENT

Forms of government vary considerably among the three Oneida branches. The Oneidas in Ontario, Canada, instituted a traditional form of government upon their arrival in the 1840s. A tribal council was established on the basis of the three traditional Oneida clans, Wolf, Bear, and Turtle. Each appointed a sachem and deputy to the tribal council. The council was coordinated with the Iroquois council at Six Nations Reserve in Canada. The Ontario Oneidas maintained this traditional system of hereditary leadership until 1934, when considerable internal tribal factionalism consumed the tribe, and the Canadian government imposed an elective form of government to resolve ongoing internal tribal conflict. The Ontario band became governed by a tribal leader and 12 council members elected at-large for two-year terms. The government manages tribal business and activities concerning housing, road maintenance, education, and welfare. The Handsome Lake Longhouse Religion continued to be a strong influence for the Ontario group among the minority not accepting the elected form of government.

The Wisconsin Oneidas essentially dissolved their government following the loss of lands in the early twentieth century. With prospects of some lands being restored, the tribe organized an elected form of government in 1937 under the Indian Reorganization Act (IRA) of 1934. They adopted an IRA constitution and established the Business Council to govern themselves. The tribe became available for certain federal grants and loans, setting the basis for future economic growth. The Business Council is composed of nine members elected every three years.

The New York Oneidas, based on the remaining small land base has experienced significant political strife in the later twentieth century between one faction favoring an elective form of government and the other favoring a more traditional form based on hereditary clans.

INDIVIDUAL AND GROUP CONTRIBUTIONS

EDUCATION

Educator Norbert S. Hill Jr. (b. 1946) was born in Warren, Michigan near Detroit. His father was an Oneida/Mohawk and his mother a Canadian Cree. His father, involved in Indian activism, founded the North American Indian Club, which provided support for urban Indians. While a youth, Hill with his family moved to the Wisconsin Oneida Reservation near Green Bay. Hill earned a B.A. from the University of Wisconsin–Oshkosh in 1969 and later an M.A. in guidance and counseling from the same institution. After serving as assistant to the dean of students at University of Wisconsin-Green Bay, Hill became director of the American Indian Education Opportunity Program at the University of Colorado, where he continued his graduate studies. Hill became chair of the Oneida education committee in the early 1970s, which led to a career of community service stressing the role of education in the improvement of tribal well-being. Hill started the noted magazine *Winds of Change* in 1986 and edited a book of historical and contemporary Indian quotes titled *Words of Power*. In the 1990s, Hill became board chairman for the proposed Smithsonian National Museum of the American Indian, overseeing its development. He also served as executive director of the American Indian Science and Engineering Society (AISES) from 1983 into the 1990s. Among the honors Hill has received are the Chancellor's Award at the University of Wisconsin–Oshkosh in 1988 and in 1994 a Rockefeller fellowship and an honorary doctor of laws degree from Cumberland College in Kentucky. Hill's brother Robert, also a member of the Oneidas, served as chairman of the Oneida tribe, then as chairman of the National Indian Gaming Commission. His first cousin is noted poet Roberta Hill Whiteman.

FILM, TELEVISION, AND THEATER

Film actor Graham Greene (b. 1950) has found success in both Canada and the United States. Greene, a full-blooded Oneida, was born on the Iroquois Six Nations Reserve in southwestern Ontario. Before becoming an actor, Greene worked at a number of different jobs, including stints as a steelworker in high-rise construction, a civil technologist, and a draftsman. He also worked as an audio technician for rock 'n' roll bands and owned his own recording studio in Hamilton, Ontario. He began his career in television, film, and radio in 1976. Greene lived for a short time in Britain in the early 1980s, where he performed on stage. Upon his return to Canada, Greene was cast in the British film *Revolution*, starring Al Pacino and directed by Hugh Hudson. Greene is perhaps best known for his performance in *Dances with Wolves*, a 1991 film that won several Academy Awards, including the award for best picture. Greene portrayed Kicking Bird, an elder who strove to protect his people from attacks by American authorities. In addition, Greene has been cast in a number of television series and is known for his work in *The Campbells*, *Spirit Bay*, *Captain Power*, *Running Brave*, *Adderley*, *Night Heat*, and *Pow-Wow Highway*. His performances not restricted to film, Greene became active on the Toronto theater scene, receiving a Dora Mavor Moore Award for best actor for his performance in the acclaimed *Dry Lips Oughta Move to Kapuskasing*, a highly successful play written by Tomson Highway, a renowned Canadian Cree playwright.

Charlie Hill, a member of the Oneida tribe of Wisconsin, is a comedian who has performed across the United States and released an album, *Born Again Savage*. He has also appeared in the movie *Harold of Orange* in 1983.

POLITICS AND GOVERNMENT

Many early leaders of the Oneidas were active in maintaining the Oneida land base or recovering lost lands in all three areas of Ontario, Wisconsin, and New York. Their stories reflect Oneida history. Sally Ainse (c. 1728–1823) led a colorful life in early Oneida history following contact with Euro-Americans. Born in the Susquehanna River region of southern Oneida traditional territory, Ainse became a fur trader, landowner, and diplomat. Sally was a trader and landowner in the Fort Stanwix area near present-day Rome, New York, until the American Revolution. Then she moved westward to British-controlled lands in the Detroit region, where she continued trading goods to American Indians for furs. Ainse became an interpreter between warring tribes and the U.S. military in the 1790s. She soon moved again, acquiring extensive lands on the Thames River near present-day Chatham, Ontario. Ainse became involved in a lengthy land dispute with the Canadian government over native land claims.

Laura Cornelius Kellogg (1880–1947), known as Minnie, was a descendent of two earlier influential Oneida leaders. She also became noted for her own oratory skills. Kellogg attended finishing school, traveled in Europe, and attended several well-known institutions such as Stanford, Columbia, Cornell, and the University of Wisconsin. Minnie was a founder of the Society of American Indians in 1911 and became a national advocate for tribal self-sufficiency. Late in her life, Minnie focused on preservation of the Oneida language and the reacquisition of lost tribal lands.

Mary Cornelius Winder (1898–1954) was an activist for Oneida rights to lands lost in the nineteenth century. While living on the Onondaga Reservation with many other displaced Oneida families, Winder operated a small grocery store. She relentlessly lobbied the U.S. government to honor its 1794 treaty with the Oneidas and for the government to grant full federal recognition to the Oneida Nation. Beginning in the 1940s, she initiated what became a 30-year successful effort before the U.S. Land Claims Commission. She and other tribal members sought recognition that the lands were inappropriately taken. However, upon victory they discovered that monetary awards alone were being offered, not return of the land itself. The Oneidas won a $3.3 million settlement, to be split between the three groups.

The second Native American appointed commissioner of the U.S. Bureau of Indian Affairs (BIA) was Robert LaFollette Bennett (b. 1912), Oneida lawyer and administrator. Bennett was born on the Oneida Reservation near Green Bay, Wisconsin, and attended the BIA's boarding school at the Haskell Institute in Kansas. Afterwards he studied law at Southeastern University School of Law in Washington, D.C., earning his law degree in 1941. Bennett served in the U.S. Marine Corps during World War II. For his legal work supporting native land claims, he received the Indian Achievement Award in 1962 and Outstanding American Indian Citizen Award in 1966. In 1966 President Lyndon B. Johnson appointed Bennett head of BIA. He left the BIA in 1969 and moved to Albuquerque, New Mexico, where he founded the American Indian Athletic Hall of Fame. Bennett was director of the American Indian Law Center at the University of New Mexico Law School from 1970 to 1975. He was recognized as Outstanding Member of the Oneida tribe of Wisconsin in 1988.

JOURNALISM

Late in the 1990s, the New York Oneida Indian Nation purchased the prominent national weekly Indian newspaper *Indian Country Today*, produced in Rapid City, South Dakota. A new enterprise, Standing Stone Media, Inc., was founded by the tribe to operate the publication. A goal of the Oneidas was to further expand circulation and represent the diverse aspects of contemporary Indian life. The Oneidas essentially took over control from the Lakota/Dakota Sioux.

LITERATURE

Poet Roberta Hill Whiteman (b. 1947) earned a B.A. from the University of Wisconsin, an M.F.A. from University of Montana, and a Ph.D. from the University of Minnesota. A member of the Oneida tribe of Wisconsin, Whiteman is a noted poet whose work has been included in *Carriers of the Dream Wheel: Contemporary Native American Poetry* (1975) and *The Third Woman: Minority Women Writers of the United States* (1980). She published her own collections, *Star Quilt* in 1984 and *Philadelphia Flowers* in 1996. Her work also appeared in *Harper's Anthology of Twentieth-Century Native American Poetry* (1988). Whiteman is noted for a very humanistic style in her poetry, addressing personal and family relationships and the relation of humans to recurrent patterns of nature.

MUSIC

Joanne Shenandoah is an internationally respected recording artist and songwriter whose material often reflects her Oneida heritage. Her releases include *Loving Ways* on Canyon Records in 1991 and contributions to an album titled *In the Spirit of Crazy Horse*, dedicated to imprisoned Indian activist Leonard Peltier. Shenandoah, whose father was an Onondaga tribal leader and jazz guitarist, has performed in Europe as well as North America, including the 1991 American Music Festival in San Francisco. Shenandoah founded Round Dance Productions, a nonprofit organization dedicated to native cultural preservation. Shenandoah has also pursued an acting career and is a writer of musical scores and soundtracks.

SPORTS

Several Oneida tribal members have been inducted into the American Indian Athletic Hall of Fame, established in 1972. Martin Wheelock played on the Carlisle football team from 1894 to 1902, earning All-American honors in 1901 and named on the "All University" team by the *Philadelphia Inquirer* in 1902. Elijah Smith participated on the Haskell football, baseball, and track teams between 1923 and 1926, setting a national collegiate record for extra points kicked. He also played baseball and football at Davis & Elkins College between 1927 and 1929. Both Smith and Wheelock were inducted into the Hall of Fame in 1980. Wilson Charles participated in track, football, and basketball at Haskell and University of New Mexico from 1927 to 1931 before becoming a member of the U.S. Olympic decathlon team in 1932. Charles was inducted into the Hall of Fame in 1972, the first year of its existence. Gordon House, of both Oneida and Navajo ancestry, was the All Armed Forces lightweight boxing champion in 1945 and became the state lightweight boxing champion in Arizona, Nevada, and Texas in 1948. House fought professionally from 1946 to 1949. He was elected to the Hall of Fame in 1985.

MEDIA

PRINT

Indian Country Today.
A prominent, nationally published weekly newspaper reporting on national news of relevance to Indian nations throughout the United States. Recently purchased and operated by Standing Stone Media, Inc. of the Oneida tribe of Wisconsin.

Address: 7831 N. Grindstone, Hayward,
    Wisconsin 54843.
Telephone: (715) 634-9672.

Kali-?-Wisaks.
Newsletter for the Oneida tribe of Wisconsin.

Address: P.O. Box 98, Oneida, Wisconsin 54155.

The Oneida.
Oneida Nation newsletter that provides tribal reservation news for the Oneida Indian Nation of New York.

Address: 101 Canal St., Canastota,
    New York 13032.
Telephone: (315) 697-8251.

Ontario Indian.
A monthly newsletter published by the Union of Ontario Indians.

Address: 27 Queen St., East, Toronto, M5C 1R5
    Canada.
Telephone: (416) 366-3527.

ORGANIZATIONS AND ASSOCIATIONS

Assembly of First Nations Resource Centre.
Extensive collection of materials on Ontario Indian tribes including tribal histories and legal histories.

Contact: Kelly Whiteduck.
Address: 47 Clarence St., 3rd Floor, Ottawa,
    Ontario K1N 9K1 Canada.
Telephone: (613) 236-0673.

Oneida Indian Nation.
Address: Genesee Street, Ames Plaza, Oneida,
    New York 13421.
Telephone: (315) 361-6300.
Online: http://www.oneida-nation.net.

Oneida of the Thames.
Address: RR#2, Southwold, Ontario N0L 2G0
    Canada.
Telephone: (519) 652-3244.

Oneida Tribe of Indians of Wisconsin.
Address: P.O. Box 365, Oneida, Wisconsin 54155.
Telephone: (920) 869-2214.

Wisconsin Indian Lawyers League.
Contact: Gerald L. Hill.
Address: P.O. Box 365, Oneida, Wisconsin 54155.
Telephone: (414) 869-2345.

MUSEUMS AND RESEARCH CENTERS

Iroquois Indian Museum and Library.
Houses and exhibits the material culture of the Oneidas and other Iroquois Confederacy tribes, exhibits modern craftwork, and offers an educational trail highlighting the ethnobotany of the region.

Contact: Christina B Johannsen or Stephanie E. Shultes.
Address: Box 7, Caverns Road, Howes Cave, New York 12092.
Telephone: (518) 296-8949.

Oneida Nation Museum.
Address: 886 Double E Road, DePere, Wisconsin 54115.
Telephone: (414) 869-2768.

Shako:wi Cultural Center.
Located on tribal lands east of Syracuse, the white pine log building houses Oneida arts and crafts and stories of the tribe's past. The Oneidas use the facility for community gatherings and public presentations.

Address: Rte. 46, New York.
Telephone: (315) 363-1424.

Six Nations Indian Museum and Library.
Houses collections of the material culture of the Oneidas and other tribes composing the Six Nations and research materials on their history.

Contact: Ray Fadden.
Address: Onchiota, New York 12968.
Telephone: (518) 891-0769.

State Historical Society of Wisconsin Library.
Excellent holdings on Indians of Wisconsin and of North America in general.

Contact: R. David Myers.

Address: 816 State St., Madison, Wisconsin 53706.
Telephone: (608) 264-6535.

SOURCES FOR ADDITIONAL STUDY

Beyond the Covenant Chain: The Iroquois and Their Neighbors in Indian North America, 1600-1800, edited by Daniel K. Richter and James H. Merrell. Syracuse, New York: Syracuse University Press, 1987.

Campisi, Jack. "Oneida." *Handbook of the North American Indians. Vol. 15: Northeast.* Edited by Bruce G. Trigger. Washington, D.C.: Smithsonian Institution, 1978.

Fenton, William M. "Northern Iroquoian Culture Patterns." *Handbook of the North American Indians. Vol. 15: Northeast.* Edited by Bruce G. Trigger. Washington, D.C.: Smithsonian Institution, 1978.

Halbritter, Ray. "The Truth About Land Claims." *The Oneida.* Vol. 7, No. 6. New York: Oneida Indian Nation, 1996.

The Oneida Indian Experience: Two Perspectives, edited by Jack Campisi and Laurence M. Hauptman. New York: Syracuse University Press, 1988.

Shattuck, George C. *The Oneida Land Claims: A Legal History.* Syracuse, New York: Syracuse University Press, 1991.

Since Pacific
Islanders had no
form of written
language for
centuries, music
was a crucial means
of expression.

PACIFIC ISLANDER AMERICANS

by
Liz Swain

OVERVIEW

The Pacific Islands region of the South Pacific Ocean is called Oceania when Australia and New Zealand are included. There are approximately 25,000 islands, atolls and islets in Oceania. Within the Pacific Islands region are the subregions of Polynesia, Melanesia, and Micronesia. The islands of Tonga, Tahiti, and Fiji are located within two of these three areas.

Polynesia means "many islands," and includes within its 5 million squares miles the Kingdom of Tonga and the Territory of French Polynesia, where Tahiti is located. Samoa and Hawaii are also found in Polynesia. The region's name comes from the Greek word *melas*, meaning black. It was so named because of the skin color of island natives.

Tonga is an archipelago of 170 islands. Its total land area is about four times the size of Washington, D.C., measuring 288 square miles (746 square kilometers). People live on 36 of Tonga's islands. The population in July 1998 was approximately 108,207. The majority of Tongans are of Polynesian ethnic origin. About 300 Europeans also live on the islands. Christianity is the primary religion, with more than 30,000 people belonging to the Free Wesleyan Church. The monarch is the head of the church, which is the Methodist Church in the United States. Other Christian religions with significant membership include the Roman Catholic and Mormon churches. Tonga's official languages are Tongan and English. The national capital, Nuku'alofa, is located on the island of Tongatapu. The national flag is primarily red. On the upper left quadrant of the flag is a white rectangle with a bright red cross on it.

French Polynesia is a territory consisting of five archipelagos. French Polynesia's 118 islands and atolls span an area slightly less than one-third the size of the state of Connecticut. French Polynesia's total land area measures 1,544 square miles (4,000 square kilometers). Tahiti is the best known island in French Polynesia. The largest of the Society Islands, it measures 33 square miles (53 kilometers). French Polynesia had a population of approximately 237,844 people in July 1998. Seventy-eight percent of the population are of Polynesian ethnic origin, 12 percent are Chinese, and a small percentage are French. Fifty-four percent of French Polynesians are Protestant, 30 percent are Roman Catholic, and 16 percent belong to other denominations. French Polynesia's official languages are French and Tahitian. Papeete, the national capital and the territory's largest city, is located on Tahiti. French Polynesia's flag consists of two horizontal red bands, with a larger white band in the center. Pictured in the white section of the flag is a blue, white and red ship. The colors are those of the French flag, and France's tricolor is displayed in French Polynesia on special occasions.

At the eastern end of Melanesia, near Polynesia, is the Republic of Fiji. This proximity led to a Polynesian influence on the culture. Although Fiji is an archipelago of 332 islands, its total area is slightly smaller than the state of New Jersey. The country's total land area measures 7,055 square miles (18,272 square kilometers). Approximately 110 of Fiji's islands are inhabited, and the population in July 1998 was approximately 802,611. Of the population, 49 percent are of Fijian ethnic origin, 46 percent are Indian, and the remaining five percent includes other Pacific islanders, Europeans, and Chinese. Fifty-two percent of the population is Christian, with 37 percent belonging to the Methodist faith. Approximately nine percent of Fijians are Roman Catholic. Indians account for the 38 percent of the population who are Hindu. There is also a Muslim minority. English is the official language in Fiji, though Fijian and Hindustani are also spoken. The nation's capital is the port city of Suva. The national flag is light blue. The British flag is depicted in the upper left quadrant; the Fijian shield appears on the right half. A lion on the shield holds a cocoa pod. Also pictured are stalks of sugar cane, a palm tree, bananas, and a white dove.

HISTORY

The history of the Pacific Islands began thousands of years ago in Southeast Asia. From 3000 B.C. to 1000 B.C., peoples left the Malay Peninsula and the Indonesian Archipelago, migrating to islands across the Pacific Ocean. They sailed in massive double-hulled canoes that held up to 200 people. With no navigation instruments, the ancestors of modern Polynesians relied on *wayfinding,* the use of nature to navigate. The navigational course was determined by observing the stars, the sun, the wave currents, and the flight pattern of birds.

The Lapita people may have reached Tonga by 3000 B.C. Artifacts confirm they were living on Tonga around 1100 B.C. Polynesians are believed to have reached Fiji by at least 1500 B.C. They were joined by Melanesians in 500 B.C. According to archaeologists, Polynesians from Tonga and Samoa settled the Marquesas Islands 2,000 years ago. Polynesians in subsequent years migrated to other areas including New Zealand and Hawaii. Artifacts found on the Society Islands indicate that Polynesians settled in Tahiti around 850 A.D.

Polynesians established a hierarchical social structure, where children inherited their father's power and social status. A chief and his descendants ruled a territory that ranged in size from a village to a region. One indication of status was a person's size. Obesity was a sign of wealth or nobility in Tonga.

Within the hierarchical governing system were power struggles. These struggles sometimes resulted in war, forcing some islanders to flee and settle other islands. Cannibalism was another aspect of war, one dictated by Fijian and Tongan religions. Captured people were sacrificed to the warrior gods. The victors ate their enemies to absorb their power and to insult the deceased and his family.

A less gruesome Polynesian tradition involved family and community life. The family extended to grandparents, aunts, uncles, and other relatives, as well as the village. Family members looked after one another, respected their elders, and shared with the community. When fishermen returned with their catch, they took what they needed and left the rest for others.

Polynesians were noted craftspeople who built boats without nails. They had no system of writing. Instead, history and traditions were relayed through songs, dance, poems, and stories. For centuries, Pacific Islanders believed that gods controlled their lives.

Pacific Island life changed dramatically in the seventeenth century when European explorers discovered the islands. Dutch navigator Jakob LeMaire reached Tonga in 1616, the first European to visit the islands. Another Dutch navigator, Abel Tasman, arrived in Fiji in 1643. English Captain Samuel Wallis reached Tahiti in 1767 and claimed it for England. A year later, French explorer Louis de Bougainville landed in Tahiti. He did not realize Wallis had been there and claimed the land for his country. France gained control of Tahiti in 1842 and made it a French colony in 1880. England gained control of Fiji, while Tonga remained an independent kingdom. In 1774, British Captain James Cook sailed through the islands, followed by British Captain William Bligh in 1789. In 1874, the Fiji islands were ceded to Britain.

Christian missionaries brought more change to the islands. In 1797, members of the London Missionary Society settled in Tonga and Tahiti. Missionaries eventually succeeded in converting Tahitians, but they left Tonga left in 1799. Catholic and Wesleyan missionaries also attempted to convert the Pacific Islanders. Wesleyan ministers succeeded in converting Tonga to Christianity. The missionary influence was seen in the nineteenth century when members of royalty converted. Fijian King Cokobau converted to Christianity in 1854. Such conversions ended cannibalism in the Pacific Islands. Missionaries also developed written forms of Pacific Islander languages that were previously nonexistent in the predominantly oral culture.

MODERN ERA

Fiji remained a British colony for 96 years. The island nation achieved full independence on October 10, 1970. The country was designated a member of the British Commonwealth with Dominion status.

Tongans proudly declare that their country was the first Polynesian kingdom, the only kingdom still remaining in the South Pacific. While the monarchy existed since the tenth century, the current dynasty was established during the nineteenth century. Power struggles in the nineteenth century led to civil war. The victorious chief took the name George when he was baptized in the Wesleyan faith, in honor of the King of England. When proclaimed the king in 1845, he became George Tupou I. Known as the father of modern Tonga, the king outlawed the worship of old gods and established a constitutional monarchy. After his death in 1893, his great-grandson, George Tupou II, ruled until 1918. George Tupou II was succeeded by his 18-year-old daughter, Salote. Queen Salote was beloved by Tongans as an intelligent, compassionate woman concerned with issues like health and medicine. She was also well-regarded internationally. The Tongan queen died in 1965, and was succeeded by her son King Tupou IV.

France gained control of Tahiti in 1842, making it a colony in 1880. The tropical paradise attracted numerous artists and writers. French artist Paul Gaughin moved to Tahiti in 1891 and immortalized the French Polynesians in his vivid paintings. In 1946, French Polynesia became a French overseas territory. France's president is the chief of state.

THE FIRST PACIFIC ISLANDERS IN AMERICA

According to an article in *Pacific Tide,* the first known Tongan in the United States was a man who came to Utah in 1924 for additional education. The Tonga man accompanied a Mormon missionary returning to the United States. The missionary went back to Tonga and returned to Utah with another Tongan man in 1936. The first Tongan family came to Salt Lake City, Utah, in 1956. This marked the beginning of a small migration of Tongans, Tahitians and Fijians.

SIGNIFICANT IMMIGRATION WAVES

Historical accounts and church records sometimes provide a more detailed look at migration and settlement patterns than government documents. This is especially true for Tongans, Tahitians and Fijians. U.S. Immigration and Naturalization Service (INS) records list immigrant admission by country of origin, with Tahiti classified as part of French Polynesia. Other government entities used the much broader classification of Asians and Pacific Islanders. This category covers people whose ancestors were the original peoples of the Far East, Southeast Asia, the Indian subcontinent, or the Pacific Islands. By examining both official documents and less formal accounts, a picture emerges of the settlement patterns of Pacific Islanders of Tongan, Tahitian, and Fijian ethnic ancestry. While more information is available about the Tongan experience in America, some could apply to Fijians and Tahitians. Three Fijians were admitted to the country in 1953, according to U.S. Immigration and Naturalization Services (INS) records. An equal number were admitted in 1954, along with three French Polynesians and one Tongan.

Waves of Tongan immigrants arrived in the United States in the 1950s and 1960s. More came during the 1970s, and there was a boom in the 1980s. According to INS records for the 1950s, the admissions records were: 71 Fijians in 1959, 14 French Polynesians in 1956, and 14 Tongans in 1958. During the 1960s, a record 368 Fijians were admitted in 1968. The low figure for annual immigration was 45 in 1967. French Polynesian immigration never rose above the 49 admissions in 1965. Tongan migration ranged from four people admitted in 1960 to a record 119 in 1966.

During the 1970s, Fijian migration ranged from 132 admissions in 1976 to 1,000 in 1979. The record year for French Polynesian migration was 1975, when 47 people were admitted. Tongan migration ranged from 133 admissions in 1976 to 809 in 1979. Fijian migration jumped during the 1980s, when admission ranged from 712 people in 1983 to 1,205 in 1987. French Polynesian migration ranged from 19 admissions in 1986 to 59 in 1984.

In the next decade, a record 1,847 Fijians immigrated to the United States in 1996. The record year for the other groups was 1991 when 1,685 Tongans and 31 French Polynesians entered. During 1997, admission was granted to 1,549 Fijians, 21 French Polynesians and 303 Tongans.

Migration for some Pacific Islanders began when the Mormon church sent students to Hawaii for higher education, and then to the United States. Others were brought to this country to work on Mormon church construction projects. Military service after World War II also brought Pacific Islanders to the United States. They settled in California and Washington, especially Southern California cities like San Diego, Oceanside, and Long Beach.

Tongans lived in large west coast cities like Los Angeles and San Francisco until the 1970s, when the national recession crippled California's economy. Tongans began moving to North Texas during the 1970s and 1980s, seeking employment near Dallas-Fort Worth Airport. Approximately 1,800 Tongans lived in the area in 1993.

According to a 1996 report to the U.S. Catholic Conference, of the approximately 20,000 Tongans in the United States, 4,500 were Catholic. The report said significant populations lived in California in Sacramento San Francisco's Bay Area and in the Southern California cities of Los Angeles, Paramount, Anaheim, Upland, and San Bernardino.

In 1992, approximately 6,000 to 8,000 Tongan Americans lived in San Francisco's Bay Area. Washington State's Asian and Pacific Islander (API) population grew 59.1% in six years, from 215,454 in 1990 to more than 342,900 in 1996. In California, the API population rose from nine percent in 1990 to 11 percent in 1996, according to a 1998 state report. That increase primarily came from migration, with 452,000 Asian and Pacific Islanders migrating to the state between 1990 and 1996. Net migration averaged 71,000 from 1991 to 1996, while the natural increase (births minus deaths) averaged 46,600. From 1993 to 1996, this

was the only group to experience positive net migration to California.

There were 7,700 Pacific Islanders living in Utah in 1990, according a state report. The total consisted of 3,611 Samoans, 1,760 Samoan and 1,334 Hawaiians.

ACCULTURATION AND ASSIMILATION

Language was the first barrier for Pacific Islanders who migrated to the United States. A limited knowledge of English caused problems when islanders sought housing, employment, health care, and legal representation. The Catholic Tongan Community of North Texas chronicled the language barrier in a 1993 report. That report was presented at a regional meeting that drew Catholic Tongans from locations ranging from San Francisco, California, to Sparks, Nevada. Those who attended concluded that bilingual educational programs were needed, along with youth-oriented programs to keep students in school and away from gangs and drugs.

Similar concerns were voiced at the 1998 Polynesian Summit conferences, organized by the state of Utah Office of Polynesian Affairs (OPA). That year, Tongans in Salt Lake City raised the issue of racism at a September meeting regarding ethnic fairness in the legal system. Some Polynesians said they were afraid to use the legal system, believing that it "works against them because of the color of their skin," according to a meeting report.

Although Pacific Islanders faced intimidating challenges to assimilation, their cultural concept of community provided valuable support. Just as the village used to help its members, assistance came from organizations such as the OPA, Catholic Tongan groups, and the Pacific American Foundation. In addition, Tongans, Tahitians and, Fijians participate in the Pacific Islander Festival, a weekend event held annually in Southern California since 1990.

TRADITIONS, CUSTOMS, AND BELIEFS

Kava (pronounced "kah-vah"), a nonalcoholic drink made with the ground root of the pepper shrub, is a ceremonial beverage for Tongans and Fijians. Called *yaqona* ("yanggona") in Fiji, the mildly intoxicating beverage is consumed during important occasions like births, weddings, deaths, and the arrival of a dignitary. Kava is also drunk socially. Etiquette requires visitors to Fijian villages to bring it to the chief. Other etiquette includes the wearing of shoes in the house. Also, it is considered rude to touch a Fijian on the head.

Centuries of island life are reflected in South Pacific legends that sometimes have some truth. According to an ancient Fijian myth, the sound of women singing lures massive turtles from the sea to hear their voices. The Calling of the Turtles is a reality that continues today. Turtles rise to the water surface to hear the singing of women villagers from Naumana on the island of Kaduva.

Another fact-based legend concerns firewalking. Fijians from the island of Bequa walk across hot rock without burning their feet. The firewalkers say the god Veli give them the power to do this. Another Fijian legend has to do with the presence of red prawns in cliff pools. Supposedly, the prawns were a gift to the daughter of a Vatulele chief. The red crustaceans disgusted her, and she had them thrown from a cliff.

Polynesian mythology traces the beginning of Tonga to the hero Maui. When Maui was fishing south of Samoa, he pulled up Tonga's islands one at a time. He walked across some islands and flattened them. The untouched islands remained mountainous.

PROVERBS

Tongan proverbs relate wisdom based on the island people's reliance on nature. The proverbs include: "There is a silver lining in every cloud"; "You will know the expert navigators when it comes to a rough time in the ocean"; and "Treat your plantation well for you are not the last person to use it".

CUISINE

While language and traditions changed as Polynesians migrated to other islands, Tongans, Tahitians, and Fijians still hold communal feasts. In an outdoor pit that Tongans call an *umu* ("oo-moo"), a whole pig is roasted with foods like chicken, fish, meat, sweet potatoes, fish and *taro* (a starchy tuber). Tongans cook the feast with taro leaves, while Tahitians and Fijians add banana leaves.

Pacific Islander cuisine includes numerous types of fish, fresh fruit like bananas and coconut, breadfruit, *cassava* (a starchy plant), and sweet potatoes. Corned beef is also popular and is cooked in Tonga with taro leaves. Tongans also combine taro with other meats, or serve it with onions or coconut milk. A favorite Tahitian dessert is *gateau a la banane* ("ga-tow a la bah-nan"), which is French for banana cake.

MUSIC

Since Pacific Islanders had no form of written language for centuries, music was a crucial means of expression. Musicians play the guitar and traditional Polynesian instruments like the *pahu* (a wood drum), ukelele, *uli uli* (small gourds), *ipu* (larger gourds), *puili* (split bamboo) and Tahitian drums made out of hollowed logs. Pacific Islander voices also unite in church choirs.

TRADITIONAL COSTUMES

Tongans wear *ta'ovala* ("tah ah vah-la"), a woven-leaf mat worn around the waist. Women sometimes wear a smaller version called a *kiekie* ("key-ah key-ah"). Ta'ovalas come in everyday and fancier varieties for special occasions.

In Tahiti, people wear a *tiare* (a hibiscus blossom) behind one ear. A flower worn behind the right ear means the man or woman is available. When placed behind the left ear, the wearer is spoken for. The tiare is also added to a crown of braided palm fronds and greenery. Fijian dancers wear skirts of shredded leaves and paint their faces for war dances.

DANCES AND SONGS

Pacific Islanders' songs and dances commemorate major events or activities, like the beaching of a canoe. A highlight of a Fijian feast is the *meke*, which combines dance, song, and performance. The Tahitian *aparima* portrays the everyday life of a young woman. During the Fijian war ceremonial dance, men holding spears dance to the tempo of bamboo sticks tapped on the ground by seated musicians.

HOLIDAYS

Christian beliefs mean that Pacific Islander Americans celebrate feast days like Christmas and Easter. Tahitian Americans in the United States may also observe the French Polynesian celebration of Bastille Day on July 14. This date is known as France's independence day in French-speaking countries. July 4 is celebrated by Tongan Americans as King Taufa 'ahau Tupou IV's birthday and a national holiday.

HEALTH ISSUES

For centuries, Pacific Islanders regarded obesity as a sign of wealth or nobility. This excess weight can lead to diabetes. Hypertension is another concern for Pacific Islanders. A 1998 California Department of Health Services report indicated that Pacific Islanders living in the state were "less likely to be aware of their hypertension [and] to be under treatment with medication" than people from other ethnic groups. The report concluded that Asians and Pacific Islanders were likely to rely on traditional remedies, perhaps because of the lack of health care providers of from their ethnic background.

Pacific Islanders face other health issues. Pacific Islander Americans have the highest mortality rates for most cancers and incidences of chronic diseases, smoking, and binge and chronic drinking. In addition, they have the lowest rate for prenatal care and immunization of children. The Oahlana Laulima project sought to address these concerns. The project's goal is a national organization to serve Pacific Americans health concerns. This will be accomplished through "advice, education, information, service and volunteer efforts." The foundation noted a connection between poor health and the cultural insensitivity of health care providers. That insensitivity would make people reluctant to seek preventive care. Economics also played a role, with access to care limited by lack of medical insurance, high costs of care, and medical treatment.

The first phase of Oahlana Laulima involved a one-year study of successful health care centers for underserved minority communities in California, Washington, Virginia, Hawaii and the District of Columbia. During the next phase, the "Family of Working Hands" in 1997 applied what they learned at the Carson Community Health Center in Carson, California.

LANGUAGE

Fijian, Tahitian and Tongan are part of the large Austronesian, or Malay-Polynesian, family of languages. Also included are languages such as Hawaiian and Samoan. During centuries of migration to other islands, the words changed. However, some similarities remain. The word for fish is *ika* in Fijian and Tongan. In Hawaiian, fish is *i'a*. Language varies within a country, too. Fiji has 300 dialects as well as the Standard Fijian language.

Fijian

In Standard Fijian, there is one sound per vowel. These are pronounced: "a" as in "father," "e" in "get," "i" in "police," "o" in "most," and "u" in "zoo." When two vowels are together, the first one is pronounced. A long vowel is marked with a line called a macron over the top. Pronunciation is lengthened. Most Fijian consonants sound the same

as English. The exceptions are: "b" is pronounced "mb;" "d" is pronounced "nd;" "th" as in "that;" "g" as in "ring;" "k," "p" and "t" are pronounced without a puff of breath; the "r" rolled as in Spanish; and "ng" as in "hunger." Common Fijian greetings and expressions include: *Ni sa yadra*—good morning; *Ni sa bula*—hello; *sa moche*—good bye; *yalo vinaka* — please; and *vinaka*—thank you.

Tongan

Tongan vowels are pronounced as follows: "a" as in "can;" "e" as in "bet;" "i" as in "in;" "o" as in "not;" and "u" as in "put." Consonants "f," "h," "l," "m," "n," and "v" are pronounced as in English, However the "k" is pronounced like the "gh" in "gherkin;" the "ng" as in "singer;" the "p" is midway between "p" and "b;" the "s" has a slight "sh" sound; and the "t" is between "t" and "d." Accent stress is usually on the last syllable. An apostrophe called a glottal stop (') represents a space and a slight pause. Common Tongan greetings and phrases include: *Malo 'e lelei*—hello; *malo tau ma'ue pongipongi ni*—good morning; *faka molemole*—please; *malo*—thank you; *fefe hake*—how are you?; and *nofo*—Good bye.

Tahitian

Tahitians vowels are pronounced as follows: "a" as the vowel in "cut"; the "e" say; an "i" in "police"; "o" as in "old"; and "u" as in flute. The consonants "f," "m," "n," and "v" are pronounced as in English. But "h" is pronounced as in "hat" unless it follows an "i" and comes before "o." An "h" in "iho" has "sh" sound. In other consanants, the "p" as pronouned in "spoon" (shorter sound); the "r" is sometimes rolled; and the "t" as in "stop." Common Tahitian greetings and phrases include: *Ia ora na*—good morning; *nana*—good bye; *maruru*—thank you; *Manuia*—cheers; *marite*—American; and *aita p'ape'a*—no problem.

FAMILY AND COMMUNITY DYNAMICS

The phrase, "It takes a village to raise a child" is not a cliché for Pacific Islanders. Children raised in Fiji, Tonga, and Tahiti are taught they are part of an extended family, one that works together for the good of the community. Tongans call this *nofo a'kainga*, which means everyone counts on one another. Cooperation starts in the home, continues at the village level and on through to the country. Children are taught to respect everyone, especially their elders. In the Tongan household, the father is head of family. Children usually remain at home until they marry.

Sometimes Pacific Islander immigrants are surprised by the differences between cultures. An 18-year-old Fijian American, Saul Brown, wrote in the 1997 Pacific Islander Festival program that growing in the United States was difficult. Growing up in Southern California, he wrote that he "felt a little embarrassed" when friends asked about the Fijian masks and other items in his home. However, Brown discovered the friends were interested in learning about his culture. Friends found the kava socials "strange but interesting." He sometimes envied theirs junk food meals of pizza and hamburgers. Another shock was discovering that people at school were not raised the way he was. "I was taught to never answer back, to always use my manners and to show respect."

EDUCATION

Parents who migrated from the Pacific Islands sometimes did not realize the importance of education in the United States. For example in the North Texas Tongan Catholic Community, one out of five students graduated from high school. Few of those went to colleges and universities. The high cost of an education was a factor, along with a lack of knowledge about financial aid.

During the 1990s, organizations such as the Utah Office of Polynesian Affairs (OPA) and The Pacific American Foundation developed programs to keep students in school. In Utah, 21.1% of Pacific Islanders dropped out of school. To lower that statistic, OPA director William Afeaki reinstated the Polynesian Young Achievers Award in 1997, which honored exceptional students. Similar programs were instituted in Southern California with tutoring and scholarships set up the Pacific American Foundation.

In San Diego, The Pacific American Foundation began concentrating on the educational needs of Pacific Islanders in Southern California, The foundation celebrated several successes in 1996. Volunteers tutored 10 students tutored for the Scholastic Aptitude Test; all enrolled in two and four-year educational institutions. A scholarship recipient graduated from Southwestern Law School. The foundation also founded a parent-student counseling program. Families of pre-teenagers learn about prerequisites and experience needed for higher education. Older students and their families learned about college financing, career counseling, grants, and loans. During 1999, the foundation worked to set up a learning center partnership program to assist the parents of Pacific American children between the ages of three and eight. The foun-

dation also worked on a program to help parents to obtain computers and software. By May of 1999, the foundation offered two scholarship programs and intensive SAT tutoring for high school juniors and seniors.

WEDDINGS

A traditional Tongan wedding is a family event. After the couple falls in love and decides to become married, the family plans and pays for the event. Special attention is paid to the elders' opinions.

A special ta'ovala is worn, made of a soft, silky *ngafi nagafi* ("gnaw-fee gnaw-fee"). This traditionally comes from Samoa to symbolize the connection with Polynesia. The ngafi nagafi is brownish-colored and decorated with feathers. Husband and wife wear the wedding ta'ovala again on the first Sunday after their marriage.

FUNERALS

For Tongan funerals, a dark brown ta'ovala is worn. The size of the ta'ovala indicates the mourner's relationship to the deceased. A larger ta'ovala signifies a closer relationship. When a relative or close friend dies, adults and children wear black. When a member of the royal family dies, Tongans wear black for a year. Families set the length of mourning times when a member dies. Tongan Americans carry on the tradition of the extended family preparing food and gathering for up to five days after the funeral.

RELIGION

The efforts of Christian missionaries in the Pacific Islands are reflected in the faiths of Pacific-Islander Americans. There are 8000 Pacific Islander members of the United Methodist Church in the United States. The church has 23 Pacific Island United Methodist congregations and 97 Pacific Island clergy. Catholics accounted for 4500 of the 20,000 Tongans living in the United States. Fijian-Americans and Tahitian-Americans are also adherents of both faiths.

While denominations vary, Pacific Islander tradition is interwoven with religious services. Worshippers value a service in their native language. Tongan-American ministers and congregation usually wear ta'ovalas.

In Tonga, where the king is the head of the church, religious observances affect the calendar. Government and shops close down for Good Friday. Tongans in the United States try to take that day off. Tongans in both countries attend services leading up to the sunrise Easter service. Government also takes a vacation that extends from the week before Christmas until the first week in January. Tongan Americans know that this is the best time to visit family in the South Pacific.

Pacific Islanders of all faiths participate in outreach programs. The Catholic St. Joseph Women's Association in San Bruno, California, was formed in 1977 to raise funds for seminarians studying for the priesthood in Tonga. In 1984, the association began issuing scholarships and awards for educational and athletic accomplishments.

EMPLOYMENT AND ECONOMIC TRADITIONS

Although the U.S. Department of Labor does not have specific employment information about Pacific Islanders, other accounts provide an economic picture that can be bleak. During the recession of the 1970s and early 1980s, Tongan-Americans began migrating to North Texas. Most who migrated found employment at the Dallas-Fort Worth Airport, primarily in food service and transportation. Others did cleaning work at the airport, office buildings, movie theaters, and restaurants. Most jobs paid minimum wage, so many Tongans worked two jobs or overtime to support their families. Children of working age were urged to find jobs to help support their families. In addition, Tongan-Americans performed yard work to supplement wages. These experiences were common to other Pacific Islanders living in the United States.

Language was often a barrier towards obtaining higher paying work. Another obstacle was the Pacific Islanders' centuries-old traditional values, which were at odds with the American idea of success. "In Tonga, people live in extended families in which everyone helps each other through agricultural gain. There are very few who hold professional jobs," Tongan Percival Leha'uli wrote in the program for the 1994 Pacific Islander Festival.

In Tonga, men are the providers, while women are the homemakers. People value the simplicity of their lives. "The idea of moving to a technological society is foreign to most Tongans," Leha'uli wrote. That situation isn't limited to Tongans. "While there is a growing number of Pacific Americans owning small businesses, it is a daily challenge just to stay afloat," David E.K. Cooper wrote in an essay on The Pacific American Foundation website. In 1999, he was president of the foundation, which strives to improve the economic outlook. The foun-

dation's Pacific American Leadership Center offered its first forum in Claremont, California, in April of 1998. The eight men and eight women who attended the two-day seminar learned how to develop leadership skills within a cultural context.

POLITICS AND GOVERNMENT

Pacific Island migration largely began after World War II. For some men, military service was the route to that migration. Although the U.S. government did not track active duty service by ethnic origin until decades later, an examination of the 1999 U.S. Department of Defense manpower records provides some information. However, these records don't provide the full picture. The military ethnic classification for active duty personnel places Tongans and Tahitians in the Polynesian category. Fijians are among the groups categorized as Melanesian.

As of March 31, 1999, the Army's ranks included 534 Polynesian men and 113 women. There were 34 male officers and five female officers. Also in that Army at that time were 102 Melanesian men and 14 women. Two men were officers. In the Navy on March 31, 1999, there were 251 Polynesian men and 46 women. Nine men and four women were officers. On duty at that time were 29 Melanesian men and 11 Melanesian women. Three Melanesian men and two women were serving as officers. On March 31, 1999, five male Polynesian officers, 56 enlisted men, and nine enlisted women were serving in the Marine Corps. Melanesians accounted for nine of the Marine Corps officers and 11 enlisted men. On duty with the Air Force on March 31, 1999 were 13 Polynesian men, and three were officers. Of the 11 Polynesian women serving, one was an officer.

A look at all branches of service indicated that the Coast Guard attracted the most Pacific Islanders, a people descended from wayfinder origins. On March 31, 1999, 795 Polynesian men served with the Coast Guard. Fifty-one were male officers. Of the 167 Polynesian women on duty, 10 were officers. At that time, 143 Melanesian men were on active duty with the Coast Guard, and six were officers. Also serving were two Melanesian women.

RELATIONS WITH FORMER COUNTRIES

It has long been a practice for people who migrate to the United States to send money home to their families. This is called a remittance, and remittances were an important source of revenue for Tonga according to the CIA 1998 *World Fact Book.*

Tonga is an agricultural-based economy. The country exports copra, vanilla, and squash pumpkins. Sugar is Fiji's chief export. Tourism is an important industry. Approximately 250,000 people visit Fiji each year. Tourism accounts for 20% of French Polynesia's gross domestic product. France began stationing military personnel in French Polynesia in 1962. Since then, a majority of the work force is employed by the military or in tourism-related jobs.

INDIVIDUAL AND GROUP CONTRIBUTIONS

ART

Manisela "Monty" Fifita Sitake (1952–) was one of three founders of the Literature and Arts Heritage Guild of Polynesia in Salt Lake City, Utah. He was born in Nuku'alofa, Tonga, and graduated from Brigham Young University in Provo, Utah, with a degree in English literature in 1984. He, Filoi Manuma'a Mataele, and Sione Ake Mokofisi started the guild in 1998 to help Polynesians with artistic talents and skills. Sitake has served as the guild president since its inception.

Sitake is also an author who writes in both Tongan and English. He prefers to write in his native tongue to preserve the Tongan language, and to encourage the importance of Polynesian literature. Sitake also plays guitar, ukulele, harmonica, and trumpet, and has recorded a compact disc mixing Tongan and western music.

Filoi Manuma'a Mataele (1968–) is vice president of the Literature and Arts Heritage Guild of Polynesia in Salt Lake City, Utah. He was born in Nuku'alofa, Tonga. He is also involved in small business and management.

JOURNALISM

Sione Ake Mokofisi (1951–) was editor in chief of *Polynesia Magazine*, the online magazine published by the Literature and Arts Heritage Guild of Polynesia. He was also a founder of the Literature and Arts Heritage guild. Born Nukunuku, Tongatapu, Tonga, he is a freelance writer/photographer and has served as the editor of *Ke Alaka'i* (on the Brigham Young University-Hawaii campus), *Alaska Sports*, and *Rugby* magazines. He worked as a reporter at Hawaii's *Northshore News*, *Anchorage Daily News*, *Alaskan Journal of Commerce*, *Alaskan Oil & Natural Resources News*, and *Tongan International*, a Tongan newspaper based in New Zealand.

He plays the guitar, ukulele, and was a member of the band, the Liahona Seven.

POLITICS

Filia (Phil) Uipi (1949–) was the first Polynesian to become a member of the Utah House of Representatives and the first Tongan to become a legislator outside of Tonga. He was born in Fotuha'a, Tonga. Upon graduating from the University of Utah Law School, Uipi was admitted to the state bar in 1986. A Republican, he was elected to two terms in the state legislature, representing District 36 from 1990 to 1994. He chaired the House Judiciary Committee during his second term. His voice was among those rallying for the establishment of the state Office of Polynesian Affairs (OPA). After leaving elected office, he served as the first chairman of the OPA's Polynesian Advisory Council. He served on other advisory boards, and by mid-1999, he was the only Tongan lawyer with a private practice in Utah.

SOCIAL ISSUES

Viliame Niumataiawalu is a longtime advocate of Fijian self-improvement and cultural awareness. He moved to Sacramento, California, in 1993 and became concerned about the plight of Fijians in America. In 1994, he founded the American Fiji Islanders Association, a nonprofit organization. Its goals included recognition of Fijian contributions and providing assistance in immigration, housing, employment, and language skills.

While working in Fiji and Australia during the 1960s, he became concerned about laborers in the business where he worked. Believing they were underpaid, he helped organize a Credit Club. Members made bi-monthly contributions into a fund that was used to provide low-interest loans for social and educational needs. When working in Utah from 1990 to 1992, he was active in the Asia and Pacific Islanders Association. He promoted education and social development for Pacific Islanders. He returned to Fiji in 1999.

MEDIA

KPOP-AM (1360).

"Ports of Paradise" is a weekly syndicated one-hour radio program featuring South Seas music from the 1920s to the present broadcast Sundays at 9 a.m. Pacific Standard Time. Syndicated broadcasts are heard in: Albany, New York, on WLAL-AM

(1190); Las Vegas, Nevada, on KLAV-AM (1230); and Anchorage, Alaska, on KKHAR-AM (590).

Contact: J Hal Hodgson, Executive Producer.
Address: P.O. Box 33648, San Diego, California 92163.
Telephone: (619) 275-7357.
E-mail: aloharn@portparadise.com.
Online: http://www.portparadise.com.

ORGANIZATIONS AND ASSOCIATIONS

Literature and Arts Heritage Guild of Polynesia.
The nonprofit guild in Utah was founded in 1998 to develop and promote the literacy and artistic talents of Pacific Islanders. The organization's goals include providing opportunities for artists to market their work and youth programs in areas such as literacy and historical traditions.

Contact: Manisela "Monty" Fifita Sitake, President.
Address: P.O. box 57978, Murray, Utah 84157-7978.
Telephone: (801) 495-3560.

The Pacific American Foundation.
The foundation was founded in 1993 as a national organization dedicated to improving Pacific Islanders' lives by helping them to help themselves. The foundation educates and provides information to decision-makers and leaders about areas of public and policies that affect Americans who trace their ancestry to the Pacific Islands.

Contact: Al Pauole, Executive Director.
Address: 1710 Rhode Island Avenue, NW, Washington, D.C. 20036-3123.
Telephone: (206) 282-4993.
Online: http://www.thepaf.org.

Polynesia, Polynesia!.
Founded in 1996, this is a nonprofit cultural heritage society that focuses on Polynesia as a connective group. The group's purpose is to promote and preserve Polynesia's culture. The organization presently offers classes, seminars, workshops and meetings to enhance cultural understanding. It also is to provides support, counseling, and assistance to needy or troubled families.

Contact: Vern Chang, President.
Address: P.O. Box 365, Fremont, Californian 94537-0365.
Telephone: (408) 972-0107.

State of Utah Office of Polynesian Affairs.
One of four offices created in 1996 by Governor Michael O. Leavitt to advocate and promote cooperation and understanding between government agencies and ethnic citizens. The governor appointed William Afeaki as the first director.

Contact: William Afeaki, Director.
Address: 324 South State Street, Fifth Floor, Salt Lake City, Utah 84111-2830.
Telephone: (801) 538-8678.

Tongan History Association.
Academic association founded in 1989. Main purpose is to study Tongan history up to the present.

Online: http://sunsite.anu.edu.au/spin/PACASSOC/TONGHIST/tonghist.htm.

MUSEUMS AND RESEARCH CENTERS

Center for Pacific Islands Studies.
Contact: Letitia Hickson, Editor.
Address: University of Hawai'i at Manoa, 1890 East-West Rd., Honolulu, HI 96822.
Telephone: (808) 956-7700.
Fax: (808) 956-7053.
E-mail: ctisha@hawaii.edu.

Polynesian Cultural Center.
The 43-acre site has re-creations of the villages of Tonga, Tahiti, Fiji and four other Polynesian islands. An open-air shopping village features arts and crafts. Cultural demonstrations include dance performances.

Contact: Lester Moore, President.
Address: 55-370 Kamehameha Highway, Laie, Hawaii 96762.
Telephone: (808) 293-3333.

SOURCES FOR ADDITIONAL STUDY

Kay, Robert F. *Tahiti and French Polynesia.* Hawthorn, Australia: Lonely Planet Publications, 1992.

Pacific Tides, November 1997.

Pacific Islander Festival Programs, Los Angeles and San Diego, California, 1991-1999.

Paulole, Al. *The Pacific American Review*, Spring 1997.

Stanley, David. *Fiji Islands Handbook*. Chico, California: Moon Publications, 1993.

Swaney, Deanna. *Tonga*. Hawthorn, Australia: Lonely Planet Publications, 1994.

Ungar, Sanford J. *Fresh Blood: The New American Immigrants*. New York: Simon & Schuster, 1995.

The United States Catholic Conference, Office for the Care of Migrants and Refugees, Washington, D.C: reports from 1993-1996.

Williamson, Robert W. *Religious and Cosmic Beliefs of Central Polynesia*. Reprinted. New York: AMS Press Inc., 1977.

PAIUTES

by
Richard C. Hanes and
Laurie Collier Hillstrom

Though Paiute populations have traditionally been small compared to other Native North American groups, several Paiutes have made key contributions to education and the arts.

OVERVIEW

The Paiute (PY-yoot) tribe is actually many different bands distributed across a large part of the western United States. Paiute means "true Ute" or "water Ute." The Paiutes call themselves Numu, meaning "People." The vast desert area used by the Paiutes extends from central Oregon southward through Las Vegas Valley to land along the Colorado River in Arizona and Southern California and eastward to southwestern Idaho. According to Catherine Fowler in *Native America in the Twentieth Century*, the numerous Paiutes bands are often recognized in three main groups: (1) the Northern Paiutes of northwestern Nevada, northeastern California, southeastern Oregon, and southwestern Idaho, (2) the Owens Valley Paiutes, who traditionally inhabited the Owens River watershed of southeastern California, and, (3) the Southern Paiutes of southeastern California, southern Nevada, northwestern Arizona, and western Utah. Paiute peoples were also historically called Snakes and Bannocks by whites and were even confused with Northern Shoshone who shared many cultural and linguistic traits, as well as overlapping traditional territories. The three main Paiute groups spoke mutually unintelligible languages of the Numic branch of the Uto-Aztecan language family.

Human population numbers had always been small when compared to surrounding regions because of the widely distributed food and water sources in this desert steppe environment. In *Native America in the Twentieth Century: An Encyclopedia*, Catherine Fowler reported that the Paiute population totaled over 11,000 in 1992, including 7,323 Northern Paiutes, 2,266 Owens Valley Paiutes, and 1,456 Southern Paiutes. Nearly half of the Paiutes lived off-reservation, often in small, federally recognized "colonies" that blended into surrounding white settlements.

HISTORY

Prior to substantial contact with non-Native peoples, the Paiutes led a highly mobile nomadic lifestyle. They ranged from the forested highlands of the Rocky Mountains westward to the Sierra Nevada Range, including the desert lowlands in between. The lifestyles of the various bands across this expansive region were largely determined by the particular foods available in the area where they predominantly lived. Most subsisted by hunting small game and gathering roots, seeds, and berries. Some Southern and Owens Valley Paiute bands used irrigation techniques and grew corn, while some Northern Paiute bands were fishermen. The extended family was the main traditional unit of social organization. Bands were composed of loose affiliations of families led by a headman selected for his abilities.

According to Bertha P. Dutton in *American Indians of the Southwest*, the Southern Paiutes moved into the Southwestern region of what is now the United States around the year 1000 A.D. The Paiutes lived for many years near the ancient Pueblo peoples already settled in the area and adopted their techniques for raising corn. Eventually the Pueblo began to leave the area. Though their early contact with European hunters and trappers in the 1820s was friendly, hostilities between the Paiutes and non-Indian intruders grew over time. Epidemics of smallpox, cholera, and other diseases swept through Paiute communities in the 1830s and 1840s. The limited contact with Euro-American explorers, fur trappers, and settlers changed abruptly when large-scale migration over the Oregon Trail began in the mid-1840s. Conflicts increased as more and more of the Paiute territory was claimed by whites. To the south, Mormons arriving from northern Utah began settling the best lands of the Southern Paiutes, including the Las Vegas Valley. Also by the 1840s the Paiutes to the north and south had acquired horses and guns and began raiding white camps and settlements. The majority of conflicts with whites took place after 1848, when the discovery of gold in California brought a flood of settlers through the center of the tribe's territory. In 1859 a major silver strike occurred at Virginia City in west-

ern Nevada. The rapid influx of miners and ranchers into the region led to hostilities with Northern Paiutes, which escalated to the Pyramid Lake War. Relatively large reservations for the Northern Paiutes were established at Pyramid Lake and Walker River in an attempt to maintain distance and peace between the Paiutes and the newcomers. However, in 1860 traders at a Pony Express station on the California Trail kidnapped and raped two Paiute girls. Tribal members responded by attacking the Pony Express station, killing five whites in the process of rescuing the girls. The Paiutes then killed 43 volunteers sent to avenge the killings. After several minor battles involving an 800-man volunteer army from California led by Colonel Jack Hays, peace with the Paiutes was restored. Most Paiutes returned to the Pyramid Lake Reservation while others withdrew further north to southeast Oregon. The military established Fort Churchill in 1860 in western Nevada to maintain peace.

During the U.S. Civil War years, when government troops were busy fighting in the East, the Paiutes continued numerous raids on ranches, farms, mining camps, and wagon trains. Following the Civil War, U.S. Army troops returned in force to the West. In Oregon, the United States established military posts in 1864 at Camp Alvord and in 1867 at Fort Harney. By 1866 the military took the offensive to end the Paiute resistance to white incursions. The escalating conflict became known as the Snake Indian War, since Northern Paiutes were often called Snake Indians by some settlers. Two war leaders, Paulina and Old Weawa, led the Paiutes in 40 skirmishes with the federal forces over a two year period before finally being forced to surrender in 1868. A treaty promising a reservation in Oregon was signed at Fort Harney with three Paiute bands, but it was never ratified by Congress. The Paiutes were forced to relocate to other reservations located elsewhere in the region. To the south, the United States and Southern Paiutes signed the 1865 Treaty of Spanish Forks. Also never ratified by Congress, the treaty was designed to the place six Southern Paiute bands on the Uintah Reservation in northern Utah. The first reservation for Southern Paiutes, the Moapa Reservation, was finally created in 1872. That same year, the almost two million acre Malheur Reservation was established in central Oregon by presidential executive order for the "free-roaming" Northern Paiutes of southeastern Oregon. However, the Malheur Reservation was returned to public ownership in its entirety following renewed, but brief, hostilities called the Bannock War in 1878. The Northern Paiute population scattered to other reservations or small communities. Many Paiute bands refused to move to the reservations already occupied by other bands. Instead, they established settlements on the outskirts of towns, where they worked as wage laborers. Two Paiute communities grew on military posts abandoned in the 1890s, Fort Bidwell and Fort McDermitt, in Oregon.

Though several large reservations (Moapa, Pyramid Lake, Walker River, Duck Valley, and Malheur) were established for the Paiutes in Nevada, Oregon, and Idaho between 1859 and 1891, by the turn of the century tribal lands had been reduced to less than 5 percent of their original territory. The government between 1910 and 1930 extended formal federal recognition and set aside modest acreage, usually 10 to 40 acres, for many of the nonreservation Paiute bands. Typical of many reservations throughout the nation, the General Allotment Act of 1887 carved up tribal lands on the larger Paiute reservations into small allotments allocated to individual tribal members and then sold the "excess" to non-Indians. The Walker River Reservation alone lost almost 290,000 acres of its best land in 1906. Around the turn of the century, many of the Owens Valley Paiutes were restricted to areas far too small to support their former way of life as the city of Los Angeles acquired former tribal lands to control water rights to the Owens River.

MODERN ERA

The Paiutes were impoverished through the loss of traditional economies, suffered population loss from disease and violent conflicts, and were removed from emerging market economies of non-Indian communities. They were also largely ignored by the U.S. government through the first three decades of the twentieth century. In the 1930s U.S. Indian policy dramatically changed again when Congress passed the Indian Reorganization Act of 1934. Native groups began to form federally recognized tribes and gain access to grants and federal services. However, inter-governmental relations declined again after World War II. Federal recognition was terminated for four of the Southern Paiute bands in 1954. This changing status discontinued health and education services vital to their well-being, in addition to the collective loss of over 43,000 acres from their land base. In yet another swing in U.S. policy, federal recognition status, as well as services were restored in 1980. Economic and cultural recovery for the Paiutes was difficult under such vacillating federal Indian policies.

Due to their location in the arid West, many Paiute bands were involved in water rights disputes throughout the twentieth century. For example, the Owens Valley Paiutes struggled to obtain enough water from the Owens River, a primary water source for the city of Los Angeles, to operate a fishery. The Paiutes of the Pyramid Lake suffered when the United States built Derby Dam as part of the Newlands Project in 1905 on the Truckee River, the primary water source for Pyramid Lake. The dam diverted almost half the river flow to a separate valley, the Carson Basin. As a result, the Pyramid Lake level dropped 78 feet by 1967, depriving cui-ui trout access to upstream spawning beds and significantly impacting tribal fisheries and waterfowl habitat on the Pyramid Lake Reservation. The cui-ui, which are central to Pyramid Lake Paiute identity, were listed under the Endangered Species Act in 1967. This helped the Paiutes regain control over their lake and fisheries. Similar water diversion plans by upstream non-Indian users severely degraded Walker River Reservation resources as well. Litigation over water rights persisted throughout much of the twentieth century with frequently unsuccessful results for the Paiutes.

SETTLEMENT PATTERNS

The Paiute population is broadly scattered, living in numerous small communities and a few large reservations. The Northern Paiutes live in at least 14 communities including: Pyramid Lake, Walker River, Fort McDermott, Fallon, Reno-Sparks area, Yerington, Lovelock, Summit Lake, and Winnemucca in Nevada; Burns and Warm Springs in Oregon; and, Bridgeport, Cedarville, and Fort Bidwell in California. Tribal memberships ranged from less than 20 individuals with the Winnemucca in 1992 to almost 2,000 with the Pyramid Lake tribe. The Owens Valley Paiute communities include Bishop, Big Pine, Lone Pine, Fort Independence, and Benton in eastern California. Their memberships in 1991 ranged from 84 at Benton to 1,350 at Bishop. Ten Southern Paiute communities include the Shivwits, Indian Peaks, Cedar, Koosharem, Kanosh, Kaibab, Moapa, Las Vegas, and San Juan. Their memberships are also small and ranged from 71 at Las Vegas to almost 300 at Moapa in 1992.

ACCULTURATION AND ASSIMILATION

TRADITIONS, CUSTOMS, AND BELIEFS

Due to their nomadic existence, most traditional Paiute homes were small, temporary huts and were made of willow poles and covered with brush and reeds. These abodes were frequently constructed near streams, where the Paiutes could fish or draw water for sustenance and irrigation.

Though marriage traditionally had no important associated rituals, the Paiutes did observe two related rituals. One was for young women at the time of their first menstrual period, and the other for young couples expecting their first child. In the menarche ritual, the young woman was isolated for four days. During this time, she observed taboos against touching her face or hair with her hands, eating animal-based foods, and drinking cold liquids. She also ran east at sunrise and west at sunset, and sat with older women of the tribe to learn about her responsibilities as a woman. After the four days of isolation, a series of rituals were performed to bring the menarche ceremony to a close. The young woman was bathed in cold water, her face was painted, the ends of her hair were singed or cut, and she had to eat animal foods and bitter herbs and to spit into a fire. The ritual for couples expecting their first child was very similar, but traditionally lasted 30 days. The pregnant woman observed the same taboos and received advice from older women, while the expectant father ran east at sunrise and west at sunset.

CUISINE

The Paiutes were a nomadic people, moving about the region to various food sources. The means of subsistence for specific Paiute bands depended to a large extent on their particular locations. In general, the Paiutes ate vegetables such as roots and rice grass, as well as berries and piñon pine nuts. Many used stones to grind seeds and nuts into flour for making bread. The Paiutes also hunted ducks, rabbits, and mountain sheep using bows and arrows or long nets. Some bands in mountainous regions fished, while others in arid desert regions dug for lizards, grubs, and insects, which were valuable protein sources. The Southern Paiutes adopted corn agriculture from the Pueblo peoples, and the Owens Valley Paiutes developed irrigation techniques to grow various crops. Many of the traditional foods are still key elements to tribal ceremonies, weddings, and other community events.

MUSIC

Typical of Native America, Paiute songs are performed by individuals or by groups in unison. A striking characteristic of Paiutes is the very limited traditional use of musical instruments. Drums, commonly used elsewhere by Native groups, were not used until after white contact. The primary traditional instruments were Shaman's rattles and sticks beaten during hand games. At Round Dances, the oldest music style in Paiute tradition, only the singer's voice is used for music. For some curing practices, healers use a small flute made of elderberry stems.

TRADITIONAL COSTUMES

Paiute men and women traditionally wore a skin breechcloth or double-apron of skin or vegetable fiber such as sagebrush bark or rushes. The cloth was suspended from a belt made from cliffrose bark or antelope skin. They also typically wore animal-skin moccasins sometimes ankle high or woven yucca or sagebrush bark sandals on their feet. In the winter, they used robes of rabbit fur strips or skin capes. Southern Paiute men and women reportedly wore twined-bark leggings and Northern Paiute men wore simple buckskin shirts. Members of some Paiute bands wore hats decorated with bird, often quail, feathers. Except in Oregon, women wore basketry hats. Throughout Paiute country men wore tanned hide hats. By the mid-nineteenth century men's shirts and leggings and women's full-length dresses were made from fringed hide, which was most likely adopted from the Ute.

DANCES AND SONGS

Popular Paiute songs are associated with hand games, Round Dances, and doctor's curing. Variations on the Round, or Circle, Dance were traditionally the most common dance form and the oldest. The Northern Paiute Hump Dance represented one variation. In a Round Dance, the participants form a circle and dance around often in a clockwise direction to music made by a singer situated in the center. A Round Dance is commonly held three times a year, during the Spring fishing season, just before fall pine-nut harvest, and during the November rabbit drives. Such dances serve to periodically affirm social unity and focus participants on the particular subsistence tasks at hand.

In 1889 Wovoka, a Southern Paiute, founded the Ghost Dance religion. In a vision, he saw the earth reborn in a natural state and returned to the Indians and their ancestors, free from white man's control. Wovoka taught his followers that they could achieve this vision by dancing, chanting, and eliminating all traces of white influence from their lives. The Ghost Dance incorporated the earlier Round Dance elements, including the lack of a percussion accompaniment.

A revival of the
traditional Ghost
Dance performed
by Paiute women.

HOLIDAYS

In addition to the popular holidays of American society, the tribes recognize special days important to their particular communities. For example, Reservation Day is celebrated by The Burns Paiute Tribe every June 13 in honor of the date the tribe received reservation lands.

HEALTH ISSUES

Until the 1930s, the Paiutes were healed by Native doctors known as *puagants*, believed to possess supernatural powers. The *puagants* each formed a magical relationship with one or more animal spirits, often using the fur or feathers of the animal to call upon the spirits to assist them in their work. By the late twentieth century, health care facilities were available to some Paiutes, often through the federal Indian Health Services (IHS). Examples of such facilities include the McDermitt Tribal Health Center in northern Nevada, the Fallon and Schurz Indian health centers in western Nevada, the Pyramid Lake Health Department in northwestern Nevada and the Owyhee Indian Health Service Hospital in southeastern Oregon.

In addition to economic development programs, projects addressing health care were a top priority among the bands. Compounded by poverty, the Paiutes suffered high rates of certain diseases, dysfunctional family relations, and substance abuse. Health screening programs were instituted where feasible. Care programs for the elderly were also implemented including regular monitoring of their well-being, in-home care, hot lunches, crafts, firewood supplies, and special housing.

LANGUAGE

The three main Paiute groups speak distinct languages of the Numic branch of the Uto-Aztecan language family. The Northern Paiutes speak a Shoshonean language, while that spoken by the Owens Valley Paiutes is related to the language of the Mono peoples of California. Members of the different subgroups have maintained their Native languages to varying degrees. The San Juan Paiutes, a Southern Paiute band whose reservation is completely within the boundaries of the Navajo Reservation in Arizona, is one of the only groups that continues to teach Paiute to children as a first language. Many other Paiute groups have actively taken steps to preserve their language. In the 1980s the Yerington Paiutes developed a dictionary and produced a series of story books and workbooks.

GREETINGS AND POPULAR EXPRESSIONS

Examples of common Numa expressions and words include: *Ku'-na O-ho'-i-gi*—around the fire; *Mu-a Tva'-i-to-a*—moonlight; *Ta-shin'-ti-ai*—cold feet; *Au*—yes; *To-a-Mi-yok*—give me the pipe; *Pa-ha-vwuk-i-num Tik-er-ru*—I am hungry; *Ta'-kavw-yu'-mu-kim*—the snow falls; *Ku-na Ma-ko-to*—to light a fire; *Ni-Tik-er'-ro-wa*—I will eat; *Hainch Ki-tum-a-r_g*—Friend, talk out!; *Ya'-ni-kin*—to laugh; *To-ya'-pi*—mountain; *Pi'-av*—female; *Wan'-sits*—antelope; *Ta'-mun*—Spring; *To-namp*—chokecherries; *Pan-so-wa'-bits*—duck; *Pun-ko-U-nish Mi-er'-ro*—the horse goes fast.

> **"T**he grandmothers have the special care of the daughters just before and after they come to womanhood. The girls are not allowed to get married until they have come to womanhood; and that period is recognized as a very sacred thing, and is the subject of a festival, and has peculiar customs."

Sarah Winnemucca Hopkins, 1883.

FAMILY AND COMMUNITY DYNAMICS

EDUCATION

Educational services were inconsistently available to the Paiutes on the various reservations and colonies. Schools were established at the Pyramid Lake and Walker River reservations in the late 1870s and early 1880s. In 1897 Indian schools were opened at Bishop and Big Pine Paiute communities and shortly afterwards at Independence. Not until after the turn of the century did other Paiute communities establish schools, from Lovelock Paiutes in 1907 to the Burns Paiutes in 1931 for the Northern Paiutes, and at Las Vegas, Shivwits, Moapa, and Kaibab between 1900 and 1940 for the Southern Paiutes. The schools lasted from only a year to decades. When local schools were not available, children were sent away, sometimes great distances, to boarding schools. The Stewart Institute, a boarding school for Nevada Indians, was established in western Nevada in 1890 and well used by Paiutes until the 1970s.

THE ROLE OF WOMEN

The most enduring Paiute tradition through all the dramatic changes of the past two centuries has been maintenance of independent and extended families as the basic social unit. Consequently, as in most Native societies in North America, women play a crucial role. For instance, besides child rearing and managing home life, women are the principal gatherers of traditional plant foods. These foods continue to provide a spiritual focal point in traditional ceremonies and feasts.

FESTIVALS

From Spring through late Fall, a series of pow wows are held around the region. These intertribal festivals include the Shoshoni-Paiute Annual Pow Wow held in July, the Veteran's Day Pow Wow held annually in November at Owyhee, Nevada, the Snow Mountain Pow Wow held in May in Las Vegas, Nevada, the Mother's Day Pow Wow held in May at Burns, Oregon, and pow wows at Bishop and Big Pine in California. Such festivals include arts and crafts shows, hand game tournaments, dancing, and traditional foods. The Paiutes commonly attend similar events hosted by tribes in surrounding regions as well, largely spurred through kinship ties.

FUNERALS

Unlike marriage which had little ceremony, funerals received considerable emphasis. A traditional funeral observance known as the Cry ceremony was introduced to the Paiutes in the 1870s. Within the next 20 years, it became pervasive in the cultures of the Owens Valley Paiutes and Southern Paiutes. The Cry took place over one or two nights after a person's death prior to the funeral, and then was repeated a year or two later as a memorial. During the Cry ceremony, two groups of singers perform song cycles known as Salt Songs and Bird Songs. The Cry ceremony remained significant throughout the twentieth century. Between the singing, people close to the deceased offer emotional speeches and give away the person's valuables to guests.

INTERACTIONS WITH OTHER TRIBES

Though the three groups differed both culturally and linguistically, today most members refer to themselves simply as Paiutes. The name Paiute means "true Ute" or "water Ute," reflecting the group's relationship to the Ute Indians of Utah. Though relations were generally good between Paiutes and Utes, in historic times the Utes became very active in

slave raids on the Paiutes, trading abducted Paiute slaves to Spanish colonists in the Southwest. The Paiutes were also closely related to the Shoshone peoples of the Northwest. Though the Owens Valley Paiutes were culturally similar to the Northern Paiutes, they spoke the language of the Mono (or Monache) peoples that lived west of the Sierra Nevada. The San Juan Paiutes, though living in fear of the Navajo to the east, actually adopted some Navajo customs regarding dress, housing, and some linguistic traits. Though generally considered Southern Paiutes, the Chemehuevi who lived along the lower Colorado River south of the Las Vegas Valley on the Arizona and California border actually shared more traits with Southern California tribes than with other Paiutes, such as floodplain farming and earthen house construction of the Mohave culture, than other Paiute cultural practices.

RELIGION

A fundamental aspect of Paiute religion is acquisition of "power," or *buha* among Northern Paiutes. The Paiutes believed in many supernatural beings that manifested themselves in elements of the natural world, such as water, thunder, and animals. *Buha* could be acquired in dreams or at cave or grave sites. Aside from healing, *buha* was sought to help control weather, sexual prowess, vulnerability in warfare, and gambling success. One powerful spirit was Thuwipu Unipugant, or "the One Who Made the Earth," who was represented by the sun. The Paiutes prayed to the spirits in order to influence them and show their respect. For example, they might pray for rain or a successful hunt.

According to Bertha Dutton in *American Indians of the Southwest*, early efforts to convert the Paiutes to Christianity were relatively successful, particularly those Paiutes who lived among the Mormons in Utah. As Catherine Fowler noted in *Native America in the Twentieth Century: An Encyclopedia*, most Paiutes attend religious services in some Christian denomination, though some also participate in Indian religious movements such as the Native American Church, the Sweat Lodge movement, and the Sun Dance.

The Paiutes made a direct contribution to one of the major nineteenth century Native American religious movements. In 1889, when most Paiutes had been pushed off of their ancestral lands and forced to live on reservations, a Southern Paiute named Wovoka founded the Ghost Dance religion, which prophesied an end to white domination. The son of Tavibo, a mystic of the Walker River Paiute band, Wovoka experienced a powerful vision during a solar eclipse. In his vision, the earth was returned to a natural state, with unfenced plains full of buffalo, no more white men, and the Indians living in harmony. Wovoka preached that in order to achieve this vision of the future, the Indians needed to rid themselves of white influence, especially the use of alcohol. He also called upon the Native peoples to pray, meditate, and dance. Within a few years, the Ghost Dance religion had spread to angry and frustrated tribes all over the West. Some tribes, like the Sioux, interpreted the Ghost Dance as a call for renewed violence against whites. Though the Paiutes refrained from resorting to violence, they embraced the Ghost Dance for many years as a form of resistance to white culture.

EMPLOYMENT AND ECONOMIC TRADITIONS

Traditionally, the Paiutes lived on an economy of hunting, fishing, and gathering. Men hunted deer, mountain sheep, and antelope. Smaller mammals, particularly jackrabbits, were captured in communal activities using large nets. Waterfowl, such as American coots, at the various large lakes were also hunted. Fish were netted or speared. Women performed extensive plant gathering, including a wide variety of roots (tubers), berries, and seeds. Pine nuts were particularly important toward the south and camas bulbs to the north. To the furthest extent south, in the Las Vegas region, agave was a key food source. Also, in the far south of Paiute country, irrigation was used to grow corn, squash, melons, sunflowers, gourds, and beans.

The various natural food sources were gathered through the year in an annual cycle necessitating a good deal of mobility. Groups would break apart into families then rejoin again seasonally. Consequently, Paiute society consisted of economically self-sufficient and politically independent families who seasonally occupied "home" tracts. The families would unite semi-annually with other families forming a camp group of 2 or 3 families. The core family unit would continually expand or contract and the camp group also changed size and composition seasonally and through the years, often foraging together and pooling resources.

Like other Native American groups who could no longer continue traditional economies, the Paiutes experienced difficulties in securing sources of income for tribal members, as well as revenue for the tribes. After relocation to reservations, the Paiutes increasingly made a living by working for wages in nearby towns or ranches. In the Owens Valley, Paiutes worked as wage laborers in the local farming and ranching economy after the 1870s and later became involved in tourism and mining operations. Elsewhere, some Paiutes raised cattle. Pyramid Lake and Walker River Paiutes were able to keep fishing, selling fish in local town markets until the 1920s when loss of water due to river diversions lowered the lakes and disrupted fish runs upstream from the lakes.

The federal Indian allotment policies from the 1890s through 1910 hit some Paiutes particularly hard, carving up reservations and placing the more economically productive lands within reservation boundaries into non-Indian ownership. As examples, the Fallon Paiutes located on the original Stillwater Reservation lost 90 percent of its land base and the Pyramid Lake Paiutes lost a 20,000 acre timber reserve. Much of the retained Paiute lands suffered cattle trespassing and poaching of big game and fish resources.

In 1965, the Southern Paiutes received approximately $7.2 million from the U.S. government in a lawsuit for almost 30 million acres of tribal lands wrongfully taken. Many bands, such as the Moapa and Kaibab, used the money as capital to improve living conditions and develop educational and employment opportunities. Also during the 1970s, five bands of Utah Paiutes formed a legal corporation, the Paiute Indian Tribe of Utah, and received a government grant to build an industrial complex.

Passage of the Indian Self-Determination and Education Act in 1974 stimulated economic development from the late 1970s into the 1990s. The act promoted Indian economic self-sufficiency through loan and grant programs. Monies from land claim settlements and federal loans led to various forms of development. Pyramid Lake, Walker River, Reno-Sparks, Las Vegas, and Fallon communities opened smoke-shops and mini-marts. At smoke-shops on tribal lands, tribes could sell cigarettes to the public without federal taxes added, making them lucrative when located near well-used routes. The Pyramid Lake Paiutes also built two commercial fish hatcheries and received revenue from issuing recreational fishing permits for the lake. Attempts at developments such as business parks, as at Big Pine, had limited success due to the isolation of tribal lands. Traditional crafts continued, such as among the

In earlier times, the Paiute tribesmen often hunted and defended themselves with the bow and arrow.

Kaibab, and a few artisans became commercially successful. Some bands have relied on grazing livestock or issuing grazing leases, including Pyramid Lake, Walker River, Fort McDermitt, and the Utah Paiutes. However, many of the Paiute communities, including Fort Bidwell, Summit Lake, Burns, and Lovelock among others, have enjoyed few successes in establishing employment opportunities and revenue sources. Still, by the latter twentieth century, most Paiute communities had successfully installed electrical and telephone services, plumbing, paved streets and built better housing. Economic plight led two Paiute bands to consider controversial projects in the 1990s. The Northern Paiute of the Fort McDermitt Reservation in Nevada discussed the possibility of building a storage facility for high-level nuclear waste on their lands, while the Southern Paiute of the Kaibab Reservation in Arizona debated whether to construct a hazardous waste incinerator. The financial rewards these projects offered the bands made them appealing, but both projects were ultimately defeated due to environmental concerns.

POLITICS AND GOVERNMENT

Traditional Paiute leadership roles recognized leaders as spokespersons, not as autonomous decision-makers and figures of authority. Decisions were frequently made in a consensus-seeking manner among all adult band members. However, the loss of traditional economies and displacement to remote reservations and colonies led to concerns in the early twentieth century regarding health care, schools, law enforcement, sanitation, housing, and utilities. In order to qualify for federal assistance and establish intergovernmental relations with the U.S. government, most Paiute bands formally organized under the 1934 Indian Reorganization Act (IRA). The IRA encouraged the formation of governments based on Western social models rather than traditional tribal arrangements. The model included tribal councils composed of elected individuals headed by a chairperson and written constitutions with by-laws. Though the IRA-formed governments became the focal point of intergovernmental relations with the United States and state governments and other non-Indian organizations, traditional leaders frequently influenced policy directions internally. In some cases the IRA stimulated factionalism within tribal politics by aligning traditional versus "progressive" elements of the membership. The contemporary councils commonly serve as business corporations, overseeing use of tribal funds and promoting economic self-sufficiency. Elections are held every two or three years. Committees of traditional leaders, including elders, often guide the course of the elected tribal council.

Four of the Southern Paiute governments in Utah (the Shivwits, Indian Peaks, Koosharem, and Kanosh) were targeted by the federal termination policies of the 1950s. The Utah bands later reorganized under the Paiute Restoration Act of 1980. The San Juan Paiutes were not able to organize is such a manner and did not gain federal recognition until 1990.

INDIVIDUAL AND GROUP CONTRIBUTIONS

Though Paiute populations have traditionally been small compared to other Native North American groups, several Paiutes have made key contributions to education and the arts. The Paiutes and their accomplishments are described below.

EDUCATION

Nellie Shaw Harner (1905-1985) was born in Wadsworth, Nevada on the Pyramid Lake Reservation. After attending the Carson Indian School in Stewart, Nevada, Harner went on to attend the Haskell Institute in Lawrence, Kansas and later received a B.A. in elementary education from Northern Arizona University in Flagstaff, Arizona, and an M.A. from the University of Nevada at Reno. Fluent in the Paiute language and keenly interested in traditional stories, histories, and lifestyles of Native Americans, Harner taught and counseled in Bureau of Indian Affairs schools in Arizona, Kansas, Nevada, New Mexico, and Wyoming. Her master's thesis, *The History of the Pyramid Lake Indians - 1842-1959*, was a key contribution to Paiute written history. Harner was named Nevada's Outstanding Woman of the Year in 1975 and spent her retirement years on the Pyramid Lake Reservation.

LITERATURE

Adrian C. Louis (b. 1945), a member of the Lovelock Paiute born and raised in Nevada, has published a number of collections of poems, including *Fire Water World* (1989), *Among the Dog Eaters* (1992), *Blood Thirsty Savages* (1994), *Vortex of Indian Fevers* (1995), and *Ceremonies of the Damned* (1997). His other work includes the novel *Skins* (1995) and another book, *Wild Indians and Other Creatures* (1996). Louis received an M.A. from Brown University and has been an instructor at the Oglala Lakota College on the Pine Ridge Reservation in South Dakota. His literary focus has been on the forced assimilation of Native culture into the dominant Western society and its ramifications, including poverty, alcohol and drug abuse, humiliation, and demoralization.

Annie Lowry (1866-1943) was also born in Lovelock, Nevada to a Paiute mother. Lowry became the subject of a book by Lalla Scott as part of the 1930 Writer's Project of the Works Progress Administration. Through the project Lowry related many Paiute traditions and events of the late nineteenth century.

Clearly one of the better known Paiute is Sarah Winnemucca (1844-1891). Winnemucca published *Life Among the Piutes: Their Wrongs and Claims* in 1883. The book is considered to be the first autobiography by a Native American woman and one of the few Indian autobiographies in the later half of the nineteenth century. Born near Humboldt Lake in northern Nevada, Winnemucca was the daughter of Paiute leader Old Winnemucca. She served as an interpreter between Paiute raiding groups and the U.S. military in 1866 and again in 1878. She was a school teacher at the Malheur and Yakima reservations in the 1870s. Following the period of armed conflict, Winnemucca began touring first the West Coast in 1879 and then the East Coast through the early 1880s giving numerous eloquent lectures on the plight of Native Americans in the Great Basin region. In 1884 she gave testimony before a U.S. Senate subcommittee on the state of the reservation system. Elizabeth Palmer Peabody, a noted education proponent in the East, met Winnemucca and encouraged her to publish her story to educate the public about governmental injustice against the Native population. The book is a blend of autobiography, ethnography, and history of the Paiute peoples between 1844 and 1883. Winnemucca also published an 1882 article on Paiute ethnography in *The Californian* journal. Winnemucca founded the Peabody Indian School in Nevada in 1884 and operated it until 1887. She was the first woman honored in Nevada with a historical marker. Her book was reprinted again in 1994 by the University of Nevada Press.

RELIGION

A Southern Paiute of the Walker River band, Wovoka (c.1856-1932) founded the Ghost Dance religion in 1889. He grew up in the area of Mason Valley, Nevada, near the present Walker Lake Reservation. His proper name means "The Cutter" in Paiute. At the time of his father's death, Wovoka was taken into the family of a white farmer named David Wilson and was given the name Jack Wilson, by which he was known among local American settlers.

ORGANIZATIONS AND ASSOCIATIONS

Benton Paiute Reservation.
The reservation located in Owens Valley of eastern California is 160 acres in size with over 80 members in 1991.

Address: Star Route 4, Box 56-A, Benton, California 93512.
Telephone: (760) 933-2321.

Big Pine Reservation.
The reservation located in Owens Valley of eastern California is 279 acres in size with over 400 members in 1991.

Address: P.O. Box 700, Big Pine, California 93513.
Telephone: (760) 938-2003.

Bishop Reservation.
The reservation located in Owens Valley of eastern California is almost 900 acres in size with 1,350 members in 1991.

Address: 50 Tu Su Lane, Bishop, California 93514.
Telephone: (760) 873-3584.

Bridgeport Paiute Colony.
The colony holds 40 acres of land in rural southeastern California not far from the Nevada border.

Address: P.O. Box 37, Bridgeport, California 93517.
Telephone: (760) 932-7083.

Burns Paiute Tribe.
In 1897 homeless Northern Paiutes who had gathered around Burns, Oregon were provided 115 allotments of land. In 1972 Congress created a 750 acre reservation. The band gained federal recognition in 1968.

Address: HC-71 100 Pa-Si-Go Street, Burns, Oregon 97720.
Telephone: (541) 573-2088.

Cedarville Rancheria Community Council.
The small tribal community holds 17 acres of land in northeastern California near the Nevada boundary.

Address: P.O. Box 126, Cedarville, California 96104.
Telephone: (530) 279-2022.

Fallon Paiute-Shoshone Tribe.
Consisting of a 3,500 acre reservation and 70 acre colony in west-central Nevada, the lands were first set aside in 1907 and 1917, respectively.

Address: 8955 Mission Road, Fallon, Nevada 89406.
Telephone: (775) 423-6075.

Fort Bidwell Paiute.
Located in the far northeastern corner of California near the Oregon state boundary, the tribe holds over 3,300 acres of land established by executive order.

Address: P.O. Box 129, Fort Bidwell, California 96112.
Telephone: (530) 279-6310.

Fort Independence Reservation.
The reservation located in Owens Valley of eastern California is over 350 acres in size.

Address: P.O. Box 67, Independence, California 93526.
Telephone: (760) 878-2126.

Fort McDermitt Paiute and Shoshone Tribe.
With the headquarters located four miles southeast of McDermitt, Humbold County, Nevada, much of the 35,000 acres of tribal land also lies in Malheur County, Oregon. The first 20,000 acres were set aside in 1936.

Address: P.O. Box 457, McDermitt, Nevada 89421.
Telephone: (775) 532-8259.

Inter-Tribal Council (ITC) of Nevada.
The Council was formed in 1964 to give the small, scattered Indian communities in the state of Nevada a larger voice in socio-political issues and economic development. The ITC has managed housing, Public Health Service, and other programs for the tribes.

Address: 680 Greenbrae Drive, Suite 280, Sparks, Nevada 89431.
Telephone: (775) 355-0600.

Kaibab Paiute Tribe.

The tribe holds a 120,000 acre reservation in the "Arizona Strip" area of Arizona north of Grand Canyon National Park.

Address: HC65, Box 2, Fredonia, Arizona 86022.
Telephone: (520) 643-7245.

Las Vegas Paiute Tribe.

The tribe holds 10 acres of land with the city limits of Las Vegas, Nevada set aside in 1912, and another 3,850 acres north of the city reserved by Congress in 1983.

Address: One Paiute Drive, Las Vegas, Nevada 89106.
Telephone: (702) 386-3926.

Lone Pine Reservation.

The reservation located in Owens Valley of eastern California is over 230 acres in size.

Address: P.O. Box 747, Lone Pine, California 93545.
Telephone: (76) 876-5414.

Lovelock Paiute Tribe.

The Tribe holds 20 acres in the town of Lovelock, Nevada in west-central Nevada, the lands were first set aside in 1907 and modestly expanded in 1910.

Address: P.O. Box 878, Lovelock, Nevada 89419.
Telephone: (775) 273-7861.

Moapa Paiute Band of the Moapa Indian Reservation.

Shortly after an 1873 Presidential Executive Order established a two million acre reservation, Congress severely reduced it to 1,000 acres in 1875. Since 1980, Congress added back slightly over 70,000 acres. The reserve is located approximately 55 miles northeast of Las Vegas, Nevada.

Address: P.O. Box 340, Moapa, Nevada 89025.
Telephone: (702) 865-2787.

Owens Valley Paiute-Shoshone Board of Trustees.

Though each of four Paiute bands in the Owens Valley region of southeastern California have their own governments, a common board oversees their activities on a regional basis. The four include colonies of several hundred acres each totaling over 1,740 acres at Bishop, Big Pine, Lone Pine and Fort Independence, established between 1902 and 1915. Another Paiute colony located in Owens Valley but not under authority of the Board is a 160 acre colony at Benton. The Board has operated a cultural center, recreational and educational facilities, and the Toiyabe Indian Health Project serving the entire Owens Valley region.

Address: 2301 West Line Street, Bishop, California 93514.
Telephone: (760) 873-4478.

Paiute Indian Tribe of Utah.

Composed of five separate Paiute bands, the five hold a total of over 32,400 acres of land scattered in five parcels in southern Utah.

Address: 440 North Paiute Drive, Cedar City, Utah 84720.
Telephone: (435) 586-1112.

Pyramid Lake Paiute Tribe.

The 475,000 acre reservation fully contains a 112,000 acre desert lake, Pyramid Lake.

Address: P.O. Box 256, Nixon, Nevada 89424.
Telephone: (775) 574-1000.

Reno-Sparks Indian Colony.

First established with 20 acres located in Reno, Nevada, the colony now holds almost 2,000 acres, most of it located 10 miles north of the Reno-Sparks urban area in Hungry Valley.

Address: 98 Colony Road, Reno, Nevada 89502.
Telephone: (775) 329-2936.

San Juan Paiute Tribe.

Though holding no land of their own currently, they live on the traditional lands now in the western part of the Navajo Reservation.

Address: P.O. Box 2656, Tuba City, Arizona 86045.
Telephone: (520) 283-4589.

Shoshone-Paiute Tribes of the Duck Valley Reservation.

The reservation was established by executive order in 1877 and consisted of almost 300,000 acres in the 1990s almost equally split by the Nevada and Idaho state boundary.

Address: P.O. Box 219, Owyhee, Nevada 89832.
Telephone: (775) 757-3161.

Summit Lake Paiute Tribe.
Located in far northern Nevada in Humboldt County and first recognized in 1913, the Tribe holds slightly over 10,000 acres largely set by Congress in 1959.

Address: 655 Anderson Street, Winnemucca,
    Nevada 89445.
Telephone: (775) 623-5151.

Walker River Paiute Tribe.
The Walker River Reservation, first established by executive order in 1859, now includes over 313,000 acres of tribal lands located primarily in Mineral County but also Churchill and Lyon counties of south-central Nevada.

Address: P.O. Box 220, Schurz, Nevada 89427.
Telephone: (775) 773-2306.

Warm Springs Confederated Tribes.
The tribes, holding over 640,000 acres in north-central Oregon, are composed of three tribes of which the Paiute constitute a relatively small portion.

Address: P.O. Box C, Warm Springs, Oregon 97761.
Telephone: (541) 553-1161.

Winnemucca Colony.
First recognized in 1917 when 60 acres were set aside by Presidential executive order, the trip now holds 340 acres in the northwestern Nevada town of Winnemucca.

Address: P.O. Box 1370, Winnemucca,
    Nevada 89446.

Yerington Paiute Tribe Colony and Campbell Ranch.
The Tribe holds 22 acres of colony lands adjacent to Yerington, Nevada and over 1,600 acres of land ten miles north of the south-central Nevada lands.

Address: 171 Campbell Lane, Yerington,
    Nevada 89447.
Telephone: (775) 463-3301.

MUSEUMS AND RESEARCH CENTERS

Eastern California Museum.
Extensive collections of the Owens Valley Paiute.

Contact: Bill Michael.
Address: 155 Grant Street, Box 206,
    Independence, California 93526.
Telephone: (619) 878-2411.

Museum of Peoples and Cultures.
Contact: Dr. Joel C. Janetski.
Address: 710 North 100 East, Allen Building,
    Brigham Young University, Provo,
    Utah 84602.
Telephone: (801) 378-6112.

Nevada Historical Society.
Address: 1650 North Virginia Street, Reno,
    Nevada 89503.
Telephone: (775) 688-1190.

Nevada State Museum.
Houses extensive archaeological collections from traditional Paiute territory and routinely has exhibits for the public on traditional Paiute life.

Address: 600 North Carson Street, Capitol
    Complex, Carson City, Nevada 89710.
Telephone: (775) 687-4810.

Stewart Indian Museum.
Established in 1982 after closure of the Stewart Indian Boarding School, the Museum assists research efforts of tribes and individuals and sponsors the Dat-So-La-Lee Basket Maker's Guild.

Address: 5366 Snyder Avenue, Carson City,
    Nevada 89701.
Telephone: (775) 882-1808.

SOURCES FOR ADDITIONAL STUDY

Bunte, Pamela A., and Robert J. Franklin. *From the Sands to the Mountain: Change and Persistence in a Southern Paiute Community.* Lincoln: University of Nebraska Press, 1987.

———. *The Paiute.* New York: Chelsea House, 1990.

———. "Southern Paiute." *Native America in the Twentieth Century: An Encyclopedia.* Edited by Mary B. Davis. New York: Garland Publishing, 1994.

Dutton, Bertha P. *American Indians of the Southwest.* Albuquerque: University of New Mexico Press, 1983.

Fowler, Catherine S. "Northern Paiute" and "Owens Valley Paiute." *Native America in the Twentieth Century: An Encyclopedia.* Edited by Mary B. Davis. New York: Garland Publishing, 1994.

Fowler, Don D., and John F. Matley. "Material Culture of the Numa: The John Wesley Powell Collection, 1867-1880." *Smithsonian Contributions to Anthropology*, Number 26. Washington, DC: Smithsonian Institution Press, 1979.

Steward, Julian H. "Basin-Plateau Aboriginal Sociopolitical Groups." *Smithsonian Institution, Bureau of American Ethnology*, No. 120. Reprint. Salt Lake City: University of Utah Press, 1970.

Wheat, Margaret M. *Survival Arts of the Primitive Paiutes*. Reno: University of Nevada Press, 1967.

Winnemucca, Sarah. *Life Among the Piutes: Their Wrongs and Claims*. Boston: Cupples, Upham, 1883. Reprint. Reno: University of Nevada Press, 1994.

PAKISTANI AMERICANS

by
Tinaz Pavri

Religion figures prominently in the life of Pakistani American families, and the Holy Quran and the teachings of the Holy Prophet serve as the guidelines that Pakistani Muslims follow throughout their lives.

OVERVIEW

Pakistan received its independence from British India in 1947. It was created on the basis of religious identity, so that Muslims from British India, which had an overwhelming majority of followers of the Hindu religion, would have a nation to call their own. It is bordered by India on the east, Iran and Afghanistan on the west, the great Karakoram mountain range and China on the north, and the Arabian Sea on the south. Modern-day Pakistan is divided into four major geographic divisions known as the North-West Frontier Province (NWFP), Punjab, Sind, and Baluchistan. Each of these regions has its own language and ethnic groups. The capital of Pakistan is the modern city of Islamabad, although its cultural and economic centers continue to be Lahore and Karachi.

HISTORY

Pakistan boasts the site of the famed Indus valley civilization (B.C. 2500 to B.C. 1700), including prehistoric remains at Mohenjo-Daro, near the modern Pakistani city of Larkana, and at Harappa, near the city of Lahore. The Indus valley civilization has remained an interest for archaeologists because of the society's high level of sophistication and stability over several centuries.

Pakistan's ethnic and cultural diversity has been formed through legacies of advancing Persians, Turks, Arabs, Huns, Greeks, and Mongols, most of whom practiced Islam. From about the eighth century until British dominance increased in the eighteenth century, Muslim rulers established kingdoms in northern India. As a result, many Pakistanis and others in British India converted to the religion of the new people.

When the struggle for independence from the British colonizers started in India at the beginning of the twentieth century, Hindus—followers of India's majority religion—and Muslims fought side by side for their freedom. The Indian National Congress, the political party that eventually led India to its independence, had many devoted Muslim members who were willing to give up their lives for the cause of India's freedom.

Mohandas K. Gandhi's movement of *satyagraha*, or non-violent passive resistance in the face of British oppression, formed the key to India's response to British colonization and gave shape to the drive for independence. Hundreds of thousands of Indians, both Hindu and Muslim, refused to cooperate with their British colonizers on every level of daily life—from the social to the political to the economic. Finally, the British decided that they could no longer rule over India; they formally relinquished its Indian colony in 1947.

However, as the goal of independence appeared more likely to be achieved, a section of the Muslim leadership led by Mohammed Ali Jinnah (1876-1948), who later became independent Pakistan's founder and first governor general, felt that Muslims would never be accorded equal treatment in a largely Hindu India. Because Jinnah feared political, social, and cultural subordination to the Hindu majority, he started a movement to establish a separate state based on Islam for the Indian Muslims. This group felt that in order to be truly free, Indian Muslims needed their own homeland. The independence leaders, both Hindus like Nehru and Mohandas Gandhi, and Muslims like Jinnah and Liaquat Ali Khan, who later became Pakistan's first prime minister, worked together with the British to make the transition from British India into independent India and Pakistan a reality.

When the British finally left India in 1947, two independent states, India and Pakistan, were formed. The separation was a consequence of, and resulted in, feelings of some bitterness between the two nations. Hundreds of thousands of Hindus and Muslims died in the riots that followed independence, as Muslims from India migrated to Pakistan and Hindus who lived in the newly created Pakistan streamed into India. Refugee camps were created on both sides of the border between the two countries to deal with these mass migrations.

These difficult, even tragic, beginnings that marked the two countries at their inception continued to be reflected in the relationship that has developed between them in the post-independence era. India and Pakistan have fought three wars over the years and have been involved in many other confrontations, particularly over the disputed Kashmir region that lies between the two countries and is today the scene of a protracted, three-way conflict among the Indians, Pakistanis, and Kashmiris, who are seeking independence from both India and Pakistan. However, there are also ties of a shared history and culture that bind the people of the two countries. Many Muslims who chose to remain in India have close family members who moved to Pakistan and some Hindus remained behind in Pakistan, ensuring an intertwined destiny for the two countries.

After the death of Jinnah, Pakistan was ruled by a series of army chiefs under what were called martial law regimes. Pakistan's presidents in the 1950s and 1960s were army generals who assumed the highest political office. In 1971, Pakistan was divided again as a result of ethnic insurgency in its Eastern wing, which was populated mainly by Bengali-speaking Muslims, and the subsequent war with neighboring India. As a result of this division, a new sovereign country—Bangladesh—was created; Pakistan has since recognized Bangladesh and has established diplomatic and trading relations with the new nation.

An overwhelming 98 percent of the Pakistani population are followers of Islam. There are much smaller Hindu, Christian and Zoroastrian minority communities. Pakistan is not a secular state; the state religion is Islam, and religion enters many aspects of Pakistani political and social life. There are also several distinct ethnic and linguistic groups in Pakistan, including Pathans, Punjabis, Sindhis, and Baluchis. The Pathans, also known as the Pushtoons or Pakhtoons, come from the region of the North-West Frontier Province (NWFP). They include tribes on the border of Pakistan and Afghanistan, although the community has become increasingly urbanized in recent years. The Punjabi community is the center of education and industry in Pakistan and includes both rural and urban segments within it. The Baluchis from Baluchistan were originally a semi-nomadic people; today, while many continue to follow ancient traditions, others have moved to the city of Karachi in search of employment. All these communities have their own languages. The Sindhis come from the region of Sind and are a mixture of several different ethnic groups but share a common language, Sindhi. These subcommunities, who are represented in the larger

Pakistani American community, have experienced some tension in recent times.

Pakistan has had four constitutions since 1947. Benazir Bhutto, the Harvard-educated daughter of Zulfikar Ali Bhutto, Pakistan's president from 1971 to 1977, was voted into power in 1988, in the country's first largely-free national elections. She led her father's political party, the Pakistan People's Party (PPP) to victory. She then lost the 1990 general election, but is today head of Pakistan's government once again. Under Benazir Bhutto, Pakistan has made significant strides towards the establishment of democracy, although it still faces internal threats of ethnic strife and religious fundamentalism.

EARLY IMMIGRATION

Since Pakistan only came into existence in 1947, any documentation of the life of Pakistani Americans can technically only commence from that year. However, it should be noted that Muslim immigrants from India and the region that is now Pakistan entered the United States as early as the eighteenth century, working alongside their Hindu or Sikh brethren in agriculture, logging, and mining in the western states of California, Oregon, and Washington.

In 1907, around 2,000 Indians, including Hindus and Muslims, worked alongside other immigrants from China, Japan, Korea, and Italy on the building of the Western Pacific railway in California. Other Indians worked on building bridges and tunnels for California's other railroad projects. As the demand for agricultural labor increased in California, Indians turned to the fields and orchards for employment. Muslim agricultural workers in California sometimes brought an Imam or learned man to the fields with them. The Imam proceeded to pray from the Holy Quran several times a day when the men took their breaks.

Muslims from the Indian subcontinent became successful as land tenants in the early part of the twentieth century, and leased or owned land in many California counties in order to grow rice. Many of these ventures were very successful, and many Indians, Hindu and Muslim, prospered financially as they increased their acreage and even bought small farms and orchards; however, heavy rains in 1920 devastated some rice crops and drove some Indians into bankruptcy.

Like Hindu and Sikh Indian immigrants, some Muslims chose to return to India after they had achieved some amount of financial prosperity. Many others, however, stayed, putting down firm roots in California and the adjoining western states and sometimes marrying Mexican women, since the immigration of Muslim women from the subcontinent was nonexistent.

While all Indian immigrants faced racial prejudice, Muslims from the subcontinent were also subject to added prejudice against their religion, Islam. Among the common misconceptions of the Islamic faith that existed in America during that time were those that viewed Muslims as polygamists and therefore not suitable people to be allowed to enter America; there were also calls for the expulsion of Muslims already in the country. Expulsions of Indians from the communities within which they worked were also attempted by other Euro-American workers. The Asiatic Exclusion League (AEL) was organized in 1907 to encourage the expulsion of Asian workers, including Indian Hindus and Muslims.

The immigration of Indians, Hindu and Muslim, was tightly controlled by the American government during this time, and Indians applying for visas to travel to the United States were often rejected by U.S. diplomats in important Indian cities like Madras and Calcutta. In addition, legislation was introduced in the United States that attempted to legally restrict the entry of Indians and other Asians into America as well as to deny them residency and citizenship rights. Some of these pieces of legislation were defeated, while others were adopted. For instance, a literacy clause was added to a number of bills, requiring that immigrants pass a literacy test to be considered eligible for citizenship. This effectively ensured that most Indians would not be able to meet the requirements. It was only in 1947 that Congress passed a bill allowing naturalization for Indians. Between 1947 and 1965 there were only around 2,500 Pakistani immigrants in the United States according to reports from the Immigration and Naturalization Service.

SIGNIFICANT IMMIGRATION WAVE

The largest numbers of Pakistani Americans have migrated to the United States since 1965, when the U.S. government lifted previously existing immigration restrictions and repealed quotas. Numbers of Pakistani immigrants swelled after 1970, with thousands of Pakistanis entering the United States each year since that time. Like their Asian Indian counterparts, they tended to be urban, well-educated, and professional. Many of them had come from cities like Karachi and Lahore, and were familiar with Western culture and ways of living. However, the dependents and relatives that they have since sponsored for permanent residence in and citizenship to the United States in the years after 1965 have tended to be characterized by lower levels of education.

Figures from the 1990 U.S. Census indicate that there are about 100,000 Pakistani Americans in the United States. The largest percentage, 32 percent, live in the Northeast, with 27 percent living in the South, 21 percent in the West, and 20 percent in the Midwest. States with the highest concentrations of Pakistani Americans are New York, California, and Illinois. Pakistani Americans tend to settle in large cities, in part a reflection of the large Pakistani cities of Lahore, Karachi, and Rawalpindi that a majority of the post-1965 immigrants came from, and in part a reflection of the availability of jobs. Accordingly, there are significant settlements of Pakistani immigrants in cities such as New York, Chicago, Philadelphia, and Los Angeles.

Although subgroup differences within the larger community are salient, with Pakistani Americans choosing to spend most time with members of their own ethnic and linguistic groups like Sindhis, Punjabis, and Baluchis, the community is also fairly united on a broader level.

ACCULTURATION AND ASSIMILATION

Very little has been written about the Pakistani American community. Many scholars writing about ethnic communities in the United States tend to lump the community together with the larger Asian Indian community, thereby glossing over the distinctiveness of the Pakistani Americans. For instance, in *Arab, Armenian, Syrian, Lebanese, East Indian, Pakistani and Bangladeshi Americans: A Study and Source Book* (San Francisco: E&R Research Associates, 1977), Kananur Chandras offers little distinction between the Asian Indian, Pakistani American, and Bangladeshi American communities and hence cannot be relied upon for information on Pakistani Americans. Others tend to assume, incorrectly, that Pakistani Americans, because they are overwhelmingly Muslim, can be described as a part of America's Arab Muslim community. In addition, there is no comprehensive listing of Pakistani American organizations across the United States, or a listing of the communities newspapers or other media channels.

CUISINE

There is considerable similarity between the cuisine of northern India and that of Pakistan, the entire region having experienced the same foreign invasions and cultural influences over the centuries. It is hence common to see restaurants featuring Indian and Pakistani cuisine under the same roof in the United States. However, Pakistani cuisine is quite distinctive and has many traditional dishes that are not necessarily shared with Asian Indians.

Although regional variations exist, Pakistani cuisine in general tends to be highly spiced. Spices such as cumin, turmeric, and chili powder are common with Asian Indian cuisine. In addition, Pakistani American cuisine also includes such spices as cloves, cinnamon, and cardamom, a result of Arab influence.

Meat dishes—lamb, goat, and beef—are common. It is also traditional for the meat to be kosher or *halaal*, cut in a way that ensures the slow draining of blood from the animal, for religious reasons. Also in keeping with Islamic tradition, pork is not eaten. Festive rice dishes include *pulao*, a fragrant dish of mildly spiced rice with peas or dried fruits, and *biryani*, which consists of rice and meat marinated in yogurt and spices. *Dals*, or lentils and split peas prepared in spicy sauces, are common. Whole peas like the chickpea, prepared in a flavorful sauce called *cholle* ("chollay"), are also popular. Vegetable dishes include *saag* ("sahg") or spinach and *aloo-mattur*—potatoes and peas. Unleavened breads made with white and wheat flour are eaten with many meals; these include the robust *naan*, clay-baked *roti*, and *paratha*.

Traditional Pakistani sweets include *zarda* ("zahrdah"), a sweet, yellow, rice dish, *jalebi* ("jahlaybee"), an orange-colored, fried sweet made of a sugary syrup and flour, *ladoo* ("lahdoo"), a round ball of sweetened chick-pea flour embellished with pistachios or cashews and *ras malai* ("rahs mahlaee"), a dessert made of heavy cream. Tea flavored with cinnamon and cardamom is also drunk frequently. Another way to round off a meal is to chew *paan*, which is the broad leaf of the betel plant sprinkled with a lime powder and *kaat* and can be mildly euphoric.

Most Pakistani American families eat at least one traditional meal a day, the main meal. It is prepared with fresh ingredients by the woman of the house. Although Western-style short cuts to food preparation like the use of canned or preserved substitutes are increasingly being used, cooking the main meal still remains quite a laborious chore. It is the woman who undertakes the task of cooking for the family, often with the help of daughters. It is still rare for male family members to be engaged in domestic chores like cooking and household cleaning. They would be more likely to work outdoors or be engaged in tasks like household repairs. Pakistani Americans regard the family meal as an important event in their daily lives. It is a time for the family to talk to each other about what events have transpired during the day and a time to be together and maintain contact in the face of busy individual schedules.

TRADITIONAL COSTUMES

Pakistani American men and women wear the traditional *salwar kameez* on festive occasions. The costume, consisting of a long tunic and tight or loose-fitting leggings or trousers and often including a diaphanous shawl or veil called the *dupatta* ("dooputtah") for women, is commonly made of cotton or silk. Women's costumes tend to be more colorful and intricate, often including exquisite embroidery or *zari*, a technique that involves the weaving of gold or silver thread into the cloth. It is more rare, but not unheard of, for some Pakistani women to wear the sari, the traditional costume of Asian Indian women.

Like their Asian Indian counterparts, Pakistani American women enjoy wearing gold ornaments or jewelry, including bangles, bracelets, rings, and necklaces. Simple ornaments are worn daily, while more opulent ones, with settings of precious stones, are worn at weddings and other celebrations. These precious ornaments are often passed down through the generations as family heirlooms. Often on festive occasions, *mehendi*, or the application of a paste made with henna that dries in delicate, intricate designs on the palms of the hands, is sported by some women and girls in the community.

DANCES AND SONGS

A common dance performed by women in the community on festive occasions like weddings and other celebrations is the *luddi* ("luhd-dee"). Women dance in circles while rhythmically clapping their hands. *Qawaali* ("kawalee"), a genre of music that traces its roots to Sufi Muslim devotional and mystical music and that is meant to encourage religious ecstasy among its listeners, has many adherents within the Pakistani American community, and is also drawing increasing numbers of other Americans into its fold of admirers. It generally encourages intense listener involvement and response. The best-known group performing this music that has toured America in recent times is the Pakistani group Nusrat Fateh Ali Khan and Party. Groups performing the Qawaali generally include several singers and such instruments as harmoniums and *tablas* ("tublah"), a type of drum. The *ghazal*, a mellow, emotional style of ancient Persian lyric verse set to music and sung by both men and women, is also popular among members of the community.

This photograph shows traditional Pakistani costumes.

Film music, from both popular Pakistani films and Indian films in Hindi, also has many adherents within the community, particularly first-generation and recent immigrants. Pakistani bands that combine Western rock and pop tunes with Urdu lyrics are popular at celebrations.

HOLIDAYS AND CELEBRATIONS

The International New Year is widely celebrated among members of the community. In addition, Pakistani Americans celebrate the creation of Pakistan on August 14 as Independence Day. The birthday of Jinnah, the founder of the Pakistani nation is celebrated on December 25, and Pakistan Day on March 23. Religious celebrations include *Eid-ul-Fitr*, festivities that signify the end of the month of fasting during *Ramadan*, and *Eid-ul-Azha*, a joyous observance of the pilgrimage to Mecca. Pakistani Hindus celebrate *Diwali* ("deevalee"), the festival of lights and *Holi* ("hoelee"), the festival of color that traditionally welcomes the spring.

Celebrations on such days typically include visits to friends and family, the exchange of gifts and sweets, and invitations to feasts. Traditional costumes are worn. Celebratory parades in cities and towns where there are large Pakistani American communities are increasingly being held. *Qawaalis*, *ghazals*, *mushaira* ("mooshaeera") or Urdu poetry readings, and Pakistani and Hindi films might be organized for community celebrations that might be held on festive days at the local community centers. Less common, but no less enjoyed in large cities with great ethnic diversity like New York, is the occasional cricket match that will be organized within the community or across cricket-playing communities like the Asian Indian and West Indian on holidays.

HEALTH ISSUES

Pakistani Americans take health issues seriously and consult health-care providers regularly. Family physicians are often chosen from within the community. Traditional herbal remedies might be employed to battle minor illnesses. Ayurveda and homeopathy are also employed. Ayurveda focuses on spiritual healing as an essential part of physical healing and bases its cures on herbs and other natural ingredients such as raw ginger and garlic. It emphasizes preventive healing. Homeopathy attempts to cure by stimulating the body's own defenses against the illness.

Members of the community are less likely, however, to seek help for mental health issues, a reflection of the traditionally low levels of consciousness of the subject in Pakistan and the social stigmas and skepticism that continue to be attached to it. Members of the community generally believe that families rather than institutional settings are best suited to take care of the mentally ill.

LANGUAGE

Urdu is the official language of Pakistan, although only about ten percent of all Pakistanis speak it. The majority of the population speaks regional dialects, like Punjabi, Baluchi, and Sindhi, which are taught is the nation's schools along with Urdu. Urdu is a blend of four different languages—Hindi, Arabic, Persian, and Turkish—and is also spoken by Muslims in India. It conforms to a modified version of the Persian script and is therefore written from right to left, whereas Hindi, which utilizes Devanagari script, is written from left to right. English is also used in official interaction in Pakistan.

About 30 percent of Pakistani Americans speak Urdu. A larger percentage, perhaps 50 percent, speak Punjabi. Others might speak Sindhi or Gujrati, reflecting their ethnic heritage and the regions of Pakistan from which they trace their ancestry. As a result of the legacy of British colonization, most Pakistani Americans are also fluent in English. While many first-generation Pakistani Americans continue to speak their native languages at home, offspring generally speak only English but understand their parents' native tongue. Many American words that have no easy translation like subways, cable-TV or microwave oven have inevitably entered everyday Pakistani American communication.

GREETINGS

Pakistani Americans salute each other with the traditional Islamic greeting *Salaam Aleikum* ("sahlaam alaykoom")—Peace be with you. The response to that greeting, conveying the same meaning, is *Aleikum Salaam*. Another common phrase is *Inshallah* ("insha-allah")—God willing.

FAMILY AND COMMUNITY DYNAMICS

Pakistani American families, like their Asian Indian counterparts, tend to be tightly knit and patriarchal. In the case of the early immigrants, often only males had formal educations, and they became the sole breadwinners. The nuclear family is most common, but members of the extended family like grandparents, aunts, and uncles visit frequently and for long periods of time. Siblings and close relatives are encouraged to visit America and are provided with financial and emotional support should they decide to eventually immigrate to the United States. The family, both immediate and extended, is the focus of existence for many Pakistani Americans. Many leisure activities for Pakistani Americans tend to be family and community oriented. Pakistani Americans prefer to reside in areas where there are other Pakistani American families who provide them with a sense of community. Since family ties are so strong, they also try to live close to relatives so that frequent visits are possible.

Most first-generation Pakistani American women continue to fulfill traditional female roles, choosing to take care of the home and family rather than pursuing demanding careers. Second-generation Pakistani American women tend to be more resistant to traditional roles, but the pressures for conformity within the Pakistani community are still quite strong. Some young women report that this results in their "doing it all"—pursuing a demanding career as well as taking on the major responsibility of running the house and caring for the daily needs of the family.

Traditional and religious values are very important to Pakistani Americans, and children are taught their history and culture at an early age. Special classes are held on weekends to teach children these aspects of their identity. Such classes include religious and language education. As is the case with many Muslims, religion tends to provide the guidelines by which the lives of many Pakistani Americans are lived. Dating is discouraged, and marriage between Pakistani Americans within the larger community in general and within the ethnic subcommunities in particular, with parental approval, is actively encouraged. Family and community members are widely consulted in selecting prospective marriage partners for young people. In recent times, there has been some tension between Pakistani American immigrant parents and their American-born children, as children question the need for parental involvement in questions of partner selection and ask for the freedom to date individuals of their choice.

On the whole, education is highly valued among Pakistani Americans. Many first-generation males came to the United States with high levels of education and proceeded to study even further in the United States. The value of education was then transmitted to their children. Both girls and boys are encouraged to study hard, but it is often understood that it will finally be the male's responsibility to be the major financial provider for his family.

As is the case with Asian Indians, Pakistani Americans mingle with their American counterparts or with members of other immigrant ethnic groups in work situations, but often choose to spend their leisure time with members of their own community. Many Pakistani Americans report conflicting feelings about American culture and ways of life. While many aspects of American culture and society are admired, such as personal and political freedom, individualism, the country's achievement in science and technology, and American economic efficiency, other aspects, such as premarital relations, dating, and divorce, are shunned. Again, regional differences prevail, with the more urban immigrants from Karachi tending to be more receptive of American culture and values than the more traditional immigrants who trace their roots to the provinces and rural areas of Pakistan.

Members of the larger Pakistani community hold distinct perceptions of the different subcommunities that the community is composed of. For instance, Pakistanis tracing their roots to Lahore are generally considered to be more traditional and conservative than the more cosmopolitan, Westernized, and sophisticated immigrants from Karachi. The Sindhis and Baluchis are also considered traditional and conservative. Distinctions are also made between immigrants tracing their roots to rural Pakistan and those who have come from large urban centers.

There is some interaction with and overlap between members of the Asian Indian and Pakistani American communities. This is particularly the case with those members of both communities who have the common bond of Islam between them and who might share in prayers at the same mosques and celebrate the same religious festivals.

WEDDINGS AND FUNERALS

A Pakistani wedding is a time for great celebration. Traditional Muslims rites are observed, and friends and relatives are invited to join festivities that might stretch over several days and that include feasting on traditional foods. The legal portion of the ceremony is accomplished with the signing of the *nikaah*, or marital agreement, by the bride and groom. A *moulvi* ("moolvee"), or knowledgeable one, is present at all ceremonies and formally asks the bride and groom whether they accept each other in matrimony. The wedding is held at party centers, not in mosques, and traditional Pakistani music is played before and after the ceremony. While gifts of money and jewelry are traditionally given at weddings in Pakistan, the community in America tends to also give as gifts appliances or other household items that would be of use to the young couple. Jewelry is still frequently passed down from mother to daughter or daughters-in-law at weddings. Pakistani Hindus, on the other hand, follow the traditional Hindu ceremony, with the bride and groom circling the holy fire from three to seven times, and the priest chanting prayers.

Pakistani Americans follow Islamic rites in burying their dead. No separate cemeteries exist for the community in America; rather, available cemeteries are used. In rare cases, the body might be flown to Pakistan for burial. Only males are allowed to participate in the actual burial ceremony. Pakistani Hindus are generally cremated according to Hindu religious tradition. In this ceremony also, males are given greater prominence. A death is a time for the Pakistani community to come together to provide emotional and sometimes financial support for the bereaved family.

RELIGION

Most Pakistani Americans are devout Muslims, who pray five times a day facing the direction of the holy city of Mecca. Religion figures prominently in the life of Pakistani American families, and the Holy Quran and the teachings of the Holy Prophet serve as the guidelines that Pakistani Muslims follow throughout their lives. Families often visit the mosque once a week, usually on Friday afternoons, where the Imam leads the prayer. If it is not possible to visit the mosque for Friday prayers, Sunday prayers are another popular alternative. Children are encouraged to attend religious education classes held on weekends and during the summer vacation in substantially populated communities. Both men and women must keep their arms and legs covered while in the mosque, and covering the head is also encouraged. The sexes must sit either in separate rooms or in separate groups within the same room for the duration of the prayers.

The majority of Pakistanis belong to the Sunni sect of Islam, although a significant representation may also be found among the Shi'ite sect. Sunnis, or Orthodox Muslims, believe that the community is responsible for maintaining Islamic law. This law, or *shari'a*, is based on four sources, which in descending order of importance are: the Quran; the examples and teachings of the prophet; communal consensus (later the consensus of religious scholars) on Islamic principles and practices; and reasoning by analogy. Shi'ites, who are followers of Muhammad's cousin, Ali, believe that Muslim religious leadership descends through blood lines. They also differ from Sunnis through certain religious procedures.

In smaller towns in America where there may not be mosques within easy access, Pakistani Americans make special trips to attend the nearest one on major religious holidays and occasions. Pakistani Americans worship at mosques alongside other Muslims who might trace their ancestry to all parts of the Islamic world and to India; there are generally no separate Pakistani American mosques.

Pakistani Americans also participate in and contribute to the larger Islamic community, which includes Arab Americans and African Americans, in America. They are part of the larger community's efforts to educate the country about the ideals of Islam and the teachings of the prophet Mohammed. Pakistani Americans have played important roles in the association the Muslim Students of America (MSA), which caters to the needs of Islamic students across the United States.

Although the overwhelming majority of Pakistani Americans are Muslims, there are also Hindus, Christians, and Zoroastrians within the community. Some Hindus chose to remain in the newly created Pakistan after partition, and they form the core of the Pakistani Hindu community. Hindus are part of a religious tradition that is less structured and less formally organized than other religions like Islam and Christianity. Hinduism is a polytheistic religion, with Hindus generally worshipping many gods, including Brahma, the God of Creation, and Surya, the Sun God. The Hindu community today has access to more than 100 temples all over America, with the oldest one being in San Francisco. It is also common for Hindus in the United States to worship at home, where a small room or portion of a room may be set aside for worship and meditation.

Pakistani Christians, like Asian Indian Christians, worship at churches all over the country and share in the religious life of the dominant Christian culture in America. Zoroastrians or Parsees trace their roots to ninth-century Persia, and form a minuscule religious minority in both India and Pakistan. They have prospered in trade and the professions in both these countries, as also in America, where reports of the earliest Zoroastrians were documented as early as the turn of the century. In recent times, Pakistani Zoroastrians have come to the United States mainly from the Pakistani cities of Lahore and Karachi.

EMPLOYMENT AND ECONOMIC TRADITIONS

The profile of the Pakistani American today is dramatically different from the earliest Muslims immigrants from the Indian subcontinent, who came to the United States as manual and agricultural workers with few skills and little or no education.

Many Pakistani American males who entered the United States after 1965 were highly educated, urban, and sophisticated, and soon found employment in a variety of professions such as law, medicine, and academia. In the post-1965 wave of immigration, many Pakistanis also came to America as students who earned graduate degrees that enabled them to pursue successful careers in a variety of fields. Some members of the community immigrated to the United States with specific educational backgrounds in fields like the law but failed to find positions within that specific field because their qualifications and experience did not transfer readily to the American context. They have either retrained themselves in other professions or fields, or have had to be satisfied with accepting positions that are meant for individuals with lesser educational qualifications than they have. This is the price that some of these immigrants have paid to settle in the United States.

Most of the community today lives a comfortable, middle-class and upper-middle-class existence, although there might be some incidence of poverty among newer uneducated immigrants. These immigrants tend to take low-paying jobs involving manual or unskilled labor and tend to live in big cities where such jobs are readily available. Many Pakistani Americans also own their own businesses, including restaurants, groceries, clothing and appliance stores, newspaper booths, and travel agencies. It is common to include members of the extended and immediate family in the business.

Pakistani Americans tend to follow the residence pattern set by other Americans, in that they move to more affluent suburbs as their prosperity increases. Members of the community believe in the symbolic importance of owning homes; accordingly, Pakistani Americans tend to save and make other monetary sacrifices earlier on in order to purchase their own homes as soon as possible.

Members of the family and the larger community tend to take care of each other, and to assist in times of economic need. Hence, it would be more common to turn to a community member for economic assistance rather than to a government agency. Relatively low levels of the community are therefore on welfare and public assistance.

POLITICS AND GOVERNMENT

In the early part of this century, Muslim immigrants were actively involved, along with their Hindu Indian brethren, in the struggle for residence and citizenship rights in America. Since the second wave of immigration in 1965, the Pakistani American community has not been politically inclined, but this is now changing, with the community starting to contribute funds to their candidates of choice in both parties, and running for elected office in districts with large Pakistani American populations. In recent times, Pakistani American candidates have run for the state senate in districts of such city boroughs as Brooklyn in New York. Because the community is geographically dispersed, the formation of influential voting blocs has not generally been possible, making it difficult to for the community to make an impact on politics in this particular way. However, there are increasing efforts on the part of community leaders to ensure voter registration and involvement. Like the Asian Indians, Pakistani Americans tend to vote Democratic in larger numbers than Republican.

RELATIONS WITH PAKISTAN

Most Pakistani Americans maintain close links with relatives and friends in Pakistan. First-generation Pakistani Americans travel to their native land at least once every few years, and tens of thousands of airplane tickets are sold to Pakistani Americans every year. They often take back to Pakistan gifts of money, food, and clothing for friends and family, and donate generously to charities. Second-generation Pakistani Americans tend to travel to Pakistan less frequently as ties become attenuated. The relationship of the U.S. and Pakistani governments in the past few decades has been very close, and the Pakistani American community has benefitted from this American interest in the country of their origin.

Pakistani Americans maintain a deep interest in the society and politics of Pakistan. Funds are raised by the community in America for the different political parties and groups in Pakistan. Tensions among ethnic groups like the Sindhis, Punjabis, or Baluchis, in Pakistan tend to be reflected in interaction between these subgroups in America, but to a much lesser extent. Tensions between India and Pakistan also tend to be reflected in the relationships between Asian Indians and Pakistani Americans.

INDIVIDUAL AND GROUP CONTRIBUTIONS

ACADEMIA

Pakistani Americans have achieved success in many fields, particularly in academia, where they hold positions of respect as faculty members in many prestigious universities. Mohammad Asad Khan (1940–), a geophysicist and educator, is on the faculty of the geophysics and geodesy department at the University of Hawaii. He has also been a visiting scientist at numerous institutions, including NASA's Goddard Space Center. Altaf Wani is an associate professor of Radiology at the Ohio State University. Mazhar Ali Khan Malik is a professor of economics and engineering and founder of the Pakistan League of America (PLA). Samuel Iftikhar (1923-1991) was an Asian scholar and reference librarian at the Library of Congress, Washington, D.C. for more than 25 years. He worked mainly in the Southern Asian section of the library.

ART

Samina Quraeshi (1946–) is the director of design arts at the National Endowment for the Arts (NEA) in Washington, D.C. She holds dual Pakistani and American citizenship and is a graduate of the Yale University School of Art and Architecture. She has been a design consultant who has run her own business.

HEALTH AND MEDICINE

Dr. Salam Shahidi (1933-1992) was a leading medical researcher in the department of health, New York City. He was also vice-chairman of the Pakistan League of America (PLA) and president of a cultural organization called the National Association of Pakistani Americans. Dr. Muhammad Akhtar is currently the commissioner of Public Health in Washington, D.C., a position he assumed in 1991. He was born in Lahore, Pakistan, and has held important posts in the health departments of the states of Michigan and Missouri during the 1970s and 1980s. Dr. Amanullah Khan (1940–), a physician, served on the faculty of West Pakistan Medical School. He was a fellow in hematology and oncology at the Wadley Institute of Molecular Medicine in Dallas, Texas, between 1966 and 1969, and has been the chair of the department of immunology from 1970. He is the author of several books and has written several articles in scholarly journals in his field. Dr. Shafi Bezar, a Manhattan surgeon, is also publisher of the community newspaper Awan, and president of the Pakistan League of America (PLA). Dr. Mohammed Sayeed Quraishi (1924–) holds a doctorate from the University of Massachusetts. He has served as a member of the United Nations WHO team to Bangladesh and has been an entomologist at the Malaria Institute of Pakistan. He has served at the National Institutes of Health in Bethesda, Maryland and the National Institute of Allergy and Infectious Diseases. He is the author of many books and received the Recognition and Appreciation of Special Achievement Award by the National Institute of Health in 1988.

MEDIA

The news group bit.listserv.pakistan provides news of events in Pakistan.

PRINT

Jung.

Published in New Jersey in English and Urdu. Features articles of interest to the community and news from Pakistan.

The Minaret.

A community newspaper that features articles on community engagements, other topics of interest to the community in America and news from Pakistan. It is published in New York City.

New York Crescent.

Includes articles of interest to the community, news about social engagements involving the community in New York and the United States.

Pakistan Calling.

An English language weekly focusing on the Pakistani American community and on events in Pakistan. It is published in New York by Zafar Qureshi.

Pakistan News.

Description: Informs the general public of current political, economic, and cultural developments and events in Pakistan. Formerly Pakistan Affairs.

Address: Embassy of Pakistan, 2315 Massachusetts Avenue NW, Washington, D.C. 20008.

Telephone: (202) 939-6227.

Fax: (202)265-5184.

TELEVISION

"TV Asia."

A program often shown on international cable channels all over the United States, includes Pakistani soap operas, films, and plays. Cities like New York and Los Angeles with relatively large Pakistani American settlements have weekly Pakistani feature and news programs.

Address: TV Asia, c/o International Channel, 12401 West Olympic Boulevard, Bethesda, Maryland 20814.

Telephone: (310) 826-2429.

ORGANIZATIONS AND ASSOCIATIONS

Many associations tend to be headquartered in big cities with significant Pakistani American populations. Some associations and organizations are restricted to the interests of particular ethnic and regional communities like Punjabis or Sindhis and subsects thereof. The list that follows are pan-Pakistani organizations—those that do not distinguish on the basis of ethnic or regional groups.

Association of Pakistani Physicians (APP).

APP is an organization of Pakistani American physicians and dentists. Focuses on how to better serve the health needs of the Pakistani American community and of all Americans.

Contact: Durdana Gilani, President.

Address: 6414 South Cast Avenue, Suite L2, Westmont, Illinois 60559.

Telephone: (630) 968-8585.

Fax: (630) 968-8677.

Online: http://www.appna.org.

Muslim Students of America (MSA).

Founded in 1963 to serve as a voice for Muslim students in American universities and today has chapters in most major cities in the United States and Canada. Pakistanis have played a leading role in the organization from its inception and have held key roles in its administration. Holds conferences annually on subjects relevant to the Muslim academic community.

Pakistan League of America (PLA).

Membership ranges in the thousands. Promotes Pakistani culture in America, holds national conventions and seminars on issues of interest to the community.

Pakistan Society of Atlanta.

Promotes Pakistani culture and heritage within the United States.

Address: 1035 Bridgewater Walk, Snellville, Georgia 30278-2050.

U.S.-Pakistan Economic Council (USPAK).

Promotes trade between the United States and Pakistan. Offers information on economic and social conditions in Pakistan.

Address: 500 Fifth Avenue, Suite 935, New York, New York 10110.
Telephone: (212) 221-7070.

MUSEUMS AND RESEARCH CENTERS

American Institute of Pakistan Studies

Integral unit of Middle East Center, University of Pennsylvania. Pakistan, including language and political identity or ethnicity, ideology and culture, national integration, and cultural history.

Address: University Museum, 33rd and Spruce Streets, Philadelphia, Pennsylvania 19104-6398.
Contact: Dr. Brian Spooner, Director.
Telephone: (215) 898-7461.
Fax: (215) 573-2003.

SOURCES FOR ADDITIONAL STUDY

Balagopal, Padmini, et al. *Indian and Pakistani Food Practices, Customs, and Holidays.* Chicago, IL: The American Dietetic Association, 1996.

Helwig, Arthur and Usha M. *An Immigrant Success Story: Asian Indians in America.* Philadelphia: University of Pennsylvania Press, 1990.

Jensen, Joan. *Passage From India: Asian Indian Immigrants in North America.* New Haven: Yale University Press, 1988.

Malik, Iftikhar Haider. *Pakistanis in Michigan: A Study of Third Culture and Acculturation.* New York: AMS Press, 1989.

Melendy, H. Brett. *Asians in America: Filipinos, Koreans, and East Indians.* Boston: Twayne Publishers, 1977.

Williams, Raymond Brady. *Religions of Immigrants from India and Pakistan: New Threads in the American Tapestry.* New York: Cambridge University Press 1988.

Though Palestinian
Americans have
generally had a
smooth transition to
a new culture, many
still feel unsettled
because of tensions
in their homeland
and specifically the
lack of a Palestinian
state.

PALESTINIAN AMERICANS

by
Ken Kurson

OVERVIEW

Historical Palestine stretched from the eastern shore of the Mediterranean Sea to lands east of the Jordan River, according to commentators, and was bordered by Syria on the north and Egypt on the south. Most of this land is now controlled by or part of the State of Israel. The majority of the six million people of Palestinian descent live in Jordan, Syria, and Lebanon (a total of two and a half million), the autonomous territories of the West Bank and Gaza Strip (two million), Israel proper (approximately 750,000), or the United States (approximately 200,000).

The Middle East has long been the crossroads of major trade routes between East and West. The economic and political significance of these lands has made them the object of continual conquest by various armies since Biblical times. This has been particularly true for Palestine; the various peoples who inhabit the region today remain mired in a bitter and deadly conflict that is the direct legacy of the war and terror that proceeded almost without interruption during the first half of the twentieth century.

HISTORY

In addition to the region's significance in terms of trade and political conquest, ancient Palestine was the "Holy Land" and birthplace for two major world religions—Judaism and Christianity—and later became very significant for Islam as well. Thus, Palestine has played a tremendous role in the world's religious and cultural history.

By 1500 b.c. the culture in ancient Palestine had developed to the point where the first known alphabetic writing system was invented. During the late Bronze Age (1500-1200 b.c.) Palestine was controlled by Egypt, and many of the major cities were used by the Egyptians as administrative centers for their rule. This was also a period of great religious activity, when many temples were built and the mythology of the Canaanite gods and goddesses was inscribed in tablets.

The ancient name for Palestine was "Canaan," and the people living there before the arrival of the Israelites were known as "Canaanites." The name "Palestine" resulted from the influx of a number of so-called sea peoples, who traveled east across the Aegean sea to settle in the lands of the eastern Mediterranean in about 1200 b.c. One of these groups, the Philistines, ended up in Palestine after Ramses III refused their entrance into Egypt, and by the eleventh century b.c. they dominated Palestine's Mediterranean coast. Also during this period, the Israelites, who were nomads and farmers from Egypt, moved to the more remote highlands of the central hilly region of Palestine where they settled small villages; the ruins of approximately 250 such villages have been discovered by modern archaeologists. By 1000 b.c. the size and strength of the Israelite tribes was sufficient for them to present a challenge to the Philistines. They wrested control from the Philistines and established a kingdom led by King Saul and his successors David and Solomon, who reigned from approximately 1020 b.c. to 920 b.c. Solomon's reign represented the zenith of this period, when the capital of Jerusalem was established and the Temple constructed. Historians claim that most of the Hebrew scriptures, or Old Testament of the Bible, were composed during this time in ancient Israel.

After Solomon's death the kingdom was divided into two Hebrew states—Israel in the north and Judah (from which the name "Jew" derives) in the south—which were at war for much of the next 400 years. Judah was defeated by the Babylonians in 586 b.c., and this period saw the ascendancy of the Kings Hezekiah and Josiah (who tried to use the teachings of the Deuteronomic writers to rule according to the laws of Moses) and the Hebrew prophets Isaiah, Jeremiah, and Micah. However, the Babylonians were soon conquered by the Persians, and the whole of Palestine came under the Persian Empire.

The conquest of the Persian Empire by Alexander the Great in 332 b.c. ushered in the Hellenistic, or Greek, period in which Hebrew was supplanted by Greek and Aramaic as the dominant language. This influence remained even after Alexander's death (323 b.c.) during a period of Egyptian rule and subsequently under the Seleucid kings from Syria, who took actions to undermine Jewish customs and enforce the worship of Greek gods. The Jews rebelled under the leadership of the Maccabees in 167 b.c. and established a Jewish state, which, by the time of the Roman conquest in 63 b.c., controlled much of Palestine and had converted many to Judaism. Yet a revolt in 132 a.d. led the Romans to evict the Jews from Jerusalem and to establish the city of Aelia Capitolina on its ruins.

In 638 Muslim invaders built a mosque on the site of the ruins of the Jewish Temple in Jerusalem. Some Christians remained in isolated towns on the Mediterranean coast (such as Ramla, Jaffa, and Lydda), and in 1099 Christian Crusaders from western Europe took Jerusalem and imposed a kingdom for nearly a century. For the most part, however, the inhabitants of Palestine became Arabized, converting to Islam and speaking Arabic.

Palestine was conquered by the Ottoman Turks in 1517, whose empire dominated the region for 400 years until its demise in World War I, after-which the British controlled the region. There was a period of modernization in Palestine in the 1830s when Ibrahim Pasha established secular schooling and civil rights so that Christians and Jews could exist somewhat on a par with the Muslims. When the rural people rebelled against this secularism, the European powers forced Ibrahim out in 1840, and the Ottoman Empire regained control.

ISRAEL

In 1919 Jews represented ten percent of Palestine's population; by 1944 the number of Jews in Palestine had risen to 32 percent of the total population. Many of the Jewish immigrants came following Hitler's rise to power in 1933 and especially thereafter as refugees of the Holocaust. Their land acquisition during the mandate was aided by financial support from the Jewish National Fund, which allowed them to purchase land from Syrian absentee landholders as well as from Palestinian Arabs. The Arab farmers who had worked the land without owning it were suddenly dispossessed and forced to seek a living in the cities.

This spurred an Arab revolt, which led the British to explore the possibility of a partition of Palestine between a Jewish state and an Arab state.

Two commissions attempted fruitlessly to settle on a map that could be agreed upon, and fears that the Arabs would side with the Germans in the incipient war led the colonial government to issue a "white paper" in 1939 limiting Jewish migration to 75,000 over the next five years and guaranteeing an "independent Palestine state" within ten years. The Arabs rejected the delayed independence, and the Jews found the immigration quota unconscionable owing to the plight of the Jews in Europe. Paramilitary groups, the Irgun and the Stern Gang, carried out attacks against British installations and assassinated the British minister of state, Lord Moyne, in order to further Jewish interests.

In 1947 the U.N. General Assembly overwhelmingly passed a resolution calling for the partition of Palestine into separate Jewish and Arab states, with Jerusalem to exist under international administration. Jewish leaders accepted the plan, though they hoped to expand the borders of their state; but the Arabs rejected it on the grounds that the Jewish minority did not deserve a state at their expense, notwithstanding the atrocities committed in Europe.

Jewish leaders declared the establishment of the state of Israel on May 14, 1948, setting the scene for the first of a series of Arab-Israeli wars and military conflicts. While the Palestinian Arabs were still suffering the effects of the British suppression of their revolts a decade earlier, the surrounding Arab countries of Egypt, Syria, Jordan, and Iraq attempted a supporting invasion of Israel on May 15.

When armistices were signed between Israel and the surrounding Arab countries of Egypt, Jordan, Lebanon, and Syria in early 1949, Israel had less than a third of the population of Palestine but controlled three-quarters of its territory. The prospect of further violence spurred a mass exodus of Arabs from their homes. More than half of the 1,300,000 Arabs were living in refugee camps at the end of the war, including about 400,000 from lands designated for the Jewish state by the U.N. partition plan.

MODERN ERA

By 1967 the process of urbanization had begun in Palestine, thus undermining the traditional social institutions that had been grounded in the village and clan. An increase in literacy (owing to six years of compulsory education provided by U.N. schools) and in higher education, and a shift from an agrarian economy to one of industrial, artisan, and white-collar jobs, also led to a change in the character of the Palestinian leadership. Where until 1948 the Palestinians were generally represented by political and religious officials from the upper classes, the new movements were more populist.

Tensions over Israeli diversion of water from the Jordan River to the south of Israel led to the Arab formation of the Palestine Liberation Organization (PLO), which carried out attacks against the diversion project, prompting Israeli military reprisals against Jordan and Syria. Incidents of this kind escalated to the Six Day War in 1967, in which Israel defeated the Arab military forces and conquered the Gaza Strip and the Sinai Peninsula from Egypt; East Jerusalem and the West Bank from Jordan; and the Golan Heights from Syria. The U.N. issued Resolution 242, calling for Israeli withdrawal from these territories in exchange for peace, and this document remained central to the question of peace in Palestine for decades.

In the ensuing decades, the Israelis were generally willing to negotiate on the basis of 242 without any preconditions, though they insisted that Jordan represent the Palestinian people. Many of the more conservative Israelis argued that the lands in question were essential to the security and even existence of Israel as a buffer against the Arab's continued aggression. The Arabs refused to acknowledge Israel's right to exist and objected to the resolution's reference to the Palestinians as refugees rather than as a people with a right to a state of their own. They repeatedly called for Israeli withdrawal from the occupied territories before negotiations could begin.

The 1970s saw continued violence in Palestine, with the PLO committing terrorist acts against Israeli targets, and more radical factions targeting civilians worldwide in an effort to implicate and thus discredit the PLO. After being expelled from Jordan in 1970, the PLO established a base of operations in Lebanon from which to attack northern Israel, as well as a small state within a state, which provided various social welfare services to the Palestinians as well as the Lebanese before it was destroyed by Israeli invasions in 1982 and 1987.

In December of 1987 Palestinian resistance to the Israeli occupation, which had for some time expressed itself in demonstrations, strikes, and boycotts, coalesced into a popular uprising that has come to be known as the *intifada*, which literally means "shaking off" in Arabic. All sectors of society in the West Bank and Gaza Strip joined the acts of resistance, the most visible being the youths in the streets taking up rocks and gasoline bombs against Israeli forces. Though it was met with a brutal response, the *intifada* seemed to strengthen the Palestinian sense of resilience and self-reliance, as groups were formed in each locality to organize the resistance activities and provide medical services, food, and education to those who were in need. As it continued into the early 1990s this uprising also seemed to increase world awareness of and sympathy for the plight of the Palestinians and their call for self-determination.

The United States pressured Israel to give up its insistence on recognizing only Jordan as the Palestinians' representative, and after much diplomacy Israel finally began negotiations with the PLO as well as with individual Arab countries. In September of 1993 Prime Minister Rabin of Israel and Yasser Arafat, representing the Palestinians, signed a peace agreement that called for a five-year period of limited autonomy for the occupied territories and further negotiations on a permanent solution after three years.

The limited autonomy commenced in July of 1994 as Arafat began his administration of Gaza and the West Bank town of Jericho without an effective state apparatus or infrastructure. He also suffered from opposition by radical groups, such as the Hamas and the Islamic Holy War, which took the form of violent provocations that called into question the viability of Palestinian self-rule under present conditions. These serious questions were looming in the fall of 1994 when the Swedish Nobel committee awarded the prestigious peace prize jointly to Arafat, Prime Minister Rabin, and Foreign Minister Shimon Peres in an effort to bolster the fledgling struggle for peaceful coexistence between Jews and Arabs in the Middle East.

SIGNIFICANT IMMIGRATION WAVES

Estimates of the number of Palestinian Americans range from 100,000 to 400,000, with a number of researchers settling on 200,000 as a reasonable guess. The difficulty in determining a more precise number results in part from the fact that there has never been an actual state of Palestine that immigrants could call their country of origin. In U.S. immigration and census records up to 1920 all Arabs, Turks, Armenians, and more were classified as coming from "Turkey in Asia," and not until recently did the Immigration and Naturalization Service recognize "Palestinian" as a nationality. Palestinian immigrants may have come from within Israel or the occupied territories; one of the Arab countries that received refugees from the Arab-Israeli wars, especially Egypt, Jordan, Lebanon, and Syria; or a country to which Palestinians immigrated in search of economic opportunity.

Palestine's unique political history makes it difficult to determine exactly when the first Palestini-

ans immigrated to the United States and how many came. Most sources refer to Arab immigrants generally and indicate that while a small number of Palestinians, mainly Christian, came to the United States before 1948, the vast majority have arrived since that year.

Some Middle Eastern Arabs immigrated to the United States after 1908, the year the Ottoman Empire began requiring military service of its subjects in certain areas. The majority of these individuals were Christians, because Muslims feared losing their Islamic culture in a Western, Christian society. Increased tensions during the British Mandate and continuing Jewish migration to Palestine from Europe, however, induced Muslim Palestinian migration. The pioneers were primarily young men, although married men and some families followed when positive reports were received or when individuals returned home and displayed their success. Unlike the Christian Palestinians who preceded them, many of these immigrants sought to make money in the United States in order to return and live a more comfortable life, and often a family pooled its resources to send a member over. Though they had not been peddlers in their homeland, the vast majority of the earliest immigrants (both Christian and Muslim) took up the occupation, with some traveling across the country selling jewelry and other small items. As their numbers grew, a network of services to bring new immigrants over as well as to organize and supply the peddlers added a new level of jobs for the more experienced.

The restrictive Immigration Act of 1924 reflected the isolationism prevalent in America between the World Wars. This, in addition to the Depression in the 1930s and World War II, served to reduce immigration greatly during the second quarter of the century. But the aftermath of World War II and the Arab-Israeli war following the establishment of the state of Israel in 1948 brought greater numbers of Palestinian immigrants, most of whom were refugees.

The greatest wave of Palestinian immigration began after the Six Day War in 1967 and has continued to the present, although it peaked in the 1980s. By 1985 the Palestinian American community was estimated at approximately 90,000; by the end of the decade, the community had nearly doubled. While some Palestinian immigrants came to the United States for political reasons, the vast majority immigrated for economic and educational opportunity. Unlike early immigrants from Palestine, those who came after 1967 were much better educated as a result of the U.N.-sponsored schools and increased attendance at universities in the Mid-

John (left) and
Jacob Rantisi pose
inside their
Kenosha,
Wisconsin,
restaurant.

dle East and abroad. Thus, many in this third wave of immigrants were professionals who met the requirements of the Immigration and Nationality Act of 1965, which contributed to a "brain drain" of many of the most educated in Palestine specifically and the Middle East in general.

SETTLEMENT PATTERNS

A majority of Palestinian immigrants initially settled on the East Coast, but industrial jobs before and especially after World War II drew the Palestinian immigrants, among many others, to urban industrial centers in the Midwest and later throughout the country. Today, the largest concentrations of Palestinian Americans are in New York and parts of New Jersey, Detroit, Los Angeles, San Francisco, Chicago, Cleveland, Atlanta, Dallas-Fort Worth, and Jacksonville, Florida.

ACCULTURATION AND ASSIMILATION

One of the few studies of the Palestinian experience in the United States was published by Kathleen Christison in the *Journal of Palestine Studies* in 1989. It details how Palestinian Americans for the most part have adapted quickly and successfully to American society while retaining a remarkable level of awareness of and involvement in the culture and politics of the land from which they or their predecessors came. She argues that there is no correlation between the extent of assimilation and the level of Palestinian nationalism: those who identify most strongly with their Palestinian roots are not necessarily the least American of the group.

Alienation seems to be rare among Palestinian Americans, though it does exist for certain segments of the population. Older Palestinians who come to the United States with grown children who support them tend to be the most alienated because they do not need to learn English to survive, they tend to socialize within the group, and they generally have the least amount of contact with the rest of American culture. Women more than men are more prone to feel alienated from American society because, in many cases, they are kept from the mainstream culture so that they may perform the primary role in imparting the Palestinian culture to their children.

Others are simply more tradition-bound and guard against the effects of the more open and liberal Western society. They oppose much that is common in the dominant culture, such as open sexuality, divorce, and drugs and alcohol, for religious and cultural reasons. They worry about raising their children here, especially girls, and some even resort to sending their children back to the Middle East for education during crucial teenage years.

Many Palestinian Americans, however, retain a Palestinian identity while identifying themselves as Americans first and foremost. Christison profiles an owner of a jewelry store in Albuquerque, New Mexico, who came to America from the West Bank when he was seven and is active in local business and politics. He married a woman from his home village and is active in promoting the Palestinian cause through the American political system. He is on the American-Arab Anti-Discrimination Committee's executive committee and was one of eight Palestinian American delegates at the 1988 Democratic convention.

Though Palestinian Americans have generally had a smooth transition to a new culture, many still feel unsettled because of tensions in their homeland and specifically the lack of a Palestinian state. Studies of Palestinian Americans report that few say they have been the subject of overt discrimination based on their ethnicity. However, many say that they are often made to feel foreign, or not fully American. Certain people they encounter want to classify them as "Arab," as if this were incompatible with being an American. Some Palestinian Americans also find that they are accepted personally but that a distinction is drawn between them and their people in the Middle East. Many Americans apparently identify Palestinians with the few extremists who commit terrorist acts to publicize the plight of Palestine or to discredit by association the moderate factions they oppose. The Palestinians in the United States resent this characterization, and they often fault the media coverage of the Arab-Israeli conflict, which, in their view, does not do enough to educate the public about their history and the injustices they continue to suffer. On the other hand, the consensus is that seven years of the *intifada* and Israeli reaction to it has done a lot to dramatize the Palestinians' plight and turn public opinion toward a solution that includes a Palestinian state alongside Israel.

TRADITIONAL CLOTHING

Traditional clothing for men was fairly uniform throughout the Middle East because they did far more traveling than the women. There were various styles that characterized the villagers, townspeople, and Bedouins, but within each group the rich and poor were distinguished primarily by the quality of the fabrics. The male wardrobe generally consisted of pants, a tunic, an overgarment secured with a belt, and sometimes a vest. Both sexes covered their head as a sign of modesty and respect. Men wore a skullcap covered by a simple cloth wrapped around the head, a more elaborate turban, or a *kafiyyeh*, the scarf secured by a cord. In the United States most Palistenian men wear Western dress, although they may sometimes wear the traditional *kafiyyeh* during special occasions.

In Palestine, women traditionally wore an outfit comprising of pants, a dress, an overgarment, a jacket or vest, and a shoulder mantle. They often wore a bonnet-like hat trimmed with coins on their head. In certain areas this was replaced by a *kafiyyeh* held in place by a folded scarf. The dresses were very elaborate, at times having as many as 21 individual pieces sewn together. The colors and embroidered patterns differed from one locality to the next and evolved over time. Fine embroidered dress panels were considered works of art and as such were handed down from mother to daughter. Jewelry was also a very important part of costume in traditional Palestine, and its function went beyond that of adornment and display of wealth. Amulets were worn to ward off the dangers of the Evil Eye, which was believed to take the lives of half of the population. Usually, what the upper classes wore in gold, the lower classes reproduced with baser metals or with less elaboration, such as necklaces whose pendants did not completely encircle the neck. Many women continue to wear traditional clothing in the United States, although their most ornate garments are generally reserved for special occasions.

CUISINE

As in most Arab cultures, beans, chickpeas, lentils, and rice are the staple ingredients in a variety of Palestinian dishes. Water, oil, vegetables, and seasonings are often added to these to produce different kinds of pastes, which are usually scooped up with pita bread—a round, flat, bread with a pocket in it. Sesame seed paste or oil may be used to embellish a meal. Stews are very popular and may be made with a variety of different meats, especially lamb. Fish is also commonly eaten. Various kinds of salads and cooked vegetables complement these dishes, and one of a number of different kinds of yogurt often accompanies a meal. Desserts include such sweet pastries as *baklava*, which is made with honey and chopped nuts, as well as fresh and dried fruits. Coffee and tea are the most common beverages.

LANGUAGE

Though many Palestinians living and/or working in Israel speak Hebrew as a necessary second language, Arabic has been the language of the Palestinians since the seventh century. Arabic is the youngest of the Semitic languages. It developed a sophisticated oral tradition through the poetry of the nomadic Bedouins before it became the language of the Islamic religion and its holy text, the Koran, in the seventh century. As the Arab Empire grew, Arabic replaced the Aramaic, Coptic, Greek, and Latin languages and became the main instrument of Arab culture. The Koran, the *Arabian Nights*, and the *Muqaddama*, a fourteenth-century history of the rise and fall of civilizations, are the great masterpieces of Arabic literature.

Arabic is the native language of virtually all Arabs, from northern Africa to the Arabian Peninsula. The dialects vary widely, though a common form of Arabic called Modern Standard Arabic (MSA), which is a simplified version of the language in the Koran, facilitates communication. MSA is the main form of written Arabic throughout the Arab world, as well as the language used in radio and TV broadcasts and in most schools. Arabic has an alphabet with 28 letters.

GREETINGS AND OTHER COMMON EXPRESSIONS

Common Arabic greetings include the following (in transliteration): *issálamu alékum*—peace be upon you; *wi alékuma salám*—and upon you; *nahárik saíd*—good day; *saíd mubárak*—may your day be pleasant; *sabáh ilxér*—good morning; *sabáh innúr*—good morning of light; *misá ilxér*—good evening; *saída*—good-bye; *maássalama*—(go) with safety; *izzáy issíha*—how are you? (how is the health?); *alláh yisallímak*—may God keep you.

FAMILY AND COMMUNITY DYNAMICS

As with many other immigrant groups coming from a more traditional society to a modern Western one, the Palestinian immigrants in the first half of this century experienced a breakdown in the nature of the hierarchical and patriarchal extended family. Whether the father was away from home as an itinerant peddler or just working long hours, his authority decreased, especially in families where the mother was also involved with the family business. The influence of education and economic opportunities and American culture generally led to more nuclear families with fewer children. Women's participation in the economic sphere of the family in time reduced the number of restrictive customs. Except for some families that remained highly traditional, most Muslim women shed their veils when they emigrated, and both Christian and Muslim women generally ceased to cover their heads as they had been required to do in their former culture.

By the time of World War II, women had become increasingly independent. They were more often allowed to remain single and there was much less family control over their choices. The segregation of the sexes was mostly limited to mosques, and marriages occurred later and were usually not arranged. Many saw marriage as the opportunity to

be liberated from parental control and to establish their own identity closer to that of the mainstream culture that they had grown up with through school and the media.

Evidence suggests that in the 1990s many families encourage marriage to other Palestinians either through community organizations that foster social contacts with others in the group or even by traveling to hometowns in the Middle East to find potential spouses. Despite these efforts some inter-ethnic and inter-religious marriages take place, and in most cases this does not put insurmountable strain on relations between the generations. However, in the families that remain the most traditional, prohibitions on dating, limits on friendships with non-Palestinians, and even extensive restrictions on the style of dress are all used to limit the influence of American culture. When they exist, though, these conditions are much more likely to be applied, or more severely applied, to girls than to boys.

WEDDINGS

In Palestine, marriage required a gift to the bride's family, usually money but sometimes real estate. Weddings lasted from three days to a week, beginning with celebrations on Tuesday and followed by a procession to the groom's house on Thursday, which was accompanied by singing, drums, and the firing of guns. Islamic law permitted a man to have as many as four wives, but a second wife was usually only taken in cases where the first wife was ill or where male children were not forthcoming. In the United States, many Palestinian marriage traditions have changed somewhat in order to conform to American law. Palestinians are encouraged to marry within their ethnic community and are expected to respect their parents wishes when choosing a spouse. The ceremony itself remains a festive event and celebrations may last several days.

FUNERALS

Upon death, ceremonies are performed within 24 hours. In Palestine, professional mourners were sometimes hired. A meal for the family is prepared after the funeral, and family members and friends bring food and give condolences in the days that follow. Mourning periods last up to a year, and women sometimes cover their dresses with dark cloth.

EDUCATION

Along with the Lebanese, Palestinians have the highest education rate in the Middle East. In the

United States approximately 35 percent of Palestinian men and 11 percent of women have at least a college degree. This compares with a rate of just over 20 percent for the American adult population in general. Though they have always been aware of the politics and history of their homeland, Palestinian American students are increasingly taking an interest in studying Arab language and culture more formally in college and graduate school. A number of Palestinian or Arab organizations are also making an effort to monitor and improve the teaching of Arab history and culture in the nation's schools.

RELIGION

Although most Arab Americans are Christian—representing Eastern Orthodox, Roman Catholic, and Protestant churches—the vast majority of Palestinian Americans are Muslim, i.e., followers of Islam. Islam is a religion based on the teachings of Mohammed (c. 570-632), who called on Arabs to surrender to the will of God (Allah) and to commit themselves anew each day. Muslims have five basic religious duties, which are known as the five pillars of Islam.

First, Muslims must repeat their creed, the *shahada*: "There is no God but the one God, and Mohammed is his prophet." The second pillar, *salat*, consists of ritual prayers said five times each day while facing toward Mecca, Mohammed's birthplace. On Fridays Muslims attend a service at a mosque in which an *imam* leads the prayer and usually gives a sermon. *Zakat*, the giving of alms, is the third pillar. The fourth pillar requires the adherent to fast during the month of Ramadan, which means refraining from food, drink and sex during daylight hours. It is also customary to pray and recite the Koran at night during Ramadan. The final pillar entails a pilgrimage, or *hajj*, to the Kaaba, the holy shrine in Mecca, that is to be made at least once in one's lifetime.

The primary Muslim holiday commemorates Mohammed's birthday and involves speeches, meetings, and prayers. The sacred book of the Islamic religion is the Koran. It is believed to be the words of Allah as revealed to Mohammed at different times by the angel Gabriel. The words of previous, lesser prophets, including Moses and Jesus, were also given by Allah, but they were corrupted, and so the Koran was sent to purify the message. This message is known as the *sharia*, which provides guidance for all specific situations in life. Included are proscriptions against drinking wine, eating pork, usury, and gambling.

EMPLOYMENT AND ECONOMIC TRADITIONS

Many of the Palestinian immigrants early in the century became itinerant peddlers in the United States, selling jewelry and trinkets that could be carried easily in a suitcase. They quickly learned enough English to emphasize that their wares were authentic items from the Holy Land. As more Palestinians came over, new opportunities opened up for the more experienced to provide services related to bringing immigrants over and setting them up in business as peddlers.

The large percentage of Palestinian immigrants since the 1967 war who are educated is reflected in the increased numbers of professionals among their ranks. A study of Palestinian Arab immigrants from Israel, the West Bank, and Gaza, published in 1994, used the 1980 census to look at socioeconomic characteristics. Among the 90 percent of Palestinian American men and 40 percent of women who are in the labor force, 40 percent and 31 percent, respectively, have either professional, technical, or managerial positions. There are also large numbers in sales: 26 percent of men, and 23 percent of women. The self-employment rate for men is a significant 36 percent (only 13 percent for women), compared to 11 percent for non-immigrant men. Of the self-employed, 64 percent are in retail trade, with half owning grocery stores. In terms of income, the mean for Palestinian families in 1979 was $25,400, with 24 percent earning over $35,000 and 20 percent earning less than $10,000.

POLITICS AND GOVERNMENT

Christison's study found that while Palestinian Americans are typically not more politically active than the population at large they are very politically aware of their history and the issues facing their homeland. They are more active in social organizations, such as mosques, churches and local associations, than in political ones, though the former have strong political implications. In the absence of a Palestinian state, the unity and preservation of communities in the diaspora serve to maintain Palestinian identity.

For example, Jacksonville, Florida, has a large contingent of immigrants from the Christian town of Ramallah, in the West Bank just north of Jerusalem. This community was long a close-knit Palestinian social unit, and it was strengthened by the formation in 1958 of the American Federation of Ramallah, Palestine, which now has over 25,000

members nationwide. Until the mid-1960s the community identified primarily with its roots in Ramallah, rather than Palestine generally. George Salem, who grew up in the community, says that in the 1950s and early 1960s, "We knew we were from Ramallah; we didn't really know whether it was Jordan or Palestine or what." But this changed after the PLO was formed and especially since the Israeli occupation of the West Bank. These events, culminating in the *intifada*, have heightened Palestinian American solidarity with those in their homeland and added a sense of urgency to finding a lasting solution to the Arab-Israeli conflict.

INDIVIDUAL AND GROUP CONTRIBUTIONS

In part owing to their small numbers, and perhaps also because of their tendency, as described above, to work more quietly behind the scenes, few Palestinian Americans are widely known. However, based on their educational and professional status there are undoubtedly many Palestinian Americans in positions of prominence in various fields, such as the business leaders and Democratic National Convention delegates mentioned above.

ACADEMIA

Edward Said is professor of English and comparative literature at Columbia University in New York City; author of numerous scholarly and general interest books, including *The Question of Palestine*; he is a member of the Palestine National Council.

Born in Jerusalem in 1935, the son of Arab Christians who were Anglican, he was educated in Cairo after the family fled to that city in 1947. Regarding the politics of his homeland he has said, "My endless beef with the Palestinian leadership is that they've never grasped the importance of America as clearly and as early as the Jews. Most Palestinian leaders, like Arafat, grew up in tyrannical countries like Syria or Jordan, where there's no democracy at all. They don't understand the institutions of civil society, and that's the most important thing!"

Mohamed Rabie is another of many Palestinian Americans in academia. He has a Ph.D. in economics and taught at Kuwait University and Georgetown University before moving to the University of Houston. He has authored many books on Middle East Affairs, including *The Other Side of the Arab Defeat, The Politics of Foreign Aid,* and *The Making of American Foreign Policy*. Rabie is the president of the Center for Educational Development and a member of various social and professional associations, including the Middle East Economics Association and the Middle East Studies Association.

GOVERNMENT AND POLITICS

George Salem served as solicitor of labor in the Reagan administration. He grew up in the Jacksonville, Florida, Ramallah community described above. Even though the community had a strong identity and there were 13 Ramallah families within a three-block radius of his house, his parents discouraged him, unsuccessfully, from running for president of the student council at his high school because they feared his becoming too Americanized. He credits youth clubs and other social organizations with upholding a distinct Ramallan identity long before the turbulent events of the 1960s forged a larger Palestinian one.

MEDIA

PRINT

The American-Arab Message.
A weekly Arabic and English language paper published on Friday with a circulation of 8,700. Founded in 1937.

Contact: Rev. Imam M.A. Hussein, Publisher.
Address: 17514 Woodward Avenue, Detroit, Michigan 48203.
Telephone: (313) 868-2266.
Fax: (313) 868-2267.
E-mail: imam4@juno.com.

Journal of Palestine Studies.
A publication of the Institute for Palestine Studies and the University of California Press, it was founded in 1971 and appears quarterly with information exclusively devoted to Palestinian affairs and the Arab-Israeli conflict.

Contact: Philip Mattar, Editor.
Address: 3501 M Street, N.W., Washington, D.C. 20007.
Telephone: (800) 874-3614; or (202) 342-3990.
Fax: (202) 342-3927.
E-mail: ips@cais.com.

Middle East Monitor.
Monthly newsletter that focuses on political events in the Middle East and North Africa, paying particular attention to current political changes and economic development.

Contact: Amir N. Ghazaii, Editor.
Address: 402 Godwin, P.O. Box 236, Ridgewood, New Jersey 07450.
Telephone: (201) 670-9623.

The Other Israel.
Founded in 1983 and published four or five times per year, it seeks to promote peace between Israelis and Palestinians.

Contact: Adam Keller, Editor.
Address: 405 Davis Court, Apartment 2106, San Francisco, California 94111.
Telephone: (415) 956-6377.
E-mail: aicipp@mcimail.com.

RADIO

WGPR-FM (107.5).
Weekly programming targeting Detroit's large Arab American population.

Address: 3140 East Jefferson, Detroit, Michigan.
Telephone: (313) 259-8862.
Fax: (313) 259-6662.

WKCR-FM (89.9).
A Sunday night program "In All Languages" periodically features Arabic and addresses concerns of New York's Arabic-speaking community.

Address: Columbia University, 490 Riverside Drive, New York, New York 10027.
Telephone: (212) 854-9297.
Fax: (212) 854-9296.
E-mail: wkcr@columbia.edu.

WSOU-FM (89.5).
Approximately one hour per week of programming catering to Arab Americans.

Address: 400 South Orange Avenue, South Orange, New Jersey 07079.
Telephone: (800) 895-9768; or (201) 761-9768.
Fax: (201) 761-7593.
E-mail: wsou@lanmail.shu.edu.
Online: http://icarus.shu.edu/wsou.

ORGANIZATIONS AND ASSOCIATIONS

American-Arab Anti-Discrimination Committee (ADC).
The committee, founded in 1980, provides legal counseling and general assistance to victims of anti-Arab discrimination, and works to fight stereotypes of Arab Americans by educating the public, particularly through schools.

Contact: Albert Mokhiber, President.
Address: 4201 Connecticut Avenue, N.W., Suite 300, Washington, D.C. 20008.
Telephone: (202) 244-2990.
Fax: (202) 244-3196.
E-Mail: adc@adc.org.
Online: http://www.adc.org.

American Arabic Association (AMARA).
Individuals interested in promoting a better understanding among Americans and Arabs through involvement in charitable and humanitarian causes; supports Palestinian and Lebanese charities that aid orphans, hospitals, and schools.

Contact: Dr. Said Abu Zahra, President.
Address: 29 Mackenzie Lane, Wakefield,
   Massachusetts 01880.

Arab American Institute (AAI).

This organization was founded in 1985 to promote the interests of the Arab American community through the political system, as well as educate the public about the community's contributions to American society.

Contact: Dr. James Zogby, President.
Address: 918 16th Street, N.W., Suite 601,
   Washington, D.C. 20006.
Telephone: (202) 429-9210.
Fax: (202) 429-9214.
E-Mail: aai@arab.aai.org.

Bethlehem Association.

Promotes understanding by the American public of the Arab people, and especially the Palestinian culture.

Contact: Dr. Hanna Canawati, President.
Address: 4115 Wilkens Avenue, Baltimore,
   Maryland 21229-4725.

Palestine Aid Society of America (PAS).

Founded in 1978, the PAS works to raise American awareness of the Palestinian point of view on issues regarding the Middle East. It also provides financial aid to educational and community empowerment projects in the occupied territories.

Contact: Taleb Salhab, Executive Director.
Address: P.O. Box 130572, Ann Arbor, Michigan
   48113-0572.

Palestine Arab Delegation (PAD).

Presents the views of Palestinian Arabs in the special political committee of the United Nations during the U.N. General Assembly.

Contact: Issa Nakhleh, Chair.
Address: P.O. Box 608, New York,
   New York 10163.
Telephone: (212) 758-7411.
Fax: (212) 319-7663.

Union of Palestinian Women's Associations in North America (UPWA).

Promotes national and social self-determination and independence for Palestine; strives toward emancipation and empowerment of Palestinian and Arab women.

Contact: Maha Jarad.
Address: 3148 West 63rd Street, Chicago, Illinois
   60629-2750.
Telephone: (312) 436-6060.

MUSEUMS AND RESEARCH CENTERS

Institute for Palestine Studies.

The institute was founded in 1963 to study the Arab-Israeli conflict, as well as the Palestinian cultural and economic life in the occupied territories, particularly in Gaza.

Contact: Dr. Philip Mattar, Executive Director.
Address: 3501 M Street, N.W.,
   Washington, D.C. 20007.
Telephone: (202) 342-3990.
Fax: (202) 342-3927.
E-mail: ips-dc@ipsjps.org.
Online: http://www.ipsjps.org.

Museum of the University of Chicago Oriental Institute.

Founded in 1919 in conjunction with university archaeological work in the ancient Near East, the institute's collection contains art from Palestine.

Address: 1155 East 58th Street, Chicago,
   Illinois 60637.
Telephone: (773) 702-9521.
Fax: (773) 702-9853.
E-mail: oi-museum@uchicago.edu.

University of Pennsylvania Museum.

Founded in 1889, this museum contains materials regarding Syro-Palestinian anthropology and ethnology.

Address: 33rd and Spruce Streets, Philadelphia,
   Pennsylvania 19104.
Telephone: (215) 898-4001.
Fax: (215) 898-0657.
Online: http://www.upenn.edu/museum/.

SOURCES FOR ADDITIONAL STUDY

Christison, Kathleen. "The American Experience: Palestinians in the U.S.," *Journal of Palestine Studies*, Autumn 1989; pp. 18-36.

Clines, Francis X. "A West Bank Village's Sons Return," *New York Times*, February 15, 1988; p. A6.

Cohen, Yinon and Andrea Tyree. "Palestinian and Jewish Israeli-born Immigrants in the United States," *International Migration Review*, 28, No. 2; pp. 243-254.

Dimbleby, Jonathan. *The Palestinians*. New York: Quartet Books, 1979.

Kifner, John. "New Pride for Palestinian Americans," *New York Times*, December 12, 1988; p. A3.

Palestinian Teenage Refugees and Immigrants Speak Out, compiled by Nabil Marshood. New York: Rosen Pub. Group, 1997.

Sacco, Joe. *Palestine: A Nation Occupied*. Seattle: Fantagraphics Books, 1994.

Said, Edward. *The Question of Palestine*. New York: Times Books, 1979.

Wilkerson, Isabel. "Among Arabs in the U.S.: New Dreams," *New York Times*, March 13, 1988; p. A12.

It is often assumed
that the Panamanians
of Central America
and the South
Americans share a
common culture.
Although the
majority share a
Spanish or Por-
tuguese heritage,
they represent very
diverse peoples
who have been
incorporated into
nation-states recently.

PANAMANIAN AMERICANS

by
Rosetta Sharp Dean

OVERVIEW

A country slightly smaller than the state of South Carolina, Panama is located in Central America. Its land mass measures 29,762 square miles (77,381 square kilometers), bounded by the Caribbean Sea to the north, Colombia to the east, the Pacific Ocean to the south, and Costa Rica to the west. The climate of the area is tropical with a dry season that extends from January to May and a rainy season from May to December. Rainfall varies from 130 inches on the Atlantic coast to 68 inches on the Pacific side. Temperatures generally range between 73 and 87 degrees Fahrenheit (23-31 degrees Celsius).

Panama has a population of slightly over 2.4 million people; 70 percent are of Mestizo origin (mixed Spanish, and Indian) or mixed Spanish, Indian, Chinese, and West Indian. The rest of the population comprises various ethnic minorities, including West Indian (14 percent), white (ten percent), Indian (six percent). Most of the population is Roman Catholic, however, there are several other denominations as well as Judaic and Islamic faiths represented. The country's official language is Spanish, and its capital city is Panama City. Panama's national flag consists of four rectangles arranged lower left, blue; upper right, red; upper left, white with blue star in the center; lower right, white with red star in the center.

HISTORY

Panama was the native name of a village on the Pacific Coast of the Gulf and Isthmus of Panama. Before its discovery by the Spanish, Panama was inhabited by a large number of Amerindians. The groups lived in organized chiefdoms, depending on the area's fish, birds, and sea turtles, and on starchy root crops for food. Numbering nearly one million when the Spanish arrived in 1501, the largest group was the Cuna. The country's name, which means "land of plenty fish," may also come from the Cuna words *panna mai*, or "far away," a reply to Spaniards who wondered where to find gold. The name Panama is also believed to be a Guarani Indian word meaning "a butterfly," and also signifying a mud fish, perhaps because the flaps of the mudfish resembled the wings of a butterfly.

Panama has been subjected to numerous occupations by foreign powers since the Renaissance period. Since 1513, when the Spanish explorer Vasco Nuñez de Balboa crossed a narrow strip of land and discovered the Pacific Ocean, the Isthmus of Panama has been a major crossroad of the world, linking two great continents and separating two great oceans. His discovery opened up a shorter route to Peru and the gold of the Incas. Fortune seekers from Europe could land at Colón, cross the narrow isthmus, and set sail on the Pacific for Peru. Shortly after his discovery, Balboa was condemned for treason and put to death with the help of a former aide, Juan Pizarro, who then used the route to conquer the Incas. Panama became an important travelway and supply post for the Spanish conquistadores (conquerors).

By 1519 Spanish settlements had been established, and the king's appointed governor, Pedro Arias de Avila, had settled in the village of Panama. Under his rule, Balboa's Indian allies were killed and other Indians were enslaved. Many fled to the jungle or to the swampland and isolated islands on the northeast coast. A priest, Bartolomé de la Casas, was outraged by the Indian enslavement and persuaded Spain's government to send African slaves in their stead. By this time, many Indians had died from disease and mistreatment, while those who escaped had become isolated in the forests and swamps. The separation of Indian groups from Panamanians remains today. African slaves became so important that the British were given a contract to deliver 4,800 slaves a year for 30 years. Slave revolts moved the Spanish king to interrupt the delivery for a time.

From the beginning, the narrowness of the land inspired the idea of a canal. The Spanish, however, were disinclined to build one, wanting to keep rival fortune seekers away from the Pacific Ocean. So for 300 years the only route was a muddy jungle road from the Atlantic Ocean to the Pacific. Outsiders often attacked. British forces captured a fortress on the Atlantic, Portobello, several times, and buccaneers troubled the area in the 1600s. The Scottish attempted to begin a colony and open the land to trade in 1698, but failed due to disease and the resistant Spanish. Spain held on to the land and controlled its markets until 1740, then allowed Panamanians to trade with other countries. Panama, though, seldom had the freedom of self-rule. From 1718 to 1722 the Spanish government in Peru held authority over Panama. Spain's viceroy of Granada (who ruled Panama, Colombia, and Venezuela), assumed control in 1739. When this government was abandoned in 1819, the viceroy moved to Panama and ruled there for two years. Although Spanish occupation of Panama ended in 1821, close relations between the Spanish and Panamanians flourished; mixed marriages and the adoption of Spanish culture and language gradually molded the Spanish and Panamanians into a distinct ethnic entity. The ancestors of the modern Panamanian people managed to preserve their Spanish heritage despite governance by European and Colombian conquests. The Spanish language in Panama has survived as a member of the Romance language group. In 1821 Panama obtained independence from Spain, and joined the new republic of Greater Colombia. The French started a canal in 1879, but after 20 years of struggle with the jungle, disease, financial problems and the sheer enormity of the project, they were forced to abandon it.

The California gold rush in the 1840s renewed interest in travel between the oceans. In 1845, the United States helped build the first transcontinental railroad that crossed Panama. Meanwhile, France, Britain, and the United States explored the possibility of a canal to join the two oceans by way of either Panama or Nicaragua. In 1879 Ferdinand de Lesseps of France, and builder of the Suez Canal, began construction of a canal in Panama under a license from Colombia. However, disease (yellow fever, malaria), rain, and mud made him abandon the project. From 16,000 to 22,000 workers had died.

THE CANAL

In the early 1900s Colombians fought a civil war—the War of a Thousand Days. Colombian rebels operated from bases in Nicaragua, passing through Panama on their way to fight. The United States now had a growing interest in building a canal across Central America. In 1902, it intervened in the war and established a truce. In 1903 and 1904,

Panama declared its independence from Colombia, drew up its first constitution, and elected its first president. In 1903, the United States signed the Hay-Ban-Vanilla treaty in which the concession for a public maritime transportation service across the Isthmus was granted; the treaty also granted the United States control over strips of land five miles wide on either side of the canal. The United States did not own the Canal Zone, but the treaty of 1903 allowed it to lease the area "in perpetuity." In return the United States agreed to pay Panama $10 million plus an annual rent of $250,000, which was later increased to $1.93 million.

In 1904, the United States purchased France's rights to the unfinished canal for $40 million and began the Herculean task of carving a canal through the isthmus. Many able and dedicated men were involved in this venture. Among them were Colonel William C. Gorges, an army doctor who achieved a major triumph in wiping out yellow fever and reducing malaria. Colonel George W.

"Getting off Ellis Island, my mother was dressed up. She had been making this suit for a year to land in. And I was dressed up with handmade lace and all. It was jampacked with mostly Europeans. And most of these people were dirty, actually dirty. I was terrified."

Ayleen Watts James in 1923, cited in *Ellis Island: An Illustrated History of the Immigrant Experience,* edited by Ivan Chermayeff et al. (New York: Macmillan, 1991).

Goethals, an army engineer who later became the first governor of the Canal Zone, was put in charge of the operation in 1907. The giant excavation through the mountains of the Continental Divide at Culebra Cut, later renamed Gaillard Cut, was directed by engineer David Gaillard. After seven years of digging and construction, and the expenditure of $380 million, the Panama Canal was officially opened on August 15, 1914, and the U.S. cargo ship *Ancon* made the first transit.

After World War II, Panamanians opposed to U.S. presence in the Canal Zone demanded renegotiation of the 1903 treaty; however, the arrangement of the 1903 treaty between the United States and Panama continued until the 1960s when disputes arose over U.S. control of the canal and zone. The United States agreed to negotiate new treaties relating to the Panama Canal and the Canal Zone. The treaties, which were accepted in 1977 and signed by General Omar Torrijos Herrera, head of the Panamanian Government, and U.S. President

Jimmy Carter, stipulated joint administration of the Canal starting in 1979, and the complete return of the Canal to Panama on December 31, 1999. The treaties, which replaced the treaty of 1903, turned over to Panama the government of the Canal Zone and the territory of the Canal Zone itself, except for areas needed to operate and defend the canal. The United States remains responsible for the operation and military defense of the canal until December 31, 1999, after which it will come under complete Panamanian control.

The presence of the Canal changed lifestyles in the country. A people that had primarily earned their living as subsistence farmers now gained most of their income from the Canal. The canal employs about 3,500 United States citizens and some 10,000 Panamanians. Among the available housing areas assigned to canal employees are Balboa and Ancon on the Pacific side and, on the Atlantic side, Cristobal, Coco Solo, and Margarita. Gatun and Gamboa are communities primarily for people who work at the locks or in dredging and hydroelectric operations.

MODERN ERA

In 1988 General Manuel Noriega used his military prominence to seize control of the Panamanian government, establishing a dictatorship, which brought him great personal wealth. Previously supported by the United States, Noriega became the object of condemnation, based on evidence linking him to drug trafficking, murder, and election fraud. In an attempt to squash Noriega, the United States imposed severe economic sanctions on Panama. Although the Panamanian working class suffered from these actions, Noriega himself was virtually unaffected. In December of 1989, a U.S. invasion of Panama led to the ousting of Noriega, who officially surrendered in January 1990. He was taken to the United States and was convicted on drug charges in 1992.

THE FIRST PANAMANIANS IN AMERICA

Panamanians, among other Central Americans have a recorded presence of almost 175 years on American soil. More than one million immigrants from Central and South America have settled in the United States since 1820, but their role in the development of American society remains uncharted. The U.S. Census Bureau did not tabulate separate statistics for Panama, Central and South American nations until 1960. The number of Panamanian Americans in the United States increased slowly. In the 1830s, only 44 arrivals were recorded, but by the early twentieth century more than 1,000 came annually. After World War I, immigration tapered off. The 1940 census listed only 7,000 Central Americans; many apparently had died or returned home.

SIGNIFICANT IMMIGRATION WAVES

After World War II, the number of immigrants increased rapidly and by 1970 the Central Americans numbered 174,000. Paradoxically, the flow of emigrants from Panama was small for nearly the entire period in which there were no immigration restrictions on applicants from the Western Hemisphere, but increased dramatically after the 1965 Immigration Act, which imposed a ceiling of 120,000 admissions from the hemisphere. By 1970, Panamanians constituted one of the largest of the Central American groups in the United States. Most Panamanians were nonwhites. Women outnumbered men among Panamanian immigrants by about one-third. The number of immigrant males per 100 females was very low in the 1960s, falling to 51 for Panama. The percentage of immigrants under 20 years of age was higher for males than for females; most female immigrants were between 20 and 49, many of them service, domestic, or low-paid, white-collar workers who immigrated to earn money to send home. Since 1962 the percentage of employed newcomers who are domestic servants has remained high, ranging from 15 to 28 percent. The entry of homemakers and children after 1968 was eased by the immigration preference system favoring family reunions. As of 1990, there were approximately 86,000 people of Panamanian ancestry living in the United States.

SETTLEMENT

Most Panamanian immigrants live in New England, or on the Gulf Coast, or Pacific Coast, or in middle Atlantic or Great Lakes areas. New York City contains the largest urban population of Panamanians. A substantial number of Panamanians settled in Florida and California. Over 15,000 Panamanians lived in New York in 1970, with fewer than 600 in San Francisco. Throughout the nineteenth and twentieth centuries, the Panamanians congregated in urban areas, especially in very large metropolitan cities. In 1920, for example, when 49 percent of the U.S. population lived in rural areas, 87 percent of the Panamanians were living in cities. They gravitated to urban centers because their education, occupational skills and lifestyles were suited to urban society. Mestizo, black, and Indian Panamanians are more numerous in New York than in any other U.S. city, numbering over 17,000 in 1970. But the forces that have led these groups to one locale or another (employment opportunities, the nucleus of an ethnic community, transportation links with the homeland) are not well understood.

ACCULTURATION AND ASSIMILATION

Little is known about the early Panamanians in the United States. Indeed, in the past, insufficient knowledge of Panamanian ethnic characteristics generated misconceptions in America. For example, the U.S. Census Bureau did not tabulate separate statistics for individual Central and South American nations until 1960—the characteristics of the individual national groups were buried in aggregated immigration and census statistics.

It is often assumed that the Panamanians of Central America and the South Americans share a common culture. Although the majority share a Spanish or Portuguese heritage, they represent very diverse peoples who have been incorporated into nation-states recently. In the newer version of acculturation and cultural pluralism, an immigrant does not surrender ethnic and cultural identity to become an American. With this approach, America is viewed more realistically, with many diverse ethnic and cultural groups. This view recognizes that one of America's strengths is in its cultural diversity and that this diversity should not be denied but highly valued.

TRADITIONS, CUSTOMS, AND BELIEFS

In the city and country, Panamanians share certain values. One is *personalismo*, a belief in interpersonal trust and in individual honor. With this belief comes a distrust of organizations and a high sensitivity to praise or insult. The most valued unit is the extended family. Another universal is *machismo*, the belief in male dominance and an image of the man as strong and daring. Women are expected to be gentle, forgiving, and dedicated to their children.

Most Panamanians are Roman Catholic, but the church and state are separate and religious freedom is guaranteed by the constitution. The religious feeling of the Panamanians is reflected in their frequent celebrations of religious holidays.

HOLIDAYS

Besides Christmas Day, New Year's Day, and Easter, Panamanian Americans celebrate the Independence Day of Panama on November 3. Other holidays such as Good Friday, Mother's Day, Father's Day, Thanksgiving, and Valentine's Day are also celebrated.

FOLK DANCES

Panamanians love festivity, and during their celebrations one can see in their traditional costumes and folk dances some of the more colorful aspects of life in Panama. The national dance is the *tamborito*, in which a man and a woman, surrounded by a circle of other dancers, pretend to flirt with each other while they dance. Other couples take turns dancing in the circle. The dance is performed to the beat of the *caja* and *pujador*, drums that were originally used by slaves brought to Panama from Africa and the West Indies during the colonial period. During the dance the woman wears the *pollera*—a full long white dress decorated with embroidery, or the *montuna*—a long skirt with bright floral patterns worn with a white, embroidered, off-the-shoulder blouse. The man's costume, the *montuno*, is a long white cotton shirt, with fringe or embroidered decorations, and knee-length trousers. The *tamborito* is especially popular during Carnival, a four-day period of joyous festivity that precedes Ash Wednesday, the first day of Lent. Lively salsa—a mixture of Latin American popular music, rhythm and blues, jazz, and rock, is a Panamanian specialty.

CUISINE

Panamanians enjoy a variety of international dishes. However, food is similar to that eaten throughout Central America. Two popular dishes are *sancocho*—a soup made with meat and vegetables, and *tazajo*—ox meat beaten thin and grilled and covered with a tomato sauce. Other favorites include *ceviche* (raw fish, cured, and mixed in lime juice, with onions, red peppers, and other spices), *empanadas*, *tortillas*, and *carimanolas* (each made with ground beef that is stuffed in a corn meal or flour dough), tamales (a mixture of chicken or pork, onions, olives, and other hot or mild spices stuffed in a corn meal mixture wrapped in banana leaves, tied with string, then steam cooked). Some nutritious vegetables enjoyed by Panamanians are plantain, yellow yam, yucca, and bread fruit.

Traditionally, every meal is accompanied with rice or a variation of rice and peas or beans. The most popular drinks are *chicha fuerte*, a liquor made with a corn base, beer that comes from the *guanabana* fruit (fruit of the soursop, a tropical American tree), and a beverage called palm wine.

HEALTH ISSUES

There are no documented health problems or medical conditions that are specific to Panamanian Americans. Many families have health insurance coverage underwritten by various ethnic organizations. Like most Americans, Panamanian American business owners and professionals in private practice are insured at their own expense, while employees benefit from their employers' health plans when available.

LANGUAGE

The Panamanian dialect is distinct to its native origin in Panama. For the first generation of immigrants, regardless of the period of arrival in America, Spanish was the primary language. Subsequent generations spoke Spanish less often, eventually switching to English as their principal language.

FAMILY AND COMMUNITY DYNAMICS

During the first three decades of the twentieth century, the Panamanian American family underwent profound changes. The first immigrants were typically single males who had left their families behind temporarily to save enough money to send for them later. They settled first in apartments. Panamanians are among the one million immigrants from Central and South American to have settled in the United States since 1820. In most discussions, Panamanians are not considered apart from other Spanish-surnamed people, although they are not a homogeneous group. The number of African Panamanians, for example, can be inferred only from the count of nonwhites in the 1960 and the 1970 Census. The husband is the usual source of authority in the family.

Panamanians gather at social clubs, and organizations for the maintenance of ethnic ties; there they discuss social, political, economic problems and news from Panama. Since many Panamanian women work outside the home, economic conditions have gradually improved, and immigrants are able to purchase a home, cars, and modern appliances, or rent larger apartments in more prosperous neighborhoods.

The typical Panamanian household features Panamanian art such as the famous Cuna Indians textile *molas*, which generally depicts native wildlife and themes, the Panamanian flag, and other cultural icons displayed in a common area. Panamanians have always held the family in high esteem. Demographics show that Panamanian families usually have two or three children. In 1970, nearly 40 percent had one wage earner, 54 percent had two, and only six percent had no income earner.

WEDDINGS

Most wedding ceremonies involve two requirements: the man and woman must say that they want to become husband and wife; the ceremony must have witnesses, including the official who marries the couple. If the couple has a religious ceremony, it is conducted by a member of the clergy, such as a minister or priest. If a couple is marrying in a civil (nonreligious) ceremony, a judge or other authorized official performs it. Many couples prefer a traditional religious ceremony, though some Panamanians depart from custom. Some even write their own wedding service. The traditional wedding ceremony begins with the bridesmaids and ushers walking slowly down a center aisle to the altar. They stand on each side of the altar throughout the ceremony. The groom enters and waits for the bride at the altar. The bride then walks down the aisle with her father, another male relative, or a family friend. She wears a white dress and veil and carries a bouquet. At the altar, the bride and groom exchange marriage vows and accept each other as husband and wife. The groom puts a wedding ring on the ring finger of the bride's left hand, and the bride may also give the groom a ring. After the ceremony, the bride and groom kiss and then leave down the main aisle.

Many Panamanians follow the traditional wedding ceremonies, but certain religious groups add their own features to it. For example, different Protestant groups have their own versions of the ceremony. Many Roman Catholic weddings take place during a mass, and the bride and groom receive communion. The reception is held either at a private home, hotel, or restaurant. Guests give gifts or money at the reception or bridal shower. The reception is accompanied by music and dancing.

BAPTISMS

When a child is ready for baptism, the parents first select the godparents. The godfather—*padrino*, and godmother—*madrina*, are often the same couple who served as best man and matron of honor at the parents' wedding. The parents bring the child to the church, where the priest confers the grace of God by putting his hand on the child and then anoints the child on the forehead with blessed olive oil. The baptism is completed by sprinkling the child with holy water. It is customary to have a large or small dinner after the baptism.

FUNERALS

A death in the family is followed by a funeral. The practices include public announcement of the death, preparation of the body, religious ceremonies or other services, a procession, a burial or other form of disposal, and mourning. The body typically is washed, embalmed, and then dressed in special garments before being placed into a coffin. Many people hold an all-night watch called a *velorio*. The funeral may include prayers, hymns, and other music, and speeches called *elogio* that recall and praise the dead person. Many funeral services take place at a funeral home with the embalmed body on display. After the funeral, the mourners return with the bereaved family to their house and share food.

EDUCATION

Law requires all Panamanian children aged six through 15 to attend school, but this rule is not rigidly enforced. Particularly in rural areas, enrollment drops greatly in the secondary years as teenagers seek employment to augment their family's income. About half the secondary-age population was enrolled in 1982. The early immigrants cared very much for the children, and instilled in their children the importance of education. Many first-wave immigrants managed to obtain or to hold jobs. Encouraged by their parents, the second generation of Panamanian Americans placed more emphasis on vocational training and college education. While most newcomers are domestic, very few are agricultural or industrial laborers. In the last two decades many Panamanians have embraced professional careers, and others have become white collar workers. Subsequent generations have progressed even further in their educational and professional pursuits. As a result, Panamanian Americans have been able to make many significant contributions to American society.

INTERACTIONS WITH OTHER GROUPS

Panamanian Americans' social relations with other ethnic groups in the United Stated defy generalization. Their ties with other Hispanic groups in the United States are not well developed; but similarity of religion, lifestyle, and language often draw them together despite country of origin. Although their ethnic group boundaries are permeable and flexible, they may be rigid with respect to class and race.

Panamanian workers generally came into contact with other ethnic groups in the workplace; they began to interact with other ethnic groups as they moved into better residential areas and suburbs. All these factors, including the proliferation of mixed marriages, have contributed to the integration of Panamanians into mainstream American society.

RELIGION

Approximately 93 percent of the population nominally belongs to the Roman Catholic Church, and six percent are Protestant (Evangelical). Other religious denominations represented in Panama include Seventh-Day Adventists, Baptists, Lutherans, Presbyterians, and Unitarians, as well as the Judaic and Islamic faiths. Women are the ones who attend church with the children. In Panamanian Catholicism, much emphasis is given to the mother of Jesus, Mary, who serves as an example for the women

EMPLOYMENT AND ECONOMIC TRADITIONS

Early Panamanian immigrants and their occupational characteristics have changed little in the latter decades of the twentieth century; 30 to 40 percent are professionals and white-collar workers—highly skilled and educated persons—with very few agricultural or industrial laborers. It is estimated that Panamanians and other Hispanics represent a consumer market of between $140 billion and $190 billion, and that market will be responsible for much of the consumer market growth in the United States in the future. In addition, revenues of owned businesses were estimated to be $29.6 billion in 1990, up 48 percent from 1987. Many experts expect an upward surge in Panamanian and other Hispanic economic growth and development during the 1990s.

However, as a whole, Panamanian Americans and other Hispanics suffer from high poverty levels compared with non-Hispanics. For example, as determined by assets owned, income, employment status, education and other factors, the average net worth of a white household is about eight times that of a Hispanic household ($43,279 as opposed to $5,524).

In the private sector, Panamanian workers are active members in the nation's work force. Panamanians have had some degree of occupational upgrading during the past decade, but they are more likely than the overall work force to be employed in lower-skilled, lower-paid occupations. Most of the increases in the employment of approximately 60 percent of Panamanian women were in mid-level occupations (technical, sales, and administrative support) and the generally lower-paid service occupations. Another 15 percent of Panamanian women were employed in management and professional positions. The occupational levels among Panamanian men have been stable in the managerial, professional, technical, sales, and administrative support positions. Occupational growth for Panamanian men has been concentrated in occupations requiring intermediate skills (operators, laborers, and fabricators), which has accounted for nearly one-third of their employment.

In the federal government, Panamanian presence is evidenced throughout all departments and agencies. No longer are Panamanian Americans limited to the social service sector of government—Departments of Education, Health and Human Services, and Housing and Urban Development. They are also in the Commerce, Labor, Interior, the State Departments, and the Pentagon, as well as the White House. During the last two decades, Panamanian Americans and other Hispanics have been ambassadors to numerous Central and South American countries.

POLITICS AND GOVERNMENT

Panamanian Americans are extremely aware that their increasing numbers translate to increased political influence, and they are exerting political power that complements their growing numbers and economic influence. In addition, they are carefully identifying issues that bring a measure of political unity to their diverse population.

Although each Hispanic group has its own identity, they are finding that their commonalities provide them with a more effective political voice. In recent years Hispanic politicians have been rallying around points of commonality as their political involvement increases. Panamanian Americans have also made significant political contributions to United States foreign policy in Latin America. Domestic issues such as civil rights, affirmative action, and bilingual education have often brought them together in a unified front.

Three million Panamanian and other Hispanic voters are concentrated in six states, which, when combined, account for 173 of the 270 electoral votes needed to win a presidential election. This underscores the importance of Hispanics as a voting bloc, particularly in the Southwest. There has been a significant increase in registered Hispanic voters in recent years; and, as more young Hispanics reach voting age, Hispanic strength as a political force will increase even more significantly. Hispanic political influence is directed by such organizations as the Mexican American Legal Defense and Educational Fund (MALDEF) Puerto Rican Legal Defense and Education fund (PRLDEF), National Council of La Raza, League of United Latin American Citizens (LULAC), American G.I. Forum, Cuban National Planning Council, Inc., National Image, Inc., Puerto Rican/Latinos Voting Rights Network, and many others.

MILITARY

The military history of Panamanians and other Hispanics contains a full scope of duty and dedication. No less than 37 Hispanic Americans have received the Medal of Honor, America's highest military decoration. During the Spanish-American War, Hispanic soldiers rode with Theodore Roosevelt's "Rough Riders." Military historians estimate that a quarter to a half million Hispanics served in the armed forces during World War II. Eight Hispanics received the Medal of Honor for actions during the Korean War, and 13 were decorated for actions in the Vietnam conflict. Panamanians played active roles during United States operations in Grenada, Panama, and Saudi Arabia. As of September 1990, Hispanics accounted for 2.1 percent of all active officers. The Army officer ranks had 1.9 percent Hispanic representation, the Navy had 2.4 percent, the Marine Corps 2.4 percent, the Air Force 2.0 percent, and the Coast Guard 1.7 percent.

RELATIONS WITH PANAMA

Panamanian Americans have always been proud of their homeland and have maintained ties beyond normal relations with family or friends left behind. Cultural ties between the two countries are strong, and many Panamanians come to the United States for higher education and advanced training. In cooperation with the United States government, many Panamanian Americans provide needed resources and training and joint operations with the Drug Enforcement Agency trying to fight illegal narcotics. In addition, Panamanian Americans supported the renewal of democracy and stability in Panama, and a fundamentally strong relationship with the United States, which became severely strained by the Noriega regime during the late 1980s. Presently, some Panamanian Americans are involved in developing business ventures in Panama. There is also a steady flow of scholarly exchanges between Panama and the United States—via grants and scholarships—in which Panamanian Americans take an active role through academic organizations.

INDIVIDUAL AND GROUP CONTRIBUTIONS

Although Panamanian Americans represent only 0.4 percent of America's total population, they have made significant contributions to American popular culture and to the arts and sciences. The following sections list Panamanian Americans and their achievements:

LITERATURE

Panamanian writers did not begin to make a significant contribution to world literature until the early twentieth century. Among the most notable of this group was the poet Ricardo Miró. Panama's best-known contemporary writers are Demetrio Korsi, a poet, and Rogelio Sinan, a poet and novelist. Korsi's works are sometimes critical of United States influence on Panamanian culture. Sinan's works have a cosmopolitan tone that reflects the author's extensive travels.

MUSIC AND FILM

Lucho Azcarraga, an internationally renowned organist and composer, is best known for Panamanian folklore music. Ruben Blades is an internationally renowned singer, actor, songwriter and producer of Buscando America; noted films are *Predator II* and *The Landlord*.

SPORTS

In boxing, Panama Al Brown was a bantamweight champion in 1929; Roberto Duran became a lightweight champion in 1972 and 1978, a welterweight champion (WBC) in 1980, and a light-middleweight champion (WBA) from 1983 to 1989; Ismael Laguna was a lightweight champion in 1965 and 1970; Jorge Lujan was a bantamweight champion from 1977 to 1980; Ernesto (Nato) Marcel was featherweight champion in 1972 and retired in 1973; Eusebio Pedroza was a featherweight champion from 1978 to 1985; Enrique Pinder was a bantamweight champion (WBC) in 1972; Rigoberto Riasco was a super bantamweight champion in 1976; Hilario Zapata was a flyweight champion in 1985. Famous jockeys include Braulio Baeza, Lafitte Pincay, Heliodoro Gustines, Jorge Velasques, and Jacinto Vasquez. These jockeys have ridden at race tracks in Panama, Belmont, and Aqueduct. And in baseball, Rod Carew played in the American League.

MEDIA

PRINT

El Diario/La Prensa.
Published Monday through Friday, since 1913, this publication has focused on general news in Spanish.

Contact: Carlos D. Ramírez, Publisher.
Address: 143-155 Varick Street, New York, New York 10013.
Telephone: (212) 807-4600.
Fax: (212) 807-4617.

Mundo Hispanico.
This publication was founded in 1979 and is published twice a month in Spanish with some English and distributed free or by subscription.

Address: P.O. Box 13808, Atlanta, Georgia 30324-0808.
Telephone: (404) 881-0441.
Fax: (404) 881-6085.
E-mail: mundohispanico@mundohispanico.com.

Que Pasa Panama!
Bi-monthly newsletter that updates information on Panama and the Panamanian communities in the United States and abroad.

Contact: Fulvia Jordan, Editor.
Address: 290 Lincoln Place, Suite D-2, Grand Central Station, Brooklyn, New York 11238.
Telephone: (718) 638-0862.
Fax: (718) 638-0862.

RADIO

WAOS-AM (1460).
Operates sunrise to sunset.

Contact: Samuel Zamarron, President.
Address: c/o WAOS Radio, 5815 Westside Road, P.O. Box 746, Austell, Georgia 30001.
Telephone: (770) 944-6684.
Fax: (770) 944-9794.

WHCR-FM (90.3).
City College of New York (National Public Radio).

Contact: Frank Allan or Linda Prout.
Address: 138th and Convent Avenue, New York, New York 10031.
Telephone: (212) 650-7481.

WKAT-AM (1360).
This is a Latin-owned broadcast featuring community news as well as Hispanic music.

Contact: Julio Romero.
Address: 13499 Biscayne Boulevard, Suite 1, North Miami, Florida 33181.
Telephone: (305) 949-9528.
Fax: (305) 944-4788.

ORGANIZATIONS AND ASSOCIATIONS

Asociacion Panameno-Americana de Asistencia Social.
Address: 6081 North Kendall Drive, Miami, Florida 33156-1966.

ASPIRA Association.
Grass roots organization working to provide leadership development and educational assistance to Latino persons, thus advancing the Hispanic community.

Contact: Ronald Blackburn-Moreno, National Executive Director.
Address: 1444 I Street, N.W., Suite 800, Washington, DC 20005-2210.
Telephone: (202) 835-3600.
Fax: (202) 835-3613.

Hispanic Institute.
Address: Colombia University, 612 West 116th Street, New York, New York, 10027.
Telephone: (212) 854-4187.

Hispanic Organization of Professionals and Executives.
Address: 1625 K Street, N.W., Suite 103, Washington, D.C. 20006.

National Council of La Raza.
Founded in 1968, this Pan-Hispanic organization provides assistance to local Hispanic groups, serves as an advocate for all Hispanic Americans, and is a national umbrella organization for 80 formal affiliates throughout the United States.

Address: 810 First Street, N.E., Suite 300, Washington, D.C. 20002.
Telephone: (202) 289-1380.

Panamanian Association of the Sacramento Area.
Contact: Cecil D. Inniss.
Address: P.O. Box 1640, North Highlands, California 95660-1640.

Panamanian Social Appeal.
Contact: Lonnie M. Ritzer.
Address: 2000 Charles Center South, 36 South Charles Street, Baltimore, Maryland 21201-0000.

La Sociedad Panamena de Atlanta (Panamania Society).
Hosts a Panamanian Independence Day celebration and scholarship drive in November to provide high school scholarships for high school seniors who are Panamanian natives or of Panamanian descent.

Telephone: (404) 284-3434.

MUSEUMS AND RESEARCH CENTERS

Circulo De Arte Latinoamericano (Latin American Art Circle).
Part of the Twentieth Century Arts Society of the High Museum of Art, it sponsors artist and events at the museum and a Latin American film festival in November.

Telephone: (404) 733-4200.

Panamanian Chamber of Commerce.
Offers membership services between the southeastern United States and Panama for commercial relationships, trade missions to Panama to meet with business and government representatives, information center for trade and business development, cultural and educational exchanges, and networking opportunities for members meeting with distributors from Latin America through the Colon Free Zone.

Address: 260 Peachtree Street, N.W., Suite 1760, Atlanta, Georgia 30303.

SOURCES FOR ADDITIONAL STUDY

Chambers, Veronica. *Mama's Girl*. New York: Riverhead Books, 1996.

Dolan, Edward F. *Panama and the United States: Their Canal, Their Stormy Years*. New York: F. Watts, 1990.

The Encyclopedia of World Faiths, edited by P. Bishop and M. Darton. New York: Facts on File, 1989.

Focus on Panama, Volume 10, edited by K. J. Jones. Panama: Focus, 1981.

U.S. Bureau of the Census. *Panamanian Population in the United States: April 1990*. Washington, D.C., 1990.

Webb, S. C., et al. *A Mosaic: Hispanic People in the United States* (Report). New Orleans, Louisiana: Defense Equal Opportunity Management Institute, Topical Research Intern Program, 1991.

Wright, Almon R. *Panama: Tension's Child, 1502-1989*. New York: Vantange Press, 1990.

PARAGUAYAN AMERICANS

by
Olivia Miller

OVERVIEW

Paraguay is a landlocked country in South America slightly smaller than California. It is bordered by the countries of Brazil, Argentina, and Bolivia. The country is divided into two unequal portions by the Rio Paraguay, the third largest river in the western hemisphere and the one for which the country is named. Paraguay means the "Parrot river" (paragua -i). To the west of the river is the Chaco, an infertile and sparsely populated section that is 60 percent of the country's land area. To the east, 95 percent of the 5.2 million Paraguayans live near the major cities. The major cities include Asuncion, the capital and a commercial city and port; Encaracion, a railroad and agricultural center; Concepcion, a river port; Coronel Oviedo; and Caaguazu.

Paraguay's government is a republic with legislative, executive, and judicial branches. Paraguay's national flag consists of three large stripes (red, white, and blue) arranged horizontally, with a seal in the center of the white stripe. The seal contains the words *Paz y Justica* (peace and justice) capped by the words Republica Del Paraguay, all within two circles.

The Eastern region comprises all of the national watershed systems along with the mountain ranges of Amambay, Mbaracayu, and Caaguazu, including Cerro San Rafael, Paraguay's highest peak at 2,788 feet. The region between the Paraguay and the Parana Rivers was once covered with rain forests. However, with the expansion of lumbering and farming activities, the forests are rapidly receding. At current rates of deforestation, virtually all of eastern Paraguay is expected to be stripped of its forestry cover by the year 2005.

Paraguay is home to a diverse wildlife population, including the Chocian peccary, which was thought to be extinct. Bird watchers are drawn from all over the world in search of species such as parrots, parakeets, hyacinth macaws, and wood storks. The western region, called the Chaco, is a vast, sparsely populated wildlife habitat with a plant and animal biodiversity comparable to the Amazon. The area has unlimited ecotourism potential. The Chaco population includes the Mennonites, a religious group of German and Canadian settlers.

The majority of Paraguayans are *mestizos*, descendants of the native Paraguayans (*Guaranis*) and the Spanish colonists. A bilingual county, Paraguay boasts that its citizens are the only national group in the Western Hemisphere that speaks an aboriginal language more widely than a European language. Continuing to speak *Guarani*, the native language, is the way Paraguayans distinguish themselves from the rest of South America.

HISTORY

Before the Europeans arrived, Guaranis lived in the southeastern part of the country in semi-nomadic tribes. Several hunter-gatherer groups, known as *Guaycuru*, lived in the western Chaco area. Native Paraguayans lived on fish and wild game, supplemented with a shifting agriculture of growing maize and mandioca. They named and knew the medicinal properties of more than a thousand species of plants. With the aid of Guaraní guides, Alejo García became the first European to cross Paraguay in 1524. The Spanish explorer Juan de Salazar founded Asuncion, the present-day capital, on the Feast Day of the Assumption, August 15, 1537. The Roman Catholic church of Spain sent Jesuit missionaries to subdue and civilize the Paraguayan natives.

In 1609, the Jesuits organized about 100,000 Guaranis into communal settlements called *reducciones* and for 150 years protected the native population from exploitation attempts by incoming colonial settlers. Between the middle of the seventeenth century and the beginning of the nineteenth century, Paraguay was ruled by a succession of governors. Conflicts with the Spanish resulted in a royal decree in 1767 that banished the Jesuits.

The native Indian population gradually absorbed the Spaniards, who in turn adopted Guaraní food, language and customs. Over time, a Spanish-Guaraní society emerged, with Spaniards dominating politically, and the mestizo offspring adopting Spanish cultural values.

MODERN ERA

Paraguay declared its independence from Spain in 1811, and was ruled by José Gaspar Rodríguez de Francia, also known as "El Supremo." He sealed the country's borders and isolated Paraguay until his death in 1840. Francia's successor, Carlos Antonio López, ended Paraguay's isolation and began modernization. The first official U.S. notice of Paraguay occurred in 1845 when President James K. Polk appointed a special agent to Paraguay. Then in 1854, the United States sent a navel ship to conduct scientific research in local rivers, but Paraguayan gunners fired on it. The United States responded by sending 19 ships and 2,500 men to force Paraguayans to pay damages for the incident.

Paraguay suffered during the War of the Triple Alliance (1864-1870) against Argentina, Uruguay and Brazil. Paraguay lost territory as well as a quarter of its population. After the war, Paraguay's agricultural sector was resuscitated by a new wave of European and Argentine immigrants, but political instability continued.

A succession of presidents governed Paraguay under the banner of the Colorado Party from 1880 until 1904, when the Liberal party seized control, ruling with only a brief interruption until 1940. In the 1930s and 1940s, Paraguayan politics were defined by the Chaco War against Bolivia, a civil war, dictatorships, and periods of extreme political instability. South America's first Nazi Party branch formed in Paraguay in 1931. During World War II, Paraguay officially severed diplomatic relations with Axis countries in 1942, but did not declare war against Germany until February 1945. Paraguay joined the United Nations as a charter member in 1945.

General Alfredo Stroessner took power in May 1954, and during his 34-year reign, political freedoms were severely limited and opponents of the regime were systematically harassed and persecuted in the name of national security and anti-communism. Paraguay became progressively isolated from the world community and it remains one of the least industrialized countries in South America.

On May 9, 1993, Colorado Party presidential candidate Juan Carlos Wasmosy was elected as Paraguay's first civilian president in almost 40 years. International observers deemed this election fair and free. In May 1998, the Colorado Party candidate Raul Cubas was elected president, but he was impeached in 1999, and the president of congress,

Luis Gonzalez Macchi, next in the line of succession, became president. In March 1999, Vice President Luis Argana was assassinated, underscoring the continued political instability of Paraguay.

THE FIRST PARAGUAYANS IN AMERICA

The first Paraguayans probably arrived in America between 1841 and 1850. Early records group Paraguayans as "other" South Americans coming from countries other than Brazil, Argentina, and Peru. During those years, 3,579 "other" immigrants arrived.

SIGNIFICANT IMMIGRATION WAVES

In the nineteenth century almost ten times as many South Americans as Central Americans immigrated to the United States. The first wave of immigrants came during a civil war in 1947 and continued arriving into the 1950s. By the 1960s, one-fourth of all Paraguayans were said to be living outside Paraguay, with the majority in Argentina, Brazil, and Uruguay. Around 11,000 Paraguayans immigrated to the United States in 1979, but the numbers steadily declined to 4,000 by 1982. While some Paraguayans immigrated for political reasons or to escape civil disturbance, many were young people seeking educational opportunities to develop professional knowledge and skills and to find better jobs. Females outnumbered male immigrants slightly, and more than half of immigrants had no occupation.

Many immigrants from Paraguay were infants adopted by American families. In 1989, 254 adoptions were completed in Paraguay. In 1993, U.S. citizens adopted 405 Paraguayan infants, and in 1995, they adopted 351.

SETTLEMENT PATTERNS

The primary target residences for Paraguayan Americans included New York, Miami, and Los Angeles. Paraguayan Americans also settled in Dallas and Atlanta. Many unskilled Paraguayan Americans have taken jobs in the service industry in urban areas such as New York, Chicago, New Jersey, and Minneapolis. Paraguayan American women also accepted jobs in hotel housekeeping, for example, an employment opportunity that other Americans felt was less attractive. Others have found agricultural employment in California and in Kansas. The latter state has partnered with Paraguay in an exchange program through a non-profit volunteer organization called Partners of the Americas. Both Kansas and Paraguay are land-locked, grow cattle and wheat, and are roughly the same size and popu-

lation. A small number of Paraguayan American are professionals who immigrated in search of better pay and more stable social conditions.

Of the 80 Paraguayan Americans who became U.S. citizens in 1984, only one arrived that year. Most of these immigrants arrived eight to ten years earlier. Naturalization figures increased slightly each year from 1987 to 1996, when 420 Paraguayans became American citizens.

ACCULTURATION AND ASSIMILATION

Since about 4,000 South Americans immigrated each year from 1910 to 1930, the U.S. population now includes third and fourth generation Paraguayan Americans. U.S. Census statistics indicate that by 1979, first and second generation South Americans numbered over 350,000, with settlements concentrated in cities of the Northeast including New York and Chicago. Paraguayan Americans gravitated toward urban areas because their education, occupation skills and lifestyles matched urban life. The 1990 U.S. Census stated that approximately 5,415 people of Paraguayan ancestry lived in the United States. Of those people, 1,886 were native to Paraguay.

The Spanish influence on Paraguayan culture has prepared Paraguayan Americans to be at home in American culture. Because 70 percent of Paraguayans speak Spanish, and because of the growth of the Hispanic ethnic group in America, many Paraguayan Americans are able to communicate with less difficulty. Newsstands offer publications in Spanish, banks provide literature and automated tellers in Spanish, even Walmart offers a Spanish translation check-out procedure. Many product labels and instructions include a Spanish version and grocers offer products known and consumed by the Hispanic community.

TRADITIONS, CUSTOMS, AND BELIEFS

Because most Paraguayan Americans have a Roman Catholic heritage, their customs and traditions are similar to those of all Latin American groups, including the U.S. Hispanic community.

In general, attitudes toward community and family follow the traditional Hispanic heritage of emphasis on bonds of family loyalty. Paraguayan Americans establish kin-based mutual support by settling in communities where other Paraguayan Americans live.

Families of adopted Paraguayan children often join a local or state community of adoptive families and meet several times yearly to allow their children to meet other Paraguayans. For example, the Ninos del Paraguay Picnic of Needham, Massachusetts, gathered 625 people for its picnic in 1997. Adoptive family networks also exist in northern California, Unionville, Connecticut, Brooklyn, New York, Princeton and Fairlawn New Jersey, and Silver Spring, Maryland.

CUISINE

Paraguayan foods are simple but tasty. The most popular dishes consist of corn, meat, milk and cheese. Manioc, a starchy tuber, is the main source of carbohydrates, and is added to just about everything. The main dishes are: *Puchero, Bori-Bori, Chipa, Asado, So'o-yosopy, Locro, Guiso, Mazamorra* and the famous and popular *Chipa,* a bread made from manioc flour. The dishes are described below.

Puchero, a meat stew, is made of boiled hominy and chopped parsley, pepper, squash, carrots or tomatoes. It is flavored with garlic or onion, and thickened with rice or cornmeal dumplings called Bori. Dumplings are often used in soup dishes in South America, and Bori-Bori is a Paraguayan Dumpling Soup.

Meat dishes as well as tropical and subtropical foodstuffs play an important role in the Paraguayan diet. The most typical Paraguayan meat is Asado, a grilled barbecue. Another favorite meat dish is Guiso, made with sausage or organ meat with rice browned in oil and flavored with tomato paste and onion. Main dishes are accompanied by chunks of toasted Chipa.

Grains, particularly maize, and manioc (cassava) are incorporated into almost all meals. A typical meal includes Locro, a maize stew, mazamorra, corn mush, mbaipy so-ó, a hot maize pudding with meat chunks, and sooyo sopy, a thick soup made of ground meat and served with rice or noodles. Desserts include mbaipy he-é, a delicious mix of corn, milk and molasses. For ceremonial occasions, Sopa Paraguaya is prepared using cornmeal cooked in oil with milk, eggs, cheese, onion and other ingredients. A green tea called mate is consumed in vast quantities while mosto (sugar-cane juice) is also enjoyed.

The drink preferred by Paraguayans is a locally produced dark rum called *caña,* an alcoholic beverage made from sugar cane, and *terere,* an infusion of *yerba mate* and cold water. This mixture is sometimes flavored with medicinal herbs. It is served in *guampas* or mates (gourd) and sipped through a *Bombilla,* which is a metal straw.

TRADITIONAL COSTUMES

Clothing worn by Paraguayans is similar to that worn by other Latin American nations, though Paraguayan women favor brighter colors. Men and women wear the poncho, and women wear shawls called *rebozos.* There is no distinctive aboriginal costume. Working-class adults and children go barefoot. This is possible because the mineral-deficient soil is seldom hard or rocky. A colonial attire that is still seen on males in the rural areas is loose baggy pants called *bombachas,* and a short jacket with a neckerchief in place of a shirt. Broadbrim straw hats are worn by everyone.

Paraguayans produce and wear *Aho-poi,* fine linen cloth embroidered with threads of the same color, generally white. Aho-poi shirts, blouses, tablecloths and napkins are in great demand around the world.

DANCES AND SONGS

Fiestas always include dancing. In Paraguay, town halls and homes of the wealthy have outdoor tile or clay dance floors. Many Paraguayan dances resemble the polka as well as the waltz and the tango. Dances such as the bottle dance are much livelier. Several dancers appear on a stage while one dancer dances with a bottle on her head. During the dance, several bottles are stacked on top of each other until as many as fourteen bottles are added. Music is usually provided by a pair of guitars accompanied by the small native harp, the *arpa.*

HOLIDAYS

Prominent celebrations in addition to Christmas, New Year's Day and Easter include *Día de San Blas* (Patron Saint of Paraguay) in February, *Paz del Chaco* (End of the Chaco War) on June 12; and the *Fundación de Asunción* (Founding of Asunción) on August 15. Official holidays observed in Paraguay also include Labour Day on May 1, National Independence Day on May 15, and the Virgin of Caacupe celebration on December 8.

HEALTH ISSUES

Paraguayans have no documented health problems other than poor teeth, a problem attributed to the lack of calcium and iodine in the diet.

LANGUAGE

Guarani, the aboriginal language, is an oral language the Jesuits recorded as a written language. There are 33 signs , either single-letters or digraphs, in the

Guarani alphabet: "a," " ," "ch," "e," "ê," "g," "g̃," "~," "h," "i," "î," "j," "k," "l," "m," "mb," "n," "nd," "ng," "nt," "ñ," "o," "õ" "p," "r," "rr," "s," "t," "u," "û," "v," "y," and "ÿ." Vowel sounds are generated by a continuous, unrestricted flow of air through the mouth and nose. In Guaraní, 12 vowels are distinguished, six oral vowels and six nasal vowels. Oral vowels are generated by air flowing through the mouth, and nasal vowels are produced by air flowing through the nose. In modern Paraguayan orthography, the nasal vowels are represented with the nasal tilde (~) over the oral version of the vowel. The Guarani language has 21 consonants. Consonants are produced by restricting or stopping the flow of air through the nose or mouth by putting both lips together or touching the tongue to the teeth.

While 90 percent of Paraguayans understand the aboriginal language Guaraní, the official language of Paraguay is Spanish, which is spoken by 70 percent of the population. The number of languages listed for Paraguay is 23. Of those, 21 are living languages. Paraguayan Americans can find their way through American culture using Spanish, but first-generation Paraguayan immigrants learn English. According to the 1990 U.S. Census, 5,144 Paraguayan Americans speak a language other than English, while 2,903 Paraguayan Americans do not speak English very well.

GREETINGS AND POPULAR EXPRESSIONS

Guaraní-speaking native Paraguayans express greetings with the word "*Maitei*." For example, "Send my greeting to your mother" is "*Maitei nde sipe.*" Other forms of courtesy include "*Mba eichapa neko'e?*" which means "good morning, how are you?" The language of the Guaranis is oral and onomatopoeic and still preserves the sounds of the forest.

Hand shaking is the common greeting done on both arriving and departing. Men shake hands with other men and also with women. Women friends will embrace briefly and brush cheeks.

Two American gestures that cause offense are the "Good luck" sign made by crossing the middle finger over the index finger, and the "O.K." gesture, with thumb and forefinger forming a circle. Tilting the head backward signifies "I forgot." Winking is usually done only for romantic connotations.

FAMILY AND COMMUNITY DYNAMICS

Paraguayan Americans continue the ancient Guaraní custom of *minga*, which is the provision of mutual assistance in household and occupational needs. Family and kin are the primary focus of an individual's loyalties and identity. The family unit includes godchildren, godparents, and many other members of the extended family. Political alliances are reflected in families, while the community is of secondary importance to the family unit. Most Paraguayan Americans live in nuclear families consisting of spouses and children. These family units are smaller than those in Paraguay, where grandparents and other relatives may also live with the nuclear family. According to the 1990 U.S. Census, there were 1,191 Paraguayan American married couples with children, and only 130 single-parent households. The majority of Paraguayan American families rent their homes, but 704 own their homes.

EDUCATION

Paraguayan Americans find schools in the United States to be superior to those in Paraguay, where only six years of attendance is required. The number of schools in Paraguay is also low, and about 20 percent of the adult population is illiterate. Many immigrants are students seeking educational opportunities, or young professionals seeking professional knowledge and skill development. The 1990 U.S. Census shows that of 4,132 Paraguayan American adults 25 years old and older, 997 were high school graduates, 700 attended school through 12th grade but have no diploma, 429 have a bachelor's degree, and 653 have had some college experience. Of the 5,415 Paraguayan Americans in the U.S. population, 1,830 are enrolled in school.

THE ROLE OF WOMEN

Paraguayan women have not traditionally occupied significant positions in society outside of their family and household roles. Traditionally, women have been cast in the role of caretaker. If a marriage dissolves, the mother typically keeps the children. In Paraguay, abortion is illegal in all circumstances, even to save the life of the mother. Paraguayan women begin childbearing on average at the age of 20 years, and they average 4.4 children per household. Compared with other Latin American nations, Paraguay's fertility rate is second only to Bolivia's. According to a survey conducted by the National Demographic and Reproductive Health survey of Paraguay (known by its Spanish acronym, ENDSRO), Paraguayan women, on average, considered 3.6 children ideal. Paraguayan Americans tend to have fewer children than Paraguayans.

Women play an important role in keeping the family together. Women who seek employment outside the home do so in order to give their children a better life. Many Paraguayan American women work in service related jobs such as hotel housekeeping and restaurant staff, though some have joined the entrepreneurial ranks as restaurant owners. Some women have also pursued educational and employment opportunities. Of the Paraguayan American labor force of 4,958 individuals, employed women number 1,537. Most of these women are private wage and salary workers.

BAPTISMS

Paraguayan Americans follow the baptism practice of the Roman Catholic church, which baptizes infants. Children are highly valued by Paraguayans, and so baptism into the Catholic faith is considered the appropriate cultural step for Paraguayan Americans. Baptism is the first ceremony for a child, and the time when a godparent is chosen. Godparents are then united with parents in the parenting role. The godparents chosen should be of good character and good standing in the community. Godparents are expected to raise the child if the parents are unable. Godparents assume the cost of the baptism and are expected to give gifts on the godchild's birthday and other significant occasions.

COURTSHIP

In the past, the Latin American and Roman Catholic traditions of courtship included the close supervision of young unmarried women. But such chaperonage does not take place for Paraguayan Americans, who often meet at community Catholic Church activities or through educational pursuits.

WEDDINGS

A formal church wedding in the traditional Roman Catholic practice or a civil wedding is the norm for most Paraguayan Americans. A church wedding in Paraguay represents a major expense for the families. A fiesta is an essential part of the ceremony, and customarily it is as large and expensive as the two families can possibly afford. For the civil wedding, the families meet for a much less expensive party and barbecue.

In the rural areas of Paraguay, common-law marriages are more prevalent than formal marriages. According to the 1990 U.S. Census, only 32 Paraguayan Americans live as unmarried partners in households.

INTERACTIONS WITH OTHER ETHNIC GROUPS

As a culture, Paraguayans have accepted other ethnic groups with minimal conflict. The majority of

Paraguayans are mestizos and the population is the most homogeneous of the countries of South America. Small numbers of Europeans, including German Mennonites and Italians, immigrated to Paraguay in the nineteenth century. In the early twentieth century, Asian and Middle Eastern people also immigrated to Paraguay. Of the 5.2 million Paraguayans today, about 8000 are Japanese or of Japanese descent.

Minorities became a significant presence during the 1970s and 1980s when thousands of Koreans and ethnic Chinese settled in urban Paraguay.

RELIGION

Roman Catholicism was established as the state religion in Paraguay in 1547 with the creation of the Bishopric of Asuncion. Jesuits propagated this faith among the Guaraní people in the centuries that followed, so that the country became 97 percent Roman Catholic and 3 percent Mennonite. Paraguayan law has required that the president must be a Roman Catholic, although the 1967 Constitution guarantees freedom of religion.

For Paraguayan American families, the role of religious instruction usually falls to the mother who functions as the family representative before the church. Children are exposed to the teachings of the church and are taken to mass by their mothers. By the age of ten, children are full participants of catechism classes, confessions, and communion. Teenage boys typically drift away from church, while girls are encouraged to continue religious devotion. Paraguayan men do not consider religious devotion to be the role of men. Although the majority of Paraguayan men are baptized, religious ardor is not significant to them, as they follow the Latin American macho ideal of manhood which leaves moral and spiritual concepts to women and children.

EMPLOYMENT AND ECONOMIC TRADITIONS

Paraguay has a predominantly agricultural economy. The work force in 1995 was 1.7 million, with agriculture representing 45 percent, industry and commerce representing 31 percent, services representing 19 percent and government representing 4 percent of the work force. The principal industries are those related to cattle, such as cold storage plants, tanneries, leather goods, and manufacturing. Other important industries include textiles, cotton oil, tung, soy bean, sourmills, construction materials, cement and lime, tobacco and sugar. Paraguay's labor code allows a 48-hour work week, and forbids work by children under 12. Children from 15 to 18 years of age can be employed only with parental authorization and cannot be employed under unhealthy or dangerous conditions. Minors between 12 and 15 years old may be employed only in agriculture, family enterprises or apprenticeships. But in reality, several thousands of children, many under the age of 12, work in urban streets in informal employment.

The law also provides for a minimum wage of $240 per month, an annual bonus of one month's salary and a minimum of six vacation days a year. However, enforcement of this law is lax. U.S. investors in Paraguay provide better working and pay conditions than their national counterparts, and Paraguayan Americans in the United States are more affluent than their national counterparts. The 1990 U.S. Census shows that the average household income for Paraguayan Americans is $32,981. Additionally, 141 of the 1,773 households reported annual earnings of over $100,000. Only 76 Paraguayan American households received public assistance.

According to the 1990 U.S. Census, three-fourths of Paraguayan Americans are employed. Employment is highest in service occupations, sales and clerical positions, followed by professionals and managerial positions, and precision production and repair work. Around ten percent are self-employed.

Paraguayan American attitudes toward work are fundamentally different from the typical American. Paraguayans regard employment as a way of establishing a personal relationship more than as a source of income. The individualistic, capitalist work-ethic is considered anti-social.

In January 1995, Paraguay, Argentina, Brazil, and Uruguay became members of MERCOSUR, the "Southern Cone Common Market." With the elimination of internal tariffs on 85 percent of all goods produced by the member-countries, and total elimination scheduled for the year 2006, what may now be regarded as Paraguay's domestic market has effectively grown from some five million people to somewhere in excess of 200 million, the majority of them in the more affluent societies of Argentina and Brazil.

POLITICS AND GOVERNMENT

For Paraguayans, political parties are not a matter of personal conviction. Citizens become Liberals or Colorado at birth and allegiance is lifelong. A person claiming political neutrality is suspected of hiding true motivations. American political party affiliation by personal conviction is a very different experience for the Paraguayan American. There is no record of Paraguayan American political activity on a national scale.

MILITARY

In Paraguay, military service is compulsory, and all 17-year-old males are liable for one year of active duty. According to the 1990 U.S. Census, 14 Paraguayan Americans serve in the armed forces, 82 male civilians are veterans and 18 female civilians are veterans.

RELATIONS WITH PARAGUAY

The United States and Paraguay have an extensive relationship at the government, business, and personal level. The U.S. Government has assisted Paraguayan development since 1937. Although U.S. imports from Paraguay are only about $40 million per year, U.S. exports to Paraguay approach $1 billion per year, according to U.S. Customs data. More than a dozen U.S. multi-national firms have subsidiaries in Paraguay. These include firms in the computer, manufacturing, agra-industrial, banking, and other service industries. Some 75 U.S. businesses have agents or representatives in Paraguay, and over 3,000 U.S. citizens reside there.

The U.S. Agency for International Development (USAID) provided more than $5 million in assistance per year for Fiscal Years 1997 and 1998 and anticipates a similar level in Fiscal Year 1999. The U.S. Department of Defense provides technical assistance and training to help modernize, professionalize, and democratize the military. The Peace Corps has about 170 volunteers working throughout Paraguay on projects ranging from agriculture and natural resources to education, rural health, and urban youth development. The U.S. Information Service (USIS) is also active in Paraguay, providing information on the United States to the press and public, as well as helping arrange educational and citizen exchanges to promote democracy.

Relations between the United States and Paraguay are not always smooth. In the late 1970s, the relationship between the United States and Paraguay faltered as a result of human rights abuses and the absence of political reform. Foreign relations were also adversely affected by the involvement of some members of Stroessner's government in narcotics trafficking. A U.S. State Department report in 1996 identified Paraguay as a regional distribution and assembly center for counterfeit merchandise. The re-export trade to Brazil, catering to consumer demand for such items as electronics, audio tapes and compact discs, designer clothing and footwear had encouraged widespread piracy. In November 1998, U.S. and Paraguayan officials signed a memorandum of understanding on steps to improve protection of intellectual property rights in Paraguay. Also in 1998, a Paraguayan national was executed by the State of Virginia. The Government of the United States conveyed its apologies to the Government and people of Paraguay because the execution violated the Vienna Convention. The Paraguayan national was not told of his right to request consular assistance.

INDIVIDUAL AND GROUP CONTRIBUTIONS

Paraguayan Americans have not made significant contributions to American popular culture, or to the arts and sciences. Much of Paraguayan literature is historical or legal writing. Still, Paraguay has always attracted the attention of other cultural giants. For example, Voltaire mentions Paraguay in *Candide*, and English writers Thomas Carlyle and Richard Burton mention the isolationist policies of the country in the 19th century. America's own political humorist P. J. O'Rourke wrote that, "Paraguay is nowhere and famous for nothing," but then visited the country to cover elections, and fell in love with the country and its people.

MUSIC

Agustín Barrios (1885-1944), one of Latin America's most revered composers for the guitar. He often performed his music in full Guaraní costume, promoting himself as the Paganini of the guitar from the Paraguayan jungles. Berta Rojas, a Paraguayan guitarist and a student of Peabody Conservatory's Manuel Barruenco, performs Barrios' compositions, in the grand traditions of classical and Latinate guitar, for American audiences.

MEDIA

The growing Hispanic media in the United States makes it possible for Spanish-speaking Paraguayans to enjoy television, radio, and printed publications in the Spanish language.

PRINT

Diario las Americas.
Daily newspaper serving Hispanics.

Address: 2900 Northwest 39th Street, Miami, Florida 33142-5193.
Telephone: (305) 633-3341.

Hispanic.
A monthly magazine with features on Hispanics in the fields of education, politics, business, and the arts.

Address: 111 Massachusetts Avenue NW, Suite 410, Washington, D.C. 20001.
Telephone: (202) 682-3000.

La Nacion.
Online Paraguayan newspaper.

Online: http://www.diarionoticias.com.py/.

ORGANIZATIONS AND ASSOCIATIONS

Asociacion Nacional por Personas Mayores (National Association for Hispanic Elderly).
Association providing employment training, health, housing and economic development for Hispanic families and a national directory of social service programs that provide support to Hispanic elderly.

Address: 3325 Wilshire Boulevard, Suite 800, Los Angeles, California 90010.
Telephone: (213) 487-1922.

Friends of Paraguay.
Non-profit organization created in 1987 to establish a network of returned Peace Corps Volunteers and others interested in improving communication and information exchange in support of social, cultural, and economic development in Paraguay.

Address: P.O. Box 27028, Washington, D.C. 20038-7028.
Online: http://www.pipeline.com/~ybycui/fop.htm.

Latin American Parents Association (LAPA).
Non-profit organization in New Jersey, Connecticut, and New York. A volunteer association of adoptive parents committed to aiding people seeking to adopt children from Latin America, as well as assisting those who have already adopted. Membership is open to anyone interested in Latin American adoptions. Annual dues are $40.

Addresses of independent chapters:
LAPA Connecticut, Inc., P.O. Box 523, Unionville, Connecticut 06085 .

LAPA Maryland, P.O. Box 4403, Silver Spring, Maryland 20914-4403.

LAPA New York, Inc., P.O. Box 339, Brooklyn, New York 11234.

LAPA NJ, P.O. Box 2666, Fairlawn, New Jersey 07411.

LAPA NJ State Chapter., P.O. Box 3125, Princeton, New Jersey 08543.

Minga.

Organization working for human rights and grass-roots development in the Alto Paran region in Eastern Paraguay. Provides small grants to assist communities, emergency relief for displaced people, and seed grants for community-based sustainable development projects to fight poverty.

Members receive a newsletter and urgent action updates. Memberships are $25 for individual membership or $50 for contributing membership. Contributions are tax-deductible.

Address: 705 East Woodley Street, Northfield,
   Minnesota 55057.
Telephone: (507) 645-6435.

Paraguayan Embassy.

Paraguay maintains an embassy in the United States. Consulates are in Miami, New York, New Orleans, Chicago, Detroit, and Los Angeles.

Address: 2400 Massachusetts Avenue N.W.,
   Washington, D.C. 20008.
Telephone: (202) 483-6960.

Paraguay Hecho a Mano, Inc.

Non-profit organization meaning "Paraguay Made by Hand," focusing on the preservation of the native Paraguayan culture through education and sale and exhibition of Paraguayan crafts in the U.S.

Contact: Carol Pope.
Address: 2705 Brook View Court, Brooksfield,
   Wisconsin 53005.
Telephone: (414) 784-7917; or (414) 790-1195.
E-mail: cpope@execpe.com.
Online: http://www.data-direct.com/pham.

**Partners of the Americas: Kansas
and Paraguay.**

Non-profit, volunteer organization with headquarters in Washington DC. The state of Kansas and Paraguay are partnered. Program has developed exchanges in areas such as agriculture, citizen participation, cultural arts, international trade, emergency preparedness, health, natural resources, university, linkage, and women in development and youth.

Address: 1424 K Street N.W., #700,
   Washington D.C. 20005.
Telephone: (202) 628-3300, (800)322-7844.

Project for the People of Paraguay.

This organization has delivered four shipments of medical, dental, educational, and personal supplies to non-profit organizations and schools in Paraguay.

Offers sponsorships of Paraguayan child living in the Chacarita, Puerto Pabla, areas or Asuncion. $20 a month provides clothes, medical dental, and educational expenses for the sponsored child. Sponsors receive photos and information about the child and family they sponsor.

Address: P.O. Box 251, Avon, Minnesota 56310.

MUSEUMS AND RESEARCH CENTERS

Denver Art Museum.

Collection of Paraguayan native art that includes textiles, jewelry, paintings, sculpture, furniture and silver.

Address: 100 West 14th Avenue, Denver,
   Colorado 80204.
Telephone: (303) 640-4433.

Indiana University Main Library.

Outstanding collection of sound recordings of various Guarani groups.

Address: Bloomington, Indiana 47405.

Thomas Rivera Library.

Part of the University of California, Riverside. Possesses the best collection of Paraguayan primary materials on the West Coast.

Address: Riverside, California 92517.

SOURCES FOR ADDITIONAL STUDY

Cooney, Jerry W. *Paraguay: A Bibliography of Immigration and Emigration.* Longview, WA: J.W. Cooney, 1996.

Hanratty, Dennis M., and Sandra Meditz. *Paraguay: A County Study.* Washington, DC: U.S. Government Printing Office, 1990.

Kelly, Robert, Debra Ewing, and Stanton Doyle. *Country Review, Paraguay 1998/1999.* Houston, TX: Commercial Data International, Inc., 1998.

Roett, Riordan, and Richard Scott Sacks. *Paraguay, The Personalist Legacy.* Boulder, CO: Westview Press, 1991.

Whigham, Thomas, and Jerry W. Cooney. *A Guide to Collections on Paraguay in the United States.* Westport, CT: Greenwood Press, 1995.

PERUVIAN AMERICANS

by
John Packel

Peruvians are attracted to the political and economic stability of the United States, the work opportunities, and the chance for their children to go to school and have a better future. A majority of these immigrants have family or acquaintances established in the United States who serve as intermediaries in their transition to a new culture.

OVERVIEW

The third-largest country in South America, Peru borders Ecuador and Colombia to the north, Brazil and Bolivia to the east, and Chile to the south. At 496,222 square miles, it is larger than Spain, Portugal, and France combined. In 1993 Peru had a population of over 22 million, and its capital, Lima, was home to fully one-third. This picturesque land is divided into three main geographic regions: the *costa*, along the South Pacific; the *sierra*, or highlands of the Andes mountains; and the *selva*, or jungle, in the east.

The *costa* is a thin, mostly barren strip of desert between the ocean and the mountains. Except for a few valleys where mountain rivers have brought enough water to make farming possible, the Peruvian desert is the driest in the world, with some areas never having seen even an inch of rain in recorded history. This region is prone to earthquakes, such as the one in 1970 that killed 66,000 people. Every few years in late December a warm Pacific current called *El Niño* (the Christ child) brings serious weather conditions that have disastrous effects on Peru's fishing industry and, in turn, its economy.

The upland plateau known as the *sierra* represents about one-fourth of Peru's land and holds a majority of the country's population. Its average elevation is 13,000 feet, making the air rather thin and cold, and ten peaks top 20,000 feet. (The highest is

Mt. Huascarán at 22,334 feet.) Called the backbone of the continent, the Andes Mountains stretch from the Caribbean Sea all the way down the Pacific coast. Rivers flowing eastward to the Amazon Basin have cut scenic gorges as deep as 5,000 feet, at the bottom of which the climate becomes tropical. On Peru's southeast border with Bolivia, Lake Titicaca spans 3,200 square miles at an elevation of 12,507 feet, making it the world's highest navigable lake.

Peru's largest geographic area, the *selva* or *montaña* region, begins with the eastern slopes of the Andes and stretches eastward to include part of the Amazon River Basin's tropical rainforest. The lower elevations contain very dense vegetation and there are virtually no roads, with transportation taking place on the rivers.

HISTORY

Most anthropologists believe that the first inhabitants of the Americas crossed over from Asia during an ice age about 30,000 years ago across a land bridge connected to Alaska where the Bering Strait is now. Some of these people migrated down the Pacific coast and arrived in the Andean region about 20,000 years ago. Little is known about this time, but the first settlements were along the coast and relied mainly on fish and wild plants and animals. Agriculture probably began around 4000 b.c., and by 2000 b.c. civilization had advanced to the point where ceremonial centers were being built in coastal areas and the skill of making pottery had developed.

The early peoples of the *montaña* grew river valley plants such as peanuts, cucumbers, manioc, squash, beans, sweet potatoes, and chili peppers. Those in the tropical forests also grew cotton and plants used for medicinal purposes. The coastal peoples farmed the sea for fish, which they at times traded to those in the highlands for the grains and potatoes cultivated there. They probably did not use boats for fishing but rather cotton nets. Anchovy runs allowed for the collection of fresh fish which could by dried and ground into a meal that was preserved for months by covering it with earth. Beached whales provided the opportunity for an immediate feast, as the meat could not be stored.

Up to approximately 900 b.c. the Andean region saw a number of small states existing relatively independently. But advances in agriculture occasioned a growth in population and the first truly urban societies in Peru. These urban environments provided the structure and personnel required for a more specialized society. A measure of communication between neighbor societies helped

provide the right conditions for expansion to full-fledged empires, and a number of these rose and fell prior to the Inca empire.

The first known of these empires was the Chavín, which expanded to encompass much of northern Peru and the central coast and lasted perhaps 1500 years. In a narrow Andean valley there are the remains of Chavín de Huántar, a city with extensive architecture. The inhabitants' stone carvings, pottery, textiles, and metalwork feature a god in the form of a fierce puma, or jaguar. The Chavín people's Akaro language was the predecessor of Aymará, which is still spoken by a small minority of Peru's population today. The Chavín were also adept at farming in the mountains and cultivated maize up to elevations of 9,000 feet.

Roughly contemporary with the Chavín was the Paracas civilization in the south. Their elaborate fabrics, woven on looms from cotton and alpaca wool, are known today because they were used in a type of mummification process. The coastal heat created oven-like conditions in the tombs and dried the contents out, thus preserving them.

The Nazca people ruled to the south of the Paracas for over a thousand years beginning about 500 b.c. They also produced wondrous fabrics, but their finest work was colorful pottery featuring birds, fish, fruit, and mythological creatures. The Nazca era is best known, however, for the mysterious lines cut into the earth by scraping away sun-scorched brown rock to reveal the yellow sand underneath. These enormous patterns, some of which are five miles long, form outlines of birds, spiders, monkeys, and other unidentifiable shapes. Scientists speculate that the shapes may have had something to do with astrological studies or an ancient calendar.

The Moche River valley, on Peru's north coast, was home to the Mochicas from about 100 to 750 a.d. They were gifted engineers and developed irrigation systems employing canals and aqueducts. The Mochicas were among the first to build roads in Peru; this facilitated the movement of their armies and made possible a messenger network in which runners carried messages marked on beads. They also pioneered the use of guano—the droppings of coastal birds—as fertilizer, a practice still in use today. They harvested the guano by paddling rafts out to off-shore islands.

The Tiahuanaco culture was based near Lake Titicaca on the high plains of present-day Bolivia at an elevation of about 15,000 feet. Its capital featured a pyramid-shaped fortress called the Acapana and courts that consisted of huge platforms made from stones weighing as much as 100 tons. In about

500 a.d. the Tiahuanacans extended their influence up the coast, bringing a religion that portrayed a weeping god with bands of tears around his eyes. With the fading of this culture came a return to the rural village life of disparate tribes.

This tribal period ended around 1000 a.d. with the ascendence of the Chimu kingdom, which had grown out of the Mochica empire and spanned nearly 600 miles of coast from present-day Lima to Ecuador. The Chimu capital, Chanchan, was a meticulously laid out 14-square-mile city with 40-foot clay walls featuring intricate, repeated patterns of birds, fish, and geometrical shapes. The primary building material was large adobe brick, and huge pyramids towered above the city. The Chimu people's advanced irrigation systems included reservoirs lined with stones.

THE INCAN EMPIRE

The Incas of Peru were one of the most advanced civilizations in pre-Columbian America, rivalled only by the Mayans and the Aztecs of Mesoamerica. We know more about the Incas than their Andean predecessors because of their fateful contact with the Spanish conquistadors in the sixteenth century. Though the Incas never developed a written language, a number of Spaniards chronicled the Incan oral history and legends. One of these was Garcilasa de la Vega, who was born in Cuzco in 1540 to an Inca princess and a Spanish conquistador and governor.

One legend told of the sun-god, Inti, creating a brother and sister, Manco Capac and Mama Ocllo, on an island in Lake Titicaca. He gave them a golden staff and told them to wander until the staff sunk into the ground, at which point they would show humans how to build villages, cultivate the land, and appreciate the sun-god's wisdom. The brother and sister wandered northward through the mountains to a beautiful river valley, where Manco Capac threw the staff and it disappeared into the ground. They named the place Cuzco, "the navel of the world," and the Inca nation was born.

Manco Capac was the first of eight Incan rulers from approximately 1200 to 1400 a.d. who built a small state centered in Cuzco. The expansion to a mighty empire began after 1430, when the powerful Chanca nation to the west of Cuzco attacked the Incas. Prince Yupanqui, who had been exiled to a distant llama ranch by his father, returned and defeated the Chancas. He became the ninth Incan ruler in 1438, renamed himself Pachacuti—"he who transforms the earth"—and set about unifying the Andean tribes into a powerful empire. He expanded the empire to the point where it reached from Lake Titicaca in the southeast to Lake Junin in the northwest.

Pachacuti and his successors would first send ambassadors to a rival tribe to try to persuade them to join the prosperous nation, which had storehouses to guarantee food in times of famine. If neither this nor the sight of the Inca army won the tribe over without a battle, the Incas used their superior weaponry. This included the bola, a series of thongs with stones attached which wrapped around an enemy's legs; rocks propelled by slings swung over the head; stone clubs and double-edged wooden swords; and protective gear such as helmets, shields, and huge spans of heavy cloth, which repelled sling-stone attacks.

Pachacuti's son, Topa Inca, expanded the empire northward almost to what is now Quito, Ecuador, and then turned west toward the coast. He persuaded the Chimu people to join in the empire and then continued southward down the coast beyond Lima into the northern territories of present-day Chile, Bolivia, and Argentina. His son, Huayna Capac, became the eleventh Lord Inca in 1493 and pushed the boundaries of Inca control into the highlands of Ecuador. At this point the Inca empire was at its peak, extending 2,500 miles north to south and covering 380,000 square miles. Close to 12 million people, speaking 20 languages and comprising at least 100 distinct tribes, had been unified under the all-important Inca ruler.

When a new tribe was brought into the empire—whether peacefully or through force—Inca soldiers were stationed in the land, and then government officials, called *curacas*, arrived to take a census, divide the land according to the Inca labor structure, and teach the Quechua ("KESH-wah") language. Members of the nobility were brought back to Cuzco to learn the Incan customs, and the tribe's religious idols were taken hostage to dissuade the local people from rebelling. When conflicts arose the Incas were likely to remove the troublesome element of the local population and replace it with loyal Inca *mitimaes*, whose purpose was to set the proper example.

Essential to the Inca empire building was their vast network of roads, which grew to an amazing length of 10,000 miles. The Royal Road was carved out of the mountain walls in the high Andes. Cutting switchbacks to climb mountainsides and at times tunneling through the mountain itself, the road was as narrow as 3 feet in places but stretched from one end of the empire to the other. The coast had a companion highway, wider and straighter, that ran from the southern city of Arequipa to Tumbes in the north. Shorter roads connected these two main ones at periodic intervals spanning the empire. Rest houses called *tampus* dotted the highways and were spaced about a day's journey apart. Storage spaces were often nearby and contained supplies for the 25,000-member Incan army.

The Incas were also adept at engineering bridges over the many rivers and ravines of their mountainous land, as well as causeways over tracts of swampland. A number of the bridges continued to be used during the Spanish colonial era, including the 250-foot suspension bridge over the Apurimac River, which lasted from 1350 to 1890. The suspension bridges consisted of five braided cables, each a foot thick, made from the fibers of the maguey plant. Three of the cables formed the base of the walkway, the other two were the side rails, and all were attached to beams sunk into piles of rock and earth. Though they swayed in the wind, the bridges were crossed safely by people, pack-laden llamas, and later the Spaniards' horses. Other types of bridges included pontoons of reed boats strapped together and baskets suspended from cables which ferried people and supplies across a ravine.

These roads and bridges were used not only by the army and by pedestrians granted permission by the government, but also by those performing a function essential to maintaining the empire—the messengers known as *chasquis*. These runners carried oral messages, small packages, or *quipus* (Incan counting devices made from strings with a series of knots in them) from village to village and from the capital to all parts of the empire. Every mile or two there were two huts, one on either side of the road, which housed runners who would continue the relay on to the next station. This communication system could transmit a message 420 miles from Lima to Cuzco in just three days. This speed was critical for quelling rebellions by conquered peoples.

Also important for Incan military success was their network of fortresses, or *pucaras*. Constructed on hilltops with views of major valleys, the *pucaras* had barracks, houses, reservoirs, and a sun temple. When an enemy tribe approached, the Incas of a nearby city would flee to the fortress for protection. Machu Picchu, the most famous of these *pucaras*, was never found by the Spanish and was only rediscovered by modern explorers in 1911. Machu Picchu had terraces for farming, palaces, and an aqueduct that carried in water from a spring a mile away and channeled it down a series of 16 stone basins. Because the Incas did not use cement to hold their structures together the stones had to be cut with such precision that they would fit together snugly—so close, in fact, that even today a knife blade cannot penetrate the spaces between them.

The Incas relied on a high degree of social stratification and specialization to accomplish their military and organizational feats. Believed to be a direct descendant of the sun, the king was a divine ruler, and he had two classes of nobility serving him. The "Incas by birth," who could claim decent from Manco Capac, made up the Incas' advisory Council of Nobles and were governors and administrators of the empire's provinces. The lower "Incas by privilege" held honorary titles and served as *curacas* responsible for a specific number of people. Military heroes and the leaders of vanquished tribes often had this status conferred upon them by the ruling Inca.

In 1525, the Inca Huayna Capac died in an epidemic that may have been smallpox or the measles, diseases introduced by the Spanish for which the native population had no immunity. Because the ruler had failed to designate his successor, two of his sons shared the role for a time—Atahualpa ruling the north from Quito and Huáscar the south from Cuzco. But soon tensions broke out between the two and Atahualpa sent his father's army against Huáscar, who was defeated and later killed. This civil war lasted a number of years and severely weakened the empire at an inopportune time, for reports of strange white-faced, bearded men in "sea houses" were brought to the Inca, who thought it best to ignore them and hope they would go away.

THE SPANISH CONQUEST

In May of 1532, Francisco Pizarro, a Spaniard seeking to conquer land and plunder gold for himself and his king, landed near the coastal city of Tumbes with a force of 180 cavalrymen and foot soldiers. He was aware of the civil war and set out toward the mountain city of Cajamarca, where Atahualpa and 30,000 Incas waited. Apparently, the Inca thought that the foreigners were there to surrender. But when Atahualpa furiously rejected a Spanish priest's offer of a prayerbook and an explanation that Spain now ruled the land, a massacre ensued in which the Spaniards used crossbows, cannons, and muskets to slaughter 2,000 Incas and take their leader prisoner.

Atahualpa tried to ransom himself with the promise of enough gold and silver to fill his cell. For two months works of art made of the precious metals poured in from the surrounding areas and were melted into gold bars, 20 percent going to King Charles I and the remainder to Pizarro and his men. This did not help Atahualpa or the Incas, however, because the invaders feared a rebellion and thought it safer to have the ruler burned at the stake.

Atahualpa objected that this would deprive him of proper burial and an afterlife, and so he was given the option of being baptized a Christian and then strangled. The last king of the majestic Incan empire was killed in this manner on August 29, 1533. For a number of years Huáscar's half-brother and his sons battled the Spanish fruitlessly; the last resistor, Topa Amaru, was executed in Cuzco in 1572.

Spain ruled Peru as a viceroyalty for nearly 300 years after the conquest and regarded it more or less as a huge mine that existed to fill the crown's coffers. The Spaniards felt that as a superior culture their customs and particularly the church brought civilized society to the natives. The political and economic system they instituted to carry out their aims, called *encomienda*, granted soldiers and colonists land and mining permits, as well as the slave labor of the natives. Living and working conditions for the native Peruvians on the farms and especially in the mines were horrendous: hard labor, malnutrition (exacerbated by the Spaniards' introduction of European crops and the elimination of many native ones), and especially diseases wiped out an estimated 90 percent of the pre-conquest native population within a century.

During this colonial period Spain passed legislation attempting to protect the native population, but it was virtually ineffectual. Practices specifically outlawed—such as debt peonage, where subjects are trapped in an unending cycle of indebtedness for necessities of life which cannot be overcome through their labor—were in reality widespread. The influx of Spaniards taking advantage of these opportunities, as well as 100,000 African slaves, became part of a highly stratified society with European-born Spaniards at the top, Peruvian-born Spaniards (Creoles) next, and the urban working poor, the black slaves, and the indigenous population at the bottom.

In 1780 a descendant of the last Inca took the name Tupac Amaru and led a rebellion by the indigenous population. The rebellion began to gain wider support by condemning the corruption of colonial officials, but promptly lost it with indiscriminate attacks on Spaniards and Creoles. Ultimately, the campaign for independence resulted from conditions outside Peru and had to be led by outsiders. When Napoleon invaded Spain and imprisoned the king in 1808, the vacuum of authority allowed the Creoles in the colonial capitals set up autonomous regimes. Then between 1820 and 1824, José de San Martín and Simón de Bolívar, two generals who had liberated Argentina, Chile, Venezuela, and Colombia from Spanish rule, completed the process by adding Peru to the list. Elect-

ed president-for-life, Bolívar attempted to modernize the country by cutting taxes, funding schools, and lifting many of the worst abuses against the indigenous population, but conservative Creole opposition forced him to leave after only two years.

INDEPENDENCE AND ECONOMIC INSTABILITY

After two decades of chaos, including wars lost to Bolivia, Colombia, and Chile, General Ramón Castilla brought a measure of stability and prosperity to Peru during his control of the country from 1845 to 1862. He exploited the economic benefits of guano, a bird dung collected from islands off the coast of Peru and sold to Europe for fertilizer, as well as desert deposits of sodium nitrate, which was used to make munitions and fertilizer. The general also organized a public school system, built the country's first railroad, ended the tribute tax paid by indigenous people, and abolished slavery, which led to the importation of Chinese laborers.

Peru's defeat by Chile in the War of the Pacific (1879-1883), fought over lands with rich nitrate deposits, was a humiliating experience that led many to call for an improvement in the lot of indigenous Peruvians so that they might contribute more fully to the society. The late nineteenth and early twentieth centuries showed evidence of efforts to modernize the society and economy. Public administration was improved, the armed forces were professionalized, public education was fostered, and modern labor legislation was enacted. These contributed to the conditions that encouraged foreign investment capital in the burgeoning sugar, cotton, copper, and rubber industries. This, in turn, created an urban industrial proletariat and strengthened the middle class.

In the 1930s the Great Depression had a crippling effect on the Peruvian economy as export markets collapsed and foreign loans dried up. This situation seems to have contributed to the rise of a political movement known as the American Popular Revolutionary Alliance (APRA), which was anti-communist but borrowed from the ideologies of Marxism and Italian fascism and advocated agrarian reform, the nationalization of industry, and opposition to U.S. imperialism. APRA's leader, the formerly exiled student organizer Víctor Raúl Haya de la Torre, never won the presidency, but the party maintained a major presence in the political scene for over 40 years, both through bloody conflicts with the armed forces and through congressional coalitions in the years APRA was not banned.

The Peruvian military had long played a large role in the state, either through generals assuming the presidency or by influencing elections. In 1962, for example, a slight plurality by APRA brought a nullification of the results and the election of Fernando Belaúnde Terry a year later. From 1968 to 1975 General Juan Velasco Alvarado and the Revolutionary Government of the Armed Forces ruled in an attempt to create a new and prosperous Peru that was "neither capitalist nor communist." The general forged ties with socialist countries and made Peru a voice for third world interests. He nationalized most of the country's banks, its railroads and utilities, and many foreign corporations.

Central to this effort to control the economy and increase social justice was Velasco's land reform, which was among the most extensive in Latin America. Ninety percent of Peru's farmland had been owned by a landed aristocracy comprising just two percent of the population, so the administration appropriated 25 million acres of this land and distributed it to worker-owned cooperatives and individual families. This failed to achieve the far-ranging effects hoped, however, in part because of the insufficient amount of arable land relative to the large number of people, and also because of the absence of policies giving the poor a greater share of the benefits.

Civilian rule returned with the reelection of Belaúnde Terry in 1980 after a constituent assembly had drawn up a new constitution. The presidency was transferred peacefully in 1985 to Alan García Perez of the APRA and again in 1990 to Alberto Fujimori, a Peruvian university professor of Japanese decent who won in a run-off against the novelist Mario Vargas Llosa. Peru's poor economic performance, including inflation that soared as high as 2800 percent annually, continued to wreak social havoc. After a period of accepting austerity measures as conditions for aid from the International Monetary Fund, under García, Peru declared a severe reduction in the debt payments it would make to foreign investors and nationalized an American oil company, which resulted in a cut-off of needed credit and U.S. aid.

In addition to these economic woes, Peru suffered from social disruption caused by leftist terrorist groups and the governmental response to them. A guerrilla organization founded by university professor Carlos Abimael Guzmán Reynoso and guided by the principles of the Chinese dictator Mao Zedong, the *Sendero Luminoso* (Shining Path), specialized in assassination and the use of violent intimidation against the peasants, such as cutting off their fingers to prevent them from voting. In a period of less than 20 years, 30,000 people were killed. The Tupac Amarú movement was another group carrying out equally vicious attacks in Peru's urban areas. The coca harvests, which supplied much of the United States' huge cocaine market, also brought violence as U.S. pressure to destroy crops led to terrorist attacks on local officials by those profiting from the drug trade. In the midst of these social woes, the country's pride received a boost in 1981 when the United Nations elected a Peruvian, Javier Pérez de Cuellar, to a five-year term as Secretary General.

In 1992 President Fujimori responded to these economic and social crises by dissolving the congress and judiciary and consolidating power in a Government of Emergency and National Reconstruction, while promising to submit a revised constitution to a referendum and hold elections at some point in the future. Referred to as an *autogolpe,* or self-coup, Fujimori's takeover also involved a suspension of civil liberties. These bold moves were well-received by the public, however, and his popularity increased further when Sendero leader Guzmán was captured and the movement's stronghold on certain rural areas, such as Ayacucho, was broken. As of 1994 Fujimori was attempting to improve Peru's standing with international creditors and lending agencies and to lure foreign investment back to the country, but the task remained a daunting one.

ACCULTURATION AND ASSIMILATION

Peruvians began immigrating to the United States in small numbers early in the twentieth century, but the vast majority have come since World War II and especially in the last 20 years (when the United States has been the destination for more Peruvians than any other country). Official statistics show a Peruvian population of 162,000 in 1990, but other estimates put the number beyond 300,000. Some of the disparity may have to do with illegal immigrants who were not counted in the former number. It is more clear where the immigrants have settled. The largest concentration, over 80,000, reside in the New York metropolitan area—particularly in Paterson, New Jersey, and in the New York City borough of Queens. Peruvians are also clustered around the cities of Miami, Los Angeles, Houston, Chicago, and Washington, D.C.

Peru's social and economic crises are at the root of internal migration from rural areas to the cities, as well as immigration to the United States. Unemployment rates of over 50 percent have left many without a means to earn the basic necessities of life,

and others are chronically underemployed. An unstable political climate and especially political violence by terrorist groups have caused many to flee. Peruvians are attracted to the political and economic stability of the United States, the work opportunities, and the chance for their children to go to school and have a better future. A majority of these immigrants have family or acquaintances established in the United States who serve as intermediaries in their transition to a new culture.

In addition to the family, there are social institutions that aid the Peruvians' assimilation to American culture. The Catholic Church is important to newly arrived Peruvians because of its familiarity, the services it often extends in terms of finding work and applying for citizenship, and the opportunity it affords for meeting other Peruvians, including those of a higher social class. Also important is the broader Latino community. Peruvians benefit from sharing a language and many cultural traits with other more established groups. The travel, legal, and labor services that already exist in these communities assist newer immigrants. State social service programs are also available to the most indigent.

Peruvians from the upper class have benefitted economically from their immigration to the United States because on the whole they have been able to transfer their capital and business expertise. They range from owners of factories and large stores to accountants for major banks and corporations to agro-industrial managers. However, this group has faced major obstacles to its assimilation. Although they are well off financially, these Peruvians do not have the economic or particularly the political power they had in Peru. Yet, because of their background, they tend not to identify with the middle-class Americans whose status they share. Many try to compensate by joining relatively exclusive associations that have social gatherings for holidays and weddings.

Middle-class Peruvian immigrants did not arrive in large numbers until the 1970s, when the exodus was led by doctors and engineers. Assimilation has been relatively easy for this group, and consequently they have been labelled the "children of success." Like those from the upper class, they had been familiar with American cultural practices before their arrival. The difference was that these middle-class Peruvians did not lose any prerogatives or privileges. This group tends to maintain a stronger cultural and religious identity through participation in church and other social activities.

Peru's lower classes were the last to take advantage of the opportunities in America and have immigrated in increasing numbers since the mid-1980s. These immigrants have come from positions ranging from low-level bureaucrats to manual laborers. They have had the most difficulty assimilating on account of their tendency to lack formal education, to have a greater difficulty learning English, and to cling more tightly to their home culture. They generally live in areas of urban poverty and have a lot of pressure to send money back to families in Peru. Many in this group have only recently made the transition from rural to urban life in Peru, where they have learned or improved their Spanish in order to come here.

HEALTH ISSUES

As is the case with the nation's standard of living in general, there is a great disparity between rural and urban health care in Peru. Most health services are located in the cities; residents of Lima have the best access to health care and about 60 percent of the country's hospital beds. Only about one-third of the rural population sees a doctor even once a year. Part of this is owed to the fact that many in Peru's indigenous population are superstitious and reluctant to use Western medicine, preferring instead home remedies and in some cases even ritual magic. Respiratory diseases are common, and many diseases are spread through parasites and infection. The infant mortality rate in Peru is very high—84 per 1,000 live births—and the life expectancy of 61 for men and 65 for women is low.

A major medical catastrophe struck Peru in 1991 when an epidemic of cholera broke out. A result of dismal or nonexistent sanitation systems that left the vast majority of rural residents without clean drinking water, the cholera spread quickly to over 50,000 people and killed hundreds. Health officials estimate that only five percent of those living in rural areas have access to potable water, and in the cities the figure is a still dangerous 80 percent.

LANGUAGE

Spanish has been Peru's official language since the Spanish conquest. Approximately 80 percent of all Peruvians speak Spanish today, including some who also speak one of the indigenous languages, Quechua ("KESH-wah") or Aymará. A language that grew out of the Latin brought to Spain by conquering Romans, Spanish has a vocabulary and structure similar to other Romance languages, such as French and especially Italian. Its alphabet generally overlaps with that of English and contains 28 letters: "k" and "w" occur only in words of foreign origin, and additional letters are "ch" (as in "chest"), "ll" (generally pronounced like the English "y"), "ñ" (like the "ny" in "canyon," which comes from the Spanish cañón), and "rr" (a rolled "r" sound). The "b" and "v" are interchangeable in Spanish and are a bit softer than an English "b." The "h" is silent, and the "d" can have a soft "th" sound within a word. Spanish vowels have one primary sound, making spelling and pronunciation on sight much easier than in English: "i" (as in "feet"), "e" (as in "they"), "a" (as in "hot"), "o" (as in "low"), "u" (as in "rude"). Words ending in a vowel, "n" or "s" are accented on the next-to-last syllable, those ending in other consonants have stress on the last syllable, and any exceptions require an accent mark.

Some common greetings and expressions include the following: hola—hello; buenos días—hello, good day; buenas tardes—good afternoon; buenas noches—good night; como está usted—how are you?; adiós—good-bye; hasta mañana—good-bye (literally "until tomorrow"); hasta luego—good-bye (literally "until later"); por favor—please; grácias—thank you; feliz navidad—Merry Christmas.

When San Martín issued proclamations declaring Peru's independence in 1821, he used both Spanish and Quechua (the Incan language, also known as Runasimi) and made both official languages. Bolívar, however, did not favor Quechua, and thereafter Peruvian governments ignored the language, hoping it would die out. This changed in 1975 when, in an effort to promote cultural pride among the indigenous population as a means to increasing their stake in Peruvian society, the military government declared Quechua an official language along with Spanish. Today Quechua is the most widely spoken of any Native American language, with perhaps seven million speakers in South America. Though there is a social stigma attached to the language because virtually all of its Peruvian speakers are members of the underclass, still the two million Peruvian highlanders who speak only Quechua are proud of their linguistic and cultural heritage and have resisted the forces of Europeanization.

These are a few Quechua expressions: allillanchu ("ah-yee-YAN-choo")—how are you?; allinmi ("ah-YEEN-me")—I'm fine; maymantam ("my-MON-tom")—where are you from?; imatam sutiyki ("ee-MAH-tom soo-TEE-kee")—what is your name? The English word "jerky" comes from the Quechua word for dried meat, charki, and the Spanish coca plant, which is the source of cocaine, gets its name from the Quechua word kuka.

A smaller number of Peru's indigenous highlanders, probably about half a million, speak Aymará, the language of a tribe conquered by the Incas. Also, in the rainforests of eastern Peru the 40 or so tribes speak a number of ancient tribal languages.

FAMILY AND COMMUNITY DYNAMICS

Approximately 45 percent of Peruvians today are descendants of Peru's indigenous population, often referred to as Indian, while about 43 percent are mestizos, people of mixed indigenous and Spanish heritage. Another ten percent are of unmixed European ancestry, almost all Spanish. The blacks who are descendants of the slaves from Africa, and those whose ancestors were imported Chinese and Japanese laborers, together make up less than two percent of the population.

Spanish colonization left a legacy of social stratification that is for the most part unbroken today. Traditionally, the small Spanish upper class ruled the native and mestizo underclass. In the twentieth century a middle class of whites and some mestizos has developed, but most mestizos and almost all of the indigenous population belong to the underclass.

About half of Peru's whites belong to the elite class that runs the country's political and economic affairs. They speak Spanish and dress much like their counterparts in the rest of the Western world. Family ties are particularly important for this group because they help maintain their powerful status in the society. Whites seldom associate with people from other classes, and their children usually marry into other upper-class families. Most of these families live in the prosperous areas of Lima and the other major cities. Most of Peru's upper- and middle-class families have a varied diet consisting of meat, fish, poultry, vegetables, and cereal products. Main dishes are heavily seasoned with onions and hot peppers. Most main dishes are accompanied by rice, potatoes, and bread.

The mestizos also generally speak Spanish and dress according to Western styles. They are the group that has had the closest relations with the ruling elite, such as when they would be hired by the whites to supervise native workers in mines or on plantations. As the middle class has grown the mestizos have found other avenues for advancement, such as going to college and becoming involved in government, business, the military, and various other professions. These opportunities have not been enough, however, to raise a majority out of the underclass.

Peru's indigenous population lives predominately in the rural highlands, the coast, and the *selva*. The people are nearly all poor and lack formal education. They subsist mainly through farming and cling tenaciously to their culture. While the young often wear Western-style clothing, the older Peruvians wear more traditional handwoven garments such as ponchos and sandals. Traditional costumes are increasingly saved for special ceremonial occasions. Rural Peruvians live mainly by agriculture. On the Pacific Coast they grow rice, cotton, sugar cane, and barley for sale. Maize and rice are the food crops along with grapes, olives, and oranges. The coastal dwellers also catch pilchard and white fish. In the highlands the staple crops are maize, potatoes, barley, and wheat. The diet of the poorest Peruvians is a fairly monotonous one and often lacks complete nutritional value—potatoes, beans, corn, squash, wheat or barley soups, and occasionally fish. The highland population frequently chews the leaves of the coca plant to suppress appetite and fatigue.

All social classes and ethnicities in Peru place a great deal of emphasis on family, often extending it to include distant relatives and godparents. Frequently chosen from a superior social class, godparents are sponsors at baptisms and other rites of passage, and this relationship maintains bonds of mutual assistance between the sponsors and the child's family. Peruvian social life often revolves around the extended family, especially among the indigenous Peruvians, who may have few important social ties beyond the family. The extended family commonly serves an economic function, as well, with members working together and pooling their resources. The nuclear family tends to be male dominated, and fathers have great authority over the children even into adulthood.

Though the indigenous families tend to be less patriarchal than white and mestizo families, there, too, the husbands dominate the household. Particularly in the shantytowns around the large urban centers, known as the *pueblos jóvenes* (young towns), harsh economic conditions result in mestizo families that are more fragile than elsewhere. Many marriages among this population consist of consensual unions rather than legal marriages.

EDUCATION

Peru has made great strides this century in educating its people. Education's share of the national budget rose from three percent in 1900 to over 30 percent in the 1960s, and school enrollment increased at double the rate of population growth. The literacy rate of those over 15 years of age is 87 percent, one of the highest in Latin America. Education is free and compulsory between the ages of six and 15. However, the vast majority of the uneducated are those in rural areas where there often are not enough schools and teachers. Great disparities also exist between the sexes in terms of the quality and number of years of education. Most middle- and upper-class students attend private schools in the cities.

Peru has more than 30 national universities, though most of them are relatively new and of lesser quality. They also tend to be very political, engendering student radicals on campus. However,

San Marcos University in Lima is the country's most prestigious public university and South America's oldest, having been chartered in 1551. The National Engineering University, the National Agrarian University, and the Superior School for Business Administration are also highly regarded. The elite sectors of society tend to favor private universities, such as Lima's Catholic University, because they are less political. Peru's important research centers include the Institute of the Sea and the International Potato Center.

RELIGION

Peru's constitution guarantees freedom of religion. About 95 percent of Peru's population is at least nominally Roman Catholic, a legacy of the church's deep-rooted involvement in the country's affairs since the Spanish conquest. The state supports the church through an annual grant, and the president is involved in the selection of its hierarchy. There are also small numbers of Protestants, Jews, and Buddhists; they comprise only about one percent of the population.

There is a wide range of religious commitment, and women tend to be far more devout than men. Agnosticism is common in the cities, especially among intellectuals. Despite this, Catholicism is firmly woven into Peruvian culture. The Catholic religion is taught in public schools throughout the country, and fiestas corresponding to Church holidays are among the most important social events of the year, even in larger cities. A list of national holidays reveals religion's prominence: New Year's Day (January 1), Holy Thursday and Good Friday (variable), Labor Day (May 1), Day of the Peasant (June 24), St. Peter and St. Paul's Day (June 29), Independence Day (July 28 and 29), St. Rose of Lima, patroness of Peru (August 30), Battle of Anzamos (October 8), All Saints' Day (November 1), Immaculate Conception (December 8), and Christmas Day (December 25).

While middle-class Peruvians tend to be strict in their religious beliefs and adherence to ritual, further down the social scale one finds an increasing tendency to blend elements of superstition, folk religion (including the worship of Incan gods), and magic with formal Catholicism. Many of the beliefs and practices of ancient Peru persist in this form. A number of local shrines and icons that have survived earthquakes or other natural disasters are revered as evidence of miracles or divine intervention.

EMPLOYMENT AND ECONOMIC TRADITIONS

Peru's economy is hampered by the inefficiency and obsolescence of many of its structures. In each of the major areas of the economy there are a few productive modern enterprises outnumbered by inefficient traditional counterparts. The modern units of the economy employ about one-third of the work force but are responsible for about two-thirds of the nation's income. The modern sectors also support Peru's politically powerful middle class and its militant labor unions. Another duality in the economy exists between low-income subsistence agriculture in the sierra, and the wealth produced on the large, productive farms of the coast, in off-shore fisheries, and in the city of Lima. Few jobs are available to the more than 200,000 people who enter Peru's work force each year, with the result that fewer than half of the country's workers are fully employed.

Approximately 42 percent of the Peruvian work force is employed in agriculture, fishing, or forestry, though these sectors represent only 14 percent of the national income. Manufacturing, mining, and construction employ 18 percent of workers and generate 38 percent of the gross national product. The service sector (which includes Lima's 200,000 street vendors) employs 40 percent of Peru's workers and contributes 48 percent of the nation's income.

Peru is a net exporter of raw materials and unfinished products and a net importer of manufactured products. It also has to import much of its food because domestic production is inadequate and because transportation is severely limited by the small percentage of roads that are paved. The leading exports are petroleum, copper, silver, zinc, lead, fishmeal, and coffee. Cocaine exports are not part of official figures, but they are estimated to bring in as much foreign currency—almost all U.S. dollars—as petroleum and copper combined. The United States is Peru's largest trading partner, buying one-third of its legal exports and supplying about 40 percent of its imported goods. Japan and Germany are also major trading partners.

POLITICS AND GOVERNMENT

Peru's 1979 constitution was the first in its history to extend the right to vote to all citizens aged 18 and over without any literacy requirement, and voting was made obligatory up to age 60. The people elect the president and two vice-presidents to five-year terms, though the president may not be reelected to a consecutive term. Since 1985 a presidential candidate must get at least 50 percent of the vote or else a run-off ensues between the top three candidates. The president heads the executive department, which carries out government operations through a cabinet led by a presidentially appointed premier.

The Peruvian legislature is made up of a 60-member Senate and a 180-member Chamber of Deputies, all of whom are elected to five-year terms concurrent with the president's. The congress convenes twice a year, from April 1 to May 31 and from July 27 to December 15, and either house may initiate legislation. The president reviews legislation but has no veto power. The judicial branch consists of judges appointed by the president to terms that end at age 70. The 16 justices of Peru's highest court, the Supreme Court in Lima, are selected by the president from a list submitted by the National Justice Council.

Peru's governments have been highly centralized since Incan times, and this is still true today. There are 24 political departments plus the constitutional province of Callao. Each department is divided into provinces, which are further divided into districts. The departments and provinces are headed by prefects appointed by the president to carry out the policies dictated by the central government. The people elect local councils to govern their districts and municipalities.

At the end of 1994 President Alberto Fujimori still ruled with the virtually dictatorial powers assumed in his 1992 presidential coup, in which he suspended the congress and judiciary, ostensibly to deal more forcefully with Peru's economic and political instability. Elections were scheduled for 1995 to determine the status of the constitution and the future of the country.

INDIVIDUAL AND GROUP CONTRIBUTIONS

Peruvian Americans have contributed to American society in various ways—from the large numbers of doctors and other medical specialists, to those in education and business, to those who provide manual labor or child care. The following is a sample of Peruvian Americans who have achieved recognition in their field.

ARTS

Carlos Llerena Aguirre (1952–) is an artist and educator born in Arequipa, Peru. He received a bachelor of arts degree from the School of Visual Arts in New York City in 1979, a master's from Hunter College in 1982, and a master's of fine arts from the University of Illinois in 1994. He was an instructor at the School of Visual Arts and has been an associate professor at the University of Illinois since 1989. He is a member of the Society of Newspaper Designers and has had exhibitions of his woodcuts and engravings in Urbana, Illinois, Lima, Norway, and London.

Isaac Goldenberg (1945–) is a poet and novelist living in New York City. Born in Peru, he is the co-director of the Instituto de Escritores Latinoamerican in New York as well as the Latin American book fair. Isaac was a New York State Council of the Arts Writer in Residence in 1987-1988. His books include *La Vida Contado* (1992), *Tiempo al Tiempo* (1984), and *La Vida a Plazos de Jacobo Lerner* (1980).

Luís John Kong (1956–) maintains various roles as poet, arts administrator, and TV and radio producer. Born in Pisco, Peru, he attended college in California, receiving a B.A. in English and biology from Sonoma State University in 1982. He directed the university's intercultural center and was a producer/programmer for a bilingual public radio program. Most recently Kong has served as poet, teacher, and consultant for the California Poets in the Schools program. He received the Corporation for Public Broadcasting Silver Award for his production "En Camino" in 1989.

BUSINESS

Virginia Patricia Rebata (1953–) is a business executive with the Marriott Corporation. Born in Lima, she graduated from the University of California, Berkeley, with a B.A. in 1975 and received an M.P.A. from California State University, Hayward, in 1980. Virginia served as youth employment services director for the San Mateo (California) County Board of Education before going to work for Marriott as director of Human Resource Field Programs and Services in 1992. She established the first English as a Second Language program for Hispanics at Marriott's headquarters and received the National Alliance for Business President's Award in 1989.

GOVERNMENT AND POLITICS

Maria Azucena Arbulu (1956–) is an official in the Michigan state government. She was born in Pueblo, Colorado, and got her B.A. at Oberlin in 1978 and her M.A. in 1984 at the American Graduate School of International Management. She worked for the Detroit Board of Education and the Motorola Corporation before taking a position as international trade specialist with the state of Michigan. She now serves as the state's trade officer for Canadian operations.

JOURNALISM

Pedro M. Valdivieso (1932–) is the editor of the paper *Actualidad* in Los Angeles. He was born in Piura, Peru, and studied journalism and public relations at San Marcos University and Lima University, respectively. He edited newspapers in Lima before moving to the United States and editing *Noticias del Mundo* (Los Angeles) and *El Diario de Los Angeles*. Valdivieso has reported for Channel 34 TV in Los Angeles and is a member of the Association of Journalists in the Spanish Language and the Federation of Journalists from Peru.

LIBRARY SCIENCE

César Rodríguez (1945–) is a university librarian born in Callao, Peru. He received a B.A. from Queens College in New York City in 1970 and an M.A. from Columbia University in 1983. He was the Yale University Social Science Library's acquisition librarian from 1976 to 1986, after which he became the curator of the library's Latin American collection. Rodríguez is a member of the Latin American Studies Association and a contributor to a number of Latin American bibliographies. He served as a corporal in the U.S. Marine Corps in Vietnam from 1965 to 1969 and received three medals.

MEDICINE AND HEALTH

Graciela Solís Alarcón (1942–) is a physician and educator originally from Chachapoyas, Peru. She earned her M.D. in Peru in 1967 and an M.P.H. from Johns Hopkins University in 1972. She did her residency in Baltimore and in Peru and has been a professor at the University of Alabama at Birmingham since 1980. She is a member of the American College of Rheumatology and the American College of Physicians and has authored a number of articles in her field.

Carlos Castaneda (sometimes Castañeda) is perhaps the best known Peruvian American. While attempting a thesis on medicinal plants for the University of California, Los Angeles, in the late 1960s, he met a Yaqui (Mexican) *brujo*, or medicine man, living in Arizona and became heavily influenced by his way of life. Carlos began a series of best-selling books based on these experiences, beginning with *The Teachings of Don Juan: A Yaqui Way of Knowl-* *edge* in 1976. The books relate a hallucinogen-induced search for a non-rational reality and an attempt to become a Yaqui warrior. The author considered them anthropological field studies, and indeed they served as his master's and doctoral theses, though critics within the field of anthropology say they are more properly regarded as fiction. While Castaneda seems to be purposely elusive regarding his biographical details, he is thought to have been born in Cajamarca, Peru, in 1925. He received his B.A., M.A., and Ph.D. from UCLA in 1962, 1964, and 1973, respectively.

SCIENCE

Jaime A. Fernandez-Baca (1954–) is a physicist at the Oak Ridge National Laboratory. He earned his B.S. in Lima in 1977 before coming to the United States for a M.Sc. and Ph.D. at the University of Maryland (1982 and 1986). Fernandez-Baca has done his research at the Instituto de Energia Nuclear in Peru and at the University of Maryland. He was awarded a fellowship by the International Atomic Energy Agency in 1977 and has published numerous technical articles.

MEDIA

PRINT

Chasqui.
Scholarly journal covering Latin American literature.

Contact: David William Foster, Editor.
Address: College of William and Mary,
   Williamsburg, Virginia 23187-8795.

El Diario/La Prensa.
Founded in 1913, this Spanish-language daily has a circulation of 67,000 and includes coverage of Peru in its international pages.

Contact: Carlos D. Ramirez, Publisher.
Address: 143-155 Varick Street, New York,
   New York 10013.
Telephone: (212) 807-4600.
Fax: (212) 807-4617.

El Nuevo Herald.
This Spanish-language daily includes Peru in its coverage of South America. It was founded in 1976 and has a circulation of 98,000.

Contact: Barbara Gutierrez, Editor.
Address: Hometown Herald, 1520 East Sunrise
   Boulevard, Fort Lauderdale, Florida 33304.

Telephone: (954) 527-8940.
Fax: (954) 527-8955.

RADIO

WADO-AM (1280).
"Perú Cerca de Ti" (Peru Near You), a magazine type program featuring music, news, and tourism information related to Peru, airs on Saturdays from 7:00 p.m. to 8:00 p.m.

Address: 666 Third Avenue, New York, New York 10017.
Telephone: (212) 687-9236.
Fax: (212) 599-2161.

ORGANIZATIONS AND ASSOCIATIONS

Great Lakes Peruvian Club.
Contact: Victor Figueroa.
Address: 8752 Lilac Lane, Berrien Springs, Michigan 49103-1445.

Movimiento Popular Peru.
Founded in 1980. Provides research, informational, and educational programs. Publishes *The New Flag* (*La Nueva Bandera*), a free bimonthly newsletter.

Address: 30-08 Broadway, Suite 159, Long Island City, New York 11106.
E-mail: lquispe@nyxfer.blythe.org.

The Peruvian-American Medical Society.
This professional organization of Peruvian American doctors raises money for equipment needed by Peruvian hospitals.

Address: 313 Heathcote Avenue, Mamaroneck, New York 10543.
Telephone: (914) 381-2001.

MUSEUMS AND RESEARCH CENTERS

American Museum of Natural History.
This New York City landmark museum has a wing dedicated to South American peoples that features Peruvian civilizations, especially the Incas.

Address: Central Park West at 79th Street, New York, New York 10024.
Telephone: (212) 769-5100.
Online: http://www.amnh.org/.

University of California, Berkeley.
The Center for Latin American Studies, founded in 1956, incorporates social science and the humanities in its scope. It gives particular emphasis to the native populations of South America.

Contact: Harley Shaiken, Director.
Address: 2334 Bowditch, Berkeley, California 94720-2312.
Telephone: (510) 642-2088.
Fax: (510) 642-3260.
E-mail: hshaiken@socrates.berkeley.edu.
Online: http://www.clas.berkeley.edu.

University of California, Los Angeles.
Founded in 1959, the Latin American Center coordinates research on the region's socio-politics, environment, technology, literature, and arts.

Contact: Dr. Carlos Alberto Torres, Director.
Address: 405 Hilgard Avenue, Los Angeles, California 90095-1447.
Telephone: (310) 825-4571.
Fax: (310) 206-6859.
E-mail: moss@isop.ucla.edu.
Online: http://www.isop.ucla.edu/lac.

University of Florida, Gainesville.
The Institute for Latin American Studies was founded in 1931. It features studies in the humanities and social sciences and has a project on Aymará language and culture.

Contact: Dr. Charles H. Wood, Director.
Address: 304 Grintner Hall, P.O. Box 115531, Gainesville, Florida 32611-5531.
Telephone: (352) 392-6548.
Fax: (352) 392-7682.
E-mail: latam@nervm.nerdc.ufl.edu.
Online: http://www.latam.ufl.edu.

SOURCES FOR ADDITIONAL STUDY

Arden, Harvey. "The Two Souls of Peru," *National Geographic*, March 1982; pp. 284-321.

Blassingame, Wyatt. *The Incas and the Spanish Conquest*. New York: Julian Messner, 1980.

De Ferrari, Gabriella. *Gringa Latina: A Woman of Two Worlds*. Boston : Houghton Mifflin Co., 1996.

Dostert, Pierre Etienne. *Latin America 1994*. Washington, D.C.: Stryker-Post Publications, 1994.

Martín, Luis. *The Kingdom of the Sun: A Short History of Peru*. New York: Charles Scribner's Sons, 1974.

Monaghan, Jay. *Chile, Peru, and the California Gold Rush of 1849*. Berkeley: University of California Press, 1973.

The Peru Reader: History, Culture, Politics, edited by Orin Starn, Carlos Iván Degregori, and Robin Kirk. Durham, NC: Duke University Press, 1995.

Stavans, Ilan. "Two Peruvians: How a Novelist and a Terrorist Came to Represent Peru's Divided Soul," *Utne Reader*, July/August 1994; pp. 96-102.

Werlich, David P. *Peru: A Short History*. Carbondale: Southern Illinois University Press, 1978.

Wright, Ronald. *Cut Stones and Crossroads: A Journey in the Two Worlds of Peru*. New York: Viking Press, 1984.

POLISH AMERICANS

by
Syd Jones

Poles numbered among the earliest colonists in the New World and today, as their numbers exceed ten million, they represent the largest of the Slavic groups in America.

OVERVIEW

Poland, the seventh largest country in Europe, occupies an area of 120,727 square miles—somewhat larger than the state of Nevada. Located in east-central Europe, it is bordered to the east by Russia and the Ukraine, the Czech Republic and Slovakia to the south, Germany to the west, and the Baltic Sea to the north. Drained by the Vistula and Oder Rivers, Poland is a land of varied landscape—from the central lowlands, to the sand dunes and swamps of the Baltic coast, to the mountains of the Carpathians to the south. Its 1990 population of just over 38 million is largely homogeneous ethnically, religiously, and linguistically. Minority groups in the country include Germans, Ukrainians and Belarusans. Ninety-five percent of the population is Roman Catholic, and Polish is the national language. Warsaw, located in the central lowlands, is the nation's capital. Poland's national flag is bicolor: divided in half horizontally, it has a white stripe on the top half and a red one on the bottom. Polish Americans often display a flag similar to this with a crowned eagle at its center.

HISTORY

The very name of Poland harkens back to its origins in the Slavic tribes that inhabited the Vistula valley as early as the second millennium B.C. Migrations of these tribes resulted in three distinct subgroups: the

West, East, and South Slavs. It was the West Slavs who became the ancestors of modern Poles, settling in and around the Oder and Vistula valleys. Highly clannish, these tribes were organized in tight kinship groups with commonly held property and a rough-and-ready sort of representative government regarding matters other than military. These West Slavs slowly joined in ever-larger units under the pressure of incursions by Avars and early Germans, ultimately being led by a tribe known as the Polanie. From that point on, these West Slavs, and increasingly the entire region, were referred to as Polania or later, Poland. Under the Polanian duke Mieszko and his Piast dynasty, further consolidation around what is modern Poznan created a true state; and in 966, Mieszko was converted to Christianity. It is this event that is commonly accepted as the founding date of Poland. It is doubly important because Mieszko's conversion to Christianity—Roman Catholicism—would link Poland's fortunes in the future to those of Western Europe. The East Slavs, centered at Kiev, were converted by missionaries from the Greek church, which in turn linked them to the Orthodox east.

Meanwhile, the South Slavs had been coalescing into larger units, forming what is known as Little Poland, as opposed to Great Poland of the Piasts. These South Slavs joined Great Poland under Casimir I and for several generations the new state thrived, checking the tide of German expansionism. But from the twelfth to thirteenth centuries, the new kingdom became fragmented by a duchy system that created political chaos and civil war among rival princes of the Piast lineage. Following devastations caused by Tatar invasions in the early thirteenth century, Poland was defenseless against a further tide of German settlement. One of the last Piasts, Casimir III, succeeded in reunifying the kingdom in 1338, and in 1386 it came under the rule of the Jagiellonian dynasty when the grand duke of Lithuania married the crown princess of the Piasts, Jadwiga. Known as Poland's Golden Age, the next two centuries of Jagiellonian rule enabled Poland-Lithuania to become the dominant power in central Europe, encompassing Hungary and Bohemia in its sphere of influence and producing a rich cultural heritage for the nation, including the achievements of such individuals as Copernicus (Mikołaj Kopernik, 1473-1543). At the same time, Poland enjoyed one of the most representative governments of its day as well as the most tolerant religious climate in Europe.

But with the end of the Jagiellonian dynasty in 1572, the kingdom once again fell apart as the landed gentry increasingly assumed local control, sapping the strength of the central government in Krakow. This state of affairs continued for two centuries until Poland was so weakened that it suffered three partitions: Austria took Galicia in 1772; Prussia acquired the northwestern section in 1793; and Tsarist Russia possessed the northeastern section in 1795). By the end of the three partitions, Poland had been completely wiped off the map of Europe. There would not be an independent Poland again for a century and a half, though a nominal Kingdom of Poland was established within the Russian Empire by the Congress of Vienna in 1815. In both Russia and Germany a strict policy of suppression of the Polish language and autonomous education was enforced.

After World War I, an independent Poland was once again re-established. With Josef Pilsudski (1867-1935) as its president and dictator from 1926 to 1935, Poland maintained an uneasy peace with the Soviet Union and Nazi Germany. But with the onset of World War II, Poland was the first victim, and once again the nation was subsumed into other countries: Germany and the Soviet Union initially, and then solely under German rule. The Nazis used Poland as a killing ground to subdue and eradicate Polish culture by executing its intellectuals and nobles, and to "settle" the Jewish question once and for all by exterminating the Jews of Europe. In camps such as Auschwitz-Birkenau this gruesome strategy was put into effect, and by the end of the war in 1945, Poland had lost a fifth of its population, half of which—over three million—were Jews.

Liberation, however, did not mean freedom, for after the war Poland fell under the Soviet sphere; a communist state was set up and Poland once again had become a fiefdom to a foreign power. In 1956 Poland's workers went on a general strike in protest to Moscow's heavy-handed domination. Though brutally suppressed, the strike did force Poland's new leader Wladysław Gomułka to relax some of the totalitarian controls imposed by Warsaw and Moscow, and farms were decollectivized. Through successive leadership of Edward Gierek and General Wojciech Jaruzelski, however, the economic conditions worsened and the Poles struggled increasingly for more autonomy from Moscow. By 1980 three events had coincided that would be decisive for Poland's future: the Soviet Union was going bankrupt; Karol Cardinal Wojtyła became Pope John Paul II; and a new and illegal union, Solidarity, had been formed under Lech Wałesa. These last two especially brought Poland into international focus. By 1989, Solidarity won concessions from the government including participation in free elections. After their overwhelming victory, which brought to power their leader Lech Wałesa as President, Solidarity set up a coalition government with the communists; and with the fall of the Soviet Union, Poland along with all of central Europe, regained new breathing room in its heartland. The difficult task now confronting the country is a transformation from a centrally planned economy to a market economy, one that causes enormous dislocations including unemployment and runaway inflation.

THE FIRST POLES IN AMERICA

Poles numbered among the earliest colonists in the New World and today, as their numbers exceed ten million, they represent the largest of the Slavic groups in America. Though claims have been made for Poles sailing with Viking ships exploring the New World before 1600, there is no hard evidence to support them. By 1609, however, Polish immigrants do appear in the annals of Jamestown, having been recruited by the colony as skilled craftsmen to create products for export. These immigrants were integral in the establishment of both the glassmaking and woodworking industries in the new colonies. An early Polish explorer, Anthony Sadowski, set up a trading post along the Mississippi River which later became the city of Sandusky, Ohio. Two other names of note occur in the early history of what would become the American republic: the noblemen Tadeusz Kościuszko (1746-1817) and Casimir Pułaski (1747-1779) both fought on the rebel side in the Revolutionary War. Pulaski, killed in the battle of Savannah, is still honored by Polish Americans—Polonia as the ethnic community is referred to—by annual marches on October 11, Pulaski Day.

SIGNIFICANT IMMIGRATION WAVES

Since the times of those earliest Polish settlers—romantics, adventurers and men simply seeking a better economic life—there have been four distinct waves of immigration to the United States from Poland. The first and smallest, occasioned by the partitioning of Poland, lasted from roughly 1800 to 1860 and was largely made up of political dissidents and those who fled after the dissolution of their national homeland. The second wave was far more significant and took place between 1860 and World War I. Immigrants during this time were in search of a better economic life and tended to be of the rural class, so-called za chleben (for bread) emigrants. A third wave lasted from the end of World War I through the end of the Cold War and again comprised dissidents and political refugees. Since the fall of the Soviet Union and Poland's democratic reforms, there has been yet a fourth wave of a seemingly more temporary immigrant group, the wakacjusze, or those who come on tourists visas but find work and stay either illegally or legally. These economic immigrants generally plan to earn money and return to Poland.

The first wave of immigrants, from approximately 1800 to 1860, was largely made up of intellectuals and lesser nobility. Not only the partitioning of Poland, but insurrections in 1830 and 1863 also forced political dissidents from their Polish homeland. Many fled to London, Paris and Geneva, but at the same time New York and Chicago also received its share of such refugees from political oppression. Immigration figures are always a problematic issue, and those for Polish immigrants to the United States are no different. For much of the modern era there was no political entity such as Poland, so immigrants coming to America had an initial difficulty in describing their country of origin. Also, there was with Poles, more so than other ethnic immigrant groups, more back-and-forth travel between host country and home country. Poles have tended to save money and return to their native country in higher numbers than many other ethnic groups. Additionally, minorities within Poland who immigrated to the United States confuse the picture. Nonetheless, what numbers that exist from U.S. Immigration and Naturalization Service records indicate that fewer than 2,000 Poles immigrated to the United States between 1800 and 1860.

The second wave of immigration was inaugurated in 1854 when about 800 Polish Catholics from Silesia founded Panna Maria, a farming colony in Texas. This symbolic opening of America to the Poles also opened the flood gates of immigration. The new arrivals tended to cluster in industrial cities and towns of the Midwest and Middle Atlantic States—New York, Buffalo, Pittsburgh, Cleveland, Detroit, Milwaukee, Minneapolis, Chicago, and St. Louis—where they became steelworkers, meatpackers, miners, and later autoworkers. These cities still retain their large contingents of Polish Americans. A lasting legacy of these Poles in America is the vital role they played in the growth and development of the U.S. labor movement, Joseph Yablonski of the United Mine Workers only one case in point.

Confusion over exact numbers of Polish immigrants again becomes a problem during this period, with large underreporting, especially during the 1890s when immigration was highest. Most agree, however, that between mid-nineteenth century and World War I, some 2.5 million Poles immigrated to the United States. This wave of immigration can be further broken down to two successive movements of Poles from different regions of their partitioned

country. The first to come were the German Poles, who tended to be better educated and more skilled craftsmen than the Russian and Austrian Poles. High birthrates, overpopulation, and large-scale farming methods in Prussia, which forced small farmers off the land, all combined to send German Poles into emigration in the second half of the nineteenth century. German policy vis-a-vis restricting the power of the Catholic church also played a part in this exodus. Those arriving in the United States totalled roughly a half million during this period, with numbers dwindling by the end of the century.

However, just as German Polish immigration to the United States was diminishing, that of Russian and Austrian Poles was just getting underway. Again, overpopulation and land hunger drove this emigration, as well as the enthusiastic letters home that new arrivals in the United States sent to their relatives and loved ones. Many young men also fled from military conscription, especially in the years of military build-up just prior to and including the onset of World War I. Moreover, the journey to America itself had become less arduous, with ship-

ping lines such as the North German Line and the Hamburg American Line now booking passage from point to point, combining overland as well as transatlantic passage and thereby simplifying border crossings. Numbers of Galician or Austrian Poles total approximately 800,000, and of Russian Poles—the last large immigration contingent—another 800,000. It has also been estimated that 30 percent of Galician and Russian Poles arriving between 1906 and 1914 returned to their homelands.

The influx of such large numbers of one ethnic group was sure to cause friction with the "established" Americans, and during the last half of the nineteenth century history witnesses intolerance toward many of the immigrants from divergent parts of Europe. That the Poles were strongly Catholic contributed to such friction, and thus Polonia or the Polish Americans formed even tighter links with each other, relying on ethnic cohesiveness not only for moral support, but financial, as well. Polish fraternal, national, and religious organizations such as the Polish National Alliance, the Polish Union, the Polish American Congress, and the Polish Roman

Catholic Union have been instrumental in not only maintaining a Polish identity for immigrants, but also in obtaining insurance and home loans to set the new arrivals on their own feet in their new country. Such friction abated as Poles assimilated in their host country, to be supplanted by new waves of immigrants from other countries. Polish Americans have, however, continued to maintain a strong ethnic identity into the late twentieth century.

With the end of World War I and the re-establishment of an independent Polish state, it was believed that there would be a huge exodus of Polish immigrants returning to their homeland. Such an exodus did not materialize, though immigration over the next generation greatly dropped off. U.S. immigration quotas imposed in the 1920s had much to do with this, as did the Great Depression. But political oppression in Europe between the wars, displaced persons brought on by World War II, and the flight of dissidents from the communist regime did account for a further half million immigrants—many of them refugees—from Poland between 1918 and the late 1980s and the fall of communism.

The fourth wave of Polish immigration is now underway. This is comprised mostly of younger people who grew up under communism. Though not significant in numbers because of immigration quotas, this newest wave of post-Cold War immigrants, whether they be the short-term workers, *wakacjusze*, or long-term residents, continue to add new blood to Polish Americans, ensuring that the ethnic community continues to have foreign-born Poles among its contingent. Estimates from the 1970 census placed the number of either foreign born Poles or native born with at least one Polish parent at near three million. Over eight million claimed Polish ancestry in their background in the 1980 census and 9.5 million did so in the 1990 census, 90 percent of whom were concentrated in urban areas. A large part of such identity and cohesiveness was the result of outside conditions. It has been noted that initial friction between Polish immigrants and "established" Americans played some part in this inward looking stance. Additionally, such commonly held beliefs as folk culture and Catholicism provided further incentives for communalism. Newly arrived Poles generally had their closest contacts outside Polish Americans with their former European neighbors: Czechs, Germans, and Lithuanians. Over the years there has been a degree of friction specifically between the Polish American community and Jews and African Americans. However, during the years of partition, Polish Americans kept alive the belief in a free Poland. Such cohesiveness was further heightened in the Polish American community during the Cold War,

when Poland was a satellite of the Soviet Union. But since the fall of the Soviet empire and with free elections in Poland, this outer threat to the homeland is no longer a factor in keeping Polish Americans together. The subsequent increase in immigration of the fourth wave of younger Poles escaping difficult transition times at home has added new numbers to immigrants in the United States, but it is yet to be seen what their effect will be on Polish Americans. As yet, these recent immigrants have played no part in the power structure—not being members of the fraternal organizations. What their effect in the future will be is unclear.

ACCULTURATION AND ASSIMILATION

In a society so homogenized by the effects of mass media, such ethnic enclaves as the amorphous reaches of Polish Americans is clearly affected. Despite the recent emphasis on multiculturalism and a resurgent interest in ethnic roots, Polish Americans like other ethnic groups become assimilated more and more rapidly. Using language as a

"We wanted to be Americans so quickly that we were embarrassed if our parents couldn't speak English. My father was reading a Polish paper. And somebody was supposed to come to the house. I remember sticking it under something. We were that ashamed of being foreign."

Louise Nagy in 1913, cited in *Ellis Island: An Illustrated History of the Immigrant Experience,* edited by Ivan Chermayeff et al. (New York: Macmillan, 1991).

measure, it can be seen how quickly such absorption occurs. In a 1960 survey of children of Polish ethnic leaders, 20 percent reported that they spoke Polish regularly. By 1990, however, the U.S. census reported that only 750,000 Polish Americans spoke Polish in the home.

As part of the European emigration, Polish immigrants have had an easier time racially than many other non-European groups in assimilating or blending into the American scene. But this is only a surface assimilation. Culturally, the Polish contingent has held tightly to its folk and national roots, making Polonia more than simply a name. It has been at times a country within a country, Poland in the New World. By and large, Poles have competed

well and succeeded in their new homeland; they have thrived and built homes and raised families, and in that respect have participated in and added to the American dream. Yet this process of assimilation has been far from smooth as witnessed by one fact: the Polish joke. Such jokes have at their core a negative representation of the Poles as backward and uneducated simpletons. It is perhaps this stereotype that is hardest for Polish Americans to combat, and is a legacy of the second wave of immigrants, the largest contingent between 1860 and 1914 made up of mostly people from Galicia and Russia. Though recent studies have shown Polish Americans to have high income levels as compared to British, German, Italian, and Irish immigrant groups, the same studies demonstrate that they come in last in terms of occupation and education. For many generations, Polish Americans in general did not value higher education, though such a stance has changed radically in the late twentieth century. The professions are now heavily represented with Polish Americans as well as the blue collar world. Yet the Polish joke persists and Polish Americans have been actively fighting it in the past two

decades with not only educational programs but also law suits when necessary. The days of Polish Americans anglicizing their names seem to be over; along with other ethnic groups Polish Americans now talk of ethnic pride.

TRADITIONS, CUSTOMS, AND BELIEFS

It had been noted that clans and kinship communities were extremely important in the early formation of Slavic tribes. This early form of communalism has been translated into today's world by the plethora of Polish American fraternal organizations. By the same token, other traditions out of the Polish rural and agrarian past still hold today.

Gospodarz may well be one of the prettiest sounding words in the Polish language—to a Pole. It means a landowner, and it is the land that has always been important in Poland. Ownership of land was one of the things that brought the huge influx of Poles to the United States, but less than ten percent achieved that dream, and these were mainly the German Poles who came first when there was still a frontier to carve out. The remaining Poles were stuck in the urban areas as wage-earners, though many of these managed to save the money to buy a small plot of land in the suburbs. Contrasted to this is the *Górale*, or mountaineer. To the lowlanders of Greater Poland, the stateless peoples of the southern Carpathians represented free human spirit, unbridled by convention and laws. Both of these impulses runs through the Polish peoples and informs their customs.

An agrarian people, many Poles have traditions and beliefs that revolve around the calendar year, the time for sowing and for reaping. And inextricably linked to this rhythm is that of the Catholic church whose saints' days mark the cycle of the year. A strong belief in good versus evil resulted in a corresponding belief in the devil: witches who could make milk cows go dry; the power of the evil eye, which both humans and animals could wield; the belief that if bees build a hive in one's house, the house will catch on fire; and the tradition that while goats are lucky animals, wolves, crows and pigeons all bring bad luck.

PROVERBS

Polish proverbs display the undercurrents of the Polish nature, its belief in simple pragmatism and honesty, and a cynical distrust of human nature: When misfortune knocks at the door, friends are asleep; the mistakes of the doctor are covered by the earth; the rich man has only two holes in his nose, the same as the poor man; listen much and speak little; he whose coach is drawn by hope has poverty for a coachman; if God wills, even a cock will lay an egg; he who lends to a friend makes an enemy; no fish without bones; no woman without a temper; where there is fire, a wind will soon be blowing.

CUISINE

The diet of Polish Americans has also changed over the years. One marked change from Poland is the increased consumption of meat. Polish sausages, especially the *kielbasa*—garlic-flavored pork sausage—have become all but synonymous with Polish cuisine. Other staples include cabbage in the form of sauerkraut or cabbage rolls, dark bread, potatoes, beets, barley, and oatmeal. Of course this traditional diet has been added to by usual American fare, but especially at festivities and celebrations such as Christmas and Easter, Polish Americans still serve their traditional food. Polish Americans have, in addition to the sausage, also contributed staples to American cuisine, including the breakfast roll, *bialys*, the *babka* coffeecake, and potato pancakes.

TRADITIONAL COSTUMES

Traditional clothing is worn less and less by Polish Americans, but such celebrations as Pulaski Day on October 11 of each year witness upwards of 100,000 Polish Americans parading between 26th Street and 52nd Street in New York, many of them wearing traditional dress. For women this means a combination blouse and petticoat covered by a full, brightly colored or embroidered skirt, an apron, and a jacket or bodice, also gaily decorated. Headdress ranges from a simple kerchief to more elaborate affairs made of feathers, flowers, beads, and ribbons decorating stiffened linen. Men also wear headdresses, though usually not as ornate as the women's—felt or straw hats or caps. Trousers are often white with red stripes, tucked into the boots or worn with mountaineering moccasins typical to the Carpathians. Vests or jackets cover white embroidered shirts, and the favorite colors replicate the flag: red and white.

HOLIDAYS

In addition to Pulaski Day, which President Harry Truman decreed an official remembrance day in 1946, Polish American celebrations consist mainly of the prominent liturgical holidays such as Christmas and Easter. The traditional Christmas Eve dinner, called *wigilia*, begins when the first star of the evening appears. The dinner, which is served upon a white tablecloth under which some straw has been placed, consists of 12 meatless courses—one for each of the apostles. There is also one empty chair kept at the table for a stranger who might chance by. This vigil supper begins with the breaking of a wafer, the *oplatek*, and the exchange of good wishes; it moves on to such traditional fare as apple pancakes, fish, *pierogi* or a type of filled dumpling, potato salad, sauerkraut and nut or poppy seed torte for dessert. To insure good luck in the coming year one must taste all courses, and there must also be an even number of people at the table to ensure good health. The singing of carols follows the supper. In Poland, between Christmas Eve and the Epiphany (January 6, or "Three Kings") "caroling with the manger" takes place in which carolers bearing a manger visit neighbors and are rewarded with money or treats. In Poland, the Christmas season comes to a close with Candelmas day on February 2, when the candles are taken to church to be blessed. It is believed that these blessed candles will protect the home from sickness or bad fortune.

The Tuesday before Ash Wednesday is celebrated by much feasting. Poles traditionally fried *pq1451czki* (fruit-filled doughnuts) in order to use the sugar and fat in the house before the long fast of Lent. In the United States, especially in Polish communities, the day before Ash Wednesday has become popularized as Pączki Day; Poles and non-Poles alike wait in line at Polish bakeries for this pastry. Easter is an especially important holiday for Polish Americans. Originally an agrarian people, the Poles focussed on Easter as the time of rebirth and regeneration not only religiously, but for their fields as well. It marked the beginning of a farmer's year. Consequently, it is still celebrated with feasts which include meats and traditional cakes, butter molded into the shape of a lamb, and elaborately decorated eggs (*pisanki*), and a good deal of drinking and dancing.

HEALTH ISSUES

There are no documented health problems specific to Polish Americans. Initially skeptical of modern medicine and more likely to try traditional home cures, Polish Americans soon were converted to the more modern practices. The creation of fraternal and insurance societies such as the Polish National Alliance in 1880, the Polish Roman Catholic Union in 1873, and the Polish Women's Alliance in 1898, helped to bring life insurance to a larger segment of Polonia. As with the majority of Americans, Polish Americans acquire health insurance at their own expense, or as part of a benefits package at their place of employment.

LANGUAGE

Polish is a West Slavic language, part of the Lekhite subgroup, and is similar to Czech and Slovak. Modern Polish, written in the Roman alphabet, stems from the sixteenth century. It is still taught in Sunday schools and parochial schools for children. It is also taught in dozens of American universities and colleges. The first written examples of Polish are a list of names in a 1136 Papal Bull. Manuscripts in Polish exist from the fourteenth century. Its vocabulary is in part borrowed from Latin, German, Czech, Ukrainian, Belarusan, and English. Dialects include Great Polish, Pomeranian, Silesian and Mazovian. Spelling is phonetic with every letter pronounced. Consonants in particular have different pronunciation than in English. "Ch," for example is pronounced like "h" in horse; "j" is pronounced like "y" at the beginning of a word; "cz" is pronounced "ch" as in chair; "sz" is pronounced like "sh" as in shoe; "rz" and "z" are pronounced alike as the English "j" in jar; and "w" is pronounced like the English "v" in victory. Various diacriticals are also used in Polish: "ż," "ź," "ń," "ć," "ś," "ą," "ę," and "ł."

GREETINGS AND OTHER POPULAR EXPRESSIONS

Typical Polish greetings and other expressions include: *Dzien dobry* ("gyen dobry")—Good morning; *Dobry wieczor* ("dobry viechoor")—Good evening; *Dowidzenia* ("dovidzenyah")—Good-bye; *Dozobaczenia* ("dozobahchainya")—Till we meet again; *Dziekuje* ("gyen-kuyeh")—Thank you; *Przepraszam* ("psheprasham")—I beg your pardon; *Nie* ("nyeh")—No; *Tak* ("tahk")—Yes.

FAMILY AND COMMUNITY DYNAMICS

Typically, the Polish family structure is strongly nuclear and patriarchal. However, as with other ethnic groups coming to America, Poles too have adapted to the American way of life, which means a stronger role for the woman in the family and in the working world, with a subsequent loosening of the strong family tie. Initially, single or married men were likely to immigrate alone, living in crowded quarters or rooming houses, saving their money and sending large amounts back to Poland. That immigration trend changed over the years, to be replaced by family units immigrating together. In the 1990s, however, the immigration pattern has come full circle, with many single men and women coming to the United States in search of work.

Until recently, Polish Americans have tended to marry within the community of Poles, but this too has changed over the years. A strong ethnic identity is maintained now not so much through shared traditions or folk culture, but through national pride. As with many European immigrant groups, male children were looked upon as the breadwinners and females as future wives and mothers. This held true through the second wave of immigrants, but with the third wave and with second and third generation families, women in general took a more important role in extra-familial life.

As with many other immigrant groups, the Poles maintain traditions most closely in those ceremonies for which the community holds great value: weddings, christenings and funerals. Weddings are no longer the hugely staged events of Polish heritage, but they are often long and heavy-drinking affairs, involving several of the customary seven steps: inquiry and proposal; betrothal; maiden evening and the symbolic unbraiding of the virgin's hair; baking the wedding cake; marriage ceremony; putting to bed; and removal to the groom's house. Traditional dances such as the *krakowiak*, *oberek*, *mazur*, and the *zbójnicki* will be enjoyed at such occasions, as well as the polka, a popular dance

among Polish Americans. (The polka, however, is not a Polish creation.) Also to be enjoyed at such gatherings are the national drink, vodka, and such traditional fare as roast pork, sausages, *barszcs* or beet soup, cabbage rolls and poppy seed cakes.

Christenings generally take place within two weeks of the birth on a Sunday or holiday; and for the devoutly Catholic Poles, it is a vital ceremony. Godparents are chosen who present the baby with gifts, more commonly money now than the traditional linens or caps of rural Poland. The christening feast, once a multi-day affair, has been toned down in modern times, but still involves the panoply of holiday foods. The ceremony itself may include a purification rite for the mother as well as baby, a tradition that goes back to the pre-Christian past.

Funerals also retain some of the old traditions. The word death in Polish (*śmierć*) is a feminine noun, and is thought of as a tall woman draped in white. Once again, Catholic rites take over for the dead. Often the dead are accompanied in their coffins by strong shoes for the arduous journey ahead or by money as an entrance fee to heaven. The funeral itself is followed by a feast or *stypa* which may also include music and dancing.

EDUCATION

Education has also taken on more importance. Where a primary education was deemed sufficient for males in the early years of the twentieth century— much of it done in Catholic schools—the value of a university education for children of both sexes now mirrors the trend for American society as a whole. A 1972 study from U.S. Census statistics showed that almost 90 percent of Polish Americans between the ages of 25 and 34 had graduated from high school, as compared to only 45 percent of those over age 35. Additionally, a full quarter of the younger generation, those between the ages 25 and 34, had completed at least a four-year university education. In general, it appears that the higher socio-economic class of the Polish American, the more rapid is the transition from Polish identity to that of the dominant culture. Such rapid change has resulted in generational conflict, as it has throughout American society as a whole in the twentieth century.

RELIGION

Poland is a largely Catholic nation, a religion that survived even under the anti-clerical reign of the communists. It is a deeply ingrained part of the Polish life, and thus immigrants to the United States brought the religion with them, Initially, Polish American parishes were established from simple meetings of the local religious in stores or hotels. These meetings soon became societies, taking on the name of a saint, and later developed into the parish itself, with priests arriving from various areas of Poland. The members of the parish were responsible for everything: financial support of their clergy as well as construction of a church and any other buildings needed by the priest. Polish American Catholics were responsible for the creation of seven religious orders, including the Resurrectionists and the Felicians who in turn created schools and seminaries and brought nuns from Poland to help with orphanages and other social services.

Quickly the new arrivals turned their religious institution into both a parish and an *okolica*, a local area or neighborhood. There was rapid growth in the number of such ethnic parishes: from 17 in 1870 to 512 only 40 years later. The number peaked in 1935 at 800 and has tapered off since, with 760 in 1960. In the 1970s the level of church attendance was beginning to drop off sharply in the Polish American community, and the use of English in the mass was becoming commonplace. However, the newest contingent of Polish refugees has slowed this trend, raising attendance once again, and helping to restore masses in the Polish language at many churches.

All was not smooth for the Polish American Catholics. A largely Protestant nation in the nineteenth century, America proved somewhat intolerant of Catholics, a fact that only served to separate immigrant Poles from the mainstream even more. Also, within the church, there was dissension. Footing all the bills for the parish, still Polish American Catholics had little representation in the hierarchy. Such disputes ultimately led to the establishment of the Polish National Church in 1904. The founding bishop, Reverend Francis Hodur, built the institution to 34 churches and over 28,000 communicants in a dozen years' time.

EMPLOYMENT AND ECONOMIC TRADITIONS

As has been noted, the Polish immigrants were largely agrarian except for those intellectuals who fled political persecution, By and large they came the United States hoping to find a plot of land, but instead found the frontier closed and were forced instead into urban areas of the Midwest and Middle Atlantic states where they worked in steel mills, coal mines, meatpacking plants, oil refineries and the garment industry. The pay was low for such work: the average annual income for Polish immigrants in 1910 was only $325. The working day was long, as it was all across America at the time, averaging a ten-hour day. But still Polish Americans managed to save their money and by 1910 it is estimated that these immigrants had been able to send $40 million back to their relatives and loved ones in Russian and Austrian Poland. The amount was so large in fact, that a federal commission was set up to investigate the damages to the U.S. economy that such an outflow of funds might create.

Families pulled together in Polonia, with education coming second to the need for young boys to contribute to the annual income. The need for such economies began to decline after World War I, however, and by 1920 only ten percent of Polish Americans families derived income from the labor of children, and two-thirds were supported by the head of family. Over the years of the twentieth century—except for the years of the Great Depression—the economic situation of Polish Americans has steadily improved, with education taking on increasing importance, creating a parallel rise in Polish Americans in the white collar labor market. By 1970 only four percent were laborers; 23 percent were craftsmen.

Polish Americans have also been important in the formation of labor unions, not only swelling the membership, but also providing leaders such as David Dubinsky of the CIO and, as has been noted, Joseph Yablonski of the United Mine Workers.

POLITICS AND GOVERNMENT

Though heavily concentrated in nine industrial states, Polish Americans did not, until the 1930s, begin to flex their political muscle. Language barriers played a part in this, but more important was the fact that earlier immigrants were too concerned with family and community issues to pay attention to the national political scene. Even in Chicago, where Polish Americans made up 12 percent of the population, they did not elect one of their own to the U.S. Congress until 1920. The first Polish American congressional representative was elected from Milwaukee in 1918.

Increasingly, however, Polish Americans have begun playing a more active role in domestic politics and have tended to vote in large numbers for the Democrats. Al Smith, a Democrat and Roman Catholic who was opposed to Prohibition, was one of the first beneficiaries of the Polish American block vote. Though he lost the election, Smith received an overwhelming majority of the Polish American vote. The Great Depression mobilized Polish Americans even more politically, organizing the Polish American Democratic Organization and supporting the New Deal policies of Franklin D. Roosevelt. By 1944 this organization could throw large numbers of Polish American votes Roosevelt's way and were correspondingly compensated by federal patronage. Prominent Polish American members of congress have been Representatives Dan Rostenkowski and Roman Pucinski, both Democrats from Illinois, and Senator Barbara Mikulski, a Democrat from Maryland. Maine's Senator Edmund Muskie was also of Polish American heritage.

RELATIONS WITH POLAND

Internationally Polish Americans have been more active politically than domestically. The Polish National Alliance, founded in 1880, was—in addition to being a mutual aid society—a fervent proponent of a free Poland. Such a goal manifested itself in very pragmatic terms: during World War I, Polish Americans not only sent their young to fight, but also the $250 million they subscribed in liberty bonds. Polish Americans also lobbied Washington with the objective of a free Poland in mind. The Polish American Congress (PAC) was created in 1944 to help secure independence for Poland, opposing the Yalta and Potsdam agreements, which established Soviet hegemony in Eastern Europe. During this same time, Polish American socialists formed the Pro-Soviet Polish American Council, but its power waned in the early years of the Cold War. PAC, however, fought on into the 1980s, supporting Solidarity, the union movement in Poland largely responsible for the downfall of the communist government. Gifts of food, clothing and lobbying in Washington were all part of the PAC campaign for an independent Poland and the organization has been very active in the establishment of a free market system in Poland since the fall of the communist government.

INDIVIDUAL AND GROUP CONTRIBUTIONS

Polish Americans comprised only 2.5 percent of the U.S. population according to the 1990 census, but they have influenced the nation's sciences and popular culture in greater proportion.

ACADEMIA

Bronislaw Malinowski (1884-1942), a pioneer of cultural anthropology, emphasized the concept of culture in meeting humankind's basic needs; he taught at Yale late in his life, after writing such important books as *Argonauts of the Western Pacific* and *The Sexual Life of Savages in Northwestern Melanesia*. Linguist Alfred Korzybski (1879-1950), born in Warsaw, came to the United States in 1918; his work in linguistics focussed on the power of the different value and meaning of words in different languages in an effort to reduce misunderstanding; he founded the Institute of General Semantics in 1938 in Chicago, and his research and books—including *Manhood and Humanity* and *Science and Sanity*—have been incorporated in modern psychology and philosophy curricula as well as linguistics.

COMMERCE AND INDUSTRY

Oleg Cassini, Polish Italian, also made a name in fashion. Ruth Handler (1917–), co-founder of Mattel toy company and creator of the Barbie doll, was born to Polish immigrant parents in Colorado. William Filene (1830-1901) was born in Posen and founded Boston's Filene department store. Iowa's largest department store, Younker's, was founded by three Polish immigrant brothers—Samuel, Marcus, and Lipma Younker—in 1850. The food industry in America has also had prominent Polish Americans among its ranks. Mrs. Paul's Fish is the creation of Polish American Edward J. Piszek (1917–). Leo Gerstenzang (1923–) was a Polish immigrant from Warsaw who invented the Q-Tip cotton swab.

ENTERTAINMENT

Hollywood has had its fair share of Polish-born men and women who have helped to shape that industry, including Harry and Jack Warner of Warner Bros. Entertainers and actors such as Sophie Tucker and Pola Negri also managed to hide their ethnic roots by changing their names. The pianist and performer Liberace (1919-1987), half-Polish and half-Italian, was born Władzie Valentino Liberace. More recently, the Polish-born Hollywood and international cinematographer Hubert Taczanowski has made outstanding contributions.

LITERATURE AND JOURNALISM

Jerzy Kosinski (1933-1991), the Polish-born novelist, came to the United States after World War II; his *Painted Bird* relates the experiences of a small boy in Nazi-occupied Poland and is one of the most stirring and troubling novels to come out of that time. The poet Czesław Miłosz (1911–), naturalized in 1970, won the Nobel Prize for Literature in 1980. Born in Lithuania of Polish parents, Miłosz studied law and served in the diplomatic corps as well as establishing a name for himself as a poet before immigrating in 1960; some of his best known works are *The Captive Mind*, *The Issa Valley*, and *The Usurpers*. The cartoonist Jules Feiffer (1929–), known for his offbeat and biting wit, was born to Polish immigrant parents in the United States.

MUSIC

Leopold Stokowski (1882-1977), is just one of the musical luminaries to carry on the Ignacy Paderewski tradition; born in London of Polish and Irish parents; Stokowski, a renowned conductor, became a naturalized U.S. citizen in 1915; he was best known as conductor of the Philadelphia Orchestra for many years, and for popularizing classical music in America; his appearance in the 1940 Disney film, *Fantasia*, is an example of such popularizing efforts. The jazz drummer Gene Krupa (1909-1973), the measure for drummers long after, was also of Polish heritage; Krupa was born in Chicago and played with Benny Goodman's orchestra before forming his own band in 1943; he revolutionized the role of the drummer in a jazz band.

POLITICS AND GOVERNMENT

In addition to above-mentioned members of congress, two other recent Polish Americans have made their names in Washington. Leon Jaworski (1905-1982) was the prosecutor in the 1973 Watergate investigation of then President Richard Nixon; and Zbigniew Brzezinski, born in Warsaw in 1928 and naturalized in 1958, was an important advisor to President Carter from 1977 to 1980 on the National Security Council.

SCIENCE

The biochemist Casimir Funk (1884-1967) was, in 1912, the first to discover and use the term vitamin; his so-called vitamin hypothesis postulated that certain diseases such as scurvy and pellagra resulted from lack of crucial substance in the body; Funk also went on to do research in sex hormones and cancer; he lived in the United States from 1939 until his death. Dr. Stanley Dudrick developed the important new method of vein feeding termed IHV—intravenous hyperalimentation.

SPORTS

Many notable Polish Americans have made their names household words in baseball. Included among these are the pitcher Stan Coveleski (1888-1984) whose 17-year career from 1912-1928 earned him a place in the Hall of Fame in 1969; Stan Musial (1920–), right field, another member of the Baseball Hall of Fame, who played for St. Louis from 1941 to 1963; Carl Yastrzemski (1939–), left fielder for the Boston Red Sox, was voted to the Hall of Fame in 1989; and Al Simmons (1902-1956), born Aloysius Harry Szymanski, who played center field for the Philadelphia Athletics from 1924-1944. In football there have been numerous outstanding Polish American players and coaches, Chicago's Mike Ditka (1939–) a stand-out among these, playing as a tight end for the Bears from 1961 to 1972 and later coaching the team to a Super Bowl championship in 1985; a Hall of Fame player, Ditka has most recently worked as a television sports commentator.

VISUAL ARTS

Korczak Ziolkowski (1909-1982), an assistant to Gutzon Borglum in the monumental Mount Rushmore project in South Dakota, continued that monumental style with a 500-foot by 640-foot statue of Chief Crazy Horse still being blasted out of solid rock in the Black Hills by his family.

MEDIA

PRINT

Dziennik Zwiazkowy/Polish Daily News.
Published in Polish, it covers national and international news with a special emphasis on matters effecting the Polish American community.

Contact: Wojciech Bialasiewicz, Editor.
Address: 5711 North Milwaukee Avenue,
   Chicago, Illinois 60646-6215.
Telephone: (773) 763-3343.
Fax: (773) 763-3825.
E-mail: polish@popmailinsnet.com

Gazeta Polska.
Polish-language newspaper.

Address: 5242 West Diversey Avenue, Chicago,
   Illinois 60639.
Telephone: (312) 685-1281.
Fax: (312) 283-1675.

Glos.
Polish-language newspaper.

Contact: Andrzej Dobrowolski, Editor.
Address: 140 Greenpoint Avenue, Brooklyn,
   New York 11222.

Glos Polek/Polish Women's Voice.
Biweekly publication of the Polish Women's Alliance of America.

Contact: Mary Mirecki-Piergies, Editor.
Address: 205 South Northwest Highway, Park
   Ridge, Illinois 60068.
Fax: (708) 692-2675.

Gwiazda Polarna (Northern Star).
Published weekly in Polish, it provides national and international news for the Polish American com-

munity as well as information about Polish activities and organizations domestically.

Contact: Malgorzata Terentiew-Cwiklinski, Editor.
Address: 2619 Post Road, Stevens Point, Wisconsin 54481.
Telephone: (715) 345-0744.
Fax: (715) 345-1913.

Narod Polski.
Publication of the Polish Roman Catholic Union of America.

Contact: Kathryn G. Rosypal, Editor.
Address: 984 Milwaukee Avenue, Chicago, Illinois 60622-4101.
Telephone: (773) 278-3210 or (800) 772-8632.
Fax: (778) 278-4595.
Online: http://www.prcua.org/narod.htm.

New Horizon: Polish American Review.
Contains items of interest to the Polish community.

Contact: B. Wierzbianski, Editor.
Address: 333 West 38th Street, New York, New York 10018-2914.
Telephone: (212) 354-0490.

Nowy Dziennik/Polish Daily News.
Polish-language newspaper.

Contact: Boleslaw Wierzbianski, Editor.
Address: 333 West 38th Street, New York, New York 10018-2914.
Telephone: (212) 594-2266.
Fax: (212) 594-2383
E-mail: listy@dziennik.com or deptula@dziennik.com.

Perspectives.
A Polish American educational and cultural bimonthly.

Contact: Krystyna Kusielewicz, Editor.
Address: c/o Marta Korwin Rhodes, 7300 Connecticut Avenue, Bethesda, Maryland 20815-4930.
Telephone: (202) 554-4267.

Polish American Journal.
Official organ of the Polish Union of the United States. Published monthly, it covers national, international, and regional news of interest to Polish Americans.

Contact: Mark Kohan, Editor.
Address: 1275 Harlem Road, Buffalo, New York 14206-1960.

Telephone: (716) 893-5771.
Fax: (716) 893-5783.

Polish American Studies.
A journal of the Polish American Historical Association devoted to Polish American history and culture.

Contact: James S. Pula, Editor.
Address: 984 Milwaukee Avenue, Chicago, Illinois 60622.

Polish American World.
Published weekly, it reports on activities and events in the Polish American community and on life in Poland.

Contact: Thomas Poskropski, Editor.
Address: 3100 Grand Boulevard, Baldwin, New York 11510.
Telephone: (516) 223-6514.

Polish Digest.
Covers history of Poland, news from Poland, and Polish culture.

Contact: Leszek Zielinski, Editor.
Address: c/o Horyzonty, 1924 North Seventh Street, Sheboygan, Wisconsin 53081-2724.
Telephone: (715) 341-6959.
Fax: (715) 346-7516.

Polish Fest News.
Contact: Ray Trzesniewski, Jr., Editor.
Address: Polish Festivals, Inc., 7128 West Rawson Avenue, Franklin, Wisconsin 53132.
Telephone: (414) 529-2140.

Polish Heritage.
A quarterly review of the American Council for Polish Culture.

Contact: Wallace M. West, Editor.
Address: 6507 107th Terrace, Pinellas Park, Florida 34666-2432.
Telephone: (813) 541-7875.

Polish Heritage Society Biuletyn.
Monthly newsletter of the Polish Heritage Society; encourages the preservation and understanding of Polish and Polish American culture and history.

Contact: Pat McBride, Editor.
Address: P.O. Box 1844, Grand Rapids, Michigan 49501-1844.
Telephone: (616) 456-5353.
Fax: (616) 456-8929.

Polish Review.
Scholarly journal of the Polish Institute of Arts and Sciences of America devoted to the study of Polish history and culture.

Contact: Joseph W. Wieczerzak, Editor.
Address: 208 East 30th Street, New York, New York 10016.
Telephone: (212) 686-4164.
Fax: (212) 545-1130.

Swiat Polski/Polish World.
Published weekly in Polish.

Contact: Ewa Matuszewski, Editor.
Address: 11903 Joseph Campau Street, Hamtramck, Michigan 48212.
Telephone: (313) 365-1990.
Fax: (313) 365-0850.
E-mail: sszcze4594@aol.com.

Zgoda.
Published by the Polish National Alliance of North America, contains fraternal, cultural, sports, and general news in Polish and English.

Contact: Wojciech A. Wierzewski, Editor.
Address: 6100 North Cicero Avenue, Chicago, Illinois 60646-4385.
Telephone: (773) 286-0500.
Fax: (773) 286-0842.
E-mail: pnazgoda@ais.net.

RADIO

WBRK-AM.
Polish American Programming.

Contact: Tom Wotjkowski.
Address: 100 North Street, Pittsfield, Massachusetts 01201.
Telephone: (413) 442-1553.

WCSS-AM.
"Polka Party."

Contact: Dan Kielbasa.
Address: 6 Genessee Lane, Amsterdam, New York 12010.
Telephone: (518) 843-2500.

WEDC-AM.
"Polish Sunshine Hour."

Contact: Halina Gramza.
Address: 5475 North Milwaukee Avenue, Chicago, Illinois 60630.
Telephone: (312) 631-0700.

TELEVISION

WCIU-TV.
"Polevision," a daily two-hour show airs between 7:00 p.m. and 9:00 p.m. with programs in both Polish and English.

Contact: Robert Lewandowski.
Address: Board of Trade Building, 141 West Jackson Boulevard, Chicago, Illinois 60604.
Telephone: (312) 663-0260.

ORGANIZATIONS AND ASSOCIATIONS

American Council for Polish Culture (ACPC).
National federation of groups devoted to fostering and preserving Polish ethnic heritage in the United States.

Contact: Dr. Kaya Mirecka-Ploss, Executive Director.
Address: 2025 O Street, N.W., Washington, D.C. 20036.
Telephone: (202) 785-2320.

American Institute of Polish Culture (AIPC).
Furthers knowledge of and appreciation for the history, science, art, and culture of Poland.

Contact: Blanka A. Rosenstiel, President.
Address: 1440 79th Street Causeway, Suite 117, Miami, Florida 33141.
Telephone: (305) 864-2349.
Fax: (305) 865-5150.

Polish American Congress (PAC).
Umbrella organization for local and national Polish organizations in the United States with more than three million combined members. Promotes improved quality of life for Polish Americans and people in Poland.

Contact: Eugene Rosypal, Executive Director.
Address: 5711 North Milwaukee Avenue, Chicago, Illinois 60646-6215.
Telephone: (773) 763-9944.
Fax: (773) 763-7114.
E-mail: pacchgo@mindspring.com.
Online: http://www.polamcon.org.

Polish American Historical Association (PAHA).
Concerned with Polish Americana and the history of Poles in the United States.

Address: 984 North Milwaukee Avenue, Chicago, Illinois 60622.
Telephone: (773) 384-3352.
Fax: (773) 384-3799.

Polish Falcons of America.

Founded in 1887, the Polish Falcons have a membership of 31,000 in 143 groups or "nests." Established as a fraternal benefit insurance society for people of Polish or Slavic descent, the Falcons also took on a strong nationalist sentiment, demanding a free Poland. The society promotes athletic and educational events and provides a scholarship fund for those majoring in physical education. The Falcons also publish a bi-monthly publication in Polish, *Sokol Polski*.

Contact: Wallace Zielinski, President.
Address: 615 Iron City Drive, Pittsburgh, Pennsylvania 15205.
Telephone: (412) 922-2244.
Fax: (412) 922-5029.
Online: http://www.polishfalcons.org.

Polish Genealogical Society of America (PGSA).

Promotes Polish genealogical study and establishes communication among researchers.

Contact: Stanley R. Schmidt, President.
Address: 984 North Milwaukee Avenue, Chicago, Illinois 60622.
E-mail: PGSAmerica@aol.com.
Online: http://www.pgsa.org.

Polish National Alliance of the United States (PNA).

Founded in 1880, the PNA has a membership of 286,000 made up of nearly 1,000 regional groups. Originally founded as a fraternal life insurance society, PNA continues this original role while also sponsoring education and cultural affairs. It maintains a library of 14,000 volumes.

Contact: Edward Moskal, President.
Address: 6100 North Cicero, Chicago, Illinois 60646-4385.
Telephone: (773) 286-0500 or (800) 621-3723.
Fax: (773) 286-0842.
E-mail: pnazgoda@ais.net.
Online: http://www.pna-znp.org/index.html.

Polish Roman Catholic Union of America.

Founded in 1873, the Roman Catholic Union has a membership of 90,000 in 529 groups. Founded as a fraternal benefit life insurance society, the union sponsors sports and youth activities, and conducts language school as well as dance and children's programs. It also has a library of 25,000 volumes.

Contact: Josephine Szarowicz, Secretary General.
Address: 984 Milwaukee Avenue, Chicago Illinois 60622.
Telephone: (773) 278-3210.
Fax: (773) 278-4595.

Polish Surname Network (PSN).

Collects and disseminates genealogical information on surnames of Polish heritage. Provides fee-based research, research analysis, and translation services.

Contact: Mary S. Hartig, Executive Officer.
Address: 158 South Walter Avenue, Newbury Park, California 91320.

Polish Union of the United States.

Founded in 1890, the Polish Union has a membership of 12,000 in 100 groups. This fraternal benefit life insurance society bestows the Copernicus Award to a student excelling in astronomy. Publishes the monthly *Polish American Journal*.

Contact: Wallace S. Piotrowski, President.
Address: 4191 North Buffalo Street, Orchard Park, New York 14127-0684.
Telephone: (716) 667-9782.

Polish Women's Alliance of America.

Founded in 1898, the Polish Women's Alliance has a membership of 65,000 in 775 groups or chapters. It is a fraternal benefit life insurance society administered by women and maintains a library of 7,500 volumes on Polish and American culture and history.

Contact: Delphine Lytell, Pres.
Address: 205 South Northwest Highway, Park Ridge, Illinois 60068.
Telephone: (708) 384-1200.
Fax: (847) 384-1222.
E-mail: pres@pwaa.org.
Online: http://www.pwaa.org.

MUSEUMS AND RESEARCH CENTERS

Many public libraries, including the Los Angeles Public Library, New York Public Library/Donnell Library Center, Boston Public Library, Denver Public Library, Miami/Dade Public Library, and the Detroit Public Library, have extensive Polish language collections to serve the Polish American communities.

American Institute for Polish Culture.

Founded in 1972 to promote the appreciation for history, culture, science and art of Poland, the American Institute for Polish Culture sponsors exhibits, lectures, and research and maintains a 1,200-volume library and publishes books on history and biography.

Contact: Blank A. Rosenstiel, President.
Address: 1440 79th Street, Causeway, Suite 403, Miami, Florida 33141.
Telephone: (305) 864-2349.

Center for Polish Studies and Culture.

Founded in 1970 at St. Mary's College, the Center for Polish Studies promotes research in the teaching of Polish and arranges educational exchanges. It also maintains a library, art gallery, and a museum of artifacts from Polish Americans.

Contact: Janusz Wrobel.
Address: St. Mary's College, Orchard Lake, Michigan 48034.
Telephone: (810) 682-1885.

Kosciuszko Foundation.

Founded in 1925, the Kosciuszko Foundation is named after the Polish nobleman who fought in the American revolution. The foundation is a clearinghouse for information on Polish and American cultural affairs. Also known as the American Center for Polish Culture, the foundation has a reference library and arranges educational exchanges as well as administers scholarships and stipends.

Contact: Joseph E. Gore, President.
Address: 15 East 65th Street, New York, New York 10021.
Telephone: (212) 734-2130.

Polish Museum of America.

Founded in 1937, the Polish Museum preserves artifacts of the Polish American experience and mounts displays of costumes, religious artifacts and Polish art. It also maintains a 25,000-volume library for researchers and the Polish American Historical Association which is concerned with the history of Poles in America.

Contact: Dr. Christoph Kamyszew, Director and Curator.
Address: 984 North Milwaukee Avenue, Chicago, Illinois 60622.

SOURCES FOR ADDITIONAL STUDY

Bukowczyk, John. *And My Children Did Not Know Me: A History of the Polish-Americans*. Bloomington: Indiana University Press, 1987.

Fox, Paul. *The Poles in America*. New York: Arno Press, 1970.

Lopata, Helena Znaniecka. *Polish Americans: Status Competition in an Ethnic Community*, second edition. New Brunswick, New Jersey: Transactions Publishers, 1974; reprinted, 1994.

Morawska, Ewa. *The Maintenance of Ethnicity: A Case Study of the Polish American Community in Greater Boston*. San Francisco: R&E Associates 1977.

Renkiewicz, Frank. *The Poles in America, 1608-1972: A Chronology and Fact Book*. Dobbs Ferry, New York: Oceana Publications, Inc., 1973.

Wytrwal, Joseph. *America's Polish Heritage: A Social History of the Poles in America*. Detroit, Michigan: Endurance Press, 1961.

Zieleniewicz, Andrzej. *Poland*, translated, revised, and edited by Robert Strybel, Leonard Chrobot, Robert Geryk, Joseph Swastek, and Walter Ziemba. Orchard Lake, Michigan: Center for Polish Studies and Culture, 1971.

PORTUGUESE AMERICANS

by
Ernest E. Norden

Wherever they settled, Portuguese immigrants had to face many disconcerting changes in their new environment. Rather than living in the same town or even the same neighborhood as the rest of their family— grandparents, aunts, uncles, cousins— upon whom they could depend for help when they needed it, they found themselves alone and without the support system that the extended family could provide.

OVERVIEW

Portugal, officially called the Portuguese Republic, is the westernmost country of continental Europe. It is bordered on the east and north by Spain, with which it shares the Iberian Peninsula, and on the west and south by the Atlantic Ocean. It is about the size of Ohio, having an area of 35,553 square miles (92,082 square kilometers), and measuring 360 miles at its longest point and 140 miles at its widest. Portugal also includes the Azores (Açores) and the Madeira Islands in the North Atlantic Ocean and Macao, a tiny territory on the southern coast of China.

Portugal's current population of roughly 9.9 million people is decreasing. Major cities are the capital Lisbon, Porto, and Amadora. However, two-thirds of the people live in rural areas. Nearly 99 percent of the population is of Portuguese origin; the largest ethnic minorities include Cape Verdeans, Brazilians, the Spanish, British, and Americans. Although there is no official religion in Portugal, 94.5 percent of the people are Roman Catholic. Other Christian groups include Protestants, Apostolic Catholics, and Jehovah's Witnesses. There are small minorities of Jews and Muslims. The country's official language is Portuguese, and the national flag has a field of green on the left with a wider field of red on the right; the national emblem is centered on the line dividing the two colors. Portugal's chief products are grapes, potatoes, hogs, beef cattle, corn, sardines, tuna, textiles, paper products, electrical machinery, cork products, ceramics, and shoes.

EARLY HISTORY

The early history of Portugal saw occupation by Iberians from North Africa and then by Celts who migrated from France. Phoenicians and Carthaginians later established themselves in southern Portugal. After the Second Punic War (218-201 B.C.) the Roman domination of Portugal began. The Lusitanians, a warlike Celtic tribe under the leadership of Viriathus, fiercely opposed the Roman armies, but the latter triumphed. Roman contributions to Portugal included roads, buildings, and the Latin language, from which Portuguese developed. Portugal's name derives from Portus Cale, a pre-Roman or Roman settlement near the mouth of the Douro River, where Porto is now located. In the fifth century A.D., as Roman control of the peninsula weakened, the land was overrun by Suevi who were followed by the Visigoths. In 711 the Muslims invaded the peninsula, and Christian forces spent the next 500 years trying to expel them. To fight off the African Almoravids, King Alfonso VI of León and Castile enlisted the aid of Henry of Burgundy, whom he rewarded with the title of Count of Portucale and the hand in marriage of his illegitimate daughter Teresa. Henry's son, Alfonso Henriques, claimed the title Alfonso I, King of Portugal, in 1139. By 1179 his kingdom, occupying the northern third of present-day Portugal, was recognized as autonomous and separate from Castile.

Alfonso I and his son Sancho I reconquered the remaining Portuguese territory from the Muslims. When Sancho II died in 1248 without leaving an heir to the throne, the Count of Boulogne declared himself King Alfonso III. He was responsible for moving the capital from Coimbra to Lisbon, for lessening the power of the church in his land, and for convoking the Cortes at Leiria (1254) at which the commoners were represented for the first time.

Alfonso III's son Diniz, who ruled Portugal from 1279 to 1325, built a navy, founded the University of Coimbra (1290) which was first located in Lisbon, and showed interest in literature, shipbuilding, and agriculture, for which he came to be called the *rei lavradór* (farmer king). His wife, Elizabeth, who worked to maintain peace in Portugal, was known as the Holy Queen (*rainha santa*) and was later canonized as St. Elizabeth of Portugal. After the death of Ferdinand I in 1383, his wife Leonor Telles married their daughter Beatriz to the King of Castile. There was disagreement as to whether Beatriz should be heiress to the throne, and in 1385 the Cortes chose John, an illegitimate son of Peter I (the Cruel), a former king of Portugal, to rule as John I. John was Master of a religious-military order, the Order of Aviz.

John's son, known as Prince Henry the Navigator, utilized the resources of geographers and navigators to launch a series of explorations beyond the frontiers of Portugal. With the peninsula now reconquered from the Muslims, the Portuguese drive for expansion continued out of a desire to explore unknown lands, to seek a trade route for transporting spices from India, and to spread the Christian religion. Henry financed the expeditions that discovered Madeira and the Azores; these islands were uninhabited but were quickly colonized, and they still belong to Portugal.

Under Manuel I (1495-1521) Vasco da Gama reached India and Pedro Àlvares Cabral discovered Brazil. Manuel, who married Isabella, the eldest daughter of Spain's Ferdinand and Isabella, never realized his dream of uniting Spain and Portugal under his power. As part of his marriage contract with Isabella, he was required to rid Portugal of the Jews who had taken refuge there after being expelled from Spain. A few were allowed to emigrate, but most were forcibly converted to Christianity. Manuel's son, John III (1521-1557) established the Inquisition in Portugal. In 1580, when Portugal again found itself with no heir to the throne upon the death of Cardinal Henry, last of the House of Aviz, Philip II of Spain seized control as Philip I of Portugal (1580-1598). Portugal remained under Spain's control for 60 years until John, Duke of Bragança, defeated the Spanish and founded his own dynasty as John IV in 1640. The Portuguese had increasingly resented Spanish rule because of taxation and because the promises Philip had made to maintain Portugal's autonomy and to name only Portuguese to government posts were soon broken. Spain finally recognized Portuguese independence in 1668.

THE EIGHTEENTH CENTURY

During the eighteenth century, wealth from Brazil began to pour into the country. Gold was discovered in Minas Gerais in 1693, and Brazil became a source of diamonds beginning in 1728. Great wealth was extracted by the Portuguese, and a 20 percent tax on it maintained their monarchs. John V (1706-1750) sought to establish an absolute monarchy. His son Joseph (1750-1777) was weak and allowed his minister Sebastião José de Carvalho e Melo, the Marquis of Pombal, to run the government in a more enlightened fashion. The latter is credited with the competent governmental response to the earthquake that leveled Lisbon in 1755. Pombal also ordered the expulsion of the Jesuits in 1759 and the consequent reform of the educational system. In 1762 Spain invaded Portugal, and peace was not achieved until 1777 through the Treaty of San Ildefonso.

THE NINETEENTH CENTURY

When Napoleon declared war on England, Portugal, allied by treaties, was drawn into the struggle. In 1806 Napoleon issued a decree intended to close all continental ports to British ships, and he later invaded Portugal to ensure that his decree was carried out there. As the French army neared Lisbon, the royal family boarded British ships, which carried them to Rio de Janeiro where they remained for 14 years. Meanwhile, the Portuguese and British armies, under the Duke of Wellington, drove the French from the country. Portugal made peace with France in 1814. In 1815 Brazil's status was elevated to that of a kingdom united with Portugal. The royal family did not seem anxious to return to Portugal, and when William Carr Beresford, the British commander in charge in Portugal traveled to Brazil to convince John VI to return, the Portuguese drew up a national constitution and would not allow Beresford back into the country. John VI returned in 1821 and swore to uphold the constitution. His eldest son Peter declared Brazil independent from Portugal in 1822 and became its emperor. John VI recognized Brazil's independence in 1825. John's death in 1826 marked the beginning of a period of political strife that lasted until after mid-century, when party government was established. The main parties were the Historicals and the more moderate Regenerators. The latter part of the century was occupied with disputes over Portugal's claims to territories in Africa.

THE TWENTIETH CENTURY

In the early twentieth century, the republican movement grew in strength. In 1908, King Charles I and his heir, Louis Philip, were assassinated. King Manuel II (1908-1910) was to be the last monarch, for a republican revolution began on October 4, 1910, and Manuel was forced to seek refuge in England until his death in 1932. The revolutionary government gave the vote to adult males and drew up a constitution. It expelled religious orders from the country and disestablished the Roman Catholic church. It founded new universities in Lisbon and Porto. But the republicans were divided into many factions, and there was great political instability.

Within 15 years, 45 different regimes held the reins of government. Portugal's bad economic situation became even worse through joining the Allies in World War I (1914-1918). In 1926 the army overthrew the government and set up a dictatorship under General António Oscar de Fragoso Carmona who named António de Oliveira Salazar, an economics professor at the University of Coimbra, as his minister of finance. After his successful handling of the budget, Salazar was named prime minister in 1932. As dictator he managed to keep Portugal out of World War II; he improved the country's roads and its means of transportation; he promoted new industries and other development. However, his government was very conservative; the people enjoyed few rights and were under surveillance by the secret police. The rich enjoyed economic advantages under his regime, but the poor got poorer. Salazar suffered a stroke in mid-1968 and died two years later. Marcelo Caetano then became head of the government and liberalized many governmental policies, but he did not go far enough or fast enough for many Portuguese. Emigration increased, inflation grew, and the country faced a grave economic crisis.

In 1974 a group of military officers, under the leadership of Otelo Saraiva de Carvalho, overthrew Caetano's government; this is often called the "Captains' Revolution" because it was planned by military officers dissatisfied with Portugal's long wars to retain possession of her colonies in Africa. One of the first things accomplished by the new junta called the Armed Forces Movement (Movimento das Forças Armadas) was the granting of independence to Portuguese colonies in Africa. The government also reestablished democratic freedoms. General elections were held in 1976; the government became more stable but had to face the problems of rapid inflation and high unemployment. The constitution was revised in 1982 to limit the powers of the president. Portugal is a member of the United Nations and of the North Atlantic Treaty Organization (NATO). In 1986 Portugal became a member of the European Common Market.

THE FIRST PORTUGUESE IN AMERICA

The Portuguese came to America very early. In fact, Portuguese explorers may have reached the Antilles before Columbus. João Rodrigues Cabrillo arrived in San Diego Bay on September 9, 1542, and was the first European to explore the land that is now California. Portuguese Jews emigrated early to America as well as to other countries to escape persecution in their native land. Mathias de Sousa is the first Portuguese immigrant on record; he arrived in Maryland in 1634. Aaron Lopez, another Portuguese Jew, played an important role in introducing the sperm-oil industry to the Newport, Rhode Island, area in the eighteenth century, and Abraham de Lyon introduced the cultivation of grapes into Georgia in 1737. Portuguese from the Azores and the Cape Verde Islands manned New England's whaling ships. They signed on as low-paid laborers in order to avoid military service and to escape the poverty in which they lived at home. Many of them settled in New England, especially around New Bedford, Massachusetts.

IMMIGRATION TRENDS

Portugal has one of the highest rates of emigration in Europe; and until the middle of the twentieth century, most Portuguese emigrants (about 80 percent of them) went to Brazil. The Portuguese began to arrive in the United States in relatively large numbers around 1870. The majority of early Portugese immigrants were men from the Azores, a group of islands and islets in the North Atlantic Ocean. These men were largely recruited to work on American whaling ships. There was also immigration to the Sandwich Islands (now the state of Hawaii), where the Portuguese went originally to labor on sugar plantations. The majority of the immigrants came to the United States seeking a higher standard of living; they were not drawn by educational opportunity or political or religious freedom. Besides wanting to escape poverty, high taxes, and the lack of economic advancement at home, many males emigrated to avoid eight years of service in Portugal's army. Natural disasters also stimulated many to seek opportunities to live and work elsewhere. The drought in the Cape Verde Islands in 1904 and the volcanic eruptions and earthquakes in the Azores in 1958 sent waves of people abroad. Most of the early Portuguese immigrants to the United States were from the Azores; continental Portuguese did not start arriving in large numbers until the beginning of this century.

Once substantial immigration to the United States started, it increased steadily, peaking between 1910 and 1920. In 1917 the United States government instituted a literacy test requiring that people over the age of 16 had to be able to read and write some language at a basic level in order to settle here. Since the literacy rate in Portugal was extremely low, this test effectively barred many Portuguese from entry; of the Portuguese immigrants admitted shortly before the literacy test was instated, nearly 70 percent were illiterate. In addition, the U.S. Immigration Act of 1924 established a quota system that allowed only a small number of Portuguese

immigrants to enter per year. The Great Depression further discouraged immigration to the United States because economic advancement was the Portuguese's main goal. Emigration from the Azores increased in 1958, however, when the Azorean Refugee Act allowed 4,800 to emigrate after the volcanic destruction that took place there. Later, the Immigration and Nationality Act of 1965 abolished the quota system and consequently spurred a sharp increase in Portuguese immigration. At that time the Portuguese began to enter this country at the rate of 11,000 to 12,000 per year. This rate started to decline in the early 1980s and has now stabilized at 3,000 to 4,000 per year. Some of these have returned to Portugal either because they preferred living there or because they were unable to adjust to their new environment. Of those who returned to live in the Azores, at least, the impressions of their life in this country, which they have related to their friends and families, have created a favorable attitude toward the United States. The many Portuguese immigrants who remained here have contributed substantially to American society.

SETTLEMENT PATTERNS

At first the Portuguese tended to settle near their ports of entry. The greatest number made their homes in New England (especially in Massachusetts and Rhode Island), New York, central California, and Hawaii. A small group settled in central Illinois. The Homestead Act encouraged some Portuguese to go west to obtain ownership of land. Those who settled on the East Coast also spread into Connecticut and New Jersey, and most recent immigrants find homes in Connecticut, New York, or New Jersey. The number of Portuguese immigrants now settling in California or Hawaii has been greatly reduced. Because so many Portuguese arrived without skills or education, they tended to remain for a long time in the lower middle class or middle class unless they attained the background necessary for advancement.

ACCULTURATION AND ASSIMILATION

The Portuguese who settled in Hawaii tended to lose their ethnic identity fastest. From the sugar plantations they moved to the large cities where they became involved in trades and service industries. Others went into farming. They tended to intermarry with other ethnic groups and quickly lost their feeling of Portuguese identity.

In California there was a greater effort to maintain ethnicity. The Portuguese immigrants generally settled in rural areas where they farmed or operated dairies. They hired other Portuguese as hands on their farms, and under these semi-isolated conditions, it was easier to preserve their old customs. Fathers were the decision makers of the household. They allowed their daughters to attend school only as long as the law required; after that they kept them at home. Boys enjoyed more freedom than girls, but they also tended to quit school as soon as possible to work on the farm or dairy; and they were expected to marry Portuguese girls. When the rate of arrival of new immigrants slowed and American-born descendants far outnumbered the foreign-born Portuguese, assimilation began. Organizations such as the Cabrillo Civic Clubs, however, were formed to preserve pride in the Portuguese heritage.

The situation on the East Coast was different. There the Portuguese, mainly of rural origin, settled in urban areas. This change in environment forced family life and attitudes to change. When times were bad at the mills, women had to go to work to help support the family. In general, children were expected to leave school at the first opportunity to go to work to contribute to the family's maintenance as well. This tended to keep the Portuguese in the lower middle class, but it freed the women from their traditionally subordinate role and granted them more independence.

Wherever they settled, Portuguese immigrants had to face many disconcerting changes in their new environment. Rather than living in the same town or even the same neighborhood as the rest of their family—grandparents, aunts, uncles, cousins—upon whom they could depend for help when they needed it, they found themselves alone and without the support system that the extended family could provide. Unlike the milieu to which they were accustomed, in the United States education was compulsory for children, women were more emancipated, young people were freer to select the mates of their choice, families were more democratic rather than being dominated by the father, and a generation gap often existed within families because the young had developed better language proficiency and had attended public schools where they were exposed to the attitudes of their American peers.

TRADITIONS, CUSTOMS, AND BELIEFS

The Portuguese have a variety of folk beliefs, many of which coincide with those of other cultures. Some believe that certain people have the power of the evil eye, which endows them with the ability to cast evil spells on others by the use of their eyes. One may ward off the evil eye by making a gesture called "the fig" in which one closes the fist and sticks the thumb between the first and second fingers. For many the devil is real and has the power to work evil. The word "devil" (*diabo*) is avoided for fear of evoking him; he may also be kept away by making the sign of the cross. Fridays and the number 13 are considered bad luck. Some people trust their health to witch doctors called *curandeiros*, who attempt to cure illnesses with herbal medicines or magic. These beliefs disappear or are looked upon as superstitions as immigrants are absorbed into American society.

When people are far from their native countries, they long to preserve some of the customs from their youth that had special significance to them. Early in the twentieth century, Portuguese immigrants revived three celebrations from their homelands—the Festival of the Blessed Sacrament, the Festival of the Holy Ghost, and the Senhor da Pedra Festival.

FESTIVAL OF THE BLESSED SACRAMENT

This celebration from the island of Madeira was initiated in 1915 in New Bedford, Massachusetts. This four-day festival, which takes place the first weekend of August, has grown to be the largest Portuguese American celebration, attracting over 150,000 visitors to New Bedford each year. Throughout the festival there is entertainment, including Portuguese and American music, singing, dancing, and famous entertainers. Decorative arches are erected in the festival area and are covered with bundles of bayberry branches. Colored lights and banners are also used for decoration. Vendors sell American and Madeiran foods including *carne de espeto* (roasted meat on a skewer), *linguiça* (sausage), *cabra* (goat), *bacalhau* (codfish) in spicy Portuguese sauces, *favas* (beans), and Madeiran wine. Local groups perform Portuguese folk music and dances; fireworks and raffles add to the festivities. On Sunday, the final day of the festival, its organizers march with a band to the church for the 11:00 a.m. mass. At 2:00 p.m. there is a colorful parade that includes children in native costumes, bands, floats, and beauty queens. Although this festival includes a mass and a procession, it is basically a secular celebration meant for socializing and having fun.

FESTIVAL OF THE HOLY GHOST

This festival, celebrated in California and in New England, is modeled after an Azorean prototype. Depending on the location, it is celebrated on some weekend between Easter and the end of July. The celebration originated with Queen Elizabeth of Aragon, wife of Portugal's King Diniz, in 1296. As an act of humility, before a mass to which she had invited the poor, she gave the royal scepter to the most indigent and had the royal crown placed on his head. After the mass, the queen and other nobles served a sumptuous meal to the poor. In the modern celebration, the crown is kept in the church throughout the year. Details of the celebration vary from place to place, but sometimes a drawing is held to determine which families will have the honor of keeping the crown at their house for one of seven weeks leading up to the festival. The child of the first winner is crowned as the child-emperor/empress. Amidst a week of feasting and celebration, he keeps the crown in a place of honor in his house, surrounded by candles and flowers, and at the end of the week, he walks in a procession to the house of the second winner, and the second child-emperor/empress is crowned. The crown passes through seven successive households. A few days before the final Sunday of the festival, the priest blesses the food that has been collected for the poor, although today this food is more commonly used for a community banquet. On the final weekend there may be a special mass, procession, and a carnival or fair that includes fireworks, charity auctions, music, ethnic food, and dancing the *chamarrita*, an Azorean folk square dance.

THE FESTA DE SENHOR DA PEDRA

This festival, begun in New Bedford, Massachusetts, in 1924, is celebrated the last Sunday of August. It is also based on an Azorean festival. Its promoters emphasize the religious aspect of this celebration. After mass the image of Senhor da Pedra and those of nine other church figures are carried in procession on floats through the streets on the shoulders of the faithful. They are accompanied by a band, other church members carrying crucifixes and banners, and children wearing their first-communion outfits or dressed as angels; children also carry six smaller floats topped by the images of saints. The priest marches in the procession carrying the sacrament. As the figure of Senhor da Pedra passes, onlookers attach money to his float. One neighborhood decorates its street with sand paintings and flower petals over which the procession will pass. A carnival with public entertainment, ethnic foods—*caçoila* (marinated pork), *bacalhau*, and *linguiça*, and raffles are also part of the festival.

Other regional celebrations include the Santo Cristo festival in Fall River, Massachusetts, the Festival of Our Lady of Fatima, which commemorates the reported appearance of the Virgin in Fatima, Portugal, in 1917, and the Festival of Our Lady of Good Voyage in Gloucester, Massachusetts, during which the fishing fleet is blessed.

PROVERBS

Proverbs are popular in Portuguese culture, and many have been passed on from one generation to the next:

Não ha rosas sem espinhos—You can't have roses without having thorns too; *Amar e saber não póde ser*—Love and prudence do not go together; *Mais quero asno que me leve, que caballo que me derrube*—I'd rather have an ass that carried me than a horse that threw me off; *A caridade bem entendida principia por casa*—Charity begins at home; *A Deus poderás mentir, mas não pódes enganar a Deus*—You may lie to God, but you cannot deceive him; *Da ma mulher te guarda, e da boa não fies nada*—Beware of a bad woman, and don't trust a good one; *Aonde o ouro falla, tudo calla*—When money speaks, all else is silent; *Do mal o menos*—Of evils, choose the least.

CUISINE

Portugal's cuisine shows great variety because each of her provinces has its own specialties. Along the coast a shellfish *açorda* is popular. This is a type of soup made from soaking country bread in a broth used to boil shellfish. Just before serving, hot shellfish and chopped coriander are added, and the dish is topped off by the addition of raw eggs that poach in the hot liquid. The city of Porto is famous for its tripe recipes. Tripe stew, for example, contains tripe, beans, veal, *chouriço* or *linguiça*, *presunto* (mountain-cured ham similar to prosciutto), chicken, onion, carrots, and parsley. The city of Aveiro is know for its *caldeirada*, a fish and shellfish stew seasoned with cumin, parsley, and coriander. Around the city of Coimbra one might find *bife à portuguésa* (steak prepared in a seasoned wine sauce and covered with thin slices of *presunto* ham) and *sopa à portuguésa* (soup made of pork, veal, cabbage, white beans, carrots, and macaroni).

Cod is the most commonly served fish, perhaps as *bolinhos de bacalhau* (codfish cakes), or *bacalhau à Gomes de Sá* (fried with boiled potatoes, onions, eggs and olives). Indeed, since Portugal is surrounded on two sides by the ocean, seafood is fresh and plentiful throughout the country. *Escabeche* consists of fish pickled with carrots and onions and stored in the refrigerator for several days before serving.

The Portuguese, like the Spanish, use olive oil and garlic generously in their cuisine, but they use herbs and spices more widely, especially cumin coriander, and paprika. *Caldo verde* (green soup) is made of fresh kale, potatoes, garlic-seasoned smoked pork sausage (either *linguiça* or *chouriço*), olive oil, and seasonings. It is served with *pão de broa* (rye bread) and red wine. Tender slices of lamprey eel prepared in a spicy curry sauce is also a typical dish.

Cozido à portuguésa is a stew made of beef, chicken, and sausage boiled with chick-peas, potatoes, turnips, carrots, cabbage, turnip greens and rice. Chicken, roasted suckling pig, lamb, and goat

are also important in Portuguese cuisine. *Massa sova-da*, a delicious Portuguese sweet bread, is even commercially available in parts of the United States.

Typical desserts and confections include *pudim flan* (a baked custard topped with a caramelized sugar sauce), *toucinho do céu* ("bacon of heaven" almond cake), and *ovos moles* (a sweet mixture of egg yolks and sugar syrup), which may be served as dessert or used as icing on a cake. *Figos recheados* (dried figs stuffed with almonds and chocolate) are often served after dinner accompanied by a glass of port wine.

Portuguese wines have a good reputation. Some of the best red wine comes from Colares, the only region that still produces grapes from native European root stock. The best white wines are from Carcavelos and Buçelas. Although they are really either red or white, the so-called green wines (*vinhos verdes*), made from grapes picked before they are fully ripe, are produced in the north. They are crackling wines and have an alcohol content of eight to 11 percent. Portugal is famous for its port wine (named for the city of Oporto); it is a fortified wine whose alcohol content is 20 percent. The best ports are aged for a minimum of ten years, but some are aged for as many as 50. Madeira wine, coming from the Madeira Islands, is similar to port.

TRADITIONAL COSTUMES

The clothing worn in modern-day Portugal is similar to that worn in the United States. However, for certain festivals, traditional costumes are worn. These vary from region to region, but men often wear black, close-fitting trousers with a white shirt and sometimes a bright-colored sash or vest. On their heads they might wear a long green and red stocking cap with a tassel on the end that hangs down to one side. Women wear colorful gathered skirts with aprons and cloth shawls over their shoulders. During the festival of *tabuleiros* in the region around Tomar, the harvest is celebrated by girls clad in ankle-length, long-sleeved white cotton dresses adorned by a wide colored ribbon that goes around the waist and over one shoulder. On their heads they wear a tall crown made of bread and weighing more than 30 pounds. The crown, which is at least as tall as the girl herself, is decorated with paper flowers and sprigs of wheat and is topped by a white dove or a Maltese cross.

DANCES AND SONGS

The *fado* is a melancholy type of song from Portugal. It is performed in certain bars of Lisbon late at night and in the early hours of the morning. These songs are believed to have originated among Portuguese sailors who had to spend months or even years at sea, away from their beloved homeland. The *fado*, meaning "fate," praises the beauties of the country for which the singer is homesick or of the love that he left behind. Regional folk dances include the *chula*, the *corridinho* (a polka-like dance from southern Portugal), the *fandango*, the *tirana*, and the *vira*.

HOLIDAYS

The Portuguese celebrate the traditional Christian holidays. Their celebration of Christmas (*Dia do Natal*) includes attending midnight mass on Christmas Eve (*missa do galo*), getting together with the extended family to share a meal and converse, singing carols outside friends' homes, and displaying a manger scene. New Year's Eve is celebrated by picking and eating 12 grapes as the clock is striking midnight in order to assure 12 months of happiness in the new year. On January 6, *Dia de Reis* (Day of the Kings), gifts are exchanged. Families share a ring-shaped cake called a *bolo Rei* which contains toy figures that bring good luck if found in one's portion. During Holy Week there are processions through the streets carrying portrayals of the passion of Jesus. The most famous processions are in the cities of Covilhã and Vila do Conde. On Easter, after attending mass, the family enjoys a special meal. This may include *folar*, a cake made of sweet dough and topped with hard-boiled eggs. On Pentecost (50 days after Easter) Holy Ghost societies in the Azores provide food for the poor in the community. *Véspera de São João* (Saint John's Eve), on June 23, is a celebration in honor of St. John the Baptist. The traditions associated with this festival have to do with fire and water. People build bonfires, dance around them, and leap over their flames. It is said that water possesses a miraculous quality that night, and that contact with it or dew can bring health, good fortune, protection to livestock, marriage, or good luck. On the thirteenth of May and October, people throng to the sanctuary of Our Lady of Fatima in search of miraculous cures or the granting of a prayer. In the United States, all these celebrations have become Americanized or have been abandoned for American equivalents (for example, the *Dia das Almas* has been replaced by Memorial Day), but certain traditions may be retained by some families out of ethnic pride.

HEALTH ISSUES

Portuguese Americans have no specific health problems or medical conditions that afflict them. They take pride in their sturdiness and longevity. They have a reputation for hard work and diligence. The birth rate of Portugal is high compared to the rest of Europe and to the United States, but it has dropped in recent years. Mutual aid societies are an established tradition among Portuguese Americans. Many workers have health insurance through their employer's benefits plan; the self-employed often insure themselves at their own expense.

LANGUAGE

Portuguese is a Romance language derived from Latin. Today it is spoken by people on five continents, including about 300,000 in the United States. Linguists see its development as consisting of two main periods. The language of the twelfth to the sixteenth centuries is called Galician-Portuguese; it was essentially the same as that spoken in northwestern Spain. The language of central Portugal, between Coimbra and Lisbon, came to be considered the standard dialect, and this language, from the sixteenth century on, is called modern Portuguese.

Modern Portuguese is characterized by an abundance of sibilant and palatal consonants and a broad spectrum of vowel sounds (five nasal phonemes and eight to ten oral ones). Portuguese has an uvular "r" similar to the French "r." On occasion, unstressed vowels tend not to be pronounced, for example, *professor* is pronounced "prufsor." Portuguese has a northern and a southern dialect. The northern dialect is more conservative and has retained more traits of Galician-Portuguese; the southern one has evolved further. The Portuguese spoken in the Azores and in Madeira might be considered a third dialect. Brazilian Portuguese differs from continental Portuguese in sound (diphthongs in final positions are not nasalized, and unstressed vowels are not omitted in pronunciation), in vocabulary (words from indigenous languages have been incorporated), and in syntax.

GREETINGS AND OTHER POPULAR EXPRESSIONS

Common Portuguese greetings and other expressions include: *Bom dia* ("bong DEE-uh")—Good morning; *Boa tarde* ("BOH-uh tard")—Good afternoon; *Boa noite* ("BOH-uh noyt")—Good night; *Por favor* ("poor fuh-VOR")—Please; *Obrigado* ("o-bree-GAH-doo")—Thank you; *Adeus* ("a-DEH-oosh")—Goodbye; *Desculpe!* ("dush-KOOLP")—Excuse me!; *Como esta?* ("KOH-moo shta")—How are you?; *Saúde!* ("sa-OOD")—Cheers!; *Feliz Natal* ("Fe-LEEZ na-TA-o")—Merry Christmas; *Próspero Ano Novo* ("PRAHS-pe-roo UN-new NO-voo")—Happy New Year.

FAMILY AND COMMUNITY DYNAMICS

In the earliest years of Portuguese immigration to the United States, most of the new arrivals were young, single males or married men hoping to bring their families over when their financial condition allowed. Most Portuguese immigrants came from rural villages and were illiterate; those who settled in urban areas had great adjustments to make. Their poor educational background and their lack of marketable skills condemned them to unskilled labor. They brought with them an anti-intellectual attitude derived from their belief that the father ruled the household and the children worked under his supervision to contribute to the common good by working on the land that their family was farming. Allowing their children to spend time in school was a luxury that these immigrants could not afford. In their new environment they resisted compulsory education for the young. When they were required to send their children to school, they sent them to public schools rather than to parochial ones. After a generation or two, however, families were more financially able to allow their children to continue their education. As a result, Portuguese American families have produced many physicians, lawyers, and university professors.

Immigrants also had to make adjustments to their diets. Since many of the early arrivals lived in boarding houses, they had to acclimate quickly to American food which generally represented an improvement over the bread, codfish, beans, and wine that were staples in Portugal. On the negative side, it was more difficult and more expensive to obtain fresh fruit, vegetables, and fish in the United States than it had been in Portugal. Children had to adjust to cow's milk after having been used to goat's milk. Immigrants who settled in rural areas, however, were not subject to such sudden changes in diet and could preserve their traditional eating habits more easily.

Because they could no longer depend upon their extended family for support, Portuguese immigrants formed mutual aid societies in the United States. The first was founded around 1847. The early societies were established for men only. Each member would pay a monthly amount into the treasury of the society or periodically would be assessed; in turn he would receive benefits if he lost his job or was unable to work because of illness or disability. These societies sometimes afforded the opportunity to socialize with other Portuguese. Similar organizations for women began to appear about 20 years later.

Women, who traditionally held a subordinate position in the family and in society in Portugal, gained greater equality with men in the United States. Many of them had to leave the home to work in industries in order to help support the family. Their progress is reflected in their participation in organizations founded by Portuguese Americans. At first they did not participate at all; then they established organizations for themselves. Later they served as auxiliaries for men's organizations, and now they enjoy equal membership with men in many of these clubs.

FRAGMENTATION OF PORTUGUESE IMMIGRANT GROUPS

Portuguese immigrants tended to differentiate themselves from other Portuguese-speaking immigrants of different geographical backgrounds. The continental Portuguese, the people from the Cape Verde Islands, those from Madeira, those from the Eastern Azores, and those from the Central Azores felt little affinity for the other groups, and often rivalry existed among them despite their common language. Except for the continentals, they did not think of themselves as Portuguese but as citizens of a particular island. And Azoreans often identified with a particular city rather than with the island as a whole. In the United States, each group tended to settle in clusters to be near others with whom they felt kinship and allegiance. The various groups did not know one another well, and prejudices grew among them. They wanted little to do with one another and even ridiculed each other's dialects. The groups with lighter skin looked down upon those with darker skin. Fraternal organizations founded by one group would not admit members of the other groups. The well-educated Portuguese who belonged to a higher social class felt little in common with those of the lower classes. This internal fragmentation has lessened with time but has inhibited Portuguese immigrants from presenting a united front for their own betterment.

RELIGION

Nearly all Portuguese immigrants to the United States are Roman Catholic. However, whereas the Roman Catholic church was protected by the Portuguese government for many years, church and state are separate in the United States. Immigrants came into conflict with the church because its laws made it difficult and frustrating to try to establish a Portuguese Catholic church in a community. The church, which had to be built with money contributed by the Portuguese immigrants, could be stripped of its Portuguese identity at the discretion of the bishop. Although none was ever built in Hawaii, the mainland United States has several Portuguese Catholic churches in California and about 30 in New England. There are also a few Portuguese Protestant churches in existence. The first was a Portuguese Presbyterian church established in

Jacksonville, Illinois, in 1850. It was founded by about 130 newly arrived Madeiran Protestants who left their native land because of religious persecution and settled in this region, after having spent several years in Trinidad. Within a few years, their numbers had grown to 400. There are Portuguese Protestant churches in New England, California, and Hawaii. Many people of Portuguese descent have found a church home in nonethnic Roman Catholic churches and in mainstream American Protestant churches.

EMPLOYMENT AND ECONOMIC TRADITIONS

Portuguese immigrants who settled on the East Coast tended to find work in factories, especially in the textile mills, in whaling and fishing, and in truck farming. Some found jobs as itinerant farm workers, picking cranberries and strawberries. Women worked as seamstresses in garment shops. In California, early Portuguese immigrants participated in gold mining as well as in whaling and fishing. Many there went into various types of farming. The first Portuguese in Hawaii worked on sugar plantations but soon moved to the urban centers to work in more skilled jobs. At first the Portuguese were assigned some of the most undesirable jobs, but as their proficiency in English and their work skills and educational level improved, they rose to higher, more responsible positions. Their success in farming is demonstrated by the fact that, by 1974, 34 percent of all market milk produced in California came from Portuguese American dairies. Many Portuguese American entrepreneurs went into business for themselves and opened restaurants, hotels, and banks. Others took advantage of educational opportunities in the United States and went into the professions. They now occupy a broad spectrum of jobs and careers and are found at all social and economic levels of society.

POLITICS AND GOVERNMENT

Portuguese Americans have assimilated quietly into American society; they have tended not to use politics as a means of promoting their own welfare. They have also tended to avoid political and social protest. They are self-reliant and avail themselves of welfare programs only as a last resort. They have organized themselves, however, through mutual aid societies as well as civic, educational, social, and fraternal organizations. Some of these include the Portuguese Union of the State of California, the

Portuguese American Civic League of Massachusetts, the Portuguese Civic League of Rhode Island, the Portuguese Educational Society of New Bedford, Massachusetts, the Luso-American Education Foundation, the Luso-American Federation, the League of Portuguese Fraternal Societies of California, and the Cabrillo Civic Clubs of California. They also have served in elected governmental positions. Their political influence began early in Hawaii; in 1894 three of the 18 elected delegates to the Constitutional Convention were Portuguese. In California the first Portuguese American was elected to the state legislature in 1900. This did not happen in Massachusetts until the early 1940s.

State governments have formally recognized the contributions that some Portuguese have made to the United States. Since 1935 California has celebrated Cabrillo Day on September 28, honoring the discoverer of that state. In 1967 the state of California further proclaimed the second week in March of each year Portuguese Immigrant Week. In 1974 Massachusetts set aside March 15 as Peter Francisco Day. Peter Francisco was a boy of Portuguese origin who, during the Revolutionary War, enlisted in the Continental Army at the age of 16; his courage and patriotism earned the respect of General George Washington. There is a Peter Francisco Park in the Ironbound district of Newark, New Jersey. Portuguese Americans have served with distinction in the United States armed services since the Revolution.

INDIVIDUAL AND GROUP CONTRIBUTIONS

Although most of the Portuguese who arrived on American shores lacked education and skills, and therefore had limited ability to make significant contributions to their new land's popular culture or to its arts and sciences, there have been exceptions. Descendants of Portuguese immigrants, having had greater educational opportunity in America, have gone on to make their mark on American society. In considering their contributions, it must be remembered that Portuguese Americans constitute only a fraction of one percent of the population of the United States, and that they have achieved success in areas besides those listed below, such as business and dairy farming.

ACADEMIA

Dr. Joaquim de Siqueira Coutinho (b. 1885) was a professor at George Washington University and at the Catholic University of America. From 1910 to 1920 he was in charge of the Brazilian section of the Pan-American Union. Francis Mile Rogers (1914–) was professor of Portuguese at Harvard University where he chaired the Department of Romance Languages and Literatures. He also served as Dean of the School of Arts and Sciences and authored a number of books.

ART AND ARCHITECTURE

William L. Pereira (1909–1985) is an internationally known architect and city planner. He designed or planned such complexes as Cape Canaveral, CBS Television City, the Los Angeles Museum of Art, the Crocker Citizens Bank in Los Angeles, the Central Library at the University of California (San Diego), and the Union Oil Center. Henrique Medina and Palmira Pimental were painters in the 1930s.

FILM, TELEVISION, AND THEATER

Harold José Pereira de Faria (Hal Peary) (1908-1985) achieved fame in the title role of the series "The Great Gildersleeve," which he played for 16 years on radio and television. He also appeared in motion pictures. John Mendes (1919-1955) performed as a magician under the name of "Prince Mendes." He was also a stage, screen, and television actor. Other Portuguese American motion picture actors include Rod de Medicis and Nestor Pavie. Carmen Miranda (1914-1955), although known as "the Brazilian bombshell," actually was born in Portugal. She was a popular film star of the 1940s known for her humor, her singing, and her extravagant hats piled high with fruit. She popularized Latin American dance music in the United States. Henry da Sylva established a ballet school in Hollywood, acted in films and directed them as well.

GOVERNMENT

Joseph F. Francis and Mary L. Fonseca were senators in the Massachusetts State Legislature. João G. Mattos served in the state legislature of California. Helen L. C. Lawrence became chair of the City Council of San Leandro, California, in 1941. In that position she exercised the power of mayor. Clarence Azevedo was mayor of Sacramento, California. In 1979, Peter "Tony" Coelho of California was elected to the United States House of Representatives; he is probably the first Portuguese American to serve in the national congress. Ernest Ladeira served as President Richard M. Nixon's advisor on social welfare. He was also an assistant to

John Volpe, Secretary of Transportation. John M. Arruda was mayor of Fall River, Massachusetts, for six years.

LITERATURE

Some Portuguese immigrants recorded their experiences in their adopted country: Laurinda C. Andrade (1899–) gives a young girl's impressions in her autobiography, *The Open Door*; Lawrence Oliver (1887-1977) wrote an autobiography titled *Never Backward*; and Alfred Lewis (1902-1977) wrote an autobiographical novel, *Home Is an Island*, as well as poetry. Onésimo Almeida, who completed his university training in Portugal and then earned a Ph.D. at Brown University where he later served as professor, wrote *Da Vida Quotidiana na LUSAlândia* (1975), *Ah! Mònim dum Corisco* (1978), and *(Sapa)teia Americana* (1983). Immigrants who tell of their experiences in poetry include Artur Ávila in his *Rimas de Um Imigrante* and José Brites in his *Poemas sem Poesia* and *Imigramante* (1984). John Roderigo Dos Passos (1896-1970) is the only American novelist of Portuguese descent who has an international reputation. His works include *Manhattan Transfer* (1925) and the trilogy *U.S.A.* (1937), for which he is best known. It comprises the novels *The 42nd Parallel* (1930), *1919* (1932), and *The Big Money* (1936). He published a second trilogy titled *District of Columbia* in 1952. Jorge de Sena (1919-1978) came to the United States from Portugal via Brazil. He was a professor at the University of Wisconsin, Madison. At the University of California, Santa Barbara, he was chair of the comparative literature program. He was a well-known literary critic, poet, playwright, novelist and short-story writer. His works include the novels *O Físico Prodigioso* (translated into English as *The Wondrous Physician*) and *Sinais de fogo* as well as the short story collections *Génesis* and *Os grao-capitaes*. English readers can obtain his work *By the Rivers of Babylon and Other Stories*. The novelist and short-story writer José Rodrigues Miguéis (1901-1980) wrote fiction such as *Saudades para Dena Genciana* and *Gente da Terceira Classe*.

MUSIC

John Philip Sousa (1854-1932) was director of the U.S. Marine Band from 1880 to 1892. He then founded his own Sousa Band in 1892 which, in its over 40-year existence, became the world's most famous concert band. At the outbreak of World War I, Sousa, at the age of 62, joined the navy to train bands at the Great Lakes Naval Training Center. He is famous as the composer of such marches as

"Stars and Stripes Forever," "Semper Fidelis," "The Washington Post March," and "Hands Across the Sea." He also composed several operettas including *The Captain, The Charlatan,* and *The Queen of Hearts,* as well as several suites for piano. Ilda Stichini and Maria Silveira were opera divas in the 1930s. Raul da Silva Pereira was a composer and conductor. Elmar de Oliveira (1950–) is a violinist who, in 1978, was the first American to win the gold medal in Moscow's Tchaikovsky competition; he is now on the faculty of the Manhattan School of Music. In the field of popular music, the vocalist Tony Martin (1912–) produced many hit records between 1941 and 1957. He had his own radio show and also appeared in films. His best role was probably in *Casbah* (1948). He appeared in nightclubs in the 1970s. A general contribution the Portuguese people have made to American music is the ukulele, which originated in Madeira and is now popular in Hawaii.

RELIGION

The charismatic religious leader Marcelino Manoel de Graça (1882-1960), also known as "Sweet Daddy Grace," founded the United House of Prayer for All People in the Harlem area of New York. His congregation, made up mainly of African Americans, included over three million people. Humberto Sousa Medeiros (1915-1983), who had been bishop of Brownsville, Texas, was named to succeed Cardinal Cushing as Archbishop of Boston in 1970. He was the first non-Irish American to fill that position in 124 years. He was elevated to the College of Cardinals in 1973.

SCIENCE AND MEDICINE

José de Sousa Bettencourt (1851-1931) earned degrees in both law and medicine. He practiced medicine and taught at the San Francisco Medical School. João Sérgio Alvares Cabral (d. 1909) practiced medicine in Oakland, California. He gave free consultations to the poor and ones at reduced rate to Portuguese. He also served as editor in chief of *A Pátria,* a Portuguese newspaper published in Oakland. Mathias Figueira (1853-1930) founded the American College of Surgeons. M. M. Enos (1875-) was head of the Portuguese Association of the Portuguese Hospital of Saint Anthony in Oakland, California. He was also director of the Portuguese American Bank and taught at the National Medical School of Chicago. Carlos Fernandes (d. 1977) was director of St. John's Hospital in San Francisco.

SPORTS

Bernie de Viveiros played baseball with the Detroit Tigers and the Oakland Oaks. Manuel Gomes also was a baseball player as was Lew Fonseca (1899-1989) who played for the Cincinnati Reds, the Philadelphia Phillies, the Cleveland Indians, and coached the Chicago White Sox; he was a pioneer in the use of film to analyze players' performance during a game. In boxing, Al Melo participated as a welterweight in the Olympics in 1924. George Araujo, Johnny Gonsalves, and Babe Herman were contenders for the world boxing championships. Justiano Silva was a professional wrestler. Henrique Santos won the United States fencing championship in 1942. Tony Lema (1934-1966), also known as "Champagne Tony," was the winner of numerous professional golf tournaments. At the time of his death he ranked tenth in all-time earnings in the PGA. Tennis star Vic (E. Victor) Seixas, Jr. (1923–), won the U.S. Open Championship in 1954.

TECHNOLOGY

Abilio de Silva Greaves invented a fire-alarm system as well as devices used in aviation. In the field of textiles, Steve Abrantes invented a wool carding device, and José Pacheco Correia invented one for combing cotton. Sebastião Luiz Dias patented an irrigation control system. John C. Lobato developed a new type of army tank.

MEDIA

People who are interested in Portuguese cultural topics and would like to communicate with those having similar interests may do so through the USENET news group called soc.culture.portuguese. A game or pastime called "MOOsaico" can be played through Telnet by contacting moo.di.uminho. pt 7777. Participants explore a virtual world and talk to other players. The game may be played in Portuguese or English.

PRINT

Jornal Portugues/Portuguese Journal.
Published every Thursday in Portuguese and English; circulation of 2,500.

Contact: Maria Leal, Editor.
Address: 1912 Church Lane, San Pablo, California 94806.
Telephone: (800) 309-0233; or (510) 237-0888.
Fax: (510) 237-3790.
E-mail: portjornal@aol.com.

Luso-Americano.
Established 1928 and published every Wednesday and Friday with a circulation of 36,000—the largest outside Portugal and Brazil.

Contact: Antonio Matinho, Editor and Publisher.
Address: 88 Ferry, Newark, New Jersey 07105.
Telephone: (973) 589-4600.
Fax: (973) 589-3848.
E-mail: lusoamerican@earthlink.net.

The Portuguese Post.
Established 1986 and published every Monday; circulation 20,000.

Contact: George Valante, Editor.
Address: 283 East Kinney Street, Newark, New Jersey 07105.
Telephone: (201) 344-5652.
Fax: (201) 344-0675.
E-Mail: Rtpusapost@earthlink.net.
Online: http://www.uspn.com/post/.

Portuguese Times, Inc.
Published every Thursday; circulation 15,000.

Contact: Manuel Ferreira, Editor.
Address: 1501 Acushnet Avenue, New Bedford, Massachusetts 02740.
Telephone: (508) 997-3118.
Fax: (508) 990-1231.
Online: http://www.webx.ca/Ptimes/.

Portuguese Tribune.
Published bi-monthly. Circulation: 1,800 subscriptions plus sales in more than 250 vending locations.

Contact: Armando Antunes, Editor.
Address: P.O. Box 3477, San Jose, California 95156-3477.
Telephone: (408) 971-1615.
Fax: (408) 971-1966.

Portuguese-American Newspaper.
Semiweekly newspaper founded in 1928; for Portuguese Americans in Portuguese.

Address: 88 Ferry Street, Newark, New Jersey 07105.
Telephone: (973) 589-4600.
Fax: (973) 589-3848.

Voz de Portugal/Voice of Portugal.
Semi-monthly magazine published in Portuguese.

Contact: Lourenco Costa Aguiar, Editor and Publisher.

Address: 370 A Street, Hayward, California 94541.
Telephone: (415) 537-9503.

RADIO

WINE-AM (940).
Radio Portugal.

Address: 1004 Federal Road, Brookfield, Connecticut 06804-1123.
Telephone: (203) 775-1212.
Fax: (203) 775-6452.

WJFD-FM (97.3).
Radio Globo.

Address: 270 Union Street, New Bedford, Massachusetts 02740.
Telephone: (617) 997-2929.
Fax: (508) 990-3893.

WRCP-AM (1290).
Radio Clube Portugues.

Contact: Anthony A. Cruz.
Address: 1110 Douglas Avenue, Providence, Rhode Island 02904.
Telephone: (401) 273-7000.
Fax: (401) 273-7008.

TELEVISION

Full Channel.
Address: 57 Everett Street, Warren, Rhode Island 02885.
Telephone: (401) 247-1250.

A Nossa Gente.
Address: Heritage Cable Vision, 1636 Alum Rock Avenue, San Jose, California 95116.
Telephone: (408) 258-2800.

Portuguese American Hour.
Address: Channel 38, 46921 Warm Springs Boulevard, Fremont, California.
Telephone: (415) 656-3232.

The Portuguese Channel.
Address: Channel 20, 1501 Acushnet Avenue, New Bedford, Massachusetts 02740.
Telephone: (508) 997-3110.
Fax: (508) 996-2151.

Portuguese Television.
Address: Channel 38, P.O. Box 51, Fremont, California 94541.
Telephone: (415) 797-4219

RTP.
This Portuguese television channel can be received from the Hughes Galaxy III satellite. This is a C-band satellite with a horizontal polarization. Its position is 93.5 degrees west, and its transponder number is five.
Address: R.T.P. USA, Adams Street, Newark, New Jersey.
Telephone: (201) 344-8888.

ORGANIZATIONS AND ASSOCIATIONS

American Portuguese Society.
Founded in 1959. Promotes friendship, understanding, and cultural relations between Portugal and the United States through exhibits, seminars, and cultural exchanges. Publishes the *Journal of the American Portuguese Society* with articles in English about Portuguese culture.
Contact: Michael Teague, Director.
Address: c/o ISSI, 2 Wall Street, New York, New York 10005.
Telephone: (212) 751-1992.
Fax: (212) 688-7082.

Luso-American Education Foundation.
Seeks to perpetuate the ethnic and national culture brought to America by emigrants from Portugal; assists qualified students and others in studying and understanding Portuguese culture. Develops high school and college courses for the teaching of Portuguese language, history, and culture.
Contact: S. Bettencourt, President.
Address: P.O. Box 2967, Dublin, California 94568.
Telephone: (510) 828-3883.
Fax: (510) 828-3883.
Online: http://www.Lusaweb.com/laef/

Portuguese Continental Union USA.
Founded in 1925. A fraternal organization serving the Portuguese community.
Contact: Francisco Mendonca, Supreme Secretary/CEO.

Address: 899 Boylston Street, Boston, Massachusetts 02115.
Telephone: (617) 536-2916.
Fax: (617) 536-8301.
E-mail: upceua@aol.com.
Online: http://members.aol.com/upceua.

Portuguese Historical and Cultural Society.
Works to promote Portuguese history and culture.
Contact: Joe Souza, President.
Address: P.O. Box 161990, Sacramento, California 95816.
Telephone: (916) 392-1048.
E-mail: portucal@juno.com.

The União Portuguesa do Estado da California (UPEC).
Fraternal insurance society founded in 1880. Maintains the J. A. Freitas library with 8,000 volumes dealing with Portugal and Portuguese Americans.
Contact: Carlos Almeida.
Address: 1120 East 14th Street, San Leandro, California 94577.
Telephone: (510) 483-7676.
Online: http://www.upec.org/.

MUSEUMS AND RESEARCH CENTERS

The Oliveira Lima Library.
Located on the campus of The Catholic University of America in Washington, D.C., this is the oldest and most extensive library of materials specializing in Luso-Brazilian history and culture.
Contact: Maria Leal, Librarian; or Thomas Cohen, Curator.
Address: 6 Mullen Library, Catholic University of America, Washington, D.C. 20064.
Telephone: (202) 319-5059.
E-mail: leal@cua.edu.

Society for Spanish and Portuguese Historical Studies.
Address: Department of History, SSB 215, University of Arizona, Tucson, Arizona 85721-0027.
Contact: Helen Nader.
Telephone: (520) 621-5860.
Fax: (520) 621-2422.
E-mail: naderh@u.arizona.edu.

SOURCES FOR ADDITIONAL STUDY

Almeida, Carlos. *Portuguese Immigrants: The Centennial Story of the Portuguese Union of the State of California*. San Leandro, California: Supreme Council of U.P.E.C., 1992.

Anderson, James Maxwell. *The History of Portugal*. Westport, CT: Greenwood Press, 2000.

Cabral, Stephen L. *Tradition and Transformation: Portuguese Feasting in New Bedford*. New York: AMS Press, Inc., 1989.

Cardozo, Manoel da Silveira. *The Portuguese in America: 590 B.C.-1974: A Chronology & Fact Book*. Dobbs Ferry, New York: Oceana Publications, Inc., 1976.

Gilbert, Dorothy Ann. *Recent Portuguese Immigrants to Fall River, Massachusetts: An Analysis of Relative Economic Success*. New York: AMS Press, Inc., 1989.

Pap, Leo. *The Portuguese-Americans*. Boston: Twayne Publishers, 1981.

Ribeiro, José Luís. *Portuguese Immigrants and Education*. Bristol, Rhode Island: Portuguese American Federation, 1982.

Wolforth, Sandra. *The Portuguese in America*. San Francisco: R&E Research Associates, Inc., 1978.

PUEBLOS

by
D. L. Birchfield

No one knows when Pueblo peoples first arrived in the Southwest, but they are believed to be descended from Archaic desert culture peoples who had been in the region for thousands of years.

OVERVIEW

Pueblo peoples have lived in the American Southwest for thousands of years. Their ancient ruins, particularly Ancestral Puebloan cliff dwellings, are among the most spectacular ancient ruins in North America. By the end of the severe, prolonged droughts in the late fourteenth century they had relocated to the vicinity of their modern communities primarily located within the watershed of the upper Rio Grande River Valley in New Mexico and the watershed of the Little Colorado River in Arizona. The pueblo tribes represent several distantly related language families and dialects, and they have continued to maintain close contact with each other since the arrival of Europeans in the region in the sixteenth century. Today the 19 pueblos of New Mexico cooperate in a loose confederation called the All Indian Pueblo Council. Each pueblo is autonomous and has its own tribal government. The Pueblos have been able to retain a tribal land base, retain a strong sense of community, and maintain their languages and cultures. The name Pueblo is the same as the Spanish word for village and denotes both the people and their communal homes.

HISTORY

No one knows precisely when Pueblo peoples first arrived in the Southwest, but they are believed to be descended from Archaic desert culture peoples

who had been in the region for thousands of years. Archaeologists have developed eight classifications for Pueblo chronology. Basketmaker I spans the period prior to 100 B.C. The Basketmaker II period (100 B.C.-400 A.D.) featured beautifully woven baskets, the cultivation of corn and pumpkins, the first pit houses, and rare, crude gray pottery. The Basketmaker III period (400-700) featured the first cultivation of beans, the domestication of turkeys, the replacing of short spears and the *atlatl* with the bow and arrow, and the increased use of pottery (either gray, or with a black pattern on a white base). The Pueblo I period (700-900) featured the cultivation of cotton; pit houses became ceremonial kivas; houses were built above ground out of stone and set immediately against one another; cradle boards were introduced; and white, red, and orange ceremonial pottery was made with black or red decorations. The Pueblo II period (900-1100) featured multi-storied stone masonry apartments and an elaborate system of roads in a culture that is also known as the Ancestral Puebloan. The Pueblo III period (1100-1300) saw the Ancestral Puebloan culture reach its greatest height in communities such as Chaco Canyon and Mesa Verde; the period featured extensive trade with and the development of polychrome pottery and pots of diverse shapes. During the Pueblo IV period (1300-1540) glazing was used in pottery for the first time, but only for ornamentation, and paintings appeared on the walls of the kivas; the population centers shifted from the Colorado Plateau to the Little Colorado River and the upper Rio Grande River. The Pueblo V period (1540-present) featured the adjustments Pueblo peoples have had to make due to the arrival of Europeans in the region. By 1700 only Zuñi, Acoma, Taos, Picuris, and the Hopi had not moved their locations since the arrival of the Spanish.

The Pueblo people were visited by a number of large Spanish exploratory expeditions in the sixteenth century, beginning with Coronado in 1540. These expeditions brought diseases for which the Pueblos had no resistance and resulted in large population decreases before the Spanish finally colonized New Mexico with the expedition of Juan de Oñate in 1598. The Pueblo people suffered severe disruptions of their lives and cultures during the long Spanish colonization of New Mexico. During the

Spanish era the number of pueblos in New Mexico was reduced from somewhere between 70 and 100 pueblos to 19. The Spanish tried to force the Pueblos to convert to Christianity and exacted forced labor from them under the *encomienda* system. Many pueblos were moved or consolidated to benefit Spanish labor demands. In the mid-seventeenth century serious disputes developed between the civil and religious authorities in New Mexico, with the Pueblos caught in the middle. In 1680 the Pueblos revolted and successfully drove the Spanish out of New Mexico for more than a decade, but the Spanish returned in force and reconquered the region by 1694. The historic southward migration of the Comanches onto the Southern Plains, beginning about 1700, displaced the Eastern Apaches from the plains and greatly altered Spanish-Indian relations in New Mexico for the remainder of the Spanish colonial era. Pueblo auxiliaries were often required to fight with Spanish troops against either Apaches, Navajos, Utes, or Comanches, depending upon Spanish Indian policies and alliances at any given time. Pueblos became Mexican citizens in 1820 at the conclusion of the Mexican revolution, the only Indians in the Southwest to be granted Mexican citizenship. As Mexican citizens, Pueblos became citizens of the United States at the conclusion of the Mexican War in 1848, the only Indians in the Southwest to gain U.S. citizenship in that manner. Most Indians in the Southwest did not become U.S. citizens until the Indian Citizenship Act of 1924.

MODERN ERA

Pueblo peoples today are still to be found in their ancestral homeland, primarily along the upper Rio Grande River Valley in the state of New Mexico, along with the Hopi in northeastern Arizona and the small community of Isleta del Sur near El Paso, Texas, just across the border from New Mexico. Census figures have sometimes shown great variation from census to census for some individual pueblos, as have population reports compiled by other federal agencies, such as the Bureau of Indian Affairs Labor Force Report. In both the 1980 and 1990 census, Arizona and New Mexico ranked third and fourth, respectively, for the largest number of Indian residents within each state (Oklahoma and California have the largest Indian populations). Texas ranked eighth. The Pueblo peoples in these states and their modern tribal governments follow.

NEW MEXICO

The Acoma Pueblo is one of the 12 Southern Pueblos, located west of Albuquerque, and the oldest

continuously inhabited settlement within the United States, dating from the twelfth century. Called the Sky City, it sits atop a 350-foot mesa. Only about 50 people now inhabit the ancient town year-round. It has no electricity or running water. Most of the Acoma people live in the nearby communities of Acomita, Anzac, and McCartys.

Cochiti Pueblo, a Southern Pueblo, is located west of Santa Fe. Cochiti pueblo raises income from a variety of sources, including recreational leases of lands near Cochiti Lake, an Army Corps of Engineers project. Cochiti drums are well-known craft items made here, as well as pottery, jewelry, and storyteller figures. A portion of the original 1628 church can still be seen in the rebuilt structure.

Isleta Pueblo, a Southern Pueblo, is the largest Tiwa-speaking pueblo, composed of several communities on the Rio Grande River south of Albuquerque.

Jemez Pueblo, another Southern Pueblo, is located north of Albuquerque in an area of wilderness and is the last remaining Towa-speaking pueblo. It absorbed the Towa-speaking survivors of Pecos Pueblo when Pecos was abandoned in the 1830s. The pueblo is known historically for its baskets made of yucca fronds. While this is no longer an active art form at Jemez, some well-known jewelers, potters, and storyteller doll makers live there.

Laguna Pueblo, a Southern Pueblo located west of Albuquerque, is the largest Keresan-speaking pueblo, composed of six villages: Old Laguna, Paguate, Mesita, Paraje, Encinal, and Seama. Each town has its own fair and feast day. A rich uranium mine was located here. Now the Laguna Reclamation Project is attempting to restore the mining site.

Nambe Pueblo, is one of the eight Northern Pueblos, located north of Santa Fe in an area of scenic land formations.

Picuris Pueblo, a Northern Pueblo, located north of Santa Fe, is the smallest of the Tiwa-speaking pueblos. The original pueblo, built in the twelfth century, was abandoned after the Pueblo revolt of 1680 and was reestablished in the early eighteenth century.

Pojoaque Pueblo, the smallest of all the pueblos, is a Northern Pueblo located north of Santa Fe. A late nineteenth century smallpox epidemic almost destroyed this Tewa-speaking people. The present settlement dates from the 1930s, but ruins of the original pueblo are nearby. Also nearby are the ruins of several pueblos deserted after the Pueblo Revolt. Traditional dances were revived in 1973 after having been abandoned for about a century. Revenues from a commercial strip along the

highway makes Pojoaque one of the more affluent pueblos.

Sandia Pueblo, a small Southern Pueblo located north of Albuquerque, occupies about 26 acres near the center of the reservation. Its annual feast day is open to the public.

San Felipe Pueblo, a Keresan-speaking pueblo known for its ceremonies, is a Southern Pueblo located north of Albuquerque. Its Green Corn Dance involves hundreds of participants.

San Ildefonso Pueblo, a Northern Pueblo of Tewa-speaking pueblo famous for its pottery is located north of Santa Fe. San Ildefonso is host to the annual Eight Northern Indian Pueblos Artist and Craftsman Show.

San Juan Pueblo is the largest Tewa-speaking pueblo. A Northern Pueblo located north of Santa Fe, it was the site of the first Spanish capitol of New Mexico.

Santa Ana Pueblo, a Southern Pueblo, is located north of Albuquerque. This Keresan-speaking pueblo is often closed to the public except for several feast days during the year. Many of the residents live on farmland outside the pueblo.

Santa Clara Pueblo, is a Northern Pueblo, located north of Santa Fe. Traditional crafts are available, and tours are available for the ancient 740-room Puye Cliff Dwellings.

Santo Domingo Pueblo, a Southern Pueblo located north of Albuquerque and known for its turquoise and silver jewelry, is the largest of the eastern Keresan-speaking pueblos.

Taos Pueblo, a Northern Pueblo north of Santa Fe, is a Tiwa-speaking pueblo famous for its drums. A National Historic Site, the pueblo is heavily visited by tourists. Taos Pueblo and the nearby town of Taos were famous during the fur trapping era.

Tesuque Pueblo, a Northern Pueblo located north of Santa Fe, is listed on the National Register of Historic Places. The Pueblo Revolt of 1680 started here.

Zia Pueblo, a Southern Pueblo located north of Albuquerque, is a Keresan-speaking pueblo known for its orange-on-white pottery. The Zia sun symbol was adopted by the state of New Mexico and appears on the state flag. The pueblo overlooks the Jemez River.

Zuñi Pueblo is known for its jewelry, sold by the Zuñi Craftsmen Cooperative Association at the pueblo. There are restaurants and a tribal campground. The Hawikuh ruins, a Zuñi village abandoned after the Pueblo Revolt of 1680, are nearby. The Zuñi Pueblo is a Southern Pueblo located south of Gallup.

ARIZONA

In northeastern Arizona, completely surrounded by the Navajo Nation, the villages of the Hopi occupy approximately 1.5 million acres of reservation land. The Hopi population exceeds 9,000, found primarily near the center of the nation, with the three ancient villages on top of First Mesa, Second Mesa, and Third Mesa and the three modern communities at the foot of the mesas.

TEXAS

Just across the border from New Mexico, in Texas, is Isleta del Sur Pueblo. This pueblo was founded by Pueblo people from Isleta who fled New Mexico with the Spanish during the Pueblo Revolt of 1680.

ACCULTURATION AND ASSIMILATION

Pueblo people are at home in both their Native world and in the world of the dominant American culture. They have learned to be U.S. citizens while still remaining Pueblo. Changes, however, have been inevitable. Pueblo culture has long been multilingual. It is now rapidly becoming bilingual. In times past Pueblos might be fluent not only in the language of their pueblo, but also in one or more of the other Pueblo languages or dialects. With the arrival of the Spanish, Pueblos also learned the Spanish language. With the arrival of the Comanches in their vicinity, many Pueblos, especially those on the eastern frontier nearest the plains, learned Comanche, just as some northern Pueblos learned Jicarillan due to close relations with the Jicarilla Apache. Pueblos nearest the Navajos were apt to know Navajo. Spanish is still common among older Pueblo people. But increasingly, Pueblo young people are learning only the language of their pueblo and English. With English being a universal language within the region, and with its hold growing ever stronger by the profound linguistic influences of radio, television, print journalism, and public education, few Pueblos today learn other Native languages besides their own.

TRADITIONS, CUSTOMS, AND BELIEFS

Ceremonial dances are at the heart of Pueblo culture. Pueblo traditional dance costumes are among the most striking of any Native peoples. Kachinas are masked male dancers who are said to actually be the personages they dance. These dancers perform ceremonial rituals in the plazas on feast days and other important occasions. Ritual clowns are also a part of some ceremonials. The clowns engage in funny, sexual, and absurd behavior. Despite their antics, which are often interpreted as a reminder of foolish human behavior, clowns are sacred figures whose actions possess more profound reasons and motivations. Some ceremonials, such as the Zuñi Shalakos, feature kachinas in ten-foot high costumes. Among the Hopi, the kachinas are said to live in the San Francisco peaks near Flagstaff. They come to the Hopi for six months each year, arriving during the February Bean Dance.

LANGUAGE

Zuñi is classified as a language isolate of the Penutian Phylum. All other Pueblo languages are classified within the Aztec-Tanoan Phylum: within the Kiowa-Tanoan family are three Tanoan languages, Tiwa, Tewa, and Towa; the Hopi language is an isolate within the Uto-Aztecan family; and Keresan is an unclassified language isolate not yet assigned to any family within the phylum. Zuñi is spoken only by the Zuñi. Tiwa is spoken by Taos, Picuris, Sandia, and Isleta. Tewa is spoken by San Juan, Santa Clara, San Ildefonso, Nambe, Tesuque, and Pojoaque. Towa is spoken only by the Jemez. Keresan is spoken by Acoma, Cochiti, Laguna, San Felipe, Santa Ana, Santo Domingo, and Zia. Language can be richly expressive and descriptive, as in these Tewa constructions for the lunar cycle: Moon of the cedar dust wind (February); Moon when the leaves break forth (March); Moon when the leaves are dark green (June); Moon when the corn is taken in (September); and Moon when all is gathered in (November).

FAMILY AND COMMUNITY DYNAMICS

Pueblo culture is matrilineal and matrilocal. Children are born into the mother's clan. Wife abuse is uncommon in functioning, matrilocal cultures because the wife is surrounded by the protection of her relatives. Child custody disputes are unknown because the child is a member of the mother's clan and remains with the mother or her relatives should a marriage not endure. In the matrilocal residence pattern, related women, and their husbands and children, live in clusters of apartments within a larger structure, which is a classic description of both Ancestral Puebloan and Pueblo building requirements. There is speculation that the development of this matrilocal system of residence accounts for the change from pit houses to aboveground masonry apartments. An aspect of life for which Pueblo Indians are perhaps best-known, Pueblo dwellings are interconnected multi-level apartment-like structures made of stone and plaster or adobe bricks. Only Taos Pueblo retain this feature. The ceiling of one "apartment" serves as floor and outside courtyard for the one above it. Pueblo structures sometimes reached five stories tall, with inhabitants moving from one floor to the next via ladders that led through holes in the ceilings instead of through outside doorways. This structural design served as a safeguard against outside attacks.

Pueblos held community gatherings in pit houses, which were dug into the ground in a central location in the pueblo. A remnant of the pit house survives as the kiva, an underground chamber that is built into the apartments of the southwest. In the kivas, related men, who do not live together in matrilocal communities, meet and hold ceremonies. These groups of related men constitute a clan. The clan affords an important opportunity for maintaining ties between related men in matrilocal cultures, even though the men trace their descent through the female line.

DANCES AND SONGS

Songs and dances are significant in Pueblo life. Masks, textiles, and body painting are important aspects of Pueblo ritual. The Pueblos use gourd rattles, wooden drums, and rawhide as musical instruments for their ceremonies and dances, which are unique to each tribe and have prescribed roles for the leaders, singers, dancers, and spectators. Many dances, performed usually by men who sing and dance in line formations or in procession, are held in honor of seasonal change and related duties, such as hunting in the winter, or harvest in the autumn. Many dances relate to the bringing of rain. Most of the Pueblos perform a version of the Corn Dance and the Matachine Dance—a dance with Spanish and Mexican roots—and many perform dances in honor of buffalo or deer. Pueblo dances are among the best-known Native American customs still practiced, and many of the Pueblos allow the public to come and watch them.

HOLIDAYS

On January 6 most pueblos celebrate the Day of the Three Kings and the installation of new governors and officials. The first week in February is the Governor's Feast at Acoma. April 19-20 is the Eight Northern Indian Pueblos Spring Arts and Crafts Show at De Vargas Mall in Santa Fe. May 3 is Santa Cruz Day at Cochiti and Taos. June 13 is Grab Day at San Ildefonso, San Juan, Santa Clara, Taos, and Picuris. July 4 is the Nambe Falls Ceremonial at Nambe. July 4 is the Annual Popé Foot Race at San Juan. The last weekend in July is the Puye Cliff Ceremonial at Santa Clara. On August 5-10 all pueblos celebrate the Symbolic Relay Run. August 10 is Grab Day at Laguna and Cochiti. Mid-August is the Intertribal Indian Ceremonial in Gallup. December (date set annually) is the time for the Shalako Ceremonial at Zuñi.

RELIGION

To be Pueblo is a way of life, a world view, a part of a community, and perhaps one of the reasons that Pueblo religion is so entrenched is that there is no word for religion in the Pueblo languages. Religious beliefs are deeply interwoven in many aspects of Pueblo culture, including farming, storytelling, dances, art, architecture, and other everyday activities. Especially symbolic for the Hopi is agriculture, which carries a sacred significance and determines a great deal of their work cycles, ceremonies, and feasts. Much Hopi spirituality centers on the belief that when their ancestors emerged from the depths of the earth, they were offered their choice of foods. The Hopi chose an ear of short blue corn, symbolizing a life of hardship, humility, and hardiness, since the short blue corn is the most difficult to harvest successfully but is also the most durable. The planting and harvest of corn is in a real way the Hopi's connection to their earliest ancestors and the creation of the world. Pueblo religious ceremonies and rituals are often tied to the bringing of rain and a successful harvest; and the Pueblo still practice many of them today.

The Hopi story of the creation of the world is based on the concept of emergence, which is a common theme in Pueblo folklore and religion. The Hopi believe that their ancestors—spirit beings—migrated through three underground worlds before arriving on the earth above them—the fourth world. There they made a covenant with the spirit being Masau-u, who allowed them to remain on the land as long as they followed sacred rules that ensure harmony among people, maintain the land, and provide water needed to grow their crops. The Hopi still try to honor this sacred contract today.

Pueblos have also modified Christian teachings to make them compatible with traditional views. The result is a form of Christianity found nowhere else in the world. Pueblo Catholicism nevertheless has much in common with the experiences of Native peoples throughout Latin America who are nominally Catholics, but whose practice and beliefs are at great odds with official canon. The church is tolerant of this practice, having found, after exerting great effort, that it cannot uproot traditional Pueblo religious beliefs. The church made its greatest effort, with public hangings and whippings, in the 1660s and 1670s. In the Pueblo Revolt of 1680, 21 of the 33 Catholic priests in New Mexico were killed. The Catholic Christian influence has resulted in the creation and observance of a number of Christian holidays and feast days, which frequently coincide with traditional celebrations and the performance of traditional dances. Some pueblos observe feast days in honor of their patron saints.

EMPLOYMENT AND ECONOMIC TRADITIONS

The Pueblo people are among the most successful dry farmers in the world. They are also skilled at irrigation farming. Today many Pueblos continue the agricultural traditions of their ancestors and continue to cultivate in the same time-honored manner. Many Pueblo people are also employed in the urban areas near their homes, and many of them who now live in these urban areas return to the pueblo frequently, sometimes as often as nearly every weekend. Traditional craftwork in pottery, weaving, jewelry, and drum making are also important sources of income.

Tribal enterprise also provides jobs. The Hopi Cultural Center, with its restaurant and motel, offers some employment opportunities. At Acoma the visitor center has a restaurant, crafts shop, and a museum, and a bingo hall is nearby. Cochiti provides services for Cochiti Lake, which leases its land from Cochiti Pueblo and has a commercial center, a marina, and an 18-hole golf course. The majority of Isleta's residents work in Albuquerque, but others operate the bingo hall, grocery stores, and the campgrounds at Isleta Lakes. Laguna Industries Inc. manufactures communications shelters for the U.S. Army and is only one of a number of Laguna tribal industries. Some Lagunas found employment in the uranium mining industry and others are now finding employment in the reclamation project that is attempting to restore the mined land.

Many of Nambe's residents work in Santa Fe, in Española, or at Los Alamos National Laboratory. Others are employed by the Eight Northern Indian Pueblos Council. Picuris Pueblo Enterprise Cultural Center houses a museum, a restaurant, and a store and operates guided tours. Pojoaque generates revenue by the development of a commercial strip fronting the highway, and the pueblo also operates an official state tourist center. The Sandia Indian Bingo Parlor is one of the largest in New Mexico. Sandia also operates Bien Mur Indian Market Center and Sandia Lakes Recreation Area. At San Ildefonso there is a museum, several trading posts, a visitor center, and the annual Eight Northern Indian Pueblos Artist and Craftsman Show. At San Juan there is the Oke Oweenge Crafts Cooperative. At Santa Ana there is the Ta Ma Myia crafts shop. Santo Domingo is developing commercial property along Interstate 25, where it also operates a museum. Taos operates a horseback riding and guided tour business as well as several trading posts. Tesuque operates a bingo parlor and Camel Rock Campground. Zuñi has been a model for tribal

This Pueblo mother is taking her children out of their above ground home to go for a walk.

enterprise, taking advantage of direct federal grants through the Community Action Programs to gain administrative control of almost all of the Bureau of Indian Affairs contract services on the reservation, which now run more efficiently and with much greater community commitment and participation.

Gaming casinos have become big business for many Native American tribes. Some Pueblos, such as the Taos Pueblos, have enthusiastically embraced casinos as a source of economic opportunity. Other Pueblos, such as the Nambe, resist gaming on traditional grounds that forbid gambling. In January of 1998, Navajo voters in New Mexico, Arizona, and Utah defeated a measure that would have opened five casinos on the Navajo reservation. The vote was 54 percent against the proposal and 46 percent in favor of it. The Taos Pueblos had to struggle through legal battles to gain the right to operate casinos. In 1996, U.S. Attorney General John Kelly was forced to order the Taos Pueblo and other Indian tribes to shut down their casino operations after state supreme court decisions voided the compacts that the governors had made with the tribes because the compacts had not received legislative approval. The Taos took the case to court and eventually won the right to operate casinos. Pueblos who chose to operate gambling enterprises do so with the goal of buying sacred lands back from the government.

POLITICS AND GOVERNMENT

Under the Indian Reorganization Act of 1934, many Pueblos refused to allow their traditional form of government to be replaced by a foreign system. The tribal council system is modeled somewhat after the U.S. government, but also has much in common with the way corporations are governed. Each tribe within the United States was given the option of reorganizing under the act, and many Pueblos refused to do so. Traditional Pueblo government features leadership from different sources of strength within each community. Clans are an important force in providing leadership, and among some Pueblos specific clans have traditional obligations to provide leaders. This is true of the Bear Clan among the Hopi, the Antelope Clan at Acoma, and the Bow Clan at Zuñi. The Tewa pueblos have dual village leaders, where the heads of the winter and summer moieties each exercise responsibility for half the year. In matters of traditional religion, which encompasses much of what white people associate with government, a *cacique* among the Pueblos and a *kikmongwi* among the Hopi have serious responsibilities to the people. Along with their assistants they not only perform ceremonies but also organize hunts and the planting of crops.

Today the Hopi in Arizona and six New Mexico pueblos (Isleta, Laguna, Pojoaque, San Ildefonso, Santa Clara, and Zuñi) elect their governors and councils. In New Mexico, the All Indian Pueblo Council had its first recorded meeting in 1598 when Juan de Oñate met with 38 Pueblo leaders at Santo Domingo. Pueblo oral history recounts that the various pueblos had been working together long before the arrival of the Spanish and that secret meetings of the council were a major factor in the successful planning of the Pueblo Revolt of 1680. The All Indian Pueblo Council was formed on November 5, 1922 when Pueblo leaders assembled at Santo Domingo to meet with U.S. government officials. Its present constitution was adopted on October 16, 1965. The council is a confederation of New Mexico pueblos that seeks to protect and advance their interests, particularly regarding relations with other governments.

RELATIONS WITH THE UNITED STATES

Because Pueblos were granted full Mexican citizenship while under Mexican rule from 1821 to 1848, they automatically became U.S. citizens when the Southwest was annexed by the United States at the conclusion of the Mexican War in 1848. The Pueblos were the only Indians in the Southwest to become U.S. citizens in that manner. Pueblos had to sue to have their status as Indians recognized by the United States, which was achieved by a decision of the U.S. Supreme Court in 1916. They are now federally recognized Indian tribes. By joining together to form the All Indian Pueblo Council in

the 1920s, after a congressional investigation had revealed that 12,000 non-Pueblo claimants were living on Pueblo land, they succeeded in getting the U.S. Congress to pass the Pueblo Lands Act of 1924, which secures some of their traditional land to them. The struggle for water rights has characterized much of their relations with United States in this century. In 1975, after a 30-year struggle, Taos Pueblo succeeded in regaining its sacred Blue Lake and 55,000 acres of surrounding land in the mountains above the pueblo. This marked one of the few times that the United States has returned a major sacred site to Indian control.

INDIVIDUAL AND GROUP CONTRIBUTIONS

ACADEMIA

Ted Jojola (1951–), an educator and administrator of Isleta Pueblo descent, is known for his research on Native American culture. His numerous publications have dealt with subjects ranging from urban planning to teaching, architecture, and ethnography. He is currently a professor at the University of New Mexico. Edward P. Dozier (1916-1971) was a pioneering anthropologist, linguist, and educator who specialized in the study of the Pueblo Indians of the Southwest. He spent much of his career at the University of Arizona and was also prominent as an activist for Indian rights.

Alfonso Ortiz (1939-1998) was a well-known anthropologist, scholar, and activist whose books on Southwest Indian tribes, including *American Indian Myths and Legends* (1984) and *The Tewa World: Space, Time, Being, and Becoming in a Pueblo Society* (1969), are considered classics in anthropological scholarship. In addition to his academic work, Ortiz was president of the Association of American Indian Affairs (AAIA) in the 1970s. During his term, the organization played a central role in the return of the sacred Blue Lake to the Taos Pueblo people and the passage of the Indian Child Welfare Act, which ensured that Indian orphans are placed in Indian foster homes, among other accomplishments. Ortiz was a professor in the University of New Mexico's anthropology department from 1974 until his death.

ART

Pueblo communities have produced a number of renowned artists, including Maria Montoya Martinez (c. 1887-1980), who has been called perhaps the most famous Native American artist of all time.

In her award-winning pottery, she revived and transformed indigenous pottery into high art. Martinez was a San Ildefonso Pueblo woman who spent much of her career producing pottery with her husband and other family members, including their son Popovi Da, who became a well-known artist in his own right. Martinez and her husband displayed and demonstrated their craft at the 1904 World's Fair in St. Louis, Missouri, as well as in museums and art shows. Martinez was particularly respected for her black-on-black pottery designs, which came to be known as blackware pottery.

Helen Quintana Cordero (1915-1994) was a Cochiti Pueblo woman responsible for reviving the nearly lost art of clay dollmaking among her people. Clay dolls, typically embodying women singing to children, had been used by Southwest Indians for centuries for religious purposes and during harvest ceremonies, but this custom had declined with the arrival of white settlers in the region. Cordero specialized in what has come to be known as the "storyteller doll," drawn from her memories of her grandfather, who would gather the Pueblo children around him and tell them traditional Indian tales of the past. She was the first to use the male figure in her pioneering clay doll arrangements, which include the storyteller with up to 30 clay children dolls sitting in various positions around him.

Pablita Velarde (1918–) is a Tewa writer and artist living in Santa Clara Pueblo, and is best known for her paintings depicting numerous aspects of daily Pueblo life, including religious ceremonies, tribal government, arts and crafts, costumes, and farming. She painted murals at the Bandelier National Park in New Mexico and at the 1934 World's Fair in an authentic and detailed style that is drawn upon her knowledge and study of her ancestry. Her works are sometimes used as secondary source material for scholars researching the life of ancient Indians. Velarde was honored by the New Mexico Department of Agriculture in 1996 with its Rounders Award, which is given to "those who live, promote, or articulate the western way of life." Helen Hardin (1946-1984), a Tewa Pueblo known for her acrylic and casein designs, was a regarded as a premier artist of the Southwest. She used Native American patterns and geometric shapes in her award-winning paintings. One of the most renowned Pueblo potters is Acoma, New Mexico artist Marie Lewis-Garcia, who produces traditional Pueblo pots. Elizabeth Naranjo is also a widely recognized potter, based in Santa Clara, while Nora Naranjo-Morse of Santa Clara is a celebrated writer and potter. Among the San Ildefonso pueblo, the Martinez, Roybal, and Herrera families established strong painting and pottery traditions that have influenced such modern artists as Maria Martinez, the famed San Ildefonso Blackware potter.

FILM

Hopi producer/director Victor Masayesva, Jr., has created a feature length film, *Imagining Indians*, that succeeds in conveying Native American resentment of the appropriation of its culture for commercial purposes. *Imagining Indians* is a 90-minute film that explores many facets of what happens when Native stories, rituals, and objects become commercial commodities. Masayesva is from Hotevilla, a village of about 500 people on Third Mesa. Hotevilla was constructed, hastily, in 1906 by Hopi women, whose men had been incarcerated by the United States and moved to Alcatraz Island to prevent them from moving to southern Utah. Masayesva had never been to a town larger than Winslow, Arizona, when he went to New York City at age 15. He studied still photography at Princeton University and then began working with video. For some of the editing techniques in *Imagining Indians* he gained access to state of the art equipment, a machine for which only three were available in the United States. Masayesva has screened *Imagining Indians* in Phoenix, Santa Fe, Houston, Boston, New York, and at the University of Oklahoma. A 60-minute version has been edited for television.

LITERATURE

Pueblos have produced some of the most outstanding contemporary Native literary writers. Two of the first three Lifetime Achievement honorees of the Native Writers' Circle of the Americas have been Pueblos: Simon J. Ortiz (Acoma) and Leslie Marmon Silko (Laguna). In the early 1970s Ortiz was editor of *Americans Before Columbus*, the newspaper of the Indian Youth Council. In the 1980s he held official tribal positions as Interpreter and First Lieutenant Governor of Acoma. He has taught at the Institute of American Indian Arts, the University of New Mexico, Navajo Community College, Sinte Gleska College, San Diego State University, the College of Marin, Lewis and Clark College, and Colorado College. He edited one of the most important collections of Native literature, *Earth Power Coming*, published by Navajo Community College Press, and has written many books, among them *From Sand Creek; Going for the Rain; A Good Journey; Fightin': New and Collected Stories; The People Shall Continue;* and *Woven Stone*.

Silko has also taught at a number of universities, including the University of Arizona and the

University of New Mexico. Her work has had a profound influence on the Native literary community. Her best known works are *Ceremony*, *Storyteller*, and *Almanac of the Dead*. Both Ortiz and Silko delivered plenary session speeches at the historic Returning the Gift conference of North American Native writers at the University of Oklahoma in 1992, a conference that drew nearly 400 native literary writers from throughout the upper Western hemisphere.

Paula Gunn Allen (Laguna) is another well-known Pueblo author. She edited the anthology *Spider Woman's Granddaughters*. She has published books of fiction, *The Woman Who Owned the Shadows*; poetry, *Shadow Country*, and *Skin and Bones*; and nonfiction, *The Sacred Hoop*, and *Studies in American Indian Literatures*. Laguna poet Carol Lee Sanchez has published *Excerpt From a Mountain Climber's Handbook*, *Message Bringer Woman*, and *Conversations From the Nightmare*. Hopi/Miwok writer Wendy Rose is coordinator of American Indian Studies at Fresno City College and has held positions with the Women's Literature Project of Oxford University Press, the Smithsonian Native Writers' Series, the Modern Language Association Commission on Languages and Literature of the Americas, and the Coordinating Council of Literary Magazines. Her books include *Hopi Roadrunner Dancing*; *Long Division: A Tribal History*; *Academic Squaw: Reports to the World from the Ivory Tower*; *Lost Copper*; *What Happened When the Hopi Hit New York*; *The Halfbreed Chronicles*; *Going to War with All My Relations*; and *Bone Dance*.

Laguna educator Lee Francis, director of the American Indian Internship program at American University in Silver Springs, Maryland, is also national director of Wordcraft Circle of Native American Mentor and Apprentice Writers and is editor of its newsletter, *Moccasin Telegraph*, and of its quarterly journal. In 1994 Francis led a team of Native writers who guest edited a special Native American Literatures issue of *Callaloo* for the University of Virginia and Johns Hopkins University Press. Many other Pueblos are literary writers, including Aaron Carr, Joseph L. Concha, Harold Littlebird, Diane Reyna; Veronica Riley, Joe S. Sando, Laura Watchempino, and Aaron Yava. Some of their best early work appears in *The Remembered Earth: An Anthology of Contemporary Native American Literature*, published by the University of New Mexico Press in 1979. Some of the most recent work by a new generation of Pueblo literary figures, including Rachael Arviso, Rosemary Diaz, and Lorenzo Baca can be found in *Neon Powwow: New Native American Voices of the Southwest* (1993).

SCIENCE

Frank C. Dukepoo (1943–), a Hopi-Laguna geneticist, was the first Hopi to earn a doctorate degree. Born in Arizona, he earned a Ph.D. from Arizona State University in 1973 and has held teaching or research positions there and at San Diego State University, Palomar Junior College, and, beginning in 1980, at Northern State University. Dukepoo has also served as director of Indian education at Northern Arizona University, and held administrative positions with the National Science Foundation and the National Cancer Institute. In addition to founding and coordinating the National Native American Honor Society, which assists Native American students, Dukepoo has conducted extensive research on birth defects in Indians.

MEDIA

PRINT

Americans Before Columbus.
Address: 318 Elm Street, Albuquerque, New Mexico 87012.

Cochiti Lake Sun.
Address: P.O. Box 70, Cochiti, New Mexico 87014.

Eight Northern Pueblos News.
Address: Route 1, Box 71, Santa Fe, New Mexico 87528.

Four Directions.
Address: 1812 Las Lomas, N.E., Albuquerque, New Mexico 87131.

Indian Arizona.
Address: 4560 North 19th Avenue, Suite 200, Phoenix, Arizona 85015-4113.

Indian Life.
Address: 1664 East Campo Bello Drive, Phoenix, Arizona 85022.

Indian Voice.
Address: 9169 Coors Road, N.W., Box 10146; Albuquerque, New Mexico 87184.

Isleta Eagle Pride.
Address: P.O. Box 312, Isleta, New Mexico 87022.

Kachina Messenger.
Address: P.O. Box 1210, Gallup,
New Mexico 87301.

Keresan.
Address: Box 3151 Laguna, New Mexico 87026.

Native Peoples Magazine.
Address: 1833 North Third Street, Phoenix,
Arizona 85004.

Pueblo Horizon.
Address: 2401 12th Street, N.W., Albuquerque,
New Mexico 87102.

Southwest Native News.
Address: P.O. Box 1990, Tuba City, Arizona 86045.

Southern Pueblos Bulletin.
Address: 1000 Indian School Road, N.W.,
Albuquerque, New Mexico 87103.

Tsa'aszi'.
Address: P.O. Box 12, Pine Hill,
New Mexico 87321.

Uts'ittisctaan'i.
Address: Northern Arizona University, Campus
Box 5630, Flagstaff, Arizona 86011.

Zuñi Tribal Newsletter.
Address: P.O. Box 339, Zuñi, New Mexico 87327.

RADIO

KCIE-FM (90.5).
Address: P.O. Box 603, Dulce, New Mexico 87528.

KENN.
Address: P.O. Box 1558, Farmington, New
Mexico 87499-1558.

KGAK.
Address: 401 East Coal Road, Gallup, New
Mexico 87301-6099.

KGHR-FM (91.5).
Address: P.O. Box 160, Tuba City, Arizona 86045.

KHAC-AM (1110).
Address: Drawer F, Window Rock, Arizona 86515.

KNNB-FM (88.1).
Address: P.O. Box 310, Whitewater,
Arizona 85941.

KPGE.
Address: Box 00, Page, Arizona 80640-1969.

KPLZ.
Address: 816 Sixth Street, Parker,
Arizona 85344-4599.

KSHI—FM (90.9).
Address: P.O. Box 339, Zuñi, New Mexico 87327.

KTDB-FM (89.7).
Address: P.O. Box 89, Pine Hill,
New Mexico 87321.

KTNN-AM.
Address: P.O. Box 2569, Window Rock,
Arizona 86515.

ORGANIZATIONS AND ASSOCIATIONS

All Indian Pueblo Council (AIPC).
Serves as advocate on behalf of 19 Pueblo Indian
tribes on education, health, social, and economic
issues; lobbies on those issues before state and
national legislatures. Activities are centered in New
Mexico.

Contact: James Hena, Chair.
Address: 3939 San Pedro NE, Suite E,
Albuquerque, New Mexico 87190.
Telephone: (505) 883-7360.

Arizona Commission of Indian Affairs.
Contact: Eleanor Descheeny-Joe,
Executive Director.
Address: 1400 West Washington, Suite 300,
Phoenix, Arizona 85007.
Telephone: (602) 542-3123.
Fax: (602) 542-3223.

Center for Indian Education.
Address: Arizona State University, Box 871311,
Tempe, Arizona 85287-1311.
Online: http://www.asu.edu/educ/cie/.

New Mexico Commission on Indian Affairs.
Address: 330 East Palace Avenue, Santa Fe, New Mexico 87501.

New Mexico Indian Advisory Commission.
Address: Box 1667, Albuquerque, New Mexico 87107.

MUSEUMS AND RESEARCH CENTERS

Albuquerque Museum and the Maxwell Museum in Albuquerque, New Mexico; American Research Museum, Ethnology Museum, Fine Arts Museum, Hall of the Modern Indian, and Institute of American Indian Arts, in Santa Fe, New Mexico; Art Center in Roswell, New Mexico; Black Water Draw Museum in Portales, New Mexico; Coronado Monument in Bernalillo, New Mexico; Heard Museum of Anthropology in Phoenix, Arizona; Milicent Rogers Museum in Taos, New Mexico; Northern Arizona Museum in Flagstaff, Arizona; and the State Museum of Arizona in Tempe.

SOURCES FOR ADDITIONAL STUDY

Bruggmann, Maximilien, and Sylvio Acatos. *Pueblos: Prehistoric Indian Cultures of the Southwest*, translated by Barbara Fritzemeier. New York: Facts On File, 1990.

The Coronado Narrative: Spanish Explorers in the Southern United States, 1528-1543, edited by Frederick W. Hodge and Theodore H. Lewis. New York: Scribners, 1970.

Eagle/Walking Turtle (Gary McLain). *Indian America: A Traveler's Companion*, third edition. Santa Fe, New Mexico: John Muir Publications, 1993.

Forbes, Jack D. *Apache, Navaho, and Spaniard*. Norman: University of Oklahoma Press, 1969; reprinted with new introduction, 1994.

Gutiérrez, Ramón A. *When Jesus Came, the Corn Mothers Went Away: Marriage, Sexuality, and Power in New Mexico, 1500-1846*. Stanford, CA: Stanford University Press, 1991.

Keegan, Marcia. *Pueblo People: Ancient Traditions, Modern Lives*. Santa Fe, NM: Clear Light Publishers, 1999.

Marquis, Arnold. *A Guide To America's Indians: Ceremonials, Reservations, and Museums*. Norman: University of Oklahoma Press, 1974.

Minge, Ward Alan. *Acoma: Pueblo in the Sky*, second edition. Albuquerque: University of New Mexico Press, 1991.

New Perspectives on the Pueblos, edited by Alfonso Ortiz. Albuquerque: University of New Mexico Press, 1985.

O'Brien, Sharon. *American Indian Tribal Governments*. Norman: University of Oklahoma Press, 1989.

Ortiz, Alfonso. *The Pueblo*. New York: Chelsea House, 1994.

Sando, Joe S. *Pueblo Nations: Eight Centuries of Pueblo Indian History*. Santa Fe: Clear Light Publishers, 1992.

Trimble, Stephen. *The People: Indians of the American Southwest*. Santa Fe, New Mexico: Sar Press, 1993.

The history of Puerto Rican American assimilation has been one of great success mixed with serious problems.

PUERTO RICAN AMERICANS

by
Derek Green

Overview

The island of Puerto Rico (formerly Porto Rico) is the most easterly of the Greater Antilles group of the West Indies island chain. Located more than a thousand miles southeast of Miami, Puerto Rico is bounded on the north by the Atlantic Ocean, on the east by the Virgin Passage (which separates it from the Virgin Islands), on the south by the Caribbean Sea, and on the west by the Mona Passage (which separates it from the Dominican Republic). Puerto Rico is 35 miles wide (from north to south), 95 miles long (from east to west) and has 311 miles of coastline. Its land mass measures 3,423 square miles—about two-thirds the area of the state of Connecticut. Although it is considered to be part of the Torrid Zone, the climate of Puerto Rico is more temperate than tropical. The average January temperature on the island is 73 degrees, while the average July temperature is 79 degrees. The record high and low temperatures recorded in San Juan, Puerto Rico's northeastern capital city, are 94 degrees and 64 degrees, respectively.

According to the 1990 U.S. Census Bureau report, the island of Puerto Rico has a population of 3,522,037. This represents a three-fold increase since 1899—and 810,000 of those new births occurred between the years of 1970 and 1990 alone. Most Puerto Ricans are of Spanish ancestry. Approximately 70 percent of the population is white and about 30 percent is of African or mixed descent. As in many Latin American cultures,

Roman Catholicism is the dominant religion, but Protestant faiths of various denominations have some Puerto Rican adherents as well.

Puerto Rico is unique in that it is an autonomous Commonwealth of the United States, and its people think of the island as *un estado libre asociado*, or a "free associate state" of the United States—a closer relationship than the territorial possessions of Guam and the Virgin Islands have to America. Puerto Ricans have their own constitution and elect their own bicameral legislature and governor but are subject to U.S executive authority. The island is represented in the U.S House of Representatives by a resident commissioner, which for many years was a nonvoting position. After the 1992 U.S. presidential election, however, the Puerto Rican delegate was granted the right to vote on the House floor. Because of the Puerto Rico's commonwealth status, Puerto Ricans are born as natural American citizens. Therefore all Puerto Ricans, whether born on the island or the mainland, are Puerto Rican Americans.

Puerto Rico's status as a semiautonomous Commonwealth of the United States has sparked considerable political debate. Historically, the main conflict has been between the nationalists, who support full Puerto Rican independence, and the statists, who advocate U.S. statehood for Puerto Rico. In November of 1992 an island-wide referendum was held on the issue of statehood versus continued Commonwealth status. In a narrow vote of 48 percent to 46 percent, Puerto Ricans opted to remain a Commonwealth.

HISTORY

Fifteenth-century Italian explorer and navigator Christopher Columbus, known in Spanish as Cristobál Colón, "discovered" Puerto Rico for Spain on November 19, 1493. The island was conquered for Spain in 1509 by Spanish nobleman Juan Ponce de León (1460-1521), who became Puerto Rico's first colonial governor. The name Puerto Rico, meaning "rich port," was given to the island by its Spanish *conquistadors* (or conquerors); according to tradition, the name comes from Ponce de León himself, who upon first seeing the port of San Juan is said to have exclaimed, "¡Ay que puerto rico!" ("What a rich port!").

Puerto Rico's indigenous name is *Borinquen* ("bo REEN ken"), a name given by its original inhabitants, members of a native Caribbean and South American people called the Arawaks. A peaceful agricultural people, the Arawaks on the island of Puerto Rico were enslaved and virtually exterminated at the hands of their Spanish colonizers. Although Spanish heritage has been a matter of pride among islander and mainlander Puerto Ricans for hundreds of years—Columbus Day is a traditional Puerto Rican holiday—recent historical revisions have placed the *conquistadors* in a darker light. Like many Latin American cultures, Puerto Ricans, especially younger generations living in the mainland United States, have become increasingly interested in their indigenous as well as their European ancestry. In fact, many Puerto Ricans prefer to use the terms *Boricua* ("bo REE qua") or *Borrinqueño* ("bo reen KEN yo") when referring to each other.

Because of its location, Puerto Rico was a popular target of pirates and privateers during its early colonial period. For protection, the Spanish constructed forts along the shoreline, one of which, El Morro in Old San Juan, still survives. These fortifications also proved effective in repelling the attacks of other European imperial powers, including a 1595 assault from British general Sir Francis Drake. In the mid-1700s, African slaves were brought to Puerto Rico by the Spanish in great numbers. Slaves and native Puerto Ricans mounted rebellions against Spain throughout the early and mid-1800s. The Spanish were successful, however, in resisting these rebellions.

In 1873 Spain abolished slavery on the island of Puerto Rico, freeing black African slaves once and for all. By that time, West African cultural traditions had been deeply intertwined with those of the native Puerto Ricans and the Spanish conquerors. Intermarriage had become a common practice among the three ethnic groups.

MODERN ERA

As a result of the Spanish-American War of 1898, Puerto Rico was ceded by Spain to the United States in the Treaty of Paris on December 19, 1898. In 1900 the U.S. Congress established a civil government on the island. Seventeen years later, in response to the pressure of Puerto Rican activists, President Woodrow Wilson signed the Jones Act, which granted American citizenship to all Puerto Ricans. Following this action, the U.S. government instituted measures to resolve the various economic and social problems of the island, which even then was suffering from overpopulation. Those measures included the introduction of American currency, health programs, hydroelectric power and irrigation programs, and economic policies designed to attract U.S. industry and provide more employment opportunities for native Puerto Ricans.

In the years following World War II, Puerto

Rico became a critical strategic location for the U.S. military. Naval bases were built in San Juan Harbor and on the nearby island of Culebra. In 1948 Puerto Ricans elected Luis Muñoz Marín governor of the island, the first native *puertorriqueño* to hold such a post. Marín favored Commonwealth status for Puerto Rico. The question of whether to continue the Commonwealth relationship with the United States, to push for U.S. statehood, or to rally for total independence has dominated Puerto Rican politics throughout the twentieth century.

Following the 1948 election of Governor Muñoz, there was an uprising of the Nationalist Party, or *independetistas*, whose official party platform included agitation for independence. On November 1, 1950, as part of the uprising, two Puerto Rican nationalists carried out an armed attack on Blair House, which was being used as a temporary residence by U.S. President Harry Truman. Although the president was unharmed in the melee, one of the assailants and one Secret Service presidential guard were killed by gunfire.

After the 1959 Communist revolution in Cuba, Puerto Rican nationalism lost much of its steam; the main political question facing Puerto Ricans in the mid-1990s was whether to seek full statehood or remain a Commonwealth.

EARLY MAINLANDER PUERTO RICANS

Since Puerto Ricans are American citizens, they are considered U.S. migrants as opposed to foreign immigrants. Early Puerto Rican residents on the mainland included Eugenio María de Hostos (b. 1839), a journalist, philosopher, and freedom fighter who arrived in New York in 1874 after being exiled from Spain (where he had studied law) because of his outspoken views on Puerto Rican independence. Among other pro-Puerto Rican activities, María de Hostos founded the League of Patriots to help set up the Puerto Rican civil government in 1900. He was aided by Julio J. Henna, a Puerto Rican physician and expatriate. Nineteenth-century Puerto Rican statesman Luis Muñoz Rivera—the father of Governor Luis Muñoz Marín—lived in Washington D.C., and served as Puerto Rico's ambassador to the States.

SIGNIFICANT IMMIGRATION WAVES

Although Puerto Ricans began migrating to the United States almost immediately after the island became a U.S. protectorate, the scope of early migration was limited because of the severe poverty of average Puerto Ricans. As conditions on the island improved and the relationship between Puerto Rico and the United States grew closer, the number of Puerto Ricans who moved to the U.S. mainland increased. Still, by 1920, less than 5,000 Puerto Ricans were living in New York City. During World War I, as many as 1,000 Puerto Ricans—all newly naturalized American citizens—served in the U.S. Army. By World War II that number soared to over 100,000 soldiers. The hundred-fold increase reflected the deepening cooperation between Puerto Rico and the mainland States. World War II set the stage for the first major migration wave of Puerto Ricans to the mainland.

That wave, which spanned the decade between 1947 and 1957, was brought on largely by economic factors: Puerto Rico's population had risen to nearly two million people by mid-century, but the standard of living had not followed suit. Unemployment was high on the island while opportunity was dwindling. On the mainland, however, jobs were widely available. According to Ronald Larsen, author of *The Puerto Ricans in America,* many of those jobs were in New York City's garment district. Hard-working Puerto Rican women were especially welcomed in the garment district shops. The city also provided the sort of low-skilled service industry jobs that non-English speakers needed to make a living on the mainland.

New York City became a major focal point for Puerto Rican migration. Between 1951 and 1957 the average annual migration from Puerto Rico to New York was over 48,000. Many settled in East Harlem, located in upper Manhattan between 116th and 145th streets, east of Central Park. Because of its high Latino population, the district soon came to be known as Spanish Harlem. Among New York City *puertorriqueños*, the Latino-populated area was referred to as *el barrio,* or "the neighborhood." Most first-generation migrants to the area were young men who later sent for their wives and children when finances allowed.

By the early 1960s the Puerto Rican migration rate slowed down, and a "revolving door" migratory pattern—a back-and-forth flow of people between the island and the mainland—developed. Since then, there have been occasional bursts of increased migration from the island, especially during the recessions of the late 1970s. In the late 1980s Puerto Rico became increasingly plagued by a number of social problems, including rising violent crime (especially drug-associated crime), increased overcrowding, and worsening unemployment. These conditions kept the flow of migration into the United States steady, even among professional classes, and caused many Puerto Ricans to remain on the mainland permanently. According to U.S. Census Bureau statistics, more than 2.7 million Puerto Ricans were living in the mainland Unites States by 1990, making Puerto Ricans the second-largest Latino group in the nation, behind Mexican Americans, who number nearly 13.5 million.

SETTLEMENT PATTERNS

Most early Puerto Rican migrants settled in New York City and, to a lesser degree, in other urban areas in the northeastern United States. This migration pattern was influenced by the wide availability of industrial and service-industry jobs in the eastern cities. New York remains the chief residence of Puerto Ricans living outside of the island: of the 2.7 million Puerto Ricans living on the mainland, over 900,000 reside in New York City, while another 200,000 live elsewhere in the state of New York.

That pattern has been changing since the 1990s, however. A new group of Puerto Ricans—most of them younger, wealthier, and more highly educated than the urban settlers—have increasingly begun migrating to other states, especially in the South and Midwest. In 1990 the Puerto Rican population of Chicago, for instance, was over 125,000. Cities in Texas, Florida, Pennsylvania, New Jersey, and Massachusetts also have a significant number of Puerto Rican residents.

ACCULTURATION AND ASSIMILATION

The history of Puerto Rican American assimilation has been one of great success mixed with serious problems. Many Puerto Rican mainlanders hold high-paying white collar jobs. Outside of New York City, Puerto Ricans often boast higher college graduation rates and higher per capita incomes than their counterparts in other Latino groups, even when those groups represent a much higher proportion of the local population.

However, U.S. Census Bureau reports indicate that for at least 25 percent of all Puerto Ricans living on the mainland (and 55 percent living on the island) poverty is a serious problem. Despite the presumed advantages of American citizenship, Puerto Ricans are—overall—the most economically disadvantaged Latino group in the United States. Puerto Rican communities in urban areas are plagued by problems such as crime, drug-use, poor educational opportunity, unemployment, and the breakdown of the traditionally strong Puerto Rican family structure. Since a great many Puerto Ricans

are of mixed Spanish and African descent, they have had to endure the same sort of racial discrimination often experienced by African Americans. And some Puerto Ricans are further handicapped by the Spanish-to-English language barrier in American cities.

Despite these problems, Puerto Ricans, like other Latino groups, are beginning to exert more political power and cultural influence on the mainstream population. This is especially true in cities like New York, where the significant Puerto Rican population can represent a major political force when properly organized. In many recent elections Puerto Ricans have found themselves in the position of holding an all-important "swing-vote"—often occupying the sociopolitical ground between African Americans and other minorities on the one hand and white Americans on the other. The pan-Latin sounds of Puerto Rican singers Ricky Martin, Jennifer Lopez, and Marc Anthony, and jazz musicians such as saxophonist David Sanchez, have not only brought a cultural rivival, they have increased interest in Latin music in the late 1990s. Their popularity has also had a legitimizing effect on *Nuyorican*, a term coined by Miguel Algarin, founder of the Nuyorican Poet's Café in New York, for the unique blend of Spanish and English used among young Puerto Ricans living in New York City.

TRADITIONS, CUSTOMS, AND BELIEFS

The traditions and beliefs of Puerto Rican islanders are heavily influenced by Puerto Rico's Afro-Spanish history. Many Puerto Rican customs and superstitions blend the Catholic religious traditions of Spaniards and the pagan religious beliefs of the West African slaves who were brought to the island beginning in the sixteenth century. Though most Puerto Ricans are strict Roman Catholics, local customs have given a Caribbean flavor to some standard Catholic ceremonies. Among these are weddings, baptisms and funerals. And like other Caribbean islanders and Latin Americans, Puerto Ricans traditionally believe in *espiritismo*, the notion that the world is populated by spirits who can communicate with the living through dreams.

In addition to the holy days observed by the Catholic church, Puerto Ricans celebrate several other days that hold particular significance for them as a people. For instance, *El Dia de las Candelarias*, or "candlemas," is observed annually on the evening of February 2; people build a massive bonfire around which they drink and dance and

chant "¡Viva las candelarias!" or "Long live the flames!" And each December 27 is *El Dia de los Innocentes* or the "Day of the Children." On that day Puerto Rican men dress as women and women dress as men; the community then celebrates as one large group.

Many Puerto Rican customs revolve around the ritual significance of food and drink. As in other Latino cultures, it is considered an insult to turn down a drink offered by a friend or stranger. It is also customary for Puerto Ricans to offer food to any guest, whether invited or not, who might enter the household: failure to do so is said to bring hunger upon one's own children. Puerto Ricans traditionally warn against eating in the presence of a pregnant woman without offering her food, for fear she might miscarry. Many Puerto Ricans also believe that marrying or starting a journey on a Tuesday is bad luck, and that dreams of water or tears are a sign of impending heartache or tragedy. Common centuries-old folk remedies include the avoidance of acidic food during menstruation and the consumption of *asopao* ("ah so POW"), or chicken stew, for minor ailments.

MISCONCEPTIONS AND STEREOTYPES

Although awareness of Puerto Rican culture has increased within mainstream America, many common misconceptions still exist. For instance, many other Americans fail to realize that Puerto Ricans are natural-born American citizens or wrongly view their native island as a primitive tropical land of grass huts and grass skirts. Puerto Rican culture is often confused with other Latino American cultures, especially that of Mexican Americans. And because Puerto Rico is an island, some mainlanders have trouble distinguishing Pacific islanders of Polynesian descent from the Puerto Rican people, who have Euro-African and Caribbean ancestry.

CUISINE

Puerto Rican cuisine is tasty and nutritious and consists mainly of seafood and tropical island vegetables, fruits, and meats. Although herbs and spices are used in great abundance, Puerto Rican cuisine is not spicy in the sense of peppery Mexican cuisine. Native dishes are often inexpensive, though they require some skill in preparation. Puerto Rican

women are traditionally responsible for the cooking and take great pride in their role.

Many Puerto Rican dishes are seasoned with a savory mixture of spices known as *sofrito* ("so-FREE-toe"). This is made by grinding fresh garlic, seasoned salt, green peppers, and onions in a *pilón* ("pee-LONE"), a wooden bowl similar to a mortar and pestle, and then sautéing the mixture in hot oil. This serves as the spice base for many soups and dishes. Meat is often marinated in a seasoning mixture known as *adobo,* which is made from lemon, garlic, pepper, salt, and other spices. *Achiote* seeds are sautéed as the base for an oily sauce used in many dishes.

Bacalodo ("bah-kah-LAH-doe"), a staple of the Puerto Rican diet, is a flaky, salt-marinated cod fish. It is often eaten boiled with vegetables and rice or on bread with olive oil for breakfast. *Arroz con pollo,* or rice and chicken, another staple dish, is served with *abichuelas guisada* ("ah-bee-CHWE-lahs gee-SAH-dah"), marinated beans, or a native Puerto Rican pea known as *gandules* ("gahn-DOO-lays"). Other popular Puerto Rican foods include *asopao* ("ah-soe-POW"), a rice and chicken stew; *lechón asado* ("le-CHONE ah-SAH-doe"), slow-roasted pig; *pasteles* ("pah-STAY-lehs"), meat and vegetable patties rolled in dough made from crushed plantains (bananas); *empanadas dejueyes* ("em-pah-NAH-dahs deh WHE-jays"), Puerto Rican crab cakes; *rellenos* ("reh-JEY-nohs"), meat and potato fritters; *griffo* ("GREE-foe"), chicken and potato stew; and *tostones,* battered and deep fried plantains, served with salt and lemon juice. These dishes are often

washed down with *cerveza rúbia* ("ser-VEH-sa ROO-bee-ah"), "blond" or light-colored American lager beer, or *ron* ("RONE") the world-famous, dark-colored Puerto Rican rum.

TRADITIONAL COSTUMES

Traditional dress in Puerto Rico is similar to other Caribbean islanders. Men wear baggy *pantalons* (trousers) and a loose cotton shirt known as a *guayaberra.* For certain celebrations, women wear colorful dresses or *trajes* that have African influence. Straw hats or Panama hats (*sombreros de jipijipa*) are often worn on Sundays or holidays by men. Spanish-influenced garb is worn by musicians and dancers during performances—often on holidays.

The traditional image of the *jíbaro,* or peasant, has to some extent remained with Puerto Ricans. Often depicted as a wiry, swarthy man wearing a straw hat and holding a guitar in one hand and a *machete* (the long-bladed knife used for cutting sugarcane) in the other, the *jíbaro* to some symbolizes the island's culture and its people. To others, he is an object of derision, akin to the derogatory image of the American hillbilly.

DANCES AND SONGS

Puerto Rican people are famous for throwing big, elaborate parties—with music and dancing—to celebrate special events. Puerto Rican music is polyrhythmic, blending intricate and complex African percussion with melodic Spanish beats. The traditional Puerto Rican group is a trio, made up of a *qauttro* (an eight-stringed native Puerto Rican instrument similar to a mandolin); a *guitarra,* or guitar; and a *basso,* or bass. Larger bands have trumpets and strings as well as extensive percussion sections in which maracas, guiros, and bongos are primary instruments.

Although Puerto Rico has a rich folk music tradition, fast-tempoed *salsa* music is the most widely known indigenous Puerto Rican music. Also the name given to a two-step dance, *salsa* has gained popularity among non-Latin audiences. The *merengue,* another popular native Puerto Rican dance, is a fast step in which the dancers' hips are in close contact. Both *salsa* and *merengue* are favorites in American barrios. *Bombas* are native Puerto Rican songs sung *a cappella* to African drum rhythms.

HOLIDAYS

Puerto Ricans celebrate most Christian holidays, including *La Navidád* (Christmas) and *Pasquas*

(Easter), as well as *El Año Nuevo* (New Year's Day). In addition, Puerto Ricans celebrate *El Dia de Los Tres Reyes*, or "Three King's Day," each January 6. It is on this day that Puerto Rican children expect gifts, which are said to be delivered by *los tres reyes magos* ("the three wise men"). On the days leading up to January 6, Puerto Ricans have continuous celebrations. *Parrandiendo* (stopping by) is a practice similar to American and English caroling, in which neighbors go visiting house to house. Other major celebration days are *El Día de Las Raza* (The Day of the Race—Columbus Day) and *El Fiesta del Apostal Santiago* (St. James Day). Every June, Puerto Ricans in New York and other large cities celebrate Puerto Rican Day. The parades held on this day have come to rival St. Patrick's Day parades and celebrations in popularity.

HEALTH ISSUES

There are no documented health problems or mental health problems specific to Puerto Ricans. However, because of the low economic status of many Puerto Ricans, especially in mainland inner-city settings, the incidence of poverty-related health problems is a very real concern. AIDS, alcohol and drug dependency, and a lack of adequate health care coverage are the biggest health-related concerns facing the Puerto Rican community.

LANGUAGE

There is no such thing as a Puerto Rican language. Rather, Puerto Ricans speak proper Castillian Spanish, which is derived from ancient Latin. While Spanish uses the same Latin alphabet as English, the letters "k" and "w" occur only in foreign words. However, Spanish has three letters not found in English: "ch" ("chay"), "ll" ("EL-yay"), and "ñ" ("AYN-nyay"). Spanish uses word order, rather than noun and pronoun inflection, to encode meaning. In addition, the Spanish language tends to rely on diacritical markings such as the *tilda* (~) and the *accento* (´) much more than English.

The main difference between the Spanish spoken in Spain and the Spanish spoken in Puerto Rico (and other Latin American locales) is pronunciation. Differences in pronunciation are similar to the regional variations between American English in the southern United States and New England. Many Puerto Ricans have a unique tendency among Latin Americans to drop the "s" sound in casual conversation. The word *ustéd* (the proper form of the pronoun "you"), for instance, may be pronounced as "oo TED" rather than "oo STED." Like-

wise, the participial suffix "-ado" is often changed by Puerto Ricans. The word *cemado* (meaning "burned") is thus pronounced "ke MOW" rather than "ke MA do."

Although English is taught to most elementary school children in Puerto Rican public schools, Spanish remains the primary language on the island of Puerto Rico. On the mainland, many first-generation Puerto Rican migrants are less than fluent in English. Subsequent generations are often fluently bilingual, speaking English outside of the home and Spanish in the home. Bilingualism is especially common among young, urbanized, professional Puerto Ricans.

Long exposure of Puerto Ricans to American society, culture, and language has also spawned a unique slang that has come to be known among many Puerto Ricans as "Spanglish." It is a dialect that does not yet have formal structrure but its use in popular songs has helped spread terms as they are adopted. In New York itself the unique blend of languages is called Nuyorican. In this form of Spanglish, "New York" becomes *Nuevayork*, and many Puerto Ricans refer to themselves as *Nuevarriqueños*. Puerto Rican teenagers are as likely to attend *un pahry* (a party) as to attend a *fiesta*; children look forward to a visit from *Sahnta Close* on Christmas; and workers often have *un Beeg Mahk y una Coca-Cola* on their lunch breaks.

GREETINGS AND OTHER COMMON EXPRESSIONS

For the most part, Puerto Rican greetings are standard Spanish greetings: *Hola* ("OH lah")—Hello; ¿*Como está?* ("como eh-STAH")—How are you?; ¿*Que tal?* ("kay TAHL")—What's up; *Adiós* ("ah DYOSE")—Good-bye; *Por favór* ("pore fah-FORE")—Please; *Grácias* ("GRAH-syahs")—Thank you; *Buena suerte* ("BWE-na SWAYR-tay")—Good luck; *Feliz Año Nuevo* ("feh-LEEZ AHN-yoe NWAY-vo")—Happy New Year.

Some expressions, however, appear to be unique to Puerto Ricans. These include: *Mas enamorado que el cabro cupido* (More in love than a goat shot by Cupid's arrow; or, to be head over heels in love); *Sentado an el baúl* (Seated in a trunk; or, to be henpecked); and *Sacar el ratón* (Let the rat out of the bag; or, to get drunk).

FAMILY AND COMMUNITY DYNAMICS

Puerto Rican family and community dynamics have a strong Spanish influence and still tend to reflect

These enthusiastic
spectators are
watching the 1990
Puerto Rican Day
Parade in New
York City.

the intensely patriarchal social organization of European Spanish culture. Traditionally, husbands and fathers are heads of households and serve as community leaders. Older male children are expected to be responsible for younger siblings, especially females. *Machismo* (the Spanish conception of manhood) is traditionally a highly regarded virtue among Puerto Rican men. Women, in turn, are held responsible for the day-to-day running of the household.

Both Puerto Rican men and women care very much for their children and have strong roles in childrearing; children are expected to show *respeto* (respect) to parents and other elders, including older siblings. Traditionally, girls are raised to be quiet and diffident, and boys are raised to be more aggressive, though all children are expected to defer to elders and strangers. Young men initiate courtship, though dating rituals have for the most part become Americanized on the mainland. Puerto Ricans place a high value on the education of the young; on the island, Americanized public education is compulsory. And like most Latino groups, Puerto Ricans are traditionally opposed to divorce and birth out of wedlock.

Puerto Rican family structure is extensive; it is based on the Spanish system of *compadrazco* (literally "co-parenting") in which many members—not just parents and siblings—are considered to be part of the immediate family. Thus *los abuelos* (grandparents), and *los tios y las tias* (uncles and aunts) and even *los primos y las primas* (cousins) are considered extremely close relatives in the Puerto Rican family structure. Likewise, *los padrinos* (godparents) have a

special role in the Puerto Rican conception of the family: godparents are friends of a child's parents and serve as "second parents" to the child. Close friends often refer to each other as *compadre y comadre* to reinforce the familial bond.

Although the extended family remains standard among many Puerto Rican mainlanders and islanders, the family structure has suffered a serious breakdown in recent decades, especially among urban mainlander Puerto Ricans. This breakdown seems to have been precipitated by economic hardships among Puerto Ricans, as well as by the influence of America's social organization, which de-emphasizes the extended family and accords greater autonomy to children and women.

For Puerto Ricans, the home has special significance, serving as the focal point for family life. Puerto Rican homes, even in the mainland United States, thus reflect Puerto Rican cultural heritage to a great extent. They tend to be ornate and colorful, with rugs and gilt-framed paintings that often reflect a religious theme. In addition, rosaries, busts of *La Virgin* (the Virgin Mary) and other religious icons have a prominent place in the household. For many Puerto Rican mothers and grandmothers, no home is complete without a representation of the suffering of Jesús Christo and the Last Supper. As young people increasingly move into mainstream American culture, these traditions and many others seem to be waning, but only slowly over the last few decades.

INTERACTIONS WITH OTHERS

Because of the long history of intermarriage among Spanish, Indian, and African ancestry groups, Puerto Ricans are among the most ethnically and racially diverse people in Latin America. As a result, the relations between whites, blacks, and ethnic groups on the island—and to a somewhat lesser extent on the mainland—tend to be cordial.

This is not to say that Puerto Ricans fail to recognize racial variance. On the island of Puerto Rico, skin color ranges from black to fair, and there are many ways of describing a person's color. Light-skinned persons are usually referred to as *blanco* (white) or *rúbio* (blond). Those with darker skin who have Native American features are referred to as *indio*, or "Indian." A person with dark-colored skin, hair, and eyes—like the majority of the islanders—are referred to as *trigeño* (swarthy). Blacks have two designations: African Puerto Ricans are called people *de colór* or people "of color," while African Americans are referred to as *moreno*. The word *negro*, meaning "black," is quite common among Puerto Ricans, and is used today as a term of endearment for persons of any color.

RELIGION

Most Puerto Ricans are Roman Catholics. Catholicism on the island dates back to the earliest presence of the Spanish *conquistadors*, who brought Catholic missionaries to convert native Arawaks to Christianity and train them in Spanish customs and culture. For over 400 years, Catholicism was the island's dominant religion, with a negligible presence of Protestant Christians. That has changed over the last century. As recently as 1960, over 80 percent of Puerto Ricans identified themselves as Catholics. By the mid-1990s, according to U.S. Census Bureau statistics, that number had decreased to 70 percent. Nearly 30 percent of Puerto Ricans identify themselves as Protestants of various denominations, including Lutheran, Presbyterian, Methodist, Baptist, and Christian Scientist. The Protestant shift is about the same among mainlander Puerto Ricans. Although this trend may be attributable to the overwhelming influence of American culture on the island and among mainland Puerto Ricans, similar changes have been observed throughout the Caribbean and into the rest of Latin America.

Puerto Ricans who practice Catholicism observe traditional church liturgy, rituals, and traditions. These include belief in the Creed of the Apostles and adherence to the doctrine of papal infallibility. Puerto Rican Catholics observe the seven Catholic sacraments: Baptism, Eucharist, Confirmation, Penance, Matrimony, Holy Orders, and Anointing of the Sick. According to the dispensations of Vatican II, Puerto Ricans celebrate mass in vernacular Spanish as opposed to ancient Latin. Catholic churches in Puerto Rico are ornate, rich with candles, paintings, and graphic imagery: like other Latin Americans, Puerto Ricans seem especially moved by the Passion of Christ and place particular emphasis on representations of the Crucifixion.

Among Puerto Rican Catholics, a small minority actively practice some version of *santería* ("sahn-teh-REE-ah"), an African American pagan religion with roots in the Yoruba religion of western Africa. (A *santo* is a saint of the Catholic church who also corresponds to a Yoruban deity.) *Santería* is prominent throughout the Caribbean and in many places in the southern United States and has had a strong influence on Catholic practices on the island.

EMPLOYMENT AND ECONOMIC TRADITIONS

Early Puerto Rican migrants to the mainland, especially those settling in New York City, found jobs in service and industry sectors. Among women, garment industry work was the leading form of employment. Men in urban areas most often worked in the service industry, often at restaurant jobs—bussing tables, bartending, or washing dishes. Men also found work in steel manufacturing, auto assembly, shipping, meat packing, and other related industries. In the early years of mainland migration, a sense of ethnic cohesion, especially in New York City, was created by Puerto Rican men who held jobs of community significance: Puerto Rican barbers, grocers, barmen, and others provided focal points for the Puerto Rican community to gather in the city. Since the 1960s, some Puerto Ricans have been journeying to the mainland as temporary contract laborers—working seasonally to harvest crop vegetables in various states and then returning to Puerto Rico after harvest.

As Puerto Ricans have assimilated into mainstream American culture, many of the younger generations have moved away from New York City and other eastern urban areas, taking high-paying white-collar and professional jobs. Still, less than two percent of Puerto Rican families have a median income above $75,000.

In mainland urban areas, though, unemployment is rising among Puerto Ricans. According to 1990 U.S. Census Bureau statistics, 31 percent of all Puerto Rican men and 59 percent of all Puerto Rican women were not considered part of the American labor force. One reason for these alarming statistics may be the changing face of American employment options. The sort of manufacturing sector jobs that were traditionally held by Puerto Ricans, especially in the garment industry, have become increasingly scarce. Institutionalized racism and the rise in single-parent households in urban areas over the last two decades may also be factors in the employment crisis. Urban Puerto Rican unemployment—whatever its cause—has emerged as one of the greatest economic challenges facing Puerto Rican community leaders at the dawn of the twenty-first century.

POLITICS AND GOVERNMENT

Throughout the twentieth century, Puerto Rican political activity has followed two distinct paths— one focusing on accepting the association with the

United States and working within the American political system, the other pushing for full Puerto Rican independence, often through radical means. In the latter part of the nineteenth century, most Puerto Rican leaders living in New York City fought for Caribbean freedom from Spain in general and Puerto Rican freedom in particular. When Spain ceded control of Puerto Rico to the United States following the Spanish-American War, those freedom fighters turned to working for Puerto Rican independence from the States. Eugenio María de Hostos founded the League of Patriots to help smooth the transition from U.S. control to independence. Although full independence was never achieved, groups like the League paved the way for Puerto Rico's special relationship with the United States. Still, Puerto Ricans were for the most part blocked from wide participation in the American political system.

In 1913 New York Puerto Ricans helped establish *La Prensa*, a Spanish-language daily newspaper, and over the next two decades a number of Puerto Rican and Latino political organizations and groups—some more radical than others—began to form. In 1937 Puerto Ricans elected Oscar García Rivera to a New York City Assembly seat, making him New York's first elected official of Puerto Rican decent. There was some Puerto Rican support in New York City of radical activist Albizu Campos, who staged a riot in the Puerto Rican city of Ponce on the issue of independence that same year; 19 were killed in the riot, and Campos's movement died out.

The 1950s saw wide proliferation of community organizations, called *ausentes*. Over 75 such hometown societies were organized under the umbrella of *El Congresso de Pueblo* (the "Council of Hometowns"). These organizations provided services for Puerto Ricans and served as a springboard for activity in city politics. In 1959 the first New York City Puerto Rican Day parade was held. Many commentators viewed this as a major cultural and political "coming out" party for the New York Puerto Rican community.

Low participation of Puerto Ricans in electoral politics—in New York and elsewhere in the country—has been a matter of concern for Puerto Rican leaders. This trend is partly attributable to a nationwide decline in American voter turnout. Still, some studies reveal that there is a substantially higher rate of voter participation among Puerto Ricans on the island than on the U.S. mainland. A number of reasons for this have been offered. Some point to the low turnout of other ethnic minorities in U.S. communities. Others suggest that Puerto Ricans have never really been courted by either party in the American system. And still others suggest that the lack of opportunity and education for the migrant population has resulted in widespread political cynicism among Puerto Ricans. The fact remains, however, that the Puerto Rican population can be a major political force when organized.

INDIVIDUAL AND GROUP CONTRIBUTIONS

Although Puerto Ricans have only had a major presence on the mainland since the mid-twentieth century, they have made significant contributions to American society. This is especially true in the areas of the arts, literature, and sports. The following is a selected list of individual Puerto Ricans and some of their achievements.

ACADEMIA

Frank Bonilla is a political scientist and a pioneer of Hispanic and Puerto Rican Studies in the United States. He is the director of the City University of New York's Centro de Estudios Puertorriqueños and the author of numerous books and monographs. Author and educator Maria Teresa Babín (1910–) served as director of the University of Puerto Rico's Hispanic Studies Program. She also edited one of only two English anthologies of Puerto Rican literature.

ART

Olga Albizu (1924–) came to fame as a painter of Stan Getz's RCA record covers in the 1950s. She later became a leading figure in the New York City arts community. Other well-known contemporary and avant-garde visual artists of Puerto Rican descent include Rafael Ferre (1933–), Rafael Colón (1941–), and Ralph Ortíz (1934–).

MUSIC

Ricky Martin, born Enrique Martin Morales in Puerto Rico, began his career as a member of the teen singing group Menudo. He gained international fame at the 1999 Grammy Awards ceremony with his rousing performance of "La Copa de la Vida." His continued success, most notably with his single "La Vida Loca" was a major influence in the growing interest in new Latin beat styles among mainstream America in the late 1990s.

Marc Anthony (born Marco Antonio Muniz) gained renown both as an actor in films like *The Substitute* (1996), *Big Night* (1996), and *Bringing out* the Dead (1999) and as a top selling Salsa song writer and performer. Anthony has contributed hit songs to albums by other singers and recorded his first album, *The Night Is Over*, in 1991 in Latin hip hop-style. Some of his other albums reflect more of his Salsa roots and include *Otra Nota* in 1995 and *Contra La Corriente* in 1996.

BUSINESS

Deborah Aguiar-Veléz (1955–) was trained as a chemical engineer but became one of the most famous female entrepreneurs in the United States. After working for Exxon and the New Jersey Department of Commerce, Aguiar-Veléz founded Sistema Corp. In 1990 she was named the Outstanding Woman of the Year in Economic Development. John Rodriguez (1958–) is the founder of AD-One, a Rochester, New York-based advertising and public relations firm whose clients include Eastman Kodak, Bausch and Lomb, and the Girl Scouts of America.

FILM AND THEATER

San Juan-born actor Raúl Juliá (1940-1994), best known for his work in film, was also a highly regarded figure in the theater. Among his many film credits are *Kiss of the Spider Woman*, based on South American writer Manuel Puig's novel of the same name, *Presumed Innocent*, and the *Addams Family* movies. Singer and dance Rita Moreno (1935–), born Rosita Dolores Alverco in Puerto Rico, began working on Broadway at the age of 13 and hit Hollywood at age 14. She has earned numerous awards for her work in theater, film, and television. Miriam Colón (1945–) is New York City's first lady of Hispanic theater. She has also worked widely in film and television. José Ferrer (1912–), one of cinema's most distinguished leading men, earned a 1950 Academy Award for best actor in the film *Cyrano de Bergerac*.

Jennifer Lopez, born July 24, 1970 in the Bronx, is a dancer, an actress, and a singer, and has gained fame successively in all three areas. She began her career as a dancer in stage musicals and music videos and in the Fox Network TV show *In Living Color*. After a string of supporting roles in movies such as *Mi Familia* (1995) and *Money Train* (1995), Jennifer Lopez became the highest paid Latina actress in films when she was selected for the title role in *Selena* in 1997. She went on to act in *Anaconda* (1997), *U-turn* (1997), *Antz* (1998) and *Out Of Sight* (1998). Her first solo album, *On the 6*, released in 1999, produced a hit single, "If You Had My Love."

LITERATURE AND JOURNALISM

Jesús Colón (1901-1974) was the first journalist and short story writer to receive wide attention in English-language literary circles. Born in the small Puerto Rican town of Cayey, Colón stowed away on a boat to New York City at the age of 16. After working as an unskilled laborer, he began writing newspaper articles and short fiction. Colón eventually became a columnist for the *Daily Worker*; some of his works were later collected in *A Puerto Rican in New York and Other Sketches*. Nicholasa Mohr (1935–) is the only Hispanic American woman to write for major U.S. publishing houses, including Dell, Bantam, and Harper. Her books include *Nilda* (1973), *In Nueva York* (1977) and *Gone Home* (1986). Victor Hernández Cruz (1949–) is the most widely acclaimed of the Nuyorican poets, a group of Puerto Rican poets whose work focuses on the Latino world in New York City. His collections include *Mainland* (1973) and *Rhythm, Content, and Flavor* (1989). Tato Laviena (1950–), the best-selling Latino poet in the United States, gave a 1980 reading at the White House for U.S. President Jimmy Carter. Geraldo Rivera (1943–) has won ten Emmy Awards and a Peabody Award for his investigative journalism. Since 1987 this controversial media figure has hosted his own talk show, *Geraldo*.

POLITICS AND LAW

José Cabrenas (1949–) was the first Puerto Rican to be named to a federal court on the U.S. mainland. He graduated from Yale Law School in 1965 and received his LL.M. from England's Cambridge University in 1967. Cabrenas held a position in the Carter administration, and his name has since been raised for a possible U.S. Supreme Court nomination. Antonia Novello (1944–) was the first Hispanic woman to be named U.S. surgeon general. She served in the Bush administration from 1990 until 1993.

SPORTS

Roberto Walker Clemente (1934-1972) was born in Carolina, Puerto Rico, and played center field for the Pittsburgh Pirates from 1955 until his death in 1972. Clemente appeared in two World Series contests, was a four-time National League batting champion, earned MVP honors for the Pirates in 1966, racked up 12 Gold Glove awards for fielding, and was one of only 16 players in the history of the game to have over 3,000 hits. After his untimely death in a plane crash en route to aid earthquake victims in Central America, the Baseball Hall of

Fame waived the usual five-year waiting period and inducted Clemente immediately. Orlando Cepeda (1937–) was born in Ponce, Puerto Rico, but grew up in New York City, where he played sandlot baseball. He joined the New York Giants in 1958 and was named Rookie of the Year. Nine years later he was voted MVP for the St. Louis Cardinals. Angel Thomas Cordero (1942–), a famous name in the world of horseracing, is the fourth all-time leader in races won—and Number Three in the amount of money won in purses: $109,958,510 as of 1986. Sixto Escobar (1913–) was the first Puerto Rican boxer to win a world championship, knocking out Tony Matino in 1936. Chi Chi Rodriguez (1935–) is one of the best-known American golfers in the world. In a classic rags-to-riches story, he started out as a caddie in his hometown of Rio Piedras and went on to become a millionaire player. The winner of numerous national and world tournaments, Rodriguez is also known for his philanthropy, including his establishment of the Chi Chi Rodriguez Youth Foundation in Florida.

MEDIA

More than 500 U.S. newspapers, periodicals, newsletters, and directories are published in Spanish or have a significant focus on Hispanic Americans. More than 325 radio and television stations air broadcasts in Spanish, providing music, entertainment, and information to the Hispanic community.

PRINT

El Diario/La Prensa.
Published Monday through Friday, since 1913, this publication has focused on general news in Spanish.

Contact: Carlos D. Ramirez, Publisher.
Address: 143-155 Varick Street, New York, New York 10013.
Telephone: (718) 807-4600.
Fax: (212) 807-4617.

Hispanic.
Established in 1988, it covers Hispanic interests and people in a general editorial magazine format on a monthly basis.

Address: 98 San Jacinto Boulevard, Suite 1150, Austin, Texas 78701.
Telephone: (512) 320-1942.

Hispanic Business.
Established in 1979, this is a monthly English-language business magazine that caters to Hispanic professionals.

Contact: Jesus Echevarria, Publisher.
Address: 425 Pine Avenue, Santa Barbara, California 93117-3709.
Telephone: (805) 682-5843.
Fax: (805) 964-5539.
Online: http://www.hispanstar.com/hb/default.asp.

Hispanic Link Weekly Report.
Established in 1983, this is a weekly bilingual community newspaper covering Hispanic interests.

Contact: Felix Perez, Editor.
Address: 1420 N Street, N.W., Washington, D.C. 20005.
Telephone: (202) 234-0280.

Noticias del Mundo.
Established in 1980, this is a daily general Spanish-language newspaper.

Contact: Bo Hi Pak, Editor.
Address: Philip Sanchez Inc., 401 Fifth Avenue, New York, New York 10016.
Telephone: (212) 684-5656.

Vista.
Established in September 1985, this monthly magazine supplement appears in major daily English-language newspapers.

Contact: Renato Perez, Editor.
Address: 999 Ponce de Leon Boulevard, Suite 600, Coral Gables, Florida 33134.
Telephone: (305) 442-2462.

RADIO

Caballero Radio Network.
Contact: Eduardo Caballero, President.
Address: 261 Madison Avenue, Suite 1800, New York, New York 10016.
Telephone: (212) 697-4120.

CBS Hispanic Radio Network.
Contact: Gerardo Villacres, General Manager.
Address: 51 West 52nd Street, 18th Floor, New York, New York 10019.
Telephone: (212) 975-3005.

Lotus Hispanic Radio Network.
Contact: Richard B. Kraushaar, President.
Address: 50 East 42nd Street, New York, New York 10017.
Telephone: (212) 697-7601.

WHCR-FM (90.3).

Public radio format, operating 18 hours daily with Hispanic news and contemporary programming.

Contact: Frank Allen, Program Director.
Address: City College of New York, 138th and Covenant Avenue, New York, New York 10031.
Telephone: (212) 650-7481.

WKDM-AM (1380).

Independent Hispanic hit radio format with continuous operation.

Contact: Geno Heinemeyer, General Manager.
Address: 570 Seventh Avenue, Suite 1406, New York, New York 10018.
Telephone: (212) 564-1380.

TELEVISION

Galavision.

Hispanic television network.

Contact: Jamie Davila, Division President.
Address: 2121 Avenue of the Stars, Suite 2300, Los Angeles, California 90067.
Telephone: (310) 286-0122.

Telemundo Spanish Television Network.
Contact: Joaquin F. Blaya, President.
Address: 1740 Broadway, 18th Floor, New York, New York 10019-1740.
Telephone: (212) 492-5500.

Univision.

Spanish-language television network, offering news and entertainment programming.

Contact: Joaquin F. Blaya, President.
Address: 605 Third Avenue, 12th Floor, New York, New York 10158-0180.
Telephone: (212) 455-5200.

WCIU-TV, Channel 26.

Commercial television station affiliated with the Univision network.

Contact: Howard Shapiro, Station Manager.
Address: 141 West Jackson Boulevard, Chicago, Illinois 60604.
Telephone: (312) 663-0260.

WNJU-TV, Channel 47.

Commercial television station affiliated with Telemundo.

Contact: Stephen J. Levin, General Manager.

Address: 47 Industrial Avenue, Teterboro, New Jersey 07608.
Telephone: (201) 288-5550.

ORGANIZATIONS AND ASSOCIATIONS

Association for Puerto Rican-Hispanic Culture.
Founded in 1965. Seeks to expose people of various ethnic backgrounds and nationalities to cultural values of Puerto Ricans and Hispanics. Focuses on music, poetry recitals, theatrical events, and art exhibits.

Contact: Peter Bloch.
Address: 83 Park Terrace West, New York, New York 10034.
Telephone: (212) 942-2338.

Council for Puerto Rico-U.S. Affairs.
Founded in 1987, the council was formed to help create a positive awareness of Puerto Rico in the United States and to forge new links between the mainland and the island.

Contact: Roberto Soto.
Address: 14 East 60th Street, Suite 605, New York, New York 10022.
Telephone: (212) 832-0935.

National Association for Puerto Rican Civil Rights (NAPRCR).
Addresses civil rights issues concerning Puerto Ricans in legislative, labor, police, and legal and housing matters, especially in New York City.

Contact: Damaso Emeric, President.
Address: 2134 Third Avenue, New York, New York 10035.
Telephone: (212) 996-9661.

National Conference of Puerto Rican Women (NACOPRW).
Founded in 1972, the conference promotes the participation of Puerto Rican and other Hispanic women in social, political, and economic affairs in the United States and in Puerto Rico. Publishes the quarterly *Ecos Nationales*.

Contact: Ana Fontana.
Address: 5 Thomas Circle, N.W., Washington, D.C. 20005.
Telephone: (202) 387-4716.

National Council of La Raza.
Founded in 1968, this Pan-Hispanic organization provides assistance to local Hispanic groups, serves

as an advocate for all Hispanic Americans, and is a national umbrella organization for 80 formal affiliates throughout the United States.

Address: 810 First Street, N.E., Suite 300, Washington, D.C. 20002.
Telephone: (202) 289-1380.

National Puerto Rican Coalition (NPRC).

Founded in 1977, the NPRC advances the social, economic, and political well-being of Puerto Ricans. It evaluates the potential impact of legislative and government proposals and policies affecting the Puerto Rican community and provides technical assistance and training to start-up Puerto Rican organizations. Publishes *National Directory of Puerto Rican Organizations; Bulletin; Annual Report.*

Contact: Louis Nuñez, President.
Address: 1700 K Street, N.W., Suite 500, Washington, D.C. 20006.
Telephone: (202) 223-3915.
Fax: (202) 429-2223.

National Puerto Rican Forum (NPRF).

Concerned with the overall improvement of Puerto Rican and Hispanic communities throughout the United States

Contact: Kofi A. Boateng, Executive Director.
Address: 31 East 32nd Street, Fourth Floor, New York, New York 10016-5536.
Telephone: (212) 685-2311.
Fax: (212) 685-2349.
Online: http://www.nprf.org/.

Puerto Rican Family Institute (PRFI).

Established for the preservation of the health, well-being, and integrity of Puerto Rican and Hispanic families in the United States.

Contact: Maria Elena Girone, Executive Director.
Address: 145 West 15th Street, New York, New York 10011.
Telephone: (212) 924-6320.
Fax: (212) 691-5635.

MUSEUMS AND RESEARCH CENTERS

Brooklyn College of the City University of New York Center for Latino Studies.

Research institute centered on the study of Puerto Ricans in New York and Puerto Rico. Focuses on history, politics, sociology, and anthropology.

Contact: Maria Sanchez.
Address: 1205 Boylen Hall, Bedford Avenue at Avenue H, Brooklyn, New York 11210.
Telephone: (718) 780-5561.

Hunter College of the City University of New York Centro de Estudios Puertorriqueños.

Founded in 1973, it is the first university-based research center in New York City designed specifically to develop Puerto Rican perspectives on Puerto Rican problems and issues.

Contact: Juan Flores, Director.
Address: 695 Park Avenue, New York, New York 10021.
Telephone: (212) 772-5689.
Fax: (212) 650-3673.
E-mail: hcordero@shiva.hunter.cuny.edu.

Institute of Puerto Rican Culture, Archivo General de Puerto Rico.

Maintains extensive archival holdings relating to the history of Puerto Rico.

Contact: Carmen Davila.
Address: 500 Ponce de León, Suite 4184, San Juan, Puerto Rico 00905.
Telephone: (787) 725-5137.
Fax: (787) 724-8393.

PRLDEF Institute for Puerto Rican Policy.

The Institute for Puerto Rican Policy merged with the Puerto Rican Legal Defense and Education Fund in 1999. In September of 1999 a website was in progress but unfinished.

Contact: Angelo Falcón, Director.
Address: 99 Hudson Street, 14th Floor, New York, New York 10013-2815.
Telephone: (212) 219-3360 ext. 246.
Fax: (212) 431-4276.
E-mail: ipr@iprnet.org.

Puerto Rican Culture Institute, Luis Muñoz Rivera Library and Museum.

Founded in 1960, it houses collections that emphasize literature and art; institute supports research into the cultural heritage of Puerto Rico.

Address: 10 Muñoz Rivera Street, Barranquitas, Puerto Rico 00618.
Telephone: (787) 857-0230.

SOURCES FOR ADDITIONAL STUDY

Alvarez, Maria D. *Puerto Rican Children on the Mainland: Interdisciplinary Perspectives*. New York: Garland Pub., 1992.

Dietz, James L. *Economic History of Puerto Rico: Institutional Change and Capitalist Development*. Princeton, New Jersey: Princeton University Press, 1986.

Falcón, Angelo. *Puerto Rican Political Participation: New York City and Puerto Rico*. Institute for Puerto Rican Policy, 1980.

Fitzpatrick, Joseph P. *Puerto Rican Americans: The Meaning of Migration to the Mainland*. Englewood Cliffs, New Jersey: Prentice Hall, 1987.

————. *The Stranger Is Our Own: Reflections on the Journey of Puerto Rican Migrants*. Kansas City, Missouri: Sheed & Ward, 1996.

Growing up Puerto Rican: An Anthology, edited by Joy L. DeJesus. New York: Morrow, 1997.

Hauberg, Clifford A. *Puerto Rico and the Puerto Ricans*. New York: Twayne, 1975.

Perez y Mena, Andres Isidoro. *Speaking with the Dead: Development of Afro-Latin Religion Among Puerto Ricans in the United States: A Study into Interpenetration of Civilizations in the New World*. New York: AMS Press, 1991.

Puerto Rico: A Political and Cultural History, edited by Arturo Morales Carrion. New York: Norton, 1984.

Urciuoli, Bonnie. *Exposing Prejudice: Puerto Rican Experiences of Language, Race, and Class*. Boulder, CO: Westview Press, 1996.

After the Revolution
of December 1989,
which brought an end
to Communism in
Romania, thousands
of new immigrants of
all ages came to the
United States, and
new arrivals (legal
and illegal) continue
to enter the country.

ROMANIAN AMERICANS

by
Vladimir F. Wertsman

OVERVIEW

Romania is a country slightly smaller than the state of Oregon, measuring 91,699 square miles (237,500 square kilometers). Located in southeastern Europe, it is bounded by the Ukraine and Slovakia to the north, Bulgaria to the south, Serbia to the southwest, Moldavia and the Black Sea to the east, and Hungary to the west. Although the majority of Romanian Americans immigrated from Romania, several thousand families also came from countries bordering or adjacent to Romania, such as Moldova and Albania.

Romania has a population of slightly over 23 million people. Eighty-eight percent are of Romanian ethnic origin while the rest consist of various ethnic minorities, including Hungarians, Germans, Serbians, Bulgarians, Gypsies, and Armenians. Eighty percent of the population nominally belong to the Romanian Orthodox Church, and approximately ten percent are Catholics of the Byzantine Rite. Other religious denominations represented in Romania include Seventh-Day Adventists, Baptists, Lutherans, Presbyterians, and Unitarians, as well as the Judaic and Islamic faiths. The country's official language is Romanian, and its capital city is Bucharest. Romania's national flag consists of three large stripes (red, yellow, and blue) arranged vertically.

HISTORY

The name Romania, which means "New Rome" in Latin, was given by Roman colonists after Emperor Trajan (c.53-117 A.D.) and his legions crossed the Danube River and conquered Dacia (an ancient province located in present-day Transylvania and the Carpathian Mountain region) in 106 A.D. Although Roman occupation of Dacia ended in 271 A.D., the relationship between the Romans and Dacians flourished; mixed marriages and the adoption of Latin culture and language gradually molded the Romans and Dacians into a distinct ethnic entity. The ancestors of the modern Romanian people managed to preserve their Latin heritage despite Gothic, Slavic, Greek, Hungarian, and Turkish conquests, and the Romanian language has survived as a member of the Romance languages group.

Romania has been subjected to numerous occupations by foreign powers since the Middle Ages. In the thirteenth century, the Romanian principalities Moldavia and Wallachia became vassal states of the Ottoman Empire. Bukovina, Transylvania, and Banat were incorporated into the Austro-Hungarian Empire during the 1700s. Czarist Russia occupied Bessarabia in 1812. In 1859 Moldavia and Wallachia became unified through the auspices of the Paris Peace Conference, and Romania became a national state. At the Congress of Berlin in 1878 Romania obtained full independence from the Ottoman Empire but lost Bessarabia to Russia. In 1881, Romania was proclaimed a kingdom and Carol I (1839-1914) was installed as its first monarch.

MODERN ERA

Following the death of Carol I, his nephew, Ferdinand (1865-1927), became king and led the country into World War I against the Central Powers. Romania regained Transylvania, Banat, Bukovina and other territories after the war. In 1940, Carol II (1893-1953) was named General Ion Antonescu (1882-1946) premier of Romania, who then forced the monarch to renounce his throne in favor of his son, Michael I (1921–). Under Antonescu's influence, Romania became an ally of Nazi Germany during World War II and fought against the Soviet Union. In the last year of the war, however, Romania switched its alliance to the Soviets and, after the war ended, Antonescu was executed. In national elections held in 1947, members of the Communist party assumed many high-level positions in the new government, and King Michael I was forced to abdicate his throne. Gheorghe Gheorghiu-Dej (1901-1965) of the Romanian Communist party

served as premier (1952-1955) and later as chief of state (1961-1965). Two years after Gheroghiu-Dej's death, Nicholae Ceauşescu (1918-1989), a high-ranking Communist official, assumed the presidency of Romania.

On December 22, 1989, the Communist regime was overthrown and Ceauşescu was executed on Christmas Day. In the post-Communist years, various changes have occurred, including a free press, free elections, and a multi-party electorate bringing to power a democratic government (President Emil Constantinescu, 1996–). The pace of transforming Romania's economy into a market economy accelerated, and improved relations with the United States, Canada and other Western countries were promoted. Romania also petitioned to become a member of NATO, and its candidacy will be considered in the year 2002.

THE FIRST ROMANIANS IN AMERICA

Romanians have a recorded presence of almost 250 years on American soil. In the late eighteenth century, a Transylvanian priest named Samuel Damian immigrated to America for scientific reasons. Damian conducted various experiments with electricity and even caught the attention of Benjamin Franklin (they met and had a conversation in Latin). After living in South Carolina for a few years, Damian left for Jamaica and disappeared from historical record. In 1849, a group of Romanians came to California during the Gold Rush but, being unsuccessful, migrated to Mexico. Romanians continued to immigrate to America during this period and some distinguished themselves in the Union Army during the Civil War. George Pomutz (1818-1882) joined the Fifteenth Volunteer Regiment of Iowa and fought at such battlefields as Shiloh, Corinth, and Vicksburg, and was later promoted to the rank of Brigadier General. Nicholas Dunca (1825-1862), a captain serving in the Ninth Volunteer Regiment of New York, died in the battle of Cross Keyes, Virginia. Another Romanian-born soldier, Eugen Teodoresco, died in the Spanish-American War in 1898.

SIGNIFICANT IMMIGRATION WAVES

The first major wave of Romanian immigrants to the United States took place between 1895 and 1920, in which 145,000 Romanians entered the country. They came from various regions, including Wallachia and Moldavia. The majority of these immigrants—particularly those from Transylvania and Banat—were unskilled laborers who left their native regions because of economic depression and forced assimilation, a policy practiced by Hungarian rulers. They were attracted to the economic stability of the United States, which promised better wages and improved working conditions. Many did not plan to establish permanent residency in America, intending instead to save enough money to return to Romania and purchase land. Consequently, tens of thousands of Romanian immigrants who achieved this goal left the United States within a few years, and by 1920 the Romanian American population was approximately 85,000.

Between 1921 and 1939, the number of Romanians entering the United States declined for several reasons. Following World War I, Transylvania, Bukovina, Bessarabia, and other regions under foreign rule officially became part of Romania, thus arresting emigration for a time. In addition, the U.S. Immigration Act of 1924 established a quota system which allowed only 603 persons per year to immigrate from Romania. The Great Depression added to the decline of new Romanian immigrants to the United States; immigration figures reached their lowest level at the beginning of World War II. Romanians who did enter the country during this period, however, included students, professionals, and others who later made notable contributions to American society.

A new surge of immigrants to the United States was generated by the threat of Nazi occupation of Romania during World War II. When the Communists assumed control of the country in 1947 they imposed many political, economic, and social restrictions on the Romanian people. Refugees (who had left the country as a result of persecutions, arrests, or fear of being mistreated) and exiles (who were already abroad and chose not to return to Romania) were admitted into the United States through the auspices of the Displaced Persons Act of 1947 and other legislation passed to help absorb the flood of refugees and other immigrants from postwar Europe. Because of the abrupt and dramatic nature of their departure, the refugees and exiles (estimated at about 30,000) received special moral and financial support from various Romanian organizations—religious and secular—in America. These immigrants infused an important contingent of professionals, including doctors, lawyers, writers, and engineers into the Romanian American community, and were also more active politically. They established new organizations and churches, and fought against Communist rule in their homeland.

After the Revolution of December 1989, which brought an end to Communism in Romania, thousands of new immigrants of all ages came to the United States, and new arrivals (legal and illegal) continue to enter the country. The elimination of Communist travel restrictions, the desire of thousands of people to be reunited with their American relatives and friends, and the precarious economic conditions in the new Romania were powerful incentives to come to America for a new start in life. Among the newcomers were professionals, former political prisoners, and others who were disenchanted with the new leadership in Romania. There were also many Romanian tourists who decided to remain in America. Many of these immigrants spoke English and adjusted relatively well, even if they took lower-paying jobs than those to which their credentials or experience entitled them. However, others found neither employment nor understood the job hunting process, and returned to Romania. Still others left the United States to try their luck in Canada or South America. Those who chose to return to Europe settled in Germany, France, or Italy. According to the 1990 U.S. Census, there were approximately 365,544 people of Romanian ancestry living in the United States.

Because early Romanian immigrants were either peasants or laborers, they settled in the major industrial centers of the East and Midwest and took unskilled jobs in factories. The heaviest concentrations of Romanian Americans can be found in New York, New Jersey, Pennsylvania, Ohio, Illinois, Michigan, and Indiana. A substantial number of Romanians also settled in Florida and California. Living near the factories where they worked, first-generation Romanian Americans established communities which often consisted of extended families or of those who had migrated from the same region in Romania. Second- and third-generation Romanian Americans, having achieved financial security and social status, gradually moved out of the old neighborhoods, settling either in suburban areas or in larger cities, or relocating to another state. Consequently, there are few Romanian American communities left that preserve the social fabric of the first-generation neighborhoods.

ROMANIANS FROM THE REPUBLIC OF MOLDOVA

While most Romanian-Americans immigrated from Romania, a significant number also arrived from countries adjacent to or bordering Romania. The Republic of Moldova, known as Bessarabia before World War II, is in fact a second Romanian country. Sandwiched between Romania and the Ukraine, it occupies an area of 13,010 square miles (33,700 square kilometers). Its capital is Chisinau (pronounced Keesheenau) and the President of Moldova is Petru Lucinschi. The population of 4.5 million consists of 65% Romanians, 14% Ukrainians, 13% Russians, 4% Gagauz (Turks of Christian faith), and 2% Bulgarians. There are also smaller groups of Poles, Belorusans, Germans and Gypsies. While 98% of the population are Eastern Orthodox believers, some Moldavians are Protestant and Jewish. The official language of Moldova is Romanian (with a Moldavian dialect), and the second language is Russian. The country's flag is the same as Romania's: red, yellow, and blue vertical stripes.

During the Middle Ages, Bessarabia was an integral part of the Romanian principality of Moldavia, but it later became a tributary to the Ottoman Empire. In 1812, following the Russian-Turkish War (1806-1812), Bessarabia was annexed by Tsarist Russia until the 1917 October Revolution. In 1918, as a result of the Romanian population majority vote, Bessarabia was reunited with Romania, but in 1940, the Soviet Union, in a pact with Nazi Germany, gained control of the land. During 1941-1944, Romania recaptured the territory, but lost it one more time at the conclusion of World War II, when the Soviet Union incorporated Bessarabia under the name of the Moldovan Soviet Socialist Republic. After the fall of Communism, in 1991 the country became independent, and took the name of the Republic of Moldova. It underwent various changes (free elections, a multi-party system of government, economic reforms) before reaching an understanding in 1996 with separatist movements in two regions, Dnestr, and Gagauzia. There was also a movement for reunification with Romania, but the majority of the population opted for independence.

Immigrants from Moldova who came to America before World War II, as well as those who arrived later (about 5,000 in the 1990s) consider themselves members of the Romanian American community, using the same language, worshiping in the same Eastern Orthodox churches and preserving the same heritage. They are also fully integrated in Romanian American organizations and support the reunification of their land of origin with Romania.

MACEDO-ROMANIANS FROM BALCANIC COUNTRIES
Macedo-Romanians, also called Aromanians or Vlachs, live mostly in Albania, although they also live in Greece and Macedonia. In addition, they have lived in Yugoslavia and Bulgaria for over 2,000 years. Their history goes back to the first and second centuries A.D., when the Roman Empire included the territories of today's Romania and neighboring

Balcanic countries. It is estimated that there are about 600,000 to 700,000 Macedo-Romanians in the above mentioned countries. They know the Romanian language, but they also use their own dialect consisting of many archaisms, characteristic regional expressions and foreign influences. Macedo-Romanians consider themselves Romanian, and belong to the same Eastern Orthodox Church. In the United States, there are about 5,000 Macedo-Romanians, settled mostly in the states of Connecticut, New York, Rhode Island, New Jersey and Missouri. The first wave of immigration took place at the beginning of the twentieth century, while a second wave was recorded after World War II, and family reunifications continue to this day.

Macedo-Romanians are characterized by their hard work, the high esteem in which they keep their families and the value they place on education. They adjusted well to American life, and preserved their cultural heritage via their own organizations, ranging from Perivolea (1905-) in New York, to the Congress of Romanian-Macedonian Culture (1985-) presided by Prof. Aureliu Ciufecu of Fairfield, CT, and the Armanimea/Aromainianship (1993-) led by poet Zahu Pana. Macedo-Romanians also have their own publishing house, "Cartea Aromana" (The Aromanian Book), editor: T. Cunia, in Fayetteville, New York. It reprints Macedo-Romanian authors before World War II, and also publishes new authors. Although the younger generation of Macedo-Romanians are proud of their heritage, they display strong trends of assimilation, and tend to use English more than the language of their ancestors.

Romanian and Jewish American Regina Kohn was permitted to enter the United States because her violin playing so impressed immigration authorities at Ellis Island that they deemed her an artist. This photograph was taken on December 28, 1923.

ACCULTURATION AND ASSIMILATION

While researching data for her doctoral dissertation on Romanian Americans in 1929, Christine Galitzi Avghi, herself a Romanian, observed that "Romanians in the United States constitute a picturesque, sturdy group of newly made Americans of whom altogether too little is known" (Christine Galitzi Aughi, *A Study of Assimilation among the Romanians in the United States* [New York: Columbia University Press, 1929]; reprinted in 1969). Indeed, in the past, insufficient knowledge of Romanian ethnic characteristics generated various misconceptions in America. Some authors, such as Wayne Charles Miller, in his *A Comprehensive Bibliography for the Study of American Minorities* (1976), erroneously considered Romanians Slavs because Romania borders several Slavic countries. Other immigration

"**I** never really knew how much my ethnic background meant to me until the Romanian Revolution a few years ago. I was never ashamed of my background, I just never boldly stated it. I guess because I live in America I thought that I was just an American, period."

Veronica Buza, "My Ethnic Experience" in *Romanian American Heritage Center Information Bulletin,* September-October 1993.

studies, including Carl Wittke's *We Who Built America: The Saga of the Immigrant* (1939; revised 1967) and Joseph Hutchmacher's *A Nation of Newcomers* (1967) completely overlooked Romanians when discussing immigrants from Eastern Europe. In *American Fever: The Story of American Immigration* (1967), Barbara Kaye Greenleaf stereotyped Romanians as wearing sheepskin coats "during all seasons" even though such coats are worn by farmers and shepherds only in the winter. Romanians who had originally come from Transylvania with ethnic Hungarians (Transylvania was under Hungarian rule before World War I) were also greatly misunderstood. For some Americans, the mere mention of Transylvania and Romania evoked Hollywood images of vampires and werewolves as depicted in several film adaptations of Bram Stoker's novel *Dracula* (1897). Such misconceptions did not deter Romanian ethnic pride, however, which reached its peak during World War II. Today, as other groups are reaffirming their cultural past, Romanian Americans are doing the same.

TRADITIONS, CUSTOMS, AND BELIEFS

Romanians have a variety of traditions and lore dating back to antiquity. For example, on certain days some farmers would not cut anything with shears so that wolves will not injure their sheep. Tuesdays were considered unlucky days to start a journey or to initiate important business. A plague could be averted by burning a shirt which has been spun, woven, and sewn in less than 24 hours. Girls would not fill their pitchers with water from a well without breathing upon it first and pouring some of it on the ground (a libation to the nymph of the well). Before serving wine, drops were poured on the floor to honor the souls of the dead. A woman who did not want children would be tortured in hell. A black cat crossing in front of a pedestrian would bring bad luck. An owl seen on the roof of a house, in a courtyard, or in a tree was a sign of forthcoming bad luck, including death in the family. Such superstitions were gradually forgotten as Romanian immigrants became acculturated into American society.

PROVERBS

A wealth of proverbs from Romanian culture have survived through generations: "A good book can take place of a friend, but a friend cannot replace a good book"; "Whether homes are big or small, a child is a blessing to all"; "The cheapest article is advice, the most valuable is a good example"; "Do not leave an old good friend of yours just to please a new one"; "One thing for sure, each couple can tell, one's home is both paradise and hell"; "Idleness is the biggest enemy of good luck"; "Knowledge is like a tower in which you test and build your power"; "Modesty is the dearest jewel of a man's soul"; and "Enjoy drinking the wine, but do not become drunk by it."

CUISINE

Romanian cuisine is savory, flavorful, and stimulating to the appetite. Herbs and vegetables are used in abundance, and one-dish meals occupy an important place in the repertoire of recipes. These dishes are very nourishing, inexpensive, and easy to prepare. Romanian Americans enjoy cooking, often modifying old country recipes or creating new dishes. *Mamaliga* ("mamalíga"), considered a national dish, is a corn mush eaten with butter, cheese, meats, and even with marmalade or fruit jelly as a dessert. *Ciorba* ("chiórbá") is a popular sour soup, seasoned with sauerkraut or pickled cucumber juice. It contains onions, parsnip, parsley root, rice, and ground beef mixed with pork, and is served after the boiled vegetables are removed. *Gratar* ("gratár") is a steak (usually pork) accompanied by pickled cucumbers and tomatoes and combined with other grilled meats. Garlic is a major ingredient used in preparing the steak. *Mititei* ("meeteetáy"), which is similar to hamburgers, consists of ground beef rolled into cylindrical forms and seasoned with garlic, and is often served with *gratar*.

Sarmale ("sarmálay") is a stuffed cabbage dish prepared with pork shoulder, rice, black pepper, and chopped onion. *Ghiveci* ("gyvéch") is a vegetable stew containing carrots, potatoes, tomatoes, green pepper, onions, celery roots, eggplant, squash, string-beans, fresh peas, cabbage, and cauliflower. *Cozonac* ("kozonák") and *torte* ("tortáy") are various forms of cakes served as desserts. *Ţuica* ("tsúika") is a brandy made from plums or wheat. *Vin* ("veen") is wine and *bere* ("báyray") is beer. Romanian hosts and host-esses usually serve salads in a variety of shapes and compositions as entre dishes. Christmas dinner often consists of ham, sausages, pastry, fruits, *bere, vin*, and a special bread called *colac* ("kolák"). At Easter, lamb, ham, sausages, breads, and painted Easter eggs are prepared, and *vin* and *bere* accompany the feast.

TRADITIONAL COSTUMES

Romanian traditional, or peasant costumes, are made from handwoven linen. Women wear embroidered white blouses and black skirts (or another color, according to region) which cover the knees. The costume is completed with headscarves of various colors (older women usually wear black scarves) arranged according to age and regional traditions. The traditional costume for men consists of tight-fitting white pants, a white embroidered shirt worn over the pants that almost reaches the knees, and a wide leather or cotton belt. Men wear several types of hats according to season; black or grey elongated lambskin hats are customary during the winter and straw hats are usually worn during the summer. On festive occasions, men wear black or grey felt hats adorned with a flower or feather. Moccasins are traditional footwear for both men and women, while boots (with various adornments according to regional traditions) are worn by men. Romanian Americans wear their national costumes only on special occasions, either on national holidays celebrated in churches, at social gatherings, or while performing at local ethnic festivals.

DANCES AND SONGS

During special occasions, dancers perform the *hora* ("khóra"), a national dance in which men and women hold hands in a circle; the *sîrba* ("sýrba"), a quick, spirited dance; and the *invârtite* ("ynvyrtée-tay"), a pair dance. These dances are accompanied by popular shoutings (sometimes with humorous connotations) spoken by the leader of the dance who also invites members of the audience to join the dancers. The orchestra consists of fiddles, clarinets, trumpets, flutes, bagpipes and panpipes, drums, and the *cobza* ("kóbza"), an instrument resembling a guitar and mandolin. Popular songs are traditionally performed during social reunions both in America and Romania. The *doina* ("dóiyna"), for example, are multi-verse tunes evoking nostalgic emotions, from a shepherd's loneliness in the mountains to patriotic sentiments. The *romanţa* ("romántsa") is a romantic melody expressing deep feelings of affection.

HOLIDAYS

In addition to Christmas Day, New Year's Day, and Easter Day, Romanian Americans celebrate the birthday of the Romanian national state on January 24 and Transylvania's reunification with Romania on December 1. Romanian Americans with pro-monarchist views also celebrate May 10, which marks the ascension of Carol I to the Romanian throne. During these festivities, celebrants sing the Romanian national anthem, "Awake Thee, Romanian," written by Andrei Muresanu (1816-1863), a noted poet and patriot. Monarchists sing the Romanian royal anthem which begins with the words "Long live the king in peace and honor." A semi-official holiday similar to Valentine's Day is celebrated by lovers and friends on March 1, when a white or red silk flower (often hand-made) is presented as an expression of love.

HEALTH ISSUES

There are no documented health problems or medical conditions that are specific to Romanian Americans. Many families have health insurance coverage underwritten by the Union and League of Romanian Societies in America or by other ethnic organizations. Like most Americans, Romanian American business owners and professionals in private practice are insured at their own expense, while employees benefit from their employers' health plans when available.

LANGUAGE

The Romanian language is a Romance language derived from Latin that has survived despite foreign influences (Slavic, Turkish, Greek, and others). In fact, it has many Latin words that are not found in other Romance languages, and is more grammatically complex. Although Romanian uses the Latin alphabet, the letters "k," "q," "w," and "y" appear only in foreign words. In addition, Romanian has specific diacritical marks: "ā," "â," "í," "ṭ," "ṣ." Romanians consider their language sweet and harmonious, bringing "honey to the mouth," and are proud of its Latin origin.

For first-generation Romanian immigrants—regardless of the period they arrived in America—Romanian was the primary language. In a very short time, however, such American words as "supermarket," "basement," "streetcar," "laundry," "high school," and "subway" became infused in daily speech; thus, Romanian has evolved into an "Americanized" Romanian. Subsequent generations generally have spoken Romanian less often, eventually switching to English as their principal language. Romanian church services (including Sunday school) are still conducted in Romanian. In several cities, radio programs are broadcast in Romanian, and there are numerous Romanian-language newspapers and periodicals in circulation.

GREETINGS AND OTHER POPULAR EXPRESSIONS

Common Romanian greetings and other expressions include: *Bunā seara* ("bóona seàra")—Good evening; *Bunā ziua* ("bóona zéeoóa")—Good day; *Salut* ("salóot")—Greetings, hello; *La revedere* ("la rayvaydáyray")—Good-bye; *Noroc bun* ("norók bóon")—Good luck; *Mulṭumesc* ("mooltsóomesk")—Thank you; *Felicitāri* ("feleecheetáry") —Congratulations; *La multzi ani* ("la múltzi ánee")—Happy New Year; *Sárbātori fericite* "(sarbatóry fayreechéetay")—Happy Holidays (this greeting is used at Christmas time, for there is no expression like Merry Christmas in Romanian); *Hristos a inviat* ("Khristós a ynveeât")—Christ has Risen (a greeting used at Easter), the reply is *Adevārat a inviat* ("adevarát a ynveeát")—In truth He has risen; *Sānātate* ("sanatátay")—To your health, (spoken when raising a toast).

FAMILY AND COMMUNITY DYNAMICS

During the first three decades of the twentieth century, the Romanian American family underwent profound changes. The first immigrants were typically single males or married men who had left their families behind temporarily in order to save enough money to send for them later. They lived in crowded boarding houses and often slept on the floors. On Sundays and holidays, they congregated in saloons or restaurants and at church. Later, Romanian immigrants gathered at the headquarters of mutual aid societies and fraternal organizations where they discussed news from Romania, read or wrote letters, and sang religious or popular songs. Meanwhile, the boarding houses evolved into cooperatives in which a boarder provided his own bed and shared all operating expenses (rent, utilities, food, and laundry services) with the other residents.

As Romanian immigrants became better accustomed to the American way of life, they adopted higher standards of living, prepared more nutritious meals, and engaged in such recreational activities as sports and movie-going. Since most women worked outside the home, economic conditions gradually improved, and the immigrants were able to purchase a home, cars, and modern appliances, or were able to rent larger apartments in more prosperous neighborhoods. The typical Romanian household features Romanian embroidery or rugs, the Romanian flag, and other cultural icons, which are displayed in a common area.

Romanians have always held the family in high esteem and are generally opposed to divorce. Although the first wave of immigrants consisted of large families, subsequent generations chose to have fewer children, a trend that could be attributed to economic factors. Early immigrants cared very much for their children, did not permit child labor, and instilled in their children the importance of education. While approximately 33 percent of the Romanian immigrants who came to America before World War I were illiterate, many of them managed to learn English or improve their education to obtain or to hold jobs. Encouraged by their parents, second-generation Romanian Americans placed more emphasis on vocational training and college education.

While maintaining their place in the industries where their parents worked, second-generation Romanian Americans gradually switched from unskilled to skilled occupations. Others became white collar workers, and many embraced professional careers. Subsequent generations went even further in their educational and professional pursuits. Romanian Americans made such progress that for several decades few of the adult members of this group had less than a high school education. The professional ranks of Romanians (those educated at American universities) were substantially enlarged by the thousands of professionals who immigrated to the United States after World War II, and in the years following the Revolution of 1989. As a result,

Romanian Americans were able to make many significant contributions to American society.

WEDDINGS

The bridal shower, a social custom that was never practiced in Romania, has evolved into an often gala affair attended by both sexes. Prior to the wedding ceremony, bans are announced for three consecutive Sundays so that impediments to the marriage—if any—can be brought to the attention of the priest. After that, the couple selects the best man and maid (or matron) of honor, both of whom are called *naşii* ("nashée"), usually a husband and wife or a sister and brother. In most cases, the *naşii* later serve as godparents to the couple's children.

On the day of the wedding, the bridal party meets in the bride's home and leaves for the church, where the groom is waiting along with the best man. In the church there is no instrumental music, and the bridal procession is made in silence. The bride is brought to the altar by her father or another male member of the family, who then relinquishes her to the groom. The ceremony is begun by the priest, assisted by a cantor or church choir that sings the responses. After receiving affirmative answers from the couple about their intention to marry and their mutual commitment, the priest blesses the wedding rings and places them in the hands of the bride and groom. Then, metal or floral crowns are placed on the heads of the couple so that they can rule the family in peace, harmony, and purity of heart. The bride and groom then take three bites of a honey wafer or drink wine from a common cup, which symbolizes their bountiful life together. Finally, the hands of the couple are bound together with a ribbon to share all joys and sorrows together, and the couple walks three times around the tetrapod (a small stand displaying an icon), symbolizing the eternity of their union and obedience to the Holy Trinity. The crowns are removed with a blessing from the priest, who then concludes the ceremony with a few words of advice for the couple. The reception is held either at a private home, hotel, or restaurant. Instead of gifts, guests give money at the reception, which is collected by the *naşii* who publicly announce the amounts received. The reception is accompanied by music and dancing, including popular Romanian songs and folk dances.

BAPTISMS

When a child is ready for baptism, the parents first select the godparents, or *naşii*, who are often the same couple that served as best man and matron of honor at the parents' wedding. The *naşii* bring the child to the church, where the priest confers the grace of God by putting his hand on the child. Then, the priest exorcises the child by breathing on the child's forehead, mouth, and breast. The godmother, or *naşa* ("násha"), renounces the service of Satan in the child's name and promises to believe in Jesus Christ and serve only Him. In front of the altar, the priest anoints the child with the "oil of joy" (blessed olive oil) on the forehead, breast, shoulders, ears, hands, and feet. The baptism is completed by dipping the child three times in a font or by sprinkling with holy water. Immediately after the baptism follows confirmation, which consists of a new anointment of the child with *mir* (pronounced "meer," meaning holy chrism), a mixture of 33 spices blessed by the bishop, on the forehead, eyes, nose, mouth, breast, ears, hands, and feet. It is customary to hold a dinner after the baptism, where guests usually bring gifts in the form of money.

FUNERALS

A death in the family is announced by the ringing of church bells three times a day (morning, noon, and evening) until the day of the funeral. Prayers for the dead are recited by the priest and the Gospel is read during the wake, called *saracusta* ("sarakóosta"). At the church, the funeral service consists entirely of singing; with the assistance of the cantor and choir, the priest sings hymns and prayers for the dead. The priest bids farewell to the family in the name of the deceased and asks for forgiveness of sins against family members or friends. At the cemetery prayers are recited and the Gospel is read. Before the coffin is lowered into the grave, the priest sprinkles soil on top of it and recites the following: "The earth is the Lord's, and the fullness thereof." Later, the deceased's family offers a *pomana* ("pomána"), which is either a complete meal or sandwiches and beverages. The purpose of the funeral is to remember the dead, and to seek forgiveness of his or her sins. At least six weeks following the burial, a memorial service called *parastas* ("parastás") is offered. During the *parastas*, the priest recites a few prayers for the deceased, and a large cake-like bread is then cut into small pieces and served with wine in the church's vestibule. After being served, the mourners recite "May his (or her) soul rest in peace" and reminisce about the person who had passed away.

INTERACTIONS WITH OTHER ETHNIC GROUPS

Romanian Americans began to interact with other ethnic groups as they moved into better residential areas and suburbs. Romanian Orthodox believers

established relationships with Orthodox Serbians, Greeks, Russians, and Ukrainians by attending their churches. Similarly, Romanian Catholics were drawn to Hungarian or Polish Catholics, while Romanian Baptists established friendly relations with Serbian, Croatian, and Bulgarian Baptists. Romanian workers came into contact with other ethnic groups in the workplace. All of these factors—including the proliferation of mixed marriages—contributed to the integration of Romanians into mainstream American society.

RELIGION

The first Romanian American churches, St. Mary's Orthodox Church (Cleveland, Ohio) and St. Helen's Catholic Byzantine Rite (East Cleveland, Ohio), were founded in 1904 and 1905, respectively. These churches also served as community centers where immigrants spent a good part of their social life. The vast majority of Romanian American churchgoers are Eastern Orthodox, with a membership of about 60,000 organized into 60 parishes under two canonical jurisdictions. Forty-five parishes are

subordinated to the Romanian Orthodox Episcopate of America, headed by Bishop Nathaniel Pop. Fifteen parishes—the majority of which are located in Canada—are under the Romanian Orthodox Missionary Episcopate of America, led by Archbishop Victorin Ursache (1912–). The Catholic Church of the Byzantine Rite has 15 parishes, serving approximately 4,000 Romanian members. The church is led by Vasile Puşcaş, the first Byzantine Rite bishop in America. The number of Romanian Protestants is approximately 2,500; most of them are Baptists. The first Romanian Baptist church was founded in Cincinnati, Ohio, in 1910; at present there are nine Romanian Baptist churches and smaller groups of Romanian Seventh-Day Adventists and Pentecostals under various jurisdictions.

The Romanian Orthodox church and the Catholic Church of the Byzantine Rite are essentially sister churches with a common history, liturgy, customs, and traditions. Both follow the teachings of the Apostles but differ in their interpretation of the Pope's infallibility. Members of the Byzantine Rite church believe in the infallibility of the Pope when he speaks *ex cathedra* on faith and morality, while

Orthodox followers contend that any person or council in the church is not infallible. Those who embraced the dogma of papal infallibility switched allegiance from the Eastern Orthodox church to the Vatican in 1697 but have preserved all other features and disciplines of the Eastern church. Both churches adhere to the Nicene Creed, and the Liturgy is based on the text of Saint John Chrysostom (c.347-407 A.D.), modified by Saint Basil the Great (c.329-379 A.D.). There are seven Sacraments: Eucharist, Baptism, Confirmation, Penance, Matrimony, Holy Orders, and Anointing of the Sick. In the Romanian Orthodox church, the Anointing of the Sick is administered by three priests and may be given to the healthy to prevent illness. Services in both churches are conducted in Romanian accentuated by song and chants. The cathedrals are richly decorated with icons and images of the saints, although carved images are forbidden. The altar is located in the center of the sanctuary, and a screen or partition called an iconostasis separates the sanctuary from the rest of the church. Only priests and deacons can enter the sanctuary; other parishioners are not permitted to cross beyond the iconostasis.

Orthodox and Byzantine Rite priests usually wear black cassocks, but gray and brown are also permitted. During the Liturgy, vestments are colorful and ornate; while a priest's headdress is a cylindrical-shaped black hat, bishops wear a mitre, a crown made of stiff material adorned on top with a cross and various small pictures or icons. At the top of the pastoral scepter are two intertwined serpents surmounted by a cross or an image of a saint. Former liturgical colors (black, red, white) are not observed in modern times. Orthodox priests are permitted to marry before ordination, but only unmarried priests can become bishops. Deacons, subdeacons, and readers assist the priests during services. Clergy and laity (nonclergy) take part in the administration of the church and in the election of the clergy in Orthodox churches, while Byzantine Rite priests are appointed by their bishops.

Romanian Protestant churches conduct their services in the same manner as their American coreligionists, employing Romanian pastors who are subordinated to various local American jurisdictions. Their predecessors were trained by American missionaries in Romania during the nineteenth century.

EMPLOYMENT AND ECONOMIC TRADITIONS

Because early Romanian immigrants settled in the eastern and midwestern regions of the United States, they found work in such industries as iron, rubber, and steel manufacturing, coal mining, meat packing, and automotive assembly. They were assigned the heaviest and dirtiest jobs, as was the custom with all newly arrived immigrants. After accumulating work experience and perfecting their English language skills, some Romanians advanced to more responsible positions. Immigrants who settled in California were employed as gardeners, fruit gatherers and packers, and in freight transporters, while Macedo-Romanians often held jobs as waiters in the hotel and restaurant industries. About nine percent of Romanian immigrants settled in Colorado, North and South Dakota, Idaho, and Wyoming; they became involved in agriculture and ranching either as farm owners or as managers. Romanians were also employed as tailors, bakers, carpenters, and barbers, establishing their own small businesses in Romanian American neighborhoods. Romanian women found employment in light industry, such as cigar and tobacco manufacturing, or as seamstresses. Younger women became clerks or office secretaries, while others worked as manicurists or hairdressers in beauty salons. Many Macedo-Romanian women took jobs in the textile industry. Some Romanians with entrepreneurial skills opened travel agencies, small banks, saloons, boarding houses, and restaurants.

POLITICS AND GOVERNMENT

The formation of the Union and League of Romanian Societies of America (ULRSA) in 1906 marked the beginning of Romanian political activity on a national scale. Founded in Cleveland, Ohio, ULRSA brought together dozens of mutual aid and cultural societies, clubs, fraternities, and other groups committed to preserving Romanian ethnicity. It provided insurance benefits, assisted thousands of Romanians in completing their education, and taught newly arrived immigrants how to handle their affairs in a democratic way. As ULRSA gained more power and prestige, its leaders were often "courted" by local and national politicians to enlist political support from the Romanian American community.

The leadership of ULRSA (with a few exceptions) has traditionally held a neutral and unbiased position in American politics. Despite this neutrality, however, many Romanians, especially those who immigrated to America prior to World War II, have pro-Democratic sentiments, while the majority of postwar immigrants and refugees with strong anti-Communist sentiments tilt more toward the Republican party. A small group of Romanian

American socialists—primarily workers from Cleveland, Chicago, Detroit, and New York—founded the Federation of the Romanian Socialist Workers of the United States in 1914 and later merged with the pro-Communist International Workers Order (IWO). Many Romanian Americans also joined local labor unions for the practical reason that they could not obtain work otherwise. Later, as employment opportunities improved, they participated in union activities according to their specific interests, benefits needs, and preferences.

MILITARY

During World War I, several hundred Romanian volunteers from Ohio and other states enrolled in the American Expeditionary Force in Europe on the French front. Many of these soldiers received commendations for bravery. Over 5,000 Romanian Americans served in the American Armed Forces during World War II and over 300 died in combat. Lieutenant Alex Vraciu of East Chicago, Indiana, destroyed 19 Japanese planes in 1944; Cornelius and Nicholas Chima, brothers from Akron, Ohio, were the only Romanian American team to fly a combat plane in 1944. Florea Busella of Glassport, Pennsylvania, was the first Romanian American woman to enroll in the Navy's WAVES in 1942, and Lieutenant Eleanor Popa, a registered nurse from Ohio, was one of the first American military women to enter Tokyo, Japan in 1945. Romanian Americans were also represented in significant numbers during the Korean and Vietnam Wars and many were promoted to officer ranks. Nicholas Daramus became the first Romanian American to be promoted to the rank of full commander in the U.S. Navy in 1977.

RELATIONS WITH ROMANIA

Romanian Americans have always been proud of their homeland and have maintained ties beyond normal relations with family or friends left behind. Before and during World War I, Romanian Americans exposed Hungarian persecution of Transylvanians in their newspapers and many organizations called for the unification of Transylvania and Romania. They also gave generous donations of money, food, and clothing for Romania's orphans, widows, and refugees. In 1919 Romanian Americans submitted a Four-Point Motion to the Peace Conference, calling for the reestablishment of Romania's territorial borders (including Transylvania and other regions formerly held by foreign powers), equal rights for ethnic minorities, and the establishment of a democracy based on principles adopted in the United States.

In the 1920s and 1930s many Romanian Americans actively supported the National Peasant Party founded in Transylvania against anti-democratic political forces. Prominent Romanians such as Queen Marie (1875-1938) visited Romanian American communities, and the Romanian government sent a group of students to complete their studies at various American universities. After World War II, Romanian Americans sent food, medicine, and clothing to refugees and other types of aid to help Romania's devastated economy.

During the years of Communist dictatorship, Romanian American groups sent a formal memorandum to President Harry Truman protesting the mass deportations of Romanians by Soviet troops in 1952, and in 1964 called upon President Lyndon B. Johnson to exert pressure on the Communists to release Romanian political prisoners and provide exit visas for individuals desiring to join relatives in the United States. Many Romanian Americans who held pro-monarchist views sought the restoration of Michael I, who was forced by the Communists to abdicate in December 1947. Romanian American Catholics vehemently opposed the suppression of their church in Romania beginning in 1948, when bishops and priests were arrested and murdered, and church property was confiscated. Many Romanian Catholics were deported.

Romanian Americans continue to aid their native country during difficult times through the auspices of the Union and League of Romanian Societies in America, the International Red Cross, and other philanthropic organizations. Presently, some Romanian Americans are involved in developing business ventures in Romania, given the precarious conditions of the country's economy and unfamiliarity with the capitalist system. There is also a steady flow of scholarly exchanges between Romania and United States—via grants and scholarships—in which Romanian Americans take an active role through the Romanian Studies Association of America, the American Romanian Academy of Arts and Sciences, and other academic organizations.

INDIVIDUAL AND GROUP CONTRIBUTIONS

Although Romanian Americans represent only one-eighth of one percent of America's total population, they have made significant contributions to American popular culture and to the arts and sciences. The following sections list Romanian Americans and their achievements.

ACADEMIA

Mircea Eliade (1907-1986) was a renowned authority on religious studies, mythology, and folklore. His many publications include *The History of Religions: Essays in Methodology* (1959) and *Zalmoxis, the Vanishing God: Comparative Studies in the Religions and Folklore of Dacia and Eastern Europe* (1972). Many of Eliade's works have been translated into several languages. Nicholas Georgescu-Roegen (1906-1994) pioneered mathematical economics and influenced many American economists through his *Analytical Economics: Issues and Problems* (1966). Georgescu-Roegen was considered by his peers "a scholar's scholar and an economist's economist." Mathematician Constantin Corduneanu edits *Libertas Mathematica*. Romance philologist Maria Manoliu-Manea served as president of the American Romanian Academy of Arts and Sciences for many years.

FILM, TELEVISION, AND THEATER

Jean Negulesco (1900–) directed *Singapore Woman* (1941), *Johnny Belinda* (1948), *Titanic* (1953), and *Three Coins in a Fountain* (1954), and was also known as a portrait artist. Television actor Adrian Zmed (c. 1954–) costarred with William Shatner in the police drama "T. J. Hooker" (1982-1986). In theater, Andrei Șerban (1943–) adapted and directed classical plays at LaMama Theater in New York City, while Liviu Ciulei (1923–) is best known for directing classical works.

JOURNALISM

Theodore Andrica (1900-1990) edited and published two successful periodicals, the *New Pioneer* during the 1940s, and the *American Romanian Review* during the 1970s and 1980s. Both publications featured articles on Romanian American life, traditions, customs, and cooking, and documented the achievements of Romanian Americans. Andrica also served as editor of the *Cleveland Press* for 20 years. The Reverend Vasile Hațegan (1915–) of the Romanian Orthodox Church wrote several articles on Romanians residing in New York City, while the Reverend Gheorghe Mureșan of the Romanian Catholic Byzantine Rite Church proved to be a gifted editor for Catholic publications. John Florea (1916–) of *Life* magazine and Ionel Iorgulescu (1918–) of *Redbook* magazine were outstanding photographers during the 1940s and 1950s. For 25 years, broadcaster Liviu Floda of Radio Free Europe hosted programs discussing human rights violations by the Communist regime in Romania. Floda interviewed hundreds of personalities, helped reunite refugee families with American relatives, and wrote dozens of articles on various subjects for Romanian Americans and foreign-language journals.

LITERATURE

Peter Neagoe (1881-1960) was the first major Romanian American author. In such novels as *Easter Sun* (1934) and *There Is My Heart* (1936), he depicted the lives of Transylvanian peasants in realistic detail. Mircea Vasiliu (an illustrator) wrote *Which Way to the Melting Pot?* (1955) and *The Pleasure Is Mine* (1963), in which he humorously recounts his experiences as an immigrant. Eugene Theodorescu's *Merry Midwife* and Anișoara Stan's (1902-1954) *They Crossed Mountains and Oceans* (1947) also focus on immigrant life in America. Moreover, Stan published *The Romanian Cook Book*, which remains a prototype of Romanian cookery and cuisine. Eli Popa edited and translated *Romania Is a Song: A Sample of Verse in Translation* (1967), a bilingual collection of Romanian classical and folk poetry, and modern verse by Romanian American poets. Andrei Codrescu (1946–), a poet, novelist, and journalist, has added new dimensions to contemporary Romanian American literature through such books as *The Life and Times of an Involuntary Genius* (1975), *In America's Shoes* (1983), and several others which delineate anti-Communist sentiments in Romania and the immigrant experience in America. Silvia Cinca, leading author, published *Comrade Dracula* (1988), *Homo Spiritus: Journey of Our Magic*, as well as several other books both in Romanian and English. She is also President of Moonfall Press in the United States.

MUSIC

George Enesco (1881-1955) was a composer, violinist, and conductor who lived in the United States before and after World War II. Enesco conducted several symphony orchestras, taught at the Manhattan School of Music in New York City, and earned fame for his "Romanian Rhapsodies," which has since been performed by many American and foreign symphony orchestras. Ionel Perlea (1901-1970) served as musical conductor of the New York Metropolitan Opera for over 20 years despite the fact that his right hand was paralyzed; he also taught at the Manhattan School of Music. Stella Roman (1905-1992), an operatic soprano, performed at the Metropolitan Opera in New York during the 1940s and 1950s, specializing in Italian opera spinto roles. Other gifted performers include Christina Caroll (1920–) of the New York Metropolitan Opera; Iosif Cristea and Gloria Vasu, both with the Boston Grand Opera Company; Yolanda Marculescu, soprano and music teacher at the University of Wisconsin at Milwaukee; Lisette Verea, operetta singer and comedienne based in New York City; and Marioara Trifan, an internationally renowned pianist. In addition, the popular tune "And the Angels Sing," which was recorded by the legendary jazz musician Benny Goodman, is in fact a Romanian folk song brought to America by Romanian immigrants.

SCIENCE AND TECHNOLOGY

George Palade (1912–) of the Yale University School of Medicine shared the 1974 Nobel Prize in medicine, for his contributions to research on the structure and function of the internal components of cells. Traian Leucutzia (1893-1970), who began his medical career in Detroit, Michigan, in the 1920s, was one of the first scientists to detect the radiation hazards of X-rays, and served as editor of the *American Journal of Roentgenology, Radium Therapy*, and *Nuclear Medicine* for several years. Valer Barbu (1892-1986) taught psychiatry and psychoanalysis at Cornell University, the New School of Social Research in New York City, and the American Institute of Psychoanalysis before and after World War II. A disciple of Karen Horney, Barbu was critical of Freudian analysis.

Constanin Barbulescu, an aeronautical engineer, devised methods of protecting aircraft flying in severe weather. He published his findings in *Electrical Engineering* and other technical journals during the 1940s. Alexandru Papana (1905-1946) tested gliders and other aircraft for Northrop Aircraft in California. Many of Papana's experiences as a test pilot were documented in *Flying* magazine.

SPORTS

Charlie Stanceu (1916-1969) was the first Romanian American to play baseball in the major leagues. A native of Canton, Ohio, Stanceu pitched for the New York Yankees and the Philadelphia Phillies during the 1940s. Stanceu was followed by Johnny Moldovan, who signed a contract with the Yankees in 1947. Gymnast Dominique Moceanu, now 18, has distinguished herself since she was 14, wimming several United States' women's national gymnastics titles. Gheorghe Muresan, 7 feet, 7 inches tall, has become a famous basketball star playing for the Washington Bullets, and has appeared as an actor in the film My Giant, with Billy Crysal.

VISUAL ARTS

Constantin Brancuşi (1856-1957) is considered by some art critics to be the father of modern sculpture. He first exhibited his works in America in 1913 at the International Exhibition of Modern Art. Many of Brancusi's pieces ("Miss Pogany," "The Kiss," "Bird in Space," "White Nigress") were acquired by the Museum of Modern Art in New York City, the Philadelphia Museum of Art, and the Art Institute of Chicago. Sculptor George Zolnay (1867-1946) created the Sequoya Statue in the United States Capitol, the Edgar Allan Poe monument at the University of Virginia at Charlottesville, and the War Memorial sculpture of Parthenon in Nashville, Tennessee. Zolnay also served as art commissioner at the 1892 World Columbian Exhibition in Chicago, Illinois. Elie Cristo-Loveanu (c. 1893-1964) distinguished himself as a portrait artist and professor of painting at New York University during the 1940s and 1950s. His portrait of President Dwight Eisenhower is on display at Columbia University. Constantin Aramescu, a Floridian, is noted for paintings on Romanian subjects. Iosif Teodorescu and Eugene Mihaescu (1937–) are illustrators for the *New York Times*, while Mircea Vasiliu (1920–), a former diplomat, is a well known illustrator of children's books. Alexandru Seceni painted icons and saints in several Romanian Orthodox churches in America and also developed a special technique of wood etching for the Romanian Pavilion at the 1939 New York World's Fair.

MEDIA

PRINT

America: Romanian News.
Organ of the Union and League of Romanian Societies in America (ULRSA). It is a monthly publication that focuses on organization activities and achievements of local ULRSA branches and features cultural news and book reviews written in English and Romanian. It is supplemented by an almanac listing important events in the Romanian American community.

Contact: Peter Lucaci, Editor.
Address: 23203 Lorain Road, North Olmstead, Ohio 44070-1625.
Telephone: (216) 779-9913.

Lumea Libera Romaneasca (Free Romanian World).
Weekly, focuses on political events in Romania, concerned with development of democracy, free

press, and elimination of Communist influences of the past. Independent orientation

Contact: Dan Costescu and Cornel Dumitrescu, Editors.

Address: P.O. Box 7640 Reko Park, New York, New York 11374.

Telephone and Fax: (718) 997-6314.

Meridianul Romanesc (The Romanian Meridian).

Weekly, news and articles concerning Romania and the Romanian American community, politics, culture, sports, tourism and other subjects. Independent orientation.

Contact: Marius Badea and George Rosianu, Editors.

Address: North State College Boulevar, Suite 107, Anaheim, California 92806.

Telephone: (908) 322-4903.

Fax: (714) 991-0364.

Romanian American Heritage Center Information Bulletin.

Organ of the Valerian Trifa Romanian-American Heritage Center (English language only). Bimonthly publication that contains articles on early Romanian American immigrants and their contributions to American society, and also features book reviews.

Contact: Eugene S. Raica, Editor.

Address: 2540 Grey Tower Road, Jackson, Michigan 49201.

Telephone: (517) 522-8260.

Fax: (517) 522-8236.

Solia (The Herald).

Published monthly in a bilingual format by the Romanian Orthodox Episcopate of America. Focuses on parish news and youth and women-auxiliary projects, but also features book reviews and produces an annual supplement listing important events and a religious calendar.

Contact: Manuela Cruga, English Language Editor.

Address: 2540 Grey Tower Road, Jackson, Michigan 49201-9120.

Telephone: (517) 522-8260.

Unirea (The Union).

Monthly bilingual publication of the Roman Catholic Diocese of Canton. Gathers news from various parishes, features a youth section, and prints book reviews. It also publishes an annual supplement listing important events, a religious calendar, and other information.

Contact: Rev. John Skala, Editor.

Address: 1121 44th Street, NE, Canton, Ohio 44714-1297.

Telephone: (219) 980-0726.

RADIO

WCAR-AM (1900).

"Ethnic and Proud," is a weekly one-hour Romanian broadcast featuring religious and community news as well as Romanian music.

Contact: Jimmy Crucian.

Address: 2522 Grey Tower Road, Jackson, Michigan 49204.

Telephone: (517) 522-4800; or, (313) 527-1111.

WNZK-AM (1900).

Religious news.

Contact: Editor, Romanian Hour

Address: 21700 Northwestern Highway, Suite 1190, Southfield, Michigan 48075.

Telephone: (313) 365-0700.

TELEVISION

TVTV (Romanian Voice Television).

Transmits news from Romania and the Romanian American community, can be viewed on International Channel in various localities (East Coast, Middle West, West Coast) via local cable television stations.

Contact: Vasile Badaluta

Address: 45-51 39th Place, Sunnyside, New York 11104.

Telephone: (718) 482-9588 or (718) 472-9111.

Fax: (718) 472-9119.

ORGANIZATIONS AND ASSOCIATIONS

American Romanian Academy of Arts and Sciences (ARA).

Founded in 1975, the ARA has a membership of 250 Romanian scholars who live in the United States. It focuses on research and publishing activities regarding Romanian art, culture, language, history, linguistics, sciences, and economics

Contact: Prof. Peter Gross.

Address: Department of Journalism, California State University, Chico, California 95929-0600.

Telephone: (916) 898-4779.

Fax: (916) 898-4839.

American Romanian Orthodox Youth (AROY).
Founded in 1950, with approximately 2,000 members, AROY functions as an auxiliary of the Romanian Orthodox Episcopate of America; cultivates religious education and Romanian culture through summer courses, retreats, sports, competitions, scholarships, and other activities.

Contact: David A. Zablo.
Address: 2522 Grey Tower Road, Jackson,
      Michigan 49201-9120.
Telephone: (517) 522-4800.
Fax: (517) 522-5907.

Association of Romanian Catholics of America (ARCA).
Founded in 1948, the ARCA promotes religious education in the tradition of the Romanian Catholic Church of the Byzantine Rite and cultural preservation, and sponsors special programs designed for youths. The Association is also involved in publishing activities.

Contact: Dr. George T. Stroia.
Address: 1700 Dale Drive, Merrillville,
      Indiana 46410.
Telephone: (219) 980-0726.

Society for Romanian Studies.
Founded in 1985, it promotes Romanian language and culture studies in American universities and colleges, cultural exchange programs between America and Romanian. Also publishes a newsletter.

Contact: Prof. Paul Michelson.
Address: Huntington College, Department of
      History, Huntington, Indiana 46750.
Telephone: (219) 356-6000.
Fax: (219) 356-9448.

Union and League of Romanian Societies of America (ULRSA).
Founded in 1906, with approximately 5,000 members, ULRSA is the oldest and largest Romanian American organization. It has played an important role in organizing Romanian immigrants and in preserving Romanian culture. Presently, the ULRSA functions as a fraternal benefit insurance organization.

Contact: Georgeta Washington, President.
Address: 23203 Lorain Road, North Olmsted,
      Ohio 44070.
Telephone: (216) 779-9913.

MUSEUMS AND RESEARCH CENTERS

Iuliu Maniu American Romanian Relief Foundation (IMF).
Has a sizable collection of Romanian peasant costumes, paintings and folk art items. It also manages a library of Romanian books that can be borrowed by mail.

Contact: Justin Liuba, President.
Address: P.O. Box 1151 Gracie Square Station,
      New York, New York 10128.
Telephone: (212) 535-8169.

Romanian Ethnic Art Museum.
Has preserved a large collection of Romanian national costumes, wood carvings, rugs, icons, furniture, paintings, and over 2,000 Romanian books, as well as English books related to Romania.

Contact: George Dobrea.
Address: 3256 Warren Road, Cleveland, Ohio
      44111.
Telephone: (216) 941-5550.
Fax: (216) 941-3068.

Romanian American Heritage Center.
Collects and preserves historical records relating to Romanian immigrants and their achievements. The collection consists of religious items, brochures, minutes, flyers, and reports donated by various Romanian American organizations, family and individual photographs, and other materials of interest to researchers.

Contact: Alexandru Nemoianu.
Address: 2540 Grey Tower Road, Jackson,
      Michigan 49201.
Telephone: (517) 522-8260.
Fax: (517) 522-8236.

Romanian Cultural Center.
A Romanian government agency similar to the United States Information Agency (USIA), has a sizable collection of Romanian books published in Romania, and a collection of folk art items. The center organizes cultural programs and assists in providing contacts in Romania.

Contact: Coriolan Babeti, Director.
Address: 200 East 38th Street, New York, New
      York 10016.
Telephone: (212) 687-0180.
Fax: (212) 687-0181.

SOURCES FOR ADDITIONAL STUDY

Hategan, Vasile. *Romanian Culture in America.* Cleveland, Ohio: Cleveland Cultural Center, 1985.

Diamond, Arthur. *Romanian Americans.* New York: Chelsea House, 1988.

Dima, Nicholas. *From Moldavia to Moldova: The Soviet Romanian Territorial Dispute.* Boulder, Colorado: East European Monographs, 1991.

Galitzi Avghi, Christine. *A Study of Assimilation among the Romanians in the United States.* New York: Columbia University Press, 1929; reprinted, 1969.

Hateganu, Vasile. "The Macedo-Romanians in America" in *Romanian American Heritage Center Information Bulletin*, March-April 1996, pp. 16-18.

Wertsman, Vladimir. *The Romanians in America, 1748-1974: A Chronology and Factbook.* Dobbs Ferry, New York: Oceana Publications, 1975.

————.*The Romanians in America and Canada: A Guide to Information Sources.* Detroit: Gale Research Company, 1980.

Winnifrith, T.J. *The Vlachs: The History of a Balkan People.* England: Duckworth, 1987.

For the most part
Russian immigrants
and their descendants
have succeeded
in assimilating
into mainstream
American life. There
are a few groups
that have avoided
acculturation and
maintained the
traditional lifestyle
they brought from
the homeland. Such
traditionalists include
the Orthodox
Christian Old
Believers and the
non-Orthodox
Molokan Christian
sect.

RUSSIAN AMERICANS

by
Paul Robert Magocsi

OVERVIEW

Since the second half of the nineteenth century, Russia has been the largest country in the world, stretching from the plains of eastern Europe across Siberia as far as the shores of the Pacific Ocean. For centuries, Russia has straddled both Europe and Asia, two continents that are divided by the Ural Mountains.

In a sense, there are two Russian homelands. One is the present-day state of Russia, which coincides with territory inhabited by ethnic Russians. The other includes territories that are beyond Russia proper but were once part of the pre-World War I Russian Empire and later the Soviet Union. Americans who identify their heritage as Russian include first-generation immigrants and their descendants who came from Russia within its present-day border; people from the Baltic countries, Belarus, and Ukraine who have identified themselves as Russians; East Slavs from the former Austro-Hungarian Empire who have identified themselves as Russians once in the United States; and Jews from the Western regions of the former Russian Empire and the Soviet Union who, aside from their religious background, identify themselves as Russians.

Much of European Russia west of the Urals was part of a medieval state known as *Kievan Rus'*, which existed from the late ninth century to the thirteenth century. During the Kievan period,

Orthodox Christianity reached Russia and that religion remained intimately connected with whatever state or culture developed on Russian territory until the twentieth century. It was in a northern part of *Kievan Rus'*, the Duchy of Muscovy, that the birth of a specifically Russian state can be found. The state-building process began in the late thirteenth century, when the Duchy of Muscovy began to consolidate its power and expand its territory. The expansion proved to be phenomenal. By the seventeenth and eighteenth centuries, the growing state included lands along the Baltic Sea, Belarus, Ukraine, Moldova, and large parts of Poland. The country's borders also moved beyond the Ural Mountains into Siberia, a vast land whose annexation together with Central Asia the Caucasus region were completed in the nineteenth century.

As the country grew, it also changed its name from the Duchy to the Tsardom of Muscovy and in 1721 it became the Russian Empire. Throughout the centuries, Muscovy/Russia functioned as a centralized state ruled by autocratic leaders whose titles changed as their power and influence grew. The grand dukes became the tsars of Muscovy, who in turn became emperors of the Russian Empire. Although the rulers of the empire were formally called emperors (*imperator*), they were still popularly referred to as tsars or tsarinas.

MODERN ERA

During World War I, Russia experienced a revolution, and in March 1917, the tsarist empire collapsed. In November 1917, a second revolution took place, led by the Bolsheviks and headed by a revolutionary named Vladimir Lenin. The Bolshevik Revolution was opposed by a significant portion of the population, and the result was a Civil War that began in 1918 and lasted until early 1921. In the end, the Bolsheviks were victorious, and in late 1922 they created a new state, the Union of Soviet Socialist Republics, or the Soviet Union. The Soviet Union consisted of several national republics, the largest of which was called Russia. Beyond the Russian republic many inhabitants, especially in the western regions of the Soviet Union, continued to identify themselves as Russians.

The new Soviet state proclaimed the establishment of Communism worldwide as its goal. It intended to achieve that goal by promoting Bolshevik-style revolutions abroad. Since many countries feared such revolutions, they refused to recognize Bolshevik rule. Thus, the Soviet Union was isolated from the rest of the world community for nearly 20 years. That isolation came to an end during World War II, when the Soviet Union, ruled by Lenin's successor Joseph Stalin, joined the Allied Powers in the struggle against Nazi Germany and Japan. Following the Allied victory, the Soviets emerged alongside the United States as one of the two most powerful countries in the world. For nearly the next half-century, the world was divided between two camps: the free or capitalist West led by the United States, and the revolutionary or communist East led by the Soviet Union.

By the 1980s, the centralized economic and political system of the Soviet Union was unable to function effectively. In 1985, a new communist leader, Mikhail Gorbachev, tried desperately to reform the system but failed. He did set in motion, however, a new revolution, bringing such enormous changes that by late 1991 the Soviet Union disappeared as a country. In its place, each of the former Soviet republics became an independent country, and among the new countries was Russia.

SIGNIFICANT IMMIGRATION WAVES

The first Russians on U. S. territory were part of Russia's internal migration. During the eighteenth century, Russian traders and missionaries crossing Siberia reached Alaska, which became a colony of the Russian Empire. By 1784 the first permanent Russian settlement was founded on Kodiak, a large island off the Alaskan coast. Soon there were Russian colonies on the Alaskan mainland (Yakutat and Sitka), and by 1812 the Russians pushed as far south as Fort Ross in California, 100 miles north of San Francisco. In 1867 the Russian government sold Alaska to the United States, and most Russians in Alaska (whose numbers never exceeded 500) returned home. Russian influence persisted in Alaska, however, in the form of the Orthodox Church, which succeeded in converting as many as 12,000 of the native Inuit and Aleut people.

Large-scale emigration from Russia to the United States only began in the late nineteenth century. Since that time, four distinct periods of immigration can be identified: 1880s-1914; 1920-1939; 1945-1955; and 1970s-present. The reasons for emigration included economic hardship, political repression, religious discrimination, or a combination of those factors.

The pre-1914 Russian Empire was an economically underdeveloped country comprised primarily of poor peasants and a small but growing percentage of poorly paid or unemployed industrial workers. European Russia also encompassed the so-called Pale of Settlement (present-day Lithuania, Belarus, Moldova, and large parts of Poland, and Ukraine). The

Taken in 1947, this photograph demonstrates the influence of American fashion on traditional Russian dress. The lace shawls of these women are called kascinkas; their high-heeled shoes are American.

Pale was the only place Jews were allowed to reside. The vast majority lived in small towns and villages in their own communities known as the *shtetl*, which were made famous in America through the setting of the Broadway musical *Fiddler on the Roof*.

Between 1881 and 1914, over 3.2 million immigrants arrived from the Russian Empire. Nearly half were Jews; only 65,000 were ethnically Russian, while the remaining immigrants were Belarusans and Ukrainians. Regardless of their ethnoreligious background, their primary motive was to improve their economic status. Many of the 1.6 million Jews who also left did so because they feared *pogroms*—attacks on Jewish property and persons that occurred sporadically in the Russian Empire from the 1880s through the first decade of the twentieth century.

While many Jews from the Russian Empire did not identify themselves as Russians, another group of immigrants adopted a Russian identity in the United States. These were the Carpatho-Rusyns, or Ruthenians, from northeastern Hungary and Galicia in the Austro-Hungarian Empire (today far western Ukraine, eastern Slovakia, and southeastern Poland). Of the estimated 225,000 Carpatho-Rusyns who immigrated to the United States before World War I, perhaps 100,000 eventually joined the Orthodox Church, where they and their descendants still identify themselves as Americans of Russian background.

The second wave of immigration was less diverse in origin. It was directly related to the political upheaval in the former Russian Empire that was brought about by the Bolshevik Revolution and Civil War that followed. Over two million persons fled Russia between 1920 and 1922. Whether they were demobilized soldiers from anti-Bolshevik armies, aristocrats, Orthodox clergy, professionals, businesspersons, artists, intellectuals, or peasants, and whether they were of non-Jewish (the majority) or Jewish background, all these refugees had one thing in common—a deep hatred for the new Bolshevik/communist regime in their homeland. Because they were opposed to the communist Reds, these refugees came to be known as the Whites.

The White Russians fled their homeland. They left from the southern Ukraine and the Crimea (the last stronghold of the anti-Bolshevik White Armies) and went first to Istanbul in Turkey before moving on to several countries in the Balkans (especially Yugoslavia and Bulgaria; other countries in east-central Europe; Germany; and France, especially Paris and the French Riviera (Nice and its environs). Others moved directly westward and settled in the newly independent Baltic states, Poland, Czechoslovakia, or farther on to western Europe. A third outlet was in the Russian far east, from where the White émigrés crossed into China, settling in the Manchurian city of Kharbin. As many as 30,000 left the Old World altogether and settled in the United States. This wave of Russian immigration occurred during the early 1920s, although in the late 1930s several thousand more came, fleeing the advance of Nazi Germany and Japan's invasion of Manchuria. During this period, approximately 14,000 immigrants arrived in the United States.

The third wave of Russian immigration to the United States (1945-1955) was a direct outcome of World War II. Large portions of the former Soviet Union had been occupied by Germany, and hundreds of thousands of Russians had been captured or deported to work in Germany. After the war, many were forced to return home. Others lived in displaced-persons camps in Germany and Austria until they were able to immigrate to the United States. During this period, approximately 20,000 of these Russian displaced persons, the so-called DPs, arrived.

Both the tsarist Russian and Soviet governments placed restrictions on emigration. In 1885 the imperial Russian government passed a decree that prohibited all emigration except that of Poles and Jews, which explains the small numbers of non-Jewish Russians in the United States before World War I. By the early 1920s, the Bolshevik/communist-led Soviet government implemented further controls that effectively banned all emigration. As for the second-wave White Russian refugees who fled between 1920 and 1922, they were stripped of their citizenship in absentia and could never legally return home. This situation was the same for the post-World War II DPs, who were viewed as Nazi collaborators and traitors by the Soviet authorities.

In contrast, the fourth wave of Russian immigration that began in late 1969 was legal. It was formally limited to Jews, who were allowed to leave the Soviet Union for Israel as part of the agreements reached between the United States and the Soviet Union during the era of détente. In return for allowing Jews to leave, the United States and other western powers expanded the economic, cultural, and intellectual ties with their communist rival. Although Jews leaving the Soviet Union were only granted permission to go to Israel, many had the United States as their true goal; and by 1985 nearly 300,000 had reached the United States.

After 1985 the more liberal policy of the Soviet government under Mikhail Gorbachev allowed anyone to leave the Soviet Union, and thousands more Jewish and non-Jewish Russians immigrated to the United States. Because Russia is an independent country with a democratically elected government, newcomers cannot justify their claim to emigrate on the grounds of political or religious persecution. This has resulted in a slowing of Russian emigration during the last decade of the twentieth century.

SETTLEMENT

Of the 2,953,000 Americans who in 1990 identified themselves wholly (71.6 percent) or partially (28.4 percent) of Russian ancestry, nearly 44 percent reside in the Northeast. The Jews, in particular, went to New York City, Philadelphia, Boston, and other large cities. The non-Jewish Russians from the Russian Empire and the Carpatho-Rusyns settled in these cities as well as Chicago, Cleveland, Pittsburgh, and the coal mining towns of eastern Pennsylvania. Nearly 5,000 members of a Russian Christian religious sect known as the Molokans settled in California during the first decade of the twentieth century. They formed the nucleus of what has become a 20,000-member Russian Molokan community that is concentrated today in San Francisco and Los Angeles.

Most White Russian soldiers, aristocrats, professionals, and intellectuals settled in New York City, Philadelphia, and Chicago. But some moved into farming communities, such as a group of Don and Kuban Cossacks who established what are still vibrant rural centers in southern New Jersey. Those who left from the Russian far east and Chinese Manchuria settled in California, especially in San Francisco and Los Angeles. The fourth wave settled almost exclusively in cities where previous Russian immigrants had gone, especially New York City. Certain sections like Brighton Beach in Brooklyn were transformed into a vibrant Russian communities by the 1980s.

While the basic settlement pattern established by the first two waves of immigrants may have been maintained, the past three decades have also witnessed migration toward the sun-belt states like Florida, as well as to California where the original Russian communities have been supplemented by newcomers from the northeast.

ACCULTURATION AND ASSIMILATION

For the most part Russian immigrants and their descendants have succeeded in assimilating into mainstream American life. There are a few groups that have avoided acculturation and maintained the traditional lifestyle they brought from the homeland. Such traditionalists include the Orthodox Christian Old Believers and the non-Orthodox Molokan Christian sect. Whether these people live in large cities like San Francisco, Los Angeles, and Erie, Pennsylvania; in rural towns like Woodburn, Oregon; or in the backwoods of Alaska, they have continued to use the Russian language at home and sometimes succeeded in having it taught in public schools. The distinct dress and religious-based lifestyle of these groups keep them at a social distance from other Americans and distinguish them

This Russian American vendor sells handicrafts from his booth in Brooklyn, New York.

from the rest of the community. A large number of White Russians, especially those of aristocratic background from the immediate post-World War I era, also found it difficult to adapt to an American society that lacked respect for the deference that Russian nobles, princes, princesses, and intellectuals otherwise had come to expect.

The Old Believers, Molokans, and White Russian aristocrats are only a small minority of the Russian American community today. But even among the vast majority who sought to assimilate, the goal was not always easy to accomplish. American society during the past 70 years has had a negative opinion of the Soviet Union and, therefore, of Russian

Americans. Russian Americans have frequently been suspected of being potential communist spies or socialists and anarchists intent on infiltrating and disrupting America's labor movement.

Even before the Soviet Union existed, immigrant workers from Russia, particularly Jews, played a leading role in organizations like the American branch of the International Workers' Organization. Leon Trotsky and Nikolai Bukharin, two of Lenin's closest associates, lived in New York City for a time where they edited a Russian-language socialist newspaper. And just before the American branch of the Red Cross was about to assist thousands of White Russians in finding refuge in the United States, authorities in places like New York led raids against the headquarters of the Union of Russian Workers and the Russian-dominated American Communist party. As a result, several thousand aliens were deported, nearly 90 percent of whom were returned to what by then had become Bolshevik-controlled Russia. It is a little known fact that as late as the 1970s some of these returnees and their descendants still maintained an identity as Americans even after living in the Soviet Union nearly half a century.

After World War II the United States was once again struck by a Red Scare, this time even more widely publicized as a result of the congressional investigations led during the 1950s by the demagogic Senator Joseph McCarthy. Again Russians and all things Russian were associated with Communism, so Russian Americans were forced to maintain a low profile, and some felt obligated to renounce their heritage.

Most recently, Russians in the United States have been linked to organized crime. With the break-up of the Soviet Union in the early 1990s, and the radical change in that country's economy, a number of speculators have tried to take advantage of the situation. Many of these new Russian businessmen have contacts or are themselves residents in Russian American communities like Brighton Beach where they carry out illegal transactions. It is common to find references in today's mainstream American media to the dangers of the Russian mafia and, by implication, of all Russians.

CUISINE

Russian Americans enjoy many traditional dishes. They prepare a variety of rich and tasty soups, which are almost always served with a dollop of sour cream, or *smetana*. Most famous is *borshch*, or borscht, made from beets, cabbage, and meat. In the summer, borscht is served cold. *Shchi*, also made from cabbage, includes as well turnip, carrot, onion, or leek, and beef. Fish soups, such as *solianka*, that include onion, tomato, cucumber, lemon, butter, and sometimes beef, are popular. Many soups also include potatoes or dumplings. The traditional dark Russian bread is made from rye, though wheat is used increasingly. Russian meals are accompanied by vodka.

LANGUAGE

Russian is the largest of the Slavic languages and is spoken today by over 250 million people. For most first-generation immigrants the Russian language was used to communicate with one's family and friends until they attained a knowledge of English. For others the Russian language took on a symbolic function and was maintained to preserve a sense of Russian identity. For these reasons, the Russian language has never died out in the United States and, if anything, the number of native speakers and publications has expanded dramatically during the last two decades.

The appearance of newspapers, journals, and books in the United States and other countries where Russians lived helped keep traditional Russian culture alive throughout much of the twentieth century. Following the onset of Bolshevik rule in late 1917, the Soviet state eventually banned all forms of cultural and intellectual activity that did not conform to Stalin's version of Communism. Even the Russian language was transformed by the deletion of several letters from the Cyrillic alphabet and the infusion of new words that reflected the changes brought about by the Soviet system. Many of these new words were really abbreviations, such as *gensek* (general secretary), *gosplan* (state plan), *kolkhoz* (collective farm), *Komsomol* (Communist Youth League), *natsmen* (national minority), *vuzy* (colleges and universities), and *zarplata* (salary). At the same time many words were eliminated, such as *gorodovoi* (police officer), *gospodin* (gentleman, Mr.), *gospozha* (lady, Mrs.), and *gubernator* (governor).

Many Russians who emigrated after the Bolshevik Revolution felt they had a moral duty to preserve the old alphabet as the medium for the "true" Russian language. As a result, until the fall of the Soviet Union in late 1991, there existed two Russian literatures: Soviet Russian literature and Russian literature abroad. Schools were also created in an attempt to preserve the Russian language for the descendants of immigrants. Since the late nineteenth century many Orthodox church parishes have had their own Russian-language

schools. This tradition is still practiced in some parishes and summer camps conducted by the Russian Scout movement. At a higher level various Orthodox churches operated Russian-language seminaries, and there were even Russian classes at university-level institutions such as the Russian Collegiate Institute in New York City (1918) and the Russian People's University in Chicago (1921). These efforts proved to be short-lived, although today there is no shortage of Russian language, literature, history, and culture courses taught at some high schools and numerous universities throughout the United States.

FAMILY AND COMMUNITY DYNAMICS

The Russian extended family structure of uncles, aunts, cousins, godparents, etc. that prevailed in villages and *shtetls* was difficult, if not impossible, to recreate in the United States. Therefore, families became more inner-directed and isolated than they had been in Russia.

There was also a decrease in the number of children. Among post-World War I White Russian émigrés, there were twice as many men as women. This meant there was a high percentage of unmarried men with no children or marriages with women of other backgrounds. Poverty and unstable economic conditions among émigrés also worked against having children. Even among the pre-World War I Russian Jewish immigration in which the number of males (56 percent) and females (44 percent) was more balanced, the number of children married couples bore was well below the American norm. Statistics from 1969 reveal that Russian American women of the first generation and their descendants had an average of 1.7 to 2.4 children, while women of comparable ages who were of English, German, Irish, or Italian backgrounds had between 2.1 and 3.3 children.

Initially, Russian immigrants strove to have their children choose marriage partners from among their own group. Among Russian Jews, the religious factor was of primary importance. Hence, descendants of pre-World War I Jewish immigrants from Russia largely intermarried with Jews or non-Jews with non-Russian origins. Non-Jewish Russians were more concerned with maintaining a Russian identity within their family, but marriages with non-Russians soon became the norm.

EDUCATION

While their family units may have been smaller than those of other Americans on average, Russian immigrants tended to place greater emphasis on education. This was certainly the case among Jews who brought a strong tradition of learning that had characterized Jewish life for centuries. Non-Jewish White Russians were intent on providing their off-spring with the highest possible education (in the Russian language, if possible) so that they could take an appropriate place in Russian society when the communist regime would collapse and they could return home. Even when it became obvious that returning to a non-communist Russia was impossible, higher education was still considered useful for adaptation to American society. It is not surprising, then, that by 1971, among Americans of nine different backgrounds (English, Scottish, Welsh, German, Italian, Irish, French, and Polish), Russians between 25 and 34 had on average 16 years of education, while all others had at most only 12.8 years.

THE ROLE OF WOMEN

In traditional Russian society, women were legally dependent upon their husbands. The Bolshevik Revolution radically changed the status of women. Under communist rule, Russian women were offered equal economic and social responsibilities, which resulted in a high percentage of females in the labor force. The majority of physicians and health care workers in general are women. In the family, however, a woman is still expected to perform domestic tasks such as cooking, cleaning, and shopping. Women have played a determining role in maintaining the cultural identity in the family, passing on knowledge of Russian language and culture to younger people and by participation in philanthropic work that affects the entire community. Among the oldest of such organizations was the Russian Children's Welfare Society Outside Russia founded in New York City in 1926 to help orphans and poor children. Today the best known is the Tolstoy Foundation, set up in 1939 by Alexandra Tolstoy (1884-1979), daughter of the famous nineteenth-century Russian novelist, Leo Tolstoy. With branches throughout the world, the Tolstoy Foundation still operates a Russian senior citizen's home and cultural center in Nyack, New York, which has helped tens of thousands Russians and other refugees settle in the United States.

RELIGION

Based on religious criteria, Russian Americans are classified in three categories: Orthodox Christians, Jews, and nominal Jews. The large pre-World War I influx of Jews from the Russian Empire consisted mainly of individuals whose lives were governed by Jewish law and tradition in the thousands of *shtetls* throughout European Russia. Whether they were of the conservative Orthodox or Hassidic tradition, attendance at the synagogue; observance of the Sabbath (from sunset on Friday to sunset on Saturday); and deference to the rabbi as community leader, characterized Russian-Jewish life. While the authority of the rabbi over most aspects of daily Jewish life could not be fully maintained in the New World, the pre-World War I Russian-Jewish immigrants maintained their religious traditions within the confines of the home and synagogue. It was their Jewishness and not any association with Russia that made them indistinguishable from the larger Jewish-American society.

"**I** felt lost, as if there was nothing to hold onto ahead of us. But having my mother and my two brothers with me, we felt we were still a family, though our life would never be the same."

Maria Oogjen in 1923, cited in *Ellis Island: An Illustrated History of the Immigrant Experience,* edited by Ivan Chermayeff et al. (New York: Macmillan, 1991).

The arrival of Russian Jews since the early 1970s stands in stark contrast to their pre-World War I predecessors. For nearly 70 years, the Soviet system frowned on Judaism and other forms of religion. Therefore, by the time of their departure, the vast majority of Soviet Jews had no knowledge of Yiddish or Hebrew and had never been to a synagogue. Living in an officially atheistic Soviet Union, many found it politically and socially expedient to forget or even deny their Jewish heritage. When it became possible for Jews to emigrate legally from the Soviet Union, many quickly reclaimed their ancestral religious identity.

These Russian-speaking nominal Jews found it difficult to relate to English-speaking religious Jews when they arrived in the United States. While a small percentage of the newcomers learned and accepted the Jewish faith while in the United

States, most follow no particular religion and have remained simply Russians or Russian Americans who are Jews in name only.

The concept of being a Russian in America is often associated with the Orthodox Christian faith. The Russian Orthodox church traces it roots to the Eastern Christian world. After the Christian church split in 1054 between the western or Latin sphere (centered in Rome) and the eastern or Byzantine-Greek sphere (centered in Constantinople, present-day Istanbul), the Orthodox church in Russia maintained its spiritual allegiance to the Byzantine east. In the second half of the fifteenth century a jurisdictionally independent Russian Orthodox church, with its main seat in Moscow, was founded. At first the church was headed by a patriarch, but after 1721 it was led by a council of bishops known as the Synod.

Eastern Christianity, and thereby Russian Orthodoxy, differed from the western Christian churches in several ways. The Divine Liturgy (not Mass) was conducted in Church Slavonic instead of Latin; priests could marry; and the old Julian calendar was retained. This meant that by the twentieth century fixed feasts like Christmas (January 7) were two weeks behind the commonly used Gregorian calendar.

Russian Orthodox church architecture both in the homeland and in the United States also had distinctive features. Church structures are based on a square floor plan (the so-called Greek cross) covered by a high central dome and surrounded by four or more smaller domes. The domes are usually finished in gold and topped by three-bar crosses. Inside the dominant element is the *iconostasis*, a screen covered by icons that separates the altar from the congregation. Some traditional churches have no pews and there is never an organ because of the Orthodox belief that only the human voice is permitted in the worship of God. Russian Orthodox priests are often clad in colorful vestments laden with gold trim. Some priests also wear long beards, which according to tradition should not be cut. Easter is the most festive of holidays when churches are packed with worshippers at midnight services, which include candlelight processions, and are followed by the early morning blessing of Easter baskets filled with food delicacies and hand-painted eggs.

Throughout its history in the United States, the Russian Orthodox church has not only ministered to immigrants from Russia, but has also functioned as a missionary church attracting new adherents. Even before Alaska was purchased by the United States in 1867, the church converted over 12,000 Aleutians and some Eskimos to Orthodoxy.

Aside from his spiritual work, the Orthodox Russian Bishop Innokentii Veniaminov (1797-1879) was also the first person to codify a written Aleut language for which he published a dictionary, grammar guide, Bible, and prayer-books.

Nearly 50,000 converts were attracted to Russian Orthodoxy during the 1890s and first decade of the twentieth century. These were Carpatho-Rusyn immigrants of the Greek or Byzantine Catholic faith living in Pennsylvania, New York, New Jersey, Ohio, and other northeastern industrial states. One of their own priests, Father Alexis Toth (1853-1909), convinced many Greek Catholic parishioners to return to the Orthodox faith of their ancestors. For his work, Toth was hailed as the father of Orthodoxy in America, and in 1994 was made an Orthodox saint.

The Russian Orthodox Church also had problems with internal divisions. Some of those divisions had occurred decades or even centuries earlier in the Russian Empire. Consequently among Russian immigrants in the United States there were Old Believers, whose movement dates from the seventeenth century, and the Molokans, whose movement emerged in the nineteenth century. The Old Believers and Molokans have been most fervent in retaining a sense of Russian identity through an active use of the Russian language in their religious services and in their daily lives.

More significant are the splits that occurred in the Russian Orthodox Church after its establishment in the United States. The divisions were the result of developments in the homeland, in particular the reaction of Russians abroad to the Bolshevik Revolution and the existence of the officially atheist Soviet Union.

During the 1920s and 1930s, three factions had developed within Russian Orthodoxy. One faction consisted of the original Russian Orthodox Church that started in Alaska before moving to California and New York. It continued to recognize formally the patriarch, whose office as head of the mother church in Russia was restored in 1917. But as long as Russia was ruled by an uncompromising Soviet government, the American branch of the church governed itself as a distinct jurisdiction known as the *Metropolia*. The second faction consisted of the post-World War I White Russian émigrés, whose numbers included some clergy and laymembers of the church who rejected the idea of a patriarch, and favored a church governed by the Synod. Those who favored rule by the Synod came to be known as the Russian Orthodox Church Abroad, or the Synod. A third group consisted of individual parishes that remained directly under the jurisdiction of the patriarch in Moscow, even though he was living in a godless Soviet communist state and was subject to governmental pressure.

Each of the three factions of the Russian Orthodox church in the United States had its own bishops, clergy, cathedrals, churches, monasteries, seminaries, publications, and supporting lay organizations. Each of the three also often denounced the others so that much of Russian community life in the United States from the 1920s through the 1960s was characterized by fierce rivalry between competing Russian Orthodox churches.

In 1970 the *Metropolia* reached an agreement with the patriarch in Moscow, was released from its formal subordination to Moscow, and became an independent body known as the Orthodox Church of America. This church is the largest of the three Russian Orthodox churches in the United States. Since 1970 the Orthodox Church of America has conducted all its services in English. The patriarchal parishes have mostly been absorbed by the Orthodox Church of America. The Synod Abroad remains staunchly Russian in terms of religious tradition and language use, and was an enemy of the Soviet Union until that state's demise in 1991.

EMPLOYMENT AND ECONOMIC TRADITIONS

The majority of Russian Jews and other Russians who arrived in the United States between the 1880s and 1914 entered the industrial labor force in the northeastern United States. This was not a particularly difficult adjustment, since 88.7 percent of Jews in European Russia in 1897 had been in manufacturing, commerce, and the equivalent of a white-collar service trade. In contrast, 63.2 percent of non-Jewish Russians worked in agriculture.

Women immigrants of Russian-Jewish background dominated America's garment industry as seamstresses in the small clothing factories and sweatshops of New York City and other urban areas in the northeast. Other Russians, including Belarusans and Carpatho-Rusyns, worked in factories in the large northeastern cities as well as in the coal mines of eastern Pennsylvania, the iron and steel factories in the Pittsburgh area, and the slaughtering and meatpacking plants of Chicago. The Russian presence was so pronounced in certain trades that they established their own unions or branches of unions, such as the Russian branch of the Union of Men's and Women's Garment Workers, the Russian-Polish department of the Union of Cloakmakers, the Society of Russian Bootmakers, and the Society of Russian Mechanics.

The White Russians who came after World War I had a much higher level of education than their predecessors. Although many took on menial jobs at first (there are countless legends of Russian aristocrats employed as waiters, taxi-drivers, or doormen at night clubs), they eventually found employment that took advantage of their skills. This was also the case among the post-World War II DPs, many of whom found their way into university teaching, federal government employment, publishing, and other jobs that reflected the Cold War interests of the United States in the Soviet Union.

The educational and skills level is highest among the most recent Russian-Jewish immigrants. As high as 46.8 percent have had a university education, and 57.6 percent have been employed in the Soviet Union as engineers, economists, skilled workers, or technicians. In the United States, most have been able to find similar jobs and improved their economic status. Among the best known, and highest paid, of the recent immigrants are several hockey players of Russian background from the former Soviet Olympic team who have become a dominant part of teams in the National Hockey League during the 1980s and 1990s.

The descendants of the large pre-World War I immigration have done very well economically. By the 1930s and 1940s, the American-born offspring of the older immigrants remained in the same industries as their parents (clothing, steel, meatpacking, etc.), although some moved into managerial or white-collar positions. The third generation began to enter professions and have become doctors, lawyers, engineers, and businesspeople in larger numbers. By 1970 the median family income for Russian Americans was nearly $14,000, which was three to four thousand dollars higher on average than the median family income among Americans of English, Scottish, Welsh, German, Italian, Irish, and French background.

POLITICS AND GOVERNMENT

Aside from their active participation in the labor movement during the early decades of the twentieth century, Russians have generally not become involved in American political life. In a sense, their labor union activity acted as a deterrent to further political work, since many were accused of being socialists or communists. In general, Russians have never formed a strong voting bloc that would encourage American politicians to solicit their support. Only in the past decade, in places like the Brighton Beach area of New York City, have local politicians like U.S. Congressman Stephen Solarz successfully courted the Russian vote.

RELATIONS WITH RUSSIA

While Russians may have avoided American politics, they did not shy away from concern with the homeland. This was particularly the case among the White Russian immigrants. The very fact that they were designated White Russians was a political statement. As refugees and political émigrés, most White Russians felt that their stay abroad was only temporary, and that they must live a Russian life while in temporary exile until the inevitable fall of the Soviet Union would allow them to return to a democratic Russia. This was the basic ideology that held the post-World War I White Russians and the post-World War II DPs together, even though they represented a wide variety of political persuasions. At one extreme some believed in the return of the monarchy. This included a woman living in the New York City area who claimed she was Grand Duchess Anatasia (1901-1918), one of the daughters of the last tsar Nicholas II Romanov who somehow had miraculously survived the mass assassination of the royal family. The legitimacy of this woman's claims were never proved or disproved.

Many rejected the monarchy and awaited the creation of a parliamentary liberal democratic state. The leader of this group was Alexander Kerensky (1881-1970), the last prime minister of Russia before the Bolshevik Revolution. He immigrated to New York City on the eve of World War II to escape the Nazi occupation of Paris where he had been living in exile. There were also regional groups like the Don and Kuban Cossacks who argued for autonomy in a future Russia, several socialist and anarchist groups on the political left, and a Russian fascist organization based in Connecticut during the late 1930s on the far right. Among the post-World War II DPs there were also those who believed in Lenin's brand of socialism, which they felt had been undermined by his successor, Joseph Stalin.

Each of these political orientations had at least one organization and publication that was closely linked to or was a branch of the same or similar émigré organization based in western Europe. Despite their various social, propagandistic, and fund-raising activities, none of these Russian-American organizations ever achieved the abolition of Soviet rule in their Russian homeland. Realizing their inability to end communist rule in Russia, some Russian Americans turned their efforts to their community in the United States and its relationship to American society as a whole. These people became concerned with the way they and their culture were perceived and depicted in America's media and public life. In response to those concerns lobbying groups, such as the Congress of Russian Americans and the Russian-American Congress, came into existence in the 1970s.

INDIVIDUAL AND GROUP CONTRIBUTIONS

ACADEMIA

Several researchers from Russia have enriched our knowledge by writing studies about their native land. In fact, much of America's present-day understanding of Russia and the Soviet Union is in large part due to the work of immigrants like ancient historian Michael Rostovtsev (1870-1972); church historians Georges Florovsky (1893-1979), Alexander Schmemann (1921-1983), and John Meyendorff (1926-1993); linguist Roman Jakobson (1896-1982); literary critic Gleb Struve (1898-1985); and historians Michael Florinsky (1894-1981), Michael Karpovich (1888-1959), Alexander Vasiliev (1867-1953), George Vernadsky (1887-1973), Aleksander Riasanovsky (1923–), and Marc Raeff (1923–).

ART

Influential Russian American artists include Gleb Derujinski, a noted sculptor, and Sergey Rossolovsky, a respected painter from Portland, Maine.

LITERATURE

Writers generally have the greatest difficulty adapting to and being accepted in a new environment, since their language is their instrument of creativity, and by its nature a foreign and inaccessible element. Nevertheless, a few Russian authors have flourished on American soil. These include Vladimir Nabokov (1889-1977), who switched from Russian to English in the late 1940s and produced many novels, including the very popular *Lolita* (1958), and the short story writer Nina Berberova. Two other authors, while continuing to write in Russian, have nonetheless enhanced their careers while in the United States. They are Josef Brodsky (1940–) and the historical novelist and social critic Aleksander Solzhenitzyn (1918–), both of whom were awarded the Nobel Prize for literature.

MILITARY

John Basil Turchin (born Ivan Vasilevich Turchinov) served in the Union army during the Civil War and was promoted to the rank of U.S. Brigadier General—the first Russian American to be elevated to such a high position.

MUSIC, DANCE, AND FILM

Classical music, opera, and ballet in the United States have been enriched for over a century by the presence of Russian composers and performers from Petr Illich Tchaikovsky and Sergei Prokofieff to Fritz Kreisler, Feodor Chaliapin, Sergei Diaghileff, Anna Pavlova, and Rudolf Nureyev, all of whom have graced America's stages for varying periods of time. Others came to stay permanently, including Serge Koussevitsky (1874-1951), conductor of the Boston Symphony Orchestra from 1924 to 1949; composers Sergei Rachmaninoff (1873-1943) and Alexander Gretchaninov (1864-1956); cello virtuoso, conductor, and musical director since 1977 of the National Symphony Orchestra, Mstislav Rostropovich (1927–); choreographer, founder of the School of American Ballet, and from 1948 to his death, director of the New York City Ballet, George Balanchine (1904-1983); and ballet dancers Natalia Makarova (1940–) and Mikhail Baryshnikov (1948). But the most famous of all was Igor Stravinsky (1882-1971), who settled permanently in New York City in 1939, from where he continued to enrich and influence profoundly the course of twentieth-century classical music. Dimitri Tiomkin was a noted composer and musical director and author of many musical scores for Hollywood films. Natalie Wood, who was born in San Francisco as Natasha Gurdin (1938-1981) was an actress in numerous American films.

SCIENCE AND TECHNOLOGY

Vladimir Ipatieff (1867-1952) was a prominent research chemist; George Gamow (1904-1968) was a nuclear physicist who popularized the big-bang theory of the origin of the universe; Wassily Leontieff (1906–) is a Nobel Prize-winning economist who formulated the influential input-output system of economic analysis; Alexander Petrunkevitch (1875-1964) wrote numerous works in the field of zoology; Igor Sikorsky (1889-1972) was an aviation industrialist and inventor of the helicopter; Pitirim Sorokin (1889-1968) was a controversial sociologist who argued that western civilization was doomed unless it attained "creative altruism"; and Vladimir Zworykin (1889-1982) was a physicist and electronics engineer who is known as the father of television.

MEDIA

PRINT

Nezavisimaya Gazeta.

Selected version of Russian daily; text in Russian; published semi-monthly in English translation. Russian online version available.

Address: 7338 Dartford Drive, Suite 9, McLean, Virginia 22102.
Telephone: (703) 827-0414.
Fax: (703) 827-8923.
Online: http://www.ng.ru/.

Novoe Russkoe Slovo/New Russian Word.

This publication is the oldest Russian daily newspaper in the world.

Contact: Andrei Sedych, Publisher.
Address: 111 Fifth Avenue, 5th Floor, New York, New York 10003.
Telephone: (212) 387-0299.
Fax: (212) 387-9050.
E-mail: ads@nrs.com.

Novyi Zhurnal/New Review.

Scholarly publication covering Russian interests.

Contact: Professor Vadim Kreyd, Editor.
Address: 611 Broadway, Ste. 842, New York, New York 10012-2608.
Telephone: (212) 353-1478.
Fax: (212) 353-1478.
E-mail: nriview@village.los.com.

Pravoslavnaya Rus.

Religious newspapaer on Russian Orthodox history and Eastern Orthodox spirituality in Russian.

Contact: Arch Bishop Laurus, Editor-in-Chief
Address: PO Box 36, Jordanville, New York 13361-0036.
Telephone: (315) 858-0940.
Fax: (315) 858-0505.
E-mail: orthrus@telenet.net.

RADIO

KTYM-AM (1460).

Operated by KMNB Media Group.

Address: 7060 Hollywood Boulevard, Suite 919, Los Angeles, California 90028.
Telephone: (323) 463-7007.
Fax: (323) 463-0917.
E-mail: webmaster@kmnb.com.
Online: http://www.kmnb.com/.

WMNB-FM (100.1).
Russian American Broadcasting Company.

Address: One Bridge Plaza, Suite 145, Fort Lee,
    New Jersey 07024.

TELEVISION

KMNB-TV.
Owned and operated by KMNB Media Group.

Address: 7060 Hollywood Boulevard, Suite 919,
    Los Angeles, California 90028.
Telephone: (323) 463-7007.
Fax: (323) 463-0917.
E-mail: webmaster@kmnb.com.
Online: http://www.kmnb.com/.

RTN.
Russian Television Network.

Address: Box 3589, Stamford, Connecticut 06903.
Telephone: (800) 222-2786.

WMNB.
    Russian American Broadcasting Company.

Address: One Bridge Plaza, Suite 145, Fort Lee,
    New Jersey 07024.
Telephone: (800) 570-2778; or (800) 772-2080.

ORGANIZATIONS AND ASSOCIATIONS

Congress of Russian Americans, Inc.
Political action umbrella group with branches
throughout the country; seeks to promote Russian
cultural heritage and to protect the legal, economic, and social interests of Russian Americans.

Contact: Katherine P. Lukin, Treasurer.
Address: P.O. Box 818, Nyack,
    New York 10960-0818.
Telephone: (914) 358-7117.
Fax: (914) 353-5453.
E-mail: pnbcra@sprynet.com.
Online: http://www.russian-americans.org.

Orthodox Church in America.
The largest church with members of Russian background; 12 dioceses throughout North America.

Address: P.O. Box 675, Route 25A, Syosset,
    New York 11791.
Telephone: (516) 922-0550.

Russian Children's Welfare Society.
Philanthropic group to help needy children of who
are immigrants or refugees, especially from Russia.

Contact: Jennifer Kaplan, Executive Director.
Address: 349 West 86th Street, New York,
    New York 10024.
Telephone: (212) 779-2815.
E-mail: main@rcws.org.
Online: http://www.rcws.org.

Russian Independent Mutual Aid Society.
Fraternal organization and insurance company to
provide workers and other policy holders with security in old age.

Contact: Alexander G. Hook, Secretary.
Address: 917 North Wood Street, Chicago,
    Illinois 60622-5005.
Telephone: (312) 421-2272.

MUSEUMS AND RESEARCH CENTERS

Immigration History Research Center.
Contact: Joel Wurl, Curator.
Address: University of Minnesota, 826 Berry
    Street, Minneapolis, Minnesota 55455.
Telephone: (612) 373-5581.
Online: http://www1.umn.edu/ihrc/.

Museum of Russian Culture.
Includes archival and published materials as well as
artifacts pertaining to Russian American life, especially in California.

Address: 2450 Sutter Street, San Francisco,
    California 94115.
Telephone: (415) 911-4082.

**New York Public Library, Slavic and
Baltic Division.**
Aside from a rich collection of printed materials on
the Russian and Soviet homeland, there is much
material on Russians in the United States from the
1890s to the present.

Address: Fifth Avenue and 42nd Street,
    New York, New York 10018.
Telephone: (212) 930-0714.

Orthodox Church in America Archives.
Includes archival and published materials on Russian Orthodox church life in North America from
the late nineteenth century to the present.

Address: P.O. Box 675, Route 25A, Syosset, New York 11791.
Telephone: (516) 922-0550.

SOURCES FOR ADDITIONAL STUDY

Chevigny, Hector. *Russian America: The Great Alaskan Adventure, 1741-1867*. Portland, Oregon: Binford and Mort, 1979.

Davis, Jerome. *The Russian Immigrant*. New York: Arno Press, 1969.

Eubank, Nancy. *The Russians in America*. Minneapolis, Minnesota: Lerner Publications, 1979.

Hardwick, Susan Wiley. *Russian Refuge: Religion, Migration, and Settlement on the North American Pacific Rim*. Chicago: University of Chicago Press, 1993.

Magocsi, Paul Robert. *The Russian Americans*. New York and Philadelphia: Chelsea House, 1989.

Morris, Richard A. *Old Russian Ways: Cultural Variations among Three Russian Groups in Oregon*. New York: AMS Press, 1991.

Ripp, Victor. *Moscow to Main Street: Among the Russian Emigres*. Boston: Little, Brown, and Co., 1984.

Studies of the Third Wave: Recent Migration of Soviet Jews to the United States, edited by Dan N. Jacobs and Ellen Frankel Paul. Boulder, Colorado: Westview Press, 1981.

Wertsman, Vladimir. *The Russians in America, 1727-1976*. Dobbs Ferry, New York: Oceana Publications, 1977.

Salvadoran immigration to the United States is a fairly recent phenomenon. The movement is small in comparison with some of the great immigration waves of the past, but it has a profound significance for both countries.

SALVADORAN AMERICANS

by
Jeremy Mumford

OVERVIEW

The smallest of the Central American states, the Republic of El Salvador measures 21,041 square kilometers—about the size of the state of Massachusetts—and has a population of approximately five million. Situated near the northern end of the Central American isthmus, it is bordered by Guatemala to the northwest, Honduras to the northeast, and the Pacific Ocean to the south. A Spanish-speaking country, El Salvador was given its name—which means "the Savior," referring to Jesus Christ—by the Spanish. Its flag consists of horizontal stripes, two blue and one white, with the national coat of arms in the center. This coat of arms contains branches, flags, green mountains, and the words "Republica de El Salvador en la America Central" and "Dios Union Libertad." Also pictured in the center of the flag are a small red liberty cap and the date of El Salvador's independence from Spain: September 15, 1821.

Two volcanic mountain ranges dominate El Salvador's landscape; they run parallel to each other, east to west, along the length of the country. Just to the north of the southern range lies a broad central plain, the most fertile and populous region of El Salvador, which includes the nation's capital city, San Salvador, and a handful of smaller cities. These urban areas have grown significantly in recent years and by the mid-1990s housed more than half the population of El Salvador. But because El Salvador's economy is largely agricultural, a considerable portion of the population remains in the countryside to work the coffee plantations and other farms.

HISTORY

Before fifteenth-century explorer Christopher Columbus discovered the New World, the land now called El Salvador belonged to the Pipil, nomads of the Nahua language group who were related to the Aztecs of central Mexico. From the eleventh century A.D., the Pipil developed their country of Cuzcatlán ("Land of the Jewel") into an organized state and a sophisticated society, with a capital city located near modern San Salvador. But during the 1520s Spanish *conquistadors*, fresh from the conquest of Mexico, invaded the land of the Pipil. Led by a general named Atlacatl, the Pipil resisted the invasion with initial success, but ultimately succumbed to the Spanish forces.

As in Mexico and the rest of Central America, the *conquistadors* created a divided society in the province they named El Salvador. A small ruling class composed of people of Spanish birth or descent grew rich from the labor of the Indian population. Intermarriage gradually softened the racial division; today the majority of Salvadorans are *mestizos*, with both Spanish and Indian ancestors. But there remains in El Salvador an extreme disparity between the powerful and the powerless, between the wealthy landowners—according to legend, the "Fourteen Families"—and the multitudinous poor.

El Salvador became independent from Spain in 1821. The ex-colony initially joined with Guatemala, Honduras, Nicaragua, and Costa Rica to form the United Provinces of Central America. But the regional federation dissolved after 20 years. Then, threatened by Mexican and Guatemalan aggression, the Salvadoran government sought to make the country part of the United States. The request was turned down. El Salvador remained independent but gradually came under the influence of American banks, corporations, and government policies. The nineteenth and twentieth centuries brought considerable political turmoil to El Salvador, with the army and the plantation owners trading places in a series of unstable regimes.

One constant in Salvadoran history has been its economy of single-crop export agriculture. In the sixteenth century El Salvador produced cacao, from which chocolate is made; in the eighteenth century it grew the indigo plant, which yields a blue dye used in clothing. Since the late nineteenth century, El Salvador's great cash crop has been coffee, although in recent decades the country has also grown cotton and sugar. El Salvador organized its economy with factory-like efficiency, consolidating land into huge plantations worked by landless peasants. As markets changed, cycles of boom and bust hit these people hard.

This unstable social order often became explosive. El Salvador has seen repeated rebellions, each one followed by massive, deadly retaliation against the poor. In 1833 an Indian named Anastasio Aquino led an unsuccessful peasant revolt. Nearly a century later, a Marxist landowner named Agustín Farabundo Martí led another. This was followed by the systematic government murder of rural Indians, leaving an estimated 35,000 dead—an event known as *la matanza*, or "the massacre."

MODERN ERA

Between 1979 and 1992, Salvadoran guerrillas waged a civil war against the government, fueled in part by the same inequities that motivated Aquino and Martí. The nation's army fought back with U.S. money, weapons, and training from American military advisors. An estimated 75,000 people died during the conflict, most of them civilians killed by the army or by clandestine death squads linked to the government (Elston Carr, "Pico-Union: 'Trial' Dramatizes Salvadoran Abuses," *Los Angeles Times*, March 21, 1993). The guerrilla war and the "dirty war" that accompanied it were a national catastrophe. But in 1992, after more than a dozen years of fighting, the army signed a peace accord with the guerrillas' Farabundo Martí National Liberation Front (FMLN). Peace has returned to El Salvador, which is now governed by a reasonably democratic constitution.

SALVADORANS IN AMERICA

Salvadoran immigration to the United States is a fairly recent phenomenon. The movement is small in comparison with some of the great immigration waves of the past, but it has a profound significance for both countries. The flight of Salvadorans from their own country was the most dramatic result of El Salvador's civil war, draining that country of between 20 and 30 percent of its population. Half or more of the refugees—between 500,000 and one million—immigrated to the United States, which was home to less than 10,000 Salvadorans before 1960 (Faren Bachelis, *The Central Americans* [New York: Chelsea House, 1990], p. 10; cited hereafter as Bachelis). El Salvador's exiled population is already changing life at home through its influence and its dollars and will undoubtedly play an important role in its future history.

Salvadoran American immigration has changed the face of foreign affairs in the United States. The flood of refugees from a U.S.-supported government forced a national rethinking of foreign policy priorities. This in turn transformed the nature of American support for the Salvadoran government and may have helped to end the war in El Salvador. Salvadoran Americans are at the center of an ongoing national debate about U.S. responsibility toward the world's refugees and the future of immigration in general.

SIGNIFICANT IMMIGRATION WAVES

The exodus of Salvadorans from their homeland was prompted by both economic and political factors. Historically, El Salvador is a very poor and crowded country. Cyclical poverty and overcrowding have led to patterns of intra-Central American immigration in the past. During the 1960s many Salvadorans moved illegally to Honduras, which is less densely populated. Tension over these immigrants led to war between the nations in 1969, forcing the Salvadorans to return home. El Salvador's civil war from 1979 to 1992 created high unemployment and a crisis of survival for the poor. As in the 1960s, many Salvadorans responded by leaving their native land.

The fear of political persecution has led other Salvadorans to seek refuge in another country. During the 1980s, death squads—secretly connected with government security forces—murdered many suspected leftists. Operating mostly at night, these groups killed tens of thousands of people during the civil war (Bachelis, pp. 41-42). At the height of the death squad movement, 800 bodies were found each month. As the frenetic pace of assassination continued, the squads resorted to increasingly vague "profiles" by which to identify members of so-called "leftwing" groups—all women wearing blue jeans, for instance (Mark Danner, "The Truth of El Mozote," *New Yorker*, December 6, 1993, p. 10). The bodies of some victims were never recovered; these people form the ranks of the "*desaparicinos*" (disappeared).

This climate of pervasive terror prompted many Salvadorans to flee their homeland. Some left after seeing friends or family members murdered or receiving a death threat; others fled violence by the guerrillas or the prospect of forced recruitment into the army. About half of the immigrants ended up in refugee camps in Honduras or in Salvadoran enclaves in Costa Rica, Nicaragua, or Mexico. The other half headed for *el Norte*—the United States.

Because they left quickly and quietly, without property or established connections in the United States, Salvadoran refugees could seldom obtain U.S. visas. They crossed borders illegally, first into Mexico, then into the United States. Refugees trekked through the desert, swam or rowed the Rio Grande, huddled in secret spaces in cars or trucks, or crawled through abandoned sewer tunnels in order to enter the United States. Many sought aid from professional alien smugglers, known as "coyotes," and were sometimes robbed, abandoned in the desert, or kept in virtual slavery until they could buy their freedom.

Once in the United States, Salvadorans remained a secret population. U.S. law provides that aliens (including illegal ones) who can show they have a tenable fear of persecution can receive political asylum and become eligible for a green card. But according to U.S. Immigration and Naturalization Service (INS) figures, political asylum was granted to very few Salvadorans: in the 1980s only 2.1 percent of applications were approved. Those who were turned down faced possible deportation. Therefore, few Salvadorans made their presence known unless they were caught by the INS.

Salvadoran refugees did not at first see themselves as immigrants or Americans. Most hoped to go home as soon as they could do so safely. In the meantime, they clustered together to maintain the language and culture of their homeland. Dense Salvadoran enclaves sprang up in Latino neighborhoods in San Francisco, Chicago, Houston, Washington, D.C., and the New York suburb of Hempstead, Long Island. Wherever a few Salvadorans established themselves, that place became a magnet for friends and relatives; about three quarters of the Salvadoran town of Intipuca, for instance, moved to Washington, D.C. (Segundo Montes and Juan Jose García Vásquez, *Salvadoran Migration to the United States* [Washington, D.C.: Center for Immigration and Refugee Assistance, Georgetown University, 1988]), p. 15; cited hereafter as Montes and Vásquez). On Long Island, outreach workers reported that the population of Salvadorans ballooned from 5,000 before the civil war to over 100,000 in 1999. However, the greatest number of refugees settled in Los Angeles, where Salvadorans soon became the second-largest immigrant community. The Pico-Union and Westlake districts of Los Angeles became a virtual Salvadoran city—by some counts second only to San Salvador.

Salvadoran refugees during the 1980s were only one current in a broad stream of Central American refugees pouring into the United States. Guatemala and Nicaragua, like El Salvador, endured civil wars during this period. Many people from those countries joined the Salvadorans seeking refuge in the United States.

The Central American influx was secret and illegal, and much of mainstream America was at first ignorant of its magnitude. But the INS kept a close eye on the situation. Many Salvadorans who were denied asylum in the States exercised their right to appeal their cases, sometimes all the way up to the Supreme Court. (Until a final decision is reached, the applicant is entitled to temporary working papers.) INS agents suddenly found a huge new bureaucratic workload dropped in their laps, for which they had little experience or funding. Many agents tried to move immigration cases along by any means necessary: intimidating Salvadorans into signing papers in English which put them on the next plane to El Salvador, or refusing asylum applications after a ten-minute interview and deporting the applicants before they had a chance to appeal (Ann Crittenden, *Sanctuary: A Story of American Conscience and the Law in Collision* [New York: Weidenfeld & Nicholson, 1988]).

The deportation of Salvadoran refugees led many liberal American activists to take an interest in the Central American influx. Disheartened by the conservative trend in America in the 1980s, these activists found a rallying point in the plight of the refugees. Some saw the Central American refugee crisis as the great moral test of their generation. Likening the deaths in El Salvador and Guatemala to the Holocaust (the systematic slaughter of European Jews by German Nazis during World War II), human rights activists in the United States felt a moral imperative to petition their government for a change in foreign policy.

American activists established a loose network to aid the refugees. Operating in clear violation of federal laws, they took refugees into their houses, aided their travel across the border, hid them from the authorities, helped them find work, and even gave them legal help. Reviving the ancient custom that a fugitive might find sanctuary inside a church and be safe from capture, the activists often housed refugees in church basements and rectories, giving birth to what later became known as "the sanctuary movement."

Throughout the 1980s the U.S. government extended very little sympathy to Salvadoran refugees. Ironically, the government only began to acknowledge the reality of Salvadoran oppression when persecution and war began to taper off in El Salvador. In 1990 a federal lawsuit brought against the INS by the American Baptist Churches (ABC) forced the agency to apply a more lenient standard

Senator Ricardo Zelada poses with two Salvadoran refugees that he is trying to make sure are receiving the aid they need, in Los Angeles, California.

to Central American asylum applications. The settlement prompted the INS to reopen many Salvadoran applications it had already denied and to approve new ones in greater numbers. By this time, however, many Salvadoran Americans had benefited from an amnesty passed in 1986, which "legalized" illegal immigrants who had entered the States before 1982.

In 1991, after years of debate on the issue, Congress awarded Temporary Protected Status to Salvadorans who had been in the United States since 1990. This status allowed qualifying Salvadorans to live and work in the States for a fixed period of time. Known as the Deferred Enforced Departure (DED), the special status was scheduled to expire at the end of 1994.

Although the war is over in El Salvador, many Salvadoran Americans are still afraid to return to their homeland. ARENA, the political party most closely associated with the death squads, was in power in the mid-1990s, and many of the conditions that brought about the war remained the same. Furthermore, Salvadoran Americans had established roots and a new livelihood in the United States. A 1990 poll found that 70 percent of Salvadorans surveyed did not intend to return to El Salvador, even if they knew they were safe (Robert Lopez, "Salvadorans Turn Eyes Homeward as War Ends," *Los Angeles Times*, December 27, 1992). However, Salvadoran Americans maintain close ties to friends and relatives at home. Within a year after the civil war ended, about 350,000 Salvadoran Americans visited El Salvador (Tracy Wilkinson,

"Returning to Reclaim a Dream," *Los Angeles Times*, May 19, 1993).

Due to poor INS records and the low profile of undocumented immigrants, statistics regarding Salvadoran immigration are notoriously unreliable. As of 1995 the total number of Salvadorans in the United States was somewhere between 500,000 and 1 million. Approximately one-third of the immigrant population were green card holders, who could apply for U.S. citizenship after five years. Between one-fifth and one-third had some form of temporary legal status. The remaining third were undocumented and therefore illegal.

ACCULTURATION AND ASSIMILATION

Assimilation is more problematic for Salvadorans in the United States than it has been for other immigrants. Most Salvadorans who have any legal status at all are asylum seekers, motivated to immigrate to the States because of fear of persecution, not a desire to become an American. Asylum laws prohibit many Salvadorans from renewing their ties to their home culture. Most asylum seekers cannot visit El Salvador, even for a loved one's funeral, without losing their legal status in the United States. (The assumption is that anyone who travels to El Salvador—whatever the reason—is not really afraid of persecution there.) Thus, many Salvadoran Americans are torn between embracing the culture of America and maintaining their Salvadoran identities.

Salvadoran Americans form an insular community—with their own social clubs, doctors, even banks—and often have little contact with outsiders. They maintain a tight network, living almost exclusively with other people from their home country, or even their hometown (Pamela Constable, "We Will Stay Together," *Washington Post Magazine*, October 30, 1994; Doreen Cavaja,"Making Ends Meet in a Nether World," *New York Times*, December 13, 1994). Many older immigrants have spent more than ten years in the United States without learning any English.

Although they immigrated largely out of fear rather than a desire for a new life, Salvadorans in the United States, especially the younger generations, are gradually becoming Americanized. While conditions have improved in El Salvador, few refugees have returned home. The United States—once a place of refuge—has become a new home for Salvadoran immigrants. To reflect the changing needs of the Salvadoran American community, the Central American Refugee Center in Los Angeles (CARECEN), one of the largest support organizations for refugees, changed its name to the Central American Resource Center (Elston Carr, "A New Direction," *Los Angeles Times*, May 9, 1993).

TRADITIONS, CUSTOMS, AND BELIEFS

El Salvador has a rich heritage of folk beliefs and customs, which evolved in a landscape of villages, fields, forests, and mountains. Salvadoran Americans seek to preserve their traditional rural culture—a difficult proposition, considering most Salvadorans settle in America's largest cities.

Salvadoran folklore is rooted in supernatural beliefs. Tales of ghosts and spirits have been passed orally from generation to generation. One such spirit is the Siguanaba, a beautiful woman who seduces men she finds alone in the forest at night and drives them mad. Slightly less dangerous are the Cadejos, two huge dogs; the black one brings bad luck, while the white one brings good luck. Another spirit, the Cipitío, is a dwarf with a big hat who eats ashes from fireplaces and strews flower petals in the paths of pretty girls. Such country legends have little meaning in a Los Angeles barrio; they are rapidly dying out among Salvadoran American children, a generation thoroughly immersed in the world of American cartoons and comic book characters.

MISCONCEPTIONS AND STEREOTYPES

Salvadoran Americans have sometimes had tense relations with their neighbors in the cities where they are concentrated. Salvadoran gangs have fought with Mexican gangs in Los Angeles, and in Washington, D.C., a city with a significant Salvadoran population, they have competed with African Americans for jobs and resources. In May of 1991, after a black policewoman shot and killed a Salvadoran man during an arrest, Salvadorans in Washington's Mt. Pleasant neighborhood rioted. This incident, however, is not necessarily representative of relations in all Salvadoran American communities.

Many cultural observers contend that mainstream America has not yet formed a distinct stereotype of Salvadoran Americans. Salvadorans have settled in neighborhoods already populated by Mexican Americans, and outsiders generally have only a vague sense of the various Latino nationalities in those neighborhoods. But Salvadorans certainly share in the widespread discrimination leveled at Latinos. In the New York borough of Brooklyn, for example, a group of white teenagers who beat up a Salvadoran man in a neighborhood park reportedly referred to him as "that Mexican."

PROVERBS

Salvadoran Spanish is rich in proverbs that reflect the country's rural landscape. While a North American might say, "Be quiet, the walls have ears," a Salvadoran would warn, "There are parrots in the field."

CUISINE

Salvadoran food is similar to Mexican food but is sweeter and milder. The foundation of the diet is cornmeal tortillas (thicker than the Mexican variety), rice, salt, and beans. The most popular national snack is the *pupusa*, a cornmeal griddle-cake stuffed with various combinations of cheese, spices, beans, and pork. *Pupusas* are served with *curtido*, a cabbage and carrot salad made with vinegar. A more substantial meal is *salpicón*, minced beef cooked with onions and chilies and served with rice and beans. For dessert, many dishes include fried or stewed bananas. *Chicha*, a sweet drink made from pineapple juice, is a popular beverage. The best Salvadoran food is found in private homes, but many Salvadoran restaurants and food stands have opened in Los Angeles and other cities where Salvadoran Americans live.

Both in El Salvador and in Salvadoran American neighborhoods, people love to buy food from street vendors. Popular street foods include *pupusas* and mango slices—spiced with salt, lime juice, red pepper, and crushed pumpkin and sesame seeds.

TRADITIONAL DRESS

Salvadorans wear the same Western-style clothing worn by most Latin Americans who are not culturally Indian. Salvadorans in the highlands, where nights can be very cold, occasionally wear brightly colored blankets of traditional Mayan design, but they call these Guatemalan blankets, underscoring their foreign origin. Around their necks, many Salvadorans wear small crosses tightly wrapped with colored yarn.

MUSIC

The most popular musical form in El Salvador is the *cumbia*, a style that originated in Colombia. A typical *cumbia* is performed with a male singer (usually a high baritone or tenor) backed by a male chorus, drums (primarily kettledrum and bass drum), electric guitar and bass, and either a brass section or an accordion. The 2/4 beat is slower than most Latin music; the baseline is heavy and up-front. A very danceable musical form, it is popular with non-Latin audiences.

Ranchera music, which originated in Mexico, is also well liked by the country people in El Salvador. In the cities, many people listen to rock and rap music from the United States. Mexican American musical styles such as *salsa*, *merengue*, and *tejano* music have become increasingly popular among Salvadorans in the United States. These and other styles from North America are also gaining more listeners in El Salvador.

HOLIDAYS

Many Salvadoran Americans celebrate Independence Day for all of Central America on September 15 of each year. The first week in August is the most important national religious festival, honoring Christ, El Salvador's patron and namesake, as the holy savior of the world. Known simply as the National Celebration, this week is marked in both El Salvador and Salvadoran American neighborhoods with processions, carnival rides, fireworks, and soccer matches.

HEALTH ISSUES

The single greatest health problem in El Salvador is malnutrition, which especially affects children. This problem is largely absent among Salvadoran Americans. Still, undocumented Salvadoran Americans are often hesitant to visit American doctors or hospitals, for fear of being reported to the immigration authorities. And many communities—including, through 1994's Proposition 187, the State of California—have sought to deny public health services to undocumented immigrants.

Partly for these reasons, some Salvadoran Americans continue to rely on traditional healers. Such practitioners, known as *curanderos*, use herb teas and poultices, traditional exercises, incantations, and magical touching to heal. Other Salvadoran immigrants are patients of Salvadoran doctors who may have received training at home but have no license to practice in the United States (John McQuiston, "Man Held for Practicing Dentistry without Degree or License," *New York Times*, December 2, 1994).

Some Salvadoran Americans carry deep emotional scars from the torture they suffered or witnessed. Many are tormented by rage, continuing fear, and guilt at escaping the violence that claimed the lives of so many of their loved ones. As a result, some members of the immigrant community suffer from depression, alcoholism, and erratic or violent behavior. Few Salvadoran Americans can afford to receive the psychological help they need to work through their traumatic experiences (Marcelo Suarez-Orozco, *Central American Refugees and U.S. High Schools* [Palo Alto: Stanford University Press, 1989]).

LANGUAGE

Spanish is the first language of almost all Salvadorans. Salvadoran Spanish is very close to the Spanish spoken in Mexico and other Central American countries; it is recognizable only by its accent.

El Salvador stands apart from neighboring countries in that its indigenous languages are virtually dead. One possible explanation for this loss lies in El Salvador's history of widespread violence against the poor. In the aftermath of the 1833 rebellion and during the *matanza* of 1932, government forces singled out Indians to be killed; out of self-protection, many Salvadoran Indians adopted Spanish language and dress during these times.

Because of their initial determination to return to El Salvador, many immigrants to America at first resisted learning English. However, bilingual education programs, particularly in Los Angeles and Washington, D.C., have been extremely helpful to Salvadoran children (Pamela Constable, "Bilingual Plan Draws Bitter Words in D.C., *Washington Post,* October 26, 1994).

FAMILY AND COMMUNITY DYNAMICS

The traditional family in El Salvador, as in Latin America generally, is large and close-knit. The father exercises final authority in all things, and together the parents maintain firm control over their children, above all their daughters. Among Salvadoran Americans, though, this pattern has begun to change. The immigration process and the vastly different conditions of life in the United States have altered Salvadoran family dynamics in dramatic and at times destructive ways.

Due to the nature of their flight to the United States, many Salvadoran refugees made the journey alone: husbands left their wives, parents their children, teenagers their families. Entire families were separated and often stayed that way. Many refugees married non-Salvadorans, sometimes for immigration benefits, and Salvadoran Americans were barred from returning home for any reason without forfeiting a request for asylum.

Some Salvadoran parents who were separated from their children for a long period of time during the immigration process found—when finally reunited as a family—that they had lost some of their traditional parental authority and control over the youngsters. Likewise, teenagers who settled in the United States alone grew into adulthood under influences very different from those they would have encountered at home. Even when families moved to America together, family dynamics inevitably changed under new cultural influences. Children learned English faster and adapted more readily to their new surroundings than their parents. They often had to translate or explain things to their parents, argue for their parents with English-speaking storekeepers, and in general become more knowledgeable and confident than their parents. This role-reversal proved painful for both generations.

Salvadoran American parents generally fear that their children may stray too far in America's permissive society. Indeed, many young Salvadoran Americans have formed gangs, especially in Los Angeles, where the culture of Latino youth gangs has deep roots. These gangs, including the nationally known Salva Mara Trucha, distribute drugs, extort money from local merchants (especially street vendors), and battle for turf with Mexican gang members (Mike O'Connor, "A New U.S. Import in El Salvador," *New York Times,* July 3, 1994; Anthony Millican, "Street Gang Shakes Down Vendors for Sidewalk 'Rent'," *Los Angeles Times,* December 27, 1992).

RITUALS OF FAMILY LIFE

Salvadoran Catholicism emphasizes all the sacraments that are practiced in other Catholic countries: baptism, confirmation, marriage in the church, communion at mass, and last rites. Other occasions are also celebrated in church, such as graduation from school and a girl's *quinceañera,* or fifteenth birthday. Still, when compared with other Central Americans, a surprising number of Salvadorans do not observe church rituals. Church weddings, for instance, are considered prohibitively expensive for the poor, and common-law marriage is frequently practiced.

One ritual of family life which is common even among the poor is *compadrazgo,* or the naming of godparents. Latin Americans of all nationalities practice this custom. They place special importance in the relationship between a child and his or her *padrino* and *madrina*—and between the parents and their *compadres,* the friends they honored by choosing them for this role.

Some rituals of the old country have been abandoned by members of the immigrant community. For instance, the traditional Salvadoran practice of interring bodies in family crypts has recently given way to a more Americanized approach to burying the dead. In the early 1980s, most Salvadoran Americans who could afford it had their bodies sent to El Salvador for burial after death, a posthumous relocation that could cost thousands of dollars. By the mid-1990s, Salvadoran Americans were beginning to reach the painful conclusion that their families would never return to El Salvador; as a result, more and more immigrants are opting for burials in the United States (Gabriel Escobar, "Latinos Making U.S. Their Home in Life and Death," *Washington Post*, July 12, 1993).

PUBLIC ASSISTANCE

Few Salvadoran American families depend entirely on public assistance; a large portion of the immigrant population is undocumented and therefore does not qualify for government benefits. However, the high rate of poverty in the community forces many to seek whatever help they can find—either through assistance for U.S.-born children or through fraudulently obtained benefits. The extent of reliance on public assistance is hard to estimate due to its underground nature.

EDUCATION

Salvadoran Americans, like many immigrants, place a high value on education as a way to advance in the world. Some Salvadorans cherish education in particular because of their ongoing struggle to achieve it at home: because the National University in San Salvador included a number of Marxist professors and students, the government closed down the campus in 1980. Some professors and students kept classes going in a variety of small buildings and private homes; all Salvadoran university students realized that they could not take access to education for granted.

In the United States access to education has been equally difficult for Salvadorans. Many schools excluded or reported undocumented students, until the U.S. Supreme Court decision in *Plyer v. Doe* (1982) established that all children, even illegal immigrants, have a constitutional right to attend public school. This issue remains controversial: California's Proposition 187, approved by voters in 1994, seeks again to exclude undocumented students from public schools.

At the university level, few institutions allow undocumented immigrants to enroll. California State is one of the few universities to admit students without proof of legal residency. Furthermore, it allows undocumented immigrants in California to pay the low tuition charged to state residents, instead of the much higher out-of-state rates. As the only major university where undocumented immigrants can enroll for less than $2000 per year, it has attracted many Salvadoran American students to its campuses in Southern California. Again, this educational route is threatened by California's Proposition 187.

RELIGION

Most Salvadorans are members of the Roman Catholic church, although various evangelical Protestant denominations, including Baptists, Seventh-Day Adventists, Assemblies of God, and Mormons, also have Salvadoran adherents. In addition, a small number of Salvadorans are Jewish or Muslim, stemming from late nineteenth-century immigration from the Middle East.

Salvadoran Catholicism bears the strong influence of liberation theology, a Catholic school of thought that evolved in Latin America during the 1960s and 1970s. Liberation theology teaches that Christianity is a religion of the poor. The movement encouraged impoverished Salvadorans to form Christian communities—or "base communities"—to improve their lives. Dedicated both to Bible study and to mutual aid in the secular world, these communities organized credit unions, cooperative stores, labor and peasant unions, and political activist groups.

Liberation theology received an important boost from the approval of the 1968 Latin American Bishops' Conference in Medellín, Colombia. In the late 1970s Salvadoran Archbishop Oscar Romero, though originally selected for his conservative views, became an important patron of the new theology. Young priests carried the message to the Salvadoran countryside with an evangelical fervor, but a shortage of priests in El Salvador necessitated an increase in the involvement of the Catholic laity. Base communities sprang up both in the cities and the country.

Liberation theology's success in organizing the poor had a profound impact on Salvadoran politics. The movement brought new political ideas to the countryside, as the universities did to the cities. Many of the peasants who comprised the rural left during the civil war—guerrillas, farmworker federation members, activists who demonstrated in San Salvador—traced the origins of their political consciousness to participation in a base community.

The Salvadoran army was well aware of the effects of the new theology. Starting in the 1970s, it targeted Catholic organizers for harassment and death. In March of 1980 Archbishop Romero was assassinated while saying mass; the murder was attributed to a right-wing death squad. Nine months later, four U.S. churchwomen who were working in El Salvador were killed, causing outrage in the States. And in November of 1989, six Jesuit priests and two women were killed on the San Salvador campus of the Jesuit-run Central American University.

Salvadoran American Catholics have not reproduced the full-fledged base communities that they left behind in El Salvador. However, many Salvadoran Americans are members of progressive Latino Catholic congregations, influenced by liberation theology and Vatican II, which advocate social justice and self-empowerment among the poor. These same congregations have a history of activity in the sanctuary movement, helping their Salvadoran members gain a foothold in the United States.

In addition to the Catholic church, several evangelical Protestant denominations have Salvadoran churches. These communities were founded throughout the Salvadoran countryside during the twentieth century by missionaries from the United States. In the 1970s and 1980s the evangelical sects increased their missionary efforts, in particular through the influence of American military advisers on soldiers in the Salvadoran army. Both in El Salvador and in the States, Salvadoran evangelicals tend to be more socially and politically conservative than Catholics.

EMPLOYMENT AND ECONOMIC TRADITIONS

Salvadorans have often been referred to as "the Germans of Central America" because of their strong work ethic (Walter LaFeber, *Inevitable Revolutions* [New York: Norton, 1993], p. 10). Salvadorans in the United States are among the hardest-working immigrants, working enough hours at low-paying jobs to send about $800 million home every year.

Although many Salvadoran refugees worked on the land before immigrating to the United States, few of them settled in America's rural areas. In this respect, Salvadorans differ from newly arrived Mexican Americans, many of whom engage in migrant farm labor; Salvadoran immigrants are instead concentrated in unskilled urban jobs that do not require English.

Many Salvadoran American men work in hotel and restaurant kitchens, especially in Los Angeles. Others work as day laborers in the building trades.

Many Salvadoran American women work as nannies and maids. Both men and women perform cleaning and janitorial services in hotels, commercial buildings, and homes. Some Salvadorans also work as unlicensed street vendors of food and goods, a line of work which is illegal in Los Angeles and other cities but is nevertheless tolerated and in fact contributes to the life and economy of the city.

Although Salvadoran Americans toil in the lowest-paying sectors of the American economy, they are slowly but inexorably becoming more prosperous. They work long hours, save a great deal, and are gradually moving from the inner cities to the suburbs.

Because the majority of Salvadoran Americans continue to toil in the lowest-paying sectors of the American economy, tens of thousands of these immigrants remain in both urban and suburban ghettoes, alienated from the communities around them. Many live in overcrowded shared or partitioned housing and struggle to get ahead while they support families back in El Salvador. Others, however, are becoming more prosperous, and are participating members of the communities in which they live.

Salvadoran American income is of vital importance to El Salvador. Salvadoran Americans, even those who are poor, have an incentive to send money to family and friends in El Salvador because a U.S. dollar buys much more there than in the States. In all, they send approximately $800 million back home per year—close to $1000 per person. These payments, known as remittances, are the largest source of income for El Salvador—larger than either coffee exports or U.S. government aid. For this reason, El Salvador is sometimes said to have a "remittance economy" (Montes and Vásquez, p. 15). It is in part because of this contribution to the economy at home that Salvadoran politicians lobby Washington for permanent status for Salvadoran Americans.

Salvadoran Americans have also brought large numbers of American consumer goods to El Salvador. By 1994 far more homes in El Salvador had color televisions, stereos, and other modern equipment than they did 15 years earlier. In this way, too, Salvadoran Americans have transformed the texture of life in El Salvador.

In addition to gifts and remittances, Salvadoran Americans have extensive investments in their home country. They may not plan to return permanently, but many are keeping the option open. According to one report, two-thirds of new housing built in San Salvador is bought by Salvadoran Americans (Tom Gibb, "Those Who Didn't Flee Rely on U.S.," *San Francisco Chronicle*, August 30, 1993. Taking as its model the role American Jews played in the growth of Israel, the Los Angeles agency El Rescate hopes to establish a bank that will allow expatriates to invest directly in Salvadoran development (Robert Lopez, "A Piece of the Pie," *Los Angeles Times*, September 19, 1993).

POLITICS AND GOVERNMENT

The Salvadoran American community has not been a significant political force either in the United States or at home. However, the size, concentration, and organization of the community suggest that this may change in the future. Most Salvadoran Americans are not U.S. citizens and therefore do not have the right to vote in elections. Salvadorans do not have nearly as much influence with the political establishment as voting constituencies have. In Los Angeles, for instance, there is a stark contrast between the U.S.-born Chicano neighborhoods of East L.A. and the Pico-Union and Westlake neighborhoods, populated by immigrant Mexicans and Central Americans. The former have many community centers, legal services, and social workers; the latter have very few (Hector Tobar, "No Strength in Numbers for LA's Divided Latinos," *Los Angeles Times*, September 1, 1992). This situation is slowly changing, however: Carlos Vaquerano, the Salvadoran community affairs director of CARECEN, was named to the board of Rebuild L.A., organized to help the city recover from the L.A. riots in 1992 (Miles Corwin, "Understanding the Riots," *Los Angeles Times*, November 16, 1992).

One area of U.S. politics in which Salvadoran Americans have played an important role is in legislation regarding their immigration status. In the debate leading to the passage of Temporary Protected Status for Salvadoran refugees and the extensions of that status, Salvadoran organizations lobbied politicians and brought their cases of persecution to the press. At first, refugee organizations were run by Americans, and Salvadorans often appeared in public only with bandannas over their faces. Gradually, Salvadorans and other Central Americans began to take charge of the refugee organizations and assume a higher public profile.

Salvadoran Americans have also contributed significantly to labor union activity. Many refugees fought for the right to organize under repressive conditions in El Salvador, and they brought dedication, even militancy, to American unions. In a 1990 Los Angeles janitors' strike, for instance, Salvadoran union members continued to march and demonstrate even under the threat of police violence. And Salvadoran street vendors in Los Angeles have organized to improve their precarious situation (Tracy Wilkinson, "New Questions Arise for Salvadorans in Los Angeles," *Los Angeles Times*, January 12, 1992).

RELATIONS WITH EL SALVADOR

Most Salvadoran Americans are not active in or outspoken about Salvadoran politics. Those U.S. organizations most actively involved in Salvadoran politics (such as the Committee in Solidarity with the People of El Salvador, CISPES) have attracted little participation by Salvadoran Americans themselves. The immigrants' own organizations have focused not on politics at home, but on relief and jobs in immigrant communities throughout the United States. This relative indifference to home politics may be surprising, given the political passions that have long raged in El Salvador; but the majority of Salvadoran Americans seem interested in putting the hatred of the past behind them.

While the most ideologically committed of the Salvadoran refugees settled in Mexico, Nicaragua, or Costa Rica, those who settled in the United States focused on survival and building a community. Refugees who fled the government and refugees who fled the guerrillas have a lot in common; many will not even discuss their political beliefs, lest it disrupt the fragile solidarity of the refugee community. Furthermore, many Salvadorans on the left became active in politics because of the desperate poverty and class war in El Salvador; when they arrived in the United States, where it seemed for the first time possible to escape poverty through hard work, their political commitment sometimes melted away.

Salvadorans outside El Salvador are not permitted to cast absentee ballots in that country's elections. The majority of the refugee community is thought to favor the left, and the absence of their votes is believed to have helped the right-wing party ARENA win the Salvadoran presidency in 1989 and 1994 (Lisa Leff, "At Peace but Uneasy, Salvadorans Vote Today," *Washington Post*, March 20, 1994).

The relative lack of political influence among Salvadoran Americans is not necessarily permanent. Salvadoran immigrants are densely concentrated in a few cities, and they have a strong infrastructure in refugee organizations. As more Salvadorans become U.S. citizens, the immigrant community will probably play a larger role in local and regional politics. And given their economic contribution, they will almost certainly come to exert more influence in El Salvador.

INDIVIDUAL AND GROUP CONTRIBUTIONS

ARTS

Claribel Alegría (1924–), the most famous living Salvadoran writer, was born in Nicaragua but moved with her family to El Salvador at an early age. She studied at George Washington University in Washington, D.C., and has since visited the United States on a regular basis. With her U.S.-born husband, Darwin Flakoll, she has lived in various parts of the world—particularly Spain and Nicaragua—but she considers herself a Salvadoran. Her autobiographical poetry and fiction (some written in collaboration with her husband) is very popular among both Salvadorans and Salvadoran Americans and provides a rich portrait of bourgeois life in a provincial Salvadoran city.

Many Salvadorans involved in their country's political strife have recorded their feelings in poetry; one such writer, Miguel Huezo Mixco (1954–), was a guerrilla soldier who composed and published verses during campaigns against the army (Mirrors of War [New York: Monthly Review Press, 1985], p. 147).

Dagoberto Reyes, a Salvadoran painter and sculptor, immigrated to Los Angeles in the early 1980s. His sculpture "Porque Emigramos" ("Why We Immigrate") was commissioned to stand in Los Angeles's MacArthur Park.

Alvaro Torres, a popular singer of Spanish-language romantic ballads, was born in El Salvador and lived in Guatemala and Mexico before moving to the United States. José Reyes, another popular Salvadoran musician, also lives in the United States.

Christy Turlington (1969–) is an internationally known supermodel. The daughter of a Salvadoran mother, she began modeling at the age of 14. She has appeared on the runways of Paris, Milan, and New York, in the pages of every major fashion magazine, and has contracts with Maybelline, Calvin Klein, and Vidal Sassoon. Turlington is also a noted animal rights activist and has raised money for Salvadoran causes.

EDUCATION

Jorge Catán Zablah (1939–), a Salvadoran who received his Ph.D. from University of California at Santa Barbara, is the chairman of the Spanish Department at the Defense Language Institute in Monterey, California.

GOVERNMENT AND POLITICS

Colonel Nicolás Carranza is an infamous Salvadoran American who commanded El Salvador's Treasury Police in the early 1980s. He has been accused of organizing and overseeing many of the clandestine death squads that operated during those years. In 1988 the Nation reported that he was living in Kentucky, supported by active duty pay from the Salvadoran military and an annual stipend from the CIA.

SPORTS

Hugo Perez, a midfielder on the U.S. national soccer team, immigrated from El Salvador to Los Angeles as a child. The second-highest all-time scorer on the U.S. team, he contributed to America's unexpectedly competitive performance in the 1994 World Cup. During World Cup matches played at Pasadena, California, Salvadoran Americans were among the most vociferous fans of the U.S. team. Waldir Guerra (1967–), another great Salvadoran soccer player who learned his craft in L.A.'s highly competitive Salvadoran soccer leagues, immigrated to the United States from his hometown of San Vicente, El Salvador, at age 16. He was a star in college and professional soccer in California and later returned to El Salvador to play professional soccer there. A member of the Santa Ana team, he is considered the second-best player in all of El Salvador.

MEDIA

Most Salvadoran Americans rely on the general Spanish-language media in the United States, which is largely produced by Mexicans, Puerto Ricans, and Cubans. There are very few media outlets geared specifically toward Salvadoran Americans.

RADIO

KPFK-FM (90.7).
Pacifica Radio for Southern California, broadcasts a radio show for Salvadorans hosted by Carlos Figueroa, who has also worked with the FMLN's Radio Venceremos in El Salvador.

Address: 3729 Cahuenga Boulevard West, North Hollywood, California 91604.
Telephone: (818) 985-2711.
E-mail: kpfk@pacifica.org.
Online: http://www.kpfk.org/.

TELEVISION

KMET-TV, Channel 38.
This Los Angeles station airs a 30-minute daily

show focusing on Salvadoran American news and culture, hosted by José Trinidad.

Contact: Laura Cohen, Public Relations Director.
Telephone: (213) 469-5638.

ORGANIZATIONS AND ASSOCIATIONS

Central American Refugee Center (CARECEN).
Address: 91 North Franklin Street, Suite 211, Hempstead, New York 11550.
Telephone: (516) 489-8330.
Fax: (516) 489-8308.
E-mail:carecen@pb.net.
Online: http://www.icomm.ca/carecen/.

Central American Resource Center (CARECEN).
Founded in 1983 as Central American Refugee Center. A relief organization for refugees, CARE-CEN has evolved into a community self-help and advocacy organization for Central Americans. Though largely staffed by non-Central Americans, its director is Salvadoran American. The Los Angeles office has changed its name from the Central American Refugee Center to the Central American Resource Center. CARECEN has independent offices in several U.S. cities.

Contact: Robert Lovato, Executive Director.
Address: 1636 West Eighth Street, Los Angeles, California.
Telephone: (213) 385-1638.

Centro Presente.
A community center for Central Americans in the Boston area.

Address: 54 Essex Street, Cambridge, Massachusetts.
Telephone: (617) 497-9080.

El Rescate.
Established in 1981, El Rescate provides legal, educational, and community economic development services to Central American refugees in the Los Angeles area.

Contact: Oscar Andrade, Director.
Address: 1340 South Bonnie Brae Street, Los Angeles, California.
Telephone: (213) 736-4703.

Interfaith Office on Accompaniment (IOA).
Works to support the refugees and displaced communities of El Salvador. Aims to enhance moral, political, and economic development by sending interfaith delegations and church volunteers to assist the Salvadoran people.

Contact: Lana Dalbert, Chair.
Address: 1050 South Van Ness Avenue, San Francisco, California 94110.
Telephone: (415) 821-7102.

MUSEUMS AND RESEARCH CENTERS

Central America Resource Center (CARC).
This Texas organization releases a bimonthly English-language newsletter with political and cultural news from Central America, selected and translated from a variety of Spanish-language news sources. It also maintains a library and archive in its Austin office. Not to be confused with the social service organization CARECEN.

Address: 2520 Longview, Austin, Texas 78705.
Telephone: (512) 476-9841.

Hemispheric Migration Project, Center for Immigration Policy and Refugee Assistance, Georgetown University.
This project sponsors and publishes research on various population movements within the Americas, including the migration of Central Americans to the United States.

Address: Box 2298, Hoya Station, Washington, D.C. 20057.
Telephone: (202) 687-7032.

SOURCES FOR ADDITIONAL STUDY

Bachelis, Faren. *The Central Americans.* New York: Chelsea House, 1990.

Constable, Pamela. "We Will Stay Together," *Washington Post Magazine,* October 30, 1994.

Crittenden, Ann. *Sanctuary: A Story of American Conscience and the Law in Collision.* New York: Weidenfeld & Nicholson, 1988.

Mahler, Sarah J. *Salvadorans in Suburbia: Symbiosis and Conflict*. Boston: Allyn and Bacon, 1995.

Montes, Segundo, Juan Jose, and García Vásquez. *Salvadoran Migration to the United States: An Exploratory Study*. Washington, D.C.: Center for Immigration Policy and Refugee Assistance, Georgetown University, 1988.

Suarez-Orozco, Marcelo. *Central American Refugees and U.S. High Schools*. Palo Alto: Stanford University Press, 1989.

U.S. Senate Committee on the Judiciary. Subcommittee on Immigration and Refugee Affairs. *Central American Migration to the United States*. Washington, D.C.: Government Printing Office, 1990.

SAMOAN

by
Paul Cox

AMERICANS

Samoans have an expansive view of familial bonds. A Samoan *a'iga* or family includes all individuals who descend from a common ancestor.

OVERVIEW

The Samoan archipelago consists of 15 inhabited islands in the South Pacific that are located approximately 14 degrees south latitude and between 171 and 173 degrees west longitude. The archipelago is a politically divided one. The eastern group of islands is known as American Samoa, a U.S. territory with a population of 41,000. The total land area of American Samoa is 77 square miles and includes seven major islands: Tutuila (which includes the territorial capital of Pago Pago), Aunu'u, Ta'u, Ofu, Olosega, Swains Island, and Rose Atoll. American Samoa is administered by an elected governor and territorial legislature as well as a non-voting delegate to the U.S. House of Representatives. The native-born residents of American Samoa are considered American nationals. While they do not pay U.S. income taxes or vote in U.S. presidential elections, they may serve in the U.S. armed services.

The western half of the archipelago comprises Western Samoa, an independent country. These islands have a total population of 182,000 and a total land area of 1,104 square miles. Western Samoa includes four inhabited islands: Upolu (which houses Apia, the nation's capital), Manu'a, Apolima, and Savaii, which is the largest but also the most underdeveloped of these islands. A former United Nations protectorate under the administration of New Zealand, Western Samoa is a member of the British Commonwealth.

Samoan weather is usually hot and wet, with a mean temperature of 79.5 degrees fahrenheit and heavy annual rainfall. In the city of Apia, for instance, annual rainfall measures about 80 inches.

The number of Samoans living outside of Samoa easily exceeds the combined population of both American and Western Samoa. Large populations of expatriate Samoans can be found in Auckland, New Zealand; Honolulu, Hawaii; Los Angeles, California; San Francisco, California; and Salt Lake City, Utah. Smaller groups have settled in Wellington, New Zealand; Sydney, Australia; Laie, Hawaii; Oakland, California; and Independence, Missouri. Most older expatriate Samoans are immigrants, although many of their offspring are natural-born citizens of their host countries. Regardless of birthplace, however, peoples of Samoan descent are linked by a distinctive cultural heritage that continues to flourish on those South Pacific islands.

HISTORY

The Samoan islands were colonized between 500 and 800 B.C. by an oceanic people distinguished by their production of Lapita pottery—a unique pottery form named after one of the original sites of pottery shard discovery in Melanesia. Based on archaeological, botanical, and linguistic evidence, it seems almost certain that the ancestors of the Samoans originated in Indo-Malaysia, spent several centuries living along coastal areas of New Guinea, and then colonized Samoa and Tonga, another island in the Pacific Ocean. It is unclear whether Samoa or Tonga was colonized first, but it was within these archipelagos that Polynesian culture developed from its Lapita roots. Over time the descendants of these original immigrants colonized other regions, including Tahiti and other areas of eastern Polynesia, the Marquesas, Hawaii, and New Zealand. The ancestors of the Polynesians brought with them a group of agricultural plants distinguished by a variety of tree crops that produced nuts and fruits (including breadfruit) and a set of starchy tuberous crops, including taro and yams. Once in Samoa, the Lapita potters developed a material culture characterized by a few large stone fortifications, early attempts at irrigation, and a startling talent for producing highly finished boat timbers.

The quality of the ship timbers produced by the Samoans did not escape notice. Indeed, the first European accounts of Samoa speak admiringly of the work of the islands' inhabitants in this respect. The quality of Samoan boats suggested an easy facility with tools of iron, according to the journals of Jacob Roggeveen, the first European to discover Samoa. Roggeveen happened upon the islands in 1722 during his ill-fated voyage from the Netherlands to New Ireland. He recorded that the Samoan seamen were a sturdy, healthy group, although he mistook their tattoos for paint. Although he traded a few nails for coconuts, Roggeveen was unable to entice any of the Samoans to board his ship. Concerned about the lateness of the season and the poor anchoring terrain, Roggeveen decided not to attempt a landing.

The second European explorer to visit Samoa, Louis Antoine de Bougainville, named the archipelago the "Navigator Islands" in honor of the superb sailing vessels manned by the natives. "Their canoes are made with a good deal of skill, and have an outrigger," he wrote. "Though we ran seven or eight knots at this time, yet the [canoes] sailed round us with the same ease as if we had been at anchor."

After sighting Bougainville's ship, the Samoans sent out a party in a canoe to meet him. Bougainville reported they "were naked, excepting their natural parts, and shewed us cocoa-nuts and roots." The "roots" presented to Bougainville were likely those of *Piper methysticum*, used in Samoa to make *kava*, a beverage that is consumed on ceremonial occasions. The present of both coconuts and *kava* to Bougainville constituted a *sua*, or ceremonial offering of respect to a traveling party. *Kava* roots were also ceremonially presented to the next European to visit Samoa, the French explorer La Perouse, on December 6, 1787. The presentation of *Piper methysticum* roots was accompanied, per usual Samoan practice, by soaring rhetoric that added considerably to the ambience of the *kava* ceremony.

Unfortunately, the La Perouse expedition met with tragedy when 11 members of the crew were later killed by Samoans. The French claimed the attack was unprovoked, although they admitted the attack came after they had fired muskets over the heads of a few Samoans to persuade them to release a grapnel rope to a long boat. Later reports indicated that the massacre occurred after the French shot and killed a Samoan attempting to steal an iron bolt. Verification of this report came from the missionary J. B. Stair, who wrote that the massacre occurred after the French had hoisted a Samoan up a mainstay of a long boat by the thumb in retribution for a petty theft (Stair, *Old Samoa*, 1897). Regardless of the root cause of the altercation, La Perouse fostered a myth of barbarity about the Samoans in its wake, bitterly remarking in his memoirs that he would leave the documentation of Samoan history to others.

The massacre of the French sailors from the *Astrolabe* in 1787 gave the Samoans a reputation for savagery that deterred future European exploration of the islands, except for a few brief contacts such as the visit of that H.M.S. *Pandora* in 1791. Only a few whalers and warships called at Samoan ports for the next number of years.

In 1828 Tongan Wesleyan missionaries arrived in Samoa, but they had little success in their proselytizing endeavors. In 1830, however, John Williams sailed the *Messenger of Peace* to Savaii under the guidance of a Samoan convert from Rarotonga. He first traveled to Sapapalii village, home of Malietoa, the highest-ranking chief in Samoa. During an interview on the ship, Williams obtained permission from Malietoa to land Tahitian and Rarotongan missionaries in Samoa. In addition, he secured a commitment from Malietoa to avail himself of the missionaries' teachings.

Williams returned to Samoa in 1832 to find the new Christian faith thriving. Other religious groups were quick to follow. In 1835 Peter Turner formally established the Wesleyan mission on Manono island. Proselytizing activities proceeded at a fast pace, particularly when George Pratt and Charles Wilson of the London Missionary Society translated the Bible into Samoan.

Although the missionaries were explicitly instructed by Williams to confine their activities to the religious sphere, the impact of the European missions on Samoan culture was rapid and profound. Samoans abandoned their former religious beliefs and made dramatic changes to central cultural practices. Warfare as an instrument of political change was discarded, as was polygamy, abortion, "indecent" dances, and certain common articles of clothing (such as the *titi*, a skirt made from *Cordyline terminalis* leaves). The missionaries introduced new agricultural plants and practices, new items of clothing (*siapo* or tapa cloth), and new forms of housing construction. In only a few years, a fundamental restructuring of traditional Samoan society had taken place. *Faifeau* or ministers played a new and pivotal role in this culture, a respected status that continues to this day.

Later, other *papalagi* (foreigners) with less evangelical interests visited Samoa. The U.S. Exploring Expedition visited and mapped Samoa in 1839. Commander Charles Wilkes appointed the son of John Williams as American Vice-Consul. In 1845 George Pritchard joined the diplomatic corps in Apia as British Consul. Both Williams and Pritchard avoided native intrigues and concentrated on assisting in the naval affairs of their respective countries.

The geopolitical importance of Samoa grew over time due to its proximity to southern whaling grounds and the unparalleled harbor of Pago Pago. In 1857 the German firm of Godeffroy greatly expanded copra trade, establishing a regional center in Samoa. This led to the establishment of a German consulate in 1861. This increased interest in Samoa created significant tensions between the three colonial powers on the island. Samoa was finally partitioned between the east (Eastern Samoa) and the west (German Samoa) during the 1880s.

American Samoa was eventually ceded by the chiefs of Tutuila and Manu'a to the United States and administered by the Department of the Navy as a U.S. territory. The region was largely forgotten until the 1960s, when President John F. Kennedy told Governor John Hayden to "get Samoa moving." During the 1960s and 1970s construction on American Samoa increased dramatically. A hospital, television transmission facilities, and schools were built throughout the territory. Steps were taken to institute a popular election to determine the territorial governor, a position previously filled by appointment from Washington, D.C.

Western Samoa's development during the twentieth century was a little more dramatic. Western Samoa changed hands from German ownership to New Zealand administration during the First World War after a bloodless invasion. After the war, Western Samoa was declared a League of Nations Trust Territory under New Zealand Administration. A nascent independence movement, called the "Mau," was ruthlessly crushed by New Zealand colonial administrators. One of the leaders of this movement, a Samoan chief and a man of great wisdom and presence, Tamasese, was shot and killed by New Zealand armed forces during this conflict. Later, though, New Zealand assumed a more benign role in Western Samoa, assisting the country as it prepared for independence in 1962. Today, Western Samoa is led by a parliament and prime minister, with His Highness Malietoa Tanumafili II acting as the ceremonial Head of State.

ACCULTURATION AND ASSIMILATION

Immigration of Samoans to New Zealand, Australia, and the United States accelerated during the 1950s. Western Samoa, with its historically close ties to New Zealand, sent a number of scholarship students to pursue college degrees in New Zealand. American Samoa saw many of its citizens enroll in U.S. military services. Samoans who chose to pursue ecclesiastical endeavors were often educated by Anglicans in London. Others entered Catholic seminaries in the South Pacific and studied in

Rome, while those who became local leaders in the Church of Jesus Christ of Latter-day Saints (Mormon) traveled to Utah. All these experiences overseas encouraged growing numbers of Samoans to emigrate from Samoa to these distant countries. Since the initial wave of the Samoan emigration overseas numerous second-generation Samoans have been born not on the islands but in their new country. In the 1990 census of the United States, over 55,000 Americans reported themselves to be of Samoan descent. Approximately 26,000 of the respondents resided in California, with another 15,000 in Hawaii, and 2,000 in Utah. But the influence of Samoan Americans has spread far beyond these limited regions.

The contributions made by Samoan Americans have been many and diverse. The courage and valor of Samoan soldiers became legendary during the Korean conflict and the Vietnam war. Prowess on the athletic field led to significant recognition for Samoan Americans in the sports of college and professional football, New Zealand rugby, and even Japanese Sumo wrestling. Samoan American political leaders such as Faleolemavaega Eni Hunkin, who served as staff council for the House Subcommittee on National Parks and Lands and later as the American Samoan delegate to the United States Congress, and Governors Peter Coleman and A. P. Lutali have played an increasingly visible role in formulation of U.S. policy in the Pacific rim.

Many recent immigrants from Samoa, though, have been forced to pursue low-paying jobs as untrained laborers. Others have been forced to rely on governmental entitlement programs for support. A few members of the Samoan community are undocumented aliens who are legally, linguistically, and culturally isolated from their host countries.

As a group, Samoans in America face all the tensions and difficulties encountered by other immigrant groups as they enter new homelands. Many older Samoans, particularly those from Western Samoa, speak English haltingly. Yet in areas of significant Samoan population concentration, even Samoan Americans who are fluent in English have faced considerable prejudice. Just as in the time of the La Perouse expedition, Samoans have in some areas gained unwarranted reputations as perpetrators of violent crime. The involvement of small numbers of Samoan youth in gang activity has led some to dismiss all young Samoan Americans as hoodlums. Such prejudice can have devastating consequences: even impartial observers concede that there have been instances when it has been difficult for a person of Samoan descent to receive a fair criminal trial in Hawaii.

In New Zealand, Hawaii, California, and Utah there is now a reawakening and organization of expatriate Samoan communities in an attempt to reach out to younger people of Samoan ancestry and inform them of the traditional ways and cultures. Samoan culture, while based largely on hospitality, is at times mystifying to Westerners as well as to the offspring of expatriate Samoans who know little of the ways and language of their ancestral home. Scholars are also sometimes confused, and as a result Samoan culture has been the topic of much controversy. In *Coming of Age in Samoa*, Margaret Mead argued that Samoan adolescents are spared the *sturm und drang* of American adolescence. She argued that, unlike their counterparts in Western cultures, young people in Samoa pass relatively easily through adolescence. Her views have been challenged by the anthropologist Derek Freeman, who argued that, contrary to the easy-going Samoan nature portrayed by Mead, Samoan culture is hierarchical, power-conscious, and occasionally violent.

The nature of Samoan society is considerably more complex than either camp may wish to admit. Unlike Mead's assertion that Samoans are a "primitive" people, Samoan culture is elaborate and sophisticated and is exemplified by Samoan rhetorical skills, which are considerable. Samoan villages are equally complex in their structure, with a plethora of different levels of *matai*, or chiefs. Villagers are related in various complex ways from a series of common descent groups.

CUISINE

Samoan cuisine is fairly bland and varies little. Samoans eat two or three meals a day consisting of boiled taro or rice cooked with coconut milk, fresh fish, breadfruit, and usually some form of tinned or fresh meat. Fruit, although plentiful in the island, is seldom eaten during the mealtime. Raw Samoan cocoa—which for many visitors is an acquired taste—orange leaf tea, lemon grass tea, or coffee is usually served with meals. Samoans do not usually engage in conversation while eating, since the hosts typically do not eat until the guests have finished their meals. Many Samoans have, in recent years, strayed from the traditional diet of starchy roots and fruits to a more westernized diet. The medical community believes that this dietary change has translated into a high incidence of diabetes among Samoan people. Although in traditional villages Samoans tend to be very trim in appearance, in some expatriate communities obesity is common, possibly as a result of a more sedentary lifestyle.

CLOTHING

Clothing in Samoa consists of a *lavalava*, a single piece of cloth that is worn as a wrap-around skirt by both men and women. Brightly colored floral print shirts or blouses, or in more informal settings, T-shirts, complete the typical outfit. In remote villages some women go without tops while washing clothes or performing other household tasks. While Samoans prefer colorful floral designs in both their *lavalava* and tops, darker colors are preferred on formal occasions. In such instances, Samoan men often wear a lavalava made from suit cloth material. Such a formal *lavalava*, when combined with leather sandals, white shirt, tie, and suit coat, is considered appropriate dress whether attending a funeral or hosting government dignitaries. In such settings women will wear a *pulu tasi*, a sort of *mu'umu'u* designed by the early Christian missionaries. On Sundays, Samoans prefer to wear white clothing to church.

Although Samoan concepts of personal modesty may differ from western concepts, they are very important to Samoans. The area between the calf of the leg and the thigh is considered to be especially inappropriate for public exhibition. Many traditional Samoan villages ban beach wear such as bikinis and swimming suits. Some even ban women from wearing trousers.

While the appearance and garb of Samoan women are subject to a range of cultural restrictions, full-body tattoos are common on Samoan men. The tattooing process is prolonged and painful. It is believed by Samoans to be a means of helping men appreciate the prolonged labor pains involved with childbirth.

HOLIDAYS

Both American Samoa and Western Samoa celebrate their respective national holidays. Christmas, Easter, and other religious holidays are also of great significance to Samoans. In addition, the second Sunday of October is celebrated by most denominations as "White Sunday." On this day, the service revolves around memorized recitations by children. After the service, Samoan children are waited upon by the adults of their family, served a festive meal, and presented with gifts.

HEALTH ISSUES

Samoans have a traditional system of healing that plays a very important role in Samoan culture. Traditional Samoan healers use a variety of massage treatments, counseling techniques, and herbal preparations to treat illness. Recent scientific analy-

sis of Samoan healing practices show them to have some degree of empirical justification: a large number of plants used by Samoans for medical purposes demonstrate pharmacological activity in the laboratory. The National Cancer Institute, for instance, recently licensed the new anti-HIV compound prostratin, which was discovered in a Samoan plant used by traditional healers.

Samoans believe that there are some illnesses that cannot be cured by Western medicine. These include illnesses of the *to'ala*, the reputed center of being located beneath the navel, and cases of spiritual possession. *Musu*, a psychiatric illness of young women characterized by a nearly autistic withdrawal from communication, has been treated successfully in New Zealand by traditional healers. Samoan healers exist and practice, albeit covertly, in most expatriate Samoan communities.

Samoans believe that the major sources of disease are poor diet, poor hygiene, and interpersonal hostility. Since Samoa is a consensus culture with a heavy emphasis on responsibility and family, many believe that an individual who does not support his family, who does not shoulder the responsibilities of village life, and who otherwise does not participate in traditional culture, has a high risk of becoming ill. Linguistic isolation complicates some medical interaction with the older Samoans, but in general Samoans are appreciative of Western medicine and responsive to prescribed courses of medical treatment.

Samoan Americans are particularly susceptible to high rates of diabetes and other illnesses associated with a high-fat diet and decreased patterns of physical activity. As a population, though, Samoans show lower cholesterol levels than would be expected given their diet and patterns of obesity. Coconut oil, which is very rich in saturated fats, plays an important part in the Samoan diet. Many Samoan delicacies such as *palusami* (young taro leaves with coconut cream) are cooked in coconut cream. Such a diet, combined with sedentary lifestyle, is a key contributor to cardiovascular illness.

American Samoa maintains a fine hospital, the L.B.J. Tropical Medical Center in Fagalu, near Pago Pago. The Western Samoa National Hospital at Moto'otua is a fine facility as well, especially for a developing country. When necessary, difficult cases are referred by L.B.J. and Moto'otua to hospitals in Honolulu and Auckland, respectively.

LANGUAGE

The Samoan language is an ancient form of Polynesian dialect. It consists of three basic types of language. Common Samoan is the Samoan language of commerce and normal village interactions, while Respect Samoan includes honorific terms used for others of equal or greater rank. The third language type employed by Samoans, Rhetorical Samoan, is a set of proverbial, genealogical, and poetic allusions.

Samoan vowels are pronounced very simply; the French approach to their vowel pronunciation is similar. Consonants are nearly identical to English consonants with two exceptions: the glottal stop indicated by an apostrophe is an unaspirated consonant produced in the bottom of the throat that can best be approximated as the break in the English expression "oh oh." Thus the Samoan word for "thank you,"—*fa'afetai*—is pronounced "fah-ah-fay-tie." The Samoan "g" sound is also difficult for some foreigners to master. It is pronounced similarly to the "ng" in "sing along;" the Samoan word for gun—*faga*—is thus pronounced as "fah-ngah." The "n" sound is pronounced as "ng" by Samoans as well. Finally, in colloquial Samoan, the "k" sound is pronounced instead of the "t;" hence *fa'afetai* becomes "fa'afekai." Samoans, however, do not like foreigners to use colloquial pronunciation. In Samoan words all syllables are given equal timing with a slight accent placed on the penultimate syllable.

The following are several common Samoan greetings and their English translations: *talofa*—hello; *fa'afetai*—thank you; *tofa*—goodbye; *malo*—congratulations; *lau afioga*—your highness (high chief); *lau tofa*—your highness (orator); *lau susuga*—sir.

RHETORIC

Ceremonial Samoan may be one of the most complex rhetorical forms known on the face of the earth. Eloquent oratory has long been an integral part of the Samoan culture. In the case of a village or district dispute, the victor is often the side represented by the most eloquent orator. Oratorical ability in Samoa is a treasured commodity because it has historically brought its finest practitioners prestige, cultural influence, and material goods.

The importance of rhetoric in Samoa has even been institutionalized in the Samoan system of chiefdoms. In Samoan culture there are two types of chiefs: high chiefs, who function very much as the corporate executive officers of the village; and orators or "talking chiefs" who speak for the village in its dealings with others. Samoan orators are expected to memorize an amazing array of information, including the historical events of Samoa, an exhaustive list of Samoan proverbial expressions, and the genealogies of most of the major families in Samoa. Orators are also expected to be able to speak with power and eloquence in an extemporaneous fashion.

Listening to Samoan oratory at a *kava* ceremony can be an awe-inspiring experience. Sophisticated allusions to ancient events, nuanced proverbial expressions, and powerful political insights are combined with extensive references to the Bible and the genealogies of those present to produce an exquisitely cerebral poetic work. Samoan oratory is delivered in a cadence and clarity of voice that is clear and ringing. Frequently speeches are yelled out as a sign of respect to visitors. Unfortunately, this oral tradition, the highest of all Samoan arts, is the art form most inaccessible to foreigners. Very little Samoan formal rhetoric has ever been translated into English.

FAMILY AND COMMUNITY DYNAMICS

Samoans have an expansive view of familial bonds. A Samoan *a'iga* or family includes all individuals who descend from a common ancestor. Samoan familial ties are complex and highly interwoven, but also very important; all Samoans are expected to support and serve their extended families. Each extended family has one or more chiefs who organize and run the family.

Family pride is a central part of Samoan culture as well. Individuals in Samoan villages fear breaking village rules not only because of any individual consequences but because of the shame it might bring

to their family. In cases of serious transgression, the entire family may be penalized by the village council. In extreme cases the transgressor's chief may be stripped of his title and the family disinherited from the land. The fear of shaming one's extended family thus serves as a potent deterrent in the culture. This philosophy extends not only to transgressors but also to victims. An offense committed against anyone, particularly elderly individuals—who are revered in Samoan society—or young women, may be seen as an offense to the victim's entire family. In contrast to western philosophies that laud individualism, Samoan culture emphasizes the importance of family ties and responsibility.

In Samoan culture, serious offenses may be redeemed by an *ifoga* (a lowering). This is a ceremony that reflects deep contrition on the part of the perpetrator. In an *ifoga*, all of a transgressor's extended family and village will gather before dawn in front of the residence of the offended or injured party. There they will sit covered by fine mats as the sun rises. They remain in that position until forgiven and invited into the house. They then present fine mats, pigs, and cash as evidence of their contri-

tion. There is no Western equivalent to an *ifoga*, but performance of an *ifoga* in western Samoa, even for a serious crime, will often result in waiver or dramatic reduction of the criminal penalties that would have otherwise been assessed.

The Samoan concept of family has profound economic consequences. All Samoans are expected to provide financial support for their families. Many expatriate Samoans routinely send a large portion of their earnings back to their relatives in Samoa. Such foreign remittances constitute a significant portion of the income of Western Samoa. Although such remittances are a godsend for the relatively weak economy of Western Samoa, there is concern that the third generation of expatriate Samoans may become so assimilated into western cultures that this practice will not survive.

COURTSHIP

While older Samoans enjoy the regard in which they are held, younger members of the culture grapple with the complicated process of courtship. In remote villages dating is frowned upon. The culturally acceptable way for young men and young women to meet each other is for the young man to bring presents and food to the young woman's family and to court his intended in the presence of the woman's family. In traditional villages, even slight deviation from this pattern may place the young man at some risk of physical harm from the young woman's brothers.

Romantic affairs are, of course, difficult to transact. Typically an intermediary called a *soa* (go-between) is used to communicate the amorous intentions of a young man to the *soa* of the young woman. If romantic interest is reciprocated, young men and young women will visit surreptitiously at night under the cover of darkness. Such liaisons, however, are fraught with danger should the young woman's brothers discover them. Brothers in traditional Samoan culture consider it their familial duty to aggressively screen out unwarranted suitors or inappropriate attempts to court their sister without parental supervision.

Physical contact between the sexes, including kissing and hand holding, is considered to be in poor taste in public. Even married couples avoid physical contact in public. These traditional practices, however, have changed as Samoan culture has become more westernized. In Pago Pago and Apia, boys and girls date, attend dances, take in films, and socialize in most of the ways common to Western countries. However, any offense to a young woman, including swearing, is still taken as a deep offense by a young woman's brothers and may result in violence.

MARRIAGE AND CHILDREN

Marriage has become more common since the advent of Christianity, but in Samoa many people live together and even raise children without the benefit of marriage. This custom, called *nofo fa'apouliuli*, sometimes functions as a sort of trial marriage in which a Samoan tests the relationship before settling on a single partner.

Illegitimacy does not have the same negative connotations in Samoan culture that it does in other cultures. Children are warmly welcomed into a family and are frequently raised by grandparents or other relatives as their own offspring. In general, children within the Samoan family have a great deal of mobility. It is not uncommon in Samoa for children to be raised by people other than their biological parents. In many cases children are raised by members of extended family or even friends. All children are, regardless of their genetic relationship to the husband and wife in the family, treated equally and expected to assist with family chores.

Until approximately age seven boys and girls are reared in nearly identical fashion in Samoan culture. But girls from eight to ten years old are expected to play major roles in caring for other infant children. It is not uncommon in Samoan villages to see eight- or nine-year-old girls packing a six-month-old baby on their hip. Once boys and girls approach puberty deep cultural taboos take effect that preclude their continued close association. Past puberty, brothers and sisters are not allowed to be alone in each other's presence.

CEREMONIES

In Samoa infant children and their mothers occupy special status. New mothers are usually presented with *vaisalo*, a rich drink made of grated coconut, coconut milk, manihot, and the grated flesh of the vi apple. On occasion fine mats may also be presented to the mother.

A Samoan wedding typically involves feasting, dancing, and much merriment. Weddings are generally held in accordance with local customs or ecclesiastical protocols, followed by a large reception for the bride and groom.

Conveyance of a chiefly title is another noteworthy cultural event in Samoa. Typically the family of the chief-to-be will prepare kegs of corned beef, fine mats, money, and other items with which to "pay" the village granting the title. Visitors to the ceremony are also hosted in extravagant fashion. Extended and sophisticated rhetoric is exchanged by orators representing the various families in attendance and includes analysis of the genealogical provenance of the title. In some villages the candidate for the chief position is wrapped in a fine mat tied with a bow; he becomes a chief when the bow is untied. Many times paper currency is placed in an ornamental fashion in the chief's headdress. All chief ceremonies, however, regardless of village, culminate in the *kava* ceremony wherein the candidate drinks *kava* for the first time as the new chief. Invitation to attend a chief investiture ceremony or *saufa'i* is a signal honor, one rarely granted to foreigners.

Conveyance of a chiefly title is far more than an honorific. Individuals in the group immediately adopt the chief's title as their own first name. All people in the village, other than the immediate family, refer to the new chief by the new title. Furthermore, in traditional Samoan culture all the dependents of the new chief use the chief's title as their new last name.

Once established, the new chief is expected to attend village councils, act with a sense of decorum and dignity, support village activities via manual labor and cash donations, and behave with the interests of his family and village foremost in his mind. As a member of the village chief council, the new chief will participate in decisions reached in consensus with the other chiefs. Some chieftains in Samoa also have special titles such as *Malietoa*, *Tamasese*, *Tupuola*, or *Salamasina*. These titles have national significance. Individuals bearing such titles should be treated as the equivalent of European monarchs.

The conveyance of chief's titles has become a difficult business for expatriate Samoans since in traditional Samoan culture all chief's titles are tied to an identifiable piece of land in Samoa. Expatriate Samoans seeking titles usually must return to Samoa for the ceremonies. In New Zealand some chief investiture ceremonies have been held. However, titles so conferred outside of Samoa are controversial within Samoa. Infrequently, diplomats, aid workers, and other foreign visitors are granted honorific titles that have no validity in terms of Samoan land relationships and are not recognized by the Lands and Title Court. Exceptions to this arrangement are rare but do occur. Although nearly all chiefs are men, several women hold chiefly titles, and in at least one case a village conferred a valid title, registered with and recognized by the Land and Titles Court, on a Samoan-speaking foreigner.

Samoan funerals include important demonstrations of high Samoan culture. In a funeral the extended family of the bereaved prepares money, fine mats, kegs of corned beef, pigs, and case goods to present to visitors at the funeral. Visitors attend with a single palm leaf held aloft in front of them. On arrival at the home of the bereaved, the orator representing the visitors stands outside the hut, addresses the dead person with an honorific string of titles, and then speaks to everyone present. After the speech the visitors are invited to sit and wait as other visitors trickle in. The funeral concludes with an orator who acts as a representative for the bereaved family. The orator speaks before distributing gifts to the visitors.

At funerals and chief investiture ceremonies a great deal of cash and a large number of fine mats—which may take up to six months to complete—exchange hands. In some instances, more than 2,000 fine mats and as much as $20,000 may be redistributed.

MANNERS

The Samoan culture is very hospitable to foreigners. Usual expectations of strict formal behavior and rigorous rhetoric are suspended for visitors. Knowledge of a few simple courtesies, however, will help ensure goodwill in such settings. When entering a Samoan house or cultural event, it is important to quickly glance to see if other people are wearing shoes. It is usually considered disrespectful to walk across a mat in a Samoan house with shoes on. Shoes can be removed and left at the door. When walking in front of anybody one should bend low and say *Tulou* ("too-low").

When entering a room or assembly of Samoans in a cultural setting it is considered good manners to walk around the room and shake each person's hand, smiling and looking them in the eyes. *Talofa* ("tah-low-fah") is the greeting. After greeting everyone present, the visitor should sit where directed. It is considered rude in Samoan culture to stand while addressing someone who is sitting.

It is important to accept whatever hospitality is offered by Samoans. Hence, if everyone is seated on a mat on the floor but the visitor is offered a chair, the visitor should sit on the chair. If seated on the floor a visitor should cross his legs and avoid pointing his feet at anyone. If this position becomes uncomfortable the visitor can place a mat over his extended legs.

The presentation of *kava* is considered to be the highest symbol of respect that can be granted to a visitor. If presented with a cup of *kava*, one may drip a few drops on the ground (symbolic of returning goodness to the earth) and say *Ia manuia* ("ee-ah mahn-wee-ah"), which means "let there be blessings." At that point one can either drink from the cup or return it to the server.

The acceptance of gifts is important in Samoa. No gift offered by a Samoan should be refused. Such refusal might be considered an indication of displeasure with the person presenting the gift. The most common gifts are those of food or mats. Gifts are frequently given as an indication of the status or prestige of both the giver and the receiver. Gifts are given without expectation of reciprocation. During dancing or other fundraising activities, however, cash donations are usually welcomed. It is also considered good manners to publicly offer a significant cash payment to an orator who has given a speech of welcome or greeting.

Samoan culture also features several rules of etiquette concerning food. Never eat in front of a Samoan without offering to share your food. When served by others, it is important to show due respect to the food. While the meal does not have to be eaten in its entirety, the food itself should be handled and treated with respect, since it represents the finest that the hosts can provide.

Display of negative emotions, particularly irritation, anger, or other hostility, is considered to be in very bad taste and a sign of weakness. Samoans treat each other with extraordinary politeness even under difficult circumstances. One who exercises decorum even under stressful circumstances receives high marks in Samoan culture.

EDUCATION

Samoans value education very highly. For a developing country Western Samoa has an astonishingly high rate of literacy—approximately 98 percent. In traditional villages education is first received at a minister's school, where children are taught to read. Later they attend elementary and secondary schools. The emphasis in Samoan education is largely on rote memorization.

Differences in educational philosophy can be found from island to island, however. Western Samoan students, for instance, pursue an education that in many ways resembles the system taught in New Zealand, while children in American Samoa receive an education that resembles, in many respects, the curriculum taught on the American mainland. In Western Samoa the best schools are frequently operated by churches. Some of the Catholic schools are particularly prestigious.

Although there is a community college in American Samoa and two university campuses in Western Samoa, many Samoans pursue higher education either in New Zealand or the United States. Many Samoan Americans major in education, law, or other social sciences.

RELIGION

In Samoa religion plays a huge role that remarkably has been ignored by many anthropologists studying Samoan culture. The Samoan culture is a pious one. Most families in Samoa conduct a nightly *lotu* or vespers service in which the family gathers together, reads from the Bible, and offers prayers. Prayers are offered at every meal. Church attendance in Samoa is almost universal; the major denominations on the islands are Anglican, Methodist, Catholic, and Mormon. Ministers of religion occupy a status in Samoa tantamount to that occupied by high chiefs and are granted extraordinary deference.

Religion in the Samoan setting, however, has a unique Polynesian twist. Most Samoan Americans prefer to organize and participate in Samoan-speaking congregations, with some accommodation made for their non-Samoan speaking offspring. Singing in a Samoan congregation is enthusiastic and beautiful. The Samoan Bible, which was translated directly from Greek, is quoted extensively in most Samoan services. By and large, Samoans are far more familiar with Bible scripture than their Western counterparts.

POLITICS AND GOVERNMENT

Since American Samoans do not vote in national elections and the region has been administered in a fairly bipartisan manner by the Department of Interior, it is difficult to assess Samoan American political leanings. Hawaii, which has been traditionally a strong bastion for the Democratic party, is home to many Samoans, but many Samoan Americans live in the staunchly Republican areas of Orange County, California, and Utah as well. Given their relatively small numbers, however, it is unlikely that any unified voting behavior on their part would have more than local political significance.

Minimum wage laws are a constant concern to those who live on American Samoa. The islands received a waiver from obeying the minimum wage law due to the havoc that implementation would likely create for the tuna canneries in American Samoa. In 1997 the waiver was replaced by a board which will use industry standards and fairness to set the minimum wage in American Samoa. Union involvement appears to be fairly minimal among Samoan workers.

Western Samoa has a lively political climate, with much jousting and intrigue between the different political parties. There continues to be, in some circles, discussion of a possible unification of the two Samoan regions into a single independent country. Few American Samoans appear to be in favor of this idea. Their resistance to Samoan unification is driven not only by the tremendous economic disparity between American Samoa and Western Samoa, but also because of different cultural trajectories. Thus, while there are significant cultural and linguistic similarities between Western and American Samoa, unification seems unlikely. Instead, many Western Samoans seek to immigrate to American Samoa. Some have even joined the U.S. armed forces.

INDIVIDUAL AND GROUP CONTRIBUTIONS

The following individuals have made significant contributions to American society. Frank Falaniko,

Jr. (1956–) is a landscape construction engineer and president of Green City, Inc.; Eni Faauaa Hunkin Faleomavaega, Jr. (1943–) is a government official; Al Noga (1965–) played professional football with the Minnesota Vikings and the Washington Redskins; and Mavis Rivers (c. 1929-1992) was a jazz vocalist who joined her father's band during World War II and sang with the Red Norvo combo, George Shearing, and Andre Previn.

MEDIA

American Samoa maintains a television station that produces local programming under the direction of the territorial government. Three channels are broadcast throughout American Samoa. These carry American network programming in the evening and locally-produced educational programming in the daytime. Western Samoa has recently begun a television production facility as well.

Both American and Western Samoa operate several radio stations. In Western Samoa 2AP is the national radio station and the major means of communication with individuals in remote villages. Every evening messages reporting deaths, births, conferences, or other family news are aired on 2AP as a way of informing people who have no other ready access to information on developments and events on the islands. Samoan-language radio programs are also broadcast by radio stations in Auckland, Honolulu, and Salt Lake City.

PRINT

Samoa News.
Address: P.O. Box 909, Pago Pago, American Samoa 96799.
E-mail: editor@samoanews.com.
Online: http://www.samoanews.com/.

ORGANIZATIONS AND ASSOCIATIONS

Polynesian Cultural Center (PCC).
Presents, preserves, and perpetuates the arts, crafts, culture, and lore of Fijian, Hawaiian, Maori, Mar-

quesan, Tahitian, Tongan, Samoan, and other Polynesian peoples.
Address: 55-370 Kamehameha Highway, Laie, Hawaii 96762.
Telephone: (808) 293-3333.
Online: http://www.polynesia.com/.

MUSEUMS AND RESEARCH CENTERS

Major libraries on Samoa are the O. F. Nelson Memorial Library in Apia, the Oliveti Library in Pago Pago, the Turnbull Library in Wellington, and the Bernice P. Bishop Library in Honolulu. Major museum collections of Samoan items can be found at the Dominion Museum in Auckland, New Zealand, the Bernice P. Bishop Museum in Honolulu, the Lowie Museum in Berkeley, and the Ethnological Museum in Basel, Switzerland.

SOURCES FOR ADDITIONAL STUDY

Baker, P. T., J. M. Hanna, and T. S. Baker. *The Changing Samoans: Behavior and Health in Transition.* Oxford: Oxford University Press, 1986.

Cox, P. A., and S. A. Banack. *Islands, Plants and Polynesians: An Introduction to Polynesian Ethnobotany.* Portland: Dioscorides Press, 1991.

Davidson, J. M. "Samoa and Tonga," in *The Prehistory of Polynesia.* Cambridge: Harvard University Press, 1979.

Fox, J. W., and K. B. Cumberland. *Western Samoa.* Christchurch, New Zealand: Whitcombe and Tombs, 1962.

Freeman, D., and Margaret Mead *Samoa: The Making and the Unmaking of an Anthropological Myth.* Cambridge: Harvard University Press, 1981.

Kennedy, P. M. *The Samoan Tangle: A Study in Anglo-German-American Relations.* Dublin: Irish University Press, 1974.

> While Saudi Arabia and the United States are linked because of a mutually beneficial relationship over oil, the two countries do not always agree on issues. Significantly, Saudi Arabia and the United States have differed in foreign policy stances regarding Israel and the Middle East.

SAUDI ARABIAN AMERICANS

by
Sonya Schryer

OVERVIEW

Saudi Arabia measures 899,766 square miles (2,331,000 square kilometers), and comprises four-fifths of the Arabian Peninsula. It is roughly one-third the size of the United States. Saudi Arabia is bounded by the Red Sea to the west; Iraq, Jordan, and Kuwait to the north; the Gulf of Arabia, Qatar and the United Arab Emirates to the east; Oman to the southeast; and Yemen to the southwest. Saudi Arabia's official language is Arabic and the capital city is Riyadh.

While population figures vary, the United Nations estimated that 20 million people lived in Saudi Arabia in 1998. One quarter of the population were foreign workers, half of them Arab. There was a small contingent of Westerners, many of whom worked in the oil industry and for international businesses.

Saudi Arabia is home to the holy cities of Mecca and Medina. These cities have special significance for Muslims the world over. Islam, the national religion of Saudi Arabia, requires that all Muslims able to do so make a pilgrimage to Mecca at least once in their lifetimes. Islam is tightly interwoven into all facets of Saudi life, including government, law, education, dress, marriage, and family. Members of religions other than Islam, including foreign workers, are not permitted to exercise their faith publicly, nor may anyone attempt to convert a Muslim. The Saudi flag, green with white Arabic script, proclaims the first pillar of Islam: "There is no God but Allah and Muhammad is His Messenger." Below these words is a saber.

HISTORY

From 4000 B.C. through biblical times, trade routes that linked modern India, China, Africa, and the Middle East crossed the Arabian Peninsula. Mecca lay on one of the more prominent routes, providing service to Egyptian caravans. The Arabians themselves were broken up into various clans who traced their lineage to Abraham and his son Ishmael.

The prophet Muhammad (c. 570 A.D.-632 A.D.), himself a merchant in Mecca, founded Islam in 622 A.D. and unified most of the Arabian Peninsula in his lifetime. The momentum of Islam led to the conquering of central Asia, northern Africa, and Spain within one hundred years of the death of Muhammad. In practical terms, the widespread observance of Islam improved business relations among regions because Islamic standards of fair dealing practices were respected, regardless of ethnicity, national origin, or language. While Jews and Christians of conquered lands were tolerated as "People of the Book," they were also taxed more heavily than converts to Islam. During the Middle Ages, Arabia enjoyed a scientific, artistic, intellectual, and cultural preeminence unmatched in Europe until the Renaissance. Arabia's decline in subsequent years led to conquest by the Ottoman Empire and its weak control, which extended from the beginning of the sixteenth into the early twentieth century.

MODERN ERA

Abdul Aziz Ibn Saud, more simply known as Ibn Saud, founded the Kingdom of Saudi Arabia on the of September 23, 1932. King Ibn Saud consolidated his control through military conquests, advantageous marriages, and the support of the Wahhabi Movement, founded by the religious reformer, Muhammad Ibn Abd al-Wahhab (1703-1792). Wahhab had studied various religious practices and traveled widely before returning to the Najd, a region of central Arabia surrounded by desert on three sides. There he aligned himself with the al-Saud family, who maintained leadership in the Najd.

The Wahhabi Movement was puritanical and fierce in its demand that Muslims live by an exacting interpretation of the Koran, the holy book of Islam, and of the teachings of the prophet Muhammad. Wahhabism required conformity, piety, and governmental or military enforcement of Islamic law. Among other tenets, Wahhabism decried any action, including the adoration of saints, which competed with the monotheism of Islam. The Wahhab/Saud dynasty shaped the moral and political landscape of sixteenth century Arabia. Its control stretched beyond the geographical boundaries of the Arabian Peninsula, and its influence permanently asserted itself in the Najd.

King Ibn Saud drew his authority by ruling in consult with the ulama (religious scholars), an indispensable aspect of public leadership in Wahhabi philosophy. As his ancestors had done, he fused political leadership with religious ideology. In 1933, oil was discovered in Saudi Arabia, and the Saudi monarchy used this wealth to bring Arabia to the forefront of global economics.

THE FIRST SAUDIS IN AMERICA

The first Saudis in the United States came as ambassadors and staff to the Saudi Arabian Embassy in Washington, D.C., in the mid-1940s. In 1999, the Information Department of the embassy was unaware of any regular Saudi citizens who had lived in the United States for extended periods before the end of the Second World War.

SAUDI ARABIAN STUDENTS IN THE UNITED STATES

Following World War II, young Saudi men began coming to the United States to obtain higher educations. Saudi Arabia's oil wealth allowed the government to sponsor these students financially. As of 1999, they were provided with tuition money, funds for room and board, clothing, medical care, one round trip plane ticket to visit Saudi Arabia each year, and other benefits. Bonuses were given to those studying in scientific or technical fields.

Saudi men were encouraged through economic incentives to marry, and to take their families with them, and therefore reduce feelings of isolation and culture shock. One incentive included tuition money for a man's spouse to study as well. Unmarried Saudi women were required to have a chaperone to travel outside of Saudi Arabia, also as of 1999, although ultimately a woman's family could choose not to chaperone her. According to editor Richard Nyrop, in his book *Saudi Arabia: A Country Study*, "[t]he vast majority [of Saudi students] remained deeply committed to the Saudi values surrounding religion as well as family and social life. The one area where there were measurable changes of opinion was in the attitudes toward women and women's role in society."

When universities in Saudi Arabia began opening in the 1960s, the number of Saudi students abroad decreased. This pleased conservative groups, who were concerned about sending so many young people out of the country, particularly to non-Muslim nations. In 1984, approximately 10,000 Saudis were studying outside of Saudi Arabia. More than half were women. In 1991-92, this figure dropped to 5,000, with half studying at universities in the United States. In 1999, the Saudi Arabian Embassy in Washington, D.C. estimated that 5,000 Saudis were studying in the United States, and that the majority were male.

The close political and economic relationship between Saudi Arabia and the United States led to a number of generous educational grants on behalf of the Saudi government. In April of 1976, Saudi Arabia presented the University of Southern California with an endowment in the amount of one million dollars to establish the King Faisal Chair of Islamic and Arab Studies. At that time, more than 150 Saudi students were matriculating at the University of Southern California.

In 1999, there were 25 Saudi Student Houses, supported by the embassy and the Saudi Cultural Mission, across the United States. In October of 1997, the Saudi Student House at Indiana State University held a "Saudi National Day," which featured traditional food, dancing, a fashion show, displays, slides and videos. At Michigan State University, a Saudi Student House was established in April of 1996 to provide Islamic, educational, social, and athletic services; in 1999 it reported 70 members. Saudi students also congregated at mosques and Islamic centers, many of which received support from the embassy.

Academically, Saudi students were diverse, researching a wide variety of topics at the masters and doctoral levels. In the late 1970s, a majority were studying the social sciences, and subsequent dissertations on the community of Saudi students constitute a substantial body work about their experiences. Examples of researched topics include Abdullah Ahmed Oweidat's Ph.D. dissertation entitled "A Study of Changes in Value Orientation of Arab Students in the United States" (University of Southern California, 1981). He studied Saudi and other Arab students and found that those who had resided in the United States for at least three years demonstrated values similar to those held by Americans, which were significantly different Arab students who had recently arrived to the United States. Another Ph.D. dissertation, by Abdullah Muhammad Alfauzan, researched how Saudi Arabian students in the United States viewed women's participation in the work force in Saudi Arabia. He found that Saudi students in the United States possessed more liberal viewpoints than their counterparts in Saudi Arabia.

Among many other topics, Saudi students have also written dissertations on agriculture, Arabian art, student teaching in Saudi Arabia, advertising dollars in the media in Saudi Arabia, and the relationship between job characteristics and quality of work life in a Saudi Arabian hospital. Much of their work provided academia in the United States with information that was underutilized or not available to American researchers.

SETTLEMENT PATTERNS

Citizens of Middle Eastern countries have been immigrating to the United States since the late nineteenth century. Middle Eastern Muslims did not begin to immigrate in great numbers, however, until after World War II. Many Arab American organizations, Muslim and Christian, have since established themselves in the United States. They have developed student groups, scholarship networks, newspapers, magazines, television programming, restaurants, cultural centers, and traveling museum exhibits. Saudi Arabians, as well as the Saudi government, have made financial contributions to Muslim organizations. Nevertheless, the relatively small Saudi community, and the low number of Saudis who choose to live permanently in the United States, has limited uniquely Saudi-American cultural developments.

In the 1990 census, only 4,486 U.S. citizens reported that they were of Saudi Arabian descent. Saudi Arabians reported living in 42 of the 50 United States. The greatest number, 517, resided in California. There were five additional states that reported over 200 Saudi Arabians: Colorado, Florida, Pennsylvania, Texas, and Virginia.

There are a variety of reasons why so few Saudi Arabians chose to permanently relocate to the United States. Among these were the wealth of Saudi Arabia, the religious faith and pride of Saudis who found it difficult to maintain an Islamic lifestyle in the United States, and a lack of factors motivating citizens to leave Saudi Arabia. Saudis are also required to obtain an exit visa from their government in order to leave Saudi Arabia, and they must provide a reason to get it. The limited number of marriages between U.S. and Saudi citizens may also have contributed to the low number of Saudi immigrants and Saudi Americans.

Political dissent and dissatisfaction with the restrictions of living in an orthodox Muslim society were among the factors that encouraged migration.

The U.S. Immigration and Nationality Act of 1965, which established preferential treatment for educated immigrants, also encouraged a limited number of Saudis to seek U.S. citizenship. Those Saudi Arabians who did settle permanently in the United States were commonly well educated and lived near cities where they held professional jobs.

Due to the number of Saudi families in the Washington, D.C. metropolitan area, there were enough children of primary and secondary school age to establish the Islamic Saudi Academy in Alexandria, Virginia, in 1984 (other Muslim children are also permitted to attend). The government of Saudi Arabia funded the academy to provide an academic, religious and Arabic curriculum. It services 1,150 children in kindergarten through the 12th grade and sits on 100 acres.

ACCULTURATION AND ASSIMILATION

PROVERBS

There are many Saudi Arabian proverbs, both secular and religious. Examples of the secular include: "He who knows not and knows not he knows not is a fool. Shun him;" "He who knows not and knows he knows not is simple. Teach him;" "He who knows and knows not he knows is asleep. Wake him;" "He who knows and knows he knows is wise. Follow him;" "He who loves thinks others are blind; the others think he is crazy;" "Better a thousand enemies outside the house than one inside;" and "He who has health has hope; and he who has hope, has everything."

Proverbs from the prophet Muhammad include: "Riches are not from abundance of worldly goods, but from a contented mind;" "Let go of the things of which you are in doubt for the things in which there is no doubt;" and "God is beautiful and He loves beauty."

Koranic proverbs include: "Whatever good you have is all from God. Whatever evil, all is from yourself" and "God will not change the condition of men until they change what is in themselves."

CUISINE

Traditional Saudi Arabian cuisine is similar to other Middle Eastern foods in that it favors lamb, rice, and a wide variety of vegetables and spices. Because of the Islamic prohibition against pork, it is absent from all Saudi cooking. Both *Gahwah*, a coffee of unroasted beans and cardamom, and tea, are very popular.

In the United States, Saudi women prepare traditional dishes and learn to work with American foods. In 1999, the Information Department of the Saudi embassy was unaware of a single Saudi restaurant in the United States, but reported that many Saudis enjoy the cuisine of other Middle Eastern countries and frequent their restaurants. Sensitive to the desires of Saudi expatriates, Saadeddin Pastry Limited, headquartered in Riyadh, ships Saudi pastries and sweets worldwide for holidays, weddings, and other special occasions.

MUSIC

Saudi music, secular or religious, was not being produced in the United States as of 1999, however, it has become more accessible through various music providers such as Amazon.com on the World Wide Web. Individual import companies, including Caravelle Fine Middle Eastern Imports, also advertise their ability to provide Saudi music in the United States. Increasing interest in Arabic music led to the publication of several books on the topic, including the translation of Habib Hassan Touma's *The Music of the Arabs*.

TRADITIONAL COSTUMES

Traditional Saudi clothing for men consists of a *thobe*, a long sleeved, loose-fitting garment that covers the body from neck to ankles. Thobes are sewn of cotton or wool and may be plain white or very colorful with fine embroidery work. A headpiece is also customary, designed to protect against the elements. For special occasions, Saudi men may wear a *bisht*, a gold-edged cloak, over the thobe.

Women's fashions are varied, not confined to traditional Saudi Arabian garb. Jeans and heels are not unheard of. In public, all women are required to wear the *abaya*, a black garment that covers them from head to foot. A variety of veils are worn as well. At the very minimum, they cover a woman's hair and neck, although veils that cover a woman's face entirely are also used, particularly in the holy city of Mecca. The Saudi Arabian police force, named the Committee for the Propagation of Virtue and the Suppression of Vice (often called the religious police), enforce a dress code and may cite or arrest women appearing under-clothed in public.

While in the United States, most male Saudi students adopt Western standards of dress, including fashionable name brands as well as jeans, T-shirts and the like. Many Saudi women do not wear the abaya while in the United States, and some do not wear a head covering at all, although most do.

A family's religious piety influences how a woman will dress after arriving in the United States. In conservative settings such as the mosque, or for celebrations, both men and women are more likely to wear traditional clothing.

DANCES AND SONGS

Khaleegy (meaning "gulf"), a popular Saudi women's dance, is characterized as fast and exciting. It is often performed at women's parties in a special dancing costume known as the *thobe al nasha'ar*, and associated songs speak of the beauty of the dancer, often mentioning her hair. Muhammad Abdou was a popular singer of songs typifying this style in Saudi Arabia in the 1990s. In the United States, the khaleegy came to be included in the repertoires of dancing groups such as the Jawaahir Dance Company of Minneapolis, Minnesota.

HOLIDAYS

The nation of Saudi Arabia recognizes two religious holidays, both of which are celebrated by Muslims the world over. The first is *Eid Al-Fitr*, which marks the end of the month of *Ramadan*, and lasts for seven days. Fasting during the Arabic month of Ramadan is a required practice of all adult Muslims in good health, although menstruating women are excused. Due to fasting, government offices, businesses, and schools in Saudi Arabia operate for fewer hours each day throughout the month. Few Muslims of any nationality in the United States are able to take time away from their jobs during Ramadan. Eid Al-Fitr is celebrated at mosques and Islamic centers with special dress, meals, and prayers. Giving *zakat* (alms) at the end of Ramadan is also a religious requirement. Muslims who do not live near mosques often travel to them for holidays. In January of 1999, approximately 14,000 Muslims gathered to celebrate Eid Al-Fitr at the Expo Center in Chantilly, Virginia.

The second Islamic religious holiday is called *Eid Al-Adha*. It celebrates the end of the *Haj* and lasts for 10 days. The Haj is a pilgrimage to Mecca required of all adult Muslims at least once in their lives, if they are able. Due to the lunar nature of the Arabic calendar, known as the *Hijra* calendar, Eid Al-Fitr and Eid Al-Adha do not fall on the same days each year in the Western world. September 23rd, the day Saudi Arabia was declared an independent nation, is often recognized as well.

HEALTH ISSUES

Sickle cell disease, most commonly known in the United States to affect Africans and African Americans, affects several other groups, including Saudi Arabians. In 1999, with the assistance of the King Faisal Specialist Hospital and Research Center in Riyadh, Saudi Arabia, worldwide collaborative research was being conducted to examine additional risk factors pertaining to Saudis with sickle cell disease.

In 1998, Suzanne Toombs Mallery finished her Ph.D. dissertation entitled "Zar Possession as Psychiatric Diagnosis: Problems and Possibilities" at the Fuller Theological Seminary in Pasadena, California. Mallery reported that *Zar Possession* was classified in the Diagnostic and Statistical Manual of Mental Disorders IV of the American Psychiatric Association as a culture-bound phenomenon. She found that this illness primarily afflicted women in North Africa and the Middle East, including Saudi Arabia, and was characterized by somatic and emotional symptoms such as headaches, seizures, chronic pain, infertility, generalized and persistent depression, apathy and crying.

The United States has had a long-term relationship with Saudi Arabia in the areas of medical research and care. In the 1960s through to the 1980s, Saudi Arabia developed and instituted expansive medical coverage for its citizens, built hospitals, and trained physicians. The United States assisted in this process, and as a result, some Saudi doctors were trained in the United States. In 1999, Saudi Arabia presented George Mason University in northern Virginia with a 1.1 million dollar grant to train 12 Saudi nurses for 15 months. Moreover, Saudi Arabia continues, as of 1999, to host and recruit doctors from around the world.

LANGUAGE

Arabic is the national language of Saudi Arabia, but English is commonly used in business transactions, particularly with foreigners. There were ten large newspapers operating in Saudi Arabia in 1992, all privately owned; seven were printed in Arabic and three in English. English is commonly taught in the public schools, and sometimes French is offered in private academies.

The most common greeting in the Arabic language is "*Assalaamu alaikum,*" which means "Peace be upon you." This is often combined with kisses to the right and left cheek. "Hello" in Arabic is "*Marhaba,*" How are you?" is "*Keef Halek,*" and Good morning is "*Sabah Al Kair.*" "*Eid Mubarak*" is spoken to wish someone a happy holiday.

FAMILY AND COMMUNITY DYNAMICS

EDUCATION

In 1970, the literacy rate for Saudi Arabian boys was 15 percent, for girls a mere 2 percent. In the 1970s and 1980s, the public education system in Saudi Arabia experienced massive growth. As a result, by 1990 the literacy rate for boys was 73 percent and 48 percent for girls. In 1998, according to the United Nations Educational, Scientific and Cultural Organization, males attended approximately 9.0 years of schooling, and females attended about 8.4 years.

In the 1990s, public education was free, noncompulsory, heavily grounded in religion, and conducted separately for males and females. Initially, there was resistance to educating girls, but it was quickly overcome and secondary school graduation rates for females met and exceeded that of males in the early 1990s. The higher graduation rate for young women came despite their comparatively fewer years of education. Due to the rapid growth in women's education over the past decades, the 1990s saw a high demand for female teachers.

Technical, vocational or university education is available after the completion of secondary school in Saudi Arabia. In the 1990s it was a stated aim of the government to replace the high numbers of foreign workers in the country with Saudi nationals. The sponsorship of Saudi students at institutions of higher education in other countries often involves a number of years of work for the government upon return.

BIRTH AND BIRTHDAYS

Saudi Arabia had one of the highest birth rates in the world in 1998. The World Health Organization estimated that the average number of children born to each woman was 5.8, compared to 2.0 for American women. Many Muslims choose to name their children after the prophet Muhammad and his wives and companions, or other Koranic figures. According to tradition, alms are frequently given after the birth of each child as a way of giving thanks. On the seventh day after a child's birth, a celebration similar to an American baby shower is often held at the home of the child's grandmother. Family and friends gather, candles are lit, cheers are made, and often the child is named on this occasion. Subsequent birthdays are usually not celebrated.

THE ROLE OF WOMEN

Women in Saudi Arabia lead lives much more tied to domestic affairs than do American women. By law, women are not allowed to drive, bicycle, or use any form of public transportation without a male escort. They do not venture into public without a male escort, usually a family member. Women are not allowed to travel outside of Saudi Arabia without the express permission of their fathers of their husbands.

In 1997, according to the United Nations Secretariat and International Labor Office, 7 percent of Saudi women over the age of 15 were "economically active," compared with 79 percent of men. Female workers were concentrated in areas where they served other women, such as nursing, teaching, or staffing women's banks and stores. By Islamic law, a woman's money is her own, including any inheritance she may acquire, and the dowry she receives when she marries. Her husband is responsible for her maintenance, regardless of her personal wealth.

Saudi women retain their last name after marriage, but their activities are regulated by their families and by religious law. Men are legally allowed up to four wives, although technically a woman must agree to her husband's subsequent marriages. The discord often caused by such arrangements discourages most men from attempting them.

Per statistics of the World Health Organization in 1998, maternal mortality rates for Saudi women were 130 per 100,000 pregnancies, compared to 12 in the United States. According to other reports in 1997-98, the ratio of women to men in Saudi Arabia was in the lowest 10 percent worldwide, at 81:100. The average age at marriage for Saudi women was 21.7 years, compared to 25.6 years for men. Contraceptive use among married women was reported at 14 percent, and births to married teenagers were reported at 8 percent. As of 1999, women were not allowed to participate in politics in any official way.

COURTSHIP AND WEDDINGS

Courtship is unknown in Saudi Arabia. Men and women do not "date," and marriage is often arranged by the couple's parents. More liberal parents allow their children greater opportunity to select their spouses.

Islamic marriages, while a very serious matter for all involved, are not a sacrament. Marriage is a contract, and while certain aspects are immutable, both parties contribute to the contract according to their needs and desires. For instance, a woman may request the right to travel in her marriage contract. Wedding parties are usually separate for the bride and groom, taking place in different locations and even on different nights. Divorce is permissible as a last resort, but the importance placed on marriage and the family keeps the divorce rate low.

Young Saudi men and women living with their families in the United States often experience a greater degree of freedom, boys more so than girls, but adolescents are unlikely to get to know members of the opposite sex. For reasons discussed earlier, Saudi Arabians are unlikely to permanently settle in the United States, and Saudi children, even if born there, expect to return to their parent's homeland.

Saudi men living alone in the United States as students are more likely to return to Saudi Arabia to find a wife than to marry an American woman. In Islam, males are legally permitted to marry any woman "of the Book," meaning Jews and Christians, as well as fellow Muslims, but family preferences for other Arabs often hold sway. Some Saudi men have married American women and returned with them to Saudi Arabia. In 1999, the American Embassy was aware of about 500 American women residing in Saudi Arabia as the wives of Saudi citizens. Often, the geographical and cultural transition is difficult or impossible for a couple to make. When marriages fail, American women have few resources. Boarding a plane, train, or bus, with or without their children, is impossible unless they have their husband's consent. Problems such as these, as well as drastic cultural differences, have limited the number of marriages between Saudis and Americans.

Saudi men living in the United States who do not wish to return to Saudi Arabia to marry do have other options when seeking a spouse. In the 1990s, the Islamic Society of North America (ISNA), headquartered in Plainfield, Indiana, maintained an electronic database of persons seeking to marry. Through it, Muslims living in the United States and Canada were able to locate potential spouses with whom they could share Islamic values. The restrictions for Saudi women desiring to marry non-Saudis are severe. As of 1999, they were required to get a kingly dispensation to marry anyone not from Saudi Arabia, Qatar, Kuwait, Bahrain, Oman, or the United Arab Emirates. In 1999, the American Embassy was aware of four Saudi women married to American men. For these reasons, Saudi men and women living in the United States are unlikely to marry Americans, thereby eliminating one aspect of Americanization: The cross-cultural marriages that have played key roles in helping to establish other ethnic communities in America.

FUNERALS

In Islam, as with most other religions, there exist observances surrounding death and the dead. After death, a body is bathed three times, the last time with scented oil. Men are washed by men and women by women, except in the case of married persons. Prayers are said during the bathing process and the body is wrapped in a white shroud. If a person dies in the morning, they must be buried that same day. If they die in the afternoon, they must be buried by the following morning. No embalming materials are used. The dead are buried five or six feet deep, on their right side, with their head facing Mecca. Coffins are allowed, but more often the person is put to rest only in their shroud. Ornate coffins, tombs, or headstones are prohibited.

Prayers are recited throughout the burial ceremony. Most frequently, God is praised, forgiveness is asked for the person's sins, and a prayer is recited for all Muslims. Forgiveness is not asked for the sins of children, as they are considered blameless. One prayer for the deceased, first recited by the prophet Muhammad and listed in Gardens of the Righteous: Riyadh as-Salihim of Imam Nawawi (trans. Muhammad Zafrullah Khan. London: Curzon Press, 1975), is as follows: "Allah, do forgive him and have mercy on him and make him secure and overlook his shortcomings, and bestow upon him an honored place in Paradise, and make his place of entry spacious, and wash him clean with water and snow and ice, and cleanse him of all wrong as Thou dost clean a piece of white cloth of dirt, and bestow upon him a home better than him home and family better than him family and a spouse better than his spouse, and admit him into Paradise, and shield him from the torment of the grave and the torment of the Fire." Muslims in the United States have established graveyards in their communities to observe these rites.

RELIGION

As the birthplace of Islam and the home of the holy cities of Mecca and Medina, Saudi Arabia has reported a 100 percent Muslim population. The vast majority of the population follows *Sunni* Islam as it is practiced in accordance with the Wahhabi Movement. Sunni Muslims follow the teachings of the Koran and the example of the prophet Muhammad (the sunna consists of the personal customs and habits of the prophet Muhammad). *Shi'a* ("sect") Muslims are made up of a distinct group whose roots can be traced back to the time following the death of the prophet Muhammad, when political control of the Islamic community was undecided due to factionalism among Muhammad's followers. The primary difference between the two groups is that Sunni Muslims recognize a *caliph* (leader), who maintains military and political authority in Muslim societies. Shi'as recognize an imam (religious leader) descended directly from the prophet Muhammad and Ali (the first imam) as a person of military, political, and religious authority, such that he is sinless and pure. There are various sects among the Shi'a Muslims as well. A third, distinct group of Muslims, some Sunni and some Shi'a, are known as *Sufis*. Sufis follow a mystical path to discipline the mind and body through spirituality and asceticism.

Islamic law is known as *shari'a* (shari'a literally translates to "the way to the water whole" but also means "the right path"), and it is the official constitution of Saudi Arabia, based in large part on the Koran. The Koran includes many stories present in the Torah and the bible, and is considered by Muslims to be God's direct, undiluted message. It has not changed since it was written down by companions of the prophet Muhammad. All facets of life are governed in the Islamic system, which does not dwell on differences of ethnicity, class, or caste, instead bringing people together through an all-encompassing, monotheistic faith. The teachings of Islam include clear instructions on such varying topics as marriage, family and criminal law, inheritance rights, business, banking, and individual deportment.

Islam has a dual meaning, indicating both submission to God and peace. There are five pillars of Islam, all of which must be practiced by Muslims.

1. Belief in and profession of the *shahada* (testimony): "There is no God but Allah and Muhammad is His messenger." These are the words on the flag of Saudi Arabia. 2. *Salat* (prayer). Muslims pray five times daily in the direction of Mecca, with each occurrence having its own name and time frame. A ritual washing of the face, nose, mouth, ears, hands and feet is required before the prayer to purify the supplicant. The salat is a highly ritualized requirement, unlike Christian prayers that may rely heavily on requests for intercession and personal confessions. A period directly after the salat, known as the dua, is appropriate for personal prayers. 3. Zakat (alms-giving). Zakat is required of every adult Muslim to assist the community, including orphans, widows, and the poor. It is not looked at as a gift, rather a person gives zakat as their wealth and good fortune were given to them by God. 4. The fast of Ramadan, the ninth month of the Islamic calendar. Fasting consists of abstention from food, drink, and sexual activity during the hours between sunrise and sunset. Fasting is required of all adults who are physically able, except for women who are menstruating. These women must make up missed days during other times in the year. The ill, those nursing or pregnant, and those who are traveling can also make up missed days later in the year. The fast of Ramadan is ended with a large celebration known as *Id al-Fitr* (breaking of the fast). 5. Haj (pilgrimage) is the last pillar of Islam, and it requires that all Muslims who are able make a pilgrimage to Mecca at least once in their lives. Haj is made in the month after Ramadan.

EMPLOYMENT AND ECONOMIC TRADITIONS

In 1933, huge oil fields were discovered in Saudi Arabia. That same year, Saudi Arabia gave an oil concession to the Standard Oil Company of California. By 1938, when mining began, it was estimated that Saudi Arabia possessed 25 percent of the world's oil supply. King Ibn Saud, and subsequent rulers, were faced with turning an isolated country, almost completely ignored by the Western industrializing nations, into a global economic force. Among other concerns was their desire to obtain the economic benefits of oil production, but not to corrupt Saudi Arabia with Western values.

Saudi Arabia needed an ally who could train their workers to get the oil out of the ground, or it would be forever at the mercy of foreign technicians and the prices they set. King Ibn Saud met with President Theodore Roosevelt aboard the USS *Quincy* in Egypt in 1945. Ultimately, the United States agreed to train Saudi workers, many of whom, in the beginning, had to first be taught to read, and to pay for the oil that resulted from their joint efforts. The enormous influx of money and technical advances lifted Saudi Arabia into the modern twentieth century faster, perhaps, than has happened to any other industrializing society. Worldwide, other businesses are entering into arrangements with Saudi firms.

POLITICS AND GOVERNMENT

The authority of the ruling family was challenged several times in the latter half of the twentieth century. One of the more dramatic incidents was the capture by religious fundamentalists of the al-Haram, or Great Mosque, in Mecca in 1979. More than 200 people lost their lives during the two week stand off. Also in 1979, the newly installed Iranian government called for the overthrow of the Saudi monarchy, claiming that they no longer ruled with

Islamic authority. During the Iran-Iraq war, which raged from 1980-1988, the Saudi government supported Iraq financially for fear of Iranian domination in the Middle East.

Saudi Arabia's close political ties with the United States, born of the economic relationship created by oil, led to their support of Operation Desert Shield in 1990-1991. Although disturbed by the presence of non-Muslim and female soldiers on Arab land, the Saudis accepted over 700,000 troops from 37 nations to forge the attack against Iraq. The Persian Gulf War (1991) led to domestic unrest in Saudi Arabia, when reform-minded citizens and human rights organizations sought to relax the rigorous methods and policies of the Saudi government.

While Saudi Arabia and the United States are linked because of a mutually beneficial relationship over oil, the two countries do not always agree on issues. Significantly, Saudi Arabia and the United States have differed in foreign policy stances regarding Israel and the Middle East. This led to the oil embargo of the early 1970s.

MILITARY

Ties between the United States and Saudi Arabia led to their joint efforts during the Persian Gulf War. Differences in foreign policy, though, specifically as they relate to Israel and the Middle East, have limited military cooperation. This did not prevent the enrollment of ten Saudi cadets at the State University of New York's Maritime College at Fort Shuyler in 1999.

MEDIA

PRINT

Saudi Arabia is often referred to in the American media concerning business issues. There is also a variety of publications concerning Arab Americans. But there are not any large publications specific to Saudis in the United States. The Press Release Network of Dubai, United Arab Emirates, provides press release services for U.S. and Middle Eastern firms in the United States to more than 200 journals and news organizations in the Middle East, including the Saudi Press Agency.

RADIO AND TELEVISION

Saudi Students Radio and TV (SSRT), Colorado State University.

Mission was to provide audience with information about Saudi Arabia and its achievements in all areas; provide broadcasting services that are important to Saudi students at Colorado State university, such as lectures and seminars; and to provide daily news that serves community.

ORGANIZATIONS AND ASSOCIATIONS

Royal Embassy of Saudi Arabia.
Address: 601 New Hampshire Ave. NW, Washington, DC 20037.
Telephone: (202) 342-3800.

Islamic Saudi Academy.
Address: 8333 Richmond Highway, Alexandria, VA 22309.
Telephone: (703) 780-0606.

The Saudi Arabian Cultural Mission to the USA (SACM).
Address: 2600 Virginia Ave. Suite # 800, Washington, DC 20037.

SOURCES FOR ADDITIONAL STUDY

Al-Farsy, Fouad. *Modernity and Tradition: The Saudi Equation.* New York, NY: Routledge, Chapman and Hall, Inc., 1990.

Braswell, George W., Jr. *Islam: Its Prophet, Peoples, Politics and Power.* Nashville, TN: Broadman and Holman Publishers, 1996.

SCOTTISH AND SCOTCH-IRISH AMERICANS

by Mary A. Hess

Unlike the Scotch-Irish, who emigrated individually, the Scots emigrated in groups, which reflects their early organization in clans.

OVERVIEW

Scotland occupies roughly the northern one-third of the British Isles; its area is 30,414 square miles (78,772 square kilometers), or about the size of the state of Maine. A fault line separates the country into the northern Highlands and the southern Lowlands, the agricultural and industrial center of the country. In addition, there are several island groups offshore, notably the Hebrides, Shetland, and Orkney Islands. Two-thirds of the nation's population of 5,100,000 live in the Lowlands, most near the country's two largest cites—Edinburgh, the Scottish capital, and Glasgow. The other major cities of Dundee and Aberdeen reflect Scotland's major industries, particularly fishing and shipbuilding, and its strong ties to maritime commerce. The name Scotland derives from a Gaelic word for "wanderer."

Although the Highlands occupy a greater land mass than the Lowlands, they are more sparsely populated. There are also distinct cultural differences between the two. Highlanders, who were organized in family groups called clans, share a mostly Celtic culture and many are still Roman Catholic; whereas the Lowlanders are mostly Presbyterian, and speak Scots, which is an English-based language.

A land of considerable natural beauty, Scotland is surrounded on three sides by water—the Atlantic Ocean to the north and west, and the

North Sea to the east. Deep and narrow inlets known as *firths* penetrate the coastline of Scotland, while inland are distinctive glacial lakes known as lochs, the most famous of which is Loch Ness, the home of the fabled "Nessie," a prehistoric creature said to live in the deepest part of the lake.

HISTORY

The earliest recorded history concerning the Scots comes from the Romans, who controlled southern Britain in the first century A.D. In 84 A.D., the Romans defeated the tribal armies of Scotland in battle but they were unable to conquer the people. In an attempt to isolate the fierce "barbarians," the Roman emperor Hadrian built a massive stone wall, the remains of which are still visible traversing northern England just south of the Scottish border. By the 600s, four tribal groups had emerged: the Angles of the Southeast, related to the Germanic tribes settling England at the time; the Britons of the southwest, a Celtic people related to the Welsh; the Picts, also Celtic, who dominated the Highlands; and the Scots, a Celtic group that settled the western islands and cost from nearby Ireland. Christianity, brought by missionaries such as St. Ninian and St. Columba, spread slowly among the tribes beginning in about 400.

Following the Viking invasions of the 800s and 900s, the four tribes gradually united under Scottish kings such as Kenneth MacAlpin, who brought the Scots and Picts together in 843 and is often called the first king of Scotland. His descendants succeeded in gaining limited control over rival kings and the feuding clans (groups of families related by blood). One king who briefly unseated the dynasty was Macbeth of Moray, who killed Duncan, a descendant of MacAlpin, in 1040. Eventually, the Scots gave their name to the land and all its people, but the kings often ruled in name only, especially in the remote Highlands where local clan leaders retained their independence.

In 1066 Norman invaders from France gained control of England. Powerful new English rulers such as the thirteenth century's Edward I, who was called "the Hammer of the Scots," gained influence over the Scottish kings and helped shape culture in the Lowlands. Still the Scots resisted English dominance, often allying with England's enemy, France. One brief period of glory came when Robert Bruce, a noble, gained the Scottish crown and wiped out an English army at Bannockburn in 1314. Bruce's daughter married Walter the Steward (steward was a high office of the royal administration). This led to *Stewart*, later spelled *Stuart*, becoming the name of Scotland's royal house.

The English and Scottish royal houses had become closely connected through marriage. On Elizabeth's death in 1603, Mary's son James IV, already king of Scotland, ascended the throne of England. The Catholic Stuart monarchs faced trouble in both England and Scotland as the religious disputes between Catholics and Protestants wreaked the land. His coronation as James I of England settled Scotland's fate, for it was during his reign that the Plantation in Ulster relocated Lowland Scots in an attempt to reconstruct Ireland as a Protestant country. James's son, Charles I, was executed in 1649 by Oliver Cromwell's Protestant regime; after the Stuarts' restoration to the throne, James II was replaced by his Protestant daughter Mary and her husband William of Orange in 1688. While rebellions continued in Scotland, the union of crowns marked the beginning of an increasing bond between Scotland and her more powerful neighbor. The Treaty of Union (1707) formalized the political connection by incorporating Scotland's government into that of England. This created the United Kingdom and laid the foundation for the British Empire—to which the Scots would contribute greatly in coming centuries.

Political turmoil continued in Scotland during the 1700s with rebellions led by James Stuart (son of James II), who was backed by France and Spain—England's Catholic enemies. The most important of these "Jacobite" (from *Jacobus*, Latin for James) campaigns occurred in 1715 and in 1745, when James' son Charles also surprised Britain by invading from Scotland. These failed attempts engendered a vast body of romantic legend, though, particularly around the figure of Charles, called "Bonnie Prince Charlie" or the "Young Pretender" (claimant to the throne). The Jacobites found more support among the fiercely independent Highlanders, who had remained largely Catholic, than among the stern Protestant Lowlanders. The Scots retained their distinctive character, however, even as they contributed to Britain's prosperity and worldwide power.

THE SCOTCH-IRISH

The Scotch-Irish trace their ancestry to Scotland, but through Northern Ireland, which also belongs to the British Empire. Northern Ireland, which is composed of six counties—Antrim, Armagh, Cavan, Down, Monaghan, and Tyrone, occupies an area of 5,452 square miles (14,121 square kilometers), or a territory somewhat larger than the state of Connecticut. Its capital and largest city is Belfast, where approximately one-fifth of the country's population of 1,594,000 resides.

The Scotch-Irish descend from 200,000 Scottish Lowland Presbyterians who were encouraged by the English government to migrate to Ulster in the seventeenth century. Trying to strengthen its control of Ireland, England tried to establish a Protestant population in Ulster. Surrounded by native hostility, though, the group maintained its cultural distinction. The same economic pressures, including steadily increasing rents on their land, frequent crop failures, and the collapse of the linen trade, coupled with the belief in greater opportunity abroad, caused many Scotch-Irish to leave for the American colonies during the eighteenth century. It is estimated that nearly two million descendants of the Scotch-Irish eventually migrated to the American colonies.

IMMIGRATION

From 1763 to 1775, 55,000 Scotch-Irish from Ulster and 40,000 Scots arrived in America. Since Scotland was able to pursue its own colonies in the New World, several small colonies were established in the early seventeenth century in East Jersey and South Carolina. These colonies were primarily for Quakers and Presbyterians who were experiencing religious persecution by the then Episcopalian Church of Scotland. Although some Scots were transported to America as prisoners or criminals and were forced into labor as punishment, many voluntarily settled in America as traders or tobacco workers in Virginia. However, the political persecution of the Jacobite sympathizers, combined with economic hard times, forced many Scots to emigrate. Unlike the Scotch-Irish, who emigrated individually, the Scots emigrated in groups, which reflects their early organization in clans. They became a significant presence in the New World, settling in the original colonies with a particularly strong presence in the Southeast.

Many Scotch-Irish joined the mass migrations to the New World brought on by the Potato Famine of the 1840s. Substantial numbers of Scots also immigrated to the United States in the nineteenth century to work in industry. Throughout the twentieth century, immigration would rise when economic conditions in Scotland worsened; this was especially true during the 1920s when an economic depression hit Scotland particularly hard. Because British law then prohibited skilled workers to leave the country, many Scotch-Irish laborers found their way to the United States through Canada.

SETTLEMENT PATTERNS

Because of profound doctrinal differences with New England's Congregationalism, the Scotch-Irish Presbyterians opted for the religious freedom of William Penn's colony; and the earliest settlements there were near Philadelphia in the 1720s. They reached as far west as Pittsburgh before finding greater opportunities in the southern colonies. The Scotch-Irish and Scots alike were strongly represented in the push westward, though, and their participation in military campaigns was significant. Darien, Georgia, was founded by Highland Scots in service to General James Oglethorpe, and their assistance was invaluable in protecting the British colonies of the Southeast from the Spanish in Florida. These Highland Scots strongly protested against the institution of slavery in the colony, setting a precedent for strong anti-slavery sentiment that stood against the Scotch-Irish planters and English colonists who were eager for slavery to help build the colony and amass fortunes.

> **"People who had come to this country in the earlier years had told me, you'll be sorry when you get to Ellis Island. But I wasn't really sorry, I was just maybe upset a little bit. What upset me the most was having to go through so many people's hands and take such a long time."**
>
> Mary Dunn in 1923, cited in *Ellis Island: An Illustrated History of the Immigrant Experience,* edited by Ivan Chermayeff et al. (New York: Macmillan, 1991).

Today the descendants of the Scotch-Irish number over six million, with about five million identifying themselves as descended from Scottish ancestry. In the 1990 U.S. Census "Scotch-Irish" was the eleventh most populous ethnic group, followed by "Scottish." The states reporting the highest concentration of Scotch-Irish are California, Texas, North Carolina, Florida, and Pennsylvania. Those claiming Scottish descent are also most populous in California, then Florida, Texas, New York, and Michigan. The issue of descent is somewhat confused since not all historians and social scientists count Scotch-Irish as a culturally distinct group. For the purposes of the 1990 census, "Scotch-Irish" was included as a classification that was a single, rather than a multiple, response to the question of national origin. Also, a significant number of African Americans and Native Americans claim Scotch-Irish ancestry.

ACCULTURATION AND ASSIMILATION

The Scots people were among the first European settlers, and along with the other colonists from the British Isles, helped create what has been recog-

nized as the dominant culture in America, namely, white and Protestant. By working hard and seizing the opportunities of a rapidly growing country, many Scottish immigrants were able to move up rapidly in American society. Unaffected by barriers of race, language, or religion, they earned a reputation for hard work and thrift that was greatly admired in the young republic. Perhaps the most notable among this group is one of America's most successful immigrants—the industrialist Andrew Carnegie. After arriving in America at the age of 13, he worked first in a cotton mill, then as a superintendent for the Pennsylvania Railroad. By shrewd investments, he parlayed his Carnegie Steel Com-

pany into a huge fortune. In his famous essay, "The Gospel of Wealth," he described his rationale for philanthropy—Carnegie donated hundreds of millions of dollars to build public libraries, endow universities, and fund scholarships. His most famous gift is one of New York's most beautiful public buildings, Carnegie Hall, which has hosted the world's most distinguished performers in the lively arts. Carnegie believed that wealth acquired by hard work should be shared with society, but on his terms; for example, Carnegie was bitterly opposed to unionization in his steel plants and was behind the murder of strikers in the Homestead Strike at his plant in Homestead, Pennsylvania, in 1892.

Scots are relatively unscathed by any ethnic stereotyping; however, the phrase, "cold as Presbyterian charity" reflects the long standing belief that Scots are dour and stingy. This seems to be lessening, although brand names such as "Scotch Tape" reinforce the idea that to be Scottish is to be thrifty. There is also the persistence of the "hillbilly" legend, which portrays Appalachian residents as ill-clad, unshod bumpkins fond of brewing "moonshine" (bootleg whiskey). This image became

widespread with the "Lil' Abner" comic strip drawn by Al Capp beginning in 1932; the strip reached 60 million readers and became first a Broadway musical and then a film in 1959. In the 1960s, a CBS television series, "The Beverly Hillbillies" and its spin-offs "Petticoat Junction" and "Green Acres" furthered the image of rural people as simpletons. The dignity of most rural Southern life has emerged, however, with the publication of the "Foxfire" books in the 1970s, and the efforts of folklorists to preserve and document a vanishing way of life. Appalshop, a rural arts and education center in Whitesburg, Kentucky, exemplifies the effort to preserve the Scottish and Scotch-Irish heritage of Appalachia on film and also recorded music.

The figure most associated with the best aspects of this tradition is the pioneer Daniel Boone (1734-1820), whose life has been celebrated in song and story, as well as movies and television. Daniel Boone was a trailblazer and patriot who continues to capture the imaginations of Americans. Other famous Scots who immigrated to America were Flora MacDonald, the woman who saved the life of "Bonnie Prince Charlie" by hiding him from his pursuers. Imprisoned by the English until she became too troublesome as a symbol of Jacobite sentiment, she was pardoned and immigrated to North Carolina. John Muir, Scottish-born naturalist (1838-1914), was reared as a strict Calvinist, and reacted to a near loss of his eyesight in an accident by a spiritual quest for the natural world. He began a walk on foot across the continent, and fiercely advocated the preservation of the wilderness; he influenced President Theodore Roosevelt to become a conservationist. The national parks are a tribute to his foresight and love of America's natural beauty.

There is a cliché about "the wandering Scot" which contains an essential truth—that Scottish people have both a wanderlust and a strong affection for Scotland. This attachment can be seen today in the celebration by Americans of their Scottish and Scotch-Irish roots, which often means both a consciousness of ethnicity as well as taking a journey to discover their ancestral heritage. Many genealogical firms in Great Britain and Ireland specialize in helping these Americans trace their ancestry. A family crest, a tartan tie, or an interest in traditional customs is a demonstration of pride in their ethnic identity.

TRADITIONS, CUSTOMS, AND BELIEFS

Scottish and Scotch-Irish customs include the *shivaree* (an elaborate courting ritual that involves the serenading of the bride outside her window) and square dancing. The square dance began with reels and other dances enjoyed by the nobility and was transformed to the present popularity of line dancing—steps done to music often featuring the most Scotch-Irish of instruments, the fiddle. Today's "Texas Two-Step" and "Boot-scooting" evolved from ancient ritual dances.

Scots enjoy large "gatherings of the clan," which celebrate their heritage and offer opportunities to meet others who share membership in the clan. Most states with a large Scottish and Scotch-Irish population (such as New York and Michigan) have "Highland Games," which feature sports such as "tossing the caber," in which men compete to toss a heavy pole the farthest distance. Bagpipe music is a very important part of this celebration, as it is at any celebration of clan identity. North Carolina, which has one of largest concentrations of people of Scottish descent, hosts the biggest gathering at Grandfather Mountain each July. Campbells mingle with MacGregors and Andersons, while enjoying Scotch whisky and traditional cuisine.

CUISINE

Main Scottish staples are oatmeal, barley, and potatoes. Oatmeal is made into a porridge, a thick, hot breakfast cereal traditionally seasoned with salt. Barley is used primarily in the distillation of Scotch whiskey, now a major source of export revenue. Potatoes ("tatties") are most often eaten mashed. There is also the traditional *haggis* (a pudding made from the heart, liver, and other organs of a sheep, chopped with onions and oatmeal and then stuffed into a sheep's stomach and boiled). This unique meal, served with tatties and "a wee dram" (small portion of whiskey), has taken its place with the tartan and the bagpipes as a national symbol. Scots also enjoy rich vegetable soups, seafood in many forms, beef, oatcakes (a tasty biscuit), and shortbread (a rich, cookie-like confection).

TRADITIONAL DRESS

The famous Scottish kilt, a knee-length skirt of a tartan pattern, was created by an Englishman, Thomas Rawlinson, who lived in the 1700s. The older kilts were rectangles of cloth, hanging over the legs, gathered at the waist, and wrapped in folds around the upper body. The blanket-like garment served as a bed-roll for a night spent outdoors. Aside from the kilt, fancy "highland" dress includes a *sporan* (leather purse on a belt), stockings, brogues (shoes), dress jacket, and a number of decorative accessories. The plaid is a length of tartan cloth draped over the shoulder and does not properly refer to the pattern, which is the tartan. Women's fancy dress is simpler, though elegant, consisting of a white cotton blouse, perhaps with embroidered patterns, and a silk tartan skirt. Her version of the plaid, a tartan also in silk, is hung over the shoulder and pinned in place with a brooch. This finery, like the tartans, is mostly an invention of the modern age but has become traditional and it is taken quite seriously. The tartan shows up elsewhere, commonly worn on ties, caps, and skirts—even on cars and in the costumes of young "punk rockers" in Edinburgh and Glasgow.

MUSIC

There is considerable Scottish influence in the field of country and folk music, directly traceable to the Scots ballad—a traditional form in which a story (usually tragic) is related to the listener in song. The ballad (e.g. "Barbara Allen") originated as an oral tradition, and was brought to the southeastern United States by immigrants who preserved the form while adapting melody and lyrics to suit their purpose. Instruments, especially the fiddle and harp,

Bagpipe music is a very important part of "Highland Games" type celebrations, as it is at any celebration of clan identity.

have been transformed into unique sounding relations such as the hammered dulcimer, pedal steel guitar, and electric mandolins, and are the staples of today's country music, particularly bluegrass, which emphasizes the heritage of country music in its traditional origins in Scotland and Ireland.

HOLIDAYS

Most Scottish holidays are those celebrated throughout Great Britain; however, two holidays are unique to Scotland: Scottish Quarter Day, celebrated 40 days after Christmas, and the commemoration of St. Andrew, patron saint of Scotland, on November 30. A sentimental holiday is the birthday of poet Robert ("Robbie") Burns, born January 25, 1759, who is perhaps best known to Americans for the perennial New Year's anthem, "Auld Lang Syne." The Scotch-Irish also celebrate July 12, the anniversary of William of Orange's victory over the Catholics at the Battle of the Boyne in 1690, with parades.

HEALTH ISSUES

Health concerns are primarily determined by economic factors, and especially by location. Having found, for the most part, economic security due to generations of residence and the economic advantage of an early arrival in America, many Scots and Scotch-Irish are insured through their employers, are self-employed, or have union benefits. The great exception is in Appalachia, where poverty persists despite the initiatives of John F. Kennedy and Lyndon B. Johnson's "War on Poverty" in the 1960s.

The dominant industry of the area, coal mining, has left a considerable mark on the health of Scottish and Scotch-Irish Americans. Black lung, a congestive disease of the lungs caused by the inhalation of coal dust, disables and kills miners at a high rate. This and chronic malnutrition, high infant mortality, and low birth weight remain the scourge of mountain people. West Virginia, Kentucky, and Tennessee still have pockets of poverty as a result of high unemployment and isolation. The pattern of early marriage and large families is still typical, as is a significant problem with domestic violence.

LANGUAGE

The Scotch-Irish are unlikely to share speech patterns and the characteristic burr (a distinctive trilled "r") with the Scots. However, linguists who have studied Appalachian accents have found continuity in usage and idiom that can be shown to originate in Scottish phrases. Occasionally remnants of the Scottish idiom survive in words such as "dinna" which means "don't," as in "I dinna ken" (I don't know), but this is increasingly rare as even isolated mountain hollows in the South are penetrated by mass media and its homogenizing influence.

FAMILY AND COMMUNITY DYNAMICS

Traditional family structure, especially in the Highlands, centered around the clan. There are about 90 original clans. Many of the clan names are prefixed by "Mac," meaning "son of." The clans have loosely defined territories, and prolonged wars, often spanning generations, were once common between clans. The most famous feud was that between the Campbells (who supported the English) and the MacDonalds (Jacobites). Even today there are MacDonalds who will not speak to Campbells and vice-versa. Large clans enrolled smaller ones as allies, and the alliances also became traditional. The adjective "clannish," derived from the Gaelic *clann* (descent from a common ancestor) perfectly describes the sentimental attachment that Scottish Americans feel concerning extended family and heritage. The origin of this term is the tendency of Scots to migrate with their clan and settle in the same location. This tendency was so pronounced that in parts of Kentucky and Tennessee, relatives adopted the use of their middle name as a surname since all their kin shared a common last name. One of the most infamous examples in America of the Scottish tendency to clannishness is the Hatfield and McCoy feud of the 1880s in the Tug River Valley along the West Virginia and Kentucky border. The murderous vendetta lasted years and involved disputes over a razorback hog, a romance between a Hatfield son and a McCoy daughter, and various other affronts to family dignity. After nationwide publicity, the feud was finally ended in 1897 after the execution of one of the Hatfields and the jailing of several other participants. However, the phrase, "feuding like the Hatfields and McCoys" is still a part of the American vocabulary.

Gatherings were purposeful and practical in frontier America, as in the "quilting bee," which allowed women to enjoy each others' company while creating a patchwork quilt—the essence of thrift. Various small pieces of fabric were sewn together in patterns to create a beautiful and utilitarian bed covering. Today many of these quilts are treasured by the descendants of the women who made them. Quilting is a popular craft that has enjoyed an ever-widening appreciation both as a hobby and folk art; quilts are often displayed in museums, and one of the best collections can be seen in Paducah, Kentucky, home of the American Quilting Society. Another traditional community activity is that of the barn raising and the subsequent dance—a tribute to the pioneer spirit that built America. Neighbors cooperated to erect barns and celebrated their hard work with fiddle music and a square dance late into the night. These gatherings helped shape community in rural areas such as the Midwest and the West.

RELIGION

The traditional dividing line between the Scotch-Irish and the Irish has been religion. While Irish immigrants have been primarily Catholics, the Scotch-Irish are followers of John Knox and John Calvin. The belief in predestination of the soul had a powerful effect on the shaping of the Scots' psyche. The original plantation of Scots in Ulster, which was motivated by economic hard times as much as by politics, was an attempt by England to subdue the native Catholic population. England thereby politicized religion when it initiated the discord between the two groups, a discord that still plays itself out in Northern Ireland. When the Potato Famine of the 1840s caused the Scotch-Irish to migrate to the New World, they brought their faith with them, retaining a tradition that stood them in good stead in the largely Protestant country. Although in Scotland the Church of Scotland was an austere entity, not given to large churches or displays of wealth, it gradually gave way to grand affirmations of material success in America. Today the Presbyterian church still plays a significant role in American religious life. The stirring hymn "Onward Christian Soldiers" (1864) exemplifies the Scottish heritage reflected in today's church: "Onward Christian soldiers / Marching as to war / With the Cross of Jesus / Going on before!" Written first as a children's hymn, it became a favorite in Protestant churches.

EMPLOYMENT AND ECONOMIC TRADITIONS

Scots and Scotch-Irish have been drawn to the land as farmers and herders just as in their home country. Highland Scots, in particular, were attracted to mountain areas that resembled their homeland, and replicated their lives as herders and small scale farmers wherever possible. Others were drawn to work in heavy industry, such as the steel mills and coal mines. The nation's railroads provided employment for many, and in the case of Andrew Carnegie, provided a step up in his career as a capitalist. Many sought higher education and entered the professions at all levels, particularly as physicians and lawyers. For others, isolated in Appalachia or the rural South, hard times during the Great Depression brought scores of Scotch-Irish to the factories of Detroit and Chicago, where they labored in the auto plants and stockyards. Poverty returned for many of these people as plants shut down and downscaled in the 1960s, creating so-called "hillbilly ghettoes" in major Northern industrial cities. Generations of poverty have created an underclass of displaced Southerners which persists as a social problem today. Author Harriette Arnow, born in 1908, wrote movingly of the plight of these economic migrants in her novel *The Dollmaker* (1954). Scottish and Scotch-Irish Americans have, of course, assimilated to a high degree and have benefited much from the opportunities that class mobility and a strong work ethic have brought them.

POLITICS AND GOVERNMENT

Not until the 1970s would Scottish nationalism be a significant force in British politics; nonetheless, in 1979, Scottish voters rejected limited home rule in a referendum. There is a significant presence of Scottish nationalists today despite the historic, economic and cultural ties to Britain.

Scottish and Scotch-Irish Americans have been involved with U.S. government from the founding of the Republic. As landholders and farmers, they were very much the people Thomas Jefferson had in mind as participants in his agrarian democracy. From legislators to presidents, including President Bill Clinton, the passion of Scottish people for government has been felt in America. Presidents who shared this heritage include Andrew Jackson (1767-1845), Ulysses S. Grant (1822-1885), Woodrow Wilson (1856-1924), and Ronald Wilson Reagan (1911–).

MILITARY

Both Scots and the Scotch-Irish were a significant presence in the American Revolution and the Civil War. The divided union was embodied by Generals "Stonewall" Jackson and Jeb Stuart for the Gray and George B. McClellan for the Blue. Many Scots had settled on the frontier and moved westward seeking land and opportunity, and pressed forward to the West, particularly Texas, Oklahoma, and the Gulf Coast. Texas in particular was a land of opportunity for the land-hungry Scots—Sam Houston and his fellows were among the intrepid settlers of that diverse state. They fought the Comanches and settled the Plains, creating a legend of Texan grit and determination not unlike the reputation of their Scottish forebears. The Alamo in San Antonio is a symbol of the tenacity of the Scotch-Irish who were prominent among the defenders of the Texas Republic.

Highland Scots and their descendants (who typically settled in the mountains) were active in the anti-slavery movement, while it was more common for the Lowland Scots and the Scotch-Irish to be proslavery. This created a major rift in the mid-South and the lowland areas, which clung to slavery while the highlands in large part chose the Union during the Civil War. Scots and Scotch-Irish have figured prominently in all the major political parties in American history, and were perhaps most identified as a group with the Populist movement which reached its peak in the 1890s and united farmers for a short time against perceived economic injustice. The South and Midwest were the stronghold of the populists, led by men like Tom Watson and Ignatius Donnelly. Scots and Scots-Irish were also a major force in the union movement, exemplified by the agitation for workers rights in the textile mills of the Southeast and the mines of West Virginia and Kentucky, marked by serious outbreaks of violence and strikes. "Which side are you on?" was a question often heard in these conflicts. Filmmaker Barbara Kopple documented this long and bloody struggle in her prize-winning film, *Harlan County, USA* (1977).

Since the breakup of the so-called Democratic "Solid South", it is difficult to predict how Scottish and Scotch-Americans vote. In addition, because of assimilation, it would be unlikely that there would be a "Scots vote" or "Scotch-Irish vote."

INDIVIDUAL AND GROUP CONTRIBUTIONS

DANCE

Isadora Duncan (1878-1927) was a major innovator in modern dance, creating a unique expression based on Greek classicism and a belief in liberating the body from the constrictive costumes and especially footwear of classical ballet; her flowing draperies and bare feet made her the sensation of her day; her colorful life story is chronicled in her autobiography, *My Life* (1926).

FILM, TELEVISION, AND THEATER

The influence of Scottish and Scotch-Irish Americans in the performing arts stretches from Oscar-winning directors like Leo McCarey (1898-1969), whose films *Going My Way* (1944) and *The Bells of St. Mary's* (1945) are considered classics in Hollywood sentimentality, to the remarkable Huston family whose careers span much of the history of the motion picture in America. Walter (1884-1950), his son John (1906-1987), and John's daughter Angelica (1951–) have all won Academy Awards. Walter Huston was a memorable character actor, perhaps best remembered for one of his son John's best films as a director, *The Treasure of the Sierra*

Madre (1948); granddaughter Angelica was directed by her father in three films, notably *Prizzi's Honor* (1985) for which she won as best supporting actress. John Huston's last film, *The Dead*, a 1987 adaptation of James Joyce's story, also starred Angelica and was scripted by her brother Danny. James Stewart (1908–), one of Hollywood's most famous and beloved citizens, is well known for classics such as *Mr. Smith Goes to Washington* (1939), *It's a Wonderful Life* (1947), and *Rear Window* (1954). One of his leading ladies (in *The Philadelphia Story*, 1940) is Katharine Hepburn, (1907 –) a strong-willed and talented actress who portrayed the doomed Mary, Queen of Scots in *Mary of Scotland* (1936). Hepburn, daughter of a prominent Connecticut physician and his wife, a suffragist and birth control activist, has enjoyed a long and honored career on stage and screen; she won three Academy Awards and was nominated for eight. Another remarkable career was that of Fred MacMurray, an actor known for films such as *Double Indemnity* (1944)—a tense *film noir*—and *The Apartment* (1960), was also known as a comic actor. He made a successful transition to Walt Disney films such as *The Absent Minded Professor* (1961) and became a television icon in the 1960s as the widowed father in the popular sitcom "My Three Sons." Two singers, Gordon MacRae (1921–) and John Raitt (1917–), enjoyed Broadway success that transferred to Hollywood musicals; both are known for their portrayal of Curley in *Oklahoma!* (which depicts customs such as the *shivaree* and the barn dance).

LITERATURE

Writers who have enriched American literature include: Robert Burns (1759-1796), the beloved Scots poet; Sherwood Anderson (1876-1941), author of the pathbreaking novel, *Winesburg, Ohio* (1919); North Carolinian Thomas Wolfe (1900-1938), whose novel, *Look Homeward, Angel* (1929) has been called "the great American novel." Carson McCullers (1917-1967), author of *Member of the Wedding* (1946) and *Reflections in A Golden Eye* (1941), is one of the South's most important novelists. Ellen Glasgow's (1873-1945) best novel, *Vein of Iron* (1935), concerns the fortunes of Ada Fincastle, the daughter of a hardy Scotch-Irish family of Virginia in the early part of the twentieth century. Larry McMurtry, whose novels *The Last Picture Show* and *Lonesome Dove* have enjoyed tremendous success after filmed versions have captured fans for the prolific writer's view of his home state and its rich history.

MUSIC

Michael Nesmith (1943–), son of Bette Nesmith Graham, became famous as a songwriter and performer with the 1960s rock group, the Monkees. Bonnie Raitt (1950–), daughter of John Raitt, is a popular Grammy-winning singer and a noted interpreter of the blues.

SCIENCE

Cyrus McCormick (1809-1884), an immigrant from Ulster, invented the reaper. Samuel Morse (1791-1872), who revolutionized communications with the telegraph and Morse Code, was also an accomplished portrait painter and a founder of Vassar College in 1861; in 1844, he sent the famous message "What hath God wrought?" from Washington to Baltimore, and between 1857 and 1858 he collaborated with entrepreneur Cyrus Field (1819-1892) in laying the first transatlantic cable. Field later established the Wabash Railroad with financier Jay Gould. A particularly enterprising Scotch-Irish woman, Bette Nesmith Graham (1924-1980), born in Dallas, Texas, died with a net worth over $47.5 million; a poor typist, she devised a product that would cover mistakes and in so doing created "Liquid Paper"—a correction fluid. Claire McCardell (1905-1958) revolutionized fashion design and dance with the invention of the stretch leotard; a pioneer in women's ready-to-wear clothing, she also created the affordable and practical "popover," a wrap-around denim housedress, and the "Moroccan" tent dress.

VISUAL ARTS

Scottish and Scotch-Irish craftsmen and artists are similarly prominent. Gilbert Stuart (1755-1828), perhaps America's best-known portrait artist, was of Scottish heritage (his paintings of George Washington provide the definitive image of the "father of his country" for many Americans), as was Scots-born portrait artist John Smibert (1688-1751), and sculptor Frederick MacMonnies (1863-1937), whose graceful public sculptures adorn the New York Public Library, among many other locations (his Columbian fountain at the World's Columbian Exposition of 1893 was one of the most celebrated artistic achievements of that fair). Another is Duncan Phyfe, craftsperson (1768-1854), whose name is well-known to generations of Americans who cherish the tables, chairs, and cabinets he created, as well as inspiring imitators of his work—the apex of the Federalist style.

MEDIA

The American Scottish Gazette.

Published by the American Scottish Foundation, Inc.

Address: 575 Madison Avenue, New York, New York 10022.
Telephone: (212) 605-0338.
Fax: (212) 308-9834.
E-mail: Edward@un.org.
Online: http://americanscotfoundation.com/amerscot/welcome.htm.

Calling All Scots.

Publication of the American Scottish Foundation, Inc.

Address: 545 Madison Avenue, New York, New York 10022.

Claymore.

Newsletter of Scottish information and services published by the Council of Scottish Clan Associations, Inc.

Address: Route 1, Box 15A, Lovettsville, Virginia 22080-9703.
Telephone: (703) 822-5292.
Online: http://www.tartans.com/cosca/index.htm.

Highlander.

A magazine of Scottish heritage.

Contact: Angus J. Ray, Editor.
Address: 560 Green Bay Road, Winnetka Illinois 60093.
Telephone: (800) 607-4410; or (847) 784-9660.
Fax: (847) 784-9661.

Scotia.

An interdisciplinary journal of Scottish studies.

Contact: William S. Rodner.
Address: Old Dominion University, Department of History, Arts and Letters Building, Norfolk, Virginia 23529.
Telephone: (804) 683-3933.
Fax: (804) 683-3241.

Scottish Banner.

Covers Scots in North America and Scotland. Intended for Scottish expatriates and descendants.

Address: P.O. Box 3065, Seminole, Florida 33775.

Telephone: (800) 729-8951; or (727) 394-0924.
Fax: (727) 394-1294.
E-mail: scotbanner@aol.com.
Online: http://www.scotbanner.com.

RADIO AND TELEVISION

TNN (The Nashville Network).

The Nashville Network is a 24-hour cable country music channel. Programming is primarily geared toward performance; programming includes recorded videos and talk shows, with a strong regional emphasis toward the South and West. "The Grand Ole Opry," a radio/television simulcast of the weekly performances of leading country music performers from Nashville's Ryman Auditorium, airs each Saturday evening at 8:00 p.m. on TNN and on a syndicated network of radio stations as well. Begun in 1925, it is the nation's oldest radio program.

WFAE.

"The Thistle and The Shamrock," a weekly Celtic music and cultural appreciation program, featuring thematically grouped presentations on Scottish, Irish and Breton music. Carried nationally on National Public Radio.

Contact: Fiona Ritchie.
Address: 1 University Place, Charlotte, North Carolina 28213.

ORGANIZATIONS AND ASSOCIATIONS

American Scottish Foundation.

An organization that promotes Scottish heritage through Scotland House, a cultural center in New York City, and a newsletter, *Calling All Scots*.

Contact: Alan L. Bain, President.
Address: 545 Madison Avenue, New York, New York 10022.
Telephone: (212) 605-0338.
Fax: (212) 308-9834.
Online: http://www.americascottfoundation.com.

Association of Scottish Games and Festivals.

Provides information for its members on Highland Games held in the United States; compiles statistics and maintains a computer database.

Contact: Robert McGregor, President.
Address: 47 East Germantown Pike, Plymouth Meeting, Pennsylvania 19462.
Telephone: (215) 825-7268.

Fax: (215) 825-8745.
E-mail: ligdir@aol.com.

Council of Scottish Clans and Associations.
Provides information on clan organizations for interested individuals or groups and maintains files of clan newsletters, books, etc. Meets each July at Grandfather Mountain.

Contact: Robert McWilliam, President.
Address: Route 1, Box 15A, Lovettsville, Virginia 22080-9703.
Telephone: (703) 822-5292.
Online: http://www.tartans.com/cosca/index.htm.

Scotch-Irish Foundation.
Members are of Scotch-Irish descent; the foundation compiles records and bibliographic materials on the Scotch-Irish. Affiliated with the Scotch-Irish Society of the United States on America.

Address: 201 Main Street, New Holland, Pennsylvania 17557.
Telephone: (717) 354-4961.
Fax: (717) 355-2227.

Scotch-Irish Society of the United States of America.
An organization of persons of Scotch-Irish heritage; sponsors the work of the Scotch-Irish Foundation.

Contact: Ian Stuart, Esquire.
Address: Box 181, Bryn Mawr, Pennsylvania 19010.

MUSEUMS AND RESEARCH CENTERS

There are significant collections on Scotch-Irish and Scottish heritage to be found in university collections; notable ones include the Robert Louis Stevenson Collection at Yale University, the Robert Burns Collection at the University of South Carolina at Columbia, and a new archive of Scottish materials to be housed in Durham, North Carolina, under the sponsorship of North Carolina Central University. There is an important genealogical collection housed at the Ellen Paine Odum Library in Moultrie, Georgia.

SOURCES FOR ADDITIONAL STUDY

Colley, Linda. *Britons: Forging the Nation 1707-1837*. New Haven: Yale University Press, 1992.

A Companion to Scottish Culture, edited by David Daiches. London: Edward Arnold, 1981.

Dobson, David. *Scottish Emigration to Colonial America, 1607-1785*. Athens: University of Georgia Press, 1994.

Finlayson, Iain. *The Scots*. New York: Atheneum, 1987.

Jackson, Carlton. *A Social History of the Scotch-Irish*. Lanham, Maryland: Madison Books, 1993.

Johnson, James E. *The Scots and Scotch-Irish in America*. Minneapolis, Minnesota: Lerner Publications, 1966; reprinted, 1991.

Lehmann, William C. *Scottish and Scotch-Irish Contributions to Early American Life and Culture*. Port Washington, New York: Kennikat Press, 1978.

Leyburn, James G. *The Scotch-Irish*. Chapel Hill: The University of North Carolina Press, 1962.

McWhiney, Grady. *Cracker Culture: Celtic Customs in the Old South*. Tuscaloosa: University of Alabama Press, 1988.

Parker, Anthony W. *Scottish Highlanders in Colonial Georgia: The Recruitment, Emigration, and Settlement at Darien, 1735-1748*. Athens: University of Georgia Press, 1997.

Rethford, Wayne, and June Skinner Sawyers. *The Scots of Chicago: Quiet Immigrants and Their New Society*. Dubuque, Iowa: Kendall/Hunt Pub. Co., 1997.

SERBIAN AMERICANS

by
Bosiljka Stevanović

Even though Serbian immigrants tended to live in closely knit, homogeneous colonies, they were never so totally isolated as to prevent any penetration of American influence, and that interaction inevitably led to changes in many aspects of their lives.

OVERVIEW

Located in the southeast portion of the former Yugoslavia, Serbia, which occupies 34,116 square miles, is the largest of the former Yugoslavia's six republics. Included in its territory are the autonomous provinces of Kosovo and Vojvodina. Serbia is bordered by Hungary to the north, Romania and Bulgaria to the east, Macedonia and Albania to the south, Bosnia-Herzegovina to the west, and Croatia to the northwest. Serbia's population of 11.2 million consists of 64 percent Serbs, 14 percent Albanians (mostly in the Kosovo region), 6 percent Montenegrins, and 4 percent Hungarians. Other groups include Germans, Gypsies, Romanians, Slovenians, and Turks. About 65 percent of the population belongs to the Eastern Orthodox church, 19 percent are Muslim, and 5 percent are Christian. The country's flag consists of three equal horizontal stripes: blue, white, and red (from top to bottom). The capital city is Belgrade. The official language is Serbian.

HISTORY

The Serbs settled in the Balkans in the seventh century during the reign of the Byzantine Emperor Heraclius (610-41 A.D.). The Serbs are Slavs, whose prehistoric home had been in the general area of today's Byelorussia and Ukraine. In the sixth century A.D. the Slavs began to leave their land, dispersing themselves to the north, east, west, and south. The Serbs went south, and became known as the South Slavs, or Yugoslavs.

The earliest and the most powerful principalities, or states, were Zeta (located in modern-day Montenegro) and Raska (located in present-day Kosovo). The earliest significant rulers of Zeta were Mutimir (829-917), during whose reign the Serbs accepted Christianity; Cheslav (927-960), an enlightened ruler who created a strong state; and Voislav (1034-1042), who was successful in asserting Zeta's statehood from Byzantium. His son Michael followed (1050-1082), and during his reign the church broke into two: the Western church, or the Roman Catholic church, and the Eastern Orthodox church, headed by a Patriarch and with Constantinople as its papal seat.

In time, Zeta weakened and Raska achieved great political and military power. The ascension to the throne of Raska by the Grand Zupan Stefan Nemanja (1114-1200) marks one of the most important events in Serbian history. Founding the Nemanjić Dynasty, which was to rule for the next 200 years, he ushered in the Golden Age of Serbian medieval history. An able politician and statesman, Stefan Nemanja ruled from 1168 to 1196, consolidating his political power within the state, undertaking Serbia's territorial expansion, and achieving independence from Byzantium. Religiously, however, Serbia became irreversibly tied to the Eastern rites and traditions of Byzantium. In 1196 he called an assembly of nobles and announced his abdication in favor of his son Stefan Prvovencani, or Stefan the First Crowned. Stefan married Anna Dondolo, the granddaughter of the Venetian Doge Enrico Dondolo, thus securing his power. In 1217 Pope Honorius III sent his legate with a royal crown for Stefan, who became Stefan Prvovencani, or the First Crowned. The crowning confirmed the independence of Serbia, and also brought about the recognition of the Serbian state as an European state.

King Stefan then turned his attention to the creation of an independent and national church. His brother Sava undertook numerous diplomatic missions before he was able to attain this goal, and in 1219 he was consecrated as the First Archbishop of the Serbian Autocephalus (autonomous) Church. This event marks another cornerstone in Serbian history and Serbian Orthodoxy, for in 1221 Archbishop Sava was able to crown his brother King Stefan again, this time according to the religious rites and customs of the Eastern Orthodox Church.

Saint Sava is one of the most sacred and venerated historical figures in the minds and hearts of Serbs. Aside from contributing enormously to edu-

cation and literacy in general, Saint Sava, together with King Stefan, wrote the first Serbian literary work, a biography of their father.

As the Serbian medieval state matured politically, it also developed a solid and prosperous economy. The state's Golden Age, reached its apogee during the reign of Czar Dušan Silni, Emperor Dušan the Mighty (1308-1355). An extremely capable ruler, he secured and expanded the Serbian state, while richly endowing the Serbian Orthodox Church, which was the center of learning and artistic creativity, predating even the beginnings of the Italian Renaissance. He elevated the head of the church to the Patriarchy, and consolidated the internal affairs through the Emperor's *Zakonik*, the written Code of Laws, unique at that time in Europe. Emperor Dushan's accomplishments were such that Serbs today continue to draw inspiration and solace from the national pride and glory achieved during his time.

The Battle of Kosovo Polje ("The Field of Blackbirds") on June 28, 1389, fought between the Ottoman Turks led by Sultan Murad I (1319-1389), and the Serbs led by Czar Lazar (1329-1389) changed the course of Serbian history for centuries to come, for the Serbian defeat was followed by 500 years of Turkish rule and domination. Over the centuries Serbia remained totally isolated from the rest of Europe, and could not participate in the enormous political changes or cultural and industrial progress unfolding in other European states.

The land and all other natural resources became the Sultan's domain. The Turks became landowners called *sipahis*, while the Serbs were reduced to the status of *raya*, the populace who worked the land they previously had owned; their labor was called *kulluk*, a term which to this day denotes the work of slaves. Every four years the countryside was raided; small Serbian male children were forcibly taken from their families and brought to Istanbul, where they were raised and trained to become Janissaries, the Ottoman's elite military unit. Another particularly distasteful practice was the use of economic pressures to convert people to Islam.

In 1804 Karadjordje (Black George, or Karadjordjević) Petrovic (1752-1817), a merchant, led the First Serbian Uprising against the Turks. Severe Turkish reprisals caused many Serbian leaders to escape north to Vojvodina, where the monasteries at Fruska Gora became Serbian cultural strongholds. Among those who escaped was Miloš Obrenović (Milosh Obrenovich) (1780-1860), a local administrator, who emerged as the leader of the Second Serbian Uprising against the Turks in 1815. In 1829 Serbia was granted autonomy by the Turkish Sultan under a hereditary prince. A lengthy feud between the Karadjordjević and Obrenović dynasties ensued.

Serbia's struggle to establish itself as an independent nation in the nineteenth century was marked by many changes of rulers and forms of government, until a monarchy was established in 1882, followed by a constitutional monarchy in 1903. Serbia also emerged as the strongest Balkan state at the conclusion of the First Balkan War against the Ottoman Empire in 1912, when Serbia, Montenegro, Greece, and Bulgaria formed an alliance (the Balkan League) and defeated the Turks.

MODERN ERA

Fearing Serbia and her leading role in the determination to rid the Balkans of all foreign domination, the Austro-Hungarian government systematically pressured Serbia both politically and economically, until the tensions between the two nations led to the events that ignited World War I. When Archduke Franz Ferdinand and his wife, Sophie, chose to review the troops in Sarajevo on St. Vitus Day, June 28, 1914—the most sacred date of the Serbian calendar, commemorating the Battle of Kosovo—a small secret association called "Young Bosnia" had Gavrilo Princip, one of its members, carry out the assassination of the Archduke and his wife. Austria, accusing Serbia of complicity, responded with an immediate ultimatum, compliance with which would have presented a serious threat to the sovereignty of Serbia. Having just fought two Balkan Wars, and not wanting to get involved in another conflict, Serbia offered a compromise. Austria rejected these terms and declared war on Serbia on July 28, 1914, precipitating World War I.

Although heavily outnumbered and drained of resources from the just concluded Balkan Wars, the Serbian army initially fought successfully against Austria-Hungary, but the addition of the German army to the Austrian side tipped the balance against Serbia. Eventually, the ravaged Serbian army had to retreat through Albania toward the southern Adriatic Sea, where the remnants were picked up by French war ships. After being reconstituted and reequipped, this newly strengthened Serbian army broke through the Salonika Front in late 1916, and over the next year and a half successfully fought its way north, culminating in the recapture of Belgrade in October of 1918. This victory significantly contributed to the final collapse of the dual Austro-Hungarian monarchy.

The physical destruction of Serbia had been staggering, but the growing significance of the Pan Slavic movement led to the establishment of the Kingdom of the Serbs, Croats, and Slovenes, including Bosnian Muslims and Macedonians, later renamed Yugoslavia ("the land of the South Slavs") by the country's king, Alexander Karadjordjević (1888-1934).

Despite the 1934 assassination of King Alexander in Marseille, the country prospered as a result of increased trade and growing industrialization. This period was brought to a sudden halt by the bombing of Belgrade on April 6, 1941, which preceded the invading armies of Nazi Germany. The Yugoslav defenses collapsed within two weeks and the country was dismembered. Some parts of Yugoslavia were ceded to Italy, Hungary, and Bulgaria; the remaining areas were divided into two occupation zones: one German, consisting of Serbia proper; the other Italian, consisting of Montenegro and Dalmatia. In less than a week after the beginning of hostilities, an Independent State of Croatia was established as a satellite to the Axis Powers, headed by Ante Pavelić, the leader of the Croat Ustaši (Ustashi) Party.

The government and King Peter II fled to London. Some Serbian troops withdrew to the mountains and organized themselves as guerrillas, under the leadership of Colonel Draža Mihailović, and became known as the Yugoslav Army in the Homeland, or more popularly, Četnik (Chetnik), from the word ceta, meaning a small fighting group. Promoted to general and named Minister of War by the government in exile, Mihailović's aim was to fight alongside the Allies in order to defeat the Axis powers, to liberate his country, and to restore democracy.

After Germany attacked the Soviet Union in June 1941, the Yugoslav Communists, under the leadership of Josip Broz Tito, formed another guerrilla movement, which they called the National Liberation Movement, or Partisans. It soon became clear that the Serbs had to fight not only the Germans, but also the Partisans and the Ustashi, who were joined by two Muslim divisions from Bosnia. The Ustashi instituted a reign of terror which led to a massacre of 500,000 to 700,000 Serbs, as well as 50,000 Jews and 20,000 Gypsies. To counter Mihailović's guerrilla attacks, the Germans used reprisals against the civilian population, taking 50 hostages for every soldier killed, and 100 for every officer; thus, in one instance alone they executed 7,000 Serbs in a single day (October 21, 1941) in the city of Kragujevac, including schoolchildren driven out of their classrooms that morning.

Tito's Partisans, conducting a campaign of anti-Chetnik propaganda, gained the support of the Allies, who withdrew their endorsement of

Mihailović's Chetniks. Operating mainly in Ustashi territory, namely Croatia and the mountain ranges of Bosnia-Herzegovina, the Partisans were joined by many Serbs who were attempting to escape Ustashi terror. However, the communists did not have the support of the Serbian population at large.

Emerging victorious at the end of the war, Tito set out to further secure the power of the Communist Party and his own. Purging the country of its enemies, the new government tried and executed General Draža Mihailović. After the redrawing of the internal borders, Tito's Yugoslavia became a federation of six republics: Serbia, Croatia, Slovenia, Bosnia-Herzegovina, Montenegro, Makedonija, and two autonomous provinces: Kosovo and Vojvodina, which were carved out of the larger Serbia.

After Tito's death in 1980, Serbia was ruled by a collective presidency until the ascension to power of Slobodan Milosevic. He became president of Serbia in 1990 and president of the Federal Republic of Yugoslavia (including Serbia and Montenegro) in 1997. Under his leadership, the country has been involved in genocidal wars against Slovenia (1992), Croatia (1992-1993), Bosnia and Herzegovina (1992-1996), and Kosovo (1998-1999). From 1992 until 1999, hundreds of thousands were killed and more than 2 million people—mostly Albanians—became refugees in neighboring countries. The intervention of the United Nations and NATO military forces, including 78 days of bombing Serbia in the spring of 1999, brought the Kosovo conflict to an end. Afterward, the International War Crimes Tribunal in The Hague indicted Milosevic and four of his associates as war criminals.

Montenegro, Serbia's partner in the Federal Republic of Yugoslavia, has a population of 650,000, about two-thirds of whom are Montenegrin Serbs. Montenegro has adopted a pro-Western political position. During the Kosovo crisis, 50,000 Albanians received refuge in this territory.

MAJOR IMMIGRATION WAVES

While the earliest Serbian immigrants came to the United States after 1815, the largest wave of immigration took place from 1880 to 1914. There were arrivals between the two world wars followed by refugees and displaced persons after World War II. Lastly, arrivals since 1965 have included the influx resulting from current events in the former Yugoslavia. Generally speaking, it is difficult to determine the exact number of Serbs who came to America in the early waves of immigration because immigration records often did not distinguish between various Slavic and, especially, South Slav-

ic groups. The term Slavonic was most often used in recording immigrants from the various parts of the Eastern Europe. Church records are more helpful in distinguishing the Serbs, for these documents clearly state religious orientation of the parishioners. In addition, census statistics compiled before World War I had further confused the issue by listing immigrants by their country of origin. Thus, the Serbs could be included with the Croats, Slovenians, Austro-Hungarians, Turks, Bulgarians, or Romanians, or simply listed as Yugoslavs after 1929, when the kingdom of the Serbs, Croats, and Slovenes was renamed Yugoslavia. According to the 1990 U.S. Census figures, there are 116,795 Americans of Serbian origin living in the United States. It is impossible to tell, however, how many out of the 257,995 who in 1990 reported Yugoslavian origin actually have Serbian ancestry. It can safely be assumed that the total number of Serbian Americans today might vary from 200,000 to 350,000 and up to 400,000, according to some estimates. By American standards, this is a rather small immigrant group.

The smallest numbers of Serbian immigrants came from Serbia proper. The people there still worked large family land that formed collectives called zadruga, which provided enough economic stability to entice them to stay. In addition, the emergence of Serbia as an independent nation during the nineteenth century offered hope for more political stability.

The historical map of the Balkans in the early 1800s explains the pattern of Serbian immigration. The Serbs who came to America at that time were from the areas which were under the domination of either Austro-Hungarian or the Turkish Empire.

Because the Austrian Empire was constantly subjected to Turkish invasions, it encouraged Serbian families to settle along the frontiers dividing the two powers, giving them land, religious, economic, and political freedom. In exchange, the Serbs agreed to protect the border areas against the Turks and to build fortifications in peacetime. The Austrian Emperor Ferdinand I (1503-1564) officially recognized this agreement in 1538, and granted self-government to the Serbian villages. In 1691 Emperor Leopold I (1640-1705) signed the "Privilegija," a document which granted the same rights to the Serbs who had fled to the Vojvodina region. Thus, a number of generations of Serbs formed a "buffer population" between the Austro-Hungarian and Turkish Empires. Therefore, the first Serbs to leave their native land for America were from the military frontier areas—Kordun, Krajina, Luka, Slavonija, Vojvodina, Dalmatia, and other coastal areas—precisely the areas where generations earlier had taken refuge from Turkish reprisal. Serbs from Dalmatia were actually the first ones to emigrate because of the close proximity to the sea and relative ease of transportation offered by the steam operated ships.

Poverty and ethnic and religious persecutions were behind the decisions to leave one's village, family, and way of life for America, whose allure as the land of opportunity appealed to able-bodied young men. In 1869 the Austrian Emperor dissolved the age-old agreement with the Granicaris. The Serbs felt betrayed by the Emperor, and in the words of Michael Pupin, who came from Vojvodina, they felt "delivered to the Hungarians," who then subjected them to a severe campaign of Magyarization, insisting on officially use of the Hungarian language in schools and courts, as well as seeking to convert them to Roman Catholicism.

The greatest numbers of Serbs arrived during the peak period of immigration to America between 1880 and 1914 from Austro-Hungarian Croatia, Slavonia, and Vojvodina, as well as from Montenegro. Although the overwhelming majority of Serbian immigrants were uneducated, unskilled men in their prime working years—mostly peasants from the countryside—they did not come to America particularly to be farmers, and they did not intend to stay. Instead, they wanted to remain in the United States long enough to earn money enabling them to return home and improve the lives of their families, in keeping with a practice called *pečalba* (pechalba). They settled in the mining areas of Pennsylvania, Ohio, West Virginia, northern Minnesota, Montana, Nevada, Arizona, and Colorado, as well as in the big industrial cities of Pittsburgh, Cleveland, and Chicago, working in steel mills and related industries. Others found works with the major meat-packing companies in Chicago, Milwaukee, Kansas City, Omaha, and St. Paul, and in the lumber industries in the Pacific Northwest. The Serbian motto *čovek mora da radi*, "a man has to work" served them very well in this country.

ACCULTURATION AND ASSIMILATION

It can be argued that assimilation into American life and society's acceptance of the new immigrants was uneven at best. On the one hand, some Serbs were impressed by the freedom and openness of the Americans as well as by the opportunities available to all. On the other hand, late nineteenth-century Americans, feeling threatened by the large numbers of new immigrants from southern and eastern Europe, increasingly expressed anti-immigrant sentiment. The Immigration Restriction League founded in Boston in 1894 attempted to achieve the curbing of this type of immigrant tide by advocating the literacy test, which required immigrants over 16 years of age to be literate. Since the eastern and southern Europeans were less literate than their counterparts from northern and western Europe, it was clear where the actions of the League were going to lead. The immigration laws from 1921 and 1924 established a national origins system and set annual quotas for each nationality based on the percentage of the total of that nationality already living in America. This was based on the 1890 and 1910 census, which respectively assigned a two percent and a three percent annual quotas, or 671, and later 942, per year for all immigrants from Yugoslavia.

The majority of the earlier Serbian immigrants endured the hardships and found that the degree of freedom and the opportunities available to them in America were worth staying for. However, the Great Depression of the 1930s adversely affected the old Serbian immigrant communities. Discouraged, many returned to their homeland.

The immigrants who arrived after 1945 were refugees from World War II. Among their numbers were former army officers and soldiers who had either been prisoners of war or attached to the Allied Forces; people deported to Nazi Germany as slave-laborers; and supporters of General Mihailović during the Civil War who fled following the communist takeover. Many Serbs, therefore, found a new home in America under the Displaced Persons Act of 1948 and the Refugee Relief Act of 1953.

The differences between this wave of Serbian immigration and the previous ones are substantial. The new immigrants came mainly from the urban areas in Serbia proper rather than the rural areas outside Serbia; they came for political reasons rather than economic reasons, and tended to see themselves as emigres rather than immigrants; they were on the whole highly educated members of the middle and upper classes, many among them had considerable social status, and they came to join already well established Serbian communities. Politically minded, many also saw this country as a safehouse in which to develop strategic operations in opposition to the Yugoslav communist state, rather than a new homeland.

Recent immigration resulting from the economic and political failures of the communist system reverts to being motivated by the economy once again, but does not offer the sense of cohesiveness experienced by earlier groups. Until the

Jelena Mladenovic
lights a candle
during the
Orthodox Easter
service at the
Serbian Orthodox
Cathedral in
New York.

dissolution of Yugoslavia beginning in 1991, the newest immigrants had come and gone freely between America and Serbia. Some worked for American companies, some for Yugoslav companies in the United States, and many, after staying abroad for a number of years went back to Yugoslavia with hard currency and marketable skills.

In America, the Serbian churches maintain parish Sunday schools where children learn the language, customs, and traditions of their ancestors. The Serbian Orthodox Diocese at the St. Sava Monastery in Libertyville, Illinois, runs a summer camp as well as the parish school. The children of immigrants have mostly attended public schools, and in the early days it was often the case that these children were the only source of information about American culture and history for Serbian adults.

ORGANIZATIONS

In the early stages of Serbian immigration, fraternal mutual aid societies and insurance companies preceded the church as the centers of Serbian American community life. These were formed for eco-

nomic reasons, as the new arrivals needed to find ways to protect themselves against the hazards of dangerous and life-threatening work in mines, foundries, or factories. In the early years the Serbs readily joined other Slavic groups, such as the Slavonic Benevolent Organization founded in San Francisco in 1857, which served all South Slavs.

In time, Serbian immigrants formed their own organizations, starting as local groups, lodges, assemblies, and societies whose goals were the preservation of culture, social welfare, and fraternal sentiment. The first such organization was the Srpsko Crnogorsko Literarno i Dobrotvorno Društvo (Serbian-Montenegrin Literary and Benevolent Society) founded in San Francisco in 1880, then Srpsko Jedinstvo (Serbian Unity) in Chicago in 1894. Other societies followed and began to form federations, such as the Srpsko Crnogorski Savez (Serbian-Montenegrin Federation) whose headquarters were in Butte, Montana, and which ceased to exist because most of its members left to fight in the Balkan Wars (1912-1913) and in World War I.

In the eastern section of the United States, eight Serbian lodges, which were part of the Russ-

ian Orthodox Society, formed their own organization in McKeesport, Pennsylvania, in 1901. Originally called Srpki Pravoslavni Savez-"Srbobran" (Serbian Orthodox Federation-"Srbobran"), it became known in 1929 as Srpski Narodni Savez (Serbian National Federation, SNF), when other organizations joined it, such as Savez Sjedinjenih

Srba-Sloga (Federation of United Serbs-"Concord"). The last organization to join this federation was Srpski Potporni Savez-"Jedinstvo" (Serbian Benevolent Federation-"Unity") from Cleveland, Ohio, in 1963. The events around this merger produced an atmosphere of "politicking," which provided the Serbian American communities with an arena all their own, and although somewhat outside from the mainstream of American political life, it served to reinforce their Serbian identity.

The SNF, whose headquarters were and still are in Pittsburgh, Pennsylvania, was first an insurance organization, evolving into the single most important Serbian organization. Its founder, Sava Hajdin, said at one point: "We never wished our federation to be only the association of benevolent societies. We wished it to be the matrix of Serbianism in America and the bastion of the idea of St. Sava." Indeed, the humanitarian side of its work included the cooperation with other organizations to provide aid to Serbia during both world wars. After the war, the federation sent relief to refugees and prisoners of war, and sponsored thousands of new immigrants.

On the cultural level, since 1906 the SNF has been publishing its weekly bilingual newspaper, "Amerikanski Srbobran;" it provides scholarships and maintains a fund for printing and free distribution of Serbian primers, used by young people to learn the language of their ancestors. It sponsors well-attended events, such as tournaments for soccer, tennis, golf, and bowling, as well as a three-day "Serbian Days" celebration each summer. In the last decade or so it has been actively raising funds for the building of St. Sava Cathedral on Vrachar Hill in Belgrade, and lastly, it is very much involved in providing humanitarian help in the latest conflict.

The oldest and largest Serbian patriotic organization is the Srpska Narodna Odbrana (Serbian National Defense). Organized in 1914 in New York by Michael Pupin, it recruited volunteers for World War I, and also sent large monetary aid to Serbia. Inactive in the 1920s and 1930s, the organization was revived during World War II by the great Serbian poet and diplomat-in-exile, Jovan Dučić (1871-1943). Declaring its support for the Cetniks of General Mihailović, who instituted a campaign of guerrilla warfare in Yugoslavia, the SND began a radio program in Chicago, and published the periodical *American Serb* from 1944-48.

After the war the SND sent food and relief supplies to thousands of Serbs dispersed in various displaced persons camps, and provided scholarships to Serbian students. In cooperation with the Serbian Orthodox Diocese and Srpska Bratska Pomoć (Serbian Fraternal Aid) the SND brought thousands of displaced persons to America. Much to their chagrin, the sponsors discovered that the new immigrants were politically very much at odds with each other, and soon the ill effects were felt in the organization. Attempts were made to bring back some unity, and in 1947 the SND sponsored an All-Serb Congress in Chicago. The Serbian

National Committee was formed, headed by Konstantin Fotić (Constantin Fotich) the former Yugoslav Ambassador to the United States. Another conference was held in Akron, Ohio, in 1949, during which the Serbian National Council was formed. The highly respected Bishop Nikolaj Velimirović, himself a refugee, attended, but failed to end the discord. In the 1960s the then president of the organization, Dr. Uroš Seffer (Urosh Seferovich), and his followers sided with Bishop Dionisije's autonomous Serbian church, while the supporters of the church in Belgrade organized their own American Serbian National Defense. Srpska Narodna Odbrana survived this turmoil and still publishes *Sloboda (Liberty)*.

Women's organizations among Serbian Americans are various groups of sisterhoods known as Kolo Srpskih Sestara, or Serbian Sisters Circles. They were organized in the beginning of the twentieth century in Pittsburgh, Cincinnati, and Chicago. The federation of Circles of Serbian Sisters was formed in 1945 when representatives of more than thirty sisterhoods met in Libertyville, Illinois. They are active in fundraising activities and support children's camps and charities. Being closely associated with the Serbian church, they, unfortunately, were affected by the schism in the church.

ART AND POPULAR CULTURE

Music is a very important role in the Serbian American community. The early Serbian immigrants from the Military Frontier areas brought with them their native mandolin-like string instrument called a tamburica (tamburitza), which varies in five different sizes and ranges. George Kachar, one of the first teachers of tamburitza in America, brought the love for his music from his homeland to a small mining town in Colorado, where he taught during the 1920s. His most remarkable students were four Popovich brothers who later became famous as the Popovich Brothers of South Chicago. Having started by traveling from community to community, they gained prominence by delighting Serbian American audiences for sixty years with their art, while also achieving national recognition by appearances at the White House and by participating in the "Salute to Immigrant Cultures" during the Statue of Liberty celebrations held in 1986.

During the annual Tamburitza Extravaganza Festival, as many as twenty bands from around the country perform for three days, with performers undoubtedly vying for the Tamburitza Hall of Fame in St. Louis, Missouri. The new students and performers are actively recruited and trained by the

Duquesne University Tamburitzans, which maintains a folklore institute, grants scholarships for promising students, and makes good use of the enthusiasm generously shared by the junior team called "Tammies." A few active tamburitza manufacturers in the United States continue to assure an adequate supply of this favorite instrument.

The immigrants who came to America after World War II brought in a different style of music performed on accordions. Drums, keyboards, and the amplified modern instruments came into use in the last few decades. These musical groups mostly play the newly composed folk music, which combines traditional instruments, melodies, and styles with modern instruments, lyrics, and production techniques. Generally speaking, be they older or newer immigrants, the Serbs sing of love and death, of parting and hope, of the tragedy that accompanied them throughout their history, and of the heroic deeds that helped them triumph over adversity. One of the most beloved and nostalgic songs is *Tamo deleko*, "There Far Away," referring to the distance of the homeland.

Serbian American choirs, performing mainly at social functions, were formed early on, such as the Gorski Vijenac (Mountain Wreath) Choir in Pittsburgh in 1901, and the Branko Radičević Choir in Chicago in 1906. There were no church choirs in the early part of the twentieth century, until Vladimir Lugonja (1898-1977) founded the Serbian Singing Foundation of the USA and Canada (SSF) in 1931 as an antidote to the Great Depression. Many choirs joined in, connected with the church parishes, and totaled thirty by World War II. Their membership in the federation was contingent on their singing in church. Since 1935, the federation has been sponsoring annual concerts and competitions where both secular and liturgical music are performed. A number of Serbian priests have come from the ranks of the SSF; many are well known directors and conductors such as Adam Popovich, Director of South Chicago's SLOBODA. A respected veteran of the Serbian American choir movement, Popovich and his choir performed at the White House for Dwight D. Eisenhower's presidential inauguration.

The *gusle*, another symbol of Serbianism, is a string instrument similar to a violin. Gusle musicians have used it since the earliest days of the Serbian kingdom in accompanying the chanting of epic poetry. Although this instrument is capable of rendering only a few melancholy notes, the *guslar*, or bard, manages to evoke myriad emotions. During the Ottoman period of Serbian history the *guslari* traveled from village to village bringing news and keeping alive ancient Serbian heroic epics and ballads, which played a role of utmost importance in the development and preservation of the Serbian national conscience and character.

The *kolo*, meaning the circle, is the Serbian national dance, and by extention the Serbian American dance. Danced in a circle as well in a single line, the dancers hold each other's hands or belts, and no one, from teenagers to grandparents, can resist the lively tunes and sprightly motions. A good number of folk dancing ensembles throughout America has kept alive the rich repertoire of folk dancing, and it is difficult to imagine any kind of Serbian celebrations without a performance of one such ensemble.

CUISINE

Serbian cuisine over the centuries has adopted the tastes and flavors of the Middle Eastern, Turkish, Hungarian, and Austrian foods. Roast suckling pig and lamb are still very much appreciated and served on festive occasions. Serbs are also fond of casserole dishes with or without meat; pies (consisting of meat, cheese, or fruit); all kinds of fried foods, and an assortment of cakes, cookies, and condiments that rival the displays in Vienna and Budapest.

A few representative dishes would be *šarma*, stuffed cabbage, made from leaves of sour cabbage, or from wine leaves, and chopped beef or veal, often in combination with chopped pork, onions, smoked meat for added flavor; Serbs especially appreciate *gibanjica*, or *pita gibanjica*, a cheese pie made with feta or cottage cheese (an American substitute for the cheese used in the homeland), or the combination of both, butter, filo pastry leaves, eggs, and milk. *Ćevapčići*, the summer time favorite for cookouts, are small barbecued sausage-like pieces, prepared from a combination of freshly chopped pork, lamb, veal, and beef, and served with raw onions.

Serbs like to drink wine, beer, and especially the plum brandy called *šljivovica*, which is the national drink, made from *šljiva*, or plums, the Serbian national fruit. Another word for šljivovica is *rakija*, which is once-distilled plum brandy; twice-distilled šljivovica is called *prepečenica*. Serbs drink at all kinds of celebrations: weddings, baptisms, and krsna slavas; and every raised glass is accompanied with the exclamation: Živeli, or "Live long." It is not surprising that many Serbs found California to be the perfect place for continuing the family tradition of growing grapes to produce wine, or plums for šljivovica.

TRADITIONAL COSTUMES

Serbian traditional clothing consists of richly embroidered, colorful garments, which are worn today only by the dancers in the folkloric dance ensembles, or perhaps at other events inspired by folk motives, such as picnics, harvests, or church festivals. Each region has its own particular motives and ways of wearing these costumes, making it easy to discern one from another. The typical costume for women from Serbia proper consists of a fine linen blouse richly embroidered with floral or folk motifs; a vest called a *jelek*, cut low under the breast, made of velvet, embroidered with silver and gold thread, and worn tightly around the waist; an ample colorful skirt accompanied by an embroidered apron and a white linen petticoat worn longer than the skirt to show off the hand-crocheted lace; knitted and embroidered stockings; and a pair of handmade leather slipper-like footwear called *opanci*. The hair is long and braided; the braids are sometimes worn down the back or twisted in a bun around the head.

The costume for men consists of a head cap called a *šajkača*, a white linen shirt, a wool jacket, and pants (The jacket is short with sober decorations and the pants are worn tight around the knees.) A richly decorated sash is tied around the waist. Knitted and embroidered socks and *opanci* (leather shoes) are worn on the feet. The fabrics used were always homegrown, spun, or woven, and the costumes were made at home. The early immigrants stood out in an American crowd by the way their clothes looked, which provided an easy target for ridicule. Today, these costumes have given way to standard dress, and if still in existence, are brought out only at folk festivals.

LANGUAGE

The Serbian language is part of the Slavic language group to which belong Russian, Ukrainian, Polish, Czech, Slovak, Croatian, Bulgarian, and Macedonian. In the seventh century two Greek missionaries, Cyril and Methodius, created the Slavic alphabet, called the Cyrillic, which is still used by the Russians, Serbs, Ukrainians, Bulgarians, and Macedonians. The Old Slavonic, or Staroslovenski, was the original literary language of all the Slavs. It evolved into the Church Slavonic, or Crkvenoslovenski, which in turn engendered the Serb Church Slavonic, the Serb literary language up until the nineteenth century.

In the early nineteenth century Vuk Srefanović Karadjić (1787-1864), who become known as the father of the "modern" Serbian language, reconstructed the alphabet to conform it phonetically with the oral language, thus recognizing the spoken language as the literary language; this resulted in reawakening Serbian culture in general. He published the first Serbian dictionary in 1818, and collected and published volumes of epic and lyrical poetry that had survived in the oral tradition in the Serbian countryside. His voluminous correspondence is an important political and literary document.

Immigrants were confronted with the modification of their language as it came into contact with English, resulting in the incorporation of many English words into everyday use, especially those that were needed to communicate in a more complex society and did not exist in their rural vocabulary. Another American influence can be seen in the fact that many immigrants changed their names for simplification. Often the changing of names was done by either the immigration officers at the time of entry into the United States, or by the employers at the factories or mines who were not accustomed to dealing with complicated Slavic names. At other times, the immigrants themselves opted for simple American names, either for business reasons, or to escape being a target for ridicule. Also, some changes were the result of the immigrants' desire to show loyalty to their adopted country; thus, the names were either simply translated—Ivan into John, Ivanović into Johnson—or the diacritical marks over the letters "ć" and the "š" were dropped and replaced by English-sounding equivalents such as Sasha for Saša and Simich for Simić. About 25 percent of all Serbian Americans declared Serbian as their mother tongue in the 1990 U.S. census.

GREETINGS AND OTHER COMMON EXPRESSIONS

Some basic greetings and sayings in Serbian include: *dobro jutro* ("dobro yutro")—good morning; *dobar dan* (pronounced as written)—good day; *dobro veče* ("dobro vetche")—good evening; *zdravo* (pronounced as written)—greetings; *hvala* ("khvala")—thank you; *dobro došli* ("dobro doshli")—welcome

FAMILY AND COMMUNITY DYNAMICS

Although Serbian immigrants tended to live in closely knit, homogeneous colonies, they were never so totally isolated as to prevent any penetration of American influence, and that interaction inevitably led to changes in many aspects of their lives. Their children and grandchildren only rarely adhere to the old ways, and as a result the immigrant heritage becomes a strange mixture of old-country and American cultural elements.

In their homeland the immigrants had been primarily farmers; all the family members lived together in a *zadruga*, a large family cooperative where everyone worked on the family land, maintaining strong family ties, as well as observing a strict hierarchical order from the head of the *zadruga*, called *straresina*, down to the youngest child. In America, each family member's occupation could be different, leading to less interdependence among the family members, without, however, destroying the closeness of family ties. To a great extent Serbian and Serbian American households still include grandparents, or other elderly relatives needing care and help. It is also a common practice to have grandparents care for the young children while the parents are working, as well as take charge of housekeeping in general. Elderly parents (or close relatives) live out their lives at home surrounded by their children and grandchildren. The structure of a typical Serbian American family also retains close relationships with the extended family—aunts, uncles, and cousins—going back a few generations, thus placing emphasis on strong emotional ties as well as offering a good family support system.

RELIGION

The Serbs accepted Christianity in the ninth century due to the work of the two Greek brothers, missionaries from Salonika, Cyril and Methodius, also called "Apostles of the Slavs." Since that time, and especially since the 1219 establishment of the Serbian Orthodox Autonomous church by King Stefan Prvovencani, the Serbs have strongly identified their religion with their ethnic heritage. *Srpstvo*, or being Serbian, expresses this concept of the Serbian identity as encompassing the nation, its historic heritage, church, language, and other cultural traditions. Serbian communal life in the United States mainly evolved and, to a large degree, still revolves around the church parish.

Orthodoxy, which means "correct worship," partly differs from other Christian practices in that priests are allowed to marry and in its use of the Julian calendar, which is 13 days behind the Gregorian calendar. Thus, for example, the Serbs celebrate Christmas on January 7th instead of December 25th.

Serbian churches, both in America and in the homeland, feature the Altar, a carved Iconostasis, and richly painted icons. A pedestal called *Nalonj*, placed at a respectable distance from the altar, is used to exhibit the icon of the Saint the particular church is named after, and upon entering the church everyone stops there to make the sign of the cross and kiss the icon.

The first Serbian churches in America were established in Jackson, California, in 1893, followed by McKeesport, Pennsylvania (1901), and Steelton, Pennsylvania (1903). At that time all Serbian churches were under the jurisdiction of the Russian Orthodox church, although served by Serbian priests. The first American-born Serbian Orthodox priest, the Reverend Sebastian Dabovich (1863-1940), the son of a Serbian pioneer in California, was appointed head of the Serbian mission in the United States by the Patriarch in Moscow in 1905.

In 1919 a separate Serbian Orthodox Diocese in North America and Canada was created under the leadership of the Reverend Mardary Uskokovich (d. 1935), who later became the first bishop of the new Diocese, establishing his seat in Libertyville, Illinois, in 1927. From 1940 to 1963 the Diocese was headed by Bishop Dionisije Milivojević. During World War II the Diocese was instrumental in arranging for the immigration of refugees, as well as placing refugee priests. The Diocese published the first English language Serbian newspaper, the *Serbian Orthodox Herald*. In 1949 the Clergy Association of the Serbian Orthodox Diocese of the United States and Canada formed their united headquarters in Pittsburgh, Pennsylvania. *Orthodoxy* was their official publication.

In 1963 the Serbian Diocese of North America suffered a painful schism and split into two groups: one wanted an independent Serbian Orthodox church in America; the other insisted on keeping the alliance with the Patriarchy in Belgrade. The immigrant community became bitterly divided. The old settlers felt that the primary role of the church was to uphold Orthodoxy and to maintain the spiritual life in the communities, while the newer immigrants saw the need to defend themselves against the Communist threat.

The church remains divided, although it officially reconciled during the Holy Liturgy jointly celebrated on February 15, 1992, by the Patriarch Pavle of Belgrade and the Metropolitan Irinej, the head of the Free Church in America, whose seat is in New Gracancia (Third Lake, Illinois). The two contending factions have worked on a new church constitution, a document expected to be administratively complete in 1995 and intended to seal the reunification.

The two most important religious holidays of the year for Serbian Americans are *Božić* (Christmas), and *Uskrs* (Easter). Both are celebrated for three days. Bozich starts with *Tucindan* (two days before Christmas) when a young pig is prepared to be barbecued for Christmas dinner, or *Božićna večera*. On the day before Christmas—called *Badnji*

Dan—the *badnjak*, or Yule Log, is placed outside the house, and the *pečenica*, or roasted pig, is prepared. In the evening straw is placed under the table to represent the manger, the Yule log is cut and brought in for burning, and the family gathers for a Lenten Christmas Eve dinner. *Božićni Post*, the Christmas Lenten, is observed for six weeks prior to Christmas, during which a diet without milk, dairy products, meat, or eggs is maintained. This strict observance is practiced by fewer people today, as most are willing to fast only for a week prior to Christmas.

On Christmas Day, *česnica*, a round bread, is baked from wheat flour. A coin placed inside the bread brings good luck throughout the year to the person who finds it. The family goes to church early on Christmas Day, and upon return home the most festive meal of the year is served. The father lights a candle and incense, and says a prayer. The family turns the *česnica* from left to right and sings the Christmas hymn *Rozdestvo Tvoje*, which glorifies the birth of Christ. The cesnica is broken and each member of the family receives a piece, leaving one portion for an unexpected guest. Each person kisses the person next to him three times with the greeting *Hristos se rodi*, "Christ is born," and receives in reply *Vaistinu se rodi*, "Indeed He is born."

In America, the burning of the *badnjak* is done at church after Christmas Eve mass, and an elaborate Lenten Christmas Eve dinner is served in the parish hall for those who wish to participate.

Traditionally, three Sundays before Christmas are dedicated to the family: *Detinjci*, the Children's Day; *Materice*, the Mother's Day; and *Očevi*, Father's Day. On each of these days the celebrants are tied to an object and their release is obtained with a gift.

Uskrs (Easter), is considered the holiest of holidays, and is celebrated from Good Friday to Easter Sunday. A seven-week Lenten period is observed, also without fish, meat, eggs, milk, or dairy products, which is practiced today in altered fashion as well. *Vrbica*, or Palm Sunday, is observed on the last Sunday before Easter when the willow branches are blessed and distributed to all present. This service is rendered especially beautiful and significant by the presence of children, dressed in fine new clothes worn for the first time, with little bells hanging from their necks on Serbian tricolor ribbons—red, blue, and white—waiting for the whole congregation to start an outside procession encircling the church three times.

Easter celebrations cannot be conceived without roasted lamb and colored eggs. The eggs symbolize spring and the renewal of the life cycle as well as *Vaskrsenje*, the Easter Resurrection. Each color as well as each design has a specific meaning in this age old folk art form of egg decorating.

The Easter Mass is the most splendid one. The doors of the iconostasis, which remained closed until the symbolic moment of *Hristovo Voskresenje*, or "Christ's Resurrection," open wide; the church bells ring, and the priest dressed in his gold vestments steps forward. The congregation sings a hymn of rejoicing, and a procession led by the banner of Resurrection encircles the church three times while the worshippers carry lit candles. The greetings *Hristos voskrese*, "Christ has risen," and *Vaistinu voskrese*, "He has risen indeed," are exchanged three times.

The most important Serbian tradition is the yearly observance of *Krsna Slava*, the Patron Saint's Day. This uniquely Serbian religious holiday, reminiscent of the prehistoric harvest festivals, is celebrated once a year in commemoration of the family's conversion to Christianity, when each family chose its patron saint, which derived from the custom of worshipping protective spirits. Passing from father to son, this joyous holiday is observed with friends and family enjoying sumptuous foods, often with music and dancing as well. The central elements which enhance the solemnity of *Krsna Slava* are: *slavska sveca*, a long candle which must burn all day; the votive light lit in front of the icon representing the picture of the family patron saint; and incense burning. Two foods are specially prepared: *koljivo*, or sometimes called *zito*, made with boiled wheat, sugar, and ground nuts; and *krsni kolač*, which is a ritual round bread baked solely for this occasion. It is decorated with dough replicas of birds, wheat, grapes, barrels of wine, or whatever else an inspired mother of the family can think of, aside from the obligatory religious seal representing the cross and the symbolic four S's: *Samo Sloga Srbina Spasava*, "Only Unity Will Save the Serbs." The priest visits the homes and conducts a ceremony in which the *kolač* is raised three times symbolizing the Holy Trinity. He and the head of the family cut a cross on the bottom of the *kolač* into which a little wine is poured to symbolize the blood of Christ.

Every year on June 28 the Serbs commemorate *Vidovdan*, or Saint Vitus Day. One of the most sacred holidays, it commemorates a defeat on June 28, 1389, when the Serbs led by Czar Lazar lost their kingdom to the Turks in the Battle of Kosovo Polje (Field of Blackbirds). The heroism and death of Czar Lazar and his Martyrs who died that day for *krst casni i zlatnu slobodu*, or the "venerable cross and golden freedom," is commemorated in epic songs and celebrated each year by churches and communities across America. The Serbs might be the only people who celebrate a disastrous defeat as a national holiday, but what they are really celebrating is the ability to withstand adversity. For the last 600 years the Serbs have maintained the tradition of respecting their ancestors for living out the old proverb *bolje grob nego rob*, or "better a grave than a slave." To Serbs in America and in the homeland Kosovo Polje is a sacred national site.

Kumstvo, or godparenthood, is another tradition deeply embedded in the Serbian culture. The parents of an unborn child choose a *kum* or a *kuma* (a man or a woman to be a godparent), who names the baby at the baptismal ceremony. The godparents also have the responsibility of ensuring the moral and material well being of the child if need be, and are considered very close family.

Some customs are remnants of pagan days and were inspired by the closeness with nature: in June, when daisies are abloom in the fields, young girls of marrying age make wreaths that they hang outside their houses. A young man confesses his love by taking the wreath away, leaving the young woman to hope that it should only be the right one. The *dodola*, or the rain dance, is another example; a young girl dressed in flowers, plants, and grasses, goes from house to house singing a prayerful chant, which is supposed to bring rain. Helpful housewives drench her with buckets of water and small gifts.

Beliefs derived from superstitions are many, such as: a black cat crossing the road in front of a person will bring bad luck; a horse in a dream will bring good luck; black birds are a bad omen; an itching left palm presages money.

EMPLOYMENT AND ECONOMIC TRADITIONS

Although historically Serbs have placed high value on education, early immigrants were largely illiterate or had very little education, due to their circumstances living under Turkish occupation. In America, they worked, as already stated, in predominantly heavy industrial areas. In time, they began to attend evening English-language classes offered by the adult-education programs in public schools, which proved to be enormously valuable to them, and especially to their children.

The younger generations took an increased interest in education, and slowly began to break away from the factory jobs and move to white-collar occupations. In recent decades the Serbs have gone on to higher education. Although Serbian American professionals can be found in nearly every American industry, a great many tend to opt for engineering, medicine, law, or other professions. Lately, however, more and more young people are attracted by financial service industries, such as banking, insurance, and stock brokerage. Boys and girls are educated alike, and everyone is free to set career goals to his or her own liking. The number of women in professions traditionally held by men, especially medicine and engineering, is very high among Serbs.

POLITICS AND GOVERNMENT

Although their participation in American political life has evolved slowly, Serbs have demonstrated a great deal of fervor for politics. Generally speaking, most Serbian Americans are more likely to be concerned with the government's policies and attitude toward Yugoslavia than in local politics.

World War I was the turning point in political activities and unity with other Slavic groups, and, again, such activities had more to do with the politics in the homeland rather than in America. President Woodrow Wilson encouraged Serbian, Croatian, and Slovenian leaders in America to meet and call for the union of the South Slavs then within the Austro-Hungarian Empire, and for the unification with Serbia in an independent Serbian kingdom. The creation of the Yugoslav National Council resulted, its purpose being to inform and influence the American people, as well as to recruit for war and raise money. Thousands of south Slavs joined either the Serbian army or the American army, and thousands of Serbian emigrants returned from the United States to fight for Serbia.

Of the many immigrants who arrived in the United States after 1945, many were very politically engaged and considered America as a base for pursuing political goals related to Yugoslavia. A number of political organizations were formed to reflect the differing views carried over from the mother country concerning the new regime and the affiliations with particular groups during World War II. After 1945, most of the large numbers of newcomers who joined the Serbian American community in America were Chetniks. Forming political organizations they continued their fight against Tito's communist dictatorship as best they could. Another faction, albeit much smaller in numbers, was an ultra right-wing group called Ljotićevci, party that was founded by Dimitrije Ljotić (d. 1945). These two groups polarized the attention of the Serbian American immigrants and heightened political awareness among Serbian American communities.

Many older immigrants felt overwhelmed and bewildered by the number of factions and their nuances. Some were alienated, and even others fell victim to the communist infiltration and propaganda. However, the vast majority of both the older immigrants and those who arrived after 1945 remain loyal to the American ideals of freedom and liberty.

Many men and women of Serbian descent who have joined the mainstream of American politics today as mayors, governors, and senators have testified to the fact that a degree of "American" political maturity has been reached by this ethnic group in spite of its still intense identification with their motherland, as exemplified by Rose Ann Vuich, the first woman senator from California in 1976.

Given the Serbian penchant for politics, the political issues of the former Yugoslavia have always been and are still being passionately debated among Serbian Americans. Political issues in the Balkans have always been a matter of life and death for the Serbs, who after a flourishing independence in the late Middle Ages, survived centuries of subjugation and, since the early 1800s, have gradually succeeded in the fight for freedom and the unification of their homeland.

The current conflict in the former Yugoslavia, which brought about a new period of intense political activity among Serbian Americans, was prompted by the premature recognition of the independence of Slovenia, Croatia, and Bosnia-Herzegovina, first by most of the member-states of the European community, and then by the United States on April 7, 1992. The Serbs in Croatia's Krajina Region, who had been turned into a minority by the declaration of independence on the part of Croatia, voted to secede from Croatia in 1991. In Bosnia-Herzegovina, they expressed their wishes not to live in minority status among the Muslims by boycotting the referendum for Bosnian independence held in late February 1992. They had reasons to fear for their lives again, because having sided with the Axis Powers during World War II, the fascist Croat Ustashi and their Muslim allies had conducted the systematic extermination of the Serbs. The Nazi-puppet Independent State of Croatia instituted death camps, among which Jasenovac is the most well known.

In Croatia, the resurgence of the old Nazi-Croat symbols at the onset of the conflict, including the use of the Fascist Ustashi flag, the renaming of streets and squares, blatant antisemitism, and the renaming of the national currency to "kuna," which was the currency's name during the Nazi period, are reminders of a painful and not too distant past.

These facts, coupled with the unilateral 1992 declaration of independence of Bosnia against the wishes of the Serbian minority, which represented approximately one-third of the population, effectively turning them for a second time into second class citizens after 500 years of Turkish/Muslim domination, and reviving the memories of persecutions during World War II, have politically galvanized the Serbian American community in the last several years.

Once again, the Serbian American community is at great odds with the Yugoslav President Slobodan Milošević, and to a large degree, and for the first time, with the U.S. government, which they perceive to be one-sided. The Serbs in America are now deeply disappointed, for not only have they shared American principles of freedom and justice for many centuries, but they, unlike the Croats and Bosnian Muslims, have fought with Americans and their allies through two world wars.

MILITARY

The degree of participation of Serbian Americans in the armed forces, as well as in the intelligence community, is high. During the World War I thousands of American Serbs went to Serbia, an ally, to fight, while others established a number of humanitarian organizations to send help abroad. The response was overwhelming during World War II as well. A large number distinguished themselves in battle and some were awarded the Congressional Medal of Honor.

Many Serbian Americans had distinguished careers in the military, such as Colonel Nicholas Stepanovich, U.S. Army, who had a brilliant career as a lawyer and military leader and was appointed by President Dwight D. Eisenhower to the U.S. ambassadorial staff to the United Nations; Colonel Tyrus Cobb, U.S. Army, who served in Vietnam both in war and in peace missions. The recipient of the Defense Superior Service Medal, Colonel Cobb was appointed to the National Security Council and was selected by President Ronald Reagan to accompany him on summits to Geneva, Moscow, and Iceland. Many other Serbian Americans served in the Office of Strategic Services (later known as the Central Intelligence Agency [CIA]), including Nick Lalich, George Vujnovic, and Joe Veselinovich. The Vietnam War and the Persian Gulf War have also claimed Serbian American decorated heroes as well, such as Lance Sijan, for whom a building is named at the U.S. Air Force Academy in Colorado Springs, Colorado.

LABOR UNIONS

The labor movement and the labor unions in America found some of their staunchest supporters among the Serbs. Having worked very hard to earn their living and having given strength and youth to their new homeland, they felt, as many other Americans did, that strong unions presented opportunities to rectify many poor work situations. They were active with the United Mine Workers of America, the American Federation of Labor, the Congress of Industrial Organizations, and the Textile Workers Union of America, among others. The contributions of the Serbs to the labor movement are numerous, as exemplified by Eli Zivkovich, who organized the story of the unionization of textile workers in North Carolina as depicted in the film *Norma Rae*.

Related to the labor movement and union organizing is the work done by Serbian Americans in the field of labor laws as exemplified by the tireless efforts of Robert Lagather, an attorney. The son of a mine worker and a miner himself as a young man, Lagather had a deep commitment to improving the working conditions in the mines, and the role he played in the Federal Mine and Safety and Health Act of 1977 testifies to his determination and dedication.

INDIVIDUAL AND GROUP CONTRIBUTIONS

The contributions of Serbian Americans were best summarized by Jerome Kisslinger: "[From] the Louisiana oyster fishermen of the 1830s and the California innkeeper of the 1850s to the Pittsburgh steel worker of 1910, the political refugee of the 1950s and the engineer today, Serbians have proved themselves to be more than a colorful fringe on our (American) social fabric—they are woven into its very fiber."

ACADEMIA

Political science professor Alex N. Dragnich (1912–) served in the Office of Strategic Services during World War II and as the Cultural Attache and Public Affairs Officer in the American Embassy in Yugoslavia. Dragnich wrote extensively on Serbian subjects; his latest publication is entitled *Serbs and Croats: The Struggle in Yugoslavia* (1992).

FILM, TELEVISION, AND THEATER

Actor Karl Malden (born Mladen Sekulovich in 1913) received an Academy Award for his performance in *A Streetcar Named Desire* in 1951 and was nominated for a second Oscar in 1954 for his work in *On the Waterfront*. Malden is best known for his starring role in the television series "The Streets of San Francisco," and for his series of television commercials for American Express.

Actor John Malkovich (1954–) founded the Steppenwolf Theatre Company in Chicago. An accomplished film actor as well, Malkovich appeared in such films as *Dangerous Liaisons*, *In the Line of Fire*, and *Places in the Heart*, for which he received an Academy Award nomination.

Steve Tesich (born Stoyan Tesich in 1942) is a well-known screenwriter, playwright, and novelist who received an Academy Award for Best Screenplay in 1979 for *Breaking Away*. His other screenplays include *Eleni*, *The World According to Garp*, and *Passing Game*.

LITERATURE

Novelist and publishing executive William (Iliya) Jovanovich (1920–) has written many works, including *Now, Barabbas* (1964), *Madmen Must* (1978), and *A Slow Suicide* (1991). Jovanovich is also the president and chief executive officer of Harcourt Brace Jovanovich.

Poet and translator Charles Simic (1938–) was awarded the 1990 Pulitzer Prize for Poetry for his collection, *The World Doesn't End*.

POLITICS

Born in 1795 as Djordje Sagić in a Serbian settlement in western Hungary, George Fisher came to America in 1815, having agreed to become a bond servant upon his arrival. He jumped ship at the mouth of Delaware River in order to escape his pledge, and was named Fisher by the bystanders who watched him swim ashore. He then wandered from Pennsylvania to Mississippi to Mexico and eventually to Texas, where he joined in the battle for independence from Mexico; helped to organize the first supreme court of the republic; and held a number of positions in the Texas state government. Fisher also published a liberal Spanish-language newspaper. In 1851 he went to Panama, and from there to San Francisco. While in California he served as secretary of the land commission, justice of the peace, county judge. He finished his wandering and wondrous life as the council for Greece in 1873.

Awarded the GOP Woman of the Year Award in 1972, Helen Delich Bently (1923–) is currently a congresswoman from Maryland. Rose Ann Vuich, served in the California State Senate from 1976 to 1992 and received the Democrat of the Year Award in 1975. Joyce George (1936–), attorney and politician, was appointed U.S. Attorney from the

Northern District of Ohio by President George Bush in 1989.

SCIENCE

Nikola Tesla (1856-1943), "the electrical wizard," astonished the world with his demonstration of the wonders of alternating current at the World Columbian Exposition in Chicago in 1893; in the first half of the twentieth century, this became the standard method of generating electrical power. Tesla also designed the first hydro-electric power plant in Niagara Falls, New York. Having introduced the fundamentals of robotry, fluorescent light, the laser beam, wireless communication and transmission of electrical energy, the turbine and vertical take-off aircraft, computers, and missile science, Tesla was possibly the greatest inventor the world has ever known. His work spawned technology such as satellites, beam weapons, and nuclear fusion.

Michael Idvorsky Pupin's (1858-1935) scientific contributions in the field of radiology include rapid X-ray photography (1896), which cut the usual hour-long exposure time to seconds; the discovery of the secondary X-ray radiation; and the development of the first X-ray picture used in surgery. His other interests covered the field of telecommunications. The "Pupin coil," which uses alternate current, made long distance telephone lines and cables possible. He also invented the means to eliminate static from radio receivers as well the tuning devises for radios. Pupin successfully experimented with sonar U-boat detectors and underwater radars, as well as the passage of electricity through gases. In addition to his scientific contributions, Pupin was a prominent Serbian patriot. He tirelessly campaigned on behalf of Serbia during World War I. In his Pulitzer Prize-winning autobiography *From Immigrant to Inventor* (1925) Pupin stated: "[I] brought to America something ... which I valued very highly, and that was: a knowledge of and a profound respect and admiration for the best traditions of my race ... no other lesson had ever made a deeper impression upon me." The Pupin Institute at Columbia University was founded in his memory.

Milan Panić (1929–) founded ICN Pharmaceuticals, Inc. in Pasadena, California. At one time his company employed 6,000 people, with sales of over $150 million. In 1992 Panić served as the Prime Minister of Yugoslavia.

SPORTS

Professional basketball player Pete Maravich (1948-1987) was perhaps best known as "Pistol Pete" Maravich.

VISUAL ARTS

John David Brčin (1899-1982) was a sculptor who immigrated to America in 1914. Drawing his inspiration from American subjects, Brcin sculpted busts of President Abraham Lincoln, Mark Twain, and many others. He also created large reliefs depicting scenes from American history.

MEDIA

PRINT

Amerikanski Srbobran (The American Serb Defender).
Published by the Serb National Federation since 1906, this is the oldest and largest circulating Serbian bilingual weekly newspaper in the United States, covering cultural, political, and sporting events of interest to Serbian Americans.

Contact: George Martich, President.
Address: 1 Fifth Avenue, seventh floor,
   Pittsburgh, Pennsylvania 15222.
Telephone: (412) 642-7372 or (800) 538-SERB.
Fax: (412) 642-1372.
E-mail: snf@serbnatlfed.org.

Glasnik Srpskog Istoriskog Kulturnog Društva "Njegoš" (Herald of the Serbian Historical-Cultural Society "Njegoš").
Founded in 1959, this historical and literary review is published biannually.

Contact: Draško Braunović, Editor.
Address: 774 Emroy Avenue, Elmhurst,
   Illinois 60126.
Telephone: (630) 833-3721.

Serb World U.S.A.
A continuation of *Serb World* (1979-1983), this bimonthly, illustrated magazine was established in 1984. It features articles about Serbian American immigrants' cultural heritage and history, as well as other topics relating to Serbian Americans.

Contact: Mary Nicklanovic-Hart
Address: 415 E. Mabel St., Tucson,
   Arizona 85705-7456.
Telephone: (602) 624-4887.

Serbian Studies.

Founded in 1980, this scholarly journal is published biannually by the North American Society for Serbian Studies. It offers broad coverage of history, political science, art, and the humanities.

Contact: Ljubica Dragana Popovich, Editor.

Address: Dept. of Fine Arts, Station B, Box 1696, Vanderbilt University, Nashville, Tennessee 37235.

Telephone: (615) 322-2831.

Sloboda (Liberty).

Founded in 1952 by the Serb National Defense Council of America, this publication is an illustrated biweekly featuring articles on Serbian history and culture.

Address: 5782 N. Elston Avenue, Chicago, Illinois 60646.

Telephone: (773) 775-7772.

Srpska Borba (The Serbian Struggle).

Monthly journal published by the Serbian Literary Association (Srpsko Literarno Udruženje) since 1953. It features articles on political, social, historical, and cultural topics.

Address: 448 Bari Avenue, Chicago, Illinois 60657.

Telephone: (773) 549-1099.

RADIO

"Serbian Radio Hour" ("Srpske Melodije I Novosti"), WCPN-FM 90.3, Cleveland, Ohio.

Weekly three-hour program featuring Serbian music and news, especially from Belgrade, Pale, and Knin.

Contact: Djordje Djelić, Director.

Address: 6364 Pearl Road, Cleveland, Ohio 44130.

Telephone: (216) 842-6161.

Fax: (216) 842-6163.

"Serbian Radio Program," KTYM-AM 1460 and KORG-AM 1190.

Program is broadcasted twice a day on Saturdays, featuring world news, special reportage from Belgrade, Pale, and Knin and music of Serbian origin.

Contact: Veroljub Radivojević, Director.

Address: 23128 Gainford Street, Woodland Hills, California 91364.

Telephone: (818) 222-5073.

Fax: (818) 591-9678.

ORGANIZATIONS AND ASSOCIATIONS

Belgrade Club, Inc.

Founded in 1982. A non-profit membership organization engaged in such cultural programs as lectures on art and art history, and film screenings. Publishes a quarterly bulletin covering the arts.

Contact: Donya-Dobrila Schimansky, President.

Address: P.O. Box 6235, Yorkville Station, New York, New York 10128.

Serb National Federation (SNF).

Founded in 1906, the SNF has lodges throughout the United States and Canada. Its activities transcend business interests to include sponsoring and promoting many programs from sports to scholarship within the Serbian American community.

Contact: George Martich.

Address: 1 Fifth Avenue, Seventh floor, Pittsburgh, Pennsylvania 15222.

Telephone: (412) 642-7372 or (800) 538-SERB.

Fax: (412) 642-1372.

E-mail: snf@serbnatlfed.org.

Online: http://www.serbnatlfed.org/.

Serbian American Affairs Office (SAAO).

Established in 1992, SAAO serves as a clearinghouse for information and research on current events occurring in the former Yugoslavia, and arranges guest appearances on radio and television stations across the United States.

Contact: Danielle Sremac, Director.

Address: P.O. Box 32238, Washington, D.C., 20007.

Telephone: (202) 965-2141.

Fax: (202) 965-2187.

Serbian Cultural Club "St. Sava" (Srpski Kulturni Klub "Sv. Sava").

Founded in 1951, this organization has chapters throughout the United States and abroad. Activities promote Serbian culture and political awareness among the host nations and the hosts' culture among the Serbs.

Address: 448 Barry Avenue, Chicago, Illinois 60657.

Telephone: (773) 549-1099.

Serbian National Defense Council of America (Sprska Narodna Odbrana).

Established in 1941 with chapters throughout the United States and abroad. Activities focus on political and cultural Serbian interests.

Contact: Slavko Panović, President.
Address: 5782 N. Elston, Chicago, Illinois 60646.
Telephone: (773) 775-7772.
Fax: (773) 775-7779.

MUSEUMS AND RESEARCH CENTERS

North American Society for Serbian Studies.

Founded in 1980 within the framework of the American Association for the Advancement of Slavic Studies (AAASS) to research and promote Serbian literature, history, and culture. Attracts Serbian scholars from the United States, Canada, and Mexico, who meet at annual conferences of the AAASS. (Note: The address of this organization varies according to the location of the president, elected for a one year term during the conference.)

Contact: Radmila J. Gorop, President
Address: Department of Slavic Studies, Columbia University, New York, New York 10027.
Telephone: (212) 854-3941.

SOURCES FOR ADDITIONAL STUDY

Kisslinger, J. *The Serbian Americans.* New York: Chelsea House, 1990.

Pavlovich, Paul. *The Serbians: The Story of a People.* Toronto: Serbian Heritage Books, 1988.

Radovich, Milan. "The Serbian Press" in *The Ethnic Press in the United States: A Historical Analysis and Handbook.* Westport, CT: Greenwood Press, 1987, pp. 337-351.

Singleton, F. *A Short History of the Yugoslav Peoples.* Cambridge, MA: Cambridge University Press, 1993.

SICILIAN AMERICANS

by
Laura C. Rudolph

The main areas of Sicilian settlement in the United States included the major industrial centers of the country including New York, New Jersey, Massachusetts, California, Illinois, and some parts of the South, including Louisiana and Texas.

OVERVIEW

Located off the tip of the Italian peninsula, Sicily is the largest island in the Mediterranean Sea and measures 9,920 square miles (25,700 square kilometers). As a result of its close proximity to both Italy (separated by the Strait of Messina by less than two miles) and North Africa (separated by less than 100 miles), Sicily has traditionally been regarded as a bridge between Africa and

Europe. Officially considered one of the regions of Italy, Sicily has nevertheless enjoyed regional autonomy with extensive powers of self-government since 1946.

Sicily is comprised of nine provinces: Agrigento, Caltanissetta, Catania, Enna, Messina, Palermo, Ragusa, Siracusa, and Trapani, as well as numerous adjacent islands including the Egadi Islands, the Aeolian Islands, the Pelagie Islands, and the Ustica Islands. The terrain is largely mountainous with Europe's largest volcano, Mount Etna, representing the highest peak at 3,260 meters. The capital of Sicily is Palermo, which has a population of 500,000 and is the largest city in Sicily.

Sicily's ethnically diverse population of slightly over five million people reflects centuries of foreign rule. The major ethnic groups include native Sicilians, Arabs, Greeks, Spanish, and northern Italians. Although the vast majority of Sicilians are Roman Catholics, there are smaller numbers of Greek Orthodox Christians.

HISTORY

Sicily's strategic location in the Mediterranean has prompted centuries of invasion and occupation by foreign powers and closely parallels the rise and fall of virtually every empire since the eighth century B.C. The name "Sicily" is thought to have originated with the Sikels, one of three peoples who occupied Sicily during the Neolithic Age. Thereafter, during the seventh and eighth centuries B.C., the Greeks established colonies, including Messina, Syracuse, and Gela, under which Sicily flourished culturally. Although the Carthaginians arrived at roughly the same time as the Greeks, they were confined to the northwest of the island and exerted a lesser influence on the island. However, by the third century B.C. the Greek Empire declined and the Romans established control, which lasted until the fifth century A.D. Sicily was subsequently occupied by the Ostrogoths, the Byzantines, and the Arabs.

Sicily flourished once again under Norman rule, which began around 1000 A.D. Frederick II's reign (1211-1250) produced an outpouring of literary, scientific, and architectural works, representing a cultural peak. After his death, however, Sicily passed into the hands of France, an oppressive occupation that ended with the bloody "Sicilian Vespers" revolt in 1282. Thereafter, for the better part of the next six centuries, the Spanish ruled Sicily, with periodic occupation from other countries. Weary from years of invasion, the Sicilians rallied under Giuseppe Garibaldi, who won control of the island in 1860. The Sicilians enthusiastically supported the unification of Italy, which was completed during the *Risorgimento* of 1860-1870. The unification with Italy did not, however, prove particularly beneficial to Sicily. Quickly deemed part of "the Southern problem," the Sicilians were forced to endure military conscription and a heavy tax burden. The *mafioso* (or mafia), an underground element often linked with criminal activity, quickly became a stronghold of power in Sicily. Efforts on the part of the Sicilians to revolt against the new laws were quickly suppressed, often brutally.

MODERN ERA

Tensions remained between northern and southern Italy into the early part of the twentieth century. In the 1920s Benito Mussolini came into power in Italy and established Fascist control. Mussolini waged unofficial war on the Sicilian *mafioso*, and official war against the Allies during World War II. Sicily proved crucial to the Allied effort and was successfully conquered in the July-August 1943 campaign. The Allied victory forced Mussolini's fall

from power, and following the war a large separatist movement was begun in Sicily, which agitated for its own rule. Although the Sicilians were not able to achieve this goal, they were not wholly unsuccessful. Sicily remained a region of the newly created Republic of Italy, but it was granted regional autonomy in 1946. However, social, political, and economic problems continued to plague the region. High illiteracy and unemployment rates, coupled with natural disasters, served to reinforce rather than lessen the poverty of the Sicilians. And, freed from the restrictive measures of Mussolini's regime, the *mafioso* quickly regained a large portion of power in Sicily. In the last part of the twentieth century, serious efforts were made to lessen the influence and control of the mafia and to rejuvenate the economy.

THE FIRST SICILIANS IN AMERICA

Sicilians have a recorded presence of over 300 years on American soil. In the late seventeenth century, the brothers Antonio and Tomaso Crisafi sailed to America. By 1696 Antonio Crisafi was in charge of the Onondaga fort, located in what is now New York State. On the West Coast in southern California, an early missionary named Father Saverio Saetta (a Jesuit), was involved in early efforts to convert the Native Americans to Christianity. He perished at the hands of the natives in 1695. Sicilian immigration remained relatively slow until the latter part of the nineteenth century. However, several Sicilian immigrants distinguished themselves in the decades leading up to that time. During the Civil War, Enrico Fardell was commissioned a colonel in the Union Army and was rapidly promoted to brigadier general for distinguished services. Father Venuta, a former professor from the University of Palermo, built the Church of St. Joseph and several school buildings in New Jersey shortly after the Civil War.

SIGNIFICANT IMMIGRATION WAVES

The first significant wave of Sicilian immigrants to the United States began in the late 1880s. Before 1880 less than 1,000 Sicilians immigrated to America per year. But by 1906 over 100,000 Sicilians left for the States in that year alone. Ultimately, out of the 4.5 million Italians that immigrated to the United States between the years 1880 and 1930, one out of every four was a Sicilian. The immigrants represented virtually every area in Sicily. The numbers would have been higher but for the passage of the U.S. Immigration Act of 1924. The Act reduced the number of persons allowed to immigrate to the United States from Italy to 3,845.

The surge of Italian immigrants to the United States happened for several reasons. After the unification of Italy was completed in 1870, Sicilians were confident their lot would improve after centuries of *la miseria*. However, they were soon disillusioned. Sicily suffered a series of agricultural crises, which precipitated a sharp drop in the grain and citrus markets. The discovery of sulfur in America greatly reduced Sicily's role in foreign market. In addition, there was widespread economic exploitation of the Sicilians, who were heavily taxed under the new government. Eventually the Sicilians banded together against the intolerable conditions, largely in the form of peasants' and workers' organizations termed mutual aid societies (*mutuo soccorso*). The mutual aid societies contributed in part to the formation of the *Fasci*, a Socialist-directed movement. By the 1890s, the *Fasci* movement was a powerful force, with revolts that were increasingly threatening to those in power. Between the years 1892 and 1894, the *Fasci* was forcibly suppressed by the government and ordered to disband. Many of the former leaders of the movement fled to the United States, while other immigrants responded to the deteriorating economic conditions, from which they saw no relief.

SETTLEMENT PATTERNS

The main areas of Sicilian settlement in the United States included the major industrial centers of the country including New York, New Jersey, Massachusetts, California, Illinois, and some parts of the South, including Louisiana and Texas. The heaviest concentrations of Sicilian Americans were in New York, Chicago, Boston, New Orleans, and San Francisco, where jobs for unskilled workers were readily available. Sicilians also migrated to rural areas such as Bryant, Texas, where over 3,000 Sicilians had settled by the 1890s.

This generation of Sicilian immigrants tended to cluster together in groups according to the regions from which they had emigrated. In New York City those emigrating from the village of Cinisi huddled together on East 69th Street, while larger sections like Elizabeth Street contained emigrants from several different areas including Sciacca and Palermo. Sicilians from fishing villages settled in Boston on the North Street, while others settled in San Francisco's North Beach. Many of the districts were soon regarded as "Little Italys." Sicilians in Chicago congregated in an area known as "Little Sicily," and those in New Orleans lived in a district dubbed "Little Palermo."

While large proportions of Sicilian Americans continue to live in urban areas, subsequent generations of Sicilian Americans gradually moved away from the old neighborhoods. Economic prosperity has enabled many to own their own houses in the suburbs, a fulfillment of the dreams of their immigrant grandparents.

ACCULTURATION AND ASSIMILATION

Many of the earliest immigrants from Sicily were young males or heads of households who intended to work for a short time in the United States before returning to Italy. After several years of working, over half would eventually send for their families and permanently establish themselves in various cities across the country. In a "chain migration" other families from the village would then immigrate to the same area. There was subsequently little assimilation at first, even among Sicilians who had emigrated from different regions. The early Sicilian immigrants held fast to the various dialects and celebrations of their native villages. Many never learned to speak English at all, and there was little intermarriage with other immigrant groups. Sheltered from the larger culture, the "Little Sicilies" that the immigrants created mimicked the world they had left behind. Mutual aid societies like the Caltanisetta (Sicily) Society in Baltimore and the Trinacria Fratellanza Siciliana in Chicago aided the immigrants with housing, employment, and general acclimation. Sicilian cuisine and entertainment could be found in virtually every Sicilian settlement area. Sicilian dances and songs were performed at the local music halls, in addition to a number of puppet shows, a traditional Sicilian entertainment. Agrippino Manteo's widely popular "Papa Manteo's Life-Size Marionettes" attracted large Sicilian audiences throughout the early part of the twentieth century. Weekly newspapers like the *Corriere Siciliano* (The Sicilian Courier) brought the Sicilian immigrants news from Sicily.

The Sicilians' seemingly stubborn resistance to assimilation was fueled in part by the hatred they aroused in their new country. Many Americans believed Sicilians were an "inferior race" destined to remain in ignorance and poverty. The prejudice that this belief encouraged generated a vicious cycle of limited economic and educational opportunities. Foremost among those who spurned the Sicilians were the earlier arrivals from northern Italy. The traditional animosity between the northern and southern Italians spilled over into the new land. Northern Italians, who had a greater number of skilled laborers among them, were therefore more likely to land higher-paying jobs than Sicilians, the majority of whom were peasants. Furthermore, northern Italian immigrants were more established in the New World and had begun to achieve a relative degree of prosperity. They were reluctant to be lumped with the newly arrived Sicilians, who they had long considered inferior to them. Consequently, they struggled to disassociate themselves from the Sicilian immigrants. In many instances the northern Italians would move out of neighborhoods when the Sicilians began to populate them. A 1975 article by F. Ianni and E. Reuss in *Psychology Today* quotes a northern Italian immigrant: "Trust family first, relatives second, Sicilians third, and after that, forget it."

"To this day, some Sicilians who also believe in the Evil Eye try not to forget to put their first stocking on the left leg, in order to ensure a day of good luck. And if, while praying at midnight, they should hear the baying of a dog, they will expect *male notizia* (bad news)."

"Southern Italian Folklore in New York city" (*New York folklore Quarterly,* v. XXI, 1965).

But if the northern Italians were suspicious and dismissive of the Sicilians, then the rest of America was openly hostile. Sicilians were labeled "dirty," "diseased," and "political anarchists" and were accused of introducing a criminal element into the United States, namely the Mafia. The notorious underworld activities of Sicilian Americans such as Charles "Lucky" Luciano were duly reported in newspapers across the United States. The image of the Sicilian "mobster" had devastating consequences for all Sicilians. Numerous innocent Sicilians were charged and convicted of heinous crimes, usually with flimsy circumstantial evidence to support their cases. When the jury system failed to convict, citizens took matters into their own hands. A case in point occurred in 1891 in New Orleans, Louisiana, where 11 Sicilians were lynched by a mob of "good citizens" outraged at the not-guilty verdict returned in a trial. Similar incidents on a smaller scale occurred in other towns throughout Louisiana well into the next century.

Given the amount of hatred these first Sicilian immigrants encountered in the New World, it is not surprising that they preferred to remain in sheltered enclaves surrounded with familiar village dialects and customs. Even as other immigrants began to consider themselves "Americans," Sicilians continued to identify themselves by their particular villages. Neither were they entirely sure of their place in the emerging Italian American culture. Although the United States grouped Sicilians under the category of "Italians," Sicilians were reluctant to do so. The unification with Italy and Sicily was less than 100 years old, and the bitterness it had wrought ran deep among Sicilians. However, second- and third-generation Sicilian Americans were less concerned with such distinctions and were more apt to label themselves "Italian Americans."

Ultimately, Sicilian immigrants followed an assimilation pattern similar to northern Italians, albeit at a noticeably slower rate. As educational opportunities increased, so too did economic opportunities. As with Italian Americans overall, Sicilians proved they were "American" in the fullest sense of the word during World War II. Sicilian Americans were able to provide crucial military aid, particularly during the Sicilian campaign of 1943. World War II marked something of a turning point as second-and third generation Sicilians achieved financial security and social acceptance. Although images of mafia lords continue to dog the Sicilians, they are far from being the victims of hatred and discrimination they once were.

TRADITIONS, CUSTOMS, AND BELIEFS

Sicilians have a variety of traditions, many of which are derived from quasi-religious beliefs. For example, according to an old folk belief, bread made during the first three days of May will result in mold and roaches throughout the house. The origins of this tradition can be traced to a legend about a woman making bread who denied a crumb to a beggar and was generous to devils masquerading as knights. This mistake resulted in the dangers inherent in making bread during the first three days of May.

Other traditions and customs are traced back to an agricultural lifestyle. Sicilians would ritually taste every new product that came from the earth while reciting the words, "Whatever I eat today, may I eat it next year." Dried figs were left in a basket and were not touched until the feast day of St. Francis of Assisi, in the belief that moths would ruin them unless they were protected by the saint. There was also a lingering belief in forms of witchcraft: a belief in the "evil eye" and the need for an exorcist for a person whose soul has been overtaken by devils. Many of the agricultural traditions and customs were difficult to transfer to the industrial New World and disappeared with immigration.

PROVERBS

Many proverbs from Sicilian culture have survived through the generations: With a rooster or without a rooster, God will still make the dawn; Nothing scratches my hand like my own nails; The war is lost for too much advice; The words of your enemies can make you laugh, but those of a friend can make you cry; Crooked wood is straightened with fire; You can't have meat without the bone; Do not be too sweet lest you be eaten, do not be too sour lest you be shunned; He who digs a grave for his brother falls in it himself; If it doesn't stain, it soils; A person eating must make crumbs; A rock offered by a friend is like an apple; A fish starts smelling bad from the head.

CUISINE

Sicilian cuisine is savory and flavorful, and reflects the influence of a diverse cultural inheritance. An Arab influence is particularly noticeable. The food is hot and spicy, and eggplants, olives, pine nuts, and capers are plentiful, along with the ubiquitous pasta and tomatoes.

Some of the main dishes include: *pasta con le sarde* (sardines, raisins, pine nuts, and capers); *frittedda* (peas, fava beans, and artichokes); *pasta con pescespada* (pasta with swordfish); *pasta con le melanzane* (pasta and eggplant); and *cuscus* (Sicilian couscous). Special dishes include the *ragu Siciliano delle feste* (Sicilian feast day ragout). The Sicilians are also known for their desserts, including their *gelato Siciliano* (Sicilian ice cream) and *cannoli*, a fried pastry stuffed with ricotta cheese and candied fruit. *Cassata* is also made with ricotta and candied fruit, in addition to almond paste and sponge cake, and *martorana* is a form of marzipan for which Sicilians are well known.

The grinding poverty that characterized Sicily in the early decades of the twentieth century forced Sicilians to exist at a mere sustenance level. It is ironic that many of the Sicilian peasants were unable to enjoy many of the foods unique to their region until they emigrated to the United States and could afford to do so. Food became a central part of the immigrants' lives and found a prominent place in many of the religious and cultural celebrations. Toward the end of the twentieth century there was a renewed interest in Sicilian cooking, and recipe books became easily accessible.

TRADITIONAL COSTUMES

The traditional costumes of Sicilian women are made of dimity bodices, red and dark blue (or white and dark blue) striped skirts of homewoven cloth, striped aprons, calfskin slippers with pointed toes, dark blue stockings, and kerchiefs of cotton wrapped around the neck and bosom. Men wear white cotton hose, homewoven cloth shirts with wide collars, heavy shoes, and a wide-brimmed hat made out of palm leaves. The festival dress of women consists of a dark blue velvet bodice, a silk skirt, dark blue stockings, a white twill mantlet, striped leather shoes, with ties of black ribbon in the front, a silver hair clasp, filigree drop earrings, numerous finger rings, and necklaces of coral and amber. The men wear a dark blue velvet suit, a white cotton cap, a red cotton sash, and two handkerchiefs of red, yellow, or green. Sicilian Americans do not wear traditional dress anymore except at special occasions.

DANCES AND SONGS

Sicilians have many unique songs, the majority of which celebrate agricultural and religious themes. For instance, during the olive harvest or grape gathering certain songs would be sung for each stage of the harvesting process. Many of the folk songs are mournful, haunting melodies, but other songs are quite ribald. The traditional instruments are bagpipes, reed flutes, drums, and wind instruments. Several songs combine dancing and singing, like the *Aria of the Fasola*, in which a man and woman sing to each other. Some of the traditional dances include *The Nail, The Polyp, The Tarascon, The Capona,* and *The Fasola*, which is a lot like the Neapolitan *tarantella*. Sicilian dances and songs were a vibrant part of the entertainment found in the communities of the first Sicilian immigrants. Gradually they were replaced with more Americanized forms of entertainment like motion pictures. However, traditional Sicilian songs and dances can still be heard at celebrations and special occasions.

HOLIDAYS

Along with traditional Catholic and American holidays like Christmas Day, New Year's Day, and Easter Day, Sicilians also celebrate several feast days. Sicilian immigrants brought with them their *feste*, which honor the patron saints of the various villages from which they had arrived. The *feste* marked not only a day of celebration, but reinforced the ties the immigrants still had to their native villages. Immigrants from Palermo honored Saint Rosalia, immigrants from Catania honored Saint Agatha, and still others honored Saint Gandolfo, Saint Joseph, and Saint Anthony. Lavish processions complete with parades, fireworks, and traditional Sicilian songs and dances characterized the *feste*. Nor were the festivals limited to the honoring of the patron saints of the villages. Immigrants from Palermo continued the practice of honoring Madonna del Lume (Holy Mother of Light) in San Francisco. A procession would lead down to the Fisherman's Wharf for the ancient Blessing of the Fishing Fleet, after which celebrations with music and dancing would take place. The *feste* celebrations of the Sicilian immigrants continue to be held today, and are equally lavish, if not more so. Many celebrations, like the annual *feste* honoring St. Joseph in New Orleans, are eagerly anticipated and attended by all groups and not just those of Sicilian ancestry.

HEALTH ISSUES

Sicilians are naturally robust and have not been prone to any particular health problems. Illnesses did occur during immigration, however. Accustomed to the mild climate and open spaces of Sicily, the immigrants fared badly among the crowded conditions of city tenements. The closeness of their living space and lack of fresh air was both mentally and physically harmful. Many of the Sicilians suffered from depression or were victims of the various diseases that all too often swept through entire city blocks of tenements. Sicilians were especially vulnerable to tuberculosis and many of them returned to Sicily gravely ill. During the mass migration, there were so many immigrants returning to die that several villages in Sicily set up sanitariums to receive them. As they began to move out of the tenements, later generations of Sicilian Americans were no longer exposed to the conditions that bred disease. Like most Americans, later generations of Sicilian Americans are able to take advantage of the medical insurance offered by their employers.

LANGUAGE

Although the official langue of Sicily is Italian, the Sicilians have a fully developed language, complete with regional dialects (*parrati*) of their own. The Sicilian language derives from Latin and reflects the influence of many centuries of occupation. Many of their words have Greek, Arab, French, or Spanish origins. The spelling is fundamentally phonetic and the stress falls on the next to last syllable unless indicted by an accent mark. The vowels are pronounced as follows: the Sicilian "a" is pronounced like the English "a" in "father;" "e" like "e" in "west"; "i" like "ea" in "feast"; a short "i" like "i" in "fit"; "o" like "aw" in "saw"; and "u" like "o" in "do."

Most of the consonants are pronounced the same as in English, with a few exceptions: "e" before "e" or "i" is pronounced like the "ch" in "church"; "c" before "a, o, or u" is pronounced like the "k" in "kite"; the "h" is always silent; and both letters in double consonants must be distinctly pronounced. Interestingly, there is no future tense.

Some of the earlier Sicilian immigrants never learned to speak English at all; many, however, adapted their Sicilian to the English language to form a hybrid language composed of both Sicilian and English words. The children of the immigrants usually spoke both English and Sicilian. Most Sicilian Americans converted to the English language by the end of the twentieth century. However, there was a growing sense of alarm that the cultural heritage of their language would be lost to Sicilian Americans. Various organizations were subsequently formed to promote the study of the language.

GREETINGS AND OTHER POPULAR EXPRESSIONS

Common Sicilian greetings and other expressions include the following: *milli grazii*—many thanks; *cuntenti di canuscirivi*—glad to meet you; *addiu*—goodbye; *una bona idea*—a good idea; *sì, daveru*—yes, indeed; *scusatimi*—excuse me; *pir favuri*—please; *mi chiamu*—my name is; *saluti*—health; *santa*—saint; *cu piaciri*—with pleasure; *benissimu*—fine; *bon*—good; *cuntenti*—content; *oggi*—today; *dumani*—tomorrow; *amicu*—friend; and *gentillissimu*—very kind.

FAMILY AND COMMUNITY DYNAMICS

In Sicily, the family was a strong defense against the desperate and unrelieved poverty that characterized life. Each family member contributed to the all-encompassing and often heartbreaking effort to survive. First loyalties were reserved for the closest kin (*casa*). This was an economic necessity as each family competed with other families for survival. Resolutely patriarchal, the family deferred to the father on every decision. But the mother's role in the family was also important; while she did not possess an equal share of the authority, she nevertheless had the important task of running the household. Children were expected to share in the responsibilities of maintaining the household from an early age.

A new emphasis was placed on extended relatives during the immigration process. Although the economic competition in Sicily fostered less of a sense of cooperation beyond the *casa*, a distinction was generally made for a second tier of kin (*parenti*). While the *parenti* played a peripheral role in Sicily, they became an important factor in immigrants' lives, in many cases becoming the first link in a migration chain. The *parenti* provided much needed emotional and financial support, eventually commanding almost as much loyalty as the *casa*.

Many Sicilians, however, felt that family loyalty as a whole suffered as a consequence of migration to the United States. The early Sicilian immigrants attempted to duplicate traditional Sicilian family patterns in the New World. Men continued to exert the greater share of authority, at least on the surface, while the women ran the households. Children continued to contribute to the economic support of the family from an early age. However, there were important changes that occurred with migration. Frequently the women, both wives and daughters, worked outside of the home. Mothers could no longer supervise their children in the manner they were accustomed to in Sicily. First the children went to school, and from there they were pulled out as soon as possible to go to work. As the children of the immigrants began to absorb American ways, they felt increasingly resentful of the expectations of their parents. The children began to question the old ways, such as automatically turning over their wages to their parents. The parents in turn felt betrayed by what they felt was the children's lack of respect for the family.

The gap between the immigrants and their children continued to widen and foster tensions as the children grew more "Americanized." As these first immigrants passed on, however, traditional Sicilian family values gradually waned and the distinctions that marked a Sicilian family became less apparent. Nevertheless, *la famiglia* continues to play an important role in the lives of Sicilian Americans today.

EDUCATION

Since the first Sicilian immigrants were primarily agricultural workers, a good education was not necessarily among the skills they valued highly. In Sicily, basic survival was of primary importance, and children were expected to start contributing from an early age. The transfer of a child from the fields to a school threatened the family's survival. Nor were schools easily accessible to the larger majority of Sicilians; only the wealthy were able to take advantage of the limited opportunities. There was consequently a high illiteracy rate among agricultural workers in Sicily, which remained true as late as the twenty-first century.

These early Sicilian immigrants brought with them their indifference toward education. Their skepticism increased along with the wariness they felt towards the American values being taught to their children in the schools. Sicilian immigrants were often resentful their children attended school at all, and they placed little emphasis on study time. Children frequently had part-time jobs in addition to their schoolwork, which lessened their chances of success in an educational setting. Since they had limited educational opportunities, the children consequently had limited economic opportunities and they were soon caught in a web of poverty.

After World War II, the children and grandchildren of these immigrants were largely cognizant of the need for education. By this time, Sicilians were acclimated to the extent that they no longer felt threatened or intimidated by American schools. They utilized the G.I. Bill and took advantage of the increased educational opportunities. Like the majority of America, Sicilian Americans strive to provide their children with a college education.

THE ROLE OF WOMEN

Sicilian immigrants carried with them a fixed set of rules concerning women's roles within the patriarchal household. Fathers perceived a fierce obligation to protect the chastity of their daughters and when the daughters were old enough to marry, they were protected and dominated by their husbands. Wives and daughters stayed strictly within the boundaries of running the households and did not work outside of the home. Such a system could not be maintained in the United States. When it was possible, wives continued to work in the house, and their daughters helped them cook, clean, and care for the younger children. But many women, even unmarried women, were forced from sheer economic necessity to work outside of the home. The women worked in factories, in the garment industry, and in the South they worked in the fields alongside the men.

The old patriarchal system clashed with the new expectations and roles for women. Fathers were unable to supervise the activities of their daughters in the manner to which they had been accustomed. At school, daughters learned "American ways" that were considered unsuitable and compromising to their chastity by Sicilian standards. In increasing numbers the daughters desired additional education beyond the household arts. Sicilian men were not in the habit of considering education—any formal education—important for females and they were reluctant to begin doing so. Gradually, the role of the Sicilian American woman has undergone a revision. Like many women in America, Sicilian women now demand educational and career opportunities. In many cases, however, the transition has generated stress and conflict within the families.

WEDDINGS, BAPTISMS, AND FUNERALS

The importance of weddings, baptisms, and funerals has not diminished among later generations of Sicilian Americans. As an extension of their religious faith, these events are observed in the manner of Roman Catholicism, combined with elements that are more traditional than religious. They also tend to be lavish and expensive, especially the weddings. The majority of expenses fall on the daughter's family, but in view of the rising costs of weddings, some families are beginning to allocate expenses a little more evenly. However, because of the importance placed on the event, it is not considered inappropriate if a family goes into debt to pay for the wedding. The celebrations begin early; the bride is given several showers before the wedding, where she receives gifts and money. Male friends and relatives of the groom thrown him stag parties. The weddings are generally all-day celebrations and the ceremony is followed by a large reception. Earlier immigrants continued the tradition of large guest lists, subsequent generations of Sicilian Americans have considerably cut down the number of invited guests.

Like weddings, baptisms are very special to Sicilian Americans. The role of godparent is chosen very carefully, for that role represents a substantial investment of time and money to the person chosen. The baptism is performed as soon after the birth as possible; traditionally, an unbaptized baby was susceptible to the devil. The godparents furnish the clothing the baby wears during the ceremony. Among the more traditional, a religious medal is sometimes included to ward off the "evil eye." After the ceremony, parties are held, which generally last until the evening.

After a death occurs in a Sicilian American family, there is an outpouring of food, flowers, and money from friends and relatives. The grief is shared with the family and everyone, even distant kin, is expected to pay respects. During the wake, which can last up to three or four days, the casket is left open, and the mourners can kneel and say a prayer. Relatives are arranged in the importance of closeness to the deceased for the funeral and the funeral procession to the cemetery. Sicilian American funerals have given way to some American traditions such as cutting the length of the wake, but in general the funerals tend to be more openly emotional and elaborate than American funerals.

RELIGION

Sicilians have a long history of religious activity in the New World. As early as the seventeenth century, Catholic missionaries sailed to the West Coast in an effort to convert Native Americans to Christianity. One of these missionaries was Father Francesco Mario Piccolo, who joined Father Chino in California in 1689. Father Piccolo became a part of the exploration journey through Lower California and soon proved an apt mapmaker. He was appointed "visitor of missions" in 1705 and spent forty years in California before his death there in 1729. Father Saverio Saetta was also instrumental in early missionary efforts.

The Jesuit missionaries, however, had little in common with the Sicilian immigrants that arrived en masse between 1880 and 1920. While the vast majority of Sicilian immigrants were Roman Catholics, many of their religious beliefs were based on a mixture of Catholicism, paganism, and superstition. Tied to an agricultural world, their semi-religious traditions and customs had been celebrated for centuries, virtually untouched and unchallenged from the unrest provoked in other countries during the Protestant Reformation. Their faith was an important extension of their local identity and the *feste* honoring the patron saints of their villages were sacred rituals. Helpless and vulnerable against the elements, the superstitions, saints, and magic their folk religion provided them with helped to ease the uncertainties and anxieties of their rural lifestyle.

Early Sicilians brought their folk religion with them to the New World. The sheltered village enclaves allowed the Sicilians to continue practicing their religion as they were accustomed to in Sicily. Each village continued the practice of the *feste*, and many held fast to their belief in witcheries such as the "evil eye." The Irish Catholics were appalled at the Sicilians' treatment of the Catholic faith, as were the Protestants. In their eyes, the Sicilians' festival processions and worship of saints smacked of paganism and idolatry, and to the Protestants it represented the worst of Catholic excess. In addition, the Sicilians were unaccustomed to regular attendance at church or confessions, and entertained a general distrust for clergy members. Catholicism was a major part of the Sicil-

A Greek Orthodox Archbishop spreads incense during a special celebration at New York's Central Park bandshell. While most Sicilian Americans are Roman Catholic, a small percentage are Greek Orthodox Christians.

ians' lives, but they were not particularly interested in formal or structured practice.

Tensions ran high between Sicilian Catholics and Irish Catholics. The Irish largely controlled the American Catholic churches, and they resented the Sicilians' potential encroachment. Eventually the Sicilians founded their own parishes, where they could practice their faith as they chose. Immigrants from the area of Palermo founded the Chapel of Saint Rosalia, while those from Patti founded Saint Mary of Tyndaris Sicilians from other villages quickly followed suit. There the Sicilians were free to practice the folk religion of their villages. Second and third generation Sicilians, however, gradually phased out most of the more superstitious and supernatural elements of the Old World and preferred to practice religion in more conventional ways. The younger generation found the folk elements an old-fashioned and embarrasing reminder of their parents' and grandparents' immigrant status. In general, the *feste* honoring the various patron saints are still celebrated, but they can and should be labeled as cultural rather than religious celebrations.

EMPLOYMENT AND ECONOMIC TRADITIONS

Because the first Sicilian immigrants generally were unskilled laborers, the jobs they found in America were of the lowest sort. They worked in factories, operated pushcarts, worked on the railroads, dug tunnels, worked at construction sites, worked on the docks, and cleaned streets. The Sicilians in New Orleans worked in the sugarcane fields, while those in San Francisco and Boston gravitated toward the waterfront, where they fished for trade. Sicilian women worked mainly in the garment trade, in factories, or alongside their husbands in the fields. Only a fortunate few men were artisans in Sicily, and those few fared much better. Skilled laborers were able to find jobs as carpenters, masons, bakers, and plumbers.

In many ways early Sicilian immigrants were exploited, sometimes even before they left Sicily. A type of labor recruitment system evolved in which a *padrone* (a fellow Sicilian that operated as a middle man between the immigrants and American bosses) lured Sicilian men over to America with the promise of paid passage and a guaranteed job. In this way the *padrone* provided American companies with large numbers of employees for which they were paid handsomely. The Sicilians, however, were charged high interest for the "loan" of their passage money and were treated as slaves by their new employers.

The road to financial security was long and difficult. Since the families hovered near the poverty level, their children had to leave school early in order to supplement their parents' income. As there was no chance of learning a trade, the children, like their parents, were unable to rise above the status of unskilled laborer. There were exceptions, however, like Vincenzo La Rosa, who founded the La Rosa Macaroni Company in 1914. Likewise, Salvador Oteri built a successful wholesale fruit business, and Giuseppe Caccioppo founded the Grandview Dairy, Inc. in 1901. All three men amassed millions. But the majority of the Sicilians found it difficult to break out of the cycle, a problem that was exacerbated by the Great Depression. However, Sicilians benefited from the economic prosperity following World War II. Third and fourth generation Sicilians of these first immigrants are represented in virtually every professional field, including medicine, law, higher education, and business.

POLITICS AND GOVERNMENT

Many of the first Sicilian immigrants expected to return to Sicily after they had earned an appropriate amount of money. While the naturalization rate was low for Italians in general, it was even lower for those from Sicily. These Sicilian immigrants cared little about American politics or governmental policies; they were more inclined to stay abreast of the political situation in Sicily. Sicilian immigrants were not apathetic toward politics, however. Many of them had been active members of the *Fasci* movement and were well acquainted with political activity.

Ultimately, it was the type of work the immigrants found in America that brought them to the political forefront with their push toward organized labor. The Sicilians became heavily involved in the struggle for labor unions, a role that earned them the label of "anarchists." However, unsafe working conditions, low pay, and long hours had begun to take their toll on American workers long before the Sicilian mass immigration began. The rapidly expanding capitalist economy in the early twentieth century further widened the gap between American "bosses" and workers. America was ripe for union activity, but the efforts thus far had proved ineffectual. As the initial success of the *Fasci Siciliano* had proved, the

Sicilians were well-versed in organizing workers. The immigrants brought this knowledge with them to Amerca at precisely the time when organized labor was ready for their experience.

The Lexington Avenue strike that took place during the first decade of the twentieth century was an early example of the Sicilians' ability to organize workers. Salvatore Ninfo and other Sicilians successfully agitated for safer working conditions and shorter hours for their work digging subway tunnels. Giovanni Vaccaro led a series of successful cigar strikes in Tampa, Florida, between 1910 and 1920. The Clothing Workers of America Union organized similar strikes, including the big strike of 1919, which was led in great part by "Nino" Capraro. Nor was the push for organized labor restricted to Sicilian American men. Capraro's wife, Maria Bambache Capraro, played a vital role in the needleworkers' strike in 1919.

As naturalization rates increased, Sicilian Americans began to switch from radical union activity to formal politics. During the 1920s and 1930s Sicilians voted primarily Democratic. In addition, they began to send Sicilian Americans into office including the first Italian representative to Congress, Vincent Palmisano (1882-1953), a Democrat from Maryland. Sicilians have since then been elected to most offices on the local, state, and national levels. In 1986 President Ronald Reagan appointed Antonin Scalia to the Supreme Court, a powerful symbol of the acceptance of Sicilian Americans into the political mainstream. While there has been a general shift in political alliance from Democratic to Republican, Sicilian Americans do not favor one party over the other to any great extent.

MILITARY

Sicilian Americans have been represented in the American military in every war from the Civil War to the Persian Gulf. During World War I, many Sicilians had only recently immigrated and there was not a widespread enlistment. Sicilians proved their military worth, however, during World War II, when the island of Sicily played a vital role in the Allied victory. Prior to the Sicilian campaign of 1943, enlisted Sicilian Americans like Max Corvo were able to provide valuable linguistic and technical information that proved beneficial to the campaign.

RELATIONS WITH SICILY

A large number of Sicilians immigrated to the United States in order to escape the terrible economic and political conditions in Sicily. Many Sicilians believed they would eventually return to Sicily. The earlier "return immigrants" cared little about American culture and maintained strong ties with Sicily. But by the time the immigrants had established a firm presence in America, they found themselves alienated from their Sicilian relatives, who called them *Americani*. While the first Sicilian Americans continued to visit their relatives in Sicily, they were increasingly estranged from the Old World Sicilians.

Subsequent generations of the first Sicilian Americans were more committed to American culture and found little in common with their relatives in Sicily. However, some descendants of early Sicilian Americans were interested in exploring their Sicilian roots in an effort to learn more about the culture their immigrant forebears had left behind. Toward the end of the twentieth century, a renewed interest in Sicilian customs and traditions helped fuel a celebration of the distinctiveness of the Sicilian heritage. Currently the City University of New York (CUNY) has a foreign exchange program for students wishing to study in Sicily.

INDIVIDUAL AND GROUP CONTRIBUTIONS

ACADEMIA

Pietro Bachi (1787-1853) was the first to teach the Italian language at Harvard University, his tenure commencing in 1825. Bachi also wrote several books on the Italian, Spanish, and Portugese languages including *A Grammar of the Italian Language* (1829). Like Bachi, Luigi Monti (1830-1914) also taught Italian at Harvard and, like Bachi, he contributed to the academic world with *A Grammar of the Italian Language* (1855). He later became the American consul at Palermo, where he penned his experiences in his book *Adventures of a Consul Abroad* (1878). Josephine Gattuso Hendin became a professor of American literature at New York University. Her book *The World Around Flannery O'Connor* (1970) was highly lauded as was her book *Vulnerable People: A View of American Fiction Since 1945* (1978). She later published a book titled *The Right Thing to Do* (1988), which draws heavily upon her experiences of growing up in a Sicilian household.

FILM

Director Frank Capra (1897-1991) is best known for his nostalgic, optimistic "Capra-esque" movies such as: *It Happened One Night* (1934); *Mr. Deeds Goes to Town* (1936); *You Can't Take It With You*

(1938); *Mr. Smith Goes to Washington* (1939); *Arsenic and Old Lace* (1944); and *It's A Wonderful Life* (1947). Capra was recognized with three Oscars for Best Director, in addition to an Oscar for Best Documentary for his propaganda series *Why We Fight* (1942). Ben Gazzara (1930-) has appeared in *The Strange One* (1957); *Anatomy of a Murder* (1949); and *Husbands* (1970) in addition to his television work on the series *Arrest and Trial* (1963-1964) and *Run for Your Life* (1965-1968). Al Pacino (1940-) has won much acclaim for his portrayal of the stereotypical "Mafia" role. He is perhaps best known for his role in *The Godfather* (1972), for which he received a Academy award nomination for best supporting actor, and for his role in *The Godfather Part II* 1974), for which he received a nomination for best actor. He was also nominated for his performances in *Justice for All* (1979); *Dick Tracy* (1990); and *Glengarry Glen Ross* (1992). He won the Academy award for best actor for his work in *Scent of a Woman* (1992).

MUSIC

Frank Sinatra (1915-1998), recorded more than 800 songs including "I'm Walking Behind You" (1953); "I've Got the World on a String" (1953); "From Here to Eternity" (1953); "Learnin' the Blues" (1955); "Chicago" (1957); "Witchcraft" (1957); and "Nice 'N' Easy" (1960). In the 1940s he began to appear in motion pictures and was soon commanding starring roles. His film credits include *Anchors Aweigh* (1945); *On the Town* (1949); and *From Here to Eternity* (1953), for which he won the best supporting actor award. He also appeared in *The Manchurian Candidate* (1962). He was the recipient of numerous honors, including the Kennedy Center Honors for life achievement in 1983 and the Medal of Freedom in 1985. Nick LaRocca (1889-1961) contributed to the emergence of jazz. He was an inspired cornet player and founded the original "Dixieland Jazz Band." "Livery Stable Blues" and "Tiger Rag" are two of his better-known songs. Natalie Merchant (1963-) achieved international success with her popular rock band the "10,000 Maniacs." By 1987 the band had reached the Top 40 with their acclaimed album *In My Tribe*. In 1995 Merchant launched a solo debut album, *Tigerlily*. The album was well received and the song "Carnival" from that album reached the Top 10. She released a second solo album *Ophelia* in 1998.

SPORTS

Tony Canzonerie (1908-1959) held the featherweight (1928), lightweight (1930-1933, 1935-

1936), and junior welterweight (1931-1932, 1933) world championships in boxing and is considered one of the most fearless, aggressive boxers of all time. He was elected to the Hall of Fame in 1956. Joe DiMaggio (1914-1999), known as the "Yankee Clipper," was one of the most beloved and baseball players. Among his many achievements, he set a record in 1941 with a 56-game hitting streak, won three American League Most Valuable Player awards, and was voted into the Hall of Fame in 1955.

MEDIA

Numerous newspapers and radio broadcasts existed during the years of the Sicilian mass immigration. But as the assimilation of Sicilians into American culture became more complete, the news and radio sources gradually disappeared. While there are no newspapers or radio shows specifically targeted to Sicilian American audiences, the World Wide Web has allowed a growing number of interested Sicilian Americans to access the Sicilian newspapers and live Sicilian radio.

ORGANIZATIONS AND ASSOCIATIONS

Arba Sicula (AS).
Founded in 1979, the organization focuses on the promotion and preservation of the Sicilian language, literature, and culture. In addition to the two journals and two newspapers they publish annually, the Arba Sicula (translated as "Sicilian Dawn") sponsors Sicilian language festivals and special Sicilian-American events.

Contact: Dr. Gaetano Cipolla, President.
Address: Modern Foreign Language Dept., St.
  John's University, Jamaica, New York 11439.
Telephone: (718) 990-6161.

Club Siciliano.
Founded in 1996 on the World Wide Web, the Club Siciliano seeks to preserve and bring about an awareness of the Sicilian culture and heritage. The website provides a listing of Sicilian-American business connections.

Address: P.O. Box 691, Bowling Green Station,
  New York, New York 10006.
E-mail: lsiciliani@aol.com.

Order Sons of Italy (OSIA).
Founded in 1905, the Order Sons of Italy focuses on the preservation of the cultural heritage of Italian Americans, including those of Sicilian ancestry.

Contact: Phillip R. Piccigallo, National Director.
Address: 219 East Street N.E., Washington,
  D.C. 20002.
Telephone: (202) 547-2900.

The National Italian American Foundation (NIAF).
An organization dedicated to protecting and preserving the Italian American heritage and culture, and to strengthing the ties between the United States and Italy.

Contact: Dr. Mario Lombardo.
Address: 1860 19th Street, N.W., Washington,
  D.C. 20009.
Telephone: (202) 387-0600.

MUSEUMS AND RESEARCH CENTERS

Balch Institute for Ethnic Studies.
Houses a formidable library containing valuable information and resources on multicultural groups in the United States, including Sicilian Americans.

Contact: Pamela Nelson, Curator.
Address: 18 South Street, Philadelphia,
  Pennsylvania 19106.
Telephone: (215) 925-8090.

The Center for Migration Studies.
Contains documents relating to the historical and sociodemographic aspects of Sicilian immigrants.

Contact: Dr. Lydio Tomas, Director.
Address: 209 Flagg Place, Staten Island,
  New York 10304.
Telephone: (718) 351-8800.

Immigration History Research Center (IHRC).
Located at the University of Minnesota, the IHRC is a valuable archival source for Siciian Americans; the collection includes newspapers, books, and manuscripts.

Contact: Joel Wurl, Curator.
Address: 826 Berry Street, St. Paul,
  Minnesota 53114.
Telephone: (612) 627-4208.

SOURCES FOR ADDITIONAL STUDY

Customs and Habits of the Sicilian Peasants, edited by Rosalie Norris. London: Associated University Presses, 1981.

Gabaccia, Donna. *From Sicily to Elizabeth Street*. Albany: State University of New York Press, 1984.

————. *Militants and Migrants: Rural Sicilians Become American Workers*. New Brunswick, NJ: Rutgers University Press, 1988.

Johnson, Colleen Leahy. *Growing Up and Growing Old in Italian-American Families*. Rutgers University Press, 1985.

Mangione, Jerre, and Ben Morriale. *La Storia: Five Centuries of the Italian American Experience*. New York: HarperCollins, 1992.

Sammartino, Peter, and William Roberts. *Sicily: An Informal History*. New York: Cornwall, 1992.

The effects of the
racism experienced
by African Americans
and other immigrants
to the United
States have been
minimized because
many Sierra Leonean
Americans are highly
educated and use
English as a first or
second language.

SIERRA LEONEAN AMERICANS

by
Francesca Hampton

OVERVIEW

Sierra Leone is located on what was once called the "Rice Coast" of West Africa. Its 27,699 square miles are bordered by the republics of Guinea to the north and northeast and Liberia to the south. It encompasses areas of heavy rain forest, swamp, plains of open savanna, and hill country, rising to 6390 feet at Loma Mansa (Bintimani) in the Loma Mountains. The country is sometimes referred to in abbreviated form as "Salone" by immigrants. The population is estimated at 5,080,000. Sierra Leone's national flag consists of three equal horizontal bands of color with light green at the top, white in the middle, and light blue on the bottom.

This small country includes the homelands of 20 African peoples, including the Mende, Lokko, Temne, Limba, Susu, Yalunka, Sherbro, Bullom, Krim, Koranko, Kono, Vai, Kissi, Gola, and Fula, the latter having the largest numbers. Its capital, Freetown, was founded as a refuge for repatriated slaves in the eighteenth century. There are also small numbers of Europeans, Syrians, Lebanese, Pakistanis, and Indians in residence. Some 60 percent of Sierra Leoneans are Muslims, 30 percent are traditionalists, and 10 percent are Christian (mostly Anglican and Roman Catholic).

HISTORY

Scholars believe that the earliest inhabitants of Sierra Leone were the Limba and the Capez, or

Sape. As the Mandingo Empire fell under the assault of the Berbers, refugees, including the Susus, Limba, Konos, and Korankos, entered Sierra Leone from the north and east, driving the Bullom peoples to the coast. The Mende, Kono, and Vai tribes of today are descended from invaders who pushed up from the south.

The name Sierra Leone derives from the name Sierra Lyoa, or "Lion Mountain," given to the land in 1462, by the Portuguese explorer Pedro Da Cinta when he observed its wild and forbidding hills. Within Sierra Leone, the Portuguese constructed the first fortified trading stations on the African coast. Like the French, Dutch, and Brandenburgers, they began to trade manufactured goods, rum, tobacco, arms, and ammunition for ivory, gold, and slaves.

In the early part of the sixteenth century, all of these peoples were invaded repeatedly by the Temne. Like the Kissis, the Temne are a Bantu people speaking a language related to Swahili. They moved south from Guinea after the breakup of the Songhai empire. Led by Bai Farama, the Temnes attacked the Susus, Limbas and Mende, as well as the Portuguese and created a strong state along the trade route from Port Loko to the Sudan and Niger. They sold many of these conquered peoples to the Europeans as slaves. In the late sixteenth century the Susus, who were converting to Islam, revolted against the Christian Temnes and set up their own state on the Scarcies River. From there, they dominated the Temnes, converting many of them to Islam. Another Islamic theocratic state in the northwest was established by the Fulas, who often attacked and enslaved nonbelievers among the Yalunka.

Taking advantage of the warfare, British slavers arrived on the Sierra Leone River during the late sixteenth century and erected factories and forts on Sherbro, Bunce, and Tasso islands. These islands were often the last view that Sierra Leoneans had of their native land before being sent into slavery in the Americas. European slave agents hired African and mulatto mercenaries to help them capture villagers or purchase them as debtors or prisoners of war from local chiefs. Relations between these groups were not always friendly. In 1562, Temne warriors reneged on a deal with a European slave trader and drove him away with a fleet of war canoes.

As controversy over the ethics of the slave trade arose in Britain, the English abolitionist Granville Sharp convinced the British government to repatriate a group of freed slaves onto land purchased from Temne chiefs on the Sierra Leone peninsula. These first settlers arrived in May of 1787 in what would become the capital of Sierra Leone, Freetown. In 1792, they were joined by 1200 freed American slaves who had fought with the British army in the American Revolutionary War. Unhappy with the land that they had been offered in Nova Scotia at the war's conclusion, these black loyalists sent ex-slave Thomas Peters on a protest mission to Britain. The Sierra Leone Company, now in charge of the new colony, helped them return to Africa.

The arrival of these ex-slaves marked the beginning of a culture uniquely influential in West Africa called *Creole*, or "Krio." Along with a steady influx of native Sierra Leoneans from the interior tribes, more than 80,000 other Africans displaced by the slave trade joined those in Freetown during the next century. In 1807, the British parliament voted to end the slave trade and Freetown soon became a crown colony and an enforcement port. British naval vessels based there upheld the ban on slave trading and captured numerous outbound slavers. The Africans released from the holds of slave ships were settled in Freetown and in nearby villages. In a few decades this new Krio society, who were English- and Creole-speaking, educated and predominantly Christian, with a sub-group of Yoruba Muslims, began to influence the whole coast and even the interior of West Africa as they became teachers, missionaries, traders, administrators and artisans. By the middle of the nineteenth century, according to the *Encyclopedia of Africa South of the Sahara*, they had formed "the nucleus of the bourgeoisie of late nineteenth-century coastal British West Africa."

Sierra Leone gradually gained its independence from Britain. Beginning in 1863, native Sierra Leoneans were given representation in the government of Freetown. Limited free elections were held in the city in 1895. Sixty years later the right to vote was extended to the interior, where many tribes had long traditions of participatory decision-making. Full independence was granted to Sierra Leone in 1961. As a new tradition of elective democratic government became firmly established throughout the country, interior tribes such as the Mende, Temne, and Limba gradually regained a dominant position in politics.

MODERN ERA

Sierra Leone's first years as an independent democracy were very successful, thanks to the benevolent leadership of her first prime minister, Sir Milton Magai. He encouraged a free press and honest debate in Parliament and welcomed nationwide participation in the political process. When Milton Magai died in 1964, he was succeeded by his half-brother, Albert Magai, head of the Sierra Leone People's Party (SLPP). Attempting to establish a one-party state and accused of corruption, the SLPP lost the next election in 1967 to an opposition party, the All People's Congress (APC), led by Siaka Stevens. Stevens was unseated briefly by a military coup but returned to power in 1968, this time with the title of president. Although popular in his first years in power, Stevens lost much influence in the latter years of his regime through his government's reputation for corruption and the use of intimidation to stay in power. Siaka Stevens was succeeded in 1986 by his hand-picked successor, Major General Joseph Saidu Momoh, who worked to liberalize the political system, restore the faltering economy, and return Sierra Leone to a multi-party democracy. Unfortunately, events on the border with Liberia in 1991 defeated Momoh's efforts and ushered in what has become almost a full decade of civil strife.

Allied with the Liberian forces of Charles Taylor's Patriotic Front, a small group of Sierra Leonean rebels calling themselves the Revolutionary United Front (RUF) crossed the Liberian border in 1991. Distracted by this rebellion, Momoh's APC party was overthrown in a military coup led by Valentine Strasser, leader of the National Provisional Ruling Council (NPRC). Under Strasser's rule, some members of the Sierra Leonean army began to loot villages. Large numbers of villagers began to die of starvation as the economy was disrupted. As the army's organization weakened, the RUF advanced. By 1995, it was on the outskirts of Freetown. In a frantic attempt to hold onto power, the NPRC hired a South African mercenary firm, Executive Outcomes, to reinforce the army. The RUF suffered significant losses and were forced to retreat to their base camp.

Strasser was eventually overthrown by his deputy, Julius Bio, who held long-promised democratic elections. In 1996, the people of Sierra Leone chose their first freely elected leader in three decades, President Ahmad Tejan Kabbah. Kabbah was able to negotiate a peace agreement with the RUF rebels, but the results were short-lived. Another coup rocked the country, and Kabbah was overthrown by a faction of the army calling itself the Armed Forces Revolutionary Council (AFRC). They suspended the constitution and arrested, killed, or tortured those who resisted. Diplomats throughout Sierra Leone fled the country. Many Sierra Leonean citizens launched a campaign of passive resistance to the AFRC. The brutal stalemate was broken when troops from Nigeria, Guinea, Ghana, and Mali, part of the Economic Council of West African States Monitoring Group (ECOMOG), routed the AFRC and restored Kabbah to power in 1998.

Although the AFRC was defeated, the RUF remained a destructive force. The RUF embarked on a campaign of renewed terror called "No Living Thing." According to testimony reprinted on a Sierra Leone website, on June 11, 1998, Ambassador Johnnie Carson told the U.S. House of Representatives subcommittee on Africa "The RUF threw [a five-year-old boy who survived] and 60 other villagers into a human bonfire. Hundreds of civilians have escaped to Freetown with arms, feet, hands, and ears amputated by the rebels." The ambassador also reported accounts that the RUF has forced children to participate in the torture and killing of their parents before being drafted as soldier trainees. A fragile peace agreement was eventually brokered between the Kabbah government and the RUF to end the fighting in Sierra Leone.

While many still hope for a better future, the violence in Sierra Leone during the 1990s has severely damaged Sierra Leonean society. Between one and two million Sierra Leoneans were internally displaced and almost 300,000 have sought refuge in Guinea, Liberia, or other countries, including the United States. The traditional, rice-farming villagers of the interior have become more alienated from the better-educated, wealthier elite of Freetown. Ethnic hostilities between elements of the majority Mende, the Temne, and other groups, have worsened because of the civil war.

THE FIRST SIERRA LEONEANS IN AMERICA

In the film *Family Across the Sea*, anthropologist Joe Opala presents several proofs connecting Sierra Leone to a unique group of African Americans whose way of life centers on the coasts and Sea Islands of the Carolinas and Georgia. These are the Gullah, or (in Georgia) Geechee, speakers, descendants of slaves imported from Barbados or directly from Africa to work rice plantations along the southeast coast of the United States beginning in the eighteenth century. It is estimated that approximately 24 percent of slaves brought into the area came from Sierra Leone, prized by buyers in Charleston specifically for their skills as rice farmers. Professor Opala has found letters establishing the facts of this regular commerce between South Carolina plantation owner Henry Lawrence and Richard Oswald, his English slave agent resident on Bunce Island in the Sierra Leone River.

Between 1787 and 1804, it was illegal to bring new slaves into the United States. However, a second infusion of 23,773 Africans came into South Carolina between 1804 and 1807, as new cotton plantations on the Sea Islands began to expand their need for labor, and landowners petitioned the South Carolina legislature to reopen the trade. Africans from Sierra Leone and other parts of West Africa continued to be kidnapped or purchased by renegade slavers long after the importation of Africans was made permanently illegal in the United States in 1808. The coastlines of South Carolina and Georgia, with their numerous rivers, islands, and swamps, provided secret landing sites for the underground sale of slaves. The fact that Sierra Leoneans were among these slaves is documented by the famous court case of the *Amistad*. In 1841, illegally captured Mendes, Temnes, and members of other tribes managed to take control of their slave ship, the *Amistad*. The *Amistad* eventually reached American waters and those on the ship were able to secure their freedom after the U.S. Supreme Court ruled in their favor.

SIGNIFICANT IMMIGRATION WAVES

During the 1970s, a new group of Sierra Leoneans began to enter the United States. Most were granted student visas to study in American universities. Some of these students chose to remain in the United States by obtaining legal residence status or marrying American citizens. Many of these Sierra Leoneans are highly educated and entered the fields of law, medicine, and accountancy.

In the 1980s, an increasing number of Sierra Leoneans entered the United States to escape the economic and political hardships in their homeland. While many continued to pursue their education, they also worked to help support family members at home. While some returned to Sierra Leone at the end of their studies, others sought resident status so that they could continue to work in the United States.

By 1990, 4,627 American citizens and residents reported their first ancestry as Sierra Leonean. When civil war swept through Sierra Leone during the 1990s, a new wave of immigrants came to the United States. Many of these immigrants gained access through visitor or student visas. This trend continued between 1990 and 1996, as 7,159 more Sierra Leoneans legally entered the United States. After 1996, some refugees from Sierra Leone were able to enter the United States with immediate legal residence status, as beneficiaries of the immigration lotteries. Others received the newly established Priority 3 designation for refugees with close family links in the United States. The United Nations High Commission for Refugees estimates that for 1999, the annual number of Sierra Leoneans resettled may reach 2,500.

SETTLEMENT PATTERNS

Large numbers of Gullah-speaking American citizens, many of who are of Sierra Leonean descent, continue to live in the Sea Islands and the coastal areas of South Carolina and Georgia. Some islands with significant populations are Hilton Head, St. Helena, and Wadmalaw. In the decades before the American Civil War, many Gullah/Geechee-speaking slaves attempted to escape from their South Carolina and Georgian plantations. Of these, many went south, taking refuge with the Creek Indians in Florida. Along with the Creeks and other embattled tribes, they created the society of the Seminoles and retreated deeper into the Florida swamps. Following the Second Seminole War, which lasted from 1835 to 1842, many Sierra Leoneans joined their Native American allies on the "Trail of Tears" to Wewoka in Oklahoma territory. Others followed Wild Cat, the son of Seminole chief King Phillip, to a Seminole colony in Mexico across the Rio Grande from Eagle Pass, Texas. Still others remained in Florida and assimilated into Seminole culture.

The largest concentration of Sierra Leonean immigrants lives in the Baltimore-Washington, D.C., metropolitan area. Other sizable enclaves exist in the suburbs of Alexandria, Fairfax, Arlington, Falls Church, and Woodbridge in Virginia, and in Landover, Lanham, Cheverly, Silver Spring, and Bethesda in Maryland. There are also Sierra Leonean communities in the Boston and Los Angeles metropolitan areas, and in New Jersey, Florida, Pennsylvania, New York, Texas, and Ohio.

ACCULTURATION AND ASSIMILATION

The Gullah/Geechee people were able to preserve some of their original language, culture, and identity for a number of reasons. First, unlike most other enslaved African peoples, they managed to remain together in large concentrations. This was initially a result of their expertise as rice planters at a time when few white laborers had these skills. Buyers sought out Sierra Leonean captives in the slave markets specifically for this ability. According to Opala, "It was African technology which created the intricate dikes and waterways which transformed the low country marshes of the southeast coast into thousands of acres of rice farms." A second reason for the preservation of Gullah culture in America was that the slaves had a greater resistance to malaria and other tropical diseases than whites. Lastly, there were large numbers of Sierra Leoneans living in the South. In St. Helena Parish, for example, the population of slaves in the first ten years of the nineteenth century grew by 86 percent. The ratio of blacks to whites in Beaufort, South Carolina was almost five to one. This ratio was higher in some areas, and black overseers managed whole plantations while the owners resided elsewhere.

As the American Civil War ended in 1865, opportunities for the Gullah to buy land in the isolated Sea Islands were far greater than for African Americans on the mainland. Although the parcels rarely exceeded ten acres, they allowed their owners to avoid the type of sharecropping and tenant farming that characterized the lives of most African Americans during the Jim Crow years. "The 1870 Census shows that 98 percent of St. Helena's population of 6,200 was black and that 70 percent owned their own farms," wrote Patricia Jones-Jackson in *When Roots Die*.

Since the 1950s, however, Gullahs residing on the Sea Islands have been adversely affected by an influx of resort developers and the construction of bridges to the mainland. On many islands where the Gullah once represented an overwhelming majority of the population, they now face minority status. However, there has been a resurgence of interest in Gullah heritage and identity, and strong efforts are being made to keep the culture alive.

Recent immigrants from Sierra Leone, while scattered over a variety of states, tend to congregate in small communities for mutual support . Many socialize or celebrate customs that bring them together regularly. The re-emergence in some cases of family and tribal support networks has made the transition to a new country easier than it might have been. The effects of the racism experienced by African Americans and other immigrants to the United States have been minimized because many Sierra Leonean Americans are highly educated and use English as a first or second language. Although it is not uncommon for newer arrivals to work two or three jobs to support themselves and their families in Sierra Leone, others have been able to attain respect and professional status in a variety of well-paid careers. Sierra Leonean Americans have also benefited greatly from the friendship and support of many former Peace Corps volunteers who served in Sierra Leone beginning in the 1960s.

TRADITIONS, CUSTOMS, AND BELIEFS

In Sierra Leone, it is considered rude to look directly into the eyes of a social superior. Therefore, commoners do not look directly at their rulers, nor do wives look directly at their husbands. When a farmer wishes to start working at a new site, he may consult a sorcerer (Krio, *lukin-grohn man*). If devils are found to be in possession of an area, they might be placated with a sacrifice such as rice flour or a bell suspended from a frame on a cord of white satin. The first soft rice of a harvest is beaten to make flour *gbafu* and set out for the farm's devils. This gbafu is then wrapped in a leaf and put under a *senje* tree or a stone for sharpening machetes, as it is believed that this stone also contains a devil. Another custom is designed to ward off the *kaw kaw* bird, which is a large bat, that is considered to be a witch that sucks the blood of small children. To protect a child, a string is tied around its torso and charms are hung from it with verses from the Koran wrapped in leaves. The Krios also have their own wedding custom. Three days before a wedding, a bride's prospective in-laws bring her a calabash containing a needle, beans (or copper coins), and kola nuts to remind her that she is expected to be a good housewife, look after their son's money, bring him good luck, and bear many children.

The Gullah/Geechee tradition of making *fanner*, which are flat, tightly woven, circular sweetgrass baskets, is one of the most visible links between that culture and West African culture. These baskets have been sold in city markets and on the streets of Charleston since the 1600s. In Sierra Leone, these baskets are still used to winnow rice. Another holdover from West African tradition is the belief that recently deceased relatives may have the power to intercede in the spirit world and punish wrongs.

PROVERBS

A rich variety of proverbs exist in the Sierra Leonean languages, and witty exchanges of proverbs are a conversational tradition. Krio, the most common language spoken by Sierra Leoneans, contains some of the most colorful proverbs: *Inch no in masta, kabasloht no in misis*—An implication knows its master (just as) a dress knows its mistress. This proverb is used to warn people that you are aware they are speaking about you. *Ogiri de laf kenda foh smehl*—Ogiri laughs at kenda on account of its smell. (Kenda and ogiri, when uncooked, are both rank-smelling seasonings). *Mohnki tahk, mohnki yehri*–Monkey talks, monkey listens. (Persons who think alike will understand one another). *We yu bohs mi yai, a chuk yu wes* (Kono)—An eye for an eye, a tooth for a tooth. *Bush noh de foh trwoe bad pikin*—Bad children may not be thrown into the bush. (No matter how bad a child may act, he can't be disowned by his family.) A Temne proverb runs, "The snake that bites a Mende man gets turned into soup for the Mende man."

CUISINE

Rice is still a staple both in Sierra Leone and among immigrants to the United States. Another common staple is cassava prepared with palm oil in stews and sauces. This is often combined with rice, chicken, and/or okra and may be eaten at breakfast, lunch, or dinner. Among the Gullah of the Sea Islands, rice also forms the basis of all three meals. It is combined with different meats, gumbos, greens, and sauces, many still prepared and eaten according to the old traditions, although, unlike in Sierra Leone, pork or bacon is a frequent addition. A popular Gullah recipe is Frogmore Stew, which contains smoked beef sausage, corn, crabs, shrimp, and seasonings. Sierra Leoneans also enjoy Prawn Palava, a recipe that contains onions, tomatoes, peanuts, thyme, chili peppers, spinach, and prawns. It is usually served with boiled yams and rice.

MUSIC

With its colorful mixture of African and Western cultures, Sierra Leonean music is extremely creative and varied and forms an essential part of daily life both in Freetown and the interior. The instruments are dominated by a great variety of drums. Drumming groups may also include a lively mix of castanets, beaten bells, and even wind instruments. Sierra Leoneans from northern parts of the country, the Korankos, add a type of xylophone, the *balangi*. Another popular instrument is the *seigureh*, which consists of stones in a rope-bound calabash. The seigureh is used to provide background rhythm. Longer musical pieces are guided by a master drummer and contain embedded signals within the overall rhythm that indicate major changes in tempo. Some pieces may add the continuous blowing of a whistle as a counterpoint. In Freetown, traditional tribal music has given way to various calypso styles that incorporate Western instruments such as the saxophone. In the United States, many Sierra Leonean music and dance traditions are kept alive by the Ko-thi Dance Company of Madison, Wisconsin. Groups like the Beaufort, South Carolina, Hallelujah Singers perform and record traditional Gullah music.

TRADITIONAL COSTUMES

Costumes worn by members of the Krio culture have a Victorian flavor. Western dress from school uniforms to suits may also be worn in a strict British style or with creative variations and brighter colors. Among working-class men in Freetown, vividly patterned shirts and shorts predominate. Men from the interior villages may wear only a loincloth or dress in elegant white or brightly colored robes that sweep along the ground. Headgear is also common and may consist of wrapped cloth in a Muslim style, western style hats, or ornate circular caps. Among women, *cabbaslot* dresses, which are long and have puffed sleeves, are sometimes popular. Tribal women generally favor wrapped headgear and a two-piece costume that consists of a skirt, or *lappa*, and a blouse, or *booba*. The way in which these garments are worn varies according to tribe. In the Mende culture, for example, the *booba* is tucked in. Among the Temne, it is worn more loosely. Mandingo women may sport a double ruffle around a lowered neckline and sometimes wear their blouses off-shoulder.

DANCES AND SONGS

One hallmark of Sierra Leonean culture is the incorporation of dance into all parts of life. A bride may dance on her way to the home of her new husband. A family may dance at the grave of one who has been dead three days. According to Roy Lewis in *Sierra Leone: A Modern Portrait*, "The dance is ... the principal medium of folk art; it is the one which European influences are least likely to affect. There are dances for every occasion, for every age and both sexes." Because rice serves as one of the foundations of Sierra Leone's economy, many dances incorporate the movements used to farm and harvest this crop. Other dances celebrate the actions of warriors and may involve dancing with swords and catching them out of the air. *Buyan* is the "dance of happiness," a delicate interchange between two teenage girls dressed entirely in white and wearing red kerchiefs. The *fetenke* is danced by two young boys, moving heel to toe and waving black scarves. At times, whole communities may come together to dance in celebration of the Muslim festival of *Eid-ul-Fitri* or the culmination of Poro or Sande secret society initiations. These dances are usually led by master drummers and dancers. For Sierra Leonean Americans, dancing continues to be a defining part of many gatherings and a joyful part of daily life.

HEALTH ISSUES

Sierra Leone, like many tropical countries, is home to a variety of diseases. Because of the civil war, which destroyed many health care facilities, health conditions have worsened in Sierra Leone. Advisories issued in 1998 by the Centers for Disease Control warned travelers to Sierra Leone that malaria, measles, cholera, typhoid fever, and Lassa fever were prevalent throughout the country. The World Health Organization continues to recommend vaccinations for yellow fever for those who enter the country and warns that exposure to insects can result in filariasis, leishmaniasis, or onchocerciasis, although the risk is low. Swimming in fresh water may bring exposure to the schistosomiasis parasite.

Another health issue affecting the Sierra Leonean American population has been the controversy surrounding the practice of female circumcision. Seventy-five percent of Sierra Leonean women are said to uphold the practice which involves removing the clitoris, as well the labia majora and minora of prepubescent girls, often in unhygienic conditions and usually without anesthetic. Organizations such as the National Council of Muslim Women and the secret Bondo Society defend the practice. A leading spokesperson for female circumcision, Haja Isha Sasso, argues that "the rite of female circumcision is sacred, feared and respected. It is a religion to us." Josephine Macauley, a staunch opponent of female circumcision, remarked in the *Electronic Mail & Guardian* that the practice is "cruel, unprogressive and a total abuse of the children's rights." Many prominent Americans have criticized the practice, calling it genital mutilation not circumcision, and some Sierra Leonean women have sought refuge against it.

LANGUAGE

Because of its long colonial association with Britain, Sierra Leone's official language is English, and most Sierra Leonean Americans speak it as a first or second language. Fifteen other tribal languages and numerous dialects are also spoken. These languages fall into two separate groups. The first is the *Mande* language group, which resembles Mandinka in structure, and includes Mende, Susu, Yalunka, Koranko, Kono, and Vai. The second group is the *semi bantu* group, which includes Temne, Limba, Bullom (or Sherbro), and Krim. The melodic Krio language is also widely spoken by Sierra Leonean Americans. Krio was created in Freetown from a blend of various European and tribal languages. With the exception of the passive voice, Krio utilizes a full complement of verb tenses. The grammar and pronunciation of Krio is similar to many African languages.

The language spoken by the Gullah/Geechee people of coastal South Carolina and Georgia is very similar to Krio. The Gullah language retains a great deal West African syntax and combines English vocabulary with words from African languages such as Ewe, Mandinka, Igbo, Twi, Yoruba, and Mende. Much of the grammar and pronunciation of the Gullah languages has been modified to fit African patterns.

GREETINGS AND OTHER POPULAR EXPRESSIONS

Some of the more popular Gullah expressions include: *beat on ayun*, mechanic—literally, "beat on iron"; *troot ma-wt*, a truthful person—literally, "truth mouth"; *sho ded*, cemetery—literally, "sure dead"; *tebl tappa*, preacher—literally, "table tapper"; *Ty ooonuh ma-wt*, Hush, stop talking—literally, "tie your mouth"; *krak teet*, to speak—literally, "crack teeth" and *I han shaht pay-shun*, He steals—literally, "His hand is short of patience."

Popular Krio expressions include: *nar way e lib-well*, because things are easy with him; *pikin*, an infant (from picanninny, anglicized from the Spanish); *pequeno nino*, little child; *plabba*, or *palaver*, trouble or the discussion of trouble (from the French word "palabre,"); and *Long rod no kil nobodi*, A long road kills no one.

FAMILY AND COMMUNITY DYNAMICS

Family and clan relationships are extremely important to Sierra Leoneans living in the United States. According to Roy Lewis, "What belongs to one, belongs to all, and a man has no right to refuse to take in a relative or share his meal or his money with a relative. This is the African social tradition." In traditional villages, the basic social unit was the *mawei*, or (in Mende) *mavei*. The mawei included a man, his wife or wives, and their children. For wealthier men, it might also include junior brothers and their wives and unmarried sisters. Wives were lodged, whenever possible, in several houses or *pe wa*. If wives lived together in a house, the senior wife supervised the junior wives. Since polygamy is illegal in the United States, these marriage customs have created a serious problem in some immigrant households. In a few cases, the polygamous relationships have been continued secretly or on an informal basis.

Generally, a Sierra Leonean man has a special relationship to his mother's brother, or *kenya*. The kenya is expected to help him, especially in making his marriage payment. In many cases, the man marries the kenya's daughter. The father's brothers are respected as "little fathers." His daughters are regarded as a man's sisters. Sisters of both parents are considered "little mothers," and it is not uncommon for a child to be raised by nearby relatives rather than by his own parents. To varying degrees, Sierra Leoneans in the United States have maintained connections to clans, and several support groups based on ethnic or chieftaincy affiliations have formed, such as the Foulah Progressive Union and the Krio Heritage Society.

Within the Gullah/Geechee community, spouses brought into the community from the outside world are often not trusted or accepted for many years. Disputes within the community are largely resolved in the churches and "praise houses." Deacons and ministers often intervene and try to resolve the conflict without punishing either party. Taking cases to courts outside the community is frowned upon. After marriage, a couple generally builds a house in or nearby the "yard" of the husband's parents. A yard is a large area that may grow into a true clan site if several sons bring spouses, and even grandchildren may grow up and return to the group. When the dwellings consist of mobile homes, they are often placed in kinship clusters.

EDUCATION

Education is highly valued within the Sierra Leonean immigrant community. Many immigrants enter the United States with student visas or after earning degrees from British universities or from Fourah Bay College in Freetown. Recent immigrants attend school as soon as economic stability of the family is achieved. Many Sierra Leonean immigrant children also receive education in their cultural traditions through initiation into the cross-tribal Poro (for boys) and Sande (for girls) secret societies.

Some members of the Gullah/Geechee peoples have earned college degrees at mainland universities. As the Sea Islands have become increasingly developed, mainstream white culture has had a tremendous impact on the Gullah educational system. However, Gullah language and traditions are still energetically preserved and promoted by organizations such as the Gullah/Geechee Sea Island Coalition and by the Penn Center at Penn School on St. Helena Island.

BIRTH

Although most Sierra Leonean American births now occur in hospitals, the delivery of a child traditionally took place far from men, and the mother would be assisted by the women of the Sande society. After the birth, soothsayers were consulted to speak about the child's future and offerings were made to the ancestors. Regardless of family religion, a Sierra Leonean infant is presented to the community one week after birth in a ceremony called *Pull-na-door* (put out the door). Family members gather to name the child and celebrate its arrival into the world. In preparation, beans, water, chicken, and plantain are put on stools and on the floor overnight as offerings to the ancestors. The child is often suckled until the age of three. Twins may be considered to have special powers and are both admired and feared.

THE ROLE OF WOMEN

Women generally occupy lower positions than men in Sierra Leonean society, although there are instances of women being selected as chief of the Mende culture. When a women is chosen to be chief, she is not allowed to marry. However, she is permitted to take consorts. Women can also attain a high position in the Bundu, a woman's society which guards the rites of circumcision, or the Humoi Society, which guards kinship rules. Unless she is a senior wife, a woman has relatively little say in a polygamous household. In traditional culture, women in their early teens are generally wedded to men in their thirties. Divorce is permitted, but children are often required to live with the father. It was the custom in the Mende culture that a widow, although she might follow Christian burial rites, could also make a mudpack with the water used to wash the husband's corpse and smear herself with it. When the mud was washed off, all of her husband's proprietary rights were removed as well, and she could marry again. Any woman who does not marry is looked on with disapproval. In the United States, the status of Sierra Leonean women is improving as some attain college degrees and professional status.

COURTSHIP AND WEDDINGS

Sierra Leonean marriages traditionally have been arranged by the parents with the permission of the Humoi Society, which enforced the rules against incest in the villages. In Sierra Leone such an engagement could even be made with an infant or small child, called a *nyahanga*, or "mushroom wife." A suitor made a marriage payment called a *mboya*. Once betrothed, he took immediate responsibility for the girl's education, including the payment of fees for her Sande initiation training. A girl might refuse to marry this man when she came of age. If she did so, however, the man must be repaid for all expenses incurred. Among poorer men and immigrants to the United States, courtship frequently begins with friendship. Cohabitation is permitted, but any children who are born into this relationship belong to the woman's family if a mboya has not been paid.

Relationships outside of marriage are not uncommon in polygamous situations. For men, this can mean the risk of being fined for "woman damage" if he is caught with a married woman. When a couple who is in an extramarital relationship appears in public, the man refers to the woman as his *mbeta*, which means sister-in-law. When they are alone together, he may call her *sewa ka mi*, loved one, and she may call him *han ka mi*, sigh of mine.

When a husband is ready to take possession of his wife and the bride price has been paid, it was the Mende custom for the girl's mother to spit on her daughter's head and bless her. The bride was then taken, dancing, to her husband's door. In the United States, especially among Christians, a Western-style wedding may be performed.

FUNERALS

According to Krio custom, the burial of a person's body does not represent the end of the funeral service. The person's spirit is believed to reside in a vulture's body and cannot "cross over" without conducting additional ceremonies three days, seven days, and 40 days after death. Hymns and wailing begin at sunrise on those days, and cold, pure water and crushed *agiri* are left at the gravesite. There are also memorial services held for a departed ancestor on both the fifth and tenth anniversary of death. The Gullah believe that it is very important to be buried close to family and friends, usually in dense woods. Some families still practice the old tradition of placing articles on the grave that the dead person might need in the afterlife, such as spoons and dishes.

INTERACTIONS WITH OTHER ETHNIC GROUPS

In the United States, Sierra Leoneans commonly marry and make friends outside of their own clan. Friendships are usually formed with other African immigrants, as well as former Peace Corps volunteers who once served in Sierra Leone. Among the Gullah people, there has been a long association with various Native American peoples. Over time, the Gullah intermarried with descendants of the Yamasee, the Apalachicola, the Yuchi, and the Creeks.

RELIGION

An essential element in all Sierra Leonean spiritual traditions is the respect and homage paid to ancestors. In the ongoing conflict between good and evil forces, ancestors can intervene to advise, help, or punish enemies. Evil human beings or deceased persons who were not correctly helped to "cross over" may return as harmful spirits. Villagers must also contend with a large variety of nature spirits and other "devils." Sierra Leonean American immigrants retain these beliefs to varying degrees. Of the major tribes, the Temnes, the Fulas, and the Susus are largely Muslim. Most Krio are Christians, mainly Anglican or Methodist.

The Gullah are devout Christians, and churches such as the Hebrew United Presbyterian and the Baptist or African Methodist Episcopal form the center of community life. One specifically African belief, however, is retained in a tripartite human being consisting of a body, a soul and a spirit. When the body dies, the soul may go on to heaven while the spirit remains to influence the living. The Gullah also believe in voodoo or hoodoo. Good or evil spirits may be summoned in rituals to offer predictions, kill enemies, or perform cures.

EMPLOYMENT AND ECONOMIC TRADITIONS

Since the Civil War, Gullah/Geechee communities in the southern United States have traditionally relied on their own farming and fishing activities in order to earn a living. They sell produce in Charleston and Savannah, and some take seasonal jobs on the mainland as commercial fishermen, loggers, or dock workers. During the 1990s, life on the Sea Islands began to change as developers started to build tourist resorts. A dramatic rise in land values on some islands, while increasing the worth of Gullah holdings, led to increased taxes and many Gullah were forced to sell their land. Increasingly, Gullah students have become a minority in local schools and discover that, upon graduation, the only jobs available to them are as service workers at the resorts. "Developers just come in and roll over them and change their culture, change their way of life, destroy the environment and therefore the culture has to be changed, " remarked Emory Campbell, former director of the Penn Center on St. Helena Island.

In large metropolitan areas, where the majority of immigrants from Sierra Leone have settled, many Sierra Leoneans have earned college degrees and entered a variety of professions. New immigrants often come to the United States with a strong desire to succeed. Sierra Leoneans commonly take entry-level jobs as taxi drivers, cooks, nursing assistants and other service workers. Many go on to higher education or start their own businesses, although the responsibility to support family members at home can slow their progress toward these goals.

POLITICS AND GOVERNMENT

Few Sierra Leonean immigrants have served in the U.S. military, although Gullah/Geechee men did participate in military service during the Vietnam War. Sierra Leonean immigrants remain very interested in the political turmoil that has devastated their homeland. Many Sierra Leonean Americans continue to send financial support to their relatives back home. Numerous organizations have been formed to try to assist Sierra Leoneans. Sierra Leonean Americans have also created several Internet sites to disseminate news about the latest events within their home country. The largest site is the Sierra Leone Web. Since a 1989 visit by then-President Momoh to the Sea Islands, there has been a marked increase in interest among the Gullah in their Sierra Leonean roots. Before the outbreak of the civil war, Sierra Leonean Americans returned often to their homeland and were welcomed as long-lost relatives.

INDIVIDUAL AND GROUP CONTRIBUTIONS

ACADEMIA

Dr. Cecil Blake was an Associate Professor of Communication and Chairperson of the Department of Communication at Indiana Northwest University. Marquetta Goodwine was a Gullah historian, associated with the Afrikan Cultural Arts Network (AKAN). She also wrote and produced "Breakin da Chains" to share the Gullah experience in drama and song.

EDUCATION

Amelia Broderick was the United States Information Services Director at the American Cultural Center. She was an American citizen who has served as a former diplomat to New Guinea, South Africa, and Benin.

JOURNALISM

Kwame Fitzjohn was an African correspondent for the BBC.

LITERATURE

Joel Chandler Harris (1848-1908) wrote a number of books, including: *The Complete Tales of Uncle Remus, Free Joe, and Other Georgian Sketches* and *On the Plantation: A Story of a Georgia Boy's Adventures During the War.* Yulisa Amadu Maddy (1936–) wrote *African Images in Juvenile Literature: Commentaries on Neocolonialist Fiction* and *No Past, No Present, No Future.*

MUSIC

Fern Caulker wa the founder of the Ko-thi Dance Co in Madison, Wisconsin. David Pleasant was a Gullah music griot and African American master drummer.

SOCIAL ISSUES

Sangbe Peh (Cinque) was well-known in the United States for his leadership in the takeover of the slave ship *Amistad* in 1841. In the U.S. Supreme Court, with the help of ex-president John Quincy Adams, he successfully maintained the rights of Sierra Leoneans and other Africans to defend themselves against illegal capture by slave smugglers.

John Lee was the Sierra Leonean Ambassador to the United States, and was a lawyer, diplomat, and businessman who owned Xerox of Nigeria.

Dr. Omotunde Johnson was the Division Head in the International Monetary Fund.

MEDIA

PRINT

The Gullah Sentinel.
Established by Jabari Moteski in 1997. 2,500 copies are distributed bi-weekly throughout Beaufort County, South Carolina.

TELEVISION.

Ron and Natalie Daisie, known for live presentations of Sea Island folklore, recently created a children's series, *Gullah Gullah Island*, for the Nickelodeon Television Network.

ORGANIZATIONS AND ASSOCIATIONS

Friends of Sierra Leone (FOSL).

FOSL is a non-profit membership organization incorporated in Washington, D.C. Formed in 1991 by a small group of former Peace Corps volunteers, FOSL has two missions: 1) To educate Americans and others about Sierra Leone and current events in Salone, as well as about her peoples, cultures and history; 2) To support small-scale development and relief projects in Sierra Leone.

Contact: P.O. Box 15875, Washington, DC 20003.
E-mail: FOSL@erols.com.

Gbonkolenken Descendants Organization (GDO).

The aim of the organization is to help develop the Gbonkolenken Chiefdom in the Tonkolili South Constituency through education, health projects, and food relief for its residents.

Address: 120 Taylor Run Parkway, Alexandria, Virginia 22312.
Contact: Jacob Conteh, Associate Social Secretary.
E-mail: Saxss@aol.com.

Koinadugu Descendant Organization (KDO).

The aim and objectives of the organization are 1) to promote understanding among Koinadugans in particular and other Sierra Leoneans in North America in general, 2) to provide financial and moral support to deserving Koinadugans in Sierra Leone, 3) to come to the aid of members in good standing whenever the need arises, and 4) to foster good relationship among all Koinadugans. The KDO is currently undertaking to secure medicines, food, and clothing for the victims of conflict in Koinadugu District in particular and Sierra Leone in general.

Contact: Abdul Silla Jalloh, Chairman.
Address: P.O. Box 4606, Capital Heights, Maryland 20791.
Telephone: (301) 773-2108.
Fax: (301) 773-2108.
E-mail: sillaj@tidalwave.net.

The Kono Union-USA, Inc. (KONUSA).

Was formed to: educate the American public about the culture and development potential of the Republic of Sierra Leone; develop and promote programs of the Kono District in the Eastern Province of the Republic of Sierra Leone; and undertake educational, social, and cultural enrichment programs that shall benefit the members of the organization.

Contact: Aiah Fanday, President.
Address: P. O. Box 7478, Langley Park, Maryland 20787.
Telephone: (301) 881-8700.
E-mail: fanday@aol.com.

Leonenet Street Children Project Inc.

Its mission is to provide foster care for orphaned and homeless child victims of war in Sierra Leone. The organization works with the government of Sierra Leone, interested NGO's, and individuals to meet this end.

Contact: Dr. Samuel Hinton, Ed.D., Coordinator.
Address: 326 Timothy Way, Richmond, Kentucky 40475.
Telephone: (606) 626-0099.
E-mail: eadhintn@acs.eku.edu.

The Sierra Leone Progressive Union.

This organization was founded in 1994 to promote education, welfare, and cooperation among Sierra Leoneans at home and abroad.

Contact: Pa Santhikie Kanu, Chairman.
Address: P.O. Box 9164, Alexandria, Virginia 22304.
Telephone: (301) 292-8935.
E-mail: slpu@juno.com.

The Sierra Leone Women's Movement for Peace.

The Sierra Leone Women's Movement for Peace is a division of the parent organization based in Sierra Leone. The United States division decided that their first priority is to aid in the education of children and women affected by this senseless rebel war. Membership is open to all Sierra Leonean women, and support from all Sierra Leoneans and friends of Sierra Leone is welcomed.

Contact: Jarieu Fatima Bona, Chairperson.
Address: P.O. Box 5153 Kendall Park, New Jersey, 08824.
E-mail: fatima_bona@ap.org.

The Worldwide Coalition for Peace and Development in Sierra Leone.

This group is a non-membership coalition of individuals and organizations formed for these two reasons only: 1) To propose a peace plan that ends the current rebel war, reforms the structure of the government, and aids public administration with techniques to end corruption and prevent future conflicts or wars. 2) To develop an economic plan that will boldly and significantly raise the quality of life in Sierra Leone.

Contact: Patrick Bockari.
Address: P.O. Box 9012, San Bernardino, California 92427.
E-mail: patbock@mscomm.com.

TEGLOMA (Mende) Association.
Contact: Lansama Nyalley.
Telephone: (301) 891-3590.

MUSEUMS AND RESEARCH CENTERS

The Penn School and the Penn Community Services of the Sea Islands.
Located on St. Helena Island, South Carolina, this institution was established as a school for freed slaves. It now promotes the preservation of Gullah culture and sponsors the annual Gullah festival. It also sponsored an exchange visit to Sierra Leone in 1989.

SOURCES FOR ADDITIONAL STUDY

Encyclopedia of Africa South of the Sahara, John Middleton, Editor-in-Chief. Vol. 4. New York: Charles Scribner's Sons, 1997.

Jones-Jackson, Patricia. *When Roots Die, Endangered Traditions on the Sea Islands*. Athens: University of Georgia Press, 1987.

Wood, Peter H., and Tim Carrier (Director). *Family Across the Sea* (video). San Francisco: California Newsreel, 1991.

Acculturation, assimilation, and intermarriage have made inroads into Sioux traditional family and community relationships. The more isolated and rural portions of the population tend to be more traditional.

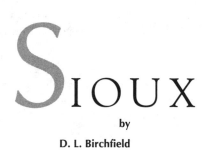

Sioux

by
D. L. Birchfield

Overview

The Siouan-language peoples comprise one of the largest language groups north of Mexico, second only to the Algonquian family of languages. Many Siouan-language peoples are no longer identified as Sioux, but have evolved their own separate tribal identities centuries ago, long before contact with non-Indians. The name Sioux originates from a French version of the Chippewa *Nadouessioux* (snakes). The immense geographical spread of Siouan-language peoples, from the Rocky Mountains to the Atlantic Ocean, from the Great Lakes to the Gulf of Mexico, attests to their importance in the history of the North American continent—most of that history having occurred before the arrival of non-Indians. Those known today as Sioux (the Dakota, the Lakota, and the Nakota), living primarily in the upper Great Plains region, are among the best-known Indians within American popular culture due to their participation in what Americans perceive to have been dramatic events within their own history, such as the Battle of the Little Big Horn in the late nineteenth century. American students have been told for more than a century that there were no survivors, despite the fact that approximately 2,500 Indian participants survived the battle. The lands of the Sioux have also been a focal point for some of the most dramatic events in the American Indian Movement of recent times, especially the 71-day occupation of Wounded Knee, South Dakota, in 1973, which brought national media attention to the Pine Ridge Reservation. Sioux writers, poets, and political leaders are today among the most influential leaders in the North American Native American community of nations, and the Sioux religion can be found to have an influence far beyond the Sioux people.

HISTORY

The Sioux had the misfortune of becoming intimately acquainted with the westward thrust of American expansion at a time when American attitudes toward Indians had grown cynical. In the East and Southeast, from early colonial times, there was much disagreement regarding the nature of the relations with the Indian nations. There was also a constant need to have allies among the Indian nations during the period of European colonial rivalry on the North American continent, a need that the newly formed United States felt with great urgency during the first generation of its existence. After the War of 1812, things changed rapidly in the East and Southeast. Indians as allies became much less necessary. It was the discovery of gold in 1828, however, at the far southern end of the Cherokee Nation near the border with Georgia that set off a Southern gold rush and brought an urgency to long-debated questions of what the nature of relations with the Indian nations should be.

Greed for gold would play a pivotal role in the undermining of Sioux national independence. At mid-century streams of men from the East first passed through Sioux lands on their way to the gold fields of California. They brought with them smallpox, measles, and other contagious diseases for which the Sioux had no immunity, and which ravaged their population by an estimated one-half. Later, in the 1870s, the discovery of gold in the heart of *Paha Sapa* (the Black Hills), the sacred land of the Sioux, brought hordes of miners and the U.S. Army, led by Lieutenant Colonel George Armstrong Custer, into the center of their sacred "heart of everything that is" in a blatant violation of the Treaty of Fort Laramie of 1868.

The Sioux had no way of knowing about the process that had worked itself out in the East and Southeast, whereby, in direct contravention of a U.S. Supreme Court decision (*Worchester vs. Georgia*), Indians would no longer be dealt with as sovereign nations. No longer needed as allies, and looked upon as merely being in the way, Indians entered a perilous time of being regarded as dependent domestic minorities. Many Eastern and South-

ern Indian nations were uprooted and forced to remove themselves beyond the Mississippi River. By the time American expansion reached Texas, attitudes had hardened to a point at which Texans systematically expelled or exterminated nearly all of the Indians within their borders; however, Sam Houston, during his terms as president of the republic of Texas and as governor of the state of Texas, unsuccessfully attempted to accommodate the needs of Indians into Texas governmental policy.

To the Sioux in the second half of the nineteenth century, the U.S. government was duplicitous, greedy, corrupt, and without conscience. The Sioux watched the great buffalo herds be deliberately exterminated by U.S. Army policy; and within a generation they found themselves paupers in their native land, with no alternative but to accept reservation life. They found it impossible to maintain honorable, peaceful relations with the United States. At first, attempts were made to acculturate the Sioux, to assimilate them out of existence as a separate people; then in the mid-twentieth century, the government attempted to legislate them out of existence through an official policy of "termination" of Indian nations. Only within recent decades have there been attempts on the part of the U.S. government to redress past wrongs. In the 1960s, under the occasional prod of court decisions and a national consciousness focused on civil rights legislation for minorities, attempts were made to recognize and respect significant remaining vestiges of Indian sovereignty. Finally, by legislation in 1979 Indians were allowed to openly practice their religions without threat of criminal prosecution. The gains have not come without bloodshed and strife, however, especially in the lands of the Sioux and especially during the mid-1970s—a time of virtual civil war on the Pine Ridge Reservation. Alarmed by the bold actions and the extent of the demands by some groups of Indians, particularly the American Indian Movement (AIM), the U.S. government tried to slow the pace of change by exploiting differences between the more acculturated Indians and the more traditional Indians. Since that time, much healing has occurred; but the question of what the nature of the relations between the Native peoples of this continent and the people of the United States will be remains open.

MODERN ERA

Federally recognized contemporary Sioux tribal governments are located in Minnesota, Nebraska, North Dakota, South Dakota, and Montana. According to the 1990 census, South Dakota ranked eleventh among all states for the number of Indians represented in its population (50,575, which was 7.3 percent of the South Dakota population, up from 6.5 percent in 1980). Minnesota ranked twelfth with a reported total of 49,909 Indians, or 1.1 percent of its population (up from 0.9 percent in 1980). Montana ranked thirteenth with a reported total of 47,679 Indians, or 6.0 percent of its population (up from 4.7 percent in 1980). North Dakota ranked eighteenth with a reported total of 25,917 Indians, or 4.1 percent of its population (up from 3.1 percent in 1980). Nebraska ranked thirty-fifth with a reported total of 12,410 Indians, or 0.8 percent of its population (up from 0.6 percent in 1980).

Many Native Americans from these areas have migrated to urban industrial centers throughout the continent. Contemporary estimates are that at least 50 percent of the Indian population in the United States now resides in urban areas, frequently within the region of the tribal homeland but often at great distances from it. Other populations of Sioux are to be found in the prairie provinces of Canada.

ACCULTURATION AND ASSIMILATION

Beginning in the late nineteenth century the U.S. government attempted to force the Sioux to assimilate into American culture. The prime weapon of cultural genocide as practiced by the United States was a school system contracted to missionaries who had little regard for traditional Sioux culture, language, or beliefs. Sioux children, isolated from their families, were punished if they were caught speaking their native tongue. Their hair was cropped, and school and dormitory life was conducted on a military model. Many children attended the school located at Flandreau, South Dakota. Some Sioux children were removed to schools in the East, to Hampton Institute in Virginia, or to the Indian school at Carlisle, Pennsylvania, while others attended the Santa Fe Indian School and the Haskell Institute in Lawrence, Kansas. Throughout this ordeal, the Sioux were able to retain their language and religion, while learning English and adjusting to the demands of American culture. Some Sioux began attaining distinction early in this process, such as physician Charles Eastman. Today, the Sioux people are at home in both worlds. Sioux intellectuals and academicians, such as noted author Vine Deloria Jr., and poet and scholar Elizabeth Cook-Lynn, who also edits *Wicazo Sa Review*, a scholarly journal for Native American Studies professionals, are leaders within their respective fields within the North American Native American community.

TRADITIONAL CRAFTS

The Sioux are skilled artisans at beadwork, quillwork, carving, pipe making, drum making, flute making, and leatherwork of all kinds—from competition powwow regalia to saddles and tack. These are crafts that have been handed down from generation to generation. Intertribal powwow competitions, festivals, and tribal fairs bring forth impressive displays of Sioux traditional crafts. A large tribal arts and crafts fair is held annually at New Town, North Dakota, September 17-19.

DANCES AND SONGS

Summer is the most popular season for powwows. Intertribal powwows featuring dance competitions are the ones at which visitors are most welcome. A number of powwows tend to occur annually on the same date. Powwows are held at a number of communities in South Dakota on May 7, including the communities of Wounded Knee, Kyle, Oglala, Allen, and Porcupine. A Memorial Day weekend powwow is held by the Devil's Lake Sioux at Fort Totten, North Dakota. Powwows are held in mid-June at Fort Yates, North Dakota, and at Grass Mountain, South Dakota. Powwows are held July 2-4 at La Creek, South Dakota; July 2-5 at Cannon Ball, North Dakota; July 3-5 at Spring Creek, South Dakota, at Greenwood, South Dakota, and at Fort Thompson, North Dakota; July 14-16 at Mission South Dakota; July 15-16 at Flandreau, South Dakota; July 17-19 at New Town, North Dakota; July 21-23 at Cherry Creek, South Dakota; July 28-30 at Little Eagle, South Dakota; and the last weekend of July at Belcourt, North Dakota. August and September are also popular months, with powwows held at Lake Andes, South Dakota, each weekend during the first half of August; at Fort Yates, North Dakota, August 4-6; at Rosebud, South Dakota, August 11-13; at Bull Head, North Dakota, August 13-15; at Bull Creek and Soldier Creek, South Dakota, September 2-4; and at Sisseton, South Dakota, and Fort Totten, North Dakota, over the Labor Day holiday.

HOLIDAYS

The Spotted Tail Memorial Celebration is held in late June at Rosebud, South Dakota. July 1-4 is the date of the Sioux Ceremonial at Sisseton, South Dakota. The Sioux Coronation is held in early October at Fort Totten, North Dakota. Tribal fairs are held July 23-25 at Fort Totten, North Dakota; August 7-9 at Lower Brule, South Dakota; August 21-23 at Rosebud, South Dakota; August 27-29 at

Eagle Butte, South Dakota; and Labor Day weekend at Devils Lake and Fort Totten, North Dakota.

HEALTH ISSUES

All of the health problems associated with poverty in the United States can be found among the contemporary Sioux people. Alcoholism has proven to be especially debilitating. Many traditional Indian movements, including AIM, have worked toward regaining pride in Native culture, including efforts to combat alcohol abuse and the toll that it takes among contemporary Native peoples.

LANGUAGE

The Iroquoian language family, the Caddoan language family, the Yuchi language family, and the Siouan language family all belong to the Macro-Siouan language phylum, indicating a probable divergence in the distant past from a common ancestor language. Geographically, the Iroquoian family of languages (Seneca, Cayuga, Onondaga, Mohawk, Oneida, and Wyandot—also known as Huron), are found in the Northeast, primarily in New York state and the adjacent areas of Canada, and in the Southeast (Tuscarora, originally in North Carolina, later in New York; and Cherokee, in the Southern Appalachians, and later in Oklahoma). The Caddoan language family includes the Caddo, Wichita, Pawnee, and Arikara languages, which are found on the central Plains. Yuchi is a language isolate of the Southern Appalachians.

Members of the Siouan language family proper are to be found practically everywhere east of the Rocky Mountains except on the southern Plains and in the Northeast. On the northern Plains are found the Crow, Hidatsa, and Dakota (also known as Sioux) languages. On the central Plains are found the Omaha, Osage, Ponca, Kansa, and Quapaw languages; in Wisconsin one finds the Winnebago language; on the Gulf Coast are the Tutelo, Ofo, and Biloxi languages; and in the Southeast one finds Catawba. The immense geographical spread of the languages within this family is testimony to the importance of Siouan-speaking peoples in the history of the continent. They have been a people on the move for a very long time.

Oral traditions among some of the Siouan-speaking peoples document the approximate point of divergence for the development of a separate tribal identity and, eventually, the evolution of a separate language unintelligible to their former kinspeople. Siouan-speaking peoples of all contemporary tribal identities, however, share creation stories

accounting for their origin as a people. They come from the stars, which can be contrasted, for example, with the Macro-Algonkian phylum, Muskogean-speaking Choctaws who emerged from a hole in the earth near the sacred mother mound, *Nanih Waiya*. It can be contrasted also with the Aztec-Tanoan phylum, Uto-Aztecan-speaking Hopi, who believe they have ascended upward through successive layers of worlds to the one they presently occupy.

Siouan-speaking peoples also exhibit a reverence for the number seven, whereas Choctaws hold that the sacred number is four. There are fundamental cultural differences between Native American peoples whom Europeans and Americans have considered more similar than different. For example, the Macro-Siouan phylum, Iroquoian-speaking Cherokees and the Macro-Algonkian phylum, Muskogean-speaking Choctaws have both been categorized by non-Indians as members of the so-called "Five Civilized Tribes" due to similarities in their material culture; whereas knowledgeable Choctaws consider the Cherokees to have about three too many sacred numbers.

Today the Sioux language consists of three principal, mutually intelligible dialects: Dakota (Santee), Lakota (Teton), and Nakota (Yankton). The Sioux language is not restricted to the United States but also extends far into the prairie provinces of Canada. The Sioux were also masters of sign language, an ancient vehicle of communication among peoples who are native to the North American continent. The Sioux language can be heard in a video documentary (*Wiping The Tears of Seven Genera-*

tions, directed by Gary Rhine and Fidel Moreno, Kafaru Productions, 1992), which records interviews with a number of Sioux members of the Wounded Knee Survivors' Association, as they relate what their grandparents told them about the 1890 massacre at Wounded Knee.

FAMILY AND COMMUNITY DYNAMICS

The basic unit of traditional Sioux family and community life is the *tiyospaye*, a small group of related families. In the era of the buffalo, the *tiyospaye* was a highly mobile unit capable of daily movement if necessary. A *tiyospaye* might include 30 or more households. From these related households a headman achieved the position of leadership by demonstrating characteristics valued by the group, such as generosity, wisdom, fortitude, and spiritual power gained through dreams and visions. Acculturation, assimilation, and intermarriage have made inroads into Sioux traditional family and community relationships. The more isolated and rural portions of the population tend to be more traditional.

In traditional Lakota community life, fraternal societies, called *akicitas*, are significant within the life of the group. During the era of the buffalo when Lakota society was highly mobile, fraternal societies helped young men develop leadership skills by assigning them roles in maintaining orderly camp movements. Membership was by invitation only and restricted to the most promising young men. Another kind of fraternity, the *nacas*, was composed of older men with proven abilities. The most important of the *nacas* societies, the *Naca Omincia*, functioned as something of a tribal council. Operating by consensus, it had the power to declare war and to negotiate peace. A few members of the *Naca Ominicia* were appointed *wicasa itancans*, who were responsible for implementing decisions of the *Naca Ominicia*. Many vestiges of traditional Lakota community organizational structure have been replaced, at least on the surface, by structures forced upon the Lakota by the U.S. government. One important leader in the society was the *wicasa wakan*, a healer respected for wisdom as well as curative powers. This healer was consulted on important tribal decisions by the *wicasa itancans*, and is still consulted on important matters by the Lakota people today.

RELIGION

The Sun Dance, also known as the Offerings Lodge ceremonial, is one of the seven sacred ceremonials of the Sioux and is a ceremonial for which they have come to be widely known. The most famous Sun Dance occurs in early August at Pine Ridge. The Sun Dance takes place in early July at Rosebud, and at other times among other Sioux communities. The ceremonials, however, are not performed for the benefit of tourists. Attendance by tourists is discouraged.

No American Indian religion has been more closely studied or more widely known than the Sioux religion, partly due to the appeal of John Niehardt's book, *Black Elk Speaks,* in which he recorded his interviews with the Sioux spiritual leader earlier this century. Another reason for its prominence is because the American Indian Movement adopted many of the practices of the Sioux religion for its own and carried those practices to many areas of the continent where they had not been widely known. The so-called New Age movement within American culture has also become captivated by the religious practices of the northern Plains Indians, primarily the Cheyenne and the Sioux (practices that are largely foreign to Indians in many other areas of the continent, but which are perceived by many Americans as representative of Indians in general). Yet, until by act of Congress, the American Indians Religious Freedom Act of 1978, the practice of Indian religions was a crime in the United States.

The practice of many Native American religions throughout the continent was forced underground in the late nineteenth century as news spread about the massacre of 153 unarmed Minneconjou Sioux men, women, and children by the U.S. Army at Wounded Knee on the Pine Ridge Reservation on December 29, 1890. The Minneconjous, camped at Wounded Knee Creek, had been holding a Ghost Dance, attempting to fulfill the prophecies of the Paiute visionary Wovoka. While fleeing their own agency after the murder of Sitting Bull, they tried to reach what they perceived to be the safety of the protection of Chief Red Cloud at Pine Ridge, who was on friendly terms with the U.S. government.

Perhaps because the massacre at Wounded Knee was one of Sioux people on Sioux land, the Sioux have been strong contemporary leaders in asserting the religious rights of Native peoples. These efforts have also been vigorously pursued on behalf of incarcerated Native Americans, where penal authorities in practically every state historically have been contemptuous of the religious rights of Native American inmates.

While the ceremonials of the Sioux, the Sun Dance, the Sweat Lodge, and other aspects of their religion may be foreign to many other Native Americans (for example, the sweat lodge, a religious ceremonial among the Sioux, is merely a fraternal and communal event among the Choctaws and many other Native peoples), one aspect of the Sioux religion is nearly universal among North America's Indians—the sanctity of land and the reverence for particular sacred lands. For the Sioux and for the Cheyenne, the sacred land is *Paha Sapa*, known in American culture as the Black Hills, and their major contemporary struggle is to regain it. They have won a decision from the U.S. Indian Claims Commission that *Paha Sapa* was taken from them illegally by the United States, and that they are entitled to $122 million in compensation. The Sioux have rejected the award of money, which, being held in trust for them, has now accumulated interest to a total of more than $400 million. They are not interested in money; they want Paha Sapa; and there is precedent for their demand. In 1970 Congress passed, and President Richard Nixon signed, legislation returning Blue Lake—the sacred lake of Taos Pueblo—and 48,000 surrounding acres to Taos Pueblo. This was the first return of land to Indians for religious purposes by the United States.

EMPLOYMENT AND ECONOMIC TRADITIONS

In the late nineteenth and early twentieth centuries the U.S. government tried to force the Sioux to become farmers. Cattle ranching, however, has become more important to them and many Sioux derive some economic benefit from the cattle industry. Sioux have distinguished themselves on the professional rodeo and all-Indian rodeo circuits.

Sioux reservations are isolated from urban industrial centers, have attracted very little industry, and experience some of the highest levels of unemployment and the highest levels of poverty of any communities within the United States. For example, on the Cheyenne River Reservation in the mid-1980s, unemployment averaged roughly 80 percent and 65 percent of all families were living on less than $3,000 per year. Many Sioux have found it necessary to leave their communities to find employment. Like many Indian reservations, various agencies of the U.S. government and programs funded by the government account for the largest percentage of jobs. Extractive industries also provide some employment, but the economic benefits go largely to non-Indians, and many traditional Sioux refuse to participate in economic activities that scar and pollute their land. The discovery of uranium on Sioux lands, which has raised questions regarding if and how it should be extracted, has been a divisive issue within Sioux communities.

POLITICS AND GOVERNMENT

The structure and operation of the contemporary government of the Lakota tribal division of the Sioux serves as an example of that of other Sioux governments. The contemporary national government of the Lakota nation is the National Sioux Council, which is composed of delegates from the Lakota reservations at Cheyenne River, Standing Rock, Lower Brule, Crow Creek, Pine Ridge, Rosebud, Santee, and Fort Peck. The council meets annually to discuss matters affecting the entire Lakota nation. It is based on the traditional model of Lakota government, where the headman of each band represented the band's tribe, and the headman of each Lakota tribe represented the Greater Sioux Council. Essentially a federal structure, it also functions by the imposition of vote counting rather than consensus—a quintessential American Indian method of decision making.

Each contemporary Lakota reservation is governed by an elected tribal council. The organization of the Cheyenne River Reservation tribal council, for example, is a supreme governing body for the Cheyenne River Sioux. It is empowered to enter into negotiations with foreign governments, such as the government of the United States, to pass laws and establish courts, appoint tribal officials, and administer the tribal budget. Certain kinds of actions by the tribal council, however, are subject to the authority of the secretary of the interior of the U.S. government, a reminder that the Sioux are not alone in their land. The council consists of 18 members, 15 of which are elected from six voting districts (the districts being apportioned according to population), and three who are elected at large— the chairperson, the secretary, and the treasurer. The council elects a vice-chairperson from among its members. Each tribal council member reports to the district tribal council for the district from which the council member was elected. These district councils are locally elected.

To vote or hold office at Cheyenne River one must be an enrolled tribal member and meet residency requirements. For enrollment, one must be one-quarter blood or more Cheyenne River Sioux and one's parents must also have been residents of the reservation. However, a two-thirds vote of the tribal council may enroll a person of Cheyenne River Indian blood who does not meet either the blood quantum or the parental residency requirements. To vote, one must meet a 30-day residency

requirement; to hold office, the residency requirement is one year.

THE "INCIDENT AT OGLALA"

No other event typifies the problems encountered by traditional Indians in seeking the redress of long-standing grievances with the United States more than the 71-day siege of Wounded Knee in 1973, known as the "Incident at Oglala." When the siege ended in May of 1973, and when no network correspondents remained to tell the world what was happening on the Pine Ridge Reservation, traditional Indians and supporters of the American Indian Movement (AIM) endured a reign of terror that lasted for more than two years. Frightened by the takeover of the Bureau of Indian Affairs building in Washington, D.C., and by the occupation of Wounded Knee, the mixed-blood leadership of the Oglala Lakota tribal government moved to crush political activism on the reservation while the AIM leadership was in court. Federal authorities allowed and funded heavily armed vigilantes, called goon squads (Guardians of the Oglala Nation), who

patrolled the roads and created a police state. Freedom of assembly, freedom of association, and freedom of speech ceased to exist. Violence reigned. Drive-by shootings, cars run off the road, firebombings and murders became the norm.

During one 12-month period there were more murders on the Pine Ridge Reservation than in all the other parts of South Dakota combined. The reservation had the highest per capita murder rate in the United States. By June of 1975 there had been more than 60 unsolved murders of traditional Indians and AIM supporters. The FBI, charged with solving crimes on Indian reservations, took little interest in the killings. But when two FBI agents were killed near the community of Oglala on the Pine Ridge Reservation on June 26, 1975, 350 FBI agents were on the scene within three days.

Two FBI agents, new to the area and unknown to its residents, were dressed in plain clothes and driving unmarked cars; they reported that they were following a red pickup truck, which they believed contained a man who was wanted for stealing a pair of boots. The vehicle actually contained a load of explosives destined for an encampment of about a dozen members of the AIM, not far from the community of Oglala. When the two FBI agents followed the red pickup off the road and into a field, to a point within earshot of the encampment, a firefight erupted between the two FBI agents and the occupants of the vehicle, who have never been identified. Armed only with their handguns, the agents attempted to get their rifles out of the trunks of their cars, and in so doing exposed themselves to the gunfire. Hearing the shooting, and thinking themselves under attack, men and women from the encampment came running, carrying rifles. They took up positions on a ridge overlooking the vehicles; when fired at, they returned the fire. Within a few minutes a third FBI agent arrived but not before the first two FBI agents lay dead near their vehicles. The red pickup fled the scene, but it had been seen and reported, and the report preserved in the records of FBI radio transmissions. The AIM members on the ridge from the encampment, went down to the vehicles and discovered the bodies of the two FBI agents. Bewildered and frightened, they fled the area on foot, under heavy fire, as law enforcement authorities began arriving *en masse*, but not before an Indian man lay dead—shot through the head at long range. The two FBI agents, already wounded, had been shot through the head at point blank range.

The full fury of the FBI descended on Pine Ridge Reservation. The director of the FBI appeared on television and announced a nationwide search for the red pickup. In the months that followed, the FBI was unable to find the red pickup or its occupants. Three men who had been at the AIM encampment that day, Darrelle Butler, Bob Robideau, and Leonard Peltier, were arrested and charged with killing the two FBI agents. No one was ever charged with killing the Indian. Peltier, in Canada, fought extradition. Butler and Robideau, however, were tried and acquitted by a jury that believed they had acted in self-defense and that they had not been the ones who executed the wounded agents. The fury of the government then fell on the third defendant, Leonard Peltier. The United States presented coerced, perjured documents to the Canadian authorities to secure Peltier's extradition from Canada. At the trial, the red pickup truck now became a red and white van, like the one to which Leonard Peltier could be linked. FBI agents who had filed reports the day of the shooting, reporting the red pickup, now testified differently, saying their reports had been in error. The government now claimed that the two dead FBI agents who had reported that they were following a red pickup did not know the difference between a red pickup and a red and white van.

With the first trial as a blueprint for everything it had done wrong in the courtroom, the government found a sympathetic judge in another jurisdiction who ruled favorably for the prosecution, and against the defense, disallowing testimony about the climate of violence and fear on the reservation, and effectively thwarting the defense of self-defense. Also, by withholding the results of crucial FBI ballistics tests, which showed that Leonard Peltier's weapon had not fired the fatal shots, the government got a conviction against Peltier. He was sentenced to two life terms in the federal penitentiary. A recent documentary (*Incident At Oglala: The Leonard Peltier Story*), through interviews with numerous participants, examines in detail the events of the day the two FBI agents were killed, and the government case against Peltier, revealing that in a fair trial Peltier would have been acquitted, as Butler and Robideau were, and that the nature of his involvement was the same as theirs.

INDIVIDUAL AND GROUP CONTRIBUTIONS

ACADEMIA

Sioux author, professor, and attorney Vine Deloria, Jr. (1933–), has been one of the most articulate speakers for the recognition of Indian political and religious rights. Born at Standing Rock on the Pine Ridge Reservation, he holds degrees in divinity from the Lutheran School of Theology and in law from the University of Colorado. His writings include *Custer Died For Your Sins* (1969), *We Talk, You Listen: New Tribes, New Turf* (1970).

LITERATURE

Sioux poet, author, and professor Elizabeth Cook-Lynn (1930–), born on the Crow Creek Reservation, is a granddaughter of Gabriel Renville, a linguist who helped develop Dakota dictionaries; a Dakota speaker herself, Cook-Lynn has gained prominence as a professor, editor, poet, and scholar; she is emeritus professor of American and Indian studies at Eastern Washington State University, and in 1985 she became a founding editor of *Wicazo Sa Review*, a bi-annual scholarly journal for Native American studies professionals; her book of poetry, *Then Badger Said This*, and her short fiction in journals have established her as a leader among American Indian creative voices. Virginia Driving Hawk Sneve, a Rosebud Sioux, is the author of eight children's books and other works of historical nonfiction for adults; in 1992 she won the Native American Prose Award from the University of Nebraska Press for her book *Closing The Circle*. Oglala Sioux Robert L. Perea (1944–), born in Wheatland, Wyoming, is also half Chicano; a graduate of the University of New Mexico, he has published short stories in anthologies such as *Mestizo: An Anthology of Chicano Literature* and *The Remembered Earth*; in 1992 Perea won the inaugural Louis Littlecoon Oliver Memorial Prose Award from his fellow creative writers and poets in the Native Writers' Circle of the Americas for his short story, "Stacey's Story." Philip H. Red-Eagle, Jr., a Wahpeton-Sisseton Sioux, is a founding editor of *The Raven Chronicles*, a multi-cultural journal of literature and the arts in Seattle; in 1993, Red-Eagle won the Louis Littlecoon Oliver Memorial Prose Award for his manuscript novel, *Red Earth*, which is drawn from his experiences in the Viet Nam War. Fellow Seattle resident and Sioux poet, Tiffany Midge, who is also enrolled at Standing Rock, captured the 1994 Diane Decorah Memorial Poetry Award from the Native Writers' Circle of the Americas for her book-length poetry manuscript, *Diary of a Mixed-Up Half-Breed*. Susan Power, who is enrolled at Standing Rock, gained national attention with the 1994 publication of her first novel, *The Grass Dancer*.

VISUAL ARTS

Yankton Sioux graphic artist Oscar Howe (1915-1984) has become one of the best known Native American artists in the United States. Known as *Mazuha Koshina* (trader boy), Howe was born at Joe Creek on the Crow Creek Reservation in South Dakota. He earned degrees from Dakota Wesleyan University and the University of Oklahoma, and was a professor of fine arts and artist in residence at the University of South Dakota for 15 years. His work is characterized by poignant images of Indian culture in transition and is depicted in a modern style.

MEDIA

PRINT

Lakota Times.
Address: 1920 Lombardy Drive, Rapid City, South Dakota 57701.

Oglala Nation News.
Address: Pine Ridge, South Dakota 57770.

Paha Sapa Wahosi.
Address: South Dakota State College, Spearfish, South Dakota 57783.

Rosebud Sioux Herald.
Address: P.O. Box 65, Rosebud, South Dakota 57570.

Sioux Journal.
Address: Eagle Butte, South Dakota 57625.

Sisseton Agency News.
Address: Sisseton BIA Agency, Sisseton, South Dakota 57262.

Standing Rock Star.
Address: Box 202, Bullhead, South Dakota 57621.

Three Tribes Herald.
Address: Parshall, North Dakota 58770.

Wicazo Sa Review.
Address: Route 8, Box 510, Rapid City, South Dakota 57702.

Wotanin-Wowapi.
Newspaper of the Fort Peck Assiniboine and Sioux tribes.

Contact: Bonnie Red Elk, Editor.
Address: Box 1027, Poplar, Montana 59255.
Telephone: (406) 768-5155.
Fax: (406) 768-5478.

RADIO

KCCR-AM (1240).
Address: 106 West Capitol, Pierre, South Dakota 57501.

KEYA-FM (88.5).
Address: P.O. Box 190, Belcourt, North Dakota 58316.
Telephone: (701) 477-5686.
Fax: (701) 477-3252.

KILI-FM (90.1).
Address: P.O. Box 150, Porcupine, South Dakota 57772.
Telephone: (605) 867-5002.
Fax: (605) 867-5634.

KINI-FM (96.1).
Address: P.O. Box 149, St. Francis, South Dakota 57572.
Telephone: (605) 747-2291.
Fax: (605) 747-5791.

KLND-FM (89.5).
Address: P.O. Box 32, Little Eagle,
South Dakota 57639.
Telephone: (605) 823-4663.

ORGANIZATIONS AND ASSOCIATIONS

Cheyenne River Sioux.
Sioux tribal divisions represented on this reservation include the Sihasapa, Minneconjou, Sans Arcs, and the Oohenonpa.

Contact: Gregg J. Bourland, Chairman.
Address: P.O. Box 590, Eagle Butte,
South Dakota 57625.
Telephone: (605) 964-4155.
Fax: (605) 964-4151.

Crow Creek Sioux.
The Sioux on this reservation include descendants of a number of Sioux tribal divisions, including the Minneconjou, Oohenonpa, Lower Brule, and Lower Yanktonai.

Contact: Harold "Curly" Miller, Chairman.
Address: P.O. Box 50, Fort Thompson,
South Dakota 57339.
Telephone: (605) 245-2221.
Fax: (605) 245-2470.

Devils Lake Sioux.
The Sioux on this reservation include Assiniboine, Pabaksa, Santee, Sisseton, Yanktonai, and Wahpeton Sioux.

Address: Sioux Community Center, Fort Totten,
North Dakota 58335.
Telephone: (701) 766-4221.
Fax: (701) 766-4854.

Flandreau Santee Sioux.
Represented are descendants of the Santee Sioux who separated from the Mdewakanton and Wahpekute Sioux in 1870 and settled at Flandreau in 1876.

Contact: Thomas Ranfranz, President.
Address: Flandreau Field Office, Box 283,
Flandreau, South Dakota 57028.
Telephone: (605) 997-3871.
Fax: (605) 997-3878.

Fort Belknap Sioux.
Represented are the Assiniboine-Sioux and Gros Ventre.

Address: P.O. Box 249, Harlem, Montana 59526.
Telephone: (406) 353-2205.
Fax: (406) 353-2797.

Fort Peck Assiniboine-Sioux.
Represented are the Assiniboine-Sioux, closely related to the Yanktonai.

Address: P.O. Box 1027, Poplar, Montana 59255.
Telephone: (406) 768-5155.
Fax: (406) 768-5478.

Indian Center.
Address: 5633 Regent Avenue North,
Minneapolis, Minnesota 55440.

Indian Center.
Address: Box 288, Yankton,
South Dakota 57078.

Indian Community Center.
Address: 2957 Farnum, Omaha,
Nebraska 68131.

Indian Student Association.
Address: University of Minnesota,
Minneapolis, Minnesota 55455.

Lower Brule Sioux.
Represented are the Lower Brule and Yanktonai Sioux.

Contact: Michael Jandreau, Chairman.
Address: P.O. Box 187, Lower Brule,
South Dakota 57548.
Telephone: (605) 473-5561.
Fax: (605) 473-5605.

Lower Sioux.
Represented are the Mdewakanton and Wahpekute divisions of the Santee Sioux.

Address: Route 1, Box 308, Morton,
Minnesota 56270.
Telephone: (507) 697-6185.
Fax: (507) 697-6110.

Oglala Sioux.
Represented are predominantly Oglala Sioux, also Brule Sioux and Northern Cheyenne.

Contact: Harold D. Salway, President.
Address: P.O. Box H, Pine Ridge,
South Dakota 57770.
Telephone: (605) 867-5821.
Fax: (605) 867-5659.

Prairie Island Sioux.
Represented are the Mdewakanton division of the Santee Sioux.

Address: 5750 Sturgeon Lake Road, Welch,
     Minnesota 55089.
Telephone: (612) 385-2536.
Fax: (612) 388-1576.

Rosebud Sioux.
Represented are the Oglala, Oohenonpa, Minneconjou, Upper Brule, Waglukhe, and Wahzhazhe Sioux.

Contact: Norman G. Wilson, President.
Address: P.O. Box 430, Rosebud,
     South Dakota 57570.
Telephone: (605) 747-2381.
Fax: (605) 747-2243.

Santee Sioux.
Represented are the Santee Sioux, including Mdewakanton, Wahpekute, Sisseton, and Wahpeton.

Contact: Arthur "Butch" Denny, Chairman.
Address: Route 2, Niobrara, Nebraska 68760.
Telephone: (402) 857-2302.
Fax: (402) 857-2307.

**Sioux Tribes of South Dakota
Development Corporation.**
Promotes employment opportunities for Native Americans; offers job training services.

Address: 919 Main Street, Suite 114, Rapid City,
     South Dakota 57701-2686.
Telephone: (605) 343-1100.

Sisseton-Wahpeton Sioux.
Represented are the Sisseton Sioux.

Contact: Andrew J. Grey, Sr., Chairman.
Address: P.O. Box 509, Niobrara, Nebraska 68760.
Telephone: (605) 698-3911.
Fax: (605) 698-7908.

Skakopee Sioux.
Represented are the Mdewakanton division of the Santee Sioux.

Address: 2330 Sioux Trail, Prior Lake,
     Minnesota 55372.
Telephone: (612) 445-8900.
Fax: (612) 445-8906.

South Dakota Commission on Indian Affairs.
Address: Pierre, South Dakota 57501.

Standing Rock Sioux.
Represented are predominantly the Teton Sioux, including Hunkpapa and Sihasapa, but also including Lower and Upper Yanktonai.

Contact: Charles W. Murphy, Chairman.
Address: P.O. Box D, Fort Yates,
     North Dakota 58538.
Telephone: (701) 854-7202.
Fax: (701) 854-7299.

Upper Sioux Community.
Represented are predominantly the Sisseton and Wahpeton divisions of the Santee Sioux, but Devil's Lake, Flandreau, and Yanktonai Sioux are also included.

Address: P.O. Box 147, Granite Falls,
     Minnesota 56241.
Telephone: (612) 564-2360.
Fax: (612) 564-3264.

Urban Sisseton-Wahpeton Sioux.
Address: 1128 Fifth Street, N.E., Minneapolis,
     Minnesota 55418.

Yankton Sioux.
Represented are the Yanktonai Sioux tribal division.

Address: P.O. Box 248, Marty, South Dakota 57361.
Telephone: (605) 384-3804.
Fax: (605) 384-5687.

MUSEUMS AND RESEARCH CENTERS

Museums that focus on the Sioux include: the Minnesota Historical Society Museum in St. Paul, Minnesota; the Plains Indian Museum in Browning, Montana; the Affiliated Tribes Museum in New Town, North Dakota; the Indian Arts Museum in Martin, South Dakota; the Land of the Sioux Museum in Mobridge, South Dakota; the Mari Sandoz Museum on the Pine Ridge Reservation, South Dakota; the Sioux Indian Museum in Rapid City, South Dakota; and the University of South Dakota Museum in Vermillion.

SOURCES FOR ADDITIONAL STUDY

Incident At Oglala: The Leonard Peltier Story (video documentary), directed by Michael Apted, narrated by Robert Redford. Carolco International N.V. and Spanish Fork Motion Picture Company, 1991.

Lakota: Seeking the Great Spirit. San Francisco: Chronicle Books, 1994.

Marquis, Arnold. *A Guide to America's Indians: Ceremonials, Reservations, and Museums.* Norman: University of Oklahoma Press, 1974.

McClain, Gary (Eagle Walking Turtle). *Indian America: A Traveler's Companion,* third edition. Santa Fe, New Mexico: John Muir Publications, 1993.

Native America: Portrait of the Peoples, edited by Duane Champagne, foreword by Dennis Banks. Detroit: Gale Research, 1994.

Neihardt, Hilda. *Black Elk and Flaming Rainbow: Personal Memories of the Lakota Holy Man and John Neihardt.* Lincoln: University of Nebraska Press, 1995.

Neihardt, John. *Black Elk Speaks: Being the Life Story of a Holy Man of the Oglala Sioux.* Lincoln: University of Nebraska Press, 1961.

O'Brien, Sharon. *American Indian Tribal Governments* (Civilization of the American Indian Series). Norman: University of Oklahoma Press, 1989.

Paha Sapa: The Struggle for the Black Hills (video documentary), directed by Mel Lawrence. HBO Studio Productions, 1993.

Ross, A.C. *Mitakuye Oyasin [We Are All Related].* Denver, CO: Wicóni Wasté, 1997.

Wiping the Tears of Seven Generations (video documentary), directed by Gary Rhine and Fidel Moreno. Kifaru Productions, 1992.

> Slovak immigrants
> exemplified the
> pattern evident
> among most ethnic
> groups in the United
> States: they adjusted
> to American society
> and preserved some
> traditions and values
> while altering others.

SLOVAK AMERICANS

by
June Granatir Alexander

OVERVIEW

Slovakia is at the crossroads between eastern and western Europe. It is bordered by Poland to the north, Hungary to the south, the Czech Republic to the west, and Ukraine to the east. Although a small country, with a land mass of 18,919 square miles, Slovakia's topography varies widely. Its territory includes rugged mountains, dense forests, and low fertile plains. The vast Carpathian mountain range that stretches along Slovakia's northern border also juts into central Slovakia. In this central region the Tatras, which cap the Carpathian system, reach altitudes as high as 8,711 feet. The capital, Bratislava, is located in southwestern Slovakia on the Danube River.

Slovakia's population is 5,297,000. Although the country is ethnically diverse, Slovaks are the overwhelming majority accounting for 4.5 million (85.6 percent) of the inhabitants. The populace also includes approximately 600,000 (10.8 percent) Hungarians and 79,500 (1.5 percent) Gypsies. The remaining population consists primarily of Czechs, Jews, and Carpatho-Rusyns. The official language is Slovak.

Slightly more than 60 percent of Slovakia's inhabitants are Roman Catholic while 8.4 percent are Protestant. Although most ethnic Hungarians belong to the Reformed church, Lutherans constitute the country's largest Protestant denomination. Other faiths include Judaism, Greek Catholic, and

Orthodox. The religion of an estimated 27.2 percent of the population is either unidentifiable (17.5 percent) or atheist (9.7 percent).

HISTORY

Throughout most of its history modern-day Slovakia was not an independent country. Its inhabitants were subject peoples of multi-national empires. When the Austro-Hungarian Empire collapsed in 1918, Slovaks joined with Czechs to create an independent Czechoslovakia. Except for a short period of independence during World War II (1939-1945), Slovakia remained part of that multi-national state until 1993.

The history of Slovakia reaches back to the fifth and sixth centuries when Slavic tribes migrated into the region south of the Carpathian Mountains. These ancestors of modern-day Slovaks established villages and developed an agricultural economy in the Middle Danube Basin. In the mid-ninth century Slavs from Bohemia, Moravia, and the Danube region united to form the Great Moravian Empire, which comprised most of latter-day Czechoslovakia, southern Poland, and western Hungary. The empire was the first unification of Czech (Bohemian and Moravian) and Slovak peoples. In the 860s Christianity was introduced into the empire. In 907 Magyars, a semi-nomadic people from the northeast, invaded the empire and established the Kingdom of Hungary, which incorporated modern-day Slovakia. The collapse of the Great Moravian Empire split the Czechs and Slovaks, and they stayed separate for the next one thousand years. Until 1918 the Slovak lands remained part of Hungary, but the region was known as Upper Hungary, not Slovakia.

During the fifteenth century, the Protestant Reformation spread into Upper Hungary, and most Slovaks converted to the Lutheran faith. In 1526, after the Ottoman Turks conquered the southern section of its kingdom, Hungary became part of the Hapsburg Empire. During the Counter-Reformation which accompanied Hapsburg rule, most Slovaks returned to Roman Catholicism, although a significant minority remained Protestant.

MODERN ERA

In the nineteenth century Slovaks and Hungary's other ethnic minorities were subjected to Magyarization, an official policy of forced assimilation. The government made Magyar (Hungarian) the official language and outlawed all other languages. It closed schools and adopted other measures to abolish ethnic cultures in Hungary. By the early twentieth century, the Magyarization policy had enjoyed significant success in Upper Hungary. In general, Slovaks living in the region did not view themselves as a separate people.

World War I opened the way for dismembering the Austro-Hungarian Empire and letting its subject nationalities create independent countries. As a result the Czech and Slovak lands were united, and Czechoslovakia was created on October 28, 1918. Many Slovak supporters of an independent Czechoslovakia had envisioned the new state as a federation of two independent people. Instead, the country's constitution established a centralized government with a single capital city, Prague. Instituting a centralized government, instead of a system that granted Slovaks autonomy, led to tensions between Czechs and Slovaks in the 1920s and 1930s. As result of the Munich Agreement (1938) and Hitler's invasion of Czechoslovakia in March 1939, Slovakia's political leaders declared Slovakia independent. Independent Slovakia was in reality a puppet government of Germany.

In 1945 Slovakia and the Czech lands were reunified. In postwar elections the Communist Party enjoyed significant victories, and in 1948 party leaders engineered a coup and took over the government. For the next 40 years Slovakia remained part of Czechoslovakia and under communist control. In 1969 the government granted Slovakia autonomy within the country and designated Bratislava as the capital city. In the fall of 1989 Slovaks joined Czechs in the Velvet Revolution that toppled the communist-controlled government in December. In April 1990 Czechoslovakia was renamed the Czech and Slovak Federative Republic. The first free elections since 1945 occurred in June 1990. As reforms and measures to privatize the economy were introduced, relations between Czechs and Slovaks became strained. After the June 1992 elections, Czech and Slovak government officials decided that the two regions should separate. Because it was achieved without bloodshed or serious animosities, the breakup of the former Czechoslovakia is often called the Velvet Divorce. On January 1, 1993, Slovakia became independent. Slovakia's first prime minister was Vladimir Meciar.

IMMIGRATION

A few Slovaks immigrated to the United States before the American Civil War but their numbers were small. Large-scale Slovak immigration to the United States began in the late 1870s, steadily increased during the following two decades, and peaked in 1905 when 52,368 Slovaks entered. Slovak immigration declined precipitously during World War I and started up again after hostilities ended in 1918. The movement came almost to a complete halt in the 1920s when American immigration laws virtually stopped East European immigration into the United States. According to immigration records 480,201 Slovaks entered the country between 1899 and 1918. The 1920 census found that there were 274,948 foreign-born Slovaks in the United States. Slovak immigrants and their children totaled 619,866.

Statistics on Slovak immigration, however, are imprecise, and it is difficult to determine the number that actually immigrated to the United States. Before 1899 U.S. immigration officials listed immigrants by country of birth. Thus, until 1899 Slovaks were recorded as Hungarians. Even after immigrants were enumerated by nationality, the Magyarization policies had been so effective that many Slovaks did not identify themselves as such. Also, perhaps one-third of the Slovaks who came to the United States were not immigrants but instead migrants. Often called "birds of passage," they worked temporarily in America and then returned to Europe. They wanted to earn money to buy property in their homeland. It was common for Slovaks to make several trips between the United States and Upper Hungary. At least 19 percent of the Slovaks who entered an American port from 1899 to 1910 had been in the United States one or more times before. Not until 1908 did immigration officials subtract the number of immigrants leaving from the total numbers entering the United States. Still, it is clear that temporary migrants formed an especially large contingent of the early stages of the Slovak immigration and remained a common feature of the movement. Between 1908 and 1910, for example, 80,797 Slovaks entered the United States while 41,726 left. Its temporary nature also affected the composition of the Slovak immigration. Most Slovak immigrants were unskilled laborers, and men typically outnumbered women by more than two to one. Between 1899 and 1910, 266,262 Slovak males and 111,265 Slovak females entered the United States.

Over time, many birds of passage decided to stay in America and sent for their families. The reasons for staying varied. Some were unable to save enough money to buy land and in some regions of their homeland no land was available. Others decided that America promised a better future while others married and decided to stay. Whatever their motives, between 1880 and the mid-1920s probably between 450,000 and 500,000 Slovaks moved permanently to the United States.

Slovak immigrants were committed to saving money and fulfilling obligations to families left behind. As a result they routinely sent money to Europe. In 1899 alone more than $4 million was channeled to the Slovak region of Hungary. The determination to save money, compounded by the fact that so many Slovaks were males who had come alone, influenced living standards. In general, Slovaks tried to live cheaply. Laborers often roomed in boardinghouses where they could get a bed and daily meals for as little as ten dollars per month. These boardinghouses were typically run by Slovak immigrants, a husband and wife who either owned or rented a large house. For these Slovak families, taking in boarders became an important source of additional income.

Slovak immigration began during a period when anti-foreign sentiment was on the rise in the United States. The response by Americans to Slovaks reflected the common anti-foreign attitude. Furthermore, the desire by Slovaks to live cheaply, the large number of males, and their concentration in unskilled industrial jobs reinforced beliefs that immigrants were creating social and economic problems for the United States. Slovaks were not usually singled out as presenting special problems. Since Slovaks did not have a separate identifiable homeland and most Americans did not know that there was a Slovak people, they often referred to Slovak immigrants simply as Slavs, Slavic, Slavish, or by the pejorative terms Hunky or Bohunk. Based on their geographic origin, Slovaks fell into the general category of undesirable immigrants. Judging persons from both eastern and southern Europe as biologically and intellectually inferior and a threat to American society, some native-born Americans demanded that these "undesirables" be barred from the country. The immigration laws of the 1920s that curtailed southern and east European immigration severely reduced the number of Slovaks who could enter the United States. Between 1929 and 1965 American quotas permitted only 2,874 persons from Czechoslovakia to immigrate annually to the United States. In the decades after immigration restriction went into effect, Slovaks were lost in popular perceptions and culture, as they were lumped into generalizations about the massive turn-of-the-century immigration.

Slovak Americans rank as the second largest Slavic group in the United States. The 1990 census revealed that 1,882,897 Americans claimed Slovak descent: 1,210,652 listed Slovak as their "first ancestry," and another 672,245 designated it as "second." Nearly three-fourths (74.7 percent) of Americans acknowledging some Slovak descent resided in the Northeast and Midwest. Less than .03

percent of the 1990 Slovak American population was foreign born, and 74 percent of these immigrants had come before World War II.

SETTLEMENT

Slovaks gravitated to areas where industries were expanding and needed unskilled labor. More than half the Slovak immigrants went to Pennsylvania and primarily to the milltowns and coal mining districts in the state's western region. Other popular destinations included Ohio, New Jersey, New York, and Illinois. Slovaks "chain migrated," that is they went to places where previous Slovak immigrants already lived. Between 1908 and 1910 an astounding 98.4 percent of Slovaks entering the country were joining relatives or friends.

ACCULTURATION AND ASSIMILATION

Slovak immigrants exemplified the pattern evident among most ethnic groups in the United States: they adjusted to American society and preserved some traditions and values while altering others. Values and beliefs that Slovaks brought with them were rooted in their rural past and reflected the concerns of agricultural communities. Slovaks placed great value on owning property and a home. They valued the family and the honoring of family obligations.

TRADITIONS, CUSTOMS, AND BELIEFS

Slovaks were a deeply religious people. Some religious holy days were customarily observed with village processions while others were less dramatic. On some saints' feast days Slovak villagers came together as a community to pray for a favor associated by legend with a saint. For example, on the feast of Saint Mark (April 25) they prayed for rain and good weather during the upcoming growing season. Although Slovaks were fervently religious, their beliefs and customs were a blend of folklore and superstitions linked to the Christian calendar. A vast array of superstitions permeated their culture. For example, Slovaks performed rituals to rid or protect their villages from demons and witches.

Slovaks also carried out numerous rituals, especially during the Christmas season, which they believed foretold their future. On November 30 at the beginning of the season they poured lead into

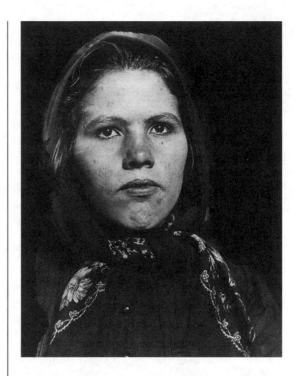

This Slovak woman's photograph was taken shortly after her arrival at Ellis Island.

boiling water and relied on the shape of the cooled droplets to make predictions about the forthcoming year. Young women had several rituals that they believed might reveal who their husbands would be. On Christmas Eve Slovaks cracked nuts and used the condition of the meat as an indicator of what the upcoming year might hold for them. They also took measures that they hoped would control the future. On Christmas Eve, the head of the household gave food from the dinner table to the family's animals in the hope of ensuring the livestock's health.

TRADITIONAL COSTUMES

The typical folk costume for women consisted of a puffed-sleeve blouse, a vest, a short but full skirt, an apron, a bonnet or headscarf, and calf-high boots. Male costumes included a hat, a shirt overlaid with a vest, trousers, and boots. Men's trousers, typically form-fitting but occasionally flared, were usually white with colorful embroidery. Both male and female folk costumes made of homespun cloth and sheepskin were multi-colored and featured intricate embroidery. Specific styles, colors, and items included in the attire varied from village to village and from region to region. In fact, peasant costumes could be so distinctive that they simultaneously indicated a person's village and religion. A headdress also revealed a woman's marital status. In the United States, Slovak folk costumes have become nostalgic or quaint artifacts worn only for interethnic or Slovak events.

CUISINE

Soup is a staple of the Slovak daily diet. Cabbage, potatoes, and dumplings, all prepared in a variety of ways, are regular fare on Slovak tables. Meat, especially in Slovakia's poorer eastern region, was not a common ingredient in soups or main dishes; though some traditional dishes served throughout Slovakia are meat-based. *Klobasa* (a sausage with garlic) and *holubky* (cabbage leaves stuffed with pork, rice, and onions) are the most popular. Duck and chicken are reserved for special occasions, but for particularly festive celebrations goose is preferred. Although desserts are not part of the daily diet, Slovak culinary specialities include several filled *kolacy* (sweet yeast baked goods). The most popular *kolac* contains prune, ground nut, or crushed poppyseed fillings. Depending on the filling, *pirohy* (small dumplings) are served as main dishes or as desserts.

Slovaks attach great importance to serving traditional foods on Christmas and Easter, the only major holidays observed by Slovaks in both the homeland and the United States. Although in regional variations, several dishes served at Christmas and Easter are considered authentic Slovak cuisine. On Christmas Eve the main dishes consist of *bobalky* (bite-size rolls in either sauerkraut and butter or in a poppyseed sauce) and a special mushroom soup. Traditional Easter specialties include Slovak *paska* (a sweet, yeast bread with raisins) and homemade *hrudka* also known as *syrek* (a bland, custard-style imitation cheese).

HOLIDAYS

In their Slovak homeland, the celebration of Christmas and Easter was an event for both family and village. While Slovak American Christmas celebrations have taken on American features with a greater emphasis on gifts and a midday turkey dinner, many Americans of Slovak descent adhere to the custom of the family coming together for traditional Slovak foods on Christmas Eve. Visiting family during both the Christmas and Easter seasons has also remained an obligatory custom among Slovak Americans.

HEALTH ISSUES

Neither Slovak immigrants nor their descendants have unique health problems. The 1990 census data indicate that average rates of disability among both young and elderly Slovaks are the same as for most other ethnic groups in the United States. The same is true for the number of Slovaks institutionalized. Immigrants and subsequent generations did suffer from afflictions characteristic of other working-class Americans, especially at the turn of the century. In addition to a high rate of tuberculosis, workers were killed or permanently maimed in industrial accidents. Some Slovaks who toiled in mines have been stricken with the respiratory problems that afflict that segment of workers.

Slovaks had local folk remedies. It has not been documented how extensively immigrants practiced these folk cures or how long they persisted in the United States. Although no systematic study of Slovak health attitudes has been done, there is no evidence that folk cures had any real impact on Slovak health practices in the United States.

LANGUAGE

Slovak belongs to the Slavic language group. Although similar to other Slavic languages, especially Czech, Slovak is linguistically distinct with its own grammar and vocabulary. Slovak has three dialects (western, central, and eastern) that roughly correspond with geographical areas in Slovakia. Each dialect also has numerous local and regional variations. Slovak, like other Slavic languages, has diacritical marks that govern the pronunciation of both consonants and vowels. The accent is on the first syllable.

The roots of the Slovak language predate the introduction of Christianity in the ninth century, but it did not become a written language until centuries later. The first serious attempt to codify a Slovak literary language occurred in the late eighteenth century. This early version was later rejected for one codified in the mid-1840s based on the central Slovak dialect.

Slovak was the primary language spoken among immigrants and between them and their children. The language has not persisted among successive generations in the United States. Several factors contributed to this decline. First, children gave way to the pressure in American society to abandon foreign languages. Second, immigrants were often barely literate. Although they taught their children, especially the older sons and daughters, to speak Slovak they could not teach them to read and write the language. Slovaks established parochial schools where language instructions were provided, but these classes often either proved inadequate or students did not remain in school long enough to become literate in Slovak. However, Slovak is taught in various Sunday schools for children and in universities, including the University of Pittsburgh. Several American libraries have Slovak-language collections.

The Slovak language was modified slightly in the United States as English, or modern, technical terms were introduced into the vocabulary. The absence of diacritical marks in English meant that either the spelling or the pronunciation of many Slovak names was changed. For example, a person with the name Karcis (pronounced "Kar-chis") had the option to change the pronunciation to the English ("Kar-kis") or keep the pronunciation and change the spelling to Karchish.

GREETINGS AND OTHER POPULAR EXPRESSIONS

Common Slovak greetings include: *Dobre rano* ("dobre rahno")—Good morning; *Dobry den* ("dobre den")—Good day; *Dobry vecer* ("dobre vecher")—Good evening; *Dobru noc* ("dobroo nots")—Good night; *Prosim* ("prosem")—please, if you please, excuse me; *Dakujem* ("djakooyem")—Thank you; *Dobru chut'* ("dobroo kootye")—Eat well!, bon appetit!; *Na zdravie* ("nazdravye")—To [your] health!, cheers! (a toast); *Vesele Vianoce* ("veseleh veanotse")—Merry Christmas.

FAMILY AND COMMUNITY DYNAMICS

Immigration is a disruptive process, especially for families. Although chain migration meant that Slovaks typically went to where relatives and friends had already settled, families were temporarily torn apart. Men immigrated alone, lived in boardinghouses, and later summoned their families or fiancees to join them. The process also worked in reverse as children emigrated first and then sent for elderly parents left behind in Europe. Although Slovaks typically maintained a close-knit family system, by mid-twentieth century Slovak Americans were moving from cities to suburbs. During the latter decades the third and fourth generations were also moving from dying milltowns to metropolitan regions.

Marriage patterns influenced family and community dynamics. For the immigrant generation, the norm was marriage between Slovaks. The second generation followed the same trend into the 1920s and 1930s, but by the post-World War II era interethnic marriages proved more common. Dating patterns differed from generation to generation and even within the same generation. Immigrants recalled that, for them, dating in the United States was limited to events sponsored by Slovak fraternals, churches, or social groups. Attending religious services and sharing in a family dinner also were

common among couples. By the mid-1920s the Slovak youth had adopted the dating practices common among their American peers. They enjoyed dances, movies, amusement parks, and other entertainment characteristic of the changing contemporary popular culture.

Both traditional culture and religious values combined to make divorce uncommon among Slovak immigrants. Reliable data on divorce rates for specific ethnic groups are unavailable but, given general trends in the United States, the empirical evidence suggests that dissolutions involving Slovaks surely rose in the latter part of the twentieth century.

WEDDINGS

Weddings were lengthy affairs that, depending on the village's size, could involve nearly all the inhabitants. Preparatory rituals for the marriage, the ceremony, and subsequent celebrations could last a week. During the festivities, usually three days after the actual marriage ceremony, the bonneting of the bride took place. A bonnet was placed on her head, and she was accepted as a married woman.

BAPTISMS

Christening the newborn traditionally occurred within a few days of birth but godparents were selected long before the child was born. Slovaks chose godparents carefully because these persons were expected to assume responsibility for the child's welfare should misfortune befall the parents. Following both Protestant and Catholic ceremonies, the celebrators retired to the home of the parents or godparents to partake in a celebratory feast. In some areas, after a son's birth or christening a bottle of *slivovica* (plumb brandy), was buried only to be retrieved and consumed on his wedding day.

FUNERALS

Proper burial of the dead was a ritual that spanned several days. The deceased's body usually lay in his or her home for two days, and on the third a procession of villagers accompanied the coffin to the cemetery for burial. Deaths also triggered a host of superstitions. Immediately following a person's demise, Slovaks covered all the mirrors and closed all the windows in the deceased's home. They believed that these measures would prevent the dead from returning.

EDUCATION

Slovak culture traditionally did not place a high emphasis on education. The Hungarian government's Magyarization policy, together with the agricultural nature of Slovak society, worked against developing a culture that valued formal education. Between 24 percent and 30 percent of the turn-of-the-century Slovak immigrants over the age of 14 could neither read nor write. Those who had attended school had gone for only a few years. With this background many immigrant parents, especially during the pre-World War I era, did not hesitate to put their children to work at early ages. In the 1920s more Slovak children regularly attended school and more completed 12 years of education. Nevertheless, Slovak parents generally advocated practical learning over an education in the sciences or liberal arts. Rather than stressing social mobility, both first- and second-generation parents typically encouraged children to get a secure job even if that meant working in a factory. The value system of both first- and second-generation Slovaks placed women in the traditional role of wife, mother, and homemaker; therefore, education was considered even less valuable for daughters than for sons.

The tendency to downplay formal education did have an impact. Based on the 1990 census nearly 21 percent of native-born Slovak Americans over the age of 24 had not received a high school diploma. This percentage undoubtedly includes a significant number of elderly persons who were forced to leave school in the earlier half of the century. Americans of Slovak descent have attended college but not in large numbers. In 1990 only 14.3 percent (123,341) of Slovak Americans older than 24 had a bachelor's degree from a four-year college, and 6.3 percent (54,008) had an associate's degree. Census figures also showed that only 7.5 percent (64,998) of this age group held a professional, master's, or doctoral degree. However, the data also reveal that more than one-half (52.6 percent) of Slovak Americans who received a bachelor's degree continued their education and obtained an advanced degree. Fewer Slovak American women than men have received college degrees. Women represented only 42.4 percent (52,237) of the Slovak Americans with a bachelor's degree, while men accounted for 57.6 percent (71,104). The discrepancy between men and women who received advanced degrees is more pronounced. Only 37.5 percent (5,196) of the Slovak Americans with professional degrees in 1990 were women while the percentage of men accounted for 62.5 percent (8,668). Women with doctorates represented 19.6 percent (1,072) of the total while men claimed 80.4 percent (4,391).

The stress on traditional roles for Slovak women has influenced their educational achievements and community activities. During World War II, Slovak women led local drives to sell war bonds and helped raise money for the International Red Cross and other relief projects. Otherwise, Slovak American women have typically limited their activities to their churches, fraternals, schools, and community events.

RELIGION

Early Slovak immigrants included Catholics, Lutherans, and Calvinists, but the majority of Slovaks were Roman Catholic. The first Slovak Roman Catholic churches were founded in 1885 in Hazleton, Pennsylvania, and Streator, Illinois. During the next four decades Slovak Catholics established nearly 250 churches in the United States. The universality of the Latin mass and Catholic theology meant that Slovaks continued to practice their religion as they had done in their homeland. But immigrants also had to observe holy days and laws unique to the American Catholic Church. The requirement that individual congregations pay all church expenses was the most significant difference between Slovak Catholic churches in Europe and the United States. Because parishes had to be self-supporting, lay organizations sponsored numerous fund-raising social events, and ethnic churches became centers of community activities.

A small number of Slovak Byzantine rite Catholics also migrated to the United States. They organized a few churches but more often they cooperated with other Byzantine rite Catholics, especially Carpatho-Rusyns, to found ethnically mixed parishes. Byzantine rite Catholics professed the same creed as followers of the Roman rite, and both were under papal authority. However, services in the Byzantine rite were conducted in Old Church Slavonic, which used the Cyrillic alphabet. The fact that Byzantine rite clergymen could marry while Roman rite priests could not became a significant difference in the United States. Having a married clergy created problems for Byzantine rite Catholics because some American bishops refused to accept wedded priests in their dioceses. This refusal caused some Byzantine rite Catholic Slovaks to join an Orthodox church.

Lutherans comprised the second largest body of Slovak immigrants. They organized their first congregation in 1883 in Freeland, Pennsylvania, and during the next half century Slovak Lutherans established more than 70 congregations and missions. In 1902 Slovak Lutherans formed their own synod, an executive and judicial body made up of clergy and laypersons. Conflicts developed when the Slovak Synod became affiliated with the Evangelical Lutheran Synodical Conference of America in 1908. Some Slovak Lutheran clergy and laypersons refused to adopt liturgical changes subsequently demanded by the conference and, as a result, serious divisions developed. Continued disagreements over liturgical and theological principles led to the formation of the Slovak Zion Synod in 1919, which affiliated with the United Lutheran church in America in 1962. Most Slovak Lutherans belong to congregations associated either with the Lutheran Church of America or the Synodical Conference.

Only a small number of Slovak Calvinists immigrated to the United States. A few of these Protestants affiliated with Reformed churches but most became Presbyterians. They founded 15 Slovak Presbyterian churches. A tiny number of Slovak immigrants converted to other Protestant religions, primarily to the Congregational church. In 1916, there were three Slovak Congregational churches and another that included both Czechs and Slovaks. These four churches had only 308 adult members.

Slovak churches survived for decades as ethnic institutions while experiencing some change. By the 1930s Slovak Protestant churches were introducing English into their services. Catholics continued to use Latin until the 1960s when the Catholic church began to use the vernacular. As the immigrant generation died and their descendants moved out of ethnic neighborhoods, some Slovak churches declined or were taken over by new immigrant groups. Nevertheless, in cities and small towns especially in Pennsylvania, Ohio, New York, and New Jersey, vibrant Slovak Lutheran and Catholic churches still exist.

EMPLOYMENT AND ECONOMIC TRADITIONS

Eighty percent of Slovak immigrants had been common or farm laborers in their homeland. Having few skills Slovaks found jobs as manual laborers in heavy industries, especially in steel and allied industries that produced durable goods. A large number of Slovaks also toiled in coal mines. In 1910 surveys revealed that 82 percent of Slovak males labored as miners or in iron and steel mills. Some Slovak women were employed as domestics, but in cities they often worked in food processing plants. Fewer employment opportunities existed for women in small milltowns. Those who were unable to find domestic service jobs typically remained unemployed and helped at home until they married. Widows and married women often ran boardinghouses where they cooked and did the laundry for residents.

The majority of second-generation Slovak males followed their fathers' paths and became industrial laborers, although some did enter the professions or acquired skills. Subsequent generations have deviated from this course. The 1990 census found that only 5.7 percent of Slovak Americans were self-employed while the vast majority remained wage and salary workers; however, in the type of jobs they differed from their parents or grandparents. In 1990 only 26 percent of Slovaks had jobs in manufacturing, mining, and construction. Most Slovaks were employed in white-collar jobs.

The evidence does not yet indicate what impact corporate downsizing has had on Slovak Americans holding white-collar positions but the process has clearly affected laborers. The closing of plants in the industrial Northeast and Midwest has adversely affected second- and third-generation Slovaks, especially persons beyond middle age. Still, the unemployment rate of 4.4 percent among Slovak Americans is below the national average. The median income for Slovak families in 1989 was just over $40,000, and only 3.7 percent had incomes below the poverty level.

POLITICS AND GOVERNMENT

Slovak involvement in politics has changed over the decades. At the turn of the century few immigrant workers regularly participated in political activities. Such involvement was typically limited to leaders of Slovak fraternal societies. Founded to provide insurance, disability benefits, and unemployment compensation, and to stimulate ethnic consciousness among Slovaks, fraternals also encouraged or required members to become American citizens. Fraternal leaders believed that having a membership composed mainly of American citizens would enhance the fraternals' political clout. These organizations worked hard to influence legislation that affected immigrants. They also became involved in American domestic issues, especially those that concerned working-class Americans. During the 1930s, fraternals actively lobbied for social security, unemployment benefits, minimum-wage/maximum-hours legislation, and the legalization of unions. Slovak immigrants and their children helped organize and joined unions, especially in the steel and mining industries where so many of them worked. In his powerful novel, *Out of This Furnace* (1941), Thomas Bell, a second-generation Slovak, vividly describes the work experiences and union activities of Slovaks in western Pennsylvania where he grew up during the Great Depression.

An accurate picture of the political activities of Slovak immigrants and successive generations is difficult to discern. In 1920 when citizenship data was recorded by "country of birth" only 45.8 percent of persons from Czechoslovakia had become American citizens and could vote. During the 1930s the New Deal programs drew working-class Slovaks to the Democratic Party. Through the 1950s Slovaks seemed to remain loyal to the Democratic Party in state and local elections but the pattern in national elections is less clear. In 1960 John F. Kennedy's Catholicism and Cold War liberalism attracted Slovak American Catholics. The specific voting patterns and political activities of Slovak Americans during the following three decades have not been

> **"I**dentification with an ethnic group is a source of values, instincts, ideas, and perceptions that throw original light on the meaning of America."

Michael Novak, an American philosopher and theologian of Slovak descent, from his *The Rise of the Unmeltable Ethnics,* 1972.

studied, but empirical evidence suggests that the same religious, class, regional, and related differences that divide the country's population and influence political behavior in general also fragment Americans of Slovak descent. In geographic areas where Slovaks have concentrated, they have been elected to local and state offices. But only one Slovak American has been elected to the United States Congress—Joseph M. Gaydos (1926–), who represented Pennsylvania's twentieth district from 1968 through 1992.

RELATIONS WITH SLOVAKIA

Slovak organizations also became involved in the politics of their homeland. Specifically to counter the Hungarian government's intensified Magyarization efforts, in 1907 Slovak journalists and national fraternal leaders organized the Slovak League of America. During World War I, the league and Slovak fraternal societies worked to secure American and international support for the creation of an independent Czecho-Slovakia. Their activities included lobbying American politicians and trying to influence public opinion. The league and its supporters pressured Thomas Masaryk, the future first president of Czechoslovakia, into signing the Pitts-

burgh Agreement on May 30, 1918. The document ostensibly provided for Slovak autonomy within the newly created state. According to the agreement's provisions Slovakia was to have its own independent administration, parliament, and court system. The Pittsburgh Agreement subsequently became one of the most controversial documents in Czechoslovakia's history. Its provisions were not incorporated into Czechoslovakia's constitution, and a centralized government was established instead. During the 1920s and 1930s several Slovak American organizations tried unsuccessfully to persuade Czechoslovakia's government to implement the Pittsburgh Agreement. During the Cold War, Slovak organizations actively supported American policies and those of other countries that opposed the totalitarian government in Czechoslovakia.

MILITARY

The precise number of Slovaks who served in World War I cannot be determined. Military records for the period after 1920 categorize Slovaks and Czechs together as Czechoslovaks. According to the 1990 census, 6,566 persons, including 635 women, of Slovak ancestry were serving in the United States military.

INDIVIDUAL AND GROUP CONTRIBUTIONS

The Americanization of names as well as intermarriage among ethnic groups precludes identifying many persons of Slovak ancestry who have made a significant contribution to American society or to the arts, sciences, education, industry, and government.

AEROSPACE

Astronaut Eugene Cernan (1935–) participated in Gemini space flights and Apollo-Saturn moon missions; his father came to the United States from Kysuce in Slovakia.

ART AND ENTERTAINMENT

Andy Warhol, (1928-1987), pop artist, famous for his paintings of soup cans and other modern art, was the son of immigrants who came to the United States from Slovakia in 1913. Actor Jack Palance (1920–) received the 1991 Academy Award for best supporting actor for his role in *City Slickers.*

LITERATURE

Thomas Bell (1903-1961), originally Belejcak, was a second-generation Slovak author of six novels; his best and most famous novel, *Out of This Furnace*, vividly portrays the life of Slovak immigrants, their children, and grandchildren from the turn of the century into the Great Depression of the 1930s. Michael Novak (1933–), author of *Naked I Leave*, is also a theologian and conservative commentator who received the 1994 Templeton Prize for Progress in Religion. Paul Wilkes (1938–) is also a noted writer.

MILITARY

In World War I, Michael Kocak (1882-c.1918), who was born in Gbely in western Slovakia, received both an Army and a Navy Congressional Medal of Honor; he singlehandedly and under fire eliminated a German machine-gun nest and then organized 25 French colonial troops and led them in a successful attack on another machine-gun position. Michael Strank (d. 1945), a Slovak who came to the United States in 1922, was one of the six men immortalized by the famous photograph of the raising of the American flag atop Mount Suribachi, Iwo Jima, on February 23, 1945; the U.S. Marine Corps Memorial monument located adjacent to Arlington National Cemetery is based on that photograph.

SPORTS

George Blanda (1927–) is a professional football legend. Chicago Black Hawks star Stan Mikita (1940–) was born in Slovakia.

MEDIA

PRINT

Fraternally Yours, Zenska Jednota.
A monthly publication of the First Catholic Slovak Ladies Association.

Contact: Dolores J. Soska, Editor.
Address: 24950 Chagrin Boulevard, Beachwood, Ohio 44122.
Telephone: (216) 464-8015.
Fax: (216) 464-8717.

Jednota (Union).
A monthly publication of the First Catholic Slovak Union.

Contact: Anthony X. Sutherland, Editor.
Address: 1011 Rosedale Avenue, Middletown, Pennsylvania 17057.

Telephone: (717) 944-0461.
Fax: (717) 944-3107.

Narodne noviny.
A monthly publication of the National Slovak Society.

Contact: Lori Crowley, Associate Editor.
Address: 2325 East Carson Street, Pittsburgh, Pennsylvania 15203.
Telephone: (412) 488-1890.

Nedelni Hlasatel.
Newspaper published in Czech and Slovak.

Contact: Josef Kucera, Editor.
Address: 5906 West 26th Street, Cicero, Illinois 60804.
Telephone: (708) 863-1891.
Fax: (708) 863-1893.

Slovak v Amerike.
Contact: John A. Holy, Editor.
Address: 1414 Main Avenue, Clifton, New Jersey 07011-2126.
Telephone: (201) 812-0554.
Fax: (201) 812-0554.

Zornicka.
A monthly publication of the Ladies Pennsylvania Slovak Catholic Union.

Contact: Cecilia Gaughan, Editor.
Address: 69 Public Square, Suite 922, Wilkes-Barre, Pennsylvania 18701.
Telephone: (717) 823-3513.

RADIO

WCPN-FM (90.3).
"Slovak Radio Hour" is a weekly one-hour cultural program that also includes local Slovak community items.

Contact: Vlado E. Mlynek.
Address: 8211 Essen Avenue, Parma, Ohio 44129.
Telephone: (216) 884-3705.

WEDO-AM (810).
"McKeesport Slovak Radio Hour" is a weekly one-hour program that features folk music, news from Slovakia, and local Slovak community items.

Address: Midtown Plaza Mall, 516 Sinclair Street, McKeesport, Pennsylvania 15132.
Telephone: (412) 664-4431.

WERE-AM (1300).

"Slovak Radio Program" is a weekly one-hour cultural program that also includes local Slovak community items.

Contact: Johanna Oros.
Address: 1041 Huron Road, Cleveland,
   Ohio 44124.
Telephone: (216) 696-1300.

WMBS-AM (590).

"Slovak Hour" is a weekly one-hour program featuring music and news.

Contact: Rudolph Faix.
Address: 82 West Lafayette Street, Uniontown,
   Pennsylvania 15401.
Telephone: (412) 438-3900.

WPIT-AM (730).

"Western Pennsylvania Slovak Radio Hour" is a weekly one-hour program that features folk music and local Slovak community items.

Address: 200 Gateway Towers, Suite 1615,
   Pittsburgh, Pennsylvania 15222.
Telephone: (412) 281-1900.

ORGANIZATIONS AND ASSOCIATIONS

First Catholic Slovak Ladies Association (FCSLA).

Founded in August 1892, the FCSLA is a religious fraternal organization that provides insurance benefits to more than 105,000 members. It also promotes the preservation of Catholicism and ethnic culture among Slovak American Catholics.

Contact: Maryann Johanek, President.
Address: 24950 Chagrin Boulevard, Beechwood,
   Ohio 44122.
Telephone: (216) 464-8015.

First Catholic Slovak Union of the U.S.A. and Canada (FCSU).

Founded in September 1890, the FCSU is a religious fraternal organization that provides insurance benefits to more than 88,300 members. It promotes the preservation of Catholicism and ethnic culture among Slovak American Catholics. The FCSU also operates an orphanage and a publishing house, the Jednota Press, in Middletown, Pennsylvania.

Contact: Kenneth A. Arendt, National Secretary.

Address: 6611 Rockside Road, Cleveland,
   Ohio 44131-2398.
Telephone: (216) 642-9406.
Fax: (216) 642-4310.

National Slovak Society (NSS).

Founded in 1890, the NSS is a secular fraternal organization that provides insurance benefits to more than 13,700 members. It also promotes the preservation of ethnic culture among Slovak Americans.

Contact: David G. Blazek, President.
Address: 2325 East Carson Street, Pittsburgh,
   Pennsylvania 15203.
Telephone: (412) 488-1890.

Slovak Catholic Sokol (SCS).

Founded in 1905, the SCS is a religious organization that provides insurance benefits to nearly 41,400 members. It promotes athletic and gymnastic programs as well as the preservation of Catholicism and ethnic culture among Slovak Americans.

Contact: Steven M. Pogorelec, Supreme Secretary.
Address: 205 Madison Street, Passaic,
   New Jersey 07055.
Telephone: (973) 777-2605.
Fax: (973) 779-8245.

Slovak League of America.

Founded in 1907, the Slovak League is a secular organization that promotes the preservation of Slovak culture in the United States. It also provides funds for projects to assist cultural and religious institutions in Slovakia.

Contact: John A. Holy, Secretary-Treasurer.
Address: 205 Madison Street, Passaic,
   New Jersey 07055.

MUSEUMS AND RESEARCH CENTERS

Balch Institute for Ethnic Studies.

Institute has Slovak books and periodicals. Its manuscript collections include some fraternal and organizational records as well as papers of a few Slovak Americans.

Contact: Joseph Anderson, Librarian.
Address: 18 South Seventh Street, Philadelphia,
   Pennsylvania 19106.
Telephone: (215) 925-8090.

Immigration History Research Center.
Located at the University of Minnesota, it is the largest repository in the world of materials on immigrants from eastern and southern Europe. Among its holdings are Slovak newspapers, fraternal and non-fraternal publications, and books. Its manuscript collections include the records of several Slovak organizations, fraternal societies, churches, and prominent persons.

Contact: Joel Wurl, Curator.
Address: 826 Berry Street, St. Paul,
 Minnesota 55114.
Telephone: (612) 627-4208.

Jankola Library and Archives Center.
This is the largest Slovak Library in the United States with more than 30,000 volumes. It also contains manuscript collections and Slovak artifacts.

Contact: Sister Martina Tybor.
Address: Danville Academy, Danville,
 Pennsylvania 17821.
Telephone: (717) 275-5606.

Jednota Museum and Archives Center.
This museum houses books, Slovak memorabilia, costumes, and artifacts. It also contains First Catholic Slovak Union publications and materials as well as records from some local FCSU lodges.

Contact: Edward Tuleja.
Address: Rosedale and Jednota Lane, Middletown,
 Pennsylvania 17057.
Telephone: (717) 944-2403.

Slovak Institute.
This institute has extensive holdings of books, newspapers, periodicals, and other documents related to Slovak immigration and life in the United States.

Contact: Reverend Father Andrew Pier.
Address: 2900 Martin Luther King Jr. Drive,
 Cleveland, Ohio 44104.
Telephone: (216) 721-5300.

Slovak Studies Association
Independent, nonprofit association, located at Illinois Benedictine College. Research focuses on Slovak Culture.

Address: Benedictine University, 5700 College
 Road, Lisle, Illinois 60532.
Telephone: (630) 829-6000.
Fax: (630) 960-1126.

E-mail: fmikula@ben.edu.
Online: http://www.ben.edu/.

Slovak World Congress (SWC).
Seeks to make known the history and aspirations of Slovak people and strives to preserve cultural heritage and provide those of Slovak descent with a sense of their historical background.

Contact: Vida Capay, Secretary General.
Address: 1243 Islington Avenue, Suite 805,
 Toronto, Ontario, Canada M8X 1Y9.
Telephone: (416) 503-1918.

SOURCES FOR ADDITIONAL STUDY

Capek, Thomas Jr., "The Slovaks in America," in his *The Cech (Bohemian) Community of New York.* New York: Czechoslovak Section of America's Making, 1921; reprinted, San Francisco: R & E Research Associates, 1969; pp. 77-93.

Hudak, Andrew F., Jr. *Slovaks in Florida.* Winter Park, FL: Agency DaVel, 1991.

Krause, Paul. *The Battle for Homestead, 1880-1992: Politics, Culture, and Steel.* Pittsburgh: University of Pittsburgh Press, 1992.

Slovak Pride: Family Names & Ancestral Villages. Rochester, NY: Slovak Heritage & Folklore Society International, 1996.

Slovaks in America: Historical and Cultural Studies: A Bicentennial Study, compiled by Joseph Krajsa, et al. Middletown, Pennsylvania: Jednota Press, 1978.

Stasko, Jozef. *Slovaks in the United States of America: Brief Sketches of Their History, National Heritage, and Activites.* Cambridge, Ontario: Good Books Press, 1974.

Stolarik, M. Mark. *Growing Up on the South Side: Three Generations of Slovaks in Bethlehem, Pennsylvania, 1880-1976.* Lewisburg, Pennsylvania: Bucknell University Press, 1985.

————. *The Slovak Americans.* New York: Chelsea House, 1988.

The belief that the American and Slovenian cultures at their best are not only compatible but complement and enrich each other seems to appeal to large numbers of Slovenian Americans who have visited the country of their ancestors.

SLOVENIAN AMERICANS

by
Edward Gobetz

OVERVIEW

Slovenia measures 7,896 square miles (20,256 square kilometers), which is slightly less than Massachusetts or half the size of Switzerland. About two-thirds of Slovenia is located in the Alps, the remaining third gradually melts into the Pannonian Plains. Correspondingly, the climate of tiny Slovenia is Mediterranean along the Adriatic Sea, alpine in the mountains, and continental (Central European) in the plains. Bordering on Italy to the west, Austria to the north, Hungary to the east, and Croatia to the south, Slovenia has a population of just a little over two million. In 1999, about 92 percent of the population are Slovenians. The largest minority groups are Serbo-Croatians (2 percent), Hungarians, Italians, and Gypsies. Roman Catholicism is the predominant religion. The flag consists of three equal horizontal stripes—from top to bottom—of white, blue, and red with a blue and white (sky and mountain) coat of arms in the upper left side corner. The capital is Ljubljana. The official language is Slovenian. Milan Kucan has been the president since 1990.

Slovenians, the westernmost Slavic people, have always been geographically and culturally a part of Central Europe rather than of the Balkans. Outside of Slovenia, significant Slovenian communities live in Italy and Austria, and a small community exists in Hungary. Slovenia is sometimes confused with Slavonia (a region in Croatia) or Slovakia. Since its independence in 1991, intensified tourist and other economic relations with Western countries, and admission as a member of the European Union, the country has received more attention.

HISTORY

While most historians believe that Slovenia was settled between 568 and 650 A.D., this has been challenged by a group of writers who argue that Slovenians are descendants of an ancient West Slavic people called Veneti, Vendi or Wends—a people that predate the Romans. All scholars agree that Slovenians settled in present-day Slovenia by 650 A.D. They enjoyed a brief independence at the dawn of their known history when they developed a form of representative democracy, which was well known to several leading figures, including Thomas Jefferson; this ancient Slovenian democracy was, according to Harvard historian Crane Brinton in the *Catholic Historical Review*, a variable that "went into the making of modern Western institutions."

After allying themselves with the Bavarians against the warlike Avars and jointly defeating them in 743, the northern Karantanian Slovenians lost their independence to their Bavarian allies who refused to leave, and a year or two later to the Franks who subdued the Bavarians. After the mysterious disappearance of Prince Kocelj, the Slovenians of Pannonia came under the rule of a Frankish overlord in 874. For over a millennium the Slovenian people were under the political administration of their more powerful neighbors: the Bavarians, the Franks, the Holy Roman Empire, and the Austrian Empire.

The Christianization of the Slovenians had been conducted by missionaries from Aquileia (now in northern Italy) and Salzburg (then an ethnically mixed territory). The most famous missionaries were the Irish bishop St. Modestus in the mid-eighth century who labored in Karantania, and the brothers St. Cyril and St. Methodius from Salonica who spread the Christian faith in Slovenian Pannonia in the late 860s and 870s and established a seminary to educate Slovenian boys for the priesthood.

In addition to constant Germanization pressures, which began with the Christianization process, the Slovenians suffered almost two centuries of sporadic Turkish raids, especially from 1408 to 1578. An estimated 100,000 Slovenians perished and an equal number of young boys and girls were taken to Turkey where boys were trained as Turkish soldiers (*janizaries*) and the girls were put into harems. In 1593, however, the united Slovenian and Croatian forces decisively defeated the Turks in the battle of Sisak, Croatia. Due to the leadership of Count Andrej Turjaški (Andreas of Turjak, Slovenia), the threat of subsequent Turkish raids on Slovenian lands was considerably diminished. Slovenians were also involved in numerous uprisings against the exploitative foreign nobility, the most famous of which was the joint Slovenian-Croatian revolt of 1573 in which over a third of the revolutionaries perished in battle, while many of the survivors were tortured and executed. Although German-speaking Austrians and Germans wanted to Germanize the Slovenians in order to establish a secure land-bridge to the Adriatic and the Mediterranean Seas, the bulk of Slovenians resisted bribes and threats, occasionally gaining genuine friends and supporters, thus preserving their ethnic and cultural identity.

Slovenians learned to read and write as early as the 860s. The Slovenians established the Jesuit College in Ljubljana in 1595, *Academia operosorum*—the first Slovenian Academy of Arts and Sciences—in 1673, and *Academia philhamionicorum* in 1701. They created a beautiful literature, culminating in the poetry of Dr. France Prešeren (1800-1849), and in the prose of Ivan Cankar (1876-1918), and share with the Scandinavians the reputation of being the best-read people of Europe. They have also made numerous contributions to the world, including Jurij Slatkonia, who became the first regular bishop of Vienna in 1513 and founded the internationally acclaimed Vienna Boys choir. Many prominent scholars and scientists were Slovenian, including: Joseph Stefan (1835-1893), a physicist and author of Stefan's fourth-power law, who was also one of the many Slovenian rectors of the University of Vienna; Frederic Pregl (1869-1930), father of micro-analysis and Nobel prize winner in chemistry in 1923; Leo Caprivi (Kopriva; 1831-1899), the chancellor of Germany in 1890s; Kurt von Schuschnigg (Sušnik; 1897-1977), the last chancellor of Austria prior to Hitler's Anschluss; Misha Lajovic (1921–), the first immigrant and the first non-Anglo-Saxon federal senator of Australia; and Dr. Aloysius M. Ambrožič (1930–), the first immigrant and Slavic archbishop of Toronto, the largest Catholic diocese of Canada.

MODERN ERA

A part of Austria until 1918 and then Yugoslavia, with a period of German and Italian occupation and the brutal communist revolution between 1941 and 1945, Slovenia organized the first free post-war elections in the spring of 1990. Slovenia declared independence from the Federation of Yugoslavia on June 25, 1991, and after inflicting surprising defeats on the communist-led Yugoslav Army under the leadership of defense minister Janez Janša, achieved peace on July 7, 1991. On December 23, 1991, the Slovenian Constitution was adopted. On January 15, 1992, while Christian Democrat Lojze Peterle was prime minister, the European Commmunity led by Christian Democratic governments recognized independent Slovenia. On May 22, 1992, Slovenia became a permanent member of the United Nations. Subsequently, constant democratic development and a successful market economy were recorded. Slovenia is aspiring to become a NATO (North Atlantic Treaty Organization) member, and its admission will be considered in the year 2002.

"The first night in America I spent, with hundreds of other recently arrived immigrants, in an immense hall with tiers of narrow iron-and-canvas bunks, four deep.... The bunk immediately beneath mine was occupied by a Turk.... I thought how curious it was that I should be spending a night in such proximity to a Turk, for Turks were traditional enemies of Balkan peoples, including my own nation.... Now here I was, trying to sleep directly above a Turk, with only a sheet of canvas between us."

Louis Adamic in 1913, cited in *Ellis Island: An Illustrated History of the Immigrant Experience,* edited by Ivan Chermayeff et al. (New York: Macmillan, 1991).

THE FIRST SLOVENIANS IN AMERICA

The first proven settler of mixed Slovenian-Croatian ancestry was Ivan Ratkaj, a Jesuit priest who reached the New World in 1680. He was followed by Mark Anton Kappus, S. J., who came to America in 1687 and distinguished himself as missionary, educator, writer, and explorer. In the 1730s Slovenians and Croatians established small agricultural settlements in Georgia. A number of Slovenian soldiers fought in George Washington's revolutionary forces. Between 1831 and 1868, the Slovenian-born scholar, missionary, and bishop, Frederic Baraga, labored on a vast 80,000 square mile piece of virgin territory, including parts of Michigan, Wisconsin, Minnesota, and Canada, where he and his followers built some of the first churches and schools. Father Andreas Skopec (Skopez) reached Fryburg, Pennsylvania, in 1846 and was joined by several of his Slovenian compatriots. Other Slovenian settlements followed in the mining town of Calumet, Michigan, in 1856, the farming community of Brockway, Minnesota, in 1865, and several rural areas in Michigan, Illinois, and Iowa. Settlements were also established in Omaha, Nebraska, in 1868, Joliet, Illinois, in 1873; New York City in 1878, and Cleveland, Ohio, in 1881. Following the missionaries and other trailblazers, the largest numbers of Slovenian immigrants reached America between 1880 and World War I, particularly from 1905 to 1913, although the exact numbers are impossible to pinpoint because Slovenians were then shown either as Austrians or jointly with Croatians, or under a number of other broader labels.

The 1910 census reported 183,431 persons of Slovenian mother tongue, 123,631 "foreign-born" and 59,800 born in America. These numbers are clearly an underestimate of the actual Slovenian population since descendants of earlier settlers often no longer knew Slovenian. Many Slovenians coming from Austria tried to escape the anti-Slavic prejudice by identifying themselves as Austrians, and many who should have been reported as Slovenian appeared under such general headings as Slav, Slavic, Slavish, or Slavonian. The actual number of Americans of Slovenian descent was probably somewhere between 200,000 and 300,000. The underestimate was even more pronounced in the 1990 census, which listed only 124,427 Americans of "Slovene" ancestry. Since the ancestry was the identifying criterion, including persons with single and multiple ethnic ancestry, regardless of whether or not they knew the Slovenian language, the actual numbers of Slovenian Americans has been growing approximately to the same extent as the total population of the United States.

SETTLEMENT

From the very beginning, Slovenian immigrants have been widely scattered in many states. However, despite the underestimates, the U.S. census probably identifies correctly the states with the highest concentration of Slovenian Americans. Ohio, where about 40 percent live, is the unrivaled leader, with greater Cleveland as the home of the largest Slovenian community. It is followed by Pennsylvania, with about 12 percent, and Illinois with less than ten percent. Minnesota and Wisconsin each have a little over five percent Slovenian population, followed in descending order by California, Colorado, Michigan, Florida, New York, Texas, Indiana, Washington, Kansas, and Maryland. There is, however, no single American state in which Slovenians have not been represented in the 1990 census.

ACCULTURATION AND ASSIMILATION

Until 1918 the bulk of Slovenian immigrants were Slovenian by ethnicity and Austrian by citizenship or statehood. They usually knew German, which facilitated their adjustment in the American work place where, at that time, many foremen were from German-speaking countries. Yet, the American population began to differentiate between genuine German Austrians, other German-nationality members, and various non-German ethnic groups, including the Slovenians who were looked down upon as inferior and given such pejorative labels as "Polacks," "Hunkies," and "Bohunks." Residents of cities with larger settlements of immigrants became aware of further subdivisions and reserved "Hunkies" for Hungarians, "Bohunks" for Czechs and Slovaks, and "Grainers" or "Grenish" (a corruption of the term "Krainers," i.e., from the Slovenian province of Krain, Kranjska, or Carniola) for Slovenians. Numerous accounts and studies suggest that for over half a century after 1880 there was strong anti-Slavic and anti-Slovenian prejudice in America. Although Slovenians were not included among the 40 "races" or ethnic groups whose hierarchical position in America has been studied since 1926 by means of the Bogardus Social Distance Scale, statistical scores and narrative reports in leading textbooks suggest that there was an intense and widespread prejudice against all Slavic groups.

Initially most Slovenians coped with the problems of being low-status or despised strangers in a foreign land by establishing their own ethnic communities, including churches, schools, and business establishments. They also organized self-help groups such as fraternal societies, social and political clubs, and national homes as their new community centers. A high degree of self-sufficiency among Slovenians helped them adjust relatively well within their own ethnic community and facilitated adjustment in the American work place and in society at large. Many applied the leadership skills they had learned in their ethnic neighborhoods to wider American society, rising from club or lodge officers to become members of city councils, mayors, and other American political, business, and civic leaders. With few exceptions this piecemeal adjustment to America seemed to proceed remarkably well. Similarly, the Slovenians avoided being on welfare; in times of crises they helped each other.

Slovenian Americans have acquired English with impressive speed and facility. They have been anxious to own homes, often with vegetable and flower gardens. Approximately 48 percent of Slovenian refugees bought their homes after being in America on the average of ten years. Yet, in the spirit of a pluralistic, multicultural America, many are anxious also to preserve the best elements of their ethnic culture. Since the 1970s there has been an unprecedented surge of interest in Slovenian music (especially the accordion as the national instrument), language, genealogy, history, culture, customs, folklore, and other aspects of Slovenian heritage. The belief that the American and Slovenian cultures at their best are not only compatible but complement and enrich each other seems to appeal to large numbers of Slovenian Americans who have visited the country of their ancestors.

CUISINE

Slovenian immigrant women and many of their descendants traditionally have been excellent cooks and bakers; many of their culinary specialties are sold in ethnic communities today at fund raising projects. Some of the most popular goodies include *potica*, which is as Slovenian as apple pie is American. Among the usual varieties are walnut, raisin, and tarragon *poticas*. Apple, cherry, apricot, cheese, and other varieties of *štrudel* are also tempting delicacies, as are *krofi*, the Slovenian variety of doughnuts, and *flancati*, a flaky, deep-fried pastry. Dumplings (*cmoki* and *štruklji*), meat-filled or liver-filled for soups, are also popular, as well as those filled with apricots, plums, finely ground meat, or cheese, which can be served as the main meal, or as dessert. In addition to all kinds of chicken and other meats, the Carniolan sausage (*kranjske klobase*) and for Easter, "filled stomach" (*želodec*) are also favorites. Slovenian wines have won many international prizes and some Slovenian Americans continue to make their own wine, even if they no longer grow their own grapes. Slovenians in the "old" country traditionally have been known for their hospitality.

TRADITIONS, CUSTOMS, AND BELIEFS

In several Slovenian communities some group-specific customs survive. One of these is *miklavževanje*, celebrations of *sv. Miklavž* or the old St. Nick's feast when the good saint, dressed up as a bishop and accompanied by angels and *parkelji* (little devils), visits Slovenian communities, exhorts children to be good, and distributes gifts, usually from a throne put in the center of the stage. Vintage festivals (*trgatve*) at recreation farms or parks and in national halls attract merrymakers, with dancing or socializing under clusters of tempting grapes; those who reach for them and are caught by the "police," are

taken to the "court" and sent to a "jail" where all can see their sad "fate." Then, a loved one pays the ransom or fine, which is used for a worthy cause, while the "thief" (or *tat*) is set free. There is also *martino-vanje*, a public celebration of St. Martin's feast when the good saint changes lowly grape juice into tasty wine. This is another good opportunity for socializing, a banquet with wine-tasting, and a dance of waltzes and polkas. Concerts and festivals, plays and sports events, bazaars and exhibits, benefit brunches, lunches, and suppers all keep Slovenians in ethnic communities busy and happy.

HOLIDAYS

June 25 is celebrated to mark the country's independence from the former Yugoslav Federation. Slovenian Americans also celebrate New Year's Day, Catholic Easter and Christmas, as well as the feast days of various saints in the Catholic calendar.

HEALTH ISSUES

Slovenian culture has emphasized the value of good health. One of the most frequently quoted sayings states, "*Zdravje je največje bogastvo*"—"Health is the greatest wealth." Following the Czech lead, the most influential Slovenian youth organizations, which often included "youngsters" 50 or 70 years old, were the Eagles (*Orli*) and the Falcons (*Sokoli*). They adopted an ancient Roman guideline as their own slogan,"*Mens sana in corpore sano*"—"A heathy mind in a healthy body," paying attention to devel-

opment of both good character and physical fitness. Active participation in athletics, gymnastics, walks, hikes, mountain climbing, and a variety of sports, including skiing, contribute to good health. Alcohol consumption and smoking, on the other hand, have been among the unhealthy practices in which large numbers of Slovenians indulge.

In America, overcrowded boarding houses and life in depressing urban areas with air, water, and noise pollution contributed a new variety of health hazards for early immigrants. In places such as steel mills and coal mines, occupational risks lurked for workers. Many often experienced unavoidable accidents, increased air pollution, extremes of heat and cold, and pollution with coal dust resulting in black lung disease that drastically shortened the life of countless miners. In some mining towns, from Pennsylvania to Wyoming, there is an alarming absence of older men; and their widows survive with nothing but their modest homes and low retirement pensions to compensate them for their families' share in building a more prosperous America.

As working and living conditions have generally improved, and some good health habits learned in childhood have persisted, the health and mental health of Slovenian Americans is now comparable to that of other Americans. It is unclear whether or not home remedies, such as a small pharmacy of medicinal herbs that many Slovenian immigrant households maintained, have been among the contributing factors to better health. A conclusion of "slightly better" than "national health" was reached by Dr. Sylvia J. O'Kicki, who examined a group of

Slovenian Americans with comparable cohorts selected from the National Health Interview Survey of 1985. She states in *Ethnicity and Health* that "when the group of Slovene Americans without any regard to the level of ethnicity is compared to the national American sample they differ favorably in health status and the practice of health behaviors.... Those who are actively involved in the heritage and traditions of the ethnic group report a more favorable health status and practice of more favorable health behaviors."

In general, there was a remarkable resilience among earlier immigrants who were confronted by adverse conditions and problems that few could imagine today. Post-World War II refugees also went through years of deprivations, hardships of camp life, and a series of new problems in a strange new country, which often left them physically and emotionally exhausted and penniless. Some of them even survived death camps such as Dachau; two of them, Milan Zajec and Frank Dejak, miraculously escaped from a communist mass grave.

LANGUAGE

Slovenian is a Slavic language that utilizes the Latin alphabet. It is also the language of the oldest preserved written documents of any Slavic people, the so-called *Brižinski spomeniki* (the Freising Monuments), dating from 1000 A.D. Prlmož Trubar published the first printed books in Slovenian starting in 1551, less than a century after the invention of the Guttenberg press. Through the millennium of incorporation into German-speaking lands the Slovenian language was the pivotal vehicle of Slovenian culture, consciousness, identity, and national survival. Because the Slovenians were few in number they were anxious to preserve their mother tongue while simultaneously learning other languages.

Slovenians have long been noted for their exceptional linguistic skills. For example, many Slovenian missionaries in America preached in five or more languages. Several colleges and universities teach the Slovenian language: University of Illinois, Indiana University, University of Kansas, Kent State University, Ohio State University, and the University of Pittsburgh. There are also several libraries with Slovenian language collections, which contributes to preservation of the language. About 30 percent of all Slovenians in the United States are bilingual—English and some Slovenian—but the younger generation tends to use English to the exclusion of their ancestors' language.

The Slovenian writing system is phonetically precise in that a letter, with very few exceptions, has the same sound. Most letters are the same as in English (except that Slovenian lacks the letters "w" and "y") and many letters have the same sound as in English. For the rest, the following pronunciation guide may be of help: "a" is pronounced as in art; "e" as in get (never as in eve); "i" as in ill (never as in like); "o" as in awe; "u" as in ruler (never as in use); "c" as in tsar (never as in cat); "i" as the "ch" in church; "g" as in go (never as in age); "j" as the "y" in yes (never as in just); "lj" as "lli" in million; "nj" as the "gn" in monsignor; "š" as in she; "z" as in zipper; and "ž" as the "ge" in garage.

GREETINGS AND OTHER POPULAR EXPRESSIONS
Dobro jutro—good morning; *dober dan*—good day; *dober večer*—good evening; *dobrodošli*—welcome; *jaz sem (Janez Zupan)*—I am (John Zupan); *to je gospod (gospa, gospodična) Stropnik*—this is Mr. (Mrs., Miss) Stropnik; *kako ste*—how are you; *hvala, dobro*—thank you, well; *na svidenje*—so long; *zbogom*—goodbye; *lahko noč*—good night; *prosim*—please; *hvala*—thank you; *na zdravje*—to your health; *dober tek*—enjoy your meal; *vse najboljše*—the best of everything; *oprosite*—excuse me; *čestitke*—congratulations; *kje je*—where is; *kje je restavracija (hotel)*—where is a restaurant (hotel); *kje je ta naslov*—where is this address; *me veseli*—I am pleased; *žal mi je*—I am sorry; *sem ameriški Slovenec (ameriška Slovenka)*—I am an American Slovenian; *vse je zelo lepo*—everything is very nice; *Slovenija je krasna*—Slovenia is beautiful; *še pridite*—come again; *srečno pot*—have a happy trip!

FAMILY AND COMMUNITY DYNAMICS

Until World War I, men usually emigrated first; after they had saved enough money, they arranged for their wives or sweethearts to follow. Early entrepreneurs, such as owners of boarding houses, restaurants, and saloons, also lured many young women to come and work for them in America; however, the men were anxious to marry them as soon as they could get to know them. As in Slovenia, divorce among Slovenian Americans has been extremely rare, although it has recently increased especially in ethnically and religiously mixed families. In general, immigrant parents are anxious for their children to marry someone from their own ethnic and religious group, although ethnic homogamy has been decreasing among members of American-born generations.

Until recently, Slovenians have also frowned upon putting their parents or elderly relatives into homes for the aged. Since employment of women has increased and families have become more mobile, an increasing proportion of the elderly are now being placed into homes for the aged. Extended families were common among early immigrants, while nuclear families prevail today. Increasingly, children move away from their parental homes once they are permanently employed, believing that this is expected in America. However, many parents still prefer to have their children live at home until marriage and save money for their own home. The oldest child is often expected to be more responsible and a role model for younger children; the youngest child is widely believed to be given most affection by all, although actual differences by order of birth are now probably comparable to those of American families. Women have played a pivotal role not only as homemakers but also in Slovenian ethnic churches, language schools, charity projects, and increasingly in political campaigns. There is a Slovenian proverb: "*Žena tri vogle podpira*"—"The woman supports three corners [of a four-corner home]."

WEDDINGS

Young people have adopted such American wedding customs as showers. However, they often still prefer huge ethnic weddings with hundreds of guests in attendance, delicious meals, and Slovenian varieties of pastries.

FUNERALS

At wakes and funerals, organizations to which the deceased belonged are represented; occasionally there are honor guards in uniforms or national costumes. After the funeral all guests are invited to a meal to show the bereaved family's appreciation for their attendance and to ease the transition for the family and community deprived of one of its members.

RELIGION

Coming from a country with strong Catholic traditions where hills and valleys are dotted with many beautiful, century-old churches, most Slovenian immigrants cling to their religious roots. They have built their own churches and other religious institutions all over America. Following the example of the missionaries, priests and seminarians came from Slovenia, and American-born descendants of immigrants gradually joined the clergy. Since 1924 the Slovenian Franciscan Commissariat of the Holy Cross in Lemont, Illinois, has played a pivotal role among Slovenian Catholics in America. It established the Mary Help of Christians Shrine (with a replica painting from Brezje, Slovenia)—the most popular Slovenian pilgrimage in North America. It comprises a monastery and seminary, a high school, a retreat house, the Alvernia Manor for the Aged, annual *Koledars*, with a Slovenian Cultural and Pastoral Center of Lemont scheduled for completion in 1994. It also publishes the religious monthly *Ave Maria*. In 1971 a Slovenian Chapel of Our Lady of Brezje was dedicated inside the National Shrine of the Immaculate Conception in Washington, D.C., becoming another significant Slovenian religious landmark in America.

Many Slovenian parishes have been struggling for survival in recent years, mostly because of the changing nature of neighborhoods, the flight of Slovenian population to the suburbs, increased Americanization and secularization of the younger generation, and the lack of Slovenian priests. In very rare instances, ethnic churches that have closed have been replaced by new ones in new neighborhoods, as happened in Milwaukee-West Allis, Wisconsin, or in Bridgeport-Fairfield in Connecticut.

There is also a small number of Slovenian Protestants who refer to themselves as Windish. Although numerically small, this community has long used a Slovenian dialect in interaction, its services, and its press, and has displayed considerable ethnic and religious vitality, as exemplified by St. John's Windish Lutheran Church in Bethlehem, Pennsylvania, and a few other Slovenian Protestant institutions.

Many Slovenians worship in other American Catholic parishes, while an extremely small number have joined other religions. Geographic and social mobility and intermarriage have caused the absorption into other Catholic churches. The children of young couples are frequently enrolled in local Catholic schools, which means that their parents also join the usually non-Slovenian parish. Many of these people still return to Slovenian parishes on special occasions—Christmas and Easter, annual festivals, celebrations of holidays, Corpus Christi processions, Palm Sunday festivities with Slovenian *butare* (ornamented bundles of branches). St. Mary's Parish in Cleveland even presents the Passion liturgy in Slovenian, all conducted by school children in biblical attire (ranging from Roman soldiers to Mary and Christ).

EMPLOYMENT AND ECONOMIC TRADITIONS

With the exception of missionaries, priests, and some 6,000 to 10,000 ideological dissenters, especially post-World War II refugees from Marshall Tito's communism, the bulk of Slovenians in America were economic immigrants. As in most groups, they tended to come from the poorest areas and most economically disadvantaged families. With the exception of persons who wanted to avoid being drafted, a few adventurers, socialist or other political dissenters, post-1947 refugees, and farm laborers have also immigrated in significant numbers.

The earliest immigrants often took advantage of the open lands and homesteading, and established such Slovenian pioneer farming communities as St. Stephen's and St. Anthony's in Minnesota, or later Traunik in Michigan. Many immigrants initially intended to return to Slovenia after they had earned enough money to establish themselves in their native country. When the land became more difficult to obtain, however, the major wave of Slovenian immigrants settled in industrial cities and mining towns where their unskilled labor earned them meager wages.

It is impossible to discover an exact breakdown of employment since Slovenians were shown as Austrians or Yugoslavs, or combined with Croatians or South Slavs on most documents. While Slovenians were better educated than other South Slav groups, the statistical distribution was probably more favorable for them than shown. The available data on the South Slavs in general are nevertheless suggestive. Thus, in 1921, 42 percent of the South Slavs were workers in steel, iron, and zinc mines, smelters, and refineries; 12 percent worked in the coal mines; 6.5 percent in the lumber industry; six percent in stockyards, and five percent in fruit growing; chemical works, railroads, and electrical manufacturing employed four percent each; professions accounted for 3.5 percent, and farming for only three percent.

Considerable numbers of Slovenian immigrants, however, soon became skilled workers. In the early decades of the twentieth century many Slovenian Americans worked in the automobile industry in Detroit, Toledo, Cleveland, and Pittsburgh. They were also well represented in the hat industry in New York. They were highly appreciated and much sought-after because of their skill and experience, having learned the trade in their home country. Included in this group were both men and women. Thus, hat making, especially straw-hat making, was a group-specific skill that many Slovenians found useful in their American employment. Other skills survived as useful hobbies: home-building and carpentry skills; butchering, sausage making, and meat-processing skills; wine making; and apiculture, which helped many Slovenian immigrants provide honey for family and friends. Women were highly skilled cooks, bakers, and gardeners, and canned large quantities of fruit and vegetables. Habits of hard work, honesty, frugality, and mutual help, particularly in times of hardship, helped Slovenian immigrants survive and succeed in a strange land.

Today, Slovenian Americans can be found in all occupations. Many are now professionals; others own businesses, agencies, and factories; still others are workers, foremen, or executives with large American companies. As research on Slovenian contributions to America shows, a large number of Slovenian Americans have achieved positions of leadership and prominence in American society.

POLITICS AND GOVERNMENT

Like other ethnic groups, Slovenian Americans were targeted by American politicians as soon as they had become citizens and were able to vote. As a rule, Slovenian Americans were attracted to the Democratic Party, viewed as the party of the working class people. Republicans have recently won a substantial number of adherents. Rising from minor political positions, such as ward leaders and members of council, Slovenian American politicians now increasingly reflect the American political spectrum, including a presidential candidate.

Slovenian American congressional representatives include John A. Blatnik (1911–) from northeastern Minnesota, who served from 1947 to 1975; he was succeeded by James L. Oberstar (1934–); Ray P. Kogovesk (1941–), was elected from Colorado in 1978; Philip Ruppe (1927–) represented Michigan between 1967 and 1979. The last was a Republican while the others were Democratic. While very few Slovenians are attracted to independent candidates, there was a substantial number of Slovenian American Democrats for Republican Ronald Reagan.

In numerous towns, such as Ely, Eveleth, Chisholm, and Gilbert in Minnesota, Slovenian Americans have long been strongly represented on city councils, and as mayors of such larger communities as Euclid and Wickliffe, Ohio. Slovenian candidates were also elected mayor in such cities as Portland, Oregon, and Indianapolis, Indiana, where the proportion of Slovenian voters was insignificant. In Cleveland, the city with the largest number of Slovenians in America, Slovenians have long served as ward leaders, council members, and heads of various branches of municipal government. They also served in Cleveland as judges, a chief of police, a council president, and a mayor. Frank J. Lausche first won national attention as a fearless judge who, and the help of Gus Korach, a Slovenian worker, broke up the widespread organized crime and corruption in a true-life drama that resulted in local and national publicity.

MILITARY

Slovenian Americans have been well represented in the military. Slovenian immigrant Louis Dobnikar, serving on the destroyer *Keamey*, was the first Clevelander and one of the first 11 Americans to be killed during World War II. John Hribar, a volunteer marine from Krayn, Pennsylvania (named after Kranj, Slovenia), was one of several Slovenian heroes of Iwo Jima. At least seven Slovenian Americans became generals, including three-star general Anthony Burshnick of the U.S. Air Force and four-star general of the U.S. Army Ferdinand Chesarek. The Archives of the Slovenian Research Center of America also contain materials on six Slovenian American admirals (with the seventh still being researched), including Ronald Zlatoper who received his fourth star in 1994.

RELATIONS WITH SLOVENIA

Slovenian Americans have not established permanent lobbying organizations in Washington, D.C., but they frequently have used existing societies and institutions, *ad hoc* committees, or temporary councils or unions to advocate or support various causes on behalf of their home country. These include: the Slovenian League, Slovenian National Union, and Slovenian Republican Alliance during World War I; various relief committees, the Union of Slovenian Parishes, and Slovenian American National Council during World War II; the Slovenian American Council, which substantially supported the first free elections that toppled the communist dictatorship in Slovenia in 1990. A special *ad hoc* committee, Americans for Free Slovenia, together with scores of other organizations and institutions, especially the *American Home* newspaper, the Slovenian Research Center of America, and thousands of individuals, helped secure the American recognition of independent Slovenia in 1992. For several decades after World War II, the Slovenian Language section of Voice of America Information Agency, played an important role by bringing objective information to its listeners in Slovenia.

INDIVIDUAL AND GROUP CONTRIBUTIONS

Slovenia, despite its small size, has made many important contributions to the world.

ACADEMIA

Emil Mrak, chancellor of University of California at Davis, and Frederick Stare, founder of Harvard University's Department of Nutrition, were America's foremost authorities on nutrition. John Nielsen (Sesek) was a leading metallurgist; Joseph Koffolt was a leader in chemical engineering; Anton Peterlin was a leader in macromolecular chemistry; Stephen Malaker was prominent in nuclear physics and cryogenics; Robert A. Pucel contributed to microwave science and technology; Anton Mavretic and Mark Dragovan distinguished themselves in astronomy; and Daniel Siewiorek was a leader in computer architecture.

AERONAUTICS

Max Stupar, an early designer and manufacturer of airplanes, was considered the father of mass airplane production. Dr. August Raspet, a noted inventor and designer of modern airplanes, was president of American Aerophysics Institute. Adrian Kisovec invented the Convertiplane-Rotafrx models. Dr. Ronald Sega became the first Slovenian astronaut.

ARCHITECTURE

Araldo Cossutta, who designed L'Enfant Plaza in Washington and numerous landmark buildings throughout America and in Europe, won, with I. M. Pei, the 1968 Architectural Firm Award. Alexander Papesh became America's foremost designer of stadiums, including the Robert F. Kennedy Stadium in Washington, D.C. Simon Kregar won national awards for design of industrial buildings.

ART

Slovenian American artists include Gregory Prusheck, Michael Lah, Stephen Rebeck, France Gorse, Donald Orehek, Lillian Brulc, Lucille Dragovan, Frank Wolcansek, John Hapel, Paul Kos, Bogdan Grom, three generations of Prazens, Joseph Opalek, Nancy Bukovnik, and Gary Bukovnik, Emilia Bucik-Razman, Miro Zupancic, Joseph Vodlan, Erica Bajuk, Vlasta Radisek, August Pust, and Damian Kreze, to mention but a few.

FILM, TELEVISION, AND DANCE

Among movie and television personalities, Laura LaPlante and Audrey Totterare are part Slovenian. Also Slovenian are actors George Dolenz and Frank Gorshin; ballerinas Veronica Mlakar of the New York City Ballet Theater and Isabella Kralj of Chamber Dance Theater in Milwaukee. Anton Schubel was director of the International Ballet Company in New York; Milko Sparemblek, a Slovenian immigrant, served as ballet director of Metropolitan Opera at Lincoln Center; Charles Kuralt, widely known as a CBS correspondent and a capable writer, has also recently discovered his Slovenian roots.

LITERATURE

Karl Mauser (1918-1977) was an author whose work was translated into German, French, and Spanish. Frank Mlakar (1913-1967), author of the acclaimed novel, *He, the Father*. Louis Adamic (1899-1951), whose widely translated books have been included as Book-of-the-Month Club and *Obras Famosas* selections, became a pioneer of multiculturalism in America with the publication of his *From Many Lands*, *My America* and *A Nation of Nations*.

MISSIONARIES

There is also a proud, if seldom known, record of contributions made to America by Slovenian missionaries. Mark Anton Kappus, a Slovenian-born Jesuit missionary, scholar, and superior of Jesuit missions in the enormous territory of Sonora and Pimeria Alta in northern Mexico and southern Arizona, came to America in 1687 and returned to Europe in 1701 to report that California was not an island, as it then had been generally believed; the most prominent Slovenian missionary was Frederic Baraga, who from 1831 to 1868, labored among Native Americans of the Upper Great Lakes region on an enormous territory of over 80,000 square miles and wrote several books, including Indian dictionaries and grammars still in use today. In numerous areas of Michigan, Wisconsin, Minnesota, and elsewhere Slovenian missionaries built the first churches and schools; they pioneered in the establishment of dioceses of Marquette, Duluth, and St. Cloud; they secured financial support from several European courts and religious organizations, while importing to America shipments of seedlings, vestments, and religious art.

MUSIC

Notable musicians include: Grammy Award-winning Polka King of America, Frankie Yankovic; the "Polka Ambassador" Tony Petkovsek; Polka Priest Frank Perkovich; America's Tamburitzan King Professor Mat Gouze; Metropolitan Opera singer Anton Schubel, who was also the talent scout for Carnegie Hall where he gave concerts with finalists of his nationwide auditions, among them his 13-year-old discovery Van Cliburn; Ivan Zorman, Dr. Sergij Delak, and Dr. Vendelin Spendov, who enriched Slovenian American music with their compositions; and John Ivanusch, known as the Father of Slovenian Opera in America; Paul Sifler is an internationally known organist and composer of such works as *Despair and Agony of Dachau*; Professor Raymond Premru's *Concerto for Orchestra* was selected in 1976 for the famous Cleveland Orchestra's Bicentennial Program conducted by Lorin Maazel.

POLITICS

Senator Tom Harkin, whose mother was a Slovenian immigrant, was one of the 1992 presidential candidates; he pioneered legislation on behalf of the disabled. George Voinovich served as mayor of Cleveland and governor of Ohio. Ludwig Andolsek was a U.S. Civil Service commissioner. John Blatnik, U.S. congressional representative from Minnesota from 1946 to 1974, chaired the Congressional Public Works committee and authored legislation that opened the St. Lawrence Seaway, established the current interstate highway system, and initiated standards for clean air and water.

SCIENCE AND TECHNOLOGY

Frederic Pregl pioneered the field of organic chemistry; Hermann Potočnik Noordung, a pioneer in space science, authored the first scientific book on manned space travel and had a considerable impact on the development of American space program. John Bucik's car of the future was one of America's leading attractions at the New York World Fair in 1964-1965. Dr. France Rode co-invented HP-35 pocket calculators, which Richard Nixon's party took to China as an example of modern U.S. technology.

SPORTS

Notable sports figures include: football players Tony and Mike Adamie, Randy Gradishar, Mark Debevc, Don Vicic, and Ken Novak; baseball players Frank Doljack, Joe Kuhel, Al Vidmar, Walter Judnich, and Al Milnar; bowlers Charles Lausche, Marge Slogar,

Mary "Whitey" Primosh Doljack, "Stevie" Rozman Balough, Sophie Rozman Kenny, Andrew Stanonik, Vince Bovitz, and Jim Stefanich; the Marolt brothers in skiing; Olympic swimmer Ann Govednik; Vicki Foltz (Šega); long-distance running champion; and Hubby Habjan, National Golf Professional of the Year (1965); Eric Heiden, winner of five gold medals at the Winter Olympics of 1980; Peter Vidmar, U.S. team captain and winner of two gold medals and a silver medal in the 1984 Olympics, was the highest scoring gymnast in U.S. history (with a 9.89 average).

MEDIA

PRINT

Amerika Domovina (The American Home).

This was published under a variety of names, starting as Narodna beseda (The Word of the People) in 1899. Privately owned and long a Slovenian-language daily, it is now a bilingual weekly newspaper, with about 3,000 subscribers. It publishes news about Slovenian communities and individuals, various ethnic affairs, and Slovenian reprints. It is the only one of the many non-fraternal Slovenian newspapers that has survived to this day.

Contact: Jim Debevec, Publisher and English Section Editor; or, Dr. Rudolph Susel, Slovenian Language Section Editor.
Address: 6117 St. Clair Avenue, Cleveland, Ohio 44103.
Telephone: (216) 431-0628.

Amerikanski Slovenec (American Slovenian).

This is the oldest Slovenian paper, published without interruption since 1891. Since 1946, when it merged with the Glasilo KSKJ (Herald of KSKJ), it has been an official organ of KSKJ, the American Slovenian Catholic Union. While most of the materials published pertain to activities of the KSKJ, it also carries a variety of news and comments of ethnic and general human interest. It is currently a bilingual (English and Slovenian) biweekly, with 10,700 subscribers.

Contact: Robert G. Gibbons, Editor.
Address: 708 East 159 Street, Cleveland, Ohio 44110.
Telephone: (216) 541-7243.

Our Voice—Glas ADZ.

This is a biweekly bilingual official organ of American Mutual Life Association (AMLA). While Clevelandska Amerika (now Ameriška Domovina) was chosen as the official organ of what was then Slovenska Dobrodelna Zveza (Slovenian Benefit Society), the seventh convention approved the establishment of its own official organ and the first issue was published early in 1932. In addition to news items about AMLA's lodge activities, Our Voice publishes many reprints from Slovenian magazines, both in Slovenian and English languages, and numerous photographs of banquets, parties, and other social and cultural affairs.

Contact: Dr. Rudolph Susel, Editor.
Address: 19424 South Waterloo Road, Cleveland, Ohio 44119.
Telephone: (216) 531-1900.

Prosveta (Enlightenment).

Long a Slovenian daily, it is now an English weekly organ of the Slovene National Benefit Society (SNPJ), devoted predominantly to news items about the fraternal organization and its local lodges and their activities. It also publishes selected items of Slovenian and general human interest, including news on various cultural programs and reprints from Slovenia. By 1994, the Slovenian language entries have been reduced to a single weekly page or less. Prosveta has 20,000 subscribers.

Contact: Jay Sedmak, Editor.
Address: 247 West Allegheny Road, Imperial, Pennsylvania 15126.
Telephone: (412) 695-1100.

Zarja—The Dawn.

This is the official organ of Slovenian Women's Union (SžZ) and was established as its monthly magazine in 1928. This bilingual magazine, with 6,500 subscribers, remains the only surviving Slovenian American monthly magazine. It is rich with news items about activities of its sponsoring organization, as well as with articles on Slovenian American families, with an emphasis on the role of mothers, and on Slovenian heritage.

Contact: Corinne Leskovar, Editor.
Address: 431 North Chicago Street, Joliet, Illinois 60432.
Telephone: (815) 727-1926.
Fax: (312) 268-7744.

RADIO

WCSB-FM (89.3).

"Songs and Melodies from Beautiful Slovenia" presents a rich variety of Slovenian songs and music, community news and news from Slovenia, excerpts from Slovenian literature, Sunday spiritual thoughts, special occasion programs, interviews, and political commentaries, all in the Slovenian language. It is currently broadcast on Sundays, 9:00 to 10:00 a.m., and on Wednesdays, 6:00 to 7:00 p.m.

Contact: Dr. Milan Pavlovčič, Producer.
Address: WCSB, Cleveland State University, Rhodes Tower, Room 956, Cleveland, Ohio 44115.
Telephone: (216) 687-3523.

WELW-AM (1330).

Tony Petkovsek's radio program broadcasts Slovenian and other polka music daily, 3:30 to 5:00 p.m., in addition to providing current community news and news from Slovenia, interviews, and radiothons in support of charitable and civic causes. Together with the Cleveland Slovenian Radio Club it has also organized annual Tony's Thanksgiving Polka Parties, which have been among the best attended Greater Cleveland community affairs.

Contact: Tony Petkovsek, Producer.
Address: 971 East 185 Street, Cleveland, Ohio 44119.
Telephone: (216) 481-8669.

WKTX-AM (830).

"Slovenia Radio" presents Slovenian and other ethnic music, together with Slovenian and English broadcasts of community news, commentaries, and transmission of news from Slovenia. It is aired on Saturdays, 9:00 to 10:00 a.m.

Contact: Paul M. Lavrisha, Producer.
Address: 6507 St. Clair Ave., Cleveland, Ohio 44103.
Telephone: (216) 391-7225.

WYMS-FM (89.9).

"Slovenian Radio Cultural Hour" presents customs, literature, songs, and music of Slovenia, together with programs dedicated to special cultural topics and news items about the Slovenian community and Slovenia. It has been conducted since 1963 by Vladislav and Isabella Kralj. The program is currently broadcast each Saturday from 11:00 a.m. until 12:00 p.m.

Contact: Vladislav Kralj, Producer.
Address: 690 Meadow Lane, Elm Grove, Wisconsin 53122.
Telephone: (414) 785-2775.

ORGANIZATIONS AND ASSOCIATIONS

American Mutual Life Association (SDZ).
Organized in 1910, it functions through 40 lodges, with a total of 12,769 members in Ohio. In addition to non-profit insurance programs and promotion of Slovenian traditions and customs, the association lists the following activities: Christmas parties for children, bowling and golf tournaments, family day picnics, clambakes, anniversary banquets honoring 50-year members, scholarship award banquets, and Christmas open house for lodge officers and board members.

Contact: Joseph F. Petric, Jr., Secretary.
Address: 19424 South Waterloo Road, Cleveland, Ohio 44119.
Telephone: (216) 531-1900.
Fax: (216) 531-8123.

American Slovene Polka Foundation.
Established in 1988, aims to preserve the American Slovene Polka style of dance. Organizes festivals, maintains a National Polka Hall of Fame, and collects memorabilia and artifacts related to the history of Polka.

Contact: Fred Kuhar, President.
Address: Shore Cultural Centre, 291 E. 22nd St., Euclid, Ohio 44123.
Telephone: (216) 261-3263.

American Slovenian Catholic Union (KSKJ).
Established in 1894 as a self-help organization which would also strive to preserve and promote Catholic and Slovenian heritage, while helping its members to be active American citizens, has 28,685 members and is the largest Slovenian Catholic organization in USA. Like SNPJ, it functions through local lodges scattered throughout America, but is coordinated by a national board of directors and an executive committee. It provides to its members payments of death and sickness benefits, scholarships, low-interest loans; it promotes friendship and true Catholic charity and conducts numerous religious, educational, cultural, recreational, and social activities.

Contact: Robert M. Verbiscer, Chief Executive Officer; or Anthony Mravle, Secretary/Treasurer.
Address: 2439 Glenwood Avenue, Joliet, Illinois 60435.
Telephone: (815) 741-2001.

Progressive Slovene Women of America (PSWA).

Founded in 1934, it has 575 members, and its purpose is: to arouse interest in knowledge; to improve social and economic conditions of women, family, and humanity in general; to promote familiarity and understanding of New and Old World cultures; and to encourage members to be good citizens and useful members of society. A philanthropic and service organization, it raises money for humanitarian/cultural causes.

Contact: Florence Unetich, National President.
Address: 19808 Arrowhead Avenue, Cleveland, Ohio 44110.
Telephone: (216) 481-0830.

Slovene National Benefit Society (SNPJ).

Founded in 1904, it is currently, with about 40,000 members, the largest Slovenian American organization. Once a stronghold of labor movement, with some prominent socialists among its leaders, it is now administered mostly by American-born, English-speaking leaders of Slovenian descent. As a non-profit fraternal benefit society, it offers low-cost insurance, tax-deferred savings plans, scholarships, pageants and debutante balls, singing and music circles, Slovenefests and other heritage programs, and a wide variety of various other benefits and activities, athletic, cultural and social projects, and recreational facilities.

Contact: Joseph C. Evanish, National President.
Address: 247 West Allegheny Road, Imperial, Pennsylvania 15126.
Telephone: (800) 843-7675.
Fax: (412) 695-1555.
E-mail: snpj@snpj.com.
Online: http://www.snpj.com.

Slovenian Women's Union (SžZ).

Organized in 1926, this organization of 6,100 members has united American Slovenian women of Catholic orientation. Fraternal activities are organized on local (lodge), regional and national basis and include scholarship and educational programs, heritage projects, visits of sick members and paying tribute to deceased members, numerous charity and athletic projects, tributes to honorees such as mothers of the year; uniformed, baton-twirling drill teams, cooking classes and contests.

Contact: Olga Ancel, National Secretary.
Address: 431 North Chicago Street, Joliet, Illinois 60432.
Telephone: (815) 727-1926.

MUSEUMS AND RESEARCH CENTERS

Museum of the Slovenian Women's Union of America.

The museum has a collection of Slovenian memorabilia, books, pictures, slides, records, Slovenian national costumes, and handicrafts. It also functions as a gift shop where various Slovenian items, including books and souvenirs, can be purchased.

Contact: Mollie Gregorich.
Address: 431 North Chicago Street, Joliet, Illinois 60432.
Telephone: (815) 723-4514.

Slovenian Heritage Center.

The center has a museum with three specified categories. One is dedicated to Slovenia alone, with maps, coats of arms, books, pictures, and artifacts. The second covers the Slovenian American history and houses a library of Slovenian and Slovenian American authors. The third area deals with the SNPJ history and also serves as a lecture and conference room.

Contact: Lou Serjak.
Address: 674 North Market, East Palestine, Ohio 44413.
Telephone: (412) 336-5180.

Slovenian Research Center of America, Inc.

This organization is dedicated to research, education, exhibits, publications, and information service on Slovenian heritage. An American and international network of Slovenian volunteer associates assist in research on Slovenian contributions to America and the world, establishing the richest contemporary collection of its kind. Other areas of research include activities and integration of Slovenian immigrants and their descendants, and their organizations.

Contact: Dr. Edward Gobetz, Director.
Address: 29227 Eddy Road, Willoughby Hills, Ohio 44092.
Telephone: (440) 944-7237.
Fax: (440) 289-3724.

SOURCES FOR ADDITIONAL STUDY

Anthology of Slovenian American Literature, edited by G. Edward Gobetz and Adele Donchenko.

Willoughby Hills, Ohio: Slovenian Research Center of America, 1977.

Arnez, John. *Slovenian Community in Bridgeport, Connecticut*. New York: Studia Slovenica, 1971.

Gobetz, G. Edward. *Adjustment and Assimilation of Slovenian Refugees*. New York: Arno Press, 1980.

Govorchin, Gerald Gilbert. *Americans from Yugoslavia*. Gainesville: University of Florida Press, 1961.

Prisland, Marie. *From Slovenia to America: Recollections and Collections*. Milwaukee: Bruce Publishing, 1968.

Slovenian Heritage, Volume I, edited by Edward Gobetz. Willoughby Hills, Ohio: Slovenian Research Center of America, 1980.

Velikonja, J. and R.L. Lencek, eds. *Who's Who of Slovene Descent in the United States*. New York: Columbia University Press, Society of Slovene Studies, 1995.

The cultures of South Africa are more rich in colorful terminology than they are in proverbs. The nation's various black ethnic groups have a wide array of piquant expressions, but so too does the white population, and there is much crossover between cultures in this regard.

SOUTH AFRICAN AMERICANS

by
Judson Knight and
Lorna Mabunda

OVERVIEW

South Africa is a nation of 471,445 square miles (1,221,043 square kilometers), slightly smaller than the combined areas of Texas, New Mexico, and Arizona. As its name implies, it is located at the southern tip of Africa, with Namibia to the northwest; Botswana to the north; and Zimbabwe, Mozambique, and Swaziland to the northeast. The nation of Lesotho is entirely contained within South Africa, one of the few places on earth where such a phenomenon occurs. As for the western, southern, and eastern boundaries of South Africa, these are formed by oceans. The Atlantic lies to the west, and the Indian Ocean to the south and east. A line along the twentieth parallel east, near Cape Agulhas, forms the boundary between the two oceans.

The population of South Africa, almost 43 million people in 1998, is extremely diverse ethnically, and indeed ethnic divisions form a central theme of South African history and culture. Racially the nation is 75 percent black; 14 percent white; 9 percent "Colored," a term designating persons of mixed racial heritage; and 2 percent Asian. Ethnically these groups are further divided, with the largest black minorities comprised of 5.6 million Xhosa, 5.3 million Zulu, and 4.2 million Sotho. Of the nation's 6 million whites, about 3.6 million are of Afrikaner heritage, and 2.4 million are English. The 3.6 million Coloreds come from a variety of origins, their ethnic makeup a mixture of white, black, and Asian ancestry. Finally, there is the Asian population, of which Indians—one of the largest communities outside of India itself—make up the majority.

Sixty-eight percent of South Africa's population is Christian, and another 29 percent is made up of persons, mostly black, who adhere to traditional religions. The other 3 percent consists of Jews, as well as the predominantly Hindu Indian population. As a further mark of its ethnic diversity, South Africa has 11 official languages, including Afrikaans, English, Ndebele, and Sotho. With such a mixture of peoples, it is perhaps fitting that South Africa has three capitals, one for each branch of government: Cape Town (legislative), Pretoria (executive), and Bloemfontein (judicial). The national flag, adopted in 1994 to replace the orange, white, and blue stripes of the old South African standard, is also fitting in its multicolored character. A green stripe shaped like a capital letter Y, with the ends opening to the left, dominates the flag. It is bordered in white on one side, with a red trapezoid in the upper right and a blue one in the lower right. To the left is a black triangle bordered in gold.

HISTORY

The earliest known inhabitants of South Africa were Pygmies and Khoisan. The latter, speakers of the so-called "click language," included the Hottentot or Khoi people, and the San or Bushmen. The Khoisan, hunter-gatherers with a rich oral tradition who produced some of Africa's most striking rock art, arrived in the area many thousands of years ago, but were ultimately displaced by the Bantu peoples. The Bantu, a large language group whose common characteristic is their word for "people," *bantu*, originated in and around what is now Nigeria in about 1200 B.C. Though they did not develop a written language, they were an Iron Age civilization whose higher level of technological advancement gave them dominance over the native peoples of southern Africa. Ultimately they seized the best land, forcing the Pygmies into the less desirable rain forest while the Khoisan retreated to the Kalahari Desert. By the fourteenth century A.D., most of southern Africa belonged to the Bantu.

The first Europeans arrived a century later, when the Portuguese reached the Cape of Good Hope in 1488. Explorer Bartholomeu Dias (c. 1450-1500) actually called it the Cape of Storms, and only later did it receive its more optimistic-sounding name. Permanent white settlement began in 1652, with the establishment of a Dutch supply station at the Cape. Subsequent decades saw an influx of slaves from the West Indies; French Protestant refugees known as Huguenots; and German dairy farmers and missionaries.

In 1806, the British seized the Cape of Good Hope, which they named the Cape Colony. The Boers or Afrikaners, as the descendants of the Dutch called themselves, ceded the Cape to Great Britain in an 1814 treaty. By 1836, the Boers of the Cape had become so dissatisfied with British rule that some 16,000 undertook a mass migration inland which came to be known as "The Great Trek." Their seizure of Bantu lands led to conflict with the Zulu tribe, who under the leadership of the legendary chieftain Shaka (c. 1787-1828) conquered most of what is now Natal Province. King Shaka was assassinated by his half-brothers in 1828, however, and the Boers defeated his successors at the Battle of Blood River in 1838.

The Natal became the site of sugar cane plantations, which saw the arrival of large numbers of indentured Indian laborers beginning in about 1860. The Boers discovered precious resources in their area—diamonds in 1867, and gold in 1882—and thereafter South Africa would be famous for its vast natural wealth. However, it would also be famous for conflict, with the next stage of political tension in the region centering around British ambitions to conquer the entire land. The Boers had founded two republics, the Transvaal or South African Republic in 1852 and the Orange Free State two years later. Britain annexed the Transvaal in 1877, and in 1880 the two sides went to war. Results of the First Anglo-Boer War (1880-81) were inconclusive, and this led to the Second Anglo-Boer War (1899-1902). The latter, sometimes simply known as the Boer War, was not merely the first important military conflict of the twentieth century. It established British imperial power in the region as an unshakable reality, and also saw the first use of modern concentration camps. In 1910 the former Boer states merged with Cape Province and Natal to form the Union of South Africa.

MODERN ERA

As a part of the British Empire, South Africa took part in World War I, its principal action being the seizure of German Southwest Africa. In 1919, following the end of the war, South Africa received a mandate to the former German colony, the present-day nation of Namibia. It fought against Nazi Germany in World War II as well, but around the same time, a new political ideology arose among South

African whites which called for separation of the races—for which the Afrikaans word is *apartheid*.

Apartheid had its roots in the long Boer tradition of ethnic separation, inculcated during the hard years of the Great Trek and thereafter, but it had other antecedents as well. It could not have existed without the Afrikaner labor movement, a group which at one point adopted a slogan which symbolizes the mixture of socialist and racist ideas which went into Apartheid: "Workers of the world unite and fight for a white South Africa!" Eager to maintain their job status against encroachment by the black majority, who would work for lower wages, white labor unions supported the new policy, and the British tradition of self-rule for nations within the Empire allowed it to take hold. The establishment of apartheid became official with the victory of the Nationalist Party in 1948, but the ideology of Apartheid had been forming for many years, with the ideas of Hendrik Verwoerd (1901-66) forming an intellectual basis.

Among the areas of principal concern in both the theory and practice of apartheid were labor; the vote, whereby a virtually all-white franchise was established; land and municipal segregation, with minorities segregated into areas variously called homelands or Bantustans; and separate educational facilities. These steps were followed by so-called "petty apartheid," which established a set of practices even more severe than those that prevailed in the American South prior to the Civil Rights movement of 1960s. Public transportation, restrooms, and even beaches and park benches were segregated. In 1950, the Nationalist-dominated parliament of South Africa passed the Group Areas Act, establishing residential and business sections in urban areas for each of the four recognized races: Whites, Blacks, Coloreds, and Asians. Existing "pass laws" that required blacks to carry documents authorizing their presence in restricted areas were strengthened as well.

Growing Afrikaner resistance to British rule led to a decision, through a 1960 referendum among whites, to give up status as a British dominion. A new republic was born on May 31, 1961, and South Africa withdrew from the British Commonwealth. The 1960s and 1970s saw an increase in laws relating to apartheid, along with growing unrest among the black population—and increasing worldwide disapproval of South Africa. Laws forbade most social contacts between races; restricted races to certain jobs; curtailed black labor unions; and abolished non-white—including Asian and Colored—participation in the national government. Political rights of the black majority were confined to partic-

ipation in tightly controlled urban councils in the townships, or in the ten ethnically distinct, government-created homelands. Though each of these ten homelands retained varying degrees of autonomy, Bophuthatswana, Ciskei, Transkei, and Venda were granted independence, though South Africa was the only nation on earth to recognize them as independent nations.

The first major anti-apartheid riots broke out at Sharpeville, where government troops killed 69 black protesters. A series of riots in 1976 led to the deaths of some 600 blacks, and the murder of resistance leader Stephen Biko (1946-1977) in 1977 led to increased tension. Around this time, world concern over apartheid resulted in a number of actions. South Africa was banned from many international cultural exchange programs, and after 1960, its athletes were not allowed in the Olympic Games and other international competitions. The United Nations imposed an arms embargo, and passed resolutions condemning apartheid. A widespread popular reaction in the West, simmering for several decades, exploded in the 1980s, with anti-apartheid protests on many college campuses. A number of artistic works, ranging from British novelist Graham Greene's 1977 novel *The Human Factor* to an array of songs by recording artists, registered the disapproval with which most Europeans and Americans regarded apartheid. Under pressure from stockholders, many foreign banks and multinationals broke their South African ties, and many in the United States called for full economic divestiture from South Africa. Meanwhile, South Africa was embroiled in wars with the Communist governments of nearby Angola and Mozambique during much of the 1980s, and also fought a sustained conflict with the Southwest African People's Organization (SWAPO) in Southwest Africa, which it had retained as a colony against international protests.

Significant changes to apartheid first came in 1983, when a new constitution extended the vote to Asians and Coloreds. Two years later, the government repealed laws banning interracial sex and marriage. Progress was the result not only of organized groups, both of leading figures both black and white. One notable figure was Archbishop Desmond Tutu (1931–), who in 1986 won the Nobel Peace Prize and called on all Western nations to apply economic sanctions against South Africa as a means of forcing an end to apartheid. Even more prominent was Nelson Mandela (1918–), leader of the African National Congress (ANC). Jailed since the early 1960s, Mandela was an important symbol of the anti-apartheid movement, as the ANC was the principal political organization. Whites prominent in the anti-apartheid movement included

Helen Suzman (1918–), an outspoken member of parliament, and Communist leader Joe Slovo (1926-1995).

As the nation tottered toward civil war, President P. W. Botha (1916–) in 1986 ordered an end to pass laws and allowed blacks to take an advisory role in government. But he also launched attacks against ANC strongholds in neighboring countries, and a massive strike by some 2 million black workers in 1988 helped lead to his resignation in 1989. Under the administration of F. W. de Klerk (1936–), the government removed its ban on the ANC and released Mandela in 1990. In 1991, de Klerk announced plans to end apartheid, and in 1994 the nation held free elections in which the ANC won the majority, making Nelson Mandela the first president of the "new" South Africa. The end of apartheid has not brought an end to tension in the country, however. Fighting between the ANC and the Zulu Inkatha Party has killed thousands, and many whites have fled the country. Racial tensions between blacks and other groups has continued as well.

SIGNIFICANT IMMIGRATION WAVES

It is difficult to discern patterns of South African immigration to the United States prior to the mid-twentieth century. This is true for a number of reasons, and—in a pattern typical of all matters South African—these reasons differ according to ethnic group. Before the end of apartheid in the early 1990s, immigration by white South Africans, either of Afrikaner or British heritage, was in very small numbers. Most were immigrants of conscience who fled their nation's repressive system, in many cases under orders from the government or at least threats from the police. White immigrants were typically of English heritage, since it was in the very nature of Afrikaner identity to stay put: this indeed was integral to the mentality which spawned apartheid. Then, of course, there were the black immigrants, who also were fleeing apartheid, though not simply as a matter of conscience but rather for survival. Immigration by blacks was limited as well, but again for different reasons: though the standard of living for blacks in South Africa was higher than for most people living on the African continent, economic conditions still made immigration difficult.

The end of apartheid, of course, brought significant waves of white emigration, but the white exodus from South Africa in the 1990s was not as severe as many had predicted. Mandela, who stepped down from the presidency in 1999, sought to retain as many whites as possible, and urged mul-

tiracial policies in an attempt to counteract a potential black backlash against former oppressors. Nonetheless, racism has remained a powerful force in South Africa, a factor which could motivate migrations in the future. This racism is not simply white against black, though that has continued, albeit in reaction to government policy rather than as a part of that policy. Yet as the *Africa News Service* reported in 1999, much of the racism is black on black. South Africa has always been a net "importer" of people, with much higher immigration than emigration, but according to the *News Service* report, black hostility towards other Africans increased in the 1990s: "South Africans even have derogatory ways of referring to black foreigners: *makwerere*—the local name given to insects that survive on cow and human feces; or *girigamba*: people from nowhere."

SETTLEMENT PATTERNS

Of the whites who left South Africa in the years leading up to and following the end of apartheid, most did not go to the United States. They were far more likely to settle in Australia or New Zealand, countries which share South Africa's British heritage. Furthermore, the climate in Oceania is similar to that in South Africa, and the location of these countries far south of the Equator means that the seasonal changes—summer at the beginning of the calendar year, and winter in the middle of the year—are similar to those in South Africa. In 1989, M. J. Polonsky and others presented "A Profile of Emigrants from South Africa: The Australian Case" in *International Migration Review*. Polonsky et al. found that South African immigrants in Australia shared several characteristics: high levels of technical skill; significant professional qualifications; families with young children; and little or no financial assets remaining in South Africa—thus indicating a decision to leave the country for good. White South Africans also settled in Britain and Canada. Thus a 1998 article in the Canadian magazine *Maclean's* reported that "South African doctors are still flocking to Canada, seeking a foreign haven from rising crime, a falling currency, and wrenching changes to the health-care system."

As for those whites who have moved to the United States, both before and after the end of apartheid, a relatively large number have settled in Midwestern states such as Minnesota and Illinois. Thus some stores in Chicago, for instance, sell Marie biscuits, cookies often served by South Africans with tea. There are also pockets of South African immigrants on the East Coast, in areas such as Atlanta, which has a large population of South

African Jews. A number of South Africans have also settled in Mid-Atlantic states such as Maryland, and in New York.

Throughout the western United States, for instance in Arizona, California, and in the Pacific Northwest, there are small South African populations, though it would be hard to discern a pattern to such settlements. Unlike, say, the Irish, South Africans in general—both white and black—have tended to come to America individually rather than in large groups. Thus they can be found throughout the country.

ACCULTURATION AND ASSIMILATION

Whether in the 1990s or before, immigrants from South Africa seemed to bear an invisible A as a mark that set them apart—an A that stood for apartheid. This was true not only of white but of black immigrants, and issues from South African life have tended to carry over to life in the United States. Thus in 1989 Mark Mathabane (1960–), a black writer and immigrant who settled in North Carolina, wrote in the autobiographical *Kaffir Boy in America*: "I marveled at the reach of apartheid: it could influence the way people thousands of miles away thought, felt, and acted; it could silence them at will; it could defeat them without a shot being fired." Sheila Roberts, a white writer who moved to Michigan in part because she opposed apartheid, wrote that "From the beginning I was seen by American friends and colleagues as not only an authority on South Africa but also a representative of the 'opposition.'" It is ironic, given their complex and multifarious heritage, that South Africans of all groups have been thus stereotyped and reduced to a mere political identity. The same ethnic diversity that has often made South Africa a focal point of tension has also produced a richly varied culture.

TRADITIONS, CUSTOMS, AND BELIEFS

It is important to note that Afrikaners consider themselves Africans, not Europeans. Interestingly, Afrikaners and South African blacks share much of the same folklore, and indeed, in a further detail which illustrates the racial complexity of South Africa, many of those shared traditions can be traced to Asian roots. There are, for instance, *goel* or ghost stories originated by indentured laborers from India and Malaysia, tales adopted by whites and blacks alike. Many of these stories revolve around the harsh southeastern wind, known as the "Cape Doctor," that blows over Cape Town in the summertime. In contrast to Afrikaners, English South Africans have a cultural heritage more tied to that of Great Britain—a heritage shared by British, Australians, New Zealanders, and Canadians—rather than to that of southern Africa.

Of course the Zulu, Xhosa, and Sotho peoples each have multifaceted cultural traditions all their own. According to Zulu myth, at one time people did not die, but simply continued living, and thus in Zulu culture, old age is seen as a blessing. A Zulu legend recounts how the Creator told a chameleon to go and tell the people of the world that they did not have to die; but the chameleon took so long to do the job that finally the angered Creator sent a lizard in his place to tell them that indeed they would die. The lizard got his work done faster, and it is only for this reason that death exists.

Like the Zulu and indeed like most groups of people throughout the world, the Xhosa have their own tales of human origins, which in their case revolves around a heroic Adam figure known simply as Xhosa. There is a large body of Xhosa folktales, called *intsomi*, as well as praise poems or *isibongo* regarding the adventures of past heroes. The Xhosa have several interesting dietary restrictions: women are typically not supposed to eat eggs, and a man is not supposed to drink milk in a village where he might later take a wife.

The Sotho, known as excellent horsemen, are distinguished by their bright blankets and cone-shaped hats. An example of the latter appears on the flag of Lesotho, whose population is primarily Sotho. The Sotho tradition also includes praise poems and folk tales, one of the most prominent of which is a tale concerning a boy named Santkatana, who saves the world by killing a giant monster.

PROVERBS

The cultures of South Africa are more rich in colorful terminology than they are in proverbs. The nation's various black ethnic groups have a wide array of piquant expressions, but so too does the white population, and there is much crossover between cultures in this regard. Many ethnicities, for instance, recognize *tom* as a word for money. *Bundu*, a variant of *boondocks*, is the South African term for what Australians would call the "Outback"; and whereas Americans go "four-wheeling," South Africans go *bundu-bashing* in a four-wheel drive vehicle. South Africans share a number of expressions with colloquial British English, including *ta* as a slang term for "thanks." Salty insults include *brak*, meaning a dog or mongrel. *Gatvol* is an off-color term meaning "fed up," as in "I'm *gatvol* with this traffic," and an expression for dismissing a request—something like "forget it," only stronger—is "Your *mal auntie*."

CUISINE

As in many other aspects of South African life, the national cuisines are as varied as the ethnic groups. Afrikaners favor a meat-and-potatoes diet that includes items such as *boerewors*, a sausage made of pork; *putu pap*, a type of porridge; and *brai* or barbecue. English South Africans, as one might expect, eat a diet similar to that of the British, though with local variations such as *bredies*, or stew. Vegetable dishes are often mixtures, such as spinach and potatoes, or roasted, sweetened pumpkin. The Zulu diet places a heavy emphasis on products of the cow, including beef and milk products such as *amasi*, or curdled milk. Mealie-meal, or cooked corn meal, and yams are also favorites. Among the Xhosa, goat, mutton, and beef are popular, as are corn and bread. Particularly notable is a spicy hominy dish called *umngqusho*. Coloreds eat *bredies*, and enjoy an Indian-style meat pastry called *samoesas*.

South African culture, obviously, is full of many and varied terms for items of food. There are, for instance, Marie biscuits, a hard, dry cookie made for dipping in tea. Cream crackers, light and puffy sweets, are also popular. Other favorite dishes include *morogo* or *imifino*, a wild leaf stew; *bobotie*, a minced beef curry; *bitlong*, which is dried meat similar to jerky; a fried bread called *vetkoek*; and *sosaties*, which are made of marinated lamb and apricots. Meals may be washed down with homemade beer, fine wines, coffee, or *mechow*, a drink made from corn meal. A strong English tea called Red Bush tea is very popular, as are Chinese and Indian teas. These are often sweetened with condensed milk.

MUSIC

The range of peoples, cultures, and traditions in South Africa is reflected in the diversity of the nation's music, and traditional music, though confined to more rural areas, continues to influence contemporary urban forms. Traditional instruments include homemade horns, drums, and stringed instruments, and among neo-traditional styles are variants on the indigenous music of the Ndebele, Pedi, Shangaan, Sotho, and Zulu. For example, the Tsonga are associated with the *mbila*, a traditional instrument played along with drums and horns; often Tsongan music is used to accompany the tribe's traditional dance forms. From the countryside have come such forms as *mbube*, a complex choral gospel music.

In the 1930s, *marabi* became very popular. Like its cousin, American big band jazz, *marabi* is a characterized by the repetition of short melodic phrases. *Kwela* gained popularity in the 1940s, with its distinctive blend of homemade guitar, saxophone, and pennywhistle. By the 1960s, whites too had become avid fans of township jazz, which had sprouted into *kwela*'s instrumental music and *mbaqanga*, a vocal jazz style. The Cape Malays developed their own Cape jazz, marked by strains of Eastern sounds from their Indonesian heritage. The social upheaval of the 1960s and 1970s, however, prompted many artists to leave the country. Self-imposed exile brought international fame to some, including Miriam Makeba (1932–), Hugh Masekela (1939–), and Abdullah Ibrahim (1934–).

In the 1980s, the townships gave birth to their own brand of pop music. Just as the heavily synthetic sounds of new wave splashed through the Western world, "township music" was punctuated by synthesizers and drum machines, though it maintained the vocal harmonies for which South Africans are famed. South African music also got a boost on the world scene when American pop singer Paul Simon teamed up with *a cappella* group Ladysmith Black Mambazo for his highly acclaimed album *Graceland* in 1986. In the 1990s, vocal artistry developed into the praise poetry of rap and hip-hop, which borrows from American styles to create uniquely South African forms. Another style that developed in the 1990s was *kwaito*, which blends traditional sounds with those of house music, rhythm and blues, and hip-hop.

TRADITIONAL COSTUMES

Though black South Africans in urban areas tend to dress in a fashion indistinguishable from that of whites, their traditional costumes are much more colorful and varied. Zulu men, for instance, sport the *amabheshu*, a type of apron of goatskin or leather worn at the back. Beads are common among men, women, and children, and popular items for men are frilly goatskin bands worn on both arms and legs.

The Xhosa, too, are known for the striking attire, including blankets with detailed patterns, which both men and women wear as shawls. The Sotho also have their brightly colored blankets, worn as coats, but these are typically store-bought since they have no tradition of hand-making these items. In areas north of Johannesburg, a great influence of the Ndebele is evident. The Ndebele are famous for their beadwork and the geometric designs that they paint on their houses. Indians and other Asians, of course, have their own styles of dress associated with their cultures. For the most part, however, South Africans wear Western-style clothing, and following the example of President Mandela, attire tends to be comfortable and casual, even for business meetings.

DANCES AND SONGS

Singing and dancing is a significant part of black South African traditional life, and praise poems form an important element in their songs. The Xhosa practice group singing and hand-clapping, but have also borrowed from Western styles introduced by missionaries. An example of the missionaries' influence, which centered around Christian hymns, is the hymn-like "Nkosi Sikele' iAfrika" or "God Bless Africa," written by a Xhosa schoolteacher in 1897. It later became South Africa's national anthem.

A popular song among Afrikaners is "Daar Kom Die Alabama," or "There Comes the *Alabama*." The song celebrates the C.S.S. *Alabama*, a Confederate raider which pursued the U.S.S. *Sea Bride* all the way to Cape Town in August 1863. All of Cape Town, is it said, came out to greet the ship from far-off America.

HOLIDAYS

South Africans celebrate a number of secular and religious holidays. These include the following, some of which are national public holidays: Family Day, April 5; Freedom Day, April 27, commemorating the first day on which black South Africans were allowed to vote; Worker's Day, May 1; Youth Day, June 16, in honor of protestors killed during riots in the Soweto township in 1976; National Women's Day, August 9; Heritage Day, September 24; Reconciliation Day, December 16; and Boxing Day or the Day of Goodwill on December 26.

English and/or Afrikaners celebrate Founder's Day on April 6, the anniversary of the founding of the Cape Colony in 1652; Republic Day, on May 31, anniversary of the declaration of the Republic of South Africa in 1961; Kruger Day on October 10, the birthday of early Afrikaner leader S. J. P. Kruger (1825-1904); and the Day of the Vow on December 16, which commemorates the Boer defeat of the Zulu in 1838.

Religious holidays include Good Friday, along with the non-religious Easter Monday holiday;

Ascension Day in April or May; and Christmas. New Year's Day, of course, is also a holiday.

LANGUAGE

South Africa has 11 official languages: Afrikaans, English, Ndebele, Northern Sotho, Southern Sotho, Swati, Tsonga, Tswana, Venda, Xhosa, and Zulu. Though none of the major languages is spoken by a majority of the populace, 98 percent of South Africans use at least one of them as their home or first language. Most blacks, in fact, are multilingual, speaking their tribal languages along with English and possibly Afrikaans, which at one time was a school requirement.

Accommodating such a plethora of languages has been a challenge, and indeed the June 16, 1976, riots at Soweto began as a protest by black students against the use of Afrikaans as the medium of instruction in black schools. At the time, Afrikaans was predominantly the language used to conduct matters of politics and internal administration, while English was used to communicate with the outside world in matters of business and science.

In the new South Africa, television broadcasts can be heard in the most prevalent languages: English, Sotho, Xhosa, Zulu, and Afrikaans. Radio broadcasts are even more varied. English, however, remains the principal language used by most people, with the other languages primarily confined to regions where native speakers predominate.

FAMILY AND COMMUNITY DYNAMICS

The subjects of family and community, as applied to South Africans in general—and particularly to South Africans in America—are closely tied to the complex political and racial history of South Africa itself. For South Africans in America, the legacy of apartheid has continued to be haunting, though of course not to the degree that it was prior to the early 1990s. In part because of their troubled national past, many South Africans living in America still feel a sense of connectedness to the old country in a way that many other immigrant groups may not. This affects family and community relations, tending to strengthen the bonds of Afrikaner to Afrikaner and black South African to black South African.

For English South Africans, on the other hand, this dynamic has not been so strong, simply because their accents make many of them indistinguishable, as far as most Americans were concerned, from

British or Australians. Yet this, too, has created tensions within families. Thus Sheila Roberts wrote of her son, "By the time he was twelve and able to understand the full infamy of South African racism, he grew so ashamed of his South African heritage that he not only began inventing a different past for himself, but he expected me not to tell people I was from South Africa. Rather, I should say I was from Britain: my accent would carry the lie. At times I went along with his request if he was with me, particularly if there was not much opportunity for a following conversation in which I would have to fabricate an intricate and unlikely past. Other times I would resist. I didn't like the lie."

BIRTH AND BIRTHDAYS

In Zulu traditional culture, a birth is celebrated by the sacrifice of animals to ancestors. Also important is a young girl's puberty ceremony, signifying the fact that she has come of age and is eligible for marriage. The Xhosa have much more intricate coming-of-age ceremonies for both sexes. Boys are segregated from the rest of the group for several weeks, during which time their heads are shaved and they undergo a number of rituals such as the smearing of white clay over their entire bodies. This rite of passage culminates with circumcision. As for girls, they are also separated from the group, though for a shorter period, and during this time the community celebrates with dances and animal sacrifices. The Sotho have similarly complex rituals surrounding puberty and circumcisions, which are performed on girls as well as boys.

English and Colored South Africans celebrate birthdays in a manner familiar to most Americans brought up in Anglo-Saxon traditions. The same is true of Afrikaners, though birthday parties are perhaps a bigger part of life than they are with other groups. This is the case in particular with regard to one's twenty-first birthday celebration, at which the young person is presented with a key to symbolize their passage into maturity.

THE ROLE OF WOMEN

Afrikaners are known for their highly conservative views, not only regarding racial relations, but also with regard to women's roles. This in part comes from a strong fundamentalist religious tradition, which arose from a strict interpretation of family guidelines provided by the Apostle Paul in the New Testament. In the 1990s, however, employment opportunities for Afrikaner women increased, a change accompanied by a decline in the practice of gender separation which typified many social interactions among Afrikaners.

Gender relations in black South African ethnic groups have also been characterized by patriarchy. The Xhosa, for instance, have a tradition of polygamy, and the man is king in the typical Xhosa home, a fact also true among the Zulu. The latter have their own polygamous tradition, one that today even extends to dating: thus it is not uncommon for a young Zulu man to have several girlfriends. As for English, Colored, and Asian families, these all tend to be more or less traditional and patriarchal, depending on the family and the degree to which they embrace cosmopolitan or Western lifestyles.

BAPTISMS

Baptisms, of course, are not a factor in the tribal life of black South Africans: though a large number of the latter tend to be Christians, the religion is of course an import, and thus plays little role in the traditional culture. The same is true of Asians. Almost all newborn Afrikaners are baptized, and infant baptism plays a significant role in the lives of English and other South African groups—including blacks—who embrace either the Anglican or the Catholic faiths.

COURTSHIP

In the past, gender relations among Afrikaners were conducted according to highly conservative guidelines. Thus males and females spent much of their time apart, and when a young man of appropriate age took an interest in a girl, courtship was formal and traditional. Should the young man wish to marry, it was incumbent on him to ask the girl's father for her hand in marriage. On three Sunday mornings prior to the wedding, the couple's name would be read in church, and if there were no objections, the marriage would be performed. This practice had declined by the 1990s, however, and courtship was conducted more along lines familiar to American and European youth.

Courtship among Coloreds has tended to be highly formal as well, in part because apartheid-era laws banning interracial dating required people of both sexes to be highly circumspect. Arranged marriages have played a significant in lives of South African groups ranging from Asian Indians to Sotho. The Zulu, on the other hand, have their own traditional courtship practices which deviate somewhat from the patriarchal standard typical of most tribal societies. Thus a Zulu girl is the one who initiates contact by sending a "love letter"—actually, a string of beads whose colors each carry specific meanings—to the young man who interests her. The Xhosa have perhaps the most relaxed practices, with boys and girls typically meeting at dances, some of which last all night.

RELIGION

Religions among persons of South African origin fall into three broad categories: Judeo-Christian, traditional and tribal faiths, and Asian religions. The latter is by far the smallest group, in South Africa at least if not among immigrants, with the majority being made up of Indian Hindus. A small portion of South Africans are Muslims, Buddhists, or Jains.

Among Afrikaners, the Reformed Church of Holland, a Protestant denomination that arose during the 1600s, is a significant factor. Reformed Church beliefs, however, have been mixed with Calvinism to make up the Afrikaner's unique brand of Protestantism. Apartheid was justified in part by virtue of the fact that John Calvin (1509-64) himself supported separation of the races, as well as a strong role for the church in government.

English, Coloreds, and black South African Christians typically belong to either the Anglican or the Catholic churches. The prominent role of Bishop Tutu, an Anglican minister, illustrates the more interracial character of these churches in contrast to the Afrikaner version of the Reformed Church. The 1980s and 1990s saw the rise of charismatic movements, which place an emphasis on healing and other powers of the Holy Spirit, primarily among black South Africans. Finally, there is a significant community of Jewish South Africans, many of whom have immigrated to the United States.

Although large numbers of Xhosa, Zulu, and members of other black ethnic groups have accepted Christianity, traditional beliefs have not died out, and in many cases are mingled with Christian practices. Adherents to the Xhosa traditional religion worship a supreme being called uThixo or uQamata, and the Zulus a deity named uNkulunkulu ("The Very Big One.") In both cases, the supreme being has little role in the personal lives of believers, but rather acts primarily as creator. The Sothos' worship of Modimo is mingled with ancestor worship, and indeed ancestors play a significant part in most traditional black African faiths.

EMPLOYMENT AND ECONOMIC TRADITIONS

A number of South African entrepreneurs have established successful businesses throughout the United States. Atlanta is a case in point. Goldberg's Deli on Roswell Road is practically across the street from Avril's Exclusives, a car detailing shop. Both are owned and operated by Jewish immigrants from South Africa, as are numerous other businesses within a small radius in the prosperous northern sector of the city.

Atlanta is also the home of Firearms Training Systems, Inc, or FATS, a facility for training law enforcement, military, and security personnel in the use of firearms through simulations of real-world situations. Its founder was South African race-car driver Jody Scheckter, who in 1979 won the Formula One championship for Ferrari. "There was a lot more tinkering than profiting in the early days," Scheckter told the *Atlanta Journal-Constitution*. Geoff Lonsdale, Scheckter's head of European operations, gave *Corporate Location* quite a different appraisal of Scheckter's entrepreneurial abilities: "He runs this company like he drives cars—flat out." Perhaps because of his Afrikaner origins, it was natural for Scheckter to develop contacts in the Netherlands, whose Ministry of Defence is a significant FATS client. By 1996, when Scheckter sold FATS to a New York-based investment firm, its annual revenues had reached $65 million.

Seattle entrepreneur Paul Suzman is another South African success story. One of the first things that impressed him when he initially visited the United States in 1971, Suzman told *Nation's Business,* was the fact that commerce in America operated 24 hours a day. "That was something that stuck in my mind," he said, "this incredible 24-hour energy." A mushroom farmer in South Africa, he established a farm in the Pacific Northwest, and went on to open a highly successful bakery that a *Nation's Business* headline characterized as "Paul Suzman's $2 Million Hobby."

POLITICS AND GOVERNMENT

In his 1989 memoir *Kaffir Boy in America,* Mark Mathabane recalled staying at "the I-House," a dormitory for international students in New York City. There he experienced tension with fellow black South Africans and others of African origin, he wrote, when he "made it known that I would not isolate myself from other students out of some false sense of black pride or solidarity." He also met two white South Africans active in the United Democratic Front (UDF), an anti-apartheid group support-ed by Mandela, Tutu, and others. From them, Math-abane learned "about the shock of finding them-selves reviled by Americans as racist simply because they were white South Africans . . . . But what was even more shocking to [them] was being shunned by most black South Africans at I-House." He lis-tened to them expressing their frustrations, then told them, "I consider you brothers, too. But remember that to people in whom apartheid has bred paranoia, your very connection with the UDF is reason to be wary of you since all the opposition groups in South Africa, particularly the UDF, are full of government informants."

Sheila Roberts also encountered the hostility that often greets white South Africans in America, a fact illustrated by an incident that occurred when she was buying tickets to a movie with her son in Lansing, Michigan, in 1986. The theatre clerk noticed her accent and asked where she was from, and "As soon as I said, `South Africa,' my son walked away, ashamed as always at any reference to our country. The young woman looked at me with cold curiosity. As she handed me the tickets, she announced that `we' should nuke `that place.' Then she used a catch-phrase from the Vietnam War, though she was too young to know where it came from. She said we should turn it into a parking lot."

Both Mathabane and Roberts were perplexed by the ignorance of Americans with regard to the situation in South Africa. In Roberts's case, this revolved around her treatment as a representative of all white South Africans, or of the white opposi-tion to apartheid. Mathabane, on the other hand, was frustrated by situations such as a discussion he had in the 1970s with an American who asked him, "What exactly is apartheid?" "I could hardly believe my ears," Mathabane wrote. "Phillip, an American, a college student, the product of what I thought was the best educational system in the world, did not know what apartheid was. What on earth was being taught in American schools?"

During the 1980s, of course, Americans sud-denly became aware of the situation in South Africa, but most responses tended to be based in emotion rather than intellect, with Roberts's the-atre clerk being an extreme example. And though former South Africans opposed to apartheid natu-rally applauded their neighbors' growing awareness, it did little to address the complex social problems in America—or South African immigrants' equally complex feelings about their home country. Roberts experienced a situation typical of many immigrants, with her children readily becoming assimilated while her own heart remained tied to the motherland. "The idea of returning" to South Africa, she wrote, "stayed with me as a consoling, if impossible, escape through the hard years of my children's teens."

INDIVIDUAL AND GROUP CONTRIBUTIONS

FILM, TELEVISION, THEATER

Athol Fugard is a playwright who has written such plays as *Boesman and Lena*, *Master Harold and the Boys*, *Sizwe Bansi is Dead*, *Statements*, and *Valley Song*; John Kai has been seen acting in such films as *Ghost and the Darkness*, *Soweto Green*, *Sarafina*, *An African Dream*, *Master Harold and The Boys*, and *The Grass Is Singing*.; Actor Winston Ntshona has been seen in such movies as *Tarzan and the Lost City*, *The Air up There*, *Perfume of the Cyclone*, and *A Dry White Season*; Actor Zakes Mokae has por-trayed many different characters in movies such as *Krippendorf's Tribe*, *Vampire in Brooklyn*, *Dust Devil*, *Percy and Thunder*, *A Rage in Harlem*, *A Dry White Season*, *The Serpent and the Rainbow*, and *Master Harold and the Boys*.

LITERATURE

Perhaps the most famous South African American literary figure was not a writer at all: rather, he inspired works such as *A Rush of Dreamers* by John Cech, a novel published in 1997. The figure in ques-tion was Joshua Norton, a Jewish South African who settled in San Francisco, where he proclaimed him-self Norton I, Emperor of the United States and Pro-tector of Mexico. An amused and indulgent city honored him as royalty throughout his life.

A more traditional South African American literary figure is Sheila Gordon (1927–), author of fiction and nonfiction, both for adults and juvenile readers. Most South African American writers, however, have tended to write nonfiction: thus Meyer Fortes (1906-83) wrote a number of works in the social sciences, as has anthropologist Philip V. Tobias (1925–), while physicist Gerrit L. Verschu-ur (1937–) has concentrated on the natural sci-ences. Mary Lillian Miles (1908–) has authored a number of devotional works; and Johan Theron (1924–), who for many years worked with the United Nations (UN), has served as editor of UN documentation. Nancy Harrison (1923–), an American citizen though she resides in England, wrote an acclaimed biography of Winnie Mandela (1936–), the controversial wife of Nelson Mandela who later became estranged from her husband.

MEDIA

Juluka.

A bimonthly magazine containing news of interest to South Africans in America.

Address: P.O. Box 34095, Bethesda, Maryland 20827.

ORGANIZATIONS AND ASSOCIATIONS

South African Club of Atlanta.
E-mail: inquiry@saclubatl.org.

South African USA Network.
Telephone: 1-800-SAUSANT.
E-mail: Info@sa-usa.com.

Southern African Development Community.
E-mail: sadc-usa@sadc-usa.net.
Online: http://www.sadc-usa.net/.

Springbok Club of Northern California.
Address: 1227 Oakshire Court, Walnut Creek, California 94598.

Springbok Club of Southern California.
Address: P.O. Box 3573, Mission Viejo, California 92690.

Springbok Southern Africa Club—Phoenix, Arizona.
Telephone: (602) 926-6859.
E-mail: 107775.3667@compuserve.com.

SOURCES FOR ADDITIONAL STUDY

Mathabane, Mark. *Kaffir Boy in America: An Encounter with Apartheid.* New York: Scribner, 1989.

Roberts, Sheila. "An Incomplete Replacing: The White South African Expatriate." In *Displacements: Cultural Identities in Question,* edited by Angelika Bammer. Bloomington: Indiana University Press, 1994, pp. 172-81.

SPANISH AMERICANS

by
Clark Colahan

Strong believers in the value of their culture, Spanish Americans make every effort to keep the language alive in the home.

OVERVIEW

Similar in climatic zones, area, and population to California, Spain occupies the greater part of the Iberian peninsula in southwestern Europe. Spain's Latin name, Hispania (Land of Rabbits), was given by Carthaginian settlers at the dawn of recorded history. Colonized by a series of important civilizations, it became heir to the cultures not only of Carthage but also of Greece and Rome. It was the home country of legionaries, several emperors, and philosophers, including Seneca, the founder of Stoicism. Later, with the fall of the empire, it was settled by Germanic Visigoths, then Arabs and Moors. As the center of the first world empire of the modern era, Spain imposed its culture and language on peoples in many parts of the globe. By the beginning of the twenty-first century it is estimated that there will be more people in the world who speak Spanish (330 million) than English.

Although politically unified since the reign of the Catholic monarchs Ferdinand and Isabel in the late fifteenth century, Spain continues to be divided by regional loyalties. Individual Spaniards, whether living in Spain or abroad, usually think of the *patria* (the fatherland) not as the entire nation, but rather as the area of the country where they were raised. This tendency has not diminished in recent years; in fact, the government has moved toward a less centralized form of rule by dividing the country into *autonomías* (autonomous areas) linked to Madrid (Spain's capital city) in a loose federalism that accommodates and even encourages more local control than the country has known for centuries.

Among the major regions in Spain are Castile, which includes the capital city of Madrid; Cataluña, which includes the city of Barcelona; Andalucía, which includes Seville; Extremadura; Galicia; and the Basque Country.

While centralist regimes of the past favored a standard national language, the Spanish government today encourages the schooling in and general use of regional dialects and languages. Galicians, for example, who occupy the northwest corner of the peninsula, speak Gallego. It is a language that reflects in vocabulary and structure the region's proximity to Portugal, to the south, and Castile, to the east. Residents of Cataluña speak Catalan, a Romance language that shares many features with other Romance languages such as Spanish and French but that is distinct from them. In Castile, the country's central region, the residents speak Castellano, which is also the language of most Latin American countries and, outside of Spain, is commonly thought of as the standard Spanish language.

Basques, who call themselves Euskaldunak, meaning "speakers of Euskera," occupy a small area of Spain known as the Basque Country; the Basque word for this region is Euzkadi. Located in the north central part of the country, and no more than 100 miles long in any direction, Euzkadi is considered by its inhabitants as part of the same ethnic nation found across the border in southwestern France. In contrast to Gallego, the Basque ancestral language, Euskera, appears unrelated to any other dialect in Spain or elsewhere, with the possible exception of some vocabulary items found in the area of the Black Sea. Basque culture is considered the oldest in Europe, predating even the prehistoric arrival of the Indo-European peoples.

Today, with the exception of enclaves on the north coast of Morocco, the Spanish empire is gone; it has been replaced by a constitutional monarchy modeled on the British system. While emigration is currently at low levels, from 1882 to 1947 some five million Spaniards emigrated (eventually about 3.8 million of those returned to Spain). Half went to Argentina, which, as a large, sparsely populated country, took active measures to attract Europeans; historically, Argentina is second only to the United States in the number of all immigrants received. A number of Spanish immigrants settled in Cuba, a colony of Spain until the Spanish-American War in 1898, and many Spaniards moved to what is now the United States.

EMIGRATION FROM SPAIN

In the first century of Spain's presence in the New World, many of the explorers and soldiers came from Andalucía (in the South) and Extremadura (in the West), two of the poorest regions of the country. The early and lasting influence of these immigrants explains why the standard dialect spoken today in the Western Hemisphere retains the pronunciation used in the South, instead of the characteristics of the older variant still spoken by those living north of Madrid. In the nineteenth and twentieth centuries the region that has produced the most emigrants has been Galicia, together with similar parts of Old Castile that border it on the south. During most of this time Galicia has been an isolated, un-industrialized corner of the peninsula. Its inheritance laws either divided farms among all the siblings in a family, resulting in unworkably small *minifundios*, or denied land entirely to all but the first born. In either case the competition for land was intense, compelling many Galicians to seek their fortunes elsewhere.

Adjoining Galicia to the east on Spain's north coast is Asturias, which also sent large numbers of immigrants overseas. Until the nineteenth century its economic situation was similar to that in Galicia, but it later became a national leader in industrial development based on coal mining, metal working, and ship building. The above-average level of occupational skills possessed by the Asturian immigrants contributed significantly to the characterization of Spanish immigrants as highly skilled workers.

The southern provinces of Spain, which include Almería, Málaga, Granada, and the Canary Islands, have been another major source of Spanish immigration to the United States. A number of factors combined to compel citizens to leave these regions: the hot, dry climate; the absence of industry; and a *latifundio* system of large ranches that placed agriculture under the control of a landed caste.

Basques have also immigrated to the United States in large numbers. Traditionally both hardy mountain farmers as well as seafaring people, they may have reached the coasts of the New World before Columbus. Basques stood out in the exploration of the Americas, both as soldiers and members of the crews that sailed for the Spanish. Prominent in the civil service and colonial administration, they were accustomed to overseas travel and residence. Another reason for their emigration besides the restrictive inheritance laws in the Basque Country, was the devastation from the Napoleonic Wars in the first half of the nineteenth century, which was followed by defeats in the two

Carlist civil wars. (*For more information about the Basque, and immigrants to the United States from this region, please see the essay on Basque Americans*)

SIGNIFICANT IMMIGRATION WAVES

In colonial times there were a number of Spanish populations in the New World with governments answerable to Madrid. The first settlement was in Florida, followed by others in New Mexico, California, Arizona, Texas, and Louisiana. In 1598, when the first New Mexican town was established, there were about 1,000 Spaniards north of Mexico; today, their descendants are estimated at 900,000. Since the founding of the United States, an additional 250,000 immigrants have arrived either directly from Spain or following a relatively short sojourn in a Latin American country.

The earliest Spanish settlements north of Mexico (known then as New Spain) were the result of the same forces that later led the English to come to that area. Exploration had been fueled in part by imperial hopes for the discovery of wealthy civilizations. In addition, like those aboard the Mayflower, most Spaniards came to the New World seeking land to farm, or occasionally, as historians have recently established, freedom from religious persecution. A substantial number of the first settlers to New Mexico, for instance, were descendants of Spanish Jews who had been compelled to leave Spain.

Immigration to the United States from Spain was minimal but steady during the first half of the nineteenth century, with an increase during the 1850s and 1860s resulting from the social disruption of the Carlist civil wars. Much larger numbers of Spanish immigrants entered the country in the first quarter of the twentieth century—27,000 in the first decade and 68,000 in the second—due to the same circumstances of rural poverty and urban congestion that led other Europeans to emigrate in that period. In 1921, however, the U.S. government enacted a quota system that favored northern Europeans, limiting the number of entering Spaniards to 912 per year, an amount soon reduced further to 131.

The Spanish presence in the United States continued to diminish, declining sharply between 1930 and 1940 from a total of 110,000 to 85,000. Many immigrants moved either back to Spain or to another Hispanic country. Historically, Spaniards have often lived abroad, usually in order to make enough money to return home to an enhanced standard of living and higher social status. In Spanish cities located in regions that experienced heavy emigration at the beginning of the twentieth century, such as the port city of Gijón in Asturias, there are wealthy neighborhoods usually referred to as concentrations of *indianos*, people who became rich in the New World and then returned to their home region.

Beginning with the Fascist revolt against the Spanish Republic in 1936 and the devastating civil war that ensued, General Francisco Franco established a reactionary dictatorship that ruled Spain for 40 years. At the time of the Fascist takeover, a small but prominent group of liberal intellectuals fled into exile in the United States. After the civil war the country endured 20 years of extreme poverty. As a result, when relations between Spain and most other countries were at last normalized in the mid-1960s, 44,000 Spaniards immigrated to the United States in that decade alone. In the 1970s, with prosperity emerging in Spain, the numbers declined to about 3,000 per year. Europe enjoyed an economic boom in the 1980s, and the total number of Spanish immigrants for the ten years dropped to only 15,000. The 1990 U.S. census recorded 76,000 foreign-born Spaniards in the country, representing only four-tenths of a percent of the total populace. In contrast, the largest Hispanic group—Mexicans born outside the United States—numbered over two million, approximately 21 percent.

SETTLEMENT PATTERNS

Five areas of the United States have had significant concentrations of Spaniards: New York City, Florida, California, the Mountain West, and the industrial areas of the Midwest. For nineteenth-century immigrants, New York City was the most common destination in the United States. Until 1890 most Spaniards in this country lived either in the city itself, with a heavy concentration in Brooklyn, or in communities in New Jersey and Connecticut. By the 1930s, however, these neighborhoods had largely disintegrated, with the second generation moving to the suburbs and assimilating into the mainstream of American life.

At the end of the nineteenth century, Florida attracted the second largest group of Spaniards in the country through its ties to the Cuban cigar industry. Most of the owners of factories were originally from Asturias, and in the second half of the century they immigrated in substantial numbers, first to Cuba, then later to Key West, and eventually Tampa, taking thousands of workers with them. Several thousands of their descendants still live in the vicinity.

California is also home to descendants of southern Spanish pineapple and sugar cane workers who had moved to Hawaii at the beginning of the twentieth century. The great majority of those

immigrants moved on to the San Francisco area in search of greater opportunity. In Southern California's heavy industry, there have been substantial numbers of skilled workers from northern Spain.

The steel and metalworking centers of the Midwest also attracted northern Spaniards. In the censuses of 1920, 1930, and 1940, due to sizable contingents of Asturian coal miners, West Virginia was among the top seven states in number of Spanish immigrants. Rubber production and other kinds of heavy industry accounted for large groups of Spaniards in Ohio, Illinois, Michigan, and Pennsylvania. With the decline of this sector of the American economy in the second half of the twentieth century such centers of industry have largely lost their drawing power, accelerating the dispersal and assimilation of these Spanish communities.

ACCULTURATION AND ASSIMILATION

The decrease in the flow of Spaniards to the United States in recent decades, combined with their ability and willingness to form part of both the Hispanic sector and the society at large, has largely obscured any specifically Spanish presence in the States. As the European segment of the American Hispanic population, and therefore in some ways the least different from the country's predominantly European cultural and racial origins, they are often perceived as less alien than Latin Americans, and are more readily accepted into American society.

SPANISH CHARACTERISTICS

Because of the widely divergent traits of the several Spanish regions, any descriptions of Spanish character can only be approximate. During the last 100 years Spanish writers have engaged in national soulsearching and debate, spurred in part by the country's disastrous loss to the United States in the Spanish-American War of 1898. Early analysts, like philosopher Ortega y Gassett and literary historian Américo Castro, questioned what it was that separated Spain from its European neighbors. Since 1975 the stress has been on reintegrating Spain into the family of nations that it led at the beginning of the modern era. One trait the discussion has demonstrated is that Spaniards often hold strong opinions at variance with those of other Spaniards. Still, some points of agreement emerge.

Castilians have an austere mystical tradition that goes hand in hand with the region's image of itself as a heroic and Christian civilizer of a world empire. In contrast, Andalucians, in the South, are often censured by those living to the north for their decidedly more outward religiosity, highly visible in Holy Week processions.

A number of factors combined to make the warrior class Spain's dominant sector in centuries past. Like the Castilian hero of the *Poem of the Cid*, members of that class made a practice of limiting their work to warfare and politics, leaving the more intellectual professions to the powerful Jewish minority, and the beginnings of modern industry and agriculture to the vanquished Muslims. When these two minorities were expelled from the country—the Jews in 1492 and the Muslims in 1610—the activities associated with them were considered somewhat tainted. The resulting social pattern was that of advancement through family connections and government service rather than commercial or intellectual distinction.

In the eighteenth century, there were efforts at Europeanization as the Bourbons, the French royal family, came to the Spanish throne with ideas of Enlightenment reform. Growing acceptance of scientific and democratic ideals closed much of the gap between Spain and the rest of Europe in the nineteenth century, though segments of both the aristocracy and the common people continued to resist such notions. These ideals were the focus of civil friction and wars for two-and-a-half centuries, finally emerging victorious only with the democracy established upon the death of Franco in 1975.

Features of a knightly ruling class still indirectly influence Hispanic societies, including those in the United States. These features include a firm grounding in family and other personal relations, a thorough *personalismo* that leads to loyalty in business and politics and to friendships in personal life. *Personalismo*, especially among males, is felt to be deeper and more common than among Anglos and is felt to provide greater security for one's self and family than the provisions of government.

The Spanish work ethic is compatible with the values of both pre- and post-industrial Europe. While often working long, intensive hours, Spaniards have generally not felt work itself to be a pursuit that will guarantee either success or happiness. Instead, leisure has a primary value: it is used to maintain essential social contacts and is identified with upward social movement. Another element of the Spanish character is an aristocratic concern with a public image in harmony with group standards, even if at variance with the private reality. As in other cultures that motivate people through the fear of shame rather than the sting of guilt, the achievement of these goals is substantially validated through the opinions held by others. This notion is exemplified by the Spanish phrase *¿Qué dirán?* (What will they say?).

Stereotypes of Spanish immigrants derive in part from the *leyenda negra*, the "black legend," created and spread by the English in the sixteenth and seventeenth centuries when the two countries were rivals for European domination. Revulsion is expressed at the alleged cruelty of bull fighting, a sport that is believed by supporters to exalt individual worth through the demonstration of almost chivalric courage. Other stereotypical images, including exaggerated ideas of wild emotional intensity, create the misperception of Spain as the land of the tambourine and castanets, fiery flamenco dancing, and the reckless sensualism of Bizet's opera heroine, Carmen. Most of these elements are only connected, and in a much attenuated degree, with the southern region, Andalucía. As in matters of religion, northern Spaniards often view the character of life in their own regions as profoundly different.

CUISINE

Spanish food varies from region to region, though the use of olive oil instead of butter is widespread. Seafood is also a common element of Spanish meals; few parts of the peninsula are without daily deliveries of fresh fish and shellfish from the coast, and these items are the featured ingredients in the rice-based casserole of the Mediterranean coast called *paella*. Much of the agriculture in the South is involved with olive production, and a typical dish of the southern zone is *gazpacho*, a thick, cold tomato and vegetable soup originally concocted to be served during the heat of the day to harvest workers. One southern town, Jérez de la Frontera, contributed to the English language the word "sherry." In the opposite corner of the country, the Galicians and Asturians drink hard cider and eat a stew called *favada*, made from two kinds of sausage, garlic, saffron, and white beans.

HOLIDAYS

Most Spanish holidays are also found in American culture through the shared influence of the Catholic church. One exception is the sixth of Jan-

uary, *Día de los Reyes Magos*, "Day of the Three Wise Men." Known in English as Epiphany (formerly Twelfth Night), this holiday has remained vital in Spain as the occasion on which Christmas gifts are given. In the United States, Spanish children usually are the beneficiaries of a biculturalism that supplies them with gifts on January 6 as well as Christmas Eve.

The most commonly pictured Spanish clothing—as in representations of the annual spring fair in Seville that served as the prototype for the California Rose Parade—is the traditional Andalucian ruffled dress for women and the short, tightly fitted jacket for men. This jacket is cut for display both while on horseback and in the atmosphere of stylized energy and romance that characterizes flamenco dancing. Throughout much of Spain, however, holiday attire is based on everyday work clothes, but richly embroidered and appointed. The western region surrounding Salamanca has an economy based on cattle raising, and the extravagantly large hat and embroidered jacket worn by that province's *charros* were passed on to the Mexican cowboys.

FLAMENCO

Though known throughout the world as a "Spanish" style of music and dance, flamenco is mainly associated with the southern region of Andalucía, where Arabic and Gypsy influences are strong. Flamenco music is characterized by rapid, rhythmic hand clapping and a specialized form of guitar playing. The dancing that accompanies this music is typically done in duet fashion and includes feet stomping and castanet playing. Dancers generally wear the traditional Andalucian costumes described above: ornate, ruffled dresses for women and short, tightly fitting jackets for men. Although flamenco has not become widely popular in America, it can be found—especially in restaurants in major urban areas that have significant Spanish American populations.

LANGUAGE

As Spanish becomes more and more the second language in the United States, the American-born generations of families that emigrated from Spain have been increasingly likely to retain it in both its spoken and written forms. Current communication with Hispanic countries is highly developed, including such media as newspapers, magazines, films, and even Spanish-language television networks. Consequently immigrants arriving in recent years have found themselves less obliged to learn English than did their counterparts of 30 years ago. These newcomers integrate easily into the new Latin American communities that in several parts of the country function mainly in Spanish.

Strong believers in the value of their culture, Spanish Americans make every effort to keep the language alive in the home. Many, however, are opposed to bilingual education in the schools, a position grounded in their awareness of the need to assimilate linguistically in order to compete in an English-speaking society.

A common greeting among Spaniards is *¿Qué hay?* ("kay I")—What's new?", and *Hasta luego* ("ahsta lwego")—See you later. Spaniards can easily be distinguished from other Spanish speakers by their ubiquitous use of *vale* ("bahlay"), employed identically to the American "okay." Two commonly heard proverbs are, *En boca cerrada no entra mosca* ("en boca therrada no entra mosca")—Don't put your foot in your mouth (literally, "If you keep your mouth shut you keep out the flies"), and *Uvas y queso saben un beso* ("oobas ee keso saben un beso")—Grapes and cheese together taste as good as a kiss. A customary toast before drinking is *Salud, dinero y amor, y tiempo para disfrutarlos* ("saluth, deenayro, ee ahmor, ee tyempo pahra deesfrutahrlos")—Health, wealth, and love, and time to enjoy them.

FAMILY AND COMMUNITY DYNAMICS

FAMILY STRUCTURE

The structure of the Spanish family has come to resemble the American and European pattern. Grandparents often live in their own house or a retirement home; women frequently work outside the home. The obligation of children to personally care for elderly parents, however, is somewhat stronger among Spaniards—even those raised in the United States—than among the general American population; a parent often lives part of the year with one child and part with another. The traditional practice of one daughter not marrying in order to live with and care for the parents during their last years has not been maintained in this country. The traditional pattern of Hispanic mothers being completely devoted to their children—especially the boys—while fathers spent much of their time socializing outside the home has diminished. Despite various changes within the family structure that broadened women's roles, most community leaders are men.

At one time, young Spanish women were allowed to date only when accompanied by a chaperon, but this custom has been entirely discarded. Family pressure for a "respectable" courtship—a vestige of the strongly emphasized Spanish sense of honor—has been largely eroded in both Spain and the United States. Long engagements, however, have persisted, helping to solidify family alliances while children are still relatively young, and giving the couple and their relatives a chance to get to know each other well before the marriage is formally established.

Because careers outside the home are now the norm for Spanish women, differences in the schooling men and women pursue are minimal. A large segment of the community stresses higher education, and, in line with the sharper class distinctions that differentiate Spain from the United States, professional pursuits are highly respected. A significant number of Spanish physicians, engineers, and college professors have become successful in the United States.

COMMUNITY LIFE

Spanish communities in the United States, in keeping with their strong regional identification in Spain, have established centers for Galicians, Asturians, Andalucians, and other such groups. Writing in 1992, Moisés Llordén Miñambres—the specialist in emigration patterns from Spain—regarded this as a given, a natural condition, and referred in passing to the "ethnic" grouping of recent Spanish emigrants reflecting the individual characteristics of the "countries" from which they come. But these were certainly not the only type of community organizations to spring up in the United States; a variety of clubs and associations were formed. The listing by Llordén Miñambres shows 23 in New York City, eight in New Jersey, five in Pennsylvania, four in California, and lesser numbers in Indiana, Ohio, Illinois, Massachusetts, Michigan, New York State, Rhode Island, Vermont, and Florida.

Llordén Miñambres divides these organizations into several categories. Beneficent societies, such as the Unión Benéfica Española of New York, have aimed to provide charitable help for the needy, bury the poor, and provide information and recommendations to Spanish immigrants. Mutual aid societies, such as the Española de Socorros Mutuos "La Nacional," founded in New York in 1868, began as examples of trade union associations, and were important in providing families with medical care and help in times of economic crisis. The members of educational and recreational societies usually were drawn from among the more successful members of the local Spanish community; activities included literary readings and musical performances, banquets, and dances. There have also been athletic associations, such as the Sporting Club of New York; Spanish chambers of commerce; and purely cultural associations that set up lectures, museums, and plays, such as the Club Cervantes in Philadelphia. And finally, there have been associations based on religious and political beliefs, such as those that supported the Spanish Republic during and after the Fascist uprising.

RELIGION

Many Spanish Americans are less active in Catholic church activities than was common in past generations in Spain; they rarely change their religious affiliation, though, and still participate frequently in family-centered ecclesiastical rituals. In both Spain and the United States events such as first communions and baptisms are felt to be important social obligations that strengthen clan identity.

EMPLOYMENT AND ECONOMIC TRADITIONS

Since Spanish American entrance into the middle class has been widespread, the employment patterns described above have largely disappeared. This social mobility has followed logically from the fact that throughout the history of Spanish immigration to the United States, the percentage of skilled workers remained uniformly high. In the first quarter of the twentieth century, for example, 85 percent of Spanish immigrants were literate, and 36 percent were either professionals or skilled craftsmen. A combination of aptitude, motivation, and high expectations led to successful entry into a variety of fields.

POLITICS AND GOVERNMENT

With the outbreak of the Spanish civil war in 1936 a number of intellectual political refugees found asylum in the United States. Supporters of the overthrown Spanish Republic, which had received aid from the Soviet Union while under attack from fascist forces, were sometimes incorrectly identified with communism, but their arrival in the United States well before the "red scare" of the early 1950s spared them the worst excesses of McCarthyism. Reacting against the political climate in Franco's Spain, Spanish Americans have tended to vote Democratic. Until the end of the dictatorship in Spain in 1975 political exiles in the United States actively campaigned against the abuses of the Franco regime. They gained the sympathy of many Americans, some of whom, during the war, formed the Abraham Lincoln Brigade and fought in Spain against the Fascists.

INDIVIDUAL AND GROUP CONTRIBUTIONS

ART AND HUMANITIES

Among the political refugees from the Spanish civil war was Pablo Casals (1876-1973), an internationally celebrated cellist. In addition to his lyrically beautiful playing, he was known for his adaptations of Spanish folk music, especially from his own region of Cataluña. He was also active in efforts to help other victims of the civil war.

Similar in terms of political position was the novelist Ramón Sender (1902-1982); after fleeing the Franco regime to Mexico and then Guatemala, he finally settled in the United States. Professor of Spanish literature at the University of New Mexico, University of Southern California, and University of California, he published in this country under the pen name of José Losángeles. He is well known for his depiction of the impact of political events on human lives, as in the short novel *Requiem por un campesino español* (*Requiem for a Spanish Peasant*). He managed to keep a sense of humor throughout the aftermath of the Spanish civil war, and humor is paramount in his Nancy novels in which the protagonist is a typical American undergraduate student.

The poet Angel González (1925–), an Asturian from a republican family who experienced the civil war as a child, has been the clearest and most honored lyrical voice to describe the emotional fatigue and near despair of life under the Franco dictatorship. Living in the United States but traveling frequently throughout the Hispanic world from the 1960s until 1992, he taught during most of that period at the University of New Mexico and has now retired in Spain.

His colleague at the same university is the novelist Alfred Rodriguez (1932–), winner of literary prizes in both Spain and the United States, including the Spanish government's *Golden Letters* award for outstanding Spanish-language narrative written in the United States. Born in Brooklyn to immigrants from Andalucía, he sojourned in Spain during the bleakest years that followed the civil war. His work continues the classic Spanish tradition of the picaresque tale, a penetrating and grimly humorous exploration of the strategies for survival in decayed or traumatized societies.

SCIENCE AND INDUSTRY

Neurologist Luis García-Buñuel (1931–) was born in Madrid and immigrated to the United States in 1956. He has headed neurology services in several American hospitals, and since 1984 has been chief of staff at the Veterans Administration Medical Center in Phoenix. Thomas García-Borras (1926–), a leading figure in the American heating oil business, was born in Barcelona and arrived in the United States in 1955. In 1983 he published *Manual for Improving Boiler and Furnace Performance*, and he is the president of U.S. Products Corporation in Las Vegas.

MEDIA

PRINT

El Diario/La Prensa.
A major newspaper founded in 1913.

Contact: Carlos D. Ramírez, Publisher.
Address: 143-155 Varick Street, New York, New York 10013.
Telephone: (212) 807-4600.
Fax: (212) 807-4617.

La Gaceta.
A community newspaper.

Contact: Roland Manteiga, Editor and Publisher.
Address: P.O. Box 5536, Tampa, Florida 33675.
Telephone: (813) 248-3921.
Fax: (813) 247-5357.
E-mail: lagaceta@aol.com.

Geomundo.
A magazine on travel, geography, and natural science.

Contact: Elvira Mendoza, Editor.
Address: De Armas Publishing Group, Vanidades Continental Building, 6355 Northwest 36th Street, Virginia Gardens, Florida 33166-7099.
Telephone: (305) 871-6400.
Fax: (305) 871-4939.

RADIO

WADO-AM (1280).
Known as "La Campeona."

Address: 666 Third Avenue, New York, New York 10017.
Telephone: (212) 687-9236.

WAMA-AM (1550).
Address: 5203 North Armenia Avenue, Tampa, Florida 33603.
Telephone: (813) 875-0086.

WKDM-AM (1380).
Address: 570 Seventh Avenue, Suite 1406, New York, New York 10036.
Telephone: (212) 704 - 4090.

WLCH-FM (91.3).
Address: Spanish American Civic Association, 30 North Ann Street, Second Floor, Lancaster, Pennsylvania 17602.

Telephone: (717) 295-7760.
Fax: (717) 295-7759.
Online: http://www.wlch.org/.

TELEVISION

Telemundo.
Contact: Henry R. Silverman, President.
Address: 1740 Broadway, 18th Floor, New York, New York 10019.
Telephone: (212) 492-5500.

Univisión.
Contact: Deborah Durham, Washington Bureau Chief.
Address: 444 North Capitol Street, N.W., Suite 601-G, Washington, D.C. 20001; or 9405 Northwest 41st Street, Miami, Florida 33178.
Telephone: (202) 783-7155; or (305) 471-3900.

ORGANIZATIONS AND ASSOCIATIONS

Hispanic Institute.
Offers lectures and concerts, maintains archives on Spanish and Portuguese literature and linguistics, and publishes a journal of literary criticism entitled *Revista Hispánica Moderna Nueva Epoca*.

Contact: Susana Redondo de Feldman, Director.
Address: 612 West 116th Street, Columbia University, New York, New York 10027.
Telephone: (212) 854-4187.

Música Hispana.
Presents concerts of Spanish, Latin American, and classical chamber music, disseminates information about Hispanic music, and offers referral services to musicians and composers.

Contact: Pablo Zinger, Director.
Address: 600 West 111 Street, 3E-1, New York, New York.
Telephone: (212) 864-1527.

Repertorio Español.
Presents and tours Spanish classic plays, contemporary Latin American plays, *zarzuela* (Spanish light opera), and dance.

Contact: Gilberto Zaldívar, Producer.
Address: 138 East 27th Street, New York, New York 10016.
Telephone: (212) 889-2850.

Twentieth Century Spanish Association of America (TCSAA).

Individuals interested in the study of twentieth-century Spanish literature.

Contact: Luis T. Gonzalez-del-Valle, Executive Secretary.

Address: University of Colorado at Boulder, Department of Spanish and Portuguese, McKenna Language Building, Campus Box 278, Boulder, Colorado 80309-0278.

Telephone: (303) 492-7308.

Fax: (303) 492-3699.

Unión Española de California.

Organizes cultural events from the traditions of Spain.

Contact: Julián Miguel, President.

Address: 2850 Alemany Boulevard, San Francisco, California 94112.

Telephone: (415) 587-5115.

MUSEUMS AND RESEARCH CENTERS

Hispanic Society of America.

Free museum exhibits paintings, sculpture, ceramics, textiles, costumes, and decorative arts representative of the Hispanic culture.

Contact: Mitchell A. Codding, Director.

Address: 613 West 155th Street, New York, New York 10032.

Telephone: (212) 926-2234.

Fax: (212) 690-0743.

Online: http://www.hispanicsociety.org/.

Southwest Museum.

Collections include artifacts from the Spanish colonial and Mexican eras.

Contact: Thomas H. Wilson, Director.

Address: 234 Museum Drive, Los Angeles, California 90065.

Telephone: (323) 221-2164.

E-mail: info@southwestmuseum.org.

Online: http://www.southwestmuseum.org/.

SOURCES FOR ADDITIONAL STUDY

Fernández-Shaw, Carlos. *The Hispanic Presence in North America from 1492 to Today, M.* translated by Alfonso Bertodano Stourton and others. New York: Facts on File, 1991.

Gómez, R. A. "Spanish Immigration to the United States," *The Americas,* Volume 19, 1962; pp. 59-77.

McCall, Grant. *Basque Americans.* Saratoga, California: R & R Research Associates, 1973.

Michener, James A. *Iberia: Spanish Travels and Reflections.* Greenwich, Connecticut: Fawcett, 1968.

Pereda, Prudencio de. *Windmills in Brooklyn.* [New York], 1960.

"Spaniards," in *Harvard Encyclopedia of American Ethnic Groups.* Cambridge, Massachusetts: Harvard University Press, 1980; pp. 948-950.

SRI LANKAN AMERICANS

by
Olivia Miller

Learning is so valued within Sri Lanka that a solemn ritual, the *akuru kiyaweema* ceremony, takes place to commemorate a child's mastery of the first letter when he or she is old enough to manipulate fingers, usually around age three.

OVERVIEW

The Democratic Socialist Republic of Sri Lanka, formerly Ceylon, is an island in the Indian Ocean approximately 20 miles off the southeastern tip of India. It occupies an area of 25,332 square miles, which is about the size of West Virginia, and has a population of 8.8 million. Sri Lanka means the "resplendent land." Sri Lanka has an equatorial climate, with little seasonal temperature variation. An agricultural country whose chief crop is rice, Sri Lanka is known for spices such as cinnamon, cardamon, nutmeg, pepper, and cloves. Tea, rubber, and coconuts are also important exports. Sri Lanka is also a major exporter of precious and semi-precious stones. The capital city is Colombo.

Seventy-four percent of Sri Lanka's citizens are of Sinhalese origin, while the rest of the population belongs to various ethnic minorities, including Sri Lankan Tamils (12.7 percent), Indian Tamils (5.5 percent), Muslims (7 percent), Burghers, Malays, Parsis, and Vaddhas. Seventy percent of the population is Buddhist, 15 percent is Hindu, eight percent is Islamic, and seven percent is Christian. The country's official languages are Sinhala and Tamil, but English is also spoken throughout Sri Lanka. Sri Lanka's national flag is yellow with two panels. The smaller hoist-side panel has two equal vertical bands of green (hoist side) and orange; the other panel is a large, dark red rectangle with a yellow lion holding a sword and a yellow *bo* leaf in each corner; the yellow field appears as a border that goes around the entire flag and extends between the two panels.

HISTORY

Serendib, the old Arab name for Sri Lanka, is the source of the word "serendipity," which means "making happy discoveries by chance." Sri Lanka has also been called Ceylon, Teardrop of India, Resplendent Isle, Island of Dharma, and Pearl of the Orient, names that reveal its richness and beauty, and the intensity of affection which it has evoked. The actual origins of the Sinhalese are shrouded in myth. Sri Lanka has had a continuous record of settled and civilized life for more than two millennia. Most historians believe that the Sinhalese came to Sri Lanka from northern India during the sixth century B.C. Buddhism and a sophisticated system of irrigation became the pillars of classical Sinhalese civilization, which flourished in the north-central part of the island from 200 B.C. to 1200 A.D. The first major literary reference to the island is found in the great Indian epic, the *Ramayana* (Sacred Lake of the Deeds of Rama), thought to have been written around 500 B.C.

Portuguese traders, in search of cinnamon and other spices, seized Sri Lanka's coastal areas beginning in 1505 and spread Catholicism throughout the island. In 1658 the Dutch conquered the Portuguese and took control of Sri Lanka. Although the Dutch were ejected by the British in 1796, Dutch law remains an important part of Sri Lankan jurisprudence. In 1815, the British defeated the King of Kandy, last of the native rulers, and created the Crown Colony of Ceylon. The British established a plantation economy based on tea, rubber, and coconuts. In 1931, the British granted Ceylon limited self-rule. On February 4, 1948, Ceylon became an independent nation.

MODERN ERA

Sri Lanka, which celebrated 50 years of independence in 1998, is one of southern Asia's oldest and most stable democracies. Sri Lankan politics since independence have been strongly democratic. Two major parties, the United National Party and the Sri Lanka Freedom Party, have generally alternated rule. In 1972, a new constitution was introduced which changed the country's name from Ceylon to Sri Lanka, declared it a republic, made protection of Buddhism a constitutional principle, and created a weak president appointed by the prime minister. In 1978, the Republic of Sri Lanka became the Democratic Socialist Republic of Sri Lanka. The ruling party introduced a new constitution based on the French model, a key element of which was the creation of a strong presidency.

Sri Lanka has made significant progress in evolving from a socialist, centralized economy to a more open and free market-oriented economy and society. It has relatively high economic growth, high literacy rates, and low fertility and mortality rates. Agriculture remains the primary source of income for Sri Lanka's predominantly rural population. Unsustainable agricultural and logging practices have resulted in substantial land degradation and reduction in the size of forest reserves. Sri Lanka was one of the first countries to develop a National Environmental Action Plan for biodiversity conservation, protection of coastal zones, forestry, and land and water management.

Since its independence 50 years ago, Sri Lanka has been plagued by hostilities between the majority Sinhalese and the minority Tamils. Since 1983, a civil war waged by Tamil separatists in the country's north and east region has claimed over 55,000 lives and severely damaged the economy. The war is largely confined to Sri Lanka's northeastern province, which is six to eight hours by road from the capital. However, terrorist bombings directed against politicians and others have occurred in Colombo and elsewhere in the country. For the past 15 years, the Sri Lankan government has fought the Liberation Tigers of Tamil Eelam (LTTE), an insurgent organization fighting for a separate state for the country's Tamil minority. In May of 1997, the fighting intensified after the government launched a major offensive aimed at opening a land route to the Jaffna peninsula through LTTE-controlled territory in the north. The offensive resulted in approximately 5,000 casualties on both sides and the displacement of tens of thousands of citizens. The unresolved ethnic conflict in the north and the east is the key issue that prevents Sri Lanka from attaining its development potential.

THE FIRST SRI LANKANS IN AMERICA

The earliest Sri Lankans to enter the United States were classified as "other Asian." Immigration records show that between 1881 and 1890 1,910 "other Asians" were admitted to the United States. It is unlikely that many of these were from Sri Lanka. In 1975, immigration records classified Sri Lankans as a separate category for the first time. That year, 432 Sri Lankans immigrated to the United States.

SIGNIFICANT IMMIGRATION WAVES

Since the outbreak of hostilities between the government and armed Tamil separatists in the early 1980s, several hundred thousand Tamil civilians have fled Sri Lanka. By 1996, 63,068 were housed in refugee camps in south India, another 30,000-40,000 lived outside the Indian camps, and more than 200,000 Tamils have sought political asylum in the West. According to 1996 U.S. Immigration and Naturalization records, 1,277 Sri Lankans were naturalized. Of this group, 615 had arrived in 1995 and 254 had arrived in 1994, compared with only 68 arrivals in 1993 and 17 before 1985. Sri Lankan refugees admitted to the United States in 1991 (54) and in 1993 (62) contrasted with typical yearly admissions of two in 1989 and six in 1992. This increase coincided with an escalation of ethnic violence in Sri Lanka in the years of high refugee admission to the United States. During the 1980s, an average of 400 Sri Lankans immigrated to the United States each year. In 1998, 322 Sri Lankans were winners of the DV-99 diversity lottery. The diversity lottery is conducted under the terms of Section 203(c) of the Immigration and Nationality Act and makes available 50,000 permanent resident visas annually to persons from countries with low rates of immigration to the United States.

SETTLEMENT PATTERNS

According to the 1990 U.S. Census, there were 14,448 Americans with Sri Lankan ancestry. Of 554 Sri Lankans admitted to the United States in 1984, 117 were 20 and younger, 127 were ages 20 to 29, and 169 were ages 30 to 39. Many Sri Lankans settle in large cities such as Chicago, Los Angeles, New York, Newark, and Miami that already have Sri Lankan and Indian communities. Sri Lankan Americans who practice Hinduism are likely to settle near an established Hindu community. The same holds true for Sri Lankan Buddhists. For example, when Buddhist monk Venerable Wipulasara arrived in America in 1993, he joined the Buddhist Asian-American community of 30,000 in Tampa Bay, Florida.

ACCULTURATION AND ASSIMILATION

While many Sri Lankans come to America prepared earn advanced degrees and move into good jobs, they are shocked at how quickly life moves in their new country. For Venerable Wipulasara in Tampa, meditation had to come between running errands, buying groceries and taking courses at the local high school to improve his English. Wipulasara created a *vihar*, a small Buddhist temple, in his apartment. Another concession Wipulasara made to American culture was to change the color of his light orange robe because people confused him with highway workers who also wore light orange.

Second-generation Sri Lankans are almost completely Americanized. Parents often send their children to religion courses. Nathan Katz, chairman of the religious studies department at Florida International University in Miami told the *St. Petersburg Times* that "most immigrants come to America and more or less lead the life they want until they have children. Then they want them to learn the old values." Young people often help each other with the assimilation process. An alliance of students who grew up in the United States but are children of people from India, Sri Lanka, Nepal, and other nations formed the Atlanta-based United Indian Student Alliance, hosting yearly conferences attended by more than 1,000 students from 30 universities.

TRADITIONS, CUSTOMS, AND BELIEFS

Learning is so valued within Sri Lanka that a solemn ritual, the *akuru kiyaweema* ceremony, takes place to commemorate a child's mastery of the first letter when he or she is old enough to manipulate fingers, usually around age three. An astrologer determines every detail of the ceremony: the time of day it should take place, which way the child should sit, and what colors should be worn. The person who teaches the first letter to the child must be an educated, respected person who knows and loves the child. The child and teacher sit together on a mat and the teacher lights a brass lamp. Milk, rice, and Sri Lankan sweetmeats are set out in precise order, along with the slate on which the child will scrawl the letter. Usually it is "Ah," the first letter of the alphabet.

Sri Lankans are extremely superstitious when it comes to numbers. For example, no piece of jewelry is made with even-numbered stones. Odd numbers are always considered lucky, with the number seven thought to be particularly magical. Kandyan bridal jewelry consists of seven pendants.

The traditional Sri Lankan meal is served with all dishes on the table at once: rice, fish and meat curries, soup, vegetables and accompaniments. Each guest takes a serving of everything onto the right hand. The food should not touch the hand above the middle knuckles, and the left hand does not make direct contact with the food but is used to pass and serve dishes.

PROVERBS

Sri Lankan culture has several sayings and proverbs, drawn from various cultures who once ruled the country, as well as from the dominant religions of Buddhism and Hinduism. The following come from the Buddhist tradition: A defrocked monk will be unable to mix with society; Whatever you love, you are its master. Whatever you hate, you are its slave; If one speaks with a pure mind, happiness will follow him like one's shadow that never leaves; O man, correct thine own self first, then turn to guide others; A wise man shall not let himself get tarnished; May all beings be well and happy, may there be peace on earth and goodwill among men; He prayeth best that loveth best , all things both great and small. "Any coconut leaf will win" is a traditional Sri Lankan saying to the effect that a party can nominate a coconut leaf and the loyal villages will vote for it. A popular saying from the Hindu Deepavali festival is "Hatred will never cease by hatred; hatred ceases by love alone."

CUISINE

In spite of its tiny size, Sri Lanka boasts an amazing variety of spicy foods and styles of cooking, reflecting the diversity of its ethnic communities. The most noticeable influences have been Portuguese, Dutch, Moor, and Malay. Since ancient times, other cultures have traded with Sri Lanka for the spices that grow there. Some of the world's best cinnamon, cloves, and many other spices are indigenous to Sri Lanka. Sri Lankan cuisine is distinguished from that of its neighboring countries by its spices, which are fast-roasted before they are ground and added to the food. Sri Lankans use two different curry powders. One is referred to as plain curry powder and is similar to the Indian yellow curry powder. The other is referred to as black or roasted curry powder and is used for meats. Along with curry, food is seasoned with hot red peppers, tamarind, garlic and ginger, cardamon, cinnamon, curry leaves, fenugreek and tiny black mustard seeds. Red chili peppers were introduced to Sri Lanka by the Portuguese. Modern-day Sri Lankan food has Indian, Portuguese, Dutch, and even a touch of British flavor mixed in. Because foods spoil quickly in Sri Lanka's tropical location, most foods are cooked in liquids to ensure that all ingredients are cooked thoroughly. Rice is eaten at least once a day, usually with very hot curry.

Coconut milk, the liquid obtained from squeezing the meat of the coconut, is central to Sri Lankan cooking. Almost every dish is prepared in coconut milk. *Sambols* are hot, spicy relishes. *Seeni Sambol* is a sweet, hot onion dish. Coconut Sambol, or *Pol Sambol*, as it is known in Sri Lanka, is probably the country's most popular dish. It is made from onion, coconut, and red chili and is served in every home and restaurant. Another favorite dish is *egg hoppers*. Egg hoppers, traditionally a breakfast food, are made of a rice and coconut batter to which an egg is added while being cooked in a pan that looks like a wok.

Ambul Thiyal is a traditional fish preparation that can be kept without refrigeration for several days. This dish is prepared by placing a fish in a clay pot over an open fire, replacing the lid with another clay pot containing firewood or tinders, and cutting the fish into cubes. Chopped green chilies and bay leaf are then added. The *goraka* is ground and mixed with a little water. Salt and pepper are added to the goraka and poured onto the fish in an earthenware pot. The dish is cooked over a moderate flame until it is very dry.

TRADITIONAL COSTUMES

Sri Lankan men did not wear garments on their upper body prior to the sixteenth century. This distinction was reserved for royalty and warriors, who wore protective clothing or armor. The lower garment, the *dhoti*, was worn from the waist to below the knees. Ancient Sinhalese garments, especially those of the upper classes, were divided and neatly arranged in folds horizontally. During very cold weather, a mantle would be worn over the usual dress.

During ancient times, Sinhalese women did not cover the upper part of their bodies. Middle-class women wore only a cloth around their hips while at home, and used another piece of cloth to cover their shoulders when they went outdoors. Upper-class women were often bare-breasted, although heavily bejeweled, and their lower-class female attendants wore a breast-band.

With the arrival of the Portuguese in the early sixteenth century, Sinhalese dress underwent a dramatic change. Sri Lankan men quickly adopted the types of shirts, trousers, socks, and shoes worn by Portuguese settlers. Prior to this time, only upper class Sinhalese wore shoes. In the Kandyan kingdom, women wore a short frock with sleeves that covered the arms. The frock was made of fine white calico wrought with blue and red thread in flowers and branch designs. Both Kandyan men and women wore jewelry. The men wore gold chains, pendants, girdles, and finger rings. Women wore chains, pendants, girdles and rings in addition to earrings, (*kundalabharana*), anklets (*pa-salamba*), bracelets, and toe-rings (*pa-mudu*).

From the sixteenth to nineteenth centuries, respectable women covered their upper bodies while women of the low castes and the untouchables (*Rodi*) were prohibited from doing so. On their lower bodies, women wore a garment that was similar to a dhoti. For upper-class women, this garment extended to the ankles. Upper-class women also wore more elaborate lower garments in an array of colors. Women in the lower classes were usually naked from the waist up, and their lower garments did not extend below their knees. During the seventeenth century, upper-class men wore doublets of white or blue calico around the middle torso, a white one next to the skin, and a blue one over the white, with a blue or red sash at the waist. A knife with a carved handle inlaid with silver protruded from the garment folds at the chest.

DANCES AND SONGS

Bharata natyam is one of the classical dance forms of Sri Lanka and India. During this dance a sari-clad feminine figure, covered with jewels and flowers, strikes a graceful pose. In Sri Lanka, announcements of *Arangetram*, the traditional first performance by a young artist, are published every month. A bharata natyam performance on stage is a composite art form combining the elements of space management, stagecraft, music, and the presentational aspects of the artist, including makeup, color and sartorial elegance, rhythm, and dramatic content.

Sri Lanka is also known for Devil Dances, dramatic rituals performed by masked dancers who represent demons and characters like *Nag Ruska*, the King of the Cobras, and *Gurulu Raska*, the King of Birds. Dancers are trained from around age ten by their elders. The dance lasts throughout one night and is accompanied by the *Yak bera*, the devil drum. The most well-known of the Devil Dances is the *Sanni Yakuma*, when 18 demons of disease are summoned around a sick person's house.

Sri Lankan music was heavily influenced by India. W. D. Amaradeva, known as Sri Lanka's greatest singer and composer, mixed North Indian (Hindustani) classical music and Sinhala folk music associated with dance, drama, ritual, and social customs. Buddhist chants and narrative styles are also a part of Sri Lanka's musical heritage. *Baila* is a genre of music borrowed from the Portuguese. Baila is still the music of choice at middle-class parties.

HOLIDAYS

The one national holiday celebrated by all Sri Lankans is Independence Day on February 4. The full moon day of each month, Poya Day, is also considered a holiday. In addition, Sri Lankan Americans celebrate a wide variety of Buddhist, Hindu, Christian, and Muslim festivals and holidays, according to one's own religious preferences.

For Buddhists, the month of May is the most important full moon holy day of the entire year. On this day, Gautama Buddha was born, gained enlightenment, and passed away. Sri Lankan Buddhists celebrate this holiday by attending religious ceremonies at temples and decorating their homes with lanterns made of colored paper and sticks. Buddhists celebrate the New Year in March or April with coconut games and pillow fights. During October and November, Hindus in Sri Lanka and the United States celebrate *Deepavali*, or the festival of lights, which symbolizes the destruction of forces of darkness and evil and the re-enthronement of the light of God in individual and collective hearts.

LANGUAGE

Sinhala and Tamil are official languages in Sri Lanka. The Sinhalese are the largest ethnic group in the country, comprising 74 percent of the population, in 1981. Sinhala is an Indo-Aryan language genetically related to such major south Asian languages as Hindi and Bengali. As a descendant of Sanskrit, the language of the Mahabharatha and Ramayana, Sinhala is also related to European languages such as Greek and Latin. Two varieties of Sinhala are commonly distinguished, the literary and colloquial; agreement between the verb and the subject is found only in the literary variety. It is likely that groups from north India introduced an early form of Sinhala when they migrated to Sri Lanka around 500 B.C., bringing with them the agricultural economy that has remained dominant during the twentieth century. From ancient times, however, Sinhala has included a large number of words and constructs that were borrowed from Tamil, and modern speech includes many expressions from European languages, especially English. There are 12 Sinhala vowel sounds and there are also double vowels, which are extended sounds. Double consonants are split to finish the previous syllable and begin the following syllable. Tamils and most Muslims speak Tamil, part of the South Indian Dravidian linguistic group.

GREETINGS AND POPULAR EXPRESSIONS

The palms clasped together, with a gentle bow of the head and the word "*Ayubowan*," meaning "Wishing you a long life," is the traditional welcome used by Sri Lankans. "*Shaaa*" is an exclamation of pleasure and surprise, as one might say upon seeing a beautiful sight. "*Ayi yoo*" or "*appoo*" are exclamations of unpleasant surprise, used for everything from hearing a bit of gossip to witnessing an auto wreck. An expression that originated in village culture and continues to be used by modern Sri Lankans is "*Koheede Yanne?*" meaning "Where are you going?" In village life, everyone is always interested in where people are heading on the road.

FAMILY AND COMMUNITY DYNAMICS

The caste system is used to create social divisions within Sri Lanka. The Goyigama caste of the Sinhalese, traditionally associated with land cultivation, is dominant in population and public influence. In the lowlands of Sri Lanka, however, other castes based on commercial activities are influential. The Tamil Vellala caste resembles the Goyigama in its dominance and traditional connection with agriculture, but it is completely separate from the Sinhalese caste. Within their separate caste structures, Sinhalese and Tamil communities are fragmented through customs that separate higher from lower orders. These include elaborate rules of etiquette and a nearly complete absence of intercaste marriages. However, differences in wealth arising from the modern economic system have created wide class cleavages that cut across boundaries of caste, religion, and language. Because of all these divisions, Sri Lankan society is complex, with numerous points of potential conflict.

Sri Lankan Americans abandon caste restrictions when they acclimate to American lifestyles. Maintaining caste distinctions is not possible for the most part in business and social settings. Sri Lankan Americans live in single family units without relatives, although relatives may migrate to the same community.

In Sri Lanka, among all ethnic and caste groups, the most important social unit is the nuclear family of husband, wife, and unmarried children. Even when economic necessity forces several families (in Sinhala, *ge*; in Tamil, *kudumbam*) or generations to live together, each wife has her own cooking place and prepares food for her own husband as a sign of the individuality of the nuclear family. Among all sections of the population, however, relatives of both the wife and the husband form an important social network that supports the nuclear family and encompasses the majority of its important social relations. The kindred (*pavula*, in Sinhala) of an individual often comprise the group with whom it is possible to eat or marry. Because of these customs, local Sinhalese society is highly fragmented, not only at the level of ethnic group or caste, but also at the level of kindred relations.

The divisions between the castes are reaffirmed on a daily basis, especially in rural areas, by many forms of language and etiquette. Because each caste uses different personal names, and many use slightly different forms of speech, it is often possible for people to determine someone's caste as soon as that person speaks. Persons of lower rank behave politely by addressing their superiors with honorable formulas and by removing their headgear. A standard furnishing in upper-caste rural houses is a low stool (*kolamba*), provided so that members of lower castes may take a lower seat while visiting. Villages are divided into separate streets or neighborhoods according to caste, and the lowest orders may live in separate hamlets.

EDUCATION

Sri Lankan Americans are highly educated. Most immigrants have completed some college and many have advanced degrees. Until colonial times, the educational system in Sri Lanka was designed primarily for a small elite. Since independence in 1948, Sri Lanka has also made important gains in education, reaching near universal literacy and primary school enrollment rates. Children from age five to ten attend primary school; from age 11 to 15 they attend junior secondary school (terminating in the Ordinary Level Examination); and from age 16 to 17 they attend senior secondary school (terminating in the Advanced Level Examination). Those who qualify can go on to the university system, which is completely run by the state. In the late 1980s, there were eight universities and one university college with over 18,000 students in 28 faculties, plus 2,000 graduate and certificate students. However, improvements in the educational system created economic difficulties because many graduates were qualified for jobs that did not exist. Women, who made up only about 25 percent of the labor force in the 1980s, were particularly affected. Many Sri Lankans who settle in the United States do so in search of better employment opportunities.

THE ROLE OF WOMEN

Since the country's independence in 1948, Sri Lankan women have gained legal rights to education and employment. Prior to 1921, the female literacy rate among Christians in Sri Lanka was 50 percent, among Buddhists 17 percent, among Hindus 10 percent, and among Muslims only 6 percent. After independence, women entered the educational system in equal numbers with men. A continuing problem in all fields of technical education was extreme gender differentiation in job training; women tended to enroll in home economics and teaching courses rather than in scientific disciplines.

Although there are no legal impediments to the participation of women in politics or government, social mores within some communities limited women's activities outside the home for most of the twentieth century. In August of 1994, voters elected a parliament that chose a female prime minister for only the third time in the country's history. In November of 1994, a woman was elected president for the first time. Eleven women held seats in the parliament. In addition to the prime minister and the minister for women's affairs, four deputy ministers are women. Although the constitution provides for equal employment opportunities in the public sector, women have no legal protection against discrimination in the private sector, where they sometimes are paid less than men for equal work. Also, they often experience difficulty in rising to supervisory positions and face sexual harassment. Women constitute approximately one-half of Sri Lanka's work force. Women have equal rights under national, civil, and criminal law. However, issues related to family law, including divorce, child custody, and inheritance, are adjudicated by the customary law of each ethnic or religious group. In 1995, the government raised the minimum age of marriage for women from 12 to 18 years. Muslims, however, were allowed to continue their customary marriage practices.

COURTSHIP

The kinship system of Sri Lanka, like those in most countries of southern Asia and the Middle East, follows the pattern of preferred cross-cousin marriage. This means that the most acceptable person for a man to marry is the daughter of his father's sister. The most suitable partner for a woman is the son of her mother's brother. Parallel cousins—the son of the father's brother or the daughter of the mother's sister—tend to be improper marriage partners. Special kinship terminology exists in both Tamil and Sinhalese for relatives in preferred or prohibited marriage categories. In many villages, people spend their entire childhoods with a clear knowledge of their future marriage plans and live in close proximity to their future spouses. The ties between cross-cousins are so close, in theory, that persons marrying partners other than their cross-cousins may include

a special ritual in their marriage ceremonies during which they receive permission from their cousins to marry an outsider. The system of cross-cousin marriage also allows control over property.

Although all marriages are arranged, children can decline the mate that is chosen by their parents. In rural areas, marriages have traditionally been arranged between teenagers. The average age at marriage has been increasing in the last decades of the twentieth century. This is attributed to the longer periods of time that are needed to obtain a college education and establish a stable career.

WEDDINGS

In rural areas of Sri Lanka, traditional marriages did not require legal registration or a ceremony. The couple simply started living together, with the consent of their parents, who were usually related. Most Sri Lankan families have limited financial resources and do not spend large sums on wedding parties. Wealthier families, especially in urban areas, have a ceremony. The bride may receive a substantial dowry, determined beforehand during negotiations between her family and her future in-laws. Matchmakers and astrologers pick the time for the marriage.

Late twentieth-century wedding ceremonies have been influenced by British and Western culture. Brides wear white, carry flowers, and are preceded by bridesmaids and flower girls as in the typical wedding of the. This contrasts with the Kandyan Sinhalese (more traditional upland dwellers named after the Kingdom of Kandy) bride in her traditional costume of the Osariya (*sari*) and the complementing regalia. The Kandyan bride tries to dress lavishly, typically wearing a grand sari with gold and silver thread, pearls, stones, beads, and sequins.

The bridal headgear, the *nalalpata*, is a headband with a gold gem-studded forehead plate, and was traditionally worn by a ruler. The nalalpata was tied to the forehead of a young prince during a ceremony. A Sinhala wedding is the only time that the nalalpata is worn. It is placed on the middle of the forehead with one stem extending down the middle parting of the hair, and another two branches extending across the forehead up to the ear. Traditionally, the nalalpata was a piece of jewelry embedded in red stones.

The bride wears a mass of chains at the neck. *Padakkam*, or pendants, are the important part of the chains. Starting from the nalalpata pendant, each successive chain shows off pendants with Sinhala designs. The *peti malaya* is the last and longest chain encircling the rest. Peti malaya means a garland of flowers or petals. The design of the pendants may vary. The *agasthi malaya* is a chain made of agate. Some chains have seeds placed at intervals along the chain. The *seri valatu* is a broad bangle with three smaller bangles joined together. The earrings, known as *dimithi*, have the shape of an overturned cup with tiny pearls dangling from two ear-studs. Some brides wear armlets to ward off bad luck.

INTERACTIONS WITH OTHER ETHNIC GROUPS

According to United Nations statistics, Sri Lanka ranks second in the world in human rights violations. Sri Lankans fight bitterly along ethnic lines. In Sri Lanka, the different ethnic communities live in separate villages or sections of villages. In towns and cities, they inhabit different neighborhoods. The fact that primary education is in either Tamil or Sinhala effectively segregates the children of the different communities at an early age. Ethnic segregation is reinforced by fears that ethnic majorities will try to dominate positions of influence and repress the religious, linguistic, or cultural systems of minorities. Sinhalese are the dominant ethnic group within Sri Lanka. However, they often feel intimidated by the large Tamil population in nearby India. The combined Tamil populations of India and Sri Lanka outnumber the Sinhalese at least four to one.

The ethnic groups of Sri Lanka have been in conflict with each other since the nineteenth century. Ethnic divisions are not based on race or physical appearance, although some Sri Lankans claim to be able to determine the ethnicity of a person by his facial characteristics or color. There is nothing in the languages or the religious systems in Sri Lanka that officially promotes the social segregation of ethnic groups. Because historical circumstances have favored one or more of the groups at various times, hostility and competition for political and economic power are today's reality. However, Sri Lankan Americans peacefully voice their ethnic differences through fund-raising and political lobbying efforts.

RELIGION

Sri Lanka is a multi-religious country of Buddhist, Hindu, Christian and Muslim followers. The various religious groups practice their faiths in separate communities that are allowed to express their religious convictions. Buddhists constitute the majority with 69.3 percent. Theravada Buddhism (one of two types of Buddhism) was introduced to Sri Lanka in the third century B.C. from India, when a branch of the sacred bo tree under which the Buddha attained enlightenment was brought to the island.

According to legend, the tree that grew from this branch is near the ruins of the ancient city of Anuradhapura in the north of Sri Lanka. The tree is said to be the oldest living thing in the world and is an object of great veneration. There is no central religious authority in Theravada Buddhism, and the monastic community has divided into a number of orders with different styles of discipline or recruitment. The modern orders originated in the eighteenth century.

EMPLOYMENT AND ECONOMIC TRADITIONS

According to U.S. naturalization statistics, of the 1,277 Sri Lankans who became U.S. citizens in 1984, 575 had occupations ranging from professional specialties (414) to laborers and service industry workers (110). No occupation was listed for 702 immigrants. Most Sri Lankan Americans are highly educated professionals who come to the United States seeking employment opportunities. Many start their own companies and become well-known in their industries. For example, Sri Lankan American entrepreneurs formed an organization among South Asian businessmen called the Indus Entrepreneurs that aims to provide a support network for entrepreneurs.

Sri Lanka has a developing, mixed public and private economy based on agriculture, services, and light industries. Agriculture accounts for approximately one-fourth of the gross domestic product (GDP) and employs two-fifths of the workforce. Services are the largest sector of the GDP and employ one-third of the workforce. Foreign banks were allowed to open "offshore" branches in Sri Lanka in 1979 as part of a government effort to promote the country as an international financial center for South Asia. In 1990, a successful new stock exchange was founded. All exchange controls on current account transactions were eliminated and more than 40 state firms were privatized. The development of a capitalist economy in Sri Lanka led to the development of a new working class. These upwardly mobile, primarily urban professionals formed a new class that transcended divisions of race and caste. This class, particularly its uppermost strata, was educated in Western culture and ideology.

POLITICS AND GOVERNMENT

Large numbers of educated Sri Lankans, both Sinhalese and Tamil, lived in the United States, Britain, and Western Europe during the 1970s and 1980s. Tamils in the United States played a role in publicizing the plight of their countrymen in the American media and provided the militant movement with financial support. For example, the *Sacramento Bee* reported on the efforts of a Sri Lankan American professor at Sacramento State University who is a member of the Tamil minority. He works in the United States to help end the bloodshed in Sri Lanka by urging the U.S. government to end military support for the Sri Lankan government. The Tamil Nadu Foundation, Inc., lobbies for Tamil goals and seeks to influence U.S. policies towards Sri Lanka. An increasing number of Western countries have sharply criticized Sri Lanka's dismal human rights record.

ORGANIZATIONS AND ASSOCIATIONS

Association of Sri-Lankans in America.

Serves as liaison between Americans of Sri-Lankan origin and the U.S. Department of State. Participates in aid programs to Sri-Lanka; promotes Sri-Lankan ethnic values in the United States and seminars on Sri-Lankan issues. Makes travel arrangements for Sri Lankan dignitaries visiting the United States. Maintains charitable program; conducts research. Provides children's services; compiles statistics; maintains speakers' bureau.

Contact: Jay P. Liyanage, Chairman.
Address: 2 East Glen Road, Denville,
New Jersey 07834.
Telephone: (973) 627-7855.
Fax: (973) 586-3411.

Friends of Sri Lanka in the United States.

FOSUS was started by a group of Sri Lankan expatriates living in the Washington, D.C., metropolitan area whose primary concern is the eradication of Tiger (Tamil) terrorism.

Address: P.O. Box 2479, Kensington
MD 20891-2479.
E-mail: fosus@hotmail.com.

Sri Lankan Association at Mississippi State University.

Helps all incoming Sri Lankan students to orient themselves to Mississippi and aids new Sri Lankans in any way they can.

Address: P.O. Box 2626, Mississippi State,
MS 39762.

Sri Lankan Association of Texas A&M.

Organization of students, faculty, and staff and their families of Sri Lankan origin attached to the Texas A & M University. Any member of the university community with an interest in Sri Lanka can become an associate member. Promotes unity, culture, and spirit among Sri Lankans and fosters understanding of Sri Lankan culture among the university community.

Contact: Primary Advisor: Dr. John P. Nichols.
Address: College Station, TX 77843.
Telephone: (409) 845-3211.

Sri Lankan Association of University of Maryland.

Promotes intellectual, social, and cultural interaction among those connected with the University of Maryland, as well as developing leadership skills.

Contact: Manjula Gunawardane, President.
Address: University of Maryland, College Park,
MD 20742.
Telephone: (301) 871-5138.

Sri Lanka Student Association at Oklahoma State University.

Non-profit, non-political, educational, and cultural organization that reaffirms Sri Lankan national objectives of Unity, Faith, and Discipline, fosters friendship, goodwill, cooperation, and understanding among the Sri Lankan students.

Contact: Arthur Webb, Staff Advisor.
Address: College of Arts and Sciences, 202 Life
Sciences East, Oklahoma State University
Stillwater, OK 74078.
Telephone: (405) 744-5658.

Sri Lankan Student Association of Virginia Tech.

Formed in the year 1996; consists of eight members to provide a common forum for Sri Lankan students studying at Virginia Tech; also promotes Sri Lanka.

Address: Virginia Tech. Blacksburg, VA 24061.

MUSEUMS AND RESEARCH CENTERS

The Tamil Nadu Foundation, Inc.

Formed in 1974 to assist Tamil people through scholarships and relief projects. Addresses the plight of Sri Lankan Tamils. Sponsors an annual conference.

Contact: Paul C. Pandian, Texas chapter.
Address: 10636 Cox Lane, Dallas, TX 75229.
Telephone: (214) 350-5094.

SOURCES FOR ADDITIONAL STUDY

De Silva, Chandra Richard. *Sri Lanka: A History*. New Delhi: Vikas, 1987.

Ratnapala, Nandasena. *Sinhalese Folklore, Folk Religion, and Folk Life*. Dehiwala, Sri Lanka: Sarvodaya Research, 1980.

Ross, Russell R. *Sri Lanka: A Country Study*. Washington, DC: Library of Congress Federal Research Division, 1990.

Wright, Gillian. *Sri Lanka*. Lincolnwood, IL: Passport Books, 1994.

SWEDISH AMERICANS

by
Mark A. Granquist

Swedish immigrants made a fairly quick and smooth transition to life in their new country and most became quickly Americanized. As a northern European people, the Swedes shared with Americans a common religious and social heritage, and a common linguistic base.

OVERVIEW

The Kingdom of Sweden is a constitutional monarchy that is located on the eastern half of the Scandinavian peninsula in Northern Europe. It measures 173,648 square miles (449,750 square kilometers), sharing the Scandinavian peninsula with Norway to the west and north. Across the Baltic Sea, Sweden borders Finland, Estonia, Latvia, and Lithuania to the East, Poland, Germany, and Denmark to the south.

As of 1992, Sweden had a population of 8,602,000. The vast majority are ethnic Swedes, with minorities of Laplanders (Sami), Finns, Estonians, Latvians, Norwegians, and Danes, and, in the late twentieth century, immigrants from southeastern Europe and the Middle East. Virtually all Swedes officially belong to the Lutheran State Church of Sweden; there are smaller groups of Pentecostalists, Methodists, Covenant, Baptists, and Roman Catholics. The country's official language is Swedish, and the capital is Stockholm. The Swedish flag is a yellow cross on a medium blue field.

HISTORY

The Swedes are descended from the Gothic tribes that moved into Sweden following the melting glaciers, probably during the Neolithic period. The various Gothic settlements were centered in eastern Sweden and the island of Gotland in the Baltic. During the Viking period (800-1050 A.D.) the Swedes pushed eastward into Russia, and were trading as far south as the Black Sea. In Russia, the Swedes (labeled by the Slavs as the "Rus") ruled many areas, especially in the trading town of Novgorod. By about 1000, most of central and eastern Sweden was united in the kingdom of the Svear, although this was disputed by their powerful neighbors, the Danes and the Norwegians. Christianity was introduced to the Swedes by St. Ansgar in 829, although it was slow to take hold and was not fully established until the late twelfth century, under the rule of King Eric IX. Medieval Sweden was slowly incorporated into the European world, and began to form the political and social structures characteristic to its society even up to this day. King Magnus VII was able to unite Norway and Sweden under his rule in 1319, but the arrangement was unstable and did not last. In 1397 Norway and Sweden were united with Denmark, under the rule of the Danish Queen Margaret in the Union of Kalmar. Sweden felt slighted in the Danish-dominated Union, however, and after a Danish massacre of Swedish nobles in 1520, the Swedes rose against the Danes and, led by King Gustav Vasa, freed themselves from Danish rule in 1523. King Gustavus Adolphus fought for the Protestants during the 30 Years War (1618-1648), and gained possessions for Sweden in northern Germany; King Charles X gained further territory in Poland and the Baltic States. Sweden's age of glory ended with the rise of Russia, which defeated the Swedes in the Northern War (1700-1721). Sweden lost Finland to Russia in 1809, but received Norway in compensation in 1814 (a union that lasted until 1905). During the nineteenth century, Sweden underwent economic, social, and political transformation that only partially offset a large-scale immigration to North America. In the twentieth century, Sweden has maintained its political and military neutrality, and has become one of the most highly developed industrialized countries in the world, with stable politics and an extensive social welfare system.

SIGNIFICANT IMMIGRATION WAVES

In 1638, during Sweden's era as a European power, a Swedish merchant company founded the colony of New Sweden in Delaware. This became an official Swedish colony under the leadership of Governor Johan Printz, but struggled because of indifference from the Swedish government; the colony never prospered, reaching a total of only about 500 inhabitants. In 1655 the Dutch took the colony by force; the Dutch were in turn defeated by the English 11 years later. A Swedish-speaking enclave existed in the Delaware River valley until the nine-teenth century, however. Swedes played a role in early U.S. history. They were a force in the Revolutionary War. John Hanson of Maryland was the first president of the United States Congress from 1781-1782. Trade and adventure brought a number of Swedes to America in the early national period, but this immigration was rather limited.

Serious emigration from Sweden to America began after 1840, and this flow became a torrent after 1860. From 1851 to 1930, more than 1.2 million Swedes immigrated to America, a number that represented perhaps 25 percent of the total population of Sweden during this period. The country had one of the highest rates of emigration of all of the European nations. The rates of immigration to America fluctuated from year to year, however, reflecting economic conditions in both Sweden and America. The first great wave arrived between 1868 and 1873, as famine in Sweden and opportunity for land in America drove 100,000 Swedes, mainly farm families, from their homeland. They relocated primarily in the upper Midwest. The largest wave of immigrants, approximately 475,000, arrived between 1880 and 1893, again due to economic conditions. This time not only farm families emigrated, but also loggers, miners, and factory workers from the cities. The American Depression of 1893 slowed Swedish immigration until the first decade of the twentieth century, when 220,000 Swedes came to America. World War I halted emigration, and improved economic conditions in Sweden kept it to a trickle after 1920.

The immigration of Swedes to America during the nineteenth century was a movement of youth— young Swedes leaving their homeland for improved economic opportunity in America. The first waves of immigration were more rural and family oriented, but as the immigration progressed this pattern changed; young single men (and later women) left Sweden to find employment in American cities. Economic advancement was the primary reason they emigrated. There were those who resented the political, social, and religious confinement of nineteenth-century Sweden, of course, but research has shown that the overwhelming motivation driving the emigrants westward over the Atlantic was economic.

SETTLEMENT PATTERNS

The patterns of Swedish immigrant settlement changed during the course of the nineteenth century, varying with economic conditions and opportunities. The initial wave of immigration in the 1840s and 1850s was directed toward rural areas of Illinois and Iowa, especially the Mississippi River valley and Chicago. In the 1860s and 1870s immigration shifted toward Minnesota and the upper Midwest, and the Swedish population of Minneapolis grew substantially. In the 1880s rural migration spread to Kansas, Nebraska, and the Dakotas. With the changing complexion of immigration later in the century (more single youth heading toward urban areas) came the growth of immigration to the East and West Coasts. Significant Swedish-American centers were established in Connecticut, Massachusetts, and Maine in the East, and Washington and California in the West, along with a Swedish colony in Texas. By the turn of the century, Swedish Americans were about 60 percent urban; Chicago was the second largest Swedish city in the world, followed by Minneapolis, New York City, Seattle/Tacoma, Omaha, and San Francisco. Smaller cities with a concentration of Swedes included Worchester, Massachusetts, Jamestown, New York, and Rockford, Illinois. By 1930 Swedish America (first- and second-generation Swedish Americans) had peaked at 1.5 million people; secondary internal migrations had dispersed the Swedes around the country. The 1990 census reported that almost 4.7 million Americans claimed some Swedish ancestry (making it the thirteenth largest ethnic group), with almost 40 percent in the Midwest, 30 percent in the West, and 15 percent each in the South and Northeast. California leads all states with 590,000 Swedish Americans, followed by Minnesota (535,000), Illinois (374,000), Washington (258,000), and Michigan (194,000).

INTERACTIONS WITH SETTLED AMERICANS

Swedish immigrants were generally well accepted by mainstream America and tended to blend in easily with their neighbors, especially in the Midwest. Coming from a Protestant, northern European country, the Swedes were seen as desirable immigrants. Overall, they were a literate, skilled, and hard-working group, and found employment on farms and in mines and factories. Young Swedish women were especially sought as domestic servants in American homes. In many areas, especially in the upper Midwest, Swedes settled in close proximity to other Scandinavian and German immigrants. Despite some ethnic frictions, these European immigrants had a dominant influence on the culture and society of the region.

ACCULTURATION AND ASSIMILATION

In general, Swedish immigrants made a fairly quick and smooth transition to life in their new country and most became quickly Americanized. As a north-

ern European people, the Swedes shared with Americans a common religious and social heritage, and a common linguistic base. Swedish immigrants settled over a wide range of areas. Because they were drawn mostly to cities, rather than tight-knit rural settlements, they were immersed immediately in American culture. In addition, there was a growing interest in, and influence from, America in nineteenth-century Sweden. During the years prior to 1914, the Swedish American community was continually replenished by newcomers; however, World War I brought with it anti-foreign attitudes, which resulted in a drastic drop in emigration and forced the Swedish American community to Americanize rapidly.

The concept of Swedish America furthered the acculturation process. In an essay in *The Immigration of Ideas*, Conrad Bergendoff described the community as "a state of thinking and feeling that bridged the Atlantic." In this enclave, which existed from the Civil War until the Great Depression, first- and second-generation immigrants created their own society, helping one another make the transition to a new culture. After World War I this community was rapidly integrated into the larger American society. The most telling indicator of this was the transition from the use of Swedish to English. By 1935 the majority of Swedish Americans primarily spoke the language of their new home.

With assimilation and acculturation, though, came a renewed interest in Swedish history and culture as children and grandchildren of immigrants sought to preserve some of the traditions of their homeland. Many institutions dedicated to this preservation were established: historical and fraternal societies, museums, and foundations. It was this dynamic that historian Marcus Hansen observed in his own generation, and which prompted his famous axiom, "What the son wishes to forget, the grandson wishes to remember." (Marcus Lee Hansen, *The Problem of the Third Generation Immigrant*, Rock Island, Illinois: Augustana Historical Society, 1938; p. 9).

INTERACTION WITH OTHERS

The Swedish immigrants interacted most readily with other Nordic-American groups, namely Danes, Norwegians, and Finns. There was a close affinity with the Finns, many of whom were Swedish-speaking settlers from western Finland (Sweden had ruled Finland from the Middle Ages until 1809). There was a special, good-natured rivalry between the Swedes and the Norwegians in America, which still results in quite a few "Swede" and "Norwegian" jokes. Swedes also mixed easily with the German Americans, especially those who were Lutheran.

These Swedish
American children
are dressed in
traditional costume
for a fair.

CUISINE

Swedish American cooking is quite ordinary; traditional dishes represent the cooking of the Swedish countryside, which is heavily weighted toward meat, fish, potatoes, and other starches. In the area of baked goods, however, Swedish American cooks produce delicious breads, cookies, and other delights. The holiday seasons, especially Christmas, are times for special ethnic dishes such as *lutefisk* (baked cod), meatballs, and ham, which are arranged on a buffet-style Smorgasbord table, surrounded by mountains of baked goods, and washed down with gallons of strong, thick Swedish coffee.

TRADITIONAL DRESS

The immigrants did not have a particularly distinctive way of dressing, and generally adopted the clothing styles of their new homeland. Some brought with them the colorful, festive clothing representative of their region of Sweden, but such ethnic costumes were not worn often. The distinctive regional festive dress of nineteenth-century Sweden has, however, been revived by some Americans of Swedish descent, seeking to get in touch with their roots. This dress is sometimes worn for ethnic celebrations or dance competitions.

HOLIDAYS

Along with the traditional holidays celebrated by Americans, many Swedish Americans celebrate two additional holidays. Along with other Scandina-

vians, Swedes celebrate the summer solstice, or Midsummer's Day, on June 21. This is a time for feasting and outdoor activities. In many areas of Swedish America this day is celebrated as "Svenskarnas dag" (Swedes' Day), a special festival of Swedish American culture and solidarity, with picnics, parades, and ethnic activities. December 13 is Saint Lucia Day. Remembering an early Christian saint who brought light in the darkness of the world, a young woman is selected to be the "Lucia bride." Dressed in a white gown with a wreath of candles on her head, she leads a procession through town and serves special breads and sweet rolls. The Luciafest is an important holiday leading into the celebration of Christmas.

HEALTH ISSUES

America in the nineteenth century was often a dangerous place for immigrants; many worked hazardous jobs, and health care was frequently lacking. As the Swedish American community began to form, various immigrant groups, especially the churches, established medical and other types of organizations to care for the arriving Swedes. Hospitals, clinics, nursing homes, sanitariums, and orphanages were all a part of the network of care for the immigrants. Especially in the urban centers of the Midwest, Swedish American medical institutions remain in operation to this day.

Some Swedish immigrants and their Swedish American descendants sought medical careers, receiving their training mainly in the United States. After completing their education, some returned to Sweden to practice there. The only significant Swedish influence on American medicine was in the field of physical therapy, where techniques from Sweden were introduced into American medical centers.

There are few diseases or conditions that seem to be specific to the Swedish American community; problems that are prominent in Sweden, such as heart disease, depression, and alcoholism, are also seen within the Swedish American community, as well as in the rest of the United States.

LANGUAGE

Swedish is a North Germanic language, related to Norwegian, Danish, and German. There are no significant linguistic minorities in Sweden. Into the modern period there were some dialects present in various regions of the country, but by the twentieth century these variations had largely disappeared. Swedish uses the standard Roman alphabet, along with the additional vowels "ä," "ö", and "å." The language is pronounced with a particular "sing-song" lilt, and in areas of heavy Scandinavian settlement in the United States (especially the upper Midwest) this lilt is apparent among English-speaking descendants of the Scandinavian immigrants.

For the immigrants in America, Swedish remained the standard language, especially at home and at church, but the settlers soon learned enough English to manage their affairs. Some picked up a fractured combination of English and Swedish, which was derisively called "Swinglish." As the cultural world of Swedish America developed, English words and expressions crept into the community and a distinctive form of American Swedish developed that maintained older linguistic traditions of the Sweden of the 1860s and 1870s. The immigrant community was divided over the question of language, with some urging the retention of Swedish, and others seeking a rapid transition to English. For many older immigrants, especially of the first generation, English remained a very foreign language with which they were not comfortable. Swedish remained the language of the churches and social organizations, but the transition to English was rapid especially among the children of the immigrants. By 1920 English was beginning to replace Swedish in the immigrant community. Bilingual approaches were a temporary measure in many immigrant organizations, in order to meet the needs of both younger and older members of the immigrant community.

GREETINGS AND OTHER COMMON EXPRESSIONS

Common Swedish greeting and other expressions include: *God morgon* ("goo mor-on")—Good morning; *God dag* ("goo dahg")—Good day, or good afternoon; *God afton* ("goo ahf-ton")—Good evening; *God natt* ("goo naht")—Good night; *På återseende* ("poh oh-ter-seh-en-deh")—I'll be seeing you; *Adjö* ("ah-yoe")—Good-bye; *Hur står det till?* ("hewr stohr deh teel")—How are you?; *Tak* ("tahk")—Thanks!; *Förlåt* ("foer-loht")—Excuse me; *Var så god* ("vahr soh goo")—You're welcome; *Lycka till!* ("leuk-kah teel")—Good luck; *Vi ses i morgon* ("vee sehs ee mor-on")—See you tomorrow.

FAMILY AND COMMUNITY DYNAMICS

When the first wave of immigrants came from Sweden to America in the 1840s and 1850s, the settlers traveled in large groups composed of entire families and led by a pastor or other community leader.

These groups established the beginnings of the ethnic communities that are still today identifiably Swedish American. Family and social structures became the bedrock of the larger community, and often these communal settlements maintained the characteristics and customs of the areas in Sweden from which the immigrants had come.

Swedish America was thus founded on a tight communal and familial structure, and these characteristics were present both in rural and urban settlements. But this pattern was soon altered by a number of factors, including the increased immigration of single young people, the geographical dispersion of the Swedish immigrants, and secondary migrations within the United States. Although Swedish Americans rarely inter-married (and then usually

"**M**ost dear to me are the shoes my mother wore when she first set foot on the soil of America. You must see these shoes to appreciate the courage my parents had and the sacrifices they made giving up family and security to try for a better life, but not knowing what lay ahead. We came to this country as many others did, POOR! My mother's shoes tell a whole story."

Birgitta Hedman Fichter, 1924, cited in *Ellis Island: An Illustrated History of the Immigrant Experience,* edited by Ivan Chermayeff et al. (New York: Macmillan, 1991).

only with other Scandinavian American groups), Swedes assimilated rapidly into American society, and by the second or third generation were indistinguishable from the general Anglo-American population. Their family patterns and social organization also became indistinct from that of the wider populations.

EDUCATION

Because of widespread literacy in nineteenth-century Sweden, Swedish immigrants were almost universally literate (at least in Swedish), and education was of primary importance to them. They eagerly embraced the American public school system, enrolling their children and organizing their own public schools wherever they were lacking. Swedish immigrants saw education as the primary means for their children to advance in America. Besides participating in the formation of public institutions of higher education (the University of Minnesota is one good example), Swedish Americans also formed their own private colleges; many remain

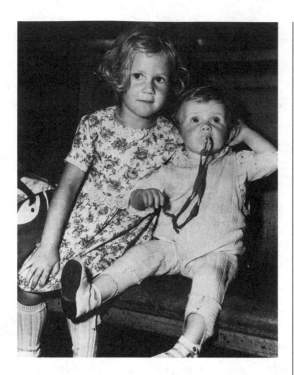

today, including Augustana College (Rock Island, Illinois), Gustavus Adolphus College (St. Peter, Minnesota), Bethany College (Lindsborg, Kansas), Uppsala College (East Orange, New Jersey), North Park College (Chicago, Illinois), and Bethel College (St. Paul, Minnesota). Other colleges and secondary schools operated for a time in the immigrant community, but many of these did not survive. Swedish American churches founded most of these schools, along with theological seminaries to train their own pastors. Literary and publishing activities were strong in the immigrant communities; presses brought forth streams of newspapers, journals, and books representing a broad spectrum of Swedish American opinions.

RELIGION

The Church of Sweden, the official state church of the country, is a part of the Lutheran family of Protestant Christianity and is by far the largest religious institution in Sweden. Having converted to Christianity rather late in the medieval period, Sweden early on joined the Protestant Reformation of the sixteenth century. Under the direction of King Gustav Vasa the Catholic church organization in Sweden was transformed to Lutheranism, which became the official religion of the state. In fact, until the mid-nineteenth century it was illegal for Swedes to be anything *but* Lutheran, or to engage in private religious devotions or study outside of Church sponsorship. The priests of the Church of Sweden were civil servants. Besides their religious

duties these priests kept the citizenship and tax records, and functioned as the local representatives of governmental power. This state church system was prone to abuse and stagnation, and many Swedes, both clergy and laity, sought to reform and renew the church.

In the eighteenth and nineteenth centuries a movement called Pietism made its way from Germany into Scandinavia, seeking to reform the church and the lives of individual believers. Stressing personal conversion and morality, the Pietists were critical of the State Church and pressed for reform of both the church and the government. They also sought a change in governmental policy to allow for more freedom of religious expression in Sweden, including religious practice outside the Church of Sweden. Over the course of the century many of the changes proposed by the Pietists were enacted by the church and the government.

It is from this religious background that Swedish immigrants came to America. They were officially Lutheran, but many were unhappy with state church Christianity in Sweden and sought different forms of religious expression. A few early immigrants came to America to escape religious persecution. For the vast majority, however, the motivation for emigration was economic, although they welcomed the chance to worship in their own way. Some found other forms of Protestantism were more to their liking, and they formed Swedish Baptist and Swedish Methodist groups, which in turn exported these movements back to Sweden.

In the 1840s and 1850s various Swedish Americans began religious activities among their fellow immigrants. Notable names include: Gustav Unonius (Episcopalian); Olof and Jonas Hedstrom (Methodist); Gustaf Palmquist and F. O. Nilsson (Baptist); and L. P. Esbjörn, T. N. Hasselquist, Erland Carlsson, and Eric Norelius (Lutherans). In 1851 the Swedish American Lutherans organized as part of an American Lutheran denomination, but they later broke away to form the independent Augustana Synod, the largest religious group in Swedish America. The Baptists and Methodists also formed their own denominational groups, related to their American counterparts. The growth of these groups was fueled by the waves of immigrants after 1865, and the denominations struggled to keep up with the demand for pastors and congregations.

The Augustana Synod practiced a Lutheranism influenced by Pietism. Other immigrants thought that Augustana was still too Lutheran, and sought a freer type of Christian organization that relied more heavily on Pietist traditions. Both within and outside Augustana congregations these immigrants formed

Mission Societies that were the core of future congregations. During the 1870s and 1880s, despite the wishes of Augustana leaders, this movement broke away from Augustana and Lutheranism, forming independent congregations. The movement eventually yielded two other Swedish American denominations, the Swedish Mission Covenant Church (1885) and the Swedish Evangelical Free Church (1884). These two groups, along with the Lutherans, Methodists, and Baptists were the largest religious groups in the Swedish American community.

The immigrant religious denominations were easily the largest and most influential organizations within Swedish America. These groups soon began to form congregations, schools, hospitals, nursing homes, orphanages, and seminaries to serve the needs of their community. Much of the cultural and social life of the immigrant communities was channeled through the churches. Still, these religious groups only formally enrolled about 20 percent of all immigrants with 70 percent in Augustana and the remaining 30 percent in the other denominations. The churches reached out beyond their membership to serve many others in the immigrant community, but some Swedes chose to join American churches or to join no church at all. It was a tremendous change for these immigrants, leaving the state church for a system where they had to intentionally join and financially support a specific congregation.

These immigrant churches weathered acculturation and assimilation better than other immigrant institutions. Most churches made the transition to English during the 1920s and 1930s and continued to grow in the twentieth century. Augustana joined with other American Lutherans in 1962, the Methodists merged into American Methodism in 1942, and the Evangelical Free Church began to encompass other Scandinavian free church movements in 1950. The Baptist General Conference and the Evangelical Covenant Church remain independent organizations. Many of the congregations and colleges of these immigrant religious groups retain a strong interest in their ethnic heritage.

EMPLOYMENT AND ECONOMIC TRADITIONS

A common stereotype of nineteenth-century Swedish immigrants was that they were either farmers and agricultural laborers in the rural areas, or domestic servants in urban areas. There was a grain of truth in this stereotype since such occupations were often filled by newly arrived immigrants. For the most part, Swedish immigrants were literate, skilled, and ambitious, quickly moving up the employment ladder into skilled positions or even white-collar jobs. Many Swedes exhibit a streak of stubborn independence and, accordingly, most sought economic activities that would allow them to work with their own talents and skills. For some this meant work within the Swedish American community, serving the needs of the immigrants. For others this meant independent work in the larger American community as skilled workers or independent businesspeople in low-capital, high-labor fields such as wood and metal work, printing, and building contracting.

At the turn of the twentieth century, Swedish American men were employed in agriculture (33 percent), industry (35 percent), business and communication (14 percent), and as servants and laborers (16 percent). Among women, common occupations included servants and waitresses (56 percent), and seamstresses or laundresses (13 percent), with smaller groups of laborers and factory workers. As the Swedes adapted to American society, their employment patterns began to emulate that of the society as a whole, and they moved into educated positions in teaching, business, and industry.

Coming from a country that in the nineteenth century was largely rural, many Swedish immigrants were attracted to America by the prospect of free or cheap agricultural land, mainly in the upper Midwest or Great Plains states. By 1920 there were over 60,000 Swedish American farmers in the United State on more than 11 million cultivated acres, and five out of six of these farmers owned their land. Swedish American farmers were industrious and intelligent and soon picked up American agricultural methods for use on their farms. For the most part, the older agricultural techniques from Sweden were not applicable to American farms, and Swedish Americans made few unique contributions to American agriculture. Later immigrants often headed to the forests and mines of the upper Midwest and increasingly to the Pacific Northwest. Here they worked as lumberjacks and miners, two professions that were common in Sweden.

In the urban areas, Swedish Americans were best known for their skilled work in construction trades, and in the wood- and metal-working industries. Swedish contractors dominated the construction business in the Midwest; at one point it was estimated that 80 percent of the construction in Minneapolis and 35 percent in Chicago was carried out by Swedes. The Swedish contractors also employed many of their fellow immigrants as carpenters, plumbers, masons, and painters, providing vital employment for new arrivals. Over half the Swedish American industrial workers in 1900 were occupied in wood and metal working. In addition, Swedes were represented in the printing and graphics, as well as the design industries.

Swedes were also employed in the engineering and architecture fields, with many designing industrial and military machinery. Two Swedish Americans, Captain John Ericsson and Admiral John Dahlgren, revolutionized American naval power during the Civil War with their invention of the ironclad warship and the modern naval cannon, respectively. Other technical achievements and inventions of Swedish Americans include an improved zipper (Peter Aronsson and Gideon Sundback), the Bendix drive (Vincent Bendix), an improved disc clutch (George William Borg), and xerographic dry-copying (Chester Carlson). Swedish Americans have also made notable contributions in publishing, art, acting, writing, education, ministry, and politics.

POLITICS AND GOVERNMENT

Sweden has a long history of representative government, with the nobles, the clergy, and the peasants all represented in the Swedish Parliament. This tradition was never overcome, even by the most autocratic of Swedish kings. At the beginning of the nineteenth century the voting franchise in Sweden was rather limited, although this changed drastically toward the end of the century.

One of the reasons Swedes came to America was to experience greater political freedom and to help shape their local communities. Swedish Americans from the old Delaware colony were active in the politics of colonial America, and were elected to the legislatures of Delaware and Pennsylvania. The Swedes were also generally on the American side of the Revolutionary War and remained politically active when it ended. John Morton (1724-1777) of Pennsylvania was a delegate to the Continental Congress, and voted for and signed the Declaration of Independence in 1776. John Hanson (1715-1783) of Maryland was one the leading political figures of that state, and was elected to the Continental Congress three times. In 1781 Hanson was elected by Congress as the first president of the United States in Congress Assembled, or the chief executive of Congress, before the office of the presidency was established.

Through the early national period Swedish Americans usually favored the Democrats over the Whigs, but later they broke with the Democrats over the issue of slavery. Swedish Americans

became enthusiastic supporters of the newly rising Republican party and of Abraham Lincoln. The Swedes' relationship with the Republican party became so firm and widespread as to be axiomatic; it was said that the average Swedish American believed in three things: the Swedish culture, the Lutheran church, and the Republican party. In the late nineteenth century Swedes became a powerful force in local Republican politics in the upper Midwest, especially in Minnesota and Illinois. In 1886 John Lind (1854-1930) of Minnesota became the first Swedish American elected to Congress. Lind uncharacteristically switched to the Democratic party, and was then elected the first Swedish American governor of Minnesota in 1898.

Not all Swedish Americans subscribed to the Republican philosophy, of course. Many immigrants, especially those who arrived in the later waves, were strongly influenced by socialism in Sweden, and brought this philosophy with them to America. Swedish American socialists founded their own organizations and newspapers, and became active within the American socialist community. Most of this socialistic activity was local in nature, but some Swedes became involved on a national level. Joe Hill (Joel Hägglund) was a celebrated leader in the Industrial Workers of the World, but was accused of murder and executed in Utah in 1915.

Although socialism was a minority movement among the Swedish Americans, it did reflect many of their concerns. Swedes tended to be progressives within their parties. They believed strongly in the right of the individual, were deeply suspicious of big business and foreign entanglements, and pushed progressive social legislation and reforms. One of the early leaders in this movement was Charles Lindbergh, Sr. (1859-1924), father of the aviator, who was elected as a Republican to Congress from Minnesota in 1906. In Congress he espoused midwestern Populist ideals, opposed big business interests, and spoke forcefully against American involvement in World War I. After the war, many Scandinavians in Minnesota left the Republican party for the new Farmer Labor party, which adopted many of the Populist ideals common among the Swedes. Magnus Johnson was elected as a Farmer Labor senator from Minnesota in 1923, and Floyd Olson served that party as governor of Minnesota from 1931 to 1936. Many Swedes left the Republican party in 1932 to vote for Franklin D. Roosevelt in the presidential election, and some remained in the Democratic party. A split occurred within the Swedish American community after Roosevelt's presidency, and that division exists to this day. Urban Swedish Americans are evenly divided between the Democratic and Republican parties, while rural Swedish Americans remain overwhelmingly Republican.

As with many ethnic immigrant groups, Swedish Americans have been under-represented in national politics, with about 13 senators and 50 representatives, mainly from the Midwest. On the state level there have been at least 28 governors (10 in Minnesota), and many state and local officials. Modern Swedish American politicians have included Governors Orville Freeman (Minnesota), James Thompson (Illinois), and Kay Orr (Nebraska), Senator Warren Magnusson (Washington), and Representative John B. Anderson (Illinois). Swedish Americans have achieved notable success on the Supreme Court, including the appointment of two chief justices, Earl Warren and William Rehnquist.

UNION ACTIVITY

As small independent farmers and business owners, Swedish Americans have not been overwhelmingly involved in American union activities. Many in skilled professions in the wood and metal industries were involved in the formation of craft unions. In addition, given the Swedish domination of the building trades in the Midwest, there were many who became involved with the construction trade unions, most notably Lawrence Lindelof, president of the International Brotherhood of Painters and Allied Trades from 1929 to 1952. Some Swedish American women were involved in the garment and textile unions; Mary Anderson joined a trade union as a shoe stitcher in Chicago, was hired by the International Boot and Show Workers Union, and eventually was appointed director of the U.S. Department of Labor's Women's Bureau.

MILITARY

Swedish Americans have fought for America in all of its wars, from the Revolution to the present day. During the Revolutionary War, Swedes from Maryland and Delaware fought, for the most part, on the revolutionary side, some in the Army, but many more in the new American Navy. About 90 Army and Navy officers from Sweden came over temporarily to fight on the American side, either directly with American troops, or more typically, with French forces (Sweden was allied with France at the time). One of these officers, Baron von Stedingk, who would become a field marshal in the Swedish Army and Ambassador to Russia.

At the start of the Civil War the Swedish American population numbered about 20,000, and their enthusiasm for Lincoln and the northern cause is seen in the fact that at least 3,000 Swedes served in the Union army, mainly in Illinois and Minnesota regiments. A number of others served in the Union navy, and it was here that Swedish Americans were best known. Admiral John Dahlgren was in command of a fleet blockading southern ports, and introduced a number of modern advances in the area of naval weaponry. Captain John Ericsson, a naval engineer, developed the North's first practical ironclad ships, which fought with great effectiveness and revolutionized naval architecture. The Swedish-American population in the South at the time was concentrated mainly in Texas, and their numbers were small, although some did enlist to fight for the Confederacy.

Leading up to World War I, Swedish American sympathies were typically with Germany, although the strongest sentiments were toward neutrality and isolationism, as espoused by Charles Lindbergh, Sr. When the United States did enter the war on the Allied side in 1917, however, many Swedish Americans rushed to show their patriotism by enlisting in the Army and by buying war bonds. In the 1920s and 1930s, Swedes generally returned to their isolationist and neutralist ways, and Charles Lindberg, Jr. took up this cause where his father left off. However, another famous Swedish American, writer Carl Sandburg, forcefully urged American intervention in Europe against the Nazis, writing many articles and works opposing the German regime. In both World Wars many Swedish Americans served with great distinction, including Major Richard Bong, who received the Medal of Honor in 1944 for destroying 36 Japanese planes in combat. Given their general engineering and technical expertise, many Swedish Americans rose to positions of importance in command, such as John Dahlquist, deputy chief of staff to General Eisenhower, and Arleigh Burke and Theodore Lonnquest, who eventually rose to the rank of admiral in the Navy. Many other Swedish Americans rose to prominence in the defense industry, especially Philip Johnson who headed Boeing Aircraft Company during World War II.

RELATIONS WITH SWEDEN

Swedish Americans have historically been very interested in the development of Sweden, and a lively correspondence is still maintained between Swedes on both sides of the Atlantic. Modern Sweden is a dramatically different country than the one the immigrants left; while Swedish Americans often have a hazy impression of a backward, rural country, reality is quite different. The Sweden of the twentieth century has often been characterized as taking the "middle way," a neutral, socialist country between the capitalist West and the communist East, ruled for most of 50 years by the Social Democratic party. Some Swedish Americans have applauded the changes that have occurred in modern Sweden, while others have deplored them. During the Vietnam era of the 1960s and 1970s relations between Sweden and the United States were somewhat strained, but the rapport between the two nations has improved significantly since then.

INDIVIDUAL AND GROUP CONTRIBUTIONS

Even though Swedish Americans represent only a small fraction of the total American population, many have made notable contributions to American life and culture.

BUSINESS

Many Swedish Americans have made names for themselves in American business. Eric Wickman (1887-1954) founded Greyhound Corporation and built it into a national enterprise. Charles R. Walgreen (1873-1939) started the national chain of drugstores, and Curtis Carlson parlayed business and service sectors into the Carlson Companies, which operates hotels (Marriot), restaurants, and travel agencies. John W. Nordstrom of Seattle founded the department store chain that bears his name. Some Swedish Americans rose through the ranks to become leaders in American industry, including Eric Mattson (Midland National Bank), Robert O. Anderson (Atlantic Richfield), Rudolph Peterson (Bank of America), Philip G. Johnson (Boeing), and Rand V. Araskog (ITT).

EXPLORATION

One of the best known of all Swedish Americans is the aviator Charles Lindbergh, Jr. (1902-1974); his father and namesake was a congressman and politician, but the younger Lindbergh is known for the first solo flight across the Atlantic in 1927; a national hero, Lindberg served as a civilian employee of the War Department. Another famous explorer was Edwin (Buzz) Aldrin (1930–), the Apollo 11 astronaut who in 1969 was the second person to step on the moon.

FILM, TELEVISION, AND THEATER

The most famous Swedish immigrant in this field was Greta Garbo (1905-1990) who was born in Sweden and came to the United States in 1925; enigmatic, Garbo made 24 films in the United States, after which she abruptly retired and sought seclusion from public view. Other Swedish American actresses have included Viveca Lindfors, Ann-Margaret (Olson), Gloria Swanson, and Candace Bergen—the daughter of Edgar Bergen (1903-1978), well known for his ventriloquism on television. Other Swedish American actors have included Werner Oland and Richard Widmark.

LITERATURE

Although Swedish Americans produced a vast quantity of written literature, some of it was written in Swedish and is unknown outside the immigrant community. With the coming of the second and third generations, however, Swedish Americans have produced a number of writers in English who have earned national reputations. The most famous of these authors was Carl Sandberg (1878-1967), who produced nationally known poetry and novels, but whose most famous work is his four-volume biography of Abraham Lincoln, a work which won Sandberg a Pulitzer prize. Another contemporary Swedish American writer in Nelson Algren (1909-1981), who has written extensively about the hard realities of urban and working class life.

MUSIC

The most famous Swedish American composer is Howard Hanson (1896-1981) who grew up in the immigrant community of Wahoo, Nebraska; for many years Hanson was director of the Eastman School of Music in Rochester, New York, and he is one of the best known twentieth-century American composers of serious classical music. A number of immigrants from Sweden have become important singers of classical music and opera. Best known of all of was Jenny Lind (1820-1887), referred to as the "Swedish Nightingale," she was already famous in Europe when P. T. Barnum brought her to America in 1850 for the first of over 90 concerts in three years; Lind took America by storm; eventually she returned to Europe, but gave generously in support of charities within the Swedish American community. Following Lind to America were such singers as Christiana Nilsson, lyric tenor Jussi Björling, and soprano Birgit Nilsson.

SCIENCE

Many Swedish Americans have become distinguished in the field of science, especially in chemistry and physics. Carl David Anderson (1905–) won a Nobel prize in Physics for his discovery of positronic particles. Another Nobel prize winner is Glenn Seaborg (1912–), who in 1951 won in chemistry for his work with transuranium elements.

VISUAL ARTS

The most widely known Swedish American painter is Birger Sandzén (1871-1945), who lived and worked in the rolling prairies of central Kansas around Lindsborg; his works are found in many museums in Europe and America. A more recent artist, known for his "Pop" art, is Claes Oldenburg (1929–). Other notable artists have included Henry Mattson, John F. Carlson, and Bror Julius Nordfeldt. In sculpture, the best known Swedish American is Carl Milles (1875-1955), who has achieved international fame for his work, especially for his outdoor sculpture; Milles studied with August Rodin in Paris, and went on to be artist-in-residence at Cranbrook Academy of Art in Michigan.

MEDIA

PRINT

Norden News.
Newspaper in Finnish and Swedish.

Contact: Erik R. Hermans, Editor.
Address: P.O. Box 2143, New York, New York 10185-0018.
Telephone: (212) 753-0880.
Fax: (212) 944-0763.

Nordenstjernan Svea.
Established in 1872, this weekly is one of the few remaining Swedish American newspapers, printed in English and Swedish.

Contact: Alvalene Karlsson, Editor.
Address: P.O. Box 4587, New York, New York 10163-4587.
Telephone: (212) 490-3900.
Fax: (212) 490-5979.
E-mail: ed@nordstjernan.com.

Svenska Amerikanaren Tribunen.
Established in 1876, this newspaper is published in Swedish and English.

Contact: Jane Hendricks, Editor.
Address: 10921 Paramount Boulevard, Downey, California 90241.

Sweden and America.
Published by the Swedish Council of America, this quarterly contains general news and articles about Swedish Americans and about developments in Sweden, and is the most widely circulated periodical about Swedish Americans.

Contact: Teresa Scalzo, Editor.
Address: 2600 Park Avenue, Minneapolis, Minnesota 55407.
Telephone: (612) 871-0593.
Fax: (612) 871-8682.

Swedish-American Genealogist.
This quarterly is published by the Swenson Swedish Immigration Research Center and contains articles on genealogical research, local and family history.

Contact: Dr. James E. Erickson, Editor.
Address: 7008 Bristol Boulevard, Edina, Minnesota 55435-4108.
Telephone: (309) 794-7204.
E-mail: j.erickson@nr.cc.mn.us.

Swedish-American Historical Quarterly.
Published by the Swedish-American Historical Society, this periodical contains articles on the history and culture of Swedish Americans.

Contact: Byron Nordstrom, Editor.
Address: Gustav Adolphus College, Department of History, St. Peter, Minnesota 56082.
Telephone: (507) 933-7435.
Fax: (507) 933-7041.

Vestkusten.
Ethnic newspaper in Swedish and English.

Contact: Bridget Stromberg-Brink, Managing Editor.
Address: 237 Ricardo Road, Mill Valley, California 94941-2517.
Telephone: (415) 381-5149.
Fax: (415) 381-9664.
E-mail: vestkust@well.com.

ORGANIZATIONS AND ASSOCIATIONS

American Swedish Historical Foundation.
Founded in 1926, this group maintains a museum, library, and archives on Swedish American culture and history, and sponsors exchange programs and cultural events. It also publishes an annual *Yearbook*, and other occasional publications.

Contact: Birgitta W. Davis, Acting Director.

Address: 1900 Pattison Avenue, Philadelphia,
    Pennsylvania 19145-5901.
Telephone: (215) 389-1776.
Fax: (215) 389-7701.
E-mail: ashm@libertynet.org.
Online: http://www.libertynet.org/ashm/.

American Swedish Institute.

Founded in 1929, the American Swedish Institute
seeks to preserve the Swedish cultural heritage in
America. The institute, housed in the mansion of a
former Swedish American journalist, offers classes,
activities, exhibits, concerts and workshops, along
with a library and archives.

Contact: Bruce N. Karlstadt, Director.
Address: 2600 Park Avenue, Minneapolis,
    Minnesota 55407.
Telephone: (612) 871-4907.
Fax: (612) 871-8682.
Online: http://www.americanswedishinst.org/.

Swedish-American Historical Society.

Founded in 1950, the society is dedicated to the
preservation and documentation of the heritage of
Swedish Americans. Publishes a quarterly journal,
Swedish-American Historical Quarterly and *Pioneer
Newsletter* as well as books in this area.

Contact: Timothy J. Johnson.
Address: 5125 North Spaulding Avenue, Chicago,
    Illinois 60625.
Telephone: (773) 583-5722.
E-mail: kanders3@northpark.edu.

Swedish Council of America.

Formed in 1973, the Swedish Council of America is
a cooperative agency that coordinates the efforts of
over 100 different Swedish American historical,
cultural, and fraternal organizations. The Swedish
Council publishes a monthly magazine called *Sweden and America*, which is a useful forum for current
Swedish American activities.

Contact: Roger Baumann, Exec.Dir.
Address: 2600 Park Avenue, Minneapolis,
    Minnesota 55407.
Telephone: (612) 871-0593.
Fax: (612) 871-8682.
E-mail: swedcoun@swedishcouncil.org.
Online: http://www.swedishcouncil.org/.

United Swedish Societies/Svenska
Central Forbundet.

Federation of 50 Swedish American organizations.

Contact: Harry Hedin, President.

Address: 20 Bristol Avenue, Staten Island,
    New York 10301.
Telephone: (718) 442-1096.
Fax: (718) 442-5376.

Vasa Order of America.

Founded in 1896, it is the largest Swedish American
fraternal organization in America with over 31,000
members in 326 lodges nationwide.

Contact: Gladys Birtwistle.
Address: 43 Holden Street, Warwick,
    Rhode Island 02889.
Telephone: (401) 739-3530.

MUSEUMS AND
RESEARCH CENTERS

American Swedish Historical Museum.

This museum collects and displays artifacts and documents of Swedish Americans to preserve the
Swedish American culture. The building is modeled
after a seventeenth-century Swedish manor house.

Contact: Birgitta W. Davis, Acting Director.
Address: 1900 Pattison Avenue, Philadelphia,
    Pennsylvania 19145-5901.
Telephone: (215) 389-1776.
Fax: (215) 389-7701.
E-Mail: ashm@libertynet.org.
Online: http://www.libertynet.org/ashm.

American Swedish Institute Museum.

This museum provides exhibits and activities for and
about Swedish Americans, including displays of the
Institute's collections, as well as traveling exhibits.

Contact: Bruce Karlstadt, Director.
Address: 2600 Park Avenue, Minneapolis,
    Minnesota 55407.
Telephone: (612) 871-4907.
Fax: (612) 871-8682.
Online: http://www.americanswedishinst.org.

Augustana Historical Society.

Preservation of both literary and non-literary materials relating to Swedish immigration to the United
States, the history of Augustana College and its
relation to the Lutheran Church, and cultural
exchange between the campus and Sweden.

Address: Augustana College Library, 639 Thirty-
    Eighth Street, Rock Island, Illinois 61201.
Contact: Harold Sundelius, President.
Telephone: (309) 794-7317.
Fax: (309) 794-7230.

Bishop Hill.
Located in Western Illinois, this is a fully preserved folk museum, dedicated to preserving the life of the pioneer Swedish immigrants in America. Founded in 1846, Bishop Hill was the home of a religious communal settlement organized by Erik Jansson; though the communal settlement collapsed after Jansson's death, a community remained. In the twentieth century the Bishop Hill Heritage Association began restoring the settlement to its original condition.

Contact: Morris Nelson, President.
Address: P.O. Box 1853, Bishop Hill, Illinois 61419-0092.
Telephone: (309) 927-3899.
Fax: (309) 927-3010.

Swedish American Museum Center of Chicago.
Located in Andersonville, an area of historical immigrant settlement, this museum collects and displays artifacts and documents of Swedish immigration, maintains an archives, and sponsors special exhibits and activities.

Contact: Kerstin Lane, Executive Director.
Address: 5211 North Clark Street, Chicago, Illinois 60640.
Telephone: (312) 728-8111.

Swenson Immigrant Research Center.
Situated on the campus of Augustana College, this center has a large collection of historical documents, records, and artifacts on Swedish Americans in the country. The Swenson center is especially good for genealogical and historical study.

Contact: Dag Blanck, Director.
Address: Augustana College, Box 175, Rock Island, Illinois 61201.
Telephone: (309) 794-7204.

SOURCES FOR ADDITIONAL STUDY

American-Swedish Handbook, eleventh edition, edited by Christopher Olsson and Ruth McLaughlin. Minneapolis: Swedish Council of America, 1992.

Barton, H. Arnold. *A Folk Divided: Homeland Swedes and Swedish Americans, 1840-1940.* Carbondale: Southern Illinois University Press, 1994.

Bergendoff, Conrad. "The Role of Augustana in Transplanting of a Culture Across the Atlantic," in *The Immigration of Ideas: Studies in the North Atlantic Community,* edited by J. Iverne Dowie and J. Thomas Tredway. Rock Island, Illinois: Augustana Historical Society, 1968.

Carlsson, Sten. *Swedes in North America 1638-1988: Technical, Cultural, and Political Achievements.* Stockholm: Streiffert and Co., 1988.

From Sweden to America: A History of the Migration, edited by Harald Rundblom and Hans Norman. Minneapolis: University of Minnesota Press, 1976.

Hasselmo, Nils. *Swedish America: An Introduction.* Minneapolis: Brings Press, 1976.

Kastrup, Allan. *The Swedish Heritage in America.* St. Paul, Minnesota: Swedish Council of America, 1975.

Letters from the Promised Land: Swedes in America, 1840-1914, edited by H. Arnold Barton. Minneapolis: University of Minnesota Press, 1975.

Ljungmark, Lars. *Swedish Exodus,* translated by Kermit Westerberg. Carbondale: Southern Illinois University Press, 1979.

Scott, Franklin. *Sweden: The Nation's History,* revised edition. Carbondale: Southern Illinois University Press, 1988.

Scott, Larry E. *The Swedish Texans.* University of Texas Institute of Texan Cultures at San Antonio, 1990.

Swedish Life in American Cities, edited by Dag Blanck and Harald Runblom. Uppsala: Centre for Multiethnic Research, Uppsala University, 1991.

Since the Swiss
came from western
Europe's oldest
democracy and
have forged a
national unity out
of ethnically diverse
constituencies, they
find American
culture compatible
with their own.

Swiss

by
Leo Schelbert

AMERICANS

OVERVIEW

Switzerland lies in the central part of the Alps, a 500-mile-long European mountain range, which stretches westward from France's Riviera into what was northern Yugoslavia. Four main passes (Grimsel, Furka, St. Gotthard, and Oberalp) allow passage from Northern Europe across the Alps to Italy, making Switzerland a country of transit. The country covers 15,941 square miles and borders Germany to the north, France to the west, Italy to the south, and Austria and the Principality of Liechtenstein to the east. The Swiss nation is a confederation of 26 member states called cantons, and the nation's capital is Bern, a city that began about 1160 and was officially founded in 1191. The national flag consists of a square red field with a white equilateral cross at its center.

In 1992 Switzerland counted 6.9 million inhabitants, including one million foreign nationals. The country is ethnically diverse, indicated by its four language groups. Religiously the Swiss people are nearly evenly divided between Catholics and Swiss Reformed, but there are also small groups of other Christian denominations and other faiths.

HISTORY

The Swiss Confederation emerged in the late thirteenth century from an alliance of three regions: the modern-day cantons Uri, Schwyz, and Unterwalden. The so-called *Bundesbrief* of 1291 documents their alliance. In it the three regions pledge mutual support to keep internal order and to resist aggression. The Confederation grew by wars of conquest and by alliances arranged with important towns located at the access routes of the passes to Italy, such as Luzern, Zürich, and Bern. By 1513, 13 cantons had united the rural population with the urban elite of artisans and entrepreneurs. Both groups were intent on gaining and preserving independence from the nobility, a unique development in European history. The Confederation's defeat at the battle of Marignano in upper Italy in 1515 ended the nation's expansion. This loss led to the gradual emergence of armed neutrality, a basic feature of Switzerland's political tradition. However, the Reformation split the people into Catholic and Swiss Reformed hostile camps and nearly destroyed the Confederation.

MODERN ERA

During the seventeenth and eighteenth centuries increasingly smaller oligarchies came to power in the Swiss cantons but were overthrown in 1798 in the wake of the French Revolution. In 1848, after five decades of foreign intervention and internal uncertainty, a new constitution was adopted. The previous system of autonomous states became one federal state, though the people remain the actual sovereign. The Swiss are called upon to vote on numerous issues several times a year. This process occurs either by constitutional requirement or more often by initiative and referendum which, given a sufficient number of signatories, force the government to submit issues to the popular vote. The executive branch, called *Bundesrat*, consists of seven members chosen by Parliament and acts as a unit. The presidency is an honorary position and rotates annually. The legislative power rests with citizens of voting age and with a Parliament, divided into a Council of States (*Ständerat*) and a National Council (*Nationalrat*). In addition, the cantons and over 3,000 communes (*Gemeinden*) have preserved their autonomy and decide numerous issues by popular vote. The Swiss are involved in political decision-making throughout the year on the local, cantonal, and federal level.

Neutrality in foreign affairs and universal military service of men are considered central to the Swiss political tradition, which may have kept the country out of two devastating world wars. Switzerland's economy, however, is fully dependent on the export of quality products and on special expertise in finance as well as the production of machinery, pharmaceuticals, watches, and precision instruments.

SWISS IN BRITISH NORTH AMERICA

The first known Swiss in what is now the territory of the United States was Theobald von Erlach (1541-1565). In 1564 he was a leading member of a French attempt to create a permanent foothold in North America. He perished when some 900 French soldiers were shipwrecked by a hurricane in September 1565, and killed by the Spanish. Some "Switzers" also lived at Jamestown during the regime of Captain Smith. In 1657 the French Swiss Jean Gignilliat received a large land grant from the proprietors of South Carolina. In 1710 some 100 Swiss joined Christoph von Graffenried (1661-1743) who founded New Bern in present-day North Carolina.

Between 1710 and 1750, some 25,000 Swiss are estimated to have settled in British North America, especially in Pennsylvania, Virginia, and South Carolina. Many were members of the Reformed church and were actively recruited by entrepreneurs such as Jean Pierre Purry (1675-1736), the founder of Purrysburg, South Carolina. About 4,000 Swiss Mennonites settled in Pennsylvania, many of whom had first gone to the Palatinate from which the next generation emigrated in search of fertile, affordable land and greater toleration of their creed.

In the late 1750s an influential group of French Swiss officers in the British service assumed leadership roles in the fight against indigenous peoples resisting white incursions into the trans-Appalachian West, the French, and the insurgent colonials. In the middle decades of the eighteenth century a group of Swiss Jesuits labored in the Southwest of the present United States to promote the northward expansion of New Spain.

SWISS IMMIGRATION 1820 TO 1930

Between 1798 and 1850, about 100,000 Swiss went abroad (the proportions between temporary and permanent migrations cannot be determined) and some 50,000 foreigners located in Switzerland. Between 1850 and 1914 those leaving the Confederation numbered about 410,000, those entering it from abroad about 409,000. Those leaving were attracted by the newly conquered lands taken from indigenous peoples in Australia, New Zealand, and in the Western Hemisphere by expanding neo-European nations such as Argentina, Brazil, or the United States. The emigrants seem to have been rooted in the lure of faraway lands or in the desire to escape parental control, intolerable marriages, or oppressive village traditions.

Between 1820 and 1930, some 290,000 people went from Switzerland to the United States. About

12,500 arrived between 1820 and 1850; some 76,500 between 1851 and 1880; and some 82,000 in the 1880s. Between 1891 and 1920, about 89,000 arrived and nearly 30,000 in the 1920s. No reliable figures exist for Swiss return migration, but it was numerically substantial. For instance, nearly 7,000 of the more than 8,200 Swiss of military service age who had gone to the United States returned to Switzerland between 1926 and 1930.

"**M**y mother had to try and keep track of us. She finally took us and tied us all together so that we would stay together. And that's the way we came off the boat."

Gertrude Schneider Smith, 1921, cited in *Ellis Island: An Illustrated History of the Immigrant Experience,* edited by Ivan Chermayeff et al. (New York: Macmillan, 1991).

In the first half of the nineteenth century large numbers of Swiss settled in the rural Midwest, especially in Ohio, Indiana, Illinois, and Wisconsin, and after 1848 in California. Some 40 percent of Swiss went to urban areas such as New York, Philadelphia, Cincinnati, Chicago, St. Louis, San Francisco, and Los Angeles. In 1920, for instance, New York counted 9,233 Swiss, Chicago 3,452, San Francisco 2,105, and Philadelphia 1,889. As to states, in 1930 California numbered 20,063 Swiss, New York 16,571, New Jersey 8,765, and Wisconsin, Ohio, and Illinois some 7,000 each.

The socio-economic status of newcomers from Switzerland spanned the spectrum from well-to-do to the poor. A sample analysis from 1915 of 5,000 Swiss men in the United States yielded the following distribution: a third belonged to the lower income and status groups; approximately 44 percent were solidly middle class; and about 22 percent were well situated.

NINETEENTH CENTURY SETTLEMENTS

In 1804 a special grant of Congress enabled a group of French Swiss winegrowers to settle on the Ohio and establish the town of Vevay, Indiana. This viticulture, which they had hoped to introduce as a permanent feature into the Midwestern economy, became insignificant by mid-century and was replaced by the cultivation of maize and other staples. In 1817 and 1825 Swiss Mennonites founded the agricultural settlements Sonnenberg and Chippewa in Ohio, respectively, and in 1838 Berne, Indiana; the latter remains conscious of its Swiss origin. By the efforts of the Köpfli and Sup-

piger families the town of Highland emerged in southern Illinois in 1831 and eventually attracted some 1,500 Swiss settlers. In the same decade John August Sutter (1803-1880) established New Helvetia in California, then still under Mexican sovereignty. When gold was discovered on his property in 1848, thousands of goldseekers overran his extensive domain, and the city of Sacramento was platted, and became California's capital in 1854.

In 1825 several Swiss, who had joined Lord Selkirk's Red River colony in Canada in 1821, settled at Gratiot's Grove northeast of Galena, Illinois. In 1845 New Glarus was founded in southern Wisconsin's Green County, today the best known settlement of Swiss origin. Numerous Swiss also settled in the towns of Monroe, Washington, and Mount Pleasant. In 1848 Bernese Swiss established Alma on the Mississippi, which counted some 900 Swiss in 1870. A French Swiss group connected with the Protestant Plymouth Brethren established a community in Knoxville, Tennessee, in the same year.

In the spring of 1856 a group of Swiss and Germans established a Swiss Colonization Society in Cincinnati, Ohio, to create a culturally homogeneous settlement. After an extensive search Tell City was laid out in 1858 on the Ohio River in Perry County, Indiana. In the post-Civil War era Helvetia was founded in West Virginia in 1867 as a result of active recruitment by that state. In the 1880s Peter Staub (1827-1904) initiated the settlement of Grütli in Grundy County, Tennessee. During the same decade 1,000 Swiss who had converted to Mormonism went to Utah and settled mainly at Midway near Salt Lake City and at St. George on Utah's southwestern border. Between 1870 and 1914 several thousand Italian Swiss went to California where they established vineyards and dairy farms.

IMMIGRATION SINCE 1930

The Great Depression and World War II diminished Swiss immigration. Between 1931 and 1960 some 23,700 Swiss arrived, and 29,100 between 1961 and 1990. Many of these Swiss did not stay permanently. They were mainly professionals and business people employed in American branches of Swiss firms. The 1980 census counted 235,355 people of single, and 746,188 of multiple Swiss ancestry. In 1990 there was a total of 607,833 persons of Swiss ancestry of whom 35,900 (5.9 percent) were Swiss-born, and of these 57.6 percent were naturalized.

ACCULTURATION AND ASSIMILATION

Although Swiss in the United States are often mistaken for German, French, or Italian, their involvement in American life has been quite extensive. Since the Swiss came from western Europe's oldest democracy and have forged a national unity out of ethnically diverse constituencies, they find American culture compatible with their own. For instance, when John J. Zubly, a delegate to the Second Continental Congress, published the widely distributed pamphlet *The Law of Liberty* in 1775, he appended "A Short and Concise Account of the Struggles of Swisserland for Liberty" to it. He paralleled the Swiss with American colonials, the Austrian emperor with the British king, and viewed their struggle as the same quest for liberty.

TRADITIONS, CUSTOMS, BELIEFS

Although Switzerland is a highly industrialized country with a powerful financial and industrial elite involved in global markets, Swiss culture remains identified with an idealized rural tradition. In New Glarus, a major tourist attraction in southern Wisconsin, a William Tell and Heidi festival is held each year. The chalet, a house style of rural origin, remains identified with the Swiss, although it is common only in certain Swiss regions.

Yodeling and the Alphorn, again native only to some rural Swiss regions, continue to serve as emblems of Swiss culture as do the various *Trachten*—colorful and often beautifully crafted garb for women and men. *Trachten* originate in distinct regions, but tend to become fused into a blended version, sometimes mixed with Tyrolian or Bavarian motifs. The so-called Swiss barn is also widely found in Pennsylvania and some midwestern states. It is built into an incline with a large entrance to the hayloft on an upper level and the entrances to the stables on the opposite lower level. The dominance of rural motifs in Swiss American culture points to a central feature of Swiss self-interpretation: Switzerland's origins are shaped by the traditions of rural communities. Their emblems symbolize Swiss culture however far removed they might be from modern day Swiss and Swiss American reality.

CUISINE

Predictably, Swiss cuisine varies according to ethnic influences. Another historic division is equally telling, however: that between country and city. Thus, two dishes eaten today by all Swiss are the simple cheese fondue, eaten for centuries by Swiss in rural regions, and veal with a sauce of white wine and cream, formerly enjoyed by city dwellers. Cheese, however, is popular in almost any form. As for other regional cuisine, German areas favor pork, often accompanied by *rosti*, a dish of diced potatoes mixed with herbs, bacon, or cheese, and fried to a golden brown.

HEALTH ISSUES

Swiss Americans follow general trends in Western medicine and health care. People in rural areas have remained connected with healing traditions based on telepathic methods and herbs and herbal ointments. In mental health the influence of Carl Gustav Jung (1875-1961) has been significant. Jung viewed mental problems as soluble in part by a skillful evocation of symbols shared by all in a postulated collective subconscious that transcends cultural boundaries. Numerous Jung Institutes of the United States promote Jungian ideas, which also have influenced American literary scholarship.

LANGUAGE

Some 73 percent of Swiss speak High German and in everyday life forms of various Low German dialects, *Schwyzerdütsch* (Swiss-German); 20 percent speak French and several regional dialects (five percent Italian, and one percent Romansh, which is divided into three groups called *Rhaeto-Romontsch*, *Oberhalbsteinisch*, and *Ladin*). Most Swiss learn as their first language a regional and older form of German, French, or Italian, which remains the principal form of communication. Since the establishment of formal schooling, however, Swiss children learn a new, yet related, language such as High German, standard French or standard Italian. The children of the Romansh region learn German or French. To enter a different linguistic world was, therefore, for most Swiss immigrants not a new experience, and they mastered multiculturalism with relative ease.

GREETINGS AND OTHER POPULAR EXPRESSIONS

Depending on their local origin Swiss greet each other in many forms. Widespread among German Swiss is *Grüezi* ("groitsee") or *Grüezi wohl*, derived from [*Ich*] *grüsse dich*—I greet you; also the French-derived *Salü* ("saly") and *Tschau* from the Italian *Ciao*, used both when first meeting and at its conclusion. In Raetoromontsch people say *Bien Dí* ("biandee")—Good day; on parting the French Swiss will use the form *a revere* for the standard French *au revoir* and the German Swiss *uf wiederluäge* ("oof weederlooaga")—See you. In German-speaking rural Switzerland the standard form for goodbye is still widespread, *Bhüet di Gott*—May God protect you.

FAMILY AND COMMUNITY DYNAMICS

Swiss family life is well-regulated and conservative. Few women hold careers outside the family, and young people tend to be cooperative and well-behaved. The Swiss American family is indistinguishable from other American families, which have changed from a patriarchal to an egalitarian and child-centered outlook. The Swiss American family is predominantly middle class. According to the 1990 census the median income of Swiss American families was over $42,000 and only 3.8 percent had an income below the poverty line. Over 40.3 percent of the 153,812 owner-occupied Swiss American housing units were mortgage-free and 46.5 percent had two wage earners in the family.

Swiss Americans recreate organizations they have known at home for mutual support as well as for enjoyment and social contact. They celebrate August 1 as the Swiss national holiday and commemorate important battles of the fifteenth century Swiss struggle for independence with parades, speeches and conviviality. At such events there is yodeling, singing, flag throwing—an artful throwing and catching of a Swiss flag on a short handle high into the air, and sometimes a reading of the *Bundesbrief* of 1291. The festivities also include traditional dishes such as *röschti* (hash browns), and *bratwurst*, in addition to dancing and the playing of folk music on the accordion, clarinet and fiddle.

RELIGION

Swiss immigrants belong to various religions. The first Swiss to arrive in North America in large numbers were the Swiss Mennonites, a group that derived from the Anabaptist communities of the Radical Reformation of the 1520s. They rejected infant baptism, thus declaring the whole of ecclesiastical Christendom as heathen. They also repudiated the state as symbolized by the sword and the oath. The Swiss Mennonite settlements that emerged in Pennsylvania and Virginia in the first half of the eighteenth century were expert in farming, and formed congregations of some 25 to 30 families. Each religious community was semi-autonomous and guided by a bishop and by preachers and deacons who were not specially schooled. The only full members were adults who had proven their faith by a virtuous life, the demands of the community, and accepted baptism as a symbol of submission to God's will. Rules set by the religious leaders ordered the manner of dress, forms of courtship, the schooling of children, and dealings with the outside world. If a member failed to conform, the person would be banned and avoided even by the next of kin. In the late nineteenth century many Mennonite congregations—influenced by the Dutch Mennonites, American Protestantism, and American secular culture—

gave up the older traditions. They moved into towns and took up occupations increasingly removed from farming. Only some conservative Swiss Mennonites and Amish still hold on to the sixteenth-century forms of their creed.

Numerous Swiss immigrants belong to the Swiss Reformed church, as formulated by Huldrych Zwingli (1484-1531). He adapted Christian doctrine to the needs of a rising urban bourgeoisie. Municipal power increased, monastic institutions were secularized, and the rule of the urban elites strengthened. Many members of the Swiss Reformed church settled in colonial Pennsylvania, Virginia, and the Carolinas. Their views and ecclesiastical organization were similar to those of Presbyterians, with whom they easily merged.

Some 50,000 Swiss Catholics arrived in the United States after the 1820s, including about 20,000 Italian Swiss who settled in California between 1887 and 1938. Depending on their language, Swiss Catholics joined either German, French, Italian, or ethnically undefined American parishes. They found, however, a very different parish organization in the United States that curtailed the Swiss practice of lay jurisdiction over secular affairs.

Several Swiss religious orders were actively engaged in establishing the Catholic church in the United States. In 1842 Franz von Sales Brunner (1795-1859) introduced the Order of the Precious Blood into Ohio. In 1852 monks from the ancient Benedictine monastery of Einsiedeln founded St. Meinrad, Indiana, the nucleus of the Swiss Benedictine Congregation of the United States formed in 1881. In 1956 the congregation united some 12 foundations with 645 monks. Benedictine sisters were also deeply involved in promoting Catholic education and charity. Anselma Felber (1843-1883) established a community at Conception, Missouri, which later moved to Clyde. Gertrude Leupi (1825-1904) founded a convent in Maryville, later transferred to Yankton, South Dakota.

EMPLOYMENT AND ECONOMIC TRADITIONS

In the eighteenth century Swiss immigrants were mainly farmers and artisans. Like other German-speaking newcomers, their methods of farming differed from those of the English. Mennonite and Amish farmers fenced their properties, built stables for their cattle, sometimes even before their houses, and tilled well-manured fields. By the mid-eighteenth century they also had developed the Conestoga wagon, a large, heavily built structure that was suited for the arduous trek across the Alleghenies.

The occupational profile of Swiss immigrants reflected the general trends of Western economies. A statistical analysis for the years 1887 to 1938 counted 42 percent in the industrial work force; 25 percent in agriculture; 6.5 percent in commerce; 4.5 percent in the hotel and restaurant business; and 4.3 percent in the professions. A large percentage of Swiss immigrants also worked as domestics.

Viticulture was introduced into the Midwest by French Swiss farmers and was also extensively practiced by Italian Swiss from Canton Tessin who went to California in large numbers after the 1870s. Bernese Swiss used their expertise in dairy farming, especially in Wisconsin. Nicolas Gerber (1836-1908), for instance, opened a Limburger cheese factory in New Glarus in 1868, as did Jacob Karlen (1840-1920) in nearby Monroe in 1878. Gottlieb Beller (1850-1902) developed a system of storage that allowed cheese production to remain responsive to fluctuating market demand. Leon de Montreux Chevalley (1854-1926) founded butter, cheese, and condensed milk factories in Portland, Oregon. Jacques Huber (1851-1918) introduced silk manufacturing to New Jersey; by 1900 he had established a firm with plants in Union City, Hackensack, and other cities of the mid-Atlantic states. Albert Wittnauer (1856-1908) used his Swiss training in watchmaking to establish a successful business in New York City.

By 1900 world-renowned firms such as Nestlé had established plants in the United States. The Swiss pharmaceutical companies Ciba-Geigy, Hoffmann-La Roche, and Sandoz emerged in the twentieth century as important forces in the United States economy and diversified their productive activities. Aargauische Portlandcement-Fabrik Holderbank Wildegg, a Swiss cement company, incorporated in 1912 with original seat in Glarus, Switzerland, and introduced superior, cost-efficient cement production into North America and dominates today's cement market.

POLITICS AND GOVERNMENT

In the eighteenth century Geneva was an autonomous city-state, but allied with the Swiss Confederation. The writings of two of its citizens influenced the founders of the United States engaged in creating a new governmental structure. Jean Jacques Rousseau (1712-1778) expounded the idea that government rested on a social contract.

Jean Jacques Burlamaqui (1694-1748) stressed in his *Principles of Natural and Political Law* that a government should guarantee its citizens secure happiness.

The relations between the United States and Switzerland have been generally friendly, but not without tensions. At times outsiders view Swiss neutrality and direct democracy as inefficient; yet Switzerland's neutral stand allows it to represent American interests in nations with which the United States has broken off diplomatic ties.

INDIVIDUAL AND GROUP CONTRIBUTIONS

The Swiss have had easy access to all aspects of life in the United States, although most did not come to public attention. The selection given below features a few according to field of endeavor.

ARCHITECTURE

William Lescaze (1896-1969), born and educated in Geneva, Switzerland, moved to the United States in 1921 and rose to prominence as a builder of skyscrapers; he also authored several treatises on modern architecture. In bridge-building Othmar Ammann (1879-1965), born in Feuerthalen, Canton Schaffhausen, achieved world renown; after studies in Zurich he went to New York City in 1904 and in 1925 was appointed chief engineer of the Port Authority of New York; he built the George Washington and other suspension bridges noted for innovative engineering and bold and esthetic design.

ARTS

Mari Sandoz (1896-1966), the daughter of Swiss immigrants, published several works of enduring value, among them the biography of her father, titled *Old Jules*, and a biography of Crazy Horse, the noted leader of the Sioux; her works reveal not only an unusual understanding of the world of the white settlers, but also of the mental universe of indigenous peoples such as the Sioux and Cheyenne. Jeremias Theus (1719-1774) worked in Charleston, South Carolina, as a successful portrait painter. Peter Rindisbacher (1806-1834) produced valuable paintings documenting his family's move to Canada's Red River colony in 1821 and to Wisconsin in 1826; his works featuring Native Americans are also highly valued for their accuracy. The same holds for the numerous works of Karl Bodmer (1809-1893) who served for 13 months as pictorial chronicler for the Prince zu Neuwied's journey to the Upper Missouri in 1832. Fritz Glarner (1899-1972), like Bodmer a native of Zurich, began working in New York in 1936 where, influenced by Mondrian, he created works in the style of constructivism.

BUSINESS AND INDUSTRY

At age 19 Lorenzo Delmonico (1813-1881) from Marengo, Canton Tessin, went to New York and opened the Delmonico Hotel in 1843 which popularized continental European cuisine in American cooking.

MEDICINE

Adolf Meyer (1866-1950), born in Niederwenigen, Canton Zurich, was influential in American psychiatry; after studies at European universities he worked in various American psychiatric institutions and insisted on the study of symptoms, on bedside note-taking, the counseling of the families of patients, and their further care after discharge; in 1898 he published a classical work on neurology and after 1910 chaired the department of psychiatry at Johns Hopkins Medical School and also directed the Henry Phipps Clinic. Henry E. Sigerist (1891-1957) taught at Johns Hopkins University from 1932 to 1942, directing its Institute of History and Medicine; he had previously been a professor at the University of Leipzig, Germany, and emerged as a leading historian and as an advocate of socialized medicine.

MILITARY

In the American Revolution John André (1751-1780), born in Geneva, Switzerland, and an officer in the British army, was captured as a spy in 1780 and hanged by the revolutionaries; the British honored his bravery by a tomb in Westminster Abbey. At the end of the Civil War another Swiss named Henry Wirz (1823-1865) was also hanged for his alleged crimes as commander of the Confederacy's Andersonville Prison where some 12,000 Union soldiers perished; his responsibility for the terrible conditions at Andersonville remains controversial.

MUSIC

Rudolf Ganz (1877-1972), who immigrated to the United States in 1900, became an influential pianist, the conductor of the St. Louis Symphony Orchestra from 1921 to 1927, and president of the Chicago Musical College of Roosevelt University from 1933 to 1954. The composer Ernest Bloch (1880-1957) of Geneva, Switzerland, taught and wrote music at various American institutions of the Midwest and the West Coast; among his works the orchestral poems titled *Helvetia, America,* and *Israel* intimate his threefold cultural orientation. In film William Wyler (1902-1981), born in Mulhouse, France, of Swiss parents, became one of Hollywood's most respected directors; his *Ben Hur* won an Oscar for him as well as for 11 of his actors. The singer, actor, and television producer Yul Brynner, actually Julius Brynner (1915-1985), was of Swiss and Mongolian descent; he starred in various movies, among them *The King and I.*

POLITICS

In the 1770s John Joachim Zubly (1724-1781) of St. Gallen, Switzerland, emerged as a leading critic of the British; he was an ordained Swiss Reformed minister, a member of the Georgia Provincial Congress, and delegate to the Second Continental Congress; yet he rejected independence and viewed the union between the colonies and Great Britain as sacred and perpetual; on his return to Georgia he was tried and ended his life in obscurity. Albert Gallatin (1761-1849) became successful in the early years of the American republic; he arrived from Geneva in 1780 and eventually moved to western Pennsylvania where he entered politics; he was elected to the state legislature in 1792 but was disbarred by the Federalists; he served instead in the House and emerged as a leader of Jefferson's party; from 1801 to 1813 he served as secretary of the treasury, then as diplomat in France, England, and Russia; after his retirement from politics he became a scholar of Native American languages, co-founded New York University, and was a leading opponent of the War against Mexico in 1847. Another lead-ing Jeffersonian was William Wirt (1772-1834), the son of Swiss immigrants; he was a noted orator and jurist and served as attorney general of the United States from 1817 to 1829. Emanuel Lorenz Philipp (1861-1925) rose to prominence in Wisconsin politics, which he entered in 1903; he served as governor from 1915 to 1921 and promoted cooperation between farmers, workers, and business.

RELIGION

Michael Schlatter (1716-1790) from St. Gallen, Switzerland, went to Pennsylvania in 1746 and there organized numerous parishes of the Swiss Reformed Church. Johann Martin Henni (1805-1881) became in 1875 the first Catholic archbishop of Milwaukee; he was born in Misanenga, Canton Graubünden, went to the United States in 1828, became vicar general of the diocese of Cincinnati and editor of the *Wahrheitsfreund,* the first Catholic German-language newspaper. Philip Schaff (1819-1893) of Chur, Canton Graubünden, was a major historian of church history at Union Theological Seminary in New York for 25 years; he was a strong advocate of Christian ecumenism, author of numerous scholarly works, and stressed the historical approach to questions of theology.

SCIENCE

Ferdinand Hassler (1770-1843) was born in Aarau, Switzerland, and studied in Jena, Göttingen, and Paris, then accepted an appointment as professor of mathematics and natural philosophy at West Point; his 1807 plan for a coastal survey of the United States was began in 1817 and the precision of Hassler's work makes it still valid today. Louis Rodolphe Agassiz (1807-1873) became internationally known as a scientist and explorer; born in Motier, Canton Fribourg, he studied the natural sciences at various European universities and published a major work on fish and proposed the theory of a previous ice age he went to Boston in 1846, undertook scientific expeditions to South America, and was appointed to the chair of zoology and geology at Harvard University; there he began work on his influential ten-volume *Contributions to the Natural History of the United States;* his son Alexander Agassiz (1835-1910) also became a noted natural scientist in his own right. A pioneer in the ethnology and archeology of the American Southwest was Adolphe Bandelier (1840-1914); he was born in Bern, Switzerland, went with his family to Highland, Illinois, in 1848, and returned to Switzerland in 1857 to study geology at the University of Bern; on his return he did extended research in Mexico and the American

Southwest, later also in Bolivia, and authored numerous studies on Native American cultures of those regions.

TECHNOLOGY

Machinist John Heinrich Kruesi (1843-1899), born in Heiden, Canton Appenzell, joined Thomas A. Edison in Newark, New Jersey, in the early 1870s and transformed Edison's ideas into workable instruments; in 1887 he became general manager and chief engineer of the Edison Machine Works in Schenectady. The Swiss Louis Joseph Chevrolet (1878-1941) came to the United States in 1900, became a successful racing car champion, winning the 500-mile Indianapolis race in 1919; in 1911 he co-founded the Chevrolet Motor Car Company in Detroit, but soon left the enterprise; in 1929 he built a workable airplane engine, and later designed a helicopter.

MEDIA

PRINT

Swiss American.

Published by North American Swiss Alliance; explores shared ethnic and bi-cultural interests of the Swiss American community.

Address: 2590 Lakeside Avenue, N.W., Canton, Ohio 44708.
Telephone: (216) 456-1983.

Swiss American Historical Society Review.

Published three times a year with a circulation of 400, this journal offers scholarly and popular articles of Swiss American interest relating to history, literature, genealogy, and personal experience.

Contact: Leo Schelbert, Editor.
Address: 2523 Asbury Avenue, Evanston, Illinois 60201.
Telephone: (708) 328-3514.

Swiss American Review.

Founded in 1860 under the name *Nordamerikanische Schweizerzeitung*, this weekly publication provides material in English, German, French, Italian, and Romansh. It has an estimated circulation of 3,000 and features news from Switzerland as well as the Swiss American communities and organizations of the United States.

Contact: Peter Luthy, Editor-in-Chief

Address: P.O. Box 1943, New York, New York 10156-1943.
Telephone: (212) 808-0505.
Fax: (212) 808-0003.
E-mail: info@goswiss.com
Online: http://www.goswiss.com

Swiss Review.

Founded in 1973, this quarterly magazine has a circulation of over 300,000. It publishes regional news from Swiss communities for the Swiss abroad, and has editions in German, French, Italian, English, and Spanish.

Contact: Gertrude Jeffries, U.S. Swiss American Editor.
Address: 1430 Cape Cod Way, Concord, California 94521.
Telephone: (510) 370-3571; or (510) 689-2740.

RADIO

Swiss Radio International.

Broadcasts via Intercontinental Short Wave transmissions daily (UTC—Universal Time): At 3:30 in German, 4:00 in English, 4:30 in French, and 5:00 in Italian; frequencies 6135, 9860, 9885.

ORGANIZATIONS AND ASSOCIATIONS

American-Swiss Association (ASA).

American and Swiss corporations and individuals interested in maintaining cultural exchange; provides forum for meetings and discussions.

Contact: Anne Yoakam, Executive Director.
Address: 450 Lexington Avenue, Suite 1600, New York, New York 10017-3904.
Telephone: (212) 878-3809.

American-Swiss Foundation.

Involves American and Swiss corporations and individuals interested in maintaining friendship and cultural exchange with Switzerland. Provides a forum for meetings and discussions. Conducts monthly events featuring Swiss and American speakers in New York.

Contact: Eugene Waering, Executive Director.
Address: 232 East 66th Street, New York, New York 10021-6703.
Telephone: (212) 754-0130.
Fax: (212) 754-4512.

North American Swiss Alliance.
Fraternal benefit life insurance society for persons of Swiss birth or ancestry.

Contact: Joan J. Spirko, Secretary-Treasurer.
Address: 7650 Chippewa Road, Room 214,
    Brecksville, Ohio 44141
Telephone: (440) 526-2257.

Swiss American Historical Society (SAHS).
Founded in 1927 it is today the only national organization. Formerly located in Chicago, it moved to Madison, Wisconsin, in 1940; it became dormant in the 1950s, but was reactivated in 1963 under the leadership of Heinz K. Meier (1929-1989). It publishes the *SAHS Review* three times a year, holds annual and occasional regional meetings, and supports the SAHS Publication Series with Lang Publishers, New York.

Contact: Prof. Erdmann Schmocker, President.
Address: 6440 North Bosworth Avenue, Chicago,
    Illinois 60626.
Telephone: (773) 262-8336.
Fax: (773) 465-5292.

MUSEUMS AND RESEARCH CENTERS

Archives of the Archabbey St. Meinrad.
This collection houses 13 volumes of transcripts of materials located at the Benedictine Abbey of Einsiedeln, Switzerland, relating to St. Meinrad's founding in 1854. Despite the fire of 1887 that destroyed valuable sources, letters of the founding generation and extensive correspondence with other monasteries and ecclesiastical institutions are preserved and provide insight into the Benedictine dimension of transplanted Swiss Catholicism.

Address: St. Meinrad College and School of
    Theology, St. Meinrad, Indiana 47577.
Telephone: (812) 357-6566.

Balch Institute for Ethnic Studies.
Dedicated to preserving and documenting the multicultural heritage of the United States, this organization also houses a collection on the Swiss, including papers of the Swiss American Historical Society.

Contact: Ira Glazer, Director.
Address: 18 S Street, Philadelphia,
    Pennsylvania 19106.
Telephone: (215) 925-8090.

Lovejoy Library.
Located at Southern Illinois University in Ewardsville, this library houses the Highland, Koepfli, and Suppiger Collections. The materials highlight the founding and evolution of the Highland settlement, which began in 1831, as well as the Swiss in Illinois. They are complemented by materials at the Madison County Historical Museum, also at Edwardsville, and by the Illinois Historical Survey Library at the University of Illinois at Urbana.

Mennonite Historical Library.
Located at Bluffton College, this library has an extensive collection of works on Swiss Mennonite history, and of Swiss Mennonite and Amish family histories and genealogies.

Contact: Harvey Hiebert, Librarian.
Address: 280 West College Avenue, Bluffton,
    Ohio 45817.
Telephone: (419) 358-3272.

New Glarus Historical Village.
This attraction presents artifacts from its early history in several, thematically arranged buildings. An exhibition hall features the town's history and special exhibits of Swiss American interest.

Contact: Bill Hoesly, President.
Address: P.O. Box 745, New Glarus, Wisconsin
    53574-0745.
Telephone: (608) 527-2317.

SOURCES FOR ADDITIONAL STUDY

American Letters: Eighteenth and Nineteenth Century Accounts of Swiss Immigrants, edited by Leo Schelbert. Camden, Maine: Picton Press, 1995.

Basler, Konrad. *The Dorlikon Emigrants: Swiss Settlers and Cultural Founders in the United States,* translated by Laura Villiger. New York: Peter Lang, 1996.

A Frontier Family in Minnesota: Letters of Theodore and Sophie Bost, 1851-1920, edited and translated by H. Ralph Bowen. Minneapolis: University of Minnesota Press, 1981.

Gratz, Delbert L. *Bernese Anabaptists and Their American Descendants.* Scottdale, Pennsylvania: Herald Press, 1953.

Kleber, Albert. *History of St. Meinrad Archabbey 1854-1954.* St. Meinrad, Indiana: St. Meinrad Archabbey, 1954.

Schelbert, Leo. "On Becoming an Emigrant: A Structural View of Eighteenth and Nineteenth Century Swiss Data," *Perspectives in American History*, Volume 7. Cambridge, Massachusetts: Harvard University Press, 1973; pp. 440-495.

The United States and Switzerland: Aspects of an Enmeshment; Yearbook of German American Studies 1990, Volume 25, edited by Leo Schelbert. Lawrence: University of Kansas for the Society for German American Studies, 1991.

Syrian Americans

by
J. Sydney Jones

New arrivals in America from Greater Syria ranged from seekers of religious freedom to those who wished to avoid Turkish conscription. But by far the largest motivator was the American dream of personal success.

OVERVIEW

Modern Syria is an Arab republic of southwest Asia, bordered by Turkey to the north, Iraq to the east and southeast, Jordan to the south, and by Israel and Lebanon to the southwest. A small strip of Syria also lies along the Mediterranean Sea. At 71,500 square miles (185,226 square kilometers), the country is not much larger than the state of Washington.

Officially called the Syrian Arab Republic, the country had an estimated population in 1995 of 14.2 million, primarily Muslim, with some 1.5 million Christians and a few thousand Jews. Ethnically, the country is comprised of an Arab majority with a large number of Kurds as a second ethnic group. Other groups include Armenians, Turkmen, and Assyrians. Arabic is the primary language, but some ethnic groups maintain their languages, especially outside of the urban areas of Aleppo and Damascus, and Kurdish, Armenian, and Turkish are all spoken in various areas.

Only about half of the land can support the population, and half of the population resides in cities. The coastal plains are the most heavily populated, with the cultivated steppe to the east providing wheat for the country. Nomads and semi-nomads live in the huge desert steppe in the far east of the country.

Syria was the name of an ancient territory, a strip of fertile land that lay between the eastern

Mediterranean coast and the desert of Northern Arabia. Indeed, ancient Syria, Greater Syria, or "Suriya," as it was sometimes called, was for most of history synonymous with the Arabian peninsula, encompassing the modern nations of Syria, Lebanon, Israel, Palestine, and Jordan. However, after partition in the First World War and independence in 1946, the country was confined to its present boundaries. This essay deals with immigrants from Greater Syria and the modern state of Syria.

HISTORY

From ancient times, the area that came to be known as Syria had a succession of rulers, including Mesopotamians, Hittites, Egyptians, Assyrians, Babylonians, Persians, and Greeks. Pompey brought Roman rule to the region in 63 B.C., making Greater Syria a Roman province. The Christian era brought centuries of unrest until the Islamic invasion of 633-34 A.D. Damascus surrendered to Muslim troops in 635; by 640 the conquest was complete. Four districts, Damascus, Hims, Jordan, and Palestine, were created, and relative peace and prosperity, as well as religious toleration, were the hallmark of the Umayyad line, which ruled the region for a century. The Arabic language permeated the region at this time.

The Abbasid dynasty, centered in Iraq, followed. This line, which ruled from Baghdad, was less tolerant of religious differences. This dynasty disintegrated, and Syria fell under the control of an Egyptian line based in Cairo. The culture flourished in the tenth and eleventh centuries, though the Crusaders made European incursions to recapture the Holy Land. Saladin took Damascus in 1174, effectively expelling the Crusaders from their occupied positions, and established centers of learning, as well as built trading centers and a new land system that stimulated economic life.

Mongol invasions during the thirteenth century wracked the region, and in 1401 Tamerlane sacked Aleppo and Damascus. Syria continued to be ruled from Egypt during the fifteenth century by the Mameluk dynasty until 1516, when the Turkish Ottomans defeated Egypt and occupied all of ancient Syria. Ottoman control would last four centuries. The Ottomans created four jurisdictional districts, each ruled by a governor: Damascus, Aleppo, Tripoli, and Sidon. Early governors encouraged agriculture by their fiscal system, and cereals as well as cotton and silk were produced for export. Aleppo became an important center for trade with Europe. Italian, French, and English merchants began to settle in the region. Christian communities were also allowed to flourish, especially during the seventeenth and eighteenth centuries.

By the eighteenth century, however, Ottoman rule was beginning to weaken; Bedouin incursions from the desert increased, and general prosperity and security declined. A brief period of Egyptian domination was again replaced by Ottoman rule in 1840, but tensions were growing between the religious and ethnic groups of the region. With the massacre of Christians by a Muslim mob in Damascus in 1860, Europe began to intervene more in the affairs of the moribund Ottoman Empire, establishing an autonomous district of Lebanon, but leaving Syria for the time under Ottoman control. Meanwhile, French and British influence gained in the region; the population steadily westernized. But Arab-Turk relations worsened, especially after the Young Turk revolution of 1908. Arab nationalists then came to the fore in Syria.

MODERN ERA

In World War I, Syria was turned into a military base of the Ottoman Empire, which fought with the Germans. However, nationalist Arabs, under Faysal, stood along side the British, with the legendary T. E. Lawrence and Allenby. After the war, the region was ruled for a time by Faysal, but a French mandate from the League of Nations set the newly partitioned region under French control until independence could be arranged. In fact, the French had no interest in such independence, and it was only with the World War II that a free Syria was finally established. British and Free French troops occupied the country until 1946, when a Syrian civilian government took over.

There were manifold challenges for such a government, including the reconciliation of a number of religious groups. These included the majority *Sunni* Muslim sect with the two other dominant Muslim groups, the *Alawites*, an extreme *Shi'ite* group, and the *Druzes*, a pre-Muslim sect. There were also Christians, divided into a half dozen sects, and Jews. Additionally, ethnic and economic-cultural differences had to be dealt with, from peasant to westernized urbanite, and from Arab to Kurd and Turk. The colonels took over in 1949 with the failure of a civilian government made up mostly of Sunni landowners. A bloodless coup brought Col. Husni as-Zaim to power, but he was, in turn, soon toppled.

A series of such coups followed, as did an abortive union with Egypt from 1958 to 1961. Increasingly, governing power rested with the Pan Arabist Ba'th Socialists in the military. On March 14, 1971, Gen. Hafiz al-Assad was sworn in as president of the titular democracy after seizing power from Col. Salah al-Jadid. Assad has remained in power since that time, enjoying a measure of popularity from nationalists, workers, and peasants for his land reform and economic development. As recently as 1991, Assad was re-elected in a referendum.

Modern Syrian foreign policy has largely been driven by the Arab-Israeli conflict; Syria has suffered several defeats at the hands of the Israelis. The Syrian Golan Heights remains a contentious issue between the two countries. Arab relations were strained by Syria's support of Iran against Iraq in the ten-year Iran-Iraq War; Syrian-Lebanese relations have also proved to be a volatile issue. Syria continues to maintain over 30,000 troops in Lebanon. During the Cold War, Syria was an ally of the USSR, receiving arms aid from that country. But with the fall of Communism, Syria turned more to the West. With the Iraqi invasion of Kuwait, Syria sent troops to aid in the U.N.-led liberation of Kuwait. During its long reign, the Ba'th regime has brought order to the country, but largely at the cost of true democratic government; foes of the government are harshly repressed.

THE FIRST SYRIANS IN AMERICA

It is difficult to discuss the time periods and numbers of early Syrian immigration to America because the name "Syria" has meant many things over the centuries. Before 1920, Syria was in fact Greater Syria, a chunk of the Ottoman Empire that stretched from the mountains of southeastern Asia Minor to the Gulf of Aqaba and the Sinai Peninsula. "Syrian" immigrants were therefore as likely to hail from Beirut or Bethlehem as they were from Damascus. A further complication in official records results from past Ottoman rule of the region. Immigrants might have been classified as Turks at Ellis Island if they came from Syria during the Ottoman period. Most often, Syrian-Lebanese are confused with immigrants from the modern state of Syria. However, it is probable is that there was little Syrian or Arab immigration in any significant numbers until after 1880. Moreover, a number of immigrants who came during and after the Civil War returned to the Middle East after earning sufficient funds to do so.

Until World War I, a majority of "Syrians" came in fact from the Christian villages around Mount Lebanon. Estimates of the number of early immigrants run between 40,000 and 100,000. According to Philip Hitti, who wrote an authoritative early history titled *The Syrians in America*, almost 90,000 people from Greater Syria arrived in the United States between 1899-1919. He further noted that at the time of his writing, in 1924, "it is safe to assume that there are at present about 200,000 Syrians, foreign-born and born of Syrian parents, in the United States." It is estimated that between 1900 and 1916, about 1,000 official entries a year came from the districts of Damascus and Aleppo, parts of modern-day Syria, or the Republic of Syria. Most of these early immigrants settled in urban centers of the East, including New York, Boston, and Detroit.

Immigration to the United States occurred for several reasons. New arrivals in America from Greater Syria ranged from seekers of religious freedom to those who wished to avoid Turkish conscription. But by far the largest motivator was the American dream of personal success. Economic improvement was the primary incentive for these early immigrants. Many of the earliest immigrants made money in America, and then returned to their native soil to live. The tales told by these returning men fueled further immigration waves. This, in addition to early settlers in America sending for their relatives, created what is known as *chain immigration*. Moreover, the world fairs of the time — in Philadelphia in 1876, Chicago in 1893, and St. Louis in 1904 — exposed many participants from Greater Syria to the American lifestyle, and many stayed behind after the fairs closed. Some 68 percent of the early immigrants were single males and at least half were illiterate.

Though the number of arrivals was not large, the effect in the villages from which these people emigrated was lasting. Immigration increased, reducing the number of eligible males. The Ottoman government put restrictions on such emigration in effort to keep its populace in Greater Syria. The United States government helped in this effort. In 1924, Congress passed the Johnson-Reed Quota Act, which greatly reduced immigration from the eastern Mediterranean, though by this time, Syrians had migrated to virtually every state of the union. This quota act created a hiatus to further immigration, one that lasted over forty years until the Immigration Act of 1965 opened the doors once again to Arab immigration. Another wave of immigration thus started in the mid-1960s; more than 75 percent of all foreign-born Arab Americans identified on the 1990 census came to this country after 1964. According to that same census, there were about 870,000 people who identified themselves as ethnically Arab. Immigration statistics show 4,600 immigrants from modern Syria arrived in the United States from 1961-70; 13,300 from 1971-80; 17,600 from 1981-90; and 3,000 alone in 1990. Since the 1960s, ten percent of those emigrating

These Syrian American children are all from immigrant families that settled in New York's Syrian Quarter.

from the modern state of Syria have been admitted under the refugee acts.

SETTLEMENT PATTERNS

Syrians have settled in every state, and they continue concentrate in urban centers. New York City continues to be the largest single draw to new immigrants. The borough of Brooklyn, and in particular the area around Atlantic Avenue, has become a little Syria in America, preserving the look and feel of ethnic business and traditions. Other urban areas with large Syrian populations in the east include Boston, Detroit, and the auto center of Dearborn, Michigan. Some New England as well as upstate New York communities also have large Syrian communities as a result of the peddlers who plied their trade in the region and stayed on to open small mercantile operations. New Orleans has a significant population from the former Greater Syria, as does Toledo, Ohio and Cedar Rapids, Iowa. California received an increasing number of new arrivals since the 1970s, with Los Angeles county becoming the hub of many new immigrant Arab communities, among them a Syrian American community. Houston is a more recent destination for new Syrian immigrants.

ACCULTURATION AND ASSIMILATION

Several factors combined to promote the rapid assimilation of early Syrian immigrants. Primary among these was that instead of congregating in urban ethnic enclaves, many of the first immigrants from Greater Syria took to the road as peddlers, selling their wares up and down the Eastern seaboard. Dealing daily with rural Americans and absorbing the language, customs, and mannerism of their new homeland, these peddlers, intent on making business, tended to blend in rapidly with the American way of life. Service in the military during both World War I and World War II also hastened assimilation, as did, ironically, the negative stereotyping of all immigrants from the eastern Mediterranean and southern Europe. The traditional clothing of the first arrivals made them stand out from other recent immigrants, as did their occupation as peddlers — the very omnipresence, of Syrian immigrants, despite their relatively low numbers vis-a-vis other immigrant groups, led to some xenophobia. New immigrants thus quickly Anglicized their names and, many of them being Christian already, adopted more mainstream American religious denominations.

This assimilation has been so successful that it is challenging to discover the ethnic antecedents of many families who have become completely Americanized. The same is not true, however, for more recent arrivals from the modern state of Syria. Generally better educated, they are also more religiously diverse, with greater numbers of Muslims among them. In general, they are not overeager to give up their Arab identity and be absorbed in the melting pot. This is partly a result of renewed vigor of multiculturalism in America, and partly the result of a different mentality in the recent arrival.

TRADITIONS, CUSTOMS, AND BELIEFS

Family is at the heart of Syrian tradition and belief systems. An old saying has it that "myself and my brother against my cousin; myself and my cousin against the stranger." Such strong family ties breed a communal spirit in which the needs of the group are more determinant than those of the individual. In contrast to traditional American society, the Syrian young saw no need to break away from the family in order to establish their own independence.

Honor and status are important in all Arab societies, particularly among men. Honor can be won through financial achievement and the exertion of power, while for those who do not achieve wealth, respect as an honest and sincere man is an essential. The virtues of magnanimity and social graciousness are integral to Syrian life, as ethics reinforced by Islamic codes. The downside to these virtues is, as Alixa Naff pointed out in *Becoming American: The Early Arab Immigrant Experience*, a tendency toward "overstatement, equivocation, intractability, intense emotionalism, and at times, aggressiveness." Women are to be protected by the man who is head of the household. Such protectiveness was not initially seen as oppressive, but rather as a sign of respect. Oldest sons also play a significant role in this family structure.

Much of this traditional system has unraveled with life in America. The old system of village communal aid often breaks down in the fast-paced world of America, setting families on their own with both parents in the work force. The fabric of the tightly knit family has definitely loosened in an environment which encourages so much individual achievement and personal freedom. As a result, much of the sense of family honor and the fear of family shame, social mechanisms at work in Syria itself, have diminished among immigrants in America.

CUISINE

It is difficult to separate specifically Syrian foods from those made popular by the Greater Syrian population. Such standard fare in America as pita bread and crushed chick pea or eggplant spreads, *hommos* and *baba ganouj*, both come from the former Syrian heartland. The popular salad, *tabouli*, is also a Greater Syrian product. Other typical foods include cheeses and yogurts, and many of the fruits and vegetables common to the eastern Mediterranean, including pickles, hot peppers, olives, and pistachios. While pork is forbidden to followers of Islam, other meats such as lamb and chicken are staples. Much of Syrian food is highly spiced and dates and figs are employed in ways not usually found in typical American food. Stuffed zucchini, grape leaves, and cabbage leaves are common dishes. A popular sweet is *baqlawa*, found all over the eastern Mediterranean, made from *filo* dough filled with walnut paste and drizzled with sugar syrup.

MUSIC

Arabic or Middle Eastern music is a living tradition that spans some 13 centuries. Its three main divisions are classical, religious, and folk, the last of which has been expanded in modern times into a newer pop tradition. Central to all music from Syria and Arab countries are monophony and heterophony, vocal flourishes, subtle intonation, rich improvisation, and the Arab scales, so different from those of Western tradition. It is these characteristics which give Middle Eastern music its distinctive, exotic sound, at least to Western ears.

"**I**n the first place, I wasn't learning the language. To spare me embarrassment as well as to expedite conversation between us, my Syrian friends were speaking to me in my own tongue. In the packing plant it was no better, for most of the workers around me were foreigners like myself. When they talked to each other they used their own language; when they talked to me they used profanity."

Salom Rizk, *Syrian Yankee*, (Doubleday & Company, Garden City, NY, 1943).

Maqam, or melodic modes, are basic to music of the classical genre. There are set intervals, cadences, and even final tones to these modes. Additionally, classical Arabic music uses rhythmic modes similar to medieval Western music, with short units that come from poetic measurements. Islamic music relies heavily on chanting from the Koran and has similarities to Gregorian chant. While classical and religious music have regular characteristics throughout a vast amount of land and culture, Arabic folk music reflects individual cultures Druze, Kurdish, and Bedouin, for example.

Musical instruments used in classical music are primarily stringed, with the *ud*, a short-necked instrument similar to the lute, being the most typical. The spike-fiddle, or *rabab*, is another important stringed instrument that is bowed, while the *qanun* resembles a zither. For folk music, the most common instrument is the long-necked lute or *tanbur*. Drums are also a common accompanying instrument in this vital musical tradition.

TRADITIONAL COSTUMES

Traditional clothing such as *shirwal*, which are baggy black pants, are reserved exclusively for ethnic dance performers. Traditional dress is almost completely a thing of the past for Syrian Americans, as well as native Syrians. Western dress is typical now both in Syria and the United States. Some Muslim women wear the traditional *hijab* in public. This can consist of a long-sleeved coat, as well as a white scarf that covers the hair. For some, the scarf alone is sufficient, derived from Muslim teaching that one should be modest.

HOLIDAYS

Both Christian and Muslim Syrian Americans celebrate a variety of religious holidays. Adherents of Islam celebrate three main holidays: the 30-day period of fasting during the daytime hours known as *Ramadan*; the five days marking the end of Ramadan, known as *'Eid al-Fitr*; and *Eid al-Adha*, "The Feast of Sacrifice." Ramadan, held during the ninth month of the Islamic calendar, is a time, similar to the Christ-

ian lent, in which self-discipline and moderation are employed for physical and spiritual cleansing. The end of Ramadan is marked by 'Eid al-Fitr, something of a cross between Christmas and Thanksgiving, an ebullient festival time for Arabs. The Feast of Sacrifice, on the other hand, commemorates the intervention of the Angel Gabriel in the sacrifice of Ishmael. According to the *Koran*, or *Quran*, the Muslim holy book, God asked Abraham to sacrifice his son Ishmael, but Gabriel intervened at the last moment, substituting a lamb for the boy. This holiday is held in conjunction with the Pilgrimage to Mecca, an obligation for practicing Muslims.

Saints' days are celebrated by Christian Syrians, as are Christmas and Easter; however, the Orthodox Easter falls on a different Sunday than the Western Easter. Increasingly, Arab Muslims are also celebrating Christmas, not as a religious holiday, but as a time for families to get together and exchange gifts. Some even decorate a Christmas tree and put up other Christmas decorations. Syria's independence day, April 17, is little celebrated in America.

HEALTH ISSUES

No medical conditions are specific to Syrian Americans. There are, however, incidences of higher-than-average rates of anemia as well as lactose intolerance in this population. Early Syrian immigrants were often turned back by immigration officials because of trachoma, a disease of the eye particularly prevalent in Greater Syria of the day. It has been pointed out, also, that Syrian Americans tend to rely on solving psychological problems within the family itself. And while Arab medical doctors are common, Arab American psychologists and psychiatrists are more difficult to find.

LANGUAGE

Syrians are Arabic speakers who have their own dialect of the formal language, one that separates them as a group from other Arab-speaking peoples. Sub-dialects can be found their dialect, depending on the place of origin; for example Aleppo and Damascus each has a distinctive sub-dialect with accent and idiomatic peculiarities unique to the region. For the most part, dialect speakers can be understood by others, especially those closely related to the Syrian dialect such as Lebanese, Jordanian, and Palestinian.

There was once a rich profusion of Arab newspapers and magazines in the United States. However, the rush to assimilate, as well as the decreased number of new immigrants because of quotas led to the decline of such publications and of spoken Arabic. Parents did not teach their children the language and thus, their linguistic traditions were lost within a few generations in America. Among newer immigrants, however, language traditions are stronger. Arabic classes for young children are once again common, as well as Arabic church services held in some churches and sight of Arabic in commercial signs advertising Arab businesses.

GREETINGS AND POPULAR EXPRESSIONS

Syrian greetings often come in triplets with response and counter-response. The most typical greeting is the casual, Hello, *Marhaba*, which elicits the response *Ahlen*—Welcome, or *Marhabteen*, Two hellos. This can earn the counter-response of *Maraahib*, or Several hellos. The morning greeting is *Sabaah al-kehir*, The morning is good, followed by *Sabaah an-noor*– The morning is light. The evening greeting is *Masa al-kheir* responded to with *Masa n-noor*. Greetings understood throughout the Arabic world are *Asalam 'a laykum* —Peace be with you—

followed by *Wa 'a laykum asalaam*–Peace be upon you, too.

The formal introduction is *Ahlein* or *Ahlan was Sahlan*, while a popular toast is *Sahteen May* your health increase. How are you? is *Keif haalak?*; this is often responded to with *Nushkar Allah*–We thank God. There are also elaborate linguistic differentiations made for gender and for salutations made to a group, as opposed to an individual.

FAMILY AND COMMUNITY DYNAMICS

As has been noted, Syrian American families are generally closely-knit, patriarchal units. Nuclear families in America have largely replaced the extended family of the Syrian homeland. Formerly, the oldest son held a special position in the family: he would bring his bride to his parents' house, raise his children there, and care for his parents in their old age. Like much else about traditional Syrian life styles, this custom has also broken down over time in America. Increasingly, men and women share a more equal role in Syrian American households, with the wife often out in the workplace and the husband also taking a more active role in child rearing.

EDUCATION

A tradition of higher education was already in place with many immigrants of the old Greater Syria, especially those from the area around Beirut. This was in part due to the preponderance of many Western religious institutions established there from the late nineteenth century onward. Americans, Russians, French, and British operated these establishments. Immigrants from Damascus and Aleppo in Syria were also accustomed to institutions of higher education, though generally the more rural the immigrant, the less emphasis was placed on his or her education in the early Syrian American community.

Over time, the attitude of the Syrian community has paralleled that of America as a whole: education is now more important for all the children, not just the males. College and university education is highly prized, and in general it has been shown that Arab Americans are better educated than the average American. The proportion of Arab Americans, for example, who in the 1990 census reported attaining a master's degree or higher, is twice that of the general population. For foreign-born professionals, the sciences are the preferred area of study, with large numbers becoming engineers, pharmacists, and doctors.

THE ROLE OF WOMEN

Though traditional roles from Syria do break down as the longer families stay in the United States, women are still the heart of the family. They are responsible for the house and raising the children, and may also assist their husbands in business. In this respect, the Syrian American community is different from American families. An independent career for Syrian and Arab women in America is still the exception rather than the norm.

COURTSHIP AND WEDDINGS

Just as gender roles still hold sway in the work force, so to do the traditional values regarding dating, chastity, and marriage. More conservative Syrian Americans and recent immigrants often practice arranged marriages, including endogamous (within group) ones between cousins, which will benefit the prestige of both families. Courtship is a chaperoned, heavily supervised affair; casual dating, American style, is disapproved of in these more traditional circles.

Among more assimilated Syrian Americans, however, dating is a more relaxed situation and couples themselves make the decision to marry or not, though parental advice weighs heavily. In the Muslim community, dating is allowed only after a ritual engagement. The enactment of a marriage contract, *kitb al-kitab*, sets up a trial period for the couple months or a year in which they get accustomed to one another. The marriage is consummated only after a formal ceremony. Most Syrian Americans tend to marry within their religious community, if not their ethnic community. Thus an Arab Muslim woman, for example, unable to find an Arab Muslim to marry, would be more likely to marry a non-Arab Muslim, such as an Iranian or Pakistani, than a Christian Arab.

Marriage is a solemn vow for Middle Easterners in general; divorce rates for Syrian Americans reflect this and are below the national average. Divorce for reasons of personal unhappiness is still discouraged within the group and family, and though divorce is more common now for assimilated Syrian Americans, the multiple divorce-remarriage pattern of mainstream America is frowned upon.

In general, Syrian American couples tend to have children earlier than Americans, and they tend to have larger families as well. Babies and younger are often coddled, and boys are often given more latitude than are girls. Depending upon the level of assimilation, boys are brought up for careers, while girls are prepared for marriage and child rearing. High school is the upper limit of education for many girls, while boys are expected to continue their education.

RELIGION

Islam is the predominant religion of Syria, though most of the early emigrants from Greater Syria were Christian. More modern immigration patterns reflect the religious make-up of modern Syria, but the Syrian American community is made up of a hodge-podge of religious groups from Sunni Muslims to Greek Orthodox Christians. Islamic groups are divided into several sects. The Sunnite sect is the largest in Syria, accounting for 75 percent of the population. There are also Alawite Muslims, an extreme sect of the Shi'ites. The third largest Islamic group is the Druzes, a breakaway Muslim sect which has roots in earlier, non-Islamic religions. Many of the early Syrian immigrant peddlers were Druze.

Christian denominations include various branches of Catholicism, mostly of the Eastern rite: Armenian Catholics, Syrian Catholics, Catholic Chaldeans, as well as Latin-rite Roman Catholics, Melkites, and Maronites. Additionally, there are Greek Orthodox, Syrian Orthodox, Nestorians, and Protestants. The first Syrian churches built in New York between 1890 and 1895 were Melkite, Maronite, and Orthodox.

Religious affiliation in Greater Syria was equivalent to belonging to a nation. The Ottoman developed a so-called millet system, a means of dividing citizens into political entities by religion. Such affiliation, over the centuries, became a second theme of identity, along with family ties, for Syrians. Though all Middle Eastern religions share common values such as charity, hospitality, and respect for authority and age, the individual sects compete with one another. The differences between the various Catholic faiths are not major dogmatic ones; for example, the churches differ in their belief in papal infallibility, and some conduct services in Arabic and Greek, others only in Aramaic.

As noted, the earliest Syrian immigrants were largely Christian. Currently there are 178 churches and missions in America serving the Orthodox. Discussions between Orthodox and Melkite priests are being held for a possible reuniting of the two faiths. Melkite, Maronite, and Orthodox churches confirm and baptize the faithful and use wine-soaked bread for the Eucharist. Often, ceremonies are done in English to serve the assimilated membership. Popular saints for the Maronites are St. Maron and St. Charbel; for the Melkites, St. Basil; and for the Orthodox, St. Nicholas and St. George.

Though some Muslims and Druzes arrived in the early waves of immigration, most have come since 1965. In general, they have found it more difficult to maintain their religious identity in America than have Christian immigrants from the same region. Part of Muslim ritual is praying five times a day. When no mosque is available for worship, small groups get together and rent rooms in commercial districts, where they can hold mid-day prayer.

EMPLOYMENT AND ECONOMIC TRADITIONS

Naff pointed out in *Becoming American* that if a Syrian immigrant's goal was to gain wealth, peddling was the means to earn it. The writer noted that "90 to 95 percent arrived with the express purpose of peddling notions and dry goods and did so for a period in the immigrant experience." Young men from villages all over Greater Syria immigrated in the late-nineteenth century in hopes of getting rich quick in the relatively lucrative endeavor of door-to-door peddling in America's under-served hinterland. Such work had obvious advantages for immigrants: it took little or no training and investment, a limited vocabulary, and provided instant if meager remuneration. Eager Syrian immigrants were herded into ships and headed off to "Amrika" or "Nay Yark," and many of them ended up in Brazil or Australia as a result of unscrupulous shipping agents.

America at the time was in transition. As few rural families owned carriages, peddlers were a common sight at the turn of the twentieth century. Carrying articles from buttons to suspenders to scissors, such peddlers were the distribution system of many small manufacturers. According to Naff, "These petty roving entrepreneurs, thriving in the age of great capitalistic merchandising, seemed like something suspended in a time warp." Armed with their backpacks and sometimes with carriages full of goods, these enterprising men plied their trade on back roads from Vermont to North Dakota. Networks of such peddlers spread across America to every state and helped account for the distribution of settlement of Syrian Americans. While the Syrians were not unique in peddling, they were different in that they stuck primarily to backpack peddling and to rural America. This resulted in the far-flung communities of Syrian Americans, from Utica, New York to Fort Wayne, Indiana, to Grand Rapids, Michigan and beyond. Muslims and Druzes were among these peddlers, too, though in fewer numbers. The largest of these early Muslim groups was centered in Providence, Rhode Island, from which its members peddled up the eastern seaboard. Large

This young Syrian American man is selling drinks in the Syrian Quarter in New York City.

Druze communities could be found in Massachusetts, and by 1902, Muslim and Druze groups could be found in North Dakota and Minnesota and as far west as Seattle.

Many immigrants used peddling as a step up toward earning their own businesses. It has been reported that by 1908, there were already 3,000 Syrian-owned businesses in America. Syrians soon also filled positions in the professions, from doctors to lawyers to engineers, and by 1910, there was a small group of Syrian millionaires to give proof to the "land of opportunity." Dry goods were a particular Syrian specialty, especially clothing, a tradition that can be seen in the modern clothing empires of Farah and Haggar, both early Syrian immigrants. The auto industry also claimed many early immigrants, resulting in large communities in Dearborn and near Detroit.

Later immigrants tend to be better trained than the first wave of immigrants. They serve in fields from computer science to banking and medicine. With cutbacks in the auto sector in the 1970s and 1980s, factory workers of Syrian descent were particularly hard hit, and many were forced to go on public assistance, an extremely difficult decision for families for whom honor is synonymous with self-reliance.

Looking at the Arab American community as a whole, its distribution in the job market reflects fairly closely that of American society in general. Arab Americans, according to the 1990 census, do appear to be more heavily concentrated in entrepreneurial and self-employed positions (12 percent versus only 7 percent in the general population), and in sales (20 percent as against 17 percent in the general populace).

POLITICS AND GOVERNMENT

Syrian Americans were initially quiet politically. Collectively, they never belonged to one political party or the other; their political affiliation reflected the larger American population, with business owners among them often voting Republican, blue-collar workers staying with the Democrats. As a political entity, they traditionally have not had the clout of other ethnic groups. One early issue that roused Syrian Americans, as it did all Arab Americans, was the 1914 Dow case in Georgia, which established that Syrians were Caucasians and thus could not be refused naturalization on the grounds of race. Since that time, second-generation Syrian Americans have been elected to offices from judgeships to the U.S. Senate.

Syrian American political action of the mid- to late-twentieth century has focussed on the Arab-Israeli conflict. The partitioning of Palestine in 1948 brought behind-the-scenes protests from Syrian leaders. After the 1967 war, Syrian Americans began to join political forces with other Arab groups to try and affect U.S. foreign policy regarding the Middle East. The Association of Arab University Graduates hoped to educate the American public as to the real nature of the Arab-Israeli dispute, while the National Association of Arab Americans was formed in the early 1970s to lobby Congress in this regard. In 1980 the American Arab Anti-Discrimination Committee was founded to counteract negative Arab stereotyping in the media. In 1985 the Arab American Institute was founded to promote Arab American participation in American politics. As a result, smaller regional action groups have also been organized, supporting Arab American candidates for office as well as candidates sympathetic to the Arab American viewpoint in international and domestic affairs.

INDIVIDUAL AND GROUP CONTRIBUTIONS

It should be noted that there is not always a clear distinction between places of origin when dealing with Syrian immigration history. For individuals as well as for immigration records, the confusion between Greater Syria and modern Syria poses some difficulties. However, the following list is mostly comprised of individuals who either arrived in the first wave of Greater Syrian immigration or were the offspring of such immigrants. Thus, in the largest possible sense, these notable individuals are Syrian American.

ACADEMIA

Dr. Rashid Khaldi of the University of Chicago and Dr. Ibrahim Abu Lughod have both become well known commentators in the media on issues dealing with the Middle East. Philip Hitti was a Syrian Druze who became a prominent scholar at Princeton and a recognized expert on the Middle East.

BUSINESS

Nathan Solomon Farah established a general store in New Mexico Territory in 1881, later becoming a developer in the region, fostering the growth of both Santa Fe and Albuquerque. Mansur Farah, arriving in America in 1905, began the trouser manufacturing company that still bears the family name. Haggar, of Dallas, also started as a Syrian business, as did the food-processing company of Azar, also in Texas, and Mode-O-Day, founded by the Malouf family of California. Amin Fayad, who settled in Washington, D.C., was the first to establish a carryout food service east of the Mississippi. Paul Orfalea (1946–) is the founder of Kinko's photocopying chain. Ralph Nader (1934–) is a well-known consumer advocate and candidate for U.S. president in 1994.

ENTERTAINMENT

F. Murray Abraham was the first Syrian American to win an Oscar, for his role in *Amadeus*; Frank Zappa was a well known rock musician; Moustapha Akkad directed *Lion in the Desert* and *The Message* as well as the *Halloween* thrillers; Casey Kasem (1933–) is one of America's most famous disc jockeys.

GOVERNMENT SERVICE AND DIPLOMACY

Najib Halaby was defense advisor during the Truman and Eisenhower administrations; Dr. George Atiyeh was appointed curator of the Arabic and Middle East section of the library of Congress; Philip Habib (1920-1992) was a career diplomat who helped negotiate an end to the Vietnam War; Nick Rahal (1949–) has been a U.S. congressman from Virginia since 1976; Donna Shalala, a prominent Arab American woman in the Clinton administration, has served as Secretary of Health and Human Services.

LITERATURE

William Blatty (1928–) wrote the book and screenplay to *The Exorcist*; Vance Bourjaily (1922–), is the author of *Confessions of a Spent Youth*; the poet Khalil Gibran (1883-1931), was the author of *The Prophet*. Other poets include Sam Hazo (1926–), Joseph Awad (1929–), and Elmaz Abinader (1954–).

MUSIC AND DANCE

Paul Anka (1941–), writer and singer of 1950s popular songs; Rosalind Elias (1931–), soprano with the Metropolitan Opera; Elie Chaib (1950–), dancer with the Paul Taylor Company.

SCIENCE AND MEDICINE

Michael DeBakey (1908–) pioneered bypass surgery and invented the heart pump; Elias J. Corey (1928–) of Harvard University, won the 1990 Nobel Prize for Chemistry; Dr. Nadeem Muna developed a blood test in the 1970s to identify melanoma.

MEDIA

PRINT

Action.
International Arabic newspaper printed in English and Arabic.

Contact: Raji Daher, Editor.
Address: P.O. Box 416, New York, New York 10017.
Telephone: (212) 972-0460.
Fax: (212) 682-1405.

American-Arab Message.
Religious and political weekly founded in 1937 and printed in English and Arabic.

Contact: Imam M. A. Hussein.
Address: 17514 Woodward Ave., Detroit, Michigan 48203.
Telephone: (313) 868-2266.
Fax: (313) 868-2267.

Journal of Arab Affairs.
Contact: Tawfic E. Farah, Editor.
Address: M E R G Analytica, Box 26385, Fresno, California 93729-6385.
Fax: (302) 869-5853.

Jusoor (Bridges).
An Arabic/English quarterly that publishes both poetry and essays on the arts and political matters.

Contact: Munir Akash, Editor.
Address: P.O. Box 34163, Bethesda, Maryland 20817.
Telephone: (212) 870-2053.

The Link.
Contact: John F. Mahoney, Executive Director.
Address: Americans for Middle East Understanding, Room 241, 475 Riverside Drive, New York, New York 10025-0241.
Telephone: (212) 870-2053.

Middle East International.
Contact: Michael Wall, Editor.
Address: 1700 17th Street, N.W., Suite 306, Washington, D.C. 20009.
Telephone: (202) 232-8354.

Washington Report on Middle East Affairs.
Contact: Richard H. Curtiss, Executive Editor.
Address: P.O. Box 53062, Washington, D.C. 20009.
Telephone: (800) 368-5788.

RADIO

Arab Network of America.
Broadcasts one to two hours of Arabic programming weekly in urban areas with large Arab American populations, including Washington, D.C., Detroit, Chicago, Pittsburgh, Los Angeles, and San Francisco.

Contact: Eptisam Malloutli, Radio Program Director.
Address: 150 South Gordon Street, Alexandria, Virginia 22304.
Telephone: (800) ARAB-NET.

TELEVISION

Arab Network of America (ANA).
Contact: Laila Shaikhli, TV Program Director.
Address: 150 South Gordon Street, Alexandria, Virginia 22304.
Telephone: (800) ARAB-NET.

TAC Arabic Channel.
Contact: Jamil Tawfiq, Director.
Address: P.O. Box 936, New York, New York 10035.
Telephone: (212) 425-8822.

ORGANIZATIONS AND ASSOCIATIONS

American Arab Anti-Discrimination Committee (ADC).

Combats stereotyping and defamation in the media and in other venues of public life, including politics.

Address: 4201 Connecticut Avenue, Washington, D.C. 20008.

Telephone: (202) 244-2990.

Arab American Institute (AAI).

Fosters participation of Arab Americans in the political process at all levels.

Contact: James Zogby, Executive Director.

Address: 918 16th Steet, N.W., Suite 601, Washington, D.C. 20006.

Arab Women's Council (AWC).

Seeks to inform the public on Arab women.

Contact: Najat Khelil, President.

Address: P.O. Box 5653, Washington, D.C. 20016.

National Association of Arab Americans (NAAA).

Lobbies Congress and the administration regarding Arab interests.

Contact: Khalil Jahshan, Executive Director.

Address: 1212 New York Avenue, N.W., Suite 300, Washington, D.C. 20005.

Telephone: (202) 842-1840.

Syrian American Association.

Address: c/o Tax Department, P.O. Box 925, Menlo Park, California, 94026-0925.

MUSEUMS AND RESEARCH CENTERS

The Faris and Yamna Naff Family Arab American Collection.

Contact: Alixa Naff.

Address: Archives Center, National Museum of History, Smithsonian Institution, Washington, D.C.

Telephone: (202) 357-3270.

SOURCES FOR ADDITIONAL STUDY

Abu-Laban, Baha, and Michael W. Suleiman, eds. *Arab Americans: Continuity and Change.* Normal, Illinois: Association of Arab American University Graduates, Inc., 1989.

El-Badry, Samia. "The Arab Americans," *American Demographics*, January 1994, pp. 22-30.

Kayal, Philip, and Joseph Kayla. *The Syrian Lebanese in America: A Study in Religion and Assimilation.* Boston: Twayne, 1975.

Saliba, Najib E. *Emigration from Syria and the Syrian-Lebanese Community of Worcester, MA.* Ligonier, PA: Antakya Press, 1992.

Younis, Adele L. *The Coming of the Arabic-Speaking People to the United States.* Staten Island, NY: Center for Migration Studies, 1995.

TAIWANESE AMERICANS

by
J. Sydney Jones

The usual stereotype of the Taiwanese engineer or computer scientist is not necessarily the norm. There have also been large numbers of blue-collar workers in service and garment industries. Also, more women are now immigrating to the United States.

OVERVIEW

Taiwan is also called Nationalist China or the Republic of China, and is located 100 miles from the mainland of China. An island country about twice the size of New Jersey, it measures 13,892 square miles (35,990 square kilometers). The Taiwan Strait, formerly known as the Straits of Formosa, separates Taiwan from the southeastern Chinese province of Fujian. A mountainous country, especially in the eastern two-thirds of the island, Taiwan also has jurisdiction over 22 islands in the Taiwan group and a another 64 in the Pescadores Archipelago to the west. To the north of Taiwan is the East China Sea with the Ryukyu Islands, Okinawa, and Japan; to the south is the Baishi Channel in the South China Sea separating Taiwan from the Philippines; to the east is the Pacific Ocean. The Japanese Current helps give Taiwan a moderate year-round climate, and because the island is situated in the tropical and subtropical zones, the summer monsoon season ensures an ample water supply. The capital of the republic is Taipei, and the island's major industries are textiles, electronics, machinery, shipbuilding, and agriculture.

One of the most densely populated places on earth, Taiwan is inhabited by 21.5 million people, a majority of whom live on the low plain of the western part of the island. Of these, only 330,000 are non-Chinese, the aboriginal inhabitants of the island related to Malay people of Indonesia,

Malaysia, and the Philippines. Of the remaining majority, 85 percent are descendants of early Chinese immigrants to the island, mostly from the provinces of Fujian and Guangdong, and primarily of the Fujianese and Hakka ethnic groups. These latter are the so-called "guest people" who migrated to Guangdong from Henan in central China and then moved on to Taiwan, beginning in the sixteenth century. The remaining 14 percent of the population are made up of "mainlanders," Chinese from a variety of mainland provinces who were either born in China or are descendants of families who fled the Communist Chinese armies after the Second World War. Most of the population speaks Mandarin Chinese, the national language. The second largest language group is Taiwanese, or *Hokkien*, spoken by Hakka and Fujian natives, and based on the Minnan dialect of southern Fujian. Many Hakka also speak their own dialect, while mainlanders speak a variety of mainland Chinese dialects in addition to Mandarin.

Daoism and Buddhism are the major religions of Taiwan. A blending of the philosophical tenets of Confucianism with these two major religions resulted in a hybrid religion, often referred to as Chinese popular religion. Christianity is also represented, and though it is a relatively minor religion, it has a strong influence in the spheres of education and health care. There are also some Muslims living in the urban areas of the country.

HISTORY

The derivation of the Chinese word Tai-wan is unknown, though its literal meaning is "terraced bay." Until the sixteenth century, Taiwan was primarily inhabited by its native Malayo-Polynesian population. In Chinese records prior to the Han dynasty (206 B.C.- 222 A.D.), Taiwan was referred to as Yangchow, then later Yinchow. In 239 A.D., the Chinese emperor sent an expeditionary force to explore the island, one of the bases for Beijing's current claim of sovereignty over the island. However, no permanent base was settled on the island. Several centuries later, more missions were sent to the island. The island was clearly identified in court records of the Ming dynasty, charted by the explorer Cheng Ho in 1430 and given its current name, Taiwan. Despite this, few Chinese ventured across the treacherous waters of the Straits of Formosa. The island was largely an operational base for Chinese and Japanese pirates.

In the sixteenth century, foreign contacts began. The Portuguese passed by the island en route to Japan in 1517, dubbing it *Ilha Formosa*, or Beau-tiful Island. The Dutch followed, establishing a settlement in southwestern Taiwan in 1624, as did the Spanish, who settled at Chi-lung in the north. The Dutch East India Company encouraged Chinese migration in order to increase agricultural production, and the numbers of Fujianese and Hakka settlers grew to some 200,000 by the end of the Dutch period. In 1642 the Dutch seized the Spanish settlements in the north; they were in turn expelled in 1661, victims of events on mainland China.

With the fall of the Ming dynasty in 1644, the Manchus of the Qing dynasty consolidated and enlarged their rule of mainland China, moving south of the Great Wall to bring all of China under their control by 1683. During these turbulent years, many Chinese fled to Taiwan to escape the Manchus, just as centuries later, Nationalist forces would flee there to avoid the Communist onslaught. Taiwan thus became a center of Chinese resistance to the Manchus, and Ming diehards continued to fight on. One supporter was Zheng Cheng-gong, also known as Koxinga, a half-Japanese supporter of the Mings, who led an army of 100,000 troops and 3,000 junks. Ultimately, Koxinga turned against the Dutch in Taiwan, expelling them and establishing a Ming-style dynasty on the island. This government in exile lasted until 1683, when the Manchus invaded Taiwan, making it part of the empire to be administered by Fujian province. Two hundred years later, Taiwan became a separate province of China.

The centuries of relative peace and prosperity under Manchu control led to dramatic increases in population on the mainland, as new emigrants swelled its population. The aboriginal population was increasingly relegated to the mountainous regions of the east of the island. Rice and sugar imports to China had become staple products of the island. As European interest in the China trade grew in the nineteenth century, two treaty ports were opened in 1858, Tainan and Tanshui, the latter just downstream from Taipei. Peking began to take more notice of its rebellious province to the west, but its years of misrule there had sown the seeds of distrust in Taiwan. In 1884 Peking reorganized rule on the island, sending Liung Ming ch'uan to administer it, which he did capably. In 1886, Taiwan was made an independent province, with Taipei its capital city.

MODERN ERA

In 1894, China went to war with Japan over Korea, and quickly lost the conflict, as well as its province of Taiwan in the ensuing treaty. For the next fifty years, the Japanese occupied Taiwan, who carried out a policy of Japanization of Taiwan's people and culture. Japanese was the language of instruction, bureaucracy, and business. Initially, the island became a rice and sugar provider for Japan. By the 1930s, industrialization involving textiles, chemicals, and machinery was made possible by relatively cheap hydroelectric power on the island. Though a repressive regime, Japanese control did improve sanitation on the island, as well as the educational system. With the onset of World War II, Taiwan was used as a Japanese staging area for invasions of Southeast Asia. In 1945, with the defeat of Japan, Taiwan was returned to China, under uncertain status. Chiang Kai-shek, of the Nationalist party, sent military forces to the island in October 1945 and replaced Japanese officials with those of the Republic of China.

Nationalist rule was not popular, as it maintained the same oppressive system. The Nationalists, involved in a civil war with the communists, viewed the Taiwanese as traitors for not having opposed the Japanese during the war. Unrest led to rebellion in 1947, which was brutally put down by the mainland government, with the loss of Taiwanese lives estimated at 10,000. It would take several decades to repair the damage done to mainlander-Taiwanese relations as a result of this massacre. The *er er ba* event, as it is known, from the Chinese for the date of the onset of the trouble, took place on February 28, 1947. In the 1990s, some amends were made to the families of the victims, and February 28 became Peace Day in Taiwan.

Communist forces under Mao Tse-tung defeated the Nationalist forces on the mainland in 1949, and Chiang Kai-shek along with his government and a portion of his army fled to Taiwan to set up a government in exile. Though there was no love lost between the Taiwanese and the Nationalists, the former could do little but absorb the newcomers. Mao's forces were on the brink of invasion, when the Korean War broke out in 1950. The U.S. Seventh Fleet was sent to the Taiwan Strait to protect Taiwan from attack. For the next two decades, the Republic of China, or Nationalist China, became the China in U.S. foreign relations, and Chiang, running an autocratic regime in Taiwan, dreamed of eventually returning to the mainland. In the bipolar world of the Cold War, Taiwan maintained a precarious independence just 100 miles off the coast of the People's Republic of China. Partly with the help of American aid, partly with a policy of import substitution, Taiwan grew into a manufacturing power. By the 1960s, it was exporting to the West in vast quantities: textiles, electronic equipment, and machinery all helped to fuel an 11 percent annual growth rate in the economy between 1960 and 1973.

In 1971, the United States normalized relations with Communist China, the People's Republic of China, and Taiwan lost its seat at the United Nations. Official diplomatic relations were established between the People's Republic and the United States in 1979. In Taiwan, equally dramatic changes were taking place. With the death of Chiang Kai-shek in 1975, his son Chiang Ching-kuo took power and attempted to cultivate a more populist image. Martial law was finally lifted in 1987, a year before his death. Lee Teng-hui, a native Taiwanese, became his successor. Between 1988 and 1996, Lee oversaw liberal changes in the political process, and in 1996, Lee became the first popularly elected president. Meanwhile, the threat from Communist China remains; Chinese military exercises in 1997 and 1998 were thought to preface a possible invasion of the island. Taiwan continues to perform a delicate balancing act, attempting to normalize relations with the People's Republic, while at the same time insuring its own independence.

THE FIRST TAIWANESE IN AMERICA

Mainland Chinese immigrants began coming to the United States in significant numbers about a century before the Taiwanese. These early immigrants, largely from Guangdong province, came to the West Coast during the boom of the Gold Rush. However, large numbers of these immigrants soon spurred a backlash of anti-Chinese sentiment. Discriminatory laws such as the exclusion act against the Chinese in 1882 denied them the right of entry to the United States simply based on ethnicity and race. Only with the defeat of Japan in World War II, in which China and the U.S. were allies, was there an effort to take the exclusionary laws off the books. Early quotas for Chinese and Asians in general were low, but the doors were once again open. In 1965, President Lyndon Johnson signed the Hart-Celler Act, which allowed for an annual quota of 20,000 Chinese, as well as for the entry of family members as non-quota immigrants.

Taiwanese immigration was influenced by these legal difficulties. The first Taiwanese immigrants came between the end of World War II and 1965, and were made up mostly of students continuing their education at American universities, mainly on the East and West Coasts, and in certain places in the Midwest, such as Chicago. The numbers of these were low, and some stayed on after graduation to find careers in the United States. Early Taiwanese immigrants also included wives of servicemen stationed in Taiwan after the Korean War. A third group of early immigrants sought better economic conditions and opportunities than they could find at home. These people often ended up working in Chinese restaurants or in service industries. Many such early immigrants felt isolated from the general Chinese American population by cultural tradition and by language, for Cantonese was the language of many Chinese immigrants of these period, as opposed to the Taiwanese or Mandarin spoken by immigrants from Taiwan.

SIGNIFICANT IMMIGRATION WAVES

After the 1965 Immigration Act, more Taiwanese came to the United States, aided by the new legislation, which gave priority to those with vital skills. Individuals with technical and scientific skills found easier admittance to the United States, as well as those in such needed occupations as hotel and restaurant work. This second wave of immigration lasted from 1965 to 1979. Once the United States recognized mainland China, however, relations with Taiwan became more informal. Immigrants since 1979 have had increased difficulties as they hold passports from a "nonexistent" nation. In 1982, Taiwan was given a quota of 20,000 immigrants, and many of these were students or trained professionals for whom there were insufficient jobs in Taiwan. A brain drain from Taiwan ensued, including students who, having completed their studies in the United States, decided to stay on. Not only were more job opportunities available in America, but young men of draft age could also avoid compulsory military service in Taiwan.

The Immigration Act of 1990 established preferences for those willing to invest in new business in the United States. Other factors in Taiwanese immigration since 1979 have been the increase of educational opportunities in the United States, as well as the uncertain position of Taiwan with respect to China. With the increased productivity of Taiwan in the 1980s, a class of transnational business people was created. Called *taikongren* or "astronauts," these business representatives shuttle back and forth between the United States and Taiwan, while their families reside in the former.

Numbers of Taiwanese immigrants to the United States are not easily calculated, since U.S. Census figures group all of the approximately 1.65 million Chinese Americans (as of 1990) in one category. These include American-born Chinese, as well as immigrants from China, Hong Kong, Singapore, Southeast Asia, and Taiwan. From 1984 to 1999, it is estimated that some 200,000 Taiwanese have immigrated to the United States, with numbers averaging about 13,000 per year. In 1994, 10,032 Taiwanese came to the United States, while about 54,000 immigrants were admitted from mainland China. In both cases, the overwhelming majority of immigrants listing an occupation were professionals, technicians, or managers. However, the usual stereotype of the Taiwanese engineer or computer scientist is not necessarily the norm. There have also been large numbers of blue-collar workers in service and garment industries. Also, more women are now immigrating to the United States.

SETTLEMENT PATTERNS

Large communities of Taiwanese Americans are scattered throughout the United States, but are concentrated primarily in California and on the East Coast. In California, Taiwanese communities are particularly prevalent in Los Angeles, San Jose, and San Francisco. In the greater Los Angeles area, for example, the town of Monterey Park has been called "Little Taipei", because of its large Taiwanese population. Other suburban Southern California communities with a high Taiwanese population can be found throughout the San Gabriel valley. Of the 10,032 Taiwanese immigrants in 1994, nearly half, 4,862, settled in California, with upwards of 3,000 in the Los Angeles-Orange Country area alone. San Jose, San Francisco, and Oakland accounted for another 1,500 immigrants. In the east, large communities can be found in the Flushing-Queens area of New York, while in Texas, Houston draws Taiwanese immigrants.

The flow of capital from Taiwan follows these immigrants, and as a result they have been able to revitalize some failing communities and culturally influence others. The Taiwanese presence is evident in the cities where they settle. Instead of the Chinatowns of old, Taiwanese immigrants create islands of Taiwanese culture amid suburbia, with all-Chinese shopping malls and strip malls offering everything from Chinese food shops to bookshops and pharmacies. All signs are in Chinese characters mixed with English in a kind of international linguistic melange; entering these malls is like being instantly transported to Taiwan itself. This is especially true for communities such as those in California at Monterey Park and San Jose, where the Taiwanese community has its own clubs, churches, newspapers, and churches. This is also the case in larger urban areas, such as Flushing in Queens, New York, where the Taiwanese are just one part of a larger multicultural blend including Pakistanis, Indians, Koreans, and Thais.

ACCULTURATION AND ASSIMILATION

Like many other immigrants from Asia, the Taiwanese tend to settle in areas with large numbers of their fellow countrymen. Families and networks of mutual aid are set in place in the United States just as they were in Taiwan. Thus the Taiwanese American community tends to remain cohesive, preserving its values, language, and cultural traditions amid the bustle of contemporary American life, but they are no longer segregated into the Chinatowns of old. As Hsiang-shui Chen pointed out in *Chinatown No More,* a study of Taiwanese immigrants in Queens, "the new Chinese immigrants do not live in isolated Chinese communities. Like the old Chinese immigrants, they have developed a complex organizational life, but it does not include all immigrants, and the new Chinese community in Queens has no hierarchical structure." Though the Taiwanese immigrant may own a business or hold a job in an inner city of San Jose or Los Angeles or Houston, "they are likely to have homes elsewhere," according to Franklin Ng in his study, *The Taiwanese Americans* (Ng, 1998:22). Thus the new Taiwanese immigrant community is looser than earlier Chinese ones, while preserving much of the mutual aid that characterized those communities.

TRADITIONS, CUSTOMS, AND BELIEFS

Taiwanese traditions are a unique blend of the groups that have occupied the island state. There are instances of Fujian culture, of traditions from Guangdong, and of customs from Japan as a result of the fifty-year occupation by that country. These traditions have also been heavily influenced by Western trends, as Taiwan itself is a modern economic power. Thus, immigrants coming to the United States have generally found a middle ground between East and West for their belief systems.

Concepts relating to nature, time, and space are a joining of two worlds: the Chinese sense of harmonic living in tune with the natural order, and the Western scientific, materialistic worldview. Ancient belief systems revolved around the *Dao,* or the Way, the manner in which humans live in harmony with the natural world. The traditional belief in *qi,* or life force, leads to a view of a world divided into polar opposites, yin and yang, as represented in such dichotomies as male-female, cold-hot, dry-wet, light-dark. Additionally, the world is seen as comprised of five elements: fire, wood, air, water, and earth. Seasons and relationships are determined by the ebb and flow of opposites and of the five ele-

ments. The tradition of *fengshui,* wind and water, is an ancient Chinese science that seeks harmony in interior and exterior design and architecture by balancing yin-yang and allowing for proper flow of qi. This tradition has gained popularity outside of the Taiwanese and Chinese community, resulting in a popularization of fengshui principles in much of the Western world as well.

A unique perception of time also informs Taiwanese life, in which both the lunar calendar and Western Gregorian calendar is used. The latter solar calendar is employed in business, school, and public life, while for determining festivals and religious observances, the lunar calendar is used. Based on the phases of the moon, the lunar calendar has 12 months, with 24 solar divisions, and is 11 days shorter than the Western calendar year. The lunar calendar and almanacs are also used to determine auspicious and inauspicious days for doing various endeavors, from starting a business, to getting married. Some Taiwanese believe that certain days are unlucky: the third, seventh, thirteenth, eighteenth, twenty-second, and twenty-seventh days of the lunar month, for example, are held by some to be bad luck days. The first and fifteenth of each lunar month are not good days to wash one's hair. Such old beliefs, however, are dying out among the younger generation of Taiwanese.

Another widespread belief among Chinese and Taiwanese is the taboo of number four, which sounds very much like the word for death. Buildings often exclude a fourth and even a fourteenth or twenty-fourth floor to avoid possible bad luck, a custom similar to that regarding the number thirteen in Western societies. Many other beliefs revolve around the play of homonyms. It is bad luck to share a pear, *li*, because that word sounds like the Chinese word "to separate." Breaking an object, the person will quickly say *Sui sui ping an*, a play on the word for "pieces" and "year after year," turning the bad situation into a wish for eternal happiness. Similarly, at Chinese New Year, the character for luck or happiness will be taped to windows upside down: the word for "down" sounds similar to that for "to come," meaning luck or happiness will come to you. Gift giving is fraught with peril, for some presents are to be avoided; umbrellas, as the Chinese word for them sounds too close to the word for separation or departure, and clocks, which sound like the expression for attending a funeral.

"[W]hen my oldest was ready for school, we came to the United States. When I came to this country, I heard about all the divorces and I was kind of scared. I wanted to save money in case my husband kicks me out, so I can go somewhere."

Su-Chu Hadley, cited in *American Mosiac: The Immigrant Experience in the Words of Those Who Lived It,* Joan Morrison and Charlotte Fox Zabusky (E.P. Dutton, New York, 1980).

PROVERBS

Taiwanese culture is rich in proverbs, many of them appearing in pairs and presenting opposite views of the same advice. Thus, to "give somebody wood on a snowy day," is to provide timely aid, while to "add flowers to a large bouquet" means to do something unnecessary. Similarly, advice about just desserts is served up in the following pair: "Bad persons always get their comeuppance; if they have not yet it is only a matter of timing;" and "Good persons always get a reward. Wait, it will come." The idea that trouble follows trouble is expressed in "The roof always leaks on a rainy day," and doing something unnecessary is parodied in "Painting feet on a snake."

CUISINE

Taiwanese cuisine is largely influenced by Fujian cooking, an Eastern style adapted to a lighter cuisine which employs more seafood. Japanese influences in this style of cooking include the substitution of vegetable oil for traditional Fujian lard to create more delicate dishes. Other popular methods of cooking include barbecuing and the use of hot-pots, in addition to pan frying, boiling, and stir-frying.

Taiwanese cooking employs a wide assortment of foodstuffs, from meats such as beef and pork, to poultry and all sorts of seafood. Noodle dishes and soups are popular, as are boiled dumplings, *shuijao*, prepared with crabmeat in addition to the usual pork and leek stuffing. Seafood is used in such delicacies as oysters in black bean sauce, prawns wrapped in seaweed, cucumber crab rolls, and clam and winter melon soup. Taiwan, with is tropical and subtropical climate, grows fruits and vegetables in abundance. Most popular fruits include papaya, mango, pineapple, melons, and citrus, while vegetables are asparagus, eggplant, pea pods, Chinese cabbage and mushrooms, *bok choy*, and leafy greens of the spinach family. Bean curd in various guises is also used. Buns, cakes, and bread are also more numerous in Taiwanese cuisine than in other parts of China, a result of Western influence in Shanghai. Beverages such as beer and rice wine, *sake*, are typical, as is Western style soda, but tea continues to be an omnipresent beverage among Taiwanese.

Some food is sold only at certain times of the day or year. For example, steamed buns and the clay-oven rolls called *shaobing* are sold only in the morning; some bread and tofu are sold in the afternoon and evening. The best time to find spring rolls is in April; moon cakes are available during the Mid-Autumn Festival; and the Dragon Boat Festival heralds delicious rice dumplings, *zongzi*. Other foods, such as snake and tiger, are now rare, used primarily for medicinal purposes.

The Taiwanese use chopsticks. It is a skill most children learn by the time they are five. Deep, curved Chinese spoons in plastic or porcelain are also used instead of Western cutlery. Knives are usually unnecessary at table as meat is diced or sliced in preparation. It is customary for the eater to hold the rice bowl close to the mouth, scooping the rice in with chopsticks, which are placed on the table or the rim of the rice bowl, and never pointing down into the bowl a sign of bad luck.

MUSIC

Music provides a ceremonial and entertainment function in Taiwanese society, both in the United States and in Taiwan. Music the dead to their burial, heralds marriages and birthdays, and also provides the framework for Chinese opera and puppet plays. An ancient musical system, Chinese music uses a scale of seven notes, but focuses on five core tones with two changing tones. These five tones are in turn tied to the Chinese concept of the five basic elements. The Taiwanese musical tradition follows that of the classical Chinese model, and in addition has its own folk traditions. Popular instruments include the *zither* with 25 strings and movable bridges, *se*, and the *chin*, another stringed instrument.

Three different types of musical ensembles are employed at festive or ritual occasions, each tracing its development back to bands that would accompany high officers in imperial times. Drums are an integral part of traditional Taiwanese music, and for special occasions, a drum pavilion or *guting* is played, comprising several sorts of gongs, cymbals, and drums, as well as the double-reeded pipe called *suona*. *Bayin* ensembles, employing eight sounds, are used for weddings and funerals with a guting following. A third type of amateur folk ensemble plays *beiguan* music at temples for a god's or goddess's birthday.

Taiwanese produce stars on the Mandarin and Taiwanese pop music scenes. Teresa Teng was one such popular singer, known all over East Asia and beloved by immigrant communities in the United States.

Folk songs and ballads have become more popular, inspired by both aboriginal music and Japanese musical styles. Taiwanese also listen to Western music in all its forms.

TRADITIONAL COSTUMES

The *chi pao* is the traditional wear for women, a long, high-collared dress with a side slit. The chi pao is generally made of silk, brocaded with designs or plain, as is desired. Such dresses are for formal occasions, though a shortened version is also used for less formal wear. The *chan sang* is similar; it literally means "long clothes," but is loose-waisted in comparison to the chi pao, and was formerly worn by men as well.

DANCES AND SONGS

Taiwanese traditional dance is ritualistic, emphasizing formal, stiff body movements with the feet kept close to the ground. Such dances are seen in folk celebrations and rituals, and in opera, where each movement is highly symbolic, telling of emotions, or time and space changes. In traditional drama, there is often a chaotic, swirling, acrobatic blend of fight and dance: armies clash, or monks attack devils. This latter form of dance is closely related to Taiwan's martial art, *guoshu*, of which there are many varieties.

Folk dance traditions are strong among Taiwanese, the lion dance and the dragon dance being the most typical. In ancient times, such dances, employing drums, masks, and animated movements, were performed to bring rain or avoid plagues. Modern performances of the lion and dragon dance are intended to bring good luck or liven up festive occasions. The dragon mask and costume in particular are works of folk art in themselves, the entire body of the dancer covered in colorful fabric. Contemporary choreographers have attempted to blend some of this folk tradition with the elements of modern dance, creating a uniquely Taiwanese form of ballet.

HOLIDAYS

Taiwanese Americans observe all the formal holidays of the United States: Christmas, New Years, Thanksgiving, Fourth of July, and Easter. In addition, they have several festivals that are peculiar to the lunar calendar and have a seasonal significance. The most important festival, for all Chinese Americans, is the celebration of the Lunar New Year, which is tied to the coming of spring and thus also known as *chunjie* or "spring festival." The advent of the new year is a time for house-cleaning, after which no more should be done for the first days of the new year, or good luck may be swept away. Red is the dominant color: red paper with calligraphic wishes for good luck or good health will be hung; festive red clothing is worn at gatherings. New Year's Day is a time for family to come together, to give gifts and to visit close friends. Special foods are prepared, and much of these are determined again by similarity in sound to words representing good luck or wealth. For example, fish, *yu*, is a popular dish because it sounds the same as the word for "abundance." Parades and dramatic performances take place over many days, before and after Chinese New Year.

The Lantern Festival, *dengjie*, takes place on the fifteenth day of the Lunar New Year and traditionally marks the end of New Year celebrations. In the United States this festival marks the beginning of spring banquets given by many Taiwanese organizations. A summer festival, the Dragon Boat Festival honors the death of a popular poet and minister of the Zhou dynasty of China (403-221 B.C.), who committed suicide in the Mi Lo River as a protest against government corruption. Legend has it that villagers attempted to recover his body with a flotilla of boats; modern-day boat races in Taiwan honor the day. The same legend tells that the people threw rice dumplings into the river to feed the fish, thus keeping them from eating the corpse of the poet. Today, Taiwanese Americans often eat zongzi at this festival, a sort of glutinous rice pudding or dumpling wrapped in bamboo leaves and stuffed with pork, beans, and other ingredients. The Mid-Autumn Festival, *zhongchiu jie*, is celebrated on the fifteenth day of the eighth lunar month, when the full moon is supposed to represent family harmony; the abundance of autumn harvest is often displayed as an offering to the moon goddess. Paste-filled moon cakes are baked at this time, made from lotus or melon seeds, or various beans. Some U.S. cities have organized street fairs to celebrate Mid-Autumn.

HEALTH ISSUES

There are no health issues peculiar to the Taiwanese population. A healthy diet is a part of the culture, owing to the five-element way of thinking and of the yin-yang dichotomy. Categories such as wet and dry, hot and cool, go into preparing a menu. The balance of such opposites is thought to be vital to good health. There is a heavy reliance on non-Western forms of medical therapy such as acupuncture.

LANGUAGE

Taiwanese Americans speak a variety of languages, but Mandarin Chinese is generally their first language, known as *kuo yu*, or "national dialect." This derives from Beijing Mandarin and is about as similar to that dialect as American English is to British English. The various ethnic groups comprising the Taiwanese community have their own dialects. The native Taiwanese dialect is spoken by the Fujian and Hakka, and is based on the Minnan dialect of southern Fujian province. Some Hakka also speak their own dialect. But generally speaking, Taiwanese all speak the four-tone Mandarin dialect. Romanization of Chinese characters is still done in the Wade-Giles system, though Taiwan is beginning to change such romanization to the pinyin system in use on the mainland. Thus Peking, the capital of communist China, is Beijing. Taipei, Taiwan's capital in the Wade-Giles system, is Taibei in pinyin.

Taiwanese Americans often mix English with Chinese, especially in written language. Thus, shop signs will often combine intricate characters with English words. In larger urban areas, Chinese language radio and television stations provide listeners and viewers with programming in Mandarin or Cantonese dialects.

GREETINGS AND OTHER POPULAR EXPRESSIONS

Common greetings and other expressions include: *Tsao* (tsow)—Good morning; *Ni hao ma* (knee how ma)—How are you; *Tsao chien* (tsow chyen)—Good-bye, see you later; *Pai tuo* (pie twa), Please;

Hsieh hsieh (shye shye) thanks; *Pu ko chi* (pookócheh) You're welcome; *Tai hau le* (tie how le) Great, wonderful.

FAMILY AND COMMUNITY DYNAMICS

Confucian values place a premium on family values and family cohesion. Clans and lineages both played significant roles in Chinese history, and in the Taiwanese American community such bonds continue to so. Whereas the extended family of three generations under one roof was once the norm in Taiwanese society, the emphasis in recent years in both Taiwan and the United States has been on the nuclear family. No longer are many children needed as they were in rural, agricultural times. Now the emphasis is on smaller families with fewer children. Often Taiwanese Americans have left family members behind; mothers and fathers remain in Taiwan while sons and increasingly daughters come to the United States to build a new life. Relations are continued via telephone, the Internet, and by periodic visits. It is common for members of an extended family to live together, however, such as in cases of a young man or woman living with relatives while attending college.

Within the family, Chinese kinship terms are observed. Grandparents are *zufumu* if they are the parents of the father, *waizufumu* if they are mother's parents. An older brother is *gege*, a younger one *didi*. *Jiejie* is an older sister while *meimei* is a younger one. Such nomenclature also extends to uncles and aunts to determine which side he or she is on (mother's or father's) and their rank of seniority in the family. Such strict labeling eventually breaks down among Taiwanese families living in America.

Depending on the economic and educational status of families, roles are more or less traditional vis-à-vis husband and wife. Among blue-collar workers, though they are likely to have a double-household, the male-female roles are more traditional and the husband will be the more dominant partner. In professional families, the roles tend to be more equal and the higher level of income affords both parents more time with their children. In general, Taiwanese Americans experience fewer divorces than other American families, partly a result of the extended kinship bonds and the overlapping social relationships in the community. Long-term separations, however, in which the husband is forced for economic reasons to leave his family in the U.S. while he shuttles back and forth to Taiwan, strain marriages.

The Taiwanese American is cohesive. Self-help within the Taiwanese American community helps new arrivals to establish themselves, to start businesses, and to find jobs. Networking is a fact of life in all cultures; Taiwanese Americans form familial bonds and groupings in specialized organizations and clubs to look out for one another.

EDUCATION

Education is highly valued by Taiwanese Americans. Many immigrants come to the United States with university and post-graduate degrees and the value of a college education is instilled in succeeding generations. With competition stiff and available spaces low in Taiwanese universities, many come to the United States to study. Preparation for college begins in kindergarten. Often parents will purchase a home contingent upon it being in a good school district. Children learn from an early age the importance of doing well in school, of getting good grades so that they can get into a good college later on. Many Taiwanese children take preparation courses for the SATs and practice writing essays for college admissions officers. In Taiwanese families, the parents are very involved in all aspects of their children's education. Favored places of enrollment are such California universities as UC Berkeley, UCLA, or Stanford. The Asian population at Berkeley is upwards of 60 percent of the total.

BIRTH AND BIRTHDAYS

The mother is given especially nutritious foods both before and after giving birth. Whereas in earlier times, and still to a great extent on mainland China and in Taiwan, the birth of a boy has been the greatest wish of parents, now Taiwanese Americans rejoice at the birth of children of either sex. The one-month birthday is a time for special celebrating; birthdays are generally celebrated following the Western calendar.

THE ROLE OF WOMEN

In Taiwan, women tended to be subordinated, largely ruled over by the male members of the *jia* or extended family unit. Though divorce is rare in Taiwan, the wife's failure to produce a male child was one reason for separation. Times are changing in Taiwan, and among Taiwanese Americans. The educational disparity between women and men is decreasing, and women are often in the work force.

WEDDINGS

The courtship and weddings of Taiwanese Americans are no longer the elaborate, lengthy affairs they are in Taiwan, where there is a "greater engagement," or *dading*, during which gifts are exchanged between both families and the dowry is presented. Still, weddings are joyous occasions and are considered an important rite of passage. The ceremony itself may be civil or religious, but it is always followed by a banquet. The couple is generally presented with gifts of envelopes filled with money. Sometimes there may be banquets both in the United States and in Taiwan, if the parents of either of the couple live there. For a time, there was also the practice of sending the bride back to Taiwan for a cooking class.

FUNERALS

Rites given at funerals depend upon the religious affiliation of the deceased. Funerals are a time for demonstrating respect for ancestors and publicly displaying status in the family. While these intricate kinship roles and patterns have partly broken down in the United States, funerals are still solemn affairs. Red may be worn by some to ward off the negative influences of death or to celebrate the long life and descendants of the deceased.

INTERACTIONS WITH OTHER ETHNIC GROUPS

Confucian cultural tradition emphasizes accomplishment over race or ethnicity. Thus Taiwanese do well in the multicultural environment found in the United States and have generally gotten along well with other ethnic minorities. Taiwanese immigrants have been resented, however, especially where they have settled in large numbers in a certain area, such as in Monterey Park in California or in Flushing in Queens, New York. Taiwanese Americans are generally successful, and such resentment is tends to come from those groups who have not fared as well in the United States. Also, coming from a rich culture with ancient traditions, Taiwanese Americans do not take it for granted that all aspects of life in the United States are better than in Taiwan. Taiwanese do not cast off their heritage in a rush to assimilate. Such an attitude can cause friction with other ethnic minorities.

RELIGION

Among Taiwanese Americans there is a rich diversity of religions. Some, as in Taiwan itself, are Christian. This is a distinct minority in Taiwan, about one million faithful, divided between Roman Catholic and Protestant churches. A larger percentage of Taiwanese Americans are Christian than in Taiwan, partly because these churches provide a social gathering point for immigrants. Protestants outnumber Catholics in these, and a large group of Taiwanese Americans belongs to evangelical or fundamentalist Baptist churches. Presbyterian is another popular denomination, where services are often given in Mandarin or in Taiwanese dialect. The full panoply of services is available at such churches, including Bible study for the young and social functions such as dinners and talks.

Other Taiwanese Americans favor the traditional religions of Taiwan and of China. These consist of Buddhism, Daoism, Confucianism, and a hybrid popular religion. The popular religion is a blend of the other three faiths, plus ancestor worship and the belief in certain local gods and goddesses. For newcomers to the United States, religious affiliation can provide an important networking resource. Taiwanese Buddhists follow the *Mahayana* school, similar to the Buddhism of Japan, Korea, and Vietnam. Buddhism in particular has made rapid growth in recent years, establishing new temples in Los Angeles, San Francisco, Houston, and New York. This growth reflects the increasing popularity Buddhism is enjoying in Taiwan itself, with adherents growing six-fold in the years from 1983 to 1995. Xi Lai Temple, a Buddhist temple near Monterey Park, California is a particularly noteworthy in this respect. It is the largest overseas temple of Foguanshan center in Taiwan, a Zen Buddhist center. Completed in 1988, it cost $26 million and is a colorful and stunning architectural presence, attracting faithful and tourists alike. One hall alone has ten thousand golden Buddhas. It speaks for the presence of Buddhism in the United States, as do the Jade Buddha Temple in Houston and the Zhuangyen Monastery in Carmel, New York.

The popular religion is represented in the United States by various temples built for the gods and goddesses. These include *Tudigong*, or the God of the Earth, *Guanyin*, the Goddess of Mercy, and *Mazu*, the Goddess of the Sea. One such temple, to Mazu, was built in San Francisco starting in 1986. These churches and temples all include functions beyond religion: there are activity halls for lectures as well as instruction in Chinese language.

Religious observance is not restricted to formal temples and churches, however. Many Taiwanese Americans will have shrines in their homes and observe lunar festivals, activities that bond the community to folk traditions and religious practices.

EMPLOYMENT AND ECONOMIC TRADITIONS

Taiwanese Americans are generally seen as consisting only of well-educated professionals. Of the 10,032 Taiwanese immigrants admitted to the United States in 1994, for example, almost three-quarters of those reporting occupations were in the professional, technical, executive, administrative, or managerial classes. In general, Taiwanese do come better prepared than the older, pre-1949, mainland Chinese immigrant: they tend to be better educated, have a profession, and know some English. Yet that is only part of the picture; 6,084 of the ten thousand plus in 1994 reported no occupation. Many are blue-collar workers working in restaurants and in the garment industry.

Many Taiwanese investors also settle in the United States, encouraged by the Immigration Act of 1990. This Act created preferences not only for those with key professional skills, but also for investors who could create employment opportunities in the United States by investing funds here. It is important for Taiwanese to start up their own business, no matter how small, for these are signs of success in Chinese society. However, as the U.S. economy slowed in the 1980s and early 1990s, there was a reverse migration of Taiwanese professionals forced to take research or teaching positions in Taiwan's high-tech industries and universities, leaving their families in the United States. With the East Asia economic crunch of the late 1990s, and with improved economic conditions in the United States, this situation has been somewhat rectified.

POLITICS AND GOVERNMENT

Since the United States officially established diplomatic relations with the People's Republic of China in 1979, Taiwan has held a precarious position as an independent country. Much of the political activity of Taiwanese Americans, therefore, has been focussed on American public and political opinion regarding Taiwan. Despite American insistence that it no longer officially supports an independent Taiwan, the U.S. Congress did pass the Taiwan Relations Act authorizing continued social and economic ties with the island nation. Various Taiwanese American political organizations have been monitoring U.S.-Taiwanese relations. The World United Formosans for Independence organization, established in 1970 in Dallas, Texas, promotes a free and democratic Taiwan and publishes the *Taiwan Tribune* to further this goal. The Formosan Association for Public Affairs in Washington

D.C. closely monitors legislation affecting Taiwan and Taiwanese. Taiwanese sovereignty is also the aim of the lobbying group, Taiwan International Relations, centered in Washington, D.C., while human rights is the focus of the Formosan Association for Human Rights, located in Kansas.

RELATIONS WITH TAIWAN

Taiwanese Americans maintain close relations with their former country, as many of these immigrants have family members in Taiwan. Frequent visits to both countries take place. Many groups continue to monitor the political situation within Taiwan, and welcomed the increasing democratization witnessed in the 1990s. Thus, with the end of martial law in 1987, and the reforms of Chiang Ching-kuo and Lee Teng-hui, Taiwanese Americans have been encouraged to expect a stronger voice for the people in Taiwan.

INDIVIDUAL AND GROUP CONTRIBUTIONS

As Franklin Ng noted in his book, *The Taiwanese Americans*, this group, despite having a short history in this country and consisting of a relatively small percentage of the population, has made "a significant presence" (Ng 1998:121). "Most came after the immigration changes in 1965," Ng observed, "but they have already helped to alter the U.S. cultural landscape." The Taiwanese Americans have helped to redirect U.S. focus on the Pacific Rim and many of them in business have become "cultural brokers in penetrating the markets of Asia" (Ng 1998:121). Taiwanese have brought capital and investment with them, and are particularly prominent in academia. But they have also become skilled workers in businesses in Silicon Valley, valuable researchers in medicine, talented artists in film and music, and one is even an astronaut. The following is a list of individual Taiwanese Americans notable for their achievements.

ACADEMIA AND EDUCATION

Chang-lin Tien (1935-) is both a renowned educator as well as administrator, serving as chancellor of the University of California, Berkeley from 1990 to 1997. Born in Wuhan, China, Chang and his family fled to Shanghai in 1937 and to Taiwan in 1949. He graduated from National Taiwan University in 1955 in mechanical engineering and received his M.A. and Ph.D. at Princeton in mechanical engineering. Conducting research at Berkeley in thermal radiation, he quickly made a name for himself, becoming a Guggenheim fellow in 1965-66 and an Alexander von Humboldt Foundation fellow in Germany in 1979. In 1988 he became vice-chancellor at the University of California, Irvine, and then returned to Berkeley two years later as its chancellor. Other prominent Taiwanese Americans in academia include Chen Hui Lee (1929-), is a professor at the University of Wisconsin-Steven Point who has authored 30 technical papers about forest genetics and tree improvements; Jian-min Yuan (1944-), a professor at Drexel University and author of more than 85 professional papers in the fields of molecular, chemical, and atomic physics as well as chaos theory; Ko-ming Shih (1953-), a professor of computer engineering at Mercer University, Macon, GA; Tsay-jiu Brian Shieh (1953-), an associate professor at the Univesity of Texas, Arlington, whose research is in compound semiconductor device modeling and vacuum microelectronics; Yuch-ning Shieh (1940-), a professor at Purdue who has published over 40 papers on oxygen, carbon, and sulfur isotope geochemistry in rocks and minerals; Yung-way Liu (1955-), an associate professor at the University of Delaware and well known research mathematician; Ray H. Liu (1942-), program director, University of Alabama at Birmingham, author of books and over 50 articles on mass spectrometry and clinical chemistry, and editor of *Forensic Science Review*; Cynthia C. Hsieh (1961-), technical services librarian at Columbia College and Chinese American activist and author; William Wei-lien Chang (1933-), well-known pathologist, formerly of West Virginia University, and author of numerous research articles in cell population kinetics and colon cancer; Tsan-kuo Chang (1950-), professor at the University of Minnesota and author of *The Press and China Policy: The Illusion of Sino-Soviet Relations, 1950-84*; and Kong-cheng Ho (1940-), associate professor of neurology at the Medical College of Wisconsin and author of 66 publications on Alzheimer's disease and the development of the brain.

ADMINISTRATION AND BUSINESS

Elaine Chao (1952-) is a former director of the Peace Corps and the United Way of America, and is married to Senator Mitch McConnell of Kentucky; Dean Shui-tien Hsieh (1948-), is a pharmaceutical company executive in Pennsylvania; Helen Kuan Chang (1962-), is a public relations director for San Jose Convention and Visitors Bureau; Jennifer Jen-huey (1964-), is an architect in San Francisco; Paul P. Hung (1933-), is an executive for

Wyeth-Ayerst Labs; John Chau Shih (1939-), is president of S Y Technology, Van Nuys, CA; and Yeou-chuong Simon Yu (1958-), is engineering manager for Monolith Technologies, Tucson, AZ.

FILM, TELEVISION, AND THEATER

Ang Lee (1954-) is a film director and producer who came to the United States in 1978 to study at the University of Illinois at Urbana-Champaign, changing his career goal from acting to film directing because of lack of fluency in English. His 1985 film, *Fine Line,* was selected as the best film at the New York University Film Festival of that year. Finding funding from a Taiwanese production company, he made *Pushing Hands* in 1992, a film that became a box-office success in Taiwan and won Golden Horse Award. The film was released in the U.S. in 1994. By far his best-known films are the *Wedding Banquet* (1993) and *Eat Drink Man Woman* (1994). He also directed the movie version of Jane Austen's *Sense and Sensibility,* a film nominated for seven academy awards. In addition, he directed the acclaimed 1997 movie, *The Ice Storm.* Doug Chiang (1962-) is a visual effects arts director at Industrial Light and Magic, the special effects company founded by George Lucas. Chiang was responsible for creation and design of *Death Becomes Her,* which won an Oscar in 1992. He has also won both an Academy Award and a British Academy Award for his work at Industrial Light and Magic. Chiang led the design team that provided the special effects for *Star Wars I: The Phantom Menace,* released in 1999.

JOURNALISM

Phoebe Eng (1961-) is an attorney and a founder of *A. Magazine,* a periodical devoted to Asian American issues with a readership of about 100,000. The magazine also reports on the media and the manner in which it covers Asian Americans and Asian American issues. In 1999, Eng wrote *Warrior Lessons,* an examination of what it means to be an Asian woman in America.

MUSIC

Cho-liang Lin, renowned violinist, is on the faculty of Julliard School.

SCIENCE AND TECHNOLOGY

Yuan-tse Lee (1936-) is a Nobel Prize winner in chemistry. The son of a well-known painter in Taiwan, Lee opted for science over art, attending Berkeley in 1962 and working at Harvard University designing a mass spectrometer that could identify the paths of different ions as they separated. This work in the deflection and identification of the ions in chemical reactions won Lee the Nobel Prize in Chemistry in 1986. Paul Chu (1941-) has conducted researches in superconductivity that have earned him world-wide fame; David Ho (1952-) is a medical researcher whose work on the use of AZT in AIDS treatment won him a "Man of the Year" citation on the cover of Time magazine in 1995; Edward Lu is a NASA astronaut.

MEDIA

PRINT

There are several daily newspapers that publish nationally, aimed at a general Chinese American audience. In addition, some newspapers are linked to Taiwan in direct and indirect ways. The World Journal, for example, is affiliated with the media magnate Tih-wu Wang and his United Daily News of Taipei.

The Chinese Press.
Address: 15 Mercer St., New York, NY 10013.
Telephone: (212) 274-8282.

International Daily News.
Established in 1981; featuring news of the Taiwanese American community.
Address: 870 Monterey Pass Rd., Monterey Park, CA 91754.
Telephone: (213) 265-1317.

Sampan.
The only bilingual newspaper in New England serving the Asian community; published twice monthly.
Address: 90 Tyler St., Boston, MA 02111.
Telephone: (212) 426-9492.

Sing Tao Daily.
Address: Sing Tao Newspapers Ltd., 103-105 Mott Street, New York, NY 10013.
Telephone: (212) 431-9030.

Taiwan Economic News.
A quarterly magazine seeking to promote business relations between the U.S. and Taiwan.
Address: U.S.A.-Republic of China Council, 200 Main St., Crystal Lake, IL 60014.
Telephone: (815) 459-5875.

Taiwan Today.

A bimonthly newsletter with notes of events and happenings of interest to Friends of Free China.

Address: Friends of Free China, 1629 K St., Washington, DC 20006.

Taiwan Tribune.

Address: P.O. Box 1527, Long Island, NY 11101.
Telephone: (718) 639-7201.

World Journal.

Address: 231 Adrian Rd., Millbrae, CA 94108.
Telephone: (415) 982-6161.

RADIO

Global Communication Enterprises, New York; Huayu Radio Broadcast, San Francisco.

KALW-FM (91.7).

Cantonese simulcast of evening news and a Chinese community hour on Saturday evenings.

Contact: Alan Favley, Program Coordinator.
Address: 2905 21st St., San Francisco, CA 94110.
Telephone: (415) 648-1177.

KAZN-AM (1300).

Broadcasts programs in several Asian languages, including Chinese.

Contact: Shirley Price, Vice President.
Address: 800 Sierra Madre Villa, Pasadena, CA 91107.
Telephone: (818) 352-1300.

KMAX-FM (107.1).

Religious programming with weekend Chinese shows.

Contact: Linda Johnson Hayes, General Manager.
Address: 3844 Foothill Blvd., Pasadena, CA 91107.
Telephone: (213) 681-2486.

KUSF-FM (90.3).

Chinese news programming every morning.

Contact: Chinese Today Communication.
Address: P.O. Box 5673, South San Francisco, CA 94083.
Telephone: (415) 386-5873.

WKCR-FM (89.9).

Broadcasts a three-hour Chinese variety show each Saturday morning.

Contact: Carl Biers, Program Director.
Address: Columbia University, 108 Ferris Hall, New York, NY 10027.
Telephone: (212) 854-5223.

TELEVISION

Chinese World Television, New York; Hong Kong Television Broadcasts, U.S.A., Los Angeles; United Chinese TV, San Francisco; Hua Sheng TV, San Francisco; Pacific TV Broadcasting Co., San Francisco.

KCNS-TV (38).

Programming in Cantonese and Mandarin.

Contact: Jim Paymar, General Manager.
Address: 1550 Bryant St., San Francisco, CA 94103.
Telephone: (415) 863-3800.

KSCI-TV (18).

Some Chinese programming.

Contact: Rosemary Fisher-Dannon, Executive Vice-President.
Address: 12401 W. Olympic Blvd., West Los Angeles, CA 90064-1022.
Telephone: (213) 478-1818.

KTSF-TV (26).

Chinese news programming and a Friday night movie in Chinese.

Address: 100 Valley Dr., Brisbane, CA 94005.
Telephone: (515) 468-2626.

ORGANIZATIONS AND ASSOCIATIONS

Many Taiwanese American organizations have been founded to promote Taiwanese-U.S. relations and to promote a free Taiwan. Others have been formed around business and professional themes and concerns.

Formosan Association for Human Rights (FAHR).

A national organization to monitor and promote human rights on Taiwan, with 16 chapters and a monthly newsletter.

Contact: Ken S. Huang, President.
Address: P.O. Box 81384, Memphis, TN 38152.

Formosan Association for Public Affairs (FAPA).

Attempts to affect U.S. policy vis-à-vis Taiwan. Chapters in 22 states and publishes a newsletter eight times annually.

Contact: J.P.C. Blaauw, Director.
Address: P.O. Box 15062, Washington, DC 20003.
Telephone: (202) 547-3686.

North America Taiwanese Professors' Association (NATPA).

Professors and senior researchers of Taiwanese origin or descent. Encourages educational exchange and cultural understanding among the Taiwanese and other peoples worldwide. Promotes scientific and professional knowledge. Seeks to further the welfare of Taiwanese communities in North America and Taiwan. Sponsors research and lectures on topics related to Taiwan.

Contact: Frank Chang, President.
Address: 5632 South Woodlawn Street, Chicago, Illinois 60637.
E-mail: FCHIANG@mail.lawnet.fordham.edu.
Online: http://www.natpa.org.

Taiwanese Association of America (TAA).

Promotes friendship and welfare among Taiwanese Americans and those concerned with Taiwanese human rights.

Contact: Mr. Chiang, President.
Address: P.O. Box 3302, Iowa City, IA 52244.
Telephone: (319) 338-9082.

Taiwan Benevolent Association of California.

Address: 2225 W. Commonwealth Ave., No. 301, Alhambra, CA 91801.
Telephone: (818) 576-8368.

Taiwan Chamber of Commerce.

Address: 870 Market St., Suite 1046, San Francisco, CA 94102.
Telephone: (415) 981-5387.

MUSEUMS AND RESEARCH CENTERS

Chinese Historical Society of America.

Devoted to the study of the Chinese people in the United States from the nineteenth century to the present, and to the collection of their relics.

Contact: Ted Wong, President.
Address: 650 Commercial St., San Francisco, CA 94111.
Telephone: (415) 391-1188.

Institute of Chinese Studies Library.

Holdings of 1500 volumes on Chinese peoples and cultures.

Contact: James A. Ziervogel, Director.
Address: 1605 Elizabeth St., Pasadena, CA 91104.
Telephone: (818) 398-2320.

SOURCES FOR ADDITIONAL STUDY

Ahern, Emily Martin, and Hill Gates, eds. *The Anthropology of Taiwanese Society*. Stanford: Stanford University Press, 1981.

Copper, John F. *Taiwan: Nation-State or Province?* Second edition. Boulder: Westview Press, 1996.

Davison, Gary Marvin, and Barbara E. Reed. *Culture and Customs of Taiwan*. Westport, Connecticut: Greenwood Press, 1998.

Harrell, Stevan, and Huang Chün-chieh, eds. *Cultural Change in Postwar Taiwan*. Boulder: Westview Press, 1994.

Hsiang-shui Chen. *Chinatown No More: Taiwan Immigrants in Contemporary New York*. Ithaca, New York: Cornell Univesity Press, 1992.

Ng, Franklin. *The Taiwanese Americans*. Westport, Connecticut: Greenwood Press, 1998.

THAI AMERICANS

by

Megan Ratner

The Thai family is highly structured, and each member has his or her specific place based on age, gender, and rank within the family. They can expect help and security as long as they remain within the confines of this order.

OVERVIEW

The Kingdom of Thailand was known as Siam until 1939. The Thai name for this nation is Prathet Thai or Muang Thai (Land of the Free). Located in Southeast Asia, it is somewhat smaller than Texas. The country covers an area of 198,456 square miles (514,000 square kilometers) and shares a northern border with Burma and Laos; an eastern boundary with Laos, Kampuchea, and the Gulf of Thailand; and a southern border with Malaysia. Burma and the Andaman Sea lie on its western edge.

Thailand has a population of just over 58 million people. Nearly 90 percent of the Thai people are Mongoloid, with lighter complexions than their Burmese, Kampuchean, and Malay neighbors. The largest minority group, about ten percent of the population, is Chinese, followed by the Malay and various tribal groups, including the Hmong, Iu Mien, Lisu, Luwa, Shan, and Karen. There are also 60,000 to 70,000 Vietnamese who live in Thailand. Nearly all people in the country follow the teachings of Buddhism. The 1932 constitution required that the king be a Buddhist, but it also called for freedom of worship, designating the monarch as "Defender of the Faith." The present king, Bhumibol Adulyadei, thus protects and improves the welfare of the small groups of Muslims (five percent), Christians (less than one percent), and Hindus (less than one percent) who also worship in Thailand. The Western name of the capital city is Bangkok; in

Thai, it is *Krung Thep* (City of Angels) or *Pra Nakhorn* (Heavenly Capital). It is the seat of the Royal House, Government, and Parliament. Thai is the official language of the country, with English the most widely spoken second language; Chinese and Malay are also spoken. Thailand's flag consists of a broad blue horizontal band at the center, with narrower bands of stripes above and below it; the inner ones are white, the outer ones red.

HISTORY

The Thai have an ancient and complex history. Early Thai people migrated south from China in the early centuries a.d. Despite the fact that their former kingdom was located in Yunnan, China, the Thai, or T'ai, are a distinct linguistic and cultural group whose southward migration led to the establishment of several nation states now known as Thailand, Laos, and Shan State in Myanma (Burma). By the sixth century a.d. an important network of agricultural communities had spread as far south as Pattani, close to Thailand's modern border with Malaysia, and to the northeastern area of present-day Thailand. The Thai nation became officially known as "Syam" in 1851 under the reign of King Mongkrut. Eventually, this name became synonymous with the Thai kingdom and the name by which it was known for many years. In the thirteenth and fourteenth centuries, several Thai principalities united and sought to break from their Khmer (early Cambodian) rulers. Sukothai, which the Thai consider the first independent Siamese state, declared its independence in 1238 (1219, according to some records). The new kingdom expanded into Khmer territory and onto the Malay peninsula. Sri Indradit, the Thai leader in the independence movement, became king of the Sukothai Dynasty. He was succeeded by his son, Ram Khamhaeng, who is regarded in Thai history as a hero. He organized a writing system (the basis for modern Thai) and codified the Thai form of Theravada Buddhism. This period is often viewed by modern-day Thais as a golden age of Siamese religion, politics, and culture. It was also one of great expansion: under Ram Khamheng, the monarchy extended to Nakhon Si Thammarat in the south, to Vientiane and Luang Prabang in Laos, and to Pegu in southern Burma.

Ayutthaya, the capital city, was established after Ram Khamheng's death in 1317. The Thai kings of Ayutthaya became quite powerful in the fourteenth and fifteenth centuries, adopting Khmer court customs and language and gaining more absolute authority. During this period, Europeans—the Dutch, Portuguese, French, English, and Spanish—began to pay visits to Siam, establishing diplomatic links and Christian missions within the kingdom. Early accounts note that the city and port of Ayutthaya astonished its European guests, who noted that London was nothing more than a village in comparison. On the whole, the Thai kingdom distrusted foreigners, but maintained a cordial relationship with the then-expanding colonial powers. During the reign of King Narai, two Thai diplomatic groups were sent on a friendship mission to King Louis XIV of France.

In 1765 Ayutthaya suffered a devastating invasion from the Burmese, with whom the Thais had endured hostile relations for at least 200 years. After several years of savage battle, the capital fell and the Burmese set about destroying anything the Thais held sacred, including temples, religious sculpture, and manuscripts. But the Burmese could not maintain a solid base of control, and they were ousted by Phraya Taksin, a first-generation Chinese Thai general who declared himself king in 1769 and ruled from a new capital, Thonburi, across the river from Bangkok.

Chao Phraya Chakri, another general, was crowned in 1782 under the title Rama I. He moved the capital across the river to Bangkok. In 1809, Rama II, Chakri's son, assumed the throne and reigned until 1824. Rama III, also known as Phraya Nang Klao, ruled from 1824 through 1851; like his predecessor, he worked hard to restore the Thai culture that had been almost completely destroyed in the Burmese invasion. Not until the reign of Rama IV, or King Mongkut, which began in 1851, did the Thai strengthen relations with Europeans. Rama IV worked with the British to establish trade treaties and modernize the government, while managing to avoid British and French colonialization. During the reign of his son, Rama V (King Chulalongkorn), who ruled from 1868 to 1910, Siam lost some territory to French Laos and British Burma. The short rule of Rama VI (1910-1925) saw the introduction of compulsory education and other educational reforms.

MODERN ERA

In the late 1920s and early 1930s, a group of Thai intellectuals and military personnel (many of whom had been educated in Europe) embraced democratic ideology and were able to effect a successful—and bloodless—*coup d'etat* against the absolute monarchy in Siam. This occurred during the reign of Rama VII, between 1925 and 1935. In its stead, the Thai developed a constitutional monarchy based on the British model, with a combined military-civilian group in charge of governing the country. The country's name was officially changed to Thailand in 1939 during prime minister Phibul Songkhram's government. (He had been a key military figure in the 1932 coup.)

Japan occupied Thailand during World War II and Phibul declared war on the United States and Great Britain. The Thai ambassador in Washington, however, refused to make the declaration. Seri Thai (Free Thai) underground groups worked with the allied powers both outside and within Thailand. The end of World War II terminated Phibul's regime. After a short stint of democratic civilian control, Phibul regained control in 1948, only to have much of his power taken away by General Sarit Thanarat, another military dictator. By 1958, Sarit had abolished the constitution, dissolved the parliament, and outlawed all political parties. He maintained power until his death in 1963.

Army officers ruled the country from 1964 to 1973, during which time the United States was given permission to establish army bases on Thai soil to support the troops fighting in Vietnam. The generals who ran the country during the 1970s closely aligned Thailand with the United States during the war. Civilian participation in government was allowed intermittently. In 1983 the constitution was amended to allow for a more democratically elected National Assembly, and the monarch exerted a moderating influence on the military and on civilian politicians.

The success of a promilitary coalition in the March 1992 elections touched off a series of disturbances in which 50 citizens died. The military violently suppressed a "pro-democracy" movement on the streets of Bangkok in May 1992. Following the intervention of the king, another round of elections was held in September of that year, when Chuan Leekphai, the leader of the Democrat Party, was elected. His government fell in 1995, and the chaos that resulted along with the nations large foreign debt led to the collapse of the Thai economy in 1997. Slowly, with help from the INM, the nation's economy has recovered.

SIGNIFICANT IMMIGRATION WAVES

Thai immigration to America was nearly nonexistent before 1960, when U.S. armed forces began arriving in Thailand during the Vietnam war. After interacting with Americans, Thais became more aware of the possibility for immigration to the United States. By the 1970s, some 5,000 Thais had emigrated to this country, at a ratio of three women to every man. The largest concentration of Thai immigrants can be found in Los Angeles and New York City. These new immigrants consisted of professionals, especially medical doctors and nurses, business entrepreneurs, and wives of men in the U.S. Air Force who had either been stationed in Thailand or had spent their vacations there while on active duty in Southeast Asia.

In 1980 the U.S. Census recorded concentrations of Thai near military installations, especially Air Force bases, in certain U.S. counties, ranging from Aroostook County (Loring Air Force Base) in Maine to Bossier Parish (Barksdale Air Force Base) in Louisiana and New Mexico's Curry County (Cannon Air Force Base). A few counties with a larger military presence such as Sarpy County in Nebraska, where the Strategic Air Command has been headquartered, and Solano County, California, where Travis Air Force Base is located, became home to larger groups. Fairly large concentrations of Thai were also found in Davis County, Indiana, the location of Hill Air Force Base, Eglin Air Force Base in Okaloosa County, Florida, and Wayne County, North Carolina, where Seymour Johnson Air Force Base is located.

The Thai Dam, an ethnic group from the mountain valleys of northern Vietnam and Laos were also counted as immigrants of Thai ancestry by the U.S. Census Bureau, though they are actually refugees from other countries. They are centered in Des Moines, Iowa. Like other Southeast Asian refugees of this area, they have coped with problems of housing, crime, social isolation, and depression. Most of them are employed, but in low-paying menial jobs that offer little in the way of advancement.

During the 1980s, Thais immigrated to the United States at an average rate of 6,500 per year. Student or temporary visitor visas were a frequent venue to the United States. The main attraction of the United States is the wide array of opportunities and higher wages. However, unlike people from other countries in Indochina, none whose original homes were in Thailand has been forced to come to the United States as refugees.

In general, Thai communities are tightly knit and mimic the social networks of their native land. As of 1990, there were approximately 91,275 people of Thai ancestry living in the United States. The greatest number of Thais are in California, some 32,064. Most of these people are clustered in the Los Angeles area, some 19,016. There are also high numbers of people whose temporary visas have expired who are believed to be in this area. The homes and businesses of Thai immigrants are dispersed throughout the city, but there is a high concentration in Hollywood, between Hollywood and Olympic boulevards and near Western Avenue. Thais own banks, gas stations, beauty parlors, travel agencies, grocery stores, and restaurants. Further exposure to the English language and American culture has caused the population to disperse somewhat. New York, with a Thai population of 6,230 (most in New York City) and Texas with 5,816 (primarily Houston and Dallas) have the second and third largest Thai populations, respectively.

ACCULTURATION AND ASSIMILATION

Thai Americans have adapted well to American society. Although they maintain their culture and ethnic traditions, they accept the norms as practiced in this society. This flexibility and adaptability has had a profound effect on first-generation American-born Thais, who tend to be quite assimilated or Americanized. According to members of the community, the young people's acceptance of American ways has made these new changes more acceptable to their parents, facilitating relations between "established" Americans and newcomers. With the high concentration of Thais in California and recent efforts to define who is and is not "native," members of the Thai community have expressed fears that there may be problems in the future.

Although many traditional beliefs are retained by Thai Americans, Thais often try to adjust their beliefs in order to live in the United States comfortably. Thais are often perceived as too adaptable and lacking in innovation. A common expression, *mai pen rai*, meaning "never mind" or "it doesn't matter," has been seen by some Americans as an indication of Thais' unwillingness to expand or develop ideas. Also, Thais are often mistaken for Chinese or Indochinese, which has led to misunderstandings, and offended Thais since Thai culture is bound up with Buddhism and has its own traditions, different from Chinese culture. In addition, Thais are often assumed to be refugees rather than immigrants by choice. Thai Americans are anxious that their presence be seen as a benefit, not a burden, to American society.

TRADITIONS, CUSTOMS, AND BELIEFS

Thais do not shake hands when they meet. Instead, they keep their elbows at their sides and press their palms together at about chest height in a prayer-like gesture called *wai*. The head is bent in this greeting; the lower the head, the more respect one shows.

Children are supposed to *wai* adults and they receive an acknowledgement in the form of *wai* or a smile in return. In Thai culture the feet are considered the lowest part of the body, both spiritually and physically. When visiting any religious edifice, feet must be pointed away from any Buddha images, which are always kept in high places and shown great respect. Thais consider pointing at something with one's feet to be the epitome of bad manners. The head is regarded as the highest part of the body; therefore Thais do not touch each other's hair, nor do they pat each other on the head. A favorite Thai proverb is: Do good and receive good; do evil and receive evil.

CUISINE

Perhaps the greatest contribution from the small Thai American community has been their cuisine. Thai restaurants remain a popular choice in large cities, and the Thai style of cooking has even begun to appear in frozen dinners. Thai cooking is light, pungent, and flavorful, and some dishes can be quite spicy. The mainstay of Thai cooking, as in the rest of Southeast Asia, is rice. In fact, the Thai words for "rice" and "food" are synonymous. Meals often include one spicy dish, such as a curry, with other meat and vegetable side dishes. Thai food is eaten with a spoon.

Presentation of food for the Thai is a work of art, especially if the meal marks a special occasion. Thais are renowned for their ability to carve fruit; melons, mandarins, and pomelos, to name just a few, are carved in the shapes of intricate flowers, classic designs, or birds. Staples of Thai cuisine include coriander roots, peppercorns, and garlic (which are often ground together), lemon grass, *nam pla* (fish sauce), and *kapi* (shrimp paste). The meal generally includes soup, one or two *kaengs* (dishes that include thin, clear, soup-like gravy; though Thais describe these sauces as "curry," it is not what most Westerners know as curry), and as many *krueng kieng* (side dishes) as possible. Among these, there might be a *phad* (stir-fried) dish, something with *phrik* (hot chili peppers) in it, or a *thawd* (deep-fried) dish. Thai cooks use very few recipes, preferring to taste and adjust seasonings as they cook.

TRADITIONAL COSTUMES

Traditional clothing for Thai women consists of a *prasin*, or a wrap-around skirt (sarong), which is worn with a fitted, long-sleeved jacket. Among the most beautiful costumes are those worn by dancers of classical Thai ballet. Women wear a tight-fitting under jacket and a *panung*, or skirt, which is made

These Thai American girls are working on a Tournament of Roses Parade float of a dragon.

of silk, silver, or gold brocade. The *panung* is pleated in front, and a belt holds it in place. A pailletted and jeweled velvet cape fastens to the front of the belt and drapes down behind to nearly the hem of the *panung*. A wide jewelled collar, armlets, necklace, and bracelets make up the rest of the costume, which is capped with a *chadah*, the temple-style headdress. Dancers are sewn into their costumes before a performance. The jewels and metal thread can make the costume weigh nearly 40 pounds. Men's costumes feature tight-fitting silver thread brocade jackets with epaulets and an ornately embroidered collar. Embroidered panels hang from his belt, and his calf-length pants are made of silk.

His jewelled headdress has a tassel on the right, while the woman's is on the left. Dancers wear no shoes. For everyday life, Thais wear sandals or Western-style footwear. Shoes are always removed when entering a house. For the last 100 years, Western clothing has become the standard form of clothing in Thailand's urban areas. Thai Americans wear ordinary American clothes for everyday occasions.

HOLIDAYS

Thais are well known for enjoying festivities and holidays, even if they are not part of their culture; Bangkok residents were known to take part in the Christmas and even Bastille Day celebrations of the resident foreign communities. Thai holidays include New Year's Day (January 1); Chinese New Year (February 15); Magha Puja, which occurs on the full moon of the third lunar month (February) and commemorates the day when 1,250 disciples heard the Buddha's first sermon; Chakri Day (April 6), which marks the enthronement of King Rama I; Songkran (mid-April), the Thai New Year, an occasion when caged birds and fish are set free and water is thrown by everyone on everyone else; Coronation Day (May 5); Visakha Puja (May, on the full moon of the sixth lunar month) is the holiest of Buddhist days, celebrating Lord Buddha's birth, enlightenment, and death; Queen's Birthday, August 12; King's Birthday, December 5.

LANGUAGE

A member of the Sino-Tibetan family of languages, Thai is one of the oldest languages in East or Southeast Asia. Some anthropologists have hypothesized that it may even predate Chinese. The two languages share certain similarities since they are monosyllabic tonal languages; that is, since there are only 420 phonetically different words in Thai, a single syllable can have multiple meanings. Meanings are determined by five different tones (in Thai): a high or low tone; a level tone; and a falling or rising tone. For example, depending on the inflection, the syllable *mai* can mean "widow," "silk," "burn," "wood," "new," "not?" or "not." In addition to the tonal similarities with Chinese, Thai has also borrowed from Pali and Sanskrit, notably the phonetic alphabet conceived by King Ram Khamhaeng in 1283 and still in use today. The signs of the alphabet take their pattern from Sanskrit; there are also supplemental signs for tones, which are like vowels and can stand beside or above the consonant to which they belong. This alphabet is similar to the alphabets of the neighboring countries of Burma, Laos, and Kampuchea. Compulsory educa-tion in Thailand is up to the sixth grade and the literacy rate is over 90 percent. There are 39 universities and colleges and 36 Teachers Training Colleges in Thailand to meet the needs of thousands of secondary school students who want higher educational attainment.

GREETINGS AND OTHER COMMON EXPRESSIONS

Common Thai greetings are: *Sa wat dee*—Good morning, afternoon, or evening, as well as good-bye (by the host); *Lah kon*—Good-bye (by the guest); *Krab*— sir; *Ka*—madam; *Kob kun*—Thank you; *Prode*—Please; *Kor hai choke dee*—Good luck; *Farang*—foreigner; *Chern krab* (if the speaker is male), or *Chern kra* (if the speaker is female)—Please, you are welcome, it's all right, go ahead, you first (depending on the circumstances).

FAMILY AND COMMUNITY DYNAMICS

Traditional Thai families are closely knit, often incorporating servants and employees. Togetherness is a hallmark of the family structure: people never sleep alone, even in houses with ample room, unless they ask to do so. Virtually no one is left to live alone in an apartment or house. As a consequence, Thais make few complaints about academic dormitories or the dormitories provided by factories.

The Thai family is highly structured, and each member has his or her specific place based on age, gender, and rank within the family. They can expect help and security as long as they remain within the confines of this order. Relationships are strictly defined and named with terms so precise that they reveal the relation (parental, sibling, uncle, aunt, cousin), the relative age (younger, older), and side of the family (maternal or paternal). These terms are used more often in conversation than the person's given name. The biggest change that settlement in the United States has brought has been the diminishing of extended families. These are prevalent in Thailand, but the lifestyle and mobility of American society has made the extended Thai family hard to maintain.

SPIRIT HOUSES

In Thailand, many houses and buildings have an accompanying spirit house, or a place for the property guardian spirit (*Phra phum*) to reside. Some Thais believe that families living in a home without a spirit house cause spirits to live with the family, which invites trouble. Spirit houses, which are usually about the same size as a birdhouse, are mounted on a pedestal and resemble Thai temples. In Thailand, large buildings such as hotels may have a spirit house as large as an average family dwelling. The spirit house is given the best location on the property and is shaded by the main house. Its position is planned at the time of the building's construction; then it is ceremonially erected. Corresponding improvements, including additions, are also made to the spirit house whenever modifications are made to the main house.

WEDDINGS

Arrival in the United States has brought an increase in self-determined marriages. Unlike other Asian countries, Thailand has been far more permissive toward marriages of personal choice, though parents generally have some say in the matter. Marriages tend to take place between families of equal social and economic status. There are no ethnic or religious restrictions, and intermarriage in Thailand is quite common, especially between Thai and Chinese, and Thai and Westerners.

Wedding ceremonies can be ornate affairs, or there may be no ceremony at all. If a couple lives together for a while and has a child together, they are recognized as "de facto married." Most Thais do have a ceremony, however, and wealthier members of the community consider this essential. Prior to the wedding, the two families agree on the expenses of the ceremony and the "bride price." The couple begins their wedding day with a religious ritual in the early morning and by receiving blessings from monks. During the ceremony, the couple kneels side by side. An astrologer or a monk chooses a favorable time for the couple's heads to be linked with joined loops of sai mongkon (white thread) by a senior elder. He pours sacred water over their hands, which they allow to drip into bowls of flowers. Guests bless the couple by pouring sacred water in the same way. The second part of the ceremony is essentially a secular practice. Thais do not make any vows to one another. Rather, the two linked but independent circles of the white thread serve to symbolically emphasize that the man and woman have each retained their individual identities while, at the same time, joining their destinies.

One tradition, practiced primarily in the countryside, is to have "sympathetic magic" performed by an older, successfully married couple. This duo lies in the marriage bed before the newlyweds, where they say many auspicious things about the bed and its superiority as a place for conception. They then get off the bed and strew it with symbols of fertility, such as a tomcat, bags of rice, sesame seeds and coins, a stone pestle, or a bowl of rainwater. The newlyweds are supposed to keep these objects (except the tomcat) in their bed for three days.

Even in cases in which the marriage has been sealed by a ceremony, divorce is a simple matter: if both parties consent, they sign a mutual statement to this effect at the district office. If only one party wants the divorce, he or she must show proof of the other's desertion or lack of support for one year. The divorce rate among Thais, both officially and unofficially, is relatively low compared to the American divorce rate, and the remarriage rate is high.

BIRTH

Pregnant women are not given any gifts before a baby is born so as to keep them from being scared by evil spirits. These evil spirits are thought to be the spirits of women who died childless and unmarried. For a minimum of three days to a month after birth, the baby is still considered a spirit child. It is customary to refer to a newborn as frog, dog, toad, or other animal terms that are seen as helpful in escaping the attention of evil spirits. Parents often ask a monk or an elder to select an appropriate name for their child, usually of two or more syllables, which is used for legal and official purposes. Nearly all Thais have a one-syllable nickname, which usually translates as frog, rat, pig, fatty, or many versions of tiny. Like the formal name, a nickname is intended to keep the evil spirits away.

FUNERALS

Many Thais consider ngarn sop (the cremation ceremony) the most important of all the rites. It is a family occasion and the presence of Buddhist monks is necessary. One baht coin is placed in the mouth of the corpse (to enable the dead person to buy his or her way into purgatory), and the hands are arranged into a wai and tied with white thread. A banknote, two flowers, and two candles are placed between the hands. White thread is used to tie the ankles as well, and the mouth and eyes are sealed with wax. The corpse is placed in a coffin with the feet facing west, the direction of the setting sun and of death.

Dressed in mourning black or white, the relatives gather around the body to hear the sutras of the monks who sit in a row on raised padded seats or on a platform. On the day that the body is cremated, which for persons of high rank can be as long as a year after the funeral ceremony, the coffin is carried to the site feet first. In order to appease the spirits who are drawn to the funeral activities, rice is scattered on the ground. All the mourners are given candles and incense bouquets. As tokens of respect for the deceased, these are thrown on the funeral pyre, which consists of piles of wood under an ornate paste pagoda. The most exalted guest then officiates at the cremation by being the first to light this structure. The actual cremation that follows is attended by the next of kin only and is usually held a few yards from the ritual funeral pyre. The occasion is sometimes followed by a meal for guests who may have traveled from far away to attend the ceremony. On that evening and the two following, monks come to the house to chant blessings for the departed soul and for the protection of the living. According to Thai tradition, the departed family member is advancing along the cycle of death and rebirth toward the state of perfect peace; thus, sadness has no place at this rite.

EDUCATION

Education has traditionally been of paramount importance to Thais. Educational accomplishment is considered a status-enhancing achievement. Until the late nineteenth century, the responsibility for educating the young lay entirely with the monks in the temple. Since the beginning of this century, however, overseas study and degrees have been actively sought and highly prized. Originally, this sort of education was open only to royalty, but, according to Immigration and Naturalization Services information, some 835 Thai students came to study in the United States in 1991.

RELIGION

Nearly 95 percent of all Thais identify themselves as Theravada Buddhists. Theravada Buddhism originated in India and stresses three principal aspects of existence: *dukkha* (suffering, dissatisfaction, "disease"), *annicaa* (impermanence, transiency of all things), and *anatta* (non-substantiality of reality; no permanence of the soul). These principles, which were articulated by Siddhartha Gautama in the sixth century b.c., contrasted with the Hindu belief in an eternal, blissful Self. Buddhism, therefore, was originally a heresy against India's Brahman religion.

Gautama was given the title Buddha, or "enlightened one." He advocated the "eight-fold path" (*atthangika-magga*) which requires high ethical standards and conquering desire. The concept of reincarnation is central. By feeding monks, making regular donations to temples, and worshipping regu-

larly at the *wat* (temple), Thais try to improve their situation—acquire enough merit (*bun*)—to lessen the number of rebirths, or subsequent reincarnations, a person must undergo before reaching Nirvana. In addition, the accumulation of merit helps determine the quality of the individual's station in future lives. *Tham bun*, or merit making, is an important social and religious activity for Thais. Because Buddhist teachings emphasize philanthropic donations as part of achieving merit, Thais tend to be supportive of a wide range of charities. The emphasis, however, is on charities that assist the indigent in Thailand.

Ordination into the Buddhist order of monks often serves to mark the entry into the adult world. Ordination is for men only, though women can become nuns by shaving their heads, wearing white robes, and obtaining permission to reside in the nun's quarters on grounds within the temple. They do not officiate at any rituals. Most Thai men *Buat Phra* (enter the monkhood) at some point in their lives, often just prior to their marriage. Many only stay for a short period, sometimes as little as a few days, but in general they remain for at least one *phansa*, the three-month Buddhist Lent that coincides with the rainy season. Among the prerequisites for ordination is four years' education. Most ordinations occur in July, just before Lent.

The *thankwan nak* ceremony serves to strengthen the *kwan*, or the soul, the life essence, of the person to be ordained. During this time, he is called a *nak*, which means dragon, referring to a Buddhist myth about a dragon who became a monk. In the ceremony, the *nak's* head and eyebrows are shaved to symbolize his rejection of vanity. For three to four hours, a professional master of ceremonies sings of the mother's pain in giving birth to the child and emphasizes the many filial obligations of the young man. The ceremony concludes with all relatives and friends gathered in a circle holding a white thread and then passing three lighted candles in a clockwise direction. Guests generally give gifts of money.

The following morning, the *nak*, dressed in white (to symbolize purity), is carried on the shoulders of his friends under tall umbrellas in a colorful procession. He bows before his father, who hands him the saffron robes he will wear as a monk. He leads his son to the abbot and the four or more other monks who are seated on a raised platform before the main Buddha image. The *nak* asks permission for ordination after prostrating himself three times to the abbot. The abbot reads a scripture and drapes a yellow sash on the *nak's* body to symbolize acceptance for ordination. He is then taken out of view and dressed in the saffron robes by the two monks who will oversee his instruction. He then requests the ten basic vows of a novice monk and repeats each as it is recited to him.

The father presents alms bowls and other gifts to the abbot. Facing the Buddha, the candidate then answers questions to show that he has met the conditions for entry into the monkhood. The ceremony concludes with all the monks chanting and the new monk pouring water from a silver container into a bowl to symbolize the transference of all merit he has acquired from being a monk to his parents. They in turn perform the same ritual to transfer some of their new merit to other relatives. The ritual's emphasis is on his identity as a Buddhist and his newfound adult maturity. At the same time, the rite reinforces the link between generations and the importance of family and community.

Thai Americans have accommodated themselves to the environment here by adapting their religious practices when necessary. One of the most far-reaching of these changes was the switch from lunar calendar days to the conventional Saturday or Sunday services that are offered in the United States.

EMPLOYMENT AND ECONOMIC TRADITIONS

Thai men tend to aspire to military or civil service jobs. Rural women have been traditionally engaged in running businesses, while educated women are involved in all types of professions. In the United States, most Thais own small businesses or work as skilled laborers. Many women have opted for nursing careers. There are no Thai-only labor unions, nor do Thais particularly dominate one profession.

POLITICS AND GOVERNMENT

Thai Americans tend not to be active in community politics in this country, but are more concerned with issues in Thailand. This reflects the general insulation of the community, where there are specific delineations between northern and southern Thais and where intercommunity outreach with other groups has been almost nonexistent. Thai Americans are quite active in Thai politics and they keep an active watch on economic, political and social movements there.

INDIVIDUAL AND GROUP CONTRIBUTIONS

Many Thai Americans work in the health-care industry. Boondharm Wongananda (1935-) is a noted surgeon in Silver Spring, Maryland, and the executive director of the Thais for Thai Association. Also worthy of mention is Phongpan Tana (1946–), the director of nurses in a Long Beach, California hospital. Several other Thai Americans have become educators, company executives, and engineers. Some Thai Americans are also beginning to enter the field of American politics; Asuntha Maria Ming-Yee Chiang (1970–) is a legislative correspondent in Washington, D.C.

MEDIA

TELEVISION

THAI-TV USA.
Offers programming in Thai in the Los Angeles area.

Contact: Paul Khongwittaya.
Address: 1123 North Vine Street, Los Angeles, California 90038.
Telephone: (213) 962-6696.
Fax: (213) 464-2312.

ORGANIZATIONS AND ASSOCIATIONS

American Siam Society.
Cultural organization that encourages investigation of art, science, and literature in relation to Thailand and its neighboring countries.

Address: 633 24th Street, Santa Monica, California 90402-3135.
Telephone: (213) 393-1176.

Thai Society of Southern California.
Contact: K. Jongsatityoo, Public Relations Officer.
Address: 2002 South Atlantic Boulevard, Monterey Park, California 91754.
Telephone: (213) 720-1596.
Fax: (213) 726-2666.

MUSEUMS AND RESEARCH CENTERS

Asia Resource Center.
Founded in 1974. The center includes among its holdings 15 drawers of clippings on East and Southeast Asia, from 1976 through the present, as well as photograph files, films, video cassettes, and slide programs.

Contact: Roger Rumpf, Executive Director.

Address: Box 15275, Washington, D.C. 20003.
Telephone: (202) 547-1114.
Fax: (202) 543-7891.

Cornell University Southeast Asia Program.
The center concentrates its activities on the social and political conditions in Southeast Asian countries, including the history and culture of Thailand. It studies cultural stability and change, especially the consequences of Western influences and offers Thai lessons and distributes Thai cultural readers.

Contact: Randolph Barker, Director.
Address: 180 Uris Hall, Ithaca, New York 14853.
Telephone: (607) 255-2378.
Fax: (607) 254-5000.

**University of California, Berkeley
South/Southeast Asia Library Service.**
This library contains a special Thai collection in addition to its substantial holdings on the social sciences and humanities of Southeast Asia. The entire collection comprises some 400,000 monographs, dissertations, microfilm, pamphlets, manuscripts, videotapes, sound recordings, and maps.

Contact: Virginia Jing-yi Shih.
Address: 438 Doe Library, Berkeley, California 94720-6000.

Telephone: (510) 642-3095.
Fax: (510) 643-8817.

Yale University Southeast Asia Collection.
This collection of materials centers on the social sciences and humanities of Southeast Asia. Holdings include some 200,000 volumes.

Contact: Charles R. Bryant, Curator.
Address: Sterling Memorial Library, Yale University, New Haven, Connecticut 06520.
Telephone: (203) 432-1859.
Fax: (203) 432-7231.

SOURCES FOR ADDITIONAL STUDY

Cooper, Robert, and Nanthapa Cooper. *Culture Shock*. Portland, Oregon: Graphic Arts Center Publishing Company, 1990.

Statistical Yearbook of the Immigration and Naturalization Service. Washington, D.C.: Immigration and Naturalization Service, 1993.

Thailand and Burma. London: The Economist Intelligence Unit, 1994.

TIBETAN AMERICANS

by
Olivia Miller

The chant of Tibetan monks is recognized around the world as the music of Tibet. The Tibetans cultivated multiphonic singing, in which a singer intones three simultaneous notes, creating a complete chord.

OVERVIEW

Tibet is officially known as the Tibet Autonomous Region of the People's Republic of China. Located in the highlands of southwest China, Tibet is approximately 14,800 feet above sea level. It has a land area of 463,320 square miles, which is twice the size of Texas, and is home to five million people. With a history dating back to 127 B.C., Tibet was an independent country until 1949, when it was invaded and occupied by the People's Republic of China.

Lhasa is Tibet's capital and only major city. Tibetan is the language spoken by most of the province's native peoples, even though Chinese is recognized as the official language. Until 1949, Tibet's national religion was Lamaism Buddhism, which was headed by the Dalai Lama. The Dalai Lama is revered by Tibetans as the spiritual and political leader of the nation. The current Dalai Lama lives in exile in India, where he heads a community of 120,000 Tibetan refugees. He leads an international campaign to regain Tibet's freedom and received the Nobel Peace Prize in 1989 for his efforts. Until the early 1980s, Tibet was virtually inaccessible to Westerners.

The Tibetan flag consists of a yellow border around alternating vertical bands of blue and red. The center of the flag contains a snow-capped mountain peak with a yellow sun above. Below the peak are two swirling jewels that are held between two lions facing each other.

HISTORY

According to tradition, Tibetans trace their ancestry to the copulation of an ape, a manifestation of wisdom, and an ogress, a form of the goddess Tara, whose offspring gave birth to the Tibetan people. Monkey gods are part of the religious folklore of India and other Buddhist countries. Chinese scholars claim that Tibetans descended from the Quiang, nomadic shepherds of western China who first appeared around 1000 B.C. During its history, Tibet has ruled parts of China, India, Nepal, central Asia, and the Middle East. The Tibetan nation gained world prominence in the sixth and seventh centuries as a silk and spice trading center. The Mongolians under Genghis Khan conquered Tibet during the Middle Ages, but bestowed political power on the head of the *Lamanists* Buddhist organization. In the seventeenth century, China gained sovereignty over Tibet and ruled until the British invaded in 1904. At the Anglo-Chinese convention in 1906, the Chinese again were recognized as the sovereign power in Tibet. By 1907, the governments of Britain and Russia agreed not to interfere in Tibetan affairs. The Tibetans rebelled against China in 1912 and expelled all Chinese officials.

"[O]ne night the Chinese Communists came there. They were shooting guns, machine guns, you know. So we were all scared. There were eight hundred of us in that monastery–it was a small monastery for Tibet. Only six of us made it away."

Labring Sakya, cited in *American Mosaic: The Immigrant Experience in the Words of Those Who Lived It,* Joan Morrison and Charlotte Fox Zabusky, (E.P. Dutton, New York, 1980).

MODERN ERA

The People's Republic of China invaded Tibet in 1949 and, after defeating the small Tibetan army, established control of the province. For nearly ten years after the Chinese invasion, the Dalai Lama remained in Tibet. In 1959, the Tibetans rebelled against the Chinese. The People's Liberation Army crushed the uprising, killing more than 87,000 Tibetans. The Dalai Lama, members of his government, and roughly 80,000 Tibetans escaped from Tibet. They sought political asylum in India, Nepal and Bhutan, and announced the formation of a Tibetan government-in-exile. The government of India welcomed the Tibetan refugees, but did not grant recognition to the Dalai Lama's government-in-exile. Since 1959, fifty-four refugee settlements have been established in India, Nepal, and Bhutan.

More than 1.2 million Tibetans died as a result of the Chinese invasion and occupation of Tibet. The United Nations passed three resolutions on Tibet in 1959, 1961, and 1965 expressing concern over human rights violations. The Tibetan government-in-exile has been reorganized along democratic principles in order to preserve Tibetan culture and education, and seek the restoration of Tibet's freedom. Tibetan people throughout the world consider this government- in-exile, which is based in Dharamsala, India, to be the sole legitimate government of Tibet.

The Chinese military presence in Tibet is estimated to number around 500,000 uniformed personnel. China is also believed to have stationed approximately 90 nuclear warheads in Tibet. China's North-west Nuclear Weapons Research and Design Academy, which is located in Tibet's north-eastern area of Amdo, is reported to have dumped an unknown quantity of radioactive waste on the Tibetan plateau. In 1999, various pro-Tibet organizations protested the World Bank's funding of China's WPRP project, which involved the transfer of about 61,775 non-Tibetan settlers into Tibet. The Chinese government has actively encouraged Chinese emigration to Tibet and Tibetans have become a minority within their own country.

By the late 1990s there were over 120,000 Tibetans in exile, including more than 5,000 living outside of the Indian subcontinent. Large numbers of Tibetans continue to leave their country in order to escape Chinese persecution. Many of these exiles have sought the assistance of the United Nations High Commission for Refugees (UNHCR), foreign donor agencies, and the governments of India, Nepal, and Bhutan.

SIGNIFICANT IMMIGRATION WAVES

The earliest Tibetans immigrating to the United States were classified as "other Asian," and immigration records show that between 1881 and 1890, 1,910 "other Asians" were admitted. It is not known how many of these were from Tibet. The Chinese occupation of Tibet in 1949 prompted an exodus of Tibetans, most of who settled in neighboring India, although some came to the United States as refugees. Refugees are considered non-immigrants when initially admitted into the United States but are not included in non-immigrant admission data. Therefore, ancestry records are the most revealing indicators of the Tibetan American population. According to the 1990 U. S. Census, there were 2,185 Americans with Tibetan and other Asian ancestry. Most, if not all, Tibetan Americans have arrived as refugees. The Refugee Act of 1980 allowed refugee admission of persons for whom the United States expressed humanitarian concerns. Transportation arrangements to the United States are usually made through the International Organization for Migration. Refugees are expected to repay the cost of their transportation. At the port of entry, the Immigration and Naturalization Service admits the refugees officially to the United States and authorizes employment.

As part of the Immigration Act of 1990, 1,000 displaced Tibetans were given special immigrant visas and have since resettled throughout the United States. The 18 Tibetans who entered in 1993 as refugees had not been granted asylum by 1997, according to a U. S. State Department report. Tibetans, classified as citizens of China, were not eligible to participate in the 1998 DV-99 diversity lottery. The diversity lottery is conducted under the terms of Section 203(c) of the Immigration and Nationality Act and makes available 50,000 permanent resident visas annually to persons from countries with low rates of immigration to the United States.

SETTLEMENT PATTERNS

The majority of Tibetan Americans have settled in southern California, where Tibetan Buddhism is the fastest growing branch of Buddhism. Forty percent of all Buddhists in the United States live in California. Approximately 90 Tibetan families are scattered throughout southern California, most of them assisted by the Los Angeles Friends of Tibet Association. The Tibetan American community is close-knit and supportive.

ACCULTURATION AND ASSIMILATION

Many Tibetan Americans keep their cultural tradition of having only one name. Like other refugees with limited education, Tibetan Americans often take menial jobs in the community. However, unlike other refugees, Tibetan Americans often receive extensive aid from local organizations because the plight of Tibetans is widely publicized. For example, the Tibetan Association of Ithaca, New York, and Area Friends of Tibet sponsors an annual Week of Tibet, with events that celebrate Tibetan culture, foods, folk dancing, and fund-raising for Tibetan causes. Similarly, the Tibetan Cultural and Community Service Center (TCCSC) of California provides social services and referrals to the Tibetan

This Tibetan American Buddhist is attending a Lollapalooza concert.

community. Many Tibetans across the nation have received housing and clothing assistance, financial and legal assistance, and immigration and citizenship training from the TCCSC. The TCCSC also provides counseling to Tibetans so that they can become self-reliant, which is an important step toward eventual self-determination. The TCCSC has been recognized as a member of the Asian Pacific Planning Council and honored by the City of Los Angeles and the California Assembly.

TRADITIONS, CUSTOMS, AND BELIEFS

Tibetans do not use surnames, preferring single or double first names. For men, a middle name is given by the *lama*, a Buddhist holy man. Tibetans throw *tsampa*, roasted barley flour, into the air to celebrate marriages, birthdays, New Year's Day, and all other important events. The tradition dates from the seventh century, when it was a formality at the enthronement of kings. At New Year's celebrations, two people would meet. One person would make an offering, then take a pinch from the tip of a mound of tsampa and throw it into the air, yelling, "*Tashi Delek*." The person receiving the offering would then recite: "Tashi Delek, good fortune and good health, May you achieve unchanging happiness, and may it ever increase." Throwing tsampa in the air is an expression of good wishes for one's own and others' happiness and for the overcoming of all obstacles.

Many of the Tibetans' values are established through their Buddhist beliefs. *Vajras* (prayer wheels

that are spun clockwise), bells, and beads are important in Tibetan Buddhism. Vajras may have nine, five, or three spokes. The upper sets of spokes of a five-spoked vajra symbolize the five wisdoms of Buddhism. A bell can be eight, twelve, sixteen, eighteen or twenty-two finger-widths in height. Its base must be round, above which is a vase surmounted by the face of the goddess Prajnaparamita. Above these are a lotus, a moon disc, and finally a vajra. The hollow of the bell symbolizes the wisdom recognizing emptiness. The clapper represents the sound of emptiness. The eight lotus petals are the four mothers and four goddesses, and the vase represents the vase containing the nectar of accomplishment.

Paired with the vajra, the bell represents wisdom, and as wisdom and method are an undivided unity, so the vajra and bell are never parted or employed separately. Beads are mainly used to count *mantras* (prayers). Beads made of bodhi seed or wood can be used for many purposes, such as counting all kinds of mantras. The string common to all beads should consist of nine threads, which symbolize Buddha Vajradhara and the eight Bodhisattvas. The large bead at the end stands for the wisdom that recognizes emptiness and the cylindrical bead surmounting it, emptiness itself; both symbolize having vanquished all opponents.

PROVERBS

Tibetans liberally sprinkle proverbs into daily conversations as a substitute for slang phrases. Proverbs have balance and rhythm, but do not rhyme. Some examples include the following: Whatever happiness is in the world, it has arisen from a wish for the welfare of others; Whatever misery is in the world, it has arisen from a wish for our own welfare; Look not on the height of the mountain, but look at the size of the mountain (tackle the problem where you are); Those who do not love comfort can do 100 deeds, those who cannot love hardship cannot do one deed; If one does not cross the doorstep's sill, one cannot arrive anyplace; A braggart has no courage; Muddy water has no depth; Having eaten together, you should agree in counsel (sharing food together has a special significance of friendship); The life of all living beings is like the bubbles of water; The stripes of wild beasts are on the outside, the stripes of man are on the inside; When the blind escorts the blind, both fall into the river; The ants do not accept each other's lineage (ants touch feelers to ascertain whether friend or foe); If one desires misery, let him buy an aged horse; If one is not happy inside, one's work cannot be done outside; If the mouth and stomach are considered first, then promise and debts follow later; One mouth, two tongues (means two-faced); If one is without soup on earth, of what use is a ladle in heaven?; After calling a dog, one should not beat him; A hoe digs, a broom sweeps (everything has its proper use); and When a man becomes old, he thinks of his homeland.

CUISINE

Tibetan restaurants are now found in many U. S. cities. Tibetan foods are practical reflecting the nomadic and often severe lifestyle of Tibetans. Cuisine tends toward oils, dough, spices, and meats that are usually boiled, then stir-fried. *Tsampa* is a flour ground from highland barley that is mixed with tea or butter. A typical Tibetan dinner begins with spicy cold appetizers followed by a main course of several hot dishes accompanied by noodles or dumplings. *Momo* are steamed dumplings made with onion, cumin, garlic, minced lamb or beef, and soya sauce. *Then thuk* is a noodle soup made with fresh spinach, onion, garlic, ginger, and meat. *Shamday* is a Tibetan curry made with bean thread noodles, ginger, onion, turmeric, lamb or beef, potatoes, and a handful of seaweed. *Sha-balé* is a deep-fried dough surrounding beef or lamb to form meat pockets seasoned with onion, ginger, garlic, cumin, and soya sauce.

MUSIC

The chant of Tibetan monks is recognized around the world as the music of Tibet. The Tibetans cultivated multiphonic singing, in which a singer intones three simultaneous notes, creating a complete chord.

Chanting is accompanied by musical instruments unique to the area such as the *dranyem*, a traditional stringed instrument. The most unusual Tibetan ritual instruments are long, copper *rag-dung* trumpets. These straight, conically bored natural horns vary in length from 3 to 20 feet. They are produced in sections that can be telescoped for portability. Each horn has a fairly shallow cup mouthpiece and, like the Western bugle, is capable of producing different tones. These horns are used to play a drone for chanting, sometimes in thirds or fifths. There are also smaller hand trumpets with dragon heads at the bell end. The players tend to concentrate on one note from which they slide up and down. Tibetan copper curved horns, about 15 inches long, are also played at Buddhist celebrations.

Tibetan wind bells are hand-crafted, solid brass wind bells used to keep devils away from the home. The handbell and the *dorje* are the principal ritual objects of Tantric Buddhism. Traditionally they are used together, the bell in the left hand, the *dorje* in the right. Representing the passive and active qualities that reach perfection only when united, they function as the *yin* and *yang* in the Chinese tradition. The handbell and *dorje* also represent the union of wisdom and compassion, which is enlightenment. These bells produce an incredible sound when rubbed with a playing stick or when rung.

Tingsha are miniature cymbals that are used to encourage "hungry ghosts" to accept offerings. Tibetans believe that by relieving the ghosts' hunger and making an offering, their suffering is diminished. Enlightenment can be achieved only when all suffering is eliminated. *Tingsha* have exceptional resonance and sound, excellent for musical accents, healing or spiritual practice. Singing bowls are traditionally struck to produce a complex and beautiful sound that is designed to aid meditation. They are also filled with water, rice, or flowers as offerings to the deities. When circled with a playing stick, singing bowls hum in a voice full of wonderful harmonics and overtones. They are made from a mixture of five to seven metals, hand-turned on a lathe, then hammered to the desired hardness and pitch. Mantras are recited as the bowls are made and, according to Tibetan legend, are absorbed into the metals. These mantras are then released when the bowl is played.

TRADITIONAL COSTUMES

Traditional Tibetan costumes are made from the wool of yaks or sheep. Fabric is woven in relatively narrow widths and long lengths, cut and assembled side-to-side for garments, blankets and other textile uses. The decoration of textiles is achieved by *plangi* (tie-dying). Typical patterns, often used in various combinations, include circles inscribed with crosses, multicolored stripes, and Buddhist motifs. The use of strong colors is commonplace. Costumes from royal or urban circles in Tibet and Bhutan may be similar in form to the garments of nomadic citizens. However, royal costumes are made of silk and decorated with exquisitely fine, difficult, woven designs.

Most Tibetans wear the *nambu*, a wool sash about eight inches wide, usually white for poor people and colorful for the wealthy. Many Tibetans also use yak hide boots. These knee-high boots are slit in the back and tied at the top with a colorful garter. The upper portions of the boots are made of leather, felt, or cloth and are often red in color. Men also wear pouches on the right side of their belts to hold a small knife and a pair of chopsticks.

The headdress is the chief adornment for Tibetan women. Because symbols of family wealth are often worn in the hair, married women wear more ornaments than unmarried women. The traditional headdress has a wooden framework covered with coral, pearls, amber, and turquoise. Tibetan women wear jewelry, including bangles, bracelets, and earrings, that are so large that the holes in their earlobes may be an eighth of an inch in diameter. Nomadic Tibetan women smear black ointment on their faces to protect themselves from the harsh climate.

Costumes for rituals usually include a mask, called *Ba*. Masks serve various functions for the Tibetan people. Some are hung in temples or used in ritual ceremonies, while others are used in theatrical performances. The faces on the masks range from deities to men and animals, with the expressions carved to display a certain characteristic such as honesty, harshness, greed, or humor. According to tradition, masks of Buddha may appear in either benevolent or wrathful manifestations. The *Rdo-rje-gro-lod*, the Wrathful Guardian Deity, and the *Bhairava Vajra*, the fearful Guardian Deity, are commonly seen in mask design since they symbolize the two deities' doctrines of "wrath" and "fear."

DANCES AND SONGS

Tibetan dance celebrates an enchanted world of wizards, demons, singing maidens, dancing yaks, acrobatic dances, thunderous horns, and lilting melodies. Two times per year, the great Lama Dances are celebrated. Mahakala Bernagchen is the protector of a lineage honored by the dance ceremony held every year on the twenty-ninth day of the twelfth Tibetan month. The second dance ceremony is held on the tenth day of the fourth month

Four ceremonial

dancers of a

Kalachakra

Initiation, a Tibetan

Buddhist ritual in

Madison,

Wisconsin

to celebrate Guru Rinpoche, who brought Buddhism to Tibet in the eighth century. During the sixth month of the Tibetan calendar, the people dress in festival costumes and jewelry and congregate around their local monastery for special festivities. For these colorful and fascinating ceremonies, all the dancers wear elaborate silk brocade costumes with unusual, unique deity masks. Other Tibetan dances include the *Via bo Shana*, the black hat dance, which is performed by three people. *Ronshu Chinen* is a dance performed by the people of northeastern Tibet. *Agi Ulu*, a harvest dance from southwestern Tibet, is the dance of the maiden *Ulu*.

HOLIDAYS

Tibetan holidays are mostly Buddhist celebrations. Across the United States, there are roughly 1,100 Buddhist meditation centers serving 1.5 million Buddhists. There are more than 100 different types of Buddhism represented in the United States, and Tibetan Americans have ample opportunities to celebrate Buddhist holidays. Public holidays in Tibet include: January 1, Western New Year's Day,

February (for three days), Tibetan New Year's Day; also February (for three days), the Chinese Spring festival; May 1, Labour Day; May 4, Youth Day, June 1, Children's Day; and August 1, Army Day.

HEALTH ISSUES

Tibetan medicine is a tradition that has been practiced for over 2500 years and is still used today. Tibetan medicine, which is called *gSoba Rig-pa*, is a science of healing based on the use of herbs and precious metals. Because Tibetan medicine is effective in its treatment of chronic diseases such as rheumatism, arthritis, ulcers, chronic digestive problems, asthma, hepatitis, eczema, liver problems, sinus problems, anxiety, and problems connected with the nervous system, the Western medical community is now examining it.

LANGUAGE

Since the Chinese invasion and conquest of Tibet, Chinese has been the official language of commerce and government. It is also the primary language taught in Tibetan schools. But native Tibetans continue to speak their native language. The Tibetan language bears little resemblance to the languages of neighboring China and India. Tibeto-Burman, a language of the Sino-Tibetan family, is based on a form of Sanskrit that originated in India during the seventh century. Sino-Tibetan languages are a family of languages spoken from northeast India eastward to Taiwan and from China southward to the Malay Peninsula. Sino-Tibetan is generally divided into two large subfamilies: the Sinitic, comprising Mandarin, Cantonese, and the other languages of China; and the Tibeto-Burman, the best-known members of which are Tibetan and Burmese. The Tibeto-Burman subfamily, although it encompasses more languages than the Sinitic, and is spoken by a wider variety of ethnic groups, is more difficult to classify. Most linguists recognize four main Tibeto-Burman branches, divided into roughly nine groups. The Tibeto-Burman languages are spoken in Tibet, Nepal, Burma, western China, and the Assam State in India. Sino-Tibetan languages are distinguished from western language families by two main traits: isolating or monosyllabic characters and the use of tones.

Tibetan is most closely related to Burmese and to other spoken dialects of Himalayan peoples, but the written script was adapted from Indian writing. The Tibetan alphabet has 30 letters arranged in eight classes. There are five vowel sounds: "a," "i," "u," "e," "o," pronounced according to the general pronunciation in Latin. There are very few words beginning with any vowel sound, and those are either of Sanskrit origin, interjections, or corrupted words.

GREETINGS AND POPULAR EXPRESSIONS

Tashidelek means "hello" in Tibetan. An old Tibetan custom sometimes used today is to greet a person by sticking the tongue out and down the face. This was done as a sign of respect for someone of higher social standing, and it was sometimes repeated at the end of every sentence in a conversation. Most Tibetan expressions and greetings relate to Buddhism. Buddha is always referred to, even in passing, as the "victoriously consummate one" because he won perfection after a long and continuous struggle with worldly desires.

FAMILY AND COMMUNITY DYNAMICS

Nomadic Tibetan family life was structured to preserve their livelihood from tending yaks and surviving on the mountains of Tibet. Young children assumed duties essential to the family's survival. The Chinese conquest of Tibet brought dramatic changes to nomadic family life. Nomadic families were restricted to only one child per household, were stripped of individual ownership of herds and were reorganized into a communal structure. In the Tibetan refugee community in India, the concept of family takes on a greater significance as a way of preserving of Tibetan culture. Most families include several children and often extended relatives. Tibetan Americans maintain strong family bonds. Even if it takes many years, a Tibetan American refugee will work to be reunited with other family members.

EDUCATION

The United States Information Agency provides scholarships for Tibetan students and professionals to study in the United States. Over 140 students participated in the program between 1988 and 1997, and almost all returned to India and Nepal upon completion of their studies to assist Tibetan refugee communities there.

Chinese is now the first language in Tibetan schools. Under Chinese authority, Tibetans are provided with inferior schools and untrained teachers. In independent Tibet, monasteries and nunneries, numbering over 6,000, served as schools and universities, fulfilling Tibet's educational needs. In the late 1990s the Tibetan government-in-exile protested to Chinese officials about inadequate school conditions. Only 45 per cent of the children of school age go to primary schools. In Tibet, the best schools are in Lhasa, Shigatse, Gyangtse, Chamdo, Silling, Kyigudo, Dartsedo, and Dechen. But these schools are meant primarily for the children of Chinese citizens. In the Chinese government-funded urban schools, there are separate classes for the Chinese and Tibetan students. The Tibetan government-in-exile allocates 65 percent of its annual budget to the education of Tibetan children. About 92 percent of Tibetan children in exile, aged 6 to 17, attend schools, with about 84 percent of them enrolled in Tibetan schools. Education in exile has produced Tibetan medical doctors, administrators, Ph.D., engineers, post-graduate teachers, journalists, social workers, lawyers, and computer programmers.

THE ROLE OF WOMEN

Historically, women in Tibet owned land and conducted business with a status equal to that of men except in the spiritual arena, where nuns (*anis*) are regarded as inferior to monks. In some Tibetan monasteries, women are not allowed to enter the chapel out of fear that spirits may be offended. Traditional Tibetan society practiced polyandry, whereby a woman could legally be married to two or three men, usually brothers, simultaneously. The practice developed as a way to prevent land divisions, but was discontinued by the 1990s.

Following China's occupation of Tibet in 1959, thousands of women protested by organizing the Tibetan Women's Association (TWA). The organization was brutally suppressed by Chinese soldiers. In 1984, Tibetan women in exile in India and Nepal reorganized the organization. The TWA's main objective is to raise public awareness of the abuses faced by Tibetan women in Chinese-occupied Tibet. Through extensive publicity and interaction in national and international affairs, TWA alerts the international community to the gender-specific human rights abuses committed against Tibetan women in the form of forced birth control policies, such as sterilizations and abortions, and restrictions on religious, political, social, and cultural freedoms. In 1987, the TWA launched the Tibetan Nuns Project to assist newly exiled nuns with shelter, food, and clothing.

Eleven Tibetan nuns arrived in the United States in April 1999 to conduct a ten-month tour to call attention to the Chinese takeover of Tibet. Temporarily settled in Nevada County, California, the Tibetan native nuns came from the refugee community in Nepal. They were educated in the exile settlements before taking to the road to benefit Tibet through their contact with Americans.

WEDDINGS

For Tibetans, a wedding is a social event between two communities. The maternal uncle of the bride is the most honored figure at the wedding and presides over the event. In the early morning, the groom's wedding party comes to invite the bride for the wedding ceremony. Guided by her chaperone, the bride is carried piggy-back through her village gate by her older brother. If the bride does not have a brother, she can pick someone as the brother figure. Her wedding party, her close friends and relatives, escort them to the wedding ceremony. The scene is very animated, both by music and by the crying of the bride and her female companions. As the bride is taken away, her villagers line up along their way and sing. The bride's head is covered with a red veil, and her feet do not touch the ground when she leaves her village. Upon arrival, the leader of the bridal party, the maternal uncle, sprinkles sacred water at the entrance of the groom's village. Then there is a ceremony for open-

ing the wedding wine. The bridal party reaches the groom's house, and the bride and her chaperone (maid of honor), dressed exactly alike, sit side-by-side to wait for the groom. The groom must select the true bride, to whom he will have sent certain items as the symbol of their relationship during courtship, usually rings, bracelets or necklaces. The groom is expected to identify their symbolism and lift off the veil without making a mistake.

After the ceremony uniting the couple, the *longda*, also called the "fortune horse" or the "paper horse," is thrown in the air. The *longda* is a woodblock-printed horse on paper about two inches wide and four inches long, a tradition from the Tibetan Sacred Horse worship. At weddings or festivals, many Tibetans bring the *longda* with them to a sacred or high-peaked mountain and throw several *longda* into the air, letting the wind blow them high and far, like horses running swiftly and serenely. The *longda* brings humans' wishes to the gods

The wedding guests and participants then form a huge circle, dancing the *Guozhan* wedding dance. An interesting aspect of this wedding custom is that the newlywed couple cannot spend their wedding night together. After the wedding ceremony, the bride is accompanied by her chaperone, even if staying overnight with the groom's family. The next day, they return to the bride's family and stay at their house for a couple of days. Later, after returning to the groom's home, the couple is finally united.

FUNERALS

Typically, Tibetans do not bury their dead. Tibetans cremate their dead or bury them in a sky funeral, considered the only way to ensure rebirth. Specially trained monks hack the body to pieces, grind the bones and flesh, and feed this to the vultures bit by bit. Sky burial sites are located on hills near monasteries.

INTERACTIONS WITH OTHER ETHNIC GROUPS

Tibetans have a long history of political and cultural conflict with China. There is considerable animosity between the Han Chinese living in Tibet and ethnic Tibetans. When Chinese officials have visited the United States, Tibetan Americans have organized protests that have resulted in arrests.

RELIGION

Buddhism encompasses the cultural values and social structure of the Tibetan people. However, Buddhism was preceded by Bön, Tibet's earliest religion, which was founded by Shenrab Miwo of Shangshung in western Tibet. Bön was a religion that involved the violent worship of local mountain and lake spirits. Magic and ritual, including animal sacrifice, was strongly emphasized. With the advent of Buddhism, the Bön religion diminished in influence, although it is still practiced in some areas of Tibet.

Before the Chinese takeover of Tibet, Buddhist monasteries, temples, and hermitages were found in every village and town throughout Tibet. Every Tibetan home had an altar. In 1959 there were a total of more than 6,259 monasteries, with about 592,558 resident monks and nuns. These religious centers housed tens of thousands of statues and religious artifacts made of gold, silver, and other metals studded with jewels. Besides texts on Buddhism, these centers were storehouses of works on literature, medicine, astrology, art, and politics of the Tibetan people.

From 1949 to 1979, China discouraged the practice of any religion in Tibet and many religious artifacts were confiscated. Many of these artifacts were taken to China and destroyed. The majority of monasteries and nunneries in Tibet were also closed. By 1976, only eight monasteries remained in Tibet. Out of Tibet's total of 6,259 monasteries and nunneries, only about eight remained by 1976.

EMPLOYMENT AND ECONOMIC TRADITIONS

Tibet is 70 percent grassland, and animal husbandry is the occupation of most of the workers in the agrarian economy. The lifestyle is very harsh, with few amenities. Tibetan Buddhist monks are supported by their communities as well as by service jobs. Tibetan Americans work as dairymen, gardeners, and farm laborers. Many Tibetan Americans are Buddhist religious workers. As educational opportunities open for Tibetans, occupational choices beyond the service and manual labor markets are emerging.

POLITICS AND GOVERNMENT

Tibetan associations and lobbying efforts are highly organized in the United States. Holiday Inn Worldwide, which has been faced with an international boycott of its hotel chain since 1993, announced in 1998 that it would not renew its management contract in Tibet, a contract that had been beneficial to the Chinese government. The Holiday Inn's decision aided the growing movement to return control

of Tibet's economic affairs to Tibetans. The city of Berkeley, California, passed legislation in the late 1990s which prohibited the city from associating with corporations or individuals that conducted business in Tibet without permission from the Tibetan government-in-exile. The campaign was joined by a coalition of over 50 organizations worldwide. The boycott attracted major grassroots support and celebrity interest and was highlighted at a Tibetan Freedom Concert in New York City.

RELATIONS WITH TIBET

The United States considers the Tibet Autonomous Region a part of the People's Republic of China. This long-standing policy is consistent with the view of the entire international community, including all of China's neighbors. No country recognizes Tibet as a sovereign state. The United States' acceptance of China's claim of sovereignty over Tibet predates the establishment of the People's Republic of China. However, the United States Congress, through the Foreign Relations Regulation Act in 1991, declared that "Tibet, including those areas incorporated into the Chinese provinces of Sichuan, Yunan, Gansu, and Qinghai, is an occupied country under the established principles of international law whose true representatives are the Dalai Lama and the Tibetan Government in exile as recognized by the Tibetan people."

Because the United States does not recognize Tibet as an independent state, officials cannot conduct diplomatic relations with the representatives of Tibetans in exile. However, the United States does maintain contact with a wide variety of representatives of differing political groups inside and outside China with views on Tibet. The United States has urged China to respect Tibet's unique religious, linguistic, and cultural traditions, as well as the human rights of Tibetans as it formulates its policies for Tibet. The United States encourages China and the Dalai Lama to hold serious discussions aimed at resolving their differences.

The United States provides humanitarian assistance to Tibetan refugees in India and also contributes to the U.N. High Commission for Refugees (UNHCR) to assist Tibetans in Nepal. Most U.S. government funding to the refugees in India has gone to the Tibet Fund, a U.S. private voluntary organization which underwrites assistance programs for Tibetan refugees in India. Such programs support reception centers, preventive health care, and income generating projects and also supply basic food, clothing, and clean water.

In 1998, President Clinton requested that China's president hold talks with the Dalai Lama in a live broadcast during a U.S.-China summit. The Chinese government condemned President Clinton for meeting with the Dalai Lama and warned that U. S. relations with China would suffer as a result. In the United States, a strong pro-Tibetan movement continues to organize benefit concerts, festivals, museum exhibitions, and academic research to preserve Tibetan culture and resist Chinese aggression. In 1999, *The Art of Happiness*, a book of Buddhist doctrines and common sense written by the Dalai Lama, became a *New York Times* best seller.

INDIVIDUAL AND GROUP CONTRIBUTIONS

Rinjing Dorje, is a folklorist, storyteller, and author of books on Tibetan humor and culinary arts, including *Food in Tibetan Life*.

MEDIA

PRINT

Tibet Monitor.
Monthly publication of the Tibetan Rights Campaign.
Address: 4649 Sunnyside Ave. N, #323 Seattle, WA 98103.
Telephone: (206) 547-1015.
Fax: (206) 547-3758.

Tibet Environment and Development Newsletter.
Bi-monthly published by International Campaign for Tibet.
Address: 1825 K St. NW Suite 520, Washington, DC 20006.
Telephone: (202) 785-1515.
E-mail: ict@peacenet.org.

Tibet Press Watch.
Bi-monthly published by International Campaign for Tibet.
Address: 1825 K St. NW Suite 520, Washington, DC 20006.
Telephone: (202) 785-1515.
E-mail: ict@peacenet.org.

ORGANIZATIONS AND ASSOCIATIONS

The United States has a strong base of regional, state, and local organizations that support the Tibetan freedom movement, many of which are named "Friends of Tibet." Selected national and international organizations are listed below.

American Religious Committee for Tibet.
Organization of interfaith leadership dedicated to the right of the Tibetan people to maintain and nurture their distinctive heritage.
Address: Office of the Dean, The Cathedral of St. John the Divine, 1047 Amsterdam Ave., New York, NY 10025.
Telephone: (212) 316-7493.

International Campaign for Tibet.
A nonprofit, membership organization founded in 1988 to promote human rights and democratic freedoms in Tibet. Monitors current developments in Tibet and reports the information to the U.S. Congress, human rights organizations, and the media. The Campaign networks with non-governmental organizations and Tibet support groups to support initiatives for peaceful resolutions to the Tibetan issue.
Contact: John Ackerly, Director.
Address: 1825 K St. NW Suite 520, Washington, DC 20006.
Telephone: (202) 785-1515.
E-mail: ict@peacenet.org.

International Committee of Lawyers for Tibet.
Provides legal research and drafting to assist Tibetans.
Contact: Eva Herzer , President.

Address: 2288 Fulton Street, #312, Berkeley, CA 94704.
Telephone: (510) 486-0588.
E-mail: iclt@igc.apc.org.

International Tibet Independence Movement.
Contact: Larry Gerstein.
Address: PO Box 2325, Bloomington, IN 47402.
Telephone: (800) 276-8588 or (317) 579-0914.
E-mail: Rangzen@aol.com.

Students for Tibet.
A network of student-run Tibet support groups on college campuses nationwide. Co-sponsored by the International Campaign for Tibet and the U.S. Tibet Committee.

Address: 545 Eighth Avenue, 23rd Floor, New York, NY 10018.
Telephone: (212) 594-5898.

Tibet Fund.
Purposes are to: assist in the preservation of Tibetan culture; further ongoing development of Tibetan arts and sciences; promote Tibetan contributions to the modern world. Funds Tibetan institutions in exile such as the Tibetan Medical Institute, the Institute of Higher Tibetan Studies, and the Tibetan Institute of Performing Arts, in addition to Tibetan Buddhist monastic institutions now reestablished in India and Nepal. Maintains speakers' bureau; conducts charitable program; compiles statistics.

Contact: Rinchen Dharlo, President.
Address: 241 East 32nd Street, New York, New York 10016.
Telephone: (212) 213-5011.
Fax: (212) 779-9245.
E-mail: tibetfund@tibetfund.org.
Online: http://www.tibetfund.org.

Tibet Society.
Scholars, students, researchers, libraries, institutes, and organizations having an interest in the languages, history, religion, and other aspects of life in Tibet and Central Asia. Serves as a forum and center of research information on Tibetan studies and affairs. Transfers charitable donations to various refugee aid groups in India.

Contact: Mr. Thubten J. Norbu, Founder.
Address: 157 Goodbody Hall, Bloomington, Indiana 47405.
Telephone: (812) 855-2233.
Fax: (812) 855-7500.

US Tibet Committee.
Independent human rights organization of Tibetan and American volunteers promoting public awareness of the current political situation in Tibet through lectures, conferences, demonstrations, and letter writing campaigns. USTC has chapters in 18 states.

Contact: Sonam Wangdu, Chairman.
Address: 241 East 32 St., New York, NY 10016.
Telephone: (212) 213-5011.
E-mail: ustcsft@igc.apc.org.

MUSEUMS AND RESEARCH CENTERS

The Cleveland Museum of Art.
Permanent collection of Himalayan art including Tibetan paintings.

Address: 11150 East Boulevard, Cleveland, OH 44106-1797.

The Costume Institute of The Metropolitan Museum of Art.
Has collection of Tibetan native costumes.

Address: 1000 Fifth Avenue at 82nd Street, New York, NY 10028.
Telephone: (212) 879-5500.

Jacques Marchais Museum of Tibetan Art.
Museum resembles a small Tibetan mountain temple tucked away from the world. Terraced sculpture gardens, a lily and fish pond, and a distant view of the lower Hudson Bay are setting for Tibetan, Nepalese, Tibeto-Chinese, and Mongolian artifacts from the seventeenth to the nineteenth centuries or earlier. Metal figures of deities and *lamas*, as well as *thangka* paintings.

Contact: Barbara Lipton.
Address: 338 Lighthouse Avenue Staten Island, NY 10306.
Telephone: (718) 987-3500.

Los Angeles County Museum of Art (LACMA).
One of the most comprehensive collections of Himalayan art, including 75 Tibetan and Nepalese *thangkas*, and Tibetan paintings that once belonged to Giuseppe Tucci, one of the few to enter Tibet in the middle of the twentieth century. He collected important works of art at various sites in Tibet and is probably the most important twentieth-century Tibetan scholar.

Contact: Janice Leoshko, Associate Curator, Indian and Southeast Asian Art.

Address: 5905 Wilshire Blvd., Los Angeles, CA 90036.

Museum of Fine Arts, Boston.
Permanent collection of Tibetan Art.

Address: 465 Huntington Ave., Boston, MA 02115.
Telephone: (617) 267-9300.

The Newark Museum.
Has completely recreated the interior of a Tibetan monastery in its galleries.

Address: 49 Washington Street, Newark, NJ 07101-0540.
Telephone: (973) 596-6529.

Office of Tibet.
Collection of films and videos on Tibet.

Address: 241 E. 32nd Street, New York, NY 10016.
Telephone: (212) 213-5010.

Virginia Museum of Fine Arts.
The Tibetan and Nepalese galleries showcase collections of opaque watercolors on cloth or palm leaf.

Address: 2800 Grove Avenue, Richmond, VA 23221-2466.
Telephone: (804) 367-0844.

SOURCES FOR ADDITIONAL STUDY

Batchelor, Stephen. *The Tibet Guide: Central and Western Tibet*. Boston: Wisdom Publications, 1998.

Beek, Steve Van. *Tibet*. Singapore: APA Publications Ltd., 1994.

Feigon, Lee. *Demystifying Tibet*. Chicago: Ivan R. Dee, 1996.

TLINGIT

by
Diane E. Benson ('Lxeis')

Tlingit people
believe that all life
is of equal value;
plants, trees, birds,
fish, animals, and
human beings are all
equally respected.

OVERVIEW

Alaska is a huge land mass that contains many different environments ranging from the frigid streams and tundra above the Arctic circle to the windy islands of the Aleutians to the mild rainy weather of southeast Alaska. Alaska consists of over 533,000 square miles, with a coastline as long that of the rest of the continental United States. The southern end of the Alaska coastline, a region known as Southeast Alaska, is home to the primary Tlingit (pronounced "klingit") communities. This area covers the narrow coastal strip of the continental shore along British Columbia; it is similar in size and shape to the state of Florida, but with few communities connected by road. Tlingit communities are located from just south of Ketchikan and are scattered northward across islands and mainland as far as the Icy Bay area. Tlingit people also occupy some inland area on the Canadian side of the border in British Columbia and the Yukon Territory. The mainland Tlingit of Alaska occupy a range of mountains from 50 to 100 miles inland. The northern portion of Tlingit country is glacial with the majesty of the Fairweather and Saint Elias mountains overlooking the northern shores of the Gulf of Alaska. Fjords, mountains that dive into the sea, islands, and ancient trees make up most of this wet country that is part of one of the largest temperate rain forests in the world.

The total population of Alaska is just under 600,000. Approximately 86,000 Alaska Natives, the indigenous peoples of Alaska, live there. The Tlingit population at time of contact by Europeans is estimated to have been 15,000. Some reports include the Haida in population estimates, since Tlingit and Haida are almost always grouped together for statistical purposes. Today, Tlingit and Haida Central Council tribal enrollment figures show a total of 20,713 Tlingit and Haida, of which 16,771 are Tlingit. Most of the Tlingit population live in urban communities of southeastern Alaska, though a significant number have made their homes all across the continent. Euro-Americans dominate the Southeast population, with the Tlingit people being the largest minority group in the region.

EARLY HISTORY

The name Tlingit essentially means human beings. The word was originally used simply to distinguish a human being from an animal, since Tlingits believed that there was little difference between humans and animals. Over time the word came to be a national name. It is speculated that human occupation of southeast Alaska occurred 11,000 years ago by Tlingit people. Haida people, with whom the Tlingit have frequent interaction, have only been in the area about 200 years, and the Tsimpsian migrated only recently from the Canadian interior mainland.

Tlingit legends speak of migrations into the area from several possible directions, either from the north as a possible result of the Bering Sea land bridge, or from the southwest, after a maritime journey from the Polynesian islands across the Pacific. Oral traditions hold that the Tlingit came from the head of the rivers. As one story goes, Nass-aa-ge-yeil' (Raven from the head of the Nass River) brought light and stars and moon to the world. The Tlingit are unique and unrelated to other tribes around them. They have no linguistic relationship to any other language except for a vague similarity to the Athabaskan language. They also share some cultural similarity with the Athabaskan, with whom the Tlingit have interacted and traded for centuries. There may also be a connection between the Haida and the Tlingit, but this issue is debated. Essentially, the origin of the Tlingit is unknown.

Tlingit people are grouped and divided into units called *kwan*. Some anthropological accounts estimate that 15 to 20 *kwan* existed at the time of European contact. A *kwan* was a group of people who lived in a mutual area, shared residence, intermarried, and lived in peace. Communities containing a Tlingit population may be called the *Sitka-kwan*, the *Taku-kwan*, or the *Heenya-kwan*, depending on their social ties and/or location. Most of the urban communities of Southeast Alaska occupy the sites of many of the traditional *kwan* communities. Before the arrival of explorers and settlers, groups of Tlingit people would travel by canoe through treacherous waters for hundreds of miles to engage in war, attend ceremonies, trade, or marry.

Through trade with other tribes as far south as the Olympic Peninsula and even northern California, the Tlingit people had established sophisticated skills. In the mid-1700s, the Spaniards and the British, attracted by the fur trade, penetrated the Northwest via the Juan de Fuca Islands (in the Nootka Sound area). The Russians, also in search of furs, invaded the Aleutian Islands and moved throughout the southwestern coast of Alaska toward Tlingit country. The Tlingit traders may have heard stories of these strangers coming but took little heed.

FIRST CONTACT WITH EUROPEANS

Europeans arrived in Tlingit country for the first time in 1741, when Russian explorer Aleksey Chirikov sent a boatload of men to land for water near the modern site of Sitka. When the group did not return for several days, he sent another boat of men to shore; they also did not return. Thereafter, contact with Tlingit people was limited until well into the 1800s.

Russian invaders subdued the Aleut people, and moving southward, began their occupation of Tlingit country. Having monopolized trade routes in any direction from or to Southeast Alaska, the Tlingit people engaged in somewhat friendly but profitable trading with the newcomers until the Russians became more aggressive in their attempts to colonize and control trade routes. In 1802 Chief Katlian of the Kiksadi Tlingit of the Sitka area successfully led his warriors against the Russians, who had set up a fort in Sitka with the limited permission of the Tlingit. Eventually the Russians recaptured Sitka and maintained a base they called New Archangel, but they had little contact with the Sitka clans. For years the Tlingit resisted occupation and the use of their trade routes by outsiders. In 1854 a Chilkat Tlingit war party travelled hundreds of miles into the interior and destroyed a Hudson Bay Company post in the Yukon Valley.

Eventually, diseases and other hardships took their toll on the Tlingit people, making them more vulnerable. In a period between 1836 and 1840, it is estimated that one-half of the Tlingit people at or

near Sitka were wiped out by smallpox, influenza, and tuberculosis. At about this time, Americans came into Tlingit country for gold, and in the process sought to occupy and control the land and its people. The Tlingit loss to disease only made American occupation more swift, and Americans became firmly established in the land with the 1867 Treaty of Purchase of Alaska. The Tlingit continually fought American development of canneries, mines, and logging, which conflicted with the Tlingit lifestyle. Disputes between the Americans and the decreasing Tlingit people proved futile for the Tlingit, since Americans displayed impressive military strength, technology, and an unwavering desire for settlement and expansion. The destruction of the Tlingit villages of Kake in the 1860s and of Angoon in 1882 by the American military (due to a disagreement involving the death of two Native people) further established American power and occupancy.

THE LAND CLAIMS PERIOD

The Treaty of Cession (1867) referred to indigenous people of Alaska as "uncivilized tribes." Such desig-

nation in legislation and other agreements caused Alaska Natives to be subject to the same regulations and policies as American Indians in the United States. Statements by the Office of the Solicitor in the U.S. Department of Interior in 1932 further supported the federal government's treatment of Alaska Natives as American Indians. As a result, Tlingit people were subject to such policies as the 1884 First Organic Act, which affected their claims to land and settlements, and the 1885 Major Crimes Act, which was intended to strip tribes of their right to deal with criminal matters according to traditional customs. By the turn of the century, the Tlingit people were threatened politically, territorially, culturally, and socially.

In response, the Tlingit people organized the Alaska Native Brotherhood (ANB). The ANB was founded in Sitka in 1912 by nine Tlingit and one Tsimpsian. The ANB's goals were to gain equality for the Native people of Southeast Alaska and to obtain for them the same citizenship and education rights as non-Natives. In 1915, due to the efforts of the ANB (and the newly organized Alaska Native Sisterhood), the territorial legislature adopted a position similar to the Dawes Act to allow Natives to become citizens, provided that the Natives became "civilized" by rejecting certain tribal customs and relationships. As a result, few Native people became citizens at this time; most did not become American citizens until the U.S. Congress adopted the Citizenship Act of 1924.

Tlingit people also actively pursued the right to vote. Unlike many Alaska Native people at the time who wanted to continue living as they had for many generations, Tlingit leaders sought increased political power. In 1924, William Paul, a Tlingit, won election to the Territorial House of Representatives, marking the beginning of a trend toward Native political power.

In 1929 the ANB began discussing land issues, and as a result Congress passed a law in 1935 allowing Tlingits and Haidas to sue the United States for the loss of their lands. By this time large sections of Tlingit country had become the Tongass National Forest. Glacier Bay had become a National Monument, and further south in Tlingit country, Annette Island was set aside as a reservation for Tsimpsian Indians from Canada. In 1959—the same year that Alaska was admitted as a state—the Court of Claims decided in favor of the Tlingit and Haida for payment of land that was taken from them. The Tlingit-Haida land claims involved 16 million acres without a defined monetary value; an actual settlement took years to conclude. In 1971, the Alaska Native Claims Settlement Act (ANCSA) was passed, which called for the settlement of all claims against the United States and the state of Alaska that are based on aboriginal right, title, use, or occupancy of land or water areas in Alaska.

Tlingit individuals did not receive title to lands as a result of ANCSA. Instead, lands claimed by southeast Natives under this act were placed under the control of the ANCSA-established regional corporation, Sealaska, and the ANCSA-established village corporations. Some village corporations had the option to provide individuals with land in some cases, but most villages designated the land for future development.

The Native Allotment Act of 1906 did result in some Tlingit lands being placed in the hands of individual Tlingits. This law provided for conveyance of 160 acres to adult Natives as long as no tract of ground contained mineral deposits. Only a few allotments were issued in southeast Alaska. The Native Townsite Act of 1926 also provided only for the conveyance of "restricted" title lands, meaning such property could not be sold or leased without the approval of the Secretary of the Interior. Despite these gains, lands re-obtained this way by the villages or by individuals failed to sufficiently meet the needs of a hunting and fishing people.

The issues of Native citizenship, their right to vote, fishing and fishing trap disputes, and the activities of ANCSA contributed to the rising tensions between the Tlingit and the newcomers. In the 1930s, 1940s, and 1950s, it was not uncommon to see signs that read "No Indians Allowed" on the doors of business establishments. The Alaska Native Brotherhood did much to fight these prejudices and elevate the social status of the Tlingit and Haida people as American citizens. Today, although Tlingit people are much more accepted, their fight for survival continues. Their ability to subsist off the land and sea is constantly endangered by logging, pulp mills, overharvesting of the waters by commercial fisheries, government regulations, and the area's increasing population.

ACCULTURATION AND ASSIMILATION

Throughout the nineteenth century, many Tlingit communities were affected by the influx of various industries. Fish canneries were established in Sitka and Klawock, gold mining began at Windham Bay, and a Presbyterian mission station was constructed at the place now known as Haines. New settlements like Juneau (1880) and Ketchikan (1888) dramatically changed Tlingit lands and economic systems. A mixed cash-subsistence economy developed, changing traditional trade and material acquisition systems. Missionary schools determined to acculturate the Tlingit and other Alaska Natives instructed the Tlingit in English and American ways and denied the indigenous students access to their traditional language, foods, dances, songs, and healing methods. Although change was overwhelming and Americanization pervasive, Tlingit clan structures remained intact, and traditions survived in the original communities. At the turn of the century it was not uncommon for southeast factories to employ clan leaders to prevent disputes and keep order between their employees and the Native communities.

The destruction and death brought on by disease caused many to abandon their faith in the shaman and traditional healing by the turn of the century. Smallpox and other epidemics of the early nineteenth century recurred well into the twentieth century. A number of communities, including Dry Bay and Lituya Bay, were devastated in 1918 and thereafter by bouts of influenza. Important and culturally fundamental traditional gatherings, or potlatches, became almost nonexistent in Tlingit country during the tuberculosis epidemics of the 1900s. These epidemics caused hundreds of Tlingit and other southeast people to be institutionalized; many of those who fell victim to these diseases were subsequently buried in mass graves. Tlingit people turned to the churches for relief, and in the process many were given new names to replace their Tlingit names, an important basis of identity and status in Tlingit society. Demoralization and hopelessness ensued and worsened with the government-sponsored internment of Aleut people in Tlingit country during World War II. Some Tlingit families adopted Aleut children who had been orphaned as a result of widespread disease and intolerable living conditions.

When they were established, the Alaska Native Brotherhood and Sisterhood accepted acculturation as a goal for their members, believing that the abandonment of cultural traditions was in the peoples' best interest. Their organizational structure, however, reflected a traditional form of government to manage tribal and clan operations. Social and clan interactions and relationships continue to exist to this day despite all outside influences and despite the marked adaptations of Tlingit people to American society. The relatively recent revival of dances, songs, potlatches, language, and stories has strengthened continuing clan interactions and identities.

TRADITIONS, CUSTOMS, AND BELIEFS

Tlingit people believe that all life is of equal value; plants, trees, birds, fish, animals, and human beings are all equally respected. Clans and Clan Houses have identifying crests; a clan is equally proud whether its crest is a killer whale or a snail. There are no recognized superior species. When any "crested" living being dies, homage is expected, and appropriate respects are paid. Today, some communities of the southeast are still very sensitive to this tradition.

Tlingit people do not tolerate misuse or misappropriation of their crests, names, songs, designs, stories, or other properties. Each crest has stories and songs associated with it that belong to the crest and thereby to its clan. Ownership recognition of these things among the Tlingit is profound. Almost a century ago, two clans began a dispute over who owned a particular crest. This conflict is discussed in detail in Frederica de Laguna's 1972 work, *Under Mt. St. Elias: The History and Culture of the Yakatat Tlingit*. The issue developed into a social, political, and legal battle that ensued for decades, and in many ways

remains unresolved. Using a killer whale song, story, or crest design without acknowledging the owning clan or without its permission, for example, can be considered stealing. Crest ownership sometimes conflicts with American notions of public domain. This conflict, along with a growing interest by the general public in Tlingit art and culture, has raised concerns among the clans about how to protect their birthrights from distortion and acquisition.

Tlingits demand that respect be shown toward other individuals and clans. When a person feels insulted by another, payment must be made by the person or clan who was responsible for the insult, or a process performed to remove the damage publicly. If this does not happen, bad feelings persist, negatively affecting relationships between clans. In the old ways, if a Tlingit person was seriously harmed or murdered by another Tlingit person, the "eye for an eye" philosophy would determine punishment: someone from the opposing clan would have to die. Today, that philosophy is adapted to remain within legal boundaries. Criminal cases are tried strictly by American law, but the family of the perpetrator is subject to social ostracism. Payment by the perpetrator's clan to the harmed clan for the wrongdoing is also conceivable.

Many newcomers to Tlingit country, including some missionaries, erroneously reported that the Tlingit people worshipped totems, idolized animals or birds as gods, and held heathen rituals. As a result some religious leaders instructed their Native congregations to burn or destroy various elements of their art and culture, and a good deal of Tlingit heirlooms were destroyed in this way. These misconceptions undermined the complexity and power of Tlingit culture and society.

POTLATCHES

Potlatches are an integral part of Tlingit history and modern-day life. A potlatch is a giant feast that marks a time for showing respect, paying debts, and displaying wealth. Tlingit people give grandly at potlatches to raise their stature. The respect and honor held toward one's ancestry, name, house crest, and family, and the extent of one's wealth might determine how elaborate a potlatch would be; these ceremonies are not, however, forms of worship to any gods. Potlatches are given for various reasons and may be planned for years in advance. The most common potlatches given today are funeral potlatches, the 40-Day Party, memorial potlatches, adoption potlatches, naming potlatches, totem-pole-raising potlatches, and house- or lodge-building potlatches.

A person's death requires a three-stage potlatch process to properly attend to the deceased person's transfer to the spirit world or future life. The first potlatch includes the mourning and burial of the deceased, lasting from one to four days. George Emmons reports in his book *The Tlingit Indians* that this process traditionally took four to eight days. During this time, the body is prepared for cremation or burial (which is more common today). Attendees sing songs of grief; sometimes the family fasts. Feasts are prepared for guests of the opposite clan (see below for explanation of opposite clans); afterward the person is buried. During the second stage, a party is held for the deceased person's clan. The third stage, or memorial potlatch, which can take place at any time, usually occurs about a year later. The memorial potlatch is a ritual process of letting go emotionally of the deceased. It marks the final release of the deceased to their future life as well as the final mourning, speeches, and deceased person's clan's payments to the opposite clan. The conclusion of the potlatch is a celebration of life and happy stories and song.

Sometimes less elaborate potlatches are held to give names to youngsters, or to those who have earned a new or second name. Naming potlatches may be held in conjunction with a memorial potlatch, as can adoption potlatches. Adoption ceremonies are held for one or more individuals who have proven themselves to a clan by their long term commitment to a Tlingit family or community and who have become members of the clan. The new members receive gifts and names, and are obligated from that day forward to uphold the ways of that clan. For whatever reason potlatches are held, ceremony is ever present. Participants wear traditional dress, make painstaking preparations, give formal speeches in Tlingit and English, and observe proper Tlingit etiquette.

CUISINE

The traditional diet of the Tlingit people relies heavily on the sea. Fish, seal, seaweed, clams, cockles, gum boots (chitons—a shell fish), herring, eggs and salmon eggs, berries, and venison make up the primary foods of most Tlingit people. Fish, such as halibut, cod, herring, and primarily salmon, (king, reds, silver, and sockeye) are prepared in many forms—most commonly smoked, dried, baked, roasted, or boiled. Dog, silver, humpy, and sockeye salmon are the fish best utilized for smoking and drying. The drying process takes about a week and involves several stages of cleaning, deboning, and cutting strips and hanging the fish usually near an open fire until firm. These strips serve as a food source throughout the year, as they are easily stored and carried.

The land of southeastern Alaska is abundant with ocean and wildlife, and because of this the Tlingit people could easily find and prepare foods in the warmer seasons, saving colder months for art, crafts, and elaborate gatherings. Today, although food sources have been impacted by population and industry, the traditional foods are still gathered and prepared in traditional ways as well as in new and creative ways influenced by the various ethnic groups who have immigrated into the area, especially Filipino (rice has become a staple of almost any Tlingit meal). Pilot bread, brought in by various seafaring merchants, is also common as it stores well, and softens, for the individual, the consumption of oil delicacies such as the eulochon and seal oils. Fry-bread is also an element of many meals and special occasions. Other influences on diet and food preparation besides standard American include Norwegian, Russian, and Chinese foods.

Other foods of the Tlingit include such pungent dishes as *xákwl´ee*, soap berries (whipped berries often mixed with fish or seal oil), seal liver, dried seaweed, fermented fish eggs, abalone, grouse, crab, deer jerky, sea greens, *-suktéitl´*—goose tongue (a plant food), rosehips, rhubarb, roots, *yaana.eit* (wild celery), and *s´ikshaldéen* (Hudson Bay tea).

TRADITIONAL GARMENTS AND REGALIA

Traditionally Tlingit men and women wore loincloths and skirts made of cedar bark. Because of the rainy weather in southeastern Alaska, raincoats were worn, which were also made from natural elements such as spruce root or cedar bark. Today, Tlingit people no longer wear loincloths and cedar bark skirts, dressing very much as other contemporary Americans. Although modern, Tlingit people display their clan or family emblem on clothing or through jewelry, as has been the custom for centuries.

The most distinctive form of ceremonial dress prior to Americanization and still the most admired is the Chilkat robe. Although called the Chilkat robe after the Chilkat tribe of Tlingit who specialized in weaving, its origin is Tsimpsian. The robe is made from mountain goat wool and cedar bark strips and generally exhibits an emblem of the clan. This garment takes a weaver one to five years to make. The technique not only involves a horizontal weaving similar to that found in other cultures, but also a symmetrical and circular (curvilinear) design as well. This complex art form came dangerously close to extinction in the twentieth century, but through the perseverance of individuals in and outside the tribe there are now several weavers, elder and younger, in Tlingit and other northwest nations today. This is also true of the recently revived art of the Raven's Tail robe, another complexly woven garment of black and white worn over the shoulders in the same cape fashion as the Chilkat robe. Raven's Tail weaving of geometric and herring bone patterns is a skill that had not been practiced in nearly two centuries, but with the resurgence of cultural interest is now being practiced throughout the

This photograph shows Tlingit Indians in traditional dress.

northwest coast. Chilkat and Raven's Tail weaving is also used to make leggings, medicine bags, dance purses, dance aprons, tunics, and shirts.

In 1982 the Sealaska Heritage Foundation in Juneau began what is called *Celebration*. It occurs every even year as a gathering to celebrate culture. At Celebration today, many Chilkat robes can be seen. Chilkat robes are never worn as daily dress, but are worn with pride at potlatches, celebrations, and sometimes for burial, if the person was of a particular social stature. Chilkat robes are a sign of wealth, and traditionally if one owned such an item, he was generally a clan leader of great prestige. Giving away a Chilkat robe meant greater glory since only the wealthiest could afford to be so generous.

Modern regalia today consists primarily of the button blanket, or dancing robe, which although time consuming and expensive to make, is much more available to the people than the Chilkat or Raven's Tail robe. Russian influence played a great part in the evolution of the button blanket, since trade provided the Tlingit people with felt of usually red, black, or blue from which the button blanket is made. These robes are often intricately decorated with one's clan emblems through appliqué variations and mother of pearl (shell) button outlines or solid beading of the design. These robes are worn to display one's lineage and family crest at gatherings, in much the same way as the Chilkat robe.

Robes of any type are almost always worn with an appropriate headdress. Headdresses can be as varied and simple as a headband or as intricate and rich as a carved cedar potlatch hat, displaying one's crest, decorated with color, inlaid with abalone shell, and finished with ermine. Russian influence inspired the sailor style hat that many women wear for dancing. These are made of the same felt as the button blanket and completed with beaded tassels. Ornamentation traditionally included some hair dressing, ear and nose piercing, labrets, bracelets, face painting, and tattooing. Most of these facets of adornment are practiced today, excluding the labret.

The formal dress of the Tlingit people is not only a show of power, wealth, or even lineage, but is an integral part of the social practices of the Tlingit. Tlingit people practice the respect of honoring the opposite clan and honoring one's ancestors in the making and handling of a garment. Importance is placed also on the maker of the garment, and the relationship of his or her clan to the clan of the wearer. Dress in Tlingit culture is an acknowledgment of all who came before.

HEALTH ISSUES

Existing traditional health-care centers consist primarily of physical healing through diet and local medicines, although this practice is rather limited. A few people today still use teas brewed from the devil's club, Hudson bay tea leaves, roots, leaves, and flowers of various plants that cleanse the body, boost the immune system, and even heal wounds and illnesses. Overall, the Tlingit people primarily use modern medical treatment through the existing federally established health-care systems.

Contemporary health-care methods are only marginally effective. Some of the Tlingit believe that people have a relationships with spirits, can communicate with animals and birds, and can learn from all life forms. Those who vocalize these experiences or abilities, however, feel vulnerable about being labelled as mentally ill. Still considered a radical idea by most modernized Tlingit and mental health specialists, this aspect of Tlingit culture is only now beginning to be discussed.

Health problems among the Tlingit are not much different than they are with other Alaska Native peoples. Extensive and continuous Indian Health Service data demonstrate their susceptibility to such illnesses as influenza, arthritis, hepatitis, cancer, and diabetes. Alcoholism is a more common disease that has taken its toll on the people, and although suicide is not as high amongst the Tlingit as it seems to be in more northern Native communities, it too has caused havoc and despair for some Tlingit communities. Providing social and emotional support for individuals as well as for the family

structure has become a concern for health-care professionals and concerned tribal citizens. Since the Alaska Natives Commission's 1994 report was released stressing the link between health and culture, more and more communities are discussing the psychology of various forms of cultural and social oppression and how to recover spiritually, mentally, and physically.

LANGUAGE

The Tlingit language is a tone language that has 24 sounds not found in English. Tlingit is phonemic in that the difference in meaning between words often depends entirely on tone. Much of the Tlingit language is guttural and some of the sounds are similar to that of German. Almost all Alaska Native languages have guttural or "back-in-the-mouth" sounds. Tlingit is unique in that it is not only guttural but has glottalized stops and a series of linguistically related sounds called glottalized fricatives. The sounds of Tlingit are difficult and varied and include not only the more familiar rolling and drawn out vowel sounds and deeper guttural sounds, but also pinched and air driven sounds with consonants which are "voiceless" (except for the "n" sound, as in "naa"). Many of the consonants have no English equivalents.

In the nineteenth century, the first attempts were made to communicate in Tlingit through writing. The Russian Orthodox Church through Bishop Innocent (Veniaminov) created the first alphabet for the Tlingit language and developed a Tlingit literacy program. The Orthodox Church supported bilingual education in its schools, but the Americans discouraged it, and ultimately sought to suppress the use of the language completely. It was not until the 1960s that a Native language literacy movement was resumed through the efforts of such linguists as Constantine Naish and Gillian Story. These linguists created the Tlingit alphabet that is more commonly used today.

Unlike the English alphabet of 26 letters, the Tlingit language has at least 32 consonants and eight vowels. The alphabet was created with not only the familiar lettering of English but also with periods, underlines on letters, and apostrophes to distinguish particular sounds. For example; the word *yéil* means Raven, and *yéil'* (with the apostrophe) means elderberry.

Tlingit grammar does not indicate concern with time, whereas English conveys some sense of time with almost any verb usage. Tlingit verbs may provide the information about an action's frequency or indicate the stopping or starting of an action. The grammatical and phonological features of the language make it a difficult one to learn if it has not been taught since birth, but it is not impossible. Unfortunately, due to past efforts to suppress the language there are not many young speakers, although the need to keep the language alive is crucial. The need to maintain indigenous languages is urgently stated in the 1994 *Final Report of the Alaska Natives Commission:* "At the core of many problems in the Alaska Native community are unhealed psychological and spiritual wounds and unresolved grief brought on by a century-long history of deaths by epidemics and cultural and political deprivation at others' hands; some of the more tragic consequences include the erosion of Native languages in which are couched the full cultural understanding, and the erosion of cultural values."

GREETINGS AND COMMON EXPRESSIONS

Tlingit people do not use such greetings as hello, good-bye, good afternoon, or good evening. Some common expressions are: *Yoo xat duwasaakw*—my name is; *Gunalchéesh*—Thank you; *Yak'éi ixwsiteení*—It's good to see you; *Wáa sá iyatee*—How are you (feeling?); *Wa.éku.aa?*—Where are you going?; and *Haa kaa gaa kuwatee*—It's good weather for us.

FAMILY AND COMMUNITY DYNAMICS

Tlingit society is divided into two primary ("opposite") clans or moieties, subclans or clans, and houses. The moieties are Raven and Eagle, and all Tlingits are either Raven or Eagle by birthright. The structure is matrilineal, meaning each person is born with the moiety of their mother, which is typically the opposite of the father: If the mother is Eagle, then the father is Raven or vice versa. Traditionally moiety intramarriage was not allowed even if the two Ravens or two Eagles were not at all blood related. Today, although frowned upon, moiety intramarriage occasionally occurs without the social ostracizing of the past.

Clans exist under the Raven moiety and the Eagle moiety. Clans are a subdivision of the moieties; each has its own crest. A person can be Eagle and of the Killer Whale or Brown Bear Clan, or of several other existing clans; Ravens may be of the Frog Clan, Sea Tern Clan, Coho Clan, and so forth. Houses, or extended families, are subdivisions of the clans. Prior to contact houses would literally be houses or lodges in which members of that clan or family coexisted. Today houses are one of the ways in which Tlingit people identify themselves and their relationship to others. Some examples of houses include the Snail House, Brown Bear Den House, Owl House, Crescent Moon House, Coho House, and Thunderbird House.

Tlingits are born with specific and permanent clan identities. Today these identities and relationships are intact and still acknowledged by the tribe. Biological relationships are one part of the family and clan structure; the other is the reincarnate relationships. Tlingit social structures and relationships are also effected by the belief that all Tlingits are reincarnates of an ancestor. This aspect of Tlingit lineage is understood by the elders but is not as likely to be understood and acknowledged by the younger Tlingit, although clan conferences are being held to educate people about this complex social system.

In Tlingit society today, even though many Tlingits marry other Tlingits, there exists a great deal of interracial marriage, which has changed some of the dynamics of family and clan relationships. Many Tlingit people marry Euro-Americans, and a few marry into other races or other tribes. Some of the interracial families choose to move away from the Tlingit communities and from Tlingit life. Others live in the communities but do not participate in traditional Tlingit activities. A few of the non-Tlingit people intermarried with Tlingit become adopted by the opposite clan of their Tlingit spouse and thereby further their children's participation in Tlingit society.

Traditionally boys and girls were raised with a great deal of family and community support. The uncles and aunts of the children played a major role in the children's development into adulthood. Uncles and aunts often taught the children how to physically survive and participate in society, and anyone from the clan could conceivably reprimand or guide the child. Today the role of the aunts and uncles has diminished, but in the smaller and dominantly Tlingit communities some children are still raised this way. Most Tlingit children are raised in typical American one-family environments, and are instructed in American schools as are other American children. Tlingit people place a strong importance on education and many people go on to receive higher education degrees. Traditional education is usually found in dance groups, traditional survival camps, art camps, and Native education projects through the standard education systems.

RELIGION

Traditionally, spiritual acknowledgment was present in every aspect of the culture, and healing involved the belief that an ailing physical condition was a manifestation of a spiritual problem, invasion, or disturbance. In these cases, a specialist, or shaman-ixt', would be called in to combat spirit(s) yéiks, or the negative forces of a witch or "medicine man." Today, anyone addressing such spiritual forces does so quietly, and most people are silent on the subject. The Indian Religious Freedom Act was passed in 1978, but to date has had little effect other than to provide some legal support for Tlingit potlatch and traditional burial practices.

Institutionalized religion, or places of worship, were not always a part of the traditional Tlingit way of life, although they are now. The Russian Orthodox and Presbyterian faiths have had the longest and most profound impact on Tlingit society and are well established in the Tlingit communities. Other religions have become popular in southeast Alaska, and a few Tlingit people are members of the Jehovah Witnesses, the Bahai's, and the fundamentalist Baptist churches.

EMPLOYMENT AND ECONOMIC TRADITIONS

The Tlingit economy at time of contact was a subsistence economy supported by intense trade. The cash economy and the American systems of ownership have altered the lifestyle of Tlingit people dramatically; however, many Tlingits have adapted successfully. Job seekers find occupations primarily in logging and forestry, fishing and the marine industry, tourism, and other business enterprises. Because of the emphasis on education, a significant number of Tlingit people work in professional positions as lawyers, health-care specialists, and educators. The Sealaska Corporation and village corporations created under ANCSA also provide some employment in blue collar work, office work, and corporate management. Not all positions within the corporations are held by Tlingit and Haida, as a large number of jobs are filled by non-Natives. The corporations provide dividends—the only ANCSA compensation families receive for land they have lost, but these are generally rather modest. Some of the village corporations have produced some hefty lump sum dividends out of timber sales and one-time sale of NOL's (net operating losses) sold to other corporations for tax purposes, but these windfalls are infrequent.

Since the ANCSA bill passed in 1971, differences in wealth distribution among the Tlingit have arisen that did not previously exist. Some of the Tlingit people are economically disadvantaged and have less opportunities today to rely on subsistence for survival. Welfare reliance has become an all-too-common reality for many families, while those in political and corporate positions seem to become more financially independent. As a result shareholder dissension has increased annually and become rather public.

POLITICS AND GOVERNMENT

Tlingit and Haida people have been and continue to be very active in both community and clan politics and tribal governments as well as in state and city issues. Many Tlingits since the 1920s have won seats in the Territorial legislature, setting in motion Tlingit involvement in all aspects of politics and government. Tlingit activist and ANS leader Elizabeth Peratrovich made the plea for justice and equality regardless of race to the territorial legislature on February 8, 1945 that prompted the signing of an anti-discrimination bill. Her efforts as a civil rights leader became officially recognized by the State of Alaska in 1988 with the "Annual Elizabeth Peratrovich Day." She is the only person in Alaska to be so honored for political and social efforts.

The ANCSA-created corporations wield a great deal of political power, and Tlingit and Haida corporate officials are often courted by legislators and businessmen. The corporations are a strong lobby group in Alaska's capital since they not only control lands and assets but represent over 16,000 Tlingit and Haida shareholders. Tlingit people cast their individual ballots based on their own choices and results show they tend to support the Democratic party. Tlingit people running for office also tend to run on a Democratic ticket.

The Indian Child Welfare Act of 1978 provided the first real means for traditional Tlingit law to be practiced and recognized by American government. Since 1978 several tribal courts have been created and tribal judges placed. A very active tribal court exists in Sitka with Tlingit judges presiding over civil matters brought before the court. Tribal courts in Tlingit country are not yet active in determining criminal cases as might be found in other tribal courts of the continental United States, but tribal councils are considering such jurisdiction. Tribal councils and tribal courts are much more a part of the communities than they were 20 years ago, and many issues today are addressed and resolved by Tlingit communities at this level.

Although no statistics are immediately available, many Tlingit men have fought in the World Wars, Korea, and Vietnam. Tlingit participation in the U.S. armed forces is common and generally supported by the families and their communities.

INDIVIDUAL AND GROUP CONTRIBUTIONS

In the twentieth century the Tlingit people have made many contributions. The following mentions some notable Tlingit Americans and their achievements:

ACADEMIA

Elaine Abraham (1929–), bilingual educator, was the first Tlingit to enter the nursing profession. In her early years she cared for people on the Navajo reservation during a diphtheria epidemic, and in Alaska, patients of tuberculosis and diphtheria during a time when many indigenous tribes feared modern medicine. Thereafter she served in major hospital supervisory positions and initiated such health programs as the original Southeast Health Aid Program and the Alaska Board of Health (now called the Alaska Native Health Board). An outstanding educator, she began as assistant dean of students at Sheldon Jackson College and was appointed vice-president in 1972. In Fairbanks she cofounded the Alaska Native Language Center and went on to become Vice-President of Rural Education and Extension Centers (1975). Abraham also established the Native Student Services office for Native students while teaching the Tlingit language at the Anchorage Community College. Her work in student services and indigenous understanding continues as Director of Alaska Native Studies for the University of Alaska in Anchorage.

GOVERNMENT

Elizabeth Peratrovich (1911-1958), civil rights activist, is recognized by Alaskans for her contributions to the equal rights struggle in the state of Alaska. February 17 is celebrated as Elizabeth Peratrovich Day. She is also listed in the Alaska Women's Hall of Fame (1989) and honored annually by the Alaska Native Sisterhood (which she served as Grand Camp President) and by the Alaska Native Brotherhood. Roy Peratrovich (1910-1989), Elizabeth's husband, is also honored by the Alaska Native Brotherhood and other Alaskans for his dedication to bettering the education system and for actively promoting school and social integration. His efforts frequently involved satirical letters to the newspapers that stimulated controversy and debate.

William L. Paul (1885-1977) began as a law school graduate and practicing attorney and became the first Alaska Native and first Tlingit in Alaska's territorial House of Representatives. He contributed to equal rights, racial understanding, and settlement of land issues. Frank J. Peratrovich (1895-1984) received a University of Alaska honorary doctorate for public service, serving as the Mayor of Klawock and as a territorial legislator in the Alaska House and Senate. He was the first Alaska Native not only to serve in the Senate but also to become Senate President (1948).

Andrew P. Hope (1896-1968) was an active politician and contributed to the advancement of Tlingit people and social change. He was instrumental in the development of the Alaska Native Brotherhood (ANB) and was one of Alaska's few Native legislators. Frank See (1915–) from Hoonah was also a notable legislator, mayor, and businessman, as was Frank Johnson (1894-1982), a teacher, legislator, and lobbyist. Frank Price was also elected to the territorial legislature.

LITERATURE AND ORATORY

Nora Marks Dauenhauer (1927–), poet, scholar, and linguist, has dedicated her work to the survival of the Tlingit language; she has stressed the importance of story in culture. Besides such published works in poetry as *The Droning Shaman*, she has edited a number of works with her husband, Richard Dauenhauer, including the bilingual editions of Tlingit oral literature, *Haa Shuka, Our Ancestors: Tlingit Oral Narratives* (1987), and *Haa Tuwunaagu Yis, for Healing Our Spirit: Tlingit Oratory* (1990). Together they have developed Tlingit language instruction materials, *Beginning Tlingit* (1976), the *Tlingit Spelling Book (1984)*, and instructional audio tapes. She has written numerous papers on the subjects of Tlingit language oratory and culture, and she has co-authored many other articles. Another active writer is Andy Hope III, essayist, poet, and editor of *Raven's Bones Journal*.

Orators and storytellers in Tlingit history and within the society today are numerous, but some of the noteworthy include Amy Marvin/Ḵooteen (1912–); Chookan Sháa, who also serves as songleader and as a lead drummer for the Mt. Fairweather Dancers; Robert Zuboff/Shaadaax' (1893-1974) traditional storyteller and humorist; Johnny Jackson/Gooch Éesh (1893-1985), storyteller, singer, and orator; and Jessie Dalton/Naa Tlaa (1903–), an influential bilingual orator. Another well-respected orator was Austin Hammond/ Daanawáak (1910-1993), a traditions bearer and activist. Hammond dedicated a song to the Tlingit people just before he died for use in traditional gatherings and ceremony as the Tlingit national anthem.

PERFORMANCE AND DANCE

A widespread interest in Tlingit dancing, singing, and stories has generated the revival and development of a large number of traditional performance groups. The renowned Geisan Dancers of Haines have scheduled national and international engagements as have Kake's, Keex' Kwaan Dancers, and Sealaska Heritage Foundation's, NaaKahidi Theatre. Other major dance groups include the Noow Tlein Dancers of Sitka, led by Vida Davis, the acclaimed children's group, Gájaa Héen Dancers of Sitka, and the Mt. Fairweather Dancers (led for many years by the late T'akdeintaan matriarch, Katherine Mills). Other notable performance groups include the Tlingit and Haida Dancers of Anchorage, the Angoon Eagles, the Angoon Ravens, the Marks Trail Dancers, the Mt. Juneau Tlingit Dancers, the Mt. St. Elias Dancers, the Seetka Kwaan Dancers, the Killerwhale Clan, the Klukwan Chilkat Dancers, and the Klawock Heinya Dancers.

Gary Waid (1948–), has bridged the Western stage and traditional performance for nearly two decades, performing nationally and internationally in such productions as *Coyote Builds North America*, (Perseverance Theatre, as a solo actor), and *Fires on the Water* (NaaKahidi Theatre, as a leading storyteller); he has also performed in educational films such as *Shadow Walkers* (Alaska State Department of Education and Sealaska Heritage Foundation). Besides performing regularly in Alaska and on tour, Waid performed in New York with *Summer Faced Woman* (1986) and *Lilac and Flag* (1994), a Perseverance Theatre Production coproduced with the Talking Band. He also performs Shakespeare and standard western repertoire. David Kadashan/Kaatyé (1893-1976) was an avid musician in both Tlingit and contemporary Western music during the big band era, and became a traditional orator and song leader of standing. Archie James Cavanaugh is a jazz musician and recording artist, best known for his album *Black and White Raven* (1980), with some selections recorded with the late great Native American jazz saxophonist, Jim Pepper.

VISUAL ARTS

Nathan Jackson is a master carver who has exhibited his works—totem poles, masks, bentwood boxes and house fronts—in New York, London, Chicago, Salt Lake City, and Seattle. His eagle frontlet is the first aspect of Native culture to greet airline passengers deplaning in Ketchikan. Two of his 40-foot totem poles decorate the entrance to the Centennial Building in Juneau, and other areas display his restoration and reproduction work. Reggie B. Peterson (1948–) is a woodcarver, silversmith, and instructor of Northwest Coast art in Sitka, sharing his work with cultural centers and museums.

Jennie Thlunaut/Shax´saani Kéek' (1890-1986), Kaagwaantaan, award-winning master Chilkat weaver, taught the ancient weaving style to others, and thereby kept the art alive. Jennie has woven over 50 robes and tunics, and received many honors and awards. In 1983 Alaska's Governor Sheffield named a day in her honor, but she chose to share the honor by naming her day Yanwaa Sháa Day to recognize her clanswomen. Emma Marks/Seigeigéi (1913–), Lukaax.ádi, is also acclaimed for her award-winning beadwork. Esther Littlefield of Sitka has her beaded ceremonial robes, aprons, and dance shirts on display in lodges and museums, and a younger artist, Ernestine Hanlon of Hoonah creates, sells, and displays her intricate cedar and spruce basket weavings throughout southeast Alaska.

Sue Folletti/Shax´saani Kéek' (named after Jenni Thlunaut) (1953-), Kaagwaantaan, silver carver, creates clan and story bracelets of silver and gold, traditionally designed earrings, and pendants that are sold and displayed in numerous art shows and were featured at the Smithsonian Institute during the Crossroads of the Continents traveling exhibit. Other exceptional Tlingit art craftsmen include Ed Kasko; master carver and silversmith from Klukwan, Louis Minard; master silversmith from Sitka; and developing artists like Norm Jackson, a silversmith and mask maker from Kake, and Odin Lonning (1953–), carver, silversmith, and drum maker.

MEDIA

PRINT

Naa Kaani.
The Sealaska Heritage Foundation Newsletter; provides updates on Sealaska Heritage Foundations cultural and literary projects. English language only.

Address: 1 Sealaska Plaza, Suite 201, Juneau, Alaska 99801.

Raven's Bones Journal.

A literary newsletter; contains reports and essays on tribal and publication issues along with listings of Native American writers and publications. (English language only.)

Contact: Andy Hope III, Editor.
Address: 523 Fourth Street, Juneau, Alaska 99801.

Sealaska Shareholder Newsletter.

A bimonthly publication of the Sealaska Corporation. The primary focus is on corporate and shareholder issues, but also reports on Tlingit, Haida, and Tsimpsian achievements and celebrations. Each issue provides a calendar of cultural, corporate, and social events. (English language only.)

Contact: Vikki Mata, Director of Corporate Communications.
Address: 1 Sealaska Plaza, Suite 400, Juneau, Alaska 99801-1276.
Telephone: (907) 586-1827.

RADIO AND TELEVISION

KTOO-FM.

A local radio and television broadcast station; does a 15-minute Native report five mornings a week. "Raincountry," a weekly program on television deals with Native affairs in Alaska focusing on issues in Tlingit country and the southeast as a whole. On Mondays the station airs the "Alaska Native News," a half-hour program, and Ray Peck Jr., Tlingit, hosts a radio jazz show. No Tlingit person is otherwise on staff for these programs.

Contact: Scott Foster.
Address: 224 Fourth Street, Juneau, Alaska 99801.
Telephone: (907) 586-1670.

ORGANIZATIONS AND ASSOCIATIONS

Alaska Native Brotherhood (ANB)/Alaska Native Sisterhood (ANS).

ANB (founded in 1912) and ANS (founded in 1915) promote community, education, and justice through a governing grand camp and operating subordinate camps (local ANB and ANS groups). Native education and equal rights are some of the many issues addressed by the membership, as are Tlingit and Haida well being and social standing.

Contact: Ron Williams, President.
Address: 320 West Willoughby Avenue, Juneau, Alaska 99801.
Telephone: (907) 586-2049.

Central Council of the Tlingit and Haida Indian Tribes of Alaska (CCTHITA).

Founded in 1965. Provides trust services through Bureau of Indian Affairs (BIA) to Tlingit and Haida people and Tlingit and Haida villages in land allotment cases, operates health and tribal employment programs, and issues educational grants and scholarships.

Contact: Edward Thomas, President.
Address: 320 West Willoughby Avenue, Suite 300, Juneau, Alaska 99801-9983.
Telephone: (907) 586-1432.

Organized Village of Kake.

Founded in 1947 under the Indian Reorganization Act. Contracts with the Bureau of Indian Affairs (BIA) to provide services to the tribe such as counseling referral, general assistance, assistance in Indian Child Welfare Act (ICWA) issues, education and cultural development, scholarships, and housing improvement. Through a Johnson O'Malley BIA contract they provide supplemental education and culture/language classes. The organization also handles its own tribal land trust responsibilities.

Contact: Gary Williams, Executive Director; or, Henrich Kadake, President.
Address: P.O. Box 316, Kake, Alaska 99830.
Telephone: (907) 785-6471.

Sitka Tribe of Alaska (STA).

Chartered in 1938 under the Indian Reorganization Act as the Sitka Community Association, STA is a federally recognized tribe and operates contracts under the Bureau of Indian Affairs (BIA). STA has an extensive social services program, providing counseling, crisis intervention, employment services, housing improvement, youth and education programs, economic development, and historic preservation. STA also supports a tribal court.

Contact: Ted Wright, General Manager; or, Larry Widmark, Tribal Chair.
Address: 456 Katlian Street, Sitka, Alaska 99835.
Telephone: (907) 747-3207.

Yakutat Native Association (YNA).

Founded in 1983. Provides family services to the tribe through Bureau of Indian Affairs (BIA) contracts. YNA's Johnson O'Malley program provides dance instruction, runs a culture camp in the summer, and is in the processes of developing a language program.

Contact: Nellie Valle.
Address: P.O. Box 418, Yakutat, Alaska 99689.
Telephone: (907) 784-3238.

MUSEUMS AND RESEARCH CENTERS

Alaska State Museum.
Houses a varied collection of southeast Alaska Indian art, with elaborate displays of traditional Tlingit regalia, carvings, artifacts, and totem designs.

Address: 395 Whittier Street, Juneau, Alaska.
Telephone: (907) 465-2901.

Sheldon Jackson Museum.
Houses Tlingit regalia, a canoe, a large spruce root basket collection, and other traditional items and artifacts including house posts, hooks, woodworking tools, bentwood boxes, and armor. The museum also contains a large variety of Aleut and Eskimo art. The museum's gift shop sells baskets and other Tlingit art.

Address: 104 College Drive, Sitka, Alaska 99835.
Telephone: (907) 747-8981.

Sheldon Museum and Cultural Center.
Shares the history of Haines, the gold rush era, and Tlingit art in the displays. The center provides books and flyers on different aspects of Tlingit art and history, as well as live demonstrations in traditional crafts.

Address: P.O. Box 623, Haines, Alaska 99827.
Telephone: (907) 766-2366.

Southeast Alaska Indian Cultural Center.
Displays a model panorama of the Tlingit battles against the Russians in 1802 and 1804, elaborate carved house posts, and artifacts. The center shows historic films and has a large totem park outside the structure. Classes are conducted in Tlingit carving, silversmithing, and beadwork, and artists remain in-house to complete their own projects.

Address: 106 Metlakatla, Sitka, Alaska 99835.
Telephone: (907) 747-8061.

Totem Heritage Center.
Promotes Tlingit and Haida carving and traditional art forms and designs by firsthand instruction. The center maintains brochures and other information on artists in the area as well as instructional literature.

Address: City of Ketchikan, Museum Department, 629 Dock Street, Ketchikan, Alaska 99901.
Telephone: (907) 225-5600.

SOURCES FOR ADDITIONAL STUDY

Case, David S. *Alaska Natives and American Laws*. University of Alaska Press, 1984.

Cole, Douglas. *Captured Heritage: The Scramble for Northwest Coast Artifacts*. Seattle: University of Washington Press, 1985.

Dauenhauer, Nora Marks, and Richard Dauenhauer. *Haa Ḵusteeyí, Our Culture: Tlingit Life Stories*. Seattle: University of Washington Press; and Juneau, Alaska: Sealaska Heritage Foundation, 1994.

Dauenhauer, Nora Marks, and Richard Dauenhauer. *Haa Tuwunáagu Yís, for Healing Our Spirit: Tlingit Oratory*. Seattle: University of Washington Press; and Juneau, Alaska: Sealaska Heritage Foundation, 1990.

Emmons, George Thornton. *The Tlingit Indians*. Seattle: University of Washington Press, 1991.

Garfield, Viola E., and Linn A. Forrest. *The Wolf and The Raven: Totem Poles of Southeastern Alaska*. Seattle: University of Washington Press, 1993.

Jonaitis, Aldona. *Art of the Northern Tlingit*. Seattle, Washington: University of Washington Press, 1986.

Langdon, Steve J. *The Native People of Alaska*. Anchorage, Alaska: Greatland Graphics, 1987.

Samuel, Cheryl. *The Chilkat Dancing Blanket*. Seattle: Pacific Search Press, 1982.

Steward, Hilary. *Looking at Totem Poles*. Seattle: University of Washington Press, 1993.

TONGAN AMERICANS

by
Amy Cooper

Though many
Tongans feel that
residence in the Unit-
ed States relieves
them from the social
obligations to village
chiefs and others,
visiting Tongan chiefs
and their families are
welcomed with
gifts and exclusive
treatment.

OVERVIEW

Tonga is an archipelago of 150 tropical islands located in the South Pacific Ocean, 36 of which are inhabited. The islands experience a cool season between May and December, and a warm season between December and May. The total land area is approximately 290 square miles. Together, the islands are known as the Kingdom of Tonga, or *Pule'anga Fakatu'i'o* and the capital is Nuku'alofa. Tonga is ruled by a constitutional monarchy that was established in 1875 and is headed by a King and a Privy Council. The population is composed of approximately 101,300 people, over 90 percent of whom are of Polynesian descent. The population is relatively homogeneous, though some Americans and people of other nations who are involved in Tonga's popular tourist trade also live on the islands. There are three primary social classes in Tonga: the King; a nobility made up of 33 families; and commoners.

HISTORY

Tongans are descended from Malaysians who settled on the main island group of Tongatapu about 3,000 years ago. Beginning in the 10th century, they were ruled by a line of sacred kings and queens called the Tu'i Tonga. The sovereign transferred power to his brother under the title of Tu'i Ha'a Takalaua in 1470. In 1600, power was transferred to the Tu'i

Kanokipolu, from whom the current rulers are descended.

The Dutch were the first to visit the islands. Jacob Le Maire arrived in 1616 and Abel Janszoon Tasman followed in 1643. In contrast to his predecessors' short stints in the islands, Captain James Cook visited the Tongans several times between 1773 and 1777. He named the Tongan islands the Friendly Islands because of the warmth shown him by the native inhabitants. In 1826, the Methodist Mission successfully introduced Christianity to Tonga, and Marists introduced Roman Catholicism in 1842. Leader Taufa'ahau, who converted to Methodism in 1831, ended the unrest and took the title King George Tupou I in 1845 and ruled until 1893. During his reign, Tonga was unified and became an independent nation, establishing its constitution in 1875. Germany, Great Britain and the United States all recognized Tonga's independence in 1876, 1879 and 1888, respectively.

George I was succeeded by his great-grandson, George II. Under George II's reign, Tonga renounced its independence in return for protection from German invasion. In 1900, it became a British protectorate, agreeing to conduct all foreign affairs through a British counsul and giving Britain veto power over its foreign policy and finances. Queen Salote Tupou III ruled from George II's death in 1918 until her death in 1965 and was succeeded by her son, who became Taufa'ahau Tupou IV. It was during his reign that Tonga became a fully independent nation, regaining control from Britain on June 4, 1970.

SIGNIFICANT IMMIGRATION WAVES AND SETTLEMENT PATTERNS

In 1990, Tongan immigrants to the United States numbered approximately 17,600 people. Tongons are considered Pacific Islanders, the smallest ethnic group represented in the country. Tongan Americans are often confused with Samoans and Hawaiians, and have only been enumerated distinct from Asians and Hawaiians since 1980. It is important to note that, in 1980, there were only 6,200 Tongan Americans. The Tongan American population rose 184 percent in ten years due to continued immigration. Mormon missionaries have been most instrumental in encouraging Tongan immigration to the United States. The Mormon Church has assisted Tongans in immigration to the United States by providing student and work visas, employment, and the opportunity for Tongans of marriageable age to meet spouses.

Tongans first came to Laie, Hawaii in 1916. The number of immigrants increased dramatically at the end of World War II when they came as labor missionaries for the Hawaiian Temple, Church College and the Polynesian Cultural Center. On mainland America, Tongans have settled primarily on the west coast, with 45 percent of Tongans living in Los Angeles and the San Francisco Bay area. Over 22 percent live in Salt Lake City or Provo. Tongan law guarantees each male eight acres of land, but Tongan men who leave the islands lose their right to land, thereby freeing land rights for other islanders. However, a shortage of land has resulted in increased immigration since the 1970s.

ACCULTURATION AND ASSIMILATION

HOLIDAYS

Because Tongan Americans are Christian, they celebrate the Christian holidays of Christmas and Easter. They also celebrate the traditional New Year's Day (called *Ta'u Fo'ou*) during which children go caroling, singing hymns for friends and neighbors. Tongans celebrate Sunday School Day (called *Faka Me*), which is something like a first communion celebration. *Faka Me* is celebrated on the first Sunday in May and gives the children in the church an opportunity to dress in new clothes specially made for the occasion. The families attend church and then host a feast for the children. Another important holiday is Tonga Emancipation Day, celebrated on June 4 in commemoration of Tongan independence from Britain, which was gained in 1970.

DANCES AND SONGS

Tongans have a strong heritage of poetry, set to dance and music. The *lakalaka* is a formal, traditional line dance performed by both men and women that uses commemorates people, historical events and places. New dances and songs are composed and choreographed for special occasions by Tongan poets. A more informal type of music is called *hiva kakala* (love songs). Young women perform solo dances (*tau'olunga*) to these songs at fund raisers. The paddle dance (*me'etu'upaki*) features dancers who carry paddle-shaped boards painted or carved with abstract representations of the human body. Other popular dances include the *kailao*, which is a war dance, and the *ma'ulu'ulu* which is an action dance similar to the *lakalaka*, but is performed while seated. Tongans have also developed a high form of harmonization for hymns.

LANGUAGE

Tongan and English are both considered official languages of Tonga, and therefore much of the population is bilingual. English is considered a second language, and schools primarily teach Tongan. Linguistically, Tongan is related to Samoan and other Polynesian languages. Among immigrant cultures, Tongans have the highest degree of native language spoken in American households. Second generation Tongan Americans are generally more fluent in English.

FAMILY AND COMMUNITY DYNAMICS

Both Tongan island communities and Tongan American communities are generally organized around large family units called *kainga*. The *kainga* encompass all blood relatives and can include people other than blood relations. Tongans see themselves as members of several overlapping groups of descent, and each person has a rank within the family structure. In this complex system, Tongans trace descent through both the mother's and father's lineage, called unilineal descent, and have social obligations to both groups.

Tongan households are large and include many generations and relations. Aunts, uncles, cousins and others may all, at some time or another, live under the same roof, for the household can shift, depending on the needs of work, marriage or education. Tongans have very specific obligations to each family member, depending on rank. Though many Tongans feel that residence in the United States relieves them from the social obligations to village chiefs and others, visiting Tongan chiefs and their families are welcomed with gifts and exclusive treatment. Tongans rely on the status that their ties to the chiefs provide, and hold strongly to the protocol of social obligations. Many Tongans are also tied to large social groups, including church groups (probably the most important), sports groups, and community associations.

CELEBRATIONS

Many different family celebrations are marked in similar ways. Birthdays, weddings, funerals, graduations and chiefly installment ceremonies are celebrated within families by the exchange of painted *tapa* cloth (a cloth made of bark), pandanus mats and feasts. Women provide the *koloa*, or ceremonial wealth, which is normally redistributed at the next event. Men provide the food for the feast. Recently, as a replacement for the traditional cloth and mats, women have begun to create quilts as *koloa*. This enables Tongans who have immigrated to the United States or other countries to participate in traditional exchanges more easily, because of the difficulty in obtaining *tapa* cloth and mats outside of Tonga.

THE ROLE OF WOMEN

Tongan women symbolically rank lower than their husbands, but are ranked higher than their brothers. A brother and all of his children are especially obligated to support his sister and her children. Tongan women spend much of their time in same-sex groups, providing child care, participating in sports and organizing church activities.

RELIGION

Christian missionary activity has taken place since 1797 and has had a great impact on the Tongan culture. Most Tongan Americans are Christian, and are primarily Methodist. In Tonga, 47 percent of families belong to the Free Weselyan Church. Sixteen percent of Tongans are Roman Catholic, 14 percent belong to the Free Church of Tonga, and nine percent are Mormon.

EMPLOYMENT AND ECONOMIC TRADITIONS

Tonga's economy is still agriculturally based, but there is a growing pattern of middle class Tongans who have been educated abroad who have started small businesses. Tonga also has a thriving tourist trade. Tongans living abroad in the United States, New Zealand or Australia, often send money to family members still living on the islands. *Kainga* participate in resource sharing characteristic of the traditional redistributive economy in Tonga. This economy is based on three core values: *'ofa* (love), *faka'apa'apa* (respect) and *fuakavenga* (responsibility). Family groups rely on traditional economic cooperation to raise money for such important occasions as weddings, funerals, graduation and home building. Tongan American family groups regularly participate in this tradition, though they are not geographically near their families. Thus, the social structure necessitates that a Tongan American living in Provo, Utah, or Los Angeles, California, fulfill an economic obligation to a relative still living in Tonga. The same Tongan American may receive goods from Tonga for an event in the future.

Tongans are generally not college educated. The 1990 census shows that most Tongan Americans are working class, employed in service occupations and technical support. Men and women are employed at almost the same rate.

MEDIA

The Tonga Chronicle.
This online newspaper provides news from Tonga and includes an archive of back issues..

Address: PO Box 197 Nuku'alofa, Kingdom of Tonga.

E-mail: tk@pacificforum.com.

Online: http://www.netstorage.com/kami/tonga/news.

Tonga Page.
Personal website that provides photographs, maps, facts, and links about Tonga.

Online: http://user.cs.tu-berlin.de/~minibbjd/tonga/index.html.

Tonga Online.
Professional website that provides current news and information about Tonga.

E-mail: kami@ender.netstorage.com.
Online: http://www.tongaonline.com.

Organizations and Associations

Maui Tongan Association.

A local organization supporting Tongans in Maui.

Address: PO Box 5103, Kahului, HI 96733-5103.

National Tongan American Society.

Founded in 1994, this group supporting Tongan Americans has annual membership dues of $20.

Address: c/o Ivoni M. Nash, 1175 W. 4515 S, Number 61, Salt Lake City, Utah 84123.

Pacific Islanders Cultural Association (PICA).

Supports Pacific Islanders in Northern California. Includes information on all Pacific Islands, links, the Northern California Outrigger Canoe Association, and Pacific Island News sources.

Address: PO Box 31238 San Francisco, CA 94131.

Telephone: (415) 281-0221.

E-mail: webmaster@pica-org.org.

Online: http://www.pica-org.org.

Polynesian Cultural Center (PCC).

This organization, founded in 1963, seeks to preserve Polynesian cultures, and provides information and education about arts, crafts and lore. Sponsors several recognition awards and funds the Institute for Polynesian Studies at the Brigham Young University—Hawaii campus.

Address: 55-370 Kamehameha Hwy., Laie, HI 96762.

Telephone: (808) 293-3333 or (800) 367-7060.

Sources for Additional Study

Barkan, Elliott Robert. *Asian and Pacific Islander Migration to the United States: A Model of New Global Patterns*. Westport, CT: Greenwood Press, 1992.

Levinson, David. *Ethnic Groups Worldwide: A Ready Reference Handbook*. Phoenix, AZ: Oryx Press, 1998.

"Tonga" in *Encyclopedia Britannica Online*. http://www.eb.com:180/bol/topic?eu=127827&sctn =5 [Accessed June 1, 1999].

Despite Trinidad and Tobago's culturally diverse people, the family, regardless of ethnic background, fulfills certain basic roles. In the United States, it is the family's responsibility to maintain traditions and enforce strong family values in the community.

TRINIDADIAN AND TOBAGONIAN AMERICANS

by
N. Samuel Murrell

OVERVIEW

Located on the northeastern coast of Venezuela, the Republic of Trinidad and Tobago comprises the two most southerly islands in the West Indies. Tobago, which lies 20 miles northeast of Trinidad, measures only 117 square miles. Trinidad, which has a land mass of 1,865 square miles, is about the size of Delaware. The Republic's capital, Port of Spain, is an important commercial center, producing beer, rum, plastics, lumber, and textiles. Chief exports of Trinidad and Tobago include oil, sugar, citrus fruit, asphalt, and coffee.

Trinidad and Tobago have approximately 1.27 million residents, most of whom live on Trinidad. While the population of Tobago is predominantly black, Trinidad supports several ethnic groups, including Asian Indians (40.3 percent), blacks (39.6 percent), Europeans, Chinese, and Lebanese (one percent). The remaining 18 percent includes individuals of mixed heritage. Roman Catholics (29.4 percent), Hindus (23.8 percent), Protestant Christians (12 percent), Anglicans (10.9 percent), and Muslims (5.8 percent) are the dominant religious groups of the islands.

The Republic's national flag has a black diagonal band edged with white on a red background. Trinidad and Tobago's national anthem "Side By Side We Stand" echoes the country's commitment to racial and ethnic diversity: "Forged from the love of liberty, / In the fires of hope and prayer, / With boundless faith in our destiny, / We solemnly declare. / Side by side we stand. / Islands of the blue Caribbean sea, / This is our native land. / We pledge our lives to thee, / Here every creed and race / Finds an equal place, / And may God bless our nation."

HISTORY

The history of Trinidad and Tobago is one of invasion, conquest, and colonization. On July 31, 1498, Christopher Columbus discovered the islands, which were inhabited by about 40,000 native peoples (Arawaks and Caribs) whom he called Indians. Columbus named the larger island Trinidad, in honor of the Holy Trinity, and called Tobago (the legendary island of *Robinson Crusoe*) Concepcion. The islands' native population began disappearing, largely from exposure to European diseases and poor treatment, shortly after the founding of the first city, San Josef de Quna (Saint Joseph), in 1592. By 1783 the native population was reduced to less than 1,490 people and by 1800 they were virtually extinct.

Trinidad remained an underdeveloped outpost for almost 200 years until the King of Spain issued the Cedular of Population in 1783 and began enticing planters to migrate to Trinidad with their slaves. In 1791 thousands of French colonists, fleeing the French Revolution in Saint Domingue, settled in Trinidad, bringing enslaved Africans with them. While Trinidad was largely ignored during the early years of colonization, Tobago fell to a number of European explorers. The island passed through the hands of Great Britain, France, Holland, and other invading European countries at least 22 times during its history, until it was finally ceded to Britain in 1814. In January 1889 Trinidad and Tobago united as one nation under British rule. Africans were brought to Tobago as slaves in the early 1600s but were not imported into Trinidad in great numbers until the early 1700s. After the British government abolished slavery in 1834, Asian Indian and Chinese laborers were brought to Trinidad as indentured servants. Between 1842 and 1917, over 170,000 Asian Indians, Chinese, and Portuguese (from Madeira) were enticed into working on the islands' vast plantations. Lured by the fertile soil and unexplored natural resources, many former American slaves migrated to the island as well. Consequently, by 1900 more than 70,000 blacks had settled in Trinidad and Tobago.

MODERN ERA

Trinidad and Tobago was governed by British royalists and dominated by Scottish, French, and Spanish colonists until its independence in 1962. Prior to independence, non-whites had little or no voice in government affairs. After World War I, however, they began protesting through strikes and demonstrations organized by such civil rights leaders as Arthur Cipriani, Uriah Buzz Butler, and others involved with the powerful Oil Field Workers Trade Union and the Manual and Metal Workers Union.

In 1947 the British Government plotted the formation of a West Indian federation, which came to fruition in 1958. They chose Port of Spain as the capital. The federation was designed to foster political and cultural solidarity and to break down economic barriers among the islands. The federation collapsed in 1961, however, when Jamaica seceded from the union, becoming an independent nation. Trinidad and Tobago attained independence on August 31, 1962, and became a republic within The Commonwealth in 1976. In 1965 Trinidad and Tobago joined the Organization of American States (OAS) and the Caribbean Free Trade Area (Carifta) which was renamed the Caribbean Community (Caricom) in 1974. Trinidad and Tobago enjoyed substantial prosperity from the 1960s to the early 1980s due to the success of the oil industry, but prices plummeted in the late 1980s, sending the country into a serious recession.

THE FIRST TRINIDADIANS AND TOBAGONIANS IN AMERICA

Trinidadian and Tobagonian immigration to the United States, which dates back to the seventeenth century, was spasmodic and is best studied in relation to the major waves of Caribbean immigration. The first documented account of black immigration to the United States from the Caribbean dates back to 1619, when a small group of voluntary indentured workers arrived in Jamestown, Virginia, on a Dutch frigate. The immigrants worked as free people until 1629 when a Portuguese vessel arrived with the first shipload of blacks captured off the west coast of Africa. In the 1640s Virginia and other states began instituting laws that took away the freedom of blacks and redefined them as chattel, or personal property. Trinidad, like many other islands in the British West Indies, served as a clearinghouse for slaves en route to North America. The region also acted as a "seasoning camp" where newly arrived blacks were "broken-in" psychologically and physically to a life of slavery, as well as a place where they acquired biological resistance to deadly European diseases.

SIGNIFICANT IMMIGRATION WAVES

Since the turn of the twentieth century, there have been three distinct waves of Caribbean immigrants into the United States. The first wave was modest and lasted from about 1900 to the 1920s. Between 1899 and 1924, the number of documented, English-speaking Caribbean immigrants entering the United States increased annually from 412 in 1899 to 12,245 in 1924, although the actual number of Caribbean residents in the United States was probably twice as high. Immigration fell substantially after 1924 when the U.S. government established national quotas on African and Caribbean countries. By 1930 there were only 177,981 documented foreign blacks in the United States—less than two percent of the aggregate black population. Approximately 72,200 of the foreign blacks were first-generation emigrants from the English-speaking Caribbean.

Most Trinidadians and Tobagonians who entered the United States during that period were industrial workers, civil servants, laborers, and former soldiers disillusioned by the high unemployment rate in Trinidad and Tobago after World War I. The number of new arrivals dropped significantly during the Great Depression (1932-1937) when more blacks returned to the Caribbean than came to the United States. Only a small number of professionals and graduate students migrated to America prior to World War II, some with the intention of staying for a short time on a student or worker's visa, and others planning to remain permanently.

The second and weakest immigration wave from the Caribbean to the United States was rather sporadic and occurred between the late 1930s and the passage of new immigration policies in the 1960s. As late as the 1950s, the number of Trinidadians and Tobagonians arriving in the United States was low in comparison to other foreign countries. This was partially due to the passage of the 1952 McCarran-Walter Act, which reaffirmed the quota bill and further restricted Caribbean immigration to America. The differential treatment of African and Caribbean peoples by immigration authorities, in contrast to Europeans, also discouraged the migration of Trinidadians and Tobagonians. After the Republic achieved independence in 1962, only 100 Trinidadian and Tobagonian immigrants were permitted to enter the United States annually.

Still, a small group, mainly from Trinidad's middle class, migrated between the waning of the Depression and the changing of U.S. immigration laws. This group consisted mainly of white-collar workers, students, and people joining their families already living in the United States. With the open-ing of a U.S. Naval Base on Trinidad in 1940, Trinidadian and Tobagonian military personnel were stationed in the U.S. Virgin Islands and Florida, and some served under U.S. and British command in Europe. After World War II, some of these soldiers migrated to America in search of jobs and improved economic opportunity. Because of laws restricting immigration, only 2,598 documented Trinidadian and Tobagonian immigrants entered the United States between 1960 and 1965.

The third and largest wave of Caribbean immigration began in 1965 and continues into the present. It was greatly influenced by the American civil rights movement, which exposed the racism inherent in U.S. immigration policy. The 1965 Hart-Cellar Immigration Reform Act, which established uniform limits of no more than 20,000 persons per country annually for the eastern hemisphere, enabled Trinidadian and Tobagonian immigrants to seek legal immigration and naturalization status in larger numbers. A clause in the Act of 1965, which gave preference to immigrants whose relatives were already U.S. citizens and therefore capable of sponsoring immigrants, also encouraged many Trinidadian and Tobagonian residents to migrate to the United States.

From 1966 to 1970, 23,367 Trinidadian and Tobagonian immigrants, primarily from the educated elite and rural poor classes, legally migrated to the United States. From 1971 to 1975, the figure climbed to 33,278. It dropped to 28,498 from 1976 to 1980, and only half that amount between 1981 and 1984, when the Reagan administration began placing greater restrictions on U.S. immigration policy. Less than 2,300 Trinidadian and Tobagonian immigrants arrived in 1984 and that number scarcely increased during President Reagan's second term of office. A few European-Trinidadians migrated during the latter half of the twentieth century, primarily because they were loosing their grip on political power in the Republic with the rise of nationalism and independence. The majority of those immigrants came to the United States because Britain had restricted immigration from the Commonwealth islands to the British Isles. A larger number migrated in the late 1980s when oil prices fell, sending the Republic into a deep recession. Trinidadians and Tobagonians are now the second largest group of English-speaking immigrants in the United States.

SETTLEMENT

A total of 76,270 Trinidadians and Tobagonians, who reported at least one specific ancestry, are documented in the 1990 U.S. Census. Of this number, 71,720, or 94 percent, of the aggregate are first generation Trinidadian Tobagonian Americans, and the remaining 4,550 are of the second generation. There were 58,473 such persons in the northeast, 1,760 in the midwest, 18,215 in the south, and 3,822 in the west. Regionally, there were 3,746 Trinidadian and Tobagonian immigrants in New England, 48,727 in the middle Atlantic, 1,523 in east north central United States, 237 in the west north central, 15,096 in the south Atlantic, 549 in east south central, 2,570 in the west south central, 446 in the mountain region, and 3,376 in the Pacific region. The largest percentage of Trinidadians and Tobagonians live in the northeast and the smallest percentage in the midwest. They ranked sixth in the 1965-1980 census report of newcomers into New York City, and rank eighth in the city's 15 largest ethnic groups. By 1982, over half of the Trinidadians and Tobagonians in America resided in New York City.

According to the 1990 Census, the six states that have the largest Trinidadian and Tobagonian populations are: New York (42,973), Florida (7,500), Maryland (4,493), New Jersey (4,245), California (3,100), and Massachusetts (2,590). Family connections, employment opportunities, racial tolerance, access to higher education, and weather conditions are some of the reasons given for the heavy concentration of Trinidadian and Tobagonian immigrants on the eastern seaboard.

ACCULTURATION AND ASSIMILATION

Trinidadian and Tobagonian immigrants generally select one of two options: they either make a quick livelihood in the United States before returning home, or they join American society permanently, usually immersing themselves in black culture and working for the betterment of African American and Caribbean American communities. Many of the early Trinidadians and Tobagonians aged 35 and older did return to their native land. Later immigrants often chose the second option and increasingly became part of the distinctly Caribbean community in New York City and Florida.

Trinidadian and Tobagonian immigrants have had to adjust in a number of ways while assimilating into American society. First, those who are permanent residents must adjust nationally, which often means giving up their Trinidad and Tobago citizenship and strong ties to Caribbean nationalism for American citizenship and values. Secondly, they must adjust to the cultural traditions, social roles, and stereotypes of the racial and ethnic groups with which they identify. Trinidadian and Tobagonian immigrants of the first and second waves arrived in the United States at the height of Jim Crow segregation and, consequently, suffered tremendous racial prejudice. Even though they came from a society where racial categories and stereotypes were not unknown, they resented having to fight virtually every social, political, and economic issue in American society. Third, they must adjust to severe variations in weather patterns, particularly in the north, which, for older generations, is especially difficult. Some immigrants have also had to adjust to life in some of America's roughest neighborhoods. Although friends, relatives, and other sponsors advise them of dangerous neighborhoods, many become casualties of urban crime. Traditionally "safe" Caribbean neighborhoods in New York City, for example, have become battle zones for gangs and drug dealers. Moreover, Trinidadian and Tobagonian immigrants living in non-Caribbean communities often feel isolated; they carry the dual burden of speaking with a foreign accent and being visibly identifiable as a minority in a European-based society. Finally, these immigrants come from a country where they represented the majority and many of them were highly respected leaders. In the United States, however, they must adjust to their new status of "resident aliens."

TRADITIONS, CUSTOMS, AND BELIEFS

Trinidad and Tobago is a multi-faceted country with a perfusion of customs and traditions that meet to form the "Trinibago" culture. Two of the most dominant cultures in Trinidad and Tobago are mixed-black (often called Creole) and Asian Indian. The first is a mixture of African, English, Spanish, and French cultures. Spanish influence is evident in the islands' music, festivals (especially the Parang festival), and dance. Even though France never occupied Trinidad, French planters on the island left their unmistakable mark in terms of language, religion, and class consciousness. The Republic's Asian Indian culture is celebrated through *Divali* (Festival of Lights), *Hosay* (Muslim New Year festival), East Indian music, and various philosophical beliefs and practices foreign to western cultures. For example, everyone is expected to take off their shoes at the door before stepping inside an Indian Muslim house, and new homes are often blessed in a special ceremony. There are rites for conception, birth, puberty, marriage, death, and the planting and harvesting of crops.

CUISINE

Trinidadians and Tobagonians have retained many of their cooking traditions in the United States, although eating habits have changed somewhat to better suit America's fast pace. Breakfast often varies from a full meal to a very light one and may include fresh coconut water and coconut jelly. Because Trinidad and Tobago is a highly Westernized nation, oatmeal, cornflakes, cocoa, coffee, and rolls are also common breakfast foods. Lunches and dinners generally consist of meat, rice, green vegetables, and fruits. One popular Trinidadian and Tobagonian dish is *pelau*, or rice mixed with pork or chicken and various local vegetables. *Calaloo* (a green, leafy vegetable that is served cooked) is sometimes combined with taro, dasheen, or tania leaves, okra, pumpkin, and crab to make a dish called calaloo and crab. Other popular dishes are dumpling and pig-tail or cow-heel soup, *souse* (well-cooked pickled pigs feet), and chicken stew. Most dishes contain meat or fish, although many of the favorites in Trinidad and Tobago (manicou, tatoo, venison, armadillo, lappe, quenk, duck, shark, flying fish, shrimp, kingfish, chip-chip, and cascadou) are not readily available in the United States. Such vegetables as pumpkin, cabbage, onion, and *melongene* (eggplant) are also well liked. Coconut ice cream and fruits are popular Trinidadian and Tobagonian desserts. Many meals, especially during special occasions, are served with *mauby* (a drink made from the bark of a tree), Guinness stout, and Carib and Stag beers.

Asian Indian dishes of Trinidad and Tobago include *roti* (usually made of beef, chicken, or goat with potatoes and spices wrapped in flat bread), *dalpori* (balled spiced dough usually accompanied by a sauce), channa, and curry goat. Two special dishes of Tobago are curry crab and dumplings and *accra*, which is seasoned salt fish pounded and shaped into small cakes and fried. Some foods are eaten seasonally, in keeping with harvest time and religious traditions. Trinidadians and Tobagonians in the United States often substitute their native dishes with American foods, and prepare traditional foods only when dining with family or during special occasions.

TRADITIONAL COSTUMES

In their homeland, Trinidadians and Tobagonians wear a variety of clothing suited for the tropics. In the United States, however, only people of Asian Indian descent have retained their unique cultural dress. Blacks from the Republic have no special costumes, except for carnival dress, which cuts across racial and ethnic lines. Carnival costumes are elaborate and costly, ranging in form, shape, size, design, and taste; some festival clothing is simply massive and requires the support of cars and trucks, while other pieces may consist of loin cloths and beads. Carnival costuming in Trinidad and Tobago and in New York City (where a Carnival takes place every year) is an extremely expensive cultural and commercial affair, providing department, fabric, hardware, and other stores with hundreds of millions of dollars in revenue every year. Designers Peter Minshall, Peter Samuel, and Edmond Hart are especially well-known in the United States for their costume talents.

DANCES AND SONGS

In New York City and Miami it is not uncommon to hear *paring* (music sung in Castilian) and *chawta* (Asian Indian drumming and vocals) in predominantly Caribbean neighborhoods. But the most popular Trinidadian and Tobagonian music in the United States is calypso and *soca* (a derivation of calypso). These sounds are known for their fast beat, heavy percussion, and social expression.

Calypso originated in Trinidad among African slaves in the 1800s. Although it has its roots in African oral traditions, it was sung in French dialect until 1883 when calypsonians began singing in English. Calypsonians play an important role in Caribbean society, functioning as poets, philosophers, and social commentators within social, political, and religious circles. The Mighty Sparrow's "Jean and Dinah," which won the Carnival crown in 1956, represents the linkage between calypso, society, culture, and politics. Sparrow's 1962 calypso, "Model Nation," captures the feelings of Trinidadians and Tobagonians toward their newly achieved status of independence: "The whole population of our little nation / Is not a lot; / But, oh what a mixture of races and culture / That's what we got; / Still no major indifference / Of race, color, religion, or finance; / It's amazing to you, I'm sure, / We didn't get our independence before."

During the 1980s, calypso also became a forum for discussing women's rights. Although they may be less popular than The Mighty Sparrow, such female calypsonians as Singing Francine, Lady Jane, Twiggy, and Denise Plummer have established their voices in Trinidadian and Tobagonian society. Their message is two-fold: women should not tolerate abuse and men should treat women as equals, especially in domestic partnerships.

Trinidad and Tobago is known for its lively rhythmic dances set to the tunes of calypso and steelband music. Immigrants from the Republic perform a variety of dances, including ballet, folk danc-

ing, limbo, wining, hula hoop, *gayelle* (stick dancing), and *mocojumby* (a costumed dancer on stilts). Jump up, a celebrative, emotionally charged, and physically exhausting dance, has a free-for-all style, and is usually performed during Carnival.

HOLIDAYS

Special holidays celebrated by Trinidadians and Tobagonians include: Emancipation Day (August 1), Independence Day (August 31), Republic Day (September 24), and Boxing Day (December 26). Other popular festivals in Trinidad and Tobago are *Phagwa* (honoring the Hindu god Lord Krishna), *Divali* (a Hindu celebration with millions of lights honoring Mother Laskami), and *Hosay* (the Muslim New Year festival). However, Carnival is perhaps the best known of Trinidadian and Tobagonian holidays; it takes place from Friday through Tuesday before Ash Wednesday of the Lenten season.

Carnival was introduced to Trinidad by the French as an urban festival celebrated by the upper class until emancipation. It then became a festival for all classes, allowing people to break from their normal routine and, through calypso, indirectly attack and ridicule the government. Preparation for this festival begins immediately after Christmas and Panorama (the Grand Steel Drum tournament), or one week before Carnival. On the first night of Carnival there is a "pan around the neck" competition. The "junior carnival" takes place on Saturday and the "panorama finals" on Saturday night. On Sunday night, able calypsonians vie for the title of

"calypso monarch" at the *Dimanche Gras*, and the "King and Queen of Carnival" are named. (In 1994 Americans were able to view the *Dimanche Gras* via satellite.) Monday and Tuesday see lots of "carnivalling," or dancing and masquerading with fantastic costumes. On the final day of Carnival, celebrants drink and dance to the point of exhaustion.

In the United States Carnival is a method by which Trinidadian and Tobagonian immigrants maintain their Afro-Caribbean heritage. It was first celebrated in New York in the 1920s as a privately sponsored indoor family affair during the pre-Lenten season, but later evolved into New York City's Labor Day Carnival (called West Indian Day Carnival). The celebration, modeled after Trinidad and Tobago's Carnival, is one of the largest scheduled street events in New York, rivaling Saint Patrick's Day and Macy's Thanksgiving Day Parades. The celebration, held since 1969, was first organized by Jesse Wattle on the streets of Harlem and was moved to the Eastern Parkway in Brooklyn a few years later by Rufus Gorin. The festival features four nights of concerts, a steel band contest, and children's pageants on the grounds of the Brooklyn Museum. The Labor Day Carnival climaxes with a lengthy procession on the Eastern Parkway. Its overall purpose is to promote unity among Caribbeans and Americans.

PROVERBS

Many of the proverbs in Trinidad and Tobago are European in origin but some sayings from Afro-

Caribbean and Asian Indian cultures have been preserved as well. British-inspired proverbs include: In for a penny, in for a pound; A penny wise and a pound foolish; and, Make hay while the sun shines. Popular Afro-Caribbean sayings include: Do not cut you nose to patch you bottom; If you see you neighbor house catch fire wet yours; No money no love; A man who cannot rule his house is *tootoolbay*; What you head consent you bottom pay for; and Don't dance with two left feet. Two common Asian Indian proverbs are: Corn "nuh" grow where rain "nuh" fall; and Don't trust you neighbor unless you neighbor trusts you.

HEALTH ISSUES

There are no documented medical problems unique to Trinidadians and Tobagonians in the United States or in Trinidad and Tobago. A few cases of leprosy were found in Trinidad and Tobago but these were isolated and did not pose a national threat to either the Republic or the United States. During the 1970s, alcohol and drug abuse was relatively low but it has increased steadily in the last decade. In 1987 alcoholism was named the most serious drug abuse problem in the nation with marijuana and cocaine following close behind.

The average life expectancy in Trinidad and Tobago is 73 years for women, and 68 years for men. Major causes of death among adults include heart disease, cerebrovascular disease, malignant neoplasms, and diabetes mellitus. The infant mortality rate is relatively low; 17 of every 1,000 babies die in their first year. In the United States, life expectancy among Trinidadians and Tobagonians has decreased somewhat due to socio-economic, health, and crime conditions. Most Trinidadians and Tobagonians use either free or low-cost medical care provided by the government of Trinidad and Tobago, and, compared to other developing countries, they enjoy relatively good health. Some families living in the United States have health insurance coverage through their jobs. The unemployed must depend upon the good will of others and the U.S. government.

LANGUAGE

As a former British colony, the official language of Trinidad and Tobago is English, although Hindi is also spoken widely in Indian communities, both in the Republic and in the United States. French, Spanish, and English patios are also common, as well as Hindustani, a dialect of Phojpuri Hindi. Trinidadians and Tobagonians speak English with a wide variety of accents and innovations due to the impact of Spanish, French, Indian, and African languages. The styles of English therefore range from standard British English, usually spoken in formal conversations, to the more common Trinidad English, a mixture of Spanish, French, British, and African. It must be noted, however, that no sharp break exists between Trinidad English and standard English.

GREETINGS AND OTHER POPULAR EXPRESSIONS

Trinidadian and Tobagonian greetings include: "Wah happenen day?" (casual); "How is the daughter doing?" (casual); "Take care daughter" (goodbye to a young woman friend); "Good morning" (with a heavy accent on morning); "good evening;" "good night;" "Merry Christmas;" "Happy holiday;" "Happy Birthday;" "Happy Easter" (Some Christians say "Christ is Risen"); "Happy New Year;" "Good luck;" and "God's speed." Some devout Hindus and Muslims greet with the name *Krishna* or *Allah*, respectively.

FAMILY AND COMMUNITY DYNAMICS

Despite Trinidad and Tobago's culturally diverse people, the family, regardless of ethnic background, fulfills certain basic roles. In the United States, it is the family's responsibility to maintain traditions and enforce strong family values in the community. Traditionally, Trinidadian and Tobagonian men were the sole providers of income for their families while women were held accountable for raising children and managing the home. Since the mid-1970s, however, family planning and sexual abuse legislation have enabled Trinidadian and Tobagonian women to enjoy the same educational, professional, and proprietorial rights as men. Many of these women have entered traditionally male-dominated fields such as medicine, law, and journalism. In the United States, where two-income families are often the rule rather than the exception, Trinidadian and Tobagonian women often work as office clerks, nurses, and domestics. They also participate in community government, money management, and child care.

Trinidadian and Tobagonian immigrants with legal status are often active in civic and political affairs and take a keen interest in their children's education by joining the Parent Teacher Association, attending school board meetings, and participating in neighborhood watch programs. There is a high literacy rate among Trinidadian and Tobagonian immigrants in the United States, resulting from the high premium they place on education. In fact, they are often critical of the American education system, which contrasts sharply with the strong British educational system of their homeland. Some Trinidadian and Tobagonian immigrants try to shield their children from racism and miseducation by sending them to private schools either taught or founded by Caribbean people. St. Mark's Academy, founded in Crown Heights, New York, in 1977 by a Guyanese man, has educated hundreds of Caribbean students, many of whom are now leaders in their communities.

WEDDINGS

In ancient Indian traditions, Hindu authorities prescribed eight different forms of marriages, or *ashrams*, but only two of these were ever practiced among Trinidadian and Tobagonian Asian Indians. The more traditional of these, which is no longer practiced, was called *aqua* (matchmaker) and dictated that parents choose their children's partners. Such marriages took place at a young age, usually puberty because it was believed that postponing the wedding of a daughter for too long would bring bad luck. The ritual itself (*panigrahana* and *homa*) involved performing a *saptapadi* (a seven-steps ritual) around a fire. While the selection process occurred when the children were very young, the couple usually did not know their mate's identity until they became teenagers. In most traditional Hindu weddings, the groom is not allowed to see his bride until late in the ceremony, after she exchanges her yellow sari for a red one.

In modern times, Hindu marriages involve bargaining between the two sets of parents and a change of status for the bride and groom. Often there is a short preliminary ceremony, or *chheka*, during which the family priest and the father of the bride travel to the house of the prospective groom to deliver a dowry. By accepting the token sum, the groom is obligated to marry the young woman. The main ceremony takes place at the bride's home, and friends and relatives assist in setting up the *mantro* (nuptial tent). The wedding is followed by a large reception, with music, jokes, singing, chanting, beating drums, and the throwing of oil, rice, and flowers in the air. Often there is another ceremony and feast at the groom's home. Muslim marriages allow the groom up to four wives but Hindu weddings join only two people and their families. Because of their legal entanglements and non-Christian nature, Muslim marriages were not recognized in Trinidad and Tobago before 1930, and Hindu weddings were not considered legal before

1946. In the United States, Trinidadian and Tobagonian Muslims and Hindus marry according to U.S. laws but retain some of their ceremonial traditions.

Most Afro-Caribbean weddings follow Christian traditions. There is an engagement period which lasts from a few months to many years. Traditionally, the bride's parents were responsible for supplying the bride's dress and the cost of the reception, and the groom and his parents provided the ring and the new home. In the United States this practice varies. In some cases, the parties are already living together and the wedding ceremony only legalizes the relationship in the eyes of the law and the community. In Trinidad and Tobago, young working women occasionally rent a flat and invite a man to live with them. Lovers who are strict Christians, however, generally do not live together before marriage. In the wedding ceremony, the bride wears white, symbolizing chastity, and large numbers of people are invited to observe the event. In Trinidad and Tobago, most wedding receptions are community events, marked by large quantities of food and rum.

BAPTISMS

Trinidadians and Tobagonians generally practice two forms of baptism: infant baptisms and adult baptisms. Among the more traditional Christian denominations (Catholics, Anglicans,

Lutherans, Presbyterians, and Methodists), infants are baptized by sprinkling water on their heads. When they reach the age of accountability, a confirmation ceremony is performed. In other Protestant Christian and Afro-centric Christian traditions, the infants are blessed at a dedication ceremony and baptized after their faith in Christ is confessed voluntarily. The subjects are dipped into a river, the sea, or a baptismal fount near the sanctuary by a minister or an elder of the Church. Shangoes and Spiritual Baptists often dip blind-folded individuals three times into the river or sea. Some of these baptismal practices operate underground in the United States.

FUNERALS

Because of the multifaceted nature of its religious culture, Trinidad and Tobago have many different funeral practices. Since Hindus believe that death cannot harm the immortal soul, a dying person is administered a tulsi leaf and water. Asian Indians in Trinidad and Tobago began cremating their dead after 1930 and the practice was carried over to the United States. The funeral is an elaborate ceremony and males may shave their heads, leaving only a lock of hair in the center, on the tenth day of mourning for an immediate family member.

Afro-centric religions (Obeah, Shango, and Shouter Baptist) and Christians bury their dead after performing special rites or conducting a formal funeral church service. A Catholic priest recites the last rites to a dying member of the Church and may offer mass for a soul that may have departed to purgatory before making peace with God. On the night before the funeral, there is a wake for the dead, during which friends and family come to offer condolences, sing dirges, and drink rum. Afro-centric religions have a Nine Night service to ensure that the shadow of the deceased does not return on the ninth evening after death to visit family members. This practice is occasionally performed after Christian, Muslim, and Hindu deaths as well.

INTERACTION WITH OTHER ETHNIC GROUPS

Given their peculiar circumstances, Trinidadians and Tobagonians have adjusted remarkably well to American society by establishing strong social, religious, economic, and political ties with both black and white communities and institutions, a dualism which often puzzles many African Americans. Both Trinidadian and Tobagonian immigrants and native-born blacks often misunderstand one another as a result of stereotypes and misconceptions. This often leads to interracial conflict. Nonetheless, in Crown Heights, Flatbush, and other New York City neighborhoods, Trinidadians have some of the largest churches and most successful businesses in the black community, and are a vital part of the city's economy.

RELIGION

Because of British, Spanish, and French influences, most Trinidadian and Tobagonian citizens are associated, in some way, with Christianity. People of Asian Indian descent on the islands practice Hindu and Islam. Still, a small number of people (nine percent) follow the African-centered religions of Shango, Rada, Spiritual Baptist, Obeah, and Rastafari. Shango and Spiritual Baptist, also known as "Shouters," are the two most common Afro-centric religious traditions, although Rastafari is growing in popularity. Trinidadian Shango, which is part of the legacy of African traditional culture and religion, incorporates a mixture of Catholic rituals and elements of African spiritual beliefs. Spiritual Baptists place great emphasis on participatory worship, while the Shango religion focuses on animal sacri-

fices, drums, and supernatural manifestations. "Obeah people," sometimes called "shadow catchers," believe they have supernatural powers and can control the spirits of the living and the dead. Followers of this religion believe that they can harness a shadow by forcing it to do specific protective tasks. Because of the negative stigma that other religious groups and the general Trinidadian and Tobagonian public have attached to these folk religions, it is difficult to tell how many immigrants are Spiritual Baptist, Shango, or Obeah followers in the United States. In order to be inconspicuous, many followers of such religions meet in private.

EMPLOYMENT AND ECONOMIC TRADITIONS

Economically, Trinidadian and Tobagonian experiences in the United States have been mixed. Individuals who are not living in America legally, as well as those who are waiting for legal status, tend to be exploited by employers and landlords. Conversely, legal immigrants from Trinidad and Tobago, who are often well educated, work in a variety of occupations.

POLITICS AND GOVERNMENT

Caribbean people have been active in American politics since the early 1800s. After slavery was abolished in the British West Indies in 1834, a number of Trinidadians, Jamaicans, and Barbadians supported the African repatriation movement and worked for the abolition of slavery in collaboration with their black counterparts in the United States. This political activity led to what became known as the Pan-African Movement, supported by W.E.B. DuBois, Marcus Garvey, and others. The Trinidad-born attorney, H. Sylvester Williams, who had ties to the United States, was one of the leaders of the first Pan-African Congress which met in London in 1900.

During the 1920s, Caribbean immigrants were drawn to Socialist and Black Nationalist groups in the United States; the majority of the members in Marcus Garvey's Universal Negro Improvement Association were from the West Indies. Caribbean American political activity reached a new level in the mid-1930s when Trinidadian and Tobagonian immigrants began playing an important role in the Democratic party in New York. Mervyn Dymally, a Trinidadian immigrant, founded the Caribbean Action Lobby to mobilize ethnic ties into a political interest group focusing on international and local relations. The first black to serve as Lt. Governor in

California and the first foreign-born person elected to the U.S. Congress, he was a leading proponent for aid to the English-speaking Caribbean. Other notable politicians were Maurice Gumbs, the founder of The Harriet Tubman Democratic Club, and Ernest Skinner, who ran for City Council in Flatbush, New York, in 1985. While Skinner lost the election, he paved the way for other West Indian Americans.

George Padmore, the great pan-Africanist who was highly decorated in Ghana, founded the International African Service Bureau. In the 1930s and 1940s Padmore, C.L.R. James, and Eric Williams joined W. E. B. DuBois and others in criticizing foreign interference in Africa and discrimination against blacks in the United States. In the 1960s Trinidadian Stokely Carmichael (1941- ; also known as Kwame Toure), a black nationalist and civil rights organizer, served as a major force behind the Student Nonviolent Coordinating Committee (SNCC). His two books, *Black Power Politics of Liberation in America* and *Stokely Speaks: Black Power Back to Pan-Africanism*, are highly regarded in political circles. In the late 1960s, the Black Power Movement in the United States attracted the Caribbean's urban poor and many organizations were formed throughout Trinidad and Tobago using its slogan. Among these were the Black Panthers, the African Unity Brothers, the African Cultural Association, and the National Freedom Organization.

MILITARY

Trinidad's rich deposit of oil and its strategic location have attracted many foreign powers over the years, most notably the United States. In 1940 President Franklin Delano Roosevelt leased three strategic military bases in British-Caribbean territories (one of which was Trinidad and Tobago) from Winston Churchill's British government. The Americans then built a sizable air strip in Port of Spain and a superb naval installation at Trinidad's well-placed deep-water harbor at Chaguaramas Bay. These actions resulted in increased employment and major development projects (through the U.S. Navy and Public Works Department), including the building of roads and bridges for wartime operations, and the recruitment of many Trinidadians and Tobagonians by the U.S. Navy during World War II. Furthermore, American interest in the Republic eased the immigration process to the United States. Many Trinidadian and Tobagonian immigrants who have become naturalized U.S. citizens continue to serve in the U.S. military, though in smaller numbers than during World War II. Because few of these individuals identify themselves

as Trinidadian and Tobagonian immigrants, it is difficult to accurately access their number in the U.S. armed forces.

RELATIONS WITH TRINIDAD AND TOBAGO

The government of Trinidad and Tobago does not allow for Trinidadians and Tobagonians to hold dual citizenship abroad. Therefore, naturalized U.S. citizens do not vote in the Republic's elections. Nonetheless, whether they are U.S. citizens or temporary residents, most Trinidadian and Tobagonian immigrants maintain constant communication with their home country. They read the *Trinidad Guardian*, the *Punch*, the *Bomb*, the *Express*, and other national papers and watch news programs broadcast over satellite dishes. Temporary residents also vote in Trinidad and Tobago's general elections and remit funds regularly to family and relatives in the Republic.

Historically, the U.S. government has maintained good diplomatic relations with Trinidad and Tobago, which in recent years has received federal loans to recover from its economic recession. In spite of strained diplomatic relations between the U.S. government and the late Prime Minister, Eric Williams, over the closing of the U.S. naval base in Chaguaramas in the 1970s, the oil boom in Trinidad (between the 1960s and the early 1980s) kept Trindadians and Tobagonians among America's favorite peoples of the Caribbean Basin.

INDIVIDUAL AND GROUP CONTRIBUTIONS

Trinidadians and Tobagonians have enriched American culture in many ways. The following individuals are most notable.

ACADEMIA

Trinidadian and Tobagonian Americans were among the first blacks to enter American academy. Eric Williams, the late Prime Minister of Trinidad and Tobago and Vice Chancellor of the University of the West Indies, taught at Howard University and gave lectures at several other distinguished American colleges and universities. His books *Capitalism and Slavery* and *Columbus to Castro* have been reprinted dozens of times since they were first published in the 1940s and continue to attract interest in the United States. The works of C.L.R. James (one of Trinidad and Tobago's first political philosophers) and Stokley Carmichael, have likewise inspired political thinking on American campuses.

FILM, TELEVISION, THEATER, AND VISUAL ARTS

Errol John is an internationally acclaimed actor and playwright who produced the well-known *Moon On A Rainbow Shawl*. Geoffrey Holder (1930–), an outstanding American producer, director, and choreographer was born in Port of Spain and has lived in the United States for over 50 years. In 1975 he won a Tony Award for directing and designing costumes for *The Wiz*. Other Trinidadian artists who are well known in the United States include: Boscoe Holder, Noel Vauctrosson, Pat Chu Foon, painter M. P. Aladdin, and sculptor Francisco Caballo.

JOURNALISM

Trinidadians have been involved in American journalism since the early 1800s. The literary genius and political scientist C. L. R. James edited the *International African Opinion* and wrote many books on Caribbean and American history and politics. One of James' most renown works is *Black Jacobins*, which documents the black struggle in the Haitian Revolution. John Stewart, a popular Trinidadian writer who did his undergraduate and graduate study in the United States, was also a lecturer for California State University.

LITERATURE

Several of Trinidad and Tobago's most brilliant minds have left their indelible marks on North American and Caribbean literature. V. S. Naipaul (Vidiadhar Surajprasad), Trinidad's premier novelist, is well known in the United States as a prolific writer of nonfiction and fiction whose works often address violent race relations. Born in Trinidad in 1932, he has studied, traveled, lectured, and written in the United States. Among his nonfiction writings are the following: *Finding the Center, Among the Believers, The Return of Eva Peron with the Killings in Trinidad, India: A Wounded Civilization, The Overcrowded Barracoon, The Loss of El Dorado, An Area of Darkness, Middle Passage*, and *A Turn in The South*. This last book gives an elegant, but disturbing first-hand encounter of the darker side of American race relations and racial injustice in Atlanta, Charleston, Selma, Birmingham, Tallahassee, Nashville, Tuskegee, and other southern cities. Naipaul's fiction is equally impressive and includes: *The Enigma of Arrival, A Bend in the River, Guerrillas, In a Free State, A Flag on the Island, The Mimic Men, Mr. Stone and the Knights Companion, A House for Mr. Biswas, Miguel Street, The Suffrage of Elvira* and *The Mystic Masseur*, and more recent works.

Lynn Joseph, a Trinidadian-born author who migrated to the United States during her college years, writes children books for Trinidadians and Tobagonians in the United States and the Caribbean.

MUSIC

Trinidadian Tobagonian American Denise Plummer became the World's Calypso Queen in 1992-1993. Billy Ocean (1950–), a well-known Trinidadian recording artist from London, won fame in the United States with the hit single "Caribbean Queen." Many less well-known Trinidadians and Tobagonians have studied and taught classical music and dance in American colleges and universities. Carol LaChapelle, for example, is a highly regarded educator who teaches choreography at the School for the Performing Arts in New York City.

SPORTS

Trinidad and Tobago's primary sports are cricket and soccer but basketball, netball, table tennis, track and field, golf, horse racing, and water sports are also popular. Among the Republic's most famous athletes is Kareem Abdul-Jabbar (1947–), born Ferdinand Lewis Alcindor, Jr., a first-generation Trinidadian American who became one of the greatest centers in basketball history and was named Most Valuable Player by the National Basketball Association six times. Lesley Stewart and Claude Noel were well-known boxers who lived in the United States and had many title fights in Las Vegas, Atlantic City, and elsewhere. Sir Larry Constantine, who lived for a short time in the United States, was one of the world's greatest cricket players. Hasley Crawford, a sprinter who lived and trained in the United States, was a 1978 Olympic gold medalist for Trinidad and Tobago.

MEDIA

There are many periodicals, papers, radio stations, and television networks in the United States that cater to the Caribbean population.

PRINT

Cimmarron.

A quarterly journal established in 1985 by the City University of New York's Association of Caribbean Studies to discuss and publish issues of importance to Caribbean Americans.

Enquiry.

A quarterly publication established in 1970 by Trinidad & Tobago Association; contains items of interest to the West Indian community.

Contact: C. J. Mungo, Editor.

Address: 380 Green Lanes, London, N4, England.

Everybody's.

A New York magazine, founded in 1977 by a Grenadian who lived in Trinidad and New York, it reflects the demographic interest and views of the American Caribbean community.

New York Carib News.

Founded in 1981, it is a weekly newspaper tabloid that covers Caribbean politics in New York.

RADIO

KISS-FM, WBLS, and 95.2.

These New York stations play calypso at designated hours.

WLIB.

A New York Caribbean radio station that plays music from Trinidad and Tobago and other countries.

TELEVISION

CSN, the Caribbean Station Network.

This station is a major news center in New York.

ORGANIZATIONS AND ASSOCIATIONS

Caribbean Community (CARICOM).

Governments of Antigua and Barbuda, Bahamas, Barbados, Belize, Dominica, Grenada, Guyana, Jamaica, Montserrat, Saint Christopher-Nevis, Saint Lucia, Saint Vincent and the Grenadines, and Trinidad and Tobago. Objects are to promote cooperation and understanding among member states; integrate the economies of member states through the Caribbean Common Market; coordinate the foreign policies of member states; harmonize the policies of member states concerning commerce, health, education, and social affairs. Maintains reference library of 50,000 books, periodicals, and archival material. Publishes *CARICOM Perspective* three times a year.

Contact: Edwin W. Carrington, Secretary General.

Address: Bank of Guyana Building, P.O. Box 10827, Georgetown, Guyana.

Telephone: (2) 69281.

There are a number of important Trinidadian and Tobagonian organizations in the United States: Trinidad Alliance; Caribbean Action Lobby (founded by Mervyn Dymally); West Indian American Day Carnival Association (founded by Rufus Gorin in New York); West Indian Cricket Club (with branches in Ohio, New York, Washington, D.C., Florida, and other states); Brooklyn Council for the Arts, and Trinidad and Tobago-New York Steel Band Club. There is also the Caribbean American Chamber of Commerce and the Caribbean American Media Studies Inc., which is dedicated to the study and dissemination of information about recent West Indian immigrants.

MUSEUMS AND RESEARCH CENTERS

Carib Culture Center.

Contact: Laura B. Moreno, Assistant Director.

Address: 408 West 58th Street, New York, New York 10019.

Telephone: (212) 307-7420.

SOURCES FOR ADDITIONAL STUDY

Bird, Adrian Curtis. *Trinidad Sweet: The People, Their Culture, Their Island.* Port of Spain, Trinidad, West Indies: Inprint Caribbean, 1992.

Foner, Nancy. *New Immigrants in New York.* New York: Columbia University Press, 1987.

Gordon, Monica, and Suzanne Michael. *Emerging Perspectives on the Black Diaspora.* Maryland: University Press of Americans Inc., 1990.

Kasinitz, Philip. *Caribbean New York.* New York: Cornell University Press, 1992.

Kessner, Thomas, and Betty Boyd Caroli. *Today's Immigrant.* London, England: Oxford University Press, 1982.

Langley, Lester. *The United States and the Caribbean in the Twentieth Century.* Georgia: The University of Georgia Press, 1985.

Sander, Reinhardt W. *The Trinidad Awakening: West Indian Literature of the 1930s*. Connecticut: Greenwood Press, 1988.

Sowell, Thomas. *American Ethnic Groups*. Massachusetts: The Urban Institute, 1978.

Williams, A.R. "The Wild Mix of Trinidad and Tobago," *National Geographic*, 185, No. 3, March 1984; pp. 66-88.

Worthman, O. C. *Contemporary American Immigration*. Boston: Twayne Publishers, 1982.

TURKISH AMERICANS

by
Donald Altschiller

In Turkey family life centers around the male head of the household as he is the one who traditionally provides for his family. Children are expected to obey their parents, even after reaching adulthood, and must also show respect for all persons older than themselves, including older siblings.

OVERVIEW

Slightly smaller than Texas and Louisiana combined, Turkey straddles both Europe and Asia, bordering Greece, Bulgaria, Armenia, Georgia, Azerbaijan, Iran, Iraq, and Syria. Its location on two continents has been a crucial factor in its variegated history and culture. The country's area of almost 300,000 square miles includes almost 10,000 square miles of European Turkey, known as Thrace, and approximately 290,000 square miles of Asian Turkey, known as Anatolia or Asia Minor. Lying between the Black Sea and the Mediterranean, modern Turkey spans bustling cosmopolitan centers, pastoral farming communities, barren wastelands, placid Aegean islands and steep mountain ranges.

Turkey's population is estimated at 59 million people, with an annual growth rate of 2.5 percent. Istanbul, Ankara, and Adana are the largest cities. The population has been a racial melting pot since prehistoric days. Settled or ruled by Hittites, Gauls, Greeks, Macedonians, and Mongols, Turks became the decisive influence, introducing a Mediterranean-Mongoloid admixture into the country's ethnic composition. It is difficult to describe the appearance of an average Turk. The individual may be blond and blue-eyed or round-headed with dark eyes or hair. Some Turks have long-headed Mediterranean looks while others possess Mongoloid features with high cheekbones.

Almost 98 percent of the population is Muslim. Turkey, however, is a secular state and Jews and Christians can fully practice their religious faiths. Kurds, who are also mainly Muslims, are the largest ethnic minority in Turkey. Other minorities include Greeks, Armenians, and Jews.

HISTORY

The Turks, who did not arrive in the Anatolian Peninsula until the eleventh century, are relative newcomers to a land that had seen many successive civilizations before their arrival. Beginning around 2000 b.c., pre-Hittites, Hittites, Phrygians, Lydians, Persians, Greeks, and Romans had lived or ruled in the region. After the collapse of Roman power in the west about 450 a.d., Anatolia became the heartland of the Byzantine Empire (a Greek continuation of Roman rule in the eastern Mediterranean).

Originally nomadic peoples from the steppes of Central Asia, Turkish tribes began moving west toward Europe around the first century a.d. In the middle of the 400s, the first group, known as the Huns, reached western Europe. Others established kingdoms in Turkestan and Persia before the 900s, by which time they had converted to Islam. In the late 900s a new Turkish dynasty, the Seljuqs, came to power in Turkestan and then Persia, from where they began to make incursions into Anatolia in the early 1000s. In 1071 the Seljuqs crushed the Byzantine army at Manzikert in eastern Anatolia, capturing the emperor himself. This important battle marked the effective end of Byzantine power in Anatolia, and the beginning of Turkish dominance.

The main branch of the Seljuqs continued to rule in Persia and Mesopotamia (Iran and Iraq), while another branch known as the Seljuqs of Rum (Rome), quickly penetrated the entire Anatolian Peninsula. Of the original population, some fled to Constantinople or the west, a few remained Christian under the generally tolerant rule of the Muslim Turkish tribes, but over the centuries most converted to Islam. Gradually, too, these former Christians, mostly Greek or Armenian speakers, began to speak Turkish, melding with the dominant Turks, whom they had originally outnumbered.

During the 1100s the Seljuqs contended with the Byzantines and with Christian Crusaders from Europe for control in Anatolia, especially along the Aegean coast, from which the Byzantines and the Crusaders had driven the Turkish tribes for over 200 years. The strongly centralized Seljuq state reached the peak of its power in the early 1200s; shortly thereafter local internal revolts, combined with the Mongol invasions from the east, began to erode its authority. By the early 1300s it had collapsed completely.

Of the ten local emirates, or kingdoms, that arose in Turkish Anatolia after the Seljuq's disintegration, one quickly came to preeminence: that of Osman, who ruled in northwestern Anatolia and founded the Osmanli or Ottoman dynasty. Osman's son, Orhan, expanded his father's dominions in Anatolia and in the 1350s undertook the first Ottoman conquests in Europe, wrestling several towns in eastern Thrace from the Byzantines and crushing the Bulgars and Serbs in battle. His successors Murad and Bayezid continued the string of Asian and European conquests.

By the early 1400s the territory of the once mighty Byzantine Empire had been reduced to a small island of land around Constantinople surrounded by Ottoman territory. As Ottoman power had increased, so had the pomp of those who wielded it. Murad, for example, had taken the title *sultan* (meaning "authority" or "power"), rather than the less majestic *bey* or *emir*, which were military ranks. Ottoman capitals also became increasingly grand. Muhammad II undertook a massive building program in Constantinople, constructing houses, baths, bazaars, inns, fountains, gardens, a huge mosque, and an imperial palace. He also encouraged the original inhabitants who had fled to return— Jews, Greeks, and Armenians, many of whom were craftsmen, scholars, or artists—and made trade agreements with Venetian and Florentine merchants. Renamed Istanbul, the city became a hub of culture and commerce.

The Ottoman Empire reached its peak under Muhammad's great-grandson, Suleiman, who took power in 1520. During his rule, the vast Ottoman Empire controlled huge areas of northern Africa, southern Europe, and western Asia. Shortly after Suleiman's death in 1566, however, Ottoman might began to wane. A series of military defeats, internal conflict, and the Empire's inability to successfully counter European political, scientific, and social developments resulted in the loss of most of its territory outside Anatolia. After World War I, when Turkey was defeated by the Allies, its position was further weakened.

MODERN ERA

Mustafa Kemal (1881-1938), a Turkish World War I hero later known as "Ataturk" or "father of the Turks," organized the Turkish army, drove the Greeks from Turkey, and founded the Republic of Turkey in 1923. After assuming the office of president, Ataturk began a series of revolutionary reforms which transformed Turkey into a modern nation. In a symbolic break with the Ottoman past, he moved the capital from Istanbul to Ankara, the heartland of his nationalist movement. Ataturk replaced religious law with civil, criminal, and commercial laws based on those of Switzerland. Ataturk also encouraged Turks to dress like Europeans. He outlawed the wearing of the *fez* and even promoted ballroom dancing at state functions.

Language reform also transformed the political culture of the country in revolutionary ways. Ataturk changed the Islamic call to prayer from Arabic to Turkish and replaced the Arabic alphabet, in which Turkish had been written, with a modified Latin alphabet. Historians believe that language reform was generally a positive development. Literacy is now more commonplace. Modern Turkish is apparently more adaptable to scientific and technical language than Ottoman Turkish and the language gap between economic classes has also been reduced.

From a one-party system under Ataturk's Republican Peoples' Party, Turkey's government evolved into a parliamentary democracy which, despite interference from the military in the early 1970s, has largely managed to maintain its independence from the powerful army.

SIGNIFICANT IMMIGRATION WAVES

The history of Turkish American immigration to the United States is not well documented and is generally unknown. Although many immigrants came to America to flee religious or political persecution, the primary motivation of many Turks was economic or educational opportunity.

Precise statistics on Turkish American immigration are difficult to obtain. According to U.S. government statistics, the number of immigrants from the Ottoman Empire was minuscule from 1820 through 1860, averaging less than 20 per year. The majority of these individuals (86 percent) returned to Turkey following the establishment of the Republic by Ataturk. Although about 360,000 immigrants from Ottoman Turkey came between 1820 and 1950, only an estimated 45,000 to 65,000 immigrants were Muslim Turks. The majority of arrivals were from the numerous ethnic minorities in the Ottoman Empire, primarily Greeks, Armenians, Jews, and Syrians.

Some historians believe that a large percentage of early Turkish Americans were illiterate but their literacy rate was much higher than that of the Ottoman Empire. According to historian Talat Sait Halman, most of the well-educated immigrants in this group eventually returned to Turkey but the less-educated remained in the United States. These remaining Turks, some studies indicate, retained their Turkish customs throughout the 1940s and 1950s without assimilating into the lifestyle of their newly adopted country.

Unlike the earlier wave of immigrants, the post-World War II generation was highly educated and included almost 4,000 engineers and physicians. These numbers would have undoubtedly been higher but strict U.S. immigration regulations—which were enforced from the mid-1920s until 1965—placed an annual quota of 100 on Turkish immigrants. Again, many of these professionals returned to Turkey after living in the United States for a brief period.

Since the 1970s, the number of Turkish immigrants has risen to more than 2,000 per year. Members of this most recent immigrant group vary widely. Many opened small businesses in the United States and created Turkish American organizations, thus developing Turkish enclaves, particularly in New York City. Still others came for educational purposes. Estimates of the total population of Turkish Americans vary widely, ranging from 100,000 to 400,000.

SETTLEMENT PATTERNS

From the beginning of Turkish immigration to the United States, many immigrants have settled in or around large urban centers. The greatest number have settled in New York City, Boston, Chicago, Detroit, Los Angeles, San Francisco, and Rochester. Other concentrations of Turkish Americans may be found along the East Coast in Connecticut, New Jersey, Maryland, and Virginia, and some have ventured into Minnesota, Indiana, Texas, and Alabama. Many of these communities are served by various local community associations. Membership totals are hard to obtain but range from 50 members to almost 500 members.

ACCULTURATION AND ASSIMILATION

The early Turkish immigrants were almost entirely male. In the culture of Anatolian Turkey, men did not feel comfortable bringing their wives and families until they were able to plant secure economic roots in the United States. Many Americans, however, believed that the Turks were prohibited from bringing their wives because of other reasons. According to Frank Ahmed, author of *Turks in America: The Ottoman Turk's Immigrant Experience*, the *Salem Evening News* falsely claimed that the

Heripsima Hovnanian is welcomed to the United States by 31 members of her family in this 1961 photograph. A bill signed by President Kennedy enabled her to enter the country.

Turks did not bring their wives because of Islamic religious strictures. The newspaper wrote extensively about the sizable Turkish community on the North Shore of Boston, including the towns of Peabody, Salem, and Lynn.

These immigrants often settled into rooming houses. Frequently, a Turk would rent the house and sublease rooms to his fellow countrymen. Although the accommodations were spare, the newly arriving immigrants somewhat replicated their village life. They ate Turkish food (pilaf, lamb, vegetable dishes) and slept on mattresses without a bedstead.

Although they were hardworking and industrious, many Turks did not escape the prejudice frequently directed at newcomers. Occasionally, they were called "Ali Hassans" or "Abdul Hamids" and some newspapers would ridicule the "terrible Turk" or Islam. Among the Turks, however, there was much tolerance for Turkish minorities, especially Turkish Jews, who were fully accepted and respected by their recently arriving compatriots.

Turks obtained work in factories in New York, Detroit, and Chicago and also in the New England leather industry. Sizable numbers worked in Massachusetts, in the leather factories of Lynn and Salem and the wire factories of Worcester. Forced to work long hours at low pay in unsanitary and unsafe conditions, some Turkish workers were involved in strikes against management, who generally viewed the Turks as "good workers."

Because of the precarious situation in Turkey and concern for their families, most Turks—one estimate was 35,000—stayed for a decade or less and then returned to their Anatolian villages before the Great Depression. A small number of Turks stayed in the United States, learned English, and married American women. According to one estimate, only a few hundred remained in this country.

As a result, the diminished Turkish American community became more close-knit. Social life revolved around coffee houses and benevolent societies. In Peabody, Massachusetts, coffee houses on Walnut Street became a congregating place for the Turks living in the area. It was here that community members would exchange news about their villages while sipping Turkish coffee and noshing on sweet pastry.

CUISINE

Turkish food is widely regarded as one of the world's major cuisines. It is noted for its careful preparation and rich ingredients. A typical Turkish meal begins with soup or *meze* (hors d'oeuvres), followed in succession by the main course (usually red meat, chicken, or fish), vegetables cooked in olive oil, dessert, and fresh fruit. Turkish coffee completes the feast and is served in small cups.

Favorite soups include wedding soup, which combines chicken and beef broth, eggs, lemon, and vegetables; lentil soup, which flavors the basic bean with beef broth, flour, butter, and paprika; and *tarhana* soup, which is made with a dried preparation of flour, yogurt, tomato, and red pepper flakes. Although most meals begin with soup, tripe soup—featuring a sauce of vinegar and garlic—is served after a complete dinner and is usually accompanied by alcoholic drinks.

Borek, which is a pastry roll filled with cheese or ground meat, and *dolma,* made from stuffed grape leaves, green pepper or eggplant are most often served prior to the meal. The *meze* tray features salads and purees, but may also include eggplant, caviar, lamb or veal, fried vegetables with yogurt sauce, and a wide variety of seafood.

The main course sometimes consists of seafood, which may be grilled, fried, or stewed. *Kofte* (meatballs) are another specialty, served grilled, fried, or stewed with vegetables. Fresh vegetables are widely used, served either hot or cold. Vegetables cooked with olive oil are essential to Turkish cuisine. Eggplant, peppers, green beans, and peas are the primary vegetables cooked with olive oil, which is also used as a main ingredient in salads. Rice pilaf, which sometimes contains currants and pine nuts, is served as a side dish. Buttermilk, made of yogurt and water, is preferred with meat dishes. *Rakl,* a drink similar to anisette, is often consumed as an alternative to wine.

The final touch to a meal is a tray of fresh fruits, including peaches, apples, pears, raisins, figs, oranges, and melons. Dessert treats include: *baklava,* a flaky pastry dipped in syrup; *bulbul yuvasi,* thin pastry leaves with walnut filling and lemon peel syrup; *sekerpare,* sweet cookies; and *lokma,* Turkish fritters. Puddings are also popular, including *muhallebi,* milk pudding, and *sutlac,* rice pudding.

At the beginning or end of a meal, it is customary to hear "Afiyet Olsun," which means, "May what you eat bring you well-being." To praise the chef, one says "*Elinize saglik,*" or "Bless your hands."

TRADITIONAL COSTUMES

Along with his many other reforms, Ataturk succeeded in making Western-style dress, at least among men, widespread in Turkey. Consequently, Turkish Americans dress no differently than most other Americans. Ataturk also outlawed the traditional *fez,* a brimless, cone-shaped, red hat and made brimmed felt hats mandatory, because with them on men could not touch their foreheads to the ground in prayer. Traditional dress for women requires that they be covered from head to foot. Most Turkish garments are made from wool. The *kepenek,* a heavy hooded mantle shaped from a single piece of felt, sheltered herders from the rain and cold, as well as served as a blanket and tent.

HOLIDAYS

Turkey observes both civil and religious holidays. While dates for civil holidays are determined by the same calendar used in the United States, religious holidays are set by the Muslim lunar calendar, resulting in observance on different days each year. Offices of the Turkish government are closed on all these days, and frequently a day or two before or after as well. In the United States many Turkish Americans celebrate New Year's Day on January 1 and National Sovereignty and Children's Day on April 23. This holiday commemorates the founding of the Grand National Assembly in 1923. At the same time, Ataturk proclaimed it a day to honor children, making it a unique international holiday. Ataturk's birthday is honored on May 19 (officially known as Ataturk Memorial and Youth and Sports Day) and his death is commemorated on November 10. In Turkey, this day is marked by a national moment of silence throughout the nation at precisely 9:05 a.m., the time of Ataturk's death. Victory Day (August 30) celebrates the victory over the Greeks in 1922 and Turkish Independence Day (October 29) recognizes the proclamation of the Republic by Ataturk in 1923. A unique American tradition, begun on April 24, 1984, is Turkish American Day, during which Turkish Americans march down New York's Fifth Avenue.

INTERACTIONS WITH OTHERS

There are many conflicts between Turkish Americans and Armenian Americans, stemming from the tragic genocide of an estimated 1.5 million Armenians by Turks perpetrated more than 70 years ago. Between 1973 and the mid-1980s, Armenian terrorist organizations assassinated several Turkish diplomats in Los Angeles and Boston. These violent actions declined by the late 1980s.

LANGUAGE

Like Mongolian, Korean, and Japanese, Turkish is part of the Ural-Altaic linguistic group. More than 100 million people living in Turkey and Central Asia speak Turkic languages. During the Ottoman era, Turkish was written in Arabic script, from right to left. Ottoman Turkish borrowed heavily from other languages, and its varying forms of Arabic script made it difficult to use.

Ataturk eliminated Arabic script, substituting the Latin alphabet with some letter modifications to distinguish certain Turkish sounds. Many Arabic and Persian loan words were removed, while words from European languages were phoneticized. The alphabet consists of 29 letters—21 consonants and eight vowels. Six of these letters do not occur in English. Turkish has no genders and there is no distinction between he, she, and it. The Turks are very expressive and often use "body language" to communicate.

There are several Turkish American organizations and community centers in the United States that teach the Turkish language to the children of Turkish Americans. Despite this effort, relatively few second- and third-generation Turkish Americans speak Turkish, a trend that will greatly affect the future of this community.

GREETINGS AND OTHER COMMON EXPRESSIONS

Common expressions among Turks and Turkish Americans include: *Merhaba*—Hello; *Gun aylin*—Good Morning; *Iyi aksamlar*—Good Evening; *Nasilsiniz*—How are you?; *Iyiyim*—I'm fine; *Tessekkur ederim*—Thank you; *Saatler olsun!*—May it last for hours! (said to one after a bath, shave, or haircut); *Gecmis olsun!*—May it be in the past! (said in case of illness).

FAMILY AND COMMUNITY DYNAMICS

In Turkey family life centers around the male head of the household as he is the one who traditionally provides for his family. Children are expected to obey their parents, even after reaching adulthood, and must also show respect for all persons older than themselves, including older siblings. Parental authority in Turkey is so great that parents often arrange for the marriages of their children. The extended family is of extreme importance in Turkey as family members often work in the same business. Men dominate in community affairs. Women are expected to manage the household. In the United States, while the roles of men and women have changed somewhat, the Turkish American family remains close-knit.

There are many political factions in Turkey, which are often reflected in the Turkish American community. All Turkish Americans, however, are united in their concern for Turkey and take great pride in their ethnic heritage. Many Turks living in the United States refuse to abandon their Turkish citizenship. Those who do apply for American visas are generally ostracized by the community.

RELIGION

Most Turkish Americans practice Islam, or "submission to god." In 610 a.d., according to Muslim belief, the angel Gabriel ordered Muhammad to recite the Word of God as it was delivered to him. This was the same basic message that had earlier been revealed to the Jews and later to the Christians, but the Word had been misinterpreted over the years and had to be restated. Over a period of 22 years, Muhammad received revelations from the angel, revelations incorporated in the Muslim holy book, the *Koran*. This is a detailed guide to behavior toward God, fellow humans, and the self. Islam therefore provides the basis of personal identity and social life to its followers.

There are five basic requirements of the faith known as the Pillars of Islam: Confession that there is "no god but God" and that Muhammad is the messenger of God; Daily prayer (five times); Giving of alms; Fasting in daylight hours for the Muhammadan month of *Ramadan*; and, Pilgrimage to Mecca at least once in a lifetime.

Prayers are said five times daily wherever one finds oneself, but on Friday the community gathers at the mosque for noon prayer. The religion also bans the eating of pork, drinking alcohol, gambling, and usury (lending money with excessive interest). There are also specific laws concerning marriage, divorce, and inheritance. In some representations, art representing human figures is discouraged. The prophet Muhammad is never portrayed unless veiled, even in motion pictures.

Islam is further divided into two major sects: *Sunni* and *Shi'ite*. Most Turkish Americans, as well as the majority of Muslims in general, are *Sunni* Muslims. They believe that the community as a whole is the guardian and guarantor of Islamic law. This law, shari'a, is based on four sources, which in descending order of importance are: the *Koran*, the examples and teachings of the prophet, communal consensus on Islamic principles and practices, and reasoning by analogy. In later years the consensus was reduced to a consensus of religious scholars. This four-pronged determinant of the law provides great unity, but also provides for a variety of interpretations. Perhaps the most graphic example of this is the treatment of the law relating to modesty among women. In some places this law is accommodated by the wearing of a veil in public; in others, simply by avoiding male company when possible; and in others, is left to the discretion of local leaders.

In the United States, many Turkish Americans worship in Arab or Pakistani mosques. Very few have converted to Christianity or Judaism. One notable exception is Halouk Fikret (1895-1965), who was born to a prominent Muslim family in Turkey, immigrated to the United States, and, in the 1920s, became a Presbyterian minister.

EMPLOYMENT AND ECONOMIC TRADITIONS

Early Turkish immigrants to the United States were predominantly from Turkey's rural community. They settled in large, industrial cities and found employment as unskilled laborers. The majority came to earn money so that they could improve their economic situation and that of their families in Turkey. After the 1950s, a well-skilled and highly educated class immigrated to the United States, the majority being medical doctors, engineers, and scientists. Today, Turkish Americans are visible in virtually every field. The majority are professionals and enjoy a middle-class lifestyle.

POLITICS AND GOVERNMENT

Before the 1970s, there was very little Turkish American involvement in American politics. The Turkish invasion of Cyprus in 1974, however, mobilized many individuals because of U.S. government support for the Greeks. Nonetheless, the small Turkish American community was not able to counter the influence of the much larger and more powerful Greek American organizations. Turkish Americans proudly point to Turkey's membership in NATO and its military and political support of the U.S. government during the 1991 Persian Gulf War.

INDIVIDUAL AND GROUP CONTRIBUTIONS

Turkish Americans have made numerous contributions to American society, particularly in the fields of education, medicine, and science. Others, including Tunç Yalman, artistic director of the Milwaukee Repertory Theater, and Osmar Karakas, who was awarded the 1991 National Press Award for the best news photograph, have contributed significantly to the arts. The following individuals are especially notable.

MUSIC

Arif Mardin (1932–) is one of the major popular music producers and arrangers in America. His clients include Aretha Franklin, the Bee Gees, Carly Simon, Roberta Flack, and Bette Midler. Born into a prominent Istanbul family, he received a scholarship and B.A. in music at Boston's Berklee School of Music in 1958. After briefly meeting Ahmet Ertegun at the Newport Jazz Festival, he joined Atlantic Records and is currently its Vice President.

Chief Executive Officer of Atlantic Records, Ahmet Ertegun (1924–) is an influential force in the music business. The son of Turkey's ambassador to the United States, he attended St. John's College in Annapolis, Maryland. The young Ahmet always loved jazz, especially the music of black musicians. He and his brother Nesuhi promoted jazz concerts in Washington, D.C., at locales ranging from the Jewish Community Center, the National Press Club, and even the Turkish embassy. Duke Ellington and Lester Young attended some of these informal jazz sessions. He soon invested $10,000 with a record collector friend and started Atlantic Records. Now, four decades later, it is a conglomerate worth $600 million. Ertegun has been dubbed the "Greatest Rock 'n' Roll Mogul in the World."

SCIENCE AND MATHEMATICS

Feza Gursey (1921-1993) was the J. Willard Gibbs Professor Emeritus of Physics at Yale University. He contributed major studies on the group structure of elementary particles and the symmetries of interactions. Professor Gursoy helped bridge the gap between physicists and mathematicians at Yale. He was the winner of the prestigious Oppenheimer Prize and Wigner Medal.

MEDIA

PRINT

ATS Bulletin.
Quarterly newsletter of the American Turkish Society.

Address: 850 Third Avenue, New York, New York 10022.
Telephone: (212) 319-2452.

Turkish Newsletter.
Monthly publication of the Turkish American Association.

Contact: Inci Fenik, Editor.
Address: 1600 Broadway, Suite 318, New York, New York 10019.
Telephone: (212) 956-1560.

The Turkish Times.

Biweekly newspaper of the Assembly of Turkish American Associations. Covers Turkish American issues with news articles, editorials, and business information.

Contact: Dr. Ugur Akimci, Editor.
Address: 1602 Connecticut Avenue, Suite 303, Washington, D.C. 20009.
Telephone: (202) 483-9090.

ORGANIZATIONS AND ASSOCIATIONS

American Turkish Friendship Council (ATFC).

Devoted to increasing understanding of commerical, defense, and cultural issues involving the United States and Turkey; provides information on the history and economical and social advancement of Turkey.

Contact: G. Lincoln McCurdy, Executive Director.
Address: 1010 Vermont Avenue, N.W., Suite 1020, Washington, D.C. 20005.
Telephone: (202) 783-0483.

American Turkish Society (ATS).

Founded in 1949, the ATS has a membership of 400 American and Turkish diplomats, banks, corporations, businessmen, and educators. It promotes economic and commercial relations as well as cultural understanding between the people of the United States and Turkey.

Contact: Lara Tanbay, Executive Director.
Address: 850 Third Avenue,18th Floor, New York, New York 10022.
Telephone: (212) 583-7614.
Fax: (212) 583-7615.
E-mail: ameriturk@aol.com.

Assembly of Turkish American Associations (ATAA).

Founded in 1979, the ATAA has approximately 10,500 members and coordinates activities of regional associations for the purpose of presenting an objective view of Turkey and Turkish Americans and enhancing understanding between these two groups.

Contact: Guler Koknar, Executive Director.
Address: 1601 Connecticut Avenue, N.W., Suite 303, Washington, D.C. 20009.
Telephone: (202) 483-9090.
Fax: (202) 483-9092.
E-mail: assembly@ataa.org.
Website: http://www.ataa.org/.

Federation of Turkish-American Associations (FTAA).

Founded in 1956 and composed of about 30 local organizations of Turkish Americans, it works to advance educational interests and to maintain and preserve knowledge of Turkey's cultural heritage.

Contact: Egemen Bagis, Executive Director.
Address: 821 United Nations Plaza, Second Floor, New York, New York 10017.
Telephone: (212) 682-7688.
Fax: (212) 687-3026.
E-mail: info@ftaa.org.
Website: http://www.ftaa.org/.

Turkish American Association (TAA).

Founded in 1965, the TAA has approximately 15,000 members and promotes cultural relations between the United States and Turkey.

Contact: Inci Fenik, Secretary.
Address: 1600 Broadway, 48th Street, Suite 318, New York, New York 10019-7413.
Telephone: (212) 956-1560.
Fax: (212) 956-1562.

Turkish Women's League of America (TWLA).

Founded in 1958, the TWLA comprises Americans of Turkish origin united to promote equality and justice for women. The organization encourages cultural and recreational activities to foster relations between the people of Turkey, the United States, and other countries, including the new Turkish republics of the former Soviet Union.

Contact: Ayten Sandikcioglu, President.
Address: 821 United Nations Plaza, Second floor, New York, New York 10017.
Telephone: (212) 682-8525.
Fax: (212) 215-5310.

SOURCES FOR ADDITIONAL STUDY

Ahmed, Frank. *Turks in America: The Ottoman Turk's Immigrant Experience.* Greenwich, Connecticut: Columbia International, 1986.

Halman, Talat Sait. "Turks," *Harvard Encyclopedia of American Ethnic Groups.* Cambridge, Massachusetts: Harvard University Press, 1980.

Hostler, Charles Warren. The Turks of Central Asia. Westport, CT: Praeger, 1993.

Spencer, William. *The Land and People of Turkey.* New York: J.P. Lippincott, 1990.

UGANDAN AMERICANS

by
Olivia Miller

Religious tolerance is an important aspect of present-day Uganda. Christians, Muslims, Jews, Hindus, and others practice their religion freely.

OVERVIEW

The Republic of Uganda is bordered by Sudan to the north, Kenya to the east, Lake Victoria, Tanzania, and Rwanda to the south, and Congo (formerly Zaire) to the west. The name Uganda is the Swahili term for Buganda, the homeland of the nation's largest ethnic group, the Baganda. British colonizers adopted the name when they established the Uganda Protectorate, centered in Buganda, in 1894. Uganda has great natural beauty, with an incredible variety of mammal species and birds. Winston Churchill called the country the "Pearl of Africa." Uganda's tropical forests, tea plantations, rolling savannahs, and arid plains are home to half of Africa's bird species.

Uganda's land area is 91,459 square miles (236,880 square kilometers), about the size of Oregon, and it lies across the equator. Its topography varies from the lush and fertile shores of Lake Victoria in the southeast to semidesert in the northeast. Uganda is fairly flat but high, with an average altitude of 3,280 feet above sea level. The capital city, Kampala, is on the shores of Lake Victoria. The White Nile, flowing out of the lake, winds through much of the country.

Uganda's population of 21 million is made up of a complex and diverse range of peoples, including the Baganda, Langi, Acholi, Pygmy, Europeans, Asians, and Arabs. The Baganda make up the largest portion of the population, about 16.7 percent. English is the official language, and many people speak Swahili and Arabic as well. There are more than 40 indigenous languages. Sixty-six percent of the population are Christian, evenly divided between Catholic and Protestant, 16 percent are Muslim, and 18 percent follow indigenous belief systems. The flag has six horizontal stripes—two each of black, yellow, and red—with the national emblem, the crested crane, in a centered white circle.

HISTORY

The ancestors of today's Bantu-speaking people, who include the Baganda and other groups, were likely the earliest occupants, about the fourth century A.D., of the low-lying plateau north of Lake Victoria. The population gradually moved southwest and developed a way of life based on farming and herding. Kingdoms of the Baganda, Bunyoro, Toro, Ankole, and Busoga peoples emerged, and they remained strong from the fourteenth century until the nineteenth century. Uganda's inland location kept it isolated from Arab and European trading until the nineteenth century. When Arab traders reached the interior of Uganda in the 1830s, they found several kingdoms with well-developed political institutions dating back several centuries. Buganda dominated the region, while Bunyoro was its greatest rival.

The first traders came in search of slaves and ivory. In the 1860s, British explorers arrived, seeking the source of the Nile River. Protestant missionaries arrived in 1877, followed by Catholic missionaries came in 1879. Baganda converts to Christianity and Islam clashed with their ruler and eventually overthrew him. The kingdom then separated along Catholic and Protestant lines. This weakening of Buganda came during a period in which European interest in the area was growing. Imperial powers from Europe soon attempted to conquer Buganda and its neighbors. After the Treaty of Berlin in 1890 defined the various European countries' spheres of influence in Africa, Uganda, Kenya, and the islands of Zanzibar and Pemba became British protectorates, and colonial agents established the Uganda Protectorate in 1894.

Colonial administrators introduced coffee and cotton as cash crops and adopted a policy of indirect rule, giving the traditional kingdoms autonomy, but favoring the recruitment of Baganda tribespeople for civil service. Few Europeans settled permanently in Uganda, but Pakistanis, Indians, and Goans arrived in large numbers. Agricultural production increased dramatically during World War I, and during the 1920s and 1930s. In the 1930s and 1940s, native Ugandans began to agitate for economic and political self-determination. In the mid-1950s schoolteacher Milton Obote, a member of the Langi people, created a loose coalition that led Uganda to independence in 1962.

MODERN ERA

In October 1962, with the coming of independence, ethnic and regional rivalries beset newly formed political parties. Obote, assisted by his army chief of staff Idi Amin, crushed the opposition, and became president, abolishing the Bagandan monarchy. Obote rewrote the constitution to consolidate virtually all powers in the presidency, and then began to nationalize, without compensation, $500 million worth of foreign assets. Obote fled after a military coup in 1971, and Uganda endured eight years of mass murder and destruction under the government of Idi Amin. Amin's main targets were the Acholi and Langi tribespeople, the professional classes, which included intellectuals and entrepreneurs, and the country's 70,000-strong Asian community. In 1972, all Asians were given 90 days to leave the country with nothing but the clothes that they wore. The economy disintegrated because the Asian population had been the backbone of trade, industry, and health care. The education system suffered lasting damage. Government-sanctioned brutality became commonplace. Amin went to war with Tanzania in 1978, then fled Uganda the following year, when the Tanzanian military pushed into the heart of his country. In 1980, Milton Obote returned from exile to resume control. Between half a million and a million people perished during the reigns of Amin and his successors from 1971 to 1986. Armless, legless, and facially disfigured torture victims survive in the population today.

Rebels drove Obote from office in 1985. Yoweri Kaguta Museveni, leader of the National Resistance Army, set up a new government in January 1986. Museveni stated his goal of bringing peace and security to Uganda. He won strong support from citizens. About 300,000 Ugandan refugees returned from across the Sudanese border.

In the 1990s, Uganda worked to recover from two decades of instability and civil war. A new constitution was ratified on July 12, 1995. Museveni won democratic, nonpartisan elections in 1994, and again in 1996. International leaders saw the 1996 elections as Uganda's final step towards rehabilitation, and U.S. President Bill Clinton visited the country. At the end of the twentieth century, Uganda had set up new economic development projects and export initiatives, and renewed its commitment to education and social services. However, at the same time, it faced a severe epidemic of acquired immune deficiency syndrome (AIDS). About 20 percent of Uganda's population was infected with the AIDS virus. By 1998, more than a million Ugandans had died of AIDS.

THE FIRST UGANDANS IN AMERICA

The first Ugandan Americans likely arrived as slaves, seized by or traded to Arabs between 1619 and 1865. According to the 1860 census, there were 4.4 million African Americans among a total U.S. population of 36 million people. Immigration records show that 857 Africans came to the United States between 1881 and 1890.

SIGNIFICANT IMMIGRATION WAVES

Immigration records from 1975 cite Ugandans separately from other Africans and show the arrival of 859 immigrants, most fleeing Idi Amin's terror. Of note is the fact that African Asians, a group encompassing all brown-skinned people, usually Indians, Pakistanis, and Goans, are counted in a separate category from Ugandans. In 1976, 359 Ugandans arrived, and 241 came in 1977. Immigration fell to less than 150 each year in the late 1980s and early 1990s, a time of political stability in Uganda. The number of Ugandan refugees granted permanent residence status in the United States between 1946 and 1996 was generally less than 50 per year, with the exceptions of 1993, when 87 were admitted, and 1994, when 79 were admitted. Only ten Ugandan refugees were admitted in 1996. In 1998, 215 Ugandans were winners of the DV-99 diversity lottery. The diversity lottery is conducted under the terms of Section 203(c) of the Immigration and Nationality Act and makes available 50,000 permanent resident visas annually to persons from countries with low rates of immigration to the United States.

SETTLEMENT PATTERNS

Ugandan immigrants often join family members already in the United States. Immigrants with professional employment are geographically scattered, though significant communities have developed in metropolitan areas such as Atlanta, Sacramento, Dallas, and St. Petersburg. Some newly arrived Ugandans receive assistance from Catholic Social Services and other humanitarian relief agencies.

ACCULTURATION AND ASSIMILATION

Because English is Uganda's official language, many Ugandan Americans do not face significant language barriers. Refugees who lived in rural areas, however, find American culture is very different from what they left behind. American life poses challenges for those who have not seen escalators, refrigerators, traffic lights, and scan-your-own grocery checkouts. Many Ugandans immigrate for better educational opportunities.

TRADITIONS, CUSTOMS, AND BELIEFS

Ugandan culture is a mixture of various traditions and practices. In Uganda, people may break into song and dance, even in the streets, when they hear good news. If you are invited to someone's home, it is polite, but not required, to bring a gift for your host or hostess. Wives are automatically included in invitations unless it is specified otherwise. In conversation, most topics can be discussed freely, and national and world affairs and the arts are the most popular topics.

The West has traditionally viewed Ugandans as passive people. Their willing servitude and non-aggressive behavior results from centuries of tribal structure that discouraged individual self-promotion. The culture of the Baganda was authoritarian, and obedience to the king was crucial. David Lamb wrote in *The Africans* that "one's well-being depended on an allegiance to a man or a group of tribal barons, and that attachment did not include the right to question. The tradition of giving all power to a village chief, the era of colonialism, and the repressiveness of men like Obote and Amin had taught them obedience, even servitude. They had learned the art of survival."

PROVERBS

Ugandans share many proverbs with other Swahili-speaking African peoples. Several sayings reflect the experience of living among abundant wildlife. Here are examples: The country rooster does not crow in the town; Do not speak of a rhinoceros if there is no tree nearby; When two elephants fight it is the grass that suffers; The one who has not traveled widely thinks his mother is the only cook; The person who is tired will find time to sleep; Return to old watering holes for more than water for friends and dreams are there to meet you; Abuses are the result of seeing one another too often; Caution is not cowardice for even the ants march armed; Every beast roars in its own den; Haste does not result in prosperity; The hunter in pursuit of an elephant does not stop to throw stones at birds; If the hours are long enough and the pay is short enough, someone will say it's women's work; If the hyena eats the sick man, he will eat the whole one; The talker will lead the dog to the meat market; Visitors' footfalls are like medicine for they heal the sick; When the master is absent, the frogs hop into the house.

CUISINE

Most people in Uganda, except for a few who live in the city centers, produce their own food. Women and girls have sole responsibility for meal preparation. Men and boys aged 12 and older are not even expected to sit in the kitchen, which is separate from the main house. The women cook food on an open fire, using wood for fuel. Most families eat two meals a day, lunch and supper. Breakfast is just a cup of tea or a bowl of porridge.

When a meal is ready, all members of the household wash their hands and sit down on floor mats. They have to wash their hands before and after the meal because most Ugandans eat with their hands. At mealtime everybody is welcome; visitors and neighbors who drop in are expected to join the family in the meal. The women serve the food, cutting it up into small pieces for each member of the family. Sauce, which is usually a stew with vegetables, beans, butter, salt, and curry powder, is served to each person on a plate. Sometimes fish or beef stew is served.

Normally the family says a short prayer before eating. During the meal, children speak only when asked a question. It is bad manners to reach for salt or a spoon. It is better to ask someone sitting close to it to pass it. It is also bad manners to leave the room while others are still eating. Everyone shows respect by staying seated until the meal is over. Leaning on the left hand or stretching one's legs while at a meal is a sign of disrespect and is not tolerated. People usually drink water at the end of the meal. It is considered odd to drink water while eating. When the meal is finished, everyone in turn compliments the mother by saying, "Thank you for preparing the meal, madam." No dessert is served.

Ugandan main dishes usually center on beef, goat, mutton, or fresh fish and the starch that comes from *ugali*, or maize meal. *Ugali* is cooked into a thick porridge until it sets hard, and it is served in flat bricks. One of the more interesting dishes is *mkate mayai*, meaning bread eggs. Originally an Arab dish, it is wheat dough spread into a thin pancake, filled with minced meat and raw egg, and then folded into a neat parcel and fried. A staple food is *matoke*, a dish of green cooking bananas, boiled then steamed and mashed, to which water has been added. Other food crops include millet bread, cassava, sweet potatoes, white potatoes, yams, beans, peas, groundnuts (peanuts), cabbage, onions, pumpkins, and tomatoes.

Ugandans grow some fruits, such as oranges, papaws (papayas), lemons, and pineapple, and these often serve as between-meal snacks. Groundnuts are an important part of the diet. They are roasted, pounded to a pulp, and then made into a sauce that may accompany meat, *matoke*, or vegetables. Groundnut stew consists of meat strips cooked with onions and tomatoes, to which peanut butter and milk are added to create a sauce. The dish is served over rice. *Nsima* is a pasty bread-like dish made from cornmeal and water that is boiled to form a paste that is served with meat, poultry, fish, or vegetables. Ugandans also fry bananas in very hot peanut oil.

Drinks include *pombe*, a fermented banana beer, and *waragi*, a millet-based alcoholic beverage. A popular Ugandan-American dessert is peanut orange cake, made from a typical cake batter with orange peel, vinegar, and one and a half cups of peanut butter added.

MUSIC

Each tribe has its own musical history. Songs have been passed down from generation to generation. *Ndigindi* (lyre), *entongoli* (harp), *amadinda* (xylophone), and *lukeme* (thumb piano) are common musical instruments in Uganda.

TRADITIONAL COSTUMES

Uganda does not have a national costume. However, the *busuti* or *gomasi*, colorful saris, are typical clothing. The style varies from one tribe to another. For men, the *kanzu*, an ankle-length robe, used to be regarded as the national dress. It was replaced by the safari suit, then by Western-style shirts and pants.

DANCES AND SONGS

Music and dance play a large role in Ugandan culture. Each tribe has specific dances, such as the Imbalu dances of the Bagisu people on the slopes of Mount Elgon and the Runyege dances native to the area around Masindi. Traditional story songs tell tales of magic birds and animals, with songs and narrative interwoven. W. Moses Serwadda, a musician, folklorist, and faculty member at Makarere University in Uganda, compiled a book, *Songs and*

Stories from Uganda, of traditional work and game story songs and lullabies. The songs appear in the original Luganda language, with phonetic pronunciation, English translation, and an explanation of the story or purpose of each.

HOLIDAYS

Uganda celebrates many Christian holidays, including Christmas, Easter, and Good Friday. The Muslim population honors Islamic holidays. Hari Raya Puasa, the sighting of the new moon, signifies the first day of the Muslim calendar and the end of Ramadan, the fasting month. The entire country observes Women's Day in early March. There are also several holidays associated with independence and events during the civil wars: NRM (National Resistance Movement) Anniversary Day is January 26; Martyrs' Day is June 3; Heroes' Day is June 9; and Independence Day is October 9.

HEALTH ISSUES

Because Uganda has a poor health care system, Ugandans who have immigrated to America typically receive of much better health care than those in their native country. Health insurance coverage by an employer is a valued benefit of life in America. Life expectancy in Uganda in 1998 was only 37 years.

AIDS has devastated Uganda. In the 1980s, the country had the highest reported incidence of the disease, more than 15 cases per 100,000 people. By mid-1990, 17,400 AIDS cases had been diagnosed in Uganda, and the number doubled every six months. At that time officials also reported that more than 790,000 people had tested positive for the human immunodeficiency virus (HIV), which is believed to cause AIDS. They estimated this figure at 1.3 million by the year's end. Those who were HIV-positive included more than 25,000 children under the age of 15. Officials estimated that 20 percent of infant deaths in Kampala were HIV-related. Also, 22 percent of women seeking prenatal care at Kampala's Mulago Hospital, the nation's largest, were infected with HIV, as were many tuberculosis sufferers. Uganda's first confirmed AIDS deaths occurred in 1982, with seventeen deaths in the southern district of Rakai. By 1989, AIDS had occurred in every part of Uganda.

LANGUAGE

Uganda had 47 languages; 46 remain in use, while one is extinct. Many Ugandans live among people who speak other languages. Uganda's three major language groups are Bantu, Central Sudanic, and Nilotic. Uganda's population groups are usually categorized by language. Following independence, Bantu-language speakers comprised roughly two-thirds of the population. British colonizers brought their language to Uganda in the late nineteenth century. Uganda adopted English as its official language after it became independent. It is the language of business, government, and education. Most Ugandans speak an African language as well. Following independence, Bantu-language speakers comprised roughly two-thirds of the population. Swahili is especially common. Also, numerous people speak Arabic.

In Swahili, which is a Bantu language, vowels are pronounced as they are in Spanish or Italian. Every letter is pronounced. Exceptions to this rule include "dh," which is pronounced "th" as in "this"; "ny," pronounced as "ni" in "onion"; "ng," pronounced as in "singer"; "gh," pronounced as the "ch" in Scottish Loch; and "ch," pronounced as in "church." In most words, the emphasis is on the next-to-last syllable.

GREETINGS AND POPULAR EXPRESSIONS

Habari is the typical greeting, meaning "hello." *Karibu* is a Swahili expression of hospitality. Handshaking is common. When faced with problems that are annoying or even disastrous, Ugandans respond with "*Shauri ya Mangu,*" Swahili for "It is God's will."

FAMILY AND COMMUNITY DYNAMICS

Ugandan Americans tend to establish single-family homes where children learn reverence for God and their family. The choice of a marriage partners is up to the individual. Ugandan immigrants take part in community and school events in much the same way as other Americans. The children of Ugandan Americans assimilate into American culture.

Uganda has a wide variety of cultures, traditions, and lifestyles. The largest cultural group, the Baganda people, have historically emphasized blood ties through the clan system. Clan members all have at least one male ancestor in common. Clan councils once regulated many aspects of Baganda life, including marriage and land use. The British were impressed with the Baganda system of governance, and appointed members of the group to important positions during the colonial period.

Some Baganda customs have persisted into the late twentieth century. The Baganda have traditionally sent their children to live with people of higher social standing in the group. This was done to create ties between groups and to provide avenues for social mobility for their children. In the 1980s, the Baganda continued to believe this was an excellent way to prepare children for adulthood.

EDUCATION

Many Ugandans immigrated to the United States to obtain a better education. The literacy rate in Uganda in 1993 was 62 percent. While not compulsory, education is highly regarded. Education is divided into four levels: primary, seven years; lower secondary, three or four years; upper secondary, two years; and postsecondary, consisting of university, teachers' colleges, or commercial training. Traditionally, there has been a fee for primary and lower secondary schooling; thereafter, education is free. In early 1997, the Ugandan government launched the Universal Primary Education Program as a step toward free primary education for all citizens. Under this program, four children per family could attend primary school at any public school at government expense.

THE ROLE OF WOMEN

Women traditionally have been subordinate to men, despite the substantial economic and social responsibilities of women in Ugandan society. Their fathers, brothers, and husbands hold authority over them. As late as the 1980s, women in some rural areas had to kneel when speaking to a man. This was the case even though women not only had significant domestic responsibilities but also contributed to the economy through agricultural work. Polygamous marriage practices also disadvantaged women.

Women's rights groups began organizing even before Uganda became independent. In 1960, the Uganda Council of Women called for marriage, divorce, and inheritance laws to be put in writing and publicized. The violence during Idi Amin's rule created hardships for women, as public services, schools, hospitals, and markets often became inaccessible. They had to take care of their families in extreme conditions. These difficulties, however, may have forced women to become more independent. Ugandan women's activism has continued. The Uganda Association of Women Lawyers set up a legal aid clinic in early 1988 to defend women's property and custody rights. The Museveni admin-

istration promised to end discrimination against women. In 1987, Museveni appointed Joyce Mpanga minister for women and development in 1987, and she pledged that the government would improve women's wages, job opportunities, and status. In the 1990s, women became increasingly involved in government. They had five percent of the seats in parliament and five cabinet positions. There was also a woman vice president.

Women still, however, had a higher illiteracy level—55.1 percent—than men, who had a 36.5 percent illiteracy rate. Fewer women received higher education. About 45 percent of the children enrolled in primary schools were girls. Only three percent of persons attending technical institutions were female.

FUNERALS

Ugandan Americans follow the funeral customs of the United States and bury their dead in caskets after a ceremony. In Uganda, funerals take place quickly, and the dead are often wrapped in a shroud of bark cloth and buried outside of town. Family members are responsible for transporting and burying the body. In the Luwero area, only a whole body can be buried. People who found the bones of relatives killed by Amin did not bury them because of the traditional taboo associated with the burial of bones.

INTERACTIONS WITH OTHER ETHNIC GROUPS

Ugandan Americans have largely lived peaceably with other minorities. The Baganda people have a tradition of tolerance, more so than many other African societies. Even before the arrival of Europeans, many of this group's villages had residents from outside Buganda. Some had come to the region as slaves, some as migrant workers, but by the early twentieth century, many settled in as farmers. Marriage outside the Baganda ethnic group was fairly common. Also, since Uganda became independent, all governments have officially opposed discrimination based on ethnicity. However, in practice, they did not always stick to this position, as indicated by Amin's expulsion of Asians.

RELIGION

Most Ugandan Americans are Christians, as about two-thirds of Uganda's population is Christian. The remaining third practices indigenous religions or follows Islam. Before Idi Amin expelled Asians from

Uganda, many Muslims lived in Jinja, one of the places on which Mahatma Gandhi chose to have his ashes scattered. Religious tolerance is an important aspect of present-day Uganda. Christians, Muslims, Jews, Hindus, and others practice their religion freely.

About 19 percent of Ugandans follow local religions. These may include belief in a creator, as well as in ancestral and other spirits. Prayers and sacrifices convey respect for the dead, who are thought to help the living. Some religious practitioners serve as mediators between the living and the dead. In the Bunyoro region, those who worship spirits believe them to be the early mythical rulers, the Chwezi, so their faith is sometimes known as the Chwezi religion. The Lugbara people of northwestern Uganda believe ancestors influence the fate of the living and communicate with them.

In the Tepeth society in northeastern Uganda, religion and politics are intertwined. Clan elders and priests admit chosen men to a cult called Sor, which makes sacrifices in hopes of enhancing fertility, gaining favorable weather, and warding off illness. This belief system holds that both women and men receive messages from spirits, but claims women cannot see these messengers. Women, however, have the right to perform certain religious rituals.

EMPLOYMENT AND ECONOMIC TRADITIONS

Ugandan Americans sometimes have difficulty adapting to the American work ethic, which defines time as money. Ugandans value relationships and nonaggression. They are not generally financially ambitious, but are content with whatever circumstances they have. Europeans and Asians in Uganda often accused Ugandans of being culturally inferior and lazy, when in fact, their values were simply different.

Still, Ugandans in America have pursued a variety of occupations. Because agriculture is an important sector to Uganda's economy, employing over 80 percent of the work force, many Ugandan Americans have farming backgrounds. However, numerous Ugandan Americans are professionals and intellectuals who fled Amin's reign of terror. They work as physicians, in other health care specialties, as teachers, and as journalists.

POLITICS AND GOVERNMENT

Ugandan Americans have joined other Africans in organizations such as the National Summit on Africa to influence U.S. policy toward Uganda. A major piece of Africa-related legislation, the African Growth and Opportunity Act, was before Congress in 1999. The bill was designed to encourage the import of goods from sub-Saharan Africa by allowing them to come into the United States duty-free and in unrestricted quantity. The House of Representatives passed the bill in July 1999, but observers were uncertain that the Senate would pass it as well and send it to President Clinton so that he could sign it into law. African American legislators were split over the bill. Some believed it would help African workers, while others feared it would encourage multinational companies doing business in Africa to exploit these same workers.

RELATIONS WITH UGANDA

For most of the twentieth century, the United States had no significant interests in Uganda. However, some U.S. companies did business with Uganda. The U.S. government has largely avoided involvement in internal Ugandan politics. It has provided some economic aid. Ugandan leaders have sought to persuade the United States to expand this assistance. After Britain ended trade with Uganda in 1973, in response to Amin's expulsion of Asians, the United States briefly became Uganda's primary trading partner. Difficulties with the Amin administration soon led the United States to withdraw its Peace Corps volunteers and cut off economic assistance. In November 1973, after repeated public threats against U.S. embassy officials and the expulsion of Marine security guards responsible for protecting U.S. government property and personnel, the United States closed its embassy. In 1978 Congress put an embargo U.S trade with Uganda

Relations improved after Amin's fall. In mid-1979, the United States reopened its embassy. Relations with successor governments were cordial, although Obote and his administration took exception to strong U.S. criticism of Uganda's human rights situation. Relations between the United States and Uganda have been good since Museveni assumed power, and the United States has welcomed his efforts to end human rights abuses and to pursue economic reform.

In the early to mid-1980s, the United States provided about $10 million in assistance to Uganda annually, mostly in the form of humanitarian aid—such as food, medical supplies, hospital rehabilitation, and disaster relief—and agricultural equipment needed to promote economic recovery. The U.S. Agency for International Development funds a multifaceted development program at a level of about $50 million per year, both direct assistance and Food for Peace commodities. The U.S. Information Agency sponsors a cultural exchange program aiding the National Theater and other cultural institutions, bringing Fulbright professors to teach at Makerere University, and sponsoring U.S. study and tour programs for many government officials. Peace Corps volunteers in Uganda work in small enterprise development, natural resources management, and education. Museveni visited Washington in October 1987 and February 1989 for consultations with the president and members of Congress.

In 1997, two University of Florida professors attended the dedication of Uganda's Makerere-Florida Linkage House of the Center for Human Rights and Peace, which works for human rights for street people, teaches human rights courses to university students, and sponsors internships allowing students to work for in human rights organizations. The Makerere-Florida Linkage House includes facilities available to University of Florida researchers.

President Clinton visited Uganda in March of 1998 and while there announced a two-year $120 million U.S. gift to Uganda to promote education and democracy. Another $61 million was designated to go toward meals for schoolchildren. New American business activities in Uganda include Coca-Cola's opening of a bottling plant in the western part of the country in November 1998.

In March of 1999, Hutu rebels from neighboring Rwanda kidnapped 14 tourists and killed eight in the group, including two Americans, four Britons, and two New Zealanders who came to see the rare mountain gorillas of Uganda's Bwindi National Park. The U.S. government advised Americans to cancel flights to Uganda until further notice.

INDIVIDUAL AND GROUP CONTRIBUTIONS

Larry Kaggwa, professor of journalism at Howard University in Washington, D.C., is a native Ugandan and a veteran journalist and educator. He has written for the *Asbury Park Press* in New Jersey, *The Washington Post*, Hearst Newspapers, the *Oakland Tribune*, the *Los Angeles Times*, the *Hartford Courant*, the *Kansas City Star*, and the *Florida Times Union*. He has presented scholarly papers in forums across the country and is dedicated to developing daily newspapers at historically black universities. Kaggwa is adviser to the student chapter of the Society of Professional Journalists.

Namu Lwanga, a native Ugandan living in the United States, has a degree in ethnomusicology and has mastered and performs a wide variety of Ugandan traditional instruments. She also wrote, acted in and produced plays in Uganda before coming to the United States. A recipient of the 1996 Parents' Choice Award for her *Web of Tales* video, Lwanga is a storyteller, musician, and dancer who produces videos, albums, and performances that focus on Ugandan traditional movements. She won the Kenyan International Music Festival with an ensemble composition based on Uganda's war-torn past.

MEDIA

The Monitor.
The largest daily newspaper in Uganda, with a circulation of 30,000, is on the AfricaNews Website and is one of only two newspapers in Africa on the Internet.

Online: http://www.africanews.com.

ORGANIZATIONS AND ASSOCIATIONS

Permanent Mission of Uganda to United Nations.
Address: Uganda House, 336 East 45th Street, New York, New York 10017.
Telephone: (212) 949-0110.

Uganda North America Association.
Encourages fellowship among Ugandans living in North America; fosters social, cultural, and business contacts; has local chapters in major cities and sponsors an annual convention.

Contact: Sam Kiggwe, President.
Address: Atlanta Chapter, P.O. Box 54136, Atlanta, Georgia 30308.
Telephone: (770) 623-6873.
Online: http://www.angelfire.com/nj/unaa/ cmtee.html.

Ugandan Embassy.
Diplomatic representation in United States.

Contact: Chief of mission, Ambassador Stephen Kapimpina.
Address: 5909 16th Street, N.W., Washington, D.C. 20011.
Telephone: (202) 726-7100 through 7102; or (202) 726-0416.

SOURCES FOR ADDITIONAL STUDY

Cunningham, James F. *Uganda and Its People*. New York: Negro Universities Press, 1969.

Edel, May M. *The Chica of Uganda*. New Brunswick, NJ: Transaction Publishers, 1996.

Lamb, David. *The Africans*. New York: Vintage Books, 1987.

Uganda: A Country Study, edited by Rita M. Byrnes. Washington, DC: Library of Congress Federal Research Division, 1992.

UKRAINIAN AMERICANS

by
Marianne P. Fedunkiw

AMERICANS

Because the United States has modeled itself as a "melting pot" for newly arrived immigrants, Ukrainian Americans have become assimilated more thoroughly and more quickly than their neighbors to the north, the Ukrainian Canadians.

OVERVIEW

Ukraine is officially named Ukrayina, which means "borderland." After Russia, it is the second-largest country in Europe in area. It is comparable, both in population (about 52 million) and size (233,089 square miles) to France. It is bordered by the Black Sea, the Sea of Azov, Moldova, and Romania to the south; Hungary, Slovakia, and Poland to the west; Belarus to the north; and Russia to the north and northeast.

Of its population, 73 percent are of Ukrainian ethnic origin. The country's official language, since the dissolution of the Soviet Union in 1991, is Ukrainian. The capital city is Kiev, and the national flag has two broad horizontal bands of blue and yellow, the blue on top representing the sky and the yellow representing fields of wheat.

Although most of western Ukraine is agricultural—it is a country that has served as the "breadbasket of Europe"—there are large petroleum and natural gas fields as well. Major industrial products include refined sugar, iron, steel, tractors, cement, glass, paper, and fertilizer.

HISTORY

The earliest evidence of human settlement in Ukraine dates back 150,000 years. Early inhabitants of the territory included the Balkans, the Cimmerians (the first nomadic horsemen to appear in Ukraine in about 1500 to 1000 B.C.), the Scythians (early seventh century B.C.), and colonies set up by the Greek Empire (by the fourth century B.C.).

The direct ancestors of Ukraine's population today were the Slavs. The Slavs made their way into the Balkans in the early seventh century A.D. By the middle of the ninth century, however, what was to become known as Kievan Rus was still relatively underdeveloped. Much of the ensuing progress is attributed to the Varangians (or Vikings or Normans) who visited Rus in the mid-ninth century.

Following the reign of Oleh, Prince Ihor, and then his wife Olha ruled. Olha took over leadership when her husband, Ihor, was killed and their son Sviatoslav was still too young to rule. Her influence was especially apparent years later when her grandson Volodymyr became prince. Olha had converted from paganism to Christianity in 955 and, with Volodymyr, is credited with bringing Christianity to a pagan land in 988.

The reign of Jaroslav the Wise (1036-1054) is often seen as the pinnacle in the history of Kievan Rus. Among his contributions were more than 400 churches in Kiev alone, and the establishment of *Ruska pravda* (Rus' Justice), the basic legal code of the country. Jaroslav's reign was followed by a period of relative decline, beginning with feuds among his sons and grandsons. Jaroslav divided his kingdom among his sons with the idea that the eldest hold a position of seniority in maintaining unity, but Kiev declined as the political and economic center of Ukraine as each principality lived almost autonomously. Eventually Kiev fell to the Mongols in 1240, under Ogodei Khan and Batu, the latter being the grandson of Genghis.

From the latter half of the thirteenth century until the sixteenth century, Ukraine fell under the rule of first Lithuania (Grand Prince Algirdas moved in to occupy Kiev in 1362) and then Poland, led by Casimir the Great (1310-1370). Ukrainians, or Ruthenians (from Rus', as they called themselves during this period), preferred to be ruled by the Lithuanians, who treated them as equals. In 1385, to consolidate power against a growing Muscovy, an alliance between Lithuania and Poland was struck. Thus, the fourteenth and fifteenth centuries were years of struggle to keep Ukrainian lands from Poland, Hungary, and Lithuania, as well as free of the *boyars* or noblemen who tried to take control. At the heart of many of these battles was religion—since Poland was overwhelmingly Catholic and even Lithuania converted to Catholicism in 1385, the Orthodox Ukrainians were effectively shut out.

The late sixteenth and early seventeenth cen-turies were periods of recolonization in Ukraine, particularly in the provinces of Kiev and Bratslav. In 1569 the regions of Kiev, Volhynia, and Bratslav (Podillia) were annexed to the Kingdom of Poland. Another part of this development included a new society which grew out of the plains of the Dnieper River—the Cossacks. These men were free, as opposed to the serfs of the sixteenth century, and organized to fend off marauding Tatars. They ruled for decades, freeing Ukraine from Polish rule and helping to defend the country from Turkish, Tatar, and other invaders. One of the most notable of the Cossack leaders (hetmans) was Bohdan Khmelnytsky, who ruled from 1648 to 1657. During this time he led an uprising and mass peasant revolt against the ruling Poles. This led to a new ruling state with the hetman as leader and a tumultuous relationship with Russia in order to fight Poland. There was also a treaty signed with Muscovy in 1654 to help protect against invaders. After Khmelnytsky died in 1657, Ukraine's position weakened and it was eventually betrayed by its ally, Russia, who entered into an agreement with Poland which divided Ukraine between Russia and Poland.

Ukraine often tried to loosen the grip of Russia and Poland. In 1708-1709 Hetman Ivan Mazepa led the Cossacks to fight alongside Sweden's King Charles XII in the Swedish king's war with Russia's Peter I. But the Swedes and Cossacks lost, and Peter destroyed the hetman's capital and the hetmanate itself. By the late seventeenth century, in any case, not much was left of the hetmanate—only about one-third of that which Khmelnytsky controlled in his heyday as leader.

MODERN ERA

In the late eighteenth century, Russia annexed much of eastern Ukraine, taking the provinces of Kiev, Volhynia, and Podillia away from Poland, and taking the Crimea from the Turks. This transfer meant not only that the Orthodox religion could be practiced (it had been persecuted under Polish rule), but that by 1831 Russian became the official language, replacing Polish. This remained basically unchanged until 1918.

Austria gained possession of much of western Ukraine, including the province of Ruthenia and what had been Galicia, also in the late eighteenth century, and it remained Austrian land until the end of World War I. The bid for a free Ukraine was a never-ending one. A major figure was the nationalistic poet and painter Taras Shevchenko (1814-1861). This influential figure, born a serf, established the Ukrainian language as a language of literature, and his work tells the story of the glories and sufferings of the nation—all of this during a time when Ukrainian was banned from schools, books, and the performing arts.

World War I saw the Ukraine caught between the Austrians and Russia, each as potential allies against the other. By 1915-1916, little of Ukraine was left in Russian control. When the Bolsheviks overthrew the Czar and later the provisional government in 1917, Ukraine was poised for freedom. On January 22, 1918, Ukraine declared itself to be independent of Russia and used the help of German and Austrian troops to clear Russians from Ukraine. But the tenuous alliance with Germany and Austria quickly broke down, and freedom was short-lived. By April 1918 a new government, acceptable to the Germans, was set up. Galicia, which had freed itself of Austrian rule, found itself independent in 1918—but that was brief too, and it soon fell to Poland. Four years of war followed, and the new Union of Soviet Socialist Republics (USSR) reconquered Ukraine in 1922 and made it one of the original republics. Aside from being lost and rewon during the Second World War, Ukraine remained part of the USSR until the USSR was dissolved in 1991.

THE FIRST WAVE OF UKRAINIAN IMMIGRATION TO AMERICA

Although individual Ukrainians had come to the United States earlier, the first mass wave immigrated in the late nineteenth century, coinciding with the period of American industrialization. This group, numbering more than 350,000, began to arrive in 1877 as strikebreakers to work the Pennsylvania mines. Most of them came from western Ukraine, particularly the Lemko and Transcarpathian regions. In search of prosperity, they read advertisements which promised earnings ten to 20 times greater than they could hope for in the Ukraine. So they left their families, traveled to the ports of Bremen, Hamburg, Rotterdam, and Antwerp, and were packed into steerage on ships for the long journey to America.

When they reached the immigration check at Ellis Island, they waited in fear since a good number each trip were sent back. Those who made it through concentrated in the factories, steel mills, and foundries in Cleveland, Akron, Rochester, Buffalo, Syracuse, Chicago, and Detroit, as well as in Pennsylvania cities. Before World War I, 98 percent of Ukrainians settled in the northeastern states, with 70 percent in Pennsylvania. Men who had left wives and children in Ukraine first worked and then, when they could support them, brought their families over. They settled in urban villages near other Slavs, Poles, Jews, and Slovaks, seeking a sense of community to replace the one they had left. Their lives centered on the neighborhood church, saloon, general store, and boarding houses.

Unlike the Ukrainian Canadians, few of the early Ukrainian Americans farmed. By the time the first wave crossed the ocean, most of the free land had been distributed already and these new immigrants had no money to buy land. There were, however, isolated groups such as the Stundists (Baptist Evangelicals) who did farm, first in Virginia then in North Dakota. There were also small groups who chose to follow Orthodox priest Ahapii Honcharenko (1832-1916)—often considered the first nationality-conscious Ukrainian—to Alaska in the 1860s and Dr. Nicholas Sudzilovsky-Russel to Hawaii in 1895. Sudzilovsky-Russel was elected to the Hawaiian Senate in 1901 and, in this position, greatly aided more than 375 Ukrainians who were lured to Hawaii by dishonest agents and forced to work as slaves on plantations until they paid the costs of their four-month sea voyages. Eventually they were released from their contracts, and most returned to North America.

THE SECOND WAVE: BETWEEN THE WORLD WARS

This wave of immigrants, covering the period between the two world wars, was considerably smaller than the first, numbering only about 15,000. It was also different in that these were immigrants who were aware of and vocal about their nationalism and politicized to the point of infighting. Until that time, Ukrainian Americans tended to be polarized along religious lines; now there were socialists and conservatives on either end of the political spectrum. Furthermore, assimilation had gained momentum by the time of the second wave, and adjustments to clothing and language came more quickly than to the first immigrants.

THE THIRD WAVE: DISPLACEMENT AFTER WORLD WAR II

The final major wave was one of refugees following the Second World War. These often well-educated Ukrainians (including 2,000 university students, 1,200 teachers and scholars, 400 engineers, 350 lawyers, and 300 physicians) had fled their homes during the war and had little interest in returning while the Soviet government was in place. They saw both the United States and Canada as temporary homes, although most would never return to live in the Ukraine.

Most of these immigrants had spent time in the postwar refugee camps in Austria and Germany. Eight of these DP (displaced person) camps housed two-thirds of the Ukrainian refugees, with the rest in private accommodation. Between 1947 and 1951, these DPs were resettled, with the greatest number (80,000) going to the United States (30,000 went to Canada, 20,000 to Australia, and the same number to Great Britain, 13,000 to Brazil and Argentina, and 10,000 each to Belgium and France).

The DPs concentrated in large cities, particularly New York City, Philadelphia, Chicago, Detroit, Rochester, Syracuse, Buffalo, and Cleveland. They gravitated to neighborhoods where Ukrainian Americans already lived, where churches and a community infrastructure had been set up by previous immigrants. This newest group enjoyed the benefits of often being better educated, and of social assistance systems, schools, and immigrant aid societies already in place. Although educated, professionals may have had to work in menial jobs until they grasped the language and had enough money to set up as doctors, lawyers, and engineers. Some found the adjustment difficult and never returned to their professions and instead took jobs administering Ukrainian institutions and organizations, many of which were brought from Ukraine by the immigrants.

SETTLEMENT PATTERNS

Before World War II, 98 percent of Ukrainian Americans settled in the northeastern United States with almost three-quarters in Pennsylvania. Between the wars, the numbers in Pennsylvania dropped, while the Ukrainian American populations of New York and New Jersey grew (especially that of New York City) and sizable communities sprang up in Ohio and Illinois.

The 1990 Census of Population states that 740,803 individuals reported their ancestry as Ukrainian, or 0.3 percent of the total. Of those who said they were Ukrainian Americans, just over two-thirds listed it as "first ancestry." It is interesting to note that the census also gave, as ethnicity choices, Carpath Rusyn, Central European, Russian and Slavic; when many of the first Ukrainians arrived in America, they were identified with labels other than Ukrainian, including some of these choices.

The majority of Ukrainian Americans, the census notes, settled in the Northeast. The state with the greatest number is Pennsylvania (129,753 reported in 1990), followed by New York (121,113), and New Jersey (73,935). Although regionally, the fewest number of Ukrainians are to be found in the

American West, California is the fourth-ranked state with 56,211 reported in 1990.

INTERACTIONS WITH SETTLED AMERICANS

Because the first wave of Ukrainians came as strikebreakers, there was tension between them and the established English, Irish, and Welsh miners in the area. Ukrainians were also the first large group of non-English-speaking immigrants, and so they stood out as "different"—they spoke a foreign language, ate different food, and, at least upon arrival, wore different clothes. They also tended to group together, further isolating themselves from the Americans. This, however, changed quickly with the generation of children who grew up in America. It was not unusual for these children, who played in the streets with other non-Ukrainian children, to pick up the language and customs quickly and assimilate thoroughly.

Discrimination, though, was part of life at the start. Ukrainians were called "Hunkies" (having come from the Hungarian part of the Austrian empire) or "Bohunks" (a derivative of Bohemians) by those who reviled these immigrants, who were often illiterate, dirty with miner's dust, and willing to do work no one else would to get a foothold toward a better life. In fact, in his *Ukrainians in North America: An Illustrated History*, Orest Subtelny notes that this so-called "scum of Europe" were thought to be contaminating once civilized towns in Pennsylvania by forcing out those who had given stability to the area: the English, Irish, Welsh, and Scottish. In fact, in 1897 a discriminatory measure passed the state of Pennsylvania, which required that nonnaturalized American miners and workers pay an additional tax.

KEY ISSUES

The most striking issue is the state of the free Ukraine since it gained its independence in 1991, with the breakup of the USSR. The country must deal with new governments and democracy as well as with the transition to economic and social independence. Much of the infrastructure of business and government has been redesigned entirely, and Ukrainian Americans are eagerly monitoring the progress of change.

Another concern is the continuing effects of the Chernobyl nuclear disaster in eastern Ukraine in the 1980s. Considerable aid, both financial and material, has been coordinated to aid victims, particularly the orphans, of the disaster.

There has always been great interest in events "in the old country." Ukrainian American organizations based in the United States have, for decades, been formed to make political pleas on behalf of those in the occupied homeland and to send material and financial aid. This included marches on the White House protesting the Polish Occupation of Eastern Galicia in 1922 and a 1933 march by Detroit Ukrainian Americans to protest the Soviet man-made famine that year.

ACCULTURATION AND ASSIMILATION

Because the United States has modeled itself as a "melting pot" for newly arrived immigrants, Ukrainian Americans have become assimilated more thoroughly and more quickly than their neighbors to the north, the Ukrainian Canadians. This is in part because the first immigrants moved to heavily populated urban centers where they tended to get "lost" more readily among other immigrants and American citizens. As the decades have passed, too, the number of new immigrants has dropped. Couple this with the thoroughness of assimilation—in 1980, less than 17 percent of people of Ukrainian descent said Ukrainian was their primary language—and the future of the Ukrainian American community can seem uncertain.

This does not, however, mean that all is bleak. Through church, cultural, and political-business organizations, Ukrainian Americans and their children and grandchildren have places to go to celebrate their heritage. This is aided by the fact that traditionally Ukrainian Americans have not moved far from their original settlement sites in the northeastern states of Pennsylvania, New York, and New Jersey. Some of the strongest organizations, too, are those which were established early in the history of immigration. The most forward-thinking have changed with the times and deemphasized nationalist concerns in favor of drawing members with cultural, business, and social activities. Credit unions, youth organizations, and professional and business clubs are strong in the communities they serve.

MISCONCEPTIONS AND STEREOTYPES

One of the most common misconceptions about Ukrainian Americans is that they were Russians, Poles, Hungarians, or Austrians. This was the case because depending on when they arrived, Ukraine was occupied by Russia or the USSR, Poland, or the Austro-Hungarian Empire.

TRADITIONS, CUSTOMS, AND BELIEFS

Before Ukraine adopted Christianity in 988, the inhabitants believed in pagan gods who ruled over the sun, stars, and moon. Folk beliefs are still connected to the sun, stars, and moon, as well as to dreams, the seasons, and agriculture. In fact, many of the pagan customs blended, over time, with Christian beliefs. These centered on the family (e.g., birth, marriage, and funeral customs), the community, and seasonal agricultural rites.

Songs and folk tales play a significant role in these ancient customs. There are specific songs for harvest festivals, New Year's celebrations, and Christmas and Easter, all celebrating both pagan beliefs and Christian traditions. Songs and music have always been important to the Ukrainian Americans; the earliest settlers, who had little money, often spent their rare free hours gathered together playing and singing. This has continued, not only in established choirs and ensembles, but as part of Ukrainian youth groups, camps, and Saturday language classes. The language classes are also a place where children of immigrants have been taught about their country's history, geography, and culture.

Examples of ancient customs still practiced today include the spring rites and songs (*vesnianky*) and the traditions associated with the harvest or Kupalo festival in which young maidens make wreaths of wildflowers, and set them afloat in a nearby stream; their fortune is determined by the young man who retrieves the wreath while facing the spirits of the night. Often these are still practiced by Ukrainian American youth at summer camps or through youth organizations and cultural festivals.

PROVERBS

Proverbs are a rich part of the Ukrainian culture and are handed down from generation to generation: A smart man seeks all from himself, a fool looks for everything in others; Fear God—and you will not fear any person; He who thinks rarely always has time to talk; Snow falls upon a pursuit that is put off; A wise man does not always say what he knows, but a fool does not always know what he says; Life is the road to death; It is difficult to learn to thank God if we cannot thank people; The rich man is not he who has great riches but he who squanders little money; A good heart does not know pridefulness; Brotherhood is greater than riches; A black dog or a white dog is still a dog.

CUISINE

Ukrainian cooking is a robust mix of meat, vegetable, and grain dishes. It is similar to, and has been influenced by, the cuisine of Poland, Russia, Turkey, Hungary, Romania, and Moldova. Although the selection and availability of food is more varied for Ukrainian Americans than it is for Ukrainians, many of the traditional foods survive in the United States.

Breads figure prominently in both immigrant and Ukrainian households—Ukraine is, after all, known as the "breadbasket of Europe"—and particular breads such as *paska* for Easter are featured during the holidays and at weddings, often decorated with braids or birds of dough. Bread is featured as a ceremonial ingredient in all special occasions, whether to bring divine blessing to the start of a farm task, to welcome guests to a celebration, or to symbolically part with the dead at the *tryzna*, or wake.

The dishes most readily associated with Ukrainians are likely *borscht* (a soup of red beets), *holubtsi* (cabbage rolls), *pyrohy* or *varenyky* (dough dumplings filled with potatoes and cheeses, sauerkraut, or various fruits such as cherries), and *kielbassa* (smoked sausage). The potato is the most readily used vegetable in traditional Ukrainian cooking, although garlic, onions, cabbage, cucumbers, tomatoes, and beets are also staples. Mushrooms are also a common ingredient, used to spice up a meal and often included in stuffings.

The best showcase for traditional Ukrainian cuisine is the Christmas Eve meatless meal prepared for January 6 (under the Julian calendar for traditional-

ists). This meal features 12 courses, symbolic of the 12 apostles present at the Last Supper. The meal begins with *kutya* (cooked wheat, ground poppy seed, and honey) and then moves on to pickled herring or pickled mushrooms, *borscht*, one or more preparations of fish, *holubtsi* with buckwheat or rice, *varenyky* with sauerkraut or potatoes, beans with prunes, sauerkraut with peas, baked beets, mushroom sauce, and ends with a dessert of pastries— *makivnyk* (poppy seed cake), *khrusty* (fried bands of dough cookies sprinkled with icing sugar), *pampushky* (doughnuts), *medivnyk* (honey cake) or *compote* (stewed dried fruit).

There is a religious context to Ukrainian festive dinners. At Christmas, a place is set at the table to welcome the spirits of dead relatives. And at Easter, the food that makes up the ceremonial meal is taken to church in a basket decorated with the finest embroidered linens to be blessed.

TRADITIONAL COSTUMES

Although today Ukrainians dress in clothes basically indistinguishable from the rest of modern Europe, there are traditional costumes of Ukraine, which vary from region to region. In Kuvijovyc and Struk's *Encyclopedia of Ukraine*, Ukrainian folk dress is divided into five different regional forms: the Middle Dnieper region, Polisia, Podillia, central Galicia and Volhynia, and Subcarpathia and the Carpathian Mountain region.

The first region around the Dnieper River is characterized by women wearing a *plakhta* (a wrap-around skirt), a *kersetka* (a blouse with wide sleeves and a bodice), and an *ochipok* (a headdress), while the men wore cut shirts. These clothes date back to the time of the ruling hetmanate.

In Polisia the clothes date back even further, to the princely era. It is here that the well-known Ukrainian embroidered blouse ablaze with red and a colorful woven skirt is worn by the women. Men dress in a shirt worn outside their trousers and a grey woolen cap (*maherka*) or a tall felt hat (*iolomok*).

The third region, Podillia, is recognized by the women's multicolored, embroidered blouses and the men's mantle. In central Galicia and Volhynia, linen is a popular fabric, and women wear corsets and head wraps which resemble turbans. The men don caftans, felt overcoats, or jackets. Finally, one of the most recognizable and colorful costumes comes from the Carpathian Mountain region, or Lemkivschyna. Women's skirts are decorated with folds and pleats, while men wear tunics and *leibyks*—the Lemko felt vests.

The greatest showcase for native folk dress for Ukrainian Americans is at dance festivals. The swirling ribbons of color and flashes of billowing satin pants tucked into red boots mix with the linen shirts, laced leather slippers, and felt hats as dancers representing different regions of Ukraine share the stage.

DANCES AND SONGS

There is a rich history of Ukrainian music. Some of the oldest traditions survive to this day through Christmas carols, originally sung in pagan times to celebrate the first long day of the season, and the Easter songs, or *hayivky*, also known as songs of spring. There were also songs to herald the arrival of summer and the harvest.

During the era of Cossack rule, other forms of music arose. The lyrico-epic "dumas" told of the struggles of the Cossacks. Music flourished in the seventeenth and eighteenth centuries—there were even organized singing guilds. Notable composers include Semen Artemovsky, author of the opera *Zaporozhian Beyond the Danube* (written in 1863), and Mykola Lysenko (1842-1912), who collected thousands of folk songs in addition to composing original songs and operas. In the United States, the first Ukrainian American choir was organized in 1887 in Shenandoah, Pennsylvania.

Traditional instruments include the *bandura* or *kobza*, whose strings are plucked to make music; the free-reed wind instrument (*sopilka*); the stringed percussion dulcimer, or *tsymbaly*, played by hitting the strings with small hammers; and the violin.

Ukrainian folk dance differs in style and costume, depending on the region being represented and the occasion being celebrated. While dancers from central Ukraine wear bright pants, embroidered shirts, and swirling skirts and aprons, Hutsul dancers from the Carpathian mountain region wear linen trousers tucked into leather slippers and felt hats, and brandish long wooden axes over which the men leap or on which they balance the women. Dance themes deal with relations between men and women as well as particular occupations such as the dances of reapers, cobblers, coopers, and smiths.

Among the most popular dances, though, are the *hopak* and *kozachok*. The *hopak* was first danced by the Cossack of the Zaporhizian Sich in the sixteenth century and spread to the rest of Ukraine. Today it is predominantly associated with the Kiev region and incorporates both male and female dances. It is a fast-tempoed, improvised dance with complex acrobatic movements with the men leaping over one another and high into the air, while the women spin and step around them.

The *kozachok* also originated during the Cossack period in the sixteenth century. It is a folk dance with male and female roles, and often begins with a slow, melodic introduction before breaking into a quick tempo. During the seventeenth and eighteenth centuries it was performed, not only in Ukraine, but also in the royal courts of Russia, France, Hungary, and Poland. Both the *hopak* and *kozachok* are standards of Ukrainian folk dance today.

The 1920s and 1930s were decades of growth in Ukrainian dance, theater and music in the United States. A number of theaters and music halls, beginning with the first in New York City in 1924, were opened. Ukrainian American singers and dancers performed in a concert commemorating the bicentennial of George Washington's birth in 1932, and the New York Association of Friends of Ukrainian Music was created in 1934. Another highlight of the period was a performance by more than 300 Ukrainian American dancers from Vasile Avramenko's dance school at the Metropolitan Opera House in New York City in 1931.

HOLIDAYS

Ukrainian Americans all celebrate the same holidays but at different times, depending on which calendar they use. The major holidays are religious. According to the "old" or Julian calendar, Christmas is celebrated January 7, with the ritual dinner the night before. Easter cycles and falls on a different weekend each year. For those who adhere to a more modern model, Christmas and Easter would

still be celebrated in a Ukrainian church, in the respective rite, but on December 25 and whatever weekend "English Easter" falls on.

One occasion Ukrainians do not traditionally celebrate is birthdays. More important are the "name days," days during the year which are named for certain saints. For example, friends would gather to help celebrate the name day of any Stephens or Stepany on January 9 by the Julian calendar, St. Stephen's Day.

The other major holiday is on January 22, commemorating the establishment of a free Ukraine on that date in 1917.

HEALTH ISSUES

There are no known afflictions specific to ethnic Ukrainians, although the most recent immigrants from the Chernobyl area are wary of the radiation exposure they received during the reactor meltdown of the late 1980s.

To some degree, folk medicine retains its place in the community in both attitude and practice. The mentally challenged were often considered to be "God's people." Physical diseases were often driven out by squeezing or sucking or were "frightened away" by shouting or beating. Diseases could also be "charmed away" by using magic incantations and prayers or treated with medicinal plants or, more "traditionally," using baths, bleeding (using leeches or cupping), or massages. These methods tended to fall out of favor as Ukrainians were assimilated into the American mode of health care.

Ukrainians have readily joined the American medical establishment. In addition to the health-care professionals who emigrated to the United States, Ukrainian Americans are well represented in the medical fields, including dentistry and chiropractic. In fact, regional associations of physicians were quick to spring up in the major northeastern centers of Ukrainian American concentration.

LANGUAGE

Ukrainian belongs to the Slavic group of Indo-European languages. It is the second most widely spoken language of the 12 surviving members of this group. Historically, there used to exist a literary language called Old Church Slavonic which was common to all of Ukraine, in addition to the dialects of the regions. Unlike other languages such as German or English, the three main dialect groups—northern, southeastern and southwestern—are not particularly different from each other. The alphabet is made up of 33 Cyrillic characters, the last of which is a character which does not stand alone but follows various consonants to soften the sound. Each letter has a particular sound so reading is relatively simple, words being pronounced phonetically.

Ukrainian was the primary language of almost all first-generation Ukrainian Americans. Because of the political situation which they left at home, many also spoke Polish, Russian, or German. In 1980 less than 17 percent listed their primary language as Ukrainian. The Ukrainian language is taught in several universities and colleges, including Stanford University, University of Chicago, University of Illinois at Urbana-Champaign, Harvard University, University of Michigan, and Kent State University. Ukrainian language collections can be found in many public libraries including those in Denver, New York, Brooklyn, Detroit, Minneapolis, and Cleveland.

GREETINGS AND OTHER POPULAR EXPRESSIONS

Common Ukrainian greetings based upon the time of day include: *Dobredeyn*—Good day; *Dobrey ranok*—Good morning; and Dobra nych—Good night. Other often used expressions include: *Diakoyu*—Thank you; *proshu* (used both for "please" and "you're welcome"), and *dopobachynya* (literally, "until we see each other again", although more commonly translated as "goodbye"). For festive occasions the phrase *mnohaya lita* is used, which means "many happy years"; a corresponding song entitled *"Mnohaya lita"* is the standard birthday song as well as being used for toasts for any happy occasion such as an anniversary or wedding.

There are standard, specific greetings and replies for Christmas and Easter. During the Christmas season, a visitor would enter a home saying, *Christos rodevsia*—Christ is born, and the host's reply would be *Slavim yoho*—Let us praise him. At Easter the greeting changes to *Christos voskrys*—Christ has risen, and the reply changes to *Voistenu voskrys*—He is risen indeed.

FAMILY AND COMMUNITY DYNAMICS

Particularly during the early waves of immigration, men came to America, settled, and then brought over their wives and children. Those who were single, after getting a job and a place to live, often sought to start a family and tended to seek a woman who was of the same ethnic background, if only for ease of communication. With each passing generation there has been a greater tolerance and incidence of marriage outside the Ukrainian culture. Similarly, divorce was and is still relatively rare; it made little economic sense in the beginning and was forbidden in the Catholic faith to which the majority of immigrants subscribed.

Because of geography and time, finding a wife or husband was not always easy. Dating, for early immigrants, was a quick practice centered on Ukrainian community social events—these new Americans worked long hours and had relatively little free time. The couple might attend a dance in a church hall or a concert. Even today, *zabavas* (dances) are prime meetings places for young people.

Around the turn of the century, Passaic, New Jersey, had a high concentration of single Ukrainian women. Most women were employed as domestics, often far from the foundry towns in large coastal cities. Some men left a wife behind in Ukraine and married again in America. A newspaper story published in 1896 told of such a case one step more unusual—the immigrant from Galicia left a wife there and married once in New Jersey and again in Michigan. After being arrested and then returning to his wife in Ukraine, he discovered his two children had grown to number four.

Like many other European immigrants, as the first generation of Ukrainian Americans aged, they often lived with one of their children to serve as babysitters for grandchildren, thereby freeing the parents to work. This also helped to continue the culture and language, and many children went to school speaking only Ukrainian.

Although the duties may have differed, both boys and girls were expected to help with household chores, especially in households where part of the income came from taking in boarders. Considerable responsibility fell on the older siblings to take care of those younger, and much was expected of them so that they could become successful and productive American citizens.

WEDDINGS

Weddings are a major celebration beginning with the negotiations for the bride's hand in marriage. The groom's family appoints a *starosty* (negotiator), who serves as an intermediary between the families of the prospective bride and groom. Originally, this figure did much of the work, even to haggling over the dowry of the bride. Today, if couples wish to include a *starosty*, it is more a symbolic role for a close relative or family friend and often translates into serving as master or mistress of ceremonies.

Before the wedding, a shower or *divych vechir* (maidens' evening) is hosted by the close friends and relatives of the bride. These are often large gatherings of women held in community banquet halls, although today they may be smaller, more intimate affairs hosted in homes. The groom and bride attend and sit beneath a wreath, after a full meal, opening the gifts which guests have brought.

One wedding day custom that is often retained is a blessing, at the home of the bride's parents, that precedes the church wedding ceremony. The bride, groom, and members of the immediate family join a priest to bless the impending union. Then everyone moves on to the church where a ceremony, which may include a full mass, takes place. During the ceremony there are certain customs, which are still kept up, such as placing crowns or wreaths of myrrh on the heads of the pair or binding the bride's and groom's hands with a long embroidered linen called a *rushnychok* and then having the priest lead them about the altar three times. The bride may also say a prayer at the altar and give a gift of flowers to the Virgin Mary, in hopes that she will bless the bride as both wife and mother.

Ukrainian wedding celebrations are large—it is not unusual to have more than 300 guests filling a church hall or banquet room—alive with song and dance, and lots of food. At the beginning of the reception, the bride and groom are greeted with bread and salt by their godparents. The bread represents the wish that they should never know hunger and the salt that they should never know bitterness. After the greeting, the newlyweds and their attendants sit at the head table and dinner begins.

A wedding dinner today reflects the tastes of the couple and their families and can include favorite Ukrainian and American dishes—*perogies* and roast beef. Although many couples have some sort of wedding cake, they may also have a traditional *kolach*; this is a bread with decorative flour, stalks of wheat and braids of dough adorning the top. The name is derived from the word *kolo* which means a circle, a symbol of eternity.

After dinner the dancing starts. Dancing is an integral part of any Ukrainian wedding, and there are a number of traditions built around the dancing segment. At one point in the evening, the bride's veil is removed and replaced with a kerchief, symbolizing her change from maiden to married woman. As the guests watch, encircling the bride and groom, the veil is then placed by the bridesmaids on the heads of single women in the circle who dance with their boyfriends, their fiancés, or groomsmen. Some couples also choose to incorporate throwing the bouquet and garter into the festivities.

BAPTISMS

Within the first year of a baby's birth, the child is christened. Close family friends or relatives are chosen as godparents and participate in the religious ceremony. This is a festive occasion which is often followed by a banquet hosted by the new parents. The link between godparent and child is maintained throughout the child's life and often the godparents are simply referred to as *chresna* (godmother) and *chresny* (godfather) for years after.

FUNERALS

Ukrainians are ritualistic and religious in their funeral rites as well. The actual religious ceremony and burial are preceded by one or two *panachydy*. These brief evening ceremonies are held in the funeral home, and friends and family of the deceased join for a memorial service. The ceremony is conducted by a priest and ends with the singing of the funeral song, "Vichnaya Pam'yat" (Ever Remembered).

The funeral itself is a religious occasion and can include a funeral mass in a church. Family and friends then accompany the casket to the gravesite (few people are cremated) and then repair to a church or community hall or family member's home for a *tryzna* (funeral remembrance luncheon).

One of the most significant features of a Ukrainian funeral is that the memorial service is repeated 40 days after the person dies, and then again annually. There is also a festival, originally associated with the pagan cult of the dead, called Zeleni *sviata* or Rosalia, which is dedicated to visiting and celebrating the dead. It is held 50 days after Easter, and today people meet at the cemetery to have a special mass said in honor of the dead.

EDUCATION

Education for the initial immigrants was a luxury few could afford. With each new wave, Ukrainians came to the United States with more and more education. Many of the artists and professionals who arrived between the wars had been educated in Europe and, as soon as they learned English, were able to pursue their work in the United States. There was also a growing number who studied at American schools and whose children were encouraged to do the same, both boys and girls. Wherever possible, children were educated in parochial schools because religion played a large role in their lives. Those who went on to post-secondary education tended to concentrate in the professions: medicine, law, engineering, graduate studies, and the arts.

Ukrainian American students decided to establish a network based on their common ethnic background soon after the third major wave of immigration. For example, the Federation of Ukrainian Students Organization of America, based in New York City, held its first congress April 10-12, 1953. This included 22 regional and university associations of students across America.

In addition to supporting religion, Ukrainian Americans also support political causes, the arts, sports, and education. The Shevchenko Scientific Society, which was founded in the United States in 1947 and included Albert Einstein among its members in the 1950s, supports science and research activities; the Ukrainian Congress Committee of America, Inc., founded in 1940, coordinates legal and material support for Ukrainians in Europe while raising the profile of Ukraine in America; and the Ukrainian National Association of America, originally established in 1894 as a fraternal benefit society to provide insurance to Ukrainian immigrants, supports the social education and welfare of Ukrainian immigrants while providing aid to the "old country."

THE ROLE OF WOMEN

As well as raising their families, women played a large role by adding to the family income, working as domestics, taking in boarders, working in kitchens or factories, or contributing to the family business. This was hard work; for example, working as a domestic meant seven-day work weeks, almost 13 hours each day, with just Sunday evenings free.

Women were also responsible for maintaining the language and culture, specifically through festive occasions such as Christmas and Easter. The wife and mother would spend hours baking and cooking the multicourse celebratory dinners, participating in the religious life of her family and community, and serving on various women's nationalistic committees.

Many women joined the organizations whose purpose was to promote Ukrainian interests in the diaspora. In addition to joining those groups which accepted men, women also formed their own associations such as the Ukrainian National Women's League of America, Inc. (a national nonpartisan, nonsectarian organization founded in 1925), whose purpose is to unite women of Ukrainian birth and descent living in the United States to promote their common philanthropic, educational, civic, and artistic interests in addition to assisting Ukrainians in Europe, the Ukrainian Women's Alliance, and the United Ukrainian Women's Organizations of America. The first congress of Ukrainian Women in America was held in New York in 1932. Women's organizations managed to combine Ukrainian and American interests (celebrating the birthdays of female poet Lesia Ukrainka along with those of George Washington and Abraham Lincoln in February) and tended to be less insular than men's organizations.

INTERACTIONS WITH OTHER ETHNIC GROUPS

Even in their early settlement patterns, new Ukrainian immigrants tended to settle near other immigrants, particularly others from Eastern and Central Europe such as Polish, Russian, and Jewish immigrants. Because of the similarities in language (and the fact that many Ukrainians emigrated while their country was under the occupation of Russia, Poland, or Austro-Hungary), Ukrainians, Poles, and Russians could communicate easily even before they learned English. It also gave them the sense of community which they had left behind when they crossed the ocean to America.

RELIGION

Most Ukrainian Americans belong to one of two faiths, Catholic (Eastern, or Byzantine, Rite) and Eastern Orthodox. The Catholics are greater in number, almost twice as numerous as the Orthodox group. The first Ukrainian Catholic church in the United States, St. Michael the Archangel, was built in Shenandoah, Pennsylvania, in 1885 under the direction of the Reverend Ivan Volansky, an immigrant priest who had arrived the year before.

In the late nineteenth century there was a struggle within the Church and in 1899 the Reverend Volansky was called back to Lviv by his superiors, who had buckled under pressure from Vatican authorities who said that Volansky was an Eastern Rite Catholic and that the Latin Rite American Catholic bishops opposed the organization of separate Ukrainian Catholic parishes. This led some Ukrainians to switch to the Russian Orthodox faith. Finally, in 1913 the Vatican acceded to the demands of Ukrainian Catholics in the United States and established an exarchate which made all Ukrainian Catholic parishes, which numbered more than 200 at the time, a separate administrative unit which reported only to the Pope.

The Ukrainian Orthodox church in America was set up in 1928 by ex-Catholic Ukrainians. In addition, thousands of Catholic Ukrainians converted to the Russian Orthodox church after the consecrated priest of a Minneapolis parish, Alexis Toth, who was a widower, was not accepted by the Roman Catholic archbishop (because he had been married). Toth broke away to join the Orthodoxy; his 365 parishioners followed him, and tens of thousands of immigrants from Galicia, Lemkivschyna, and Transcarpathia filled out the ranks.

Ultimately, there were many battles among the dominant religious groups, which included Byzantine Rite Catholic Ruthenians/Ruthyns as they called themselves, Ukrainian Catholics, and Orthodox "Russians." Today the Ukrainian Catholic church (Byzantine Rite) and Orthodoxy remain strong in the United States.

There are also Ukrainian Protestants, including the Stundinst sect, a Baptist denomination which settled in the United States in 1890. This group settled first in Virginia and then went west to North Dakota, where they established a settlement called Kiev, named after the city in which they had lived in Ukraine.

In 1905 Ukrainian Protestants founded the Ukrainian Evangelical Alliance of North America. In 1922, the Union of Ukrainian Evangelical Baptist Churches was established to consolidate the Ukrainian Protestant parishes.

EMPLOYMENT AND ECONOMIC TRADITIONS

Most of the early immigrants of the late nineteenth century worked in the steel mills and foundries of the northeastern states. Within the ethnic urban communities where they lived, other entrepreneurial Ukrainian Americans opened grocery or general stores, butcher shops, and taverns. Women contributed to the family income by taking in boarders and doing their laundry and cooking. Overall, it was characteristic of this first generation of settlers to remain in the job, or at least the industry, with which they began.

Although their pay was not substantial, Ukrainian Americans as a group rarely took advantage of government assistance (where available) or unemployment benefits. They were also among the most law-abiding immigrants—in his *Ukrainians in North America: An Illustrated History*, Orest Subtelny notes that between 1904 and 1908, only 0.02 percent were accused of breaking any law.

By the time of the second immigration wave between the world wars, there was a shift in employment trends. Second-generation Ukrainian Americans had greater opportunity for higher education, and the second influx of immigrants tended to be better educated themselves. From that point forward, the university graduation rate grew, with medicine, law, engineering, and teaching being the principal professions. This is reflected in the growth of Ukrainian American professional and business clubs across the United States. For example, membership in the Society of Ukrainian Engineers in America grew from 82 members at the end of 1949 to 363 just five years later.

POLITICS AND GOVERNMENT

Ukrainian Americans were involved in local, state, and national politics from the earliest years of mass immigration. Dr. Nicholas Sudzilovsky-Russel was elected to and became presiding officer of the Hawaiian senate on February 10, 1901.

In 1925, George Chylak began a five-year term as mayor of Oliphant, Pennsylvania. Mary Beck (Mariia Bek), born in 1908 in Ford City, Pennsylvania, was the first woman elected to the Detroit Common Council. She served as the council's president from 1952 to 1962 and was the acting mayor of Detroit from 1958 to 1962.

In state politics, the lawyer O. Malena took a seat in the Pennsylvania legislature in 1932, the lawyer S. Jarema won a seat in the New York legislature in 1935, and Judge John S. Gonas (born 1907) took a seat in the Indiana legislature in 1936. Gonas was also a senator from 1940-1948 and a Democratic candidate for vice president in 1960.

Ukrainian Americans also garnered the attention of government rather quickly. On March 16, 1917, President Woodrow Wilson proclaimed April 21 a day "upon which the people of the United States may make such contributions as they feel disposed to aid the stricken Ruthenians (Ukrainians) in the belligerent countries," following discussion in Congress on the Ukrainian cause. And it was President Dwight D. Eisenhower who unveiled a stature of poet and nationalist Taras Shevchenko in Washington, D.C., to commemorate the 150th anniversary of the poet's birth.

Ukrainians, although some belonged to Communist organizations such as the Haidamaky (established in 1907 in New York), tend to be conservative in their politics and, therefore, tend to support the Republican party. But in 1910, the Ukrainian National Association of America (UNA) actually encouraged people to vote for the socialists since neither Republicans nor Democrats were addressing the concerns of the workers. Leftist factions included the Ukrainian Workers Association which broke away from the UNA in 1918 and the Ukrainian Federation of Socialist Parties in America. The other choice for Ukrainian Americans in the 1920s was the conservative-monarchist Sich movement.

Ukrainian Americans are also involved in supporting political change in Ukraine itself. Demonstrations were frequent in the 1920s and 1930s and included the participation of thousands of men, women, and children: the White House was picketed in 1922 on the issues of Polish occupation of Eastern Galicia; about 20,000 Ukrainian Americans marched in Philadelphia in 1930 to protest this same Polish occupation of Western Ukraine; and a 1933 march in Detroit was held to protest the Soviet-induced famine in Ukraine.

MILITARY

Early records reveal that Ukrainian Americans served in George Washington's army during the American Revolution. Mykola Bizun, Ivan Lator, Petro Polyn, and Stephen Zubley are just some of the Ukrainian names that are listed in Washington's register. There was also a group that fought in the Union Army during the American Civil War. Officers Joseph Krynicky, Ivan Mara, and Andrey Ripka served, and the Union dead included Ukrainian Americans Julius Koblansky, Petro Semen, and I. H. Yarosh. All of this, however, was relatively limited involvement since the major waves of immigration were to follow.

Most significant for the Ukrainian Americans during the years of World War I was the concurrent bid for a free Ukraine. World War I was heralded as an opportunity to defeat Austria or Russia, both of which ruled parts of Ukraine at the time. The Federation of Ukrainians in America was formed in

1915 to inform the American public about Ukrainian goals. In 1917—the same year that President Woodrow Wilson declared April 21 as "Ukrainian Day"—dreams were realized and the Ukrainian Peoples Republic was established. But Wilson supported the Russian empire, and not long after, the free Ukraine fell. In addition, many Ukrainians, particularly in Canada, were deemed to be Austrian citizens and, hence, on the wrong side; thousands were incarcerated as enemy aliens.

During World War II thousands of Ukrainian Americans served in the armed forces. Nicholas Minue of Carteret, New Jersey, was posthumously awarded the Congressional Medal of Honor for his single-handed destruction of a German machine gun position. Nestor Chylak, Jr., who went on to be an American League baseball umpire, received the Purple Heart and Silver Star and was almost blinded during the Battle of the Bulge. And Lt. Colonel Theodore Kalakula was awarded the Silver Star and two oak leaf clusters for saving medical supplies during a Japanese air raid and for his attack against the Japanese after the company commander had been wounded. Kalakula was also the first Ukrainian American graduate of West Point.

INDIVIDUAL AND GROUP CONTRIBUTIONS

Ukrainian Americans, in all areas of endeavor, have made lasting contributions to American life. Some of these individuals and their accomplishments follow.

ACADEMIA

George Kistiakovsky (1900-1982), a research chemist, immigrated in 1925 to the United States, where he became a research fellow at Princeton University, after which he joined the faculty of Harvard University in 1930. He was the author of more than 200 articles on chemical kinetic gas-phase reactions, molecular spectroscopy, and thermochemistry of organic compounds. He received many awards including the U.S. President's Medal of Merit in 1946, the Exceptional Service Award of the U.S. Air Force in 1957, and the National Medal of Sciences from the president in 1965. He also served as a consultant to the Manhattan Project, the initiative to develop the atomic bomb in the early 1940s and was appointed head of the explosives division of the Los Alamos Laboratory. In 1959 he was named Special Assistant for Science and Technology by President Dwight D. Eisenhower. Kistiakovsky's daughter, Vera (born in 1928 in Princeton, New Jersey) is an accomplished academic in her own right. She completed her Ph.D. in nuclear chemistry at the University of California, Berkeley, in 1952 and became a professor of physics at the Massachusetts Institute of Technology in 1963.

Other Ukrainian American academics include George Vernadsky, (1897-1972) a historian at Yale University from 1946-1956 and author of a five-volume history of Russian and a biography of Hetman Bohdan Khmelnytsky; Stephen Timoshenko (1878-1972), a specialist in theoretical and applied mechanics, vibration, and elasticity who taught at the University of Michigan and Stanford University from 1927 to 1960; Lew Dobriansky, (born 1918 in New York City), economist and author of *Decisions for a Better America*, published in 1960; and Myron Kuropas (born 1932 in Chicago), professor of educational foundations at Northern Illinois University and special assistant for ethnic affairs to President Gerald Ford in 1976-1977. Kuropas has written several books on Ukrainians in North America including *To Preserve a Heritage: The Story of the Ukrainian Immigration in the United States*, published in 1984.

FILM, TELEVISION, AND THEATER

Ukrainian Americans who found their way to Hollywood include director Edward Dmytryk (1908–) and Academy Award winner Jack Palance. Dmytryk directed a number of Hollywood films including *Murder My Sweet*, *Crossfire*, and *The Caine Mutiny*.

Jack Palance, born Walter Palahniuk on February 12, 1920, in Lattimer, Pennsylvania, made his first film, *Panic in the Streets*, in 1950. He began his career as a professional boxer in the 1940s after he returned from a tour of duty in the U.S. Army Air Corps. He made his stage debut on Broadway in *Silver Tassel* in 1949, and also appeared in stage productions of *Julius Caesar*, *The Tempest* and *A Streetcar Named Desire*. Among his more than 50 films are *Shane*, *Batman*, and *City Slickers*, for which he won an Academy Award as Best Supporting Actor in 1991. He had his own television series, "Bronk," in 1975, and appeared on various programs over more than four decades.

One of the most versatile individuals in Ukrainian dance and film was Wasyl Avramenko. Born in 1895 in Stebliv, Ukraine, he founded the First School of Ukrainian National Dances in Kalisz, Poland, in 1921. After he immigrated to the United States he directed performances at the Metropolitan Opera House, the 1893 World's Fair in Chicago, the White House in 1935, and took dance tours to Brazil, Argentina, Australia, and Israel throughout the 1950s, 1960s, and 1970s. He established his own dance studio in New York in 1952. Avramenko also did work in film; in 1936, he organized a Ukrainian film company and produced two movies using the texts of two Ukrainian classic plays, *Zaporozhetz Za Dunaem* (*The Cossack from Beyond the Danube*) and *Natalka Poltavka* (Natalka from Poltava).

William Tytla (1904-1968) made his mark in Hollywood animation. He was born in Yonkers, New York, and worked at Walt Disney Studios as an animator, creating Dumbo and the Seven Dwarfs before moving to Paramount, Famous Studios, and Twentieth Century-Fox, where he was director of a cartoon series including Popeye, Little Audrey, and Little Lulu.

Among others in this area of the arts were: Nick Adams, born Adamschock (1931-1968); Anna Sten, born Stenski-Sujakevich (1908-1993), star of *The Brothers Karamazov* and *Nana*; and 1940s Hollywood leading man, John Hodiak (1914-1955) who was married to actress Anne Baxter and starred in Alfred Hitchcock's *Lifeboat* with Tallulah Bankhead and *The Harvey Girls* opposite Judy Garland.

JOURNALISM

There are many Ukrainian Americans who have contributed to a rich heritage of Ukrainian-language journalism in the United States. Reverend Ivan Volansky (1857-1926) published *Ameryka*, the first Ukrainian newspaper in the United States in 1886.

Because of the rapid growth of the Ukrainian press in the United States, there are hundreds of women and men who could be listed here. A partial list includes: Cecelia Gardetska (born 1898), who worked on journals in Ukraine and America including *Nashe Zhitia* (*Our Life*) in Philadelphia and served as the head of the Department of Journalists for the Federation of Ukrainian Women's Organizations in the United States; Bohdan Krawciw (born 1904), who in addition to editing more than 15 journals and newspapers was general editor of Volume 2 of *Ukraine: A Concise Encyclopedia*, published in 1971; and Volodymyr Nestorovych (born 1893), also an editor of a number of Ukrainian-language newspapers in the United States, although he was an engineer and economist by occupation.

LITERATURE

Tania Kroitor Bishop, born Shevchuk, published *An Overture to Future Days* in 1954. This volume of poetry was written in both English and Ukrainian. Bishop also translated other works from Ukrainian into English.

A circle of young poets who called themselves the New York Group of Poets, among them Bohdan Boychuk (1927–), Patricia Kylyna (P. Warren), Yurii (George) Tarnavsky (1934–), and B. Pevny (1931–), published its first volume of modern poetry in 1959. Boychuk became a U.S. citizen in 1955 and worked as an engineer in addition to publishing plays and poetry.

MUSIC

Professor Alexander Koshetz (1875-1944) directed the first concert of Ukrainian church music to an American audience at Carnegie Hall, New York City, in 1936. Hryhorii Kytastyi (1907-1984), musical director, composer and bandurist, is the author of more than 30 melodies of Ukrainian songs for solo and choir with bandura (a traditional stringed instrument) or piano accompaniment. He directed the Bandurists Ensemble in numerous concerts throughout Europe, the United States, and Canada.

Other notables in music include: Nicholas Malko, director of the Chicago Symphony Orchestra from 1945 to 1957; Mykhailo Haivoronsky (1892-1949), composer and founder of the United Ukrainian Chorus in the United States in 1930; Paul Pecheniha-Ouglitzky (Uhlytsky) (1892-1948), double-bass player, composer, and conductor, who lived and worked in New York and was orchestrator for NBC radio; and Virko Baley (1938–), pianist, composer, champion of Ukrainian modern music and chamber music, and conductor of the Las Vegas Symphony Orchestra.

SCIENCE AND TECHNOLOGY

Aeronautical engineer Igor Sikorsky, born in Kiev in 1889 (d. 1972), immigrated to the United States and formed the Sikorsky Aero Engineering Company in 1923. This company built the S-29, the first twin-engine plane made in the United States. Sikorsky is also credited with designing the first helicopter (the VS-300, first flown in 1939) and the S-40 (the first large American four-engine clipper, built in 1931).

Michael Yarymovich (1933–) served as chief scientist of the U.S. Air Force and assistant director to the Apollo Flight Systems in the 1960s. In 1975, he was appointed Assistant Administrator for Laboratory and Field Coordination of the Energy Research and Development Adminstration.

SPORTS

Many Ukrainian Americans became successful in the National Hockey League (NHL). Terry Sawchuk (1929-1970) was elected to the Hockey Hall of Fame in 1971 with 103 career shutouts as a goalie having played 21 seasons with Detroit and Toronto. Bill Moisenko (d. 1994), a right wing for the Chicago Black Hawks, was selected for the all-star team in 1947 and scored a record three goals in 21 seconds in one 1952 game. New York Ranger teammates Walter Tkaczuk and Dave Balon were two-thirds of the NHL's highest scoring line during the 1969-1970 season. And in 1971, Johnny Bucyk, Vic Stasiuk, and Bronko Horvath formed the famous "Uke" line in the all-star game. More recently, Ukrainian American hockey players have included Mike Bossy, Dale Hawerchuk, and Mike Krushelyski.

In baseball, there was umpire Nestor Chylak, Jr. (1922-1982). Chylak was born in Peckville, Pennsylvania and studied engineering at Rutgers University before going to war from 1942 to 1946. He was nearly blinded at the Battle of the Bulge and was awarded the Silver Star and Purple Heart. His major league officiating career spanned three decades, from 1954 to 1978, when he retired as an umpire in the American League.

Football was another sport in which Ukrainian Americans excelled. Bronko (Bronislav) Nagurski (1908-1990) was a famous tackle for the Chicago Bears in the 1930s and 1940s. He helped lift the Bears from ninth to third place in the league and was an all-league player for three consecutive years. Nagurski was elected to the National Football Hall of Fame in 1951. He also made a career as a professional wrestler and won the world heavyweight title in 1937 and 1939. Charles Bednarick, center for the Philadelphia Eagles from 1949 until 1962, was elected to the National Football Hall of Fame in 1967.

Ukrainian American boxers included Steve Halaiko, a member of the 1932 U.S. Olympic team and Golden Gloves champion; and John Jadick, junior heavyweight champion in the 1930s. Wrestler Mike Mazurki (1909-1990) (born Michael Mazurski) went on to a career in films in the 1940s. In the 1960s there were golfers Mike Souchak and Steve Melnik, and soccer star Zenon Snylyk, a member of the 1964 U.S. Olympic soccer team and World Cup team.

VISUAL ARTS

Two of the best-known Ukrainian American artists celebrated their birthdays one day apart. Edward Kozak was born January 26, 1902, in Hirne, Ukraine. Having studied at the Art Academy in Lviv he immigrated to the United States, becoming a citizen in 1956. In addition to participating in exhibitions across the United States, Canada, and Europe, he has illustrated a number of books and from 1951-1954 was a performer on WWJ-TV in Detroit. He established his own painting studios in Detroit and Warren, Michigan, in 1950 and for his efforts in educational films was twice awarded first prize by the American Teachers' Association. Fellow artist Jacques Hnizdovsky, born January 27, 1915, in Pylypcze, Ukraine, studied at the Academy of Fine Arts in Warsaw and Zagreb before settling in New York City in 1949. His career has included a number of one-man shows in North America and Europe. He is best known for his woodcuts, and his work is featured in collections in the Boston Museum of Fine Arts, the Philadelphia Museum of Art, the White House, and the Museum of Modern Arts, Spain.

Another influential figure in the arts community was sculptor Alexander Archipenko (1887-1964), who settled in the United States in 1923. He opened his own art school in New York City in 1939 and served as sculptor in residence at a number of American universities. At the time of his death, he had just completed his 199th one-man exhibition.

Ukrainian American artists established their own association in 1952. More than 100 painters, graphic artists, and sculptors were part of the original group, which included Kozak, Hnizdovsky, Michael Moroz, Michael Chereshnovsky (1911–), and Nicholas Mukhyn.

Yaroslava Surmach-Mills is another well-known artist. Born in New York City in 1925, she graduated from the Cooper Union Art School and has worked as an art instructor, as art editor for *Humpty Dumpty Magazine*, and as an illustrator for numerous children's books. Her work, "Carol Singers," was chosen as a UNICEF Christmas card design in 1965.

MEDIA

PRINT

America.
Published by the Providence Association, an insurance company, it is a weekly tabloid with separate issues in Ukrainian and English, with a circulation of about 6,000. First printed in 1912, this Catholic paper covers politics, sports, and news about Ukraine and the United States.

Contact: Osip Roshka, Editor.
Address: 817 North Franklin Street, Philadelphia, Pennsylvania 19123.
Telephone: (215) 627-0233.

Narodnia Volya.
Published by the Ukrainian Fraternal Association (UFA). First printed in 1911, this weekly publication has a circulation of about 3,000. There are two editors, one for the Ukrainian pages and another for *The Ukrainian Herald*—the English-language section. The paper includes a literary section, news from Ukraine and the United States as it concerns Ukrainian Americans, and updates on the life of the Association. The UFA also publishes an English-language quarterly called *Forum* on the arts and history of Ukraine.

Contact: Nicholas Duplak, Ukrainian Editor; or
    Serge Kowalchuk, Jr., English Editor.
Address: 440 Wyoming Avenue, Scranton,
    Pennsylvania 18503.
Telephone: (717) 342-8897.

New Star Ukrainian Catholic Newspaper.
The organ of the St. Nicholas Diocese in Chicago, this bulletin of church news has a circulation of 3,500 and is published in both Ukrainian and English every three weeks.

Contact: Ivana Gorchynsky, Editor.
Address: 2208 West Chicago Avenue, Chicago,
    Illinois 60622.
Telephone: (312) 772-1919.

Svoboda.
A daily Ukrainian-language newspaper with a circulation of 14,000, it includes local and Ukrainian news stories and advertisements. A weekly English-language newspaper, *Ukrainian Weekly*, is published out of the same location.

Contact: Zenon Snylyk, Editor of *Svoboda*; or
    Roma Hadzewych, Editor of *Ukrainian Weekly*.
Address: 2200 Route 10, Parsippany,
    New Jersey 07054
Telephone: (201) 434-0237.

Ukrainian News.
Originally published in Germany in 1944, this Detroit-based paper has an international circulation. It is published weekly by the Bahriany Foundation (a foundation of writers named for Ukrainian writer and political leader Ivan Bahriany). The content includes news as well as literary articles.

Contact: Serhiy Kozak, Editor.
Address: 19411 West Warren Avenue, Detroit,
    Michigan 48228.
Telephone: (313) 336-8291.

RADIO

WCEV and WVVX.
"Ukrainian Variety Hour," hosted by Maria Chychula from 9:00 to 10:00 a.m. daily on FM 103.1, and on Monday, Wednesday, and Thursday evenings, 7:00 to 8:00 pm on AM 1450. She has been hosting these cultural radio programs since the late 1960s.

Contact: Maria Chychula.
Address: 2224 West Chicago Avenue, Chicago,
    Illinois 60622.
Telephone: (312) 278-1836.

WHLD (1270).
"Sharvan's Ukrainian Radio Program," hosted by Wasyl Sharvan for more than 45 years, is a weekly program that airs from 1:30 to 4:30 p.m. on Saturdays and includes includes commentary, news, and music.

Contact: Wasyl Sharvan.
Address: 701 Fillmore Avenue, Buffalo,
    New York 14212.
Telephone: (716) 895-0700.

WNZK.
"Song of Ukraine," "Slovo," and "Ukrainian Catholic Hour" comprise three hours of Ukrainian programming weekly for the more than 100,000 Ukrainian Americans in the metro Detroit area. "Song of Ukraine" is a commentary program, airing Tuesdays at 9:00 p.m.; "Slovo," airing Fridays at 8:00 p.m., is a program hosted by and for new immigrants; and "Ukrainian Catholic Hour," airing on Saturdays at noon, combines information, sermons, and music for Catholics of the Byzantine Rite.

Contact: Jerry Tertzakian.
Address: 1837 Torquay, Royal Oak,
    Michigan 48073.
Telephone: (810) 557-3500.

ORGANIZATIONS AND ASSOCIATIONS

Ukrainian Academy of Arts and Sciences in the United States.
Founded in 1950, it was established to organize and sponsor scholars pursuing Ukrainian studies. The facilities include a museum and library which has material on the history of Ukrainian immigration to the United States and books on Ukrainian history and literature. It also publishes a scholarly journal, *Annals of the Ukrainian Academy of Arts and Sciences*.

Contact: Prof. William Omelchenko,
Vice-President.
Address: 206 West 100th Street, New York,
New York 10025-5018.
Telephone: (212) 222-1866.
Fax: (212) 864-3977.

Ukrainian American Youth Association.

Operates summer camps and offers various cultural
and recreational activities.

Contact: Stefa Hryckowian, President.
Address: 136 Second Avenue, New York,
New York 10003.
Telephone: (212) 477-3084.

Ukrainian Catholic Church.

First parish in the United States, established in
1885 in Shenandoah, Pennsylvania.

Contact: Archbishop Metropolitan Stephen Sulyk.
Address: Archdiocese of Philadelphia,
827 North Franklin Street, Philadelphia,
Pennsylvania 19123.
Telephone: (215) 627-0143.

Ukrainian National Women's League of America.

A non-partisan, non-sectarian organization that
sponsors educational scholarships and cultural
events.

Contact: Anna Krawczuk, President.
Address: 108 Second Avenue, New York,
New York 10003.
Telephone: (212) 533-4646.
Fax: (212) 254-2672.
E-mail: unwla@worldnet.att.net.

Ukrainian Orthodox Church in America.

Founded in 1928 by Ukrainians who emigrated
from Russia, Bukovina, Galicia, and Poland.

Contact: Father F. Istochyn, Secretary to the
Archbishop.
Address: Ukrainian Orthodox Church of St.
Vladimir, 6729 North Fifth Street,
Philadelphia, Pennsylvania 19126.
Telephone: (212) 927-2287.

MUSEUMS AND
RESEARCH CENTERS

Harvard Ukrainian Research Institute.

Established January 22, 1968, with financial and
moral support from large numbers of Ukrainian
Americans, Ukrainian Studies at Harvard began
in 1957.

Contact: Prof. Roman Szporluk, Director.
Address: Harvard University, 1583 Massachusetts
Avenue, Cambridge, Massachusetts 02138.
Telephone: (617) 495-4053.
Fax: (617) 495-8097.
E-mail: huri@fas.harvard.edu.
Website: http://www.sabre.org/huri.

Shevchenko Scientific Society.

Founded in 1947 in New York City to support
research and to assist immigrant Ukrainian scholars
in adjusting to life in the United States, it was
named for the famous nineteenth-century Ukrainian poet, Taras Shevchenko. The society organizes
scientific sessions, lectures, and conferences as well
as maintaining archives and a library.

Contact: Leonid Rudnytzky, President.
Address: 63 Fourth Avenue, New York,
New York 10003.
Telephone: (212) 254-5130.

Ukrainian Center for Social Research

Independent, nonprofit research center. Examines
history, problems, and present status of people of
Ukrainian origin, focusing on demographic, social,
cultural, economic, and related issues.

Contact: Eugene Fedorenko, Director.
Address: 203 2nd Ave. New York,
New York 10003.
Telephone: (212) 477-1200.
Fax: (212) 777-7201.

Ukrainian Institute of America.

Founded in 1948, the Institute maintains a permanent exhibition of Ukrainian folk arts, sponsors lectures, concerts and conferences, and houses a
Ukrainian historical gallery. It was established with
funds from Volodymyr Dzus, a wealthy Ukrainian
industrialist.

Contact: Volodymyr Barenecki, President.
Address: 2 East 79th Street, New York,
New York 10021.
Telephone: (212) 772-8489.

Ukrainian Museum-Archives Inc.

Established in 1952, the archives emphasize the
period of the Ukrainian Revolution and Ukrainian
immigration to the United States after World War
II. The archives include about 20,000 volumes in
addition to archival materials.

Contact: Stepan Malanczuk, Director.
Address: 1202 Kenilworth Avenue, Cleveland, Ohio 44113.
Telephone: (216) 781-4329.

Ukrainian National Museum.
Established in 1958 through the merger of the Ukrainian Archive-Museum in Chicago and the Ukrainian National Museum and Library of Ontario, Canada.
Address: 2453 West Chicago Avenue, Chicago, Illinois.
Telephone: (312) 276-6565.

SOURCES FOR ADDITIONAL STUDY

Encyclopedia of Ukraine, five volumes, edited by Volodymyr Kubijovyc and Danylo Husar Struk. Toronto: University of Toronto Press, 1984-1993.

Kuropas, Myron B. *The Ukrainian Americans: Roots and Aspirations 1884-1954*. Toronto: University of Toronto Press, 1991.

Subtelny, Orest. *Ukrainians in North America: An Illustrated History*. Toronto: University of Toronto Press, 1991.

Ukraine and Ukrainians Throughout the World: A Demographic and Sociological Guide to the Homeland and Its Diaspora, edited by Ann Lencyk Pawliczko. Toronto: University of Toronto Press for the Shevchenko Scientific Society, Inc., 1994.

Ukrainians in North America, edited by Dmytro M. Shtohryn. Champaign, Illinois: Association for the Advancement of Ukrainian Studies, 1975.

Werstman, Vladimir. *The Ukrainians in America 1608-1975*. New York: Oceana Publications, 1976.

URUGUAYAN AMERICANS

by
Jane E. Spear

Although Uruguayans constituted 43 percent of all immigrants to the United States coming from Latin America and the Caribbean in the 1990s, they only made up a small part of the large U.S. Hispanic population.

OVERVIEW

Uruguay is a country in South America that measures 68,037 square miles (176,216 square kilometers), approximately the size of the state of Oklahoma. It is located along the South Atlantic Ocean coast of South America, between Argentina to the west, and Brazil to the northeast, sitting south of the Equator. The official name of Uruguay is the "Oriental Republic of Uruguay," or, Republica Oriental del Uruguay. The word Oriental refers to its eastern position on the South American continent. The republic consists of 19 departments, which are divisions similar to states. Montevideo, in the department of the same name, is the country's largest city.

Uruguay's population by 1999 was 3.2 million. Eighty-six percent of the population was of white European descent, 6 percent was black, and 8 percent was *mestizo*, an ethnic mixture of white and indigenous descent. At that time, the life expectancy was 69.3 years for men; and, 75.7 years for women. The country enjoyed a literacy rate of 95 percent of the population over the age of 15. An estimated 66 percent of Uruguayans are Roman Catholics, although Uruguayan society was secularized early in its history as an independent republic. Church and State were officially and legally separated in 1917. Less than half of the adult population regularly attended church by the late 1980s.

Other Protestant denominations coexist with and have the same legal status as the Catholic church, although Catholics are significantly in the majority. In 1856, Italian immigrants founded one denomination, the Waldensian Evangelic Church of the River Plate, or Río de la Plata, in both Uruguay and Argentina. The Waldensian church began during a religious revival near Lyon, France during the twelfth century, predating the Protestant Reformation that swept through Europe in the sixteenth century. The church is named for the founder of the movement, Valdo, or Valdesius. The 15 Waldensian churches in Uruguay join with 8 in Argentina with a total membership of 15,000.

The flag and coat of arms of Uruguay were both adopted in 1830. The sun is represented on each of them. On the flag it sits in the upper left-hand corner. The flag's nine blue stripes over a white background represent the number of divisions the country was originally divided into upon gaining independence. The symbols on the coat of arms are scales, which symbolize equality and justice; a horse and ox, which represent liberty and plenty; and the hill of Montevideo, representing strength.

HISTORY

The Charrua Indians were the largest group of indigenous inhabitants in the land area that was to become Uruguay. In 1516 when the Spanish navigator Juan Díaz de Solís landed on Uruguayan shores, the Charruas immediately killed him and his crew. Uruguay did not possess the gold, uranium, and other precious metals abundantly present in other South American countries, in demand by the Spanish conquistadors as well as other Europeans. Because of that, very few Europeans had any interest in developing settlements there. Not until Portuguese soldiers arrived from Brazil in 1680 did Europeans begin to settle permanently. The Spanish colonists who founded Montevideo in 1726 did so more to prevent Portuguese expansion into Uruguay than for an interest in the land. During much of the early to mid-1700s the Portuguese and Spanish battled for control of the entire area. By 1777, the year following the United States' declaration of independence from England, the Spanish had managed to settle most of Uruguay. It then became a Spanish colony, a section of the Viceroyalty of La Plata. La Plata included Argentina, Paraguay, and portions of Brazil, Bolivia, and Chile. The natives battled with the Europeans during this period, and were defeated. Those who escaped either death in battle or death by the hitherto unknown diseases the Europeans had brought with them retreated to the interior regions of the South American continent. This accounts for the predominance of the white race in Uruguay even in modern times.

José Gervasio Artigas was a soldier who organized his own army to fight for freedom from Spanish colonial rule. In 1811 Artigas' near-defeat of the Spaniards when he laid siege to Montevideo was thwarted when Portuguese troops arrived from Brazil and attacked the Uruguayan and the Spanish armies. Neither Artigas nor his followers would submit to Portuguese or Spanish rule, so they fled inland to neighboring Paraguay and Argentina, nearly emptying Uruguay of people. When the Spanish surrendered in 1814 and ended Spanish rule, Artigas captured Montevideo for Uruguay. Only two years later, in 1816, the Portuguese again attacked, and this time the struggle lasted four years. At that time the Portuguese made Uruguay a part of Brazil, and Artigas went into exile.

By 1825, when a group of Uruguayan patriots known as "The Immortal Thirty-Three" staged a rebellion against Brazil, the renewed fight for Uruguayan independence emerged. Their armies gained control of the countryside within months, with the support of Argentina. Due to British intervention sparked because of a blockade that threatened British trade, Argentina and Brazil recognized Uruguay as an independent republic. The country adopted its first constitution in 1830. José Fructuoso Rivera became the nation's first president. In 1835 Manuel Oribe followed as second president, but an attempt by Rivera to regain power in 1836 began a civil war. Rivera's troops, known as the Colorados, who were from the cities, and Oribe's troops, the Blancos, primarily landowners from the rural areas, fought for 16 years, until 1852, when the Colorados defeated the Blancos. The two groups eventually developed into Uruguay's two major political parties, and the struggles between the two forces continued for much of the rest of the nineteenth century, with power shifting back and forth between them. The Colorados had gained control in 1865 with Brazil's help. The Blancos subsequently received assistance from Paraguay. Brazil, Argentina and Uruguay then joined forces against Paraguay into what was called "The War of the Triple Alliance," defeating Paraguay in 1870. The Colorados became the dominant party, as immigrants flowed into Montevideo from all over South America and Europe.

MODERN ERA

While some Colorado leaders were dictators, under the rule of the liberal Colorado José Batlle y Ordóñez, Uruguay entered an era of social and governmental reform. Batlle held to democratic ideals, and advocated social justice for all. During his leadership, new laws established free education, minimum wages and workers' rights, and free medical care for the poor as well as marriage and divorce legislation. The government took benevolent control of public utilities and factories and established national banks and railroads. It was during his term in office that the church and state were officially separated.

With its stable domestic economy and social welfare programs, Uruguay prospered even during the Great Depression and World War II, when its products, especially meat and wool, were in demand by the Allies, with whom they joined forces. Uruguay had cut all diplomatic ties with Germany, Japan, and Italy in 1942 but did not declare war on them until 1945, near the end of the conflict, and no Uruguayan troops fought in World War II. When the United Nations was founded in 1945, Uruguay became a charter member.

When Uruguayans approved a new constitution in 1951 that abolished the presidency and set up a nine-member National Council of Government. The intention of the new government was to allow the Colorados and the Blancos to share power. But by the next year Uruguay's economy began to collapse. Foreign trade was no longer prosperous due to a loss of agricultural exports. Both inflation and the cost of social programs grew rapidly. The grave economic situation continued into the 1960s. Many Uruguayans left for other countries, principally Argentina, the United States, Australia, Spain, Brazil, and Venezuela. By 1967, the inefficient National Council was abolished in favor of the reestablishment of the presidential government.

Economic downturn gave rise to political unrest. One group of urban guerrillas known as the Tupamaros kidnapped and murdered many Uruguayan officials. When President Juan María Bordaberry was elected in 1972, he declared war on the Tupamaros. He crushed the movement in a few months, but by 1973 Bordaberry was president in name only. The military took control of the government and suspended the constitution. They replaced Bordaberry in 1976 with Aparicio Méndez. General Gregorio Alvarez succeeded him in 1981. At this time, many of the country's artists, intellectuals and politicians, were persecuted for espousing beliefs different from those of the military regime, and consequently went into exile abroad, mostly to Spain, the Netherlands, and Belgium. The late 1970s and early 1980s saw political unrest throughout Latin America. Uruguay maintained the highest ratio of political prisoners to its general population throughout the world while other Latin American governments also commited crimes against their people that encouraged some to flee to the United States.

Many Uruguayans who left the country for political reasons chose to return in 1984 when Julio María Sanguinetti, the leader of the Colorado Party, was elected president, signaling a return to civilian government. Sanguinetti faced all of the same problems that the nation had faced since the 1960s, only this time they were worse. Major economic problems, including inflation, foreign debt, and unemployment, were major issues. In 1989 Luis Albert Lacalle won the presidency, and the Blanco party returned to dominance. His plans to privatize companies, taking them out of government control, and his call for smaller wage increases worried the workers, who organized strikes in opposition to such plans. In 1992 the voters rejected the plans to privatize, and in 1994 Sanguinetti was reelected to the presidency.

In 1996, Uruguay XXI, a "non-state public entity" designed to develop Uruguay's economy internationally, was established by law. As Minister of Economy and Finance Luis A. Mosca explained in a special feature titled "Uruguay, A Country to Watch," in the June 5, 1998 edition of the *New York Times*, the mission of Uruguay XXI was "to foster the internationalization process of the Uruguayan economy by promoting investments and the export of goods and services within the general framework provided by the government's economic policy." In 1991, Uruguay joined Argentina, Brazil, and Paraguay to form MERCOSUR, the southern common market. Until the mid-1990s, China was the largest foreign investor in Uruguay; however, the MERCOSUR alliance began to change that. Uruguay also made agreements with Chile and Bolivia and continues to extend its economic rebuilding efforts to the other South American countries and elsewhere around the world. In addition, President Sanguinetti signed a trade agreement with President Hosni Mubarak of Egypt in 1998.

The concerns at the end of the twentieth century were over social welfare policies, such as social security and an inefficient workforce. Sanguinetti moved immediately to reform the social security system when he took office in 1994. According to Calvin Sims, writing for the *New York Times* on February 19, 1995, "The basic problem was the high ratio of people who depend on or work for the state. About 1.1 million of Uruguay's 3.1 million people are registered workers, while 700,000 people no longer in the work force receive pensions. Uruguay has more than one retired person for every two workers, and about 37 percent of the state budget goes to the bankrupt social security system." Moreover, the pace of economic reform was too slow, according to some observers. The fear remained that Uruguay, suffering from its hesitancy to privatize, would lag behind its free trade partners and neighbors Argentina and Brazil and would be unable to compete effectively. Uruguay's poor economy could lead to an increase in emigration.

THE FIRST URUGUAYANS IN AMERICA

Before the 1960s, the economy of Uruguay provided its citizens with middle-class affluence, and emmigration was limited. With a comfortable standard of living, adequate employment opportunities, a favorable social welfare and health insurance system, and democratic freedoms, the need to leave was not pressing. On the whole, even the poorest of the Uruguayans enjoyed certain benefits that kept them satisfied enough to stay in their own country. For those who left the cultural and recreational opportunities of the cities, where 85 percent of all Uruguayans lived, the proposition of going to neighboring countries such as Argentina, with its familiar language and proximity to the home country, was more appealing than moving to the United States. Those who pursued business or educational opportunities in the United States and elsewhere, often returned home, never forsaking their Uruguayan citizenship.

Two factors changed the complacency of Uruguayans. First, there were economic and political problems in Uruguay after World War II, particularly money and employment crises during the 1960s and 1970s. Second, an oppressive military regime took control of the government. Now, there were motivating factors to leave Uruguay, and the people leaving Uruguay in vast numbers were the ones that the country could least afford to lose—well-educated professionals and the young. This, too, marked the beginning of the social security crisis. As the aging population retired, and young people left the country, the burden on the country's financial resources grew. Of Uruguay immigrants from 1963 to 1975, 17.7 percent of them were aged 14 years or younger, 68 percent of them were between the ages of 15 and 39, and only 14.3 percent were over 40 years old. The continued employment problems of the late 1980s represented yet another impetus for the youth of Uruguay to seek employment and new lives elsewhere. Some of them went to the United States, but the largest population of Uruguayan emigrants continued to reside in Argentina.

SIGNIFICANT IMMIGRATION WAVES

The most significant wave of Uruguayan immigration to the United States occurred in the 1960s and 1970s. An estimated 180,000 Uruguayans left between 1963 and 1975, when the country's economy suffered a devastating slump. Then, according to statistics from the General Directorate of Statistics and Census of the Republic of Uruguay, between 1975 and 1985, during the period of oppressive military control, 150,000 Uruguayans left the country. And, as late as 1989, only 16,000 of these citizens had returned to their native country. When these two figures are added together, the emigration figure stands at approximately one-tenth of the population.

By the mid-1990s 10 percent of the U.S. population, an estimated 27 million people, was of Hispanic origin. Although Uruguayans constituted 43 percent of all immigrants to the United States coming from Latin America and the Caribbean in the 1990s, they only made up a small part of the large U.S. Hispanic population. The most successful Uruguayan immigrants went to New York City, New Jersey, and Long Island. Two other significant centers of Uruguayan American population are Washington, D.C., and Florida.

ACCULTURATION AND ASSIMILATION

Uruguayan Americans are as diverse as their native counterparts in Uruguay. For educated and sophisticated Uruguayan professionals, fitting into a cosmopolitan lifestyle in New York demanded little adjustment, except to climate. In their own country, Uruguayans of several different classes lived a Westernized, cultured existence. The large Spanish-speaking population in the United States has ensured that a variety of multilingual resources are easily at hand, thus reducing cultural adjustments due to language barriers.

TRADITIONS, CUSTOMS, AND BELIEFS

Many of the customs of other Latin American nations are observed in Uruguay. When people greet each other, they usually shake hands. Public embraces and the use of first names are used only among close friends and family members. Meetings even among friends are formal, whether in public places or corporate settings. The eased sense of time among Latin Americans is apparent among Uruguayans—meetings often do not start on time, and no one is reprimanded or considered ill-mannered for being late. Even in informal social settings polite custom requires that if invited to a Uruguayan's home, the visitor should send flowers or chocolates to the hostess ahead of time rather than at the time of the visit. Conversation in Uruguay in polite social settings does not include politics. The much-loved national pastime of football, known as soccer in the United States, is always a safe topic. Uruguayans in the United States also tend to follow Uruguayan football and their national teams.

CUISINE

Uruguayans are mainly of European descent and this is reflected in their cuisine, which is strongly influenced by Spanish and Italian cooking. Uruguayans love meat, especially beef, largely due to the large number of cattle they raise. In the 1990s, it was estimated that cattle and sheep *estancias*, or farms, took up four-fifths of the country's land. Their taste for meat is reflected in a traditional meal of *parrillada criolla*, a barbecued mixture of *chorizo*, a Latin American sausage, *riñones*, or kidneys, and strips of beef. Another meat specialty is *marcilla dulce*, a blood sausage mixed with orange peels and walnuts. *Milanesa* is deep-fried steak that has been breaded with Italian-seasoned crumbs. Because much of the population is of Italian heritage, pasta is usually served daily, and is an integral element of a good meal. Uruguayans prefer freshly made pasta to the dry pasta popular in the United States. Another dish reflecting their Italian roots is *faina*, made with chickpea flour and boiled with oil and salt, similar to polenta (boiled cornmeal) in texture.

Other favored dishes include *buseca*, which is soup made with calf's tripe, haricot or other white beans, peeled tomatoes, garlic, and Parmesan cheese. It combines Hispanic influences, from the Mexican soup *menudo*, made with tripe, hominy, and chili powder, with Italian elements, adding cheese and garlic to the soup. Potato *fritatas*, made with eggs and potatoes, and *pascualina*, a Uruguayan spinach pie made with Spanish olive oil and cheddar cheese, are two other dishes enjoyed by Uruguayans. Favorite sweet treats include *Masas surfidas*, the term given to many varieties of pastries, and *pasta frola*, a pastry cake spread with quince preserves, and varieties of fresh fruit, such as grapes and citrus fruits.

Yerba mate, or simply *mate*, is a beverage of green tea. Sometimes, a special ceremony surrounds the drinking of mate. A hollowed-out gourd or a china cup is almost filled with the green tea. A metal straw is inserted, and boiling water is then poured over the leaves. The mate is passed around to friends and family seated in a circle, with each person adding more hot water as it is passed.

Between 1973 and 1985, the period of military control, people met one another in public squares for this tea ceremony. The ceremony provided a subterfuge, allowing citizens to congregate with less fear that the military police would arrest them on charges of illegal political conspiracy.

DANCES AND SONGS

Uruguayans appreciate many forms of music, whether it comes from the popular guitar, introduced by Spanish settlers, and the songs of the *gauchos*, or from a formal orchestra. In addition to the guitar, the accordion is also played along with many of the traditional folk songs and dances. From its African slave ancestral population, *candombe* reigns as the most popular dance in Montevideo. The drumbeats of the Afro-Uruguayans reach their loudest and most festive during the Uruguayan Mardi Gras celebration.

Uruguayans enjoy opera, as well as the tango. In 1917 Uruguayan composer Gerardo H. Matos Rodríguez wrote *La Cumparsita*, a tango, a music form as loved in Uruguay as it is in neighboring Argentina, where the tango claims its home. In the United States, the Uruguayan American Chamber of Commerce was a sponsor of The Millennium Gala Concert of the Nations, featuring the Symphonicum Europae, on November 29, 1999, at the Lincoln Center New York City.

HOLIDAYS

In Uruguay, the church and state are separate, and therefore holidays are secularized (non-religious). For instance, Christmas Day is celebrated as "Family Day" rather than as a religious holiday. Other holidays that Uruguayans celebrate include Kings' Day (January 5), commemorating the visit of the Three Kings, with presents sometimes exchanged; Semana de Turismo, or Tourism Week, which coincides with Easter; Desembarco de los Treinta y Tres (Landing of the 33, April 19), commemorating the fight by 33 Uruguayan patriots for independence from Portuguese-Brazilian occupation in 1825; Labor Day (May 1); Artigas's Anniversary (June 19), celebrating the national hero José Gervasio Artigas, who began the struggle for independence in 1811; and Todos Santos, or All Souls Day, on November 2. Mardi Gras, or *Carneval*, is celebrated in Uruguay as in other Latin American countries, although not with as much vigor as it is in Rio de Janeiro in Brazil.

LANGUAGE

Spanish is the official language of Uruguay. As much as one-third of the population is of Italian descent in the coastal areas, and Italian is widely spoken in these regions. A colloquial tongue known as *Rio de la Plata* consists of Spanish with Italian influences is also used. English is taught in schools and is heard frequently, especially in the coastal areas, where tourism was flourishing at the end of the 1990s.

When adjusting to life in the United States, Uruguayans often find Spanish is the language, next to English, most frequently spoken. Because of this, some Uruguayans do not find their adjustment to life in the United States as difficult as it is for other immigrants.

FAMILY AND COMMUNITY DYNAMICS

As early as 1900, the patriarchal tradition was beginning to disappear in Uruguay. Following the legal decree making divorce legal in 1907, on which divorce could be filed by a wife on the grounds of the cruelty of her husband, and in 1912 when women needed no specific reason to file at all, women became socially emancipated. By 1919, women were allowed to keep their own bank accounts separate from their husbands, and they were already beginning to enter the workforce. Because of the other reforms of José Batlle as early as 1902, health care extended to nearly the entire population of the country.

Uruguay became country with a large middle class long before World War I. Family ties remained strong, particularly among the rural population, where birth control was not as widely practiced and the families were much larger. Also in the rural areas, some of the more traditional *machismo*, an aggressively strong masculine character associated with patriarchy, prevailed. Still, with a pronounced equality between spouses more predominant in Uruguay than in other Latin American countries, and with education considered a priority for both males and females, the tone of family life centered around the bonds of parents and children. Among the working classes, it was common to find married children in their thirties still living with their parents, and perhaps grandparents, in an extended family setting. However, among the more affluent Uruguayan Americans this practice was infrequent.

EDUCATION

At the end of the twentieth century, Uruguay had a literacy rate of nearly 95 percent for people over 15 years of age. Education is mandatory by law for children between the ages of 6 to 15 years, and public education is free to all Uruguayans through the university level. However, rural communities have only elementary-level schools, so children must go to the cities to attend high school or university. There is only one university in Uruguay, the University of the Republic in Montevideo, which has approximately 35,000 students, but there is also a teacher training institute and a nationwide system of vocational, or trade, schools. Education is prized in their native land, and consequently many Uruguayan Americans pursue education and professional careers in the United States.

BAPTISMS

Baptisms are particularly common among the rural peoples of Uruguay. Babies had godfathers, or *compadres*, who were usually of a better social class. This was part of the practice known as *compadrazgo*, which was intended to provide important social connections for the children as they grew and into their adult life. The godfather would help the godchild find employment when necessary, and the godchild would provide a vote for the godfather when necessary. Among Roman Catholic Uruguayan immigrants, each child to be baptized traditionally has two godparents, a man and a woman, charged with the task of nurturing them spiritually and assisting the parents in raising the child in the faith.

WEDDINGS

The long history of the separation of church and state in Uruguay from its independence in 1828 to even before the formal declaration of its policy in 1917 established a tradition of civil marriage in the country. From 1837, civil marriage was recognized by the government, which diminished the influence of the Catholic Church. Yet weddings, particularly among those who are practicing Roman Catholics, continue to be celebrated traditionally with both religious and civil ceremonies. Among Uruguayans in the United States, celebrations are dependent on the individual disposition of the couple and family and their religious practices.

RELIGION

The Spanish explorers brought the Roman Catholic religion with them to Uruguay. The faith did not play as important a role as it did with Uruguay's neighbors, even in the early colonial days. Uruguay's indigenous population resisted the conversion imposed upon the natives of other areas, giving the Catholic Church less influence in Uruguay. After independence in 1828, the secular influence pervaded. Still, the Catholic population enjoyed their own parochial schools and even their own political party and movements. The Union Civica del Uruguay (Civic Union of Uruguay) was founded in 1912, although it never won any significant percentage of the national vote. The party changed its name to the Partido Democrata Cristiano (Christian Democratic Party, or PDC) in 1962, along with the increasingly progressive trends of Catholicism following Vatican II. The second conference of Latin American Bishops, held in Mexico in 1979, had a radical impact on Uruguay. The bishops called for a "preferential option for the poor," inspiring Uruguayan Catholics to provide temporary hospice for the radical Tupamaros when they were given amnesty in 1985.

Other faiths represented in Uruguay include Protestantism and Judaism. Protestant denominations grew in prominence throughout the twentieth century. By the late 1980s, the Protestant population in Uruguay was estimated at two percent or slightly higher. From 1960 to 1985, the number of Protestants increased in Uruguay by 60 percent. The Jewish population of Uruguay settled primarily in Montevideo and accounted for approximately two percent of the population. Beginning in 1970, the Jewish population began to decrease, mostly due to emigration.

EMPLOYMENT AND ECONOMIC TRADITIONS

The majority of Uruguayans have long held a middle-class lifestyle, with women as likely to be in the labor force as men. Many citizens who emigrated to the United States and elsewhere left because economic conditions did not allow them to continue to maintain their affluence and secure employment. Regarding those who left Uruguay from 1963 to 1975, the following statistics were available: 12.8 percent of the emigrants were professionals, technicians, managers, and administrators; 16 percent were office employees; 12.4 percent were salespeople; and 47.6 percent were drivers, skilled and unskilled workers, and day laborers. The divisions of labor and professions for those Uruguayan Americans living in the United States were not determined officially by the U.S. government census figures.

POLITICS AND GOVERNMENT

Uruguayans, whether living at home or abroad, follow the politics of their native land. For many of the political exiles of the 1980s, democratic freedoms were crucial to their decision to leave. The return of those freedoms likewise were a major factor in their decision to return.

Uruguayans, under the direction of David P. Michaels and President Sanguinetti, formed the Uruguayan American Chamber of Commerce (UACC) in 1996 to further business and economic ties between the United States and Uruguay. The UACC has offices in Miami, Florida, and in New York City.

ORGANIZATIONS AND ASSOCIATIONS

The Embassy of Uruguay to the United States.
Contact: The Honorable Dr. Alvaro Diez de Medina, Ambassador.
Address: 2715 M Street, N.W., 3rd floor, Washington, D.C. 20007.
Telephone: (202) 331-1313.
Fax: (202) 331-8142.

Uruguayan American Chamber of Commerce.
Founded 1996.

Contact: David P. Michaels.
Address: 1710 First Avenue, Suite 333, New York, New York, 10128.
Telephone: (212) 722-6587.
Fax: (212) 996-2580.
Online: http://www.uruguaychamber.com.

Uruguayan-American Foundation (Washington, D.C., and northern Virginia area).
Contact: Mr. Mario Casilla.
Telephone: (703) 821-0614.
Fax: (703) 821-1323.

Uruguay Trade Bureau.
Contact: Minister Enriqueta Suzacq.
Address: 747 Third Avenue, 21st floor, New York, New York 10017.
Telephone: (212) 751-7137/7138.
Fax: (212) 758-4126.

SOURCES FOR ADDITIONAL STUDY

Finch, M. H. J., and Alicia Casas de Barran. *Uruguay, 102. World Bibliographical Series*. Oxford: Clio Press, 1989.

Solari, Aldo, and Rolando Franco. "The Family in Uruguay." In *The Family in Latin America*. Edited by Man Singh Das and Clinton J. Jesser. Ghaziabad, India: Vikas, 1980, pp. 46–83.

Taglioretti, Graciela. *Women and Work in Uruguay*. Paris: United Nations Educational, Scientific, and Cultural Organization (UNESCO), 1983.

Taylor, Philip B., Jr. *Government and Politics of Uruguay*. Westport, CT: Greenwood Press, 1984.

Weinstein, Martin. *Uruguay: Democracy at the Crossroads*. Boulder, CO: Westview Press, 1988.

VENEZUELAN AMERICANS

by
Drew Walker

Venezuelan Americans are great fans of baseball. Unlike other South American countries, baseball rather than soccer is the national sport.

OVERVIEW

Venezuela is situated on the northern coast of South America. It is bounded by the Atlantic Ocean and Caribbean Sea to the north, Brazil to the south, Colombia to the west and southwest, and Guyana to the east. The capital of Venezuela is Caracas, and other major cities include Valencia, Barquisimeto, Maracaibo, and Ciudad Guayana. Venezuela is the sixth-largest country in South America and has a population of about 10,800,000. The land of Venezuela can be divided into three main regions: coastal mountains, plains, and forest. The coastal mountains are confined to a small part of the north of the country, while the plains and forest areas make up most of the landscape. The Orinoco River divides the country between north and south.

HISTORY

Archaeologists estimate that the first people arrived in present-day Venezuela around 14,000 B.C. By the time the Spanish arrived at the end of the fifteenth century, there were an estimated half a million Indians living in this region, constituting a number of cultural groups and speaking languages derived from the three main linguistic families of Arawak, Carib, and Chibcha. In 1948, Christopher Columbus was the first European to arrive in Venezuela. At first assuming the land to be a large island, Columbus traveled east along the coast, where he encountered the wide mouth of the great Orinoco River. Knowing that no island could produce such a large river and outflow, Columbus realized that he was encountering a landmass much larger than he had assumed. When another explorer, Alonso de Ojeda, arrived a year later, he sailed westward along the coast. Ojeda observed houses that Indians had been built on stilts above the coastal water. These houses reminded Ojeda of the great Italian city of Venice, and he named this land "Venezuela," which in Spanish means "Little Venice." From 1500 to 1541, a series of Spanish settlements arose on the coast of Venezuela. Over the following centuries, the European and African populations in Venezuela continued to grow.

MODERN ERA

As the Spanish empire grew in South America and the Caribbean, Venezuela moved from the control of one province to the next until 1717. In that year, Venezuela was placed under the control of the viceroyalty of the Virreynato de la Nueva Granada in the Colombian city of Bogotá. Due to its difficult climate and the perceived lack of gold and other resources, Venezuela was largely ignored by the Spanish empire, while other countries such as Bolivia, Peru, and Colombia received the bulk of its attention and resources.

By the end of the eighteenth century, resistance to colonial rule in Venezuela grew. In 1806, a revolution began, headed by Francisco de Miranda. After trying to establish an alternative government in the capital city of Caracas, de Miranda was arrested and sent to Spain, where he died in prison a few years later. With the loss of Miranda, Simon Bolívar, a man who was to become the national hero of Venezuela, took control of the independence movement. Commanding a revolutionary army, Bolívar battled the Spaniards in Venezuela but did not succeed in ousting them from power. Withdrawing into Colombia and then Jamaica, Bolivar waited until 1817 to resume his battle for independence.

In 1817, Bolívar returned to Colombia and won a series of winning battles against Spanish forces. In August of 1819, Colombia became an independent nation. At a conference held later that year, Colombia, Ecuador, and Venezuela were united into one state named Gran Colombia. In 1821, Bolívar and his army defeated the Spanish in Venezuela and won its independence. He and his deputy, Antonio José de Sucre, amassed a large army which liberated Ecuador, Peru, and Bolivia by 1824. In 1829, Gran Colombia was split up into three separate countries.

Following Bolívar's death in 1830, a series of dictators ruled over Venezuela. During this time periods of civil war, political, and economic instability were frequent. It was not until the second decade of the twentieth century, when oil was discovered in Venezuela, that economic and social stability began to grow. By the end of the 1920s, Venezuela had become the largest exporter of oil in the world, yet the wealth obtained from these exports was confined to a tiny elite group while the majority of Venezuelans lived in poverty. Between 1935 and 1945, there was a great deal of civil unrest in Venezuela, as people demanded governmental reform and a more equitable distribution of Venezuela's oil wealth. In 1945, Rómulo Betancourt, the leader of the Acción Democrática (Democratic Action) party took over the government. These changes led to the creation of a new constitution in 1947 and to the election of well-known novelist Rómulo Gallegos as Venezuela's first democratically elected president. This new democratic regime had been in power only six months when a coup toppled the government, and a military officer named Marcus Pérez Jiménez took over. Pérez Jiménez was overthrown in 1958 and, through a coalition of civilians and military officers, Rómulo Betancourt was elected president. After a series of careful constitutional, economic, and social reforms, Betancourt stepped down in 1963. He was followed by a series of democratically elected presidents.

THE FIRST VENEZUELANS IN AMERICA

There is no clear record of early settlement by Venezuelans in the United States. However, many migrations between South America and the United States did occur. It is also known that many European settlers first lived in Venezuela, only to immigrate to the United States. Therefore, it is possible that many Venezuelans arrived in the United States as European immigrants from South America.

SIGNIFICANT IMMIGRATION WAVES

In the nineteenth century, nearly ten times as many South Americans as Central Americans came to settle in the United States. From 1910 to 1930, the numbers of South Americans entering the United States each year was over 4,000. Most of these people were concentrated in urban areas of the northeastern United States, Chicago, Los Angeles, and San Francisco. However, there are few definite figures as to how many of these immigrants came from Venezuela. Many Venezuelans entered the United States for schooling and remained after graduation, and they are frequently joined by relatives. Since the early 1980s, the opportunity to earn higher salaries, and economic fluctuations in Venezuela have attracted increasing numbers of Venezuelan professionals to the United States.

SETTLEMENT PATTERNS

According to 1990 census figures, the states with the most Venezuelan Americans were: Florida, with 12,362; New York, with 5,559; California, with 4,575; Texas, with 3,295; New Jersey, with 2,130; Massachusetts, with 1,403; and Maryland, with 1,257. Urban areas such as Miami, New York City, Los Angeles, and Washington, D.C., have the greatest concentrations of Venezuelan Americans.

ACCULTURATION AND ASSIMILATION

The Venezuelan American population consists of a mixture of different social groups, reflecting the diversity in their homeland. Among middle-class immigrants, some 70 percent have a combined European, Indian, and African ancestry. Approximately 21 percent of Venezuelan Americans identify themselves as white, 8 percent as black, and 1 percent as Indian. Many Venezuelan Americans are descendants of Europeans from Spain, Italy, and Portugal. Venezuelan Americans often live in Latino communities within large metropolitan areas.

TRADITIONS, CUSTOMS, AND BELIEFS

Depending on an individual's family history, his or her traditions may reflect those of several different ethnic groups. The culture of Venezuelan Americans is heavily influenced by the Spaniards. Many cultural forms found within the Venezuelan American community are also seen among Caribbean peoples and Colombian Americans. It is often difficult to separate the religious elements of Venezuelan American culture from the more secular elements.

Venezuelans have long been influenced by American and European popular culture. These influences are more important place in Venezuelan culture than in that of its neighbors, and Venezuelan immigrants place a great deal of emphasis on popular culture. Baseball is a passion for many Venezuelan Americans, and they are often loyal supporters of hometown teams. Television programs, both in Spanish and English, are a great source of entertainment for Venezuelan Americans. *Telenovelas*, or soap operas, are particularly popular.

CUISINE

Many types of traditional cuisine are found within the Venezuelan American community. Venezuelan cuisine has a good deal in common with that of other Latin American and Caribbean countries. Among the many foods enjoyed are *arepas*, which are small pancakes made from corn. Arepas are often stuffed with different fillings, including beef, shrimp, ham, sausage, eggs, salad, avocado, and octopus. Another specialty is the *empanada*, a crescent-shaped, deep-fried turnover made of cornmeal, which is stuffed with chicken (*empanada de pollo*), cheese (*empanada de queso*), or beef (*empanada de carne*). A Venezuelan dish that is often served during Christmas is *hallaca*, which consists of chopped beef, pork, or chicken with vegetables and olives. This mixture is folded into a corn dough, wrapped in banana leaves, and steamed. A popular Venezuelan drink is *tizana*, which consists of chopped fruit and fruit juice. The types of fruit that are used to make tizana include papaw, banana, watermelon, cantaloupe, orange, and pineapple.

MUSIC

The Venezuelan American community listens to many forms of traditional and popular music. Perhaps the most well known type of Venezuelan music is a rhythm called the *joropo*. Featuring the music of an accordion, harp, *cuatro venezolano* (a small, guitarlike instrument), and maracas, the *joropo* is accompanied by an energetic dance performed by couples. Venezuelan Americans enjoy a full range of popular music: rock, salsa and other Caribbean forms, pop, country, Latin jazz, and classical.

DANCES AND SONGS

The joropo musical form is accompanied by a song called "Alma Llanera," which has become the unofficial national anthem of Venezuela. Although folk dance is taught and performed by some Venezuelan Americans, most prefer modern dance. Parties, concerts, and nightclubs featuring salsa or merengue often provide Venezuelan Americans with opportunities to dance.

HOLIDAYS

For many Venezuelan Americans, Carnival is the main festival of the year. Many Venezuelan Americans visit Venezuela during Carnival to reunite with family and friends. In the United States, groups gather to celebrate with music, drinking, singing, and dancing.

HEALTH ISSUES

As a group, Venezuelan Americans possess no significant health problems. Some Venezuelan Americans prefer to visit practitioners of traditional medicine. Traditional medical remedies are readily available in many areas with large Hispanic American populations.

LANGUAGE

Although there are more than 25 Indian languages spoken in Venezuela, Spanish and English are the predominant languages of the Venezuelan American community. Most Venezuelan American children grow up using Spanish with their families and speak the language fluently. Some Venezuelan Americans speak "Spanglish," Spanish combined with a liberal usage of English words.

GREETINGS AND POPULAR EXPRESSIONS

While greetings vary among Venezuelan Americans, the standard greetings are: *Hola* (oh-la) for "Hello," *Buenas días* (boo-ay-nas dee-ahs) for "Good morning," *Buenas tardes* (boo-ay-nas tar-days) for "Good afternoon," *Buenas noches* (boo-ay-nas no-chays) for "Good evening" or "Good night."

FAMILY AND COMMUNITY DYNAMICS

Family ties are strong among Venezuelan Americans. Children are taught at an early age to view the family as the key unit of society. The heavy reliance on family ties and connections is a great strength for Venezuelan Americans, but may sometimes limit the ability of individuals to assimilate into the greater society and economy of the United States. The connection between family and community dynamics is often strong, and the pull of the family leads to concentrations of Venezuelan Americans in urban areas in which cultural, business and political networks may form that otherwise might not exist.

EDUCATION

As a group, middle-class Venezuelan Americans share a proportionately higher education level than many other Hispanic American groups. Venezuelans have not found great difficulty in achieving success in English-speaking institutions of higher education. The teaching and preservation of the Spanish language is often regarded as a family prior-

ity, and many Venezuelan Americans try to ensure their children's fluency in Spanish.

THE ROLE OF WOMEN

The role of women in the Venezuelan American community is complex and varied. Traditionally, women were expected to submit to the will of male family members, and had the tasks of housekeeping, child-raising, and the moral education of the family. In these tasks, the women of the family shared in a great deal of the labor, drawing on networks in their villages, neighborhoods, and extended families. The home was often considered the private realm of the family and women its keepers, while the public realm was the place of men. The degree of conformity to these roles varied from urban to rural settings and between classes.

Many Venezuelan American women are active in the workforce. They are engaged in a variety of professions, including business, social work, and teaching. Possessing a high degree of literacy, many Venezuelan American women and their female children have found greater opportunities than their mothers and grandmothers did in Venezuela.

BAPTISMS

Venezuelan Americans are admitted into the Catholic Church through the sacrament of baptism. Catholic doctrine states that unless a person is reborn through water and the Holy Spirit, he cannot enter into the kingdom of God. The rite begins with formal declarations made by the priest on behalf of the church, and by the parents and godparents on behalf of the child. The parents and the priest then trace the sign of the cross on the forehead of the child. The priest, parents, godparents, and those attending pray together, and several passages are read from the Scriptures. The priest then blesses the baptismal water. The parents and godparents renounce Satan and profess their faith. Water is poured over the child's head, as a sign that she or he has been cleansed of original sin. The child is then annointed with *chrism*, a consecrated oil, and placed in a white baptismal garment. A candle is lit and, after a final prayer before the altar, the priest blesses all in attendance.

COURTSHIP

Opportunities for courtship are abundant within the Venezuelan American community. Single people meet and mix at school parties, weddings, festival celebrations, and nightclubs. Groups of young men and women often meet in clubs to dance and listen to music. In most instances, young people are allowed to choose whom they wish to date. However, dating outside of one's race or social class is often frowned upon by parents and other family members.

WEDDINGS

The majority of Venezuelan Americans marriages are performed by the Catholic Church. The priest, bride, groom, and wedding party all gather before the altar. The priest welcomes the couple and the congregation. This is followed by prayers and readings from both the Old and New Testaments. After the Gospel is read, the priest delivers a homily (sermon) based on the Scripture readings. He often speaks of the mystery of marriage, the dignity of love in marriage, the grace given by the sacrament, and the responsibilities of a married couple. The rite of marriage is then performed, with marriage vows according to Catholic custom. Following the wedding Mass, a celebration is held. The wedding couple receives gifts, traditional dishes are served, and entertainment is provided. In some cases, the wedding celebration lasts for several days.

INTERACTIONS WITH OTHERS

Venezuelan Americans frequently interact with other ethnic minorities, particularly other Hispanic groups. Interaction often takes place at festivals, concerts, and religious activities. Business, community work, and politics also offer opportunities to meet other Latin American and Caribbean peoples.

RELIGION

While the vast majority of Venezuelan Americans are Catholic, their attendance at Mass and other official religious functions is infrequent when compared with other Hispanic groups. However, Venezuelan Americans are quite religious. Many Venezuelan religious traditions exist, forming a complex synthesis of the religious and the secular, the official and the unofficial. Some secular persons are often revered as "saints" because of their good works and the positive impact that they had on others. For example, Simon Bolívar is honored as a great man and pictures of him often occupy a prominent place in the homes of Venezuelan Americans.

Other important figures include Dr. José Gregorio Hernández. Hernández was a medical doctor who had an illustrious career before his death in 1918. Considered to have had an unusual ability to heal,

Hernández is venerated for inspiring health and healing. His image and story have made Hernández so famous that he is being considered for canonization as a Catholic saint. Another powerful image and figure is that of María Lionza. In a form of spirituality and imagery that mixes Catholic belief, traditional Afro-Venezuelan folk culture, and native Indian myth, the mysterious figure of Lionza is the center for many complex rituals about food, fortune, healing and safety. Lionza is referred to as "the Queen" or the "Spirit Queen" by her followers, and she, like Hernández, is seen as a figure of inspiration.

EMPLOYMENT AND ECONOMIC TRADITIONS

Venezuelan Americans are prominent in a variety of professions, particularly banking and the petroleum industry. They are often valued for their expertise in these areas. Venezuelan Americans also occupy important positions within the television, publishing, and radio industries.

POLITICS AND GOVERNMENT

Many Venezuelan Americans have established careers in local politics and government. A growing number of Venezuelan Americans are also pursuing government service on the federal level. The political allegiances of Venezuelan Americans extend across the entire spectrum of American politics.

RELATIONS WITH FORMER COUNTRY

Venezuelan Americans maintain strong ties with Venezuela. Whether in business, family, or community life, Venezuelan Americans closely monitor events within Venezuela. Visits to the homeland are relatively frequent among first-generation immigrants, and visits by Venezuelans to relatives in the United States are also quite common.

INDIVIDUAL AND GROUP CONTRIBUTIONS

ART

Carolina Herrera is a prominent fashion designer. Internationally known, Herrera was inducted into to the Fashion Hall of Fame in 1981, and received the MODA Award for Top Hispanic Designer in 1987.

Thomas Zapata (1961–) attended Lawrence University and the Pratt Institute in New York, where he received a master's degree in architecture in 1984. Zapata earned a master's degree in building design at Columbia University. He was the winner of the Collegiate Schools of Architecture National Design Award for his work on the Schibsten Ditten Project in 1989. In 1990, he received the Design Award from the Canadian National Royal Trust Office Complex. Zapata also took third prize in the National Architecture Competition.

EDUCATION

Ralph Morales is a prominent educator in the field of nutrition. Born in Los Angeles in 1940, Morales received a B.S. degree from La Sierra College in 1966, an M.S. degree from Loma Linda University in 1971, and a Ph.D. from Kansas State University in 1978. He has served as a assistant professor at Arizona State University, associate professor at the State University of New York, and a professor at San Francisco State University and California State University at Chico. Morales is noted for his many publications in the field of dietetics, and received an Outstanding Service Award from the American Dietetic Association in 1987.

FILM, TELEVISION, AND THEATER

Iliana Veronica Lopez de Gamero is a Venezuelan American who has achieved fame as a ballet dancer. Born in 1963, Lopez de Gamero has danced with the San Francisco Ballet, the Ballet Corps of the Cleveland Opera House, and as a soloist for the Berlin Opera House and the Düsseldorf Opera House. She was a finalist at the IV International Ballet Competition in Moscow in 1981, and was principal dancer of the Miami City Ballet in 1987.

JOURNALISM

Radamés Jose Soto is a notable Venezuelan American journalist. Born in 1959, he studied journalism at the University of Miami, and received a bachelor's degree in 1982. Soto worked as a news reporter for the *Los Angeles Times* from 1984 until 1986. He then pursued a career in television journalism, working for Channel 47 in New York and WPIX in New York. Soto has been nominated for the Irene Taylor Award, and won the 1989 ACE Award for best journalist. Another figure in the field of journalism is Ricardo Aranbarri. Born in 1959, he studied television production at Emerson College in Boston, from which he received a bachelor's degree in 1985. He has worked as an assistant producer for Venezolna De Television and for Venevision, and as a broadcast journalist and producer for WXTV in Secaucus, New Jersey.

MUSIC

Singer and lyricist Mariah Carey was born in New York City in 1970. Her debut album, *Mariah Carey*, soared to number one on the *Billboard* charts and remained there for more than five months. Seven million copies of the album were sold, and four singles from the album reached number one on the pop charts. Carey has released several other successful albums, and has become one of the most popular recording artists in the world.

SCIENCE AND TECHNOLOGY

Venezuelan American scientist Francisco Dallmeier (1953–) is a leading ornithologist (a biologist who studies birds). Dallmeier attended the Universidad Central de Venezuela and Colorado State University, where he received a master's degree in wildlife ecology in 1984, and a Ph.D. in 1986. Dallmeier served as director of the La Salle University Museum of Natural History from 1973 to 1977, biologist and educational coordinator for INELMECA from 1977 to 1981, program manager for the Smithsonian Institute's Man and the Biosphere Biological Diversity Program from 1986 to 1988, acting director of this program from 1988 to 1989 and then director from 1989 on. He is a prominent figure in the area of biodiversity research in the United States.

SOCIAL ISSUES

Federico Moreno (1952–) immigrated to the United States with his family in 1963. He attended the University of Notre Dame, and received a bachelor's degree in government. After teaching at Atlantic Community College and Stockton State College, Moreno attended law school and earned his law degree from the University of Miami. After two years at a private law firm, Moreno worked as a public defender. For four years, he maintained a private law practice. In 1986, Moreno became a judge in Dade County, Florida, and later served for three years as a judge in Florida's Circuit Court. In 1990, President Bush appointed Moreno to the United States District Court for the Southern District of Florida.

Ana María Distefano is a Venezuelan American and a prominent government official. Born in 1951, Distefano attended the University of Pittsburgh, where she received a bachelor's degree in 1983. After several positions in the private sector, she came to work for the United States Department of Commerce in its Minority Business Development Agency and later in the public Information Office of its Bureau of the Census. Distefano has received awards and honors from the National Association of Hispanic Journalists, the Hispanic Association of Media Arts and Science, the National Association of Black Journalists, the Public Relations Society of America, and other organizations.

SPORTS

Venezuelan Americans are great fans of baseball. Unlike other South American countries, baseball rather than soccer is the national sport. Baseball was first introduced to Venezuela as a result of the oil boom of the early twentieth century. The sport quickly spread from oil workers' camps to every city, town, and village across the country. Many Venezuelan Americans enjoy playing baseball and actively support major and minor league Venezuelan teams.

Many current and former professional baseball players in the United States are Venezuelan Americans. Among these are Luis Aparicio, one of baseball's greatest shortstops. Aparicio holds records for number of games played by a shortstop, double plays, and assists. He was Rookie of the Year in 1956 and played on All-Star teams from 1958 to 1964 and from 1970 to 1972. In 1984, Aparicio was inducted into the Baseball Hall of Fame. Dave Concepción, another talented shortstop, played with the Cincinnati Reds from 1970 to 1988, was named captain of the Reds in 1973, played in three World Series, and was a member of All-Star teams in 1972 and from 1975 to 1982.

Other Venezuelan American baseball players include: Alvaro Espinoza, an infielder who has played for the Minnesota Twins and New York Yankees; Andrés José Galarraga, a first baseman for the Atlanta Braves and 1993 National League batting champion; Ozzie Guillén, who was both the American League Rookie Player of the Year and Rookie of the Year in 1985, and a member of the 1990 American League All-Star Team; Carlos Alberto Martínez, who played for the Chicago White Sox in 1988; Carlos Narcis Quintana, who joined the Boston Red Sox in 1988; Manny Trillo, second baseman for the National League All-Star team in 1979, 1981, and 1982, National Silver Slugger team 1980 and 1981, and member of the National League All-Star Team in 1977 from 1981 to 1983; Omar Vizquel, a shortstop with the Cleveland Indians and six-time Gold Glove winner; and Bo Díaz, who appeared in five World Series games and was named to both the 1981 American All-Star team and the 1987 National League All-Star team.

VISUAL ARTS

Marisol Escobar is a prominent Venezuelan American sculptor and painter. During the 1960s, Escobar gained international fame as a sculptor. Known for her strong political commitments and overproduced eccentricity, she created works that sparked controversy, changing in inspiration and style greatly over the following decades. Escobar's works can be found both in private art collections and in art museums. In the 1990s, she continued to produce new work, and became active in public education concerning the spread and treatment of AIDS.

MEDIA

PRINT

There are eight Spanish-language newspapers published daily in the United States, each including coverage of the Venezuelan American community. Two are published in New York, two in Miami, one in Chicago, and three in El Paso, Texas. The Spanish-language newspapers that are most widely read by Venezuelan Americans are *El Diario/La Prensa* and *Noticias del Mundo*, which serve the New York area; *El Nuevo Herald* and *El Diario de las Américas* in Miami; and *El Mañana* in Chicago.

Two popular Spanish-language magazines among Venezuelan Americans are *Temas* and *Réplica*. Three English-language magazines, *Hispanic*, *Hispanic Business*, and *Hispanic Link*, are also widely read. Two bilingual magazines, *Vista* and *Saludos Hispanos*, are also well-received. Academic and professional journals of interest to Venezuelan Americans include *Americas Review*, *Hispanic Journal of Behavioral Sciences*, *Journal of Hispanic Policy*, and *Latino Studies Journal*.

RADIO

There are approximately 35 AM and 115 FM radio stations that broadcast Spanish-language programming in the United States. In addition, 75 AM and 15 FM stations dedicate significant portions of their air time to Spanish-language programming. Most of these stations include news, music, and other programs of interest to the Venezuelan American community.

TELEVISION

In many major American cities, there are television stations that broadcast exclusively in Spanish. These stations are also available to other areas through cable and satellite television. They offer a wide variety of news, entertainment, and educational programs for both Venezuelan Americans and the larger Hispanic community in the United States.

ORGANIZATIONS AND ASSOCIATIONS

Embassy of Venezuela.
Address: 2445 Massachusetts Avenue, NW, Washington, D.C. 20008.
Telephone: (202) 797-3800.

MUSEUMS AND RESEARCH CENTERS

Florida Museum of Hispanic and Latin American Art.
Address: 4006 Aurora Street, Coral Gables, Florida 33146.
Telephone: (305) 444-7060.
Fax: (305) 261-6996.
Online: http://www.latinoweb.com/museo/.

Museum of Latin American Art.
Address: 628 Alamitos Avenue, Long Beach, California 90802.

Telephone: (562) 437-1689.
Fax: (562) 437-7043.
Online: http://www.molaa.com/index.htm.

SOURCES FOR ADDITIONAL STUDY

Hispanic Policy Development Project. *The Hispanic Almanac*. Washington, DC: Hispanic Development Project, 1984.

Meier, Matt S., with Conchita Franco Serri and Richard A. Garcia. *Notable Latino Americans: A Biographical Dictionary*. Westport, CT: Greenwood Press, 1997.

Rudolph, Donna Keyse and G.A. *Historical Dictionary of Venezuela*. Lanham, MD: Scarecrow Press, 1996.

Venezuelan Democracy Under Stress, edited by Jennifer L. McCoy et al. New Brunswick, NJ: Transaction Publishers, 1994.

Wright, Winthrop R. *Café con Leche: Race, Class, and National Image in Venezuela*. Austin: University of Texas Press, 1990.

VIETNAMESE AMERICANS

by
Carl L. Bankston III

The extended family is the heart of Vietnamese culture, and preservation of family life in their new home is one of the most important concerns of Vietnamese Americans.

OVERVIEW

The Socialist Republic of Vietnam is a long, narrow, "S"-shaped country of 127,243 square miles (329,556 square kilometers). It extends about 1,000 miles from southern China southward to the Gulf of Thailand. It is bordered on the west by Laos and Cambodia and on the east by the south China Sea. At the center of the "S," Vietnam is less than 30 miles wide. The northern and southern parts of the country are somewhat wider, with the north reaching a maximum width of 350 miles.

This southeast Asian nation has a population of about 75 million people. The ethnic Vietnamese, who make up nearly 90 percent of the population, are thought to be descendants of peoples who migrated into the Red River Delta of northern Vietnam from southern China. There are also about three million members of mountain tribes, found mainly in the Central Highlands and in the Annamese Cordillera mountain chain in the north; about two million ethnic Chinese, most of whom live in large cities; about 500,000 Khmer, or ethnic Cambodians; and about 50,000 Cham, descendants of a Malayo-Polynesian people who dominated the area that is now southern Vietnam before the arrival of the Vietnamese.

Religions include Buddhism, Confucianism, Taoism, Roman Catholicism, Cao Dai (a mixture of aspects of Roman Catholicism and various Asian religions), Hoa Hao (a Vietnamese offshoot of

Buddhism), Islam, Protestantism, and animism. Most Vietnamese practice the mutually compatible religions of Buddhism, Confucianism, and Taoism. About three million are Catholics, concentrated in the southern part of the country. About one million practice the Cao Dai religion and about one million belong to the Hoa Hao sect. The number of Protestants is small, and they are mostly found among the tribesmen of the mountains, where American and European missionaries were active until recently. Almost all of the Cham are Muslims.

The country's official language is Vietnamese and the capital city is Hanoi. The official flag is red with a large yellow star in the center, but many Vietnamese Americans object to this flag, viewing it as an emblem of the communist government. They identify instead with the flag of former South Vietnam, which is yellow with three horizontal red stripes in the center.

EARLY HISTORY

Although the Vietnamese are newcomers to North America, they are heirs to a culture far older than the United States, and even older than any of the national societies of Europe. The first known historical records of the Viets in the Red River Delta of what is now northern Vietnam were written by the Chinese in the second century B.C. Vietnamese archaeologists have traced their civilization back even further, to the Phung-Nguyen culture that existed before 2000 B.C.

While the village constituted the basis of rural Vietnamese folk culture, many of the nation's formal institutions were introduced from the great neighbor to the north, China. Even the name of the country is derived from Chinese: "Viet" is a variant pronunciation of the Chinese word "Yueh", which designates the "hundred" tribes that populated the southern region of China, and "Nam," which is the same as "nan" in Chinese and means "south." Vietnam's close but troubled relations with its huge northern neighbor have shaped many of its political and social structures and have, in recent years, played a crucial role in the creation of a refugee crisis.

As the Chinese empire of the Han dynasty extended its control over the area to the south, the Viets accepted Chinese administrative designations for their territory and the local rulers were redefined as prefectural and district officers. Despite some early rebellions against Chinese rule (one in particular was instigated by the Trung sisters, who remain Vietnamese national heroes for their struggles against the Chinese in the first century A.D.), Vietnam was a part of the Chinese empire until the suc-

cessful war for independence in the tenth century. Despite the adoption of Chinese forms of government, Chinese written characters, and Chinese-style Buddhism, the Vietnamese have continued to be wary of their powerful neighbor.

Until the fifteenth century, the Vietnamese occupied only the northern part of what we now know as Vietnam. The southern portion constituted the empire of the Cham, Champa, and part of the Khmer, or Cambodian, territory. By 1471, however, under the rulers of the Le dynasty (modeled after the Chinese "emperors"), Vietnam succeeded in conquering almost the whole of Champa. This success not only brought the newly enlarged country into conflict with the Khmers, but it also gave the country its present elongated shape, wide at the top and bottom and exceedingly narrow in the middle where the mountains that run down its center approach the sea coast. This geographical feature, often described as two heads and a little body, divided the country into two regions.

MODERN ERA

While Vietnam's early history was dominated by its struggles with neighboring China, modern Vietnam has been greatly influenced by France. Vietnam's early contacts with Europe were primarily forged through Catholic missionaries, particularly Jesuits, who arrived in 1615, after they had been prohibited from entering Japan. France, as the most powerful of Catholic nations in the seventeenth century, was especially active in supporting these religious endeavors, through the Societe des Missions Etrangeres. Alexandre des Rhodes, a French Jesuit, along with some of his Portuguese colleagues, was instrumental in creating a new system of writing, which was later adopted throughout Vietnam. This form of writing became known as *quoc ngu*—national language—and uses the Latin alphabet to transcribe phonetically the Vietnamese spoken language. This system was adopted throughout Vietnam in the beginning of the twentieth century.

Through the work of missionaries, the French gained influence in Vietnam long before the arrival of a single French soldier or administrator. When a peasant rebellion, known as the *Tay-son*, reunified the country in 1788 under the rule of a rebel leader who had himself proclaimed emperor, the surviving heir of the southern Nguyen family, Nguyen Anh, sought the assistance of France. Because of the revolution in France, this claimant to the throne received only token French ships and volunteer troops that nonetheless helped him reestablish himself at Saigon in 1789. The French also constructed forts for him and trained his troops, which contributed to Nguyen Anh's success in taking control of the entire country by 1802.

Nguyen Anh's son, the Emperor Minh-mang, facilitated a revival of the Confucian religion to reestablish order in the country and to support his own position as an emperor. The spread of Catholicism presented a danger to the Confucian order in the eyes of Minh-mang, who consequently initiated a policy of persecution against Catholics in 1825.

By the nineteenth century, the French were struggling to catch up to other European countries in the competition for colonies. The French Emperor Napoleon III took up the cause of the Catholics in Vietnam and used their persecution as a pretext for invading the country. His envoys seized Saigon and the three surrounding provinces in 1862. Minh-mang's grandson, Tu-duc, had to choose between opposing a rebellion in the north and effectively fighting the French. In 1863 he officially ceded the three provinces to France and agreed to the establishment of a French protectorate over Vietnamese foreign relations. In the 1880s, following a war between France and China, which still claimed sovereignty over Vietnam, the French extended their control over the rest of Vietnam. They held the southern part, known as Cochinchina, as a colony, and central and northern Vietnam—respectively named Tonkin and Annam—as protectorates. The two latter territories were placed under the nominal rules of the emperors of the Nguyen dynasty, whom the French tightly controlled and manipulated.

As in other parts of Southeast Asia, the system of colonial domination created in the late nineteenth century was maintained until the rise of an Asian imperial power, Japan. A variety of Vietnamese nationalist movements had developed in response to French rule. The anti-imperialist stance expressed in Lenin's analysis of colonialism attracted some, including the young man who joined the French Socialist Party in 1920 and later became known by the adopted name of Ho Chi Minh. Following the surrender of France to Japan's ally, Germany, Ho Chi Minh's forces were left as the only effective resistance to Japan in Vietnam.

When Japan surrendered in August 1945, the Communist-dominated nationalist organization called the Viet Minh staged the August Revolution and easily seized power. The last of the French-controlled Vietnamese emperors, Bao-dai, abdicated and Ho Chi Minh declared the independence of Vietnam, proclaiming the creation of the Democratic Republic of Vietnam, on September 2, 1945. Japanese forces remained in Vietnam, however, and the Allies moved in to disarm them and send them home. China, still under the Nationalist government of Chiang Kai Chek, was given the task of disarming the Japanese in northern Vietnam, while the British were assigned to the territory south of the sixteenth parallel. While the Chinese allowed the Viet Minh to retain control of Hanoi and the north, the British helped the French seize control of the south and reestablish French colonial power. After the British left in January 1946 and the Chinese left in the spring of that same year, the country was again divided into north and south.

At first the French and the new Vietnamese government accepted one another, albeit uneasily, as neither was prepared for open conflict. In March 1946, Ho Chi Minh signed an agreement with the French in which he accepted the deployment of French troops in the north, while France agreed to recognize the Democratic Republic of Vietnam, on the condition that this state would remain part of the Indochinese Federation (including the parts of Vietnam under direct French rule, Cambodia, and Laos) within the French Union. Ho Chi Minh and the French also agreed to hold a popular referendum to decide whether Cochinchina should join Vietnam or remain a French colony.

France was not interested in seeing a truly independent power in Vietnam, and the Viet Minh had no desire to see their country continue under colonial rule. In late 1946 and early 1947, tensions between the two sides erupted into combat and the first Vietnam War began. In February 1947, following the Battle of Hanoi, France reoccupied Hanoi and the Viet Minh once again assumed the position of guerrillas, fighting in the mountains.

It was a long time before either side was able to gain a decisive victory. In the late 1940s France, realizing that it could not win the war militarily, added a political dimension into the conflict, accusing the Viet Minh of fighting for communism and not for independence. France created a State of Vietnam, at the head of which they placed the former emperor Bao-dai, to whom they granted more independence than what they agreed to give Ho Chi Minh in 1946. The United States and other non-communist countries quickly recognized the new Vietnamese state, while China, the Soviet Union, and other communist counties recognized the government of the Democratic Republic of Vietnam. In one single move, France succeeded in transforming their war of colonial re-conquest into an anti-communist crusade, and made an imperialist conflict into a quasi-civil one. Despite their machinations, the move did not help them on the battlefield. In the early 1950s, the growing army of the Democratic Republic of Vietnam, under the command of General Vo Nguyen Giap, began a series of offenses against the French. They achieved a famous victory at Dien Bien Phu in May 1954. The French defeat at Dien Bien Phu led to in an international conference on Vietnam in Geneva, which resulted in a cease fire and a temporary division of the country into North Vietnam, governed by Democratic Republic from Hanoi, and South Vietnam, which was entrusted to the French and their State of Vietnam with Bao-dai as the Chief of State and Ngo Dinh Diem as the Prime Minister in Saigon. Some South Vietnamese who sympathized with Ho Chi Minh's government moved north. About one million northerners, between 600,000 and 800,000 of whom were Catholics, fled south on U.S. and French aircraft and naval vessels.

Ngo Dinh Diem proved to be an energetic leader, putting down armed religious sects and criminal groups. He also demanded that France remove all its troops from Vietnam. In 1955, Diem organized and won elections that forced Bao-dai to abdicate. Diem proclaimed Vietnam a Republic with him as its first president. Supported by the United States, Diem refused to take part in the elections for national re-unification that had been promised by the Geneva Conference, which led to terrorism and other forms of resistance to his regime in many parts of South Vietnam.

RELATIONS WITH VIETNAM

Before 1975, there were almost no Vietnamese people in the United States, but the destinies of Vietnam and the United States became increasingly intertwined during the 1950s and 1960s. Since the war, the Vietnamese have become one of the largest Asian American groups. The American government began to show an interest in Vietnam during World War II, when it gave supplies and other forms of assistance to Ho Chi Minh's anti-Japanese forces. After the war, however, containment of international communism became America's primary foreign policy objective, and the Americans became increasingly dedicated to preserving the anti-communist South Vietnamese government of Ngo Dinh Diem in order to keep the North Vietnamese from taking over the whole country.

Diem was a Catholic, and he relied heavily on Catholic support, alienating the Buddhist majority. This created opportunities for the North Vietnamese-supported insurgents, who organized themselves into the National Liberation Front. Their members became known as the Viet Cong. Many volunteer agencies based in the United States, including CARE, Catholic Relief Services, and Church World Services, became active in South Vietnam in the 1950s in response to the social disruption of war. It was through these organizations that many of the South Vietnamese were first acquainted with Americans and American culture.

In 1961 President Kennedy sent military advisors to South Vietnam to assist the beleaguered Diem government. Diem became increasingly unpopular in his own country, however, and in 1963 he was overthrown by a military coup, apparently with the knowledge and consent of the American government. The new leaders of South Vietnam proved less able to maintain control than Diem and by 1965, with the South Vietnamese government on the verge of collapse, President Johnson sent in ground troops.

American military and political leaders believed they were winning the war through the end of 1967. At the beginning of 1968, the Viet Cong and North Vietnamese troops launched the *Tet* offensive, which convinced American leaders that victory, if possible at all, would not be quick or easy. It also increased the American public's opposition to the war. In 1973 the Paris peace talks ended with the United States agreeing on a timetable for withdrawing its troops and turning the war over to the South Vietnamese army. The South Vietnamese government was no better prepared to defend itself than it had been in 1965, and in April 1975 the South Vietnamese capital of Saigon fell to an invasion of North Vietnamese and National Liberation Front troops.

SIGNIFICANT IMMIGRATION WAVES

On April 18, 1975, less than two weeks before the fall of Saigon, President Ford authorized the entry of 130,000 refugees from the three countries of Indochina into the United States, 125,000 of whom were Vietnamese. This first large group of Vietnamese in America has become known as "the first wave." Those in the first wave who arrived in the mid- to late-1970s, typically had close ties with the American military and therefore tended to be the elite of South Vietnam. According to data collected by the United States Department of State in 1975, over 30 percent of the heads of households in the first wave were trained in the medical professions or in technical or managerial occupations, 16.9 percent were in transportation occupations, and 11.7 percent were in clerical and sales occupations. Only 4.9 percent were fishermen or farmers—occupations of the majority of people in Vietnam. Over 70 percent of the first wave refugees from this overwhelmingly rural nation came from urban areas.

During the months of April and May 1975, six camps opened in the United States to receive refugees and prepare them for resettlement. After refugees were interviewed, given medical examinations, and assigned to living quarters, they were sent to one of nine voluntary agencies, or VOLAGs. These VOLAGs, the largest of which was the United States Catholic Conference, assumed the task of finding sponsors, individuals, or groups who would assume financial and personal responsibility for refugee families for up to two years.

Despite the fact that many first wave arrivals were from privileged backgrounds, few were well-prepared to take up a new life in America. The majority did not speak English and all found themselves in the midst of a strange culture. The American refugee agencies attempted to scatter them around the country, so that this new Asian population would not be too visible in any one place, and so that no one city or state would be burdened with caring for a large number of new arrivals. Nevertheless, although at least one percent of the southeast Asian population in 1976 resided in each of 29 states, California had already become home to the largest number of refugees, with 21.6 percent of all the Southeast Asians in the United States.

The beginning of the first wave in 1975 was followed by smaller numbers, with only 3,200 Vietnamese arriving in 1976 and 1,900 in 1977. These numbers increased dramatically in 1978 as a result of an enlarged resettlement program developed in response to the lobbying of concerned American citizens and organizations; 11,100 Vietnamese entered the country that year. Political and economic conditions in Vietnam at this time drove large numbers of Vietnamese from their country, often in small unseaworthy boats. News of their hostile reception in neighboring countries and their sufferings at the hands of pirates created pressure in the United States to expand further the refugee program. Then in January 1979 Vietnam invaded neighboring Cambodia and the following month war broke out between Vietnam and China. As a result the number of Vietnamese admitted to the United States in 1979 rose to 44,500. Many of this second wave were Chinese citizens of Vietnam. As the war continued, the number of fleeing Indochinese rose steadily. Some were Cambodians or Laotians but Vietnam, with its larger population, was the homeland of the majority of refugees. In 1980, 167,000 southeast Asians, 95,200 of whom were Vietnamese, arrived in the United States. They were followed in 1981 by 132,000 southeast Asians, 86,100 of whom were Vietnamese.

Unlike the first refugees, the second wave came overwhelmingly from rural backgrounds and usually had limited education. Indeed, they appear to have been the least educated and the least skilled of any legal immigrants to the United States in recent history. Their hardships were increased by their time of arrival: 1980 was a year of high inflation rates, and 1981 to 1983 saw the most severe economic recession of the previous 50 years.

While first wave refugees came directly to the United States, those in the second wave tended to come through refugee camps in southeast Asia. Agencies under contract to the United States Department of State organized classes to teach English and familiarize refugees with American culture. VOLAGs were still charged with finding sponsors prior to resettlement.

By the early 1980s, secondary migration (moving a second time after arriving in the United States) had somewhat concentrated the Vietnamese American population in states with warmer weather. By 1984, over 40 percent of these refugees were located in California, mostly in the large urban centers. Texas, the state with the next largest number of southeast Asians, held 7.2 percent. This trend toward concentration continued throughout the 1980s, so that the 1990 census showed 50 percent of Vietnamese Americans living in California, and a little over 11 percent living in Texas. Other states with large numbers of Vietnamese were Virginia, Washington, Florida, New York, Louisiana, Massachusetts, and Pennsylvania.

The number of Vietnamese and other Indochinese coming to the United States never again reached the high points of 1980 and 1981. The influx did continue, however, with roughly 24,000 Vietnamese reaching America every year through 1986. Many of those leaving Vietnam for the United States in the 1980s emigrated legally through the Orderly Departure Program (ODP). This was a program formed by the governments of the United States and Vietnam, despite the fact that there were no formal diplomatic relations between the two countries, which allowed those interviewed and approved by U.S. officials in Vietnam to leave the country. Two of the groups in which the United States was particularly interested were the former South Vietnamese soldiers, who were in prisons and re-education camps, and the Amerasians, the roughly 8,000 children of American fathers and Vietnamese mothers who had been left behind at the end of the war. Although an estimated 50,000 Vietnamese were resettled in the United States through the Orderly Departure Program between late 1979 and 1987, refugees also continued to pour out of Vietnam by boat and on land, across war-torn Cambodia to Thailand.

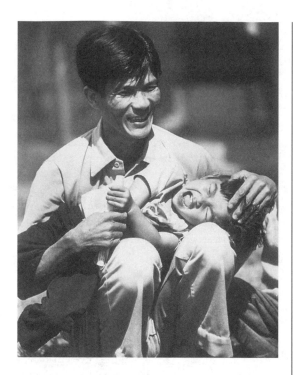

Although the number of Vietnamese to enter the United States diminished in the late 1980s and early 1990s, the group continued to grow as a part of American society. While the 1980 U.S. census placed the number of Vietnamese in this country at 245,025, the 1990 census listed 614,545. This increase of over 150 percent made the Vietnamese America's fifth largest Asian group. Because they have large families (the average number of persons in Vietnamese families in 1990 was 4.36 compared with 3.06 for white Americans and 3.48 for African Americans), by the year 2000 the Vietnamese are expected to be the third largest group among Asians and Pacific Islanders, outnumbered only by Chinese and Filipinos.

ACCULTURATION AND ASSIMILATION

When the first group of Vietnamese arrived in the United States, there was concern about how well this large group of people, from a vastly different culture with limited English and traumatic experiences of war, would fit into American society. The Vietnamese remain newcomers; nearly half are immigrants who arrived after 1980 and only 18.6 percent of Vietnamese living in the United States were born here. Despite these obstacles, their adaptation has been rapid. By 1990 almost three-fourths of Vietnamese in the United States could speak English well or very well. Only 20.5 percent did not speak English well, and only 4.7 percent could not speak English at all. There were differences between those

who arrived before 1980 and those who arrived after 1980, but both groups showed high levels of English-language ability. Among the pre-1980 immigrants, 86.9 percent reported that they could speak English well or very well and only 2.0 percent reported that they could not speak English at all. Among the post-1980 immigrants, 62.8 percent said that they could speak English well or very well, and 7.3 percent said that they could not speak English at all.

Despite the general success in adapting to the new country, many Vietnamese Americans continue to face hardships. Nearly a quarter lived below the poverty level in 1990. Moreover, many Vietnamese have had to face prejudice and discrimination from other sectors of the American population.

Maintaining Vietnamese traditions is a major concern in most Vietnamese American communities and adult Vietnamese Americans often worry that their children may be losing distinctive cultural characteristics. Since Vietnamese Americans are such new arrivals, it is difficult to judge to what extent these concerns are justified. Some Vietnamese Americans have made a conscious effort to assimilate completely into American society (for instance, by changing the last name "Nguyen" to "Newman" or "Winn"), but most retain their sense of ethnicity. Those who live in areas largely populated by Vietnamese typically remain more culturally distinctive than those who reside in suburban areas, surrounded by Americans of other ethnic backgrounds.

American views of the Vietnamese have been dominated by American involvement in the Vietnam War. Books and movies about Vietnam and the Vietnamese, such as the films *Apocalypse Now* and *The Deer Hunter*, tend to be ethnocentric, addressing the American experience in Vietnam, rather than Vietnamese life. Vietnamese Americans are often stereotyped in the popular press as chronic overachievers or desperate refugees. These stereotypes may lose some of their force as the Vietnamese presence in America continues.

CUISINE

Rice is the basis of most Vietnamese meals. In fact, the word *com* (pronounced "gum"), which means "cooked rice," is also used to mean "food" in general. In Vietnamese, to ask "have you eaten yet?" one literally asks "have you eaten rice yet?" Rice is eaten with a variety of side dishes, which are usually quite spicy. Popular dishes include *ca kho* (braised fish, pronounced "ga khaw"), *ca chien* (fried fish, pronounced "ga cheeyen"), *thit ga kho sa* (chicken braised with lemon grass, pronounced "tit ga khaw sa"), *thit bo xao* (stir-fried beef, pronounced "tit baw sow"), and *suon xao chua ngot* (sweet and sour spare ribs, pronounced "sow chewa ngawt"). Egg rolls, known as *cha gio* ("cha yaw"), are served with many Vietnamese meals and at almost all Vietnamese festive occasions. A rice noodle soup, *pho* ("fuh"), is one of the most popular breakfast and lunch foods. Vietnamese restaurants have become common in the United States, and their delicious foods are one of the most widely appreciated contributions of Vietnamese Americans to American life.

TRADITIONAL DRESS

Vietnamese men, even in Vietnam, long ago adopted western dress. Women, however, still wear the traditional *ao dai* (pronounced "ow yai") on most special occasions. The *ao dai* consists of a long mandarin-collared shirt that extends to the calves, slit at both sides to the waist. This is worn over loose black or white pants. *Ao dais* may come in many colors, and their flowing simplicity makes them among the most graceful forms of dress.

The conical Vietnamese hat known as the *non la* (literally, "leaf hat") may be seen often in areas where large numbers of Vietnamese Americans reside. Designed for protection from the hot sun of southeast Asia, the *non la* is light and provides comfortable shade when working outdoors.

HOLIDAYS

The most important Vietnamese holiday is *Tet*, which marks both the beginning of the lunar New Year and the beginning of spring. *Tet* usually falls in late January or early February. In traditional families, a ceremony may be held on the afternoon before *Tet*, during which deceased ancestors are invited to come back and spend the festival days with the living. As in the western New Year, fireworks may be heard at midnight, heralding the coming year. Several young men dressed up as a dragon, the symbol of power and nobility, perform the dragon dance on the streets or other open spaces. The dragon dance also has become an important part of the cultural exhibitions in schools and other places. On the morning of *Tet*, families awaken early and dress in their best clothes. People offer each other New Year wishes and give the children lucky red envelopes containing money. *Tet* is considered a time for visiting and entertaining guests, and non-Vietnamese are heartily welcomed to most of the celebrations and ceremonies.

Many Vietnamese Americans, especially Buddhists, also celebrate the traditional holiday of *Trung Nguyen*, or "Wandering Souls Day," which falls in the middle of the seventh lunar month. On this holiday, tables are filled with food offered to the wandering souls of ancestors. In some cases, money and clothes made of special paper may be burned at this time.

Trung Thu, or the "Mid-Autumn Festival", held on the fifteenth day of the eighth lunar month is one of the loveliest of Vietnamese holidays. Bakers in Vietnamese communities begin to prepare weeks before the festival by making moon cakes of sticky rice. People fashion lanterns of cellophane paper in many different shapes, and place candles inside. On the night of the festival, children form a procession and travel through the streets with their bright lanterns, dancing to the beat of drums and cymbals.

In 1994, Congress designated May 11 as the annual Vietnam Human Rights Day. Each year, the day is used to remind the world that Vietnam remains under communist rule and that the Vietnamese struggle for freedom continues. In 1995, Congress sponsored a rally at the Hart Senate Office building on Capitol Hill.

PROVERBS

Like the proverbs of many other peoples, traditional Vietnamese proverbs form a treasury of popular wisdom, offering insights into the society and into its beliefs about how relations among people are or ought to be. The following are a few of the countless proverbs that have been quoted by generations of Vietnamese people: Birds have nests, people have ancestors; If a branch is broken from a tree, the branch dies; Big fish eat little ones; From our own thoughts we can guess the thoughts of others; Even the fierce tiger will not devour its kittens; The city has its laws, the village has its customs; The law of the Emperor must give way before the customs of the village; The higher one climbs, the more painful the fall; Life is ten times more valuable than wealth; Chew when you eat, think when you speak.

HEALTH ISSUES

Many older Vietnamese suffer from the strains of war and exile. Younger Vietnamese, who sometimes find themselves straddling two cultures, express confusion over discrepancies between the expectations of their parents and those of the larger society. Nevertheless, Vietnamese Americans as a whole do not exhibit mental health problems that prevent them from functioning in American society.

Vietnamese Americans generally have a high opinion of the American medical establishment.

The profession of medical doctor is the most highly rated by Vietnamese Americans in terms of prestige, and it is a source of great pride to Vietnamese American parents to have a child who is a doctor or a nurse.

Tuberculosis was a serious problem among Vietnamese refugees to the United States, but they were kept in refugee camps overseas until it was determined that the disease was cured. As a result, the incidence of tuberculosis among Vietnamese Americans now appears to be very low.

LANGUAGE

Vietnamese is generally a monosyllabic language. Two or more one-syllable words may be joined together, however, usually connected by a hyphen, to form a compound word. Vietnamese is a tonal language; the meanings of words are determined by the pitch or tone at which the words are spoken. Several of these tones are also found in English, but English does not use the tones in the same way. In Vietnamese, the sound "*ma*" pronounced with a falling tone and the sound "*ma*" pronounced with a low rising tone are actually two different words. The first means "but" and the second means "tomb." There are six of these tones in Vietnamese. In modern written Vietnamese, which uses the romanized system of writing introduced by European missionaries, the tones are indicated by diacritical marks, or marks written above and below the vowel in each syllable. A word without any mark is spoken with a mid-level tone. When the word has an acute accent over the vowel, it is pronounced with a voice that starts high and then rises sharply. When the word has a grave accent over the vowel, it is pronounced with a voice that starts at a low level and then falls even lower. A tilde over the vowel indicates a high broken tone, in which the voice starts slightly above the middle of the normal speaking voice range, drops and then rises abruptly. A diacritical mark that looks like a question mark without the dot at the bottom is written over a vowel to indicate the low rising tone that sounds like the questioning tone in English. A dot written under a vowel means that the word should be pronounced with a voice that starts low, drops a little bit lower, and is then cut off abruptly. Most non-Vietnamese who study the language agree that the tones are the most difficult part of learning to speak it properly.

One of the most interesting features of Vietnamese is its use of status-related pronouns, a feature that it shares with many other Asian languages. While English has only one singular first-person, one singular second-person, and two singular third-person pronouns, Vietnamese has words that perform the function of pronouns. The word that is used for a pronoun depends on the relationship between the speaker and the person addressed. When a student addresses a teacher, for example, the word used for "you" is the respectful "*thay,*" which means "teacher." Many of the words used as pronouns express family relations, even when the Vietnamese are speaking with non-family members. Close friends are addressed as "*anh*" ("older brother") or "*chi*" ("older sister"). To address someone more politely, especially someone older than oneself, one uses the words "*ong*" (literally, "grandfather") or "*ba*" (literally, "grandmother"). In this way, the fundamental Vietnamese values of respect for age, education, and social prestige and the central place of the extended family in Vietnamese life are embodied in the language itself.

The dialect of northern Vietnam, known as *tieng bac*, is slightly different from that of southern Vietnam, known as *tieng nam*. One of the most notable differences is that the Vietnamese letter "*d*" is pronounced like the consonant "y" in the southern dialect and somewhat like the "z" in the northern dialect. Although the southern dialect is more common among Vietnamese Americans, many Vietnamese Americans who are from families that moved south in 1954 speak the northern dialect.

Although many of Vietnamese Americans speak English well and use it outside the home, the vast majority retain the Vietnamese language. In 1990, about 80 percent of those who identified themselves as Vietnamese in the U.S. census said they spoke Vietnamese at home, while another 4.7 percent said they spoke Chinese, and only 14.1 percent reported speaking English at home. Even among those who came to the United States before 1980, over 70 percent reported speaking Vietnamese at home. Vietnamese Americans generally regard their language as an important part of their cultural identity, and make efforts to pass it on to their young people.

GREETINGS AND OTHER POPULAR EXPRESSIONS

Some common Vietnamese greetings and expressions are: *Chao ong* ("jow ohm")—Hello (to an older man or to one to whom one wishes to show respect); *Chao anh*—Hello (to a male friend); *Chao ba* ("jow ba")—Hello (to an older woman); *Chao co* ("jow go")—Hello (to a younger woman); *Di Dao* ("dee dow")—Where are you going? (commonly used as a greeting); *Ong* (or *anh, ba, co,* depending on the gender and relationship of the person addressed) *manh gioi khong* ("ohm mahn yoi kohm")—Are you well? (used in the sense of the English "How are you?"); *Cam on* ("gahm ung")— Thank you; *Khong co gi* ("kohm gaw yi")—You're welcome (literally the expression means: "that is nothing!"); *Chuc mung nam moi* ("chook meung nam meuey")—Happy New Year. Since Vietnamese uses tones and also contains some sounds not found in English, the suggested pronunciations are only approximate.

LITERATURE

Until the twentieth century, the greater part of Vietnamese literature was written in Chinese characters. A smaller portion of their literature was written in *chu nom*, a writing system that uses a combination of Chinese characters to transcribe Vietnamese sounds. The Vietnamese people have a wealth of folktales that were usually passed on by storytelling, although many were collected in anthologies in chu nom. The folktales include stories about animals, fairy tales, fables with moral lessons, Buddhist legends, and stories about historical figures. There are several good collections of Vietnamese folktales in English that can be enjoyed by children and adults alike. Among these are *Under the Starfruit Tree: Folktales from Vietnam* (Honolulu: University of Hawaii Press, 1989), collected by Alice M. Terada; *The Beggar in the Blanket and Other Vietnamese Tales* (New York: Dial Press, 1970), retold by Gail Graham; and *The Wishing Pearl and Other Tales of Vietnam* (New York: Harvey House, 1969), translated by Lam Chan Quan and edited by Jon and Kay Nielsen.

The earliest works of formal literature composed in *chu nom* are poems that date from the Tran dynasty in the thirteenth century A.D. The most important early Vietnamese author, however, was Nguyen Trai, a poet of the early 1400s, who was heavily influenced by Chinese models. Ironically, Nguyen Trai served as a minister in the court of the Vietnamese ruler Le Loi (also known as the Emperor Le Thai To), who waged a successful war of liberation against China. This emperor was himself a poet and his writings are included in one of the first anthologies of Vietnamese poetry, which is still read today.

The seventeenth and eighteenth centuries were something of a golden age for narrative and lyric verse in *chu nom* characters. The six- and eight-syllable verse known as *luc-bat* became the most important and widely used literary form at this time. At the beginning of the nineteenth century, the poet Nguyen Du used the six-eight syllable *luc-bat* to compose the long narrative *Kim Van Kieu*, or the *Tale of Khieu*, which is considered the national literary masterpiece of Vietnam (translated into English by Huynh Sanh Thong and published in the United States by Yale University Press, 1983).

The early- to mid-twentieth century saw a flowering of Vietnamese literature, due largely to the spread of the *quoc ngu*, or romanized system of writing. The older Chinese-based writing system was difficult to learn and to use, and the new writing made mass literacy possible, creating new readers and writers. In the twentieth century also, western forms of literature, such as the novel, journalism, and literary criticism, took root. Two of the most popular contemporary novelists in Vietnam are Duong Thu Huong, whose novel *Paradise of the Blind* (translated into English by Nina McPherson and Phan Huy Duong, William Morrow and Co, 1993) became the first novel from Vietnam to appear in English in the United States, and Bao Ninh, *The Sorrow of War*, which also appears in English (translated by Phan Thanh Hao and edited by Frank Palmos, New York: Pantheon Books, 1995).

Vietnamese Americans, struggling to adjust to life in a new country and a new language, are only beginning to establish a literature of their own. Most Vietnamese communities have their own newspapers, which frequently offer poems and stories in Vietnamese. The memoir has become an important literary form for Vietnamese American authors attempting to reach a wider English-speaking audience. Two important memoirs by Vietnamese American authors are *The Vietnamese Gulag* (Simon and Schuster, 1986), by Doan Van Toai, and *When Heaven and Earth Changed Places* (Doubleday, 1989), by Le Ly Hayslip. The latter work has also been made into a film by Oliver Stone, and Hayslip has published a second memoir entitled *Child of War, Woman of Peace* (Doubleday, 1993). Jade Ngoc Quang Huynh's *South Wind Changing: A Memoir* (Graywolf Press, 1994), which tells of the author's youth and university education in Saigon, imprisonment in a reeducation camp, flight to America, and his efforts to become a writer, met with great critical acclaim.

FAMILY AND COMMUNITY DYNAMICS

The extended family is the heart of Vietnamese culture, and preservation of family life in their new home is one of the most important concerns of Vietnamese Americans. While American families are generally nuclear, consisting of parents and their children, the Vietnamese tend to think of the fam-

This Vietnamese
American girl is
performing at the
Lotus Festival in
Los Angeles.

ily as including maternal and paternal grandparents, uncles, aunts, and cousins. Traditionally-minded Vietnamese Americans think of all social relations on the model of family relations. Many Vietnamese Americans have taken on family patterns similar to the nuclear families of other Americans, but many of them still attempt to retain close ties with their extended families, so that even when adult children marry and leave the household, parents often encourage them to live nearby.

Older and newly arrived Vietnamese Americans often display indirectness and extreme politeness in dealing with others. They will tend to avoid looking other people in the eyes out of respect, and they frequently try not to express open disagreement with others. U.S.-born Vietnamese youth often have the mannerisms and cultural traits of other American adolescents, which sometimes leads to intergenerational conflict, and to complaints by older people that the younger people are "disrespectful."

Vietnamese American family ties are strong and their families generally remain intact, despite the strains of exile and adaptation to a new country. In the 1990 U.S. census, 84 percent of Vietnamese people over 15 years of age who had been married were still married. Only 5.3 percent were divorced and only 4.5 percent were separated.

Although Vietnamese Americans often express a distaste for public assistance, most Vietnamese families who arrive in the United States as refugees receive public assistance for about six months from the time of arrival. In 1990, about a fourth of Vietnamese American families were receiving some form of public assistance.

COURTSHIP AND WEDDINGS

Dating is almost unknown in Vietnam, where couples are almost always accompanied by chaperons, and many Vietnamese American parents feel very uncomfortable with the idea of their daughters going out alone with young men. Still, American-style dating has become fairly common among young Vietnamese Americans. Most Vietnamese Americans marry within their ethnic group, but Vietnamese American women are much more likely to marry non-Vietnamese than are Vietnamese American men.

EDUCATION

Education is highly valued in Vietnamese culture, and the knowledge attained by children is viewed as a reflection on the entire family. In a study of achievement among southeast Asian refugees, Nathan Caplan, John K. Whitmore, and Marcella H. Choy found that with both grades and scores on standardized tests, Vietnamese American children ranked higher than other American children, although they did show deficiencies in language and reading. Even Catholic Vietnamese Americans usually attend public schools. Both males and females pursue higher education. A degree in engineering is by far the most popular degree, although this occupation tends to be pursued by males more than by females.

The high value placed on learning leads a large proportion of young Vietnamese Americans to pur-

sue higher education. Almost half of Vietnamese Americans between the ages of 18 and 24 in 1990 were in college, compared with 39.5 percent of white Americans and 28.1 percent of black Americans in the same age group. High school dropout rates among young Vietnamese Americans were also lower than those of other Americans. Only 6.5 percent of Vietnamese Americans from ages 16 to 19 were neither enrolled in high school nor high school graduates, compared to 9.8 percent of white American youth and 13.7 percent of black American youth.

MALE-FEMALE RELATIONS

Vietnamese culture is patriarchal, but relations between male and female Vietnamese in the United States have become much more egalitarian. Vietnamese families strongly encourage higher education for both young men and young women. Still, almost all community leaders are men and young Vietnamese American women often voice frustration at the expectation that they should be primarily wives and mothers, even if they work outside the home.

It is common for Vietnamese American women to work outside the home (55.8 percent contribute to the labor force), but they are often employed in low-paying, marginal, part-time jobs. Although over 90 percent of the female civilian labor force for this group was currently employed in the 1990 census, only 66.6 percent were employed full-time.

RELIGION

Although Buddhism is the religion of the overwhelming majority of people in Vietnam, probably about 30 percent of Vietnamese Americans are Catholics. The rituals and practices of Vietnamese Catholics are the same as those of Catholics everywhere, but some observers, such as Jesse Nash, author of *Vietnamese Catholicism* (New Orleans, Art Review Press, 1992) have claimed that the Vietnamese Catholic outlook is heavily influenced by Confucianism.

Vietnamese Buddhists are almost always Mahayana Buddhists, the general school of Buddhism found in China, Japan, Korea, and Tibet. Vietnamese Buddhism is heavily influenced by the tradition known in Vietnamese as *Tien*, which is more commonly known in the West by its Japanese name *Zen*. This discipline emphasizes the achievement of enlightenment through meditation. Thich Nhat Hanh, a Vietnamese Zen master who was nominated for the Nobel Peace Prize by Martin Luther King, Jr., is widely known in the United States, even outside the Vietnamese American community, for his stories, poems, and sermons.

EMPLOYMENT AND ECONOMIC TRADITIONS

Vietnamese Americans may be found in almost all occupations, but they seem to show a preference for technical jobs, such as electrical engineering and machinery assembling. In the southern states along the Gulf Coast, Vietnamese fishermen and shrimpers play an important role in the fishing industry. High rates of employment have helped to earn Vietnamese Americans a reputation for being hard-working and energetic. In 1990, male Vietnamese Americans over the age of 26 had an unemployment rate of only 5.3 percent and even second-wave refugees, with an unemployment rate of only 6.3 percent, showed less joblessness than most others in the country.

About ten percent of Vietnamese Americans were self-employed in 1990. According to a United States census report on minority-owned businesses, in 1987, Vietnamese in America owned 25,671 firms, with 13,357 employees. This means that the number of Vietnamese-owned businesses had increased by about 415 percent since 1982. Of these businesses, 46 percent (11,855 firms) were in California and a little over one-fifth of these businesses (5,443) were in Texas. This remarkable growth in business ownership among Vietnamese Americans appears to have continued into the 1990s, suggesting that they are adapting well to the U.S. economy.

POLITICS AND GOVERNMENT

Vietnamese Americans are not yet heavily involved in American politics. Most Vietnamese American communities have a branch of the Vietnamese American Voters' Association, a decentralized set of grass-roots groups that functions primarily to prepare Vietnamese people to apply for U.S. citizenship and to advise Vietnamese Americans on voting in local elections.

The relationship between Vietnam and the United States is the major political issue for most Vietnamese Americans, and it is a highly divisive one. Some Vietnamese Americans favor closer relations to Vietnam, feeling that this will lead to greater prosperity for their parent country and con-

tribute to its liberalization. Others strongly oppose any relations between the United States and Vietnam, in the belief that any relations between the two countries help to support the current socialist Vietnamese government.

Young Vietnamese Americans have only begun to serve in the American military. Nevertheless, military service is popular among new college graduates. Vietnamese American cadets at the major American military academies, although few in number, have received widespread attention in the media.

Many Vietnamese Americans remain concerned with the political situation in Vietnam. In Garden Grove, California, a group of Vietnamese American youngsters formed the group "Movement for Human Rights in Vietnam by 2000." In 1999, Nguyen Dan Que, a medical doctor and former political prisoner, announced that "I am going to organise—and this is a challenge to the [Vietnamese] government—a meeting of former political prisoners in Vietnam." In April 1999, approximately 800-1,000 Vietnamese Americans rallied on Massachusetts Avenue in Washington, D.C., to express their concern about Vietnam.

Political emotions can run very high in Vietnamese American communities. In Westminster, California, Truong Van Tran, an electronics store owner in an area known as Little Saigon put up a poster of Ho Chi Minh in his shop. After a few eventless months, someone complained to Tran's nephew, who was working at the store. Tran responded with a pointed letter to a local group of anti-communist Vietnamese Americans. Soon afterward Tran faced protesters outside his store. The owner of the mall took the matter to Orange County Superior Court where the judge ordered Tran to take the poster down until she could review the matter further. In February of 1999 the court ruled that Tran had the First Amendment right to display the poster despite the mall owner's claims to his right to orderly business. When Tran returned to his store with the Ho Chi Minh poster, an angry mob of 200 Vietnamese immigrants assaulted him. Tran left the scene in an ambulance. He later told the *New York Times*, "I have a right to hang whatever picture I like in my store. I know the law in this country."

Santa Ana, California, was the site of a flap over a Vietnamese American art show. The Bowers Museum of Cultural Art put on an exhibit of Vietnamese art called "A Winding River" that contained some works that seemed to promote communism. The communist symbols and images sparked controversy and inspired many Vietnamese immigrants in the area to picket and protest the exhibit. Laura Baker, the Bowers Museum curator of Asian art, told the *New York Times* that the public protests had doubled attendance at the exhibit.

INDIVIDUAL AND GROUP CONTRIBUTIONS

Because the arrival of Vietnamese Americans is so recent, they have only begun to make their mark on American culture.

ACADEMIA

Huynh Sanh Thong is a scholar and translator of Vietnamese literature. Thong was the first editor of *The Vietnam Forum* and *Lac Viet*, two series of collections of literary works on Vietnamese history, folklore, economics and politics. Both of these collections are part of The Southeast Asian Refugee Project of the Yale Council on Southeast Asia Studies.

ART AND ENTERTAINMENT

Dustin Nguyen, born Nguyen Xuan Tri in Saigon, fled with his family to the United States in 1975 when he was 12 years old. Nguyen graduated from high school in Missouri and attended Orange Coast College in California, where he became interested in acting. He moved to Hollywood to pursue this interest and became famous for the character he played on the T.V. series *21 Jump Street* from 1986 to 1990.

JOURNALISM

Andrew Lam is an associate editor with the Pacific News Service. The son of a South Vietnamese army officer, he fled Vietnam with his family in 1975, the day before Saigon fell. He has published essays and news stories in a wide variety of publications. His memoir "My Vietnam, My America" (published in the December 10, 1990 issue of *The Nation*), gives a young Vietnamese American's reflections on his dual heritage.

MILITARY

Jean Nguyen and Hung Vu, in 1985, became the first Vietnamese immigrants to graduate from the United States Military Academy at West Point. Both had arrived in the United States just ten years earlier, unable to speak English.

MEDIA

PRINT

Most Vietnamese American communities have small Vietnamese-language newspapers with limited circulation. However, there are only a few national publications that are accessible to the public at large.

Across the Sea.
A magazine published twice a year by Vietnamese American Student Publications.

Contact: Jeffrey Hung Nguygen and Quyen Le, Editors.

Address: 700 Eshleman Hall, University of California-Berkeley, Berkeley, California 94720.

Gia Dinh Moi (New Family).
Monthly Catholic magazine in Vietnamese.

Address: 841 Lenzen Avenue, Third Floor, San Jose, California 95126-2736.

Horizons: Of Vietnamese Thought and Culture.
A magazine for Vietnamese American young adults.

Contact: Huy Thanh Cao, Editor.

Address: 415 South Park Victoria, Suite 350, Milpitas, California 95035.

International Association for Research in Vietnamese Music.
Address: P.O. Box 16, Kent, Ohio 44240.
Telephone: (216) 382-2917.
Fax: (440) 677-4434.
E-mail: iarvm@aol.com.

Journal of Vietnamese Music: Nhac Viet.
Formerly *Nhac Viet Newsletter*. Published by International Association for Research in Vietnamese Music; a research journal focusing on the music of Vietnam and Asia.

Contact: Dr. Sara Stone Miller, Editor.
Address: P.O. Box 16, Kent, Ohio 44240.
Telephone: (216) 677-9703.

Khang Chien.
A monthly Vietnamese-language magazine covering events and developments in Vietnam.

Contact: Nguyen Trong Thuc, Editor.
Address: P.O. Box 7826, San Jose, California 95150.
Telephone: (408) 363-1078.
Fax: (408) 363-1178.

Nguoi Vet.

Daily newspaper in Vietnamese.

Contact: Do Ngoc Yen, Publisher.
Address: 14891 Moren Street, Westminster, California 92683.
Telephone: (714) 892-9414.
Fax: (714) 894-1381.

Thoi Luan.

A weekly Vietnamese community newspaper.

Contact: Do Dien Duc, Publisher.
Address: 1685 Beverly Boulevard, Los Angeles, California 90026.
Telephone: (213) 483-8817.

Tin Viet.

Weekly Vietnamese community newspaper.

Contact: Nguyen Thuong Hieb, Editor.
Address: 9872 Chapman Avenue, Suite 12, Garden Grove, California 92641.
Telephone: (714) 530-6521.

Van Hoc.

A major Vietnamese American literary magazine entirely in Vietnamese.

Address: P.O. Box 3192, Tustin, California 92680.

Vietnam Daily Newspaper.

Daily community newspaper serving the greater San Francisco area.

Contact: Giang Nguyen, Publisher.
Address: 575 Tully Road, San Jose, California 95111.
Telephone: (408) 292-3422.
Fax: (408) 292-4088.

The Viet Nam Forum.

A journal published by the Southeast Asian Refugee Project of the Yale Council on Southeast Asian Studies. This project was founded as an archive for written material by refugees from Southeast Asia. The Council also publishes *Lac Viet*, a series of anthologies of works on Vietnamese history, folklore, economics, and politics.

Contact: Dan Duffy, Editor.
Address: Yale Council on Southeast Asian Studies, Box 13A Yale Station, New Haven, Connecticut 06520.

The Viet Nam Generation.

A press established for the purpose of publishing scholarship and literature about the war in Viet-

nam; it also publishes material on contemporary Vietnamese Americans.

Address: 18 Center Road, Woodbridge, Connecticut 06525.

Viet Nam Hai Ngoai.

Monthly Vietnamese magazine.

Contact: Dinh Thach Bich, Editor and Publisher.
Address: P.O. Box 33627, San Diego, California 92103-0580.

ORGANIZATIONS AND ASSOCIATIONS

Vietnamese Americans have formed a wide variety of organizations during the short time they have been a part of American society. Most of these exist to help newly arrived Vietnamese adjust to American society, but they also provide information about Vietnamese American culture, business, and other aspects of Vietnamese life in this country.

Center for Southeast Asian Refugee Resettlement.

Provides services to newly arrived Indochinese refugees.

Contact: Vu-Duc Vuong, Executive Director.
Address: 875 O'Farrell Street, San Francisco, California 94109.
Telephone: (415) 885-2743.

Federation of American Cultural and Language Communities (FACLC).

A coalition of ethnic organizations representing Americans of Armenian, French, German, Hispanic, Hungarian, Italian, Japanese, Sicilian, Ukrainian, and Vietnamese descent; works to address areas of common interest to ethnic communities; seeks to further the rights of ethnic Americans, especially their cultural and linguistic rights. Publishes quarterly newsletter.

Contact: Alfred M. Rotondaro, Executive Director.
Address: 666 11th Street, N.W., Suite 800 NIAF, Washington, D.C. 20001.
Telephone: (202) 638-0220.

National Association for the Education and Advancement of Cambodian, Laotian, and Vietnamese Americans.

Seeks to: provide equal educational opportunities for Indochinese-Americans; advance the rights of

Indochinese-Americans; acknowledge and publicize contributions of Vietnamese and other Indochinese in American schools, culture, and society; encourage appreciation of Indochinese cultures, peoples, education, and language. Facilitates the exchange of information and skills among Indochinese professionals and other professionals working with Indochinese Americans. Works toward legislative needs of Indochinese-Americans in education, health, social services, and welfare.

Contact: Ms. Kimoanh Nguyen-lam, President.
Address: 1250 Bellflower Boulevard, Long Beach, California 90840.
Telephone: (562) 985-5806.
Fax: (562) 985-4528.
E-mail: kclam@csulb.edu.

Vietnamese American Civic Organization.
Promotes the participation of Vietnamese Americans in voting and other civic activities.

Contact: Hiep Chu, Executive Director.
Address: 1486 Dorchester Avenue, Dorchester, Massachusetts 02122.
Telephone: (617) 288-7344.

Vietnamese American Cultural and Social Council.
Devoted to the social welfare of Vietnamese Americans, as well as to the maintenance of Vietnamese culture in America.

Contact: Paul Phu Tran, Executive Director.
Address: 1211 Garbo Way, Suite 304, San Jose, California 95117.
Telephone: (408) 971-8285.

Vietnamese American Cultural Organization.
Concerned with furthering Vietnamese culture and traditions in the United States.

Contact: Father Joseph Hien.
Address: 213 West 30th Street, New York, New York 10001.
Telephone: (212) 343-0762.

Vietnamese Chamber of Commerce in America.
Serves minority groups; provides help with small businesses.

Contact: Tuong Nguyen, Executive Director.
Address: 9938 Bolsa Avenue, Suite 216, Westminister, California 92683.
Telephone: (714) 839-2257.

Vietnamese Fishermen Association of America.
Represents the interests of the large number of Vietnamese Americans who fish off the Pacific and Gulf Coasts.

Contact: John Nguyen, Executive Director.
Address: 570 Tenth Street, Suite 306, Oakland, California 94607.
Telephone: (510) 834-7971.

Vietnamese Heritage Society (VHS).
Works to preserve Vietnamese culture and heritage and to increase understanding between ethnic groups.

Contact: Trang T. Le, President.
Address: 9750 West Wheaton Circle, New Orleans, Louisiana 70127.
Telephone: (504) 254-1857.

Vietnamese Senior Citizens Association.
Vietnamese individuals 50 years of age and older. Offers social and cultural assistance and fellowship to members. Sponsors community events including the Tet festival (a celebration of the Vietnamese New Year) and ceremonies commemorating Vietnamese national heroes and deceased relatives of members. Maintains cemetery for members.

Contact: Linh Quang Vien, President.
Address: 3813 Wildlive Lane, Burtonsville, Maryland 20866

Vietnam Refugee Fund.
Community and professional volunteers who provide assistance and staff programs aimed at the smooth resettlement of Vietnamese refugees into the U.S. Offers counseling, seminars in crosscultural understanding, job information and placement service, and translation and interpretation. Intervenes on behalf of Vietnamese refugees and residents in legal matters; assists in organizing citizenship classes. Operates Vietnamese-language radio program in Washington, DC, area.

Contact: Dao Thi Hoi, Coordinator.
Address: 6433 Nothana Drive, Springfield, Virginia 22150.
Telephone: (703) 971-9178.
Fax: (703) 719-5764.

SOURCES FOR ADDITIONAL STUDY

Bass, Thomas A. *Vietnamerica: The War Comes Home.* New York: Soho, 1996.

Caplan, Nathan, John K. Whitmore, and Marcella H. Choy. *The Boat People and Achievement in America: A Study of Family Life and Cultural Values*. Ann Arbor: University of Michigan Press, 1989.

Do, Hien Duc. *The Vietnamese Americans*. Westport, Connecticut: Greenwood Press, 1999.

Freeman, James M. *Hearts of Sorrow: Vietnamese-American Lives*. Stanford, California: Stanford University Press 1989.

McKelvey, Robert S. *The Dust of Life: America's Children Abandoned in Vietnam*. Seattle: University of Washington Press, 1999.

Refugees as Immigrants: Cambodians, Laotians, and Vietnamese in America, edited by David Haines. Totowa, New Jersey: Rowman & Littlefield, 1989.

Rutledge, Paul. *The Vietnamese Experience in America*. Bloomington: Indiana University Press, 1992.

Southeast Asian-American Communities, edited by Kali Tal. Woodbridge, Connecticut: Viet Nam Generation, 1992.

Tenhula, John. *Voices from Southeast Asia: The Refugee Experience in the United States*. New York and London: Holmes & Meier, 1991.

Toai, Doan Van, and David Chanoff. *The Vietnamese Gulag*. New York: Simon & Schuster, 1986.

Tollefson, James W. *Alien Winds: The Reeducation of America's Indochinese Refugees*. New York: Praeger, 1990.

VIRGIN ISLANDER AMERICANS

by
Lolly Ockerstrom

As citizens of a U.S. territory, Virgin Islanders have a relationship to the United States unlike that of other immigrant groups. Islanders claim allegiance to two distinct cultural identities, as they are simultaneously Virgin Islanders and U.S. citizens.

OVERVIEW

Known until 1917 as the Danish West Indies, the U.S. Virgin Islands rise out of the Caribbean waters 1,100 miles (1,770 kilometers) south of Miami and 40 miles (64 kilometers) east of Puerto Rico. They cover a total of 165 square miles. To the north lie the Bahamas, while to the south rests Haiti. Part of the Greater Antilles chain, the Virgin Islands are composed of 68 volcanic islands and cays, which are small islands made chiefly of coral. The three main islands are St. Thomas, St. John's, and St. Croix. All are rugged and mountainous. The British Virgin Islands of Tortola, Virgin Gorda, Anegada, and Jost Van Dyke are located farther east and cover 59 square miles.

Since the end of World War II, tourism has been the most important industry on the islands. Renowned for their breathtaking white sandy beaches, numerous cays, and exotic fauna, the Virgin Islands are a popular tourist destination, particularly for those interested in diving, sailing, and sport fishing. The average yearly temperature is 80 degrees Fahrenheit (25 degrees centigrade); trade winds help to keep the temperature moderate. By the late 1990s the population totaled 102,000, with the majority living in the capital city of Charlotte Amalie on St. Thomas. The annual rate of population growth is 2.5 percent. The population density is 76 persons per square mile.

Island mythology abounds with tales from pirate days, of Bluebeard and island ghosts, which are exploited to promote tourism. The islands also have had a long and painful history of colonialism and slavery under Danish rule. One result is that the majority of Virgin Islanders are of African descent, while the rest are of European or mixed heritage. The United States purchased the Virgin Islands in 1917 from Denmark for $25 million. The official language is English, although Spanish and Creole are also widely used. The currency is the U.S. dollar. Known as "America's Paradise," the Virgin Islands claim a culture that is Afro-Euro-Caribbean.

HISTORY

Native peoples inhabited the Virgin Islands thousands of years before Christopher Columbus came to the islands on his second voyage to the New World in 1493. The Arawaks are thought to have arrived on the islands about 100-200 A.D., while the Ciboneys came between 300 and 400 B.C. The Caribs arrived much later, about 100 to 150 years before Columbus. The Arawak and Carib Indians originated in Central America and traveled to the Virgin Islands through what is now Trinidad and the Lesser Antilles. It is not known where the Ciboneys originated. Various theories hold that they moved south from Florida, north from South America, or east from Central America. There was no firsthand contemporary study of any of these people, but twentieth-century archaeological studies have made it possible to reconstruct the social and cultural patterns of the first Virgin Islanders. Ancient *petroglyphs*, or rocks incised with figures hundreds of years ago, exist throughout the region. They have provided the only written record of these earlier times.

The Arawaks, Caribs, and Ciboneys crafted articles from stone, shell, bone, and wood. They also worked with other natural materials from the local environment, including hemp, fiber, grass, cotton, and skins, to fashion such everyday items as bowls, mortars and pestles, flints, and celts. The Arawaks and the Caribs produced pottery from yellow and red clay, although the Ciboneys do not appear to have worked in clay at all. Only the Caribs made mats from grasses. All three tribes were fish-eating cultures, and all were hunters and gatherers who crafted dugout canoes from cedar and silk-cotton trees to use for transportation. The Arawaks were the most skilled in cultivating the soil to grow crops. Of the three groups, the Caribs were the most warlike. Their principal weapons were bows used with poisoned arrows. The Arawaks preferred spears. Both the Carib and the Arawak tribes used javelins and clubs as well.

Around 1550, the native tribes were forced off the islands when Charles V of Spain declared them enemies. By the time the Danes arrived on St. Thomas in 1672, very few natives remained. The Danes established trade and commerce on the islands, developing plantations for growing sugar, cotton, coffee, and livestock, which demanded a continuous supply of cheap labor. This led to the use of indentured white servants and black slaves brought in from Africa.

The Danes ran a flourishing slave trade that began in 1672 and continued until a massive uprising on St. Croix in 1848 that ended slavery in the Virgin Islands. During that period, 100,000 people of African descent were forcibly transported to work as field laborers on Danish plantations. While most came directly from Africa, others came from neighboring Caribbean islands. It is estimated that in 1778, the slave population on St. Croix was 22,867, with another 4,634 on St. Thomas and 2,454 on St. John. Referred to as "*kamina* folk," they labored in the plantation fields. The Creole word *kamina* signified both the piece of land being cultivated and the black people who performed the work. Historian Isaac Dookhan theorized that had the Spanish not driven the native peoples from the Virgin Islands, enslaved Africans might never have been forced to come to the Virgin Islands. But the Arawaks, Caribs, and Ciboneys did vanish, and African slaves were captured and brought to the islands. As a result, as Dookhan noted, every aspect of life in the Virgin Islands was dominated by slavery. Class distinctions developed based on degrees of color, wealth, and education; a white ruling class emerged and suppressed the black laboring class; and the economy became dependent on the presence of slaves to work the plantations to produce food commodities for trade. The slave history of the Virgin Islands created difficult social conditions for all residents well into the twentieth century. However, in rereading Virgin Islands history, historians are recognizing a strong tradition of protest and resistance from which the *kamina* folk created a distinct culture of survival.

MODERN ERA

Competition from other sugar-producing nations, including European sugar-beet growers, began to have a negative impact on the Virgin Islands' plantation-based economy during the nineteenth century. Following the abolition of slavery, plantation growers hired indentured servants and other laborers. To reduce operating expenses in order to remain competitive, growers began to exploit their workers, leading to a massive labor revolt on St. Croix in 1878. Despite attempts by the Danish government to improve conditions, agriculture and trade continued to decline. At the outbreak of World War I, Denmark could no longer afford to maintain the islands. Denmark and the United States began discussions regarding the purchase of the Virgin Islands as early as 1863, but negotiations broke off when the U.S. Senate failed to ratify the purchase proposal. Talks resumed in 1914. Denmark and the United States signed treaties, and on March 31, 1917, control of the Virgin Islands was transferred to the United States.

The United States wanted the islands chiefly to defend access to the Panama Canal and to prevent the Germans from acquiring a strategic position in the Caribbean during the World War I. U.S. naval officers governed the Virgin Islands from 1917 until 1931, when the United States appointed Dr. Paul D. Pearson as the first civilian governor. He set up ambitious programs to invigorate the islands' economy. The Virgin Islands Company was established to encourage homestead farming, revive the sugar-cane industry, and improve the port of St. Thomas. But while social services improved during the first years of U.S. ownership, the Virgin Islands remained impoverished as a result of continued failures in trade and agriculture since the nineteenth century. When Herbert Hoover became the first U.S. president to visit the Virgin Islands in 1931, he characterized the islands as the "effective poorhouse" of the United States.

During World War II, the U.S. Virgin Islands took on strategic military importance as the United States routed convoys through the Caribbean. Military bases were constructed on the islands, warships were anchored in the Virgin Islands' harbors, and roads were built. Agricultural laborers left farming first for construction, then for jobs relating to tourism. Sugar production was phased out in 1966, and the Tourist Development Board was established in 1952. By 1954 more than 60,000 tourists visited the Virgin Islands, spending an estimated $4 million. When Cuba was closed to Americans in 1959, the number of tourists coming to the Virgin Islands rose to 200,000. By 1999 the number rose to two million. Tourism transformed the islanders' way of life, not always in positive ways. The rapid rise in tourism during the 1960s placed strain on the existing infrastructure, which was unable to keep up with new demands. Traditional ways of life were severely disrupted. Inadequate planning for future needs resulted in damage to the environment, racial tension, and rising crime rates. During the 1970s Virgin Islands' Governor Juan Luis and the Virgin Islands Chamber of Commerce identified crime as the islands' most severe problem. The crime rate did not begin to fall until the late 1970s.

Tax laws and subsidies favorable to industry have attracted new businesses to the islands. These include watch assembly operations, textile manufacturing, and oil refining. Immigrants from other Caribbean islands have come to the Virgin Islands seeking employment. Other newcomers, from the U.S. mainland, have come to retire. Between 1950 and 1970, the population of the Virgin Islands mushroomed from 26,665 to 63,200. By the end of the twentieth century, it had reached 102,000.

THE FIRST VIRGIN ISLANDERS IN AMERICA

The 1920s, the first full decade of U.S. ownership, were economically depressed years in the Virgin Islands. Lacking a viable economic system following the decline of plantation agriculture and trade, the islands remained impoverished. The U.S. prohibition act, in effect from 1919 to 1933, had been extended to the Virgin Islands and had hurt the rum production industry. Even after the appointment of a new governor in 1931, and the establishment of new programs to stimulate economic growth, unemployment was still widespread. In 1934 rioting broke out in St. Thomas. Whites continued to be assigned to positions of leadership and power, while black Virgin Islanders remained unemployed, adding more stress to already strained race relations. As a result, many Virgin Islanders emigrated to New York and other eastern seaboard cities in search of employment and relief from oppression.

SIGNIFICANT IMMIGRATION WAVES

As a slave-trading colony of Denmark during the seventeenth and eighteenth centuries, the Virgin Islands, then known as the Danish West Indies, were a destination for slaves and slaveowners. People who came to the islands rarely left unless they were returning to Denmark or another part of Europe. Not until after the United States purchased the islands did Virgin Islanders come to the U.S. mainland. Many Virgin Islanders who emigrated settled on other Caribbean islands such as Puerto Rico, where they found employment. Later emigrants from the Virgin Islands to the mainland United States were often students enrolled in colleges and universities. The number of Virgin Islanders coming to the continent was small. Government statistics on immigration and the Virgin Islands concentrate on the number of alien workers brought to the islands, especially during the 1970s economic boom, rather than the number of Virgin Islanders emigrating to the mainland.

These Virgin
Islander students
are taking a break
from their daily
school lessons.

ACCULTURATION AND ASSIMILATION

As citizens of a U.S. territory, Virgin Islanders have a relationship to the United States unlike that of other immigrant groups. Islanders claim allegiance to two distinct cultural identities, as they are simultaneously Virgin Islanders and U.S. citizens. Culturally, Virgin Islanders have developed art forms, clothing, cuisine, and traditions unique to their region and its Caribbean and African history. Economically, the Virgin Islands remain dependent on the United States. Politically, the relationship is troubled. The United States granted the islanders citizenship in 1927, but did not allow them a delegate to the U.S. Congress until 1972. Although Virgin Islanders are U.S. taxpayers, they are unable to vote in presidential elections because the Virgin Islands are not a state.

During the late 1960s, issues of acculturation and assimilation for many black Virgin Islanders became a reversal of the usual immigrant experience. Large numbers of whites from the U.S. mainland migrated to the island, threatening to overwhelm Virgin Islanders and their culture. Marilyn Krigger, a professor at what was then the College of the Virgin Islands, maintained that black students at the college experienced a serious crisis of identity as a result of this migration. Chief among the students' observations was that faculty members were mostly white Americans from the mainland. Public school teachers, also from the mainland, were largely unaware of local history, customs, foods, and other aspects of island life. The distinctive history and culture of the Virgin Islands became endangered. Unlike immigrant ethnic groups struggling to maintain a balance between their cultural past and their new homeland in the United States, U.S. Virgin Islanders had to struggle for cultural survival on their own land.

Separate black and white communities began to emerge as a result of economic disparities. There were great discrepancies between blacks' and whites' wages and status in business. Educational segregation developed as whites sent their children to expensive private schools out of the reach of most black Virgin Islander families. All-white residential areas appeared as well. An atmosphere of distrust and hatred arose.

For those Virgin Islanders who came to the U.S. mainland, cultural identity remained a troublesome issue. They have struggled to balance their identity as U.S. citizens with memories of Virgin Islands life. Because most black Virgin Islanders are descendants of slaves, they have tended to identify with black mainlanders.

TRADITIONS, CUSTOMS, AND BELIEFS

Culturally, Virgin Islanders belong to the larger group of Caribbean islands, which for centuries have been a crossroads for trade, commerce, and military maneuvers for people from all over the world. Many different cultures from Africa, Europe, Asia, and Australia have brought their own traditions to the Virgin Islands. These have further enriched the already complex tapestry of Caribbean island traditions.

PROVERBS

Virgin Islanders are fond of the saying, "What a *kallaloo!*" The word kallaloo actually means a soup of seaweed and greens, but islanders use the word to refer to any kind of mess. Another word frequently invoked is *limin'*, which means lying back and enjoying the day.

CUISINE

Several different cultures have left an imprint on the Virgin Islands, producing a national cuisine that represents a wide range of tastes and traditions. Seafoods, chutneys, and curries are all typical of Virgin Islands fare. Baked plantains are common, as are chicken legs, *kallaloo*, johnny cakes (unleavened fried bread), and cassava bread. *Souse*, a stew served at all festivities, is made of a pig's head, tail, and feet and flavored with lime juice. Fish is either fried or boiled and eaten with *fungi*, a cornmeal dumpling. Conch is cooked in garlic sauce and served hot or cold in salads or as a main dish, as well as in chowder or as a fritter. The native tannia root is cooked into a soup. Paté turnovers, pastries filled with spiced beef or salt fish are served at sidewalk stalls. Sugar cakes, desserts of sugar and fresh coconut, are very popular among natives and tourists alike.

More than 250 species of plants, exotic fruits, nuts, and vegetables are produced on the Virgin Islands. Among them are coconuts, grapes, soursop, mamee, custard apple, sugar apple, cashew, and papaya. Cassava, arrowroot, and sweet potatoes are also native to the Virgin Islands, as are several species of squash, beans, and cacao.

When Columbus and the Spaniards arrived in 1493, explorers introduced new foods to the islands, including sugar cane, which became one of the most important trade crops during the seventeenth and eighteenth centuries. Oregano and cumin arrived from Europe; lemons, oranges, and bananas came from the Canary Islands. The British introduced fruit buns, ginger beer, and breadfruit. The Dutch brought with them from Indonesia more spices: nutmeg, mace, cloves, and cinnamon. The French contributed methods of preserving fruits using rum, which became the drink of the Caribbean. Virgin Islands' bay rum became one of the most important export products for Islanders.

Other drinks of the Virgin Islands include *maubi*, made from the bark of the maubi tree with herbs and yeast added. Cruzan rum, one of the Virgin Islands' biggest exports, has been distilled on the island of St. Croix since the seventeenth century. Other popular island drinks are soursop, made of this fruit plus milk, water, sugar, and spices, and the piña colada.

African slaves who worked the plantations were granted plots of their own on which to grow food, and they began to incorporate food from the Virgin Islands into more familiar recipes from Africa. They cooked with plantains, yams, beans, and okra, as well as salt pork and salt fish. To add flavor, they used chili peppers, which are high in vitamins A and C. The scotch bonnet, a type of pepper grown on the Virgin Islands, is said to be more than 50 times hotter than a jalapeno. When slavery was abolished, indentured servants were brought from Asia, and they brought with them curries from East India and stir-fried cuisine from China.

MUSIC

Caribbean calypso music, steel drums, and reggae are well-known to music lovers throughout the world. The precursor of the calypso was known as *kareso*, a term most likely derived from the African word *kaiso*, which means "bravo." The word is used to signify approval for a singer. Quelbe, which is unique to St. Croix, is a percussion music made by scraping corrugated gourds. It is sometimes referred to as scratch music.

DANCES AND SONGS

The most famous folk dance of the Virgin Islands is the quadrille. A square dance of French origin, it was changed to fit local musical rhythms and tastes. The quadrille is performed by four couples and danced in rhythms of 6/8 and 2/4 times. Dancers wear period costumes: for women, dresses with layers of ruffles; for men in dark pants, white shirts, and cummerbunds. A scratch band provides music, and dancers respond to the commands of a caller. The quadrille is considered the true folk dance of the Virgin Islands. It declined in popularity during the fifties and sixties, but regained favor during the 1970s, partly through the performances of the Milton Payne Quadrille Dances of Christiansted, in St. Croix. This group formed in 1969. One year later the Mungo Niles Cultural Dancers were founded, and their goal was to promote the culture of the Virgin Islands. The group provided free weekly dance instruction throughout the Virgin Islands and went on tour to New York and Washington, D.C., during the 1980s. Other well-known dance groups include the St. Croix Heritage Dancers and the St. Croix Cultural Dancers.

HOLIDAYS

The major holiday in the Virgin Islands is Carnival, which occurs during the last two weeks of April on St. Croix and during June on St. Thomas. It has been a Caribbean tradition for many years. In the Virgin Islands, Carnival devotes the first week to calypso song competitions and the second to community activities, which include parades, marches, singing, and dancing. Streets are filled with stalls selling local foods, drinks, and produce. The festivities begin with the opening of the Calypso Tent, where song competitions take place. At the end of the first week, judges announce the new calypso king or queen, a much-sought-after honor. During the second week, attractions include the Children's Village, offering ferris wheel, merry-go-round, and other rides, and J'ouvert, a 4:00 a.m. tramp through town ending with fireworks at the harbor. A children's parade traditionally takes place on the Friday of the second week, lasting from 10:00 a.m. until 2:00 p.m. An all-day adults' parade is held the following day. Each parade is filled with dance troupes, floats, music, and exotic costumes that reflect the year's chosen theme. The famed Mocko Jumbi Dancers, wearing elaborate costumes with headdresses, perform traditional African dances on 17-foot-high stilts. They are thought to represent spirits hovering over the street dancers.

Carnival is cultural rather than religious. It boosts both local pride and the local economy, and it is financed by a government grant. The holiday's popularity waned during the first half of the twentieth century, but was revived in 1952 by a radio personality known as Mango Jones, who later served as delegate to Congress. American novelist Herman Wouk wrote of Carnival in his famed *Don't Stop The Carnival:* "Africa was marching down the main street of this little harbor town today; Africa in undimmed black vitality, surging up out of centuries of island displacement, island slavery, island isolation, island ignorance; Africa, unquenchable in its burning love of life."

Other Virgin Islands holidays are related to hurricane season. The fourth Monday in July is Hurricane Supplication Day, and it is marked by special church services in which celebrants pray for safety from the storms that at times have ravaged the islands. The holiday is thought to have originated from fifth-century English rogation ceremonies, which followed a series of storms, although Rogation Day is also a Christian feast day preceding Ascension Day. The word rogation, coming from the Latin *rogare*, means to beg or supplicate. Islanders mark the end of hurricane season in October with Hurricane Thanksgiving Day, featuring church services in which participants express thanks for having been spared during the season.

Christmas and Easter are important holidays in the Virgin Islands, as Christianity is predominant among the islands' many religious traditions. Other holidays include New Year's Day, January 1; Three Kings' Day, January 6; and U.S. Independence Day, July 4. Holidays with variable dates include Martin Luther King Day in January; Presidents' Day in February; Memorial Day in May; Labor Day in September; Columbus Day in October; and Veterans' Day in November. Residents celebrate Virgin Islands Thanksgiving in October and the U.S. Thanksgiving in November.

Several holidays honor Virgin Islands' history. During the 1990s, islanders observed Emancipation Day on July 3 to mark the date Virgin Islands slaves gained freedom from Danish colonists on St. John. The festivities, held at Coral Bay, St. John, included storytelling, games, and music, along with sales of native foods and plants. Participants characterized the celebration as a cultural and spiritual gathering. They expressed a desire to emphasize local culture and history rather than entertainment. March 31, Transfer Day, marks the day ownership of the Virgin Islands passed from Denmark to the United States. June 16 is Organic Act Day, recognizing the islands' constitution. Liberty Day, which celebrates freedom of the press, is on November 1.

LANGUAGE

The majority of Virgin Islanders speak English, although the 1990 census reported that more than 25 percent spoke a language other than English in the home. Spanish and Creole are widely spoken. Linguistic field workers also reported that islanders speak several varieties of Dutch, English, and French Creole.

FAMILY AND COMMUNITY DYNAMICS

The 1990 census found that family size in the Virgin Islands was 3.1 persons, typical of family size in the United States. The total number of households was 32,020; 23,012 of these were classified as "families." Of these, 13,197 were reported to be families in which both husband and wife were present. Family structure tends to be traditional, with men considered heads of families and women in charge of child care. Although an increasing number of women engage in paid employment, they tend to work part-time or in cottage industries, allowing them to work at home and take care of small children. Virgin Islanders have worked hard to overcome social problems related to the rapid rise in tourism and have retained pride in their distinctive history and culture. They have struggled to gain more political autonomy, but have expressed their desire for the islands to remain part of the United States.

EDUCATION

The Virgin Islands ranks among the world's most literate regions, with a 98 percent adult literacy rate, although this was not always the case. The 1990 U.S. Census reported that of 55,639 resident Virgin Islanders over the age of 25, 14,021, or 25 percent, held a high school diploma. Fifteen percent, or 8,421, held a bachelor's degree or higher. In 1995, enrollment in public elementary and secondary schools numbered almost 40,000. School attendance is compulsory between the ages of five and 16; the government provides free public education for these students. The Department of Education also provides free lunches for all public school students. In conjunction with New York University, schools of the islands conduct a teacher training program.

The College of the Virgin Islands was founded in 1962 as a junior college. In 1972 it became the University of the Virgin Islands. Located on St. Thomas, it is the only university in the islands. In 1996 the university reported enrollment of 2,949. Seventy-six percent of the students were female. This prompted discussion among islanders over why young Virgin Islands men were not seeking higher education. Jessica Dinisio reported in *Uvision* that many Virgin Islanders attributed the low number of enrollments among young men to cultural and societal pressures. Young men were expected to enter the work force and earn money. Others felt that the numbers represented a growing desire among young women to attain economic independence.

The university offers programs in agriculture and natural resources and in home economics, among other subjects. The Cooperative Extension Service produces publications and coordinates television and radio programs. Late 1990s' publications included *Agriculture and Food Fair Bulletins; Eco-Educational Tours; Protecting Your Water Quality Through a Home and Farm Assessment; Recipes for a Non-Toxic Household; Traditional Medicinal Plants of St. Croix, St. Thomas, and St. John; Growing Mangoes; A Bibliographic Guide to Agriculture in the U.S. Virgin Islands, including Danish West Indies: Origins to 1987.*

THE ROLE OF WOMEN

As in other parts of the world, gender roles in the Virgin Islands are changing as more women join the labor force. As Hilde Kahne and Janet Z. Giele have reported in *Women's Work and Women's Lives: The Continuing Struggle Worldwide,* important socioeconomic transformations have taken place in Latin America and the Caribbean since the post-World War II period, resulting in the emergence of new roles for women. Women have benefited from lower fertility rates, smaller family sizes, increased educational opportunities, and greater participation in the labor force. However, despite some gains, women in the Virgin Islands have also suffered from poverty and inequities in income. Islanders have continued to view women's earnings from work outside the home largely as supplemental income. They also continued to regard uncompensated work such as child care, cooking, and cleaning as women's work.

The rapid shift from rural to urban communities between 1940 and 1970 in the Virgin Islands and elsewhere in the Caribbean slowed somewhat in the 1970s, although by then major social and economic changes had occurred. Domestic service remains the largest occupation for Caribbean women generally, although street peddling, known as "higgling," has become more prominent in the eastern Caribbean. Higglers travel among the islands to sell fresh produce or to market handcrafted items. Women with small children frequently become employed doing piecework at home, which allows them to remain with their children, though it also enables employers to exploit women. Whatever their employment, women in the Virgin Islands are contributing increasingly to the economies of their households.

RELIGION

The Virgin Islands are primarily Christian and Protestant, but have many religious denominations, a legacy of having received many waves of immigrants from Denmark, Holland, England, France, and Africa. The principal Christian denominations are Anglican, Christian Mission, Wesleyan, Lutheran, Baptist, Methodist, Reformed and Dutch Reformed, Roman Catholic, Salvation Army, Seventh Day Adventist, Church of God in Christ, and the Apostolic Faith. Danish Lutheranism has a particularly large number of adherents. Chapels and churches representing many different faiths exist side by side in the islands. When Puerto Ricans began to come to the Virgin Islands to seek employment, they brought Catholicism with them. Moravian missionaries arrived during the colonial period of the seventeenth century, and their presence is still felt. Many Virgin Islanders are faithful readers of the Bible. Attending church services on Sundays is very much a part of island life. Gospel singing is a much-loved activity that expresses the spiritual dimensions of islanders. There is a sizable Jewish population in the islands as well.

EMPLOYMENT AND ECONOMIC TRADITIONS

Although their economy is historically agricultural, the Virgin Islands lack sufficient rain and high-quality soil to support large-scale agricultural production. On St. Croix and St. John, sorghum, fruit, and vegetables are produced, and leaves from the bay tree forest on St. John are used for making bay rum. Cattle raised on St. Croix are exported to Puerto Rico. These are small-scale operations, however. Agriculture has not supported the Virgin Islands economically since the nineteenth century. Tourism is the mainstay of the economy, with 30 percent of Virgin Islanders working in the tourist trade. The territory's largest single employer, though, is Hess Oil Virgin Islands, the biggest oil refinery in the world, located on St. Croix. Otherwise, manufacturing is on a small scale, and most products are exported to the continental United States. Exports include petroleum products, alumina, chemicals, clocks and watch parts, meat, and ethanol. Fishing in island waters is for sporting rather than commercial endeavor. The median income for Virgin Islanders in 1990 was $24,036. Virgin Islanders who come to the U.S. mainland frequently do so for the purposes of furthering their education or to seek employment in fields not found on the Virgin Islands.

POLITICS AND GOVERNMENT

The United States granted residents of the Virgin Islands citizenship in 1927. From 1917 to 1931, the islands were under the authority of the U.S. Navy. In 1931 the U.S. Department of the Interior took administrative responsibility, with the president appointing a governor. A legislature of 15 locally elected members from the three main islands has been in place since 1954. Members are elected for two-year terms. Virgin Islanders won the right to vote for their own governor in 1970, and the governor is elected for a four-year term. Since 1972 islanders have elected one delegate to the U.S. Congress. The delegate is allowed to vote on House of Representatives committees and speak in debate on the floor of the House, but is not allowed to vote on bills. Virgin Islanders may not vote in U.S. presidential elections.

Several constitutional conventions have dealt with Virgin Islands voting and legislative rights. The Organic Act of 1936, which established constitutional government for the islands, granted universal suffrage. Also in 1936, the first political party on the islands was organized. Since the purchase of the Virgin Islands by the United States, islanders have continued to agitate for more home rule. While expressing their opposition to any form of annexation by a U.S. state, islanders have also made it clear they are opposed to independence from the United States. The Virgin Islands remain an unincorporated territory rather than an autonomous territory.

Virgin Islanders tend to view themselves as islanders. Those who come to the mainland United States often think of their move as temporary. Students in particular anticipate returning to the Virgin Islands once they have completed their education, even though many express concern that employment prospects in the islands are limited.

INDIVIDUAL AND GROUP CONTRIBUTIONS

Virgin Islander artists as a whole are identified with Caribbean arts, literature, and music. Notable contributors are performing artists living in the Virgin Islands rather than on the mainland and are known locally for folk music, calypso, jazz, and blues. Studies of Caribbean literature do not concentrate on Virgin Islanders, instead offering critical readings of work by such well-known writers as Derek Walcott of St. Lucia; V.S. Naipaul of Trinidad; and Jamaica Kincaid of Antigua. Anthologies such as *The Routledge Reader in*

Caribbean Literature (1996, edited by Alison Donnell and Sarah Lawson Welsh) and the *Oxford Book of Caribbean Short Stories* (1999, edited by Stewart Brown and John Wickham) have not included Virgin Islanders among their collections. The Virgin Islands Humanities Council has published short, amateur collections of Virgin Island poetry, but Virgin Islands writers have not yet drawn critical attention to their work.

Tim Duncan (1976–) made a strong impression in his first two years of play for the San Antonio Spurs of the National Basketball Association. Only a year after graduating from Wake Forest University, Duncan won Rookie of the Year honors in 1998. In 1999 he helped lead his team to the NBA championship en route to receiving the Finals Most Valuable Player award. Other significant professional honors include: unanimous Rookie of the Year (1998), All-NBA First Team (1999), All-NBA Defensive First Team (1999).

Edward Wilmot Blyden (1832-1912) was one of the leading figures in the formation of the Pan-Africanism movement. Blyden was born in the Virgin Islands and later moved to Liberia. He served as a government official in various roles and his writings helped to form the basis of the movement.

Almeric Christian (1919–) is a pioneering lawyer and judge. Christian, born in the Virgin Islands, moved to the United States and attended Columbia University and later its law school. Upon passing the bar, Christian established a successful private practice. Eventually he was appointed a circuit court judge for the Third Circuit, and then to chief judge.

Kelsey Grammer (1945–) is one of the most popular television stars in the United States. Grammer, born in the Virgin Islands, made his television breakthrough as Dr. Frasier Crane on the hit show *Cheers*. Grammer received an Emmy Award nomination for his work on *Cheers*, and when the show ended its successful run in 1993, Grammer and NBC collaborated on the show *Frasier*. The show was a continuation of Grammer's *Cheers* character and won him several Emmy Awards.

Camille Pissaro (1830-1903) was one of the leading Impressionist painters of the late nineteenth century. Pissaro was born in the Virgin Islands, traveling to Paris for schooling. His parents eventually conceded to let him pursue his interest in painting, and in 1855 he returned to France. In the 1860's Pissaro began to paint in the Impressionist style, participating in all of the Impressionist shows between 1874 and 1886. Pissaro achieved high critical acclaim by the 1890s.

Roy Innis (1934–) is one of the foremost civil rights leaders in the United States. Innis, born on St. Croix, came to the United States and was educated at the City College of New York. In the early 1960s Innis became involved in the Civil Rights Movement and joined the Congress of Racial Equality (CORE). In 1968 he became the head of the group.

MEDIA

St. Thomas This Week (Including St. John).
Free guide published weekly by the U.S. Virgin Islands Department of Tourism.

ORGANIZATIONS AND ASSOCIATIONS

Association of Virgin Islanders Abroad (AVIA).
Shomari A. Moorehead developed the association in 1999 to provide nonresident Virgin Islanders with a way to network with one another.

Online: www.shomari.com/avia/about_avia.html.

U.S. Virgin Islands Department of Tourism.
Government office to distribute information about the Virgin Islands to tourists.

Address: 444 North Capitol Street, N.W.,
Washington, D.C. 20001.
Telephone: (202) 624-3590.

SOURCES FOR ADDITIONAL STUDY

Boyer, William W. *America's Virgin Islands: A History of Human Rights and Wrongs.* Durham, NC: Carolina Academic Press, 1983.

Dinisio, Jessica. "More Women Seek High Education than Males Including at UVI." *Uvision.* Vol. 2, no. 5. April 30, 1996.

Dookhan, Isaac. A *History of the Virgin Islands of the U.S.* Second edition. Kingston, Jamaica: Canoe Press, 1994.

Tyson, George F. and Arnold R. Highfield, eds. *The Kamina Folk: Slavery and Slave Life in the Danish West Indies.* U.S. Virgin Islands: Virgin Islands Humanities Council, 1994.

Welsh American
culture still blooms in
singing festivals,
which stem from the
traditional Welsh
eisteddfod, which
calls for Welsh
writing and oratory.

WELSH
AMERICANS

by
Evan Heimlich

OVERVIEW

Wales, the western, mountainous peninsula of the island of Great Britain, occupies an area just slightly larger than the state of New Jersey. Wales is shaped roughly like a rectangle with a section taken out of the west side—Cardigan Bay, facing Ireland across the Irish Channel. North of Cardigan Bay the island of Anglesey and the Lleyn peninsula jut westward; to the south, also stretching west, lies the larger Pembroke peninsula. Bounded by water on three sides, Wales itself constitutes a peninsula with its eastern border formed by England. Much of the terrain is mountainous. In the northwest is the rugged Snowdonia range, named for Mount Snowdon, at 3,560 feet the highest in Britain south of Scotland. Lesser mountains and hills run south through central Wales into Pembroke and the famous coalfields of South Wales.

Principal cities and towns lie mostly along the coast. Through these busy seaports come the ore and slate from Welsh mines and quarries. Notable seaports spread from Cardiff, Wales' capital and largest city, which lies on the Bristol Channel in the south, to Caernarfon ("car-nar-vin") and Bangor opposite Anglesey in the north. The Welsh climate is temperate and wet.

The country was named after its inhabitants. The Welsh trace their ancestry to two distinct groups of people—the Iberians who arrived from southwestern Europe in Neolithic times and the

Celtic tribes who arrived on the island in the late Bronze Age. Fierce fighters, they resisted the Anglo-Saxon invaders, who could not understand their language and called them *wealas* (strangers). They called themselves *Cmry* (fellow countrymen); and, although populations and cultures overlap between Wales and England, Wales and its culture remain distinct. Wales occupies about 8,000 square miles and is the size of a small New England state. Since virtually all farms are no more than 50 miles from the shore, Wales has maintained its own connections with the outside world.

HISTORY

With the collapse of Roman power in the 400s, Germanic tribes from Northern Europe began settling in southeastern Britain. Most numerous were the Angles and the Saxons, related peoples who became the English. The Celts resisted this long influx of alien settlers but were gradually pushed west. By about 800, they occupied only Britain's remotest reaches where their descendants live today: the Highland Scots, the Cornish of the southwest coast, and the Welsh. The Irish are also Celtic.

Over the coming centuries, the Welsh, isolated from other Celts, developed their own distinctive culture. However, their identity would always be shaped by the presence of their powerful English neighbors. Wales became a western refuge from the invasion and conquest by hostile tribes from Europe, as well as for puritanical dissenters against English culture. Not only did this refuge lie farther west than most conquerors could effectively extend, its geography made it inaccessible. Later, Wales became a site from which England extracted resources and prefigured the position that colonial America assumed.

The Roman empire took Wales along with Britain in the first century A.D.: "Wales, however, was always a frontier area of the Empire, and remained scarcely changed throughout the Roman period of occupation," except by the introduction of Christianity (George Edward Hartman, *Americans from Wales* [New York: Farrar, Straus and Giroux, 1978], pp. 27-28; cited hereafter as Hartman). In the fifth century A.D., early Welsh Christianity blossomed with the monasteries of St. David. Historically, in literature and legend, Germanic invaders took what is now England, isolating the Celts in the mountainous area of Wales.

In the late eighth century, Anglo-Saxon invaders—who were not yet Christians—built Offa's Dike (named after Offa, the Anglo-Saxon king of Mercia), a physical, earthen barrier to keep Welsh people from raiding eastward. This boundary still marks the separation between Wales and England.

In 1066, William the Conqueror defeated the English and, with his French-born Norman nobles and knights, took power in England and determined to subdue the unruly Welsh. Over the next century, the Normans built a series of wooden forts throughout Wales from which Norman lords held control over surrounding lands. In the late 1100s, they replaced the wooden strongholds with massive, turreted stone castles. From about 1140-1240, Welsh princes such as Rhys ap Gruffydd and Llewellyn the Great rose up against the Normans, capturing some castles and briefly regaining power in the land. After Llewellyn's death in 1240, Welsh unity weakened. The English King Edward I conquered Wales in the late 1200s, building another series of massive castles to reinforce his rule. The Welsh successfully resisted the invaders for hundreds of years, until in 1282, they were brought under the political jurisdiction of England under Edward I. Under Edward and his successors, Welsh revolts continued against the English. Most important was the rebellion of Owain Glyndwr in the 1400s. Despite his failure, Glyndwr strikes a heroic chord in Welsh memory as the last great leader to envision and fight for an independent Wales.

During the 1400s, the Welsh increasingly became involved in English affairs, taking part in the War of the Roses. In 1485, a young Welsh nobleman named Henry Tudor won the Battle of Bosworth Field against King Richard III, thus securing his claim to the English throne. The Welsh rejoiced at having a Welshman as king of England. King Henry VII, as he was called, restored many of the rights that the Welsh had lost under English occupation. Under his son, Henry VIII, Wales and England became unified under one political system. Elizabeth I, daughter of Henry VIII, was the last Tudor monarch. When she died in 1603, English language, law, and customs had become entrenched in Welsh life. Since that time, the history of the Welsh people has been closely tied to that of their English neighbors. Wales has become a highly industrialized mining region of Great Britain. About four of five Welsh people have adopted English as their language. Yet the Welsh remain a people apart, proud, independent-minded, and always conscious of their own national character.

SIGNIFICANT IMMIGRATION WAVES

As explorers, migrants, settlers, and missionaries, the Welsh people—themselves descended from Europe's seekers of western refuge—led early waves of westering Europeans to America. Myths of their ancestors' independence prompted them, as did Anglican labeling of their Christianity as Dissent. Generally, Welsh people came to the United States within waves of British migrants. Many valued religious freedom, especially Welsh emigrants whose Christianity did not conform to the Church of England. Furthermore, explorations, rich lands, and higher-paying industrial jobs lured them from Wales to America. Some important early British settlers in North America—including Pilgrims and founders of the United States—were Welsh or Anglo-Welsh, and not English at all.

Popular belief in pre-Columbian contact between Wales and the New World supported Welsh migration to America. According to this popular belief, centuries before Columbus, Welsh migrants had crossed the Atlantic, reached North America, and mixed with Indians. Thus some Welsh missionaries sought to reunite with and Christianize their long-lost cousins.

In Wales, many published reports circulated from those who claimed to have found Welsh Indians in North America. Though no one ever proved the legends, they nevertheless helped propel Welsh immigration. They also motivated important exploration. For example, in 1792 (seven years before the Louis and Clarke Expedition), John Evans, a Welsh Methodist, searched for Welsh Indians in the northern reaches of the Missouri River (David Williams, *Cymru Ac America: Wales and America* [Cardiff: University of Wales Press, 1976], pp. 7, 19); cited hereafter as Williams). Contemporary artifacts commemorate the legend. According to a plaque to Madoc ap Owain Gwynedd on the wall of the Fine Arts Center of the South in Mobile, Alabama, visitors can see where Prince Madoc, the Welsh explorer of America, is believed to have arrived with three ships. Also, the plaque of the Daughters of the American Revolution, which is located on the public strand of Mobile Bay, reads: "In memory of Prince Madoc, a Welsh explorer, who landed on the shores of Mobile Bay in 1170 and left behind, with the Indians, the Welsh language." (David Greenslade, *Welsh Fever: Welsh Activities in the United States and Canada Today* [Cowbridge, Wales: D. Brown and Sons, 1986], p. 17; cited hereafter as Greenslade). Although the various claims of the existence of Welsh-speaking Indians have not been proved, the finding (after Columbus) of Americans descended from Welsh and Indian ancestors offers some corroboration. However, even discounting the legendary Madoc, the Welsh came to the American continent early, relative to other Europeans.

After Britain's Religious Toleration Act of 1689, Welsh emigration subsided until agricultural economics motivated a late eighteenth-century wave. Welsh farmers had reaped poor harvests for years when they heard of America's expansion into the fertile Ohio valley; meanwhile in Wales, acts of British parliament enclosed commons and open moorlands. Concerned by the streams of emigrants leaving Wales, the British government passed measures to prevent skilled workmen from emigrating.

As industrialists built America's factories, skilled industrial workers migrated in large numbers from Wales to America beginning in the 1830s. Near the end of that century, skilled industrial workers mostly took over from their farming countrymen as newly arrived Welsh Americans. These workers, many of whom developed their industries, came here mostly from southern Wales, Britain's main source of coal and iron.

Knowledgeable Welsh industrialists came here to fill positions in ironworks not only as workers, but also as industrial pioneers and leaders. After David Thomas perfected techniques of burning anthracite coal to smelt iron ore, an American coal company in 1839 brought him from Wales to the great anthracite coalfields in Pennsylvania, where he developed America's anthracite iron industry. The new industry drew the Welsh by the thousands. By the beginning of the twentieth century, Scranton recorded nearly 5,000 natives of Wales, and more than 2,000 in Wilkes-Barre, who came to mine coal for David Thomas' process (Williams, p. 81). From the time of the Civil War to the end of World War I, Scranton claimed the largest concentration of Welsh people in the world outside Wales and England (William D. Jones, Wales in America: Scranton and the Welsh 1860-1920 [Scranton: University of Scranton Press, 1993], p. xvi; cited hereafter as Jones).

Another segment of Welsh American migration followed the tinplate-production industry. Glamorganshire, in southern Wales, dominated the world market as the main producer of tinplate until America, a principal market for Welsh tinplate, captured for itself the role of tinplate producer. To protect its own young tinplate industry, America's 1890 McKinley Tariff raised prices of imported tinplate, throwing the Welsh industry into a depression and effectively drawing hundreds of workers from Wales to its new tinplate works (Williams, p. 85). The Welsh American tinplate producers centered in Philadelphia and Ohio, monopolized their industrial science, and then dominated the field for several generations. Many Welsh immigrants developed into important figures of the industry business, becoming executives and capitalists in their own right (Hartman, p. 86). In addition to their major roles in the development of American coal, iron, and steel industries, Welsh Americans in the mid-nineteenth century also built the American slate industry. Immigrants from North Wales prospected for and dug America's early slate quarries along the borders between Pennsylvania and Maryland, and between New York and Vermont.

Robert D. Thomas, a Congregational minister, authored what became for the Welsh of the post-Civil War period a convenient and detailed guide-book in their own language concerning the available land opportunities in America. After its publication in 1872, *Hanes Cymry America* ("History of the Welsh in America") became popular in Wales and probably figured in encouraging further emigration.

Immigration of Welsh farmers in the closing decades of the nineteenth century swelled America's Welsh communities into the tens of thousands, until about 1890, when the immigration of Welsh farmers to America ebbed. Australia and other destinations began to draw their share of emigrant farmers from Wales who were forced from their farms because they opposed the Anglican Church in Wales. Their emigration helped to improve the harvests by balancing the Welsh population level (Hartman, pp. 75-76).

SETTLEMENT PATTERNS

At first, Welsh Americans settled in or near British colonies, among fellow Welsh Americans who shared their religious denomination, such as Baptist, Methodist, or Quaker. Many tried to found a new homeland for their people. Following the missionaries and farmers were the skilled industrial workers and artisans. Baptists led the way. John Miles, founder of the first Baptist church in Wales in 1649, suffered religious persecution as a Baptist, both before and after he led Welsh Baptists to Massachusetts in 1662. Though at first the colony refused to tolerate them, eventually Massachusetts granted them land, where they established the town of Swansea and the First Baptist Church, which stands today as the oldest Welsh church in America.

Two decades after Baptists first arrived, Welsh members of the Society of Friends, or Quakers, founded the second and much larger Welsh group settlement in America. Quakers suffered the worst religious persecutions in Wales, because they professed to value their "inner light" over Church and Bible. Many people of all classes joined the Quakers in England, among them William Penn, who supposedly had a Welsh grandfather. In 1681, Penn obtained a vast tract of territory south of New York. "He [said] that he originally intended to call it New Wales, as it was `a pretty hilly country,' but the authorities in London did not like the name, and it was called Pennsylvania" (Williams, pp. 24-25). Penn led the Quakers there, including many from Wales, and Pennsylvania became the heart of Welsh settlement.

Preacher Morgan John Rhys founded a new homeland for Welsh Americans in western Pennsylvania where they could live together and preserve their language and customs. Although Beulah, the center of the settlement that he established, has not survived, Ebensburg, its second township, has lasted. Meanwhile, Philadelphia, with its large Welsh population, soon flourished and became one of the most important cities in America.

"There was a man that came around every morning and every afternoon, with a stainless steel cart, sort of like a Good Humor cart. And the man was dressed in white and he had warm milk for the kids. And they would blow a whistle or ring a bell, and all the kids would line up, and he had small little paper cups and every kid got a little warm milk."

Donald Roberts, 1925, cited in *Ellis Island: An Illustrated History of the Immigrant Experience*, edited by Ivan Chermayeff et al. (New York: Macmillan, 1991).

American regions from New York to Wisconsin and Minnesota to Oregon offered Welsh immigrants work in their traditional occupations and drew concentrations of descendants of Welsh shepherds and dairy farmers. After the Civil War, in Wisconsin, Iowa, Minnesota, Missouri, and Kansas, men entered trades and Welsh American young women found service work in private homes. Some Welsh American fruit growers became pioneers of orchard industries in the Pacific Northwest. Copper workers came to Baltimore, silver miners to Colorado, and prospectors for gold, after 1849, rushed to California. Slate quarrymen came to New England and the Delaware Valley. Because so many Welsh immigrants were coal miners, they came in the greatest concentrations to the coal regions of Pottsville, Wilkes-Barre, and Scranton. Steelworkers came to Pittsburgh, Cleveland and Chicago. (Islyn Thomas, *Our Welsh Heritage* [New York: St. David's Society of New York, 1972], p. 27). Scranton led Welsh American communities in maintaining a Welsh American identity. On the 1990 census, two million Americans reported their ancestry as Welsh.

SETTLEMENT PATTERNS

Welsh Americans, like other British Americans, spread throughout the United States. Americans reporting Welsh ancestry on the 1990 census, in fact, divide evenly between the Northeast, Midwest, South, and West—more evenly than any other European-American group. Early Welsh American Baptists, who first settled in Massachusetts, branched out to other places. They moved to Pennsylvania because it was especially tolerant of their religion. Others bought land in what is now the state of Delaware, which they called the Welsh Tract.

Some Welsh setters sought not only toleration, but further isolation, to ensure that their children did not lose their national characteristics. To escape Anglo-Americanization, Ezickiel Hughes, of Paddy's Run, Ohio, a sponsor of Welsh immigrants, "decided to place his colony in the open waste lands of Patagonia," at the remote, under-colonized southern tip of South America, where it still exists (Williams, p. 73). Other intramigration followed economic opportunities, such as the move of the industrial town of Lackawanna from Pennsylvania to western New York. Largely accepted by dominant Anglo-Americans, Welsh Americans frequently dominated their industries; non-Welsh coal miners often complained that Welsh American supervisors favored their brethren. Irish American workers suffered categorically at the hands of some Welsh American mining bosses (Jones, p. 37).

ACCULTURATION AND ASSIMILATION

In America, as in Wales, members of this ethnic group forged their identity through their churches, language, and education. Traditional Welsh American ethnic identity, which depended also on the domination of particular fields of employment, has since flourished in singing festivals.

Especially since nineteenth-century modernization linked the Welsh to England and Welsh Americans to America, the two minority groups have acculturated to the respective cultural dominance of England and America. When England industrialized Wales, extracting its abundant coal and iron ore, it divided the inhabitants into a rural group in which Welsh was spoken and an urban group in which English was the primary language.

Late in the nineteenth century, battles over Welsh culture moved into the field of education as England prohibited Welsh public schools from teaching in Welsh. The Welsh maintained their culture, though, through their traditional Sunday schools and through nationalism. Although the Welsh fought and won from the British the legal right to use their own language in courts and schools, the use of the Welsh language declined.

Welsh traditional beliefs, attitudes, and customs stem largely from the strength and nonconformity of Welsh churches. In seventeenth- and eighteenth-century Wales, religious nonconformity preserved Welsh identity when it "arrested the inroads of Anglicanization and the complete absorption of Wales into England" (Hartman, p. 26). Although this resurgent nationalism was crucial for Welsh identity, it was less important to Welsh American identity. At Sunday Schools, Welsh churches campaigned to perpetuate the Welsh language by teaching men, women, girls, and boys to read their Bible in Welsh. Because of the Sunday School movement, many Welsh Americans became literate in their own language. Welsh culture has struggled not only against the English church, but also against the English language. The Welsh flag itself displays a red dragon who legendarily champions the ancient Welsh language. The dragon, called Y Ddraig Goch, which is said to keep the faith that "three things, yea four, will endure forever, the earth, the sea, the sky and the speech of the Cymry," leads the Welsh people "in an unending war for the perpetuation of [their] language" (Thomas, p. 49).

Welsh American communities waxed and waned with their churches. At first, as new territories opened in North America, Welsh missionary work expanded to fill the opportunities to convert new souls. In eighteenth-century Pennsylvania, Quaker, Baptist, and Presbyterian churches anchored communities in which Sunday Schools helped shaped Welsh American identities; nevertheless, these early Welsh Americans eventually became Americanized in their habits and English in their speech. During the nineteenth century, however, an increasingly Welsh-minded clergy led Welsh American congregations. Their work, coupled with frequent exchanges of visitors from Wales and between Welsh American communities, drew together a Welsh American identity which better resisted acculturation.

Toward the turn of the twentieth century, in Scranton and elsewhere, Welsh Americans acculturated. More immigrants joined occupations outside their traditional industries. The contexts of their ethnic identities also changed as Eastern European and Italian immigrants entered the coal mines: to the newcomers, Welsh immigrants and Welsh Americans seemed more similar than ever to Anglo, Yankee, or established "mainstream" Americans. Churches, organizations, and festivals sustain Welsh American culture. America's Welshness manifests itself in placenames such as Bangor, Bryn Mawr, and Haverford. Welsh American places include not only Scranton, but small towns such as Emporia, Kansas, and Cambria, Wisconsin, population 600, "a stronghold of Welshness" near Madison, which bears Welsh street signs (Greenslade, pp. 68, 87).

SONGS

Welsh American culture still blooms in singing festivals, which stem from the traditional Welsh *eisteddfod,* which calls for Welsh writing and oratory. The *eisteddfod* arose in 1568, when Queen Elizabeth commissioned a qualifying competition to license some of "the multitude of persons calling themselves minstrels, rhymers and bards" (Thomas, p. 24). At the end of the eighteenth century, Romanticism revived Welsh cultural promotion and the *eisteddfod.* Today, the United States usually sends the largest delegation of "Welshmen in Exile" to the annual *eisteddfod* in Wales. The "exiles" march in ranks by country to the singing of the Welsh nostalgic hymn, "*Unwaith Eto Yng Nghymru Annwyl*" ("Once Again in Dear Wales"). The revived *eisteddfod,* popular in Wales since 1819, features reconstructed Druidic rites, in "an atmosphere of mysticism always associated with the Celtic spirit" (Hartman, p. 143).

Since the 1830s, Welsh Americans also compete in their own *eisteddfod.* Especially in Pennsylvania, Ohio, Iowa, and Utah, strong traditions of *eisteddfod* have inspired expert choirs in their performances of Bach, Handel, Mendelssohn, and other classical composers of sacred music. Utica sponsors the oldest continuously *eisteddfod* in the United States. However, because few Welsh Americans speak or write in Welsh, Welsh Americans focused on singing and mostly replaced the *eisteddfod* with the *Gymanfa Ganu* or Welsh singing festival. The *Gymanfa Ganu* started in Wales in 1859 and spread through America by the 1920s. Unlike in Wales, where each church denomination sponsors its own *Gymanfa Ganu,* Welsh American ones include all denominations. The National Gymanfa Ganu Association of the United States and Canada, founded by Welsh Americans, represents the only successful attempt at forming an all-over national association of Welsh Americans. It originated at Niagara Falls with a gathering of 2,400

Welsh Americans and meets at key American centers each year on Labor Day.

CUISINE

Welsh cuisine uses the basic ingredients of dairy products, eggs, seafood, lamb or beef, and simple vegetables such as potatoes, carrots, and leeks. A national symbol, leeks are waved at rugby football matches by Welsh fans. The leek is Wales' most popular vegetable, being featured in soups and stews. One favorite dish, Anglesey Eggs, includes leeks, cheese, and potatoes. Welsh Rabbit (often called Rarebit by the English) combines eggs, cheese, milk, Worcestershire sauce, and beer. The rich melted mixture is poured over toast.

CLOTHING

The Welsh dress much as Europeans and North Americans do, though perhaps a bit more formally than the latter. Among young people, however, jeans, a t-shirt, and running shoes are as common in Wales as everywhere else. Traditional costumes, commonly worn at events such as an *eisteddfod,* feature colorful stripes and checks, with a wide-brimmed hat for women that looks like a witch's hat with the top half of the cone removed.

LANGUAGE

Cymraeg, the Welsh language, has long been a separate branch of Indo-European languages. It descends from Celtic and relates closely to Breton, the language of Brittany, to Highland Scots Gaelic, and to Irish Gaelic. The language looks difficult to an outsider; it also sounds strange with lilting, musical tones in which one word seems to slur into the next. And in a sense, it may—the first letter of a word may change depending on the word before it. This is called *treiglo*, and it achieves a smoothness treasured by the Welsh ear. Welsh also contains elusive sounds such as "ll" (in the name Llewellyn or Lloyd, for example), which is pronounced almost like a combination of "f," "th," and "ch," though not quite. Welsh words nearly always accent their second-to-last syllable.

The Welsh language's age and its supposed migratory path across Eurasia prompts some linguists to make extraordinary claims about etymologies of certain words. For example, the ancient name for the Caucasian chain of mountains forming an immense barrier between Europe on the north and Asia to the south, may come from the same words as the Welsh "Cau," which means "to shut up, to fence in, to encompass", and "Cas," which translates as "separated" or "insulated" (Jenkins, p. 55).

The Welsh alphabet uses the letters "a, b, c, ch, d, dd, e, f, ff, g, ng, h, I, l, ll, m, n, o, p, ph, rh, r, s, t, th, u, w," and "y" to make such words such as: *Cymru* (Wales); *Cymry* (Welsh people); *Ninnau* (We Welsh), the title of a Welsh American periodical; *noson lawen* (an informal evening of song, recitation, and other entertainment); *te bach* (light refreshments, usually tea and Welsh cakes); *cymdeithas* (society); *cwrs Cymraeg* (Welsh language course); and *bore da, syr* (good morning, sir). Welsh spelling lacks silent letters; in different words, too, the same letter nearly always has the same sound. The Welsh language, which lacks the letter "k," always sounds "c" as the English "k": thus "Celt" is pronounced "Kelt."

Celt, which first referred to "a wild or covert," and the people who lived there, became a loose term to refer to a grouping of disparate peoples living in certain areas of Great Britain. Romans called *Cymry* who lived on open plains Gauls, which the *Cymry* pronounced as Gaels, and the Saxons, in turn, as *Waels* or Wales, home of the *Waelsh* or Welsh (Jenkins, pp. 38, 40, 97).

Welsh surnames have their own story. When English law in 1536 required Welshmen to take surnames, many simply added an "s" to their father's first name. Common first names such as William or Evan (the Welsh equivalent of John) begot the common surnames of Williams and Evans.

The Welsh pride their language on its musical-ity and expressiveness, and cherish traditional oratorical skills of poets and priests. In literature, the canonization of poet Dylan Thomas is a matter of Welsh American pride. Thomas wrote and recited in Wales and America English-language poems that drew from Welsh culture and preaching styles. The art of oral storytelling which flourished in medieval Wales left as its written legacy the *Mabinogion* (translated into English by Jeffrey Gantz). Preachers of sermons mastered versions of a chanting style "marked by a great variety of intonations" called *hwyl* and each preacher characteristically followed "his own peculiar melody" through a major key to climax in a minor key (Hartman, p. 105). With their *hwyl*, Welsh preachers led congregations in fervent evangelical revivals.

RELIGION

In pre-Christian Wales, the Druids (a special class of leaders) dominated a religion in which Celts worshipped a number of deities according to rites associated with nature (Hartman, p. 27). However, Welsh and Welsh American identities have centered on religious traditions of strictness, evangelicalism, and reform. From the breach between Welsh and Anglican churches stemmed modern Welsh nationalism itself. Also, Mormonism and scattered versions of pre-Christian paganism figure in Welsh American religion.

The patron saint of the Welsh, St. David (born circa 520) "organized a system of monastic regulations for his abbey ... which became the awe of Christian Britain because of its severity of discipline" (Hartman, p. 28). St. David's Day commemorates his death. On the first day of March, Episcopalian churches such as St. David's Episcopalian Church in San Diego (the cornerstone of which comes from St. David's Cathedral in Wales) hold memorial services (Greenslade, p. 33). For all denominations of Welsh Americans, the day represents an occasion for the annual rallying of Welsh consciousness.

As Welsh churches pitted their religious fundamentalism against the English establishment, their progressivism foreshadowed contributions of Welsh Americans to American puritanism and progress. Around the year 1700, when English rule still dominated Welsh religion, the reform movement came from within the church and received its great stimulus from the pietistic evangelism introduced by John Wesley and George Whitfield. Soon these men, and Welshmen of similar beliefs, were emphasizing the necessity of abundant preaching within the church and the need for experiencing a rebirth in religious conviction as a necessary part in the salvation of the individual.

After this evangelical Methodism spread through Wales, Welsh Methodists split from Wesley and from English Methodists and followed Whitfield into Calvinism, calling themselves Calvinist Methodists. Welsh Methodists, furthermore, withdrew from the Anglican Church and precipitated a consolidation of Welsh culture. "Within a few decades, the Calvinist-Methodists, the Congregationalists, and the Baptists had won over the great majority of the masses of Wales from the established [Anglican] church," and at Sunday Schools taught Welsh people to read the Bible (Hartman, p. 33).

Welsh Christian nonconformists shared fundamentalism and puritanism, yet did not lack for internal controversy. Unifyingly, their shared religion demanded "rigid observance of the marriage vows, discouragement of divorce, austere observance of conduct of life generally" and the strict reservation of Sundays for religious activities; on the other hand, divisive religious differences arose "over the issues of church organization, Calvinism, and infant baptism" (Hartman, pp. 103-104). Congregations and denominations guarded their independence.

In America, as in Wales, Welsh churches pioneered Sunday Schools; children and adults attended separate classes in which teachers used Socratic methods of questioning. Welsh American churchgoers sang hymns and testified, respectively, on Tuesday and Thursday nights, and regularly held *gymanvas*, preaching festivals.

The first groups of Welsh converts to Mormonism came to America in the 1840s and 1850s. Mormon founder Joseph Smith converted Captain Dan Jones to the religion, then sent him on a mission to Wales. Captain Jones in turn converted thousands, most of whom resettled in Utah and contributed much to Mormon culture. As a prime example, Welsh Americans founded the Mormon Tabernacle Choir.

Since the 1960s, versions of Celtic nature-worship have gained popularity in America and Britain. Two members of the Parent Kindred of the Old Religion in Wales brought Hereditary Welsh Paganism to the United States in the early 1960s. Today, Welsh Pagans can be found in Georgia, Wisconsin, Minnesota, Michigan, California, and West Virginia. Welsh pagans form circles with names like The Cauldron, Forever Forests, and Y *Tylwyth Teg*. Members take symbolic Welsh names like Lord Myrddin Pendevig, Lady Gleannon or Gwyddion, Tiron, and Siani. Welsh pagans in America also use the Welsh language in their rituals. Although the

Druids, who led the pre-Christian Welsh religion, have not survived, some of their practices have.

EMPLOYMENT AND ECONOMIC TRADITIONS

Welsh Americans traditionally worked in farming or, during the Industrial Age, in the heavy industries of coal, iron, and steel. Because these industries had developed earlier in Wales, immigrants tended to know their work better than workers from elsewhere. Thus Welsh immigrants took leading roles in America's developing industries. Welsh American industrial bosses especially preferred to hire Welsh American workers, and more specifically, ones from their own religious denomination. As a result, Welsh Americans dominated coal mining, and many coal mines filled mostly with a particular denomination of Welsh Americans. Bosses themselves held membership in the Freemasons. Across the coal region, though only men worked as miners and bosses, boys, girls, and women worked around the mines.

POLITICS AND GOVERNMENT

George Washington once noted, "Good Welshman Make Good Americans" (Thomas, p. 27). In the founding of the United States of America, cultural history positioned Welsh immigrants as American revolutionaries. The Welsh, who already tended to resent English control, were strongly inclined toward revolution in France, Britain, and America. The United States can trace the derivation of its trial-by-jury system through England to Wales. Though it is unclear exactly where Welsh culture contributed to the founding moments of America, Welsh Americans claim the Welshness of Jeffersonian principles, especially that certain rights are inalienable, that rights not assigned to governments are reserved for the people, and that church and state must remain separate. In February of 1776, one month after the publication of Thomas Paine's *Common Sense*, a Welshman, Dr. Richard Price, published in London *The Nature of Civil Liberty*, appealing "to the natural rights of all men, those rights which no government should have the power to take away"; five months later, Welsh American Thomas Jefferson published similar ideas in the Declaration of Independence (Williams, p. 45).

For decades, nearly 75 percent of Welsh immigrants became citizens, higher than any other group

(Williams, p. 87). In accord with their religion, Welsh Americans have helped to lobby for temperance, Prohibition, and Sabbath-enforcing Blue Laws. Welsh American abolitionists included workers on the underground railroad, such as Rebecca Lewis Fussell (1820-1893), and authors such as Harriet Beecher Stowe, who wrote *Uncle Tom's Cabin*. Author Helen Hamilton Gardiner (1853-1925) joined several other Welsh American leaders in the fight for women's suffrage.

Welsh Americans also have been labor leaders. In 1871, Welsh American coal miners led their union in a historic strike in which they protested a 30 percent wage decrease, ultimately to no avail. They won only disapproval and prejudice from more established classes of Americans (Jones, p. 53).

INDIVIDUAL AND GROUP CONTRIBUTIONS

ART AND ENTERTAINMENT

Illustrator Alice Barber Stephens (1858-1932), and architect Frank Lloyd Wright (1969-1959); pioneer film-producer D. W. Griffith (1875-1948); Bob Hope (1903–); talk show host Dick Cavett (1936–); stage and screen actor Richard Burton (1925-1984); actor Ray Milland (1907-1986); actress Bette Davis (1908-1989).

EDUCATION

Elihu Yale launched Yale University; Morgan Edwards and Dr. William Richards established Brown University; Carey Thomas (1857-1935) founded and served as president of Bryn Mawr College. Catharine E. Beecher (1800-1858), sister of Harriet Beecher Stowe, founded seminaries for women. Helen Parkhurst (1887-1973), originator of the Dalton Plan of individualized student contracts, established the Dalton School in New York.

EXPLORERS

In the 1780s Jacques Clamorgan, a Welsh West Indian, whose real name was Charles Morgan, led an important scientific exploration of the West before Lewis and Clark; Clamorgan ventured up the Missouri for the fur-trading Spanish who wanted to ally with the Mandans, who seemed to be the remaining Welsh Indians. Meriwether Lewis himself was Welsh American, as was frontiersman Daniel Boone, and John Lloyd Stevens, who discovered Mayan ruins and authored travel narratives.

GOVERNMENT AND COMMUNITY SERVICE

Luther Hammond Lewis founded the Big Brother Movement. Roger Williams (born in Wales in 1599) was the first European to establish a democracy on this continent, based upon the principles of civil and religious liberty, at Providence plantations, Rhode Island. Thomas Jefferson (1743-1826), was the greatest Welsh American colonial patriot, whose ancestors came from the foot of Mount Snowden in Wales to the colony of Virginia. Another Welsh American, Gouverneur Morris (1752-1816), later wrote the final draft of the Constitution of the United States. Supreme Court Chief Justice John Marshall (1755-1835) fathered American constitutional law. Welsh American presidents of the United States include not only James Monroe and Calvin Coolidge, but moreover, Abraham Lincoln. Robert E. Lee, General of the Confederate Army, and Jefferson Davis, president of the Confederacy, also were Welsh Americans. So were Supreme Court Chief Justice Charles Evans Hughes, Secretaries of State Daniel Webster and William H. Seward, and first Lady Hillary Clinton. At least 30 state governors also were Welsh American.

LITERATURE

Emlyn Williams, actor and playwright, author of *The Corn Is Green*; Jack London (1876-1916), author of *The Call of the Wild* and *White Fang*; Kate Wiggin (1856-1923), author of *Rebecca of Sunnybrooke Farm*; and Harriet Beecher Stowe (1811-1896), author of *Uncle Tom's Cabin*.

MEDICINE

Medical scientist Alice Catherine Evans (1881-1975), first woman president of the society of American Bacteriologists; pioneer nutritionists Mary Swartz Rose (1874-1941) and Ruth Wheeler (1877-1948); as well as women's health reformer Mary Nichols. Mary Whiton Calkins (1863-1930), was the first female president of the American Psychological Association, and became the first president of the American Philosophical Association.

MILITARY

Spirited Welsh Americans led the American Revolutionary War. Robert Morris (1734-1806) financed the American effort, in which Major General Charles Lee, born in Wales in 1731, served as second in command to Washington. General "Mad Anthony" Wayne (born in 1745), a Pennsylvania-born Welsh American, fought the Battle of Monmouth.

General Isaac Shelby (born in 1750), a Maryland-born Welsh American, fought with his father, Evan Shelby, and other Welsh generals and soldiers in 1774 at the Battle of Point Pleasant, New Jersey.

MUSIC

Opera star Margaret Price; popular vocalists Shirley Bassey and Tom Jones, known as the "Welsh Elvis."

RELIGION

Welsh preacher Morgan John Rys, who came to America in 1794, preached that slavery contradicted the principles of the Christian religion and the rights of man; he also stirred controversy by preaching a sermon in which he said that no land should be taken from the Red Indians without payment.

MEDIA

PRINT

The Bard.
Published in Phoenix, Arizona, by the Annwn Temple of Gwynfyd, a circle of hereditary Welsh pagans.

Ninnau.
Monthly magazine containing news and information for Americans and Canadians of Welsh ancestry.

Contact: Arturo Lewis Roberts, Editor and Publisher.
Address: 11 Post Terrace, Basking Ridge, New Jersey 07920.
Telephone: (908) 204-0704.
Fax: (908) 221-0744.
E-mail: 73541.2554@compuserve.com.

Welsh Studies.
Address: Edwin Mellen Press, 415 Ridge Road, Box 450, Lewiston, New York 14092.
Telephone: (716) 754-2788.
Fax: (716) 754-4056.

Y Drych (The Mirror).
Monthly newspaper on Welsh social and political news; also covers Welsh events in the United States and Canada; includes regular cultural, genealogical, and Welsh-language features.

Contact: Mary Morris Mergenthal, Editor.
Address: P.O. Box 8089, St. Paul, Minnesota 55108-0089.
Telephone: (612) 642-1653.
Fax: (612) 642-0170.

Yr Enfys (The Rainbow).
Published since 1949 by Undeb Y Cymry Ar Wasgar (Wales International), it is the only international periodical for Welsh exiles.

ORGANIZATIONS AND ASSOCIATIONS

National Welsh American Foundation (NWAF).
Has bestowed charitable awards since 1980, and lobbies for a Presidential proclamation of the first of March as the official Welsh American Day.

Contact: Wilfred Greenway.
Address: 216-03 43rd Avenue, Bayside, New York 11361.
Telephone: (212) 224-9333.

Welsh American Historical Society.
Contact: Mildred Jenkins, Secretary.
Address: c/o Welsh American Heritage Museum, 412 East Main Street, Oak Hill, Ohio 45656.

Welsh Associated Youth of Canada and the United States (WAY).
Launched in 1970 to involve young Welsh Americans in their heritage; a decade later, the Welsh National Gymanfa Ganu Association board of trustees granted WAY a permanent seat.

Contact: Claire Tallman.
Address: P.O. Box 3246, Ventura, California 93006.

Welsh Harp Society of America.
Founded by the St. David's Society of Kansas City in 1984.

Contact: Judith Brougham.
Address: 4202 Clark, Kansas City, Missouri 64111.
Telephone: (816) 561-6066.

Welsh Heritage Week.
Contact: Anne Habermehl.
Address: 3925 North Main, Marion, New York 14505.
Telephone: (315) 926-5318.

Welsh National Gymanfa Ganu Association (WNGGA).
Contact: David E. Thomas.
Address: 5908 Hansen Road, Edina, Minnesota 55436.
Telephone: (612) 920-1454.

Welsh Society.

Seeks to keep alive Welsh culture and heritage; assists immigrants to the United States from Wales; maintains charitable programs.

Contact: Daniel E. Williams, Secretary.
Address: 450 Broadway, Camden,
    New Jersey 08103.
Telephone: (609) 964-0891.

MUSEUMS AND RESEARCH CENTERS

Cymdeithas Madog—The Welsh Studies Institute.
Contact: Donna Lloyd-Kolkin.
Address: 1352 American Way, Menlo Park,
    California 94025.
Telephone: (415) 565-3320.

SOURCES FOR ADDITIONAL STUDY

Ashton, E. T. *The Welsh in the United States.* Hove, Sussex: Caldra House, 1984.

Dodd, A. H. *The Character of Early Welsh Emigration to the United States.* Cardiff: University of Wales Press, 1957.

Greenslade, David. *Welsh Fever: Welsh Activities in the United States and Canada Today.* Cowbridge, Wales: D. Brown and Sons, 1986.

Hartmann, George Edward. *Americans from Wales.* New York: Farrar, Straus and Giroux, 1978.

Holt, Constance Wall. *Welsh Women: An Annotated Bibliography of Women in Wales and Women of Welsh Descent in America.* Metuchen, New Jersey: Scarecrow, 1993.

Jones, William D. *Wales in America: Scranton and the Welsh 1860-1920.* Scranton: University of Scranton Press, 1993.

Morris, Jan. *The Matter of Wales.* Oxford: Oxford University Press, 1984.

Thomas, Islyn. *Our Welsh Heritage.* Trucksville, PA: National Welsh-American Foundation, 1991 (originally published in 1972).

Thomas, R. D. Hanes. *Cymry America: A History of the Welsh in America,* translated by Phillips G. Davies. Lanham, Maryland: University Press of America, 1983 (originally published in 1872).

Williams, David. *Cymru Ac America: Wales and America.* Cardiff: University of Wales Press, 1975 (first published in 1946).

———. *A Short History of Modern Wales.* London: John Murray, Ltd., 1961.

YEMENI AMERICANS

by
Drew Walker

The role of women in the Yemeni American community is complex due to the great disproportion of males to females within the population. The position of a woman in Yemeni society varies according to her age, social class, and occupation.

OVERVIEW

Yemen (in Arabic, al-Yaman or al-Jumhuriyah al-Yamaniyah) is situated in the southwestern corner of the Arabian Peninsula. It is bordered by Saudi Arabia to the north, Oman to the east, the Gulf of Aden to the south, and the Red Sea to the west. The northern border with Saudi Arabia is part of a vast desert and remains mostly uncharted. Yemen's total land area is estimated to be around 156,000 square miles (405,000 square kilometers), which is slightly smaller than the state of California. The land of Yemen can be divided into five major regions: the highlands in the east, the eastern and northeastern desert regions, the central mountains (known as the Yemen Highlands), the western mountains, and the coastal plain found in the northwest. The population of Yemen lives in all of these zones, the altitudes of which range from sea level to more than 10,000 feet. In different areas adequate rainfall and good soil provide for significant agricultural production. Throughout the country, the temperature ranges greatly, from the hot desert to cool mountainous climates.

HISTORY

The long and rich history of Yemen extends back beyond three thousand years. From about 1000 B.C. most of the area today known as Yemen was ruled by three successive historical groups, the Mineans, the

Sabaeans, and the Himyarites. These three groups or kingdoms derived their status and wealth through the trade in spices and other products such as frankincense and myrrh. Both frankincense and myrrh were forms of gum taken from trees that covered much of Yemen's lands. These substances had medicinal properties and were highly valued in the ancient world for their ritual and healing powers. With the introduction of the camel as a means of transportation in the eleventh century B.C., large caravans carried these products from their center of production in the city of Qana (today Bir 'Ali) to the great markets of Gaza in Egypt. Also included in these caravans were gold and other fine goods that arrived in Yemen by sea from India.

The early trade of the Mineans eventually gave way to the Sabaeans around 950 B.C. As a result, the Sabaean capital of Ma'rib attained great status and became a center of early Yemeni culture. Sabaean control lasted for the next 1,400 years, and they maintained an impressive agricultural system in addition to their trade in spices and other goods. To provide irrigation for their farmlands the Sabaeans built a great dam at Ma'rib in the eighth century, which stood for more than a thousand years.

The Himyarites succeeded the Sabaeans, establishing their capital at Dhafar. Trading from the port of al-Muza on the Red Sea, the Himyarites controlled trade in the region until the first century B.C., when the Romans conquered it. The spread of Christianity in the ancient Mediterranean world diminished the popularity of ritual fragrances. The lack of demand for the region's spices combined with Roman domination eventually led to the demise of Yemeni wealth in the spice trade. By the fourth century A.D. both Christianity and Judaism had been introduced into Yemen, and the Ethiopians occupied the region from early on in that century.

In 570 A.D., after centuries of neglect, the great dam at Ma'rib broke for the last time and was subsequently abandoned by the Sabaean kingdom, which had for centuries been losing influence in the region. By this time the Himyarites had established an alliance with Persia, which led to the expulsion of the Ethiopian occupation forces. It was not long after these events that Islam came to Yemen in the early to mid-seventh century. After centuries of exploitation by Christians and Jews in Yemen, the spread of Islam was quick and decisive. The Prophet Muhammad sent his son-in-law to be governor, leading to the establishment of the mosques in Janadiyah and Sana'a', still today the two most famous mosques in Yemen. From this point on Yemen was ruled by a series of Muslim holy men and

governors known as *caliphs* and *imams*. A series of rulers from differing groups came to rule Yemen over the following centuries, founding different dynasties Most prominent among these groups was an Iraqi Shi'ite sect introduced in the ninth century known as the Zaydi.

A turning point in the history of Yemen occured around the early fifteenth century, when reputedly one Sheik 'Ali ibn 'Umar' introduced a Yemeni specialty—named coffee—as a beverage to the greater Mediterranean world. It was at this point that Yemen became an area of conflict between the Ottoman Empire, the Egyptians, and various European countries over the trade in coffee. At first providing an economic boom that lasted for centuries in some areas of Yemen, by the eighteenth century coffee was being grown and sold elsewhere around the world. The result was yet another rapid decline in the position of Yemen in the world economy.

By 1517 the Zaydi imams of Yemen could no longer resist the forces from outside and were absorbed for the first time into the Ottoman Empire, a period of domination which lasted until 1636.

MODERN ERA

In the nineteenth century Britain and other European powers began to occupy different parts of the Middle East. In 1839 the British, deciding that Yemen was of strategic value to their empire, occupied the coastal port of Aden. As the century progressed the Ottomans moved back into northern Yemen while the British fortified their presence in the south. By an agreement in 1904 that put into writing that which had existed for decades, Yemen was divided into northern and southern areas, with the Ottomans (Turks) controlling the north and the British the south. However, in 1911, following a sustained series of local insurrections, the Turks eventually granted autonomy to North Yemen under the rule of the Zaydi imam, and in 1919 the British granted autonomy of the south to Imam Yayha, who was named king. In 1925 North Yemen became an independent state.

Imam Yayha did not recognizing the distinction between north and south, and pressed hard against the British and neighboring Saudis to gain complete control over all of Yemen. Yayha eventually consolidated his power in the north and ruled until 1948, when he was assassinated. His successor and son, Ahmad, fought against the continuing presence of the British in Aden. He formed a brief alliance with Egypt and Syria, but had little success. When Ahmad died in 1962, his son Muhammed al-Badr had no sooner come to rule than he was ousted in a coup led by a military officer named Colonel Abdullah al-Sallal. Al-Sallal proclaimed Yemen a republic named the Yemen Arab Republic (YAR), and he sought control over all of Yemen's territories under this new rubric. Backed by the Saudis, the imam who al-Badr had deposed of had fled to the mountains in the north to form a royalist army. Attacking the forces of the YAR, who were backed by Egypt, these royalists waged a civil war for eight years, until the Saudis and Egyptian agreed to end their support and to arrange an election in which the people of the YAR could decide their own form of government. When this plan failed in 1966, the civil war resumed. By 1967 the Egyptians had withdrawn and YAR leader al-Sallal was overthrown and sent into exile, succeeded by Abdul Rahman al-Iryani. At this time, after years of street fighting, the British finally pulled out of Aden. Adding to the drastic changes that year, with the collapse of the YAR in the south, was the founding of a new state named the People's Republic of South Yemen on the 30th of November. Establishing a firm division between north and south by 1970, the southern government once again changed its name, to the People's Democratic Republic of Yemen (PDRY). During the 1970s the two Yemens engaged in a series of short border wars, which after much other turmoil resulted in the drafting of a constitution establishing the unification of north and south. It was not until May 1990 that the full merger finally took place, creating a unified country named the Republic of Yemen.

THE FIRST YEMENIS IN AMERICA

There is no specific record of when the first Yemeni Americans arrived in the United States. It is most likely that the first Yemenis came shortly after the Suez canal was opened in 1869. By 1890 there are records of a small number immigrating, and there are also records showing that some Yemenis obtained U.S. citizenship by fighting in the First World War.

SIGNIFICANT IMMIGRATION WAVES AND SETTLEMENT PATTERNS

Many early Yemeni immigrants first settled within pre-existing Lebanese and Palestinian communities in cities such as New York. After orienting themselves to their new surroundings many Yemenis set off for the Midwest and West, where the labor force was quickly growing. Working as farm laborers in California's San Joaquin Valley and as factory workers in Detroit, Canton, Weirton, and Buffalo, many Yemeni Americans prospered in the 1920s. During

the depression of the 1930s the flow of Yemeni immigration slowed dramatically but resumed again in greater numbers after the end of the Second World War in 1945. One route of immigration into the United States was through Vietnam, where many Yemenis had worked in warehouses, shops, and on the docks as watchmen. Through a loophole in the immigration laws, many Yemeni immigrants who were not literate in their mother tongue (which was a requirement for all immigrants entering into the United States) could bypass regulations and thus be admitted. Patterns of Yemeni immigration were often in the form of chain migration, in which already established immigrants would secure visas for their relatives in Yemen. With the elimination of a quota system for immigration in 1965, Yemenis gained easier access to entrance and work visas, leading to a great increase in the numbers of immigrants. In the years of immigration before 1970, nearly all immigrants from Yemen were adult males.

ACCULTURATION AND ASSIMILATION

The population of Yemen mainly speaks Arabic but a small number of other linguistic and cultural groups such as the Mahra, and ethnic immigrant minorities including Somalis and Ethiopians, are also represented. Religion is a major factor in the separation of Yemeni society into subgroups. Among those of the Islamic faith the Sunni sect is the largest, followed by a Shi'ite minority and an even smaller group known as the Isma'ilis. In addition to religious differences, tribal differences play an important social role. Despite the great number of younger men who emigrate abroad to work and often return with foreign practices, Yemenis maintain much of their cultural heritage.

Among Yemeni Americans cultural traditions are maintained to various degrees in the communities in which they live. In places like Detroit or New York a great deal of Yemeni cultural activity can easily be found and participated in. There is overall a strong resistance to acculturation and assimilation. Despite this resistance, however, many Yemeni immigrants adopt American customs and attitudes, which work in complex ways to modify their identities in the United States and in Yemen.

TRADITIONS, CUSTOMS, AND BELIEFS

Yemeni culture and its traditions and customs among Yemeni Americans are a rich mixture of Islamic influences and more ancient traditions and practices. Most Yemeni Americans are aware of and take great pride in the long history of their peoples. In many places Yemeni culture displays a mixture of complex traditions that are not seen in the cultures of its neighbors. Yemeni Americans are proud of the beauty of the landscape of Yemen and of their great achievements in architecture and construction, its images often decorating the walls of gathering places and homes. In addition to their traditional skill as builders, Yemeni Americans also point to a reputation for fine craftsmanship that has endured for thousands of years. Most Yemeni Americans adhere to the Islamic faith, and it is there that many of the most subtle and profound traditions, customs and beliefs are found. Christian, Jewish, and other minority influences also add to the cultural and religious diversity of Yemeni Americans.

Different social scientists have noted that within the twentieth century the practice of young men emigrating alone and working abroad after marriage has itself become a custom. Emigrating to many parts of the world, these men form what in many ways has become a key tradition in the lives of men and women in Yemeni society. Among the Yemeni American population one finds a great number of such emigrants, often between the ages of 18 and 45, who maintain economically vital links between Yemen and the United States. The sacrifice made by these emigrants is honored and respected in Yemeni society.

Another Yemeni custom practiced by Yemeni Americans, and is a part of various social situations, is the chewing of a substance called qat. Qat is the name of a seedless plant that grows up to 20 feet high and grows best between 3,000 and 6,000 feet above sea level. Its leaves are harvested throughout the year in Yemen and neighboring countries. When chewed, qat is said to have a stimulant and euphoric effect. Qat is chewed like tobacco. In the United States a bundle of qat sells for $30 to $35. It is estimated that Yemeni Americans may spend as much as $3 million a year on qat. Many Yemeni American celebrations are thought to be incomplete without it.

PROVERBS

Yemeni proberbs include: *La budd min Sana'a wa lau taal al-safr* (You must visit Sana'a, however long the journey takes); *Min ratl hakya tafham wiqya* (From a pound of talk one gets but an ounce of understanding); *Ya gharib kun adib* (A foreigner should be well behaved); *Jaarak al-qarib wa la akhuk al-ba'id* (Look to your neighbor who is near you rather than to your distant brother); *Kun namla wa takul sukr* (Work

like an ant and you'll eat sugar); *Man maat al-yaum salim min dhanb bukra* (He who dies today is safe from tomorrow's sin); *Yaddi fi fumuh wa yadduh fi 'aini* (My fist is in his mouth, but his fist is in my eye, meaning "six of one, half a dozen of the other"); *La sadiq illa fi waqt al-dhiq* (A friend in time of need is a friend indeed); *Qird fi 'ain ummuh ghaz-aal* (A monkey in its mother's eye is like a gazelle, meaning love is blind); *Lau kan al-kalaam min fidha fa al-samt min dhahab* (If speech is of silver, then silence is golden); *'Asfoor fil yadd wa la 'ashra fi al-shajarah* (A bird in hand is worth ten in a tree); *Ma ghaab 'an al-nadhr ghaab 'an al-khaatir* (Out of sight, out of mind); *Idha sahibak 'asl la talhusuh kulluh* (If you have honey, don't lick the pot clean); and *Tal'ab bi hanash wa taquluh dudah* (You play with a snake and call it a worm).

CUISINE

Yemeni Americans usually consider lunch the main meal of the day. While at home many Yemeni Americans eat the traditional way—without utensils and using bread to scoop up the food.

The national dish of Yemen, widely cooked in the United States, is *salta*. *Salta* is a heavily spiced chicken or lamb stew served with lentils, beans, chickpeas, and coriander, all on a bed of rice. Another dish is *shurba*, a more soupy stew made with lentils, fenugreek, or lamb. There are many kinds of bread, of which the most popular made-at-home bread is *khubz tawwa*. In addition, *lahuh*, a pancake-like bread made from sorghum, is eaten on special occasions. *Bint al sahn* is a sweet bread dipped in honey and clarified butter.

TRADITIONAL COSTUMES

Many Yemeni Americans wear traditional clothing around the house and at special secular and religious gatherings. Yemen is well-known and esteemed for its production of beautiful textiles and for the importation of fine textiles from around the world. Traditionally, however, these fine fabrics were often reserved for the rich, who could afford them, and garments made from them long served as markers of class and wealth. Today, however, many Yemeni Americans can afford what used to be materials that only the rich had access to.

For men of the highlands, the most distinctive and important article worn was the *djambia*, a curved dagger. Different forms of these daggers were used to distinguish classes, and each class was forbidden to wear the wrong dagger. The traditional garment of men from the Tihama area of Yemen is an embroidered skirt, or *futah*, which is wrapped around the hips and fastened with a belt. In the highlands regions a shorter, calf-length skirt was worn with a jacket, belt, and dagger.

With the exception of an outfit (introduced some fifty years ago) consisting of a black skirt, veil and head covering known as the *sharshaf* or the loose black coat known as the *abaya*, the traditional clothing of women varied a great deal. The veil is an important traditional part of women's clothing. While a controversial subject among women and between men and women today, the veil had the effect of a status symbol. Brightly colored cotton dresses with very wide long sleeves, including brass and silver adornment, were commonly worn in different areas.

DANCES AND SONGS

Music and song are varied in the Yemeni American community, and Yemeni Americans are more or less traditional in their tastes, depending on their access to different forms of music. Traditional music from Yemen, available on compact discs all over the world, consists of small-scale performances of an accompanied voice, strongly related to poetic expression. A range of instruments are used in the accompaniment, including a plucked string instrument called an *'ud*, as well as percussion instruments.

The position of Yemen as a vital crossroads between the traffic of the Indian Ocean and the Red Sea led to a great variety in musical expression. Like much of Yemeni culture, the music is often distinct from that of its neighboring Arab lands. Local accents, rhythms and modes of everyday speech and its poetic forms figure strongly in the distinctive styles of Yemeni music and song. In Yemeni American culture and in Yemen, different poetic and musical forms are used in different settings, with special forms such as *razfah* and *balah* heard at wedding celebrations, for example.

HOLIDAYS

Many Yemeni Americans gather to celebrate Yemeni holidays when possible. Among these are May 1, which is International Labor Day; May 22, which is the Yemeni Day of National Unity; September 26, which is Revolution Day; October 14, which is National Day; and November 30, Yemeni Independence Day. Of great importance to many Yemeni Americans are the religious holidays of the Islamic faith. While these holidays begin and end at different times each year, the dates for the Roman calendar year 1999 (which is the Muslim year 1420)

are listed below. The Islamic year, made up of twelve months of 29 or 30 days each, contains a total of 353 or 354 days and is based on the lunar cycle. Each month traditionally began with the sighting of a new moon.

Ramadan: December 20, 1998–January 18, 1999

The sighting of the new moon, which in the United States is monitored by the Islamic Society of North America, begins the observance of Ramadan, the most important holiday of Islam, which lasts an entire month. It is a time for inner reflection, self-control, and devotion to God. It is a personal time arranged through social means, Ramadan takes on different meanings for every individual each year of his or her life. During Ramadan Muslims are urged to read the Koran or to spend more time listening to its recitation in a mosque.

The most prominent ritual of Ramadan is the required fasting during daylight hours, which entails abstaining from food, drink, smoking, and sexual activity. Nothing may be eaten during this month between the rising and setting of the sun. If an individual is ill, traveling, or pregnant, however, strict fasting need not be observed, with the understanding that he or she will later try to make up for this lapse.

The last ten days of Ramadan are thought to be of special significance, particularly the 27th night. The end of Ramadan and the beginning of the 'Eid-ul-Fitr festival is a time for mutual congratulation and greetings. Two of the most universal Arabic greetings are '*Eid mubarak* (a blessed 'Eid) and '*Kullu am wa antum bi-khair*' (may you be well throughout the year).

'Eid-ul-Fitr: January 19, 1999

This festival, the Festival of Fast-Breaking, takes place immediately after the end of Ramadan. Often likened to Christmas, it is a time for obligatory charity and generosity. Yemeni Americans may wear holiday attire, attend a special community morning prayer, and visit friends or relatives. Although the celebration lasts three days, most of the main festivities occur on the first day.

Hajj: March 18–March 26, 1999

The *hajj* is a pilgrimage to Mecca, Saudi Arabia, when Muslims from all over the world converge on Mecca, Islam's holiest site. With roughly two million Muslims participating each year, the *hajj* is thought to be the world's largest international gathering, during which God is worshiped at the Sacred House called the Kabah. Few Yemenis in the United States undertake the *hajj*, but it is obligatory to make the pilgrimage at least once in every Muslim's lifetime; thus great efforts to attend should be made if conditions permit.

'Eid-ul-Adha: March 27, 1999

Known as the Festival of Sacrifice, 'Eid ul-Adha celebrates the commemoration of Prophet Abraham's willingness to sacrifice everything for God, including the life of his son Ishmael. God's sparing of Ishmael through the substitution of a sheep in his stead is celebrated by slaughtering an animal and distributing its meat among family, friends, and the needy. Traditionally this provided the means by which many poor Muslims were able to enjoy the uncommon luxury of eating meat during the four days of the festival.

HEALTH ISSUES

Among the health issues within the Yemeni American community, the chewing of *qat* has recently come to the forefront. Thought to have negative addictive effects, different Yemeni Americans are starting to question the wisdom of its excessive use. In addition, as in many newer immigrant communities, the issue of health insurance is perhaps the most important health care issue faced by Yemeni Americans.

LANGUAGE

The official language of Yemen and that spoken by the vast majority of Yemeni Americans is Arabic. Among the population of Yemeni Americans one can find a variety of Arab dialects, including the following: the Sanaani or Northern Yemeni dialect, spoken by some 7,600,000 in Yemen; the Ta'izzi-Adeni or Southern Yemeni dialect, spoken by approximately 6,760,000 in Yemen; the Hadrami dialect, spoken by approximately 300,000 in Yemen; the Mehri dialect spoken by nearly 58,000; and the Judeo-Yemeni dialect, spoken by approximately 1,000. In the population of Yemen overall the literacy rate is estimated to be between 25 percent and 39 percent. Amongst the literate, there is a standard form of Arabic which one finds used for education, official purposes, books, newspapers and formal speeches.

GREETINGS AND POPULAR EXPRESSIONS

Some common greetings and expressions in Arabic are as follows, and they are pronounced roughly as they are spelled: *Ahlan!* (Hello!); *Sabah il-kheyr* (Good morning); *Sabah in noor* (to return someone's wish good morning); *Keyf il-hehl?* or *Keyfek?* (How are you?); *Tamam, Ilhandulillah* or *Bi kheyr, ilhandulillah* (Fine); *It sharafna* (Nice to meet you); *Ma'assalama* (Goodbye); *Minfadlak* or *minfadlik* (Please); *Shukran!* (Thank you); *Al-fi shukr* (Thank you very much); *Na'am* (Yes); *La* (no); and *Yala!* (Let's go!).

FAMILY AND COMMUNITY DYNAMICS

In many parts of Yemen it is still not uncommon for young men of 16 years to marry, produce children, and emigrate. Spouses and children often remain behind as the money obtained from work is sent from the United States families back home. This money is often used to purchase land and help develop a homestead for the family. In the United States many male immigrants live in inner-city apartments or houses with several other men in the same situation. Whether as single men or in family groups, a great many Yemeni immigrants live in communities with high Arab populations and frequent places where Yemenis congregate.

While very important in Yemen itself, the practice of Islam takes on different degrees of importance in America, depending on one's work and living situations and access to religious centers. In areas with larger Arab populations, access to newspapers, magazines, books, and other media in Arabic help maintain a sense of community and common interest.

EDUCATION

While the educational levels of Yemeni Americans range across the spectrum, many first-generation immigrants have a standard education and are employed as laborers in farm and factory work. Knowledge of the Koran and other sacred literature is highly respected, as is higher education. Since the 1970s a growing number of Yemenis have come to the United States to pursue college degrees.

THE ROLE OF WOMEN

The role of women in the Yemeni American community is complex due to the great disproportion of males to females within the population. The position of a woman in Yemeni society varies according to her age, social class, and occupation. The practice of veiling depends on what part of Yemen she comes from. A woman's educational level has a strong influence on how she relates to older women, who are often less educated. In addition to homemaking, women have traditionally taken part in farming activities and also business ventures. Conflicts between economic necessity and tradition often arise for Yemeni American women. In more traditional families, barriers of language and customs regarding the roles of women in public can lead to an existence more cloistered and isolated than that of non-Yemeni women.

COURTSHIP AND WEDDINGS

Although the number of traditional weddings in the Yemeni American community is small, those that do take place are impressive social events. Often the match between a bride and bridegroom are still selected by their respective parents. Due to the traditional Yemeni separation of the sexes, most often a man relied on advice and information from his mother, sisters, and aunts in choosing a bride. When looking for a wife, the family of the groom helps the man determine the right candidate from his neighborhood or village or within his own family among his cousins (a practice that Islamic law allows). While the mother evaluates the women of the potential brides' families, the father does the same for the men of these families, and they discuss their impressions.

When they reach an agreement on a candidate, a date is set for the future groom and his father to visit the house of the potential bride's family in order to discuss the matter. At this time the potential bride has a chance to look at the man; if very traditional, she may serve tea to the visitors. It is often the case that the man will know very little if anything about his bride-to-be and that the young woman will know much more about him. During this meeting the father of the man asks the father of the bride-to-be if he agrees to the union. At this time it is the custom for the father of the woman to ask for time to discuss it with his wife, daughter, and other family members. After some time, if the father of the woman agrees, a time is scheduled for the ceremony of the betrothal, held on a Thursday or a Friday.

The groom and his father, accompanied by three or four male friends or relations bringing raisins, qat, and other gifts, pay a visit to the house of the father of the bride. An engagement ring is handed over to the father of the bride along with a gift of clothes for the mother and bride. Dates for the wedding are considered, and a bride price is decided upon. It is the custom that the greatest share of the bride price, which is paid by the father of the groom, is later spent purchasing jewelry and clothing for the bride. Valuables bought with this money are the bride's alone and often remain her prized possessions for many years afterward. The actual ceremony of the betrothal is quite informal, with a great deal of conversation concerning the firm promises between the two families to marry their children.

The wedding lasts for at least three days. In the presence of a scholar of Islamic law called a *qadi*, papers of marriage are signed. In this ceremony it is the custom for the groom to ask his future father-in-law "Will you give me your daughter in marriage?" The father of the bride answers, "Yes, I will give you my daughter to be your wife." The qadi then asks the father of the bride if his daughter agrees to the arranged marriage. After answering that she agrees, the groom and father of the bride clasp right hands. As they do this the qadi lays a white cloth over their hands and recites the first *sura* of the Koran known as the *fatiha*.

The celebration of the marriage is then inaugurated when the father of the groom throws a handful of raisins onto the carpet. All those present at the ceremony try to pick up as many raisins as possible—they are thought to be signs of a happy future for the newlyweds. It is another custom for all those present at the wedding to give money, whose sums are announced, one after the other, by a crier.

The most important and most public part of the wedding celebrations takes place on the Friday following the marriage ceremony. At this time a lavish feast is prepared including a variety of meats. Lunch is a big affair that day, as is the gathering of men to chew qat and socialize. Women guests often help out in the extensive preparations for the feast. After going to midday prayers in a group, the men march through the street with the groom, who is dressed in a special costume and carrying a golden sword, singing, beating drums and making merry. That afternoon the qadi joins the men and recites poems and imparts moral knowledge, interspersed with breaks of music.

While this takes place, all the women gather at the house of the bride while a makeup artist arranges the bride's hair and paints fine patterns on her hands and feet. The palms of the bride's hands and the soles of her feet are painted red with henna dye. The women eat sweets together at this time. Music is played during this gathering as well.

When the sun sets and evening prayers have ended, the men take to the street to arrange for a part of the festivities called the *Zaffa*. Standing in a line outside the house the groom, his father and his brothers face toward the groom's house. In another line stands the qadi, who gives recitations. During this time the men slowly, step by step, approach the house, all the while singing. While they are doing this all of the women climb onto the surrounding roofs trilling loudly in a high pitch, mixing with the singing of the men to make the greatest noise. When the groom gets near the house he runs and jumps over the threshold into the house, after which the guests dance for a bit and go home, ending the official part of the ceremony. If the bride has not yet arrived, she arrives soon afterward accompanied by her father, brothers, and other male relatives. At this time she enters the house of her husband she is officially a member of her new husband's family.

RELIGION

Most Yemeni Americans are Muslims. In the traditional practice of Islam, the observance of daily rituals and prohibitions are mandatory, especially the practice of praying five times a day. The first is the morning prayer. If there is a local mosque, men attend this prayer there. The morning ends with the midday prayer, which takes place when the sun has reached its highest point in the sky. After this people eat their midday meals. When the sun is at a 45 degree angle to the surface of the earth, it is time for the afternoon prayer. The next prayer of the day, the evening prayer, takes place at sunset. About an hour or more later, when the sky is completely dark, the last prayer of the day is done. When possible, Yemeni Americans make every effort to follow these prayer rituals, although in many work situations in the United States this simply cannot be done.

EMPLOYMENT AND ECONOMIC TRADITIONS

Employment and economic traditions among Yemeni Americans varied throughout the twentieth century. Earlier, in the second half of the twentieth century, many worked as factory workers in industries such as automobile manufacturing. Later, farm work became an occupation for many. More recently, Yemeni Americans have worked as small local merchants, and a number of others are working as scholars and attending universities for higher degrees. Yemeni Americans are often proud to boast of their strong work ethic.

POLITICS AND GOVERNMENT

A number of Yemenis earned U.S. citizenship by fighting for the United States in the First World War.

INDIVIDUAL AND GROUP CONTRIBUTIONS

ACADEMIA

Dr. Nasser Zawia is Assistant Professor in the Department of Pharmacology and the Division of Environmental Health at Meharry Medical College in Nashville, Tennessee. Dr. Zawia also heads various committees on drug use and is an adviser to the governor of Tennessee on the issue of drugs. Zawia's primary research focus is on the adverse effects of environmental agents on the development of the brain. Zawia also worked as a staff fellow at the National Institute for Environmental Health Sciences (NIEHS/NIH). Known for his work on heavy metals and developmental gene expression, Zawia has written extensively in the field of toxicology and is widely published in both national and international journals.

JOURNALISM

Mr. Shaker Alashwal is the founder of the Yemeni American League for college students and graduates. He is also co-editor of *Yemen News*, a community newspaper for Yemeni Americans. In addition to his work as an community organizer and editor, Alashwal is a writer who has published in local and international newspapers on issues relating to Yemen and Yemenis in America.

LITERATURE

The poet Ali Mohammed Luqman was born in Aden, in 1918. Luqman became interested in writing early, beginning to write poetry while still in his teens. In 1936 he went to India, where he attended al-Ghira Muslim University. Afterward he attended the American University of Cairo, earning a bachelor's degree in journalism in 1947. Returning to Aden, Luqman became the editor of his father's newspaper, *Fatat al-Jezira*. In 1943 he published his first collection of poetry, entitled *Overwhelmed Melody*. Luqman is noted for being the first poet to introduce Arabic poetic plays in the region of Aden. Although he produced a great deal of work in poetry, Luqman wrote in many other genres of literature. In many cases throughout his life political circumstances forced him at times to write anonymously. When political turmoil erupted in southern Yemen he moved to Taiz in northern Yemen and then to the United States, where he died in December 1979, among his wife and four sons.

SCIENCE AND TECHNOLOGY

Tawfig Jabr Hassan, MD, is a successful physician affiliated with Oakwood Hospital, in Dearborn, Michigan. Tawfig is also the city commissioner for the City of Dearborn. Abdullah Faris works as a high-tech engineer in California's Silicon Valley.

SOCIAL ISSUES

Mr. Ali Alazzani is an accomplished and well-known Yemeni activist. He has been the leader of different Yemeni and Arab American organizations. He is currently retired and acts as an educational consultant for the Department of Education for the State of California.

Saleh Muslah, M.D., M.A.C.P., was appointed consultant to the Governor John Engler of Michigan on issues concerning Michigan's Arab American communities.

Ms. Ashwaq al-Qassim was a champion of peace, a promoter of dialogue and an advocate of tolerance in and outside of the Yemeni American community. Ms. al-Qassim redefined the word "dedication" and was a great thinker on the subject of ethics. Al-Qassim was an activist, a human rights advocate, artist, and co-founder of Bosnia Link. In addition, she was a founder and a supporter of many nonprofit and non-governmental organizations.

MEDIA

Online newspapers published for the Arab American community and of interest to Yemeni Americans include the following. More information and URLs can be found in the media website for Yemen at http://www.al-bab.com/yemen/media/med.htm.

Yemeni Issues.
Newsletter of the Yemeni American League (in English).

Yemen Times.
Published weekly on Mondays (in English). Established in 1991, it has become highly influential. In 1995 the paper and its editor/publisher, Professor Abd al-Aziz al-Saqqaf, won the National Press Club's International Award for Freedom of the Press.

ORGANIZATIONS AND ASSOCIATIONS

Yemen American Cultural Center.
Address: 2770 Salina, Dearborn, MI 48120.
Telephone: (313) 841-3395.
Fax: (313) 841-3395 or (313) 843-8973.
Online: www.eli.wayne.edu/CommunityOrgs/ YemenAmCC.html.

Yemen American League Chapter and Contacts. New York.

Contact: Shaker Alashwal.
Address: 198 Court Street # 6, Brooklyn, NY 11201.
E-mail: YALNET@aol.com.
New Mexico.
Contact: Abdullah Sofan.
E-mail: Abdulla@zia.net.
Detroit.
Contact: Abdulwali Altahif, and Haffiz Azzubair.
E-mail: YALNET@aol.com.

Yemen Links on Arab.Net.
Set of links ranging from homepages of Yemeni American students to websites of Yemen newspapers.
Online: www.arab.net/links/yn/welcome.html

YemenNet.
Comprehensive news site about Yemen affairs around the world. Includes a Yemen internet search engine.
Online: www.yemennet.com.

MUSEUMS AND RESEARCH CENTERS

American Institute for Yemeni Studies.
Contact: Dr. Maria deJ. Ellis, Executive Director.
Address: P.O. Box 311, Ardmore PA 19003-0311.
Telephone: (610) 896-5412.
Fax: (610) 896-9049.
E-mail: aiys@aiys.org.

SOURCES FOR ADDITIONAL STUDY

Friedlander, Jonathan, ed. *Sojourners and Settlers: The Yemeni Immigrant Experience.* Salt Lake City: University of Utah Press, 1988.

Haiek, Jospeh R., ed. *Arab American Almanac*. 3rd edition. Glendale, CA: The News Circle Group Publishing Co., 1984.

Staub, Shalom. *Yemenis in New York City: The Folklore of Ethnicity*. Philadelphia: Balch Institute Press, 1989.

"The Yemeni Immigrant Community in Detroit: Background, Emigration, and Community Life." In Abraham, S., and Nabeel Abraham, eds., *Arabs in the New World*, Detroit: Wayne State University Press, 1983.

YUPIAT

by

Oscar Kawagley

The Yupiat people believe that everything of the earth possesses a spirit. Having a spirit means that all things possess consciousness or awareness; and having awareness means that they are mindful of who they give themselves to and how they are treated.

OVERVIEW

An estimated 86,000 Native people inhabit 87 percent of the Alaskan land mass, or 493,461 square miles. Approximately one-fourth of the Alaskan Native or Yupiat (pronounced "yu-pee-at") live in the southwest area of the state. This floodplain of the Yukon and the Kuskokwim Rivers composes the Arctic and Subarctic region. Villages are located along the Bering Sea and Bristol Bay coasts as well as the delta of the two rivers. There are approximately 21,415 Yupiat living in 62 villages, although the majority are concentrated in the villages of Bethel and Dillingham. Approximately 40 to 50 percent of the populace are non-Native in these two villages.

The Native people of Alaska migrated from Asia. Anthropologists theorize that they originated in Mongolia because their physical features resemble those of Mongoloids. According to Yupiat creation mythology, the Yupiat were created by the Raven in the area in which they are presently located.

Approximately 32 percent of Alaska Native people have migrated to Anchorage (the biggest city in Alaska) and the Matanuska-Susitna area. Most of these people are looking for opportunities for a better life and living. Many live in poverty because they do not possess marketable skills. Many Alaskan Native people are now campaigning for an educational system that respects their own languages, ways of knowing, skills, and problem-solving methods and tools. They feel this will lead to a Native state of well-being with a positive identity and cultural pride leading to self-reliance, self-determination, and spiritual strength.

ACCULTURATION AND ASSIMILATION

The Yupiat people did not readily accept education in the coastal, Yukon and Kuskokwim delta villages. The resistance was lead by shamans, village leaders, and elders. It was not the superior knowledge, weapons, or methods of non-Natives that defeated the leaders, but the diseases that members of the dominant society brought with them. The Yupiat people had no resistance to these new illnesses. The shamans, who treated ailments using spiritual methods, stood by helplessly while many of their people succumbed to these foreign diseases. Whole villages were wiped out, orphaning many children and young adults. It was during this time that the missionaries were able to establish their churches and orphanages, building schools to teach a different language and way of life. The cognitive and cultural imperialism of the dominant society forced the Yupiat to conform to this system. Under the teachings of the missionary-teachers, the youngsters were faced with corporal punishment for using their mother tongue and practicing their strange ways. Being told their language and ways were inferior mentally scarred many students. To this day, the Yupiat people suffer many psycho-social problems.

The goal of traditional Yupiat education was to teach the youth to live in harmony in the human world, as well as the natural and spiritual worlds. It was their belief that everything in the universe (plants, animals, rivers, winds, and so forth) had a spirit, which mandated respect. Everything possessing a spirit meant that everything had a consciousness or awareness, and therefore must be accorded human respect. The Yupiat did not practice pantheism; they merely treated everything with respect and honor. Such a way of life led the Yupiat to possess only that which was absolutely necessary and taught them to enjoy to the utmost the little they had. The Yupiat people have been bombarded by Western society's institutions for a little over 100 years. These strange outside values and ways have wreaked havoc with their world view. Most Yupiat are aware of who they are and where they came from, but the continuing barrage of foreign values and ideas causes confusion. The clash of Western and Yupiat values and traditions has caused many Yupiat people to suffer from a depression that is spiritual in nature. There is a need for them to regain harmony with Nature. This is what fosters their identity.

TRADITIONS, CUSTOMS, AND BELIEFS

In the past, Yupiat clothing was made from the pelts of such animals as Alaskan ground squirrels, muskrat, mink, land otter, wolf, beaver, red fox, caribou, and moose, in addition to fish and waterfowl skins. Yupiat women made parkas, pants, boots, and gloves from these skins. For special occasions, the women wore squirrel-skin parkas with many designs and tassels on them. A well-made parka shows that the owner has fine skills; if a woman with a beautiful parka is of marrying age, parents of young men assess her as a possible wife for the son.

The Yupiat people observe the Western holidays, although they practice Yupiat singing and dancing. In this way they have begun to Yupiakize many of the Western holidays. Of the several original ceremonies, it is only the Messenger Feast that is still observed. The celebration, which takes place in the spring, experienced a resurgence around 1990. None of the other traditional ceremonies are practiced anymore. The reason may be that few elders remain remember the songs and dances. All traditional ceremonies required singing songs in a prescribed order, and making changes was taboo. Often these require very elaborate paraphernalia such as masks, drums, clay lamps, food, and designated leaders with special costumes. Much time was spent in preparation for the performances. The rehearsals for traditional ceremonies were not to be observed by the villagers.

The Yupiat people have returned to practicing their songs and dances, which are a form of prayer. Since Yupiat culture is based on oral traditions, songs have been passed down from generation to generation for centuries. Five dominant ceremonies and several minor ceremonies are observed throughout the year. The dominant ceremonies are: *Nakaciuq* (Bladder Festival), *Elriq* (Festival of the Dead), *Kevgiq* (invitation ceremony), *Petugtaq* (request certain items), and *Keleq* (invitation). These were ceremonies of thanksgiving to the *Ellam Yua* (Spirit of the Universe) and Mother Earth for the many gifts. Ceremonies focus on three things: centering or balancing within oneself and with the world; reciprocation to the plants and animals that must be killed in order to live; and expression of joy and humor. All Yupiat rituals and ceremonies incorporate meditation on the integration of the human, natural, and spiritual worlds.

CUISINE

The Yupiat region is rich with waterfowl, fish, and sea and land mammals. Salmon are a staple source of food and are caught in setnets, or drifting downriver. The nets are let out of a boat perpendicular to the river shoreline and allowed to drift downriver for approximately one-half mile. When the net is pulled in, fishers remove their catch. The fish are taken to the fish camp, where they are unloaded into holding boxes. The fish are beheaded and split by the women. The split fish are hung to dry. When the surface of the flesh begins to harden, they are moved to the smoke house where they are smoked and preserved for winter use. Some of the fish are salted, frozen, or buried underground for later use. Today about half the food is supplied by subsistence activities; the other half is purchased from the commercial stores.

The tundra provides berries for making jams, jellies, and a Yupiat delicacy commonly called Eskimo ice cream—a concoction of vegetable shortening, berries, and sugar. Today there are many variations of this dessert. Yupiat women have incorporated many new ingredients, such as raisins, strawberries, dried peaches, apples, and mashed potatoes to create innovative and tasty mixtures.

HEALTH ISSUES

Traditionally the Yupiat people were a healthy people in spite of occasional famines and diseases. Presently, the two biggest problems with the growing population are water and sewage. Water from the rivers and lakes is no longer potable as a result of pollution. Wells must be drilled and sewage lagoons built, but there are inherent problems as well. The land on which this must take place is marshy and presents difficulties for control. Federal and state agencies are constantly asked to grant more funding for these activities. However, the matter becomes more problematic each year. The solutions require expensive undertakings.

Suicide among young Yupiat men is high. This is generally attributed to problems Native youth have with identity and finding a meaningful place in society. The Bethel and Dillingham region has a wide range of chronic health problems, including otitis media, cancer, cardiovascular disease, diabetes, tooth and gum disease, obesity, and sexually transmitted diseases. The Yupiat people are only now beginning to have a role in stemming these maladies.

LANGUAGE

The language of the Dillingham and Bethel regions is Yupiat. There are four dialects: Yupiat of the delta region; Cupiaq of the coastal; Suqpiaq of the Alaska Peninsula; and Siberian Yupiat of St. Lawrence Island. These dialects are becoming grammatically impoverished. There has been much debate among the Yupiat over whether their language should be taught at home or in the schools. As a result, English is becoming the dominant language. Some villages still prefer to speak primarily Yupiat and regard English as the second language. Even these villages, however, are losing pieces of language. The younger generation communicates mainly in English. For the first time in the history of the Yupiat people a generation gap is steadily widening. The Yupiat people realize their world view is imbedded in the language; that its webbing is ineluctably intertwined in the nuances, inflections, and subtleties of the words. Therefore many Yupiat people wish the language be revived, retaught, and maintained by parents, village members, and the schools.

FAMILY AND COMMUNITY DYNAMICS

According to Yupiat tradition, the father is the head of the family but the mother's role as preparer of food is equally important. She tends to the plants and animals, giving proper care and observing taboos. In Yupiat culture, plant and animal foods have consciousness and are aware of how the woman takes care of them. If pleased with the care, they give of themselves to the hunter again after reincarnation. Some of these beliefs are still observed by traditional families.

Many traditions are being lost, however, due to the pressure to make money and to satisfy advertisement-induced "needs." As with the dominant society, divorce and one-parent families are on the rise among Yupiat people. The number of single teenage mothers has increased. The nuclear family, which was once very important to Yupiat people, today is crumbling. Few Yupiat youth really know who the members of their extended family are. This knowledge was important for survival in the past.

Traditionally there was no dating among the Yupiat people. Marriages were arranged by parents. Today many Yupiat people date and fall in love. Only very traditional families arrange marriages. With new modes of transportation, such as, three- and four-wheelers, snow machines, airplanes, and boats with powerful outboard motors, Yupiat people can visit loved ones in distant villages.

In times past, men and women had very distinct roles in the village. The men were providers, the women were caregivers. Children were treasured by the parents, as they were insurance that the elders would be taken care of in later years. Father, grandfather, and males of the extended family and community educated the boys. Mothers, grandmothers, and women of the extended family and community taught the girls. It was said that the community raised the children.

EDUCATION

Today education of the young is haphazard. Many young people do not want to learn and do not see the value of traditional ways. The schools provide inferior schooling for Native youth. They graduate without mastering either the Yupiat language or English. They are usually very weak in mathematics and the sciences. Many do not pursue higher education, which accounts for the growing number of high school graduates in the villages who are unable to acclimate to the subsistence way of life and the outside world. The majority of the few who enter the universities end up as drop-outs. Only about 2.3 percent have made it through institutions of higher learning. Nevertheless, they are taxing the village need for housing, subsistence products, recreational facilities, health services, general assistance, and so forth.

All village schools are publicly funded by the state of Alaska. Ancillary funds are received from the federal government, required by such laws as the Indian Education, Johnson-O'Malley, Title VII Bilingual, and the Migratory Education acts. Today, there is a growing number of Yupiat students dropping out of elementary and high schools because they do not see any value in the knowledge and skills taught there. The cognitive and cultural imperialism of the dominant society is alive and well. Those few that do make it through the universities do not return to their villages for their new knowledge and skills cannot fit into the community nor does a position exist. It might be said that there is a brain drain from the delta. Many students who enroll in the University of Alaska system will register in education programs. When successfully completed they have the opportunity to return to their home villages to teach. Most graduate students will continue in education, working for a master's degree in administration (for a principal's certificate) or in cross-cultural education. A few will enroll in anthropology. There are very few Native students who enroll in mathematics and the sciences.

The Yupiat elders, community members, parents, teachers' aides, teachers, and university professors have been pioneers in exploring mathematics and the sciences in Yupiat thought. This effort attempts to use the Yupiat skills and ways of thinking as the basis for mathematics and sciences curricula. Yupiat people have begun to realize they have knowledge which is not understood by the dominant society. Schooling has been based on the outside world with a concomitant feeling that what the Yupiat know is of little importance. Today the Yupiat are challenging this train of thought and have taken a keen interest in changing it. They are promoting education that focuses on their language, knowledge, and skills from elementary through high school. Making their community their laboratory will edify and strengthen the identity of the Yupiat youth. This will be their most important contribution to education, arts, mathematics, sciences, industry, and government.

RELIGION

The Yupiat people believe in a *Ellam Yua* ("thlam yu-a"), a Spirit of the Universe. The most important god, however, is the Raven, the creator of earth and human beings. The Raven-god is given powers of the spirits, yet has the weaknesses of human beings. It has provided many wonderful things for the Yupiat such as the sun, moon, and stars for light, and life for all the earth's inhabitants. But the Raven possesses human frailties such as greed, making mistakes, hurting others and itself. It is the indomitable trickster and often has other animals and humans play tricks. The Raven is a survivor. It, as a pronoun designating the Raven, is fitting because it changes in form to a human, a plant, and is often a messenger in its existing form.

The Yupiat people believe that everything of the earth possesses a spirit. Having a spirit means that all things possess consciousness or awareness; having awareness means that they are mindful of who they give themselves to and how they are treated. A hunter who cares for and heeds taboos, and whose wife does the same, will be a successful provider. The animals will give of themselves to the hunter knowing that they will be well taken care of. Since the Yupiat people believe that everything in nature has a spirit, some anthropologists say that they are pantheistic. This is not the case. Because animals and other things possess spirits means they are honored and respected, but not necessarily worshipped. The purpose of this spirituality is to live in harmony with everything of the human, natural, and spiritual worlds. To live in harmony is to be balanced in living and doing things that feel right in the heart.

Medicine people were specialists among the Yupiat people. Some specialized in bone healing, others used herbs for curing diseases, still others called upon spirits of animals, such as the bear and eagle, or spiritual beings for aid. Yupiat people believed that animal spirits and spirit helpers lived on the moon. Powerful medicine people would experience out-of-body travel to the moon, the sea, the spiritual world, other villages, animal kingdoms, and other far-off places. They were citizens of two worlds—the earth and places where the spirits dwelled. They travelled readily and learned much from their experiences, which they conveyed to their village.

The Yupiat people believed human beings were inherently good, which is quite different from most modern day religions. If a person did something wrong, the community would seek out some activity to help the wrongdoer correct his or her behavior, to become rehabilitated, and again become a positive member of the community. This differs from the punishment that is dispensed by the modern-day justice system.

Since the Yupiat people had to kill living things in order to survive, they developed rituals and ceremonies to regain a sense of peace with the world and its creatures. This was their method of reciprocation to Mother Earth. The Yupiat people could never become vegetarians because they needed the animal protein and fat to live in a harsh environment.

Land is important to the Yupiat people, for human beings and spirits occupy the same space. The land is described in action words, therefore it is a process, on-going and dynamic. By careful and patient observation the Yupiat people learned how they are to interact with other people, nature, and the spirits. Nature became their metaphysic. Today, the Yupiat people are not living as close to nature and, as a result, suffer from a spiritual depression.

EMPLOYMENT AND ECONOMIC TRADITIONS

Well over 50 percent of villagers qualify for government assistance. Yupiat unemployment is as high as 80 percent in some villages. Jobs are scarce and the Alaska Native Commission claims that the few subsidized public service positions are generally occupied by transient or permanently settled non-Natives. The regional and village corporations, created by the Alaska Native Claims Settlement Act, are barely surviving, unable to develop business ventures from natural resources that are accessible to transportation and do not require a large initial capital investment. The main industries in the Bethel and Dillingham regions are seasonal fisheries and government-funded jobs. These regions are not rich in natural resources. Some small pockets of gold, platinum, and cinnabar exist. Profiting from such resources, however, conflicts with the Native concept of living in harmony with nature. Mining activities require that the surface of the environment be altered and make it unproductive for animal habitats, berries, and edible plants. Thus corporate leaders in the Yupiat community are reluctant to invest in ventures that will alter the environment.

Since the women's role requires them to stay in the village, some have assumed leadership roles as village corporations' presidents. The men's role requires them to leave the village for subsistence hunting and trapping. Traditionally a man and woman have always been a team. It makes sense that women assume some of the modern roles, which a growing number are doing. Many women have become bilingual teachers and counseling aides in the schools. Others are community health aides and practitioners. These women generally receive a rudimentary introduction to health practices, including diagnosis, medication, and emergency care from the Kuskokwim Community College in Bethel. As they advance, they receive more training. If they encounter a situation about which they know little, they call a physician in the Public Health Service Hospital in Bethel. Critical situations require the patient be transported to the hospital with one of the many local air services. The female aides with their nurturing ways and knowledge of traditional healing practices are well suited to this service. If modern treatment and pharmaceuticals do not work, the Yupiat practitioners often try Yupiat treatments. Often, the two treatments will work in concert to heal the patient. The health practitioners are the bridge between the patient and the medical doctor.

POLITICS AND GOVERNMENT

The Yupiat people were governed by egalitarianism whereby each member of the village had the same rights and responsibilities. They had a traditional council composed of elders who held meetings to address problems and issues affecting the village. They chose a chief, a servant-leader who often was the best hunter-provider in the village. The chief and council would address a problem, striving for consensus to arrive at a solution. Sometimes there would be an issue that no one agreed upon. It would be tabled for the next meeting. If, at the succeeding meeting, there still was no agreement, the matter would be dropped. The chief was kept in power as long as he or she used common sense and did not become arrogant or try to make decisions on his or her own. The chief was strictly a servant of the people and was expected to uphold their will.

Several forms of governmental entities usually operate within the modern village, which is confusing to the local people as well as agents of other institutions. Villagers and agents wonder with which entity they are supposed to work. Each village has a traditional or Indian Reorganization Act (IRA) council, a municipal office funded by the state of Alaska, a health center funded by the federal government, and a village corporation. Each has a prescribed function within the village. The IRA or tribal council was established under the auspices of the federal government, the health center is under the Yukon-Kuskokwim Health Corporation funded by the federal Indian Health Service, and the village corporation established under the Alaska Native Claims Settlement Act (ANCSA) has responsibilities for business ventures and village lands.

The Indian Self-Determination and Education Act has had the biggest impact on the Yupiat villages. This law allows the Yupiat villages to contract services operated by the federal government, including schools, social services, general assistance, child welfare, health services, and game management. Many of these services have been taken over by regional corporations or by organized clusters of villages. Funding for these activities is always a problem. The sources are consistently looking for ways to cut programs.

The Yupiat region belongs to the Alaskan Federation of Natives, Inc. (AFN), which is a statewide organization representing all Native regions. This organization functions year-round with one annual meeting of representatives from every region. They try to address all issues affecting the Alaskan Native people. They present many resolutions to various government agencies and institutions whose activities affect the Native people. The Yupiat people are always well represented. Being from a region where there are many elderly people who do not speak English, they have purchased communications technology that translates English to Yupiat for the duration of the meeting. They are the only native group to use translators. This shows the importance given to the AFN annual meeting by the Yupiat people.

The people of the Bethel and Dillingham regions vote heavily democratic. The majority of the Alaskan Native people belong to the Democratic Party.

MILITARY

Since World War II, many Yupiat men have joined the armed forces. Today, many young men are members of the Army National Guard. Most villages have a guard unit. The headquarters of the 297th Infantry Battalion is in Bethel. It provides opportunities for income as well as training. Many Yupiat young men have become officers.

MEDIA

RADIO AND TELEVISION

KYUK-AM (640) and KYUK-TV (Channel 4). Has many tapes of Yupiat songs, myths, legends and stories, and videotapes of the Yupiat people.

Contact: Joe Seibert, General Manager
Address: 640 Radio Street, Pouch 468, Bethel, Alaska 99559.
Telephone: (800) 478-3640; or (907) 543-3131.
Fax: (907)543-3130.
E-mail: joe_seibert@ddc-alaska.org.

MUSEUMS AND RESEARCH CENTERS

Alaska State Museum.
Address: 395 Whittier Street, Juneau, Alaska 99801-1718.
Telephone: (907) 465-2901.
Fax: (907) 465-2976.

Anchorage Museum of History and Art.
Address: 121 West Seventh Avenue, Anchorage, Alaska 99501.
Telephone: (907) 343-4326.

Institute of Alaska Native Arts, Inc.
Address: Box 70769, Fairbanks, Alaska 99707.
Telephone: (907) 456-7406.
Fax: (907) 451-7268.

Sheldon Jackson Museum.
Address: 801 Lincoln Drive, Stika, Alaska 99835.
Telephone: (907) 747-5222.
Fax: (907) 747-5212.

UAF Museum.
Address: 907 Yukon Drive, P.O. Box 756960, Fairbanks, Alaska 99775-6960.
Telephone: (907) 474-7505.
Fax: (907) 474-5469.

Yugtarvik Museum.
Address: Bethel, Alaska 99559.
Telephone: (907) 543-3521.
Fax: (907) 543-3596.

SOURCES FOR ADDITIONAL STUDY

Alexie, O., and H. Morris. *The Elders' Conference 1984*. Bethel, Alaska: Orutsararmiut Native Council, 1985.

Barnhardt, R. "Administrative Influences in Alaskan Native Education," in *Cross-Cultural Issues in Alaskan Education*, edited by R. Barnhardt. Fairbanks: Center for Northern Educational Research, 1977; pp. 57-63.

Bielawski, E. *Cross-Cultural Epistemology: Cultural Readaptation through the Pursuit of Knowledge* (paper presented at the Seventh Inuit Studies Conference). Fairbanks: University of Alaska Fairbanks, 1990.

Darnell, F. "Education among the Native Peoples of Alaska," *Polar Record*, 19, No. 122, 1979; pp. 431-446.

Fienup-Riordan, A. *Eskimo Essays Yup'ik Lives and How We See Them*. New Brunswick and London: Rutgers University Press, 1990.

————. *The Real People and the Children of Thunder: The Yup'ik Eskimo Encounter with Moravian Missionaries John and Edith Kilbuck*. Norman and London: University of Oklahoma Press, 1991.

Henkelman, J. W., and K. H. Vitt. *Harmonious to Dwell*. Bethel: Tundra Press, 1985.

Kawagley, O. "Yup'ik Ways of Knowing," *Canadian Journal of Native Education*, 17, No. 2, 1990; pp. 5-17.

Napoleon, H. *Yuuyaraq: the Way of the Human Being*. Fairbanks: Center for Cross-Cultural Studies, University of Alaska Fairbanks, 1990.

Oswalt, W. H. *Bashful No Longer*. Norman: University of Oklahoma Press, 1990.

————. *Mission of Change in Alaska: Eskimos and Moravians on the Kuskokwim*. San Marino, California: Huntington Library, 1963.

BOOKS

Alba, Richard D. *Ethnic Identity: The Transformation of White America*. New Haven, Connecticut: Yale University Press, 1990.

Discusses relations between white and ethnic minority groups in contemporary American society.

Albyn, Carole Lisa, and Lois Sinaiko Webb. *The Multicultural Cookbook for Students*. Phoenix, Arizona: Oryx Press, 1993.

Covers the cuisines of 122 countries, providing at least two traditional recipes per country. Glossary of terms.

Allen, James Paul, and Eugene James Turner. *We the People: An Atlas of America's Ethnic Diversity*. New York: Macmillan, 1988.

Identifies American ethnic groups on national, regional, and city scales, providing good annotations, maps, and statistical data based on the 1980 U.S. Census.

Angell, Carole S. *Celebrations Around the World: A Multicultural Handbook*. Golden, Colorado: Fulcrum, 1996.

Holidays, festivals, feasts, and other celebrations from various countries around the world. Indexes and bibliographies.

Ashabranner, Brent K. *Still a Nation of Immigrants*. New York: Cobble Hill Books/Dutton, 1993.

Illuminates recent trends in American immigration. Photographs.

Asian Americans Information Directory. Detroit: Gale Research, 1994.

Comprehensive resource covering Asian American organizations, museums, agencies, institutions, programs, services, and publications. See also *Encyclopedia of Associations*.

Axtell, Roger E., ed. *Do's and Taboos Around the World*. Third edition. New York: John Wiley & Sons, 1993.

More than 200 greetings, beckonings, farewells, terms of endearment, and other gestures of courtesy and customs culled from the cultures of 82 countries. Includes historical anecdotes.

Bernardo, Stephanie. *The Ethnic Almanac*. Garden City, New York: Doubleday, 1981.

Reference source covering 40 ethnic groups that includes statistical data, short essays, biographies, customs, and bibliographies.

Brown, Francis J., and Joseph S. Roucek. *One America: The History, Contributions, and Present Problems of Our Racial and National Minorities*. Westport, Connecticut: Negro Universities Press, 1970.

Reference book covering almost 100 ethnic groups that includes information on immigration, settlement, and major contributions, as well as statistical data and bibliographies.

Bruhn, Wolfgang, and Max Tilke. *A Pictorial History of Costume: A Survey of Costume of All Periods and Peoples from Antiquity to Modern Times Including National Costume in Europe and Non-European Countries*. Studio City, California: Players Press, 1995.

Contains excellent color illustrations of ethnic costumes from Europe, Asia, and Africa.

Buenker, John, and Lorman A. Ratner, eds. *Multiculturalism in the United States: A Comparative Guide to Acculturation and Ethnicity*. New York: Greenwood Press, 1992.

Discusses minority groups in America, focusing on pluralism and ethnic relations.

Buttlar, Lois, and Lubomyr R. Wynar. *Building Ethnic Collections: An Annotated Guide for School Media Centers and Public Libraries*. Littleton, Colorado: Libraries Unlimited, 1977.

Recommends books covering more than 50 ethnic groups.

Casey, Betty. *International Folk Dancing, U.S.A.* Garden City, New York: Doubleday, 1981.

Describes folk dancing in several European, Asian, and Latin American countries. Illustrated.

Champagne, Duane. *The Native North American Almanac: A Reference Work on Native North Americans in the United States and Canada*. Detroit: Gale Research, 1994.

Comprehensive guide covering North American tribes, their history, language, arts, education, literature, media, and prominent Native Americans.

Champion, Selwyn G. *Racial Proverbs: A Selection of the World's Proverbs Arranged Linguistically*. Second edition. New York: Barnes & Noble, 1964.

Offers hundreds of proverbs from 27 countries.

Chiswick, Barry, ed. *Immigration, Language, and Ethnicity: Canada and the United States*. Washington, D.C.: AEI Press, 1992.

Explores immigration patterns, ethnic and linguistic minorities, and language policy in both countries.

Coppa, Frank J., and Thomas J. Curran, eds. *The Immigrant*

Experience in America. Boston: Twayne Publishers, 1976.

 Provides historical coverage of European, Hispanic, and Asian immigration to the United States.

Cordasco, Francesco, and David N. Alloway. *American Ethnic Groups, the European Heritage: A Bibliography of Doctoral Dissertations at American Universities.* Metuchen, New Jersey: Scarecrow Press, 1981.

 Lists more than 1,400 dissertations that cover 30 ethnic groups.

Cordry, Harold V. *The Multicultural Dictionary of Proverbs: Over 20,000 Adages from More Than 120 Languages, Nationalities and Ethnic Groups.* Jefferson, North Carolina: McFarland, 1997.

 Proverbs from all continents, arranged by subjects in aphabetical order. Subject and keyword indexes, but lacks language and ethnic group indexes.

Countries of the World and Their Leaders Yearbook. 2 vols. Detroit: Gale Research, 1995.

 Comprehensive study of more than 200 countries that includes information on religion, education, media, and politics and government.

Daniels, Roger. *Coming to America: A History of Immigration and Ethnicity in American Life.* New York: HarperCollins, 1990.

 Historical overview of immigration and settlement patterns in the United States. Photographs.

Davis, Hillary. *Celebrate: Traditional Ethnic Entertaining in America.* New York: Crescent Books, 1992.

 Explores the folklore, festivals, cookery, and heritage of various ethnic groups.

Dinnerstein, Leonard, and David M. Reimers. *Ethnic Americans: A History of Immigration.* Fourth edition. New York: Harper & Row, 1999.

 Historical overview of immigration and ethnic relations.

Dinnerstein, Leonard, Roger L. Nichols, and David M. Reimers. *Natives and Strangers: A Multicultural History of Americans.* New York: Oxford University Press, 1996.

 Historical account of various ethnic groups in the United States and their relationships with one another. Illustrated.

Di Pietro, Robert. *Ethnic Perspectives in American Literature: Selected Essays on the European Contribution.* New York: Modern Language Association, 1983.

 Illuminates European ethnic groups. Bibliography.

Eiseman, Alberta. *From Many Lands.* New York: Atheneum, 1970.

 Documents the immigrant experiences from the past 200 years through journals, newspapers, and literature.

Encyclopedia of Associations. Farmington Hills, Michigan: Gale Group, 1999.

 Comprehensive reference source on thousands of organizations in the United States, including hundreds of ethnic organizations. Includes activities and contact information. Subject and keyword indexes.

Ferraro, Thomas J. *Ethnic Passages: Literary Immigrants in Twentieth-Century America.* Chicago: University of Chicago Press, 1993.

 Discusses the impact of emigration and immigration on twentieth-century American fiction.

Friedman, Lester D., ed. *Unspeakable Images: Ethnicity and the American Cinema.* Urbana: University of Illinois Press, 1991.

 Traces ethnic influences in American motion pictures.

Georges, Robert A., and Stephen Stern. *American and Canadian Immigrant and Ethnic Folklore: An Annotated Bibliography.* New York: Garland Pub., 1982.

 Includes coverage of 50 ethnic groups, primarily Europeans, but also Asian and African peoples.

Gold, Milton J., Carl A. Grant. and Harry N. Rivlin, eds. *In Praise of Diversity: A Resource Book for Multicultural Education.* Washington, D.C.: Teacher Corps, 1977.

 Contains essays praising various cultures and ethnic groups for their contributions to American society.

Greene, Victor R. *American Immigrant Leaders, 1800-1910: Marginality and Identity.* Baltimore, Maryland: Johns Hopkins University Press, 1987.

 Recognizes Irish, German, Norwegian, Swedish, Jewish, Polish, and Italian leaders in various fields. Bibliography.

Handlin, Oscar. *The Uprooted: The Epic Story of the Great Migrations that Made the American People.* Boston: Little Brown, 1951.

 Reference source that compares immigrant groups, emphasizing how they altered American culture.

Hayden, Carla D., ed. *Venture into Cultures: A Resource Book of Multicultural Materials and Programs.* Chicago: American Library Association, 1992.

 Discusses the culture, holidays, games, arts, crafts, dances, foods, and juvenile literature of African Americans, Asians, Arabs, Hispanic Americans, Jews, Africans, Persians, and Native Americans.

Hecker, Melvin. *Ethnic America, 1970-1977: Updating the Ethnic Chronology Series.* Dobbs Ferry, New York: Oceana Publications, 1979.

 Provides chronologies for 31 ethnic groups.

Hoerder, Dick, ed. *The Immigrant Labor Press in North America, 1840s-1970s: An Annotated Bibliography.* New York: Greenwood Press, 1987.

 Includes essays, statistical data, and bibliographies on 30 ethnic groups, most of which are European.

Hutchinson, E. P. *Immigrants and Their Children, 1850-1950.* New York: Russell & Russell, 1976.

 Comprehensive study illuminating the generation gaps within numerous ethnic groups over the past 100 years, focusing on economic, social, professional, and linguistic issues.

Jackson, Kenneth T., ed. *The Encyclopedia of New York City.* New Haven, Connecticut: Yale University Press and New York Historical Society, 1995.

 Brief articles on 60 ethnic groups in New York. Several entries lack bibliographies and pictures. Useful for quick reference.

Johnson, Michael. *The Native Tribes of North America: A Concise Encyclopedia.* New York: Macmillan, 1992.

 Guide to 400 tribes in North America, centering on identity, religion, culture, kinship, and location. Excellent Illustrations.

Kanellos, Nicolás, ed. *The Hispanic American Almanac: A Reference Work on Hispanics in the United States*. Detroit: Gale Research, 1993.

>Comprehensive reference source that examines history, religion, the arts, media, music, science, sports, education, and notable Hispanics. Illustrated.

Katz, William Loren. *The Great Migrations, 1880s-1912*. Austin, Texas: Raintree, Steck-Vaughn, 1993.

>Recounts major immigration waves from Europe, the Middle East, and Asia.

Kivisto, Peter, ed. *The Ethnic Enigma: The Salience of Ethnicity for European-Origin Groups*. Philadelphia: The Balch Institute Press, 1989.

>Addresses ethnic relations between European American groups.

Knippling, Alpana Sharma, ed. *New Immigrant Literatures in the United States: A Sourcebook to Our Multicultural Literary Heritage*. Westport, Connecticut: Greenwood Press, 1996.

>Covers authors from more than 20 language/ethnic groups and their works. Bibliographies.

Kraus, Barbara. *The Barbara Kraus International Cookbook*. Adapted and edited by Margaret Markham. New York: Perigree Books, 1991.

>Contains typical dishes from more than 100 countries. Indexed by the names of meals and by country. Bibliography.

Latham, William. *How to Find Your Family Roots*. New expanded edition. Santa Monica, California: Santa Monica Press, 1994.

>Guide for tracing ethnic backgrounds in America and abroad (180 countries).

Lee, Joan Faung. *Asian American Experiences in the United States: Oral Histories of First to Fourth Generation Americans from China, the Philippines, Japan, India, Pacific Islands, Vietnam and Cambodia*. New York: McFarland, 1991.

>Supplemental source to other sources on Asian Americans. Illustrated.

Lehman, Jeffrey, ed. *Gale Encyclopedia of Multicultural America: Primary Documents*. Farmington Hills, Michigan: Gale Group, 2000.

>Includes more than 200 documents (e.g., poems, recipes, treaties, and oral histories) on 90 ethnic groups in the United States. Illustrations, index.

Levinson, David. *Ethnic Groups Worldwide: A Ready Reference Handbook*. Phoenix, Arizona: Oryx Press, 1998.

>Covers the ethnic composition and relations of all countries from all continents. Maps and bibliographies.

Levinson, David, and Melvin Ember, editors-in-chief. *American Immigrant Cultures: Builders of a Nation*. New York: Simon & Schuster Macmillan, 1997.

>Articles on more than 170 ethnic and religious groups, accompanied by bibliographies and pictures.

Liebman, Lance, ed. *Ethnic Relations in America*. Englewood Cliffs, New Jersey: Prentice-Hall, 1982.

>Provides essays on ethnic history, immigration, and language, as well as political and legal issues.

Luis, William. *Dance Between Two Cultures: Latino Caribbean Literature Written in the United States*. Nashville: Vanderbilt University Press, 1997.

>The works and activities of ten outstanding Puerto Rican, Cuban, and Dominican authors, born and raised in the United States.

Malinowski, Sharon, and Anna Sheets, eds. *Gale Encyclopedia of Native American Tribes*. Detroit: Gale Research, 1998.

>Essays on more than 400 Native American groups, focusing on their history and current culture. Includes more than 200 stories/legends. Illustrations, maps, and multiple indexes. List of all federally recognized tribes in the United States and Canada.

Mangiafico, Luciano. *Contemporary American Immigrants: Patterns of Filipino, Korean, and Chinese Settlement in the United States*. New York: Praeger, 1988.

>Reviews settlement patterns and social adjustment.

Manoogian, Sylvia, and Natalia Bezugloff. *Directory of Language Collections in North American Public Libraries*. Chicago: American Library Association, 1986.

>Locates language collections in more than 200 libraries, arranging them by foreign language and by geographic location.

McCabe, Cynthia Jaffe. *The American Experience: Contemporary Immigrant Artists*. New York: Independent Curators; Philadelphia: The Balch Institute for Ethnic Studies, 1985.

>Examines the artistic contributions of various ethnic groups in America.

Mead, Frank S. *Handbook of Denominations in the United States*. Tenth edition. Revised by Samuel S. Hill. Nashville, Tennessee: Abingdon Press, 1995.

>Reference source that includes the religious bodies of several American ethnic groups.

Melton, J. Gordon, ed. *Encyclopedia of American Religions*. Fifth edition. Detroit: Gale Research, 1996.

>Offers comprehensive coverage of more than 1,700 religious groups.

Meltzer, Milton. *The Hispanic Americans*. New York: Crowell, 1982.

>Reference source for young people, focusing on the social and economic conditions of various Hispanic American groups.

Miller, Sally M., ed. *The Ethnic Press in the United States: A Historical Analysis and Handbook*. New York: Greenwood Press, 1987.

>Furnishes essays and bibliographies on more than 25 ethnic groups.

Miller, Wayne Charles. *A Comprehensive Bibliography for the Study of American Minorities*. New York: New York University Press, 1976.

>Covers several dozen ethnic groups (not only minorities) in short essays and bibliographies.

Miller-Lachmann, Lyn. *Global Voices, Global Visions: A Core Collection of Multicultural Books*. New Providence, New Jersey: R. R. Bowker, 1995.

>Comprehensive reference work that includes significant books on multicultural literature (e.g., fiction, non-fiction, biographies) written by American and foreign authors in English. Extensive annotations. Covers all continents.

Minority Organizations: A National Directory. Fifth edition. Chicago: Ferguson Publishing Company, 1997.

>Provides information on 9,700 organizations representing African American, Native American, Hispanic American, and Asian American groups.

Morrison, Joan, and Charlote Fox Zabusky. *American Mosaic: The Immigrant Experience in the Words of Those Who Lived It*. Pittsburgh, Pennsylvania: University of Pittsburgh Press, 1993.

Collection of experiences by American immigrants from Europe, Asia, the Middle East, South America, and South Africa.

Newman, Jaqueline. *Melting Pot: An Annotated Bibliography and Guide to Food and Nutrition Information for Ethnic Groups in America*. New York: Garland Publications, 1993.
Contains information on the food habits, cookery, and nutrition of several dozen American ethnic groups.

Palmer, Ransford R. *In Search of a Better Life: Perspectives on Migration from the Caribbean*. New York: Praeger, 1990.
Comparative study centering on the migration of Caribbean peoples to the United States, Canada, and Great Britain.

Parillo, Vincent. *Strangers to These Shores: Race and Ethnic Relations in the United States*. Sixth edition. Boston: Allyn and Bacon, 2000.
Examines America's pluralism in a multiracial society, covering more than 100 ethnic groups.

Pozzetta, George. *Folklore, Culture, and the Immigrant*. New York: Garland, 1991.
Discusses immigration, ethnicity, and acculturation in the United States.

Racinet, Albert. *The Historical Encyclopedia of Costumes*. New York: Facts on File, 1988.
Includes traditional costumes from Africa, Asia, Europe, Oceania, and North America. Illustrated.

Santoli, Al. *New Americans: An Oral History, Immigrants and Refugees in the U.S. Today*. New York: Viking Press, 1988.
Personal accounts of American immigrants from several ethnic groups.

Schon, Isabel. *A Hispanic Heritage: A Guide to Juvenile Books about Hispanic People and Culture*. Series IV. Metuchen, New Jersey: Scarecrow Press, 1991.
Includes information on several Hispanic American groups.

Schorr, Alan. *Hispanic Resource Directory, 1992-1994: A Comprehensive Guide to More Than 6,000 National, State, and Local Organizations Concerned with Hispanic Americans*. Juno, Alaska: Denali Group, 1992.
Includes information on several Hispanic American groups.

Shorris, Earl. *Latinos: A Biography of the People*. New York: W. W. Norton, 1992.
Provides Hispanic American history and biographies of notable Latinos.

Smith, Jessie Carney, and Joseph M. Palmisano. *The African American Almanac*. Eighth edition. Detroit: Gale Group, 1999.
Comprehensive reference source covering history, organizations, politics, religion, music, sports, science, the arts, and notable persons.

Sowell, Thomas. *Ethnic America: A History*. New York: Basic Books, 1981.
Includes ethnic groups from Africa, Asia, Europe, and Latin America.

Standard Periodical Directory. New York: Oxbridge Communications, 1999.
Annual directory containing English and bilingual titles that covers more than 60 American ethnic groups.

Statistical Abstract of the United States. Washington, D.C.: U.S. Bureau of the Census, 1998.
Reference source published annually that presents immigration statistics by country of origin, permanent residents, refugees, and undocumented aliens in the United States, along with comparative data dating back to the nineteenth century.

Stave, Bruce, and John Sutherland. *From the Old Country: An Oral History of European Migration to America*. New York: Twain Publishers, 1994.
Furnishes oral histories from the 1930s through the 1970s, including discussions on crossing the ocean, work, family, love and marriage, community life, and other topics.

Streep, Peg, et al, eds. *An American Christmas: A Celebration of Our Heritage from Around the World*. New York: Philosophical Library, 1989.
Explores the ethnic folklore, customs, and social life of several ethnic groups.

Takaki, Ronald T. *A Different Mirror: A History of Multicultural America*. Boston: Little, Brown & Co., 1993.
Excellent presentation of America's multicultural cosidety, its historical development, and race and ethnic relations. Illustrations, bibliography, and index.

———. *Strangers from a Different Shore: A History of Asian Americans*. Boston: Little Brown, 1989.
Investigates Chinese, Japanese, Korean, Indian, Filipino, and Vietnamese groups. Illustrated.

Thernstrom, Stephan et al. *Harvard Encyclopedia of American Ethnic Groups*. Cambridge, Massachusetts: Belknap Press/Harvard University Press, 1980.
Scholarly source covering more than 100 ethnic groups that includes discussions of immigration, settlement, organizations, religions, and major contributions. Bibliographies.

Tilke, Max. *National Costumes from East Europe, Africa and Asia*. New York: Hastings House, 1978.
Treats various ethnic groups. Color illustrations.

Tilton, Jeff Todd. *Worlds of Music: An Introduction to the Music of the World's Peoples*. New York: Schirmer Books, 1992.
Addresses Native American, African American, European, Asian, Latin American, and American (folk) music.

Upton, Dell. *America's Architectural Roots: Ethnic Groups that Built America*. Washington, D.C.: Preservation Press, 1986.
Provides examples of American ethnic architecture. Illustrated.

U.S. Census of the Population and Housing. Washington, D.C.: U.S. Bureau of the Census, 1991-1992.
Contains the latest numerical data on American ethnic groups, their geographical location, language preservation, and other relevant topics.

Veliana, Suarez, Ana. *Hispanic Media, USA: A Narrative Guide to Print and Electronic News Media in the United States*. Washington, D.C.: Media Institute, 1987.
Supplies Hispanic American newspapers, directories, and mass media information.

Waldman, Carl. *Encyclopedia of Native American Tribes.* New York: Facts on File, 1988.

> Describes 150 North American tribes, their locations, migration patterns, life styles, languages, and other relevant topics. Color illustrations.

Warren, Lee. *The Dance of Africa: An Introduction.* Englewood Cliffs, New Jersey: Prentice Hall, 1972.

> Covers several African dances. Photographs and dance instructions.

Wasserman, Fred. *Ellis Island: An Illustrated History of the Immigrant Experience.* New York: Macmillan, 1991.

> Records through photographs the experiences of individuals who entered America through Ellis Island.

Wasserman, Paul, and Alice Kennington, eds. *Ethnic Information Sources of the United States.* Second edition. Detroit: Gale Research, 1995.

> Comprehensive source covering more than 120 American ethnic groups that includes organizations, periodicals, research centers, radio, and other subjects. Bibliography.

Wasserman, Paul, et al. *Festivals Sourcebook: A Reference Guide to Fairs, Festivals, and Celebrations.* Second edition. Detroit: Gale Research, 1984.

Waters, Mary C. *Ethnic Options: Choosing Identities in America.* Berkeley: University of California Press, 1990.

> Reviews the ethnic composition of America, focusing on mixed marriages and the freedom to choose ethnic backgrounds.

Weiser, Marjorie K. *Ethnic America.* New York: Wilson, 1978.

> Supplies articles on different ethnic groups in the United States, especially Native Americans and African Americans, and their acculturation.

Wertsman, Vladimir F. *What's Cooking in Multicultural America: 400 Ethnic Cuisines at Your Finger Tips.* Metuchen, New Jersey: Scarecrow Press, 1995.

> Presents cuisines from every continent, including 120 Native American tribes. Annotated bibliographies.

———. *Career Opportunities for Bilinguals and Multilinguals: A Directory of Resources in Education, Employment, and Business.* Second edition. Metuchen, New Jersey: Scarecrow Press, 1994.

> Employment guide that identifies educational institutions specializing in languages and targets prospective employers in the United States and abroad who are interested in hiring individuals with language skills.

Westin, Jeane Eddy. *Finding Your Roots: How to Trace Your Ancestors at Home and Abroad.* New York: Jeremy P. Tarcher/Putnam, 1998.

> Guide for genealogical research in the United States and beyond.

Weyr, Thomas. *Hispanic USA: Breaking the Melting Pot.* New York: Harper and Row, 1988.

> Discusses Hispanic American culture, ethnic identity, and assimilation.

Wilde, Larry. *Larry Wilde's Complete Book of Ethnic Humor.* New York: Bell Publishing Co./Crown Publishers, 1984.

> Reveals the ethnic wisdom, expressed through humor, of various ethnic groups.

Wittke, Carol Frederick. *We Who Built America: The Saga of the Immigrant.* Revised edition. Cleveland, Ohio: Case Western University, 1967.

> Provides concise coverage of several American ethnic groups.

Wynar, Lubomyr. *Ethnic Film Strip Guide for Libraries and Media Centers.* Littleton, Colorado: Libraries Unlimited, 1980.

> Covers several dozen groups.

———. *Encyclopedic Directory of Ethnic Organizations in the United States.* Littleton, Colorado: Libraries Unlimited, 1985.

> Contains information on more than 70 ethnic groups.

Yinger, J. Milton. *Ethnicity: Source of Strength; Source of Conflict.* New York: State University of New York Press, 1994.

> Evaluates the pros and cons of ethnicity, ethnic relations, and assimilation.

PERIODICALS

EMIE Bulletin (1976–). New York: Ethnic Materials Information Exchange Round Table/ALA, Queens College Graduate School of Library and Information Studies. Quarterly.

> Multiethnic coverage featuring short articles, bibliographies, and book reviews.

Ethnic Newswatch (1992–). Stamford, Connecticut: Softline Information. Quarterly.

> CD-ROM containing articles from more than 90 ethnic and minority newspapers and magazines.

Ethnic Resource Guide (1975–). Bloomington: Ethnic Heritage Studies Program, Indiana University. Annual.

> Provides articles on African American and European groups.

Ethnic Studies Review (Explorations in Ethnic Studies) (1978–). Tempe: National Association of Ethnic Studies, Arizona State University. Monthly.

> Focuses on cultural activity of ethnic minorities and inter-ethnic group relations.

Journal of American Ethnic History (1981–). Piscataway, New Jersey: Transaction Periodicals Consortium, Rutgers State University of New Jersey. Quarterly.

> Covers multiple aspects of American immigration and ethnic history, ethnic and racial groups, and acculturation.

Melus (1973–). Huntington, West Virginia: Society of Multicultural Literature in the USA, Marshall University. Quarterly.

> Studies ethnicity in American literature and media.

Multicultural Education: The Magazine of the National Association for Multicultural Education (1993–). San Francisco: Caddo Gap Press. Quarterly.

> Examines various aspsects of multiculturalism aimed at public schools and higher education audiences.

Multicultural Review (1990–). Westport, Connecticut: Greenwood Publishers. Quarterly.

> Contains articles, book reviews, and bibliographies, providing excellent coverage of numerous American ethnic groups.

Spectrum (1965–). St. Paul, Minnesota: Immigration History Research Center. Irregular.

> Each issue has a specific theme based on the IHRC's resources and new acquisitions.

Personal names, place names, events, organizations, and various subject areas or key words contained in the *Gale Encyclopedia of Multicultural America* are listed in this index with corresponding page numbers indicating text references. Page numbers appearing in boldface indicate the chapter range of a cultural group.

immigration and settlement, 80
language, 84–85
media, 93
politics and government, 92
religions, 90–91
traditions, customs, and beliefs, 80–83
Amistad (Ship), 1613
Amistad Research Center, 817
Ammann, Jakob, 80
Ammann, Othmar, 1710
Amulets, 60
Amyotrophic Lateral Sclerosis (ALS), 760
Anabaptists, 80
Anastasoff, Christ, 297
ANB (Alaska Native Brotherhood), 1765, 1775
ANC (African National Congress), 1662–1663
Ancestral Puebloans, 1261
ANCSA (Alaska Native Claims Settlement Act of 1971), 914, 1766, 1772
Andean music, 558–559
Andersen, Morten, 521
Anderson, Marian, 49
Anderson, Mary, 1699
Andersons, Edgars, 1110
André, John, 1710
Andrica, Theodore, 1515
Angi (Ceremonial fire), 1278
Angkor period, 306
Anglo-Burmese Wars, 300
Angola, 30
Ang-Sam, Sam, 316
Anh Nguyen, 1848
Ani-Kutani, 362
Anishinabe (People), 1341
Anka, Paul, 328
Ankrah, Joseph A., 722
Antelope (Animals), 726
Anthony, Marc, 1498
Anti-Semitism, 1034–1035. *See also* Racial and cultural discrimination
Anzac Day (Holiday), 169
Ao dai (Clothing), 1853
Apache Crown Dance, 100
Apaches, **95–107**
acculturation, 99
associations, museums, and research centers, 106–107
employment and economics, 102–103
family and community, 99, 102
health, 101
history, 96–98
immigration and settlement, 98
language, 102
media, 105–106
notable individuals and groups, 103–105
politics and government, 103

traditions, customs, and beliefs, 99–100
Aparicio, Luis, 1845
Apartheid, 30, 1662–1663. *See also* Racial and cultural discrimination; Racial segregation
Aphrodite (Goddess), 488
APN (National People's Assembly), 73
Apostolic Church (Armenian), 141
Appalachia, 1573
Appiah, Kwame Anthony, 729
APRA (American Popular Revolutionary Alliance), 1435
Aquino, Benigno S., Jr., 626
Aquino, Corazon, 626
Arab American Institute (AAI), 1122, 1124, 1410, 1726
Arab American University Graduates, Inc. (AAUG), 118, 1726
Arab Americans, **108–122**
acculturation, 111–112
associations, museums, and research centers, 120–122
comparison to Lebanese Americans, 1117, 1122
differences from Chaldean Americans, 357
employment and economics, 117
family and community, 114–116
history, 108–109
immigration and settlement, 109–110
language, 113–114
media, 120
notable individuals and groups, 118–119
politics and government, 118
relations with Americans, 110–111
relations with Moroccan Americans, 1255
religion, 117
stereotypes and misconceptions, 112
traditions, customs, and beliefs, 112–113, 116–117
Arab Film Festival, 119
Arab people, 1402–1403
Arab Women's Council (AWC), 1726
Arabic (Language), 1118
Algerian Americans, 71–72
Arab Americans, 113–114
Chaldean Americans, 357
Druze, 536
Egyptians, 570
Iraqi Americans, 932
Israeli Americans, 976
Jordanian Americans, 1056–1057
Morocco, 1254
Palestinians, 1405–1406
Saudi Arabians, 1562
Syrian Americans, 1721
Yemeni Americans, 1888
Arab-Isreali conflict, 1402–1403

Arab-Isreali War, 110
Arafat, Yasser, 1403
Arai, Clarence Takeya, 1026
Aranbarri, Rocardo, 1844
Arawaks (People), 196, 687, 1001, 1490, 1864
Arbenz Guzman, Jacobo, 765
Arbeter Ring (Labor union), 1044
Arbulu, Maria Azucena, 1441
Arceneaux, Thomas J., 13
Archipenko, Alexander, 1827
Areak ka (Musical group), 311
Arenas, Reinaldo, 482
Arepas (Food), 1841
Arevalo, Juan Jose, 765
Argentina, 123–124, 130
Argentinean Americans, **123–132**
 acculturation, 125
 associations, museums, and research
  centers, 131–132
 employment and economics, 130
 family and community, 128–130
 history, 124
 immigration and settlement, 125
 language, 128
 media, 131
 notable individuals and groups, 131
 religion, 130
 traditions, customs, and beliefs, 125–127
Arguello, Roberto, 1309
Arias, Arturo, 780
Aristide, Jean-Bertrand, 807
Ariyoshi, George Ryoichi, 1026
Arizona, 95, 97, 1479–1480
Armed forces. *See* subheading of specific cultural
 group under, "notable individuals and groups,"
 e.g., Irish Americans—notable individuals
 and groups
Armed Forces movement (Portugal), 1463
Armed Forces Revolutionary Council
 (AFRC), 1612
Armenia, 133–134
Armenian (Language), 139–140
Armenian Americans, **133–146**
 acculturation, 137
 associations, museums, and research
  centers, 144–145
 employment and economics, 142
 family and community, 140
 history, 133–134
 immigration and settlement, 135–136
 language, 139–140
 media, 143–144
 notable individuals and groups, 142–143
 politics and government, 142
 relations with other Americans, 137
 relations with Turkish Americans, 1799

 religion, 141
 traditions, customs, and beliefs, 137–138
Armenian Apostolic Church, 141
Armenian Catholic Church, 141
Armenian studies (Academic discipline), 140
Armour, John David, 664
Arnarson, Ingolfur, 885
Arnerich, Mateo, 463
Arpilleras (Crafts), 382
Arranged marriages. *See also* Matchmakers
 Arab, 114
 Bangladeshi, 192
 Eritrean, 597
 Japanese, 1016
 Nez Percé, 1289
 Sierra Leonean, 1617
 Trinidadian and Tobagonian, 1789
Arrao, Claudio, 383
Arthritis, gout, 630
Artigas, José Gervasio, 1832
Artists. *See* subheading of specific cultural group
 under, "notable individuals and groups," e.g.,
 African Americans—notable individuals
 and groups
Asante (People), 722
Asawa, Ruth, 1025
Ash Wednesday, 890, 1210
Ashe, Arthur, 51
Ashkenazic Jews, 973, 1031, 1252. *See also* Israeli
 Americans; Jewish Americans
Asian American Heritage Council of
 New Jersey, 1232
Asian Immigrant Women Advocates
 (AIWA), 1085
Asian Indian Americans, **147–160**
 acculturation and assimilation, 150
 associations, museums, and research
  centers, 159
 employment and economics, 154–155
 family and community, 153
 health, 152
 history, 147–149
 immigration and settlement, 149–150
 language, 152–153
 media, 158–159
 notable individuals and groups, 156–158
 politics and government, 155
 relations with India, 155–156
 religion, 154
 traditions, customs, and beliefs, 150–152
Asim, Waheed, 24
al-Assad, Hafiz, 1716
Assembly of First Nations Resource Centre, 1362
Assimilation. *See* subheading of specific cultural
 group under, "acculturation," e.g., Armenian
 Americans—acculturation

Association of Arab American University
    Graduates, 1124
Associations and organizations. *See* subheading of
    specific cultural group under, "associations,
    museums, and research centers" e.g., Acadians—
    associations, museums, and research centers
Associations, building and loan, 506
Assumption Day (Holiday), 233
Astrology, 1226
Asturias region, 1672
Atahualpa (Incan ruler), 554, 1434
Ataturk (Turkish leader), 490, 1796–1797, 1799
Athabaskan (Language), 102, 1260, 1263
Athabaskan (People), 1764
Athletes. *See* subheading of specific cultural group
    under, "notable individuals and groups," e.g.,
    African Americans—notable individuals
    and groups
Atlantic Coast Asian American Student Union
    (ACAASU), 761
Atoka Agreement (1897), 408
Atomic Energy Commission (AEC), 914
Atsimewu drum (Musical instrument), 724
Attiyeh Foundation (AF), 1726
Attneave, Carolyn, 370
Attucks, Crispus, 47
Auctions, 86
Audubon, John James, 665, 816
Augustana Synod Church, 1696
Aung San (Burmese leader), 300
Ausbund (Hymn collection), 90
Australia, 161–165
Australia Day, 169
Australian Americans, **161–172**
    acculturation, 167
    associations, museums, and research
        centers, 171–172
    employment and economics, 170
    family and community, 168, 170
    history, 162–165
    immigration and settlement, 165–167
    language, 169
    media, 171
    notable individuals and groups, 170–171
    politics and government, 170
    religion, 170
    traditions, customs, and beliefs, 167–169
Austria, 173–174
Austrian Americans, **173–185**
    acculturation, 176
    associations, museums, and research
        centers, 184–185
    employment and economics, 180
    family and community, 179
    health, 178

history, 173–175
immigration and settlement, 175–176
language, 179
media, 183
notable individuals and groups, 181–183
politics and government, 180
religion, 179–180
traditions, customs, and beliefs, 176–178
Austro-Hungarian Compromise (1867), 867
Austro-Hungarian empire, 461, 867
Authors. *See* subheading of specific cultural group
    under, "notable individuals and groups," e.g.,
    African Americans—notable individuals and
    groups
Ava period, 299
Avila, Pedro Arias de, 1413
Avramenko, Wasyl, 1825
AWC (Arab Women's Council), 1726
AWOC (Agricultural Workers Organizing
    Committee), 633
Awooner, Kofi Nyidevu, 730
Ayarma people, 256
Ayatollah Ruhollah Khomeini, 920
Ayensu, Edward, 730
Aylwin, Patricio, 374
Aymará (Language). *See* Quechua (Language)
Ayoungman, Vivian, 248
Ayurvedic medicine, 152, 1394. *See also* Folk
    medicine
Azerbaijan, 134
Azikiwe, Nmamdi "Zik," 1314
Aztecs (People), 1298

B

Babaginda, Ibrahim, 1314
Babenberg empire, 174
Babín, Maria Teresa, 1498
Babishvili, Vladimir, 705
Baca, Lorenzo, 103
Bacalodo (Food), 1493
Bachi, Pedro, 1607
Baci rituals, 1097
Baekeland, Leo, 237
Baez, Alberto Vinicio, 1218
Baganda (People), 1808–1809
Bagels, 223
Bagration, Teymuraz, 705
Bahai (Religion), 925
Bahasa Indonesian (Language), 902
Bahasa Malaysian (Language), 1177
Baigais gads (The Year of Terror), 1102
Baila music, 1685
Bajan (Dialect), 200–201
Bakarade (Sculpture), 216
Baker, Sidney, 169

Business professionals. *See* subheading of specific cultural group under, "notable individuals and groups," e.g., African Americans—notable individuals and groups

Busk festivals, 441–442, 960–961

Button blanket, 1769

Byzantine Rite Catholicism, 347, 349–350, 1512–1513, 1640, 1823

C

Caballeros de Dimas-Alang (Organization), 632

Cabral, Amilcar, 336

Cabral, Ana Maria, 336

Cabral, João Sérgio Alvares, 1473

Cabrenas, José, 1499

Cabrera, Lydia, 481

Cachupa (Food), 338

Caciquism (Land-ownership system), 623–624

Cadiens. *See* Acadians

Cadillac, Antoine de Lamothe, 670

Cafés, 292

Cairene Arabic (Language), 570

Cajuns. *See* Acadians

Caldos, 771

Calendars, 592, 1731

California, 1391, 1465, 1523, 1673, 1730

California Gold Rush, 165, 208, 375, 388, 659. *See also* Gold mining

California State University, 1541

Caliphs (Leaders), 930

Callas, Maria, 744

The Calling of the Turtles, 1368

Caló (Language), 1200

Calvin, John, 656

Calvinism (Religion), 874, 875, 1879

Calvinist Dutch Reformed Church, 902

Calypso music, 751, 1786

Cambodia (Country), 305–308

Cambodian (Language), 312

Cambodian Americans, **305–318**
    acculturation, 309–311
    associations, museums, and research centers, 317–318
    employment and economics, 314–315
    family and community, 313
    health, 311–312
    history, 306–308
    immigration and settlement, 308–309
    language, 312
    media, 316–317
    notable individuals and groups, 312, 316
    politics and government, 316
    religion, 313–314
    stereotypes and misconceptions, 311
    traditions, customs, and beliefs, 311

Camels, 592–593

Camp McCoy, Wisconsin, 1024

Camp settlements, 3

Camp Verde Reservation, 97

Camps, concentration, 709, 1023, 1446

Canaan. *See* Israel

Canada, 248, 319–322, 668–671, 680

Canadian Americans, **319–332**
    acculturation, 323–324
    associations, museums, and research centers, 331–332
    employment and economics, 326
    family and community, 325
    health, 324
    history, 320–322
    immigration and settlement, 322–323
    language, 324–325
    media, 329–331
    notable individuals and groups, 327–329
    politics and government, 326–327
    stereotypes and misconceptions, 323–324
    traditions, customs, and beliefs, 324

Canals, 1413–1414

Cancer, 35

CANF (Cuban American National Foundation), 480

Canja de galinha (Food), 338

Cannibalism, 1365

Canoes, 823, 1342

Canoncito Navajo, 1260

Canseco, José, 482

Cantonese (Language), 394–395

Canzonerie, Tony, 1607

Cape Verde, 333–336, 341

Cape Verdean Americans, **333–344**
    acculturation, 337–338
    associations, museums, and research centers, 343–344
    employment and economics, 341
    family and community, 340
    health, 339
    history, 334–337
    immigration and settlement, 337
    language, 339–340
    media, 342–343
    notable individuals and groups, 341–342
    politics and government, 341
    relations with Cape Verde, 341
    religion, 340
    traditions, customs, and beliefs, 338–339

Capra, Frank, 994, 1607

Capraro, Nino, 1606

Cardenas-Jaffe, Veronica, 778

Cardinal, Douglas, 249

Cardoso, Fernando Henrique, 273, 281

notable individuals and groups, 435
religion, 435
traditions, customs, and beliefs, 431–433
Costumes, traditional. *See* subheading of specific
cultural group under, "traditions, customs, and
beliefs," e.g., Algerian Americans—traditions,
customs, and beliefs
Cote, Adelard, 683
Cottage industries, 91
Cotton industry, 31, 32, 568
Coucou (Food), 199
Coughlin, Charles E., 1035
Council of Energy Resource Tribes, 861
Council of Twelve, 1241
Count Roger, 1184
County of Oneida v. Oneida Indian Nation, 1355
Courtship. *See* subheading of specific cultural
group under, "traditions, customs, and beliefs,"
e.g., Acadians—traditions, customs, and beliefs
Couscous (Food), 70, 1252
Coutinho, Joaquim de Siquera, 1471
Cow industry, 12, 102
Coyotes (Illegal immigrants), 1300
CRA (Christian Reformed Church), 548
Crafts, traditional. *See* subheading of specific
cultural group under, "traditions, customs, and
beliefs," e.g., Belarusan Americans—traditions,
customs, and beliefs
Cranes (Animal), 1020
Crawfish, 6. *See also* Fish and seafood
Credit unions, 679
Creditors, 1043
Creek (Language), 443
Creeks (People), **437–449**
acculturation, 439–441
associations, museums, and research
centers, 448–449
employment and economics, 445
family and community, 443–444
health, 442–443
history, 437–439
language, 443
media, 448
notable individuals and groups, 447–448
politics and government, 446–447
religion, 444–445
stereotypes and misconceptions, 440–441
traditions, customs, and beliefs, 441–442
Cremation, 153, 1747
Creole (Language), 454, 811–812
Creoles, **450–459**
acculturation, 451–452
associations, museums, and research
centers, 458–459
Cuban history, 474
employment and economics, 456–457

family and community, 455–456
history, 451
language, 454
media, 458
notable individuals and groups, 457–458
politics and government, 457
relations with Acadians, 3, 7
religion, 456
traditions, customs, and beliefs, 452–453
Crests, 1767
Cricket (Sport), 752, 1006
Crigler-Najjar syndrome, 84
Crime. *See also* Domestic abuse; Mafia (Sicilian)
African Americans, 36
Italian Americans, 986, 988
Jamaican Americans, 1006, 1010
Russian Americans, 1525
Virgin Islands, 1865
Crisafi, Antonio, 1598
Cristo-Loveanu, Elie, 1516
CRITFC (Columbia River Inter-Tribal Fisheries
Commission), 1289, 1293
Crkvenoslovenski (Language), 1588
Croatia, 460–462, 469, 1592
Croatian (Language), 466–467
Croatian Americans, **460–472**
acculturation, 465
associations, museums, and research
centers, 472
employment and economics, 468
family and community, 467–468
health, 466
history, 461–464
immigration and settlement, 264–265
language, 466–467
media, 471
notable individuals and groups, 469–471
politics and government, 468–469
relations with Croatia, 469
religion, 468
traditions, customs, and beliefs, 465–466
Crocodile Dundee (Film), 167
Cronyn, Hume, 328
Crop cultivation. *See* Farms and farming
Crop Over celebrations, 200
Crossmas (Holiday), 891
Crowfoot (Blackfoot leader), 248
Crown Colony governments, 1001
Crown Dance, Apache, 100
Crowns (Headdress), 1468
The Crusades, 971, 1716
Cruz, Pedro dela, 636
Cruz, Victor Hernández, 1499
Cry ceremonies, 1380
CSO (Community Service Organization), 1214
Cuba, 473–475, 481

E

EAA (East Africa Association), 1063
Earl of Carlisle, 196
Earl of Pembroke, 196
East Africa Association (EAA), 1063
East Germany, 708–709, 717
East Indian Americans. *See* Asian Indian Americans
Easter
    Amish, 83
    Arab Americans, 117
    Belarusans, 224
    Bosnians, 266
    Lebanese, 1118
    Macedonians, 1166
    Mexican Americans, 1210
    Polish Americans, 1451
    Serbians, 1590
    Ukrainians, 1819
Eastern Orthodox Church
    Arab Americans, 117
    Carpatho-Rusyn Americans, 349–350
    Gypsy Americans, 801
    Lebanese Americans, 1120
    Macedonian Americans, 1168
    Romanian Americans, 1512–1513
    Ukrainian Americans, 1823
Easurk Emsen Charr, 1085
Ebonics, 36
Economic traditions. *See* subheading of specific cultural group under, "employment and economics," e.g., Amish—employment and economics
Ecuador, 553–556
Ecuador Day, 559
Ecuadoran Americans, **553–566**
    acculturation, 557–558
    associations, museums, and research centers, 566
    employment and economics, 562–563
    family and community, 560–561
    history, 554–556
    immigration and settlement, 556–557
    language, 559–560
    media, 565–566
    notable individuals and groups, 561, 564–565
    politics and government, 564
    religion, 562
    traditions, customs, and beliefs, 558–559
Edmunds Act (1882), 1236
Edmund-Tucker Act (1887), 1236
Education. *See* subheading of specific cultural group under, "family and community," or "notable individuals and groups," e.g., African Americans—family and comunity
EELC (Estonian Evangelical Lutheran Church), 607
Egg decorating, 1590

Egg hoppers (Food), 1684
Egusi soup, 1316
Egypt, 567–568, 572, 972
Egyptian Americans, **567–574**
    acculturation, 568
    associations, museums, and research centers, 573–574
    employment and economics, 572
    family and community, 570–571
    health, 569
    history, 567–568
    immigration and settlement, 568
    language, 570
    media, 573
    notable individuals and groups, 572–573
    politics and government, 572
    relations with Egypt, 572
    religion, 571–572
    traditions, customs, and beliefs, 569
Eid al-Adha (Holiday), 71, 116, 1562, 1888
Eid al-Fitr (Holiday), 116, 152, 1562, 1720, 1887
Einstein, Albert, 1047
Eisenhower, Dwight, 716
Eisteddfod (Musical tradition), 1877
Ekemode, O.J., 1322
El Dia de los Innocentes (Holiday), 1492
El Dia de los Tres Reyes (Holiday), 1494
El Norte (Film), 780
El Rescate (Organization), 1545
El Salvador, 1534–1535, 1543. *See also* Salvadoran Americans
Elderly, 812
Elia, Andrew, 63
Elia, Dimitria Tsina, 63
Eliade, Mircea, 1515
Elizabeth I, Queen, 576, 1873
Elizabeth II, Queen, 577
Elizabeth, Queen of Aragon, 1466
Elopement, 839
Emancipation Day (Virgin Islands), 1868
Emch (Healer), 1228
Emmigration. *See* subheading of specific cultural group under, "immigration and settlement," e.g., Yemeni Americans—immigration and settlement
Empanadas (Food), 378
Emperor Charles IV, 498
Emperor Dusan Silni, 1580
Emperor Haile Selassie, 614
Emperor Le Thai To, 1855
Emperor Minh-mang, 1849
Employment. *See* subheading of specific cultural group under, "employment and economics," e.g., Amish—employment and economics
Endo, Mitsuye, 1024
Endogamous marriages, 84, 114, 358. *See also* Interracial and intercultural marriages

Ukrainian American, 1820–1821
Yupiat, 1896
Folk schools, 518
Folk tales. *See* Stories and storytelling
Foods. *See* subheading of specific cultural group
    under, "traditions, customs, and beliefs," e.g.,
    Barbadian Americans—traditions, customs, and
    beliefs; specific type of food, e.g., Gumbo
Foofoo (Food), 788
Football (Soccer), 752, 770, 1834
Forbes, Kathryn, 1336
Ford, Glenn, 327
Foreign language instruction. *See* Bilingual
    education
Formosan Association for Public Affairs, 1736
Fort Apache Reservation, 97
Fort Apache Timber Company, 102
Fortresses, 1434
Fortune-telling, 797, 800–803
Forty-eighters (Immigrant group), 175, 178
Forty-niners (Immigrant group), 868, 870, 875
Four Noble Truths (of Buddhism), 314
Foustanela (Clothing), 736
Fox, Michael J., 328
Fox, William, 878
FPC (Fair Play Committee), 1024
France, 655–658
Francia, José Gaspar Rodríguez de, 1423
Francis, Lee, 1486
Franco, Francisco, 207
Frankincense, 1883
Fraternal organizations, 678, 1641
Free-Soil party, 1334
French (Language)
    Acadians, 5, 9–10
    Belgians, 233
    Canada, 324–325
    Creoles, 454
    French, 662
    French-Canadian Americans, 675
    Haitian Americans, 811
French Americans, **655–667**
    acculturation, 660
    associations, museums, and research
      centers, 665–666
    employment and economics, 663
    family and community, 662
    health, 662
    history, 656–657
    immigration and settlement, 657–660
    language, 662
    media, 665
    notable individuals and groups, 663–665
    politics and government, 663
    religion, 663
    traditions, customs, and beliefs, 661

French and Indian War, 656
French-Canadian Americans, **668–685**
    associations, museums, and research
      centers, 684–685
    employment and economics, 678–679
    family and community, 675–677
    health, 675
    history, 669–671
    immigration, 671–673
    language, 675
    media, 683–684
    notable individuals and groups, 680–683
    politics and government, 679–680
    relations with Canada, 680
    religion, 677–678
    traditions, customs, and beliefs, 673–675
French-Canadians, 3
French National Assembly, 662
French Polynesia, 1364–1366, 1371–1372,
    1777–1778
French Revolution, 657
Fruit industry, 633, 688, 845–846
Fruits, 1065. *See also* specific type of fruit, e.g.,
    Coconuts
Fujimori, Alberto, 1436
Fulani empire, 1313
Funan (Territory), 306
Funk, Casimir, 1456
Fur trade. *See* Trade and trading
Furuseth, Andrew, 1336
Fuster, Illeana, 849

G

Ga (People), 724
Ga-Adangbe (People), 724
Gage, Nicholas, 743
Gagnon, Ferdinand, 681
Gagnon, Rene A., 680
Galbraith, John Kenneth, 327
Galicia region, 1672
Gallatin, Albert, 1711
Gallaudet, Thomas, 664
Gamarra, Eduardo A., 259
Gambling and gaming, 958, 1341, 1347, 1359,
    1483
Gandhi, Indira, 148
Gangs, street, 1540
Garamendi, John, 215
Garand, John C., 682
Garbo, Greta, 1700
Garcia, Cristina, 482
Garcia, Jose, 532
García-Borras, Thomas, 1678
García-Buñuel, Luis, 1678
Garifuna (Language), 691–692, 849

Haitian Voodoo, 811, 814
Haj (Pilgrimmage), 572, 1562, 1565, 1887
al-Hakim, bi-Amrih Alla, 535, 538
Hall, Prince, 203
Hallaca (Food), 1841
Halloumi (Food), 489
Halloween, 942
Hammelsmarsch (Custom), 1155
Hammond/Daanawaa, Austin, 1774
Han dynasty, 387
Hanai (Custom), 825
Handball, 217
Handshaking, 230, 1129
Handsome Lake (Person), 1358
Haney, Enoch Kelly, 447
Hangin, John Gombojob, 1225, 1231
Hangul (Alphabet), 1080
Hanifi, Mohammed Jamil, 25
Hanihara, Masanao, 1016
Hannukah (Holiday), 976, 1036
Hansen, Marcus Lee, 520
Hanson, Anton, 609
Hanson, Howard, 1700
Hanson, John, 1698
Haozouis, Blossom, 104
Harald the Fariheaded, 885
Haraszthy, Ágaston, 868
Hardin, Helen, 1485
Hare-Hawkes-Cutting bill (1931), 625
Hari Raja (Holiday), 901
Hari Raya Puasa (Holiday), 1177
Härm, Richard, 610
Harner, Nellie Shaw, 1384
Harrell, Beatrice, 414
Harris, Joel Chandler, 1619
Harris, Wilson, 791
Harrison, Richard B., 48
Hart-Cellar Immigration Reform Act (1965),
  750, 1784
Harvest Festival (Iroquoian), 961
Harvey, Laurence, 1147
Hassa, Tawfig Jabr, 1891
Hassler, Ferdinand, 1711
Hat industry, 1653
Hataali, 1263
Hatcegan, Vasile, 1515
Hatfield and McCoy feud, 1573
Hats, 168, 256. See also name of specific hat,
  e.g., Berets
Haudenosaunee (People). See Iroquois
  Confederacy
Hausa (Language), 1317
Hausa (People), 1319
Hawaii, 627, 819–821, 1015–1016, 1464
Hawaiian (Language), 825
Hawaiian Provisional Battalion, 1024

Hawaiian Sugar Planters Association
  (HSPA), 627
Hawaiians, **819–831**
  acculturation, 821
  associations, museums, and research
    centers, 829–830
  employment and economics, 827
  family and community, 825–826
  health, 824–825
  history, 819–821
  language, 825
  media, 829
  notable individuals and groups, 829
  politics and government, 828
  religion, 826
  traditions, customs, and beliefs, 821–824
Hawayanos (People), 630
Hawkins, Benjamin, 440
Hawley, Henry, 196
Hay, James, 196
Hayakawa, Sessue, 1025
Hayakawa, S.I., 1026
Hayashi, Harvey Saburo, 1026
Hay-Ban-Vanilla Treaty (1903), 1413
Hayslip, Le Ly, 1855
HDF (Hungarian Democratic Forum), 868
Headdresses, 1769
Healing, folk. See Folk medicine
Health. See subheading of specific cultural group,
  e.g., Barbadian Americans—health
Health clinics, 773
Health insurance
  Amish, 84
  Belgian Americans, 233
  Canada, 324
  Dutch Americans, 546
  English, 584
  Irish Americans, 943
  Nicaraguan Americans, 1305
  Polish Americans, 1452
Hebrew (Language), 976, 1038
Hechicería (Folk healers), 1305
Heder (School), 1040
Heiau (Temple), 826
Heimskringla (Newspaper), 895
Helms-Burton Act, 480
Hemoglobin disorder, 490
Hemon, Aleksandar, 270
Hendin, Josephine Gattuso, 1607
Henius, Max, 521
Hennepin, Louis, 237
Henni, Johann Martin, 1711
Henri I (Haitian ruler), 806
Henriques, Alfonso, 1462
Henry, Gregory A., 791
Henry the Navigator, Prince, 1462

politics and government, 860–861
population, 1480
religion, 859–860, 1482
traditions, customs, and beliefs, 855–857
Horse ranching, 6, 1283
Horse trading, 802
Hosokawa, William K. "Bill," 1026
Hostos, María de, 1491
House, Gordon, 1362
Houser, Allan, 104
Houses and housing, 443, 536, 795
Houston, Texas, 770, 774, 776
Houston, Velina Hasu, 1026
How Stella Got Her Groove Back (Film), 809
Howe, LeAnn, 414
Howe, Oscar, 1630
Hoyt, Hugh Desmond, 785
HRF (Hungarian Reformed Federation), 875
HSPA (Hawaiian Sugar Planters Association), 627
Huaqiao (Migration), 388
Huaren (Migration), 388
Huascar del Pinal, Jorge, 779
Huayna Capac (Incan ruler), 1434
Hughes, Langston, 49
Huguenots (Protestant group), 656, 659, 663
Huiguan organizations, 391
Huks (Political group), 626
Hula (Dance), 824
Hull, Brett, 329
Human Immunodeficiency Virus (HIV). *See* Acquired Immune Deficiency Syndrome
Human sexuality, 537
Hung Vu, 1859
Hungarian (Language), 872–873
Hungarian Americans, **866–883**
    acculturation, 871
    associations, museums, and research centers, 880–882
    employment and economics, 875–876
    family and community, 873–874
    health, 872
    history, 867–868
    immigration and settlement, 868–871
    language, 872–873
    media, 879–880
    notable individuals and groups, 878–879
    politics and government, 876–877
    religion, 874–875
    stereotypes and misconceptions, 871
    traditions, customs, and beliefs, 872
Hungarian Calvinist Church, 875
Hungarian Democratic Forum (HDF), 868
Hungarian Reformed Federation (HRF), 875
Hungary, 866–868
Hungry Ghost Festival, 1177
Hunter-Gault, Charlayne, 49

Hunting. *See also* Fishing; Whaling
    Acadians, 11
    of buffalo, 243
    Hopi, 856
    Inuit, 907–908, 913
Huppah (Canopy), 1039
Hurja, Emil, 649
Hurricanes, 846
Hurricane Supplication Day, 1868
Hus, Jan, 498
Hussein, King, 1053
Hussein, Sadam, 931, 932, 934
Huston, John, 1575
Huynh Sanh Thong, 1859
Hwang, Henry, 400
Hwyl (Chanting style), 1878
Hyangga (Poetry), 1077
Hygiene, 798
Hypertension, 35, 1368
Hyun, Peter, 1086
Hyung-Soon, Kim, 1086

I

I Won't Get Married (Song), 1238
Iacocca, Lee, 994
Ibanez, María Elena, 426
IBEA (Imperial British East Africa Company), 1063
Ibos (People), 1313, 1319
Iceland, 884–886, 894
Icelandic (Language), 891
Icelandic Americans, **884–896**
    acculturation, 887
    associations, museums, and research centers, 896
    employment and economics, 893
    family and community, 892–893
    health, 891
    history, 885–886
    immigration and settlement, 886–887
    language, 891
    media, 896
    notable individuals and groups, 894–895
    politics and government, 894
    relations with Iceland, 894
    religion, 893
    traditions, customs, and beliefs, 887–891
Icelandic Lutheran Church, 893
Iceland's National Hymn (Song), 890
Icons (Religious), 1589
Id al-Fitr (Holiday), 1316
Idul Fitri (Holiday), 901
Ieyasu, Tokugawa, 1015
Ifoga (Ceremony), 1553
Iftikhar, Samuel, 1397

IRA (Indian Reorganization Act). *See* Indian
Reorganization Act of 1934 (IRA)
Iran, 918–920
Iranian Americans, **918–928**
acculturation, 921–922
associations, museums, and research
centers, 927–928
employment and economics, 926
family and community, 924–925
history, 919–920
immigration and settlement, 920–921
language, 924
media, 927
notable individuals and groups, 926–927
politics and government, 926
religion, 925–926
stereotypes and misconceptions, 923
traditions, customs, and beliefs, 923
Iraq, 929–931, 934
Iraqi Americans, **929–935**
acculturation, 932
associations, museums, and research
centers, 935
differences from Chaldean Americans, 355
family and community, 933
health, 932
history, 929–931
immigration and settlement, 931–932
language, 932
media, 934–935
relations with Iraq, 934
religion, 933–934
traditions, customs, and beliefs, 932
IRCA (Immigration Reform and Control Act
of 1986), 777, 847, 1300
Ireland, 577, 936–937, 948. *See also* Northern
Ireland
Iribarren, Rene, 383
Irish (Language), 943–944
Irish Americans, **936–953**
acculturation, 940
associations, museums, and research
centers, 951–953
conflict with Italian Americans, 991
employment and economics, 946
family and community, 944–945
health, 943
history, 936–937
immigration and settlement, 937–940
interest in Northern Ireland, 948
labor movements, 948
language, 943–944
media, 950–951
notable individuals and groups, 947, 949–950
politics and government, 947
religion, 945–946
traditions, customs, and beliefs, 940–942

Iroquoian (Language), 962–963
Iroquois Confederacy, **955–969,** 1358. *See also*
Oneidas (People)
associations, museums, and research
centers, 968–969
employment and economics, 965
family and community, 961–962, 963–964
health, 962
history, 955–958
language, 962–963
media, 968
notable individuals and groups, 966–967
politics and government, 965–966
religion, 964
stereotypes and misconceptions, 960
traditions, customs, and beliefs, 958–961
Ishtaboli (Game), 410
Islam, 1115, 1121, 1723. *See* subheading of specific
cultural group under, "religion," e.g., Iraqi
Americans—religion
Islamic Salvation Front (FIS), 69
Island Caribs (People), 687
Isleta del Sur Pueblos, 1481. *See also* Pueblos
Israel, 970–972, 977, 979, 1030, 1045, 1400–1403
Israeli Americans, **970–981.** *See also* Jewish
Americans
acculturation, 973
associations, museums, and research
centers, 981
employment and economics, 979
family and community, 977–978
health, 976
history, 970–972
immigration and settlement, 972–973
language, 976
media, 980
notable individuals and groups, 979–980
politics and government, 979
religion, 977, 978
traditions, customs, and beliefs, 974–976
Issei (People). *See* Japanese Americans
Issues, social
See subheading of specific cultural group
under, "family and community," e.g.,
Apache—family and community
Ista-Mitra (Film), 1274
Italian (Language), 990, 1602
Italian Americans, **982–999.** *See also* Sicilian
Americans
acculturation, 987–988
associations, museums, and research
centers, 997–999
employment and economics, 992–993
family and community, 990–991
health, 989
history, 982–983

immigration and settlement, 984–987
language, 990
media, 996–997
notable individuals and groups, 994–996
politics and government, 993–994
religion, 991–992
traditions, customs, and beliefs, 988–989
Italy, 982–983. *See also* Sicily
Itliong, Larry, 633
Iwamatsu, Jun Atushi, 1026
Iwamatsu, Makoto, 1025

J

Jackson, Andrew, 363, 407
Jackson County, Missouri, 1235
Jackson Heights, New York, 557
Jackson, Jesse, Sr., 48
Jackson, Nathan, 1774
Jacobites, 1568
Jacobs, Jack, 448
Jacques I (Haitian ruler), 806
Jaffrey, Madhur, 156
Jagiellonian dynasty, 1446
Jainism (Religion), 154
Jamaica, 1000–1003, 1011
Jamaican Americans, **1000–1013**
    acculturation, 1003–1004
    associations, museums, and research
        centers, 1013
    employment and economics, 1010
    family and community, 1007–1009
    health, 1006
    history, 1001–1002
    immigration and settlement, 1002–1003
    language, 1006, 1007
    media, 1013
    notable individuals and groups, 1006,
        1011–1012
    politics and government, 1010–1011
    religion, 1009–1010
    stereotypes and misconceptions, 1009
    traditions, customs, and beliefs, 1004–1006,
        1006–1007
James, C.L.R., 1792
Jani (Holiday), 1106
Japan, 1014–1015
Japanese (Language), 1019–1020
Japanese Americans, **1014–1029**
    acculturation, 1017–1018
    associations, museums, and research
        centers, 1028
    employment and economics, 1022
    family and community, 1020–1021
    health, 1019
    history, 1015

immigration and settlement, 1015–1017
language, 1019–1020
media, 1027
notable individuals and groups, 1025–1027
politics and government, 1023–1025
religion, 1021–1022
traditions, customs, and beliefs, 1018–1019
Jaroslav the Wise, 1814
Jausoro, Jim, 216
Javacheff, Christo, 296
Jay, John, 664
Jazz music, 49
JDL (Jewish Defense League), 1045
Jean, Wyclef, 816
Jean-Louis, Marc, 816
Jellebyas (Clothing), 594
Jemez Pueblos, 1479. *See also* Pueblos
Jemison, Mae C., 50
Jennings, Peter, 328
Jewelry
    Asian Indian, 151
    Eritrean, 594
    Guyanese, 790
    Jordanian American, 1056
    Pakistani American, 1393
    Palestinian, 1405
    Sri Lankan, 1684
Jewish Americans, **1030–1051**. *See also* Israeli
  Americans; Jewish people; Judaism
    acculturation, 1033–1034
    associations, museums, and research
        centers, 1049–1050
    employment and economics, 1043–1044
    family and community, 1038–1041
    health, 1037
    history, 1031–1032
    immigration and settlement, 1032–1033
    language, 1038
    media, 1048–1049
    notable individuals and groups, 1045–1048
    politics and government, 1044–1045
    relations with Israel, 1045
    relations with Israeli Americans, 978
    religion, 1041–1043
    stereotypes and misconceptions, 1034–1035
    traditions, customs, and beliefs, 1035–1037
Jewish Defense League (JDL), 1045
Jewish New Year, 975, 1036
Jewish people. *See also* Israeli Americans; Jewish
  Americans; Judaism
    Arab conflict, 1401–1403
    Austrian, 176
    Cape Verdean, 335
    Hungary, 866
    Iranian, 920
    Moroccan, 1250, 1251, 1252

Marriage engagement, 676

Marriages. *See* name of specific type of marriage, e.g., Interracial and intercultural marriages; subheading of specific cultural group under, "family and community," e.g., Amish—family and community

Marshall, Paul, 204

Marshall, Thurgood, 48

Marti, Jose, 475

Martin, Agnes, 329

Martin, Peter, 521

Martin, Ricky, 1498

Martin, Tony, 1473

Martinez, Anita, 694

Martinez, Bob, 482

Martinez, Dennis, 1309

Martinez, Maria Montoya, 1484

Martinovanje celebrations, 1650

Martyrs, religious, 80

Mary Help of Christians Shrine, 1652

Masayesva, Victor, Jr., 1485

Masjid (Gathering place), 1121

Masked dances (Cambodian), 311

Masks, face. *See* Face masks

Mason, James O., 1244

Massachusetts, 672, 673, 1875

Masses (Roman Catholic), 693

Mata, Eduardo, 1218

Mataele, Foloi Manuma'a, 1372

Matchmakers, 1039, 1183, 1789. *See also* Arranged marriages

Mate (Beverage), 126, 1835

Mathabane, Mark, 1668, 1669

Matrifocal cultures, 692, 1481

Matrilineal cultures, 102, 364, 411, 758, 1481

Mau (Samoan resistance movement), 1549

Mau Mau uprising, 1063

Maury, Matthew Fontaine, 665

Mawei (Social unit), 1616

Maximo, Antonieta, 695

Mayan
    civilization, 845
    culture, 764–765, 767
    empire, 1298
    language, 765, 773–774
    religion, 776

Maynard, Robert Clyve, 203

Mazuha Koshina, 1630

Mazzanovich, Antonio, 464

McCarran-Walter Act (1952), 111, 1017

McCarran-Warren Act (1965), 786

McCarthy, Nobu, 1025

McCoy and Hatfield feud, 1573

McDonald, Julie Jensen, 520

McFee, Malcolm, 242

McGillivray, Alexander, 439

McGuire, Peter James, 948

Meats, 6, 113, 1207, 1835. *See also* name of specific meat, e.g., Beef

Mecca (Holy city), 572, 933, 1558. *See also* Islam

Medeiros, Humberto Sousa, 1473

Media. *See* subheading of specific cultural group under, "media," e.g., African Americans—media

Medical insurance. *See* Health insurance

Medical profession, 1080

Medicine and medical issues. *See* subheading of specific cultural group under, "health," or "notable individuals and groups," e.g., Amish—health

Medicine bundles, 246

Medicine, folk. *See* Folk medicine

Mediterranean anemia, 1184

Meeting houses, Mormon, 1242

Mehta, Zubin, 157

Meidung (Amish custom), 91

Melara, Julio, 851

Melchior, Lauritz, 521

Melkite/Greek Catholic Church, 1120

Melo, Sebastião José de Carvalho e, 1462

Menarche rituals, 856, 964, 1378

Mende (People), 1617

Mendes, John, 1472

Mendez, Hermann, 779

Menehune (Legendary characters), 821

Menendez, Robert, 482

Menilek II, King, 613

Mennonites, 1708

Menor, Benjamin, 636

Mensef feasts, 1055

Mental health. *See* subheading of specific cultural group under, "health," e.g., Amish—health

Merchant, Ismail, 156

Merchant marines, 188

Merchant, Natalie, 1607

Merchants, street. *See* Street peddlers

MERCOSUR (Organization), 1833

Merengue (Dance), 1494

Mescal (Food), 99

Mescalero Apaches, 103. *See also* Apaches

Mescalero Reservation, 97

Messenger Feast, 1894

Messengers, 1434

Mestizos (People), 624, 1296, 1439

Mestrovic, Ivan, 471

Metalious, Grace DeRepentigny, 681

Methodism (Religion), 247, 1021, 1879

Metis (People), 321

Mexican American Political Association (MAPA), 1215

Mexican Americans, **1190–1221**
    acculturation, 1195–1197
    associations, museums, and research centers, 1220–1221

under, "notable individuals and groups," or "traditions, customs, and beliefs," e.g., African Americans—notable individuals and groups; specific type of music, e.g., Blues music
Musica nacional (Musical style), 559
Musical instruments. *See* name of specific type of musical instrument, e.g., Drums (Musical instrument)
Muskogean languages, 410, 443
Muskrats, 11
Muslims. *See* Islam
Mussolini, Benito, 1598
Mustard oil, 1274
Mutton, 1055
Muumuu (Clothing), 823
Myalism (Religion), 1009
Myanmar, 299–301
Myanmar Americans. *See* Burmese Americans
Mylonas, George, 742
Myrrh, 1883
Myths, 6, 1368
Myung-Whun Chung, 1086

N

NAACP (National Association for the Advancement of Colored People), 44, 53
NAACP Legal Defense and Educational Fund, 53
Naadam Festival, 1227
Naca Omincia (Tribal council), 1626
Nacas (Fraternal society), 1626
Nacatamal (Food), 1304
Nader, Ralph, 119, 1123
Nagaret (Musical instrument), 594
Nagurski, Bronko, 1827
Naipaul, V.S., 1792
Nair, Mira, 156
Nakash Brothers, 979
Nalalpata (Headdress), 1687
Nalukataq (Holiday), 910
Nam June Paik, 1086
Naming practices, 1039. *See also* subheading of specific cultural group under, "family and community," e.g., Hopis (People)—family and community
Nampeyo (Person), 862
Nanih Waiya (Choctaw mound), 405
Nanji, Azim A., 921
Napoleon (Leader), 657, 1463
Nara (People), 596
Narodni List (Newspaper), 465
Naser (Musician), 1135
Nasii (Family representative), 1511
Nasser, Gamal Abdal, 568
Nassi, Thomas, 63
Nation Elders' Program, 1359

National Assembly (Governmental body), 598
National Association for the Advancement of Colored People (NAACP), 44, 53
National Association for the Advancement of Colored People Legal Defense and Educational Fund, 53
National Association of Arab Americans, 118, 1124, 1726
National Basque Monument, 216
National Coalition for Haitian Rights, 808, 814, 815
National Council of La Raza, 1501
National Dance Theater Company (NDTC), 1012
National Day (Nigeria), 1316
National Farm Workers Association (NFWA), 633
National flags
    Costa Rican, 429
    Druze, 535
    Guamanian, 756
    Laotian, 1091
    Maltese, 1184
    Tibetan, 1751
    Uruguayan, 1832
    Wales, 1876
National Gymanfa Ganu Association, 1877
National Heroes Day, 1005
National People's Assembly (APN), 73
National Revolutionary Movement (MNR), 253
National Sioux Council, 1627
National songs, 594
National Union of Algerian Women, 73
National Union of Eritrean Women (NUEW), 597
National Urban League, 53
Nationalism and Nationalist movements
    Albanian American, 62
    Italian American, 986
    Latvian American, 1109
    Lithuanian American, 1143, 1144, 1146
    Scottish, 1575
Nationalist party (Taiwan), 1729
Nationalista party (Philippines), 625
Native American Church, 1262
Native Baptist Church, 1009
Native Hawaiians, 828
Nauvoo, Illinois, 1235
Navajo Agricultural Products Industry, 1266
Navajo Code Talkers, 1266–1267
Navajo Community College, 1264
Navajo Indian Irrigation Project (NIIP), 1266
Navajo Nation, 1260
Navajo-Hopi Land Dispute, 1268
Navajos, **1259–1271**
    acculturation, 1262
    associations, museums, and research centers, 1270–1271

P

Pa ndau (Handicraft), 841
PAC (Polish American Congress), 1455
Pachacuti (Incan ruler), 1433
Pachamama (Incan Earth Mother), 255
Pacific American Foundation, 1370, 1371
Pacific Islander Americans, **1364–1374**
    acculturation, 1367
    associations, museums, and research
      centers, 1373
    employment and economics, 1371
    family and community, 1369–1370
    health, 1368–1369
    history, 1365–1366
    immigration and settlement, 1366–1367
    language, 1369
    media, 1372
    notable individuals and groups, 1372
    politics and government, 1371
    relations with Pacific Islands, 1371–1372
    religion, 1370–1371
    traditions, customs, and beliefs, 1367–1368
Pacific Islands, 1364–1366, 1371–1372,
  1777–1778
Pacino, Al, 1607
Paczki (Food), 1451
Paczki Day (Holiday), 1451
Padakkam (Pendants), 1687
Padmore, George, 1791
Padrinos (Godparents), 770
Padrone (Supervisor), 632
Pagan period, 299
Paganism, 1591, 1879
Paha Sapa (Sacred land), 1627
Pahlavi, Shah Mohammed Reza, 920
Pahos (Prayer feathers), 857
Pai, Margaret K., 1085
Paik, Nam June, 1086
Paiutes (People), **1375–1388**
    associations, museums, and research
      centers, 1385–1387
    employment and economics, 1382
    family and community, 1380
    health, 1379
    history, 1376–1377
    language, 1379–1380
    notable individuals and groups, 1384–1385
    politics and government, 1383–1384
    religion, 1381–1382
    settlement, 1377
    traditions, customs, and beliefs, 1377–1379
Paj ntaub (Handicraft), 841
Pakistan, 18, 187–188, 1389–1391, 1397
Pakistani Americans, **1389–1399**
    acculturation, 1392
    associations, museums, and research
      centers, 1398–1399

    employment and economics, 1396–1397
    family and community, 1394–1395
    health, 1394
    history, 1389–1391
    immigration and settlement, 1391–1392
    language, 1394
    media, 1398
    notable individuals and groups, 1397–1398
    politics and government, 1397
    relations with Pakistan, 1397
    religion, 1395–1396
    traditions, customs, and beliefs, 1392–1393
Palacio, Andy, 690
Palacio, Clifford, 688, 694
Palance, Jack, 1825
Pale of Settlement, 1521
Palestine. *See* Israel
Palestinian Americans, **1400–1411**
    acculturation, 1404–1405
    associations, museums, and research
      centers, 1409–1410
    employment and economics, 1407
    family and community, 1406
    history, 1400–1403
    immigration and settlement, 1403–1404
    language, 1405–1406
    media, 1409
    notable individuals and groups, 1408
    politics and government, 1407–1408
    religion, 1407
    traditions, customs, and beliefs, 1405
Palestinian Arabs, 972
Palestinian Liberation Organization (PLO),
  972, 1402
Pali alphabet, 303
Pallais, Nadia, 1309
Palm Sunday, 1590
Paloheimo, Yrjo, 649
Pan-African movement, 1010
Pan-Albania Federation of America, 62
Panama, 1412–1414, 1419
Panama Canal, 1413–1414
Panamanian Americans, **1412–1421**
    acculturation, 1415
    associations, museums, and research
      centers, 1420–1421
    employment and economics, 1418
    family and community, 1416–1417
    health, 1416
    history, 1413–1414
    immigration and settlement, 1414–1415
    language, 1416
    media, 1420
    notable individuals and groups, 1419
    politics and government, 1418–1419
    relations with Panama, 1419

RCA (Reformed Protestant Dutch Church),
547–548
Reamker (Poem), 312
Rebane, Hans, 607, 1108
Rebata, Virginia Patricia, 1441
Rebildfest (Holiday), 518
Reconstructionist Judaism, 1043. *See also* Judaism
Red Lake Reservation, 1349
Red-Eagle, Philip H., Jr., 1630
Redemptioner immigration systems, 710
Reed, Rex, 9
Refalosa dances, 379
Reform Judaism, 1042. *See also* Judaism
Reformation, Protestant, 656
Reformed Church of Holland, 547, 1668
Reformed Protestant Dutch Church (RCA),
547–548
Refugee Act (1980), 614, 777
Refugees. *See* subheading of specific cultural group
under, "immigration and settlement," e.g.,
Laotian Americans—immigration and settlement
Reggae music, 1005
Reina, Carlos Roberto, 846
Reincarnation, 539, 839, 1748, 1771
Reindeer, 909
Reinhardt, Max, 183
Relative Friends (Film), 1274
Religion. *See* name of specific religion, e.g.,
Calvinism; subheading of specific cultural
group under, "religion," e.g., Jamaican
Americans—religion
Religious cults, 787
Religious martyrs, 80
Religious orders, 1143, 1144
Removal Act (1835), 363
Removal Treaty (1832), 446
Reno, Janet, 521
Repatriation, 32, 527, 634, 1003, 1194
Republic of Armenia, 133–134
Republic of Indonesia, 897–898, 903–904, 1175
Republican movement (Portugal), 1463
Republican party, 609, 1335, 1698
Research centers. *See* subheading of specific
cultural group under, "museums and research
centers," e.g., Arab Americans—museums and
research centers
Reservation Business Council (RBC), 1349
Resistance movements, 765–766
Reunification of Germany (1990), 709, 717
Revere, Paul, 664
Reverse migration, 640
Revolutionary United Front (RUF), 1612
Revolutionary War, American. *See* American
Revolutionary War
Reyes, Dagoberto, 1544
Reynolds, Allie P., 448

Reza, Shah, 919
Rhee, Syngman, 1073, 1075
Rhys, Morgan John, 1875, 1881
Ribaut, Jean, 658
Ribbon shirts, 1356
Ribot-Canales, Verónica, 131
Rice, 1852
    Afghan American diets, 19
    Bangladeshi American diets, 190
    Laotian cooking, 1094
    Ojibwa diets, 1343
    Sierra Leonean diets, 1615
Riel, Louis, 321, 671
Riel Rebellion, 321
Riis, Jacob A., 520
Rimur (Music), 888
Ringgold, Faith, 51
Rios Montt, Efrain, 766
Rivera, Geraldo, 1499
Rivera, José Fructoso, 1832
Rizal, Jose, 624
Road building, 598, 1433
Roberts, Sheila, 1669
Robinson, Rose, 863
Rock, Howard, 915
Rodation Days (Holiday), 502
Rodriguez, Agustin, 532
Rodriguez, Alfred, 1678
Rodríguez, César, 1442
Rodriguez, Chi Chi, 1499
Rodríguez, Paul, 1217
Rogation Day (Holiday), 233
Rogers, Francis Mile, 1472
Rogers, Will, 370
Roggeveen, Jacob, 1548
Roles of women. *See* subheading of specific cultural
group under, "family and community," e.g., Arab
Americans—family and community
Rom. *See* Gypsy Americans
Roma. *See* Gypsy Americans
Roman Catholicism. *See* subheading of specific
cultural group under, "religion," e.g., Brazilian
Americans—religion
Romani (Gypsy language), 799–800
Romania, 1504–1505, 1514
Romanian (Language), 1509–1510
Romanian Americans, **1504–1519**
    associations, museums, and research
        centers, 1517–1518
    employment and economics, 1513
    family and community, 1510–1511
    health, 1509
    history, 1505
    immigrations and settlement, 1505–1507
    language, 1509–1510
    media, 1516–1517

Uniate Church, 117
Union and League of Romanian Societies of America (ULRSA), 1513–1514
Union Civica del Uruguay (Political party), 1837
Union Nationale des Femmes Algériennes (UNFA), 73
Unions, labor. *See* Labor movements and unions
Unitas, Johnny, 1147
United Democratic Front (UDF), 1668
United Farmworkers of America (UFW), 1215
United Jewish Appeal, 1041
United Kingdom, 575–578
United States English (Organization), 1201
United States of America Constitution, 966
Universal Negro Improvement Association (UNIA), 1010
University of Asmara, 596
University of Minnesota Immigration History Research Center, 643
University of the Virgin Islands, 1869
Upphlutur (Vest), 889
Uqqals (Religious elite), 538
Uralic-Altaic (Languages), 1229
Uranium mining, 1266
Urbanization, 795, 802
Urbina, Nicasio, 1308
Urdu (Language), 1394
Uris, Leon, 112
URNG (Guatemalan National Revolutionary Unity), 766
Uruguay, 1831–1833, 1837
Uruguayan Americans, **1831–1838**
    acculturation, 1834
    associations, museums, and research centers, 1837
    employment and economics, 1837
    family and community, 1836
    history, 1832–1833
    immigration and settlement, 1834
    language, 1836
    politics and government, 1837
    relations with Uruguay, 1837
    religion, 1836–1837
    traditions, customs, and beliefs, 1834–1835
Urus-Ova (Celebration), 1227
U.S.S. General Sherman (Ship), 1072
Utah Office of Polynesian Affairs (OPA), 1370
Ute Indians, 1380

V

Vaccinations, 1241
Vajras (Prayer wheels), 1753–1754
Valdez, Luis, 1217
Valdivieso, Pedro M., 1442
Valenzuela, Arturo, 382

Vallbona, Rima de, 435
Vallee, Hubert Prior "Rudy," 680
Vallenato music, 421
Valley Bridal Dress, Macedonia, 1165–1166
Valparaiso University, 1143
Valtman, Edmund, 610
Vampira, 650
Van Biesbroeck, Georges, 237
Van de Poele, Karel, 237
Vang Pao, 842
Vanoff, Nick, 1170
Vardoulakis, Mary, 743
Varonka, Jazep, 225
Vaska, Lauri, 610
Vasquez-Ajmac, Luis Alfredo, 778
Vassallo, Paul, 1187
Vatra organization, 62
Veblen, Thorstein, 1335
Vedas (Sacred texts), 1395
Vegetables, 1799
Veils, 1887
Velarde, Pablita, 1485
Velarde, Stacey, 103
Vellam (Best Men), 60
Velorios (Funeral party), 1303
Velvet Revolution, 1635
Venezuela, 1839–1840, 1843
Venezuelan Americans, **1839–1846**
    acculturation, 1841
    associations, museums, and research centers, 1846
    employment and economics, 1843
    family and community, 1842–1843
    health, 1842
    history, 1839–1840
    immigration and settlement, 1840–1841
    language, 1842
    media, 1845
    notable individuals and groups, 1843–1845
    politics and government, 1843
    relations with Venezuela, 1843
    religion, 1843
    traditions, customs, and beliefs, 1841
Vermont, 672
Vesak (Holidays), 301
Véspera de São João (Holiday), 1469
Vetra, Gundars, 1110
Vezina, Elie, 679, 681
Vicuna, Cecilia, 383
Vidovdan (Holiday), 1590
Vientiane (Lao dialect), 1095
Viet Cong, 1850
Viet Minh, 1092, 1849
Vietnam, 1847–1850
Vietnam Human Rights Day, 1853
Vietnam War, 833–834, 1092, 1850

Vietnamese (Language), 1854
Vietnamese Americans, **1847–1862**
    acculturation, 1852–1853
    associations, museums, and research
        centers, 1860–1861
    employment and economics, 1858
    family and community, 1855–1857
    health, 1853–1854
    history, 1848–1850
    immigration and settlement, 1850–1852
    language, 1854
    media, 1859–1860
    notable individuals and groups, 1859
    politics and government, 1858
    religion, 1857
    traditions, customs, and beliefs, 1855
Vigil, Padre, 1298
Vikings, 512
Vincent, Michaelle, 815
Vincenti, Carlson, 103
Violent crime. *See* Crime
Virgin Islander Americans, **1863–1871**
    acculturation, 1866–1867
    associations, museums, and research
        centers, 1871
    employment and economics, 1870
    family and community, 1869
    history, 1864–1865
    immigration and settlement, 1865
    language, 1868
    media, 1871
    notable individuals and groups, 1870–1871
    politics and government, 1870
    religion, 1870
    traditions, customs, and beliefs, 1867–1868
Virgin Islands, 1863–1865
Visayan (Language), 630
Visual artists. *See* subheading of specific cultural
    group under, "notable individuals and groups,"
    e.g., African Americans—notable individuals
    and groups
Viveiros, Bernie de, 1473
Vizenor, Gerald, 1350
VOLAGs (voluntary agencies), 1851
Volansky, Ivan, 1823
Volleyball, 561
von Erlach, Theobold, 1705
Vööbus, Arthur, 609
Voodoo, 811, 814
Voting and voting rights
    African American, 43
    Amish, 92
    Asian Indian American, 155
    Cuban American, 476, 480
    Ecuadoran American, 564
    Finnish American, 647

    Mexican American, 1216
    Navajo, 1268
    Pakistani American, 1397
    Swiss, 1705
    Virgin Islander, 1870
Voting Rights Act (1957), 44
Vow women, 246–247
Vu, Hung, 1859

W

Wage labor, 827
Wagiameme Performing Troupe, 692, 694
al-Wahhab, Muhammad Ibn, 1559
Wahhabi movement, 1559. *See also* Islam
Wai greetings, 1744
Waid, Gary, 1774
Wajang kulit dances, 901
Wakamatsu Tea and Silk Farm Colony, 1016
Wakes, 258, 434, 944, 1303
Waldensian Evangelical Church of the River Plate,
    1831
Wales, 577, 1872–1873. *See also* Welsh Americans
Walker, William, 1297
Walla Walla Council (1855), 1283
Wallis, Samuel, 1365
Walloon (Language), 233
Walloon Belgians. *See* Belgian Americans
Wampum (Native American material), 959, 1356
Wanaragua (Dance), 691
Wanichugu Dance Company, 694
War brides, 628
War of 1812, 321
War of Independence (Algeria), 68
Ward, Russell, 167
Warhol, Andy, 352, 508
Washington, Booker T., 38, 44
Waso (Holiday), 301
Water Festival (Cambodian), 311
Watering of the Banyan Tree festival, 301
Watts race riot, 46
Wauneka, Annie Dodge, 1268
Way of the Cross (Good Friday custom), 8
Weah, George, 1135
Weaving, 1264
Websites. *See* The Internet
Weddings. *See* subheading of specific cultural
    group under, "family and community" e.g.,
    Albanian Americans—family and community
Wee'kwetset ceremonies, 1286
Weil, Theodore Alexis, 609
Weimar Republic, 709
Welch, James, 249
Welch, Raquel, 260
Welfare. *See* Government aid
Wellaamotkin (Nez Percé leader), 1283, 1292

Xieng Mieng (Person), 1096
Xiong, Lee Pao, 1099
Xiong, William Joua, 1099
Xoua Thao, 841

Y

Yang, Dao, 842
Yankoff, Peter Dimitrov, 297
Yaqona (Beverage), 1367
Yarymovich, Michael, 1826
Yasbeck, Amy, 118
Yayha, Ahmad, 1884
Yayha, Imam, 1884
Yemen, 1883–1884
Yemeni Americans, **1883–1892**
    acculturation, 1885
    associations, museums, and research
      centers, 1891
    employment and economics, 1890
    family and community, 1888–1889
    health, 1888
    history, 1883–1885
    immigration and settlement, 1885
    language, 1888
    media, 1891
    notable individuals and groups, 1890–1891
    politics and government, 1890
    religion, 1890
    traditions, customs, and beliefs, 1885–1888
Yepremian, Garo, 493
Yi dynasty, 1072
Yiddish (Language), 976, 1034, 1038
Yin Li (Calendar), 392
Yoga, 152
Yom Kippur (Holiday), 975, 1036
Yoruba (Language), 1317
Yoruba (People), 1315, 1318, 1319
Young, Brigham, 1235–1237
Young, Loretta, 1158
Young-Sam, Kim, 1074
Yule logs, 1589
Yunus, Muhammad, 193
Yupanqui, Prince, 1433
Yupiat, **1893–1899**
    acculturation, 1894
    associations, museums, and research
      centers, 1898
    employment and economics, 1897
    family and community, 1895–1896
    health, 1895
    language, 1895
    media, 1898
    politics and government, 1897–1898
    religion, 1896–1897
    traditions, customs, and beliefs, 1894–1895
Yupiat (Language), 1895

Z

Zachos, John Celivergos, 742
Zadonu Group (Organization), 730
Zadruga (Family unit), 1589
Zah, Peterson, 1268
Zakarpats'ka. See Ruthenia
Zakarpats'kan Americans. See Carpatho-Rusyn
  Americans
Zakat (Almsgiving), 571, 1565
Zanco, Charles, 513
Zapata, Thomas, 1843
Zappa, Frank, 995
Zar possession (Illness), 1562
Zatkovich, Gregory, 351
Zawia, Nasser, 1890
Zayma dances, 594
Zhongchiu jie (Holiday), 1734
Zhou dynasty, 387
Zia Pueblos, 1480. See also Pueblos
Zibergs, Jekabs, 1108
Zimdin, William, 610
Ziolkowski, Korczak, 1456
Zionism, 971
Zionist movement, 1045
Zografoff, Boris, 1170
Zohn, Harry, 176
Zorba dancing, 737
Zoroastrianism (Religion), 154, 1396
Zuberoa'ko Maskarada dances, 212
Zubly, John J., 1707, 1711
Zuckerman, Pinchas, 979
Zukor, Adolph, 878
Zul (Celebration), 1227
Zulu (People), 1661, 1664, 1667
Zuñi Pueblos, 1480. See also Pueblos
Zwingli, Huldrych, 1709